FRANKLIN D.
ROOSEVELT

His Life and Times

FRANKLIN D.

ROOSEVELT

His Life and Times

An Encyclopedic View

Edited by

OTIS L. GRAHAM, Jr.

MEGHAN ROBINSON WANDER

A DA CAPO PAPERBACK

Library of Congress Cataloging in Publication Data

Franklin D. Roosevelt: his life and times: an encyclopedic
view / edited by Otis L. Graham, Jr., Meghan Robinson
Wander.
     p.   cm.—(A Da Capo paperback)
  Reprint. Originally published: Boston: G.K. Hall, c1985.
  Includes bibliographical references and index.
  ISBN 0-306-80410-7
  1. Roosevelt, Franklin D. (Franklin Delano), 1882-1945—
Encyclopedias. 2. New Deal, 1933-1939—Encyclopedias. 3.
Presidents—United States—Biography—Encyclopedias. 4.
United States—History—1933-1945—Encyclopedias. I.
Graham, Otis L. II. Wander, Meghan Robinson.
[E807.F69 1990]   90-3609
973.917'092—dc20   CIP

*Frontispiece: Franklin D. Roosevelt, 33d president of the
United States, taking the oath of office, 4 March, 1933.*
(National Archives.)

This Da Capo Press paperback edition of *Franklin D. Roosevelt:
His life and Times* is an unabridged republication of the edition
published in Boston in 1985. It is reprinted by arrangement with
G.K. Hall & Co.

Published by Da Capo Press, Inc.
A Subsidiary of Plenum Publishing Corporation
233 Spring Street, New York, N.Y. 10013

CONTRIBUTORS

W. Andrew Achenbaum
Carnegie–Mellon University

Howard W. Allen
Southern Illinois University at Carbondale

Joseph L. Arnold
University of Maryland Baltimore County

Bernard Asbell
New Haven, Conn.

Frank Annunziata
Rochester Institute of Technology

Ellsworth Barnard
University of Massachusetts at Amherst

Michael R. Beschloss
The Dwight D. Eisenhower Institute for Historical
    Research

Gregory D. Black
University of Missouri—Kansas City

Shelley Bookspan
PHR Associates

Joseph Boskin
Boston University

James R. Boylan
University of Massachusetts at Amherst

Alan Brinkley
Harvard University

W. Elliot Brownlee
University of California, Santa Barbara

David Burner
State University of New York at Stony Brook

Helen M. Burns
Baltimore, Md.

Milton Cantor
University of Massachusetts at Amherst

Alan Cassels
McMaster University

John W. Chambers
Rutgers University

Searle F. Charles
Elgin Community College

E. Charles Chatfield
Wittenberg University

Jean Christie
Fairleigh Dickinson University

Wayne S. Cole
University of Maryland

Rebecca Conard
PHR Associates

John Milton Cooper, Jr.
University of Wisconsin—Madison

Thomas E. Cronin
The Colorado College

E. David Cronon
University of Wisconsin—Madison

Kenneth S. Davis
Princeton, Mass.

Nelson L. Dawson
The Filson Club

Ralph F. de Bedts
Old Dominion University

Leonard Dinnerstein
The University of Arizona

Justus D. Doenecke
New College University of South Florida

William R. Emerson
The Franklin D. Roosevelt Library and Museum

Richard T. Goldberg
Newton, Mass.

John W. Gordon
United States Military Academy

Otis L. Graham, Jr.
The University of North Carolina at Chapel Hill

George D. Green
University of Minnesota

Allen Guttmann
Amherst College

Samuel B. Hand
The University of Vermont

Tamara K. Hareven
Clark University

Erwin C. Hargrove
Vanderbilt University

Brice Harris, Jr.
Occidental College

Robert M. Hathaway
Washington, D.C.

Ellis W. Hawley
The University of Iowa

Jim F. Heath
Portland State University

Patricia R. Hill
Harvard University

William R. Hochman
The Colorado College

John W. Huston
United States Naval Academy

Akira Iriye
The University of Chicago

Peter Irons
University of California, San Diego

Charles O. Jackson
The University of Tennessee, Knoxville

D. Clayton James
Mississippi State University

Bernard K. Johnpoll
Florida Atlantic University

Laura Kalman
University of California, Santa Barbara

Lawrence C. Kelly
North Texas State University

Warren F. Kimball
Rutgers University

Gregory King
PHR Associates

Richard S. Kirkendall
Iowa State University

Dean Kohlhoff
Valparaiso University

Warren F. Kuehl
The University of Akron

Marc Landy
Boston College

R. Alan Lawson
Boston College

Linda J. Lear
George Washington University

Timothy Lehman
Chapel Hill, N.C.

Albert Lepawsky
University of California, Berkeley

William E. Leuchtenburg
The University of North Carolina at Chapel Hill

Nelson Lichtenstein
The Catholic University of America

Allan J. Lichtman
The American University

Francis Lippmann Loewenheim
Rice University

Robert William Love, Jr.
United States Naval Academy

Richard Lowitt
Iowa State University

Donald R. McCoy
The University of Kansas

Charles G. MacDonald
Florida International University

Michael J. McDonald
The University of Tennessee, Knoxville

Richard D. McKinzie
University of Missouri—Kansas City

Robert J. McMahon
University of Florida

Dean L. May
The University of Utah

Robert L. Messer
University of Illinois at Chicago Circle

Nathan Miller
Chevy Chase, Md.

Malcolm Muir, Jr.
Austin Peay State University

John Muldowny
The University of Tennessee, Knoxville

Craig Murphy
Wellesley College

Paul L. Murphy
University of Minnesota

Mark D. Naison
Fordham University

Gerald D. Nash
The University of New Mexico

Monica L. Niznik
Dubuque, Iowa

Charles E. Neu
Brown University

Arnold A. Offner
Boston University

James S. Olson
Sam Houston State University

Kenneth O'Reilly
University of Alaska, Anchorage

Michael A. Palmer
United States Naval Historical Center

Herbert S. Parmet
Graduate School and University Center of the City
    University of New York

Michael E. Parrish
University of California, San Diego

Forrest C. Pogue
The Dwight D. Eisenhower Institute for Historical
    Research

David L. Porter
William Penn College

E. B. Potter
United States Naval Academy

Alfred B. Rollins, Jr.
Old Dominion University

Elliot A. Rosen
Rutgers University

Paul B. Ryan
Hoover Institution on War, Revolution and Peace

John Salmond
La Trobe University

James E. Sargent
Virginia Western Community College

Michael Schaller
The University of Arizona

Lois Scharf
Case Western Reserve University

Charles Schilke
Cambridge, Mass.

Robert D. Schulzinger
University of Colorado, Boulder

Jordan A. Schwarz
Northern Illinois University

Martin J. Sherwin
Tufts University

Harvard Sitkoff
University of New Hampshire

Richard Norton Smith
Washington, D.C.

Thomas G. Smith
Nichols College

Susan Smulyan
Smithsonian Institution

Paul Soifer
PHR Associates

Thomas T. Spencer
University of Notre Dame

Bernard Sternsher
Bowling Green State University

Mark A. Stoler
The University of Vermont

Roy Talbert, Jr.
University of South Carolina

George B. Tindall
The University of North Carolina at Chapel Hill

Christopher L. Tomlins
La Trobe University

Melvin I. Urofsky
Virginia Commonwealth University

John C. Walter
Smith College

Geoffrey C. Ward
New York, N.Y.

Susan Ware
Harvard University

Philip W. Warken
United States Naval Academy

Robert F. Wesser
State University of New York at Albany

Graham J. White
University of Sydney

John Edward Wilz
Indiana University

George Wolfskill
The University of Texas at Arlington

TABLES
AND CHARTS

INTRODUCTION

The hundredth anniversary of Franklin D. Roosevelt's birth was 31 January 1982. His centennial year was marked by many events—tributes on the floor of Congress on 31 January, a splendid Smithsonian exhibit on his life and presidency, the publication of several commemorative books, and a White House luncheon hosted by President Ronald Reagan. Interest in FDR and his New Deal seemed to be increasing, not solely because of his centennial.

The long political ascendancy of the New Deal coalition and policy ideas had appeared to be at an end with the 1980 election of the candidate of antigovernmental rhetoric, Ronald Reagan. Much earlier, observers of American politics had remarked that the older New Deal solutions could no longer serve an America in vastly different circumstances. But if the New Deal was increasingly questioned as a model for an America entering her third century, Roosevelt's personal leadership looked better and better as time passed. Five presidents in a row (Kennedy, Johnson, Nixon, Ford, Carter) had failed to complete two terms, let alone establish a clear direction that could shape national policy. To the experience of young people in the 1940s who had known only one president, writer Theodore Sorenson in a book published in 1984 contrasted that of his eight-year-old daughter, who had lived during four presidencies! The national mind turned again to Franklin Roosevelt for an understanding of presidential leadership in times of confusion and crisis.

This was a time to make the Roosevelt record and personality more available to the public— hence this encyclopedia, modeled on Mark E. Neely, Jr.'s acclaimed *Abraham Lincoln Encyclopedia,* also available in a Da Capo paperback edition. The Lincoln volume had been written by one person with a masterly command of Lincoln scholarship. But Franklin Roosevelt's presidency spanned more than twelve years, engaged both domestic and international crises, and administered a federal government vastly larger than Lincoln was fated to manage. It was decided to make *Franklin D. Roosevelt, His Life and Times: An Encyclopedic View* an invitational volume, with representation from the international community of scholars dedicated to the study of American history and government in the twentieth century. Two editors came together for the assignment of compiling this book: Otis L. Graham, Jr., a scholar who has written on modern reform movements, the New Deal, and Franklin Roosevelt, and is now Professor of History at the University of California at Santa Barbara, and Meghan Robinson Wander, senior editor at a Boston publishing house.

The editors have found the compilation of this encyclopedia a voyage of discovery. Perspectives on Roosevelt, his times, and his associates have changed and will continue to do so. It is now half a century after the New Deal began, forty years since Roosevelt died. An FDR encyclopedia twenty years earlier, or twenty years from now, would tell the same story in different ways. Time and new evidence bring fresh ideas and insights. More perhaps than any other modern president, Franklin Roosevelt was elusive, never adequately encompassed by any single interpretation. We invite the reader to a rich feast of scholarship in history and biography, compiled by a diverse group of writers including the leading Roosevelt and New Deal scholars along with younger historians, writers, archivists, and journalists. The book spans Roosevelt's life and more—his lineage, youth, and education, his early political career, the polio attack, his relief and recovery programs and reform policies during the Great Depression, his role as a world leader during World War II, and his subsequent reputation. Dozens of entries sketch the careers and personalities of the people who influenced him and those who worked for him or against him. Other entries recount the major events and currents of thought that dominated his lifetime. Photographs, posters, cartoons, and other visual displays will jog the memory of older readers and perhaps bring the times alive for younger ones.

We hope that the many images, impressions, and assessments in *Franklin D. Roosevelt, His Life and Times: An Encyclopedic View* present a striking portrait of the times, career, and personality of "the Democratic Roosevelt"—the chief executive whom the Murray-Blessing survey of historians in 1982 moved upward in the ranking of U.S. presidents to second place, just behind the Great Emancipator, Lincoln himself.

President of the United States longer than any other chief executive, leader of this country through both the Great Depression and World War II, Franklin D. Roosevelt is linked with many hundreds of important political concepts, events, and public personalities of the twentieth century. In this encyclopedia we have selected 321 topics for discussion: ideologies and issues, legislation, federal agencies, political parties, interest groups, aspects of Franklin D. Roosevelt's personal life, and people of importance to him— dozens of major appointees, heads of politically active organizations, heads of state, military officers, family members, critics, and friends. The people singled out for biographical sketches were chosen not necessarily for their enduring historical importance, but because a glimpse or longer look at their relationship to FDR reveals an interesting facet of Roosevelt himself. Written about many different individuals by many different individuals, the biographical articles share a common aim: to describe briefly each profiled person's life and accomplishments before and after that person's own "Roosevelt years" while particularly illuminating the person's interaction with Franklin D. Roosevelt. The biographical sketches collectively, then, create a vivid, diffracted image of Roosevelt himself. Similarly a connection with FDR is implicit in the other topics selected for inclusion in this encyclopedia. The articles on political philosophies, events, institutions, organizations, and legislation all describe the entity in and of itself but focus on it in relation to FDR.

Our aim is to create for the reader a sense of Roosevelt's era, his political thought, and the problems that faced him as both a national and an international leader. In discussing the concepts of the period, we have in several instances chosen to use the language of that day—Negroes and Indians were the terms known to Franklin D. Roosevelt, blacks and Native-Americans were not; what today we call the defense industry was not then a vast military-industrial complex and we have placed discussion of the production of a materiél under war mobilization, a heading congruent with the perception of arms manufacture at that time.

Because Roosevelt was a very actively involved commander in chief, we have tried to draw in a number of military officers with whom he had a relationship of some substance or to whose strategic thinking he gave some attention. Individuals whose abilities Roosevelt noticed and to whom he gave benefit of his own sponsorship—his cabinet officers, the justices he appointed to the Supreme Court, and the administrators he placed at the head of his New Deal relief or reform agencies—receive separate articles; however, all important federal agencies of the era do not. The Reconstruction Finance Corporation, for example, was active and undeniably important in the 1930s, but it was not actually established under Roosevelt, so discussion of the RFC can be found under Jesse Jones, the man FDR chose to be its head. The House Committee to Investigate Un-American Activities figured much more prominently in American political life several years after Roosevelt's death, but it was founded during his administration and was a decisive factor in the fate of the WPA. In certain areas, the swiftly changing sequence of agencies or boards and their shifting purviews presented a particular challenge: to identify for the reader the essential issues and focus on some major agents or agencies of change without becoming bogged down in a swamp of administrative complexity. We attacked this problem in several ways: various farm agencies or organizations are discussed in the overview article on agriculture; a list accompanying the war mobilization essay brings order to the multitude of war agencies and boards.

In a select few instances we have encouraged an omnibus article, relatively long in the context of this book, to give shape to complex topics by an overview rather than by a series of separate discussions. The two most prominent examples are the overview of the elections in which Roosevelt was a candidate for president and the overview of Roosevelt's public reputation as perceived, analyzed, and further developed by biographers, political scientists, and historians.

So that Roosevelt the private person with his likes and personal interests may appear, we have invited essays on his reading and religion, his hobbies, his homes, his family, and his inner circle of friends, advisers, and aides. So that Roosevelt the object of public affection and honor may appear, we include description of Roosevelt stamps, portraits, memorials, and awards. To recapture as best we can his charm and charisma, we have urged the authors of the many essays to quote him often, and we have included a wealth of illustration. The illustrations present Franklin D. Roosevelt at all stages of his life, from a baby on his father's shoulder to president of the United States, photographed just days before his death receiving delegates to the not-far-distant founding conference of the United Nations Organization.

Not every biographical sketch in the book is accompanied by an illustration; some personalities not shown in a separate photograph appear elsewhere and may be traced through the index to a group photograph. The cartoons we selected do not inevitably express the point of view of the essay they accompany; in some instances we took the opportunity to show some of the controversy surrounding certain topics and to add, we hope, creative tension to the overall effect of the book. The stills from Federal Theatre Project plays scattered throughout the book are intended to serve a dual purpose: to show the variety and inventiveness of the Federal Theatre productions in that brief era of substantial government support for the arts, and to show that points of view on social and political issues such as regulation or housing and resettlement were effectively communicated to average citizens across the nation via a dramatic entertainment medium.

The bibliographic notes following the arti-cles cite important works for further reading. We encouraged the authors to be frankly evaluative in their comments on published literature, and to mention archival and unpublished material they consider significant.

A number of scholars, graduate students, archivists, and librarians gave generously of their time and knowledge to make this volume possible.

William R. Emerson, director of the Franklin D. Roosevelt Library, advised us on topics relating to military leaders and to President Roosevelt's personal life. He also mobilized the library and museum staff to contribute their expertise to the encyclopedia. The book's blend of illustrations was initially inspired by the impressive display assembled by Marguerite Hubbard at the Franklin D. Roosevelt Museum adjacent to the Roosevelt Library. Special thanks are due to Paul McLaughlin who knowledgeably guided our search through the archives' several thousand photographs to find many of the images reproduced here.

Alan Brinkley and Patricia R. Hill of Harvard University extended our invitation to write short pieces for the book to several graduate students in the history or American civilization programs there: Günther Bischof, Marc J. Dolan, William Jongeward, Peter C. Mancall, Gregory A. Mark, Charles F. McGovern, Aviel Roshwald, Miles David Samson, Charles N. Schilke, Thomas A. Schwartz, and Robert A. Wampler each contributed a set of essays to the project. Timothy Lehman at the University of North Carolina at Chapel Hill wrote many of the brief articles on domestic issues, events, and personalities. Sarah Wilkerson-Freeman and Lynn Haessly, also at University of North Carolina at Chapel Hill, efficiently researched and edited certain material.

Anne L. Rubino of the Special Collections Department at Hofstra University Library contributed the articles on FDR's hobbies; Lorraine Brown of the Institute on The Federal Theatre Project and New Deal Culture at George Mason University selected materials from that archive and composed accompanying captions to illustrate the social and political concerns of the era as dramatized in Federal Theatre productions.

Public History Research Associates of Santa Barbara, California, prepared an essential reference component of the book—the tables and charts identifying persons, organizations, events, and issues and, where pertinent, dates of significance in Franklin D. Roosevelt's personal and political career. The PHR group—Shelley Bookspan, Rebecca Conard, Gregory King, and Paul Soifer—also brought their training and good judgment as historians to the generation of a number of articles and the preparation of the cross references.

Several individuals shared their comments and ideas for articles in the early stages of the book's development. Thomas Spencer of the University of Notre Dame prepared preliminary article groupings. Nancy Cridland, history subject specialist at the Indiana University Library, and Sarah Fusfield, a former senior editor of the Academic American Encyclopedia, suggested additional topics and areas to emphasize.

Our greatest thanks are due to Robert A. Rosenbaum, who sponsored Mark E. Neely, Jr.,'s *Abraham Lincoln Encyclopedia*, the prototype of this book. To those named above, to the skillful and patient in-house editors and designers who prepared the manuscript for publication, and to the dozens of contributors who wrote for *Franklin D. Roosevelt, His Life and Times: An Encyclopedic View*, the editors extend their heartfelt thanks.

OTIS L. GRAHAM, JR.
Santa Barbara, California

MEGHAN ROBINSON WANDER
Boston, Massachusetts

CHRONOLOGY OF FDR'S CAREER

1882 Born at Hyde Park, New York, 30 January

1896 Entered Groton

1900 Entered Harvard University

1903 Harvard, A. B., 24 June

1904 Elected permanent chairman of class of 1904, Harvard

1904 Entered Columbia Law School

1905 Married Anna Eleanor Roosevelt, 17 March

1905 Toured Europe on honeymoon trip

1907 Admitted to New York bar

1907 Employed as junior clerk in law firm of Carter, Ledyard, and Milburn, New York City

1909 Member, Hudson-Fulton Celebration Commission

1910 Elected to New York State Senate, opposed by John F. Schlosser, with 52 percent of the vote, 8 November

1911 Degree of Master Mason conferred by Holland Lodge No. 8, New York City, 28 November

1912 Reelected to New York State Senate, opposed by George A. Vossler, with 62 percent of the vote, 5 November

1913 Member, Plattsburg, New York, Centennial

1913 Appointed assistant secretary of the navy, April

1914 Defeated in Democratic primary for the U.S. Senate by James W. Gerard

1915 Member, National Commission, Panama-Pacific Exposition

1918 Overseer of Harvard University through 1924

1918 Toured European naval bases, July–September

1919 Traveled to Europe to supervise dismantling of naval establishment, January–February

1920 Nominated for vice-president on ticket with James N. Cox at Democratic National Convention in San Francisco, 6 July

1920 Resigned as assistant secretary of the navy, 6 August

1920 Returned to law practice in firm of Emmet, Marvin, and Roosevelt

1920 Defeated in election for vice-president by Warren G. Harding and Calvin Coolidge, 2 November

1921 Vice-president in New York City for the Fidelity and Deposit Company of Maryland

1921 Stricken with poliomyelitis at Campobello, New Brunswick, Canada, August

1924 Formed new law practice, Roosevelt and O'Connor, resigned 1933

1924 Placed in nomination at Democratic National Convention New York governor Alfred E. Smith

1924 Managed Smith's presidential campaign, unsuccessfully

1926 *Whither Bound,* FDR's first book, published

1927 Founded the Georgia Warm Springs Foundation, therapy center for the treatment of polio victims

1928 *The Happy Warrior, Alfred E. Smith* published

1928 Again placed in nomination at Democratic National Convention Governor Alfred E. Smith

1928 Elected governor of New York, opposed by Albert Ottinger, by 50.3 percent of the vote, 6 November

1930 Reelected governor, opposed by Charles H. Tuttle, by 63 percent of the vote, 4 November

1932 *Government—Not Politics* published

1932 Elected president, major opponent Herbert Hoover, by 57.4 percent of the vote, 8 November

1933 *Looking Forward* published

1933 Shot at in assassination attempt in Miami, Florida, by Giuseppe Zangara, 15 February

1933 Inaugurated as 32nd president, 4 March

1934 *On Our Way* published

1936 Reelected president, major opponent Alfred M. Landon, by 60.8 percent of the vote, 3 November

1940 Reelected president, major opponent Wendell L. Willkie, by 54.8 percent of the vote, 5 November

1944 Reelected president, major opponent Thomas E. Dewey, by 53.5 percent of the vote, 7 November

1945 Died, Warm Springs, Georgia, 12 April; buried Hyde Park, New York, 15 April

A

Agricultural Adjustment Administration

The main agency of the New Deal for agriculture, the Agricultural Adjustment Administration (Triple-A) came out of a decade of agitation for action by the federal government to raise farm prices and restore profit to the farm business. Agitation began soon after the sharp break in farm prices in 1920. The problem resulted from the increase in farm production during World War I and the continued loss of markets, especially in Europe, after the war. A farm implements manufacturer, George N. Peek, devised a solution that gained great support from farmers, their organizations, and their congressional representatives. It proposed that the protective tariff should reserve the American market for American farmers and a government corporation should "dump" the surplus commodities on foreign markets. Congress enacted the proposal in the McNary-Haugen bills, but President Coolidge used the veto to defeat them.

Alternative proposals included recommendations that farmers free themselves from the price-depressing surpluses by cutting back on production. One advocate, Herbert Hoover, insisted that the federal government should merely advise farmers on the cuts they should make, but a group of social scientists, most notably M. L. Wilson of Montana State College, maintained that the government must go further and offer payments to farmers to take some of their acres out of production. To obtain the funds required to make such payments, Washington should tax the processors of farm products. In the 1932 campaign, Franklin Roosevelt came close to an explicit endorsement of Wilson's Voluntary Domestic Allotment Plan, and after victory, the president-elect chose an advocate of the plan, Henry A. Wallace, as secretary of agriculture.

Before the end of 1933, the plan, administered by the new Agricultural Adjustment Administration, had become the major New Deal farm policy. During Roosevelt's first hundred days, Congress authorized

Ding Darling, *New York Tribune, 2 August 1933.*
(© I.H.T. Corporation. Reprinted by permission.)

experimentation with the plan by passing the Agricultural Adjustment Act, but the legislation authorized experimentation with Peek's ideas as well, and Peek, a hero of the battle for "equality for agriculture," became the first administrator of Triple-A. It was a part of the Department of Agriculture, and Peek clashed with his superior officer, Wallace, over policy and authority. Finally, in December, FDR moved Peek to another position. He was replaced by Chester Davis, who emphasized acreage reduction as the solution to the price problems of the producers of the so-called basic agricultural commodities: wheat, corn, hogs, cotton, tobacco, rice, and milk.

Although farmers had traditionally thought of ways of expanding output and felt somewhat uncomfortable in cutting back, they did like the results. Defenders of production control, like Wallace, tried to reassure farmers and answer critics by pointing out that farmers were merely being advised to manage production as industrial corporations did in their quest for profits. For farmers, however, the most persuasive arguments were the higher prices and the government checks they received for reducing their acres devoted to crops and livestock.

Triple-A did have critics. Some charged that it was not promoting good land-use practices; others protested against the impact on the rural poor. The leader of the Socialist party, Norman Thomas, the Southern Tenant Farmers' Union, and others argued that landlords often refused to give their tenants shares of the government checks, demoted sharecroppers to day laborers so as to free themselves from any obligation to share the benefits from Washington, and cut back on the number of sharecroppers as they cut back on their cotton acreage. Hoping to use the farm program to make life more secure for sharecroppers, the Legal Division of Triple-A, headed by Jerome Frank, ruled that landowners participating in the cotton program must keep on their lands the same tenants who had resided there in 1933. The ruling infuriated Davis, who feared it would alienate planters, farm leaders, and their allies in Congress. Wallace believed he must back up his top lieutenant. Davis "purged" Frank and others, and Wallace ruled that the cotton contract merely obligated planters to keep the same number of tenants.

Another challenge to the farm program came from the processors and distributors of farm crops, but Triple-A officials had prepared themselves for it. These business people did not like the reductions in production for they had developed facilities for the handling of large volumes of commodities, and the processors also disliked the new tax that had been imposed on them. They challenged the farm law in the courts, and the U.S. Supreme Court ruled early in 1936 that the federal government did not have the authority to regulate agricultural production or to tax one group for the benefit of another. Triple-A's Program Planning Division, headed by an economist, Howard Tolley, had been seeking ways of converting Triple-A into a promoter of better land-use practices and now, in the crisis created by the Court, brought forward a plan that Congress quickly translated into the Soil Conservation and Domestic Allotment Act. It paid farmers to cut back on the production of soil-depleting crops, such as wheat and cotton, and to increase the production of soil-building crops, such as grasses and legumes. The plan seemed capable of both conserving the soil and controlling production. Tolley now took Davis's place as administrator of Triple-A.

In 1938, Congress strengthened Triple-A by passing a new Agricultural Adjustment Act. The new legislation limited the volume of farm goods that could be marketed, established the Ever-Normal Granary plan for the storage of crops, and added a program of crop insurance for wheat.

The changes from 1936 to 1938, although they also included provisions designed to give some protection to tenants, did not end criticism of Triple-A. It brought obvious benefits to farmers who produced for the market, most of whom had suffered from the low prices of the 1920s and early 1930s. But critics pointed out that farmers with the largest farms received very large payments from government, and such critics were not satisfied by the response that the production control program could not accomplish its objectives if those farmers did not participate. Sharecroppers continued to suffer. In fact, cotton planters increasingly used their government checks to buy tractors and mechanical cotton pickers that permitted them to get along with fewer croppers. After the Bureau of Agricultural Economics became the central planner for the Department of Agriculture in 1938 and Tolley became its chief, the planning agency encouraged Triple-A to do more on behalf of soil conservation and the rural poor. But the agency, now under the leadership of Rudolph "Spike" Evans, maintained its emphasis on making the farm business more profitable and was suffused with a sense of accomplishment, although farm prices, while well above 1932–33, were below desired levels.

The Second World War created a demand for the crops in the Ever-Normal Granary and altered Triple-A's mission. The agency did not lose its interest in profitable farming, but it did move away from production restraints. Production control had proven difficult, for ways of increasing output per acre were available and farmers made use of them. But now the agency's emphasis shifted to maximum production so as to meet the wartime demands for food and fiber. And, though officials had to overcome fears of glutting the market, they succeeded with their task of expanding production to the levels the new situation required.

For background information on Triple-A, consult Gilbert C. Fite, *George N. Peek and the Fight for Farm Parity* (Norman: University of Oklahoma Press, 1954), and William D. Rowley, *M. L. Wilson and the Campaign for the Domestic Allotment Plan* (Lincoln: University of Nebraska Press, 1970). Historians have focused much of their attention on the Triple-A's shortcomings. See, for example, David E. Conrad, *The Forgotten Farmers: The Story of the Sharecroppers in the New Deal* (Urbana: University of Illinois Press, 1965). For more positive accounts, consult Van Perkins, *Crisis in Agriculture: The Agricultural Adjustment Administration and the New Deal. 1933* (Berkeley: University of California Press, 1969); Roy V. Scott and J. G. Shoalmire, *The Public Career of Cully A. Cobb: A Study in Agricultural Leadership* (Jackson: University and College Press of Mississippi, 1973); and Anthony J. Badger, *Prosperity Road; The New Deal, Tobacco, and North Carolina* (Chapel Hill: University of North Carolina Press, 1980). On the war period, see Dean Albertson, *Roosevelt's Farmer: Claude R. Wickard and the New Deal* (New York: Columbia University Press, 1961).

RICHARD S. KIRKENDALL

See also Agriculture; Peek, George Nelson; Tugwell, Rexford Guy; Wallace, Henry A.; Wickard, Claude Raymond

Agriculture

Depression gripped American farm people when Franklin D. Roosevelt came to power in 1933, but his New Deal brought relief and change. Then, although World War II promoted boom conditions on the nation's farms, it also drained away a large part of the rural population.

Agriculture's depression had begun in 1920. Farm prices fell sharply that year, dropping farm income from nearly $17 billion in 1919 to less than $9 billion in 1921. Throughout the 1920s it never reached $12 billion, and in 1929 the purchasing power of farm crops was only 91 percent of the pre–World War I level. Then, the Great Depression hit farmers hard, dropping their income 60 percent, to $5 billion, while national income fell about 40 percent.

As conditions worsened, loud and at times violent protests erupted in rural America, but on election day in 1932, farmers rejected appeals from the Left and voted for the candidates of the center. The voting behavior of mid-western farmers was especially significant, for most of them had voted Republican in the past, but now they gave most of their votes to Roosevelt, hoping his promised New Deal would bring higher prices for their products.

With roots in the land, Franklin Roosevelt embraced Jeffersonian notions about the importance of agriculture. He had grown up and had his home on an attractive estate in the rich Hudson River farm country, and he liked to present himself as a farmer, although a tenant worked his land. He believed strongly in the value of farming as a way of life, as something more than just one of the ways to make money, and he assumed that farmers still possessed economic and political power, as well as being important for other reasons. In his view, an increase in farm purchasing power seemed to be the most effective way of promoting general economic recovery, just as the capture of the farm vote appeared to be a key to victory at the polls.

In power, Roosevelt sought to save and change agriculture. In May 1933, he obtained passage of the Agricultural Adjustment Act, which empowered the Department of Agriculture to press farmers to cut back on their production and employ other means to raise farm prices. The law also empowered the president to experiment with monetary policy as a means of raising prices, and a supplementary Farm Credit Act sought to protect farmers against foreclosures on their property. Farm protest erupted again in the fall of 1933 for relief had come more slowly than farmers expected. The administration responded with crop loans and storage administered by a new Commodity Credit Corporation, the distribution of some surplus commodites to the unemployed, and moderate monetary inflation. As benefits began to reach the farm and prospects brightened, they sapped the strength of the protest movement. Few farmers had revolutionary aspirations; they had protested in hopes of improvements in the farm business. The New Deal made improvements and thereby robbed the radicals of support. By 1934, farm prices and farm income were rising, and farmers were receiving checks from Washington for their participation in the production control program.

Although production control had become the central feature of the New Deal for agriculture, it was not the whole program. The Farm Credit Administration, established in 1933, greatly enlarged the volume of credit available to farmers and their cooperatives. The Tennessee Valley Administration, also established in 1933 to reconstruct a region, supplied farmers with electricity, fertilizer, and better health services, conserved soil, and withdrew poor lands from agricultural production. Other agencies, above all the State Department, worked to regain foreign markets for American farm products; still others brought relief to rural victims of depression and drought and planted shelterbelts on the Great Plains. A great success, the Rural Electrification Administration, brought into existence in 1935, made loans at low cost to nonprofit electrical cooperatives established by farmers and promoted an increase in the number of farms enjoying the many benefits of electricity from 750,000 of the 6.5 million in 1935 to 2.3 million in 1941. The Soil Conservation Service, also formed in 1935, em-

Addressed to "Mr. Franklin D. Roosevelt, Washington, D.C.," this photo postcard from a Kansas constituent de- scribed the brutally sudden onset of a 1935 dust storm. *(Courtesy FDR Library.)*

The test field of a practical operating farm, showing the dramatic improvement the use of fertilizer—in this case, TVA-produced phosphate—could make in agricultural productivity. *(Courtesy FDR Library.)*

barked upon a campaign to change the ways farmers used the land. And after the U.S. Supreme Court declared the production control program unconstitutional, Congress passed a new law in 1936 establishing a program that seemed capable of both conserving soil and controlling production without running into trouble with the Court.

In yet another move in 1935, Roosevelt established a Resettlement Administration (RA), using relief funds. Resettlement tried to improve land-use practices and help those who suffered seriously from past mistakes in the use of the land, such as destitute groups living in once-thriving but now exhausted lumbering, mining, and oil regions, sharecroppers in the South, and farmers on poor land in the drought areas and the Appalachians. In addition to efforts to rehabilitate poor rural people in the places in which they lived, the agency purchased some poor or submarginal land and resettled its occupants on better land or in new suburban communities developed by RA. It also constructed camps for migratory workers. Widespread criticism, small appropriations, and the political weakness of its clients, however, hampered RA's work.

By election day 1936, farmers were better off than they had been four years earlier, and most of them, in spite of a substantial Republican campaign, rewarded Roosevelt with their votes. In Iowa, for example, more than 60 percent of the farmers voted for him, whereas Democratic presidential candidates in the 1920s had averaged less than 30 percent. Obviously the benefits of New Deal farm programs were very persuasive.

The following year, Congress passed a Farm Security Act and the secretary of agriculture established a Farm Security Administration (FSA), substituting it for RA. The FSA embarked upon a significant series of farm programs. Over 3.5 million of the 6.5 million farms were smaller than one hundred acres, and farms of that size in most types of agriculture were too small to support a family. Also, many of the

small farmers did not own the land they worked. Under the influence of the agrarian tradition, FSA tried to improve the lot of the rural poor in various ways so as to keep them on the land. It made loans to tenants to enable them to become farm owners and to small farmers to help them enlarge and improve their farms so that they could support families. Some New Dealers and others preferred the migration of large numbers of rural people to the cities, but many recognized that there were no job openings there in the 1930s. FSA challenged the status quo and put pressure on others to match its efforts, but it clashed with other agencies that worked chiefly to serve the most substantial farmers. Its concrete accomplishments were small, in part because Congress, influenced by opposition to spending money on the rural poor, gave the agency only small sums.

In 1938, Congress strengthened the Department of Agriculture's price-raising efforts with new legislation. It authorized experimentation with Wallace's idea for an Ever-Normal Granary as well as a new scheme to cut back on the sales of farm products and a system of crop insurance. Under the Ever-Normal Granary plan, crops were stored to reassure consumers that they would have enought to eat and to guarantee farmers adequate prices. A short time later, New Dealers launched a food-stamp program to make more food available to the urban poor.

The secretary of agriculture, Henry A. Wallace, now sought to bring the several farm programs together in a coordinated attack upon the nation's varied farm problems. He elevated the department's Bureau of Agricultural Economics (BAE) to the role of central planner, and it embarked upon an ambitious attempt in 1939 and 1940 to construct a planning system involving cooperation among the national agricultural agencies, the agricultural colleges and their extension services, and the farmers. The leaders in the BAE and their allies hoped to change both farm policies and the ways in which they were made.

The activities of the BAE and the FSA alienated

the most influential farm organization, the American Farm Bureau Federation. It had provided strong support for the major New Deal farm programs, but now its leaders concluded that the Roosevelt administration had fallen under the spell of urban liberalism, that it was biased against the farmer, and that Wallace and his department were drawing away from the Farm Bureau and rejecting the view that their job was to serve the interests of commercial farmers. The officials seemed, to the Farm Bureau, too interested in the rural poor and the urban consumers. Furthermore, the department's tendency to develop committees of farmers to plan and administer farm programs seemed capable of creating groups that would replace the farm organization in the policymaking process, thereby depriving the Farm Bureau of its status as the leading representative of the farmer and providing department officials with the power to dominate farm politics and alter the orientation of farm policy. Thus, the organization, which had grown greatly during the New Deal years, embarked on a campaign to check the trends it feared and to expand its power.

The Farm Bureau, which had its strength in the Middle West and the South, apparently expressed sentiments that many farmers now felt. More than in 1932 and 1936, Roosevelt depended on city voters for his victory in the 1940 election. Most farmers in the Middle West returned to the Republican party.

The New Deal had promoted change in American agriculture. Above all, it made the federal government much more important in the lives of American farmers. The enlarged federal government made some attempts to lift out of poverty the rural people who had lived below the poverty line before the depression hit; but it emphasized helping those who had been impoverished or at least severely hurt by the depression, and it achieved considerable success in restoring the incomes of those farmers.

In the conditions brought on by World War II, some features of the New Deal for agriculture withered. The Farm Bureau pressed its campaigns against the FSA and the BAE, and Congress killed the BAE's program of state and local planning and slashed appropriations for the FSA.

The federal government, however, continued throughout the Roosevelt years to play large roles in the lives of the nation's commercial farmers. After years of encouraging them to cut back on production, Washington now employed subsidies, draft exemptions, and appeals to patriotism to persuade them to increase production, and it became a massive purchaser of farm products so as to serve needs of the American armed forces and those of the nation's allies.

The war exerted a powerful influence on agriculture and rural life. Millions of people, including many sharecroppers and farm laborers, moved off of farms to enter the armed forces or take jobs in the rapidly developing war plants and shipyards. For many of these people, wartime opportunities accomplished what the New Deal had been unable to do: the new jobs moved previously poorly employed people above the poverty line, doing so chiefly by moving them out of agriculture. Migration dropped the farm population, which had been over 30 million in 1940, by 17 percent, but the remaining farmers expanded agricultural production more than 3 percent each year by increasing their use of tractors and fertilizer and enlarging their farms. Many people who remained on the farms achieved prosperity for the first time since World War I as farm prices rose above parity and farm income soared more than 400 percent. Farmers were able to enjoy spending sprees, to pay debts, and to put money in the bank.

Despite their newfound prosperity, farmers continued to move away from Roosevelt. Winning the closest presidential election since 1916, FDR in 1944 depended even more on the urban vote than he had before. He would have lost if he had not received unusually strong support from blue-collar workers, for the Democratic vote outside the big cities, which had been dropping for several years, especially in the rural Middle West and Far West, dropped still more. In the farm belts, only the southern farmers, influenced by party tradition as well as farm policy, gave FDR the support that farmers in most places had given him in the 1930s.

The New Deal for agriculture has inspired a rich historical literature. For a discussion of one portion, see Richard S. Kirkendall, "The New Deal for Agriculture: Recent Writings, 1971–1976," in *Farmers, Bureaucrats, and Middlemen: Historical Perspectives on American Agriculture,* ed. Trudy Huskamp Peterson (Washington: Howard University Press, 1980). In *Social Scientists and Farm Politics in the Age of Roosevelt* (Ames: Iowa State University Press, 1982), first published in 1966, Kirkendall supplied a survey of the subject from the vantage point of one group of significant participants. Donald H. Grubbs in *Cry from the Cotton: The Southern Tenant Farmers' Union and the New Deal* (Chapel Hill: University of North Carolina Press, 1971) illustrates a trend in historical writing, which emerged in the 1960s, that presented the treatment of the rural poor as a key to the meaning of the New Deal, and emphasized the New Deal's shortcomings. Theodore Saloutos responded to this New Left revisionism in *The American Farmer and the New Deal* (Ames: Iowa State University Press, 1982), the most substantial survey of its subject. Historians have not devoted nearly as much attention to the agricultural history of World War II. Gilbert C. Fite's *American Farmers: The New Minority* (Bloomington: Indiana University Press, 1981) provides a good place to begin for those eager to understand the great significance of the war in American agricultural history.

RICHARD S. KIRKENDALL

See also Agricultural Adjustment Administration; Peek, George Nelson; Tugwell, Rexford Guy; Wallace, Henry A.; Wickard, Claude Raymond

Alien Registration Act (1940)
See Civil Liberties in Wartime; Espionage

Alphabet Agencies
See New Deal

America First Committee

The America First Committee was the most powerful isolationist or noninterventionist mass pressure group in the United States battling against the foreign policies of the Roosevelt administration during the fifteen months from September 1940 until the Japanese attack on 7 December, 1941.

America First grew out of an earlier student organization at Yale University led by R. Douglas Stuart, Jr., a twenty-four-year-old law student and son of the first vice-president of the Quaker Oats Company. During the summer of 1940, young Stuart won the support of prominent middle western business and political leaders. On 4 September 1940 the committee announced its formation, with its national headquarters in Chicago.

Gen. Robert E. Wood, chairman of the board of Sears, Roebuck and Company, served as national chairman of America First, and Stuart was national director. Wood, Stuart, and five others from the Middle West (mostly businessmen) formed the executive committee that shaped America First policies. A larger national committee included John T. Flynn, Hanford MacNider, William R. Castle, George N. Peek, Chester Bowles, Alice Roosevelt Longworth, Edward Rickenbacker, Kathleen Norris, Lillian Gish, and others. Among speakers at America First rallies were Democratic senator Burton K. Wheeler of Montana, Republican senator Gerald P. Nye of North Dakota, and Col. Charles A. Lindbergh. The committee financed its activities through voluntary contributions. Its national headquarters received some $370,000 from approximately 25,000 contributors.

In the fall of 1940, the committee placed advertisements in major newspapers and sponsored radio broadcasts. By November it began to organize local chapters. At its peak it had approximately 450 chapters with a total national membership of around 850,000. It won its greatest strength in the Middle West and was least successful in the South.

America Firsters believed it was more important for the United States to stay out of the European war than to ensure a British victory over the Axis. They feared that Roosevelt's steps to aid Britain short of war would prove to be steps to war. America First vigorously opposed Lend-Lease, convoys, and repeal of the Neutrality Act in 1941. It was never able to defeat any administration aid-short-of-war proposal actually put to a vote in Congress. It tried unsuccessfully to lead the debate away from the aid-short-of-war issue, which the committee always lost, and shift it to the issue of whether the United States should or should not declare war on the Axis—an issue on which it had the support of nearly 80 percent of the American people. Like Americans generally, America First focused most of its attention on the European war rather than on the Pacific.

Most in America First were patriotic citizens; they were not pro-Nazi. But during 1941 the committee came under increasing attack on the grounds that it was a "Nazi transmission belt" serving Hitler's cause. Those charges seriously undermined the effectiveness of the organization. The foreign policy debate became increasingly heated and emotional—on both sides. With the Japanese attack on Pearl Harbor, the America First Committee ceased its noninterventionist activities, dismantled its organization, and pledged support to America's war against the Axis.

Though America First and its leaders were much criticized then and later, it functioned as a vehicle through which Americans could dissent from governmental policy. In that sense, it was an agency for the democratic process in foreign affairs.

The standard scholarly history on the subject, based on research in the America First Committee records and papers, is Wayne S. Cole, *America First: The Battle against Intervention, 1940–1941* (Madison: University of Wisconsin Press, 1953). On General Wood, see Justice D. Doenecke, "General Robert E. Wood: The Evolution of a Conservative," *Journal of the Illinois State Historical Society* 71 (August 1978):162–75. For scholarly accounts of other leaders and spokesmen for America First, see Michele Flynn Stenehjem, *An American First: John T. Flynn and the America First Committee* (New Rochelle: Arlington House, 1976); Wayne S. Cole, *Charles A. Lindbergh and the Battle against American Intervention in World War II* (New York: Harcourt Brace Jovanovich, 1974); and Wayne S. Cole, *Senator Gerald P. Nye and American Foreign Relations* (Minneapolis: University of Minnesota Press, 1962).

WAYNE S. COLE

See also Isolationism; Johnson, Hugh Samuel; LaFollette, Philip Fox; Lindbergh, Charles Augustus; Peek, George Nelson; Wheeler, Burton Kendall

American Communist Party (CPUSA)

See Communism; Labor; Liberalism and Progressivism

American Federation of Labor

See Green, William; Labor; Lewis, John Llewellyn

American Guide Series

See Federal Writers' Project

American Liberty League

A politically conservative research and opinion organization, primarily devoted to opposing the New Deal and FDR. Founded on 22 August 1934, the Liberty League's stated goals were "to defend and uphold the Constitution . . . to teach the duty of government to protect individual and group initiative and enterprise, to foster the right to work, earn, save and acquire property and to preserve the ownership and lawful use of property when acquired." In practice this meant that the Liberty League opposed and attacked nearly every New Deal measure and many New Deal officials through its hundreds of publications and in speeches and appearances of its spokesmen before Congress. From its founding through the election of 1936, the Liberty League was seen as the center of conservative opposition to FDR and his policies.

The league's principal spokesmen included prominent public officials and wealthy businessmen. The league's president, Jowett Shouse, was the former Democratic party Executive Committee chairman. John Jacob Raskob, instrumental in the founding of the league, was the former director of General Motors and chairman of the Democratic National Committee. Al Smith, FDR's predecessor as governor of New York and as Democratic presidential candidate, also was a leading Liberty Leaguer. The founding of the Liberty League thus meant at least a partial alienation of prominent Democrats from FDR, an estrangement that grew more pronounced and bitter with time. Prominent Republicans in the league included Nathan Miller, head of U.S. Steel, and Irénée Du Pont, whose family eventually provided 30 percent of the league's enormous financial resources.

Despite its initial claims of being nonpartisan and nonpolitical, the league from its inception was viewed by the administration and the public as an opponent of FDR, dedicated to denouncing New Deal policies, embarrassing the president, and restoring to business the freedom it had previously enjoyed from government regulation and public accountability. Shouse and Smith both had personal grudges against FDR stemming from the 1932 campaign, but most members of the league were genuinely appalled at New Deal departures from previous constitutional, administrative, and executive methods in combating the depression. Among the league's steady barrage of often contradictory criticisms were that the New Deal was fascistic, socialistic, and communistic; that FDR was a tyrannical dictator and, alternatively, that he was a weak-minded tool of his socialistic brains trusters; that the New Deal retarded recovery; that government spending threatened to cause inflation; that regulation was based upon false economic principles; that economic planning was dangerous; and that the New Deal was an enemy of private enterprise and its bedrock, the Constitution.

Although it spent more than a half million dollars on its promotional and educational campaigns and literature, the league never gained more than 125,000 members. Its chief liability in attracting popular support was that its leadership was composed of some of the wealthiest and most powerful businessmen in the United States: the Du Ponts, Alfred Sloane of General Motors, Edward F. Hutton of General Foods, and others. The league was instantly and permanently identified with great wealth, and both the press and FDR exploited the opposition of great millionaires to the New Deal. The league's campaign to unseat FDR and restore the rule of unfettered private enterprise climaxed at a 25 January 1936 league dinner in Washington. Al Smith, the politician identified with urban and working-class Democrats, accused the New Deal of class warfare and betraying the Democratic platform of 1932 as well as the Constitution. This speech gave the administration a devastating weapon against the Liberty League—selfish big business—which the press gleefully used during the campaign. The league's popularity rapidly declined from that point. Alfred M. Landon, Republican presidential candidate of 1936, called the league's endorsement of him "the kiss of death." After the overwhelming reelection of FDR, the league ceased its public activities, and by 1940 the organization had closed.

The story of the Liberty League has been told in great detail, but with critical restraint, by George Wolfskill.

See also Conservatism; Democratic Party; Republican Party; Smith, Alfred E.

American Socialist Party
See Thomas, Norman Mattoon

American Youth Congress
See Communism

Armed Forces
See Arnold, Henry Harley; Chennault, Claire Lee; Commander in Chief; Cooke, Charles Maynard, Jr.; Eisenhower, Dwight David; Halsey, William Frederick, Jr.; Holcomb, Thomas; Joint Chiefs of Staff; King, Ernest J.; Leahy, William Daniel; MacArthur, Douglas; Marshall, George Catlett; Nimitz, Chester William; Selective Service Act; Stark, Harold Raynsford; Stilwell, Joseph Warren; War Mobilization; Pearl Harbor; World War II

Henry H. Arnold. (Courtesy FDR Library.)

Arnold, Henry Harley ("Hap")
(25 June 1886–15 January 1950)
Chief/commanding general, U.S. Army Air Corps/U.S. Army Air Forces, 1938–46. General Henry ("Hap") Arnold was born in Gladwyne, Pennsylvania, the son of a physician. After graduating from West Point in 1907, he was taught to fly by the Wright brothers in Dayton in 1911.

In his autobiography, Arnold recalled that during World War I while serving in Washington as assistant chief of military aeronautics, he knew FDR "slightly." There is no evidence, however, of any contact between Arnold and FDR while Arnold served in a variety of peacetime assignments in the twenties and thirties. In the ill-fated airmail experiment of 1934 in which Arnold commanded the Western District, FDR was dissatisfied with the air corps performance. To gain favorable publicity and demonstrate the capability of the long-range bomber, a flight of the newest B-10 bombers flew from Washington, D.C., to Alaska and returned, commanded by Arnold. The feat and the attendant publicity earned him an audience with FDR.

Arnold was assigned to Washington in 1936 as a brigadier general, and in September 1938, FDR appointed him chief of the U.S. Army Air Corps. Major General Arnold's tenure coincided with FDR's thinking that the quickest, most dramatic, and possibly most effective means of achieving demonstrable military power was though aviation. At a White House meeting on 28 September 1938, FDR authorized an Air Corps of 7,500 combat planes, an action that Arnold called the corps' "Magna Carta." This was followed by FDR's call in November 1938 for U.S. production of 20,000 planes per year, a number revised to 60,000 for 1942 and 125,000 for 1943. As Arnold became in FDR's eyes the chief military official responsible for aircraft procurement and allocation, some friction developed. The issue was conflicting jurisdiction among the various agencies involved, particularly the role of the Treasury Department. Arnold, in a White House meeting in early 1939, felt that FDR was threatening him with assignment to Guam if he failed to play ball, and for the next nine months he was taboo at the White House. During this period, he balanced the official policy of furnishing American-built aircraft to Britain and France with the need to build the air corps to meet any potential threat. The proper allocation of planes to various American military claimants as well as to U.S. Allies resulted in frequent harmonious contact between FDR and Arnold from 1939 throughout the war.

Arnold was surprised and pleased at FDR's decision to include him as a member of the Joint Chiefs of Staff, commencing with the Argentia meeting of August 1941. He continued to participate throughout the war, attending all the overseas diplomatic conferences except that at Yalta, which was precluded by Arnold's fourth heart attack. As a measure of his increasing confidence in the general's abilities, FDR directed him to proceed from the Casablanca Conference in January 1943 to Chungking to meet with Chiang Kai-shek. Arnold's discussions there concerned not only the allocation of planes to China but also the amount of tonnage to be shipped over the Hump, the types of aircraft to be utilized in China, and the jurisdictional problems occasioned by Chiang's close relations with General Claire Chennault.

Arnold had early recognized Harry Hopkins's potential to influence FDR, and so the general met frequently with Hopkins to furnish data, recommendations, and ideas outside official channels. FDR relied heavily on Arnold in aviation matters other than the military such as planning and development for postwar world expansion of civil aviation.

Arnold showed keen sensitivity to FDR's feelings and so was permitted to utilize during the war the talents of Robert Wood, former Sears, Roebuck executive, and Charles Lindbergh, the famous aviator, both of whom were persona non grata to Roosevelt because of their prewar isolationist views. FDR's respect for Arnold's abilities was represented by the airman being promoted to five-star rank along with other military leaders.

Reminiscing about the death of FDR, Arnold wrote that President Roosevelt had been not only a "great personal friend" but "one of the best friends the Air Force ever had."

For more information on Arnold, see his autobiography, H. H. Arnold, *Global Mission* (New York: Harper & Bros., 1949).

JOHN W. HUSTON

See also Joint Chiefs of Staff

Arsenal of Democracy

See Fireside Chats; World War II

Assassination Attempt of 1933

Before becoming president, Franklin Roosevelt nearly lost his life to an assassin. On the evening of 15 February 1933, the president-elect, just back from a carefree yachting trip to the Bahamas, was touring before crowds in a park in central Miami. Sitting in the back of his open car, the tanned and ebullient Roosevelt made a short speech to the twenty thousand or so who pressed close to his motorcade. As he was chatting with Chicago mayor Anton J. Cermak, who had walked up to the side of the car, a short, curly-haired man jumped up on a park bench scarcely more than thirty-five feet from Roosevelt's car and fired five quick shots from his cheap revolver. As he fired, a nearby spectator, Mrs. Lillian Cross, shook his arm and perhaps saved Roosevelt's life. Mayor Cermak fell over with what proved to be fatal wounds and a bystander, Mrs. Joseph H. Gill, was wounded seriously. Roosevelt, still sitting upright in his car seat, was unharmed. Later he recalled of that moment, "I heard what I thought was a firecracker; then several more."

As his chauffeur started to pull away, Roosevelt countermanded the Secret Service orders and directed his driver to remain at the scene long enough to attend to Mayor Cermak. The wounded man was placed in Roosevelt's car, and all the way to the hospital Roosevelt talked to Cermak and monitored his pulse. Roosevelt remained at the hospital until after 11:00 and then returned to his yacht for the night. Raymond Moley, who was with him through the evening, reported, "Roosevelt was simply himself—easy, confident, poised, to all appearances unmoved." Seemingly unshaken by this brush with death, Roosevelt had a drink, talked with friends until 2:00 A.M., and slept soundly through the night. His calm under pressure created a note of hope for a nation awaiting the new president's solution for the depression.

The would-be assassin was Joseph Zangara, a

thirty-three-year-old Italian immigrant. Some feared that his act might be part of a left-wing plot, but Zangara assured his interrogators tht he had acted alone. "I want to make it clear," he testified, "I do not hate Mr. Roosevelt personally. I hate all presidents, no matter from which country they come, and I hate all officials and everybody who is rich." Zangara, who complained of a constant pain in his stomach that may have been cancer, was later executed for having killed Mayor Cermak.

Frank Freidel devotes a chapter to this event in his *Franklin D. Roosevelt: Launching the New Deal* (Boston: Little, Brown & Co., 1973).

See also Interregnum

Assistant Secretary of the Navy
(1913–1920)

One of the most unlikely choices by President Woodrow Wilson for his cabinet in 1913 was his selection of a North Carolina newspaperman, Josephus Daniels, to be his secretary of the navy. Editor of the staunchly Democratic and pro-Wilson *Raleigh News and Observer,* Daniels knew nothing of the sea or ships. As an experienced politician, however, he believed it would be wise to select for his assistant secretary a younger man from another region of the country, preferably someone from New York or New England and perhaps with more experience in nautical matters than Daniels himself. His choice was a young state senator from New York named Franklin D. Roosevelt, whom he had first met at the Baltimore convention and who had impressed him with his progressive views and strong support for Wilson. Roosevelt accepted with unabashed enthusiasm the offer of the number two navy post.

They were an odd pair, this provincial southern editor and the patrician Ivy Leaguer from the Hudson Valley aristocracy. An experienced yachtsman, Roosevelt spoke the language of the admirals, shared most of their views about the navy, and quickly be-

Assistant Secretary of the Navy Franklin D. Roosevelt descending from a biplane at the U.S. Naval Air Station in Pauillac, France, 14 August 1916. (Courtesy FDR Library.)

came their confidant and frequently their spokesman. The secretary, on the other hand, had a landlubber's healthy skepticism of the navy professionals and was determined not to let the admirals do all of his thinking. FDR loved the seventeen-gun salute he was entitled to by his position and quickly designed an assistant secretary's flag to be flown when he was aboard ship. Daniels was uncomfortable with such pomp and often made a point of eating with the enlisted men when he visited a ship. Years later Roosevelt recalled that at first he had thought Daniels "the funniest looking hillbilly I had ever seen." Others also considered it a strange match. Republican senator Elihu Root of New York, whom Daniels consulted as a courtesy about the appointment, reminded Daniels that "whenever a Roosevelt rides, he wishes to ride in front." The prediction proved accurate, for not only was FDR a brashly self-confident young man, but he was also well aware of his cousin Theodore's use of the assistant secretary post as a springboard for glory and high office.

While Secretary Daniels quickly demonstrated that he was in charge and intended to make major policy decisions, he allowed Roosevelt considerable latitude in developing the assistant secretary's position into an important administrative office concerned with a wide variety of matters—personnel, procurement, labor relations, and the like. Unlike most government agencies of the time, the Navy Department was a large and far-flung enterprise with a substantial budget, thousands of uniformed and civilian employees, and installations and yards scattered from coast to coast. It offered ample opportunity for the development of Roosevelt's considerable administrative talents, and he relished the challenge. "I get my fingers into everything," he liked to boast.

The differing backgrounds and temperaments of the two men influenced both their relationship and the way they approached their responsibilities. Although he was fascinated by naval lore and traditions, Roosevelt had a young man's impatience with bureaucratic delay. He sometimes chafed more or less openly at what he considered his chief's overly deliberate ways and his unwillingness to make important decisions without a great deal of thought and consultation, which the younger man viewed as indecision. "J.D. is too damned slow for words," an exasperated Roosevelt complained in 1916. "Mr. D. totally fails to grasp the situation," he commented to his wife on the day war broke out in Europe in 1914. A few days later he boasted, " *I am running* the real work, although Josephus is here!"

Only later did Roosevelt come to understand and appreciate that the secretary's cautious approach was derived from his long experience with the political process. The navy had a large and growing budget, its activities were important to the economies of many communities across the country, and its affairs were accordingly of more than passing interest to many politicians in and out of Washington. Where Roosevelt felt more at home in the Army and Navy Club, Daniels enjoyed far more talking politics on Capitol Hill. He cultivated the congressional chairmen responsible for naval appropriations and carefully built up a network of supporters on both sides of the aisle. The navy's success in getting its appropriations bills through Congress unscathed was far more due to Daniels's deft political touch than to Roosevelt's Navy League preparedness speeches. In fact, the secretary's political instincts were often much sounder than his subordinate's. He vetoed FDR's use of the secretary's yacht, the *Dolphin,* to bring his family back from Campobello during a polio epidemic in 1916, waiting until after the Maine elections. Later he rejected Roosevelt's offer to arrange an early discharge for Daniels's Marine son so he could be among the first to return from France.

Although Roosevelt was a considerably more vocal big-navy advocate, in truth both men favored a substantial increase in the size of the navy, as American interests were threatened by the European war and troubles in Mexico and the Caribbean. A near pacifist, the secretary was far more reluctant than his more impetuous subordinate, however, to see the navy used in action. In April of 1917, Daniels was the last member of the Wilson cabinet to cast his vote for entry into the war, and he did so with tears in his eyes.

Daniels and Roosevelt also sometimes disagreed on naval tactics and on aspects of navy preparedness. After a number of ships were sunk by German submarines off the Atlantic coast early in 1917, FDR developed an almost irrational enthusiasm for a crash program to construct a fleet of 50-foot launches to patrol American harbors. Daniels was quite persuaded of the need to build larger 110-foot subchasers, but for once he shared the navy professionals' skepticism of the value of the smaller craft. "How much of that sort of junk shall we buy?" he complained in his diary. Roosevelt persisted, however, and one day as acting secretary he managed to authorize construction of some of the small craft, which as it turned out had no discernible role in shaping the outcome of the war.

More significant was Roosevelt's championship of the so-called North Sea mine barrage, an ambitious scheme by the navy's Bureau of Ordnance to keep German U-boats out of the North Atlantic by laying a wide belt of mine fields from Norway to Scotland. The cost and technical difficulties were enormous, and at first the British Admiralty and the head of the American naval mission in London, Adm. William S. Sims, strongly opposed the project. Always fascinated by grandiose undertakings, Roosevelt's enthusiasm for the mine barrage project knew no bounds. When he sensed that Secretary Daniels had lost interest in pressing the British further, FDR went over his head. "I know you will not mind my sending a copy of this to the President," he told Daniels in yet another memo advocating the mine barrage. To his wife he confided that he had "given the Sec'y a very stinging memorandum and sent a copy to the President." After an improved mine was developed, the British were won over, and in the spring of 1918, both navies began the herculean task of laying the mine barrage. It was still incomplete when the war ended in

November, but the mine fields probably contributed to the sagging morale of German submariners and helped provoke the Kiel mutiny in the last days of the war. Later Daniels conceded that his insubordinate assistant had been right—that not laying the mine barrage earlier was "the greatest naval error of the war."

For all his zest for his navy post, Roosevelt was well aware that it lacked a key ingredient for a future political career. At a dramatic moment in world history, when thousands of Americans were in uniform fighting overseas, FDR was stuck at a civilian desk in Washington, far from the real action. During 1918 he pressed Daniels for a commission and active duty at sea, but the secretary rightly reminded him his service in Washington was far more important than anything he could do afloat. Daniels finally approved Roosevelt's request to inspect navy bases and confer with Allied leaders in Europe in the summer of 1918, a mission that only sharpened his disappointment at not being in uniform. At his own urging, FDR again went to Europe early in 1919 to negotiate the termination of navy contracts and the disposal of surplus property, an assignment he accomplished with his usual efficiency. The two European trips would be the basis for many of FDR's war stories in future years, but they only partly assuaged his disappointment at not wearing a uniform during the conflict.

Daniels and Roosevelt both attended the Democratic National Convention at San Francisco in 1920, with the secretary housed aboard the battleship *New Mexico,* part of the Pacific fleet anchored in San Francisco Bay. The Democratic party was in political disarray, and Daniels was gloomy about its prospects. The one bright spot was the selection of Roosevelt to be the party's nominee for vice-president, with the secretary on the rostrum beaming his pride in his protégé. For nearly eight years, the two men had shared good times and bad, and their bond of affection would grow deeper in the years ahead. On the day in August 1920, when Roosevelt submitted his resignation as assistant secretary of the navy, Daniels scrawled in his diary, "He left in [the] afternoon, but before leaving wrote me a letter most friendly & almost loving wh. made me glad I had never acted upon my impulse when he seemed to take sides with my critics."

We should be glad as well, for there is no telling how differently either man's future career would have turned out if Daniels had yielded to that impulse.

The standard Roosevelt biography is the multivolume work by Frank B. Freidel, *Franklin D. Roosevelt,* of which the first volume, *The Apprenticeship* (Boston: Little, Brown & Co., 1952) covers Roosevelt's service as assistant secretary of the navy in considerable detail. Two good shorter biographies treating this period of his life are James MacGregor Burns, *Roosevelt: The Lion and the Fox* (New York: Harcourt, Brace, 1956) and Rexford G. Tugwell, *The Democratic Roosevelt: A Biography of Franklin D. Roosevelt* (Garden City, N.Y.: Doubleday, 1957). Perhaps the best work treating the complex relationship between Roosevelt and his superior, Secretary of the Navy Daniels, in the Wilson administration is the perceptive memoir by Daniels's son, Jonathan Daniels, *The End of Innocence*

(Philadelphia: Lippincott, 1954). Alfred B. Rollins, Jr., *Roosevelt and Howe* (New York: Knopf, 1962) treats Roosevelt's relationship with his longtime political adviser and confidant, Louis Howe, and includes two chapters on their work together in the Navy Department. The most detailed scholarly work on this period of Roosevelt's life is Joseph W. Coady, "Franklin D. Roosevelt's Early Washington Years, 1913–1920" (Ph.D. diss. St. John's University, 1968).

E. DAVID CRONON

See also Daniels, Josephus; Halsey, William Frederick, Jr.; Roosevelt, Theodore; Wilson, Thomas Woodrow

Atlantic Conference and Charter

The first of the many wartime meetings between President Franklin Roosevelt and Prime Minister Winston Churchill of Great Britain took place aboard naval vessels anchored in Placentia Bay, Newfoundland, Canada, 9–12 August 1941. The Atlantic Charter, a purposefully vague statement about Anglo-American goals, was the most widely known product of the talks, but their real importance lay in the public display of Anglo-American cooperation, if not quite alliance.

Both Roosevelt and Churchill believed firmly in their personal ability to persuade others—Roosevelt with charm and indirection, Churchill with a debater's logic and argumentation—and during 1940 each occasionally had expressed a desire to meet the other. But the practical origin of the Atlantic Conference (code named Riviera) lay in Harry Hopkins's trip to London in January 1941, where he had been sent by the president on what was the first of many diplomatic missions. Besides assessing Britain's over-

THE Atlantic Charter

THE President of THE UNITED STATES OF AMERICA and the Prime Minister, Mr. *Churchill*, representing HIS MAJESTY'S GOVERNMENT IN THE UNITED KINGDOM, being met together, deem it right to make known certain common principles in the national policies of their respective countries on which they base their hopes for a better future for the world.

1.   *Their countries seek no aggrandizement, territorial or other.*

2.   *They desire to see no territorial changes that do not accord with the freely expressed wishes of the peoples concerned.*

3.   *They respect the right of all peoples to choose the form of government under which they will live; and they wish to see sovereign rights and self-government restored to those who have been forcibly deprived of them.*

4.   *They will endeavor, with due respect for their existing obligations, to further the enjoyment by all States, great or small, victor or vanquished, of access, on equal terms, to the trade and to the raw materials of the world which are needed for their economic prosperity.*

5.   *They desire to bring about the fullest collaboration between all nations in the economic field with the object of securing, for all, improved labor standards, economic advancement and social security.*

6.   *After the final destruction of the Nazi tyranny, they hope to see established a peace which will afford to all nations the means of dwelling in safety within their own boundaries, and which will afford assurance that all the men in all the lands may live out their lives in freedom from fear and want.*

7.   *Such a peace should enable all men to traverse the high seas and oceans without hindrance.*

8.   *They believe that all of the nations of the world, for realistic as well as spiritual reasons, must come to the abandonment of the use of force. Since no future peace can be maintained if land, sea or air armaments continue to be employed by nations which threaten, or may threaten, aggression outside of their frontiers, they believe, pending the establishment of a wider and permanent system of general security, that the disarmament of such nations is essential. They will likewise aid and encourage all other practicable measures which will lighten for peace-loving peoples the crushing burden of armaments.*

FRANKLIN D. ROOSEVELT

WINSTON S. CHURCHILL

August 14, 1941

(National Archives.)

Roosevelt and Churchill attend divine service aboard the HMS Prince of Wales *during the Atlantic Conference, 10 August 1941.* (National Archives.)

all war effort and leadership, particularly the will to resist, Hopkins proposed a Roosevelt-Churchill meeting. The date suggested, April 1941, was pushed back as German military successes in Greece and Crete forced the prime minister to stay close to home. Then, late in July, Hopkins (again in England) .and Churchill fixed a time and place for the conference. The president preferred the Newfoundland site in order to enhance secrecy, avoid reporters, and be within easy reach of American communications and military facilities then under construction at Argentia as part of the destroyer-base lease arrangement. Moreover, that location would give Roosevelt an opportunity to travel by warship, the means he most enjoyed because of both the physical comfort and his boyish enthusiasm for the navy.

Churchill, accompanied by Hopkins who was then returning from a trip to England and the Soviet Union, crossed the Atlantic aboard the battleship *Prince of Wales.* Roosevelt, after a brief diversionary fishing trip along the New England coast to throw off reporters, sailed to Newfoundland on the cruiser *Augusta,* arriving on 7 August, two days before the British party. Both men originally intended to have a brief tête-à-tête that would give them a chance to assess each other without having to make major decisions. But the press of world events did not permit that luxury. The two leaders eventually agreed to the presence of a small staff of high-level advisers and military officers. The president, in an attempt to preserve secrecy, told only a handful about his plans and strictly forbade them to pass the word to others. As a result, the Americans arrived without having planned an overall conference strategy. Given Roosevelt's preference for personal diplomacy, that may have been just what he wanted.

The protocol and ceremonies surrounding the talks were what would be expected at a formal meeting between two major world leaders. Bands played martial airs as military personnel stood on deck in formation; Sunday church services became an opportunity to acknowledge the common culture that but-

tressed the emerging alliance; the two men exchanged memorabilia, toured each other's warships, and posed for photographers (U.S. Army cameramen had been rushed in when Roosevelt realized that Churchill had brought along two journalists despite the president's request that the press be kept away).

The public picture of growing Anglo-American unity hid some serious divergencies of policy. Churchill's dream was an unequivocal American commitment to join with Britain and declare. war on Germany. Hitler's attack on the Soviet Union had only suspended the threat of an invasion of Britain, and the likely collapse of Soviet resistance would again make England the target. Only a timely alliance with the United States could stem the German advance across the channel. Churchill reasoned, perhaps wishfully, that Roosevelt would not have suggested a conference without some such dramatic announcement in mind.

But the president came to Newfoundland determined to avoid any such commitment. He warned his advisers not to discuss the possibility of war and did the same in his talks with Churchill. Roosevelt believed that a declaration of war could not command a public consensus, and there are strong suggestions that the president himself did not yet think that full American participation in the war would ever be necessary. Churchill, eager to vindicate his American policy, reported to his cabinet that Roosevelt "had said that he would wage war, but not declare it, and that he would become more and more provocative," including forcing an "incident" at sea with German U-boats (War Cab. 84, 19 Aug. 1941, CAB 65/19, Public Record Office, London). Even if the president was that candid, which was unlike him, he did not go beyond his long-standing hope and belief that American participation could be limited to sea and air warfare. American military officers were more inclined to assume that the United States would join the fight, but even they drew back from British notions of Anglo-American intervention in places like French North Africa. The hemispheric nature of American thinking is illustrated by the military's concern about the threat of a German occupation of the Atlantic islands off northwestern Africa. Since those islands could provide a stepping-stone for an invasion of South America, the Americans asked for and received agreement on U.S. occupation of the Portuguese Azores.

On the other side of the world, the confrontation with Japan presented Churchill with both a danger and an opportunity. Continued Japanese expansion threatened resources vital to the British war effort, and Britain could not turn and defend Southeast Asia while Hitler was on the march. Yet the Pacific crisis might be a back door for American entry into the war. Roosevelt seemed more inclined to associate with Britain against Japan, and any step that brought the Americans toward alliance was desirable. According to British conference notes, the president agreed to parallel warnings to Japan that further expansion would bring an Anglo-American counteraction, even if that risked war. But the statement that finally resulted was much gentler. The British blamed Secretary of State Cordell Hull for toning down the warning, but Roosevelt's military leaders had insisted emphatically that the chance of war with Japan be avoided until the United States was militarily prepared. In the end, the president agreed merely to tell the Japanese that he would try to work out his differences with Tokyo if Japan would withdraw from Indochina.

The Atlantic Charter papered over the differences between Churchill and Roosevelt. For the president, it provided an answer to the expected cries of the anti-interventionists that he had sold out the United States to protect Britain and her empire. Moreover, the platitudes in the charter—the four freedoms were all eventually included—served to prevent the British from proposing more concrete war aims, something Roosevelt thought would only resurrect the kind of problems Woodrow Wilson faced after World War I. Churchill and Roosevelt agreed that neither nation sought additional territory and that boundary changes required consent from the peoples involved (something Stalin thought was aimed at Soviet incorporation of the Baltic states). A clause calling for respecting the rights of peoples to choose their own form of government came to be interpreted as a challenge to colonialism, even though Churchill, then and later, tried to limit the statement to nations conquered by the Axis powers. Churchill tried, unsuccessfully, to include an endorsement of a peacekeeping postwar organization, but Roosevelt backed away, preferring a vaguer statement about "policing" the world with only the chance of forming an international organization. Roosevelt's advisers, particularly Under Secretary of State Sumner Welles, tried to include a commitment to eliminate trade discrimination. Churchill correctly saw that as an attack on any sort of special trading relationships within the European empires, and with Roosevelt unwilling to push the issue, they struck a compromise that called only for equal access to raw materials. Nonetheless, broad issues of postwar policy that related to the independence of European colonies, to liberalized trade, and to international organization had been raised publicly. For better or worse, Pandora's box was opened, if only a tiny crack, and those issues eventually came to dominate the debate on the postwar world.

The standard American treatment of the Atlantic Conference is in Theodore A. Wilson, *The First Summit* (Boston: Houghton Mifflin, Co., 1969), published before the British archives were opened. Additional detail from the British side can be found in David Reynolds, *The Creation of the Anglo-American Alliance 1937–1941)* (Chapel Hill: University of North Carolina Press, 1982), and Alan P. Dobson, "Economic Diplomacy at the Atlantic Conference," *Review of International Studies* 10, no. 2 (April 1984). Memoir sources include Winston Churchill, *The Grand Alliance* (Boston: Houghton Mifflin, Co., 1951); Robert S. Sherwood, *Roosevelt and Hopkins* (New York: Harper & Bros., 1948); and a look at the human interest side of the conference by one of the journalists Churchill brought along, H. V. Morton, *Atlantic Meeting* (London: Methuen & Co., 1943). American records of the conference and its background are published in *Foreign Relations of the United States, 1941*, vol. 1 (Washington: U.S. Government Printing Office, 1958), and Warren F. Kimball, ed., *Churchill and Roosevelt: The Complete Correspondence*, 3 vols. (Princeton: Princeton University Press, 1984).

WARREN F. KIMBALL

See also Churchill, Winston Leonard Spencer; Colonialism; Foreign Policy; Hopkins, Harry L.; Personal Diplomacy; Welles, Benjamin Sumner; World War II

Atomic Bomb

From the first, nuclear fission was an international phenomenon. Discovered in Germany, publicized in Britain, harnessed in America, exploded in Japan, and coveted in Moscow, war and diplomacy shaped its history. Until the mid-1960s historians in America generally ignored the Soviet connection. But once archives were opened and it became possible to follow the inner development of Anglo-American wartime atomic energy policies, the history of the atomic bomb, especially its use against Hiroshima and Nagasaki, had to be revised. It was now obvious that decisions related to the bomb involved too many complex motivations to be covered by merely asking, was the bomb necessary to end the war before the planned November invasion?

As is often the case, new information required new and prior questions: Did postwar considerations, especially with respect to the Soviet Union, influence the formulation of Roosevelt's atomic energy policies? What effect did the legacy of Roosevelt's atomic energy decisions have on the decisions of the Truman administration? And, finally, was the decision to use the atomic bomb motivated in any way by postwar (as distinct from wartime) expectations?

In February 1939, nuclear fission was discovered in Germany by Otto Hahn and Friedrich Strassmann with the interpretive assistance of Lise Meitner and Otto Frisch. When the remarkable news was published in the British science journal *Nature*, it was obvious to nuclear physicists everywhere that, in theory at least, this discovery might be fashioned into a weapon of extraordinary power.

Scientists in every major industrial nation—including Russia and Japan as well as Britain, France, and Germany—were immediately conscious of its military potential. Roosevelt was personally informed in September by Alexander Sachs, who read aloud Albert Einstein's famous letter of 2 August (actually composed by Einstein's former assistant, the Hungarian physicist Leo Szilard), warning the president of the military implications of this discovery. It took two more years, however, before Frisch and Rudolph Peierls, two émigré physicists working in Great Britain, conceived of a method by which a bomb could be built in time to be used during the war. In accordance with an Anglo-American scientific alliance agreed to in the summer of 1940 for the "general interchange of secret technical information with the United States," the British government's MAUD (atomic

Albert Einstein
Old Grove Rd.
Nassau Point
Peconic, Long Island

August 2nd, 1939

F.D. Roosevelt,
President of the United States,
White House
Washington, D.C.

Sir:

Some recent work by E. Fermi and L. Szilard, which has been communicated to me in manuscript, leads me to expect that the element uranium may be turned into a new and important source of energy in the immediate future. Certain aspects of the situation which has arisen seem to call for watchfulness and, if necessary, quick action on the part of the Administration. I believe therefore that it is my duty to bring to your attention the following facts and recommendations:

In the course of the last four months it has been made probable - through the work of Joliot in France as well as Fermi and Szilard in America - that it may become possible to set up a nuclear chain reaction in a large mass of uranium, by which vast amounts of power and large quantities of new radium-like elements would be generated. Now it appears almost certain that this could be achieved in the immediate future.

This new phenomenon would also lead to the construction of bombs, and it is conceivable - though much less certain - that extremely powerful bombs of a new type may thus be constructed. A single bomb of this type, carried by boat and exploded in a port, might very well destroy the whole port together with some of the surrounding territory. However, such bombs might very well prove to be too heavy for transportation by air.

-2-

The United States has only very poor ores of uranium in moderate quantities. There is some good ore in Canada and the former Czechoslovakia, while the most important source of uranium is Belgian Congo.

In view of this situation you may think it desirable to have some permanent contact maintained between the Administration and the group of physicists working on chain reactions in America. One possible way of achieving this might be for you to entrust with this task a person who has your confidence and who could perhaps serve in an inofficial capacity. His task might comprise the following:

a) to approach Government Departments, keep them informed of the further development, and put forward recommendations for Government action, giving particular attention to the problem of securing a supply of uranium ore for the United States;

b) to speed up the experimental work, which is at present being carried on within the limits of the budgets of University laboratories, by providing funds, if such funds be required, through his contacts with private persons who are willing to make contributions for this cause, and perhaps also by obtaining the co-operation of industrial laboratories which have the necessary equipment.

I understand that Germany has actually stopped the sale of uranium from the Czechoslovakian mines which she has taken over. That she should have taken such early action might perhaps be understood on the ground that the son of the German Under-Secretary of State, von Weizsäcker, is attached to the Kaiser-Wilhelm-Institut in Berlin where some of the American work on uranium is now being repeated.

Yours very truly,

A. Einstein

(Albert Einstein)

The Einstein letter of August 1939 alerting President Roosevelt to the imminent development of a nuclear chain reaction in uranium, and probable exploitation of the phe- *nomenon in the construction of bombs. (Courtesy FDR Library.)*

energy) committee informed the U.S. Office of Scientific Research and Development (OSRD) of the Frisch-Peierls results. Shortly thereafter, President Roosevelt set in motion a joint Anglo-American effort to produce atomic bombs for use during the war.

The Manhattan Project, as the atomic bomb development program was known in America, was a military undertaking directed by Gen. Leslie R. Groves, U.S. Army Corps of Engineers, who had supervised the construction of the Pentagon. Stimulated by fear of a German lead in the development of this ultimate weapon conceivably capable of deciding the war, the civilian scientists labored furiously to win the race with little thought (until late in the war) about the postwar implications of their work.

On 2 December 1942, under the direction of the Italian émigré physicist Enrico Fermi, scientists at the University of Chicago's Metallurgical Laboratory conducted the first controlled nuclear chain reaction experiment. Shortly thereafter, the design and construction of the weapon got under way at Los Alamos, New Mexico, directed by the theoretical physicist J. Robert Oppenheimer. In less than 2 ½ years (an incredible feat under the circumstances), the scientists at Los Alamos achieved their goal. At 5:30 A.M. on 16 July 1945, the first atomic device exploded atop a one-hundred-foot tower in the Alamogordo desert in New Mexico. This plutonium, implosion-type bomb (similar to the one dropped on Nagasaki on 8 August) created "a searing light with the intensity many times that of the midday sun," General Groves wrote to President Truman, who was attending the Potsdam Conference at the time. (The uranium, gun-type bomb dropped on Hiroshima on 6 August was a much simpler design that did not have to be tested.)

Initially conceived by scientists as a wartime weapon developed in an imagined race against Germany, the atomic bomb was transformed by the Anglo-American leaders into a wartime instrument of postwar military and diplomatic policy. The first shocks of this subtle transformation were felt in London. Heeding the advice of his science advisers, James Conant and Vannevar Bush, and his secretary of war, Henry L. Stimson (all of whom distrusted British postwar intentions), Roosevelt sought to end the Anglo-American atomic energy partnership. "What are we going to have between the white snows of Russia and the white cliffs of Dover?" Churchill asked in shocked response.

Roosevelt's answer was to reverse his previous decision. At the Anglo-American summit conference in Quebec in August 1943, he and Churchill signed a secret agreement "governing collaboration between the authorities of the U.S.A. and the U.K. in the matter of Tube Alloys" (as the British called the atomic bomb project). The Quebec Agreement reinstated the policy of complete interchange of atomic energy information between the two countries, although the British returned as a junior rather than an equal partner. Roosevelt made no explicit commitment to an Anglo-American postwar atomic monopoly at Quebec; that would come a year later when he and Churchill signed the Hyde Park Aide-Memoire on 18 September 1944. But in the summer of 1943 he was fully aware that the prime minister intended to use the bomb as a diplomatic bargaining counter against the Soviet Union after the war.

The Quebec arrangement complemented Roosevelt's plans for maintaining order in the postwar world. Based upon the principle of peace through power, he conceived of a four-nation (United States, Great Britain, China, and the Soviet Union) regional police force "so powerful that no aggressor would dare to challenge it." Roosevelt told Arthur Sweetser, an ardent internationalist, that violators first would be quarantined and then, if they persisted in their disruptive activities, bombed at the rate of a city a day until they agreed to behave. The president told Soviet foreign minister Molotov about this idea in May 1942, and in November he repeated it to Clark Eichelberger, who was coordinating the activities of American internationalists. A year later, at the Teheran Conference, Roosevelt presented his plan to police the postwar world to Stalin. As Professor Robert A. Divine has noted, "Roosevelt's concept of big power domination remained the central idea in his approach to international organization throughout World War II."

Roosevelt did not live long enough to work out precisely how to integrate the atomic bomb into his plans for keeping the peace in the postwar world. Yet against the background of the Quebec Agreement, his police approach to peacekeeping, and the atomic energy decisions he took in 1944 at Hyde Park, he appears to have decided that a nuclear-armed Britain would be a valuable postwar ally. Just as the seapower of the Royal Navy had served America's purposes in the nineteenth century by containing European incursions into the New World, so an atomic-armed Royal Air Force would now play a similar role with respect to Soviet ambitions in Europe. If Churchill wanted the bomb to bolster Britain's otherwise weak military position after the war, Roosevelt wanted Churchill to have it to reinforce American influence. There might still be four policemen, but only two of them would have the bomb.

The bomb's national security implications, together with the international character of science, guaranteed that a nuclear arms race (presumably with the Soviet Union) would ensue if the United States and Britain emerged from the war in exclusive possession of the atomic bomb. Recognizing the need to avoid such a catastrophe, the eminent Danish physicist Niels Bohr warned Roosevelt and Churchill in 1944 that the Soviet Union probably knew about the Manhattan Project and was capable of duplicating its results. He urged them, under the circumstances, to approach Stalin before the bomb was tested and before the war ended with a proposal to develop a plan for the international control of atomic energy. But on 18 September 1944, as documented in the Hyde Park Aide-Memoire, the president and the prime minister explicitly rejected Bohr's approach. "We did not even speak the same language," Bohr said of his meeting with Churchill. Indeed, as Vannevar Bush, who favored a modified version of Bohr's initiative, ruefully

noted, the president's objective appeared to be to ignore the opportunity for international control and to use the new weapon "to control the peace of the world."

On the afternoon of 12 April 1945, Franklin Roosevelt suddenly died. That evening his vice-president, Harry S Truman, took the oath of office and assumed the formidable burdens of the presidency. Among them was the atomic bomb, a development about which he was completely ignorant. The suddenness of Roosevelt's death and Truman's lack of information effectively left atomic energy policymaking under the guidance of the advisers inherited from the late president.

Having discussed with Roosevelt in December the idea of using the new weapon as a postwar bargaining counter with the Soviet Union, Secretary of War Stimson naturally pursued the same line of reasoning with Truman in May. One important factor encouraging this notion of atomic leverage was the prevailing imbalance between American postwar objectives and current military realities in Europe. As the president's difficulties with Stalin mounted, the atomic bomb became an increasingly important consideration in the formulation of American diplomacy. The more frightful it seemed as a weapon of war, the more useful it appeared as an instrument of peace. A hint of the role the bomb would play in Truman's administration emerged in May when the president, referring to the upcoming test at Alamogordo, told Stimson that he had "postponed" the Potsdam Conference "until the 15th of July on purpose to give us more time."

The assumptions and attitudes developed during the Roosevelt years helped to guide the atomic bombs to their destinations. James F. Byrnes, secretary of state-designate, interpreted what he learned as Truman's representative on the Interim Committee (a group organized by Stimson in May 1945 as an atomic energy advisory body) to mean that the bomb "might well put us in a position to dictate our own terms at the end of the war." Discussing "further *quid pro quos* which should be established in consideration for our taking [the Soviet Union] into [postwar atomic] partnership," Truman and Stimson agreed that after the first time S-1 (as Stimson referred to the bomb) had been successfully used against Japan a fitting exchange would be "the settlement of the Polish, Rumanian, Yugoslavian, and Manchurian problems."

Having inherited as part of Roosevelt's legacy the assumption that the bomb should be used if it was ready before the Japanese surrendered, Truman, Stimson, and Brynes reasoned that such a clear demonstration of its extraordinary power would both encourage the Japanese to surrender promptly and induce the Soviets to cooperate after the war, perhaps in exchange for the neutralization of this terrifying weapon. In any case, they anticipated that the sudden, devastating use of the bomb directed at a modern urban target—"a vital war plant employing a large number of workers and closely surrounded by workers' houses" (as the Interim Committee's minutes record its recommendation)—would have a desirable "shock effect"—in Moscow as well as in Tokyo.

What was the result of the shocks caused by the destruction of Hiroshima on 6 August (where the death toll has been variously estimated to have been between 70,000 and 140,000—including 21 American POWs), and the obliteration of the industrial area of Nagasaki on 9 August (where the estimated deaths range from 35,000 to 70,000)?

In Tokyo the result was confusion and dismay. The rapid succession of crises blurred the significance of each. Two days after Hiroshima was bombed the Soviet government made good on its promise to declare war against Japan within three months after the surrender of Germany. The next day Nagasaki was destroyed. "The machinery of the [Japanese] government," Professor Robert Butow has written, "had ground to a halt [on 9 August] not because it had been damaged but because it had been thrown off balance. The factors which should have urged speedy and smooth operation had engendered exactly the opposite results." The struggle within the government between those who had been conspiring for months to end the war and those who insisted that Japan must never surrender *unconditionally*, as the Allies insisted, remained unresolved—until Hirohito, the Emperor of Japan, was asked to intervene.

In the early morning hours of 10 August, in the Emperor's bomb shelter, Premier Kantaro Suzuki startled his divided colleagues on the Supreme Council with the unprecedented announcement, "Your Imperial Majesty's decision is requested. . . ." That decision, "to accept the Allied proclamation *on the basis outlined by the Foreign Minister*," brought the war to its conclusion—*on the condition* that the United States guarantee the survival of dynasty and Emperor. That only unconditional surrender remained an obstacle to peace in the wake of the atomic bombings of Hiroshima and Nagasaki, and the Soviet declaration of war—until the government of the United States offered the necessary (albeit veiled) assurance that neither Emperor nor throne would be destroyed—suggests the possibility, which even Stimson later recognized in his memoirs, that neither bomb may have been necessary, and certainly that the second was not.

Nevertheless, the atomic bombings of Hiroshima and Nagasaki contributed to the illusion of diplomatic advantage from the bomb that has guided U.S. nuclear weapons policy throughout the cold war.

Atomic energy has attracted superb government historians in the United States and Great Britain. Anyone interested in seriously investigating its history must therefore begin by reviewing two of the best official histories written about World War II: Richard G. Hewlett and Oscar E. Anderson, Jr., *The New World, 1939/1946: A History of the United States Atomic Energy Commission*, vol. 1 (University Park: Pennsylvania State University Press, 1962) and Margaret Gowing, *Britain and Atomic Energy, 1939–1945* (London: Macmillan, 1964). They are thorough, judicious and well written, though somewhat timid about drawing out the diplomatic significance of the evidence at their disposal with respect to U.S.-Soviet relations. Herbert Feis, the author of several important volumes on the diplomatic history of World War II, wrote two books on the atomic bomb: *Japan Subdued: The Atomic Bomb and the End of the War in the Pacific* (Princeton: Princeton University Press, 1961) and *The Atomic Bomb and the End of World War II* (Princeton: Princeton University Press, 1966). In the second book, there appears a faint recognition of the importance of the Soviet Union to this issue. Conversely, in *Atomic Diplomacy: Hiroshima and Potsdam* (New York: Simon & Schuster, 1965), Gar Alperovitz overemphasizes the Soviet connection, arguing that the expectations with which Truman and Stimson invested the atomic bomb explain virtually all of American diplomacy with the Soviet Union between 23 April and 10 August 1945. In *A World Destroyed*, using documents unavailable to either Feis or Alperovitz, Martin J. Sherwin traced the development of U.S. atomic bomb policies back to their origins in the Roosevelt administration. Based on the papers of all the primary policymakers, Sherwin's book seeks to understand the full array of assumptions and motivations that led to Hiroshima and subsequently to the origins of the nuclear arms race.

MARTIN J. SHERWIN

See also Churchill, Winston Leonard Spencer; Groves, Leslie; Japan; Personal Diplomacy; Quebec Conferences; Stalin, Joseph, and the Soviet Union; Stimson, Henry L.; Truman, Harry S; World War II

Japanese emperor Hirohito in a photograph released in August 1945. (National Archives.)

Awards

As a student at Harvard, Franklin D. Roosevelt was a member of Alpha Delta Phi and served as president (editor) of the *Harvard Crimson* during his senior

Governor Franklin D. Roosevelt receiving an honorary LL.D. from Fordham University in New York, 12 June 1929. (William Fox.)

Honorary Degrees Conferred upon Franklin D. Roosevelt

1.	American University	Doctor of Laws	3 March 1934
2.	Brussels, University of (Belgium)	Doctor	30 December 1944
3.	Buenos Aires, University of (Argentina)	Doctor	28 November 1936
4.	Catholic University of America	Doctor of Laws	14 June 1933
5.	Dartmouth College	Doctor of Laws	22 June 1929
6.	Fordham University	Doctor of Laws	12 June 1929
7.	Georgia, University of	Doctor of Laws	11 August 1938
8.	Harvard University	Doctor of Laws	20 June 1929
9.	Hobart College	Doctor of Humane Letters	4 June 1929
10.	Leon, University of (Nicaragua)	Doctor	10 May 1943
11.	London, University of (England)	Doctor of Laws	18 June 1941 (Conferred 25 August 1943)
12.	Louvain, University of (Belgium)	Doctor of Laws	10 April 1945
13.	McGill University (Canada)	Doctor of Laws	16 September 1944
14.	North Carolina, University of	Doctor of Laws	5 December 1938
15.	Notre Dame, University of	Doctor of Laws	9 December 1935
16.	Oglethorpe University	Doctor of Laws	22 May 1932
17.	Oxford University (England)	Doctor of Civil Law	19 June 1941
18.	Pennsylvania, University of	Doctor of Laws	20 September 1940
19.	Pennsylvania Military College	Doctor of Laws	16 June 1920
20.	Puerto Rico, University of	Doctor of Laws	24 May 1939
21.	Queens University (Canada)	Doctor of Laws	18 August 1938
22.	Rio de Janeiro, University of (Brazil)	Doctor	27 November 1936
23.	Rollins College	Doctor of Laws	23 May 1936
24.	Rutgers University	Doctor of Laws	10 June 1933
25.	Southern California, University of	Doctor of Laws	1 October 1935
26.	Syracuse University	Doctor of Civil Law	9 June 1930
27.	Temple University	Doctor of Jurisprudence	22 February 1936
28.	Uruguay, University of	Doctor	30 November 1936
29.	Washington College	Doctor of Laws	21 October 1933
30.	William and Mary, College of	Doctor of Laws	20 October 1934
31.	Yale University	Doctor of Laws	20 June 1934

(Courtesy FDR Library)

year. He was made an honorary member of Phi Beta Kappa when he acted as marshal for his class's twenty-fifth anniversary reunion. He also served from 1918 to 1924 as a Harvard University overseer.

In 1911, Holland Lodge 8 of New York City conferred on him the degree of Master Mason. During this period, he served on various state and national commissions, including the Hudson-Fulton Celebration Commission (1909), the Plattsburg (N.Y.) Centennial (1913), and the National Commission of the Panama-Pacific Exposition (1915).

While he was governor of New York, Roosevelt received an honorary Doctor of Laws from Fordham University, 1929, and in 1931, he was elected to the Académie Diplomatique Internationale. Several other American universities awarded Roosevelt an honorary LL.D. after he became president. The Canadians, the British, and the Argentines similarly decorated the president. The University of Buenos Aires awarded FDR an honorary degree in 1936 and Queen's University, Kingston, Ontario, Canada, awarded him a Doctor of Laws degree in 1938, as did Oxford University in 1941.

Various organizations elected FDR to honorary membership or bestowed honorary medals upon him during his presidency, including the New York County Lawyers' Association, the Russian Orthodox Clubs of America, the Society of American Foresters, American Farm Bureau Federaration, the United Mine Workers, and the Cuban Red Cross.

The *New York Times* covered most of the honors bestowed upon FDR, and many are listed in the volumes of *Who's Who in America* that were published during the years of his political career.

See also Harvard Crimson

The leaders of the Rome-Berlin Axis, Benito Mussolini and Adolf Hitler (right) *in the 1930s. (National Archives.)*

Axis Alliance

Commonly known as the Rome-Berlin-Tokyo Axis, the Axis alliance was a coalition composed of Italy, Germany, Japan, and some of their satellites. It originated with the Italo-German protocols of 25 October 1936, which established a Rome-Berlin Axis as the basis of future foreign policy coordination, and the 25 November 1936 Anti-Comintern Pact between Germany and Japan, a pact Italy signed a year later. By the terms of that pact, the signatories publicly pledged cooperation against Communism and privately agreed to benevolent neutrality should any one of them become involved in a war with the Soviet Union. On 22 May 1939, Germany and Italy supplemented these agreements with the so-called Pact of Steel, a formal military alliance requiring mutual consultation and full support should either come into conflict with any other power(s). On 27 September 1940, all three countries signed the Tripartite Pact, a defensive military alliance promising mutual assistance if any signatory was attacked by a presently neutral country excluding the Soviet Union. In a series of bilateral agreements, the three nations also recognized one another's military conquests and respective spheres of influence.

American perceptions of the Axis alliance differed drastically from its reality. In the public mind, the alliance constituted a close political and military collaboration among three highly aggressive states, who were led and directed by Nazi Germany, were linked by a common fascist and militarist ideology, and were determined to conquer and divide the world. In reality, the Axis alliance was a paper coalition of three powers who neither trusted one another nor coordinated their diplomatic and military plans.

Conflicting interests as well as mutual suspicions precluded any real coordination among the three nations. Throughout the years 1936–45, each power consistently proceeded unilaterally with its own political plans and military campaigns, a situation that resulted in mutual recrimination and a fatal dispersion of Axis strength. In 1939–40, for example, Germany attacked Poland without consulting or coordinating with her Italian ally, and Rome in turn refused to join

the ensuing war until France was virtually defeated and then ignored German entreaties not to attack Greece. Although Hitler did subsequently come to Mussolini's aid, he never informed Italy or Japan of the negotiations that culminated in the 1939 Nazi-Soviet Pact or of his decision to invade the Soviet Union in 1941. These moves wreaked havoc with Japanese plans and heavily reinforced Tokyo's predilection to keep its own plans secret, to pursue an independent policy with the USSR, and to reject any possibility of close collaboration with its European allies, Hitler's post–Pearl Harbor declaration of war against the United States notwithstanding.

Fundamentally, the Axis alliance was a diplomatic ploy designed to scare potential adversaries into inactivity by the threat of a multifront, coalition war. Prior to the 1939 Nazi-Soviet Pact and the outbreak of war in Europe, this threat was directed primarily at England, France, and the Soviet Union. In the Tripartite Pact of 1940, it was directed at the United States. Hitler hoped the alliance would discourage America from aiding England in the Atlantic, while Tokyo hoped the threat of a two-front war would prevent Washington from opposing Japanese military moves in China and Southeast Asia.

Americans did interpret the Tripartite Pact as a threat of a two-front war against them, but contrary to Axis expectations they responded with even greater belligerency in both theaters. Aid to Britain increased dramatically in late 1940 and 1941, culminating in Lend-Lease and an undeclared naval war with Germany in the Atlantic. Simultaneously, Washington increased its diplomatic opposition to Japanese expansion and its economic sanctions against Tokyo. By the summer of 1941 a virtual embargo was in effect.

The essential Axis miscalculation regarding the United States was psychological. Rather than withdrawing in fear as the Axis had anticipated, Americans concluded that the Tripartite Pact was clear evidence of a Berlin-directed, worldwide conspiracy against them that required increased belligerency and massive aid to potential allies while those allies were still unconquered. The pact thus boomeranged by galvanizing both the Roosevelt administration and the public into greater recognition of potential threats and into increased efforts to prepare militarily and forge a powerful coalition against the Axis. Such efforts included Lend-Lease aid to all Axis opponents, the Atlantic Charter, combined Anglo-American war planning, and the decision to concentrate on Germany should the United States find itself in a coalition war against the Axis.

According to some scholars, the belief in a conspiracy against them also blinded Americans to the deep divisions within the Axis and the subsequent possibility of separating Japan and avoiding a war with her. By the fall of 1941 Tokyo was willing to stop its southward advance and leave the Tripartite Pact in all but name if the United States ended the embargo and gave Japan a free hand in China. But the belief that Tokyo was merely a devious German puppet, combined with fear of Allied and public reaction to such "appeasement" and a moralistic commitment to the Open Door, led Roosevelt and Hull to reject such an understanding and thereby virtually guarantee a needless war in the Pacific.

Hitler's declaration of war against the United States a few days after Pearl Harbor (a rather capricious and disastrous declaration in no way required by the terms of the Tripartite Pact) merely reinforced this belief in a Berlin-controlled conspiracy. The result was now quite positive, however, for it enabled Roosevelt to proceed with the "Germany first" strategy and his efforts to forge an effective coalition against the Axis. Throughout the war, the Tripartite Pact thus acted as a needed threat to create and maintain Allied unity, whereas in reality the Axis partners themselves continued their mistrust and lack of any real collaboration. They thereby squandered the military advantages they held in early 1942 and simultaneously prodded their opponents into real and effective collaboration that led to total victory for the Allies by 1945. The myth of the Axis alliance thus resulted only in effectively unifying their adversaries.

There is no comprehensive history of the Axis alliance. Although numerous historians have carefully examined the origins of the coalition and relations among its members, all the resulting studies are limited in terms of the years, issues, and/or number of partners analyzed. On German-Italian relations, Elizabeth Wiskemann's *The Rome-Berlin Axis* (New York: Oxford University Press, 1949) remains the most comprehensive survey. Mario Toscano's *The Origins of the Pact of Steel*, 2d rev. ed. (Baltimore: Johns Hopkins Press, 1967) and F. W. Deakin's *The Brutal Friendship: Mussolini, Hitler and the Fall of Italian Fascism* (New York: Harper & Row, 1962) are much more detailed and up-to-date, but each is limited in the number of years covered. The best analysis of German-Japanese relations up to Pearl Harbor is Ernst L. Presseisen's *Germany and Japan: A Study of Totalitarian Diplomacy, 1933–1941* (The Hague: Martinus Mihoff, 1958), while Johanna Menzel Meskill's *Hitler and Japan: The Hollow Alliance* (New York: Atherton Press, 1966) emphasizes the years 1940–45. The Anti-Comintern Pact is reproduced in Presseisen, and the Pact of Steel in Toscano. Presseisen and Meskill both reproduce the Tripartite Pact, but Meskill also provides the supplemental and secret German-Japanese notes and the Tripartite Military Agreement of 18 January 1942. Burkhart Mueller Hillebrand's *Germany and Its Allies in World War II: A Record of Axis Collaboration Problems* (Frederick, Md.: University Publications of America, 1980), a recently published work written for the U.S. Army in 1954 by a former German general, provides a brief but comprehensive summary of the lack of military cooperation among Berlin and its individual allies. Paul W. Schroeder's *The Axis Alliance and Japanese American Relations, 1941* (Ithaca, N.Y.: Cornell University Press, 1958) argues that lack of realism regarding the true nature of the Tripartite Pact led the United States into a needless confrontation with Japan. N. Bruce Russett amplifies this conclusion in his more recent *No Clear and Present Danger: A Skeptical View of U.S. Entry into World War II* (New York: Harper & Row, 1972).

MARK A. STOLER

See also Fascism; Foreign Policy; Hitler, Adolf, and Germany; Japan; Mussolini, Benito, and Italy

B

Bank Holiday

See Banking; Fireside Chats

Banking

During the Roosevelt administration, a banking crisis was surmounted, far-reaching bank reforms were enacted, and the existing banking system in the United States was preserved. When Franklin Roosevelt took office as president of the United States, he faced the challenge of an unprecedented banking crisis. Its origins lay in the 1920s when an epidemic of bank failures was symptomatic of the unhealthy state of the banking system. After the stock market crash in 1929, the use of bank funds for securities speculation was highlighted, and investigations revealed illegal activities among highly placed bankers. Public indignation was intense, and confidence in American banks fell.

Between Roosevelt's election and his inauguration, bank failures rose, panics developed, runs on banks resulted, and hoarding of gold and currency soon followed. To stem the panic and check the out-

Run on the Bank of the United States, 1933. (UPI/Bettmann Archive.)

flow of bank deposits, some state governments declared moritoria. The movement spread, but under the dual banking system in the United States wherein supervisory authority was shared by the federal government and the banking departments of the individual states, no coordinated action was possible. The people turned to Washington for relief. At the federal level, the Hoover administration ineffectively sought to control the situation, and in the Congress, bank reform legislation was divisive and failed to be enacted. As his administration drew to a close, Herbert Hoover's advisers pressed for the declaration of a national bank holiday. Hoover was reluctant to take executive action, however, without the concurrence of the president-elect. Still a private citizen, Roosevelt refused. He had neither the authority nor the inclination to cooperate. The crisis mounted. In the final hours of 3 March, it was clear that the banks must be protected against additional runs. Hoover's advisers, joined now by Roosevelt's New Dealers, continued to seek a solution, but none was found. As a last resort, they telephoned the governors of all the states that had not suspended operations, trying to induce each to declare a brief bank holiday. Finally, with the compliance of the governors of New York and Illinois, banks in all forty-eight states were closed. When inauguration day dawned, the country was devoid of banking service.

The situation called for immediate action, and the newly inaugurated Roosevelt responded accordingly. In his inaugural address, he indicted the bankers, charging that "the money changers have fled from their high seats in the temple of our civilization. We may now restore that temple to the ancient truths." He reassured the people and told them that "the only thing we have to fear is fear itself." Republicans and Democrats continued to work together to fulfill the president's promises. The next day Roosevelt issued his first proclamation. He summoned the Congress to convene in extraordinary session on 9 March, the date on which the new secretary of the treasury, William Woodin, agreed to have ready emergency bank legislation. At 1 A.M. on 6 March, he issued a second proclamation. Utilizing controversial authority provided by the Trading with the Enemy Act of World War I and basing his action on drafts previously prepared for Herbert Hoover, Roosevelt ordered a national bank holiday to extend from 6 March through 9 March "to be observed by all banking institutions" during which time all banking transactions were suspended. At the Treasury Department, there were round-the-clock meetings to work out a plan to restore confidence in the banks and provide for their reopening. Heated disagreements took place, but by 2 A.M. on 9 March, the emergency banking bill was ready for Congress. Meanwhile, encouraged by the decisive action of the president, the American people adapted themselves to the lack of banking services, and when the new Congress convened, the country was optimistically calm.

Congress convened at noon. The Emergency Banking Act was quickly introduced. No printed copies were available; the provisions were read to the members. By 4:05 P.M. the bill passed the House by a voice vote, and by 7:23 P.M. it was approved in the Senate by a vote of 73 to 7. At 8:36 that evening, Roosevelt signed it into law.

The new law legalized the action taken by the president in the previous days. It authorized the secretary of the treasury to determine which banks were sound and should reopen. It provided that Reconstruction Finance Corporation funds be made available to banks that were essentially solvent but temporarily in need so that they could reopen as quickly as possible. Unsound banks were to remain closed and be placed under the direction of conservators. Provision was made for the issuance of sufficient emergency currency to meet demands.

By presidential proclamation, the bank holiday was extended to 13 March. On 12 March, Roosevelt, in his first fireside address, spoke to the nation about the banking situation. He explained what had been done in the past few days, why it was done, and what the next steps would be. He asked the people to cooperate. The next day, banks began reopening, deposits exceeded withdrawals, and the wheels of the banking industry again turned.

Roosevelt met with severe criticism from progressives and liberals for failing to nationalize the banks. This probably could have been done, but he chose to revitalize the existing system through the use of government support. In the months that followed the crisis, he spoke frequently of a government-business partnership and urged the bankers to participate.

Roosevelt's initial plan was to adjourn the Congress after the passage of emergency legislation. The mood of the country was so favorable, however, he determined to move forward with an economic recovery program. Bank reform legislation was not part of his plan. He preferred to postpone the consideration of additional banking legislation until a later date. Nevertheless, a banking bill was introduced by Congressman Henry B. Steagall and Senator Carter Glass. Each had sponsored bank reform legislation in the previous Congress. They now joined forces to introduce the Banking Act of 1933.

The most controversial feature of the bill was a provision to establish the Federal Deposit Insurance Corporation (FDIC) to go into effect on 1 July 1934. Steagall had long campaigned for deposit insurance. Carter Glass had opposed it but now reluctantly accepted the concept. Franklin Roosevelt was against it, his opposition based on the failure of deposit guarantee laws enacted at the state level. He was joined by most bankers who thought it was an unwarranted burden on strong banks to protect the weak banks. When the bill reached the Senate floor, Arthur Vandenberg offered an amendment to insure immediately all bank deposits up to $2,500. It was widely rumored that Roosevelt would veto the bill if the Vandenberg amendment was retained. Public pressure mounted in favor of deposit insurance, and letters flowed to Washington in its support. Roosevelt recognized the political realities of the situation. Conferences took place and a compromise was reached. Deposit insurance was delayed. A temporary plan would go into effect on 1 January 1934, and a permanent plan, insuring bank deposits on a graduated scale, would begin operations the following July. The compromise was accepted, and the bill passed and was signed on 16 June 1933. The creation of the FDIC would have a far-reaching impact on American banking. It protected banks against panic, extended federal supervision over a substantially increased number of state banks, and reduced dramatically the number of bank failures.

The Glass-Steagall Act contained a number of other important bank reforms. Investment banking was separated from deposit banking. Commercial banks could no longer underwrite securities, and they were required to divorce themselves from their security affiliates within one year. Federal Reserve powers were broadened to curtail bank loans for speculative purposes and to regulate interest rates. Most significant was a shift of power from the Federal Reserve banks to the Federal Reserve Board, particularly from New York to Washington, by vesting control over open market operations in the board while giving statutory recognition to the Federal Open Market Committee.

Roosevelt had not sought bank reform legislation and withheld his support for the Banking Act of 1933 until the bill was virtually assured of passage. Nevertheless, he accepted the law with good humor, congratulating Carter Glass as the father of the best piece of legislation since the passage of his other act creating the Federal Reserve System. In later years, Roosevelt was to claim for his administration full credit for the Banking Act of 1933 and for the highly successful FDIC.

The Banking Act of 1933 provided limited remedial reforms. It was a stopgap measure, and in 1935 Franklin Roosevelt again turned to bank reform. In November 1934, he appointed Marriner Eccles chairman of the Federal Reserve Board. Eccles, a Utah banker, had come to Washington to work under Henry Morgenthau at the Treasury Department. Upon his appointment to the Federal Reserve, he quickly presented the president with a plan to reform the banking system by increasing the powers of the Federal Reserve Board and centralizing control over banking in Washington.

The Eccles proposals were incorporated with other banking legislation prepared by an interdepartmental subcommittee appointed by the president earlier in 1934. On 2 February, Roosevelt sent the administration's Banking Act of 1935 to Congress. It was an omnibus bill containing three titles—Title I related to the FDIC, Title II contained the Federal Reserve provision, and Title III contained technical amendments to the federal banking laws. Opposition was expected. It was led by Carter Glass who also worked to have the Eccles appointment defeated. The bill passed the House with little opposition, but it had a stormy passage in the Senate. Hearings were held and bankers appeared to decry political control of the Federal Reserve Board. Initially, Roosevelt seemed indifferent, but in early summer he pressed for passage. After many conferences and much compromise, a greatly altered bill finally passed the Congress. Roosevelt signed it into law on 23 August 1935.

The Banking Act of 1935 was the most comprehensive banking law since the enactment of the Federal Reserve Act in 1913. The new law provided for basic changes in the structure of the Federal Reserve System. The regional Federal Reserve banks were made subservient to the Federal Reserve Board, now to be called the Board of Governors of the Federal Reserve System. Board members were to be appointed for terms of fourteen years and the board chairman for a term of four years. Presidents of the Federal Reserve banks were to be appointed by the boards of directors of the regional banks, subject to approval of the Board of Governors. A new Federal Open Market Committee was established composed of the Board of Governors and four representatives selected from the presidents of the Federal Reserve banks. In addition, the Board of Governors was given direct control over reserve requirements, discount operations, interest rates, and open market operations. Concentration of power in the Federal Reserve Board made central banking an integral part of the American banking scene.

In his attitude and actions with respect to bank reform, Franklin Roosevelt revealed his most conservative inclinations. He chose to modify and rectify rather than build anew. He never seriously considered government ownership of the banks, nor did he call for unification of all commercial banks under the Federal Reserve System. He gave the dual banking system his support. Banking, in and of itself, held little interest for him. After the enactment of the Banking Act of 1935, he did not turn again to major bank reform. Yet the laws enacted under his administration brought American banking forward. Federal deposit insurance became a basic element of the banking system, and Federal Reserve control was firmly lodged in Washington.

The most comprehensive analysis of the banking crisis is Susan Estabrook Kennedy's *The Banking Crisis of 1933*

(Lexington: University Press of Kentucky, 1973). Arthur Ballantine, Hoover's under secretary of treasury, wrote a contemporary account, "When All the Banks Closed," in *Harvard Business Review* 26 (March 1948):129–43, as did Roosevelt's comptroller of the currency, J. F. T. O'Connor, in *The Banking Crisis and Recovery under the Roosevelt Administration* (Chicago: Callaghan, 1938). Also of interest is Marcus Nadler and Jules I. Bogen, *The Banking Crisis, The End of an Epoch* (New York: Dodd, Mead, 1933). Helen M. Burns, *The American Banking Community and New Deal Banking Reforms 1933–1935* (Westport, Conn.: Greenwood, 1974), discusses the Roosevelt bank reform measures and the impact of the banking community on those measures. A firsthand account of the Banking Act of 1935 is given in the autobiographical work by Roosevelt's chairman of the Federal Reserve Board, Marriner S. Eccles, in *Beckoning Frontiers: Public and Personal Recollections* (New York: Alfred A. Knopf, 1951). For background information on banking in the 1920s, see Eugene N. White, *The Regulation and Reform of the American Banking System 1900–1929* (Princeton: Princeton University Press, 1983).

HELEN M. BURNS

See also Eccles, Marriner Stoddard; Federal Deposit Insurance Corporation; Great Depression; Jones, Jesse Holman; Monetary Policy

Barnes, Harry Elmer
(15 June 1889–25 August 1968)

Historian and isolationist critic of Roosevelt. Harry Elmer Barnes was born and educated in New York; he graduated from Syracuse in 1913 and received his Ph.D. from Columbia in 1918. Barnes, one of the preeminent historians of his day, wrote extensively and taught at a number of institutions, including Clark University, the New School for Social Research, and Smith College. His earlier writings challenged the prevailing notion of German guilt for World War I and viewed the French and the English as no less responsible than the Germans. During the thirties, his isolationism led him to emphasize the failings of the European democracies and to urge an accommodation with Hitler. He opposed Roosevelt's foreign policies before and during World War II, when he wrote several pamphlets arguing against U.S. involvement. U.S. entry into both world wars, he later wrote, "converted the libertarian American dream of the pre-1914 days into a nightmare of fear, regimentation, destruction, insecurity, inflation, and ultimate insolvency." After the war he joined Charles A. Beard, Charles A. Tansill, and others in calling for a revisionist interpretation of the causes of the war, blaming Roosevelt's internationalist tendencies more than German or Japanese aggression.

There is no adequate biography of Barnes. His views can be found in his *Perpetual War for Perpetual Peace* (Caldwell, Idaho: Caxton Printers, 1953). Several of his pamphlets are collected in *Selected Revisionist Pamphlets* (New York: Arno Press, 1972).

Baruch, Bernard Mannes

(19 August 1870–20 June 1965)

Financial speculator, head of the War Industries Board in World War I, and unofficial economic adviser to various presidents. At the Democratic National Convention of 1932, Bernard Baruch seemed to support everybody *but* Franklin Roosevelt. The self-made millionaire had been a Democratic party stalwart since Woodrow Wilson's time, but he found Roosevelt too "wishy-washy" and secretly supported candidates like Al Smith and Newton Diehl Baker whom he found stronger. For their own parts, candidates like Smith, Baker, Albert Ritchie, and Roosevelt himself actively sought the support of an old-line Democrat like Baruch, who served as a powerful link with more influential days before the Republicans seemed to own the White House. Despite these contenders' approaches and the curiosity of other Democrats, Baruch remained silent about his preferences, preferring not to back publicly a losing candidate, as he had done in 1924 and 1928. Eventually, however, Baruch's party loyalty overcame his distaste for FDR, and he offered his services to the candidate and his counselors almost immediately after the nomination.

Whatever Roosevelt's feelings about this offer might have been, advisers like Louis Howe and Raymond Moley felt that Baruch was not to be trusted. Even if he were committed to the candidate's policies, they argued, Baruch was a living symbol of the Wall Street speculator of 1929, the preeminent villain of the time. Yet if the nominee could not fully embrace the speculator, he could not fully ignore him either; beyond his personal influence within the party, Baruch also offered the considerable financial support that the Democrats—twelve years out of power and as impoverished as the rest of the nation in 1932— desperately needed for Roosevelt to gain the presidency. A man of Baruch's considerable self-opinion would feel more than slighted if he were not asked to participate actively in the shaping of Roosevelt's campaign.

Consequently, instead of inviting him into the inner circle of his advisers, Roosevelt agreed as early as August of 1932 that Baruch should work ex officio as "professor emeritus" of the brains trust. This tendency to consult Baruch rather than rely on him held for the rest of Roosevelt's life. Although he visited "the barony of Hobcaw" (Baruch's estate in South Carolina) on several occasions during his presidency, Roosevelt's dealings with Baruch always remained distinctly cool. As for Baruch, the speculator's relationship with Eleanor Roosevelt was quite warm and much closer than with her husband, perhaps because both she and Baruch were more comfortable when working through unofficial channels.

Although he served as Roosevelt's adviser on such occasions as the World Monetary and Economic Conference in 1933, Baruch's main impact on the administration during the thirties consisted of supplying more visible personnel to head up the New Deal's various new departments; Roosevelt appointees like Hugh Johnson (chief of the National Recovery Administration) and George Peek (administrator of the Agricultural Adjustment Administration) had been Baruch's number one men for some time. Far from initiating policies, the unofficial president (as one telegram had it) usually served as critic and subsequent booster of ideas hatched by other advisers and was often treated as the in-house representative of conservative business and financial interests. After Pearl Harbor, however, the president called on Baruch increasingly for advice on the management of the wartime economy, drawing on Baruch's legendary experience as head of the War Industries Board in 1917 and 1918.

Throughout the war years, however, Baruch carefully avoided specific offices. When the president offered him control of the Office of Economic Stabilization, he refused to accept it. When the administration tried to persuade him to head the War Production Board in early 1943, he vacillated long enough to make his eventual acceptance too late to do any good, and FDR was forced to withdraw his original offer. In both cases, Baruch—although a staunch patriot—refused to serve in a position that would increase his responsibilities without proportionally increasing his ability to affect the economy.

Baruch (New York: Holt, Rinehart and Winston, 1957, 1960), two volumes of memoirs he wrote with the uncredited assistance of biographer Marquis James, are an important but often unreliable primary source, as are earlier biographies by Carter Field (New York: Harper & Row, 1944) and Harry Irving Shumway (Boston: Little, Brown, 1946), both titled *Bernard Baruch*. The most valuable works are Margaret Coit's diverting *Mr. Baruch* (Boston: Little, Brown, 1957) and two recent books, Jordan A. Schwarz's prize-winning *The Speculator: Bernard Baruch in Washington, 1917–1965* (Chapel Hill: University of North Carolina Press, 1981) and James Grant's excellent *Bernard M. Baruch: Adventures of a Wall Street Legend* (New York: Simon & Schuster, 1983).

See also Business

Bernard M. Baruch, 1919. Photographer: Lucien Swift Kirtland. (National Portrait Gallery, Smithsonian Institution.)

Beard, Charles A.

(1874–1948)

A prominent isolationist critic of FDR's foreign policy, Charles A. Beard during the 1930s was considered to be America's foremost historian with some thirty books to his name. He was born near Knightstown, Indiana, the son of a prosperous businessman. Beard graduated from DePauw University in 1898 and then continued his studies at Oxford University in England. In 1902 he returned to the United States where two years later he received his doctorate from Columbia University, which promptly appointed him to its Department of Political Science.

During his years in England, Beard was strongly impressed by socialist critiques of British government and society, and this influenced his own later work on this side of the Atlantic. With the publication in 1913 of his book, *An Economic Interpretation of the Constitution,* Beard established himself as a prominent member of the Progressive school of historians, which examined American history in the light of a radical critique of the contemporary social and political structure of America.

Although his progressive views initially inclined Beard to support Roosevelt's New Deal reforms, his isolationist tendencies eventually transformed him into a vehement critic of FDR's foreign policy. In part influenced by the 1935 Nye committee's report on the role financiers and arms manufacturers had played in embroiling America in World War I, Beard became convinced that the United States had no vital interests at stake in European political developments. He developed a doctrine of Continentalism, which presented U.S. security needs as being limited to the adequate defense of the North American continent. Ideological or economic considerations did not constitute sufficient justification for involvement in foreign wars.

From around the time of Roosevelt's 1937 quarantine speech, Beard became a sworn opponent of the president's foreign policy. He predicted that FDR would embroil the United States in war with Japan as an easy way out of the depression and called instead for the fostering of American economic self-sufficiency in order to eliminate the temptation to interfere in overseas conflicts.

Beard clung to these views despite the increasing immediacy of the danger posed to U.S. security by German and Japanese expansionism. After the outbreak of war in Europe in 1939, Beard's die-hard isolationism began to alienate many fellow liberal intellectuals in this country. During the period of 1941–45, Beard supported the actual war effort, but continued to cast doubt on the generally accepted reasons for America's involvement in the war in the first place. After FDR's death and the end of World War II, Beard devoted his energies to the unmasking of Roosevelt as a scheming politician who had served his own political ends by engineering America's entry into the war.

His rather simplistic line of argument and the narrowly personal thrust of his attacks on FDR had left Beard isolated from a large part of the American intellectual community by the time he died in 1948. Nonetheless, the posthumous influence of his work can be discerned in the writings of some of the revisionist historians of the 1960s, whose books castigated postwar American foreign policy as serving the needs of narrow economic interest groups rather than the true national interest.

For an excellent critical analysis of Beard's life and work, see Part 3 of Richard Hofstadter's *The Progressive Historians* (New York: Alfred A. Knopf, 1968). Beard's two books on Roosevelt are *American Foreign Policy in the Making, 1932–40* and *President Roosevelt and the Coming of the War, 1941* (New Haven: Yale University Press, 1941 and 1948, respectively).

Adolf A. Berle, Jr. (Courtesy FDR Library.)

Berle, Adolf Augustus, Jr.

(29 January 1895–17 February 1971)

Member of the New Deal's brains trust—advisers to FDR during the 1932 campaign and in the organization of his presidency—and an informal adviser during his first term, assistant secretary of state, 1938–44, and ambassador to Brazil, 1945. A child prodigy, Adolf A. Berle, Jr., owed his early education to his father, a Congregationalist minister who dabbled in theories of education which he applied to his four children. Born in Boston in 1895, Berle graduated from Harvard College at eighteen and Harvard Law School at twenty-one. Following a brief stint in Louis Brandeis's law firm, Berle served in army intelligence during World War I in the Dominican Republic. Assigned to the Russian section of the American delegation at the Paris Peace Conference, he achieved minor fame when he became one of the few members of the delegation to denounce the terms of the treaty publicly as a betrayal of Wilsonian ideals.

In the early twenties, while he practiced corporation law in New York for a big firm that encouraged public service activities, Berle wrote articles for liberal journals on foreign affairs, took cases involving Indian rights in the Southwest, and lived for two years at the Henry Street Settlement House on New York's Lower East Side. In 1924 he established his own firm specializing in corporation law, and in 1927 he joined the faculty of Columbia University Law School while beginning a study with economist Gardiner Means on the legal and economic consequences of contemporary behavior. The result of their collaboration, *The Modern Corporation and Private Property,* mostly written by Berle, was published in 1932. Arguing that wealth and power in America was concentrated in two hundred corporations through a host of financial devices that divorced corporations from public or stockholder control, the book became an instant classic. It described concentrated corporate power and planning and emphasized the need for federal regulation of corporations amid the social crisis of the Great Depression. Although its conclusions were not original, the book, written with great verve and timely published, achieved enduring importance.

Also in 1932, Berle formed with fellow Columbia professors Raymond Moley and Rexford Tugwell FDR's brains trust. Through his incisive intellect and ability to develop a political base in New York, Berle became the most durable of the brains trusters, advising Roosevelt long after Moley and Tugwell had moved on. A liberal who called for increasing federal intervention in the economy, Berle wrote FDR's 1932 Commonwealth Club address. In the ideological struggles of the New Deal, Berle was a prominent advocate of national planning in opposition to the antitrust atomism of the Brandeisians. Following the election, Berle eschewed several offers of positions in the administration, temporarily served as counsel to the Reconstruction Finance Corporation, and returned to New York to work with Fiorello La Guardia. La Guardia's election as mayor in 1933 was viewed as significant by Berle and FDR because of New York's importance to national recovery. As city chamberlain, Berle became the guiding hand behind financial schemes that brought New York back from the brink of bankruptcy. At the same time, Berle remained a freewheeling unofficial adviser to FDR through frequent conferences and letters that began with the jocular salutation, "Dear Caesar," from which Roosevelt in 1937 ordered him to desist. Also, Berle wrote speeches for FDR and served in brief foreign policy roles at Latin American conferences. In 1938 Berle acceded to FDR's wishes and moved to Washington as assistant secretary of state.

Known as a brilliant intellectual who did not suffer fools gladly, Berle's chief asset in Washington for FDR was his versatility. The only important State Department activity that involved him before Pearl Harbor was negotiation of the St. Lawrence Seaway with Canada, a public power project dear to FDR's heart. But by 1941 Berle had carved out a valuable niche for himself as State Department coordinator of intelligence, a post that involved him with the FBI's activities in Latin America and with the OSS's activities elsewhere. During the war he worked with antifascist and anticommunist Europeans in trying to re-create a democratic Europe. Berle consistently advocated republican self-determination for all nations, a liberalism that brought him into conflict with Nazis, fascists, communists, and imperialists—including America's British ally. Never at a loss for enemies (Felix Frankfurter had been one since Berle was his law student at Harvard), Berle found himself wrongly accused by fellow liberals during the war of impeding collaboration with the Soviet Union. Also, Secretary of State Cordell Hull resented Berle's special relationship with FDR. Nevertheless, Berle in 1944 assumed a vital task in negotiating with the British and other Allies an agreement covering postwar commercial aviation. In the midst of a major international conference on aviation in late November 1944, Roosevelt removed Berle as assistant secretary of state and asked him to go to Brazil as ambassador—where Berle was when FDR died and the war ended.

Berle spent the rest of his life in a variety of endeavors as a member of America's foreign policy establishment and an anticommunist liberal intellectual. Although an excellent speaker, Berle apparently never seriously considered a career in electoral politics. His politics was of the good-government variety that marked him as somewhat patronizing, aristocratic, and corporatist. Yet, beginning in 1947, he served for a decade as chairman of New York's Liberal party, an organization comprised mostly of Jewish social democratic labor leaders. In the 1950s he was active with Radio Free Europe and expanded his numerous alliances with social democrats in Latin America, playing a strong role in fostering democratic governments in Venezuela and Costa Rica. Within the Council on Foreign Relations and elsewhere, he advocated paying more attention to American interests in Latin America. His numerous intellectual and policy interests were also reflected in the Twentieth Century Fund, which he headed for a quarter century.

With the election of President Kennedy, Berle returned to Washington for six months in 1961 as chairman of the president's task force on Latin America and as the architect of the Alliance for Progress. He also played a role in planning the abortive Bay of Pigs invasion of Castro's Cuba in April. President Johnson used him as an adviser during the 1965 intervention in the Dominican Republic (Berle recalling ironically that he had opposed U.S. intervention there in 1918). He supported Johnson's escalation of the Vietnam War and was aghast over Columbia University demonstrations against the war—which he believed were inspired by Moscow. Berle died in 1971.

A book about Berle by Jordan A. Schwarz, tentatively entitled *Liberal: The World of Adolf A. Berle,* will be published in late 1985. The best published glimpse of Berle can be found in Beatrice Bishop Berle and Travis Beal Jacobs, eds. *Navigating the Rapids, 1918–1971: From the Papers of Adolf A. Berle* (New York: Harcourt Brace Jovanovich, 1973), which includes a diary he kept intermittently. His wife has written an engaging autobiography that idolizes Berle—*A Life in Two Worlds: The Autobiography of Beatrice Bishop Berle* (New York: Walker & Co. 1983). On Berle's relationship with FDR and his role in the early New Deal, see Elliot A. Rosen, *Hoover, Roosevelt and the Brains Trust: From Depression to New Deal* (New York: Columbia University Press, 1977); R. G. Tugwell, *The Brains Trust* (New York: Viking Press, 1968); Frank Freidel, *Franklin D. Roosevelt: Launching The New Deal* (Boston: Little, Brown & Co. 1973); and Arthur Schlesinger, Jr., *The Crisis of the Old Order, 1919–1933* (Boston: Houghton Mifflin Co., 1957). Berle himself was a prolific writer, and much of his writings are self-revealing, but none of it is a memoir. The work that he considered his crowning achievement, a judgment not shared by reviewers, and that includes several reminiscences of FDR is *Power* (New York: Harcourt, Brace & World, 1969).

JORDAN A. SCHWARZ

See also Brains Trust

Mary McLeod Bethune, 1943–44, detail of a portrait. Artist: Betsy Graves Rayneau. (National Portrait Gallery, Smithsonian Institution. Gift of Harmon Foundation.)

Bethune, Mary McLeod

(10 July 1875–18 May 1955)

New Deal official, civil rights leader. Mary McLeod Bethune, daughter of an illiterate South Carolina sharecropper, was the only one of seventeen children to go to school. She attended Moody Bible Institute in Chicago and then taught in several Presbyterian schools in the South. In 1904, she began in Florida her own primary school for blacks, which became Bethune-Cookman College in 1929; she served as its president. The depression led her to believe in political action as a remedy for the poverty faced by blacks, and she formed the National Council on Negro Women in 1935. She became a friend of Eleanor Roosevelt and a regular visitor to the White House, especially after her appointment to the Advisory Committee of the National Youth Administration. From this office Bethune pushed for nondiscriminatory policies and succeeded in funneling government funds into many black communities.

As the highest ranking black in the New Deal, Bethune met with President Roosevelt six or seven times a year and pushed privately and publicly to make the New Deal more sensitive to the issue of race. Bethune commanded considerable attention in the black community as leader of a group of black federal officials known as the Black Cabinet and as a champion for a variety of civil rights causes, including antilynching activities, the Scottsboro boys, and rights for black sharecroppers. She ended her work in Washington in 1944 and returned to Florida where she lived until her death in 1955.

The best biography of Bethune is Rackham Holt, *Mary McLeod Bethune* (Garden City, N.Y.: Doubleday, 1964). Harvard Sitkoff, *A New Deal for Blacks* (New York: Oxford University Press, 1978), discusses her connections with Roosevelt and the New Deal.

See also Black Cabinet; National Youth Administration

Biddle, Francis Beverley

(9 May 1886–4 October 1968)

Few of the New Dealers served as long and as faithfully under Franklin Roosevelt as did Francis Biddle. After a first career as a prototypical "Philadelphia lawyer," Biddle shed his Republican heritage in 1932 and left his successful law practice in 1934 to occupy a series of administrative, judicial, and legal positions in the federal government. His tenure in these posts was marked by a pragmatic liberalism that often put him at odds with ideologues of the Left and Right. Patrician by birth and casual in temperament, Biddle nonetheless left behind him a legacy of determined protection of constitutional rights, marred by occasional accommodations with pressure groups that he later regretted.

Francis Biddle was born in Paris while his parents were traveling in Europe. His father was a law professor at the University of Pennsylvania, and his maternal ancestors included Edmond Randolph, the first attorney general of the United States, a link with law and public service of which Biddle remained inordinately proud. Like Roosevelt a product of Groton and Harvard College, but unlike him an outstanding student, Biddle was graduated with honors from Harvard Law School in 1911 and was rewarded by selection to serve for a year as secretary to Supreme Court Justice Oliver Wendell Holmes.

After three years of practice in the family law firm, Biddle formed a new partnership in 1917 and spent his time until 1934 as counsel to the Pennsylvania Railroad and other major corporations and businesses. His support for Robert La Follette in 1924 and Al Smith in 1928 marked Biddle as an apostate Republican in a city and state dominated by the GOP Old Guard, and in 1932 he formally renounced his ancestral party and became a fervent New Dealer and Roosevelt acolyte.

Roosevelt first tapped Biddle for a New Deal post in 1934, appointing him as chairman of the first National Labor Relations Board. This agency, established to monitor compliance with Section 7(a) of the National Industrial Recovery Act (NIRA), "was unable to enforce its orders," Biddle later wrote, and he clashed repeatedly with Secretary of Labor Frances Perkins and Donald Richberg of the National Recovery Administration. The 1935 Supreme Court decision in the *Schechter* case, which invalidated the NIRA, ended the board's existence and Biddle's job, although he worked closely with Senator Robert Wagner to draft an enforceable labor law that created an independent agency with real enforcement powers.

Biddle returned to his Philadelphia law practice in 1935 but chafed for a return to public service. He spent several months in 1938 as chief counsel to a congressional panel set up to investigate the Tennessee Valley Authority (TVA), drawing Republican criticism for grilling Wendell Willkie, the southern utilities' lawyer, and battling with TVA chairman Arthur Morgan, who "did his best to destroy" the agency in Biddle's view.

Having resisted an appeal from Attorney General Frank Murphy in 1939 to become a federal appellate judge in Philadelphia, Biddle succumbed to Roosevelt's assurance that he would be appointed solicitor general after a brief judicial stint. Biddle loyally endured this service, although he confessed that listening to lawyers "bored" him. Roosevelt waffled on his commitment to Biddle, but after an Oval Office audience he kept his bargain. Biddle greatly enjoyed his year-long stint as the government's advocate before the Supreme Court, which he felt "combines the best of private practice and of government service." Appearing before the Court in more than twenty cases, Biddle scored his greatest success in the *Darby Lumber* case, in which the justices upheld the New Deal wages and hours law and overruled a relic of constitutional reaction, *Hammer* v. *Dagenhart,* a decision that had struck down the child labor law of the Progressive Era.

After the elevation of Attorney General Robert Jackson to the Supreme Court in 1941, Biddle was confirmed by the Senate to replace him on 5 September. The Japanese attack on Pearl Harbor shocked the country just three months later, and wartime responsibilities occupied Biddle for the next four years. His most difficult decision in this post, and one he intensely regretted, was to abandon his objections to the mass evacuation and internment of 120,000 Americans of Japanese ancestry living on the West Coast. Biddle later attributed his capitulation to his status as the "new boy" in Roosevelt's cabinet and his deference to Secretary of War Henry L. Stimson, the elder statesman "whose wisdom and integrity I greatly respected."

In directing the Department of Justice, Biddle put into practice his lifelong commitment to the rights of black Americans. Unlike Jackson, he supported the efforts of the Civil Rights Section of his department to curb the endemic brutality of southern police officers and was proud of bringing to the Supreme Court the *Screws* case, in which the justices affirmed the federal conviction of a Georgia sheriff who had murdered a handcuffed black prisoner. Biddle also approved the prosecution of local officials who used force and intimidation against members of the Jehovah's Witnesses sect.

Wartime pressures undermined Biddle's devotion to the principles of civil liberty. He authorized the prosecution of a grab bag of Nazi sympathizers and Roosevelt haters under the sedition provision of the Smith Act and tolerated illegal wiretapping and break-ins by the FBI. Biddle also pressed for the deportation to Australia of Harry Bridges, the West Coast longshoremen's union leader. Despite the earlier finding of James Landis, the Harvard Law School dean who concluded after a lengthy hearing that Bridges had not been proved to be a Communist party member, Biddle ordered a second hearing and convinced himself that Bridges was a Communist and should be deported. Although Roosevelt had political qualms about this decision, and the Supreme Court later reversed the deportation order, Biddle stuck to his position.

President Truman unceremoniously removed Biddle as attorney general six months after Roosevelt's death in 1945, softening the blow with an appointment as the American judge on the International Military Tribunal, which conducted the Nuremberg trials of Nazi war criminals. Biddle found this assignment both demanding and rewarding, but after the trials ended he felt no desire to resume either public service or private practice. "I had lost touch with the law," he later wrote in a tone of resignation. Biddle and his wife, the poet Katherine Chapin, divided their retirement years between Washington and Cape Cod until his death.

Francis B. Biddle. (Constant Collection. Courtesy FDR Library.)

Biddle's life and career have not yet attracted a biographer. In two volumes of memoirs, however, he wrote at length and with considerable objectivity about his private and public service. The first volume, *A Casual Past* (Garden City, N.Y.: Doubleday, 1961), dealt with his education and private law practice. *In Brief Authority* (Garden City, N.Y.: Doubleday, 1962) discussed his New Deal service and included perceptive comments on Roosevelt and many of his fellow New Dealers. Biddle also collected his writings on law and civil liberties in *The Fear of Freedom* (Garden City, N.Y.: Doubleday, 1951). His work on the National Labor Relations Board is addressed in Peter Irons, *The New Deal Lawyers* (Princeton: Princeton University Press, 1982). Irons also recounts Biddle's role in the internment of Japanese-Americans in *Justice at War* (New York: Oxford University Press, 1983).

PETER IRONS

See also Civil Liberties in Wartime; Internment of Japanese-Americans

Biographers and Public Reputation

By almost any standard, Franklin D. Roosevelt was a herculean figure. Four times elected president, he served as chief executive in times of great domestic and foreign crises, providing crucial leadership for the New Deal and the Grand Alliance. As a result of his policies, Roosevelt attracted intense admiration and condemnation, earning a dichotomous reputation that continued long after his death in 1945. Evaluation of President Franklin D. Roosevelt has contributed not only to an understanding of his era but to the ongoing definition of the proper role of government in America.

The contours of the Roosevelt reputation emerged even before his death. Incensed by inflationary fiscal and monetary policy, extensive regulation, and expanded bureaucracy, conservative critics accused him of taking America toward socialism. From the opposite perspective, advanced reformers and radicals on the Left decried the fact that in a time of great popular discontent, Roosevelt had not sought fundamental change, such as public ownership of banks, utilities, railroads, and key industries, or significant redistribution of wealth. In regard to foreign policy before 7 December 1941, isolationists and interventionists battled over whether Roosevelt was deceptively leading the country into foreign wars or acting too timidly to

James MacGregor Burns on Roosevelt

Holmes had been right—a second-rate intellect but a first-rate temperament. To examine closely single aspects of Roosevelt's character—as thinker, as organizer, as manipulator, as strategist—is to see failings and deficiencies closely interwoven with the huge capacities. But to stand back and look at the man as a whole, against the backdrop of his people and his times, is to see the lineaments of greatness—courage, joyousness, responsiveness, vitality, faith, and, above all, concern for his fellow man. A democrat in manner and conviction, he was yet a member of that small aristocracy once described by E. M. Forster—sensitive but not weak, considerate but not fussy, plucky in his power to endure, capable of laughing and of taking a joke. He was the true happy warrior.

Excerpted from *Roosevelt: The Lion and the Fox,* copyright 1956 by James MacGregor Burns. Reprinted by permission of Harcourt Brace Jovanovich, Inc.

shore up Britain, France, and China against aggression from Nazi Germany and militarist Japan. A clear majority of Americans, however, saw Franklin D. Roosevelt as a great reform president who, while upholding the best of American ideals, had led the country through the trials of depression, perilous international events, and finally global war.

This was certainly Roosevelt's image of himself. He saw himself in the American reform tradition, heir of Washington, Jefferson, Theodore Roosevelt, and Woodrow Wilson. When the United States went to war, some of his admirers compared him with another great wartime president, Abraham Lincoln. In establishing his image of the strong leader, Roosevelt was aided by his successful use of the press and the radio and through the agreement of photographers and political cartoonists not to use illustrations that emphasized the physical handicap he suffered after an attack of polio. Always concerned with history, Roosevelt arranged for publication of the public papers of his presidency and, more important, launched plans for the first modern presidential library-museum to house his papers and memorabilia at his birthplace and grave site in Hyde Park, New York.

Roosevelt's unexpected death in 1945 on the eve of military victory, as with Lincoln nearly a century earlier, led millions to view him as a martyr to the nation's cause. His reputation was never greater. He was by then a recognized international leader, one of the two most powerful men in the world, and a major architect of the plans for the postwar order. He had given voice to America's wartime ideals in the concepts of the arsenal of democracy, the Atlantic Charter, the four freedoms, and the United Nations. Domestically, his New Deal had benefited millions of Americans through federal relief, unemployment insurance, Social Security, minimum wage standards, collective bargaining guarantees, farm price supports, and federal mortgage programs. In addition, concrete artifacts abounded: roads, bridges, tunnels, post offices, hydroelectric dams, rural electric power lines, newly planted shelterbelts across the windswept prairies, all erected with federal funds.

Roosevelt remained a powerful symbol both of

American hopes and of national victories over economic depression and military aggression. This image was reflected in the first significant biographies written after his death by journalist John Gunther, *Roosevelt in Retrospect: A Profile in History* (New York: Harper & Row, 1950), and by historian Dexter Perkins, *The New Age of Franklin Roosevelt, 1932–1945* (Chicago: University of Chicago Press, 1957). Polls by Arthur Schlesinger in 1948 and 1962 showed that historians considered Roosevelt to be one of the three greatest presidents, surpassed only by Lincoln and Washington. The majority of Americans seem to have agreed.

It was probably inevitable that such a dynamic and popular president would offer a yardstick by which to measure his successors in the White House. Concerned with personalities, competition, and measurable results, the mass media contrasted every new president's style and success with the voters and with Congress during their first hundred days in office with that of FDR, as though there were something inherently significant in that figure. More important, his successors recognized the political appeal of the fallen president to members of the Roosevelt coalition—white working-class ethnics, blacks, and liberal intellectuals—and many of their children, a group that would remain a considerable segment of the electorate for several decades. Favorable identification with Roosevelt, even if only ritualistic obeisance, became mandatory for Democratic contenders and for the majority of Republican presidential candidates as well. As historian William E. Leuchtenburg has shown, Roosevelt cast a mighty long shadow (*In the Shadow of FDR: From Harry Truman to Ronald Reagan* [Ithaca, N.Y.: Cornell University Press, 1983]).

No one labored under the shadow more than his immediate successor, Harry S Truman. Coming unexpectedly into a presidency dominated for twelve years by FDR, Truman seemed overawed and sought counsel and support from the Roosevelt family and advisers. He also pledged to carry on his predecessor's policies. Even as he gained personal independence, however, he wooed the Roosevelt coalition by revering publicly the dead president and identifying

James MacGregor Burns on Roosevelt

"I dream dreams but am, at the same time, an intensely practical person," Roosevelt wrote to Smuts during the war. Both his dreams and his practicality were admirable; the problem lay in the relation between the two. He failed to work out the intermediary ends and means necessary to accomplish his purposes. Partly because of his disbelief in planning far ahead, partly because he elevated short-run goals over long-run, and always because of his experience and temperament, he did not fashion the structure of action—the full array of mutually consistent means, political, economic, psychological, military—necessary to realize his paramount ends.

So the more he preached his lofty ends and practiced his limited means, the more he reflected and encouraged the old habit of the American democracy to "praise the Lord—and keep your powder dry" and the more he widened the gap between popular expectations and actual possibilities. Not only did this derangement of ends and means lead to crushed hopes, disillusion, and cynicism at home, but it helped sow the seeds of the Cold War during World War II, as the Kremlin contrasted Roosevelt's coalition rhetoric with his Atlantic First strategy and falsely suspected a bourgeois conspiracy to destry Soviet Communism; and Indians and Chinese contrasted Roosevelt's anticolonial words with his military concessions to colonial powers, and falsely inferred that he was an imperalist at heart and a hypocrite to boot.

Roosevelt's critics attacked him as naïve, ignorant, amateurish in foreign affairs, but this man who had bested all his domestic enemies and most of his foreign was no innocent. His supreme difficulty lay not in his views as to what *was*—he had a Shakespearian appreciation of all the failings, vices, cruelties, and complexities of man—but of what *could be*. The last words he ever wrote, on the eve of his death, were the truest words he ever wrote. He had a strong and active faith, a huge and unprovable faith, in the possibilities of human understanding, trust, and love. He could say with Reinhold Niebuhr that love is the law of life even when people do not live by the law of love.

Excerpted from *Roosevelt: The Soldier of Freedom,* © 1970 by James MacGregor Burns. Reprinted by permission of Harcourt Brace Jovanovich, Inc., and Weidenfeld & Nicolson, Ltd.

his own domestic program, the Fair Deal, as a direct descendant of the New Deal. Dwight D. Eisenhower vehemently disagreed with many of Roosevelt's domestic policies and disliked his preachy style. Nevertheless, Ike recognized the greatness of Roosevelt's performance as commander in chief. During his final illness he wrote: "Any President, if he is to be effective, must be able to inspire people. It is an essential quality of leadership. I have often thought how fortunate it was that the two great Allies of World War II were led by two men—Churchill and Franklin D. Roosevelt—who had that ability and used it masterfully." Recognizing the need for continued bipartisan support for U.S. internationalism in the postwar world, Eisenhower remained publicly a champion of Roosevelt's internationalist legacy.

Isolationist as well as anti–New Deal, the midwestern wing of the Republican party was not reluctant to attack the late Democratic champion, particularly on foreign policy. Seeking to unseat the Democrats in the late 1940s and early 1950s, GOP politicians like senators Robert Taft, William Knowland, and Joseph McCarthy sought to encourage and utilize widespread public disappointment with postwar international developments by placing a major share of the "blame" for Russian domination in Eastern Europe as well as the later Communist victory in China upon Franklin D. Roosevelt. They argued that the president had been ill-informed and in ill-health at the Yalta Conference in early 1945 and had been duped by Stalin into recognizing expanded Communist influence in Europe and Asia. Accusations of a "betrayal at Yalta," especially when combined with ardent anticommunism, may have been effective in aiding the shift of many Democratic voters of East European and Catholic background to the Republican national ticket.

Much less effective politically were conservative Republican attacks upon Roosevelt's domestic policies. Only ardent Hooverites and other Roosevelt haters applauded a vitriolic "exposé" like *The Roosevelt Myth* (New York, 1948) in which journalist John

Flynn accused the president of leading the country toward fascism and of betraying his every friend and ideal. Nor was there much of value in the more temperate but nonetheless distorted and simplistic portrayal of FDR as a would-be socialist in *The Roosevelt Leadership, 1933–1945* (Philadelphia: Lippincott, 1955) by Edgar E. Robinson, a conservative constitutionalist and normally an objective and distinguished historian.

Although perhaps appealing to people who wished to believe it, the myth of the "betrayal" at Yalta, like the accusation of Roosevelt's fascism or socialism, bore more relationship to partisan politics than to historical accuracy, as more objective, documented accounts indicated. Although Roosevelt's health had declined by the winter of 1944–45, he was not mentally impaired (Howard Bruenn, M.D., "Clinical Notes on the Illness and Death of President Franklin D. Roosevelt," *Annals of Internal Medicine* 72 [April 1970]:579–91). Available evidence indicates he was Stalin's equal at negotiating at Yalta. Soviet domination of Eastern and Central Europe was the result of Russian policy and the fact that the Red Army occupied Eastern Europe as a result of its long drive against the *Wehrmacht*.

As Truman took an increasingly firm stand toward the Soviet Union, he claimed that he was following Roosevelt's policies and that Stalin was breaking the Yalta agreements. The conflict over the proper course and the correct analysis of the dead president's policy pitted former counselors against each other—left-wing soft-liners like Henry Wallace against hard-liners like W. Averell Harriman. Eventually, Eleanor Roosevelt and most anticommunist liberals and the

James MacGregor Burns on Roosevelt

"All that is within me cries out to go back to my home on the Hudson River," Roosevelt had said nine months before. The train, still hugging the riverbank, crossed from Poughkeepsie into Hyde Park. It was Sunday, April 15, 1945, a clear day, the sky a deep blue. Tiny waves were breaking against the river shore where the train slowed and switched off into a siding below the bluff on which the mansion stood. Cannon sounded twenty-one times as the coffin was moved from the train to a caisson drawn by six brown horses. Standing behind was a seventh horse, hooded, stirrups reversed, sword and boots turned upside down hanging from the left stirrup—symbolic of a lost warrior.

Following the beat of muffled drums the little procession toiled up the steep, winding, graveled road, past a small stream running full and fast, past the ice pond, with its surface a smoky jade under the overhanging hemlocks, past the budding apple trees and the lilacs and the open field, and emerged onto the height. In back of the house, standing in the rose garden framed by the hemlock hedge, was a large assembly: President Truman and his Cabinet and officialdom of the old administration and family and friends and retainers, a phalanx of six hundred West Point cadets standing rigidly at attention in their gray uniforms and white crossed belts. Behind the coffin, borne now by eight servicemen, Eleanor Roosevelt and her daughter, Anna, and her son Elliott moved into the rose garden.

The aged rector of St. James Episcopal Church of Hyde Park prayed—". . . earth to earth, ashes to ashes, dust to dust." Raising his hand as the servicemen lowered the body slowly into the grave, he intoned:

> "Now the laborer's task is o'er,
> Now the battle day is past,
> Now upon the farther shore
> Lands the voyager at last. . . ."

A breeze off the Hudson ruffled the trees above. Cadets fired three volleys. A bugler played the haunting notes of Taps. The soldier was home.

core of the Roosevelt coalition supported Truman's interpretation and his evolving policy of containment.

In the immediate postwar period, historical scholarship on Roosevelt's foreign policy focused not on the origins of the emerging cold war but on the resumption of the old controversy over U.S. entry into World War II. Old isolationists like Charles A. Beard, *American Foreign Policy, 1932–1940* (New Haven, Conn.: Yale University Press, 1946) and *President Roosevelt and the Coming of the War, 1941* (New Haven, Conn.: Yale University Press, 1948), and Charles C. Tansill, *Back Door to War: Roosevelt Foreign Policy, 1933–1941* (Chicago: Regnery, 1952), put forward a thesis, later reiterated by some post–Vietnam War skeptics such as political scientist Bruce M. Russett, *No Clear and Present Danger: A Skeptical View of the U.S. Entry into World War 2* (New York: Harper & Row, 1972), denying that the Axis constituted a threat to vital U.S. interests. They argued that Roosevelt deceived Americans into thinking he was pursuing peace when instead he sought to lead the United States into war in Europe. A few extremists went so far as to charge that Roosevelt had deliberately provoked the Japanese and that he knew and withheld knowledge of their plan to attack Pearl Harbor from local commanders there in order to overwhelm isolationist resistance and take the country into the war. This astonishing accusation was made by some Roosevelt detractors over the years (most recently by John Toland in *Infamy: Pearl Harbor and Its Aftermath* [San Francisco: Doubleday, 1982]) but has never been proved.

Most historians have completely rejected these hypotheses, based as they were on circumstantial evidence and on a conspiratorial theory of history that is both overly sinister and simplistic. The dominant interpretation, the internationalist or interventionist school, concluded that the Axis powers did pose a serious threat to U.S. security and international interests, particularly after the German conquest of France in 1940, and that the fundamental causes of American involvement lay in world events over which the United States actually had little control. This internationalist view came first from former administration officials like Herbert Feis, *The Road to Pearl Harbor* (Princeton: Princeton University Press, 1950) and William L. Langer and S. Everett Gleason, *The Challenge to Isolation, 1937–1940* (New York: Peter Smith, 1952) and *The Undeclared War, 1940–41* (New York: Peter Smith, 1953), and subsequently from university-based historians such as Robert A. Divine, *The Reluctant Belligerent: American Entry into World War II* (New York: John Wiley & Sons, 1965), Arnold A. Offner, *American Appeasement* (Cambridge, Mass.: Harvard University Press, 1969), Warren F. Kimball, *The Most Unsordid Act: Lend-Lease, 1939–1941* (Baltimore: Johns Hopkins University Press, 1969), and Robert Dallek, *Franklin D. Roosevelt and American Foreign Policy, 1932–1945* (New York: Oxford University Press, 1979). The scholarly debate is no longer over the wisdom of American entry into the war against Hitler's Germany, but rather over the degree of isolationist op-position and whether Roosevelt acted boldly or cautiously in educating public opinion, improvising, obtaining legislation, and manipulating certain situations, such as the undeclared antisubmarine war in the Atlantic, in order to hamper Nazi expansion before the United States became a full belligerent.

In regard to the Far East, even critics of Rooseveltian policy there, such as Paul W. Schroeder, *The Axis Alliance and Japanese-American Relations, 1941* (Ithaca, N.Y.: Cornell University Press, 1958), conclude that the president misunderstood Japan's intentions and underestimated her military strength and that his hard-line policy sought to increase the costs of the Japanese expansion and thus deter it, even though it produced the opposite result. Nor is the conspiracy theory of the Pearl Harbor disaster supported by the evidence, according to the leading scholars of the subject, Roberta Wohlstetter, *Pearl Harbor: Warning and Decision* (Stanford, Calif.: Stanford University Press, 1962), and the monumental work of Gordon W. Prange, *At Dawn We Slept: The Untold Story of Pearl Harbor* (New York: McGraw-Hill, 1981).

The opening of the Roosevelt Library in 1950 enabled scholars to launch a major investigation into the nature of the man and his relationship to his era. The framework for historical inquiry had already been established by Richard Hofstadter in *The American Political Tradition and the Men Who Made It* (New York: Knopf, 1948) in which he questioned whether Roosevelt had any ideology, liberal or conservative, or was simply a political opportunist. Hofstadter also asked if the New Deal was evolutionary rather than revolutionary. A number of other scholars sought answers to such questions, too, particularly in the massive collection of documents at Hyde Park.

Although differing in style and their assessment of the degree of change involved, this first generation of scholarly biographers and historians, nevertheless, came to the same general conclusion: that Roosevelt had played an important role as a liberal, activist president in the establishment of a governmental structure that could restrain the worst excesses of unrestricted capitalism and the business cycle and bring some of the benefits of the welfare state to America while avoiding the class conflict and totalitarianism that had plagued many other nations.

This liberal interpretation was carefully documented in a series of works. Frank Freidel, *Franklin D. Roosevelt*, 4 vols. (Boston: Little, Brown & Co., 1952–73) detailed his protagonist's childhood and early career through his first year in the White House in an expertly handled biographical approach. With a broader brush, Arthur M. Schlesinger, Jr., wrote a vivid historical narrative of the shift in national governmental leadership from Hoover to Roosevelt through 1936 in *The Age of Roosevelt*, 3 vols. (Boston: Houghton Mifflin Co., 1957–60). William E. Leuchtenburg provided the best single-volume account in *Franklin D. Roosevelt and the New Deal, 1932–1940* (New York: Harper & Row, 1963). From the perspective of a political scientist, James MacGregor Burns, *Roosevelt*, 2 vols. (New York:

Harcourt Brace Jovanovich, 1956, 1970), particularly favorable to FDR's wartime leadership, criticized him as a skilled political tactician who achieved many short-term domestic goals but failed to remold the party system for effective long-term reform. While Schlesinger emphasized Roosevelt's pragmatism, his experimentation withiin "the vital center" between poles of radicalism and reaction, Burns and Leuchtenburg focused on the increased number of organized groups—not only in business, but agriculture and labor—to which the federal government, now envisaged as a "broker state," responded under Roosevelt.

The masses of documents at Hyde Park, for all their worth, proved disappointing in terms of disclosure of the "real" FDR. Although the details of the governmental process became clearer, the inner Roosevelt continued to remain enigmatic. This was largely a result of FDR's unsystematic thought, his imprecision, and the different impressions he gave to people. Those who sought to portray a coherent concept of his thought, like Daniel Fusfeld, *The Economic Thought of Franklin D. Roosevelt and the Origins of the New Deal* (New York: Columbia University Press, 1956) and Thomas H. Greer, *What Roosevelt Thought: The Social and Political Ideas of Franklin D. Roosevelt* (East Lansing: Michigan State University Press, 1958), generally came up with little more than a collection of scattered utterances and clichés. Some valuable insights came from Bernard Bellush, *Franklin D. Roosevelt as Governor of New York* (New York: Columbia University Press, 1955) and Alfred B. Rollins, Jr., *Roosevelt and Howe* (New York: Alfred A. Knopf, 1962).

For evidence of the facile mind of the president as it dealt with daily problems, there remained probably no better accounts than the memoirs of Raymond Moley, *After Seven Years* (New York: Harper & Bros., 1939), Frances Perkins, *The Roosevelt I Knew* (New York: Viking Press, 1946), and Eleanor Roosevelt, *This I Remember* (New York: Harper & Bros., 1949). Standing in a class by themselves are the many memoir-histories by Rexford G. Tugwell, such as *The Democratic Roosevelt* (Garden City, N.Y.: Doubleday & Co., 1957) and *Roosevelt's Revolution* (New York: Macmillan, 1976), in which the disillusioned radical New Dealer continually reexamined the possibilities and realities of Roosevelt's leadership. After nearly two decades, the reputation of Franklin D. Roosevelt remained high, but like the portrait by artist Elizabeth Shoumatoff who was painting FDR when he died, the historical picture of Roosevelt remained unfinished.

The Roosevelt reputation was further bolstered by Democratic presidents who recaptured the White House from the Republicans in the 1960s, but FDR remained a protean figure, refracting attitudes and the changing circumstances of his successors. Personally ambivalent toward Roosevelt as a result of his father's criticism and Eleanor Roosevelt's personal disdain for him, John F. Kennedy nevertheless evoked his memory in order to capture the Roosevelt electoral coalition and win the presidency. Afterward, however, he felt confined by it. As he complained peevishly to Nathan Pusey, president of Harvard University: "Nate, when Franklin had this job, it was a cinch. He didn't have all these world problems. He had only to cope with poverty in the United States, but look what I've got."

More than any other president, Lyndon B. Johnson was personally as well as politically trapped in a struggle with the Rooseveltian image. He met Roosevelt only once, but when FDR died, LBJ wept openly. "He was just like a daddy to me, always," he said. His identification with Roosevelt was like that of an overly dutiful son, but also like a son, Johnson yearned not only to equal but to excel his mentor. He was exhilarated by his 1964 victory over Barry Goldwater (whom he accused of being a threat to peace and to New Deal benefits like Social Security) because he had exceeded FDR's percentage of the popular vote in 1936. He thought first of calling his Great Society program the Better Deal, and he argued, with considerable merit it seemed, that his 1965 legislation achievements—medical care, civil rights, federal aid to education, housing, and the War on Poverty—exceeded those of the hundred days. With less accuracy, Johnson claimed that his use of extensive military force in the Dominican Republic and Vietnam was in line with Roosevelt's opposition to totalitarian aggression in World War II, despite the dramatic differences and contrary to the fact that such intervention violated both Roosevelt's basic anticolonialism and his Good Neighbor policy. The majority of Americans refused to accept the analogy. In what may have been one of the last things Johnson read before his death in 1973, a Harris poll showed that respondents chose FDR over LBJ 393 to 28 when asked which recent president "most inspired confidence." In the end Johnson consoled himself by arguing that "Hoover and Roosevelt were more abused than I am."

The importance of Roosevelt's continuing popularity was not lost on Richard Nixon, who cited the former chief executive on a number of occasions, but with the hope of capturing part of his electoral coalition rather than perpetuating his liberal domestic programs. Nixon carved away white southern voters in 1968, and four years later he sought to peel away white ethnic groups in the North into what he called a "new American majority," a coalition based upon social rather than economic issues. But Nixon's plan to curtail New Deal programs collapsed as he was forced to resign in 1974 as a result of the Watergate scandal.

Like other American institutions, the Roosevelt image came under attack in the turbulence of the 1960s and early 1970s. Protests against social and economic oppression at home and abroad led many to find the roots of these problems in the relationship of government to the organized interest groups of a corporate capitalist economy. Since Roosevelt and the New Deal had been credited with the establishment of the broker state, they now received the blame for its shortcomings, its unresponsiveness to those who were poor and nonwhite and who lacked political power. The New Left critique of the developments of

Frank Freidel on Roosevelt

Many contemporaries and some later writers have considered Roosevelt an enigmatic, contradictory figure. He polarized American society; as with Theodore Roosevelt, few people were neutral in their opinions about him. Both ardent admirers and vehement haters were united in their feeling that they could not always understand him. Outwardly he was jovial, warm, and capable of seeming most indiscreet in his candor when he was not being indiscreet at all, and sometimes far from candid. He effectively communicated his friendly solicitude and emphatic self-assurance in his public appearances and radio talks; they convinced millions of people that he was a friend, indeed a mainstay. Yet toward the public and even toward those with whom he was most intimate, including his immediate family, there was an inner reserve. He seldom talked about his thinking or his plans until he had firmly made up his mind. "I am a pig-headed Dutchman," he once told Adm. William Leahy during World War II. ". . . We are going ahead with [this] and you can't change my mind" (Leahy, p. 136). On the other hand, as Edward Flynn has pointed out, "Roosevelt would adopt ideas only if he agreed with them. If he disagreed, he simply did nothing" (Flynn, p. 214). Though not sharing his thought processes, he helped build an aura of mystery and authority, and he kept power firmly to himself. Effective though these traits were when he was president, their origins lay far back in his early life. Eleanor Roosevelt wrote to one of her sons, "His was an innate kind of reticence that may have been developed by the fact that he had an older father and a very strong-willed mother, who constantly tried to exercise control over him in the early years. Consequently, he may have fallen into the habit of keeping his own counsel, and it became part of his nature not to talk to anyone of intimate matters" (Lash, p. 344).

. . . .

At the time of his death, Roosevelt was eulogized as one of the greatest figures of modern times. In the next few years, as conservatives in Congress sought to obliterate New Deal domestic programs and blamed the travail of the cold war upon Roosevelt's mistaken policies, his reputation declined. Isolationist historians in the 1940's, and "New Left" historians a generation later, found little to praise. Many other historians and biographers have been cautious both in their praise and criticism. Yet Roosevelt's popular reputation throughout the world has been little diminished. Despite adverse judgments concerning some of his policies and actions, he remains a major figure in modern history. His twelve years as president brought basic, lasting changes in both domestic and foreign policy. The government came to assume responsibility for the economic security of the American people and to be concerned with the security of peoples throughout the world. Roosevelt's "four freedoms" became a national, and to some extent an international, goal. Although, his inner reserve often baffled those closest to him, his basic character was not much different from that of a large part of the American people: a soaring idealism tempered by realism. He wrote in 1942 to Jan Smuts, "I dream dreams but am, at the same time, an intensely practical person" (*Personal Letters*, p. 1372). He has been honored for having sought noble goals, and criticized for having fallen short of them. Others fell short, too, but few had the vision of Roosevelt, who, the day before his death, worked on the draft of a speech ending, "The only limit to our realization of tomorrow will be our doubts of today." Roosevelt added in his own hand, "Let us move forward with strong and active faith."

Excerpted from "Franklin Delano Roosevelt" by Frank Freidel in *The Dictionary of American Biography*, supplement 2. ©1973 American Council of Learned Societies. Reprinted with the permission of Charles Scribner's Sons.

Jerry Doyle, New York Post, *23 April 1935.*

Arthur M. Schlesinger, Jr., on Roosevelt

There are two sorts of greatness—the foursquare, all-of-a-piece, unitary, monolithic kind, possessed by Washington, Jackson, Winston Churchill; and the glittering, elusive, pluralistic, impalpable kind, possessed by Jefferson, Henry Clay, Lloyd George, where levels of personality peel off with the delusive transparence of the skins of an onion, always frustrating the search for a hard core of personality underneath. The greatest statesman may perhaps, like Lincoln, combine both kinds: in the phrase of Archilochus, he is both hedgehog and fox. Franklin Roosevelt clearly belongs in the second category. He had, not a personality, but a ring of personalities, each one dissolving on approach, always revealing still another beneath.

Yet one cannot exhaust the Roosevelt mystery by saying that he was complicated. For, though the central core of personality remained impossible to pin down, one felt, nevertheless, beneath the dazzling variety on the surface, behind the succession of masks, a basic simplicity of mind and heart. His complexity was infinite, but it all pertained to tactics. On questions of essential purpose, he retained an innocence which was all the more baffling because of its luminous naïveté. "He sometimes tries to appear tough and cynical and flippant," Hopkins once told Sherwood, "but that's an act he likes to put on. . . .You and I are for Roosevelt because he's a great spiritual figure, because he's an idealist." This was true. It was his tactical deviousness which got him into trouble; it was the fundamental, tantalizing, intermittent but ultimately indestructible idealism which saved him.

He was complicated everywhere except in his heart of hearts. There he perceived things with elementary, almost childlike, faith. "What is your philosophy" asked the young man. "Philosophy?" Roosevelt replied. "Philosophy? I am a Christian and a Democrat—that's all." And for him, his church and his party implied a series of lucid commitments—respect for persons, respect for nature, respect for freedom. He held to these commitments with a confidence he never questioned and a serenity which never faltered.

In the end, a President of the United States must stand or fall by his instinct for the future as well as by his understanding of the past and his mastery of the present. Implanted within him, there must be an image, not necesarily—or even desirably—explicit or conscious, but profoundly rich, plastic, and capacious, of the kind of America he wants, of the vision of the American promise he is dedicated to realize, of the direction in which he believes the world is moving. Without such a sense, his Presidency will be static and uncreative. As Franklin Roosevelt's successor once put it, "The President's got to set the sights." This vision of the future becomes the source of his values; it justifies his strivings; it renews his hopes; it provides his life with its magnetic orientation.

It was this astonishing instinct for the future which above all distinguished Roosevelt, his extraordinary sensitivity to the emergent tendencies of his age and to the rising aspirations of ordinary people—a sensitivity housed at the same time within a personality and intelligence sufficiently conventional to provide in itself a bridge holding together past and future. Indeed, his very position on the breaking point between an old world and a new one gave him a special freedom and spontaneity which only a man can possess who is nourished by older values. When Roosevelt accepted the inevitability of change, he did so, not by necessity, but by conscious choice. He had made a deliberate decision, both tempermental and intellectual, in favor of adventure and experiment. "My impression of both him and of Mrs. Roosevelt," wrote H. G. Wells, "is that they are unlimited people, entirely modern in the openness of their minds and the logic of their actions." Nothing could daunt him, very little surprised him, he was receptive to everything, and not in a passive sense either, he received, not to accumulate, but to act; the future which he perceived was (this he deeply believed) to be in part his own creation. Wells summed him up: "The most effective transmitting instrument possible for the coming of the new world order. He is eminently reasonable and fundamentally implacable. He demonstrates that comprehensive new ideas can be taken up, tried out and made operative in general affairs without rigidity or dogma. He is continuously revolutionary in the new way without ever provoking a stark revolutionary crisis."

The essence of Roosevelt, the quality which fulfilled the best in him and explained the potency of his appeal, was his intrepid and passionate affirmation. He always cast his vote for life, for action, for forward motion, for the future. His response to the magnificent emptiness of the Grand Canyon was typical: "It looks dead. I like my green trees at Hyde Park better. They are alive and growing." He responded to what was vital, not what was lifeless; to what was coming, not to what was passing away. He lived by his exultation in distant horizons and uncharted seas. It was this which won him confidence and loyalty in a frightened age when the air was filled with the sound of certitudes cracking on every side—this and the conviction of plain people that he had given them head and heart and would not cease fighting in their cause.

the 1930s was suggested by Paul Conkin, *The New Deal* (New York: Harlan Davidson, 1967; 2d ed., 1975); Barton Bernstein, *Towards a New Past: Dissenting Essays in American History* (New York: Random House, 1968), pp. 263–321, and Howard Zinn, *The Politics of History* (Boston: Beacon Press, 1970). They charged that Roosevelt's program was designed to protect vested interests and power relationships and was, therefore, conservative in intent as well as result. Much of this analysis had more relevance to the 1960s than to the 1930s, but recognition of the limitations of New Deal reform by the New Left revisionists was a significant contribution to scholarship.

So was the challenge to the entire concept of broker-state liberalism (the notion that the whole community benefited from government support and coordination of organized interest groups) posed by other revisionists outside the New Left, such as Grant McConnell, *Private Power and American Democracy* (New York: Random House, 1966) and Theodore Lowi, *The End of Liberalism* (New York: W. W. Norton & Co., 1969). In addition, Roosevelt was faulted for allowing political expediency to outweigh moral imperatives, particularly in regard to minority groups. Among the instances cited in the 1960s were his refusal to advocate a federal antilynching law, his wartime authorization of the internment of Japanese-Americans, and, as documented in David S. Wyman, *Paper Walls: America and the Refugee Crisis, 1938–* 1941 (Amherst: University of Massachusetts Press, 1968); and Henry Feingold, *The Politics of Rescue* (New Brunswick, N.J.: Rutgers University Press, 1970), his excessive caution in responding to Nazi persecution and eventual extermination of millions of European Jews.

From a different, and neoconservative, perspective, Roosevelt and the New Deal underwent new assaults in the 1960s. Libertarians like Murray Rothbard in *America's Greatest Depression* (New York, 1963) and monetarists like Milton Friedman and Anna Schwartz in *A Monetary History of the United States, 1867–1960* (Princeton, N.J.: Princeton University Press, 1963) challenged federal fiscal and monetary policies as harmful rather than productive of economic recovery in the Great Depression and assailed the growing power of the national government over the economy. In the same period, the rise of the New Right intensified the old diatribe among extreme Roosevelt-haters through Finis Farr's moderate lament over *FDR* (New Rochelle, N.Y.: Arlington House, 1972) and through the virulent and specious conspiracy theories woven by Ann M. Wolf, *The Long Shadow of Franklin D. Roosevelt* (Philadelphia: Dorrance, 1974), and Anthony C. Sutton, *Wall Street and FDR* (New Rochelle, N.Y.: Arlington House, 1975).

Among the general public, Roosevelt's reputation may have been slightly hurt by the attack upon the "imperial presidency," an inflated, powerful, manipulative office misused by Johnson and Nixon to carry out unpopular, unethical, occasionally illegal activities at home and abroad. The modern presidency had its origins under Roosevelt, and both Johnson and Nixon sought to deflect criticism by arguing misleadingly that they had done nothing worse than what had been done by FDR or other presidents. While recognizing Roosevelt's issuance of misleading statements about the activity of U.S. naval destroyers in the Atlantic in 1940–41 and the use of mail openings, buggings, and other forms of surveillance on Charles Lindbergh and other isolationist leaders in the same period, a number of historians emphasized the relationship of most of these actions to national security in a world at war. The distinction was made, for example, in Arthur M. Schlesinger, Jr., *The Imperial Presidency* (Boston: Houghton Mifflin, 1973), and C. Vann Woodward, *Responses of the Presidents to Charges of Misconduct* (New York: Delacorte, 1974). Nevertheless, the events and accusations of the Vietnam and Watergate eras left the general public with increased cynicism and distrust of all political leaders.

In historical scholarship, Franklin D. Roosevelt seemed less relevant to analysis of his era two decades after his death than he had earlier. Although some scholars continued to examine particular aspects of his career, for example, Alfred H. Jones, *Roosevelt's Image Brokers* (Port Washington, N.Y.: Associated Faculty Press, 1974), and Graham J. White, *FDR and the Press* (Chicago: University of Chicago Press, 1979), most practitioners of the craft of history had departed from a focus on political leadership and the presidential synthesis in American history and increasingly turned their attention to changes in institutions. When dealing with past politics, they sought to extend the understanding of events beyond the apex of the presidency. One example of the new approach was a greater concern with lesser political figures who had a significant influence upon the formulation and implementation of public policy. Important works in this vein included histories of particular groups such as Richard Kirkendall, *Social Scientists and Farm Politics in the Age of Roosevelt* (Columbia, Mo.: University of Missouri Press, 1966), and Elliot A. Rosen, *Hoover, Roosevelt, and the Brains Trust* (New York: Columbia University Press, 1977), and biographies such as J. Joseph Huthmacher, *Senator Robert F. Wagner and the Rise of Urban Liberalism* (New York: Atheneum, 1971); Joseph Lash, *Eleanor and Franklin* (New York: W. W. Norton & Co., 1971); and Michael E. Parrish, *Felix Frankfurter and His Times: The Reform Years* (New York: Free Press, 1982).

Even monographs that attributed a significant role to Roosevelt also emphasized the influence of other persons, socioeconomic groups, and long-term attitudinal and institutional developments, as, for example, in Richard T. Polenberg *Reorganizing Roosevelt's Government: The Controversy over Executive Reorganization, 1936–1939* (Cambridge, Mass.: Harvard University Press, 1966); James T. Patterson, *Congressional Conservatism and the New Deal* (Lex-

ington: University of Kentucky Press, 1967); John M. Allswang, *The New Deal and American Politics: A Study in Political Change* (New York: John Wiley & Sons, 1978); Harvard Sitkoff, *A New Deal for Blacks* (New York: Oxford University Press, 1978); and Albert U. Romasco's study of the administration's relationship with the business community over recovery policies, *The Politics of Recovery: Roosevelt's New Deal* (New York: Oxford University Press, 1983). Another new approach that also diminished the focus on Roosevelt was the "organizational" or "institutional" school, which viewed modern American history primarily through long-term trends in organizational development. In this view, the New Deal was an acceleration within the national government of trends long underway in the public and private sectors, trends of centralization, interrelatedness, and replacement of haphazard development with deliberate social management in an increasing number of areas. This process involved bureaucratization, rationalization, increased organization along functional lines, and expanded efforts at large-scale planning. This organizational view of history was applied to the 1930s by Ellis W. Hawley in his seminal study, *The New Deal and the Problem of Monopoly: A Study in Economic Ambivalence* (Princeton, N.J.: Princeton University Press, 1966); in various essays in John Braeman et al., eds., *The New Deal*, 2 vols. (Columbus: Ohio State University Press, 1975); and in Otis L. Graham, Jr., *Toward a Planned Society: From Roosevelt to Nixon* (New York: Oxford University Press, 1976).

In the political arena, Franklin D. Roosevelt's image seemed to slip from the spotlight in the 1970s. He was largely ignored by presidents Gerald R. Ford and Jimmy Carter, and the Democrat who sought to retain his legacy, Senator Edward Kennedy of Massachusetts, was limited by personal political liabilities. Then, to almost everyone's surprise, FDR's mantle was boldly snatched away in 1980 by a right-wing Republican, a former movie actor and governor of California, Ronald Reagan.

Reagan did more than simply revive ritualistic obeisance to the memory of FDR; he made commemoration of the dead president such a centerpiece of his campaign and early administration that editorial writers at first labeled him "Franklin Delano Reagan." Yet Reagan's emulation of FDR was only rhetorical and stylistic, not substantive. He sought to use the former chief executive's confident, cheerful, theatrical style, and even FDR's own phrases (taken out of context until they seemed to indicate that Roosevelt was somehow opposed to most of his own policies) for conservative anti-Rooseveltian ends, indeed, to destroy the legacy of Roosevelt and his New Deal.

"I looked up FDR's old platform," he declared on more than one occasion, "and I discovered that it called for a restoration of states' rights and a reduction in the national budget. You know what? I'm still for that." Often Reagan would cite a sentence from a presidential message of January 1935 to prove that he and Roosevelt had the same policy toward the unemployed. He said: "Roosevelt at one time made a statement that the Federal Government had to get out of the business of—we didn't call it 'welfare' then, we called it 'relief.' " The facts are not so simple. Roosevelt did say, "The Federal Government must and shall quit this business of relief," but he said it in a message to Congress in which he called for a massive federal works program to give the able-bodied jobless not "relief" but "employment" through the biggest peacetime appropriation in the history of this or any other nation. Characteristically, Reagan neglected to mention that context or what Roosevelt said next: "The Federal Government is the only governmental agency with sufficient power and credit to meet this situation. We have assumed this task and we shall not shrink from it in the future. It is a duty dictated by every intelligent consideration of national policy to ask you to make it possible for the United States to give employment to all of these three and one half million employable people now on relief." Congress responded with a multibillion-dollar appropriation creating the WPA and NYA. To help those who were not employable, Roosevelt submitted a plan that eight months later Congress adopted as the landmark Social Security Act of 1935.

Identification with Roosevelt served Reagan in a number of ways. It allowed him to ignore his predecessors and link himself with the last president considered "great." It suggested that Reagan like FDR would launch a new era in domestic and foreign policy. Most important, it enabled Reagan to entice elements of the liberal Roosevelt coalition into a new conservative Reagan coalition (as Reagan himself had switched allegiances in the 1950s) and to do so without repudiating respect for Roosevelt, indeed, while claiming to be faithful to his memory. It was, as William E. Leuchtenburg admonished, perhaps the greatest sleight of hand of modern American politics. Within two years it appeared that even though the administration's policies were curtailing the spirit and the substance of the New Deal, Reagan had, nevertheless, managed to persuade a significant sector of the public that in both style and substance he was a latter-day FDR.

In 1982, the centennial of Roosevelt's birth came at a time when liberal Democrats were engaged in a major battle with Reagan over the legacy of the New Deal and who were the true political heirs and interpreters of Franklin D. Roosevelt. The intensity of that struggle indicated how important that legacy remained. Virtually the only agreement between the two sides was that FDR was a great president and that he deserved a specific memorial in Washington, D.C. Bipartisan agreement reached on the latter after nearly forty years of disagreement led to an authorization in 1982 for a garden wall and park to be constructed in his memory across the Tidal Basin from the Jefferson Memorial. But characteristically, as of two years later, no funds had been appropriated for its construction.

As the nation approached the fortieth anniversary of Franklin D. Roosevelt's death in 1945, it was evident that the former president had made an enduring impact both upon his successors in the White House and upon American society. A poll of historians in 1982 showed that Roosevelt had moved up to second place, just behind Lincoln, in the gallery of great presidents (*Journal of American History* 70 [December 1983]:551). In death as in life, he remained a powerful symbol of the principle that a democracy's government has a direct and immediate interest in the welfare of its citizens and can and should pursue that interest through active policies at home and abroad. Significant erosion and manipulation of that image had occurred, particularly in the wake of the 1960s and 1970s, but the sentiment appeared likely to remain a significant factor in the nation's civic culture at least until the passing of the generations whose political attitudes were shaped by Franklin D. Roosevelt and the America of the 1930s.

The strength of Roosevelt's reputation has rested on published history and biography as well as the assertions of politicians and editors and the personal memories or family heritages of millions. In scholarship, the work of the New Left and liberal revisionists has raised important questions about Roosevelt's concepts of the world, economic interests, minority groups, and the uses of power. These have become more central to the agenda of students of his role than older questions of whether Roosevelt was a conservative or liberal or whether the New Deal was evolutionary or revolutionary. To an important extent, however, historical scholarship has moved away from Roosevelt to other concerns: long term institutional and attitudinal developments rather than a particular president, even one as celebrated as Roosevelt. Consequently, with notable exceptions such as Michael R. Beschloss, [Joseph] *Kennedy and Roosevelt: The Uneasy Alliance* (New York: W.W. Norton & Co., 1980); the earlier-mentioned book by Robert Dallek on foreign policy, and William E. Leuchtenburg's innovative study of the impact of Roosevelt's reputation upon his successors in the White House, *In the Shadow of FDR: From Harry Truman to Ronald Reagan* (Ithaca, N.Y.: Cornell University Press, 1983), most scholars of late have tended to abandon the Roosevelt-centered focus on the era to biographers writing for a more popular audience. Among the latter are, for example, Kenneth S. Davis, *FDR, The Beckoning of Destiny: 1882–1928: A History* (New York: Putnam, 1972), Bernard Asbell's imaginary version of *The FDR Memoirs* (Garden City, N.Y.: Doubleday, 1973), Joseph Alsop, *FDR, 1882–1945: A Centenary Remembrance* (New York: Viking Press, 1982), a sensitive remembrance by one of Roosevelt's cousins, and Nathan Miller's mammoth portrait, *FDR: An Intimate History* (Garden City, N.Y.: Doubleday, 1983).

Recent political developments and trends in scholarship are not likely to change the general popular and historical verdict about Franklin Delano Roosevelt in any major way, at least in the near future. For all his faults and weaknesses, FDR remains, in the dominant view, a giant figure in an era of tremendous crises. His audacity, exuberance, resourcefulness, and superb political skills helped lead the nation through those turbulent times and enabled him to become the focal point of the hopes and fears of millions in peace and in war. A symbol of that era as no other single individual in America, his memory will continue to remain a part of the contemporary political scene for some time to come. He also remains one of the most important presidents in the nation's history and, in terms of his impact, one of the twentieth century's additions to the pantheon of the founding fathers.

Classics in Roosevelt scholarship include James MacGregor Burns, *Roosevelt: The Lion and the Fox.* (New York: Harcourt Brace Jovanovich, 1956), and *Roosevelt: The Soldier of Freedom* (New York: Harcourt Brace Jovanovich, 1970), an analytical biography by a leading political scientist, especially the first volume on Roosevelt's strengths and weaknesses as a domestic reform president. Frank Freidel's *Franklin D. Roosevelt*, 4 vols. (Boston: Little, Brown, 1952–73) is a detailed biographical narrative from Roosevelt's childhood to the end of the hundred days. The best one-volume account, highly readable and judicious, is William E. Leuchtenburg, *Franklin D. Roosevelt and the New Deal, 1932–1940* (New York: Harper & Row, 1963). A vivid portrayal by an activist liberal Democrat and prize-winning historian of the shift in national leadership from Hoover to Roosevelt is provided in Arthur M. Schlesinger, Jr., *The Crisis of the Old Order, The Coming of the New Deal,* and *The Politics of Upheaval,* the three volumes comprising *The Age of Roosevelt* (Boston: Hougton Mifflin Co., 1957–60). More recent works include Robert Dallek, *Franklin D. Roosevelt and American Foreign Policy, 1932–1945* (New York: Oxford University Press, 1979). Focusing on presidential leadership throughout the troubled period, Dallek maintains an admiring view of Roosevelt the diplomatist. Paul K. Conkin's *The New Deal,* 2d ed. (Arlington Heights, Ill.: Harlan Davidson, 1975) is a brief, but influential critique of the shortcomings of Roosevelt and the New Deal. A compelling analysis of the influence of Roosevelt's reputation as president upon his successors in the White House is William E. Leuchtenburg's *In the Shadow of FDR: From Harry Truman to Ronald Reagan* (Ithaca, N.Y.: Cornell University Press, 1983).

JOHN W. CHAMBERS

See also Memorials

*Hugo L. Black.
(Courtesy FDR Library.)*

Black, Hugo Lafayette

(27 February 1886–25 September 1971)

United States senator, 1927–37, Supreme Court justice, 1937–71. Born in an Alabama farmhouse, Hugo Black attended law school at the University of Alabama, graduating at the age of twenty. His first client was a black prisoner claiming back wages from a local farmer. Black won. After a few years as a small-town lawyer, including service as a police court judge and county prosecutor, Black ran successfully for the Senate in 1926. During the first years of the New Deal, while serving as chairman of a Senate investigatory committee, Black uncovered fraud and waste in connection with government airmail services. His

tireless investigation of the utility companies' lobbying campaign against the Wheeler-Rayburn Act, which abolished public utility holding companies, aided the passage of that act in 1935.

Black actively supported Roosevelt's Court-packing plan in 1937. After the resignation of Justice Van Devanter and the death of Arkansas senator Robinson (who had been promised the next court appointment), FDR named Black to the vacant seat on 12 August 1937. At the time, Roosevelt, fearing the loss of Black's vote in the Senate, remarked that he wished the new justice was twins! Immediately after his confirmation by the Senate, reports of Black's two-year involvement with the Ku Klux Klan during the twenties appeared. Black admitted his former membership but noted his quick resignation, and in a few weeks the public controversy subsided.

Black's early years on the Court were marked by his insistence that the judiciary had no power to review the sustantive merits of legislation. He fully supported the contention of New Deal proponents that the interstate commerce clause authorized national economic regulation by Congress. And he regularly rejected attempts by the states to impede federal legislation in the areas of labor relations, racial segregation, and wartime price controls.

After the war, Black became noted for his absolute construction of the First Amendment and consistently pushed for an expansion of the area of protected civil liberties. Paradoxically, he never fully accepted the Warren Court's expansion of the rights of criminal defendants. With his health failing, Black retired from the Court in September of 1971 and died a week later.

Two works by John P. Frank, *Mr. Justice Black* (New York: Knopf & Sons, 1948), and "Hugo L. Black," in *The Justices of the United States Supreme Court, 1789–1969* (New York: Chelsea House Publishers, 1969), pp. 2321–70, carry the life of the justice down to 1969. Wallace Mendelson's *Justices Black and Frankfurter: Conflict in the Court* (Chicago: University of Chicago Press, 1961) details the disputes between the jurists during the 1940s and 1950s. *Mr. Justice Black, Absolutist on the Court* (Charlottesville: University Press of Virginia, 1980) by James J. Magee concentrates on Black's judicial record during the postwar period.

See also Supreme Court of the United States

Black Americans

See Negroes

Black Cabinet

The group of black men and women appointed by Roosevelt to administrative positions. During his tenure, Roosevelt appointed a significantly larger number of blacks to administrative positions than his predecessors. Although these appointments were not at the highest levels of the administration—the members of the group could not dramatically alter the federal government's policies toward black Americans—the Black Cabinet still performed a vital function. As one historian recently commented, "They made white New Dealers marginally more sensitive to the needs of blacks; and they made the federal government seem more comprehensible and relevant to blacks."

The Black Cabinet was not a formal group created by the Roosevelt administration, but rather, an informal gathering of advisers from various New Deal agencies. The members of the group did, however, meet, often in the home of Mary McLeod Bethune; a small group also met on a less frequent basis, usually at Dr. Robert Weaver's house. In 1936 the group began to call itself the Federal Council on Negro Affairs; the press used the terms *Black Cabinet* and *Black Brain Trust*. Among the most famous members of the group were Bethune, the director of the National Youth Administration's Division of Negro Affairs from 1935 to 1943; Weaver, who served in a variety of positions, including adviser of Negro affairs in the Public Works Administration from 1933 to 1938; and William H. Hastie, assistant solicitor in the Interior Department. Not all the members of the Black Cabinet served at the same time. Indeed, one scholar has suggested that it is more appropriate to speak of several, perhaps overlapping, black cabinets that served during the president's tenure.

The Black Cabinet, because of its informal nature, did not leave many formal records. Indeed, there is some debate about the people who should be included in the group. Besides Bethune, Weaver, and Hastie, other prominent members were Edgar Brown (Civilian Conservations Corps); Roscoe C. Brown (Public Health Service); Ambrose Caliver (Department of the Interior); Joseph H. Evans (Farm Security Administration); Crystal Bird Fauset (Office of Civil Defense); Charles E. Hall (Department of Commerce); Frank Horne (Housing Authority); William I. Houston (Department of Justice); Joseph R. Houchins (Department of Commerce); Henry A. Hunt (Farm Credit Administration); Campbell C. Johnson (lieutenant colonel, Selective Service); Dewey R. Jones (Department of the Interior); Eugene K. Jones (Department of Commerce); Edward H. Lawson, Jr. (Works Project Administration); Ralph E. Mizelle (Post Office); Lawrence A. Oxley (Department of Labor); Theodore Poston (War Information Office); J. Parker Prescott (Housing); Alfred Edgar Smith (Works Project Administration); William J. Thompkins (recorder of deeds); William J. Trent (Federal Works Agency); Robert L. Vann (assistant to the attorney general); Arthur Weiseger (Department of Labor); and John W. Whitten (Works Project Administration).

The impact of the Black Cabinet is hard to determine. Through informal channels, the group had some impact on the New Deal agencies. The impetus behind certain changes, however, was often provided by Eleanor Roosevelt after a meeting with Bethune. The existence of the group apparently had some impact on the voting behavior of black Americans. As Nancy Weiss has recently argued, "The Black Cabinet was important to black people because it signified that the government was paying attention to them in ways that had never been the case before. They, in turn, found in the Cabinet a reason to look more favorably on the Democratic party." This impact, she concludes, demonstrated Roosevelt's ability to manipulate his "limited departures from past racial practices to his own political advantage."

In a final analysis, the Black Cabinet's activities must be placed into a proper historical perspective. The group did not end discrimination against blacks in the United States, but the appointment of blacks to federal positions was viewed by many at the time as an important step. It symbolized the attempt by some in the New Deal to eradicate the racial injustices in America. Although some of the members of the Cabinet attained higher administrative offices than had blacks previously, the group was circumscribed by the racial conventions of the larger society. If the Black Cabinet had only a symbolic impact on the New Deal, this must ultimately be attributed not to failings of the members of the group, but to the reluctance of a president unwilling to challenge the more intransigent elements of a still powerful segregated society.

For a recent appraisal of the Black Cabinet, see Nancy J. Weiss, *Farewell to the Party of Lincoln: Black Politics in the Age of FDR* (Princeton: Princeton University Press, 1983); in chapter 7 Weiss uses many valuable primary sources, including interviews with members of the Black Cabinet, to describe their actions. She also examines the importance of the group in political terms, seeing the impact of their symbolic value translated into political advantage by Roosevelt. Also see B. Joyce Ross, "Mary McLeod Bethune and the National Youth Administration: A Case Study of Power Relationships in the Black Cabinet of Franklin D. Roosevelt," *Journal of Negro History* 60 (January 1975):1–28; and Mary McLeod Bethune, "My Secret Talks with FDR," and Allan Morrison, "The Secret Papers of FDR," both in *The Negro in Depression and War: Prelude to Revolution 1930–1945;* ed. Bernard Sternsher (Chicago: Quadrangle Books, 1969). Ross's article stresses the necessity to focus on the "power relationships" that influenced the members of the Black Cabinet and the importance of viewing the individual's impact on a specific agency in terms of policies toward blacks. For a complete list of members of the Black Cabinet, see Mary Mace Spradling, ed., *In Black and White*, 3d ed. (Detroit: Gale Research Co., 1980), 1:83.

See also Bethune, Mary McLeod; Negroes

Black Thursday or Bloody Thursday

See Great Depression

Brains Trust

The brains trust, a group of academic advisers gathered by Franklin D. Roosevelt during the 1932 campaign, was so dubbed by *New York Times* reporter James Kieran. Though the term since has been used in the singular and applied to all the president's principal advisers, it properly belongs to three Columbia University professors, Raymond Moley, Rexford Guy Tugwell, and Adolf A. Berle, Jr. Faced by the pressures of a national campaign for the Democratic party nomination and a contest against Herbert Hoover for the presidency and unfamiliar with the economic complexities of depression causation, Roosevelt agreed to the origination of such a group in March 1932 on the suggestion of Samuel I. Rosenman, his counsel. He had, in fact, made wide use of academic expertise in crucial state matters during his gubernatorial years.

Since Raymond Moley, professor of government and public law, had already demonstrated a capacity for organization of expert advice in connection with the Governor's Commission on the Administration of Justice as well as a keen ability for speech writing in his draft of Roosevelt's statement of removal of Sheriff Thomas M. "Tin Box" Farley, Rosenman proposed that Moley should recruit the group that would advise on the campaign. The forgotten man speech, the initial Roosevelt-Moley collaboration, foretold the New Deal's ambiance, with its stress on use of the national government for the elimination of rural poverty and underpaid industrial labor. It offered a theory of depression causation that involved the restoration of farmers' purchasing power, finding the farm depression of the twenties, which affected nearly half the population, responsible for pulling down the balance of the economy.

In a lengthy 19 May 1932 memorandum for the candidate, Moley asserted that both major parties had grown conservative and stultified in the twenties and argued for a liberalized Democratic party based on progressive principles. This was the original context for his introduction of the "New Deal" catch phrase, used again by Moley in his draft of Roosevelt's acceptance speech at the Democratic National Convention in Chicago. Moley's economic proposals became important components of the New Deal program. These included provision for a large-scale relief and public works program of $2.6 billion, including direct federal relief opposed by Hoover, for both the urban and the rural sectors. Given this scale of expenditure, the budget could not be balanced except by a regressive sales tax. Moley proposed instead the creation of an emergency or extraordinary budget. Provision for the social minima included old-age pensions and unemployment insurance as a cushion against cyclical joblessness. The Moley memorandum advocated also divorcement of commercial from investment banking, regulation of securities issuance and exchanges, heavy taxation of corporate profits or "surpluses" and of inheritances, as well as the yardstick principle, meaning federal ownership and operation of power sites in the public domain as a mechanism for measurement of electric utility rates. Finally, to protect higher internal price and wage levels, Moley promoted the concept of intranationalism to shelter rising farm prices and wages from the vicissitudes of the world marketplace.

Since Roosevelt and Moley perceived the Great Depression as originating in the steep decline of commodity prices that began in 1921, they recruited a young Columbia University economist familiar with agriculture, Rexford G. Tugwell, to the group that met periodically at Albany and Hyde Park in the spring and summer of 1932. Tugwell shaped the outline of a farm program based on acreage allotments in collaboration with Henry A. Wallace, editor of *Wallace's Farmer,* and MIlburn Lincoln Wilson, an agricultural economist at Montana State College, Bozeman. The proposal, already rejected by President Hoover, found acceptance in Roosevelt's principal farm address at Topeka, Kansas, on 14 September 1932. Tugwell also introduced the concept of a concert of interests into the Roosevelt circle. It analyzed depression causation in terms of a breakdown of price and wage relationships that would require restructuring under federal mechanisms, a theory explained by Roosevelt in a speech at St. Paul, Minnesota, on 18 April 1932.

For the long term, Tugwell desired abandonment of our market economy for planning in the industrial and financial sectors, as well as in agriculture. This conception of federal overhead management by an Economic Council in the form of estimation of consumption, planning of production, allocation of capital issues, adjustment of price relationships, and formulation of a coordinated foreign policy, ventured in July 1932, was rejected on the advice of Adolf A. Berle, Jr., a month later. Berle regarded a planned economy as incapable of contemporary explication or implementation. Moley believed that "business could plan for itself."

Berle, a member of the law faculty at Columbia, was the group's third member. In 1932, he and Gardiner C. Means wrote *The Modern Corporation and Private Property,* a classic exposition of the growing concentration of control of the income stream in the hands of less than two thousand industrial managers. This required, he believed, either the evolution of industrial statesmanship or, as Berle and Moley wrote for Roosevelt's Commonwealth Club address, delivered in San Francisco 23 September 1932, the emergence of a new "economic constitutional order" which would dictate an enlarged federal role in the achievement of economic balance, a better distribution of purchasing power, the restoration of wages and employment, and the return of agriculture to prosperity.

Berle was recruited to the advisory group principally for his expertise in connection with the financial collapse that began in 1929. A long memorandum of May 1932 explained depression causation in terms of a collapse of values, caused by the liquidation initially of speculative situations and then, more ominously, of legitimate investments. Whereas individuals feared for their savings and ability to repay loans, banks feared for their own liquidity. As a result, the economy ground to a halt. Berle dealt with an array of securities and home and farm mortgages, urging that speculators in securities and vacant land could not be bailed out. But legitimate situations, such as home and farm investment, needed to be salvaged by utilization of the credit of the U.S. government. In time, the principle was applied by Roosevelt to the bank rescue and to an expansion of the Reconstruction Finance Corporation's activities.

The brains trust performed its last collaborative task in the 1932–33 interregnum in defense of their reform-recovery program. Moley, now Roosevelt's principal economic adviser, fended off a group of conservative internationalists of both parties, including Norman Davis and Henry L. Stimson, who attempted to divert the president-elect from his domestic priorities to international questions. Also, Moley served as FDR's chief aide in conferences with Herbert Hoover and his secretary of the treasury, Ogden L. Mills, intended by the outgoing president to abort the New Deal at its inception.

Just as Roosevelt never formally announced the existence of a brains trust, so its dissolution proceeded without fanfare as the circle of advisers enlarged in the presidential years and as Roosevelt required lawyers capable of legislative draftsmanship and administrative execution of his program.

The origin of the brains trust is described in Samuel I. Rosenman, *Working with Roosevelt* (New York: Harper & Bros., 1952). Rexford Guy Tugwell, *The Brains Trust* (New York: Viking Press, 1968), furnishes an insightful view into his relationship with Roosevelt in the 1932 campaign, and Raymond Moley, *After Seven Years* (New York and London: Harper & Bros., 1939), though critical, is invaluable. Adolf Berle's memoranda are reprinted in Beatrice B. Berle and Travis B. Jacobs, eds., *Navigating the Rapids, 1918–1971* (New York: Harcourt Brace Jovanovich, 1973). Tugwell's and Berle's papers are located in the Franklin D. Roosevelt Library, Hyde Park, New York, and Moley's in the Hoover Institution, Stanford, California. For a more complete discussion of the subject, see Elliot A. Rosen, *Hoover, Roosevelt, and the Brains Trust: From Depression to New Deal* (New York: Columbia University Press, 1977).

ELLIOT A. ROSEN

See also Baruch, Bernard Mannes; Berle, Adolf Augustus, Jr.; Moley, Raymond; Tugwell, Rexford Guy.

Brandeis, Louis Dembitz

(13 November 1856–5 October 1941)

Supreme Court justice, 1916–39. Louis Dembitz Brandeis was born in Louisville, Kentucky, where he excelled as a student before entering the Harvard Law School in 1875. His law school career was brilliant; he compiled a nearly perfect record and graduated in 1877, too young to qualify as class valedictorian. Brandeis began his legal career in St. Louis where he spent an unhappy interlude before being lured back

Louis D. Brandeis. (Date, photographer unknown. National Portrait Gallery, Smithsonian Institution.)

to Massachusetts in 1879 by Samuel D. Warren, Jr., a law school friend and scion of the Boston aristocracy.

Brandeis laid the foundation in Boston for his later emergence on the national scene. The new firm of Warren & Brandeis prospered. Brandeis's legal reputation rose rapidly, and his growing income, prudently invested, put him on the road to affluence. Brandeis was a Republican until 1884, and his early reform philosophy was of the genteel Mugwump variety. By the turn of the century, however, his growing zeal had put him in the forefront of New England political activists. By means of such dramatic events as the famous "Brandeis brief" in *Muller* v. *Oregon* (1908) and his involvement in the Ballinger-Pinchot controversy (1910–11), he came into a national prominence that was enhanced in Jewish circles by his intense activity in Zionist affairs.

Brandeis's evolving social philosophy emphasized the curse of bigness and was based on his distrust of power both in business and in government. This perspective appealed to Woodrow Wilson, and Brandeis became one of the chief architects of Wilson's New Freedom in the campaign of 1912. A grateful Wilson nominated Brandeis for the Supreme Court in 1916. Brandeis quickly emerged as a brilliant justice who along with Oliver Wendell Holmes, Jr., formed a minority liberal bloc during the long years of conservative judicial dominance.

Yet Brandeis was not willing to abandon his wider political interests although his judicial position imposed certain constraints. He adjusted to his position by working for liberal causes through intermediaries, the most notable of whom was the energetic Harvard Law School professor Felix Frankfurter, with whom he had begun a correspondence in 1910. The Brandeis-Frankfurter relationship deepened in the 1920s as Frankfurter steadily rose in Brandeis's estimation. From time to time over the course of many years, Frankfurter received money from Brandeis both to support his political advocacy and to relieve his own straitened financial circumstances.

The period from 1920 to 1932 was not a productive one for the Brandeis-Frankfurter collaboration because of the unfavorable political climate. The election of Franklin D. Roosevelt in 1932, however, afforded Brandeis a welcome opportunity to influence the policies of a liberal administration. Working primarily through Frankfurter, who had been cultivating Roosevelt assiduously since his 1928 gubernatorial triumph in New York, Brandeis began an effort to influence the New Deal. Roosevelt had great respect for Brandeis, calling him, partly in jest and partly, one suspects, with a kind of awe, "Isaiah." Brandeis's effort to influence the New Deal had three general aspects. He sought to place suitable people in the government, to shape particular pieces of legislation, and to persuade Roosevelt to adopt his own comprehensive recovery program.

The dramatic expansion of the federal government under Roosevelt gave Brandeis, acting through Frankfurter who was himself prolific with suggestions, an opportunity to install key people in a variety of posts throughout the government, particularly in the burgeoning New Deal administration agencies. Brandeis and Frankfurter sought positions for people who shared, in a general way, their liberal perspective, but they were more interested in commitment and competence than in any narrow political orthodoxy.

It was only natural for Brandeis, as a zealous political reformer, to show interest in the details of the administration's legislative program, though here, as with personnel matters, there were limits to what he could accomplish. His relationship to specific legislation varied from strong opposition to the National Industrial Recovery Act and the Agricultural Adjustment Act to close involvement in the details of drafting the Social Security Act.

Brandeis retained a deep suspicion of bigness in government as well as in business, so he disapproved of the centralizing tendencies of the early New Deal in 1933. He chafed at Roosevelt's vacillations in 1934 and took fresh hope from the initiatives of 1935. And yet, while Brandeis generally supported the legislation of 1935–36, he was disappointed because he thought that Roosevelt had failed to go far enough to ensure genuine recovery. Brandeis's own recovery program involved heavy taxation of the giant corporations and the superrich, which he thought would generate the revenue necessary to launch a massive public works program in order to employ the millions of workers needed to stimulate the economy and lead to recovery.

In retrospect, it is clear that 1935 was the last opportunity for major reform because Roosevelt's defeat in the bitter court fight of 1937 weakened his control of Congress. Brandeis strongly opposed the administration's attempt to pack the Supreme Court, although he had himself generally supported New Deal legislation in Court tests except in the NRA and AAA cases. Brandeis's opposition strained his relationship with Roosevelt, and by the time it was restored, the chance for bold action had passed.

From 1938 to his death, Brandeis became increasingly concerned with the rise of fascism and its implications for the Jews of Europe. He remained a close observer of world events after his retirement from the Court in 1939. During the hazardous days of 1940–41, Brandeis's disappointments with the New Deal faded; Roosevelt gained stature in his eyes as a global statesman. His historical consciousness extended from childhood memories of the Civil War to the prelude to World War II. Frankfurter reported to Roosevelt that the day before Brandeis died, he had praised FDR as "greater than Jefferson and almost as great as Lincoln."

For many years the standard biography of Brandeis has been Alpheus T. Mason's *Brandeis: A Free Man's Life* (New York: Viking Press, 1946). This work, which covers the New Deal era in a cursory fashion, has been supplemented by Lewis J. Paper's *Brandeis* (Englewood Cliffs, N.J.: Prentice-Hall, 1983), a biography enhanced by an incorporation of more recent scholarship. Indispensable for the study of Brandeis is the five-volume compilation of his letters ably edited by Melvin I. Urofsky and David W. Levy (1971–78). Allon Gal in his *Brandeis of Boston* (Cambridge: Harvard University Press, 1980) gives an illuminating analysis of his early career. Nelson L. Dawson focuses on Brandeis's impact on the New Deal in *Louis D. Brandeis, Felix Frankfurter, and the New Deal* (Hamden, Conn.: Shoe String Press, 1980) and Bruce A. Murphy has provided a general survey of the Brandeis-Frankfurter collaboration in *The Brandeis/Frankfurter Connection: The Secret Political Activities of Two Supreme Court Justices.* (New York: Oxford University Press, 1982).

NELSON L. DAWSON

See also Supreme Court; Zionism

Brussels Conference

A conference of the signatories of the Nine Power Treaty of 1922 which met from 3 November to 24 November 1937. Called for by the League of Nations on 5 October 1937, it sought "a method of putting an end to the Sino-Japanese conflict by agreement."

Following the Marco Polo Bridge incident of 7 July 1937, fighting between Chinese and Japanese armies had broken out in renewed intensity. Japan's forces had advanced deep into Chinese territory, and her bombing had devastated Chinese cities. The League's call for action coincided with FDR's quarantine speech, and the day after the speech, Roosevelt announced that the United States would participate in the conference as an "example of one of the possible paths to follow in our search for means toward peace throughout the whole world."

Despite the rhetoric of the quarantine speech, FDR quickly backed away from any decisive action. He told the American negotiator, Norman Davis, that the purpose of the conference should be conciliation. On the most important issue of economic sanctions, FDR and Secretary of State Hull were opposed. One reason for their opposition was the failure of the League, despite its condemnation of Japan, to vote any sanctions. Roosevelt also feared that the British might try to drag the United States into agreeing to sanctions. The United States, FDR told Davis, could not be seen as "a tail to the British kite." Most important, FDR thought that he lacked domestic support for any firm action. Weakened politically by the Court-packing fight and the sit-down strikes, Roosevelt felt the country would only support his leadership in "peaceful" measures against aggression. He did not consider sanctions a peaceful step.

It has been argued that London was ready to support an appeal by Washington for sanctions. Foreign Minister Anthony Eden told Parliament that in order to get the "full cooperation" of the United States, "I would travel, not only from Geneva to Brussels, but from Melbourne to Alaska." But Bradford Lee's study of unpublished British records demonstrates that Eden's voice was in the minority in the Chamberlain cabinet. The British were more worried about being maneuvered by the Americans into a position of blame for not supporting sanctions. Considering that sanctions had failed to stop the Italian conquest of Ethiopia, Prime Minister Chamberlain told Eden that one could not rely on the Americans, and he added, "On no account will I impose a sanction." The British were also preoccupied with the deteriorating European situation and did not want to endanger their Far Eastern interests by a tough stance they could not support.

Given the American and British positions, the conference was doomed from the beginning. Japan, though a signatory to the Nine Power Treaty, refused to attend. The conference closed by issuing a report of its deliberations and a statement that participatory governments would continue to explore all peaceful methods of arriving at a just settlement. The Chinese delegate, Wellington Koo, attacked the declaration as a "mere reaffirmation of principles" which could not possibly cope with the grave situation in the Far East.

The diplomatic record of the conference is available in the State Department's *Foreign Relations of the United States, The Far East*, vol. 4, 1937. The best account of American policy remains Dorothy Borg, *The United States and the Far Eastern Crisis of 1933–1938* (Cambridge, Mass.: Harvard University Press, 1964). A more sympathetic and realistic view of FDR's role is Robert Dallek, *Franklin D. Roosevelt and American Foreign Policy, 1932–1945* (New York: Oxford University Press, 1979). The British policy can be followed in the excellent study by Bradford A. Lee, *Britain and the Sino-Japanese War, 1937–1939* (Stanford, Calif.: Stanford University Press, 1973).

See also Foreign Policy

Bureau of Agricultural Economics

See Agricultural Adjustment Administration; Agriculture

Business

As the term was used during the era of Franklin D. Roosevelt, *business* had two distinct meanings. It referred, on the one hand, to the system of economic activity conducted through commercial firms for the purpose of making profits. It referred, on the other, to the profit seekers organized and acting as an interest group and in this capacity having relations with the government and other holders of political and social power. In both senses, business was an entity of major concern to Roosevelt and his administration.

As a system of economic activity, American business faced major challenges between 1933 and 1945 and yet survived these with remarkably little change in its basic structure and modes of conduct. Although the Great Depression drastically reduced the scope of economic activity and produced severe business distress, it led neither to the replacement of the existing managerial elite by a new one nor to much change in the degree of economic concentration or the group of firms exercising economic dominance. And although New Deal reform and war mobilization altered some of the environment in which business firms operated, they did relatively little to put the government into business, socialize investment decisions, or change the nature and number of business units. Indeed, the stability of the system in these regards has led some interpreters to discount the calls for change in New Deal rhetoric and see reform not only as helping to prevent change but as being managed by those intent on doing so. Impressed by the outcome, they have seen conscious efforts at system maintenance that are difficult to discern in the historical records.

What changes that did occur in the business system were primarily in the areas of personnel and public relations management and in what historians Louis Galambos and Alfred Chandler have called secondary organizations with coordinative rather than production or marketing functions. In an era of reformist critiques, growing governmental activity, and resurgent labor militancy, specialists in public relations and personnel management were much in demand and were able to institutionalize places for themselves in the corporate organization, develop new strategies for achieving their goals, and secure for their endeavors a larger share of corporate resources. And in an era when market coordination and informal cooperative substitutes were widely perceived to have "failed," there was an ongoing search for new industrial superstructures out of which came further growth and development of secondary organizations. Trade associations, in particular, became larger and more elaborate, more intertwined with governmental and corporate bureaucracies, and more likely to seek

Business Failures in the United States, 1925–1945

YEARS	TOTAL CONCERNS (1000s)	FAILURE RATE PER 100,000 CONCERNS (1000s)	AVERAGE LIABILITY PER FAILURE ($ 1000s)
1925	2113	100	20.9
1926	2158	101	18.8
1927	2172	106	22.5
1928	2199	109	20.5
1929	2213	104	21.1
1930	2183	122	25.4
1931	2125	133	26.0
1932	2077	154	29.2
1933	1961	100	23.0
1934	1974	61	27.6
1935	1983	62	25.4
1936	2010	48	21.1
1937	2057	46	19.3
1938	2102	61	19.2
1939	2116	70	12.4
1940	2156	63	12.2
1941	2171	55	11.5
1942	2152	45	10.7
1943	2023	16	14.1
1944	1855	7	25.9
1945	1909	4	37.4

Source: U.S. Bureau of the Census, *Historical Statistics of the United States, Colonial Times to 1957* (Washington, D.C.: U.S. Government Printing Office, 1960).

S. J. Ray, Kansas City Star, c. 1933–34. (Kansas City Star.)

regulatory as opposed to service roles. Institutional linkages to public power, through advisory committee systems and business-staffed commodity sections, became more prominent; and organizations devoted to consensus building within and among industries became another growth sector.

As an organized interest group, American business also continued to exhibit many of the same characteristics that it had earlier. The more fully developed organizations continued to be those based on commodity, functional, regional, or positional interests. But trying to speak for all business organizations was the U.S. Chamber of Commerce, and claiming to represent a general rather than a particular business interest were the National Association of Manufacturers and various councils and congresses of organizational leaders. Efforts to develop an all-inclusive peak association comparable to those in various European countries continued to be unsuccessful. Nor was there ever a single philosophy underlying the actions of America's organized businesspersons. Although most were distrustful of the state and equated its growth with a loss of liberty, this antistatism came in forms that ranged from free-market fundamentalism through a pragmatic acceptance of government aid to designs for a social corporatism.

These divisions within business make it difficult

to generalize about business-government relations during the Roosevelt period. Throughout, relations with some businesspersons and business groups were good, and relations with others were bad. But broadly speaking, observers then and since have seen the story of such relations as moving through three phases, marked respectively by mutual support and collaboration, antagonism and hostility, and rapprochement within a context of mutual suspicion. The overall pattern, it has been suggested, might be conceptualized as "a partnership formed, dissolved, and in renegotiation."

During the crisis of 1933, most business groups endorsed and gave initial support to the system of national economic controls established under the National Industrial Recovery Act. In the formation and implementation of such controls, they saw an opportunity to organize economic recovery or at least to erect defenses against the depression. And since the governmental leaders responsible for the passage and administration of the act were willing to let business persons function as public planners and controllers, expressions of mutual trust and admiration were much in vogue. The Roosevelt administration's initial financial policies, moreover, tended to allay fears about its "unsoundness" in that area. The Economy Act, its position on banking regulation, and its moves to contain currency inflation schemes were all in line with established views in the business community.

By 1934, however, disappointment with the performance of business planners and political pressures from other quarters had led the administration to embrace policies that growing numbers of businesspersons saw as unsound, irrational, and socially threatening. They complained particularly about the new monetary experiments, about misguided regulation of capital markets, and about the rise within the National Recovery Administration (NRA) of antibusiness zealots bent upon subjecting business to "government dictation" or rule by "labor bosses." Some helped to form the American Liberty League, dedicated to the protection of property rights from bureaucratic tyranny. Others helped to swell the ranks of the National Association of Manufacturers and turn it into a staunch foe of what was now perceived as "big government." And by early 1935 the once proadministration Chamber of Commerce had been captured by Roosevelt's critics, and the era of antagonism and hostility had begun in earnest.

During the period from 1935 to 1938 a variety of peacemakers tried to reestablish some basis for business-government cooperation, utilizing for this purpose such agencies as the Business Advisory Council in the Commerce Department, the consultative machinery attached to the Securities and Exchange Commission, and institutional survivals of the NRA system. But in general such efforts had little success. As most businesspersons saw it, the recovery programs of 1935 and 1938, with their encouragement to labor unions, increased governmental expenditures, efforts at redistribution, and populistic attacks on modern business organization, were actually re-

sponsible for continuing depression and social disorder. In their efforts to force policy changes, they used what power they could muster to hamper implementation of the programs and support Roosevelt's political opponents. And on the other side, Roosevelt managed to maintain a political base by assuming the role of a people's champion fighting special interests, associating himself with movements that were challenging the social power of business, and blaming the lack of recovery on social sabotage by "economic royalists." Despite the efforts at peacemaking and occasional breathing spells in the conflict, the dominant pattern was an ongoing state of hostility.

After 1938, however, as conservative social attitudes reasserted themselves, depression gave way to war, and wartime performance reestablished the prestige of business, a growing rapprochement did take place. Although mutual suspicions persisted, particularly during the fashioning of the prewar rearmament programs, Roosevelt made increasing use of business talent and expertise and managed to develop forms of control that were at least minimally satisfactory both to the majority of businesspersons and to their politically liberal critics. By 1943 accommodationists seeking areas of agreement rather than areas of conflict were moving back into leadership roles in the Chamber of Commerce; and urging a continuing partnership that would extend beyond the war period were such groups as the Committee for Economic Development, reconversion planners associated with

United States Gross National Product, 1929–1945 (billions of dollars)

YEAR	GROSS NATIONAL PRODUCT*
1929	103.8
1930	90.9
1931	75.9
1932	58.3
1933	55.8
1934	64.9
1935	72.2
1936	82.5
1937	90.2
1938	84.7
1939	90.4
1940	100.5
1941	125.3
1942	159.6
1943	192.6
1944	210.6
1945	213.1

*Gross national product = Market value of the output of goods and services produced by the nation's economy.

Source: U.S. Bureau of the Census, *Historical Statistics of the United States, 1789–1945* (Washington, D.C.: U.S. Government Printing Office, 1949). The Bureau of the Census obtained these data from *Survey of Current Business*, which regularly revises them to maintain comparability through time.

Talburt, New York Daily News, *3 February 1936. (Scripps-Howard Newspapers.)*

Bernard Baruch, and a new collection of war business-crats and dollar-a-year men.

From the political responses to depression and war came a growth of welfare and regulatory statism, stronger labor unions, and greater prestige for government and military administrations, all of which were resisted by the preponderance of organized businesspersons. But eventually, a growing number of them came to accept these innovations as contributing to a stronger capitalism. And even as the battles over the innovations were being fought, the reality of mutual interdependence brought not only new efforts by public and business administrators to control and use one another but also further interpenetrations of the public and private sectors and new attempts to institutionalize mutually supportive roles in social management.

A comprehensive history of American business during the Roosevelt era has yet to be written. But perceptive analyses of systematic continuities and changes can be found in Alfred D. Chandler and Louis Galambos, "The Development of Large-Scale Economic Organizations in Modern America," *Journal of Economic History* 30 (March 1970): 201–217; Chandler's essay in Stephen E. Ambrose, ed., *Institutions in Modern America* (Baltimore: Johns Hopkins University Press, 1967); and the relevant chapters in Thomas C. Cochran, *Business in American Life* (New York: McGraw-Hill, 1972). On business politics and business-government relations, see Ellis W. Hawley, *The New Deal and the Problem of Monopoly* (Princeton: Princeton University Press, 1966); George Wolfskill, *Revolt of the Conservatives* (Boston: Houghton Mifflin, Co., 1962); and the relevant essays in Joseph Frese et al., eds., *Business and Government* (Tarrytown, N.Y.: Sleepy Hollow Press, 1984).

ELLIS W. HAWLEY

See also Baruch, Bernard Mannes; Chamber of Commerce; Conservatism; Henderson, Leon; Johnson, Hugh Samuel; Jones, Jesse; Kennedy, Joseph Patrick; Regulation, Federal; Republican Party; Securities and Exchange Commission; Taxation; War Mobilization

Byrnes, James Francis ("Jimmy")

(2 May 1879–9 April 1972)

FDR's "assistant president," Franklin Roosevelt and Jimmy Byrnes, the jaunty little Irishman from South Carolina, were friends and political allies from the moment of their first meeting at the 1912 Democratic National Convention; it was in many ways an unlikely match.

Byrnes, born a few weeks after the death of his civil servant father, had been forced to drop out of school at age fourteen to help support his family. He was schooled in law and politics by running errands for a Charleston attorney and riding the backcountry judicial circuit as a court recorder. Admitted to the bar, he put together his reputation as a crusading young prosecutor and his part ownership in a local newspaper into a bid for a congressional seat, squeaking by his primary opponent by a mere fifty-seven votes. In 1910, at age thirty-one, Byrnes left South Carolina for the first time to begin his long career in Washington.

The self-made, first-term congressman from the Deep South and the young delegate from the Dutchess County gentry shared a passion and talent for politics. Ambitious, but competing in separate arenas, they could afford to help each other's rising career. Assistant Secretary of the Navy Roosevelt could count on Byrnes's support on the House Appropriations Committee. In 1920 Congressman Byrnes campaigned vigorously for the Cox-Roosevelt ticket in the face of the Harding landslide. During the period of the Republican ascendancy when both men were out of public office, Byrnes encouraged Roosevelt's political comeback as governor of New York. In 1932 Byrnes, then a senator, was among the first to publicly support Roosevelt's nomination for president.

Given this long and friendly association, it was

no surprise that Byrnes immediately became known as the president's "fair-haired boy" on Capitol Hill. During the hundred days and throughout Roosevelt's first term, Byrnes earned the title of the New Deal's "legislative ball carrier," a cloakroom wheeler-dealer who always seemed to get the administration's job done.

During the second term, differences arose over labor and civil rights issues, but the two men continued their warm personal relationship. Whether as a reward for past services or as a way out of potential difficulties, Roosevelt's appointment of Byrnes to the Supreme Court in 1941 reflected also his high regard for Byrnes's ability.

But after America's entry into the war, Byrnes left the judiciary for the executive branch. After only one term as a justice, Byrnes, in a virtually unprecedented move, resigned his seat to become, first, Roosevelt's "number 1 inflation stopper" as head of the newly created Office of Economic Stabilization and then "czar of czars" as director of the Office of War Mobilization. His commanding position over the wartime domestic economy soon earned Byrnes yet another title of Roosevelt's "assistant president for the home front." This extraordinary delegation of presidential power again demonstrated Roosevelt's confidence in Byrnes.

That confidence had limits, however. For all his legislative, judicial, and administrative ability, Byrnes apparently was not acceptable as Roosevelt's running mate. In 1940 and again in 1944, Byrnes had been judged a liability to the ticket and had been maneuvered out of the running for the vice-presidential nomination. Catholics might have resented his having left the church upon marrying a Protestant. His more recent record on sit-down strikes and civil rights legislation might have cost labor and black votes. Following his second and more bitter disappointment at the 1944 convention, Byrnes planned the earliest possible departure from the Roosevelt White House.

Partly by way of mending personal and political fences, Roosevelt, after he was safely in office for a fourth term, invited his old friend to accompany him to the Big Three summit conference at Yalta. It is also possible that Roosevelt was grooming Byrnes for a foreign policy post as either secretary of state or ambassador to the United Nations. If so, that plan was cut short by Roosevelt's death just weeks after his return from the conference.

But in the interim, Byrnes had assumed yet another role as Roosevelt's foreign policy lobbyist with Congress and public spokesman on the meaning of the Yalta agreements. That final service to the dead president helped make Byrnes secretary of state under Roosevelt's successor—a very different job after 12 April 1945. His role as Truman's chief foreign policy adviser lasted but a few months before a clash of personalities and policies forced Byrnes's resignation. In early 1947, he left Washington and national politics for good.

After publicly breaking with Truman over government spending and civil rights policy, Byrnes again

James F. Byrnes, 1940. Artist: Oskar Stoessel. (National Portrait Gallery, Smithsonian Institution. Gift of David E. Finley.)

entered politics at the state level as a staunchly conservative, anti-integrationist governor of South Carolina in the 1950s. Retiring to private life after his long and varied public career, Byrnes published an autobiography appropriately titled *All in One Lifetime.* In it he praised Roosevelt as a farsighted leader and dear friend. Privately, however Byrnes tempered that public judgment with the bittersweet observation that FDR "played upon the ambitions of men as an artist would play upon the strings of a musical instrument."

A full-scale Byrnes biography is yet to be written. His autobiography *All in One Lifetime* (New York: Harper & Bros., 1958) expands upon his earlier best-selling memoir of his involvement in foreign affairs, *Speaking Frankly* (New York: Harper & Bros., 1947). Both these works, while essential sources, are only the starting point for understanding so long and varied a life. Most published scholarly works have focused on Byrnes's brief tenure as Truman's secretary of state. Earlier aspects of his career and relationship with Roosevelt are treated in Winfred B. Moore, Jr., "New South Statesman: The Political Career of James Francis Byrnes, 1911–1941" (Ph.D. diss., Duke University, 1976) and John W. Partin, " 'Assistant President' for the Home Front: James F. Byrnes and World

War II" (Ph.D. diss., University of Florida, 1977). Byrnes's failure to gain the vice-presidential nomination is described in John W. Partin, "Roosevelt, Byrnes, and the 1944 Vice-Presidential Nomination," *Historian* 42 (November 1979): 85–100. The Roosevelt-Byrnes-Truman relationship's impact on postwar American foreign policy is discussed in Robert L. Messer, *The End of an Alliance: James F. Byrnes, Roosevelt, Truman and the Origins of the Cold War* (Chapel Hill: University of North Carolina Press, 1982).

ROBERT L. MESSER

See also Supreme Court of the United States

C

Cabinets

Franklin Roosevelt made twenty-five cabinet appointments during his administration. Of these, only Secretary of the Interior Harold L. Ickes and Secretary of Labor Frances Perkins served for the full twelve years. Henry Morgenthau, Jr., who was named treasury secretary on the death of William H. Woodin in 1934, in effect belongs in this group as well. Other Roosevelt appointees who held office for two terms or more included Secretary of State Cordell Hull (1933–44), Postmaster General James A. Farley (1933–40), and Secretary of Agriculture Henry A. Wallace (1933–40), who returned to the cabinet briefly in 1945. This longevity is striking in comparison to the dropout rate in recent administrations.

Roosevelt considered the cabinet members his of-

FDR's Cabinets

Vice-President

John Nance Garner 1933
Henry A. Wallace 1941
Harry S Truman 1945

Secretary of State

Cordell Hull 1933
E. R. Stettinius, Jr. 1944

Secretary of Treasury

William H. Woodin 1933
Henry Morgenthau, Jr. 1934

Secretary of War

George H. Dern 1933
Harry A. Woodring 1936
Henry L. Stimson 1940

Secretary of Navy

Claude A. Swanson 1933
Charles Edison 1940
Frank Knox 1940
James V. Forrestal 1944

Secretary of Interior

Harold L. Ickes 1933

Postmaster General

James A. Farley 1933
Frank C. Walker 1940

Attorney General

H. S. Cummings 1933
Frank Murphy 1939
Robert H. Jackson 1940
Francis Biddle 1941

Secretary of Commerce

Daniel C. Roper 1933
Harry L. Hopkins 1939
Jesse Jones 1940
Henry A. Wallace 1945

Secretary of Labor

Frances Perkins 1933

Secretary of Agriculture

Henry A. Wallace 1933
Claude R. Wickard 1940

ficial family, and his choices were personal. Although Raymond Moley and the president's longtime friend Louis Howe negotiated with the candidates for the first cabinet, they had little or no influence on the actual selections. On occasion, decisions were based on a personal relationship; Moley observed that George Dern, the governor of Utah, was made secretary of war (1933–36) because Roosevelt "simply liked" him. But politics were also a factor. After considering Macy's president Jesse Straus for secretary of commerce, the post went to Daniel C. Roper (1933–38), a close friend of William Gibbs McAdoo. The appointments of Republicans Henry Stimson to the War Department (1940–45) and Frank Knox as secretary of the navy (1940–44) were clearly intended to give the cabinet a bipartisan look as both the 1940 election and war neared. Perhaps because of his attitude toward the cabinet, Roosevelt found it difficult to remove even members who opposed his policies such as Secretary of War Harry H. Woodring (1936–40). Woodring was eventually forced to resign because of his objections to increased military aid to Great Britain.

Roosevelt rarely turned to the cabinet for advice on major policy questions, a fact that led Ickes to wonder what use it was to the administration. He wrote in his diary in 1935, "The President makes all of his own decisions and, so far at least as the Cabinet is concerned, without taking counsel with a group of advisers." Indeed, Roosevelt often ignored the departments completely and created agencies and committees to deal with problems he deemed important. The National Emergency Council (1934–39) tried to coordinate the work of the myriad of new agencies with that of the established departments. A related problem was his unwillingness clearly to delegate authority. Cabinet officers felt they were bypassed in areas that logically fell within their jurisdiction. At the same time, Roosevelt's practice of dividing responsibility frequently led to conflicts that fell to him to resolve.

The best source on the inner workings of the Roosevelt cabinets is Harold L. Ickes's three-volume *The Secret Diary of Harold L. Ickes* (New York: Simon & Shuster, 1953–55). Raymond Moley's *After Seven Years* (New York: Harper & Bros., 1939) and his *The First New Deal* (New York: Harcourt Brace Jovanovich, 1966) describe the selection process for the first-term cabinet. Richard F. Fenno, Jr., *The President's Cabinet: An Analysis in the Period from Wilson to Eisenhower* (Cambridge, Mass.: Harvard University Press, 1959) and Stephen Hess, *Organizing the Presidency* (Washington, D.C.: Brookings Institution, 1976) treat the cabinets in a broader comparative context.

PAUL SOIFER

See also Biddle, Francis Beverley; Black Cabinet; Cummings, Homer Stillé; Douglas, Lewis Williams; Dern, George Henry; Edison, Charles; Farley, James Aloysius; Forrestal, James Vincent; Garner, John Nance; Hopkins, Henry L.; Hull, Cordell; Ickes, Harold LeClair; Jackson, Robert Houghwout; Jones, Jesse Holman; Knox, William Franklin; Morgenthau, Henry T., Jr.; Murphy, Francis William; Perkins, Frances; Roper, Daniel Calhoun; Stettinius, Edward Reilly, Jr.; Stimson, Henry L.; Swanson, Claude Augustus; Truman, Harry S; Walker, Frank Comerford; Wallace, Henry A.; Walsh, Thomas James; Wickard, Claude Raymond; Woodin, William Hartman; Woodring, Henry Hines

Cairo Conference

(Code name Sextant), 22–26 November, 1943. World War II conference preceding the Teheran Conference, attended by President Roosevelt, Prime Minister Winston Churchill, Generalissimo Chiang Kai-shek of China, and the Anglo-American combined chiefs of staff. The meeting was held to discuss Far Eastern military operations, to enhance the symbolic importance of China in the war effort and postwar planning, and in part to meet Churchill's desire for U.S.-British talks before the Teheran Conference with Stalin. Churchill had lured Roosevelt to the Egyptian city with his tales of villas and gardens, the mysterious Pyramids, and the seclusion to be found there. The prime minister personally met Roosevelt on the latter's arrival in Cairo and took him to the large villa of Ambassador Alexander Kirk, where the president would stay while at the conference.

Roosevelt's immediate goal in the meeting was to keep China in the war. His larger concern was to bolster Chiang's importance as a member of the Big Four and to strengthen U.S.-Chinese relations in anticipation of cooperation in establishing a stable postwar system in the Far East. Roosevelt's concerns thus meshed with Chiang's, who was concerned that Allied strategy in the Far East might shift to a direct assault on Japan across the central and southwest Pacific, depriving Chiang of his monopoly on the sole alleged route for an attack on Japan. Churchill's concerns were to make Chiang the source of dissent at the meeting, for he wished to give priority to Anglo-American staff talks in preparation for the Teheran Conference dealing with the Overlord plans to invade Europe. (Roosevelt had asked Stalin to send representatives to the Cairo talks in order to avoid arousing Stalin's suspicions. The Soviet leader refused out of a concern not to antagonize Japan.) Churchill felt that Roosevelt's desire to deal with Chiang was a misplaced priority and threatened a dangerous shift of military efforts away from the major European campaign.

At the meeting, Roosevelt made China the first order of business, to Churchill's annoyance. The military talks centered around a possible operation to open up the Burma Road supply route into China. Chiang would provide support for such an operation only if the United States and Britain agreed to support amphibious operations in the Bay of Bengal. Churchill was opposed to the diversion of military forces to the Far East, thus undermining his hope for Eastern Mediterranean operations in the next year, and refused to commit British ground forces for a Burma assault. Even Roosevelt was dubious about the proposed operations, and he was irritated by Chiang's in-

Chiang Kai-shek, president of China, and Madame Chiang pose with President Roosevelt during the Cairo Confer- *ence, November 1943. (U.S. Signal Corps.)*

sistent demands; but he did give Chiang a general promise of support for the Chinese leader's military plans. Roosevelt was also instrumental in having the conference draw up a public statement, the so-called Cairo Declaration, that committed the Allies to returning to China the territories she had lost to Japan in the war. Roosevelt also agreed to seek Stalin's assent to this declaration at Teheran.

The basic results of the Cairo Conference were the general agreement to a Far Eastern operation involving Burma and the bolstering of Chiang's importance as a major ally. Despite Churchill's probable pique at these results, Anglo-American unity was reaffirmed at a Thanksgiving dinner that Roosevelt gave for the prime minister and his daughter, Sarah. Roosevelt could be pleased with the conference, but he was to find his achievements in part undone by the second Cairo Conference (3–7 December) which followed immediately the Teheran meetings with Stalin. This second conference, attended by Roosevelt and Churchill, resulted in the decision to delay the Burma operation in light of the decision made at Teheran to commit to the cross-channel invasion of Europe in late spring, 1944. Roosevelt also decided to appoint General Dwight D. Eisenhower commander of the Overlord operation while at this meeting (thus denying the post to Gen. George C. Marshall). Finally, Churchill and Roosevelt made an unsuccessful attempt to persuade the Turkish prime minister Inonu to bring Turkey into the war on the Allied side.

The best and most recent work on Roosevelt's diplomacy is Robert Dallek's *Franklin D. Roosevelt and American Foreign Policy, 1932–1945* (New York: Oxford University Press, 1979). This work can be supplemented by James MacGregor Burns, *Roosevelt: The Soldier of Freedom, 1940–1945* (New York: Harcourt Brace Jovanovich, 1970), which provides personal insights on the meeting, and by John Lewis Gaddis, *The United States and the Origins of the Cold War, 1941–1947* (New York: Columbia University Press, 1972). Older but still useful is Herbert Feis's masterful account, *Churchill, Roosevelt, Stalin: The War They Waged and the Peace They Sought* (Princeton: Princeton University Press, 1957).

See also Chiang Kai-shek; Churchill, Winston Leonard Spencer; Foreign Policy; Personal Diplomacy; World War II

Campaigns, Presidential

See Elections

Campobello

The Roosevelts spent their summers on the largest, outermost island in Passamaquoddy Bay, off the coast of Maine near the Canadian border. Politically, Campobello is part of New Brunswick, Canada, although since 1962 the island has been physically linked with Lubec, Maine, by the Roosevelt International Bridge.

In 1767 William Owen, a Welshman, acquired title to the island through a royal grant, obtained for him through the efforts of Lord William Campbell, governor of Nova Scotia. When Owen took possession in 1770, he named the island Campo Bello, thus acknowledging, in whimsical fashion, his patron as well as the island's natural beauty. The island remained a feudal estate in the hands of the Owen fam-

FDR with Tip at Campobello, 1902. (Courtesy FDR Library.)

Campobello viewed from the bay. The James Roosevelt house is at left; FDR's house is on the right. (Courtesy FDR Library.)

ily until the late nineteenth century. After John James Robinson-Owen, the fourth and last principal proprietor, died in 1874, his widow, Cornelia, sold the island to a group of American investors known as the Campobello Company. They turned the island into a summer resort, and wealthy easterners were soon escaping to one of three large hotels built between 1881 and 1883.

Franklin's parents, James and Sara Roosevelt, first visited Campobello in 1883 and soon thereafter bought ten acres overlooking Friar's Bay, where they built the family's summer home. As was the custom among patrician families in the late nineteenth century, the Roosevelts spent leisurely summers on Campobello throughout Franklin's boyhood. As a young adult, Franklin fraternized there with his peers and attended the usual complement of social activities designed to introduce eligible bachelors to proper young ladies. Eleanor first visited the Roosevelt summer cottage in 1904 in order to become better acquainted with her future mother-in-law.

Franklin and Eleanor continued to spend summers on Campobello after their marriage, acquiring a second cottage in 1909 to accommodate their growing family. The routine was interrupted however, in 1921, when FDR was stricken by poliomyelitis during a visit to the island. After that, Campobello reminded him of an unrecoverable past. Roosevelt did not return to the island until 1933, when the president, Sara, Eleanor, and three of their sons sailed up aboard a battleship for a hometown celebration of sorts. FDR made only two more visits to Campobello during his life, one in 1936 and another in 1939.

In 1963, the Hammer brothers, who then owned the Roosevelt compound, donated the property to the governments of Canada and the United States for the purpose of establishing an international historic park. The Roosevelt Campobello International Park, formally established on 22 January 1964, by joint agreement between the two countries, opened during the summer of that year. Situated on the southeast end of

the island, the 2,600 acres of Campobello Park are now a bird and animal refuge, and the cottage that Franklin and Eleanor acquired in 1909, restored by the Hammers, is open to the public.

Events that occurred at Campobello are described in many published works, but *Campobello, The Outer Island* by Alden Nowlan (Toronto: Clarke, Irwin & Co., 1975) contains a well-illustrated succinct history of the island that explains the Roosevelt connection and covers the basic information concerning the development of Roosevelt Campobello Park.

Casablanca Conference

The meeting between President Roosevelt and British prime minister Churchill in Casablanca, Morocco, 14–24 January 1943, was the first of their conferences to be held outside the Western Hemisphere. (They had met previously in Newfoundland and twice in Washington.) The location itself demonstrated the changed situation the two leaders faced. An Anglo-American invasion of Morocco and Algeria in November 1942 had destroyed the myth of an independent French government in Vichy and forced the Italians and Germans to defend French North Africa. The Casablanca Conference had been scheduled in anticipation of a quick victory of North Africa, requiring planning for the next step, but Hitler had surprised Allied strategists by sending reinforcements to Tunisia. The hoped-for December 1942 victory took until May 1943, but the plans made at Casablanca survived the delay.

Initially, Roosevelt had proposed high-level Anglo-Soviet-American military staff talks but when Churchill suggested a meeting with Soviet leader Joseph Stalin, the president quickly agreed. Stalin—his forces under siege from Leningrad to Stalingrad—declined, but by then the momentum for a summit meeting had built up, even if it was just two of the Big Three. The president's continued efforts to arrange tripartite military staff talks, even while he and Churchill were meeting, illustrates Roosevelt's fear that the Soviets would succumb to German pressure and negotiate a separate peace with Hitler. The invasion of North Africa (Operation Torch) was a pale substitute for the major European second front Stalin wanted—and thought he had been promised—even if Torch was the only practical thing to do in 1942. Moreover, the North African campaign guaranteed some sort of delay in launching that second front, and that was bound to heighten Stalin's suspicions.

Even with the Soviet Union hovering in the background like an unwelcome ghost in the attic, Anglo-American affairs dominated the Casablanca Conference. Not only was the meeting the high point of wartime cooperation between the two nations, but it marked the last time that England could and would try to retain its nineteenth-century-style role as a balance weight. Nationalism, economic growth in the United States, and economic decline in Great Britain since World War I all combined to make change inevitable. But the same combination of romanticism, assertiveness, and perseverance that had brought England to the top drove Churchill to give it one more try. That intermingling of old and new, of nineteenth and twentieth century, of Victorian England and Labourite Britain, gave the conference a unique flavor. Modern aircraft brought Churchill and Roosevelt to a North African oasis replete with caravans, camels, and colonialism. They met in a tourist hotel (the Anfa) outside the city and journeyed by automobile after the talks to the medieval trading center of Marrakesh. To most of the conferees at Casablanca, the world was still relatively simple: Hitler was the enemy, Japan would get her comeuppance, and things would go back to "normal" once those little problems were solved. The realities that would make normalcy an impossible dream were either hidden or ignored as Britons and Americans planned their future strategies. Some, like Franklin Roosevelt, foresaw the anticolonial explosion that was coming, but his attempts to sensitize his British cousins to that eventuality lacked any sense of urgency. Essentially, the conferees assumed that all they needed to do was win the war and the peace would take care of itself.

Churchill and the British military arrived in Casablanca expecting strong opposition to their proposals for an expansion of operations in the Mediterranean theater. General George C. Marshall, U.S. Army chief of staff, had long insisted that the United States and Great Britain concentrate on preparations for a cross-channel invasion, and the American navy was known to be pressing Roosevelt to shift men and supplies to the Pacific theater. If Marshall and the U.S. Navy had their way, there would not be enough left over to launch any attack in the Mediterranean.

Joint discussions about long-term strategy found all agreed on the desirability of mounting a massive cross-channel invasion, but undecided on immediate operations. All agreed that inaction in 1943 was intolerable. Not only should the pressure be kept on Germany, but Roosevelt and Churchill wanted to reassure Stalin that the delay in the second front was not a prelude to Anglo-American negotiations with Hitler. Since Marshall was inclined to believe that a major invasion of Western Europe was unfeasible until 1944, he could support recommendations to invade either Sicily or Sardinia, once the Italo-German forces were out of Tunisia. With Churchill convinced that only a major invasion and subsequent move up the Italian peninsula could satisfy the Russians, the Sicilian operation won out. The Americans insisted upon and finally received British agreement to a large-scale invasion of Burma, but that operation fell afoul of later changes in the needs of the central Pacific theater.

During the conference, which proved remarkably free of rancor, two other joint policies received approval. The first, the continued heavy bombing offensive against Germany, proved no problem as long as the Americans did not try to commit British air forces to daylight bombing. The second, the unconditional surrender declaration, provided little cause for discussion in 1943—but later became a matter of historical controversy. The idea that the Allies should demand the unconditional surrender of Germany and Japan (Italy was frequently exempted in such discussions) had cropped up early in the war, and Churchill learned of Roosevelt's support for the policy at least by August 1942. They discussed it during the Casablanca Conference, and then, in a move that Churchill later claimed surprised him, Roosevelt set forth the policy in a postconference meeting with the press. Churchill may have been surprised at the timing (there is evidence both ways on that point), but there is no doubt that he and the president had previously agreed upon unconditional surrender as a general policy. Whether or not it prolonged the war by driving the Germans to fight on with no hope of a negotiated peace is both doubtful and moot. The declaration not only reflected a strong Anglo-American desire to eliminate permanently the "German problem" but also represented a clear and unequivocal promise to the Soviet Union that, in spite of the further postponement of a cross-channel attack, the British and Americans were in the war until the complete and utter defeat of Germany. Their hope was that the Russians were equally committed.

At that same press conference, another event occurred that commanded headlines but had little real effect on the history of the Second World War. As an unplanned part of the performance, French generals Charles de Gaulle and Henri Giraud, under prodding by Roosevelt, stiffly shook hands while cameras clicked. The front-page photographs which appeared around the Allied world were misleading. Giraud, expecting to be proclaimed the leader of the Free French, had eagerly accepted an invitation to come to Casablanca. De Gaulle, aware of Roosevelt's and Churchill's unwillingness to choose between the two Frenchmen, at first refused Churchill's request and stayed in London. Only when Churchill threatened to withdraw his support from de Gaulle did the French leader reluctantly fly to Casablanca. Roosevelt, who spoke of Giraud as the eager bridegroom and de Gaulle as the unwilling bride, tried to get the two to agree to a joint temporary unified Free French command, but each refused to submit in any way to the other. Acting like snubbed royalty, de Gaulle refused to cooperate with Giraud, while the latter with equal haughtiness claimed to be above politics and interested only in liberating France. Roosevelt's annoyance centered on de Gaulle, and the president later described the Frenchman's attitude: "The day he arrived, he thought he was Joan of Arc and the following day he insisted that he was Georges Clemenceau."

The most significant decision of the entire conference was hidden in a Combined Chiefs of Staff report to Roosevelt and Churchill. The paper noted that the military had agreed to establish a combined staff in London to plan the large-scale cross-channel invasion. Headed by a chief of staff to the as then unnamed supreme Allied commander, this group began planning for the Normandy invasion.

The cooperative mood of Casablanca did not last long. The American military felt the British had conned them into a Mediterranean strategy and began to suspect them of looking for ways to avoid a cross-channel attack, particularly when the British suggested that the logical follow-up to the invasion of Sicily might be operations in the Aegean Sea, something General Marshall called "suction pump" effect. The British, on the other hand, suspected the Americans of trying to shift the main focus of the war from Europe to the Pacific. When the U.S. Chiefs of Staff Committee requested of its British counterpart a "clarification of the Casablanca decisions," the London committee commented that "while the American draft pays lip service to the offensive against the Axis in Europe, its implication is to give pride of place to the war in the Far East" (PREM 3/420/7/6–9, Public Record Office, London). Churchill scrawled "I fully concur" across the document and dated it 18 April 1943. Some of the participants in the Casablanca Conference had harbored such suspicions all along, and in less than three months the Casablanca mood had dissipated.

Even so, the Casablanca Conference was crucial to the development of Anglo-American strategy for World War II. For better or for worse, the decision to expand operations against Italy ensured that the Normandy invasion could not take place until 1944—a delay that saw the Soviets take the offensive and begin their sweep across Eastern Europe, but a delay that also guaranteed that the invasion of France would succeed and that British and American forces would liberate and occupy Western Europe. Unconditional surrender, a demand that reflected American and British thinking that Germany had to be humiliated on the battlefield in order to prevent any rebirth of "Prussian" militarism, remained a guiding principle of Anglo-American and Soviet policy. Some voices were heard later to argue that the destruction of Germany would invite further moves westward by the Soviet Union, but no one at Casablanca predicted the reversal of roles that would take place later in 1943 on the German-Soviet front. Thus, Soviet expansion was not something to fear, while the threat of a separate peace was always present. And, running like a silken thread throughout the talks, were hints of Anglo-American differences over the future of colonial empires. The Americans suspected that Churchill's plans in the Mediterranean were intended to protect Britain's interests in the Middle East, while the postwar disposition of the French Empire kept cropping up only to meet evasion and postponement from Roosevelt. Most of all, it was the end of an era for Great Britain. The decision to continue operations in the Mediterranean, which finally resulted in the invasion of Italy, was the last time that British strategy would prevail. For the rest of the war, military and political decisions reflected the interests and goals of the United States.

There is no history of the Casablanca Conference, although a small body of literature has grown up around the issue of unconditional surrender. For the conference itself, see the memoirs by Winston S. Churchill, *The Hinge of Fate* (Boston: Houghton Mifflin Co., 1950), Robert S. Sherwood, *Roosevelt and Hopkins* (New York: Harper & Bros., 1948), and Harold Macmillan, *The Blast of War* (New York: Harper & Row, 1967). Brief secondary accounts can be found in Robert Dallek, *Franklin D. Roosevelt and American Foreign Policy* (New York: Oxford University Press, 1979), and Forrest Pogue, *George C. Marshall: Organizer of Victory* (New York: Viking Press, 1973). The most lucid and readable summary of the debate over the origins and long-term effect of the unconditional surrender doctrine is Raymond O'Connor, *Diplomacy for Victory* (New York: Norton, 1971). See also the appropriate volume of the official British *History of the Second World War, Grand Strategy* subseries, and *British Foreign Policy in the Second World War* by L. Woodward, both published by Her Majesty's Stationery Office in London, England. The documents of the conference are published in *Foreign Relations of the United States, Conferences at Washington 1941–1942, and Casablanca, 1943* (Washington, D.C.: U.S. Government Printing Office, 1968), and Warren F. Kimball, ed., *Churchill and Roosevelt: The Complete Correspondence,* 3 vols. (Princeton: Princeton University Press, 1984).

WARREN F. KIMBALL

See also Churchill, Winston Leonard Spencer; de Gaulle, Charles; Eisenhower, Dwight David; Foreign Policy; Joint Chiefs of Staff; Personal Diplomacy; Stalin, Joseph, and the Soviet Union; World War II

Cash-and-Carry

See Foreign Economic Policy; World War II

Catholics

American Catholics formed an important part of Roosevelt's electoral coalition, but less because of active support of the New Deal by the church hierarchy than because of the social composition of the church's American membership. A large proportion of American Catholics were of immigrant stock (Irish, German, Italian, Eastern European) and engaged in working-class occupations. Catholics had been part of the urban Democratic constituency for decades before the 1930s. Roosevelt strengthened that traditional allegiance by appointing Catholics to positions of importance within his administration (James Farley, Marvin McIntyre, Thomas Walsh, Frank Murphy, and others) and to 25 percent of all the judicial positions he filled; by making flattering public references to papal encyclicals; by naming an unofficial envoy to the Vatican in 1940 (over the strenuous objections of many American Protestants); and by committing the government to relief and social welfare programs and to support of unionization, all of which were of particular benefit to Catholics.

But American Catholics were not, of course, a single, undifferentiated mass. The diversity of opinion within the Catholic community was clearly visible in the varied responses to the New Deal among leaders of the church. Considerable conservative opposition survived (and grew as the 1930s progressed) among both clerical and lay leaders, who were disturbed by what they considered the excessive "statism" of the New Deal. Conservative Catholics reacted with particular hostility to Roosevelt's 1933 recognition of the Soviet Union (whose atheism they detested) and what they considered the administration's inadequate response to the anticlerical policies of the government of Mexico. Conservative criticism arose not only from among members of the ecclesiastical hierarchy but from such prominent Catholic political leaders as Alfred Smith, whose hostility to the New Deal emerged from a combination of personal bitterness and ideological opposition.

The New Deal also inspired occasional criticism from the Catholic Left. The Catholic Worker movement, founded in 1933 by Dorothy Day and Peter Maurin, at times found the Roosevelt administration distressingly cautious in its support of labor organization. The erratic Father Charles E. Coughlin, the Detroit radio priest whose ideology cannot easily be classified as either of the Left or of the Right, mixed warm support of the New Deal with frequent criticisms of its inadequate commitment to financial and monetary reform. By the late 1930s, Coughlin had become one of the president's bitterest critics, although the basis of his criticism by then had shifted to embrace a harsh anticommunism and a rabid anti-Semitism.

For the most part, however, the Catholic leadership was warmly supportive of the New Deal. The American church in the 1930s had embraced a level of social and political activism without precedent in its recent history—in part as a reaction to the obvious needs of depression society and in part in response to new doctrinal stances outlined in Pope Pius XI's 1931 encyclical *Quadragesimo Anno*. In that document, Pius endorsed what was already a growing trend within the church: a renewed interest in the teachings of St. Thomas Aquinas and his injunctions to make religion the basis of opposition to unjust social conditions. Such leading Catholic liberals as Monsignor John Ryan of the National Catholic Welfare Council identified themselves prominently with the New Deal and claimed that Roosevelt's policies were embodiments of the pope's message. Catholic periodicals, ranging from the once-conservative *America* to the moderate *Commonweal* to the more radical *Catholic Worker* and *Michigan Labor Leader*, openly supported the president. "All Catholics who desire to give practical effect to the principles of social justice laid down by Pope Pius XI," *Commonweal* editorialized, "will see that . . . Roosevelt's opportunity to lead . . . is likewise the Catholic opportunity to make the teachings of Christ apply to all."

Roosevelt's identification with the labor movement in the 1930s, and in particular his support (belated though it may have been) of the Wagner Act of 1935, further strengthened his popularity among Catholics. Nearly 30 percent of the membership of the CIO, and 40 percent of its leadership, was Catholic. Some of the most prominent labor leaders of the era—Philip Murray, James Carey, John Brophy—were practicing Catholics who used papal social teachings as a basis for their activities and who identified themselves to varying degrees with the New Deal.

Strong isolationist sentiment in the late 1930s temporarily eroded Roosevelt's standing among some Catholic social groups. Isolationism emerged among some Catholics (notably those connected with the Catholic Worker movement) as an expression of radical pacifism, among others as an expression of anticommunism (which they associated with anti-internationalism), and among still others as an expression of cultural and ethnic prejudices. After Pearl Harbor, however, all but a few of these isolationists supported the administration's conduct of the war; and Roosevelt's electoral performance among American Catholics remained impressive through the 1944 election.

Two major studies of American Catholics in the New Deal era are David J. O'Brien, *American Catholics and Social Reform: The New Deal Years* (New York: Oxford University Press, 1968) and George Q. Flynn, *American Catholics and the Roosevelt Presidency* (Lexington: University Press of Kentucy, 1968). Neil Betten, *Catholic Activism and the Industrial Worker* (Gainesville: University Presses of Florida, 1976) examines Catholic involvement in the labor movement. Mel Piehl, *Breaking Bread* (Philadelphia: Temple University Press, 1982) is a study of the Catholic Worker. George Q. Flynn, *Roosevelt and Romanism: Catholics and American Diplomacy, 1937–1945* (New York: Greenwood, 1976) discusses international issues and the war years.

ALAN BRINKLEY

See also Coughlin, Charles Edward; Democratic Party; Smith, Alfred E.; Walker, Frank Comerford

Censorship

See Office of Censorship

Cermak, Anton

See Assassination Attempt of 1933; Interregnum

Chamber of Commerce, United States

National organization established in 1912 with a broad aim to promote and protect business interests. During the 1930s, the U.S. Chamber of Commerce acted as a funnel for channeling conservative opposition to Franklin Roosevelt. For a brief period at the beginning of Roosevelt's first term, however, the chamber reserved judgment on several of the New Deal legislative enactments, including the National Recovery Administration (NRA) and the Agricultural Adjustment Administration (AAA), and offered its cooperation to the administration. In September 1934, the director of the chamber wrote a statement to the president that there was "a general state of apprehension among businessmen of the country" because of the failure to balance the budget, the increasing involvement of government in private business matters, growing labor disturbances, and radical statements by members of the administration concerning the security of property. The president disagreed with the chamber's call to return to normalcy. "It is time to stop crying 'wolf' and to cooperate for recovery," Roosevelt told chamber officials.

By its annual meeting in May 1935, the Chamber of Commerce abandoned any pretense of cooperation with the New Deal: it passed a series of resolutions opposing the NRA, AAA, Wagner Act, Banking Act, Social Security Act, and Public Utilities Holding Act. The antipathy toward Roosevelt's policies did not dissipate as time passed; the chamber's magazine, *Nation's Business,* urged greater business freedom, and questionnaires administered by the chamber consistently showed an overwhelming repudiation of New Deal measures on the part of its constituent members. On his part, FDR often rebuked the chamber for its nearsighted philosophy and expressed his opinion that the organization no longer voiced the real views of business.

An early analysis of the Chamber of Commerce's position vis-à-vis Roosevelt's programs is Rinehart J. Swenson, "The Chamber of Commerce and the New Deal," *Annals of the American Academy of Political and Social Sciences* 179 (May 1935):136–43. William Wilson, "How the Chamber of Commerce Viewed the NRA: A Reexamination," *Mid-America* 44 (April 1962):95–108 sees less support for industrywide codes than was previously believed by scholars. See also George Wolfskill and John A. Hudson, *All But the People: Roosevelt and His Critics, 1933–1939* (Toronto: Macmillan Co., 1969).

See also Business

Claire L. Chennault. (Constant Collection. Courtesy FDR Library.)

Chennault, Claire Lee

(6 September 1890–27 July 1958)

Leader of Flying Tigers and commanding general, Fourteenth Army Air Force in China during World War II. Born in Texas, Chennault grew up in Louisiana and was commissioned in the U.S. Army in World War I. Earning his wings in 1919, he served in a variety of peacetime assignments flying fighter aircraft. While instructing at the Air Corps Tactical School in the 1930s, he strongly advocated increased fighter airplane firepower, speed, and range at a time when bomber development and doctrine were being emphasized. Considered a maverick, Chennault retired in 1937 and immediately departed for China, where he became an adviser to Chiang Kai-shek and trained Chinese aviators.

In October 1940 as the Japanese continued their gains in China, Chennault was dispatched to the United States to recruit an American-supported air force. Opposed by the U.S. Army Air Corps because of its need to expand at the same time it was providing assistance to Britain, Chennault nevertheless was able to convince FDR to authorize the purchase of P-40 fighters and permit American military aviators

to leave active duty to serve with the Chinese. FDR even permitted one of his closest advisers, Tommy Corcoran, to return to the private sector to assist the Chinese. By December 1941 the American Volunteer Group, known popularly as the Flying Tigers, began to score significantly against the Japanese, confirming Chennault's reputation as a brilliant tactician. Integrated into the U.S. Army Air Force on 4 July 1942 with Chennault as a brigadier general, the AVG became part of the Tenth Air Force and became the nucleus of the Fourteenth Air Force when it was formed in August 1943.

Chennault and his problems mirrored in many ways U.S. difficulties with China during World War II. FDR, anxious to keep China in the war, was inclined to build up airpower there, particularly in view of the unreliability of Chinese ground troops. Lt. Gen. Joseph Stilwell, Chennault's superior until October 1944, advocated the use of properly trained Chinese forces on the ground, but Chennault insisted to FDR, who appeared interested in the concept, that Japan could be defeated with five hundred aircraft operating from Chinese bases. The British, who were more concerned with protection or recovery of empire possessions, placed emphasis on India and Burma. Chennault consistently succeeded in getting Chiang to plead directly to FDR his case for building up air power in China, even though a major constraining factor was the requirement that all supplies to support such forces had to be flown over the Hump from India. Chennault enlisted a host of advocates to intercede with FDR, among them not only Chiang and Madame Chiang Kai-shek but T. V. Soong, Wendell Willkie, Henry Wallace, and Joseph Alsop, a young lieutenant at the time on Chennault's staff who maintained close rapport with Harry Hopkins. FDR interceded with generals Marshall and Arnold to increase tonnage over the Hump and provide aircraft to China or Chennault's forces.

Stilwell's recall in October 1944 failed to resolve Chennault's difficulties, as American success in the Pacific islands campaign and the aerial devastation of Japan by B-29s from bases outside China relegated China to a minor theater of war. After the death of FDR, Chennault realized that air power in China would not increase, and he retired in July 1945. After World War II he returned to China and started a quasi-civilian airline, Civil Air Transport, which was moderately successful before becoming the first Central Intelligence Agency "client" airline in the Far East.

Chennault's story is told in Maj. Gen. Claire Lee Chennault, *Way of a Fighter* (New York: Putnam, 1949). The ground forces account and the diplomacy are best presented in Barbara W. Tuchman's *Stilwell and the American Experience in China, 1911–1945* (New York: Macmillan Co., 1970).

JOHN W. HUSTON

See also Chiang Kai-shek; Stilwell, Joseph Warren; World War II

Chiang Kai-shek

(31 October 1887–5 April 1975)

Leader of Chinese Nationalist forces. Born in Chekiang, China, Chiang graduated from Tokyo military academy in 1907. He soon became active in the Chinese Nationalist movement, taking parts in attempts to overthrow the Manchus and then Yuan Shih-kai. In 1917, he was military aide to Sun Yat-sen. In 1924, he became commandant of the Whampoa Military Academy in Canton, a school that trained many Chinese leaders. After Sun's death, Chiang became increasingly prominent in the Koumintang party, and from 1928 on, he exercised virtually uninterrupted power within the Nationalist government.

Although formally the Chinese Revolution began when Sun Yat-sen created the Koumintang in 1924, it began in reality in 1926 when Chiang launched the Northern Expedition. Starting from Canton, Chiang captured Hankow, Kiukiang, and the Chinese section of Shanghai. Between 1927, when the Koumintang took Nanking, to 1937, when Japan attacked China, Chiang tried—often without success—to gain control over all China. He intermittently fought with various warlords as well as with Communist forces, stationed after 1935 in Yenan.

From the beginning, Chiang's fundamental relationship to Roosevelt was one of supplicant. The relationship really began in the fall of 1938, when the president commissioned Henry Morgenthau, Jr., secretary of the treasury, to arrange a $25 million loan for Chiang's government. Late in 1939, Chiang wrote Roosevelt, claiming that only economic sanctions would force Japan into a just settlement of the two-year-old war. In October 1940, Chiang sent word that continued resistance to Japan depended on five hundred American planes, American volunteers to fly them, and a single large loan. When, a month later, Chiang sought an outright alliance with the United States, Roosevelt refused, though the president did pledge $100 million credit and agreed to divert to China a hundred pursuit planes scheduled to defend the Burma Road. In January 1941, Roosevelt sent administrative assistant Lauchlin Currie to aid Chiang in his economic problems and to demonstrate American determination to provide additional assistance.

Chiang's requests grew more strident and frequent after the United States entered World War II. Roosevelt tended to make sweeping promises—including huge deliveries of matériel and planes and a major air offensive—but often could not deliver. Loans and credits were relatively easy for Chiang to come by, including half a billion dollars in the winter of 1941–42, though by 1943 Roosevelt was balking. In April 1941, the president quietly authorized the "resignation" of American military personnel to become "civilian" members of Col. Claire Chennault's Flying Tigers. In November 1941, Chiang's objection helped kill a proposed modus vivendi with Japan, though British opposition and Japanese troop movements south of Formosa were undoubtedly greater

factors. Early in 1942, Roosevelt appointed one of America's best corps commanders, Gen. Joseph W. Stilwell, chief of staff to Chiang. To compensate for the loss of the Burma Road, he pushed the development of the dangerous air route over the Hump. Other Roosevelt policies included the abolition of extraterritorial privileges and immigration exclusion and the appointment of Chiang as supreme commander of the United Powers in China, a title that conferred more status than power.

Chiang Kai-shek. (National Archives.)

Yet Roosevelt did not always accede to Chiang's requests. In November 1941, he told Chiang that America would not respond to a Japanese offensive on the Burma Road by preemptive air attacks. In August 1942, he turned down Chiang's plea that the United States foster Indian independence. More important, planes and supplies originally earmarked for China often could not get through, in part because they were suddenly rushed to other theaters and in part because the fall of Burma cut off the main supply route. Chiang, on his part, continually threatened to negotiate separately with the Japanese.

Roosevelt realized that Chiang's regime was corrupt, its army inefficient, its leader arrogant. He never envisioned Chinese territory as a major war theater. Yet he would not make American aid contingent upon reform. Among his reasons were: genuine personal respect for Chiang, a man whom he claimed in private had come up "the hard way to become the undisputed leader of four hundred million people" and who, as an enlightened modernizer, had "created in a very short time what it took a couple of centuries for us to attain"; fear of Chinese internal collapse and surrender to the Japanese; the beliefs that China could tie down several million Japanese troops and aid in launching air attacks that might bring victory cheaply, hence saving some fifty years of island hopping; hopes that China would eventually become a great power, serving in the occupation of Indochina, Korea, and perhaps Japan and in general supporting U.S. policy against that of other Pacific powers.

The high point of the Chiang-Roosevelt relationship, and the only face-to-face meeting between the two men, came at the Cairo Conference, held 22–26 November 1943. Though Roosevelt found Chiang mercurial, defensive, and heavily dependent upon his far more sophisticated wife, Soong Mei-ling, he hoped to win Chiang's confidence with assurances of membership in the Big Four and the return of Manchuria, Taiwan, and the Pescadores after the war.

In the summer of 1944, when it appeared that China was on the verge of military collapse, Roosevelt demanded that Chiang give Stilwell command over all Chinese forces. Yet when Chiang first delayed and then refused, Roosevelt acquiesced in Stilwell's removal. Of prime concern to Roosevelt was the realization that Chiang's forces could never constitute the main springboard for a major assault on Japan, American victories in the eastern Pacific, and knowledge that Russia would eventually enter the Pacific war. Yet political considerations were undoubtedly a factor, with Roosevelt not daring to risk a break with Chiang on the eve of the 1944 elections. Stilwell's replacement, Gen. Albert C. Wedemeyer, and Roosevelt's new ambassador, Patrick J. Hurley, were both far more friendly to Chiang's cause. Though Roosevelt opposed American aid to Chinese Communist forces, he hoped that Chiang would agree to a coalition government, for he saw a coalition under Chiang's control as the only way of saving his regime. After Stilwell's dismissal, Roosevelt's exchanges with Chiang became less frequent, and at Yalta Roosevelt infringed on certain Chinese territorial interests, such as Manchuria, without consulting him.

Once World War II ended, civil war broke out. It continued until 1950, when Chiang and his Nationalists were driven to the island of Taiwan, where he ruled until his death in 1975.

We have no thorough biography of Chiang Kai-shek. Herbert Feis, *The China Tangle: The American Effort in China from Pearl Harbor to the Marshall Mission* (Princeton: Princeton University Press, 1953), sees an essentially benign American policy stymied by incompetent Nationalists and malevolent Communists. Tang Tsou, *America's Failure in China, 1941–1950*, 2 vols. (Chicago: University of Chicago Press, 1963), argues that Roosevelt devoted inadequate support to making China a great power. Barbara Tuchman, *Stilwell and the American Experience in China, 1911–1945* (New York: Macmillan Co., 1970), blames Roosevelt for uncritically backing Chiang's doomed regime, and Robert Dallek, *Franklin D. Roosevelt and American Foreign Policy 1932–1945* (New York: Oxford University Press, 1979), stresses the political and ideological constraints under which Roosevelt operated. To Michael Schaller, *The U.S. Crusade in China, 1938–1945* (New York: Columbia University Press, 1979), Roosevelt misperceived rapid shifts of power within China. Christopher Thorne, *Allies of a Kind: The United States, Britain, and the War against Japan, 1941–1945* (New York: Oxford University Press, 1978), sees Roosevelt a prisoner of the exaggerated beliefs in China he held early in the war.

JUSTUS D. DOENECKE

See also Cairo Conference; Chennault, Claire Lee; Foreign Economic Policy; Japan; Open Door Policy; Personal Diplomacy; Stilwell, Joseph Warren

Child Labor

See New Deal; Wages and Hours Legislation

China

See Chiang Kai-shek; Chennault, Claire Lee; Currie, Lauchlin; Japan; Open Door Policy; Stilwell, Joseph Warren; Stimson, Henry L.

Churchill, Winston Leonard Spencer

(30 November 1874–24 January 1965)
From 1900 until his retirement from public life in 1964, Winston Churchill was a major British political

Sir Winston S. Churchill, 1946. Artist: Douglas Chandor. (National Portrait Gallery, Smithsonian Institution.)

leader. He served in the British cavalry following his graduation from Sandhurst in 1894 and fought in India and the Sudan. Those experiences served as the subject for much of his work as a journalist in the late 1890s, and that brief career became the springboard for his election in 1900 to Parliament as a Conservative. He later joined the Liberal party and remained there until the 1920s, when he again went to the House of Commons as a Conservative. During World War I he served in various cabinet posts, including a stint as first lord of the admiralty (a post similar to the U.S. secretary of the navy).

While out of the government from 1929 through 1939, Churchill developed a reputation both as an author and as a staunch opponent of Hitler's Germany. At the same time, he endeared himself to Conservatives by supporting King Edward VIII during the abdication crisis and by vehemently condemning Indian nationalism. When Prime Minister Neville Chamberlain's peace plans collapsed with the German invasion of Poland on 1 September 1939, he was forced to bring Churchill into the cabinet, once again as first lord of the admiralty. When the collapse of French resistance to Hitler brought Chamberlain's resignation, Churchill became prime minister on 10 May 1940, a post he held until July 1945, a few months after Roosevelt's death.

Franklin Roosevelt and Winston Churchill first crossed paths in 1918, when they both attended a formal dinner at Gray's Inn, one of England's prestigious legal societies. Churchill forgot the chance meeting, a slip that annoyed the president when the two next met in 1941, but Roosevelt himself had failed to even mention Churchill in letters and reports of that early trip to London.

Their personal relationship, one that helped shape the era of World War II, began on 11 September 1939. On that day, Roosevelt sent the Englishman a letter suggesting that Churchill keep "in touch personally with anything you want me to know

A message of encouragement from Roosevelt to Churchill, hand-carried from the president to the prime minister by Wendell Willkie. The lines of poetry are from Longfellow's "The Building of the Ship." (Courtesy FDR Library.)

about." The president's initiative stemmed in part from his own inclination to seek information and impressions from outside normal State Department channels. But Roosevelt also resented Prime Minister Chamberlain's open contempt for the United States and hoped to create a better relationship with a major political leader, one who might succeed to the prime ministry.

Roosevelt began the correspondence somewhat dubious about Churchill, who seemed to represent all the aspects of British aristocracy and colonialism that the president disliked and, to a degree, blamed for much of the world crisis. Churchill, for his part, had criticized some of the seeming radicalism and class conciousness of the New Deal, though he applauded Roosevelt's attacks on wealthy special interests and, in particular, the elimination of Prohibition. Despite their political differences, the similarities in their upbringing helped bridge the gap. Both had been raised primarily by their mothers, both had attended prestigious schools, both had a boyish enthusiasm for the navy, both were accustomed to a bucolic-class style of life about which they invariably romanticized. Still, had it not been for the compulsion of a common enemy—Hitler's Germany—their politics would likely have kept them apart.

The "common-law" alliance between the United States and Britain that preceded American entry into World War II was, for both Churchill and Roosevelt, a matter of necessity. The initial get-acquainted period of their relationship ended with the fall of France and Churchill's elevation to prime minister. There-

after, the English leader's main goal in his dealings with Roosevelt was to obtain active American involvement in the war, followed by a firm Anglo-American postwar partnership. From May 1940 until the Japanese attack on Pearl Harbor brought the United States into the worldwide struggle, Churchill maneuvered to involve the United States, step by step, in any way he could. American economic and military aid—cash, sales, swaps of destroyers for Western Hemisphere bases, and finally Lend-Lease—could help Britain hold out and prevent a collapse of the will to resist Hitler, but the prime minister knew that only active American participation in the war could defeat Germany.

Roosevelt, on the other hand, consistently avoided any commitment to join the fight. Like most Americans, he initially believed that Britain and France together were strong enough to hold the Germans in check. But the collapse of France changed all that, and the president responded by dramatically increasing aid to Britain. Still, even as late as the summer of 1941, Roosevelt thought, perhaps wishfully, that American military participation in the war could be limited to naval and air forces. He angered Churchill with a request that the British promise not to let their fleet fall into German hands and frustrated the prime minister with demands that Britain pay cash for goods until they had neither cash nor gold left. Such moves may have been good politics, designed to head off congressional antiinterventionists, but they also betrayed a suspicion of Britain that always lurked just below the surface. Like many Americans, Roosevelt suspected that the British always had ulterior motives, particularly when it came to money and the empire.

The German attack on the Soviet Union in June 1941 took the pressure off Britain, but the United States remained reluctant to enter the fray. Not until the Japanese attack on Pearl Harbor of 7 December 1941 did the reluctance disappear, and then only after Hitler declared war on the United States. Churchill immediately arranged a quick trip to Washington where he received the assurances he sought: the United States would follow a Europe-first grand strategy.

With American entry into the war, the Churchill-Roosevelt relationship entered a new phase. As Churchill himself put it when an adviser suggested following the same gentle approach with the Americans that Britain had used since 1939, "Oh! that is the way we talked to her while we were wooing her: now that she is in the harem, we talk to her quite differently!" With the Soviet Union besieged by German armies, Japan on the march in the Pacific, western Europe occupied by the Nazis, and North Africa and the Suez Canal threatened by Italo-German forces, Churchill and Roosevelt had no time for anything except candor and cooperation. Until the Anglo-Americans could take the offensive, theirs was a relationship of equal partnership. To be sure, Roosevelt occasionally raised issues that made Churchill bridle, particularly when the president recommended that Britain promise the Indians their independence. But most of their efforts were spent developing the economic and strategic plans that would, ultimately, spell defeat for Germany, Italy, and Japan.

It was during this period that their relationship almost ripened into friendship. Both men, as part of their overall style and diplomacy, used their personal charm and their families as a means of cementing the alliance. In the course of their extensive correspondence (they exchanged nearly two thousand cables, letters, and memoranda) and frequent meetings (they met nine times between August 1941 and February 1945), the two men established a personal relationship. They enjoyed inside jokes, regularly swapped wisecracks, and never forgot the personal touch at Christmas and on birthdays. But dry martinis and fishing trips could not eliminate their differences.

Those differences came out in the open as the Allies began to push back Hitler while Japan's Pacific advance was stymied. The successful Anglo-American invasion of French North Africa brought on a confrontation over future strategy. Churchill and his advisers, scarred by the experiences of World War I and sensitive to Britain's limited manpower, advocated a strategy of multiple attacks all around the periphery of German-held Europe from Norway to western France to Italy to Greece—a strategy that would force Hitler to disperse his limited forces and resources while having to maintain a major invasion against German-Russians. Roosevelt and his advisers insisted on a major invasion against German-held western Europe, not only because such a second front had been promised to the Russians, but because they believed it was the quickest and hence the least costly way to defeat Hitler. The president had strayed from that concept when he went against his military advisers and agreed to the North African invasion and again when he supported the move from North Africa to Sicily and then on to Italy. But by the summer of 1943, Roosevelt had gotten Churchill and the British to commit to a major cross-channel invasion and a second front by late spring 1944.

That commitment coincided with a number of major changes in the worldwide strategic situation. The Soviet victory at Kursk, coming a few months after the German surrender at Stalingrad, ended the military threat to Russia and put Stalin's forces in a position to take the offensive. Over the same period, the Anglo-American liberation of North Africa dragged on until May 1943, delaying the invasions of Sicily and Italy. Then, once the hoped-for Italian surrender came, Hitler surprised his foes by choosing to fight Rome and central Italy instead of retreating to an Alpine defense line. Meanwhile, the Americans had begun to push back the Japanese in the South Pacific and were gearing up for the island-hopping campaign that would start in the central Pacific in November. These strategic developments, combined with America's dominant role in wartime production, changed Anglo-American relations and with them, the Churchill-Roosevelt equation. Churchill's slow peripheral strategy seemed ineffective in the light of Soviet advances, the demands of the Pacific theater, and the delays in the Mediterranean. Moreover, the prime minister's attempts to promote operations in Yugo-

slavia and the Aegean Sea raised suspicions that a quick end to the war took second place to the defense of traditional British interests in the area. At the same time, Roosevelt's assessment of the probable postwar situation made him place greater emphasis on good relations with the Soviet Union.

Whatever the reasons, the Churchill-Roosevelt relationship passed from one of relative equality to an unequal partnership, with the United States playing the lead role. That new phase was marked by the president's unsuccessful attempt in May 1943 to arrange a private meeting between himself and Stalin, a conference that would have left Churchill out in the cold.

When the prime minister learned of the proposal and expressed concern, Roosevelt defended the idea by arguing that, with the British absent, Stalin would "be more frank" in discussions about the Balkans, Poland, and even the Far East. Angered by the implication that Britain was a second-class power, Churchill nonetheless acquiesced, unwilling to consider any alternative to a postwar Anglo-American entente.

As postwar planning became a higher priority, Roosevelt and his advisers, along with many other American leaders, tended to be increasingly critical of British policies, more so than of Soviet actions. For Americans to picture Great Britain as a greater threat than the Soviet Union to postwar cooperation may seem absurd, but they were not looking at the world from a cold war perspective. Many Americans tended to place responsibility for the world crisis on Britain and, to a lesser degree, France. Bolshevism, Nazism, and fascism were hated and feared, but not blamed for the collapse of the interwar order. American calls for arms control, the elimination of trade barriers, and the establishment of governments that would meet the needs and hopes of their citizens—thus ending colonialism and spheres of influence—were a critique of British greed and power politics, and it was those factors that had prevented effective international cooperation and had permitted the dictators to run amok. At the same time, the main issue for immediate postwar policies was to prevent another German-caused war, not to prevent Soviet expansion.

Not surprisingly then, sharp disagreements frequently punctuated relations between Roosevelt and Churchill after mid-1943. The president's refusal to agree to major operations in either Yugoslavia or the Aegean Sea culminated in a bitter dispute over American insistence on an invasion of southern France using the forces that could have gone to the Balkans. Roosevelt's continued suggestions that Britain divest itself of its colonial empire, particularly India and Hong Kong, infuriated the prime minister. American backing of antimonarchist politicians in Italy and criticism of British military support for the Greek monarchy highlighted what Roosevelt saw as British attempts to maintain spheres of influence and what Churchill saw as attempts to displace British interests with American ones.

Anglo-American competition, an old tradition, might not alone have broken the Churchill-Roosevelt partnership, but their differences on how to cope with

President Franklin D. Roosevelt and Prime Minister Winston Churchill at the Yalta Conference, 4–11 February 1945.   *(AP/Wide World Photos.)*

the Soviet Union in the postwar era drove a wedge between them. Churchill, working from the assumptions of centuries of experiences within the European power structure, strove to make the Soviets accept a balance that England could live with. Roosevelt, less concerned about the ideological challenge of Bolshevism, assumed that the Soviets were a major world power equivalent to or even more powerful than the British. Churchill accepted war as an undeniable fact of international reality; Roosevelt, still a Wilsonian at heart, feared that war could come again but optimistically worked to avoid if not eliminate it.

Churchill's much publicized anti-Soviet policies actually developed a good deal later than he would have us believe. As late as his Moscow (Tolstoy) Conference with Stalin in October 1944, Churchill was searching for a division of Europe into spheres of influence. Although the president and prime minister had different concepts of what a sphere of influence should be (ideas they failed to communicate to each other), each agreed that Soviet political and military influence would be paramount in eastern Europe. Yet, by the time Churchill and Roosevelt joined Stalin at the Yalta Conference (February 1945), the two Western leaders had developed divergent viewpoints on how to deal with the Soviet Union. Churchill saw an Anglo-American alliance as the best means of restraining Soviet expansion; Roosevelt placed great emphasis on building upon the cooperative relationship of the wartime coalition. The president recognized such policies might fail and often hedged his

bet—the decision not to share the atomic bomb secret with the Soviets is but one example. But he consistently tried to work with Stalin rather than confront him. In the weeks following the Yalta talks, Churchill tried to persuade Roosevelt to take a firm stand against Soviet actions in Eastern Europe, but the president refused. He told Churchill they had the ability to get tough, but he counseled patience.

Roosevelt's death and the electoral defeat of Churchill intervened before the two men had to choose between a compromise and confrontation. Perhaps Soviet policies would have eventually persuaded Roosevelt to abandon his idea of great-power cooperation and would have brought him into the Anglo-American alliance Churchill tried to create. On the other hand, Roosevelt might have persisted in his Soviet policies, which, combined with growing Anglo-American friction over colonialism and trade, might have broken the Churchill-Roosevelt relationship. Stripped of mythology, that relationship was made of the stuff that makes most alliances work, mutual self-interest. Both men never forgot that they were leaders whose first responsibility was to their own nations. But their personal contact made the wartime alliance work more smoothly than would otherwise have been possible. Regardless of the tensions and disputes that developed, theirs was a relationship characterized by more candor, more closeness, and more personal contact than international relations usually permits. Wartime alliances invariably founder when postwar politics take over, and the Churchill-Roosevelt relationship was no exception. As the war wound down, theirs was an alliance in decline, but it was also an alliance that had been victorious.

Winston Churchill and Franklin Roosevelt are central characters in any book that touches on international relations in World War II, although there is no comprehensive study of their relationship. The places to start reading are Churchill's six-volume *History of the Second World War* (Boston: Houghton Mifflin Co., 1948–53), James MacGregor Burns, *Roosevelt: Soldier of Freedom* (New York: Harcourt Brace Jovanovich, 1970), Martin Gilbert's official biography of Churchill, being published in the United States by Houghton Mifflin Co., and Warren F. Kimball, ed., *Churchill and Roosevelt, the Complete Correspondence*, 3 vols. (Princeton: Princeton University Press, 1984).

WARREN F. KIMBALL

See also Atlantic Conference and Charter; Atomic Bomb; Cairo Conference; Casablanca Conference; Colonialism; de Gaulle, Charles; Foreign Policy; Lend-Lease; Personal Diplomacy; Quebec Conferences; Stalin, Joseph, and the Soviet Union; Teheran Conference; World War II; Yalta Conference; Zionism

---

Civil Aeronautics Authority

Short-lived airlines regulatory body. On 23 June 1938, Congress created the Civil Aeronautics Authority, invested with powers of economic and safety regulation in the field of commercial aviation. E. J. Noble, a liberal Republican and founder of the Life Savers confectionery company, was appointed chairman of the five-member authority. The new agency replaced the controversial Bureau of Air Commerce, created in 1926, under the jurisdiction of the Department of Commerce.

The 1938 legislation also established an office of administrator, who was to be responsible for the executive and operational functions of the authority; Roosevelt selected Clinton Hester, formerly general counsel of the Treasury Department to fill this position. An Air Safety Board, charged with accident investigatory functions, was also created.

The complex regulatory arrangement stemmed from a five-year political struggle among Roosevelt, Congress, and the airlines industry. Earlier, in his message to Congress on 31 January 1935, Roosevelt had stated he did not approve of the concept of a permanent aviation commission, but rather that he wanted the Interstate Commerce Commission to be given full authority. By 1938, however, FDR had come to favor the formation of such an agency. The phenomenal growth of the new industry had helped convince him: whereas in 1932 the annual total of passenger miles flown by scheduled domestic airlines was 127,000, by 1938 this total had jumped to 560 million.

The Civil Aeronautics Authority had little time, however, to establish a record by which to judge its accomplishments, for Roosevelt announced a plan to transfer the functions of the administrator back to the Department of Commerce, effective 30 June 1940.

The authority and the Air Safety Board were combined into a separate agency, the Civil Aeronautics Board. The reorganization sparked bitter opposition, with major aeronautical and congressional leaders criticizing the plan as a step backward. The brief history of the authority and the Air Safety Board were extolled, and the earlier record of the Department of Commerce in the field of aviation was recalled. Critics believed the new arrangement would result in a loss of efficiency and a greater tendency for regulatory staff to be involved in partisan politics.

In making the change, Roosevelt remarked that it was part of a program for improving the organization of the government by reducing the number of administrative agencies and streamlining the task of executive management. The work of the agency is now carried out by the Federal Aviation Administration and the Civil Aeronautics Board.

There are many accounts of the birth and demise of the Civil Aeronautics Authority, but none gives much attention to Roosevelt's involvement with the agency. See Robert E. Cushman, *The Independent Regulatory Commissions* (New York: Oxford University Press, 1941) for a thorough analysis of the administrative framework. Other books contain historical background on the authority and place it in the context of earlier and later federal agencies regulating airlines, airports, and pilots: Robert Burkhardt, *The Federal Aviation Administration* (New York: Frederick A. Praeger, 1967), Donald R. Whitnah, *Safer Skyways: Federal Control of Aviation, 1926–1966* (Ames: Iowa State University Press, 1966), and John H. Frederick, *Commercial Air Transportation* (Chicago: Richard D. Irwin, 1946).

GREGORY KING

Civil Rights

See Bethune, Mary McLeod; Black Cabinet; Black, Hugo Lafayette; Civil Liberties in Wartime; Internment of Japanese-Americans; National Association for the Advancement of Colored People; Negroes; Randolph, Asa Philip; Roosevelt, Anna Eleanor; Supreme Court of the United States; Thomas, Norman Mattoon

---

Civilian Conservation Corps

Of the myriad creations of Franklin Roosevelt's New Deal, it was the Civilian Conservation Corps (CCC) that most obviously bore his personal stamp. The CCC was aimed at one of the most urgent problems facing the new president in March 1933, that of the hopelessness and despair of American young people caught in the maelstrom of depression. It was a problem starkly symbolized by the estimated 250,000 young people simply drifting about the country, "the boy and girl tramps of America," the writer Thomas Minehan called them. Roosevelt had long been concerned over the waste of American natural resources that had occurred in the previous fifty years. The depression gave him the chance to use another wasted

CCC enrollees at Camp #7–1, Halsey, Nebraska, pulling seedling ponderosa pine from the nursery, 28 October 1940.

(National Archives.)

resource, the nation's unemployed young men, in order to do something about it. The result was the CCC. Hurriedly thrown together in the first frenetic weeks of the New Deal, it lasted until 1942, perhaps the most universally applauded of all the agencies created in those years.

The basic idea of the CCC was extremely simple. Unemployed young men between eighteen and twenty-five years of age could volunteer to be placed in camps or companies of two hundred men and then put to work restoring the national domain. Because of the need for speed, it was decided to work as far as possible through existing federal departments, with a CCC director to coordinate the enterprise. The Labor Department selected the enrollees, the War Department transported them to camps, which it administered, and the Agricultural and Interior departments supervised the actual conservation projects. Each enrollee enlisted for an initial six-month period, renewable for up to two years, and was paid $30 monthly, $25 of which was sent home to his family. This basic organizational structure remained unaltered until the corps was disbanded in 1942.

The president's choice for CCC director was Robert Fechner, the conservative, southern-born vice-president of the AFL. Far from the archetypal New Dealer—he once described his position in the glistening Harvard-oriented New Deal constellation as being like that of "a potato bug among dragonflies"—Fechner nevertheless coordinated activities well enough, as well as disarming critics of the CCC's low wage rates from within the ranks of organized labor. His was an astute appointment.

The CCC quickly caught the public imagination. It grew rapidly, until at its peak, in 1935, there were more than half a million young men, plus several thousand unemployed veterans of World War I in about 2,500 camps, the bulk of which were west of the Mississippi River. Its enrollees were engaged in a multiplicity of conservation tasks, erosion control, wildlife protection, the development of national parks, the preservation and restoration of historical sites, and dam construction. By far the greatest number, however, were engaged in simple reforestation projects, and it was here that the CCC made its greatest contribution. Of all the trees planted in the United States up until 1942, 75 percent were planted by the CCC. Its importance in the history of American conservation is without question.

From 1938 till its termination, the numbers enrolled in the CCC were steadily reduced, and from 1941, its functions were narrowed to those deemed essential to the war effort. It was ended in July 1942, despite the president's vigorous dissent, a casualty of the drive to cut all federal agencies save those deemed essential to the winning of the war. By this time, more than 3 million young men, plus a quarter of a million veterans, had passed through its ranks.

Why was the CCC so popular, given its emergency nature and the fact that it could provide no permanent answer to the problems of unemployed young people in an industrial urban society? There were several reasons for this, in addition to the obvious one that it provided immediate relief for the enrollees and their families. First, it was popular in the camp localities. Camps were usually established near a small village or town, and the amount they spent in the local market provided such places with a real economic boost. Also, the benefits of CCC work were tangible, obvious, and immediate. Most people found it easy to accept the value of the tasks performed. Moreover, they liked its image. Run by the army as they were, the camps were seen as "safe," the enrollees free from the dangers of subversive ideas or unsettling attitudes. Fechner never challenged traditional racial patterns. Most CCC camps were rigidly segregated. Finally, people responded to the corps because of its links with the past. At a time when the nation was becoming distinctly urban in tone, there was something about these young men going out to work with their hands in the wilderness that appealed profoundly to romantic and nostalgic elements in the national imagination.

Though an emergency measure, the CCC lasted to become one of the New Deal's most important creations. As Arthur M. Schlesinger, Jr., has written, it "left its monuments in the preservation and purification of the land, the water, the forests, and the young men of America."

The only scholarly study of the CCC is John Salmond, *The Civilian Conservation Corps, 1933–1942: A New Deal Case Study* (Durham, N.C.: Duke University Press, 1967). Kenneth Holland and Frank E. Hill, *Youth in the CCC* (Washington: American Council of Education, 1942), is of some value, as is Conrad L. Wirth, *The Civilian Conservation Corps Program of the Department of the Interior* (Chicago: Merchandise Mart, 1944). George P. Rawick's dissertation, "The New Deal and Youth: The Civilian Conservation Corps, the National Youth Administration, the American Youth Congress" (University of Wisconsin, 1957) is also helpful. The quotation from Arthur Schlesinger, Jr., comes from the second volume of *The Age of Roosevelt, The Coming of the New Deal* (Boston: Houghton Mifflin Co., 1959), p. 340.

JOHN SALMOND

See also Conservation; Relief

CCC enrollees with felled trees. (National Archives.)

Civil Liberties in Wartime

A much less repressive civil liberties atmosphere prevailed in the World War II period than had existed in either World War I or the Civil War. Several factors explain this changed environment. Government officials and American citizens in general had learned a lesson from the earlier excesses of curtailment of free expression. The actions of contemporary European dictatorships also provided a negative example, which Americans were determined to avoid. Several months before Pearl Harbor, President Roosevelt told the press that "suppression of opinion and censorship of news are among the mortal weapons that dictatorships direct against their own peoples. . . . It would be a shameful use of patriotism to suggest that opinion should be stifled in its service."

The president's appointments to the Supreme Court and to the position of attorney general also contributed to a more liberal treatment of civil liberties. Frank Murphy, a lawyer and former governor of Michigan, set up a Civil Liberties Unit in the Justice Department to prosecute violaters of civil rights statutes. When the president elevated Murphy to the increasingly civil-liberties-conscious Supreme Court in 1940, he named Francis Biddle, another committed civil libertarian, to replace him in the attorney general post.

The pro–civil liberties atmosphere was also enhanced by emphasis on federal rather than state regulation of aliens and alleged subversives. Both the president and the attorney general were afraid that attempts to deal with these issues by states or local governments would result in confusion and open the door to vigilante activities on the part of overzealous private citizens as had happened in World War I. Here Congress took the initiative, passing in 1940 an Alien Registration Act, popularly known as the Smith Act, which required the registration and fingerprinting of noncitizens. Attorney General Biddle frequently remarked publicly that these procedures would be carried out as humanely as possible. In 1941 the Supreme Court sanctioned such federal regulation of alien activity in *Hines* v. *Davidowitz* (312 U.S. 52), a decision that overturned a Pennsylvania statute requiring aliens to register and carry identification. In a related area, the Court in *Goldman* v. *United States* (316 U.S. 129 [1942]), also sanctioned the use by the FBI of presidentially suggested wiretaps as that body investigated questions relating to national security.

Roosevelt was generally more pragmatic than resolute. As James MacGregor Burns has writen: "Like Jefferson in earlier days, he was all for civil liberties in general, but easily found exceptions in particular. . . . To be sure, Roosevelt's civil liberties derelictions were not numerous, but certainly the wartime White House was not dependably a source of strong and sustained support for civil liberties in specific situations." One such situation concerned Roosevelt's view of criticism of his wartime policies which appeared in the press. Francis Biddle, in his autobiography, recalled that in 1942 the president asked him to take action to stop such criticism. According to Biddle, "I explained to him my view of the unwisdom of bringing indictment for sedition except where there was evidence that recruitment was substantially being interfered with, or there was some connection between the speech and propaganda centers in Germany. . . . The President was not much interested in the theory of sedition, or in the constitutional right to criticize the government in wartime. He wanted this anti-war talk stopped."

The first peacetime sedition law since 1798 was enacted in 1940 as fears of internal subversion grew. Sections 2 and 3 of the Smith Act made it unlawful to advocate or teach the overthrow of the government by force or violence or to conspire with or attempt to help others to do this. Biddle, uneasy with the measure, deliberately tried to test its constitutionality in 1941 with the prosecution of the Dunne brothers, Minneapolis Trotskyites convicted of trying to overthrow the government by force. The Supreme Court, however, declined to hear the case. Several newspapers were barred from the mails on the ground that they were seditious; they all espoused near-Nazi views and included *Social Justice,* the *Gallilean,* and the *Philadelphia Herald.* One of the most notable indictments for sedition involved thirty American fascists, pro-Nazi in their statements and critical of Roosevelt whom they argued had deliberately invited the Japanese attack on Pearl Harbor. The federal court judge hearing the case died in the seventh month of a turbulent trial, and the indictment was dismissed.

The Justice Department's zealous attempts to deal with dissent arose against a background of reported espionage activities. In late 1940, blasts, which were never proven to have been caused by saboteurs, did occur at several industrial plants in the East. In June 1942, the FBI captured eight German spies off the Long Island shore, and one month later, a spy ring was broken up in the Panama Canal Zone.

The Justice Department also tried to curtail the dissenting activities of naturalized citizens, especially those of German and Italian descent, through a program of denaturalization. This involved demonstrating that their antigovernment statements proved they had obtained their citizenship illegally. The Supreme Court overturned this policy in three important cases, *Schneidermann* v. *United States* (320 U.S. 119, 1943), *Baumgartner* v. *United States* (322 U.S. 665, 1944), and *Bridges* v. *Wixon* (326 U.S. 135, 1945). Justice Murphy argued in the Baumgartner case that the naturalized citizen "does not lose the precious right of citizenship because he subsequently dares to criticize his adopted government. He has as much right as the natural born citizen to exercise the cherished freedoms of speech, press and religion."

Conscientious objectors were also treated more sensitively. The 1940 Selective Training and Service Act revealed greater liberality toward their claims. Those qualifying were required to perform noncombatant duties if conscience permitted and, if not, other work of national importance under civilian direction. Between 25,000 and 50,000 men were inducted for noncombatant service, 12,000 were as-signed to camps for work of national importance under civilian direction, 14,000 were classified but not assigned, 20,000 registrants, claiming exception as objectors, were not classified as such, and about 6,000 objectors, most of them Jehovah's Witnesses, were convicted and sentenced to prison between 1940 and 1947. In one important parallel case, the Supreme Court ruled at war's end that a pacifist who refused to bear arms but was willing to serve in the army as a noncombatant could be admitted to citizenship under the 1940 act (*Girouard* v. *United States* [328 U.S. 61, 1946]). Generally then, COs were treated with far more sensitivity than were the Japanese-Americans on the West Coast, who were lumped together, regardless of whether they were citizens or not, and sent to relocation camps.

Finally, the war produced the first conviction for treason in American history, with the Supreme Court ruling in *Haupt* v. *United States* (330 U.S. 631, 1947) that treasonous activity could include supportive actions not in themselves treasonous, thereby widening the clause for future use.

The relevant chapters on World War II in Paul L. Murphy, *The Constitution in Crisis Times* (New York: Harper & Row, 1972), and Clinton Rossiter, *Constitutional Dictatorship: Crisis Government in the Modern Democracies* (New York: Harcourt, Brace & World, 1948), place the problems of civil liberties in the context of wartime events. A good contemporary account was presented by Robert E. Cushman in "Civil Liberties in Wartime," *American Political Science Review* 37 (1943):49–56; Cushman stated that up to the time he was writing the government was doing a commendable job of protecting civil liberties but cautioned that violations could occur. James MacGregor Burns, *Roosevelt: The Soldier of Freedom* (New York: Harcourt Brace Jovanovich, 1970), portrays Roosevelt as a less than committed civil libertarian, as does Roosevelt's attorney general, Francis Biddle in his autobiography, *In Brief Authority* (New York: Doubleday & Co., 1962). A survey taken in the 1970s of historians, political scientists, journalists, former White House aides, and members of Congress, however, ranked Roosevelt high on the civil liberties scale; see Alan F. Westin and Trudy Hayden, "Presidents and Civil Liberties from F.D.R. to Ford: A Ranking by 64 Experts," *Civil Liberties Review* 3 (1976):9–35. Frank Murphy's defense of civil liberties is treated extensively in Harold Norris, *Mr. Justice Murphy and the Bill of Rights* (Dobbs Ferry, N.Y.: Oceana Publications, 1965), and somewhat less so in J. Woodford Howard, Jr., *Mr. Justice Murphy. A Political Biography* (Princeton: Princeton University Press, 1968). A more general view of the Court's civil liberties record is C. Herman Pritchett, *The Roosevelt Court* (New York: Macmillan Co., 1948).

PAUL L. MURPHY

See also Biddle, Francis Beverley; Espionage; Ickes, Harold LeClair; Internment of Japanese-Americans; Supreme Court of the United States

Civil Works Administration

The Civil Works Administration (CWA) was a federally sponsored work program operated during the winter of 1933–34 that provided work and income for a few million individuals, benefiting at least 12 million people.

By late October 1933, President Franklin D. Roosevelt knew economic recovery was occurring too slowly to employ additional millions of unemployed during the coming winter. The major thrust of the Public Works Administration, directed by Harold Ickes to stimulate construction industries, would not be felt until the spring of 1934. Harry Hopkins, director of the Federal Emergency Relief Administration (FERA), and several of his colleagues knew more relief aid would be needed. Having a strong preference for work relief rather than direct cash payments, Hopkins and his staff formulated a work relief plan to provide jobs for approximately 4 million unemployed workers for the winter months. Roosevelt quickly accepted the concept. He transferred $400 million from the Public Works Administration to the new Civil Works Administration, designating Hopkins and his FERA staff to operate the CWA. Within three weeks, over 2 million unemployed were at work on CWA projects. In February 1934, over 4 million unemployed were on the CWA payroll.

The CWA had three basic weaknesses. First, the speed needed for implementation caused confusion in placing workers on projects and in selecting projects. Second, obtainment from the Public Works Administration of the initial $400 million for CWA forced implementation of a higher wage scale than customary for semiskilled and clerical employees in a few regions of the nation. This stimulated opposition to the CWA and led to its costing more than originally intended. Third, some projects (not the majority) were of poor quality, and many projects lacked adequate supervision.

American public opinion of CWA was sharply divided. To many it was a "godsend"; to others, it was a "boondoggle." The rapid implementation necessary forced a high degree of decentralization in choosing and initiating projects. Some suppliers of goods and tools and a few local officials attempted to use CWA fraudulently and for political purposes. In several states, Hopkins had to send in outsiders to take over supervision of projects. He fought dishonesty diligently. The media reports, however, greatly overplayed the extent of graft, for the vast majority of officials were honest and reasonably resourceful. They possessed good perceptions of needed projects, and they fulfilled the goal of completing socially and economically useful projects.

The federal government and the states, the latter contributing roughly 10 percent, spent $933 million for CWA projects. The achievements included 255,000 miles of roads built or improved, 3,700 playgrounds built or improved, over 11.5 million feet of sewer pipe laid, over 800 small airports built or improved, approximately 3,000 artists and writers employed, and 50,000 teachers hired for rural schools. The Civil Works Administration was the most outstanding administrative achievement by government officials prior to the Second World War.

President Roosevelt and Hopkins terminated the CWA in the spring of 1934. The immediate crises had been successfully met. But the CWA proved to be more costly than FDR had anticipated, and both he and Hopkins were bothered by graft and corruption. The FERA was seen by Hopkins as an alternate means of expanding work relief with better planning and control possible. Roosevelt hoped the reviving economy and the Public Works Administration would increase employment. For the unemployable in need, he sought alternate means of assistance which emerged in the Social Security Act of 1935.

A very readable account of the formation of the CWA and its political difficulties is presented by Robert E. Sherwood in *Roosevelt and Hopkins: An Intimate History* (New York: Harper and Brothers, 1948). Searle F. Charles provides a useful brief overall portrait of the CWA in *Minister of Relief: Harry Hopkins and the Depression* (Syracuse: Syracuse University Press, 1963).

SEARLE F. CHARLES

See also Hopkins, Harry L.; Pendergast, Thomas J.; Relief

Cohen, Benjamin Victor
(23 September 1894–16 August 1983)

Adviser to FDR. The son of a Polish-born ore dealer, Benjamin Cohen enjoyed a comfortable youth in his birthplace, Muncie, Indiana. A studious young man, he "neglected marbles for Descartes and Spencer." Cohen received his Ph.B. from the University of Chicago in 1914; a year later, after earning the highest grades ever awarded in the school's history, he received his J.D. from the University of Chicago Law School. In 1916, he acquired an S.J.D. from Harvard Law School, where he worked under Felix Frankfurter.

Cohen then became legal secretary to Judge Julian Mack of the federal circuit court in New York. Since most important receivership cases came before Mack, Cohen soon learned the complexities of the law on corporate reorganization. When World War I began, Cohen became an attorney for the U.S. Shipping Board. War brought Cohen into contact with Louis Brandeis, and he spent 1919 to 1921 as counsel for the American Zionists. He helped to negotiate the Palestine Mandate at the Paris Peace Conference.

After the war, Cohen entered private practice in New York and quickly became known as an expert in the field of corporate reorganization. He played the stock market; according to one legend, he was so excited about the automobile stock that made him temporarily wealthy that he would point delightedly at passing Chryslers. Wealth, however, did not make Cohen insensitive to the problems of the poor; during the twenties, he also served as unpaid counsel to the National Consumers' League and, with Frankfurter, drafted a model minimum wage bill for working women which became the basis for legislation in several states.

Cohen's first contact with the New Deal came in 1933 when Frankfurter brought him to Washington along with James Landis to salvage Roosevelt's securities legislation. Cohen and Landis, aided in the evenings by Thomas Corcoran, worked feverishly for a month to rewrite the Truth in Securities Act of 1933. With Cohen at his side to advise him on technical matters, Sam Rayburn won unanimous approval for the Cohen-Landis bill in the House, and it quickly became law.

Upon Judge Mack's recommendation, Secretary of Interior Harold Ickes added Cohen to his staff as associate general counsel of the Public Works Administration from 1933 through 1934 and as counsel to the National Public Power Committee from 1934 through 1941. In the latter capacity, Cohen successfully defended the constitutionality of his Public Utility Holding Company Act against the holding companies that challenged it. An indispensable adviser to Ickes, Cohen wrote numerous speeches for the secretary and was one of the few people who could talk him out of his periodic threats to resign.

But Cohen is remembered more for his extraordinary partnership with Thomas Corcoran than for his role in keeping the Department of Interior running smoothly. The revisions to the Securities Act had brought the two men together, and they quickly became close. In Washington, they were known as "the Gold Dust Twins" (from "Let the Gold Dust Twins Do Your Work"), Frankfurter's "two chief little Hot Dogs," and the "Brain Twins." For a time, Corcoran and Cohen lived with several other government lawyers in "the Little Red House on R Street." Eventually, they took an apartment together ("the Little White House"), an arrangement that continued until Corcoran's marriage in 1941. Sam Rayburn said that, of the pair, Cohen was the brains; he was regarded as the most brilliant legislative draftsman in Washington. But Cohen shied from the limelight. The gregarious Corcoran had the influence in the White House and Congress to get the legislation that Cohen drafted passed.

Together the two men drafted the Securities and Exchange Act of 1934, the Public Utility Holding Company Act of 1935 (although Cohen opposed the controversial "death sentence" of the bill which gave the Securities and Exchange Commission the power to order the dissolution of holding companies), the Rural Electrification Act of 1935, the Fair Labor Standards Act of 1938, and numerous speeches for Roosevelt. Although some credited them with the Court-packing bill, they did not draft it. Instead they preferred a constitutional amendment that would have permitted Congress to override the Supreme Court. When the recession of 1937 began, they were among the neo-Brandeisians who successfully urged Roosevelt to adopt an antimonopoly program and to embrace deficit spending.

The New Deal's momentum was lost after 1938, and Corcoran and Cohen's influence with the president declined. With the worsening foreign situation, Cohen's attention turned to the war abroad. He was an early advocate of preparedness and aid to the Allies. He found the legal basis for the destroyers-for-bases deal and was instrumental in drafting Lend-Lease. In 1941, he left Interior to become counsel to Ambassador Winant in England. Between 1943 and 1945, he served as general counsel to the Office of War Mobilization (OWM). He helped to draft the Dumbarton Oaks agreement.

Although Cohen may have been a very well-respected individual in the nation's fractious capital, he received few rewards from FDR for his service. When Raymond Moley and Thomas Corcoran recommended Cohen for a seat on the SEC in 1934, FDR declined because he feared an anti-Semitic reaction. When Ickes suggested Cohen as under secretary of the treasury in 1938, Roosevelt questioned the advisability of appointing another Jew under Morgenthau. When Francis Biddle recommended Cohen as solicitor general in 1941, FDR told Biddle that the appointment would reopen the Court fight. As Ickes lamented, Cohen was one of Roosevelt's mainstays, but the president gave him no recognition. FDR's refusal to support Cohen as general counsel to the State Department after Dumbarton Oaks caused Cohen to resign from government service in protest, but he continued to work without pay as Byrnes's general counsel in OWM. Truman made Cohen general counsel of the State Department in July 1945 when he made Byrnes secretary of state.

Almost all of Cohen's work for the government after 1945 concerned foreign policy. He was general counsel of the State Department from 1945 through 1947, a delegate to the United Nations from 1948 through 1952, and U.S. representative on the United Nations Disarmament Commission in 1952. An early opponent of the cold war, Cohen agreed with Henry Wallace that the United States should be more cooperative with the Soviets. Cohen died in 1983 in New York.

Current Biography included a useful sketch on Cohen in 1941. Michael Parrish provided the best information on Cohen's role in drafting securities legislation in *Securities Regulation and the New Deal* (New Haven: Yale University Press, 1970). Harold Ickes wrote extensively about Cohen, his role in Interior, and his attitude toward the war in *The Secret Diary of Harold Ickes* (New York: Simon & Schuster, 1953). For Cohen's elevation to general counsel in the State Department, see "U.S. at War," *Time*, 16 July 1945. John Morton Blum discussed Cohen's advocacy of preparedness in *Roosevelt and Morgenthau* (Boston: Houghton Mifflin Co., 1972) and Cohen's position on the cold war in *The Price of Vision* (Boston: Houghton Mifflin Co., 1973). Katie Louchheim interviewed many New Dealers who discussed Cohen and his relationship with Corcoran in *The Making of the New Deal* (Cambridge, Mass.: Harvard University Press, 1983). Joseph P. Lash wrote a moving obituary of Cohen, "Ben Cohen, 'A Good Man,' " *New York Times*, 5 September 1983.

LAURA KALMAN

See also Corcoran, Thomas Gardiner

Colonialism

Of the myriad diplomatic problems facing President Franklin D. Roosevelt during the Second World War, none was more complex, contentious, or plagued by a tangle of conflicting interests than the future of the colonial empires. This issue was most immediately posed by the Southeast Asian colonies overrun by the Japanese. Nationalists in those areas and their former European imperial overlords alike looked to Washington with a curious mixture of hope and fear. Would Roosevelt, they wondered, press for colonial liberation as a measure consistent with traditional American anticolonial sentiments? Or would he instead favor a policy of colonial reconquest in line with the wishes of his European allies? As it appeared likely that U.S. troops would eventually liberate those territories from the Japanese, precedents established there would undoubtedly have a deep impact on the future course of colonial rule throughout the world. Consequently, the president's attitudes toward this question would have far-reaching implications indeed.

Much to the delight of colonial nationalists, FDR gave several strong indications during the early war years that he would place the power and prestige of the United States unequivocally behind the principle of self-determination for all peoples. At the president's insistence, the Atlantic Charter, signed by Roosevelt and British prime minister Winston Churchill in August 1941, included a commitment to the "right of all people to choose the form of government under which they will live." In a radio address to the nation on 23 February 1942, the president specified that "the Atlantic Charter not only applies to the parts of the world that border on the Atlantic, but to the whole world." His under secretary of state, Sumner Welles, echoed this theme in a Memorial Day address that same year, declaring that the war should ensure "the liberation of all people." He continued: "The age of imperialism is ended. The right of people to their freedom must be recognized, as the civilized world long since recognized the rights of an individual to his personal freedom."

American anticolonial pronouncements were not restricted merely to public addresses. On the contrary, Roosevelt and senior administration spokesmen criticized the European imperial system in numerous conversations both among themselves and with various foreign leaders, especially during the first few years of the war. The president himself often took the lead on this issue, alternately chiding British, French, and Dutch officials on past colonial practices while urging more enlightened postwar policies. His seemingly offhanded suggestion to the British that they return Hong Kong to the Chinese as a gesture of good will typified his approach, as did his repeated efforts to prod the British on the emotional issue of Indian independence.

Roosevelt's thinking in this regard represented a virtually indistinguishable blend of idealism and self-interest. On the one hand, his attitude reflected a genuine revulsion with what he viewed as the often inhumane treatment of subject peoples. His passionate remarks after visiting the British colony of Gambia in early 1942 are particularly revealing. At a subsequent press conference, he recalled that it was "the most horrible thing I have ever seen in my life." Disease was rampant, he exclaimed, and "the natives are five

thousand years back of us." Similarly, FDR expressed disgust with French colonial policy, especially in Indochina, on more than a few occasions. "France has had the country—thirty million inhabitants—for nearly one hundred years," he stormed at one point, "and the people are worse off than they were at the beginning."

At the same time, the president's concern with the plight of subject peoples was reinforced by a fear that the indefinite preservation of the colonial system would adversely affect U.S. interests in a stable and prosperous postwar world. In imperialism, Roosevelt often remarked, lay the seeds of future wars. Furthermore, the continued existence of colonial trade blocs both closed out U.S. commercial interests and represented a glaring affront to the American vision of an open postwar trading system. Roosevelt was convinced that the dismantling of the European colonial empires not only would promote the welfare of the native populations but would serve as well the cause of international peace and prosperity, a paramount objective of U.S. diplomacy.

The American commitment to colonial self-determination should not be confused with nationalist demands for immediate independence, despite the hopes of native leaders. Like Woodrow Wilson before him, Roosevelt advocated an evolutionary approach to the colonial problem. He feared that subject peoples were not yet prepared to handle the responsibilities that independence would inevitably bring in its wake. Consequently, he advocated a system of trusteeship in which the European colonial powers would prepare responsible native elites for independence during an appropriate tutelage period. This plan represented, in effect, a middle course between the twin evils of immediate independence without adequate preparation and indefinite prolongation of imperial control.

From its very inception, however, the trusteeship formula was beset with difficulties. The European nations used every opportunity to express their firm opposition to any plan that would compromise their territorial sovereignty in the colonial areas. Churchill's oft-quoted remark that he had not become the king's first minister "in order to preside over the liquidation of the British Empire" typified the angry European response to what was seen as self-interested American meddling. This reaction deeply troubled the Roosevelt administration, as it threatened not only to create severe strains within the wartime alliance but to open fissures that would jeopardize American postwar plans, plans that depended to a great extent on harmonious relations with the European colonial powers. Strong opposition from within the U.S. government itself placed another limit on trusteeship planning. The military services insisted that U.S. national security required exclusive American control over the Japanese-mandated islands in the Pacific; they feared that general acceptance of the trusteeship concept would foolishly compromise those needs. As a result of these larger political, military, and strategic concerns, the Roosevelt administration substantially modified its approach to the colonial issue. Although it never abandoned completely its interest in effecting a liberalization of colonial rule, by late 1944 the administration quietly jettisoned its trusteeship planning and informed the British, French, and Dutch that it would not contest their reassertion of sovereignty in Southeast Asia. After Roosevelt's death, the new administration of Harry S Truman continued this policy.

Foster Rhea Dulles and Gerald A. Ridinger emphasize the idealistic component of the president's colonial policy in their article, "The Anti-Colonial Policies of Franklin D. Roosevelt," *Political Science Quarterly* 7 (March 1955):1–18. Walter LaFeber argues for the intersection of U.S. ideals with concrete economic interests in the trusteeship planning for Indochina in "Roosevelt, Churchill, and Indochina: 1942–1945," *American Historical Review* 80 (December 1975):1277–95. Robert J. McMahon similarly suggests that idealism merged with self-interest in the case of the Dutch East Indies in his book, *Colonialism and Cold War: The United States and the Struggle for Indonesian Independence, 1945–49* (Ithaca, N.Y.: Cornell University Press, 1981). Gary R. Hess, Jr.'s book, *America Encounters India, 1941–1947* (Baltimore: Johns Hopkins University Press, 1971), is the most complete account of U.S. policy toward the divisive issue of Indian independence. Two broad studies, William Roger Louis's *Imperialism at Bay: The United States and the Decolonization of the British Empire, 1941–1945* (New York: Oxford University Press, 1978), and Christopher Thorne's *Allies of a Kind: The United States, Great Britain, and the War against Japan, 1941–1945* (New York: Oxford University Press, 1978), offer the most comprehensive treatment to date of the role of the colonial issue in Anglo-American diplomacy.

ROBERT J. MCMAHON

See also Churchill, Winston Leonard Spencer

Columbia University

See Brains Trust; Education

Commander in Chief

The president's position over the armed forces as set forth in Article II, Section 2, of the Constitution. President Roosevelt interpreted his authority as commander in chief in broader terms and exercised it more aggressively than any previous president. He became so absorbed in the direction of high-level military matters and so proud of his role therein during World War II that he requested his cabinet members to address him as commander in chief rather than as president and once became annoyed because Adm. Ernest J. King also used the former title as head of the U.S. fleet.

During the years 1933–38, the armed services became instruments as well as beneficiaries of the domestic programs of the Roosevelt administration: the War Department, for instance, administered the Civilian Conservation Corps; for a time the Army Air Corps handled airmail services for the Post Office Department; and considerable funds were channeled through the Public Works Administration into mili-

President Roosevelt discussing Pacific strategy with Gen. Douglas MacArthur (left), *Adm. Chester W. Nimitz, U.S.N., Adm. William R. Leahy, U.S.N.* (right) *during their meeting at Pearl Harbor, 26 July–11 August 1944.* (National Archives.)

tary and naval construction projects. A lifelong maritime enthusiast and assistant secretary of the navy, 1913–20, FDR strongly supported the creation of a two-ocean navy in the late 1930s but also became an ardent advocate of air power on the eve of World War II. Adjusting quickly to the primacy of his role as commander in chief as Hitler's armies overran much of Europe in 1939–40, Roosevelt did not hesitate to subordinate his New Deal to military preparedness, though congressional appropriations for defense increased more slowly than he wanted.

Possessing a strong sense of Britain's strategic value to American interests, the president endeavored to assist the British militarily, but in the process he provoked strong isolationist reactions in America and some uneasiness among his army and navy leaders about sending military matériel to Britain when American forces were ill equipped. During the eighteen months preceding the Pearl Harbor attack, nevertheless, FDR wielded his military powers vigorously in behalf of the defense of Britain and also to try to deter further aggression by Japan. Among other initiatives frowned upon by some of his military officials, he ordered the shipment of munitions, aircraft, and other war matériel to the United Kingdom as well as Lend-Lease supplies to China; the establishment of U.S. naval and air bases in British possessions from Newfoundland to the Caribbean; the stationing of American troops in Iceland and Greenland; the assignment of U.S. combat ships to protect British-aid convoys as far as Iceland; the embargoing of oil, scrap iron, and other strategic items in trade with Japan; and the strengthening of defenses in the Philippines with troop and aircraft reinforcements and with a revamped American-Filipino military organization under Gen. Douglas MacArthur.

Jealously guarding his authority over issues of strategy and high command, FDR in 1939 ordered the Joint Army-Navy Board and several munitions and military procurement agencies to report directly to him, bypassing the War and Navy departments. This move proved to be a harbinger, for when he founded the Joint Chiefs of Staff in early 1942 as his main military advisory body, he dealt directly with the chiefs in the strategic direction of the war, relegating the war and navy secretaries largely to departmental administration. Although sometimes deciding contrary to his military chiefs' advice, especially before mid-1943, Roosevelt developed a close rapport with them eventually and during the later stages of the war leaned heavily on the Joint Chiefs, along with close adviser Harry Hopkins, in decision making on strategy, logistics, high command, and Allied military relations.

The president's occasional overruling of his chiefs resulted partly from the seriousness with which he viewed his position as commander in chief and from his somewhat exaggerated notion of his forte in grand strategy. Some of the instances in which he made strategic decisions against the counsel of the Joint Chiefs or of the War and Navy departments were his approval of Operation Torch, the invasion of Northwest Africa in late 1942; his policy of unconditional surrender, proclaimed at Casablanca in early 1943; his prohibitions on several occasions in 1943 against showdowns by the American chiefs with their British counterparts over the latter's alleged delaying tactics regarding an Allied invasion of France; his disapproval of the Anakim and Buccaneer plans for operations in the Bay of Bengal in 1943; and his recall of Gen. Joseph W. Stilwell as commander of the China-Burma-India theater in late 1944. A respected postwar military historian found twenty-two cases in which FDR made strategic decisions against the advice of the Joint Chiefs or the War and Navy departments and another thirteen wherein the initiative in strategic decisions probably came from him. Remarkably, in many of these cases his judgment appears wiser in retrospect than that of his military advisers. Although his decisions contrary to the advice of his military chiefs have attracted considerable attention among historians, Roosevelt usually exercised his powers as commander in chief tactfully and shrewdly, rarely becoming involved in direct clashes with the Joint Chiefs as a body or as individuals.

Although he delighted in his roles as supreme soldier and grand strategist, Roosevelt at first intervened in military realms normally in support of a general political objective. During the early, dark days of the war, one of his principal aims was to preserve Britain and to build eventually a formidable coalition of Allies with an Anglo-American nucleus, thus his seeming appeasement of Churchill and the British chiefs on a temporary strategy of attrition. As the tide of war turned, a key objective of the president was to ensure the defeat of Germany as rapidly as possible and then to shift the brunt of Allies power against Japan, thus his reluctance to dwell on long-range political issues in Europe. Unfortunately Roosevelt and his military advisers often acted in 1944–45 as if postwar political planning could be postponed until the Axis powers were defeated and assumed that political and military ends could be kept separate.

Besides intervening in military strategy, Roosevelt often delved also into the Joint Chiefs' considerations of logistics and command. He sometimes unilaterally and unpredictably decided to change, say, the supply tonnage being shipped to Britain for a given month or the number of new medium bombers assigned to a particular theater, which obviously caused consternation among military planners. Usually he trusted the judgments of Marshall and King on senior command positions, though FDR reserved to himself some military appointments, notably that of Gen. Dwight D. Eisenhower to head the great Allied invasion force that struck Normandy in 1944. As commander in chief, Roosevelt also felt a strong obligation to be seen by the American servicemen; despite increasing health problems, he seemed indefatigable in his numerous travels to naval and military bases in the United States and in several overseas areas. In his role as commander in chief, too, he fervently supported some new federal agencies that made unusual and significant contributions to the defeat of the Axis, such as the Office of Strategic Services and the Office of Scientific Research and Development. Roosevelt was an early and enthusiastic believer in the military worth of the Manhattan District atomic project and of the Ultra and Magic code-breaking programs.

As war leader, FDR became for much of the citizenry an inspiring symbol of national spirit and unity, with the highest degree of manpower and economic mobilization in American history attained during the last four years of his presidency. By the time of his death, American military strength was at an unprecedented level, with over 16 million persons in uniform and with American ground, sea, and air forces possessing enormous firepower. The vigorous leadership he provided as commander in chief was crucial to the unrivaled position of military power America attained by 1945 and to the survival, at least for the duration of the war, of the grand coalition of nations committed to defeating the Axis.

The best balanced and most readable work on Roosevelt as wartime president is James M. Burns, *Roosevelt: The Soldier of Freedom* (New York: Harcourt Brace Jovanovich, 1970), especially the concise expositions on his roles as commander in chief (pp. 490–96) and as grand strategist (pp. 544–52). FDR's decisions against the advice of his military chiefs are stressed in Kent R. Greenfield, *American Strategy in World War II: A Reconsideration* (Baltimore: Johns Hopkins Press, 1963), ch. 3. William R. Emerson, "F.D.R. (1941–1945)," in *The Ultimate Decision: The President as Commander in Chief*, ed. Ernest R. May (New York: Braziller, 1960), pp. 133–77, is a soundly reasoned, generally favorable portrayal of the wartime commander in chief. The roles of Harry Hopkins, the Joint Chiefs, and Churchill in influencing Roosevelt's strategic judgments are presented largely from Hopkins's viewpoint in Robert E. Sherwood, *Roosevelt and Hopkins: An Intimate History*, vol. 2 (New York: Harper & Bros.,

1948). Roosevelt's exercise of his powers as chief of the armed services is compared to the military authority exerted by other wartime presidents in Warren W. Hassler, Jr., *The President as Commander-in-Chief* (Reading, Mass.: Addison-Wesley Publishing Co., 1971). His position in the context of civil-military relations during World War II is perceptively examined in Samuel P. Huntington, *The Soldier and the State: The Theory and Politics of Civil-Military Relations* (Cambridge, Mass.: Belknap Press, Harvard University Press, 1957), ch. 12. A treasury of primary materials on Roosevelt's involvement in strategy making is found in the U.S. State Department's series *Foreign Relations of the United States,* both in the annual volumes for 1939–45 and in the volumes on the major Allied wartime conferences.

D. CLAYTON JAMES

See also Joint Chiefs of Staff; Office of the Presidency; World War II

Commodity Credit Corporation
See Agriculture

Communism

Franklin Roosevelt's attitude toward Communism has long been a controversial issue. The first president to afford diplomatic recognition to the Soviet Union and the architect of a wartime alliance with that nation, he was criticized by some contemporaries for underestimating the Communist threat and making excessive concessions to the Soviet Union at wartime's end. Moreover, some of his opponents argued that New Deal agencies offered a comfortable home for Soviet spies and American Communist party cells.

The most extreme versions of this critique are manifestly false. At no time in his career did FDR express sympathy for Communism, domestic or international. His pronouncements on the subject invariably focused on the incompatibility of Communism with American ideals, and often lumped communism with fascism as totalitarian ideologies.

Nevertheless, it is true that Roosevelt's view of Communism lacked the passion or sense of imminent danger felt by his conservative critics. Roosevelt did not take Communists very seriously as a threat to domestic order or regard the Soviet Union (at least till the end of the war) as a dangerous, expansionist power. His administration, except briefly in the late thirties and early forties, proved unreceptive to congressional investigations of "Communist subversion" and made no systematic effort to drive Communists out of reform coalitions. Moreover, during the Popular Front Era (1935–39) and during American involvement in World War II (1941–45), lower level administration officials interacted regularly with Communists in agencies such as the WPA, the National Labor Relations Board, and the Office of Strategic Services. Finally, Eleanor Roosevelt did take a personal interest in one Popular Front organization in which Communists were quite influential—the American Youth Congress—and President Roosevelt addressed a group of its members on the White House lawn.

FDR's relatively relaxed attitude toward domestic Communism, in part, reflected a realistic assessment of the actual influence of the American Communist party (CPUSA). At no time during his presidency did the CPUSA have more than eighty thousand members. It did not elect one member to Congress under its own name. Its spheres of influence—within organized labor, among black organizations, among students and the intelligentsia—always derived from coalitions with liberals, rather than in the party's own name, and depended heavily on the continuation of liberal support.

Moreover, the Communist party, during much of Roosevelt's presidency, openly supported his domestic and foreign policies and virtually suspended agitation of "communism"—or even socialism—as a domestic political goal. Although Communists denounced Roosevelt as a "fascist" from 1932 through 1934, from the beginning of 1935 till his death (with the exception of the period between the signing of the Nazi-Soviet pact and Hitler's invasion of the Soviet Union), the CPUSA offered the New Deal critical support and endorsed Roosevelt's presidential campaigns. Moreover, much of the party's rank and file, and some of its leadership, felt a deep emotional attachment to Roosevelt for his role in standing up to fascism and for his domestic reform policies. This attachment even extended to the top leader of the CPUSA, Earl Browder, who fancied himself, especially during wartime, as an important ally of the president and who imagined himself to exert considerable influence on Roosevelt administration policies.

This Communist support for Roosevelt, it should be emphasized, only occurred when Soviet leaders encouraged its articulation. Shortly after the Nazi-Soviet pact, leaders of the Communist International ordered American Communist leaders to denounce FDR's foreign and domestic policies, and they shifted their line in response to these orders. But most Communists were much more comfortable supporting Roosevelt than opposing him. The CPUSA grew fastest when it downplayed its Communist features and functioned as the left wing of reform coalitions, and its members, who were heavily ethnic (Jewish, black, and Eastern European), felt some of the same attachments to the New Deal as their more conservative compatriots.

For his part, FDR appeared to accept the participation of Communists in domestic reform coalitions. He did not trust or admire them, but neither did he try to purge them of influence. During wartime, when Communists volunteered for service in the armed forces and intelligence services, Roosevelt administration officials grudgingly allowed them to participate. Moreover, some State Department officials sought out the advice of Communist leaders on relations with Communist insurgents in the Far East. For FDR and most of his administration, the great international danger derived from the Axis powers and the great threat to the New Deal derived from the political right. Fighting American Communism did not appear to be a priority.

Judging from an assessment of CPUSA influence, Roosevelt's low-key approach to the party appears both sensible and realistic. American Communists, despite their loyalty to the Soviet Union, posed little danger to the security and stability of the United States. Most of them were far more interested in reform than in revolution and were emotionally affected both by New Deal reforms and by Roosevelt's vigilance in combating the Axis. By 1944, Communists were endorsing Roosevelt for a third term, assigning their interest in socialism to the distant future and even dissolving the Communist party as a contribution to national unity! Under the press of American conditions, Communism proved far more vulnerable to liberalism than vice versa, and FDR's dispassionate approach toward it proved compatible with both national security interests and the progress of domestic reform.

On Roosevelt's view of Communism and the American Communist party, the best book is still James MacGregor Burns, *Roosevelt: The Lion and the Fox* (New York: Harcourt, Brace and World, 1956). On the American Communist party's changing perceptions of the Roosevelt administration and on its Popular Front and wartime alliance with American liberalism, see Joseph Starobin, *American Communism in Crisis, 1943–1957* (Cambridge, Mass.: Harvard University Press, 1972), Al Richmond, *A Long View from the Left* (Boston: Houghton Mifflin Co., 1973), and Maurice Isserman, *Which Side Are You On? The American Communist Party During the Second World War* (Middletown, Conn.: Wesleyan University Press, 1982). Isserman's book is a particularly rich source on Communist contacts with the Roosevelt administration. On the Communist party's activity in two key spheres where it possessed influence, labor and civil rights, see Bert Cochran, *Labor and Communism: The Conflict That Shaped American Unions* (Princeton: Princeton University Press, 1977), and Mark Naison, *Communists in Harlem During the Depression* (Urbana: University of Illinois Press, 1983).

MARK D. NAISON

See also Stalin, Joseph, and the Soviet Union

Concentration Camps

See Holocaust; Internment of Japanese-Americans

Congress of Industrial Organization

See Dubinsky, David; Green, William; Hillman, Sidney; Labor; Lewis, John Llewellyn

Congress, United States

During Franklin D. Roosevelt's presidency, executive-legislative relations passed through four stages. From 1933 to 1937, Congress enthusiastically endorsed Roosevelt's New Deal relief, recovery, and reform measures and pursued an isolationist foreign policy.

Between 1937 and 1939, conservative southern Democrats aligned with Republicans to stymie New Deal reforms. Congress then shifted priorities to international issues and from 1939 to 1941 supported Roosevelt's proposals to aid the Allies short of war. During World War II, Congress granted the president extensive authority, supported his defense policies, and sliced his New Deal programs. Throughout these four stages, Democrats controlled both the Senate and the House as illustrated in the table on the following page.

Congress played a largely subordinate role during Roosevelt's first term. By 1933, unemployment had soared to over 12 million workers out of jobs, farm prices had dropped drastically, and numerous businesses and banks had collapsed. In his inaugural address, Roosevelt declared "the nation asks for action, and action now" and summoned Congress into special session to enact New Deal emergency measures. Congress quickly approved the Emergency Banking Act and during the next hundred days enacted an unprecedented volume of landmark relief and recovery legislation. Roosevelt's cabinet members and brains trust deluged Congress with detailed drafts of bills. From March through June, Congress approved the Economy Act, the Civilian Conservation Corps (CCC), the Federal Emergency Relief Act, the Agricultural Adjustment Act, the Tennessee Valley Authority, the Banking Act of 1933, and the National Industrial Recovery Act. Congress in 1934 approved the Securities and Exchange Commission, the Gold Reserve Act, the Communications Act, the National Housing Act, and the Reciprocal Trade Act. These hastily passed measures, utilizing innovative concepts and improvisations, established numerous agencies, rebuilt the nation's confidence, and revived the economy. The emergency conditions, Roosevelt's immense popularity and tactical genius, and large Democratic majorities expedited the massive legislation.

Roosevelt worked effectively with Democratic congressional leaders. In the Senate, Majority Leader Joseph Robinson of Arkansas revived the Democratic caucus and attempted to make majority votes binding on all Democratic members. Speaker Henry Rainey of Illinois and Majority Leader Joseph Byrns of Tennessee directed House Democrats, while the House Rules Committee limited floor debate and permitted only committee amendments on most New Deal measures.

The 1934 congressional elections, mounting Supreme Court and business conservatism, and the radical economic and social plans of Senator Huey Long, Dr. Francis Townsend, and Father Charles Coughlin influenced Roosevelt to seek adoption of more liberal second New Deal reform legislation. In 1935 Congress approved the Works Progress Administration, the National Labor Relations Act, and the Social Security Act for the unemployed, organized labor, and aged. Democratic leadership, including senators Robinson and Pat Harrison of Mississippi and representatives William Bankhead of Alabama and Sam Rayburn of Texas, steered through the controversial Public Utility Holding Company Act, the wealth tax

Party Alignment in Congress during FDR's Presidency

		SENATE			HOUSE		
CONGRESS	YEARS	DEM.	REP.	OTHER	DEM.	REP.	OTHER
73rd	1933–34	60	35	1	310	117	5
74th	1935–36	69	25	2	319	103	10
75th	1937–38	76	16	4	331	89	13
76th	1939–40	69	23	4	261	164	4
77th	1941–42	66	28	2	268	162	5
78th	1943–44	58	37	1	218	208	4
79th	1945–46	56	38	1	242	190	2

bill, and the Guffey-Snyder Coal Act. Bankhead became speaker and Rayburn moved up to majority leader in June 1936, and Roosevelt helped his party capture unprecedented congressional majorities in the 1936 elections.

By 1937, conservative southern Democrats coalesced with Republicans against Roosevelt's second New Deal. They claimed the president infringed on legislative powers, and they lamented the rapid expansion of federal authority, the decline of states' rights, and the New Deal shift toward organized labor. Senators Carter Glass and Harry Byrd of Virginia and Josiah Bailey of North Carolina, along with representatives John O'Connor of New York, Eugene Cox of Georgia, and Howard Smith of Virginia, led Democratic resistance, while Senate and House minority leaders Charles McNary of Oregon and Bertrand Snell of New York organized Republicans.

Senate Democrats in 1937 split sharply over Roosevelt's judicial reorganization plan and party leadership. After the Supreme Court invalidated several New Deal measures, Roosevelt sought congressional authorization to increase the size of the Supreme Court. Burton Wheeler of Montana, Tom Connally of Texas, and other previously loyal Democrats protested the president's move. The Senate Judiciary Committee reported the bill unfavorably, while the conservative coalition blocked Roosevelt's plan on the Senate floor. When Majority Leader Robinson died in July, Roosevelt helped Alben Barkley of Kentucky defeat Harrison for the post and alienated southern members backing the latter.

At the 1938 session, the conservative coalition obstructed second New Deal reforms. The House Rules Committee, controlled by conservative Democrats O'Connor, Cox, and Smith, cleared bills Roosevelt opposed and stymied or changed substantially New Deal legislation. Congress approved farm legislation and the Fair Labor Standards Act after House liberals utilized a discharge petition, but killed Roosevelt's executive reorganization measure. In the 1938 congressional primaries, the president attempted to realign his party by supporting liberal challengers against incumbent conservative Democrats. Although helping defeat Representative O'Connor and reelect Senator Barkley, Roosevelt suffered major setbacks in efforts to remove senators Millard Tydings of Maryland, Walter George of Georgia, and Ellison Smith of South Carolina.

The conservative coalition by 1939 firmly controlled Congress. In the 1938 elections, Republicans gained eight Senate and eighty-one House seats. McNary persuaded Republican senators to let the divided Democrats debate key issues, while new House Minority Leader Joseph Martin of Massachusetts organized Republican opposition. In 1939 Congress slashed Works Progress Administration (WPA) appropriations, approved the Hatch Act, authorized an investigation of the National Labor Relations Board, and rejected self-liquidating projects and housing bills.

From 1933 to 1939, Congress pursued a predominantly isolationist policy toward European conflicts. The economic depression, disillusionment with World War I, and the Nye committee investigation buttressed isolationist sentiment on Capitol Hill. Roosevelt tried little to dissuade Congress from enacting the popularly supported Johnson Act of 1934 and the neutrality acts of 1935 through 1937. In early 1939, Roosevelt urged Congress to repeal the Neutrality Act of 1937 or remove the arms embargo. Southern and Border State Democrats, including many anti–New Dealers, supported the president's request. They argued that Germany and Japan threatened American security and favored strengthening

Karl Kae Knecht, Evansville Courier, 1934. The president as teacher reviews with his pupils the list of alphabet agencies. (Evansville Courier.)

Selected Legislation during FDR's Presidency

1933 (The Hundred Days)
23 January—Twentieth Amendment to the
        Constitution ratified
9 March—Emergency Banking Relief Act
20 March—Economy Act
22 March—Beer-Wine Revenue Act
31 March—Civilian Conservation Corps
        Reforestation Relief Act
12 May—Federal Emergency Relief Act
12 May—Agricultural Adjustment Act
18 May—Tennessee Valley Authority
27 May—Federal Securities Act
5 June—Gold Repeal Joint Resolution
6 June—National Employment System Act
13 June—Home Owners Refinancing Act
16 June—Banking Act of 1933
16 June—Farm Credit Act
16 June—Emergency Railroad Transportation
        Act
16 June—National Industrial Recovery Act
5 December—Twenty-first Amendment to the
        Constitution ratified (repealing
        Eighteenth Amendment
        Prohibition)

1934
11 January—Liquor Tax Act
30 January—Gold Reserve Act of 1934
31 January—Farm Mortgage Refinancing Act
15 February—Civil Works Emergency Relief
        Act
23 February—Crop Loan Act
27 March—Naval Parity Act
28 March—Independent Offices
        Appropriations Act
31 March—Philippine Independence Act
7 April—Farm Relief Act of 1934
13 April—Debt Default Act
21 April—Cotton Control Act
27 April—Home Owners Loan Act
9 May—Sugar Act
10 May—Revenue Act of 1934
18 May—Crime Control Acts (six),
24 May—Municipal Bankruptcy Act
6 June—Securities Exchange Act
7 June—Corporate Bankruptcy Act
12 June—Airmail Act
12 June—Reciprocal Tariff Act
12 June—Farm Mortgage Foreclosure Act
15 June—National Guard Act
16 June—Crime Prevention Compact Act
18 June—Free Zone Act
19 June—Communications Act
19 June—Silver Purchase Act
27 June—Railroad Retirement Act of 1934
27 June—Railway Labor Act
28 June—Taylor Grazing Act
28 June—Federal Farm Bankruptcy Act
28 June—National Housing Act
28 June—Tobacco Control Act

1935
8 April—Emergency Relief Appropriation Act
27 April—Soil Conservation Act
5 July—National Labor Relations Act
9 August—Motor Carrier Act
13 August—War Pension Act
14 August—Social Security Act
23 August—Banking Act of 1935
28 August—Public Utility Holding Company
        Act
29 August—Farm Mortgage Moratorium Act
        of 1935
29 August—Railroad Retirement Act of 1935
30 August—Bituminous Coal Stabilization
        Act
30 August—Revenue Act of 1935
31 August—Neutrality Act of 1935

1936
29 February—Soil Conservation and
        Domestic Allotment Act
29 February—Neutrality Act of 1936
20 June—Federal Anti-Price Discrimination
        Act
22 June—Revenue Act of 1936
26 June—Merchant Marine Act of 1936
30 June—Government Contracts Act

1937
1 March—Supreme Court Retirement Act
26 April—Bituminous Coal Act
1 May—Neutrality Act of 1937
22 July—Farm Tenant Act
18 August—Enabling Act
26 August—Judicial Procedure Reform Act
26 August—Revenue Act of 1937
1 September—National Housing Act

1938
4 February—Amended Federal Housing Act
16 February—Agricultural Adjustment Act of
        1938
17 May—Naval Expansion Act of 1938
28 May—Revenue Act of 1938
23 June—Civil Aeronautics Act of 1938
24 June—Food, Drug, and Cosmetic Act
25 June—Fair Labor Standards Act

1939
3 April—Administrative Reorganization Act
        of 1939
2 August—Hatch Act
4 November—Neutrality Act of 1939

1940
25 June—Revenue Act of 1940
28 June—Alien Registration Act
16 September—Selective Training and Service
        Act
8 October—Second Revenue Act of 1940
8 October—Excess Profits Tax-Amortization
        Tax Act

1941
11 March—Lend-Lease Act
18 August—Selective Service Extension Act
20 September—Revenue Act of 1941
22 December—Amended Selective Service Act

1942
30 January—Emergency Price Control Act
14 May—Women's Army Auxiliary Corps
        Act
25 June—War Labor Disputes Act
30 July—Women Appointed for Voluntary
        Emergency Service Act
2 October—Stabilization Act of 1942
21 October—Revenue Act of 1942

1943
11 March—Lend-Lease Extension Act
13 April—Army and Navy Female Physicians
        and Surgeons Act
29 April—Farm Labor Act of 1943
10 June—Current Tax Payment Act of 1943
1 July—Women's Army Corps Act
11 November—Public Health Service Act of
        1943
17 December—Repeal of Chinese Exclusion
        Acts

1944
25 February—Revenue Act of 1943
31 March—"State Rights" Soldier Vote Act
17 May—Lend-Lease Extension Act
22 June—Servicemen's Readjustment Act

West European defense to deter Hitler from invading the Western Hemisphere. Senators Connally, Claude Pepper of Florida, and Key Pittman of Nevada, along with representatives Rayburn and Luther Johnson of Texas and Sol Bloom of New York, directed repeal advocates. Republicans and many midwestern and western Democrats adamantly defended the neutrality acts. They stressed the Nye committee findings, countered that charity begins at home, and claimed the Atlantic and Pacific oceans protected the United States. The president could not persuade Congress to repeal the arms embargo, as the Senate Foreign Relations Committee refused to change the neutrality laws and the House stymied the Roosevelt-backed Bloom bill.

After World War II began in September 1939, Congress tended to support the president's internationalist measures. Roosevelt quickly summoned Congress into special session to revise the Neutrality Act. Although isolationists filibustered, Congress adopted the Neutrality Act of 1939, removing the arms embargo. In 1940 Congress approved financial aid to Finland, unprecedented peacetime appropriations, and arms sales to Western Hemisphere nations, federalized the National Guard, and passed the first peacetime Selective Service Act. Internationalists Rayburn and John McCormack of Massachusetts became house speaker and majority leader, and Roosevelt won an unprecedented third term. Following spirited debate, Congress in 1941 adopted the Lend-Lease Act, extended the service time of draftees to eighteen months, and permitted American merchant ships to be armed and sent into combat zones. After Japan attacked Pearl Harbor, Congress complied with Roosevelt's requests to declare war on Japan and Germany. Isolationists rallied behind the president to promote national unity.

During World War II, Congress readily supported the main thrust of Roosevelt's defense programs. The president needed authority to make quick political, economic, and military decisions and raise requisite defense manpower, funds, and matériel. Besides broadening and extending Selective Service and augmenting tax revenues, Congress in 1942 authorized the president to create war agencies, reorganize the executive branch, and enforce regulations and controls. Congress played a passive role as the executive branch established the War Production Board, the Office of War Mobilization, the Office of Price Administration, and the Office of Economic Stabilization.

The 1942 congressional elections revived the bipartisan conservative coalition on domestic issues. Republicans gained nine Senate and forty-four House seats, leaving Democrats a slim majority in the lower house. Conservative southern Democrats, along with

Familiar Names of Legislation

Bankhead Act—Cotton Control Act (1934)
Bankhead-Jones Act—Farm Tenant Act (1937)
Burke-Wadsworth Act—Selective Training and
    Service Act (1940)
Crosser-Dill Act—Railway Labor Act (1934)
Frazier-Lemke Act—Federal Farm Bankruptcy
    Act (1934)
Frazier-Lemke Act of 1935—Farm Mortgage
    Moratorium Act of (1935)
GI Bill of Rights—Servicemen's Readjustment
    Act (1944)
Glass-Steagall Act—Banking Act of (1933)
Guffey-Snyder Act—Bituminous Coal
    Stabilization Act (1935)
Guffey-Vinson Act—Bituminous Coal Act
    (1937)
Hatch Act—2 August 1939
Johnson Act—Debt Default Act (1934)
Jones-Connally Act—Farm Relief Act of 1934
Jones-Costigan Act—Sugar Act (1934)
Lame-Duck Amendment—Twentieth
    Amendment to the Constitution (1933)
Miller-Tydings Act—Enabling Act (1937)
Norris Amendment—Twentieth Amendment to
    the Constitution (1933)

Robinson-Patman Act—Federal Anti-Price
    Discrimination Act (1936)
Smith Act—Alien Registration Act (1940)
Smith-Connally Anti-Strike Act—War Labor
    Disputes Act (1942)
Truth-in-Securities Act—Federal Securities
    Act (1933)
Tydings-McDuffie Act—Philippine
    Independence Act (1934)
Vinson Act—Naval Parity Act (1934)
Vinson Naval Act—Naval Expansion
    Act of 1938
Wages and Hours Law—Fair Labor Standards
    Act (1938)
Wagner Act—National Labor Relations
    Act (1935)
Wagner-Crosser Railroad Retirement
    Act—Railroad Retirement Act of 1935
Wagner-Steagall Act—National Housing
    Act (1937)
Walsh-Healy Act—Government Contracts
    Act (1936)
Wealth Tax Act—Revenue Act of 1935
Wheeler-Rayburn Act—Public Utility Holding
    Company Act (1935)

Republicans, protested that newly created executive agencies infringed on legislative authority and used the war emergency to extend or institute new social and economic reforms. Special congressional committees were created to examine executive agencies, defense, small business, and gasoline and fuel shortages. Congress in 1943 terminated the WPA, the CCC, the National Youth Administration, and the National Resources Planning Board, overrode the president's veto of the antilabor Smith-Connally Act, protested his Fair Employment Practices Committee, and rejected national health insurance. In 1944 Congress overrode another Roosevelt veto, slicing four-fifths off his proposed $10 billion tax increase. Although enacting the GI Bill of Rights, Congress rejected a national service bill and let states control absentee ballots for armed forces personnel. In the 1944 elections, Roosevelt won an unprecedented fourth term and saw his party regain firmer control of the House. In early 1945, the president, recalling Woodrow Wilson's error in excluding Republicans from participation in the peace negotiations of 1918–19, was making plans to include congressional Republicans in the upcoming diplomacy of peacemaking. Cordial relations with GOP senator Arthur Vandenberg of Michigan, former isolationist who had rallied behind the president's internationalist approach, were a good omen for that postwar executive-legislative cooperation that Wilson had lacked in his battle over the Versailles Treaty and the League of Nations.

No president had made larger or more lasting changes in executive-congressional relationships than Franklin Roosevelt in his 12¼ years. The White House was now understood to be the dynamic, initiating element in the American governmental system. The president initiated most legislation, drawing upon civil service in the departments and on White House staff. Congress, lacking staff support and disunified by nature, had become the reactive, critical branch. Roosevelt did not conceal his conviction that the presidency was the more important of the two and alone spoke for all of American democracy. This assumption, as much as the liberal-conservative divisions over New Deal and wartime issues, had given president-Congress relations in the Roosevelt years a quality of intermittent warfare. He regarded both the other two branches of government as obstructionist, and in 1937–38 he moved against both of them by proposing structural reforms to allow a president to move his measures through the minefield of judicial and legislative vetoes. The Court voluntarily yielded, but Congress dug in its heels and brought the New Deal to an end. Roosevelt had moved the center of action, media attention, and responsibility from the Hill to the White House, completing the work of Theodore Roosevelt and Woodrow Wilson. But he had been denied those structural changes—executive branch reorganization, a planning board, realignment of the political parties—that might have shifted power to his end of the avenue also. Thus his last seven years were spent in a legislative deadlock that prevented him or any of his successors from carrying a major program of reforms through Congress,

until the assassination of John F. Kennedy gave Lyndon Johnson a brief opening for the Great Society.

All the following books contain pertinent information: John M. Allswang, *The New Deal and American Politics* (New York: John Wiley & Sons, 1978); Irving Bernstein, *Turbulent Years* (Boston: Houghton Mifflin Co., 1970); John M. Blum, *V Was for Victory* (New York: Harcourt Brace Jovanovich, 1977); A. Russell Buchanan, *The United States and World War II*, 2 vols. (New York: Harper & Row, 1964); James MacGregor Burns, *Roosevelt: The Lion and the Fox* (New York: Harcourt, Brace & World, 1956) and *Roosevelt: The Soldier of Freedom, 1940–1945* (New York: Harcourt Brace Jovanovich, 1970); Wayne S. Cole, *Roosevelt and the Isolationists, 1932–45* (Lincoln: University of Nebraska Press, 1983); Robert Dallek, *Franklin D. Roosevelt and American Foreign Policy, 1932–1945* (New York: Oxford University Press, 1979); Robert A. Divine, *The Illusion of Neutrality* (Chicago: University of Chicago Press, 1962), *The Reluctant Belligerent*, 2d ed. (New York: John Wiley & Sons, 1979), and *Second Chance* (New York: Atheneum, 1967); Frank Freidel, *Franklin D. Roosevelt*, 4 vols. (Boston: Little, Brown & Co. 1952–73) and *F.D.R. and the South* (Baton Rouge: Louisiana State University Press, 1965); Ellis W. Hawley, *The New Deal and the Problem of Monopoly* (Princeton: Princeton University Press, 1966); Manfred Jonas, *Isolationism in America, 1935–1941* (Ithaca: Cornell University Press, 1966); Alvin M. Josephy, Jr., *The American Heritage History of the Congress of the United States* (New York: American Heritage, 1975); William L. Langer and S. Everett Gleason, *The Challenge to Isolation, 1937–1940* and *The Undeclared War, 1940–1941* (New York: Harper & Row, 1952–53); William E. Leuchtenburg, *Franklin D. Roosevelt and the New Deal, 1932–1940* (New York: Harper & Row, 1963); *Origins and Development of Congress*, 2d ed. (Washington: Congressional Quarterly, 1982); James T. Patterson, *Congressional Conservatism and the New Deal* (Lexington: University of Kentucky Press, 1967); Richard Polenberg, *War and Society: The United States, 1941–1945* (Philadelphia: J. B. Lippincott, 1972); David L. Porter, *Congress and the Waning of the New Deal* (Port Washington, N.Y.: Kennikat Press, 1980) and *The Seventy-sixth Congress and World War II, 1939–1940* (Columbia: University of Missouri Press, 1979); Arthur M. Schlesinger, Jr., *The Age of Roosevelt*, 3 vols. (Boston: Houghton Mifflin Co., 1957–60); and Gaddis Smith, *American Diplomacy during the Second World War, 1941–1945* (New York: John Wiley & Sons, 1965).

DAVID L. PORTER

See also Conservatism; Court-packing Plan; Democratic Party; Elections in the Roosevelt Era; Election of 1934; Election of 1938; House Committee to Investigate Un-American Activities; Hundred Days; Isolationism; New Deal; Office of the Presidency; "Purge" of 1938; Rayburn, Samuel Taliaferro; Reorganization Act of 1939; Republican Party; South, The; Taxation; Temporary National Economic Committee; Wagner, Robert Ferdinand

Conservation

During the New Deal era the conservation movement reached its zenith, with Franklin D. Roosevelt, amateur forester and outdoorsman, providing leadership and support.

From colonial days, Americans had treated the continent as a land of inexhaustible resources. In 1748 Peter Kalm, a visiting Swedish naturalist, lamented their carelessness: "Their eyes are fixed upon the present gain, and they are blind to the future." Capitalistic drives, faith in Providence, and the conditions of frontier existence impelled them to "conquer" their environment. Moving West, they wore out the topsoil, turned forests into stumpland, exterminated wildlife, and on the arid Plains, ploughed up the grass that held the soil together.

In the mid-nineteenth century, a few voices cried out against the reckless destruction. Henry Thoreau scorned the enterpriser who spends his day "shearing off those woods and making earth bald before her time." In *Man and Nature* (1864), George Perkins Marsh pondered the responsibility of human beings to maintain the "harmonies of nature." Geologist John Wesley Powell pleaded for classification and appropriate management of the vast federal lands, and John Muir began to preach his belief in wilderness as manifestation of the Divine. As the frontier receded into legend, growing concern produced legislation. Primarily to safeguard water and timber supplies, New York State set aside the Adirondack Forest Preserve in 1885, and in 1891, Congress provided for forest reserves (later called national forests). A dawning appreciation of natural scenery, on the other hand, led Congress in 1872 to create Yellowstone, the first national park.

Around 1900 a movement took shape. As the rising Progressives regarded government as an instrument for various reforms, so conservationists demanded public action. Some stressed wise use of resources, a goal that distinguished them from others who valued nature in its pristine state. Preservationists and developers could often cooperate, but on occasion latent disagreement burst into bitter controversy.

Advocates of wise use captured national attention. With Theodore Roosevelt as their champion, geologist W. J. McGee, forester Gifford Pinchot, and other technicians dramatized the impact of exploitation and waste, suggested legislation, and articulated guiding principles. Following the concept of multiple-purpose management, the president's Inland Waterways Commission recommended in 1908 the creation of an executive agency that could "take account of the purification of waters, the development of power, the control of floods, the reclamation of lands by irrigation and drainage, and all other uses of the waters or benefits to be derived from their control."

Although unable to carry out this sweeping proposal, the conservationists attained some immediate objectives. As president, Theodore Roosevelt tripled the national forest system. The Newlands Act of 1902 financed irrigation works to be carried out by a Bureau of Reclamation. Technological advance had raised the issue of public—or private—generation of hydroelectricity; after years of controversy the Federal Power Act of 1920 confirmed paramount national control over potential sites on the rivers.

In 1913 nature lovers attuned to Thoreau and Muir lost a battle to prevent construction of the dam that flooded Yosemite's spectacular Hetch Hetchy Valley. They triumphed, however, when in 1916 the new National Park Service was charged "to conserve the scenery and the natural and historic objects and the wild life therein . . . by such means as will leave them unimpaired for the enjoyment of future generations."

Accusing the government of locking resources away from the people, lumber companies and mining corporations appealed effectively to ordinary citizens steeped in the frontier tradition of individual enterprise. Furthermore, as the Progressive current lost momentum, so the conservationist wave subsided. Politically, its successors in the 1920s focused on public hydropower, and Nebraska senator George W. Norris made the uncompleted federal project at Muscle Shoals, Alabama, a symbol of that cause.

As a boy roaming the family acres, Franklin D. Roosevelt observed—and hunted—birds and acquired a keen and enduring interest in forestry which led him to experiment in tree planting on the estate. In this connection, he sought the advice of professional foresters, as during his later career he would sound out the experts in various fields of conservation. When elected in 1910 to the New York State Senate, he chaired the Forest, Fish, and Game Committee and, after hearing Gifford Pinchot on the disasters caused by deforestation in China, proposed a bill that would have restricted cutting of timber on privately owned lands. Facing the hostility of lumber companies, he proclaimed in 1912 that individual liberty must yield to "the liberty of the community."

In campaigning for the vice-presidency in 1920, and especially during two terms as governor of New York (1929–33), Roosevelt made conservation a major political issue. Since, like many members of his class and generation, he believed in the superior virtue of rural living, he tried, without great success, to place unemployed men on subsistence farms. More practically and on a larger scale, he saw to it that the Temporary Emergency Relief Administration put the jobless to work on forest improvement. Further, he set on foot a pioneer study of land use and a reforestation program. Declaring that the waters of the St. Lawrence River were running "to waste," he appointed the Power Authority of the State of New York to develop the electric power "which nature has supplied us through the gift of God." (The project went into operation in the 1950s.) In the 1932 presidential campaign, he demanded yardstick public projects on certain great rivers and promised to maintain federal sovereignty over the power resources of the nation.

As president, then, Roosevelt intended to conduct an active conservation policy. Although he valued wilderness and wildlife ("yes, we must stop the slaughter of those bears!" he replied to one correspondent), depression conditions and personal predilections inclined him to emphasize development of resources for broadly economic purposes. In conservation, as in other fields, "planning" became the watchword in Washington.

With Senator Norris by his side, he announced in January 1933 that Muscle Shoals must become the nucleus of an integrated program for the entire valley of the Tennessee River; as he presented it to Congress in April, the plan would transcend electrical production and encompass "flood control, soil erosion, afforestation, elimination from agricultural use of marginal lands, and distribution and diversification of industry," and might, furthermore, lead to "like development of other great natural territorial units within our borders." Subsequently he appointed several advisory groups. One committee, instructed to study water uses in the Mississippi Valley, reported in October 1934 not only on the obvious topics but also on "agriculture and irrigation, industry and commerce, water storage, forestry, recreation and the conservation of wildlife" and on the needs of the people "who live on the land and are dependent on the water"; and it proposed "directive planning" for the valley. Less soaring of vision, the National Resources Board and its successor, the National Resources Committee, collected data on resources, helped states set up planning commissions, and advocated a six-year budget for public works.

Yet Roosevelt shied away from pressing further all-enveloping regional schemes on a no-longer-compliant Congress. Bureaucratic rivalries hampered coordination. Agencies, such as the Forest Service, the Soil Conservation Service, the Bureau of Reclamation, and the army's Corps of Engineers, pursued sometimes incompatible objectives, and each enjoyed the support of allied interest groups. The president refused the pleas of Harold L. Ickes, secretary of the interior, that he create a single Department of Conservation and rejected suggestions that he convene a major conservation conference, which, he warned, might turn into a free-for-all. In the spring of 1937, he sent to Congress a proposal for seven "regional authorities or agencies" to plan for the integrated use and conservation of water, soil, and forests, but, politically, the time had passed for such measures, and he never went to bat for the "seven little TVA's."

Nevertheless, the New Deal carried through a number of large projects based in part on the multiple-purpose principle. Roosevelt's administration completed Boulder (now Hoover) Dam on the Colorado River and, on the Columbia, constructed Bonneville and Grand Coulee, designed for flood control, irrigation, and the generation of electricity for the Northwest. (But the president was never able to fulfill his dream of harnessing the tides of Passamaquoddy in the Bay of Fundy.) The disappointing flood control bill (or Copeland Act) of 1936 did at least acknowledge the relation of upstream land use to river flow.

At the beginning of his presidency, Roosevelt proposed what became the Civilian Conservation Corps, one of the most admired of New Deal innovations. His active interest helped to add millions of acres to the wildlife refuges, national parks, and national forests. Although his suggestion of a shelterbelt to run from north to south in the Great Plains en-

countered much skepticism, the 18,600 miles of tree strips set out in eight years along the 99th meridian produced substantial benefits to crops by anchoring the soil and moderating the constant winds.

In May 1934, clouds of dirt blown from the Dust Bowl darkened the skies of eastern cities, a startling reminder of the repeated droughts that were devastating the Great Plains. In 1936 the governor of Oklahoma, calling for more federal aid, reported "forty or fifty thousand of these people that haven't anything, they are just burned out." Elsewhere, floods ravaged the Northeast and Midwest, while in the Southeast every rainfall gullied the slopes and carried topsoil to the sea.

Exploitative agriculture, conservationists insisted, had engendered catastrophe, and they set out to raise the public consciousness. For the Farm Security Administration, Pare Lorentz produced classic films, *The River,* and *The Plow That Broke the Plains,* while photographers such as Dorothea Lange recorded the ravaged country and its inhabitants. The gaunt faces, the barren ground, raised questions about a social system that ruined land and human beings. In the Agriculture Department, Rexford G. Tugwell and Lewis Gray, among others, sought to effect far-reaching reforms in land use. In its report of December 1936 (drafted largely by Gray), Roosevelt's Great Plains Committee called for a transformation of mental attitudes: the plainsman "cannot assume that whatever is for his immediate good is also good for everybody" and must realize also that he cannot " 'conquer Nature'—he must live with her on her own terms, making use of and conserving resources which can no longer be considered inexhaustible." Recommending certain measures (not in fact very radical), the committee asserted that traditional individualism must yield to an economy in which public and private agencies could cooperate in a twenty-year effort to change the uses of the land.

The administration took many constructive steps. The Taylor Grazing Act (1934) regulated grazing on the overused public ranges and withdrew much of the public domain from settlement. In all parts of the country, the Soil Conservation Service, headed by the crusading Hugh Bennett, organized farmers into soil conservation districts and helped them to employ techniques that would enrich the soil and prevent erosion. To some, however, these promising efforts failed to cope with the dimensions of the problem. As Morris L. Cooke, who had chaired the Great Plains Committee, expressed it in 1938, "We have to arouse something akin to a war psychology if we are really to make this a permanent country." By that time, however, the New Deal was fading, and soon the Second World War diverted American energies. As, coincidentally, rain returned to the Great Plains, rising prices stimulated reckless expansion of wheat acreage that, once more, destroyed soil cover and was to result during the 1950s in new storms of dust. In the years of economic "growth" that followed the war, the political climate shifted to a complacent conservatism.

Many of the New Deal conservation measures

have weathered opposition and, though often under-financed, have gained wide acceptance. The Soil Conservation Service has continued its work through periods of neglect, and in times of heavy unemployment thoughts turn to creation of another (less sexist and less racist) Civilian Conservation Corps. With dams now blocking almost every stream, vast water projects no longer inspire, and yet the electricity they provide has lightened the tasks of countless Americans. Moreover, in exposing and discussing the state of land, soil, and water, Roosevelt and the New Dealers aroused public awareness and provided opportunities for preservationists and ecological planners to be heard. Bob Marshall, forester and backpacker, persuaded the Forest Service to designate wilderness reserves, and although it was somewhat constrained by political considerations, the Great Plains Committee implied a social critique and an outlook more broadly inclusive than the aims of either developers or preservationists of the past. Thus the New Deal nourished the beginnings of a later movement.

Emerging a generation later, with the celebration of Earth Day in 1970, environmentalists attacked perils previously only dimly foreseen and promulgated values different from those that dominated the 1930s. They decried technological interference with natural processes, whether by dams, chemicals, or nuclear fission. With Aldo Leopold they called, not for management, but for adherence to a land ethic and for recognition of the human place in a community of all living things.

Despite differences, Roosevelt and other conservationists of the New Deal shared with today's environmentalists a common conviction: that the nation must exercise its responsibility to safeguard the world in which we live and preserve it for our descendants. Largely through their efforts, this has become an accepted belief of the American people.

Basic sources include Roosevelt's papers, and those of Morris L. Cooke and other associates, at the Franklin D. Roosevelt Library in Hyde Park, New York; the papers of Harold L. Ickes and George W. Norris in the Library of Congress, Washington, D.C.; and the official records of relevant government agencies, preserved by the National Archives and Records Service in Washington. In *Franklin D. Roosevelt and Conservation, 1911–1945*, 2 vols. (Hyde Park, N.Y.: National Archives and Records Service, 1957), Edgar B. Nixon has collected and published an illuminating selection of Roosevelt's correspondence and public statements, to which he has added clarifying and informative editorial notes. Among secondary works, Samuel P. Hays, in *Conservation and the Gospel of Efficiency* (Cambridge, Mass.: Harvard University Press, 1959), analyzes the utilitarian outlook of the technology-minded conservationists around Theodore Roosevelt. A. L. Riesch Owen's *Conservation under FDR* (New York: Praeger, 1983) provides a general account of its subject. In *Morris Llewellyn Cooke: Progressive Engineer* (New York: Garland, 1983), Jean Christie traces the career of a prominent adviser to Franklin Roosevelt as governor and as president. In "Roosevelt, Norris, and the 'Seven Little TVA's,' " *Journal of Politics* 14 (August 1952), William E. Leuchtenburg closely examines the internal politics of an incident that marked a turning point in regional development policies. Donald Worster's *Dust Bowl: The*

Southern Plains in the 1930's (New York: Oxford University Press, 1979) portrays a disaster, which, the author asserts, was caused less by natural forces than by the prevailing social organization and economic culture. A collection of articles, edited by Carroll Pursell, in *From Conservation to Ecology: The Development of Environmental Concern* (New York: Thomas Y. Crowell, 1973) provides a brief introduction to the various currents of thought on the environment from colonial times to the late twentieth century.

JEAN CHRISTIE

See also Civilian Conservation Corps; Ickes, Harold LeClair; Norris, George William; Pinchot, Gifford; Tennessee Valley Authority; Roosevelt, Theodore; Tugwell, Rexford Guy

Conservatism

The essence of American conservatism has always been the preservation of that which is best in established traditions. Informed conservatives are those who are committed to the wisdom and the continuity of the past; they are dubious of extravagant change. The social order, they would argue, is, in effect, organic; it cannot be discarded or recast as if it were a piece of machinery. Order and social class are natural requirements of a society where people are equal only in some moral sense. American conservatism, then, has been predicated on a commitment to order, stability, tradition, continuity, and the past over the future. This is not to say, however, that American conservatism has been a fixed body of dogma. On the contrary, conservatives have understood that society must change; change, after all, is a form of renewal and revitalization for that which is organic.

Evans, Columbus *(Ohio)* Dispatch, *16 July 1935. A strange coalition equipped with air pumps tries to inflate the New Deal.*

From the outset, that is from the American Revolution on, there has been an ongoing tension in the United States between conservatism and the professed ideals of both the Declaration of Independence and the American Revolution, ideals that carried with them commitment to equality, democracy, social change, optimism about people and their potential, and, above all else, progress. Likewise, over the years, the conservative viewpoint in American political, economic, and social life has consistently met challenges, challenges that have been encountered within a constitutional system devised to keep an effective control over a government that is presumably committed to majority rule.

The Civil War, in an important sense, was a watershed for conservatism in that it established once and for all the Constitution as the symbol of national unity. It also marked a shift in the emphasis of the debate between conservatives and their critics. With the rise of industrial capitalism in the late nineteenth century, the overriding concern on which nearly all other questions would turn was the right and the capacity of government to regulate business in the general interest of the nation. This proposition challenged a basic conservative premise that property and freedom are inseparable; separate property from private ownership and freedom would vanish. Certainly, to write about conservatism in the United States after the Civil War is to write about American business and private property and the right of government to regulate both.

Post–Civil War conservatism, what is usually described as laissez faire conservatism or social Darwinism, thus placed the emphasis on liberty; in economic matters, people must have maximum freedom. But in a situation of maximum economic freedom, an elite group, an aristocracy, would inevitably rise to the top. In the gospel of wealth, as it was often called, these aristocrats, chosen by natural selection, had not only the right but the moral obligation to be good stewards of their wealth, to be enlightened leaders in wielding political power, and to be exemplary in their private lives.

The principal implementation of these conservative principles was through the Republican party. In the post–Civil War period, the Republican party found its raison d'être in the Industrial Revolution. The party became unashamedly the party of business and eventually the party of big business. So long as the partnership produced uninterrupted material prosperity, the Republican party dominated American politics. From 1860 to 1932, there were only two Democratic administrations, those of Cleveland and Wilson. And during this long period, the Republican party controlled the Congress most of the time as well. In those seventy-two years, the Republicans controlled the Senate for sixty years and the House of Representatives for fifty years.

Although the conservative philosophy had been continually challenged throughout American history, its most serious challenge seemed to emerge from the Great Depression in the form of the New Deal. The New Deal put conservatives on the defensive; conservatives were now cast in the role of critics. Franklin Roosevelt was a "traitor to his class," and conservatives opposed him relentlessly during the 1930s. Among the more prestigious conservative critics was former president Herbert Hoover. Hoover, who labeled his brand of conservatism as progressive individualism, first developed that theme in 1922 in *American Individualism*. The individual should be given maximum freedom and the role of government was to assure the individual "liberty, justice, intellectual welfare [meaning education], equality of opportunity, and stimulation to service." As late as 1934, in *Challenge to Liberty*, Hoover, still advocating progressive individualism, was critical of the New Deal because it represented oversized omnipresent government, which stifled individualism.

Other conservative voices were raised attacking the New Deal, including prominent businessmen, the Republican party, and a host of organizations such as the Sentinels of the Republic, the American Taxpayers' League, the American Liberty League, and others.

Certainly the most ambitious of the organizations was the American Liberty League, which attracted to its ranks a substantial cross section of the leaders of American business, industry, finance, law, and the professions. In fact, in the history of the country to that time, no one organization had marshaled so much prestige, wealth, and managerial skill as the American Liberty League did in the fight against Franklin Roosevelt and the New Deal. It raised almost as much money as each of the two major parties during 1935 and 1936, and most of the funds came from a score of prominent businessmen, especially the Du Pont family.

The American Liberty League was certainly the most articulate voice for political conservatism during the decade of the 1930s, and its criticism of the New Deal was consistent with conservative thought expressed since *The Federalist* letters. Its views were the views of most conservatives and would have been applauded by a wide spectrum of the better known spokesmen for conservatism over the years, people like William Graham Sumner, John W. Burgess, Andrew Carnegie, George Santayana, Ralph Adams Cram, Albert J. Nock, H. L. Mencken, and a host of others. Criticism of the New Deal followed quite naturally from the commitment to basic conservative principles: strict construction of the Constitution, fear of a powerful federal government, an overriding need for balanced budgets, and respect for free enterprise, private property, and individualism.

The failure to unhorse Roosevelt and the New Deal did not mean that the conservative cause was left without champions. In 1937, in opposition to Roosevelt's Court-packing plan, a conservative coalition began developing in the Congress, consisting of Republicans and southern Democrats whose views, except on racial issues, were quite consistent with the Republicans. In those years before the United States became involved in World War II, the coalition fought Roosevelt to a standoff. Not only did the coalition succeed in killing the Court plan, but also a child labor bill, a stronger food and drug bill, a ship safety bill, crop insurance and other farm bills, a proposal to make the Civilian Conservation Corps permanent, an extension of the Tennessee Valley Authority to other parts of the country, the wages and hours proposal, and a reorganization plan for the executive branch. Some of this legislation later passed in much modified form.

Looking back on the New Deal, an increasing number of writers have argued that the New Deal itself was conservative in the sense that it was intended to save the system rather than seriously to amend it. This is the theme of such critics as Paul Conkin, Howard Zinn, Barton Bernstein, and Ronald Radosh. "The myth of a New Deal revolution . . . dies hard," wrote Radosh. New Deal policies, according to Radosh, "were only a change in the way of doing things. They were a means of working out new arrangements to bolster the existing order."

An interesting irony is that Roosevelt considered himself a conservative and the New Deal to be conservatism, certainly not radicalism. "The true conservative," he said, "seeks to protect the system of private property and free enterprise by correcting such injustices and inequalities as arise from it. I am that kind of conservative."

So far as the Left was concerned, it agreed with Roosevelt. The New Deal was never more than a spirited attempt to save the system. Roosevelt gave the country lots of motion, ballyhoo, and showmanship, a performance that Norman Thomas, the Socialist leader, described as trying "to cure tuberculosis with cough drops." But to conservatives, Franklin Roosevelt, who still ranks high in their demonology, was never mistaken for one of their own.

Conservatives emerged from the New Deal experience somewhat chastened. They still remained true to their familiar principles, of course. But many, perhaps most, conservatives were prepared to incorporate into their philosophy an enlarged role for government in the economy and a more enlightened attitude toward equality and civil rights. Years after the New Deal and because of its stabilizing influence and political longevity, most American conservatives—including President Ronald Reagan, who endorses a "safety net" for the poor—had finally accepted the main outlines of the welfare state.

A first-rate history and excellent apologia for the conservative position is Russell Kirk, *The Conservative Mind from Burke to Santayana* (Chicago: H. Regnery Co., 1953). Clinton Rossiter's *Conservatism in America*, rev. ed. (New York: Knopf, 1962), which received the Charles A. Beard Memorial Prize, develops an interesting conservative program for American democracy. A wide-ranging book with about half of it devoted to conservatism since World War II is Ronald Lora, *Conservative Minds in America* (Chicago: Rand McNally, 1971). George Wolfskill's *The Revolt of the Conservatives* (Boston: Houghton Mifflin Co., 1962), which received the Texas Theta Sigma Phi Award, is the definitive history of the American Liberty League. The story of Roosevelt's conservative opposition in Congress is found in James T. Patterson, *Congressional Conservatism and the New Deal* (Lexington: University of Kentucky Press, 1967).

GEORGE WOLFSKILL

See also American Liberty League; Biographers and Public Reputation; Catholics; Chamber of Commerce; Congress, United States; Democratic Party; Economic Royalists; Election of 1938; Election of 1942; Liberalism and Progressivism; Republican Party; South, The; Vandenberg, Arthur Hendrick

Constitutional Amendments

See Interregnum; Prohibition; Rayburn, Samuel Taliaferro

Consumerism

The era of the Great Depression was the second time in the twentieth century when consumer unrest became sufficiently vocal as to be called a movement, the first time having been in the early 1900s. While consumer issues seemed to arouse little concern in the 1920s except within certain professional groups such as the American Home Economics Association, an early signal of potential extensive discontent was the substantial popularity of *Your Money's Worth* (New York: MacMillan, 1927), a work written by Stuart Chase and F. J. Schlink. Once the depression made consumer problems more acute and immediate, this volume proved to be the prototype for a large number of so-called guinea-pig muckraking books designed to expose abuses in the marketplace. These works were instrumental in arousing consumer unrest.

The actual leadership of the consumer movement fell to certain groups such as Consumers' Research, Consumers' Union, and a variety of national women's organizations. The New Deal responded to the new unrest among consumers, but only in limited fashion. To be sure, at least in the early period of the Roosevelt administration there were those committed to a consumer-oriented society. Assistant Secretary of Agriculture Rexford Tugwell was one. The concept of consumer interest was also formally acknowledged in the structure of the National Recovery Administration (NRA) and the Agricultural Adjustment Administration created in 1933. Consumers were provided official representation in both agencies. Some saw this recognition as opening a significant new era, and indeed, there seemed to be some reason for optimism. In the winter of 1933–34, substantial agitation even arose for creation of a federal Department of the Consumer.

The promise was not to be fulfilled. The dynamics of the New Deal dictated otherwise. Consumer advocacy almost always took the shape of calls for reform, and of the three Rs (relief, recovery, and reform), this one clearly took last place in the priorities of Franklin Roosevelt. Moreover, the amount of influence exercised by the many competing voices who sought to make themselves heard by the FDR administration was largely dependent on their organizational power. In this the consumer was consistently at a disadvantage. The Consumers' Advisory Board (CAB) of the NRA was a case in point. It sought actively to develop a constituency through promotion of a network of consumer councils, but with limited success. Representatives of the CAB remained, in Tugwell's words, "spearheads without shafts." Finally, it is reasonable to believe that too many New Dealers, including FDR, shared the view of NRA's Gen. Hugh Johnson that consumers' interest was the public interest and, therefore, really needed no special representation. "Who is the consumer? Show me a consumer," Johnson barked in response to agitation from the CAB.

The most significant and lasting legislative contribution of the New Deal to the consumer cause was the Food, Drug, and Cosmetic Act of 1938. It would strengthen materially the powers of the Food and Drug Administration, but the five-year struggle for enactment also demonstrated the political opposition to consumer protection and the limited commitment of the president to that cause. Tugwell persuaded the president to allow introduction of reform legislation in 1933. Roosevelt later chided the assistant secretary for urging support for a new law when relief and recovery measures were waiting for passage. The president's caution increased when it appeared that the proposed new statute offended conservative congressmen, and lack of organized and unified consumer support for a revised law did not help. The congressional sponsor of the revision was Senator Royal Copeland of New York, hardly a political favorite of FDR. Thus, ultimate passage of the Food, Drug, and Comestic Act in 1938 owed little to the president.

Robert Herrmann has argued that consumerism would have gained much greater influence in the next years if the coming of World War II had not diverted public attention. The international threat doubtless did help to redirect consumer concern to other issues, but there is also reason to believe that the movement had peaked on its own by 1938. At any rate, while consumerism was always a part of the public scene during the next twenty years, it would not again reach the force it had attained in the Great Depression until that new period of social unrest that came in the 1960s.

Contemporary statements on the consumer movement of the 1930s are limited in value. The most informative commentary on the nature of consumer discontent then may be found in the guinea-pig muckraking volumes of which the best known was *100,000,000 Guinea Pigs* (New York: Vanguard Press, 1932) by Arthur Kallet and F. J. Schlink. The most systematic development of the consumer thesis was *Guinea Pigs No More* (New York: Covici & Friede, 1936) by J. B. Matthews. A very brief recent assessment of the movement is Robert Herrmann, *The Consumer Movement in Historical Perspective* (University Park: Pennsylvania State University Press, 1970). Also brief on the subject of consumerism but more comprehensive on its relationship to the New Deal is Arthur M. Schlesinger, Jr., *The Coming of the New Deal* (Boston: Houghton Mifflin Co., 1959). While directed at specific legislative reform, Charles Jackson's *Food and Drug Legislation in the New Deal* (Princeton: Princeton University Press, 1970) provides many useful insights into the Roosevelt administration and the consumer movement.

CHARLES O. JACKSON

Cooke, Charles Maynard, Jr.

(19 December 1886–24 December 1971)

Principal strategic planner for the chief of naval operations in World War II. Charles M. Cooke, Jr., was born in Fort Smith, Arkansas, graduated from the University of Arkansas in 1905, entered the U.S. Naval Academy at Annapolis in 1906, and graduated second in his class in 1910. Noted for his keen analytical mind and his reflective temperament, he retained his midshipman nickname, "Savvy," throughout his long career.

As a submarine officer, his professional competence, coupled with intellectual brilliance, foreshadowed his later reputation as a master strategist. In 1936–38, as plans officer for the commander in chief, U.S. fleet, and later, in 1939–40, as a war planning officer for the chief of naval operations, Cooke made significant contributions to preparations for the coming conflict. These included the development of the long-range submarine; the basic war plan for defeating Japan; the adoption of replenishment-at-sea techniques to keep the fleet underway for extended periods; and the prewar production of landing craft for the amphibious operations that were to characterize World War II.

In early 1942, Adm. Ernest J. King, the naval commander in chief, named Cooke as his chief planning officer, and for over three years, he played a leading role in Allied strategy. As a member of the presidential party, he accompanied King to President Roosevelt's summit conferences at Casablanca, Quebec, Cairo, Teheran, and Yalta; he was present also at the Potsdam Conference. Among his many ideas that accelerated victory was a suggestion he made to rear Adm. Forrest Sherman, the planner for Adm. Chester Nimitz. Cooke proposed to bypass Truk, the formidable Japanese base in the Carolines, and instead, attack the Marianas, using the previously captured Ulithi as a logistics base. Thus began the strategy of island-hopping by which Japanese Pacific strongholds, cut off from logistic support, were starved into impotence.

Because of his unsurpassed ability to visualize operations conducted simultaneously in the European–North African theater and in the Pacific–Far East area, Cooke exerted a strong and positive influence over major campaign plans. The fact that Roosevelt approved those strategic concepts, which originated in Admiral Cooke's fertile mind and were proposed by the Joint Chiefs of Staff, is evidence that the president appreciated his contribution.

After the war, Cooke became, successively, commander, Seventh Fleet, and commander, Naval Forces Pacific. He quickly sensed that the defeat of Japan had created a strategic vacuum that the Soviets and Chinese Communists would fill either with their own troops or with proxies, a prediction that proved accurate. Cooke also believed that those who wished for improved relations with Moscow and its satellites would be disappointed.

He retired in May 1948 to his home in Sonoma,

California, where he continued to publicize his views until his death.

Grace Person Hayes, *The History of the Joint Chiefs of Staff: The War against Japan* (Annapolis: Naval Institute Press, 1982) is an authoritative work with numerous references to Cooke's global planning. Thomas B. Buell, *Master of Sea Power: A Biography of Fleet Admiral King* (Boston: Little, Brown & Co., 1980) reflects, passim, King's admiration of Cooke. Cooke's papers, held at the Hoover Institution, Stanford University, shed light on how he viewed his career. Maurice Matloff and Edwin M. Snell, *Strategic Planning for Coalition Warfare, 1941–1942* (Washington: U.S. Government Printing Office, 1953), Maurice Matloff, *Strategic Planning for Coalition Warfare, 1943–44* (Washington: U.S. Government Printing Office, 1959), and Louis Morton, *Strategy and Command, The First Two Years* (Washington: U.S. Government Printing Office, 1962) are all balanced appraisals of Allied strategic planning with many references to Cooke.

PAUL B. RYAN

Corcoran, Thomas Gardiner

(29 December 1900–6 December 1981)

Presidential adviser. Thomas Gardiner Corcoran, Franklin D. Roosevelt's "Tommy the Cork," was born in Pawtucket, Rhode Island. His undergraduate education began in 1918 at Brown University where he majored in the classics and served as class valedictorian in 1921. He remained at Brown to earn a Master of Arts degree in English in 1922, and then enrolled at the Harvard Law School, completing his Bachelor of Laws degree in 1925. It was during his doctoral year, 1926, that he came under the tutelage of Felix Frankfurter, the man who would bring him into the Roosevelt inner circle.

Corcoran left Frankfurter in 1926 to become the law clerk and lifelong companion of Associate Justice Oliver Wendell Holmes. Under Holmes, Corcoran developed the philosophy of civil service that directed him during his subsequent career. After his year with Holmes, Corcoran joined the New York law firm of Cotton/Franklin as a law clerk. While with the firm, Corcoran developed an expertise in the fields of holding companies and securities, knowledge that served him well during the New Deal years.

In 1932 George Franklin recommended Corcoran for a position on the legal staff of President Herbert Hoover's newly created Reconstruction Finance Corporation (RFC). Corcoran remained with the RFC until 1940, maintaining an official government position there while acting unofficially as Roosevelt's adviser, friend, and political stalwart.

Although as an RFC official Corcoran became embroiled in the furor over gold buying in 1933, his major role on behalf of the New Deal that year was that of legislative draftsman. Roosevelt had chosen Felix Frankfurter to manage the redrafting of the truth in securities bill of 1933, and Frankfurter, in turn, delegated the responsibility to James Landis, Benjamin Cohen, and Corcoran, the "little Hot Dogs." Corcoran directly contributed to the writing of the first draft of the bill only and then successfully lobbied for the bill's passage through Congress. Corcoran also helped draft and defend in congressional hearings the Securities and Exchange Act of 1934.

Having gained success as a White House lobbyist, Corcoran was tapped by Roosevelt to push the public utilities holding company bill through a recalcitrant Congress in 1935 and also to assist in the drafting of the Wealth Tax Act. By this time, Corcoran had joined the ranks of Roosevelt's inner circle, enjoyed direct access to the Skipper, as he affectionately called the president, and was a regular guest at White House social gatherings where he frequently entertained with his accordion, his Irish ballads, and his Irish charm and wit.

While lobbying against the utility concerns, Corcoran was also involved in the Passamaquoddy Dam controversy in Maine. During heated debate over the utilities bill, Congressman Owen Brewster (R., Maine) accused Corcoran of threatening to stop the construction of the dam unless Brewster voted in favor of the administration's bill. Although Corcoran was exonerated, his reputation with Congress and across the nation had suffered.

During Roosevelt's first term, Corcoran established an informal "placement bureau" for bright, young lawyers. Held together by a communications network of Corcoran's design, the placement bureau members informed Corcoran of openings in the civil service, the availability of candidates, and Roosevelt's needs. Corcoran supplied FDR with lawyers for his New Deal agencies and filled other personnel needs throughout the Roosevelt presidency.

In the election year of 1936, Roosevelt utilized the versatile Corcoran as a member of his speechwriting team. Such memorable phrases as "rendezvous with destiny" earned Corcoran both a reputation for turning a phrase and a spot on the team through 1940.

During the second term, Corcoran's support for Roosevelt's policies brought him into disfavor among both Democrats and Republicans. Many opposed to the Court-packing plan of 1937 believed Corcoran to be its originator. In fact he was not, but merely assisted Roosevelt in the campaign to win support.

Before the outcry over the Court plan had diminished, Corcoran was embroiled in more controversy. He was a major force behind Roosevelt's attempt to unseat non–New Deal Democrats in the primary elections of 1938. In all but one of the contests the attempted purge failed, leaving Corcoran steeped in bad publicity. Corcoran was also held responsible for supporting economic policies of the second term that led to the Roosevelt recession, or as some called it, the Corcoran recession.

The most controversial role Corcoran assumed during the second term, however, was that of leading the "third termites" in their drive for Roosevelt's re-election in 1940. Corcoran managed the surreptitious campaign until Roosevelt publicly revealed himself as a candidate. By then Corcoran had fallen into such disfavor with conservative Washington politicos that he resigned his position with the RFC and took up residence in New York to campaign for Roosevelt out of the mainstream.

Roosevelt's reelection meant unemployment for the presidential aide, since by 1941 Corcoran was considered too serious a liability for an official government appointment. He entered the private practice of law, remained personally close to the president, and backed the early war effort through support of Claire Chennault and the Flying Tigers. Corcoran continued to practice law and to engage actively in both politics and the advising of Democratic presidents until his death in 1981.

The only in-depth study of Thomas Corcoran is Monica Lynne Niznik, "Thomas G. Corcoran: The Public Service of Franklin Roosevelt's 'Tommy the Cork'" (Ph.D. diss., University of Notre Dame, 1981; University Microfilms, Ann Arbor, Mich., no. 81–18582). Contemporary articles, such as Alva Johnson, "White House Tommy," *Saturday Evening Post* 210 (31 July 1937):5, and Blair Bolles, "Cohen and Corcoran: Brain Twins," *American Mercury* 44 (January 1938):38, are plentiful, but they suffer from the bias of the times and usually are narrow in focus. Information on Corcoran may also be found in monographs on specific New Deal topics, as in Ralph E. DeBedts, *The New Deal's S.E.C.* (New York: Columbia University Press, 1964).

MONICA L. NIZNIK

See also Cohen, Benjamin Victor

Coughlin, Charles Edward

(25 October 1891–27 October 1979)

Catholic priest, radio personality, and political dissident; prominent as an early ally and later antagonist of Franklin Roosevelt. Charles Coughlin was born to parents of Irish descent in Hamilton, Ontario, and from a very early age, he was surrounded by and immersed in the institutions of the Catholic church. He attended parish schools in Hamilton before moving on to a cloistered secondary school and college run by the Basilian Order. He remained with the order to

Father Charles E. Coughlin, "the Radio Priest," at the microphone. (Religious News Service Photo.)

train for the priesthood and was ordained in 1916. After teaching in Basilian schools in Canada for seven years, he moved to Michigan in 1923 and began work as a parish priest. Three years later, he was assigned to a new parish in the Detroit suburb of Royal Oak.

Coughlin's early months in Royal Oak were troubled by harassment from the local Ku Klux Klan and by the financial insolvency of his new Shrine of the Little Flower; and in October 1926, he arranged with a local radio station to broadcast one of his Sunday sermons in an effort to win sympathy and publicity for his parish. The warm public response encouraged him to continue his broadcasts, and by 1930 he had developed a phenomenal popularity. His weekly Sunday discourse ("The Golden Hour of the Little Flower") was being broadcast over the CBS network, and his magnetic radio personality was attracting an audience estimated to be as high as 40 million.

It was at about that time, with economic conditions rapidly worsening (in Detroit more quickly than elsewhere), that Coughlin began to turn to political subjects. At first, he focused primarily on denunciations of communism. Gradually, however, he came to attack as well the "predatory capitalists" whose greed and corruption he considered the spawning ground for revolution. In particular, he criticized the financial power of private bankers and the "tyranny of the gold standard." Over the next several years, he would wage campaigns for abandonment of the gold standard, the remonetization of silver, the nationalization of all banking and currency, and other schemes for inflation and financial reform.

In 1932, he began a relationship with Franklin Roosevelt that would continue for more than a decade. Coughlin refrained from openly endorsing Roosevelt's candidacy, but he gave every possible public indication of his support for the Democrat. After Roosevelt's victory, Coughlin attempted to position himself to play a major role in the new administration. The president and his advisers tolerated Coughlin at first, but his presumptuous boasting about (and exaggeration of) his relationship with the administration finally became too embarrassing for the White House to bear. By 1934 the president was beginning to distance himself from the priest.

There followed nearly two years of agonized reappraisals by Coughlin of his relationship with Roosevelt. At times, he affirmed in ringing terms his faith in the New Deal; at other moments, he denounced the administration stridently for its connections with Wall Street and the "international bankers" and for its failure to "drive the moneychangers from the temple." In 1935, he created a new organization, the National Union for Social Justice, to work for the election of legislators and the passage of legislation sympathetic to Coughlin's financial goals. Membership in this "people's lobby" was large and national in scope, but the union lacked any real organizational substance. Its attitude toward the president was ambiguous. Coughlin tried at times to ally himself with emerging labor organizations (particularly in the automobile industry) and with the movements of other dissident leaders (especially that of Huey Long). But his own vanity was such that he could not tolerate the prospect of sharing authority or public recognition with others, and such alliances almost invariably collapsed.

In the spring of 1936, Coughlin grudgingly recognized that his relationship with the New Deal had deteriorated beyond repair, and he set out, finally, to establish a third party of his own—in association with a motley collection of other dissidents, among them Francis Townsend, the pension crusader, and Gerald L. K. Smith, an erratic associate of the late Huey Long. The result of his efforts, the Union party, nominated North Dakota congressman William Lemke for the presidency, and Coughlin pledged to deliver 9 million votes to the ticket or retire from public life. When Lemke polled fewer than 1 million votes in the 1936 election, Coughlin announced the end of his radio career. But early in 1937, he returned to the airwaves.

The remainder of his public career consisted of a pathetic decline into bigotry and hysteria. By now vitriolic in his hatred of Franklin Roosevelt, he became increasingly reactionary in his sermons, denouncing the New Deal as a Communist conspiracy and the president as a dangerous dictator. Early in 1938, a new element appeared in his public speeches (and in the pages of his newspaper, *Social Justice*): a virulent anti-Semitism, of which there had been only fleeting signs in earlier years. At about the same time, he began to express cautious admiration for the fascist regimes of Adolf Hitler and Benito Mussolini. These excesses, along with rapidly declining public support, helped lead to the cessation of Coughlin's radio broadcasts in 1940. Early in 1942, in the aftermath of Pearl Harbor, his newspaper was banned from the mails, and Coughlin acceded to orders from his bishop to cease all political activities. For the next twenty-four years, he tended to his parish duties in Royal Oak and, after 1966, lived in retirement in a nearby suburb, where he died of a heart attack in 1979.

Coughlin's radio sermons were published by his own Radio League of the Little Flower annually from 1931 to 1936, after which they were reprinted weekly in his newspaper, *Social Justice*. There are two serious biographies, neither definitive: Charles J. Tull, *Father Coughlin and the New Deal* (Syracuse: Syracuse University Press, 1965) and Sheldon Marcus, *Father Coughlin: The Tumultuous Life of the Priest of the Little Flower* (Boston: Little, Brown, 1973). Alan Brinkley, *Voices of Protest: Huey Long, Father Coughlin, and the Great Depression* (New York: Knopf, 1982) chronicles Coughlin's ascent to prominence. David Bennett, *Demagogues in the Depression: American Radicals and the Union Party, 1932–1936* (New Brunswick, N.J.: Rutgers University Press, 1969) is a history of the origins and denouement of the Union party.

ALAN BRINKLEY

See also Catholics; Democratic Party; Union Party

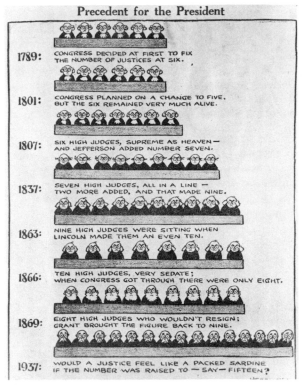

(A 1937 copyright cartoon by Herblock.)

Court-Packing Plan

In a message to Congress on 5 February 1937, Franklin D. Roosevelt recommended that if a federal judge who had served at least ten years waited more than six months after his seventieth birthday to resign or retire, the president could add a new judge to the bench. He could appoint as many as six new justices to the Supreme Court and forty-four new judges to the lower federal tribunals. Though Roosevelt claimed that he sought only to improve the efficiency of the courts by eliminating the problem of crowded federal dockets brought on by insufficient and superannuated personnel, critics accused him of seeking to remake the judiciary in order to ensure approval of New Deal laws. In the very first week they fastened on his proposal the pejorative name by which it has been known ever since—the Court-packing plan.

FDR's proposal sent shock waves through the nation, not only because of the boldness of the scheme, but because it came with almost no forewarning. To be sure, in 1935 the president had denounced the Court's "horse-and-buggy" definition of interstate commerce, and in 1936 he had charged the Court with creating "a 'no-man's-land' where no Government—State or Federal—can function." But he had not said a word about the Court in the 1936 campaign, and until the morning of 5 February not one of his congressional leaders nor any member of his cabinet save for Attorney General Homer Cummings, the chief architect of the plan, knew anything about the proposal.

Yet the crisis had been building for a long time. From the outset, the "Four Horsemen" (Pierce Butler, James McReynolds, George Sutherland, and Willis Van Devanter) had shown themselves to be adamantly hostile to New Deal emergency legislation, and in the thirteen-month period beginning in May 1935 they were joined by Owen Roberts and, not infrequently, Chief Justice Charles Evans Hughes, giving the elements hostile to the expansion of the authority of the national government a sure majority of at least 5–4 and often greater. During these months the Court struck down more acts of Congress—including the foundation stones of the early New Deal, the National Industrial Recovery Act and the Agricultural Adjustment Act—than in any such period in history.

Roosevelt believed he had no choice but to act. The Court's interpretations of the commerce clause and the taxing power indicated that it was prepared to invalidate much of the rest of the New Deal when statutes such as the Social Security Act and the National Labor Relations Act (the Wagner Act) reached it in 1937. Still worse, the president, despite his huge mandate in 1936, was inhibited from submitting new legislative proposals out of fear that they, too, would be declared unconstitutional. Though this Court was the oldest in history, not one of the justices had left the bench in all of FDR's first term, a most unusual development. It did not seem advisable for the president to rely either on the hope that a vacancy would occur or on the slow process of constitutional amendment, especially since vested interests might well block ratification of any proposed amendment.

Though the announcement of the Court-packing plan incited an angry outburst of protest, most observers agreed that the legislation was likely to be enacted, chiefly because Roosevelt had carried huge Democratic majorities in Congress in with him in 1936. Even opponents acknowledged that party discipline would get the bill through the House with votes to spare, and prospects looked almost as good in the Senate where the Republicans were reduced to only sixteen seats. At the end of March 1937, *Time* wrote, "Last week the staunchest foes of the President's Plan were privately conceding that, if he chose to whip it through, the necessary votes were already in his pockets." Doubtful Democratic senators could not justify voting against it so long as the Court continued to eradicate New Deal laws.

It required a series of actions by the Court itself to cut the ground out from under FDR's proposition. In testimony before the Senate Judiciary Committee, the chief justice demolished Roosevelt's claim that the Court was behind in its work. More important, in a series of decisions from late March through May, the Court embarked on a new course by unexpectedly upholding both the Wagner Act and the Social Security law, as well as a state minimum wage statute that closely resembled one it had struck down only a few months before. Most of the decisions came by a 5–4 vote with both Roberts and Hughes abandoning the conservatives. In May, too, one of the Four Horsemen, Justice Van Devanter, announced he was retiring from the bench, thereby giving the president the possibility of a 6–3 majority. This set of developments, especially Roberts's about-face, doomed the bill. "A switch in time," it was said, "saved nine."

But the fight was not over yet. The president did not want to accept defeat, even if clothed in victory. Moreover, he could not be sure that Roberts's conversion was permanent, and he could not take full advantage of the Van Devanter vacancy because it had been reserved for the sixty-five-year-old majority leader, Joseph T. Robinson, who, though loyal to FDR's programs, was fundamentally a conservative. So Roosevelt decided to continue the struggle by promoting a slightly modified version of the original bill. It authorized him to appoint an additional justice for each member of the Court who was seventy-five; no more than one could be named in any calendar year. Since the president would be able to appoint three justices by 1 January 1938—one to the Van Devanter slot, one for 1937, one for 1938—he lost very little in this compromise.

On 6 July 1937, the Supreme Court controversy finally reached the floor of the Senate, with the opposition forced to acknowledge that, despite all that had happened, including the switch of the Court, Roosevelt had a majority for the revised legislation. The slim margin for the measure depended, though, on personal ties that bound certain senators to the majority leader. When at the end of the first week of acrimonious debate the Senate learned the shocking news that Robinson had died of a heart attack, all hope for the proposal vanished. On 22 July, 168 days after it was first introduced, the bill was sent to committee from which it never emerged.

Though this was the worst defeat Franklin Roosevelt had ever sustained, he claimed that he had lost the battle but won the war. In truth, he lost more than a battle, for this setback strengthened an emerging bipartisan conservative coalition and helped bring the creative period of the New Deal to an end. But in another sense the president was right. The changed attitude of the Court in the spring of 1937 proved to be permanent, for the Court validated every New Deal law that came before it.

Roosevelt, denied the opportunity to make any appointments to the Supreme Court in his first term, was able before he was through to name eight justices and elevate Harlan Fiske Stone to the chief justiceship. This new Court—the Roosevelt Court as it was called—took so broad a view of the commerce and taxing powers that scholars speak of the Constitutional Revolution of 1937, for since that time the Court has not struck down a single significant piece of social legislation. Of all the many consequences of FDR's Court-packing endeavor, by far the most significant was the legitimization of the twentieth-century state.

The standard works on the Court crisis are Joseph Alsop and Turner Catledge, *The 168 Days* (Garden City, N.Y.: Doubleday, Doran, 1938), and Leonard Baker, *Back to Back* (New York: Macmillan, 1967). See, too, the essays by William E. Leuchtenburg: "The Origins of Franklin D. Roosevelt's 'Court-Packing' Plan," in *The Supreme Court*

Review: 1966, ed. Philip B. Kurland (Chicago: University of Chicago Press, 1966); "Franklin D. Roosevelt's Supreme Court 'Packing' Plan," in *Essays on the New Deal*, ed. Harold M. Hollingsworth and William F. Holmes (Austin: University of Texas Press, 1969); and "A Klansman Joins the Court: The Appointment of Hugo L. Black," *University of Chicago Law Review* 41 (Fall 1973):1–31.

WILLIAM E. LEUCHTENBURG

See also Cohen, Benjamin Victor; Congress, United States; Cummings, Homer Stillé; Hughes, Charles Evans; Interstate Commerce; Isolationism; New Deal; Office of the Presidency; Supreme Court of the United States

Cox, James Middleton

(31 March 1870–15 July 1957)

Newspaper publisher, governor of Ohio, and presidential candidate. James Cox was born in Jacksonburg, Ohio, the youngest in a farm family of seven, and earned his teaching certificate at age seventeen in Middletown, Ohio. After teaching for several years he began reporting for his brother-in-law's paper and moved to the *Cincinnati Enquirer* in 1892. After a brief stint in Washington as a private secretary to Congressman Paul Sorg, Cox returned to Ohio and purchased, on borrowed funds, the *Dayton Daily News*. There the short and stocky newspaper publisher developed a reputation for reform-minded journalism. In 1908 Cox was elected to Congress where he served without distinction until 1912 when he won election as the governor of Ohio. Cox served in this position for three terms, interrupted by electoral defeat in 1914, and established an impressive reform record. The 1920 Democratic National Convention in San Francisco nominated Cox for president on the forty-fourth ballot and one day later unanimously endorsed Franklin Roosevelt as his vice-presidential running mate.

The 1920 campaign was a disaster for Cox but not for Roosevelt. They bravely ran on Woodrow Wilson's record and his unpopular League of Nations proposal but were trounced by a nation tired of Wilsonian reform. Cox and Roosevelt toured the country, trying to upset Warren G. Harding's complacent, stay-at-home campaign. The Harding ticket won by a wide margin—404 to 127 in the electoral college—and Cox returned to his newspaper business. Roosevelt, in contrast, was flushed with the thrill of the campaign and attracted many followers in his first appearance on the national political scene.

In 1933 President Roosevelt appointed Cox as a delegate to the London World Monetary and Economic Conference and later offered a variety of other posts to his old friend and running mate. Cox, although loyal to the president, preferred to spend his later years with his newspapers and at his hunting cabin in Michigan.

There is no biography of Cox, but his autobiography, *Journal through My Years* (New York: Simon & Schuster, 1946), is a fine source. A readable but brief treatment is contained in Irving Stone, *They Also Ran* (Garden City, N.Y.: Doubleday & Co., 1943).

See also Election of 1920

Critics of the New Deal

See American Liberty League; Douglas, Lewis Williams; Federal Bureau of Investigation; Hoover, Herbert Clark; Lindbergh, Charles Augustus

Cummings, Homer Stillé

(30 April 1870–10 September 1956)

Attorney general during the Roosevelt administration. Homer Cummings was born in Chicago and educated at Yale, receiving his Ph.B. from its Sheffield School in 1891 and his L.L.B. in 1893. After law school he began practicing in Stamford, Connecticut, joining in a partnership with Charles D. Lockwood that lasted until Cummings moved to Washington in 1933. An active and lifelong Democrat, he began his political career by campaigning for William Jennings Bryan in 1896. He believed that government and law could be fashioned into tools for social justice and put this belief into practice in government service. He formulated a progressive plan for municipal services in Stamford as mayor in 1900, 1901, and 1904 and was state's attorney for Fairfield County from 1914 to 1924. In his final year in that post, he secured the dismissal of a very questionable murder charge against a vagrant, an effort that earned him the praise of the Wickersham Commission and the later celebrity of a film dramatization of the case, *Boomerang* (1947).

Cummings entered national politics as a Democratic committeeman from Connecticut in 1900, a position he kept until 1924. He narrowly lost contests for both the House and Senate, but came to prominence by delivering the keynote address at the 1920 convention and by trying to bind up the divisions at the 1924 convention. In 1932 he rallied numerous senators and congressmen to support Roosevelt's nomination, which he also furthered by helping to plan campaign tactics and by acting as floor manager at the Chicago convention. Originally slated by FDR to become governor-general of the Philippines, Cummings was selected to head the Justice Department when Thomas Walsh died in March of 1933. His six years as attorney general are among the most important and tumultuous in modern legal history. His concern with criminal justice led him to initiate the expansion of federal criminal jurisdiction and to support the buildup of the FBI. Decisions of the Supreme Court that struck down much New Deal legislation, however, dominated the first years of his tenure and greatly disturbed Cummings. After the 1936 election, Roosevelt instructed him to draft a proposal to add a judge for every one who did not retire at age seventy. The famous Court-packing proposal died under intense congressional pressure and was ultimately rendered unnecessary by a change in the direction of the Court. Cummings retired in 1939 and practiced law in Washington until his death in 1951.

No biography of Cummings has been written, and there are no recent sketches of his time as attorney general or of his relationship with FDR. A brief but dated essay introduces Carl Brent Swisher, ed., *Selected Papers of Homer Cummings* (New York: Charles Scribner's Sons, 1939). Interesting anecdotes and insights into the relationship between the president and the attorney general can be found in Frank Freidel, *Franklin Delano Roosevelt*, 4 vols. (Boston: Little, Brown & Co., 1952–73), Arthur Schlesinger, Jr., *The Age of Roosevelt*, 3 vols. (Boston: Houghton Mifflin Co., 1957–60), and James MacGregor Burns, *Roosevelt: The Lion and the Fox* (New York: Harcourt Brace Jovanovich, 1956).

See also Court-Packing Plan; Federal Bureau of Investigation

Currie, Lauchlin

(8 October 1902–)

The first economist to serve on the White House staff (1939–45). Lauchlin Currie was born in West Dublin, Nova Scotia, Canada. After undergraduate training at the London School of Economics (B.Sc., 1925) where John Maynard Keynes was an important influence on him, he came to the United States and earned a Ph.D. in economics at Harvard University (1931).

A vocal supporter of the early New Deal while teaching at Harvard (1927–34), Currie became the assistant director of the Division of Research and Statistics of the Federal Reserve Board in 1934. Here he was a leading proponent of Keynesian fiscal policy that eventually became central to Roosevelt's recovery and employment programs. In the midst of the 1937 recession, Currie pressed for additional deficit spending, particularly for housing and railroad reconstruction. Summarizing his views at this time, he has stated, "I was an advocate of relief and work relief, and feared only that by themselves they would not provide a sufficiently large deficit." His influence was reflected in the $3.75 billion Congress appropriated in June 1938 for relief and public works and the works financing bill of 1939. Roosevelt recognized Currie's value and appointed him to one of the six administrative assistant positions in the Executive Office of the President in 1939. He supported additional defense expenditures before the outbreak of World War II, headed the U.S. economic mission to China in 1941, and directed Lend-Lease aid to China as deputy administrator of the Foreign Economic Administration. Since leaving the White House in 1945, Currie has been a consultant to the government of Colombia and has lectured at American and Canadian universities.

Currie's contribution to New Deal economic policy is analyzed in Byrd L. Jones, "Lauchlin Currie, Pump Priming, and New Deal Fiscal Policy, 1934–1936," *History of Political Economy* 10 (Winter 1978):509–24, and his "Lauchlin Currie and the Causes of the 1937 Recession," *History of Political Economy* 12 (Fall 1980):303–15. Both articles include reprints of significant memoranda by Currie. Currie briefly reviews his work during the New Deal in his "Comments and Observations," *History of Political Economy* 10 (Winter 1978):541–48.

See also Banking; Chiang Kai-shek; Lend-Lease

D

Daniels, Josephus

(18 May 1862–15 January 1948)

Editor, southern reformer, cabinet member, and diplomat. Toward the end of his long life, Josephus Daniels liked to remind friends that he was probably the only man who had served under the three Democratic presidents from Grover Cleveland through Franklin Delano Roosevelt. He was too circumspect to note that he was also the only administrative superior FDR ever had. Daniels's role as chief clerk in the Interior Department in the second Cleveland administration hardly deserves mention, but his early support of the presidential aspirations of Woodrow Wilson through his newspaper, the *Raleigh* (North Carolina) *News and Observer,* as a member of the Democratic National Committee, and as director of publicity in the 1912 campaign brought him a seat in the Wilson cabinet as secretary of the navy. He was one of only three cabinet members to serve throughout both Wilson terms, and only Gideon Welles under presidents Lincoln and Johnson before him held the navy secretaryship for as long a time.

Daniels's first act as secretary-designate was to select a young progressive state senator and Wilson supporter from New York, Franklin D. Roosevelt, as his assistant secretary, the number two civilian position in the Navy Department. Two more different associates could hardly be imagined. Daniels was then slightly paunchy at fifty, Roosevelt trim and fit at thirty-one. Roosevelt's wealth and patrician background contrasted sharply with Daniels's humble yeoman origins, and his Groton and Harvard schooling far outclassed his chief's lone summer term at the University of North Carolina. An experienced yachtsman, Roosevelt loved the sea and ships and got on famously with the admirals. Secretary Daniels, on the other hand, came to Washington knowing next to nothing about the navy, and as a Jeffersonian Democrat, he instinctively distrusted the professional officer class. Yet Daniels's disarming country-bumpkin appearance concealed a shrewd mind and deft political skills that complemented Roosevelt's administrative abilities and made them a highly successful team, although it took the younger man some years to appreciate all his superior's qualities.

Daniels quickly demonstrated that he intended to be more than a figurehead navy chief. He instituted a number of personnel reforms, such as requiring sea service for promotion, and compulsory schooling for poorly educated sailors, improving the quality of the U.S. Naval Academy and opening it to enlisted men for the first time, strengthening the Naval War College, and reforming the naval prisons. He rejected a general staff system advocated by some naval officers, establishing instead the modern office of Chief of Naval Operations and a Secretary's Advisory Council of bureau chiefs. He insisted on competitive bidding on navy contracts and used navy facilities as a yardstick

Josephus Daniels, 1913. Artist: Dewitt Lockman. (National Portrait Gallery, Smithsonian Institution. Gift of Mrs. Ann Thornton.)

for manufacturing costs, eventually persuading Congress to authorize a navy-owned armor plate plant to end collusive bidding and ensure fair prices from the three private armor plate companies. After the navy shifted from coal to oil as its standard fuel during Daniels's administration, the secretary vigilantly guarded the naval oil reserves from threatened private exploitation. One of Daniels's innovations was the Navy Consulting Board, headed by the famous inventor Thomas A. Edison and composed of experts nominated by leading scientific and engineering societies, to advise on technical problems.

Some of Daniels's reforms were controversial, such as his orders abolishing the officers' wine mess and substituting left and right for port and starboard, and they made him unpopular with many naval officers and their civilian supporters in Congress and the influential Navy League. One wit remarked that at one fell swoop the secretary had jettisoned "larboard, starboard, and sideboard"! Although under Daniels the navy embarked on a major construction program in 1915, big-navy advocates distrusted the secretary as a pacifist and charged before and after the war that under his leadership the navy was inadequately prepared. Like most political hearings, the postwar congressional investigation of such charges by Adm. William S. Sims, the wartime commander of American naval forces in Europe, mostly confirmed preexisting views. Daniels's critics could not deny the navy's highly creditable performance in the war, however, and more important, the secretary always retained the respect and support of President Wilson. Assistant Secretary Roosevelt sometimes disagreed with his chief's policies and chafed at what he considered the secretary's indecision and inaction, occasionally giving quiet support to Daniels's enemies. Daniels was aware of but overlooked this disloyalty, and Roosevelt in time came to appreciate that the secretary's moves, although sometimes exasperatingly deliberate, usually succeeded because of his sound political instincts and careful groundwork. In retrospect, Daniels must be regarded as one of the most innovative and perhaps one of the few great navy secretaries.

During the Republican twenties, while Roosevelt recovered from his polio attack and began to rebuild a political career, he and Daniels, once again editing his North Carolina newspaper, kept in touch. Although they were never intimate friends, their memories of their eight years together in the Navy Department gave them an increasing regard and affection for each other. Daniels was an enthusiastic backer of Roosevelt's successful bid for the presidency in 1932. One of FDR's first acts after the election was to assure the older man he would always be "Chief" to Roosevelt and the president would continue to be "Franklin" to him, a familiarity accorded only a few old friends. Daniels hoped for a cabinet post in the new administration, perhaps the navy secretaryship again, but the president-elect had other plans for his cabinet. After declining to head a proposed new transportation agency, the seventy-year-old Daniels settled for a brand new career as ambassador to Mexico.

Initial Mexican reactions to Ambassador Daniels were decidedly cool, largely because of his key role in the bloody American occupation of Veracruz in 1914, but also because of his diplomatic inexperience and the fact that he knew not a word of Spanish. His chief redeeming merit, in the eyes of the Mexican government, was his presumed close friendship with the new American president. Yet by the end of his nearly nine years of service in Mexico City, Daniels had become one of the most popular and successful American diplomats ever to serve in that post. This was because as a lifelong progressive he warmly supported the social and economic goals of the Mexican Revolution, which, he regularly reminded his old friend in the White House, was Mexico's desperately needed version of the New Deal. Ambassador Daniels steadfastly remained an eloquent champion of neighborliness in the country whose reform policies gave President Roosevelt's Good Neighbor policy its severest test. When Mexico's land reform program affected American-owned lands, Daniels tried to distinguish between the rights of small resident American farmers and those of large absentee landowners, some of whom he regarded as exploitative and less deserving of their government's support. When Mexican president Lazaro Cardenas expropriated British and American oil holdings in 1938 after a long labor dispute Daniels believed the oil companies had mishandled, the ambassador almost single-handedly prevented a diplomatic break between the two countries, in sharp contrast with the nearly decade-long rupture in Anglo-Mexican relations that resulted from the dispute. Daniels's influence with President Roosevelt, in opposing the harder line advocated by Secretary of State Cordell Hull and Under Secretary Sumner Welles, ultimately paved the way for the settlement of all major Mexican-American differences in November 1941. This assured the United States of a friendly and cooperative neighbor to the south during World War II, unlike the hostile situation with which Daniels and Roosevelt had had to deal throughout the Wilson administration. By this time Daniels had returned home to care for his ailing wife. But once again, his association with Roosevelt had brought fortuitous results far beyond initial expectations.

Late in his life Daniels wrote five volumes of autobiography, of which three are important for an understanding of his long association with Roosevelt: *The Wilson Era: Years of Peace, The Wilson Era: Years of War,* and *Shirt-Sleeve Diplomat* (Chapel Hill: University of North Carolina Press, 1944–47). The most comprehensive biography of Daniels is Joseph L. Morrison, *Josephus Daniels Says . . . : An Editor's Political Odyssey from Bryan to Wilson and F.D.R., 1894–1913* and *Josephus Daniels: The Small-d Democrat* (Chapel Hill: University of North Carolina Press, 1962, 1966), of which the second volume deals with the Daniels-Roosevelt relationship. E. David Cronon's *Josephus Daniels in Mexico* (Madison: University of Wisconsin Press, 1960) is a scholarly treatment of Daniels's service as ambassador to Mexico in the 1930s. E. David Cronon, ed., *The Cabinet Diaries of Josephus Daniels, 1913–1921* (Lincoln: University of Nebraska Press, 1963) reproduces Daniels's scribbled diary entries during his service as Wilson's secretary of the navy.

The most detailed work on Daniels's navy service is Innis L. Jenkins, "Josephus Daniels and the Navy Department, 1913–1916" (Ph.D. diss., University of Maryland, 1960).

E. DAVID CRONON

See also Assistant Secretary of the Navy

Death of FDR

Franklin D. Roosevelt died of a cerebral hemorrhage on 12 April 1945 at 3:35 P.M. at the Little White House, his summer cottage at Warm Springs, Georgia.

The president was sitting for a watercolor by Elizabeth Shoumatoff, who had portrayed him previously. Also present in the room were two cousins, Laura Delano and Margaret Suckley, and a friend, Lucy Mercer Rutherfurd. At 1:00 P.M., according to Shoumatoff, the president said, "We've got just fifteen minutes more," which were widely reported to be his last words. Exactly fifteen minutes later, the president slumped in his chair, never to regain consciousness. Actually, during those minutes, Suckley heard him say quietly as he rubbed the back of his neck, "I have a terrific headache."

At the time of his death, the president was attended by Commander Howard G. Bruenn, a young navy heart specialist who had accompanied the president to Warm Springs, and Doctor James E. Paullin, an internist and former president of the American Medical Association, who had sped about seventy-five miles from his office in Atlanta, arriving only minutes before the death.

The state of the president's health had stirred speculation and controversy during his campaign for a fourth term in 1944 and the few months of his life thereafter. His personal physician, Rear Admiral Ross T. McIntire, surgeon general of the navy, was a specialist in eye, ear, nose, and throat ailments. FDR disdained health regimens and even conversation about health. Dr. McIntire's usual concentration on his patient's recurring sinus flare-ups pleased the president. Anna Roosevelt Boettiger, the president's daughter, who lived in the White House as his closest personal attendant during the last year of his life, told the author of her lack of confidence in McIntire's awareness of the president's general condition. After the president's death, McIntire's medical record on the president was sought by researchers, including Anna Roosevelt's subsequent husband, Dr. James A. Halsted, but the record disappeared from navy files and has never been found.

That void in available medical information enlarges the importance of an observation recorded by the funeral director, Fred Patterson of H. M. Patterson and Son, Atlanta: "On starting the embalming it was shortly discovered that he [FDR] had been a victim of arteriosclerosis which seemed to have seriously affected all of his arteries."

The years since FDR's death have not ended rumors that the president had been poisoned by Stalin's cook at the Yalta Conference, that he actually did not die at all, and so on. The most frequent "evidence" offered with these persistent rumors is that "nobody" saw the president's body because his casket was "never" opened for viewing. Actually, the casket lay in the Little White House during the morning after the death, according to Patterson, "with the lid half open and half of the inner lid closed." Fifteen years after the death, the maid of the Little White House, Lizzie McDuffie, told me, "They had the casket lying open in the living room near the president's bedroom door. There was a glass over him." Through that room that morning walked three relatives, several house and White House staff members, and military guards.

Such rumors are often a measure of the public's emotional shock brought on by the event. The shock began at 5:47 P.M. when the International News Service transmitted the shortest news bulletin in history:

Gathered before the White House, a grieving crowd watches President Roosevelt's funeral procession, 14 April 1945. (Courtesy FDR Library.)

Mourners in Washington, D.C., 14 April 1945. (Courtesy FDR Library.)

FLASH WASHN—FDR DEAD. Many people rushed to their radios after hearing a garbled hint of the news from children. That was because the flash broke into children's programs: "Front Page Farrell" on NBC, "Wilderness Road" on CBS, "Captain Midnight" on ABC, and "Tom Mix" on Mutual.

In New York City, the news poured and spread like a scalding fluid into the streets, into restaurants and bars, through subway trains jammed with rush-hour crowds. At Times Square, policemen on horse-back fought to keep crowds on the sidewalks so cars could get through.

Behind the front lines in Germany, where the U.S. Ninth Army was sweeping within fifty miles of Berlin and a hundred miles of the Russian forces at the Elbe River, Gen. Dwight D. Eisenhower, supreme commander of the Allied forces in Europe, had just finished a late-night conference in a trailer with generals George S. Patton and Omar Bradley and gone to bed. Patton and Bradley roused Eisenhower with the shocking news.

In London at about midnight, an aide brought the news to Prime Minister Winston Churchill, who was still in his study. Churchill was later to write, "I felt as if I had been struck a physical blow." In Moscow, at about 3:00 A.M., Foreign Minister Vyacheslav

Molotov, in an extraordinary gesture, visited Ambassador Averell W. Harriman at the American embassy to convey the shock of Marshal Joseph Stalin.

But before the news was given to the world at large, Vice-president Harry S Truman, relaxing at day's end with Speaker Sam Rayburn in a hideaway room of the Capitol, received a call summoning him to the White House. Minutes later in a second-floor sitting room, Mrs. Roosevelt told him the news. She then departed by plane for Warm Springs. Truman summoned the cabinet, sent for his wife and daughter, and prepared to take his oath as thirty-third president.

Late in the morning of 13 April, the president's funeral train departed Warm Springs for Washington, where a funeral service was to be held in the East Room of the White House, and thence to Hyde Park; burial services were on 15 April. On the first night of the journey, the train, moving no faster than thirty-five miles per hour, passed through the towns of the Carolinas and southern Virginia. Crowds stood for hours to catch a glimpse of the train going by, at most places whites segregated from blacks. Mrs. Roosevelt, peering from the president's beloved railroad car, the *Ferdinand Magellan*, was later to say: "I lay in my berth all night with the window shade up,

General Marshall and Admiral King arriving at Hyde Park, 15 April 1945, to pay last respects to their fallen commander in chief. (UPI/Bettmann Archive.)

looking out at the countryside he had loved and watching the faces of the people at stations, and even at the crossroads, who came to pay their last tribute all through the night. The only recollection I clearly have is thinking about 'The Lonesome Train,' the musical poem about Lincoln's death. I had always liked it so well—and now this was so much like it. I was truly surprised by the people along the way. I didn't expect that because I hadn't thought a thing about it. I never realized the full scope of the devotion to him until after he died—until that night and after. Later, I couldn't go into a subway in New York or a cab without people stopping me to say they missed the

The caisson bearing President Roosevelt's body rolls past an honor guard at Hyde Park, 15 April 1945. (Courtesy FDR Library.)

way the president used to talk to them. They'd say 'He used to talk to me about my government.' "

Bernard Asbell's book, *When F.D.R. Died* (New York: Holt, Rinehart & Winston, 1961), drew, of course, on the memoirs of leading New Deal figures and family members who were active in the Roosevelt circle at the time of his death. But certain anecdotal works by relatively minor figures were especially helpful, among them *Off the Record with F.D.R.: 1942–1945,* by William D. Hassett, a diary by FDR's staff assistant of secret wartime trips, including the final one to Warm Springs (New Brunswick, N.J.: Rutgers University Press, 1958); *F.D.R.: My Boss,* by Grace Tully, his private secretary (New York: Charles Scribner's Sons, 1949); *Thank You, Mr. President,* by A. Merriman Smith, one of only three news correspondents at Warm Springs in April 1945 (New York: Harper & Bros., 1946); and a memoir of a favorite Warm Springs personage, *Hi-Ya Neighbor,* by Ruth Stevens (New York: Tupper & Love, 1947).

BERNARD ASBELL

Declaration of War

On 7 December 1941, Japanese carrier–based bombers attacked the U.S. naval base at Pearl Harbor, Hawaii. On 8 December, President Roosevelt addressed a joint session of Congress, beginning with the famous words—"Yesterday, December 7, 1941—a date which will live in infamy—the United States of America was suddenly and deliberately attacked by naval and air forces of the Empire of Japan." The president called for congressional passage of a resolution recognizing "the state of war" which "has thus been thrust upon the United States." The Senate approved the resolution unanimously (82 to 0), the House by a vote of 388 to 1. The sole dissenter was Congresswoman Jeannette Rankin of Montana, who had also voted against the declaration of war on Germany in 1917. On 11 December, Germany and Italy—Japan's Tripartite Pact cosignatories—declared war on the United States. On 1 January 1942, the Declaration of the United Nations, drawn up at American initiative, was signed by all the major anti-Axis belligerents (numbering twenty-six at the time). This document, amounting to a formal alliance, reaffirmed the principles of the Atlantic Charter and pledged its signatories to press for total victory over the Axis powers and to avoid any separate peace or armistice agreements with the enemy.

America's entry into World War II was the culmination of a gradual process of increasing involvement in the struggle against Germany and Japan. Over the course of the previous two years, the United States had drifted from a position of neutrality in the conflict to a role as large-scale arms supplier of Britain, China, and the Soviet Union.

While insisting that his goal was to keep the country out of war, President Roosevelt was able to manipulate public opinion into supporting the step-by-step revision by Congress of the neutrality legislation that stood in the way of an all-out effort to supply Britain with war matériel. Congressional passage of the Lend-Lease bill in February 1941 provided for the shipment of massive quantities of war-related supplies to Britain as well as to other countries resisting German and Japanese aggression without any provision for repayment. In January-March 1941, staff talks between British and American officers led to agreement on a Europe-first military strategy in the event the United States became directly engaged in the world conflict. In September 1941, in response to the growing intensity of German submarine warfare, the decision was made to provide American naval escorts halfway across the Atlantic for British convoys carrying Lend-Lease supplies. Following the *Greer* incident, Roosevelt announced a shoot-on-sight policy against German U-boats in the western Atlantic.

Similarly, on the Asian front, concern over Japan's expansionist policies had led Roosevelt to furnish Chiang Kai-shek's resistance forces in China with arms and to impose ever tighter limitations on the export of vital materials such as scrap iron and fuel oil to Japan. Japan's apparent intention of attacking the rubber- and oil-rich British and Dutch possessions in Southeast Asia led to intensive eleventh-hour negotiations between U.S. secretary of state Hull and Japanese ambassador Nomura during the fall of 1941. These talks ended with Japan's surprise attack on Pearl Harbor on 7 December.

Some critics have claimed that Roosevelt deliberately allowed the U.S. forces at Pearl Harbor to be surprised so as to galvanize American public opinion into uninhibited support for entry into the war. These charges appear to be unfounded. However, it does seem apparent that Roosevelt's foreign policy would eventually have led to American involvement in the war in any case. The circumstances under which the entry was finally made happened to be particularly conducive to the creation of wholehearted public backing for the war effort.

Detailed accounts of the background to and consequences of America's entry into World War II can be found in Robert Dallek, *Franklin D. Roosevelt and American Foreign Policy, 1932–1945* (New York: Oxford University Press, 1979); Robert A. Divine, *The Reluctant Belligerent* (New York: Wiley, 1979); and Arnold A. Offner, *The Origins of the Second World War* (New York: Praeger, 1975). For the text of Roosevelt's speech before Congress of 8 December 1941, see Samuel I. Rosenman, ed., *The Public Papers and Addresses of Franklin D. Roosevelt*, 13 vols. (New York: Harper & Bros., 1938–50). The original reading copy of the speech, believed lost for forty-three years, was discovered misplaced in the Senate archives in 1984 (see *New York Times*, 2 April 1984).

See also Isolationism; World War II

Deficit Spending

See Fiscal Policy; Great Depression; New Deal; Recession of 1937–38; Temporary National Economic Committee

de Gaulle, Charles

(22 November 1890–9 November 1970)

Leader of the Free French forces during World War II. A graduate of Saint-Cyr military academy, Charles André Joseph Marie de Gaulle served with distinction in World War I. During the interwar period, he gained visibility by his strategic writings, in which he pleaded for mobile strike forces. Soon after World War II broke out, de Gaulle became Premier Paul Reynaud's under secretary of state for national defense. He opposed France's armistice with Germany and, on 16 July 1940, escaped to London, where he organized the Free French movement and attracted several French colonies to his cause.

Roosevelt would not recognize de Gaulle's Free French. Nor would he invite them to sign the United Nations Declaration of 1 January 1942. Instead he opted for maintaining diplomatic relations with Henri Philippe Pétain's Vichy regime, doing so to prevent Vichy's ships and strategic overseas territory from falling into Hitler's hands. Furthermore, Roosevelt would not give de Gaulle the date of, much less invite him to participate in, the Allied landings in North Africa. The president noted previous fighting between the Free French and Vichy forces at Dakar and Syria and feared a repetition. When the Allied commanding general, Dwight D. Eisenhower, turned political control of North Africa to Vichy military commander Admiral Jean-Louis Darlan, doing so to save lives and gain Dakar, de Gaulle was furious. The Darlan deal, he believed, not only revived a discredited Vichy regime; it was part of America's design for postwar hegemony.

Only with reluctance did de Gaulle attend the Casablanca Conference of January 1943. He complained to Churchill that he was being surrounded by American bayonets on French territory, called a plan for Anglo-American control of North Africa a violation of French sovereignty, and correctly sensed that Roosevelt envisioned a greatly reduced status for France after the war. At the initial meeting between the two men, several American armed police hid behind the curtain, ready to shoot if de Gaulle bodily assaulted the president. Roosevelt did secure de Gaulle's promise that he would cooperate with General Henri Giraud, whom Roosevelt was grooming as leader of French forces in Africa. In a much publicized photograph, de Gaulle is shown shaking hands with a man for whom he had the greatest contempt.

On the last day of the conference, Roosevelt signed the Anfa memorandum, by which the United States and Britain recognized Giraud as trustee of the French nation, through whom all Allied aid must be funneled. When, in February, Churchill learned of the document, he insisted upon amending it to include de Gaulle. Roosevelt, upon returning to the United States, mocked de Gaulle as the reincarnation of Joan of Arc and Clemenceau. Unfortunately, the word got back to the French leader.

When, in the late spring of 1943, Roosevelt heard that de Gaulle wanted to command all French

At the Allies' grand strategy conference at Casablanca in January 1943, President Roosevelt and Prime Minister Churchill meet with General Giraud (left of Roosevelt) and

General de Gaulle (left of Churchill), unfriendly rivals for leadership of the Free French. (National Archives.)

forces, he threatened to send troops and naval vessels to Dakar, doing so to prevent de Gaulle's possible rule there. Although by November 1943 de Gaulle had forced Giraud out of the all-important French Committee of National Liberation, it was only 11 July 1944, a month after D-Day, that Roosevelt granted de Gaulle's committee any real recognition, and this was limited to "temporary *de facto* authority for civil administration in France." Complete military authority remained with Eisenhower. De Gaulle's visit to Washington that same month produced superficial cordiality, though Roosevelt privately said that de Gaulle's movement would "crumble." In March 1945, Roosevelt responded affirmatively to de Gaulle's plea for military aid to Indochina. Yet Roosevelt vetoed Stalin's suggestion of inviting de Gaulle to a summit meeting, spoke disparagingly of him at Yalta, and turned down de Gaulle's invitation to meet with him in Paris. (De Gaulle similarly refused Roosevelt's invitation to come to Algiers.) At the time of Roosevelt's death, the animosity between the two men had never been greater.

Although Roosevelt was cordial in face-to-face contacts with de Gaulle, in private he made no secret of his antipathy. At one point the president referred to de Gaulle as "that 'jackenape,' " at another he said of the French leader, "He's a nut." In a communiqué to Churchill dated 17 June 1943, he called de Gaulle "a very dangerous threat to us," doing so in the belief that "he has proven to be unreliable, uncooperative, and disloyal to both our Governments." In turn, de Gaulle's hostility toward Roosevelt, although involving personal clashes, to be sure, was fundamentally based on what he saw as the president's continual undermining of him, and to him this meant disparaging the nobility of France. Roosevelt's antipathy was the more complex, and historian Arthur Layton Funk notes several factors in it. Roosevelt saw de Gaulle as a leader without followers, claiming to represent—with no legitimacy—an exhausted, confused, and defeatist nation. To encourage de Gaulle would be to encourage dictatorship, class struggle, and civil war. De Gaulle's tactics and judgment were also at issue. Examples included his quarrels with Britain following the conquest of Syria and Lebanon; the Gestapo tactics of Colonel André de Wavrin Passy's Gaullist intelligence service; vindictive anti-American editorials in the Gaullist press; the ouster of Giraud; and France's insistence upon representation on the Allied Advisory Commission. Roosevelt also envisioned United Nations trusteeships over such French areas as Indochina and Dakar, American military control over some French bases, and the postwar disarming of France.

From 1944 to 1946, de Gaulle was president of France's provisional government. In 1958, he again became president and served in that office for ten years. His rule was marked by French recognition of Algerian independence, withdrawal of French troops from the North Atlantic Treaty Organization, and a veto on British entry into the Common Market.

Milton Viorst, *Hostile Allies: FDR and Charles de Gaulle* (New York: Macmillan Co., 1965), is sympathetic to de Gaulle, as is Dorothy Shipley White, *Seeds of Discord: De Gaulle, Free France and the Allies* (Syracuse: Syracuse University Press, 1964). Arthur Layton Funk, *Charles de Gaulle: The Crucial Years, 1943–1944* (Norman: University of Oklahoma Press, 1959), makes no case for either Roosevelt or de Gaulle, but sees the conflict as inevitable as a tragedy of Euripides. Significant memoirs include *The Complete War Memoirs of Charles de Gaulle*, trans. Jonathan Griffin and Richard Howard (New York: Simon & Schuster, 1955–60); Harold Macmillan, *The Blast of War, 1939–1945* (New York: Harper & Row, 1968); and Robert D. Murphy, *Diplomat among Warriors* (Garden City, N.Y.: Doubleday, 1964).

JUSTUS D. DOENECKE

See also Casablanca Conference; Churchill, Winston Leonard Spencer; Colonialism; Eisenhower, Dwight David; Foreign Policy; Mussolini, Benito, and Italy; Personal Diplomacy; Quebec Conferences; Spanish Civil War; Stimson, Henry L.; World War II; Yalta Conference

Democratic Party

By 1932, changes were long overdue for the Democrats. An enlarged electorate was less likely to support the Grand Old Party of Civil War memory, and this set the scene for realignment. A new generation of voters, less influenced by traditions of the last century or by the sectionalism of a more provincial and rural America, was being produced by the twin forces of urbanization and immigration. As Samuel Lubell pointed out in his influential study, *The Future of American Politics*, over 6.5 million people left the nation's farms and hills between 1920 and 1930, thereby entering "the cities at roughly the same time that the children of the immigrants were growing up and bestirring themselves. The human potential for a revolutionary change had thus been brought together in our larger cities when the economic skies caved in." Out of all this emerged a new kind of Democratic party, still a "big tent," but one with clearer ideological goals.

That realignment was shaped by the impact of Roosevelt and his New Deal. Until then, the party had suffered from what Rexford Guy Tugwell has called the "poverty of ideas which only the depression seemed to relieve." Tied to the county courthouses of the South and to the big-city machines of the urban North, the Democrats were wedded far more to state organizations than to Washington, the result of a federal sytem that virtually institutionalized stability and inhibited structural modifications. Ideology was just about irrelevant. Democrats were on every side of every issue, whether it concerned tariffs, currency, internationalism, or booze. "I'm not a member of any organized political party" was the line made famous by Will Rogers. "I'm a Democrat." Positions on just about any given issue of the day were determined far more by geography and religion than by social and economic class.

The South, with the exception of some isolated counties in the interior highlands, maintained the solid Democratic allegiance that dated back to the end of post–Civil War Reconstruction. Whether for peace or war, President Woodrow Wilson could turn to Dixie for his most ardent support. Wilson's strength was indeed firmest in the rural South. Democrats were the party of both Protestant fundamentalism and the Ku Klux Klan, which had been revived in 1915 and had become more prominent by the 1920s. Not surprisingly, then, they were as likely to champion the cause of Prohibition as local political oligarchies. Centering around the county seats and the state houses, Democrats were the power brokers of a region where "popular democracy" still meant representation by a tiny controllable fraction of the white vote. A substantially commercial, industrial society remained in the future. Most of the region lacked even the presence of a local Republican organization.

Outside the South, the Democratic party had become the party of growing urban political machines that had long since learned to organize the new industrial workers who had arrived in America since the middle of the nineteenth century. Often, as in the cases of the political organization masterminded by Martin Lomasney in Boston or Tammany Hall in New York, the machines were ethnic and working class, enlisting the loyalties of recent Irish immigrants and, later, newcomers from southern and eastern Europe. At best, they had only tenuous ties to what was really a fragile national party structure. Such groups were largely unenthusiastic about identifying their interests with farmers and others in the South and West who rallied behind the Democratic absorption of William Jennings Bryan and his Populists. Their inevitable clash reached a significant highlight during the 103-ballot Democratic National Convention in New York's Madison Square Garden. That dramatic session in 1924 betrayed the party's divisions over such issues as Prohibition and the KKK, and exhausted the delegates, who settled for the presidential candidacy of a conservative Wall Street lawyer, John W. Davis.

Four years later, meeting at Houston, Democrats nominated Al Smith. Even more profoundly than had Prohibition, Smith's Roman Catholicism effectively divided the party into sectarian groups. Five southern states were sufficiently rebellious to give their electoral votes to the Republican candidacy of Herbert Hoover, their first such defection from the Democrats since Reconstruction.

David Burner has pointed out that "the claims of the party that symbolized regional tradition and white supremacy clashed for a moment with the claims of Protestant Anglo-Saxonism." In the North, a large outpouring of first- and second-generation urban voters identified with the candidate from the "sidewalks of New York," whose actual campaign was hardly less conservative than Hoover's. Most important in the long run, however, was a strengthening of the Democratic urban immigrant machines.

Roosevelt's 1932 Great Depression campaign against Hoover, then, largely hoped to unite anti-Smith Democrats with the party's power bases above the Mason-Dixon line. The seeds of what was to come were planted during that battle against incumbent Hoover, but they were hard to find. At least when Roosevelt addressed the Commonwealth Club in San Francisco, he acknowledged that changes in American society might require a more active federal government. Generally, though, once he had defeated his rivals for the Democratic nomination, he relied on such traditional themes as a lower tariff and a balanced national budget, and joined his party's new majority by favoring repeal of Prohibition. He was, he said, pleading "not for class control but for a true concert of interests." His acceptance speech comments about pruning governmental expenditures were sufficiently conservative to be repeated with approval by Ronald Reagan forty-eight years later. That address, delivered before the convention on 2 July, was also memorable for Roosevelt's declaration of "a new deal for the American people." Certainly, change seemed overdue, but precisely what change that would be was rather vague, almost as elusive as the quality of the candidate himself. Elmer Davis, the writer and radio news commentator who later headed Roosevelt's Office of War Information, considered FDR "the man who would probably make the weakest President of the dozen aspirants." Even more memorable was the observation made by journalist Walter Lippmann during the 1932 campaign: "Franklin D. Roosevelt is no crusader. He is no tribune of the people. He is no enemy of entrenched privilege. He is a pleasant man who, without any important qualifications for the office, would very much like to be President."

Such critics, of course, underestimated Roosevelt's political acumen. Even if he could have known precisely what the New Deal would and could do to effectuate relief, recovery, and reform (and he could not have), that campaign was no time for such specifics. Getting elected was far more important and utilizing the existing party structure far more essential. Thanks not only to the party's divisions but to the two-thirds requirement for the nomination, in effect for the last time during the 1932 convention, he had not become the Democratic candidate until House Speaker John Garner backed him on the fourth ballot. Garner, who made the outcome possible by releasing his delegates to avoid a deadlocked convention, became Roosevelt's vice-presidential candidate. FDR then took charge of the party's national organization, and he did so by securing the election as chairman of the Democratic National Committee a man who had served him so well in New York State, James A. Farley.

As governor, FDR had acquired just enough reputation as a reformer to be regarded warily by most local party leaders. Mayor James Michael Curley of Boston was the only well-known urban machine leader to overcome such reservations and give the candidate full-hearted support, switching from the 1928 hero, Al Smith. Local resistance enhanced the value of Farley's ability to organize the campaign on behalf of the party's national candidate. The most persuasive factor among party regulars was their confidence in Roosevelt's victory.

Roosevelt's approach to party organization was similar to his approach to the private enterprise system: he was no revolutionary in either case. But he was an activist, using the powers of the presidency for firm party leadership. "Roosevelt came as close as any man could in trying to combine the roles of Washington and Houdini," Robert A. Rutland has written. The process involved catering to the needs of all Democratic machine leaders, wooing those urban bosses who had most resisted his candidacy in the first place, and pleasing them through the expenditure of the federal largess obtained through Congress. Farley turned the traditional Jefferson-Jackson Day dinners into major fund-raising affairs. Held regionally as well as in Washington, they gathered in as many as 250,000 Democrats, some of whom paid as much as a thousand dollars for their dinners to replenish the war chests of state and local party committees.

From Capitol Hill, the New Deal extracted a flood of emergency social and economic legislation. Early efforts at forging a coalition with business interests, most notably via the short-lived National Industrial Recovery Administration, soon gave way before a greater accommodation for labor and those rendered most helpless by the Great Depression.

The first thunder came from the Right, a vehement response to such New Deal initiatives as the establishment of the Securities and Exchange Commission. Al Smith and his former campaign manager, millionaire John Raskob, joined other conservative Democrats in forming the American Liberty League. Formed before the 1934 congressional elections, the league was dominated by General Motors and Du Pont, which provoked Farley to scoff that it should be called the American Cellophane League because "first, it's a Du Pont product and second, you can see right through it." The league had just about run its course by the next presidential election, but in the process, it attracted anti–New Dealers of both parties. Smith remained a vigorous foe of his ex-colleague from New York. Repeatedly, he warned about the New Deal's "trend toward communism."

Such objections were overwhelmingly repudiated by the vote of confidence given during the congressional elections of 1934, which must still be regarded as the greatest mid-term triumph for an administration in power. Democrats overwhelmed the opposition in each house, gaining nineteen in the lower chamber and raising the Senate majority by nine for a total of sixty-nine of the ninety-six seats. Little wonder that the administration was encouraged to press ahead with its reform program.

But, from another direction, it was also pushed. In California, novelist-muckraker Upton Sinclair's End Poverty in California (EPIC) campaign had contested economic fundamentalism against an array of powerful groups, including oil, public utility, railroad, and newspaper interests. Sinclair won the Democratic primary handily. Ignored by the White House and excoriated by vehement opposition, he only narrowly lost to his Republican opponent. Sinclair might even have won if there had been a two-way race, but the EPIC campaign nevertheless emphasized the discontent of the impoverished. From California, also, came the proposal by Dr. Francis Townsend to give each American over the age of sixty two hundred dollars per month with the stipulation that that sum be spent during the next thirty days. Townsend clubs proliferated not only in California but throughout the country. Huey Long's Share Our Wealth program catapulted the Louisiana senator to national prominence and helped to push the New Deal leftward. Long and Townsend together constituted an especially strong manifestation of national protest. A Democratic National Committee survey indicated that Long himself could attract between 3 and 4 million votes in 1936 as a third-part candidate, and that included the potential for attracting 100,000 Democratic voters in New York State.

By 1935, the radio priest of Royal Oak, Michigan, Father Charles Coughlin, had become a vigorous opponent of the New Deal, denouncing the administration as the pawns of "international bankers." Coughlin's denunciation of Roosevelt's monetary policies gradually became enormously influential in Roman Catholic working-class districts, and his increasingly strident anti-Semitism exacerbated ethnic tensions during that period of economic hardship. Facing these ambitious rivals who were gathering mass followings among the discontented, Roosevelt energized the New Deal in 1935 with a change of direction. "If there was to be leadership given to the millions who still lacked economic security," Otis Graham has written, "FDR was determined to give it."

Roosevelt's reelection in 1936 followed that reorientation of the New Deal, which no longer claimed or appeared to want big business as part of the coalition. Scholars were quick to label the new realignment as FDR's second New Deal. The validity of that perception is less significant than the reality of what the voters saw that year. Voting by class divisions, ethnic and interest groups clearly supplanted the sectional character of the pre–New Deal party. Urban workers were becoming more unionized than ever. Overwhelmingly first- and second-generation non-Protestants—largely Jewish and Catholic—they joined with beleagured farmers as FDR's most loyal supporters. In what "exhibited both the quantitative and qualitative characterization of a critical election," Roosevelt solidified his revamped Democrats.

Aided by an electorate that had grown by nearly 6 million since 1932 and with black voting becoming mainly Democratic for the first time, the outcome confirmed the party's new preeminence in American politics. The outcome also reaffirmed the two-party system and the basic consensus supporting American capitalism.

The results showed the increasing importance of northern cities over the South, and the South lost out in another way: the durable two-thirds rule that governed presidential nominations at Democratic conventions. Combined with the party's divisive elements, the rule had been responsible for such prolonged agonies as the 1924 convention. With a sweetener in the form of increased representation at future conventions to states carried by the Democrats, the backers of repeal triumphed.

But the great victory did not spare Roosevelt from the realities of Democratic disunity. The fierce resistance to his 1937 plan to enlarge the Supreme Court provided leverage for his natural opponents, especially many southern Democrats. Other conservatives, encouraged by his new political vulnerability, fell behind newspaper publisher Frank E. Gannett and Amos Pinchot of the prominent Progressive family and formed the National Committee to Uphold Constitutional Government. Gannett hoped for "the creation of a new party which can have loftier ideals and finer objectives than either of the parties today." The most dramatic defiance, however, came during the congressional elections of 1938 when the president failed to "purge" all but one of the anti–New Deal Democrats he had earmarked for defeat. His New Deal had substantially realigned the parties, but he was forced to live with the incompleteness of that realignment: many Democrats, most but not all of them southerners, were not liberals and thought the New Deal had gone too far.

The 1940 campaign certainly marked the start of the conversion of the president from "Dr. New Deal" to "Dr. Win-the-War." Taking Secretary of Agriculture Henry A. Wallace as his running mate in place of Garner, Roosevelt's third nomination was virtually pro forma. The same threat of war that enabled him to break with tradition also led the Republicans to bypass its isolationists and select a political novice, Wendell Willkie. Willkie, who had opposed New Deal regulations as head of the Commonwealth and Southern electrical power holding company, gave FDR the toughest battle he had yet faced.

In that election year, Roosevelt had proceeded with the destroyers-for-bases deal with Great Britain and the peacetime draft. Inevitably, Willkie attempted to place FDR on the defensive about whether the United States would intervene in the European war. The antiwar vote had no other place to go, and so the election of 1940 saw the start of an exodus from the Democratic party by antiwar ethnic groups. Roosevelt's losses were greatest among voters of German and Italian ancestry, with some Irish Catholic defections also observable. Roosevelt retained the bulk of his coalition and, with special emphasis, those most fearful about Hitler. Although closer than his earlier victories, it was still comfortable. His electoral vote margin was 449–82 and he won 55 percent of the popular vote.

FDR's fourth nomination came in 1944, while the war was still being fought. It was less of a contest than four years earlier: the third-term tradition had been broken and there was a national emergency. An ominous indication that a conservative tide was running came with the election of the Seventy-eighth

Congress in 1942. Republican congressional candidates outpolled Democrats by 1.2 million; that had not happened since 1928, and it translated into a fifty-seat gain in the House, and nine additional senators.

Still, with the presidency itself, the admonition about not "changing horses in the middle of the stream" was especially persuasive while the Axis powers were yet to be defeated. As in 1940, the convention was held in Chicago, and the most significant decision there involved dumping Wallace from the vice-presidency and replacing him with Senator Harry S Truman of Missouri. Wallace was undoubtedly jettisoned to mollify the South, conservatives, and others who objected to his liberalism. Truman, the Border State man with his reputation enhanced by his wartime chairmanship of a committee investigating the national defense program, was the "perfect" compromise candidate. He was as acceptable to labor as to conservatives.

Opposing Roosevelt was Republican governor Thomas E. Dewey of New York. Only forty-four, Dewey had become the GOP candidate on the strength of his national reputation as a district attorney. The election was the closest of FDR's four. Roosevelt had become increasingly vulnerable for several reasons: there were reservations about his health; many of his voters were overseas and couldn't vote; and there was widespread anxiety, especially among the Polish-American community, about the Soviet presence in eastern Europe after their westward march into Germany. The president emerged with a 3.6 million popular margin and 432 electoral votes to Dewey's 99. More important than his plurality at that moment, however, was the Democratic ability to reverse the congressional trend of two years earlier. They gained twenty House seats and kept their Senate majority.

FDR, of course, was dying during that final year, and the New Deal was shelved for the duration. The big question among administration liberals was whether reforms could resume after the war. At Soldiers Field in Chicago during the 1944 campaign, Roosevelt had pledged that the government would be responsible for providing 60 million jobs.

Although a Democratic president had reshaped American politics with a New Deal and wartime leadership that brought him three reelections to the White House, he had found his party more useful for nomination than for governing. Perhaps the most productive recent scholarship of the New Deal era has concerned the delicate relationships between the administration in Washington and party leaders at state and local levels. Scholars have found that, far from dealing urban political machines a "last hurrah," as suggested by the Edwin O'Connor novel, in such cities as Pittsburgh, Kansas City, Chicago, and Boston, local party organizations remained intact or were actually strengthened. Historians addressing themselves to the political limitations faced by the New Deal have demonstrated the obstacles created by the federal system. The national administration could not, for example, despite enormous power, simply manipulate the existing party organizations of the forty-eight states and their cities. In a city like Boston, for example, Mayor Curley's Democratic machine welcomed some New Deal programs but frustrated others. In Virginia, the Democratic oligarchy was staunchly conservative. There Senator Harry Byrd's machine turned against FDR early, and resisted implementation of National Recovery Administration and federal relief programs.

The South, in fact, was the great paradox. No region of the country received more New Deal largesse. Through farm assistance, relief, and such major programs as the Tennessee Valley Administration and rural electrification, substantial aid went to the region FDR called the nation's "poorhouse." As Georgia congressman Philip Landrum recalled in an 1973 interview, "Beginning with the Roosevelt era, we had a district which lent itself to federal supports more than many other districts. Quite mountainous [and with] a lot of timber, . . . it was a perfect setup for the U.S. forest service to come in . . . and people began to look with favor on the Federal Government. It was not the big monster that it has been characterized as in other areas. . . . And for a great number of years even up to now it's very difficult to get a concentrated Republican leadership in there." FDR came into close personal contact with the South and southerners through his Warm Springs Foundation in Georgia.

Nevertheless, as in Virginia, it was in the South where resistance was greatest, where, in fact, rebellion was sharpest. Not only Harry Byrd, but such legislators as Josiah Bailey of North Carolina, Carter Glass of Virginia, and even loyal Joseph T. Robinson of Arkansas, the Democratic Senate majority leader until his death in 1937, were representatives of the region's commercial and banking interests. Inevitably, FDR's programs threatened the South's advantage as a nonunion, low-wage area attractive to new industrial capital. As Frank Freidel has pointed out, the president's attempted purge of 1938 was an "attempt to liberalize the leadership of the party's Southern wing."

In common with other presidents, before and since, FDR toyed with the notion of a political realignment, if not an entirely new party. As early as 1942, and again in 1944, the he entertained the idea of joining with Wendell Willkie in forming a liberal coalition. Through Sam Rosenman, Roosevelt even floated to his formal rival a proposal for joining his ticket in 1944 as the vice-presidential candidate. Willkie, who died in October of that year, had even contemplated becoming mayor of New York City as a springboard for his leadership of a national third party. It remains of intriguing although uncertain significance that such Roosevelt successors as Eisenhower and Nixon became equally exasperated with the prevailing two-party alignment.

The long-term catalyst may be the legacy of Roosevelt himself. With varying degrees of fortune, his coalition persisted beyond the New Deal by many years. The Democratic party may not have been exactly what FDR wanted it to be and elements of the party always had doubts about him, but his death ended those tensions. Democrats regularly celebrate his memory at nominating conventions and on the campaign trail, as historian William Leuchtenburg has traced in his *In the Shadow of FDR*. Democrats such as Senator Ted Kennedy and House Majority Leader Thomas "Tip" O'Neill were outraged in 1982 when President Ronald Reagan, on FDR's hundredth birthday, implied that Roosevelt would now be a Republican. Whatever one thinks of this dispute, it may safely be said that the election of Franklin Roosevelt in 1932 led to changes that altered the American party system and the agenda for the balance of the century.

Basic introductions to the New Deal party system can be obtained, first, from the historical context supplied by Robert A. Rutland, *The Democrats from Jefferson to Carter* (Baton Rouge: Louisiana State University Press, 1979) and, more specifically, from Otis L. Graham, Jr.'s essay, "The Democratic Party, 1932–1942," in Arthur M. Schlesinger, Jr., *History of U.S. Political Parties* (New York: Chelsea House Publishers, 1973), 3:1939–2066. The best one-volume political account is still *Franklin D. Roosevelt and the New Deal, 1932–1940* by William E. Leuchtenburg (New York: Harper & Row, 1963). More detailed and more wide-ranging coverage is available in the two volumes by James MacGregor Burns, *Roosevelt: The Lion and the Fox* (New York: Harcourt, Brace & World, 1956) and *Roosevelt: The Soldier of Freedom, 1940–1945* (New York: Harcourt Brace Jovanovich, 1970). Major studies still in progress are the three-volumes already completed of *The Age of Roosevelt* by Arthur M. Schlesinger, Jr. (Boston: Houghton Mifflin, 1957–60), and the highly detailed four volumes by Frank Freidel, *FDR* (Boston: Little, Brown & Co., 1952–73). More recently, Leuchtenburg has supplied an insightful coda to FDR's influence, *In the Shadow of FDR: From Harry Truman to Ronald Reagan* (Ithaca, N.Y.: Cornell University Press, 1983). Of great value for an understanding of the Democratic party before the New Deal are David Burner, *The Politics of Provincialism: The Democratic Party in Transition, 1918–1932* (New York: Alfred A. Knopf, 1968) and Robert K. Murray, *The 103rd Ballot* (New York: Harper & Row, 1976). Also essential and, like the preceding, helpful for this essay, is Samuel Lubell, *The Future of American Politics*, 3d rev. ed. (New York: Harper Colophon Books, 1965). Two useful volumes by FDR politicos are Ed Flynn, *You're the Boss* (New York: Viking Press, 1947) and James A. Farley, *Jim Farley's Story: The Roosevelt Years* (New York: McGraw-Hill Book Co., 1948). Roosevelt's post-1940 relationship with Wendell Willkie and contemplation of a political realignment is discussed in Burns's second volume and, more recently and with additional details, in Steve Neal, *Dark Horse: A Biography of Wendell Willkie* (Garden City, N.Y.: Doubleday, 1984). Indispensable for an account of dissenters in the 1930s are Alan Brinkley, *Voices of Protest* (New York: Alfred A. Knopf, 1982) and T. Harry Williams, *Huey Long* (New York: Alfred A. Knopf, 1969). Enlightening and often stimulating views of the relationship between the national Democratic party and local politics can be found in the following works: Robert E. Burke, *Olson's New Deal for California* (Berkeley and Los Angeles: University of California Press, 1953); Lyle Dorsett, *The Pendergast Machine* (New York: Oxford University Press, 1968); J. Joseph Huthmacher, *Senator Robert Wagner and the Rise of Urban Liberalism*

(New York: Atheneum, 1968); James T. Patterson, *Congressional Conservatism and the New Deal* (Lexington: University of Kentucky Press, 1967) and *The New Deal and the States: Federalism in Transition* (Princeton: Princeton University Press, 1969); Bruce M. Stave, *The New Deal and the Last Hurrah: Pittsburgh Machine Politics* (Pittsburgh: University of Pittsburgh Press, 1970); Charles H. Trout, *Boston, the Great Depression, and the New Deal* (New York: Oxford University Press, 1977); and Roland Young, *Congressional Politics in the Second World War* (New York: Columbia University Press, 1956). In its literature, as in other ways, the South remains distinctive and attractive to scholars. One may consult the following in relationship to the party and the region during the New Deal: William D. Barnard, *Dixiecrats and Democrats: Alabama Politics, 1942–1950* (Tuscaloosa: University of Alabama Press, 1974); Ralph J. Bunche, *The Political Status of the Negro in the Age of FDR*, ed. Dewey W. Grantham (Chicago: University of Chicago Press, 1973); Robert A. Garson, *The Democratic Party and the Politics of Sectionalism, 1941–1948* (Baton Rouge: Louisiana State University Press, 1974); Alexander Heard, *A Two-Party South?* (Chapel Hill: University of North Carolina Press, 1952); Ronald L. Heinemann, *Depression and New Deal in Virginia: The Enduring Dominion* (Charlottesville: University Press of Virginia, 1983); V. O. Key, Jr., *Southern Politics* (New York: Alfred A. Knopf, 1950); William D. Miller, *Mr. Crump of Memphis* (Baton Rouge: Louisiana State University Press, 1964); George Brown Tindall, *The Disruption of the Solid South* (Athens: University of Georgia Press, 1972); and J. Harvie Wilkinson III, *Harry F. Byrd and the Changing Face of Virginia Politics, 1945–1966* (Charlottesville: University Press of Virginia, 1968).

HERBERT S. PARMET

See also Catholics; Congress, United States; Dewey, Thomas E.; Dewson, Mary W.; Election of 1910; Election of 1928; Election of 1934; Election of 1938; Election of 1942; Elections in the Roosevelt Era; Farley, James Aloysius; Flynn, Edward Joseph; Garner, John Nance; Hague, Frank; Labor; Negroes; New Deal; Purge of 1938; Rayburn, Samuel Taliaferro; Smith, Alfred E.; the South; Truman, Harry S; Two-thirds Rule; Wagner, Robert Ferdinand; Walker, Frank Comerford; Wallace, Henry A.; Women and the New Deal

Depression of the 1930s

See Great Depression

Dern, George Henry

(8 September 1872–27 August 1936)

Secretary of war (1933–36). George H. Dern was born near Scribner, Dodge County, Nebraska. He graduated from Freemont Normal College (1888) and attended the University of Nebraska. Moving to Utah in 1894, Dern had a successful career in mining before entering politics. He was elected to two terms as governor in the strongly Republican state (1924–32). Roosevelt came to know and like Dern through the

National Governors' Conferences, and wanted him in the cabinet in some capacity. He considered the western Democrat for secretary of the interior before naming him to the War Department. Dern supervised the army's participation in the Civilian Conservation Corps, and the Corps of Engineers began several important public works projects, including the Bonneville Dam, during his tenure. Determined to maintain the autonomy of the Corps of Engineers, which he once referred to as "an agency of the legislative branch" in a letter to Roosevelt, Dern was often at odds with the administration over plans to coordinate water resource development through a single agency. During 1935 and 1936, he opposed legislation to establish a permanent National Resources Board even though the bill was strongly backed by the president.

The water policy differences between Dern and Roosevelt are briefly discussed in Arthur Maass, *Muddy Waters: The Army Engineers and the Nation's Rivers* (Cambridge, Mass.: Harvard University Press, 1951).

Dewey, Thomas E.

(24 March 1902–16 March 1971)

As unlikely a presidential candidate as ever won his party's nomination, Thomas E. Dewey, the son of a small-town newspaper editor, became a symbol of urban America, an authentic national hero before his thirty-fifth birthday, and Franklin Roosevelt's bitterest opponent in two presidential campaigns. Ironically, it was FDR himself who cleared the appointment of Dewey, a former U.S. attorney for southern New York, when Governor Herbert Lehman stalled at the prospect of anointing so politically potent a special prosecutor to scour the civic face of racket-

Governor Dewey of New York opening his presidential campaign tour in Philadelphia, 7 September 1944. (UPI/ Bettmann Archive.)

infested New York City. That was June 1935, when Dewey was a private lawyer and frequent dabbler in GOP organizations, a methodical man whose confessed ambitions were to administer a great downtown law firm and "make a hell of a lot of money." Dewey ultimately realized both dreams, but only after a twenty-year delay caused by his role in special prosecution and spectacular subsequent rise to prominence.

An admiring press dubbed him "the Gangbuster," and by 1938 he had already won fame as the nemesis of Lucky Luciano, Dutch Shultz, financier Richard Whitney, and racketeers in the garment and restaurant industries; he was, moreover, the object of Hollywood melodramas and radio serials. His fame overcame a five-to-one Democratic edge in 1937, when Manhattan voters elected him their district attorney. Dewey turned down a lucrative private offer to join John Foster Dulles's law firm to make the race. No sooner had he claimed victory than he was pursuing Jimmy Hines, a mainstay of the New Deal and Tammany Hall's most charming rogue. Influenced by a visit from Tommy Corcoran, Judge Ferdinand Pecora declared a mistrial in the Hines case, and Dewey's career seemed shattered. But New York's office-hungry Republicans drafted him anyway to run against Lehman for the governorship.

The contest was fought without quarter, Dewey drawing huge crowds as he proclaimed himself "a New Deal Republican" and vowed to clean up the tainted politics of Albany and New York City. His narrow loss to the phenomenally popular Lehman earned him an invitation to represent the GOP at the 1938 Gridiron Dinner, where he needled FDR and furthered his own budding status as would-be president. In the spring of 1939, he won a retrial of Hines. By year's end, his hat was in the presidential ring (Harold Ickes, sniping at his youth and stature, said it was really a diaper), and some polls showed him actually ahead of Roosevelt. Yet Dewey's candidacy was premature. It was dashed on the rocks of international tension and the sudden appearance of an even more unlikely contender than the thirty-eight-year-old D.A. of New York County—Wendell Willkie.

"Lowell," he snapped to a reporter at the time, "you make me sick. . . . Don't you realize that Franklin Roosevelt is the easiest man in the world for me to beat." Such pugnacity, combined with a swaggering manner and the cool precision of a courtroom advocate, won Dewey more admiration than affection. Uncertain of his own foreign policy response to the German advances and cautioned by Dulles and others against bold support for the Allies, he swept the 1940 primaries against Arthur Vandenburg and Robert Taft, only to lose the nomination to Wendell Willkie. Two years later, he came back to win New York's governorship, and soon a west wind of reform was blowing through the musty corridors of Albany.

Dewey remade the GOP in New York, discarding Old Guard conservatives and reaching out to liberals and a vast urban family of polyglot sympathies. He pressed his legislature for the first civil rights laws in the country, for new initiatives to fight cancer and renovate aging mental hospitals, for a first-of-its-kind throughway snaking north from New York City and west to the Pennsylvania line, and for generous hikes in aid to education and state employees. Simultaneously, aided by wartime restrictions on building, he squirreled away a surplus of over $600 million for public works and slashed state taxes in eleven of his twelve years as governor.

Proclaimed the natural spokesman of the new Republican breed, Dewey was easily nominated in 1944 to oppose an aging FDR. Differences over postwar policies alienated Willkie's backers, yet the candidate and his chief adviser on the subject, John Foster Dulles, could later claim credit for the birth of bipartisan foreign policy. Dewey sent Dulles at the height of the campaign to confer with Secretary of State Cordell Hull; the two men agreed to keep Roosevelt's idea for a United Nations outside the partisan debate. Later, the president himself scored a direct hit against his much-disliked rival ("the little man" in FDR's caustic phrase, or the "son of a bitch"). Declaring flatly for the UN's right to dispatch peacekeeping forces without congressional approval, Roosevelt one-upped the more cautious Dewey and, after Willkie's sudden death in October 1944, won the support of many of the dead man's warmest advocates.

By then, Dewey and the president had engaged in a more private duel. George Marshall on his own decided to appeal to the Republican candidate to withhold public discussion of Pearl Harbor and forgo the potent issue in favor of national security considerations. Dewey disbelieved Marshall's story that FDR had known nothing of the impending attack, especially since U.S. code breakers had managed to unravel Japanese directives before and since. "Instead of being re-elected," he told Marshall's emissary, "he ought to be impeached." But he kept his word, and Pearl Harbor did not emerge as a major controversy until after the president's death.

Dewey made his 1944 campaign a blunt frontal attack on "the mess in Washington," scoring points against bureaucratic mismanagement and vowing a thorough housecleaning of FDR's "tired old men." It was, he said in the closing days, a contest of "competence against incompetent bungling." Such themes did little to arouse Republican partisans, and Dewey was forced to take the gloves off in a stinging rebuke after the president himself turned the tide with his famous tribute to his little dog Fala. "Wisecracks and vilification," he charged, could not obscure Roosevelt's "sad record" of military unpreparedness, nor the AFL's own estimate of 10 million unemployed Americans seven years into the New Deal. Roosevelt might be indispensable, Dewey declared, but only to his own cabinet, political bosses in Chicago and the Bronx, and Communist leader Earl Browder.

The contest came to life, and there was talk of an upset, but on 7 November, the Roosevelt coalition summoned one final majority for "the Champ." Dewey had run Roosevelt his closest national race. FDR answered the congratulatory message of his defeated rival with chilly formality and never abandoned his distaste for the New Yorker, whose later growth prepared him for a statesmanlike but fatally flawed campaign against Harry Truman in 1948. "Everything came too early for me," Dewey admitted near the end of his life. He hadn't wanted to oppose Roosevelt at all in 1944, but timing forced his hand, too soon for voters to perceive the relaxed, even genial figure he would become afterward. An elder statesman at the age of forty-six, Dewey's chief legacy was a revitalized Republican party, its old isolationism and obstructionist role at home yielding to more moderate positions. Ironically, his greatest political effectiveness was exerted on behalf of other men: in 1952, he engineered Dwight Eisenhower's nomination and ushered in the vice-presidential career of young Richard Nixon.

Dewey died in March 1971, all but forgotten by a generation too young to recall his early fame.

The only full-scale biography of Dewey is Richard Norton Smith, *Thomas E. Dewey and His Times* (New York: Simon & Schuster, 1982), based upon the Dewey Collection at the University of Rochester plus 170 interviews with Dewey associates. Other useful references include Warren Moscow, *Politics in the Empire State* (New York: Knopf, 1948), Hickman Powell's highly favorable account of the Luciano case, *Ninety Times Guilty* (New York: Harcourt Brace & Co., 1939), Robert Ray's Ph.D. dissertation comparing the 1944 speeches of Roosevelt and Dewey (State University of Iowa, 1947), and Barry Beyer's well-researched *Thomas E. Dewey: A Study in Political Leadership* (New York: Garland, 1979). Dewey's own memoir, *Twenty against the Underworld,* is a revealing account of his career as a gangbuster; projected as the first of a two-volume series, it appeared after his death (Garden City, N.Y.: Doubleday, 1974). His 1940 speeches form the heart of Dewey's *The Case against the New Deal* (New York: Harper & Bros., 1940). A more mature work reflecting his essentially pragmatic conservatism is *Thomas E. Dewey on the Two-Party System* (New York: Doubleday, 1966), a series of lectures delivered at Princeton University in 1950 and published in the wake of Barry Goldwater's disastrous 1964 campaign.

RICHARD NORTON SMITH

See also Elections in the Roosevelt Era; Republican Party

Mary W. Dewson. (Courtesy FDR Library.)

Dewson, Mary W. ("Molly")
(18 February 1874–October 1962)

Democratic politician and head of the Women's Division of the Democratic National Committee from 1933 to 1937. Molly Dewson came to the New Deal by way of Wellesley College, the woman suffrage campaign, a stint in World War I with the Red Cross, and five years at the National Consumers' League in the 1920s. She was primarily associated with two causes throughout her career: the minimum wage and promoting opportunities for women in public life.

Eleanor Roosevelt spotted Molly Dewson as a likely recruit for Democratic politics in the 1920s when Dewson was in her mid-fifties. After a small part in the 1928 campaign, Dewson became a trusted member of the Roosevelt team through the 1940 election. She developed a warm and easy relationship with Eleanor, but got along famously with FDR as well. He liked her candor, her sense of humor, and her ability to trade sallies with male politicians. She in turn idolized his skill as a politician and his commitment to the social issues so dear to women in public life in the postsuffrage era. Molly Dewson even bore a certain resemblance to her commander in chief—a tall, gangly woman, sensibly dressed in tweeds and low shoes, with a pair of pince-nez perched on her nose.

With the full support of Franklin Roosevelt, Molly Dewson built the Women's Division of the Democratic National Committee (DNC) into a central component of the newly revitalized Democratic party. She won increased patronage for women, including Frances Perkins's nomination as secretary of labor. She worked for equal representation of men and women on all Democratic party committees; by the late 1930s, seventeen states had met this goal. She initiated the Reporter Plan for Democratic women to study the New Deal's impact on their localities and, not coincidentally, build support for FDR's reelection. With eighty thousand active Democratic women on the Women's Division roster by 1936, Dewson's political standing soared. In the 1936 campaign, the Women's Division supplied 90 percent of the DNC's campaign literature in the form of brightly colored fact sheets called rainbow fliers. This innovative tactic saved the Democratic party $1 million.

At the height of her political power, Molly Dewson returned to her old field of social welfare, serving on the three-member Social Security Board from 1937 until ill health forced her to resign in December 1938. One of her proudest memories was that she was among the several hundred guests invited to the White House following Franklin Roosevelt's funeral. Molly Dewson remained an ardent New Deal Democrat until her death in Castine, Maine, in 1962.

For biographical material, see Paul C. Taylor, "Mary Williams Dewson," in *Notable American Women: The Modern Period*, ed. Barbara Sicherman and Carol Hurd Green (Cambridge, Mass.: Harvard University Press, 1980), pp. 188–91. Susan Ware, *Beyond Suffrage: Women in the New Deal* (Cambridge, Mass.: Harvard University Press, 1981) covers Dewson's activities in the 1930s; Ware is currently writing a biography of Dewson's entire career. An unpublished autobiography by Dewson covering her New Deal years, "An Aid to the End" (1949), is available at the Roosevelt Library in Hyde Park, the Schlesinger Library of Radcliffe College, and the Library of Congress.
SUSAN WARE

See also Women and the New Deal

Dies Committee

See House Committee to Investigate Un-American Activities

Douglas, Lewis Williams
(2 July 1894–7 March 1974)
Budget director, New Deal critic, and deputy administrator of the War Shipping Administration. Born into a wealthy copper mining family in Bisbee, Arizona, Lewis Douglas shunned the mining business for a life of public service. He was educated at eastern preparatory schools and Amherst College. After graduating from Amherst in 1916, he served as an officer with the American Expeditionary Force in 1917–18. He experienced action at the front and was decorated for meritorious service and bravery.

Soon after the war, Douglas entered politics. He won a seat in the Arizona state legislature in 1923, and three years later he was elected to the U.S. House of Representatives where he served three terms. As a congressman, he was a highly principled laissez-faire Democrat who championed limited government, states' rights, low tariffs, sound money, and an annual balanced budget. President-elect Roosevelt selected the young Arizonan for the Budget directorship in February 1933.

During his two years in office, Douglas proved a stubborn steward of the public purse. He believed that reducing federal expenditures and balancing the budget would entice capital investment and revitalize the depressed economy. During the early New Deal, President Roosevelt shared that conservative view and regularly sought Douglas's advice on a variety of domestic issues. A member of a select group known as the "Bedside Cabinet," the Budget director met nearly every morning with FDR and exerted some influence on New Deal policymaking. His principal contribution during the hundred days was to draft the economy bill, enacted on 20 March 1933. That measure sought budget equilibrium by reducing veterans' pensions and federal salaries by a total of $500 million. Despite persistent efforts, Douglas could not dissuade Roosevelt from experimenting with unorthodox economic policies. When FDR abandoned the gold standard in mid-April 1933, Douglas remarked, "Well, this is the end of Western civilization." He called a currency inflation amendment to the Agricultural Adjustment Act an "insane proposal." And as an advocate of currency stabilization and international economic cooperation, he became dispirited when the president aborted the London Economic Conference in early July 1933.

Douglas's disillusionment turned to despair when Roosevelt embarked upon a policy of deficit financing. Although FDR was sincere in his commitment to economy in government and a balanced budget, he believed that those goals had to be postponed in order to fund relief and recovery measures. Douglas had few objections to direct assistance, but he vigorously opposed a large-scale public works program. Such an endeavor, he insisted, was ineffective, inefficient, and costly. Moreover, a policy of deficit spending would create huge budget gaps, impair the nation's credit, and lead to runaway inflation.

Throughout 1933 and 1934, the outspoken Budget director exhorted Roosevelt to restrain spending and balance the budget. "Lew, you are obsessed on this subject," FDR snapped. "Perhaps I am, Mr. President, but at least it is a conviction and a deep one that we cannot spend ourselves into prosperity." Unable to check Roosevelt's "mad and reckless" expenditures, Douglas resigned on 30 August 1934. Roosevelt was hurt by the resignation but eventually sent Douglas a warm letter of gratitude.

After his departure, Douglas took an executive position with American Cyanamid for three years and then served as principal (president) of McGill University from 1937 to 1939 before assuming the presidency of Mutual of New York Life Insurance Company. As a private citizen, Douglas became a leading critic of the New Deal. In books, articles, and speeches, he lashed out against government policies that he thought would lead to socialism. His criticisms subsided with the eruption of war in Europe. An internationalist, he advocated unlimited assistance to the Allies and joined interventionist groups like the Century Group and the Committee to Defend America by Aiding the Allies. During the presidential campaign of 1940, he denounced Roosevelt for attempting to violate the two-term tradition and formed an organization called Democrats for Willkie.

In May 1942 President Roosevelt asked Douglas to direct American merchant shipping as deputy administrator of the War Shipping Administration. Mindful of his past differences with the president, Douglas joked, "You know you and I disagreed once upon a time about a budget, but this budget, Mr. President, you have to balance." "Tell me, Lew, why?" FDR inquired. "Because you can't print ships." With that response, the president roared with laughter. Although Emory Land was the titular head of War Shipping, Douglas, in practice, ran the agency. Working closely with Harry Hopkins, he allocated ships and planned their use until ill health forced him to resign his post in June 1944.

Douglas resumed his public service career in the Truman administration, serving in 1945 as an adviser to General Lucius Clay in postwar Germany. In 1947 he was appointed ambassador to Great Britain, a position he filled with distinction for nearly four years. After the London mission, Douglas devoted himself to various business, civic, and charitable enterprises. Plagued by ill health all his life, he died in 1974. His remains were scattered over Jerome, the Arizona mining town where he began his career with Peggy Zinsser, his bride of fifty years.

A biography of Douglas by Robert P. Browder and Thomas G. Smith is in progress. A number of scholars have stressed Roosevelt's fiscal conservatism and Douglas's influential role in the early New Deal. Two of the best works are Frank Freidel, *Franklin D. Roosevelt: Launching the New Deal* (Boston: Little, Brown & Co., 1973) and James E. Sargent, "FDR and Lewis W. Douglas: Budget Balancing and the Early New Deal," *Prologue* 6 (Spring 1974):33–43. Douglas discussed his economic views and opposition to the New Deal in *The Liberal Tradition: A Free People and a Free Economy* (New York: D. Van Nostrand Co., 1935). The best source of information on the subject is the Lewis W. Douglas Collection at the University of Arizona. Quotations are from the Douglas Papers.

THOMAS G. SMITH

Douglas, William Orville

(16 October 1898–19 January 1980)

Supreme Court justice, 1939–75. Born in Maine, Minnesota, William O. Douglas grew up in Washington. A graduate of Whitman College and Columbia University Law School, Douglas by 1928 was a professor of law at Yale University. As a corporate law specialist, the future justice was offered a position on the staff of the newly created Securities and Exchange Commission (SEC) by Joseph Kennedy, its first chairman. In 1936 Roosevelt appointed Douglas as a commission member, and in 1937 he was named chairman. While serving with the SEC, Douglas led the fight to bring public utilities under SEC regulation and secured the reorganization of the New York Stock Exchange.

He had also gained entrance into Roosevelt's inner circle. He was a regular at FDR's poker parties and was one of the first to be told of Roosevelt's plans to run for a third term. When Justice Brandeis retired from the Supreme Court in 1939, Roosevelt, on Brandeis's recommendation, nominated Douglas to succeed him.

Douglas served on the Court until 1975 (longer than any other justice) and always sided with the liberal wing of the Court. During the FDR years, Douglas consistently voted with Justices Black and Murphy in upholding governmental regulation of economic matters. The question of the state's power to compel displays of loyalty from its citizens drove a wedge between Douglas and Felix Frankfurter and the resulting feud between the two lasted until Frankfurter's death in 1965.

An active and openly ambitious man, Douglas was not content to see his Supreme Court appointment as the climax of his career. When political considerations forced Henry Wallace from the 1944 ticket, the young justice's name was raised by FDR as a possible running mate. Although Douglas wrote to Chief Justice Stone that he would not accept the vice-presidential nomination, he hinted to others that he would run if given the chance. But little public support developed for his candidacy and Truman was selected. In 1948 Truman offered the vice-presidency to Douglas but the justice declined.

After the war Douglas supported the Warren Court's expansion of civil liberties and civil rights, laying claim to the title of the Great Libertarian. He wrote books on a wide variety of topics: travel in Arabia, Asia, and Russia; American foreign policy; and his most cherished cause, conservation. In 1965 he published *A Wilderness Bill of Rights*, arguing that the time had come for humans to stop sacrificing nature for the sour promise of industrial progress. In-

William O. Douglas, 1940. Artist: Osker Stoessel. (National Portrait Gallery, Smithsonian Institution. Gift of David Finley.)

capacitated by a stroke in early 1975, Douglas resigned from the Court on 12 November of that year and died in 1980.

Douglas's two autobiographical volumes, *Go East, Young Man* (New York: Random House, 1974) and *The Court Years* (New York: Random House, 1980), are essential to an understanding of this enigmatic man. The latter, published posthumously, is rather badly arranged. For an appreciation of Douglas's judicial record, see Vern Countryman's *The Judicial Record of Justice William O. Douglas* (Cambridge, Mass.: Harvard University Press, 1974). *Justice William O. Douglas* by James Duram (Boston: Twayne Publishers, 1981) is a balanced appraisal of the justice's contribution to American life.

See also Supreme Court of the United States

Dollar-a-Year Man

See Business

Draft

See Selective Service Act

Dubinsky, David

(22 February 1892–17 September 1982)
President of the International Ladies Garment Workers' Union (ILGWU) and cofounder of the American Labor party. Born David Dobnievski in Brest Litovsk, Russian Poland, Dubinsky left school at age eleven to become a baker's apprentice in Lodz. In 1907, after joining the Jewish socialist *Bund,* Dubinsky was arrested as a labor agitator and sentenced to exile in Siberia. Escaping, he eventually emigrated to the United States in 1911 where he became a cutter in the New York garment trades and joined Local 10 of the ILGWU in 1911. An energetic and pugnacious man, brash but unpretentious, Dubinsky attracted a powerful following among right-wing socialists in the union's New York locals. From this base he was able to advance to the presidency of the union in 1932.

With the union's fortunes at low ebb as a result both of years of socialist-communist faction fighting and of the depression, Dubinsky took full advantage of the encouragements afforded union organizing by Section 7 of the National Industrial Recovery Act (1933), and within two years had rebuilt the ILGWU. Dubinsky served on the Labor Advisory Board of the National Recovery Administration (1933–35), and in 1935 became a vice-president and member of the American Federation of Labor Executive Council. Here he combined with other advocates of industrial unionism to form the Committee for Industrial Organization (CIO), founded with the intention of agitating for the creation of industrial unions in the mass production industries.

To Dubinsky, as to other CIO leaders, the continuation of the Roosevelt administration beyond 1936 was essential if organized labor was to have any hope of adding permanently to its political and economic influence. Consequently, in 1936 Dubinsky resigned from the Socialist party and joined with John L. Lewis, Sidney Hillman, and George L. Berry (president of the International Printing Pressmen-AFL) in founding labor's Non-Partisan League to mobilize the labor vote and union money behind Roosevelt's reelection. Their success ensured the establishment of organized labor as a central actor in the New Deal coalition.

Max Danish, *The World of David Dubinsky* (Cleveland: World Publishing Co., 1957), provides an uncritical account of Dubinsky's life and career. Information on Dubinsky and the Jewish labor movement in New York is contained in Irving Howe, *World of Our Fathers* (New York: Harcourt Brace Jovanovich, 1976). On Dubinsky and the ILGWU, see "David Dubinsky, the I.L.G.W.U. and the American Labor Movement," Special Supplement, *Labor History,* Spring 1968. On labor political action, see J. David Greenstone, *Labor in American Politics* (New York: Alfred A. Knopf, 1969).

CHRISTOPHER L. TOMLINS

Dumbarton Oaks Agreement/ Conference

See Cohen, Benjamin Victor

Dust Bowl

See Conservation

E

Early, Stephen Tyree

(27 August 1889–11 August 1951)

Roosevelt's press secretary from 1933 to 1945. Early was born in Crozet, Virginia, and lived in the District of Columbia from age nine. He began his career in journalism as a member of the staff of the United Press shortly after graduation from high school. Early met Franklin D. Roosevelt in 1912 at the Democratic National Convention and maintained the acquaintance while serving as an Associated Press correspondent assigned to cover the State, War, and Navy departments during Roosevelt's tenure as assistant secretary of the navy. After serving in World War I as an infantry officer and on the staff of the servicemen's weekly, *Stars and Stripes,* and a brief career in public relations, Early began his working relationship with Roosevelt as his advance man during the unsuccessful campaign for the vice-presidency in 1920. Early returned to the Associated Press after the election and became Washington representative of Paramount News in 1927. Both posts prepared him well for his work under Roosevelt. When FDR was elected president in 1932, he made Early an assistant secretary with responsibility for press relations. In July 1937 Early received the title of secretary.

Early was the first effective press secretary. An experienced newspaperman, public relations director, and newsreel editor, he understood the demands of the new mass media and developed new, coherent policies and procedures for managing the public relations of the modern presidency. He controlled White House communications and used radio and photographs to promote the New Deal and the image of Roosevelt as a strong popular leader. However, he did not permit loyalty to FDR to affect his professional relations with reporters. He did not act as a White House "spokesman," but rather held daily news conferences to provide reporters with useful information. He defended the press to Roosevelt and always dealt candidly with reporters.

Following Roosevelt's death, Early stayed on as

Surrounding FDR at his White House desk on 4 March 1943, the tenth anniversary of his first inauguration, are Marvin McIntyre, Grace Tully, Stephen Early, and Edwin Watson (left to right). (Courtesy FDR Library.)

special assistant to President Truman, retiring in July 1945 to become vice-president of Pullman Company. He returned to the government in April 1949 and served as the first deputy secretary of defense until June 1950. His last government service was a two-day stint as press secretary in December 1950 following the death of President Truman's press secretary, Charles G. Ross. Early died of a heart attack at the George Washington University Hospital in Washington, D.C., at the age of sixty-one.

The Stephen T. Early Papers are in the Roosevelt Library, Hyde Park, New York. Two useful studies of Early are Steven E. Schoenherr, "Selling the New Deal: Stephen T. Early's Role as Press Secretary to Franklin Roosevelt," (Ph.D. diss., University of Delaware, 1975), and Richard W. Steele's brief biography in the *Dictionary of American Biography,* Supplement 5 (New York: Charles Scribner's Sons, 1977); pp. 196–97.

See also Photographs

Eccles, Marriner Stoddard

(9 September 1890–18 December 1977)

A Utah banker and businessman who came to Washington in February 1934 to work as special assistant to Treasury Secretary Morgenthau on credit and monetary matters. Eccles was named chairman of the Federal Reserve Board in November 1934, served in that capacity until 1948, and continued as vice-chairman until 1951. He then returned to business concerns in Utah, remaining active and outspoken in public affairs until his eighty-seventh year.

Marriner Stoddard Eccles was the first son of the second (polygamous) family of David Eccles, pioneer Utah entrepreneur and industrialist. When the senior Eccles died in 1912, Marriner, at age twenty-two, with barely a high school education, assumed management of the two-sevenths of his father's estate that fell to him and his eight younger siblings. By 1928 the family interests had grown to include the Utah Construction Company, Amalgamated Sugar Company, and twenty-eight First Security banks—all of major importance in the Mountain West.

Fighting successfully to keep his banks open during the early years of the depression, Eccles began to observe that the action taken by individual banks to remain solvent had the general effect of tightening the credit structure and further deepening the crisis. "Seeking individual salvation," he later wrote, "we were contributing to collective ruin." Influenced in part by the writings of popular economists William T. Foster and Waddill Catchings, he had by 1931 roughed out the logic of a compensatory fiscal policy. After offering his unorthodox views to the Senate Finance Committee's "Depression Clinic" in early February 1933, Eccles was introduced by Stuart Chase to Rexford G. Tugwell, who subsequently helped arrange Eccles's appointment to the Treasury staff in February 1934.

In the Treasury, Eccles undertook a number of assignments, but took special pride in helping to draft legislation leading to the establishment of the Federal Housing Authority. When offered the chairmanship of the Federal Reserve Board that fall, he accepted only on the condition that the president support a set of proposed changes in the structure of the Federal Reserve System, which became the basis of the Banking Act of 1935, considered by Congress concurrently with his stormy confirmation hearings. The Banking Act controversy reveals something of Eccles's populist anti-eastern bias, in that its major thrust was to wrest control of the Federal Reserve System from the New York banks and place it in the hands of the Reserve Board in Washington.

Eccles's direct manner was perhaps a factor in his never becoming an intimate of FDR. He thus found it difficult to gain access to the president during the recession crisis of 1937. His persistent advocacy of renewed government spending to counter the recession helped move the president to announce a spending program in April 1938. Shortly after the recession, Federal Reserve policy became largely subject to Treasury needs in financing the war. The Fed was finally freed from Treasury domination only in 1951, in part through Eccles's action.

Leaving the Board of Governors that year, Eccles returned to the West to direct the First Security Corporation. In the early 1960s, he became an outspoken advocate of population control, publicly criticizing the Catholic and Mormon churches for their pronatalist policy. In 1965 he announced his opposition to the Vietnam War, one of the first important American businessmen to do so.

It was during the battles over fiscal policy in the 1930s, however, that he made his most significant and lasting contribution to economic and social policy in America. Under his leadership, the Federal Reserve System was transformed from an instrument of big banking interests to an influential advocate of a compensatory policy. In 1982, the Federal Reserve Building was fittingly renamed to honor Marriner S. Eccles for his sixteen years as a major figure in the system.

Beckoning Frontiers (New York: Alfred A. Knopf, 1951), Eccles's memoir, edited by Sidney Hyman, is the starting point for understanding his public career. Eccles's tenacious, no-nonsense style comes across clearly in this book full of arresting and instructive vignettes describing Eccles's work in Washington. Less satisfactory, though covering Eccles's later years, is Sidney Hyman, *Marriner S. Eccles: Private Entrepreneur and Public Servant* (Stanford: Stanford University Graduate School of Business, 1976). Eccles is a major figure in Dean L. May, *From New Deal to New Economics: The American Liberal Response to the Recession of 1937* (New York: Garland Publishing Co., 1981), which focuses on his role in the recession crisis of 1937. Dean L. May, "The Banking Act of 1935," (manuscript in possession of the author) centers upon the roles of Eccles, Carter Glass, and New York banker George L. Harrison in the controversy surrounding the Banking Act. Arch O. Egbert has written on "Marriner S. Eccles and the Banking Act of 1935" (Ph.D. diss., Brigham Young University, 1976). Leonard J. Arrington's *David Eccles: Pioneer Western Industrialist* (Logan: Utah State University, 1975) gives information on Eccles's family background. A collection of Eccles's writings and speeches was published in 1940 as *Economic Balance and a Balanced Budget*, ed. Rudolph L. Weissman (New York: Harper & Bros., 1940).

DEAN L. MAY

See also Banking; Fiscal Policy

Economic Royalists

A phrase from FDR's acceptance speech at the Democratic National Convention of 1936; it defined the tone and issues for the campaign. On 27 June 1936, the convention waited for its nominee formally to accept renomination for the presidency and to announce the direction of his second campaign. From the platform the delegates knew that Roosevelt wanted this effort to be an affirmation of the New

Another Myth Exploded

FDR SAYS IT IS NOT AT ALL TRUE THAT HE "HAS GRILLED MILLIONAIRE FOR BREAKFAST;" THAT WHAT HE REALLY LIKES IS SCRAMBLED EGGS.

Quincy Scott, Portland Oregonian, 6 December 1938.

Deal: "We hold this truth to be self-evident—that government in a modern civilization has certain inescapable obligations to its citizens, among which are: (1) Protection of the family and home; (2) Establishment of a democracy of opportunity for all the people; (3) Aid to those overtaken by disaster." Also prefiguring Roosevelt's address was the platform's militant promise to "rid our land of . . . malefactors of great wealth."

The delegates were not disappointed when, after all the cheers had died down, Roosevelt quickly moved from a nonpartisan expression of gratitude to all who had helped in the early New Deal to attacks on those who built "new dynasties" based on "concentration of control over material things." These "economic royalists" stifled the freedom and opportunity of Americans by creating a species of "economic tyranny." In announcing that he was campaigning against concentrated economic power, he confirmed the shift in political strategy from an appeal to all groups to the construction and elaboration of what would become known as the Roosevelt coalition. The speech and the subsequent campaign also solidified the wealthy opposition to FDR and further increased the suspicions and fears the big business community had of his administration.

The acceptance speech is printed as Item 79, pages 230–36, Samuel I. Rosenman, ed., *The Public Papers and Addresses of Franklin D. Roosevelt,* vol. 5 (New York: Random House, 1938).

See also Taxation

Edison, Charles

(3 October 1890–31 July 1969)

Secretary of the navy, 1940. The son of the famous inventor, Charles Edison was born in West Orange, New Jersey. A graduate of MIT, he came into contact with FDR in 1917 when his father was appointed chairman of the Navy Consulting Board. In late 1936, Charles Edison became assistant secretary of the navy and was virtually head of the department because of the chronic illness of Claude Swanson. Edison became acting secretary on 7 July 1939 and secretary on 1 January 1940.

In his naval posts, Edison fought to retain the "flush-deck" destroyers that were due for scrapping in 1939. He also backed technological innovation, such as the high-pressure, high-temperature boiler, and pushed for reorganization of the department.

His tenure in office, however, was not the happiest. Significantly handicapped by partial deafness, Edison seemed to FDR to be dilatory in such important matters as ship construction and the establishment of the Neutrality Patrol. FDR also felt that Edison was too easily influenced by top naval officers, such as Admiral Stark. Clearly, Edison's position was temporary; indeed, on the day he became secretary, FDR told him to run for governor of New Jersey in 1940 to offset the influence of Frank Hague. Duly elected, Edison served until 1944, when he resumed his business career. He published a collection of poetry, *Flotsam and Jetsam,* under the name "Tom Sleeper" in 1967.

W. L. Langer and S. E. Gleason's *The Challenge to Isolation* (New York: Harper, 1952) and Robert G. Albion's *Makers of Naval Policy* (Annapolis: Naval Institute Press, 1980) provide sound analyses of Edison's service with the Navy Department.

MALCOLM MUIR, JR.

See also Hague, Frank

Education

In the late summer of 1890, when the James Roosevelts were traveling in Europe, they hired as governess for their eight-year-old son Franklin, and took back with them to Hyde Park, a French-speaking Swiss native named Jeanne Sandoz. She was nineteen years old, a slender slip of a girl, barely five feet tall (the boy Franklin was soon taller than she), who was hired partly because the Roosevelts wanted their son to become fluent in French but also because she was reputed to be an unusually good teacher. And so she proved to be. She had a somewhat suprising interest in physics and chemistry: the curriculum she devised for her pupil had a greater proportionate emphasis on scientific information than any he later followed. She was also quite aggressively liberal in her political views: she spoke out against the criminal selfishness of the "masters of money" and preached the Social

Several trips abroad were part of FDR's childhood education. His first transatlantic voyage was to Scotland when he was three years old. In this 1887 photograph taken of father and son in Washington, D.C., Franklin poses in his Murray clan suit. (Courtesy FDR Library.)

Gospel, striving to arouse in her charge some sense of the social responsibility, the concern for those less fortunate than he, that ought in her view to accompany his abundant privileges. She had much vivacious charm, and this enabled her to impart to the boy, whose quickness of mind and wide-ranging curiosity delighted her, a considerable measure of the enthusiastic interest she took in every subject she taught. By the time she left the Roosevelt household in early 1893, returning then to Switzerland to be married, Mlle. Sandoz had "more than anyone else . . . laid the foundations of my education," as Franklin Roosevelt wrote her forty-odd years later.

She was succeeded at Hyde Park by a male tutor, a personable young man named Arthur Dumper, from Cleveland, who was athletic and interested in nature studies and quickly became the eleven-year-old Franklin's warm friend as well as teacher. His tenure as tutor was initially intended to last a year and a half, for Franklin was scheduled to enter boarding school in September 1894, six months after his twelfth birthday. But the imperious Sara Roosevelt, whose elderly husband was by then in failing health, flatly refused to part with her darling boy at the appointed time; and so Dumper stayed on with the Roosevelts through the summer of 1896. He, too, proved an excellent teacher. In formal schooling, thanks to Dumper, Franklin rather more than kept pace with his contemporaries at Groton—and the collecting hobbies he avidly pursued enabled him to accumulate a great deal more miscellaneous information about geography, political history, and natural history than the bulk of his contemporaries had. He had started a stamp collection when he was nine, and the following year, his uncle Fred Delano presented him with a valuable stamp collection that he, Uncle

Fred, had made. In that same year he began collecting birds' eggs and nests, and on 1 January 1893, started a bird diary, which, when he discontinued it on 6 August 1896, contained seventy-nine pages of precisely reported sightings. Dumper encouraged him to begin the ambitious project of shooting, with a collector's gun his father had given him, and then mounting for exhibition a male and female of every species of bird in Dutchess County. His collection of Hudson River birds became, it has been said, the most comprehensive ever made.

At Groton School in Groton, Massachusetts, where he enrolled in September 1896 at the age of fourteen, he entered the dominion of the school's founder and headmaster, the Reverend Dr. Endicott Peabody, rector of Groton parish, and of Mrs. Peabody, a pair whose "influence . . . means and will mean more to me than that of any other people next to my father and mother," he wrote nearly four decades later.

Other Groton masters influenced him, notably black-bearded Sherrard Billings, a small man physically who, perhaps in compensation for his lack of size, preached and practiced the "strenuous life" as assiduously as did Franklin's distant cousin, Theodore Roosevelt. (Billings hero-worshiped TR, whose classmate he had been at Harvard.) It was this master who encouraged the adolescent boy into debate and public speaking and who did most at Groton to reinforce in him that sense of social responsibility and concern for the unfortunate that Mlle. Sandoz had stimulated. At his behest, Franklin joined the Groton Missionary Society and engaged in charitable activities on behalf of "poor boys" from the Boston area. Yet another master important to the boy's education was Amory Gardner, a wealthy and eccentric bachelor (Isabella Stewart Gardner of Boston, the fabulous art patroness, was Amory's aunt), who was probably the best subject-matter teacher in the school. He was a progressive educator who inveighed against narrow specializations, believing that a teacher of chemistry and physics should "know a good deal about Homer, Beethoven, Dante, and Velasquez" and that a teacher of classics should "know something of business, trigonometry . . . etc." Franklin took Greek under him and reported to his parents, "I can learn quicker & better with him than anyone else."

But the ruling force of the Groton world, dominating everything, was the man who had created that world in his own image. Few men who ever lived can have been more sure of themselves, of what they meant in the world and wanted to do in it, than Endicott Peabody. Few Americans can have been more firmly committed to essentially aristocratic principles (Groton was frankly exclusively elitist) or more absolutely certain of the moral structure of a universe ruled by God the Cosmic Headmaster with the aid of Jesus Christ, the Supreme Gentleman. And few educators can have had greater impact upon their pupils—an effect produced far more by force of a moralistic authoritarian personality and a rocklike integrity of character than by force of mind. The impact could

FDR at Groton, May 1899. (Courtesy FDR Library.)

and sometimes did shatter sensitive boys of weak character, boys who were psychologically insecure, boys who were inclined to "think too much" ("I'm not sure I like boys to think too much," Peabody once said). But upon the overmothered Franklin, whose inner resources and strength of character were remarkable and whose need for a strong, actively exemplary, firmly disciplining father could no longer be supplied by invalid James Roosevelt, the Peabody impact was a shaping, molding influence—wholly benign. It was exerted in familial ways, for the rector and his wife treated the student body as a family of a hundred boys, with each of whom they shook hands and to each spoke a good-night word at the close of every day. (The nightly ritual became a means of expressing approval or censure of a boy's conduct, for the rector's manner would vary from the cold and curt to a warmly smiling comment as he said good night.)

In the prospectus for the school that he sent out in 1883 to a select number of the elite who might wish to enroll their sons, Peabody said that Groton's purpose would be "to cultivate manly Christian character, having regard to moral and physical as well as intellectual development"—and the order in which he named the three kinds of "development" was the order of emphasis placed upon them, overall, in Groton as educational experience.

Franklin, entering III Form (the equivalent of freshman class in a normal American high school), had classes representative of the whole of the Groton curriculum so far as relative emphasis among different types of subject matter was concerned. He took Latin, Greek, algebra, English literature (Shakespeare, Grey's *Elegy,* Goldsmith's *Deserted Village,* and so on), English composition, French literature and composition, Greek and Roman history, and sacred studies, the latter taught by the rector himself and consisting of Bible and mission history. He also took a science course, the only one in all his four years in the school—and it was such science as Aristotle might have taught, being a course in zoology, with laboratory study, whose exclusive concern was with descriptive classification. In later years he took courses in political economy wherein he learned the virtues of the gold standard and free enterprise, the iniquities of bimetallism and government interference with free market operations. He did well scholastically and was in the upper fourth or fifth of his form in each of his four years.

But it was not through scholarship or any kind of intellectual brilliance that a boy gained glory at Groton. This was gained on the playing fields, in the team sports in which every boy was required to participate, or in track and field and boxing events; in none of these was Franklin Roosevelt a star performer or even a better than average one. "There has been a good deal written about Franklin Roosevelt when he was a boy at Groton, more than I should have thought justified by the impression that he left at the school," commented Rector Peabody in a later year. "He was a quiet, satisfactory boy of more than ordinary intelligence, taking a good position in his Form but not brilliant. Athletically he was rather too slight for success. We all liked him."

Harvard, where Roosevelt enrolled as a matter of course in the fall of 1900, was of considerably less importance to his education, overall, than Peabody's school had been. In several ways his freshman college year was a continuation of his Groton life. He roomed with a Groton classmate in one of the so-called Gold Coast dormitories on Mount Auburn Street, where most of his Groton classmates were close neighbors. He took his meals, not in commons, but at a Groton table in a Cambridge eating house. He went often to Groton for visits. But there was in other, and essential, ways a sharp departure from his Groton life. The college he entered was of the university Charles W. Norton (who was still president) had made—an institution with a brilliant faculty that provided an abundance of intellectual fare but that also, through a system of free electives and almost no regulation or guidance of personal lives, no emphasis on "character development," left it up to the student to partake or not of what was offered.

Franklin Roosevelt, it must be said, partook meagerly. He did not enroll in snap courses, as many of his friends did. At Harvard as at Groton he was, as Peabody had described him, "a faithful scholar," but his grades were lower than they had been at Groton (he was content with a C or low B, and seldom scored higher). None of his professors seems to have excited him greatly intellectually, and the curriculum he chose to follow had grave deficiencies as preparation for a life of intelligent awareness in twentieth-century America and especially for a public life that must deal, in decisive ways, with the adjustment of political and social and economic institutions to the energies released by scientific technology. All his courses were in political science, history, and English composition and literature, save for a course or two in Latin literature, one in paleontology, and one in French literature. He enrolled in a general introductory course in philosophy under Josiah Royce but dropped it after three weeks. He took no philosophy, no mathematics, no chemistry, no physics, no psychology, and studied no economic theory more advanced, in essence, than Adam Smith's.

But he was intensely active in extracurricular affairs and learned far more from them that was useful to him in later life than he did from his classroom studies. He tried out for football in his freshman year but was cut from the squad at the first pruning. He tried out for the crew but failed to make it, though he stroked an intramural crew in his sophomore year. He became the librarian of his club, the Fly Club, and of Hasty Pudding, and was on the library committee of the Harvard Union. But his main activity was the *Crimson,* Harvard's student newspaper, a morning daily. The intense competition for a staff position on the paper absorbed a great deal of his time and energy, which, however, were well rewarded. He became managing editor in the second semester of his third year and president of the *Crimson* in his fourth year, doing a highly creditable but far from brilliant job in this position.

Sometime toward the close of his last Harvard year he complained to his roommate that his Harvard studies had been "like an electric light that hasn't any wire. You need the lamp for light but it's useless if you can't switch it on." His implication was that Harvard was responsible for the failure to "connect up" and "switch on," and perhaps Harvard was, in part. But surely the failure was largely Roosevelt's own. His had always been and would always remain a collector's mind, broad but shallow—a mind quick to grasp bits and pieces of information but unresponsive to the challenge of unifying abstractions. He had no interest in generalizing concepts, was inclined to dismiss them as "merely theoretical." He was concerned with "facts," with concrete experiences. These were truly organized only to the severely limited degree that his very simple Christian faith and his commitment to conservation served as organizing themes. And so the fruit of his education became, for the most part, a vast collection of facts, of pieces of information, classified and cataloged but not connected into a coherent body of knowledge.

Following Harvard, he spent two years at Columbia Law School, where he failed to complete his work toward a degree after he had passed the New York bar examination. Columbia was a continuation of the pattern established at Harvard, so far as quality of academic performance was concerned. And as he learned from life, from experience, thereafter, he continued to accumulate facts and to be unconcerned about underlying patterns of meaning. He perhaps gained from this certain practical advantages as political leader: his mind remained flexible (he changed it easily) and open to experience, and he was uninhibited and undisturbed by fundamental doubts.

Perceptive accounts of Roosevelt's education by those personally associated with him are contained in Rexford G. Tugwell's *The Democratic Roosevelt* (Garden City, N.Y.: Doubleday, 1957), which is remarkably acute in its psychological analyses; Frances Perkins's *The Roosevelt I Knew* (New York: Viking, 1946), which is sensitively admiring and often penetrating psychologically if, from a historian's point of view, somewhat overly inclined to give it subject rather more than the benefit of every doubt; and Eleanor Roosevelt's *This I Remember* (New York: Harper, 1949), which is, when read with careful attention to implications, quite harshly critical at times. Full accounts of the Groton and Harvard years are given in Frank Freidel's *Franklin D. Roosevelt: The Apprenticeship* (Boston: Little, Brown & Co., 1952), and, from a different point of view and with considerable dependence on Freidel's research, Kenneth S. Davis's *F.D.R.: The Beckoning of Destiny, 1882–1928* (New York: Putnam, 1971).

KENNETH S. DAVIS

See also Groton School; *Harvard Crimson;* Peabody, Endicott; Wilson, Thomas Woodrow

Eisenhower, Dwight David ("Ike")
(14 October 1890–28 March 1969)

European theater commander in World War II. Dwight D. Eisenhower was born in Denison, Texas, and reared in Abilene, Kansas. A West Point graduate of 1915, he served ably through various tours of duty, especially in staff positions, but rose slowly in rank between the world wars. After six years on Gen. Douglas MacArthur's staff in Washington and Manila, he returned to the United States in late 1939 as a lieutenant colonel. Once he caught the attention of Chief of Staff George C. Marshall, however, his advancements in rank and responsibilities were rapid. Winning Marshall's esteem for his brilliant planning during war games in mid-1941, Eisenhower was assigned to the War Department's War Plans Division in the fall of 1941. The next spring he became head of the Operations Division of the War Department, by which time he had risen in grade to major general. While involved in war planning in Washington, Ike began to have increasing contact with President Roosevelt and by the late spring of 1942 was often joining Marshall in trying to keep FDR's strategic focus on Operation Bolero, the buildup of troops and matériel in the United Kingdom for a future invasion of the European continent.

In June 1942, Marshall selected Eisenhower over 366 other senior officers to command U.S. Army forces in the European theater, then confined to the British Isles. The next month he was promoted to lieutenant general and was appointed Allied commander for Operation Torch, the invasion of French Northwest Africa set for that autumn. During the Torch planning, Eisenhower was often contacted by FDR, especially regarding preinvasion negotiations to ensure the cooperation of French officials and troops in Northwest Africa. Eisenhower worked out an agreement with Admiral Jean Darlan of the collaborationist Vichy regime that resulted in French support, after initial resistance, when Anglo-American

Gen. Dwight D. Eisenhower confers with Field Marshal Montgomery. (Courtesy FDR Library.)

forces invaded Morocco and Algeria in November 1942. The deal provoked considerable public controversy, but Roosevelt and Marshall firmly backed Ike. Following Darlan's assassination in late December, Eisenhower again became involved in sensitive negotiations with the French, this time involving a power struggle between Generals Charles de Gaulle and Henri Giraud. Having relied upon Ike as a virtual ambassador to French Northwest Africa, Roosevelt conferred with him during the Allied conference at Casablanca in January 1943 about the delicate de Gaulle-Giraud situation. Eisenhower was influential in the decision to establish the two French generals in a dual headship over Free French forces, though de Gaulle later gained unilateral control.

Eisenhower was elevated to full general in February 1943, and three months later his forces completed the conquest of Northwest Africa with the capture of Tunisia. In July and August, his Anglo-American armies seized Sicily and invaded south Italy in September. The advance into Italy precipitated the overthrow of fascist dictator Benito Mussolini and the new Italian government's acceptance of Allied surrender terms. Again, Roosevelt entrusted Eisenhower with the early diplomatic negotiations that led to Italy's surrender. By then Ike was earning increasing praise from Roosevelt, Prime Minister Winston S. Churchill, and the Combined Chiefs of Staff for his leadership in three roles: a general who produced victories, an Allied team captain who was adept at working out differences among senior British and American officers, and a leader gifted with political shrewdness and tact who could negotiate effectively in sensitive situations. Because of the high priority he placed on the Anglo-American alliance, FDR was particularly pleased that Churchill was developing a high regard for Eisenhower.

Returning from Allied conferences at Cairo and Teheran, FDR visited with Eisenhower at his headquarters in Algeria in early December 1943 and informed him that he would command Operation Overlord, the invasion of Normandy scheduled for late spring, and would be the supreme Allied commander in the European theater during ensuing operations. The next month Ike moved to England to oversee the huge preparations for Overlord. His cross-channel assault, involving the largest invasion force in history, struck Normandy in June 1944. The Allied armies broke out of their beachheads five weeks later and began a rapid advance across north France, liberating Paris in late August. Meanwhile, another assault force landed in south France and pushed rapidly up the Rhone Valley. After repulsing a fierce German counteroffensive in the Ardennes region of Belgium in the winter of 1944–45, Eisenhower's Allied armies advanced into west Germany, crossing the Rhine in early March 1945.

Eisenhower's decision in favor of a broad- rather than a narrow-front advance into Germany led some postwar critics to charge that he thereby forfeited an opportunity to seize Berlin before the Soviet forces reached it. At the time, however, Eisenhower's position was staunchly supported by Roosevelt, Marshall, and War Department planners, and since then most American military historians, though not British, have tended to accept his judgment. Berlin was captured by the Soviet army on 2 May, and five days later Germany surrendered. Roosevelt's esteem for Eisenhower as an allied commander had grown rapidly since Torch and especially after Overlord. On the president's strong recommendation, Eisenhower was promoted to the five-star grade of general of the army in December 1944.

After serving six months as head of the American occupation forces in west Germany, Eisenhower succeeded Marshall as army chief of staff in late 1945. He held the presidency of Columbia University, 1948–51; commanded NATO forces, 1951–52; and was president of the United States, 1953–61, retiring afterward to a farm near Gettysburg, Pennsylvania.

Dwight D. Eisenhower, *Crusade in Europe* (Garden City, N.Y.: Doubleday, 1948), is his highly readable war memoirs, intended more for general readers than for scholars of the European war. More revealing and extensive are *The Papers of Dwight D. Eisenhower: The War Years,* ed. Alfred D.Chandler and Stephen E. Ambrose, 5 vols. (Baltimore: Johns Hopkins University Press, 1970). Forrest C. Pogue, *The Supreme Command* (Washington: Department of the Army, 1954), a volume in the army's history of the European operations, provides an excellent, detailed study of Eisenhower and his theater command. Another sound work on Ike as wartime leader is Stephen E. Ambrose, *The Supreme Commander: The War Years of General Dwight D. Eisenhower* (Garden City, N.Y.: Doubleday, 1970). An insightful study by Eisenhower's chief of staff is Walter Bedell Smith, *Eisenhower's Six Great Decisions* (New York: Longmans, Green, 1956). The best, as well as the most recent, work on Ike up to his White House years is Stephen E. Ambrose, *Eisenhower,* vol. 1, *Soldier, General of the Army, President-Elect, 1890–1952* (New York: Simon & Schuster, 1983).

D. CLAYTON JAMES

Election of 1910

FDR's first venture in electoral politics. The year 1910 was an opportune time for young Democrats of Franklin D. Roosevelt's background and inclination to enter politics. Across the nation the dominant Republican party was badly divided between its progressive and conservative wings. In New York State, such divisions, revolving about the reform program of the departing governor Charles Evans Hughes, had already weakened the GOP's hold in several upstate areas. In the 1909 assembly elections, for example, the Democrats had won seats in the heavily Republican counties of Clinton, Warren, Genesee, Steuben, Onondaga, and Sullivan. With the dual objective of exploiting Republican weaknesses and yet offering

FDR giving a speech in Dutchess County, New York, during his 1910 campaign for election to the New York State Senate. (Courtesy FDR Library.)

upstate New Yorkers an alternative to the Tammany-controlled state Democratic organization, Auburn independent Thomas Mott Osborne, in early 1910, spearheaded the creation of the Democratic League of the State of New York. The league quickly spread its influence on behalf of "liberal principles" through the upstate regions, including Roosevelt's Dutchess County where it enlisted as members prominent citizens like John Mack, the county's district attorney, and John Sague, mayor of Poughkeepsie.

It was John Mack who first broached to Franklin Roosevelt, then practicing law in New York City, the possibility of running for office as part of the Democratic League's effort to reconstruct the New York party free of bossism and machine control. To Mack, Roosevelt must have been a highly attractive recruit. He was youthful and handsome; he hailed from a well-to-do family with a magic name; and he was available. Bored with the law and inspired by the brilliant example of "Uncle" Theodore Roosevelt, FDR jumped at the chance. He was subsequently tendered the nomination for the state senate seat in the staunchly Republican twenty-sixth district comprising Dutchess, Columbia, and Putnam counties. It is most probable that the local Democratic organization leader, Edward A. Perkins, who was a Tammany ally, assented to the Roosevelt selection because he thought the prospects for victory were slim.

At a Democratic party conference held in Poughkeepsie on 6 October 1910, FDR was formally nominated for the New York State Senate. In a written statement, he pledged his political independence and promised to make a strenuous campaign for office. Although at first he was hardly taken seriously by press and politicians, young Roosevelt set out to visit every corner of the district. In a rented Maxwell touring car bedecked with flags, he and congressional candidate Richard Connell traveled approximately two thousand miles in the tricounty area in four weeks. Roosevelt spoke any place where people, mostly farmers, would listen to him—railroad platforms, feed lots, country stores, inns and taverns, and open fields. A novice campaigner, he nonetheless nimbly adapted himself to his audiences; he quickly developed an easy informality about his mannerisms and his speech making; he exuded self-confidence; and he often flashed a good sense of humor. His message echoed the sentiments of Osborne's Democratic League. He lambasted political bossism—Republican William Barnes and his upstate machine, especially Barnes's local ally, Lou Payn of Columbia County, as well as Tammany's Charlie Murphy, who, Roosevelt argued, should not rule the country districts. He dismissed his senatorial opponent, incumbent John F. Schlosser, as a member of the infamous "Black Horse Cavalry," that bipartisan group of legislators in Albany who opposed Hughes's reform policies. At one juncture, he even declared his support for the Republican governor's progressive program. Although Roosevelt seldom addressed specific issues, he did endorse the direct primary and called for a clean-up of the "corrupt" New York legislature. Throughout the campaign, FDR stressed efficiency and good government in the traditions of Grover Cleveland.

On election day, Roosevelt defeated his opponent by a margin of 1,140 in a total vote that exceeded 30,000. No doubt his victory was part of a national trend that saw the Democrats win control of the House of Representatives for the first time since 1892 and capture governorships in several usually Republican states, including New York. But it was also a personal triumph, for FDR compiled a larger plurality in the tricounty district than Democratic gubernatorial contender John A. Dix. In Albany, beginning in 1911, Roosevelt would thus join dozens of other independents who, like him, owed no obligation to the established party organization.

For a good discussion of Roosevelt's entry in politics, see Frank Freidel, *Franklin D. Roosevelt: The Apprenticeship* (Boston: Little, Brown & Co., 1952). Also extremely useful is Alfred B. Rollins, Jr., *Roosevelt and Howe* (New York: Alfred A. Knopf, 1962), which casts the election of 1910 in New York in the context of Osborne's Democratic League. Both the Franklin D. Roosevelt Papers (Hyde Park, N.Y.) and the Thomas Mott Osborne Papers (Syracuse University Library) contain much information on the topic.

ROBERT F. WESSER

See also State Senator of New York

Election of 1920

Franklin Roosevelt as Democratic vice-presidential candidate received national exposure during the election of 1920, which routed the Democratic party and initiated twelve years of Republican rule. Among Democrats only Roosevelt emerged from the fray in a stronger position than he entered.

Neither major party had an easy time selecting a candidate. The Republican convention chose the relatively unknown Warren G. Harding on the tenth ballot because he was an affable man who threatened no element of the party. Massachusetts governor Calvin Coolidge, who had sought the presidential nomination and was known for his handling of the Boston police strike, received the vice-presidential nomination. The Democratic nomination proved to be even more difficult. The convention was deadlocked for two days until the delegates swung to James M. Cox of Ohio on the forty-fourth ballot. Although he had never met Roosevelt, Cox selected the former assistant secretary of the navy for the vice-presidential nomination because Roosevelt balanced the ticket geographically, "was recognized as an Independent," and had "a well-known name." Tammany boss Charles F. Murphy, Roosevelt's New York State rival, reluctantly consented to Roosevelt's nomination, and the last obstacle was cleared for the popular Roosevelt to be nominated.

Cox and Roosevelt began their campaign with a flurry of activity. Soon after the convention, the running mates met for the first time to discuss campaign strategy. The meeting was friendly, and afterwards Roosevelt spoke for both men when he told a press conference that the League of Nations would be the central issue of the campaign. Cox and Roosevelt decided to visit Woodrow Wilson one week later, and before they left the White House they confirmed in writing that Wilson's proposal for a League of Nations would be the theme of their bid for office. On 7 August Cox made good on his promise when he launched his campaign with a denunciation of Republican isolationism and a promise to join the League. Two days later Roosevelt joined the election battle with a speech from his home in Hyde Park, declaring that his party stood for the "march of progress," not a return to "normal conditions" but a continued search "forward to new better days."

The Democratic and Republican campaign strategies were as different as they could be. Harding ventured off his front porch in Marion, Ohio, only late in the campaign, and Coolidge left Massachusetts for only a few short trips. In contrast, Cox traveled twenty-two thousand miles in thirty-six states and delivered nearly four hundred speeches to an estimated 2 million people. Roosevelt equaled that pace, touring nationwide and making an average of ten speeches per day. He discussed the League of Nations but emphasized economic issues, boasting, "We will drag the enemy off the front porch." Roosevelt made only one serious campaign blunder, a casual remark that "I wrote Haiti's Constitution myself," which allowed Harding to charge the Democrats with an imperial attitude toward "helpless neighbors." Otherwise Roosevelt was an effective speaker who impressed many with his vitality and his articulation of progressive ideas.

In 1920, however, the electorate preferred stability to motion. Cox and Roosevelt's fast-paced campaign, support for the League, and progressive political ideas were out of step with a nation looking for a rest from the political movement of the past two decades. Harding and Coolidge received 16 million votes to Cox and Roosevelt's 9 million, and the margin was even greater in the electoral college. For the Democratic party, the lone bright spot in the election was the emergence of Roosevelt as a leader with a national following.

The standard coverage of the topic is Donald R. McCoy, "Election of 1920," in *History of American Presidential Elections,* ed. Arthur M. Schlesinger, Jr. (New York: McGraw-Hill Book Co., 1971). Roosevelt's role in the election is detailed by Frank Freidel, *Franklin D. Roosevelt: The Ordeal* (Boston: Little, Brown & Co., 1954).

See also Cox, James Middleton; Tammany Hall

A Cox-Roosevelt campaign insignia from the presidential election of 1920. (Courtesy FDR Library.)

Election of 1928

The elections held in 1928 marked the last act of a political drama scripted by the Republican party. Since the Civil War, the GOP had largely dominated national politics in the United States. Never had Republican control seemed more secure than in 1928 as Herbert Hoover crushed Al Smith 58 to 41 percent, cracked the solid South, and entered the White House with firm majorities in both houses of Congress. The Democratic opposition was internally divided, devoid of fresh ideas, and uncertain of its own future as a viable political force.

Yet Hoover's victory in 1928 opened the door for Franklin D. Roosevelt's triumph in 1932, as the Great Engineer failed to cope with the economic distress that began in 1929. Roosevelt himself had reentered the national limelight in 1928 with an upset victory in the New York State gubernatorial campaign. Drafted at the request of Al Smith to help the national ticket carry New York, FDR succeeded where the Happy Warrior failed. Although Smith lost his home state, FDR defeated the state's attorney general Albert Ottinger by a margin of 25,000 out of 4.25 million votes cast. In eloquent testimony to the Democrats' thirst for new leadership, party luminaries hailed the eyelash winner in New York State as a surefire presidential nominee even before he spent a single day in the governor's chair.

The electoral results of 1928 were thus doubly significant to the future of American politics. They associated Herbert Hoover and the GOP with the afflictions of depression and launched the second career of Franklin Delano Roosevelt.

The presidential contest between Al Smith and Herbert Hoover has been a particular focus of scholarly attention. To many historians these presidential combatants appeared to represent the antagonism between an "old" America of Protestant, native-stock, Prohibitionist, rural dwellers and a "new" America of Catholic, foreign-stock, anti-Prohibitionist urbanites. Historians who contend that two conflicting traditions clashed in 1928 suggest that Al Smith's defeat moved millions of new Americans into the Democratic fold, foreshadowing the New Deal coalition.

In fact, 1928 was the last election of the old politics, not the first contest of the new. The realignments that broke the Republican hold over American politics began only after the advent of depression and were not rooted in the politics of the 1920s. America's Great Depression thus becomes a more significant discontinuity in the nation's political history than the now conventional wisdom would have us believe.

A two-tiered realignment of the American party system took place only after 1929. First, between 1930 and 1932 the Democrats benefited from a depression effect that swelled the ranks of party loyalists throughout the United States, but neither restored the Democrats to majority status nor reshuffled the composition of voter groupings. Second, between 1932 and 1936 Roosevelt's policies and leadership created a positive incentive for fealty to the Democratic party, especially among urbanites, blacks, young voters, and those benefiting most from his economic programs. This Roosevelt effect both established the party's national dominance and shaped the economic and social composition of the New Deal coalition.

The gubernatorial race that catapulted FDR to the forefront of party leadership emerged as part of Al Smith's strategy for victory in the bitterly fought presidential campaign. The Happy Warrior knew that he could not win without carrying New York, but feared that his hopes would be buried in an avalanche of Hoover votes from upstate counties. Of all potential nominees for governor, only Franklin D. Roosevelt possessed the qualities necessary to aid Smith north of the Bronx: personal appeal, oratorical skill, upstate Protestant roots, independence of Tammany Hall, and "the best trade name in American political life."

Neither FDR nor his mentor Louis Howe coveted the gubernatorial nomination. Both believed 1928 to be a Republican year and feared that an unsuccessful campaign would confound their presidential ambitions. On the eve of the Democratic State Convention, Roosevelt announced that his continuing quest for recovery from polio demanded two more winters at Warm Springs, ruling out any contest for governor. But FDR succumbed to a personal appeal from Al Smith combined with nomination by acclamation at the state convention.

Once nominated, FDR threw himself into the campaign with the same enthusiasm that he approached every political contest. Quickly dispelling rumors that his health was being sacrificed to Al Smith's ambition, FDR campaigned energetically throughout the Empire State. "We started in Orange County," he wrote of one campaign swing, "and we went on through Sullivan, Delaware, Broome, Steuben, and so forth, out through the Southern Tier, all the way to Jamestown. . . . And then, for good measure, we just dropped into Schenectady and spoke there earlier in the evening, and now here we are in Troy. Too bad about this unfortunate sick man, isn't it."

FDR pounded away at such progressive themes as the public development of water power, aid to labor, and parity for the farmer. He relearned New York State politics en route, ably assisted by speech writer Samuel I. Rosenman. Roosevelt blasted the GOP for their string of broken promises in both state and national politics, but scarcely even mentioned his particular Republican opponent. Although an able public official with a mildly progressive record, Attorney General Ottinger could neither match FDR's oratorical skill nor find an issue capable of igniting the enthusiasm of voters. Ironically, although Franklin Roosevelt denounced the emergence of religious bigotry in the presidential campaign, he became the unintended beneficiary of anti-Semitic votes cast against his Jewish opponent.

If religious issues lurked on the periphery of the gubernatorial campaign, they occupied center stage in the 1928 contest for the presidency. Hoover and Smith were both regarded as the leading public officials their respective parties had to offer. Hoover was the consummate bureaucrat who had transformed the Department of Commerce into a driving force of domestic policy. Al Smith, the master of practical politics, had served four terms as governor of New York State, earning a national reputation for his devotion to social welfare and government efficiency. Yet Al

Smith's Catholicism sparked far more interest in 1928 than either the accomplishments or the policies of the two campaigners.

Responses to Smith's religion preoccupied the public, commanded the attention of party leaders, and sharply skewed the voters' choices. The sectarian campaign launched against him ranged from fulminations against "Rum and Romanism" to thoughtful ruminations on the relationship between church and state in Catholic theology. A profusion of scandal sheets flooded the nation in 1928, often targeted to localities that seemed most receptive to anti-Catholic appeals. In his hometown of Hyde Park, Franklin D. Roosevelt observed, "practically all" the families served by the local post office "began in early July to receive copies of the *Fellowship Forum,* the *New Menace* and one or two similar [anti-Catholic] publications."

Although campaigners could not openly court either pro- or anti-Catholic support, each campaign sought to exploit the religious agitation. The Republican leadership offered mild denunciations of intolerance combined with an attempt to accuse Democrats of injecting religion into the campaign. The Hoover organization, moreover, neither disciplined local politicians who pandered to religious bigotry nor attempted to police their activities. The Democrats, in turn, sought to equate votes for Al Smith with support for religious toleration. "Religious prejudice has become a major issue," noted former secretary of war Breckinridge Long, "and tolerance is on our side."

Regardless of their economic position, their place of residence, their stand on Prohibition, or their ethnic heritage, Protestant and Catholic voters split more decisively in 1928 than in either previous or subsequent presidential elections. No other cleavage within the electorate stands out so distinctively in that presidential year. Both Protestants and Catholics responded to religious tensions as Smith benefited from a pro-Catholic and Hoover from an anti-Catholic vote.

If religious strife in 1928 did not durably realign the commitments of voters, it did spark an extraordinary increase in voter turnout that reversed the trend of nearly three decades. Although historians have stressed Al Smith's activation of Catholic and new immigrant voters, they have slighted the boom in Republican votes that occurred in 1928 as well. The GOP gained 5.67 million votes over 1924 compared to a gain of 6.63 million for the Democrats, despite the GOP's enormous lead over their rivals in 1924 and the correspondingly greater number of votes lost through normal attrition.

Other issues divided voters in 1928. As the first presidential candidate to challenge the Eighteenth Amendment and the Volstead Act, Al Smith garnered support from wets, while drys tended to opt for Herbert Hoover. Yet both parties deliberately obscured the Prohibition issue during the campaign, and the wet and dry controversy had less influence on voters than did religious differences.

Far more than previous Democratic candidates, Smith also garnered the votes of immigrants and first-generation Americans. Foreign-stock voters, however, did not form a relatively larger percentage of his coalition than of those forged by Progressive candidate La Follette in 1924 or by Roosevelt in 1932. Yet the composition of foreign-stock support for the Democrats shifted from 1928 to 1932, as predominantly Protestant groups figured much more prominently in the vote for FDR than in the tally for Al Smith.

Independent of religion, ethnic heritage, and Prohibition, the cleft between city and country failed to emerge as an influence on voting behavior. This finding suggests that explanations for the heavily urban character of the New Deal vote must be found in the policies and politics of the 1930s rather than in any urban-rural split that predates the great crash.

Most historians agree that the combination of domestic tranquility, international stability, and economic prosperity guaranteed a Republican victory in 1928. Yet Franklin Roosevelt and other critics believed that Smith should have exploited the uneven distribution of prosperity through "a progressive attack against the Coolidge-Hoover economic program." Instead, the reformist governor of New York State ran a cautious campaign that relied on his personal appeal to ordinary citizens and sought to propitiate business interests that feared radical changes in the status quo. Although Al Smith's 1928 tally was inversely related to a voter's economic standing, this division of the electorate reflected long-standing voter alignments rather than the issues and events of 1928.

The politics of race also figured prominently in 1928, as the Hoover campaign sought to crack the solidly Democratic South by exploiting the opponent's religion, his opposition to Prohibition, and his alleged sympathy for racial equality. "An intelligent effort is being made this year," wrote publicity chief Senator Henry J. Allen, "to give the white folks down there a chance" to support the GOP. Smith boosters responded in kind, promoting Democratic votes as necessary for the continuation of white supremacy. Although Hoover succeeded in curtailing the usual harvest of Democratic ballots in the South, the Great Depression soon shattered the dream of establishing a competitive, white-oriented Republican party in states of the Old Confederacy.

In the aftermath of Al Smith's defeat, one of FDR's correspondents confided to him that no Democrat could be elected president without first reeducating the public in favor of progressive reform. "I am thoroughly convinced that no candidate can be sold to the public outside of his immediate locality, without a campaign of education.... Since the days of the 'Full Dinner Pail,' ... the Republican party has been constantly hammering into the minds of the voters ... these slogans, backed up with constant reference in the press to 'good times,' until many, many people really believe they are living in an age of prosperity excelling all expectations." Beginning in 1929, the Great Depression reeducated the public far more quickly than anyone would have dreamed possible from the perspective of 1928. Coerced into a political comeback that he had viewed as premature, Franklin D. Roosevelt ironically found himself ideally situated as governor of New York State to exploit Herbert Hoover's failed response to economic distress.

In a path-breaking work, *The Future of American Politics* (New York: Harper & Bros., 1952), Samuel Lubell argues that Al Smith, not Franklin D. Roosevelt, forged the political alignments characteristic of the 1930s and 1940s. The sons and daughters of the new immigrants, in this view, were first drawn to the Democratic fold by Al Smith and subsequently became the backbone of the New Deal coalition. Kristi Andersen, in *The Creation of a Democratic Majority, 1928–1936* (Chicago: University of Chicago Press, 1979), updates the Lubell thesis, using an ingenious reanalysis of surveys asking individuals to recall their past voter behavior. According to Andersen, the New Deal realignment arose from the mobilization of newly eligible or previously inactive voters not yet immunized to partisan change by a previous commitment. Allan J. Lichtman, *Prejudice and the Old Politics: The Presidential Election of 1928* (Chapel Hill: University of North Carolina Press, 1979) examines both the 1928 contest and its relationship to presidential elections between 1916 and 1940. It combines quantitative and traditional approaches to historical study, developing more thoroughly many of the themes sketched in this essay. Edmund A. Moore, *A Catholic Runs for President: The Campaign of 1928* (New York: Ronald Press Co., 1956) is a narrative account of the election that stresses the sectarian campaign against Al Smith's religion.

ALLAN J. LICHTMAN

See also Democratic Party; Hoover, Herbert Clark; Republican Party; Smith, Alfred E.

Election of 1934

Dramatic congressional election victory for Roosevelt and the Democrats. President Roosevelt approached the 1934 elections not as party leader but as "president of all the people." Yet his bipartisan stance concealed his quiet involvement in several crucial states. In California, Upton Sinclair's End Poverty in California (EPIC) movement jelled into a gubernatorial campaign for the socialist novelist. Sinclair met Roosevelt at the White House, and the two parted on amiable terms. But Sinclair's radicalism frightened some New Dealers, and as election day drew near Roosevelt withdrew support from Sinclair's losing candidacy. In the Pennsylvania election between old friend and progressive Republican Gifford Pinchot and a conservative Democrat, Roosevelt adopted a hands-off policy. Faced with a choice in Wisconsin between the Progressive candidacies of Robert and Philip La Follette and the Democrat regulars, Roosevelt again took a nonpartisan stance. In other states as well, Roosevelt played a low-key role, quietly encouraging liberal candidates of either party but not breaking with the regular Democrats.

The 1934 elections gave Roosevelt a surprisingly strong vote of confidence. Normally in off-year elections the party in power loses some congressional strength, but this year proved the only modern exception. Roosevelt toured the nation in August and was pleased beyond expectations with the results, "The reception was grand and I am more than ever convinced that, so far as having the people with us goes, we are just as strong—perhaps stronger—than ever before." Election day bore out Roosevelt's assessment. With voter turnout unusually high for an off-year election, Democratic strength rose in the House from 310 to 319, while in the Senate the Democrats picked up 10 new seats to bring their total to 69. The Democrats' two-thirds Senate majority was the greatest ever held by either party, and in the House the Republicans slipped to 103 representatives, the smallest percentage in their party's history. The vote so overwhelmingly affirmed Roosevelt that journalist William Allen White proclaimed, "He has been all but crowned by the people." But the election results were more than a show of strength for Roosevelt personally; they also showed strong support for bolder policies to deal with the depression. The election campaigns evidenced an undercurrent of radical discontent, and the new Congress contained a number of new members elected on programs to the left of the president. This set the stage for a new flurry of New Deal legislation beginning in 1935.

Three standard accounts of the politics of the period, all sympathetic to Roosevelt, are William E. Leuchtenburg, *Franklin D. Roosevelt and the New Deal* (New York: Harper & Row, 1963), James MacGregor Burns, *Roosevelt: The Lion and the Fox* (New York: Harcourt, Brace & World, 1956), and Arthur M. Schlesinger, Jr., *The Coming of the New Deal* (Boston: Houghton Mifflin Co., 1958).

See also Congress, United States; Democratic Party; Elections in the Roosevelt Era; Republican Party

---

Election of 1938

This congressional election ensured the stalemate of the New Deal as Roosevelt's efforts to realign the Democratic party failed. President Roosevelt entered the election of 1938 on the defensive. Democrats could be expected to lose seats in Congress, as presidential parties always did in off-year elections (with the exception of 1934). Roosevelt's problems were confounded by the coalition of conservative Democrats and Republicans that had formed in Congress to block Roosevelt's Supreme Court reform and his executive reorganization plans. The recession of 1937–38 further weakened Roosevelt's public standing and made his coalition vulnerable to attacks from the Right. Despite all this working against him, Roosevelt thought he had a mandate from his 1936 landslide to complete the reform package of the New Deal; so he chose the 1938 election as an opportune time to rid the Democratic party of obstructionists and bring conservatives in line with the party's national platform.

Roosevelt's attempt at party realignment met

with more failure than success. He began the campaign with a cross-country train tour, stopping to speak in behalf of certain liberal Democrats while pointedly ignoring some conservative members of his own party. In New York he opposed House Rules Committee chairman John O'Connor, a persistent New Deal foe. Roosevelt's "purge" (as reporters called it) centered in the South where he spoke against powerful senators Walter George of Georgia, "Cotton Ed" Smith of South Carolina, and Millard Tydings of Maryland. Roosevelt's efforts had little noticeable effect, however; O'Connor lost and the southern trio won, with all four races being determined more by local interests than national concerns. The president's personal popularity and his appeal for realignment of the party along liberal principles could not transcend the strong localism of the voters, who seemed to resent outside intervention in what they viewed as their own affairs.

The election day results confirmed the rightward swing of public opinion. With the failure of the "purge," conservative Democrats gained strength and the Republicans nearly doubled their numbers in the House, going from 88 to 170 representatives. The GOP picked up 7 seats in the Senate and more than a dozen governorships. Some prominent liberal governors, including Philip La Follette of Wisconsin, Frank Murphy of Michigan, and Elmer Benson of Minnesota, lost, while a group of new faces emerged among Republican leaders. In Roosevelt's own New York, Thomas E. Dewey came so close to beating Roosevelt ally Herbert H. Lehman that Dewey began to be considered for national office. Most important, the New Deal coalition in Congress was decimated. Conservative Democrats who united with Republicans could stymie any Roosevelt initiative, and the new Congress began to look for ways to cut back on the New Deal. The failure of party realignment diminished Roosevelt's personal power, especially since he was in the final two years of what most expected to be his last pesidential term. Roosevelt tried to put a good face on the results, insisting that the election was not a rejection of the New Deal, but for the next two years, his New Deal remained on the defensive.

James MacGregor Burns, *Roosevelt: The Lion and the Fox* (New York: Harcourt, Brace & World, 1956) and William E. Leuchtenburg, *Franklin D. Roosevelt and the New Deal* (New York: Harper & Row, 1963) both provide a sympathetic view of Roosevelt in the election. For the conservatives' perspective, see James T. Patterson, *Congressional Conservatism and the New Deal* (Lexington: University of Kentucky Press, 1967).

See also Congress, United States; Democratic Party; Elections in the Roosevelt Era; "Purge" of 1938; Republican Party

---

Election of 1942

In the 1942 election, the Republicans scored major gains as President Roosevelt remained aloof from pol-

itics. The election presented the president with a dilemma as to the nature of his wartime leadership. To downplay politics and emphasize national unity for the sake of defeating fascism seemed the best way to ensure support for the war effort. But this nonpartisan strategy would risk the loss of support for the social gains of the New Deal and might allow conservatives in Congress to gain more power. Liberals within the administration urged Roosevelt to stress the ideological dimension of the war as a struggle for progressive social reform and the essential unity of domestic and foreign policy.

Although at other times he was carried by this argument, Roosevelt decided that in the 1942 elections, politics would be "out." He feared that to accept the political dimension of the war would alienate business leaders and jeopardize the national spirit of good will which was necessary for the success of such wartime measures as the draft, rationing, and economic controls. Thus he acted as commander in chief above the political fray and intervened only briefly in partisan politics. When Edward J. Flynn, chairman of the national Democratic party, suggested that a vote for Republicans consoled the Axis governments, Roosevelt repudiated Flynn and asked only that voters support candidates who would back up the wartime government.

Roosevelt broke his silence for only three races, two of them in his native New York. He used his influence to try to nominate a Democratic candidate for governor who would present a strong challenge to Republican candidate Thomas E. Dewey. These efforts ended in confusion and Dewey won easily. Roosevelt also spoke out against New York Republican congressman Hamilton Fish, a conservative and isolationist critic of Roosevelt, but again to no avail as Fish overwhelmed his lackluster Democratic opponent. Roosevelt spoke most eloquently for his old friend and liberal crusader, Republican senator George Norris of Nebraska. Despite the president's endorsement of him as "one of the major prophets of America," Norris lost to a conservative Democrat.

If Roosevelt was too busy with the war to engage in politics, his conservative critics were not so constrained. The Republicans attacked the continued centralization of governmental power during the war as an extension of the New Deal. They found a perfect target in the Office of Civilian Defense, an organization created to boost civilian morale, which conservatives portrayed as another New Deal social engineering scheme. The Republican-dominated press continued to picture Roosevelt as a power grabber and hinted that he might cancel future elections. Wendell Willkie, the titular head of the Republican party who shared Roosevelt's internationalism and a measure of his domestic liberalism, agreed to spend most of the campaign season touring the world as Roosevelt's representative and so left the Republican party to its more conservative elements.

The result was a resounding loss for the Democrats, even greater than the expected losses for a presidential party in an off-year election. The Republicans gained forty-six seats in the House and nine in the Senate plus several governorships. This gave the Congress of 1943 a dominant coalition of Republicans and conservative Democrats and sent a message to Roosevelt that the public was unhappy with his policies. An extremely low voter turnout, caused in part because youthful servicemen, mostly Democrats, were unable to vote, helped the Republicans, who were delighted with the results and hoped to begin to repeal the New Deal. *Fortune* magazine wrote, "The victorious candidates rode an anti-Roosevelt and an anti-Washington wave." By remaining aloof from most party politics, Roosevelt had kept his personal prestige intact, but the election cost him support for his party and his program.

Roosevelt's role in the election of 1942 is detailed by James MacGregor Burns in *Roosevelt: The Soldier of Freedom* (New York: Harcourt Brace Jovanovich, 1970). The mood of the nation is neatly summarized in John Morton Blum, *V Was for Victory* (New York: Harcourt Brace Jovanovich, 1976).

See also Congress, United States; Democratic Party; Elections in the Roosevelt Era

Elections in the Roosevelt Era, 1932–1944

Patterns of voting in the United States changed fundamentally in response to the Great Depression, the programs of the New Deal, and the personality of Franklin D. Roosevelt. Many of the characteristics of the coalition of Democratic voters that emerged in the 1930s are still discernible even in the last quarter of the twentieth century, over fifty years after FDR's first election. The elections of the 1930s and the emergence of the "Roosevelt coalition" ended a period of over three decades during which the Republican party apparently claimed the allegiance of the majority of the active electorate. Between 1896 and 1932, only one Democrat, Woodrow Wilson, was elected to the presidency, and that interruption in Republican domination probably occurred only because the progressive faction in the Republican party followed Theodore Roosevelt into the Progressive party

in 1912, thus preventing the reelection of William Howard Taft. Wilson failed to obtain support of a majority of the American electorate in either 1912 or 1916 when he was reelected; and after the Republican landslide victory in 1920, control of the Congress and the presidency remained solidly in Republican hands until Roosevelt's election in 1932.

The Roosevelt victory in 1932 was a landslide. He received 57.4 percent of the popular vote and 472 electoral votes. This shift to the Democrats seems even more overwhelming when it is recalled that the 1924 Democratic nominee, John W. Davis, polled only 28.8 percent of the vote and Alfred E. Smith of New York was overcome by the Hoover landslide of 1928. The Roosevelt victory in 1932 was made even more impressive by the success of Democratic candidates for the House of Representatives and the Senate. After the 1932 election, the Democrats controlled both Houses of Congress with substantial majorities. The Democrats won 310 seats in the House, the Republicans 117; in the Senate the distribution was 60 Democrats and 35 Republicans. The election of 1932 was the first election since 1916 which resulted in a Democratic-controlled Congress.

Although any nominee the Democrats were likely to select in 1932 could have defeated Hoover, the overwhelming election victories of Franklin D. Roosevelt and the Democratic party in subsequent elections testify to the enduring nature of public support for Roosevelt and his party. In the first national election after the enactment of the legislation of the first hundred days, the mid-term election of 1934, Democratic seats in the House of Representatives increased by 9 and the number of new Democratic senators also by 9. According to an axiom of American politics commonly held at the time, the party that won a presidential election could expect to lose the next mid-term election; thus, the Democratic victory in the election of 1934 has been interpreted ever since as a ringing endorsement of Roosevelt and the legislation of the early New Deal. The Democratic Congress elected in 1934 then enacted some of the most important legislation of the New Deal years during the second hundred days in 1935.

The election of 1936 registered an even more resounding popular endorsement of Roosevelt, the New Deal, and the Democratic party. The Republicans

Voting Behavior in Presidential Elections, 1932–1944

YEAR	TOTAL POPULAR VOTE FOR FDR	TOTAL NUMBER OF VOTES CAST	TOTAL ELECTORAL VOTE FOR FDR	PERCENT POPULAR VOTE FOR FDR
1932	22,809,638	39,738,045	472	57.4
1936	27,752,869	45,646,166	523	60.8
1940	27,307,819	49,831,786	449	54.8
1944	25,606,585	47,862,775	432	53.5

Source: John Morton Blum et al., *The National Experience*, 4th ed. (New York: Harcourt Brace Jovanovich, 1977).

FDR campaigning by train, Wilkes-Barre, Pennsylvania, 29 October 1936. (Ace Hoffman, Wilkes Barre.)

nominated Alfred M. Landon of Kansas, the only Republican governor to be elected in 1932 and reelected in 1934. Landon has been described as an effective candidate who was more liberal than his party; but Landon was no match for Roosevelt in 1936. The once dominant Republican party was engulfed again in 1936, this time by even greater margins. Roosevelt lost only two states, Maine and Vermont, and he amassed 523 electoral votes to only 8 for Landon. The popular vote was almost as overwhelming. Roosevelt won 60.8 percent of the popular vote, a margin exceeded only once in all the presidential elections since the early nineteenth century—Lyndon Johnson's majority in 1964. Democratic candidates for lesser offices in 1936 ran very well too, and Democratic ma-

Ross Lewis cartoon, Milwaukee Journal, 1939–40.

jorities in the House and Senate increased again. After 1936 in the House the Democrats controlled 331 seats and the Republicans 89; they had 76 Senate seats, compared to only 16 held by the Republicans.

Democratic successes at the polls after 1936 were not as spectacular, but the party's control of the national government continued unbroken throughout the Roosevelt years. In the 1938 mid-term election, Republicans regained several seats in the House and the Senate, and in the presidential election of 1940, the Republican nominee, Wendell L. Willkie, was more successful than Landon had been four years earlier. Several states in the Great Plains and the Midwest returned to the Republican column in 1940, when the electoral vote was 449 for Roosevelt, 82 for Willkie. Roosevelt's share of the popular vote was still a robust 54.7 percent, compared to 44.8 percent for Willkie, but the victory in 1940 hardly compared to the landslide in 1936.

During the years of World War II, election results varied little from the margins established in 1940. In the mid-term election of 1942, the Democrats retained control of the House of Representatives by only a narrow margin (218 Democrats, 208 Republicans), but the Senate remained safely in the hands of a substantial Democratic majority (58 Democrats, 37 Republicans). The Republicans nominated Thomas E. Dewey, governor of New York, in 1944; and Dewey's effort to attract voters away from Roosevelt was only slightly more successful than Willkie's had been in 1940. Dewey carried a few states in the Great Plains and Midwest plus Maine and Vermont. These states gave Dewey an electoral vote of 99; Roosevelt won 432. Roosevelt's popular majority again declined slightly to 53.4 percent, and Dewey won 45.9 percent. Democrats gained a substantial number of seats in the House of Representatives in 1944 (242 Democrats, 190 Republicans), lost 2 seats in the Senate (56 Democrats, 38 Republicans), and thus retained a solid majority in both Houses.

The Democratic share of the popular vote in the presidential election of 1944, the last election in which Roosevelt was a candidate, declined substantially in comparison to the landslides of 1932 and 1936, but the Democratic party was still very much in control of the national government until after the election of 1944. In fact, Democrats have failed to win a majority in both Houses of Congress only three times since 1932, in the elections of 1946, 1952, and 1980. A major realignment in the voting habits of the American electorate had occurred, and the Democratic party had been transformed from a bitterly divided and weak minority into the party of most Americans. Millions of voters had acquired an enduring allegiance to the Democratic party and would continue to think of themselves as Democrats, and usually vote Democratic, long after the economic crisis of the 1930s had passed into history. It is with good reason that Samuel Lubell named this political transformation the "Roosevelt revolution."

The voters who participated in the Roosevelt revolution in the 1930s were predominantly new voters.

The rate of turnout of the eligible electorate increased from less than 45 percent in the mid-1920s to about 57 percent in 1936. The total votes cast for president increased by over 70 percent between 1920 and 1936, and most of the increase in turnout benefited Roosevelt and the other Democratic candidates. Indeed, except for the election of 1928, the actual number of votes cast for Republican nominees for president between 1920 and 1936 was remarkably constant. The total vote for Alfred Landon in 1936 was 16,679,543; in 1920 Warren G. Harding won 16,333,314 votes. The point may be even more emphatically made by examining selected urban areas where the shift to the Democratic party was most pronounced. In Chicago (Cook County) between 1920 and 1936, the total votes cast for all presidential candidates increased by 64.6 percent, but the vote for Republican presidential candidates increased by only 15.8 percent. In New York County, the total vote increased 37.6 percent, the Republican vote only 15.1 percent, and the comparable figures in Philadelphia County were 91.7 percent and −11.8 percent. In nineteen cities where the first- and second-generation immigrant stock populations amounted to over one-half of the population, the Democratic vote increased by 205 percent, the Republican vote by 29 percent. Thus the Republican presidential vote totals increased slightly, but the preponderance of new votes were cast for Franklin D. Roosevelt.

The principal source of increased Democratic strength in the 1930s came from the cities, especially the industrial cities of the Northeast and the Great Lakes. Lubell called it "the revolt of the cities." These new Democrats were working-class, low-income voters—many of them first- or second-generation immigrants from Eastern and Southern Europe who had crowded into America's industrial cities in the late nineteenth and early twentieth centuries. Most of the foreign-stock population was Catholic, another large portion was Jewish; and these groups were almost certainly among the first to suffer from the rampaging unemployment of the early 1930s. Native-born, old-stock Americans of the working class and, after 1936, urban blacks, too, responded to the appeal of Roosevelt and the New Deal, but the preponderance of the new Democrats were urban foreign-stock voters.

The new Democrats of the 1930s rarely, if ever, had voted before. Most of them were recruited from the nonvoting population of the 1920s which amounted to more than half the eligible electorate. Many nonvoters were immigrants who had entered the United States before World War I but had not been naturalized until the 1920s. The children of the immigrants were growing into adulthood in the same years; and because they were young and children of nonvoting parents, they also constituted a large and growing proportion of the nonvoting electorate. A third group of nonvoters in the 1920s consisted of women who only slowly began to exercise the right to vote after the adoption of the Nineteenth Amendment in 1919. Foreign-stock women may have been more reluctant to exercise the franchise than women of native stock, and the evidence suggests that women in all socioeconomic and ethnic groups tended to vote far less frequently than men in the same groups. Thus the pool of nonvoters in the 1920s that would supply the new Democratic majority consisted predominantly of groups that only recently had become eligible to vote through naturalization, coming of age, or the Nineteenth Amendment.

A recent analysis by Kristi Andersen of the voting histories as recalled by almost fifteen thousand individuals suggests persuasively that young voters were particularly significant contributors to the surge to the Democratic party in the 1930s. These individuals were interviewed by the Survey Research Center at the University of Michigan between 1952 and 1974. In 1932 the youngest age group (twenty-one to twenty-four years), for example, was 55 percent Democratic and the entire voting population 52 percent Democratic. Four years later in 1936, the youngest age group was 61 percent Democratic, while the rest of the population recalled being only 53 percent Democratic. It also appears from this analysis of voters' recollections that many who came of age before 1928 did not vote until 1928 or afterwards and acquired a partisan identification, usually Democratic, sometime after that. Most members of a younger group that became old enough to vote after 1928 and before 1936, however, voted as soon as they were eligible, and overwhelmingly they voted Democratic.

The importance of southern voters to the New Deal majority in the 1930s cannot of course be ignored. White southerners, solidly Democratic since Reconstruction when the Democratic party had become the party of white supremacy, continued to cast their votes for Democratic candidates through the Roosevelt era and afterwards. Over 75 percent of the American black population still resided in the South in the 1930s, but most southern blacks had been disenfranchised since the late nineteenth century. As late as 1940, only about 5 percent of blacks of voting age were registered to vote in the former Confederate states. Thus, with few blacks voting in the elections of the 1930s, the South cast over 75 percent of its popular vote and all its electoral vote for Roosevelt. In 1940 the South gave Roosevelt a 73 percent majority and, again, its entire electoral vote. The South produced a nearly unanimous Democratic representation in Congress, as it had since Reconstruction. Every southern senator in 1936, for example, was a Democrat, and so were 119 of the 120 southern members of the House of Representatives. Roosevelt actually polled slightly higher percentages of the popular vote in the southern states in each of his four elections in the 1930s and 1940s than did any other Democratic nominee since the beginning of the twentieth century, but the differences were only marginal. Southern voters continued to respond to national presidential contests much as they had since Reconstruction.

Urban black voters were a small but, for the future, a very significant new component of the Roosevelt coalition. Black migration to northern urban areas since World War I had been substantial, and the northern black population approximately doubled between 1920 and 1940. Blacks who voted in northern cities evidently remained loyal to the Republican party in 1932, but in 1936 and 1940 blacks voted for Roosevelt at a rate well above that of the electorate as a whole. On the other hand, most blacks continued to show a reluctance to call themselves Democrats, and public opinion polls in 1937 and 1940 both showed that less than 45 percent of the blacks interviewed identified themselves as Democrats. It was easier for blacks to vote for Roosevelt and other Democrats in the 1930s and early 1940s than to abandon the party of Lincoln; and it was not until later that the partisan identification of most urban blacks fell into line with their voting behavior. Almost no New Deal legislation was written specifically to aid blacks, and no attack on the Jim Crow system in the South came from Roosevelt's administration; but urban blacks shared in the New Deal programs intended to aid the poor and the unemployed generally. In any case, most urban blacks switched to vote for Roosevelt and the Democrats in 1936, and they have been voting Democratic ever since.

Other important groups in the voting population were not attracted to Roosevelt and the Democratic party and remained or became Republican identifiers in the 1930s. Northeastern Protestants displayed considerable resistance to the surge to vote Democratic. Polls of voters in the 1930s show that in the northeastern states 51 percent of this group voted for Alfred Landon in 1936 and 68 percent for Wendell Willkie in 1940. The party identification of northeastern Protestants revealed a strong affinity for the Republican party, and 54 percent of the Protestants in the Northeast professed to be Republicans in a 1940 opinion survey. In the Midwest by 1940, Republican strength was also strong among Protestants. Slightly over half of the midwestern Protestants voted for Roosevelt in 1936, but four years later Willkie garnered about 61 percent of the midwestern Protestant vote. While only half of the midwestern Protestants interviewed identified themselves as Republicans, a mere 30 percent called themselves Democrats.

Aggregate election statistics suggest a similar picture. All regions of the nation displayed a substantial across-the-board shift to the Democratic party in the 1930s. Some of this shift was a deviation from a traditional attachment to the Republican party that would not endure long past 1936. As prosperity returned and the nature of the New Deal program became clearer, northern rural, more affluent, and traditional Republican areas reverted to their "normal" voting habits. In a sample of thirty rural Protestant counties in northern states analyzed by James L. Sundquist, the Democratic presidential vote increased by only 2 percent between 1920 and 1944. These counties surged into the Democratic party in 1932, but this was only a deviation. By 1944 the Republican party was almost as strong as it had been before 1932. Examination of the aggregate state vote points

to the same conclusion. The states that Roosevelt had carried in 1936 but failed to carry in 1940 and 1944 were mainly rural states in the Great Plains, the Midwest, and New England.

Republicans in the 1930s also tended to be of a higher socioeconomic status. Indeed, in the 1930s, class distinctions were probably drawn more sharply than ever before in American history. Partisan differences along socioeconomic lines existed only outside the South, however, since almost all white southerners voted Democratic. In the nonsouthern states, class voting differences were more clearly distinguishable. For example, 51 percent of those with some college education voted for Roosevelt in 1936, and in 1940 that proportion dropped to 39 percent. By contrast, those who had finished high school gave Roosevelt 60 percent of their vote in 1936 and 56 percent in 1940. Voters with less than a high school education gave Roosevelt 69 percent of their vote in 1936 and 67 percent in 1940. Those in business and the professions voted 48 percent for Roosevelt in 1936 and 31 percent in 1940. Data on voting of working-class occupations in 1936 are unavailable, but in 1940 skilled workers gave Roosevelt 57 percent of their vote, while 68 percent of the semiskilled and unskilled reportedly voted for Roosevelt. Everett C. Ladd, Jr., and Charles D. Hadley concluded in *Transformations of the American Party System* that there was in the polling data "a rather neat declension in Democratic support with movement from the lowest to the highest socioeconomic stratum, whatever the measure used" (p. 68). On the other hand, as Ladd and Hadley emphasized, class distinctions between the two parties in the 1930s often have been exaggerated. While white northern Protestants ranking in the lowest third on a measure of socioeconomic status voted 60 percent for Roosevelt in 1936, only 49 percent did so in 1940. Moreover, only 36 percent of the northern Protestants in the lowest third identified themselves as Democrats in 1940. The Republican party had greater appeal for most of the better educated and to those who were relatively well-to-do, but it also apparently retained the allegiance of most northern white Protestants, even those of very low socioeconomic standing.

The socioeconomic, ethnic, and religious composition of the urban voters who participated in the Roosevelt revolution was similar in many respects to the vote cast for Alfred E. Smith for president in 1928. This similarity was perhaps first noticed by Lubell in *The Future of American Politics.* Lubell pointed out that Al Smith carried a majority of the vote cast in the twelve largest cities in 1928. Thus, concluded Lubell, "the Republicans' hold on the cities was broken not by Roosevelt but by Alfred E. Smith. Before the Roosevelt Revolution there was an Al Smith Revolution" (p. 49). According to this argument, Al Smith, a Catholic from New York City, appealed especially to urban foreign-stock populations, and in 1928 these voters marched to the polls in unprecedented numbers to vote for him. In other words,

Lubell insisted that one of the most critical components of the Roosevelt majority actually moved into the Democratic party in 1928.

The view that an Al Smith revolution preceded the Roosevelt revolution has found its way into many accounts of this period, and often, as Sundquist has noted, the two revolutions are treated as two stages of the same realigning era. It is very probable that the shift to Al Smith in the major industrial areas in 1928 and the strength of Roosevelt in these same urban areas in the 1930s and 1940s were responses by the same groups to two very different sets of stimuli. The surge of urban foreign-stock voters to support Smith was apparently a response to Smith's personal attractiveness—to his image. But the depression after 1929 introduced a combination of new variables very different from those at work in 1928. The immigrant-stock urban workers who would have been attracted presumably to Al Smith were also among those affected immediately and most fundamentally by the depression. There is, to be sure, some evidence that tends to support the view that a small but enduring shift to the Democrats may have occurred in a few cities—Boston, Providence, Chicago, Cleveland, and perhaps Philadelphia. These modest Democratic gains seem hardly worthy of description as a revolution, however, and it is more appropriate to conclude, as did Sundquist, that "the minor realignment of 1928 in the cities can . . . be considered an episode . . . distinct from the realignment of the 1930s."

In any case, available evidence indicates that some of the new Democrats voted Democratic for the first time in 1928, some in 1932, and others later in the 1930s. The single act of voting for Al Smith in 1928 or for Roosevelt in 1932, however, probably did not convert most voters into instant partisan Democrats. It seems more correct to view the entire era between 1928 and 1944 as a period when millions of Americans, most of them of urban, immigrant-stock origins, came to think of themselves as Democrats because they gradually came to see the Democratic party as representing their interests. To quote Sundquist again, "One landslide is not a party realignment." Had Roosevelt failed, had the country experienced four more years of limited or ineffective response to the economic crisis of the 1930s similar to that provided by the Hoover administration, then surely the realignment of the 1930s would have taken a very different form. The formation of the new alignment depended upon a perception on the part of distressed voters that the New Deal was on the side of the unemployed, the poor, and the disadvantaged. It was what Roosevelt "did after he came to the Presidency," as Lubell pointed out, that persuaded most voters to become Democrats.

A discussion of major works on the elections of the Roosevelt era must begin with Samuel Lubell's *The Future of American Politics,* 3d rev. ed. (New York: Harper & Row, Colophon Books, 1965). First published in 1951, this study remains one of the most perceptive books on American politics in the 1930s and 1940s. *The American Voter* (New York: John Wiley & Sons, 1960) by Angus Campbell, Philip E. Converse, Warren E. Miller, and Donald E. Stokes focuses primarily upon voter behavior and attitudes in the 1950s, but the authors found it necessary to analyze the response of voters to Roosevelt and the New Deal as a basis for studying post–World War II voting behavior. This is a classic study that has profoundly influenced the writings on the history of American elections since its publication. James L. Sundquist, *Dynamics of the Party System: Alignment and Realignment of Political Parties in the United States* (Washington, D.C.: Brookings Institution, 1973) is an excellent history of elections in the United States since the pre–Civil War era. A major portion of this comprehensive and thoughtful book concentrates on the voter realignment of the 1930s. Everett C. Ladd, Jr., and Charles D. Hadley's *Transformations of the American Party System: Political Coalitions from the New Deal to the 1970s,* 2d rev. ed. (New York: W. W. Norton & Co., 1978) is concerned with American voting behavior since the Great Depression. Ladd and Hadley's work is indispensible to a serious study of American elections in the 1930s and 1940s. Another very useful study of American electoral behavior in the Roosevelt years is Kristi Andersen, *The Creation of a Democratic Majority, 1928–1936* (Chicago: University of Chicago Press, 1979), which argues convincingly that most new Democrats in the 1930s were new voters, not converted old Republicans. *Partisan Realignment: Voters, Parties, and Government in American History,* Sage Library of Social Research, vol. 108 (Beverly Hills, Calif.: Sage Publications, 1980) by Jerome M. Clubb, William H. Flanigan, and Nancy H. Zingale is a worthy addition to this distinguished list. Like the Sundquist study, this is an analysis of American elections since the early nineteenth century, but unlike all others cited here, except Lubell's, it is based primarily upon an analysis of aggregate election data. It is a sophisticated study of the history of American election behavior with observations and conclusions about the elections of the Roosevelt years that should not be ignored.

HOWARD W. ALLEN

See also Congress, United States; Democratic Party; Dewey, Thomas E.; Dubinsky, David; Economic Royalists; Election of 1934; Election of 1938; Election of 1942; Farley, James Aloysius; Flynn, Edward Joseph; Garner, John Nance; Hague, Frank; Hearst, William Randolph; Hillman, Sidney; Hoover, Herbert Clark; Hyde Park; Ickes, Harold LeClair; Kennedy, Joseph Patrick; Labor; Landon, Alfred Mossman; Lewis, John Llewellyn; Lippmann, Walter; Moley, Raymond; Niebuhr, Reinhold; Niles, David K.; Norris, George William; Opinion Polls; "Purge" of 1938; Republican Party; Sinclair, Upton; Smith, Alfred E.; Tammany Hall; Third Term; Truman, Harry S; Two-thirds Rule; Thomas, Norman Mattoon; Union Party; Wallace, Henry A.; Willkie, Wendell Lewis

Emergency Banking Act (1933)

See Banking; Federal Deposit Insurance Corporation; Hoover, Herbert Clark; Woodin, William Hartman

Environmental Policies

See Conservation; National Resources Planning Board; Planning

EPIC

See Sinclair, Upton

Espionage in World War II

The prevention of espionage activities and the apprehension of saboteurs was the responsibility of the Federal Bureau of Investigation and its chief, J. Edgar Hoover. The FBI's activities in this area began in the 1930s when, with war approaching in Europe, the bureau placed less emphasis on apprehending criminals and returned to its practice, dormant since the 1920s, of hunting spies. In 1936 President Roosevelt asked the FBI to covertly obtain information relating to subversive activities. FBI agents were instructed to be discreet and to keep within bounds of propriety.

In September 1939, three days after Britain and France declared war on Germany, the president issued a new directive to the bureau, requesting it to take complete charge of investigative work relating to espionage, sabotage, and violation of the neutrality regulations. Local law enforcement officials were asked to hand over to the bureau any relevant information and also to discourage private vigilante groups from becoming involved in apprehending suspected spies. Roosevelt stated to the press, "The task must be conducted in a comprehensive and effective manner on a national basis, and all information must be carefully sifted out in order to avoid confusion and irresponsibility." At the same time Attorney General Frank Murphy cautioned that the work is to be done "in a reasonable and responsible way; it must not turn into a witch hunt." In 1940 the FBI was given permission by the attorney general to wiretap telephones of suspected spies.

Congress in March 1940 reenacted the Espionage Act of 1917. This act made it a crime to make or convey false reports for the benefit of the enemy or to cause disobedience in the armed forces or to willfully obstruct recruitment or enlistment in the mili-

tary. Three months later Congress passed the Alien Registration, or Smith Act. Five million aliens were registered and fingerprinted under this measure.

One of the best known espionage incidents of the war involved eight Nazi spies captured off the coasts of Long Island and Jacksonville, Florida, in June 1942. When the story was finally pieced together, it was revealed that the spies, all native-born Germans who spoke fluent English, had been instructed to blow up designated bridges, transportation routes, and industrial plants. They had been trained at a special school near Berlin conducted by the Nazi high command. Two of the men were naturalized citizens of the United States. Upon recommendation of a special military commission appointed by the president, six were sentenced to death in the electric chair and two to life imprisonment in August 1942. The spies had applied to the U.S. Supreme Court for a writ of habeas corpus and for a dismissal of the charges against them on the ground that the handling of the case overturned the precedent established after the Civil War in the *Milligan* case (1866). The Court, meeting in special session, rejected the request.

The first conviction since 1791 of an American citizen for treason occurred in July 1942 when forty-nine-year-old Detroit restaurant owner Max Stephen was found guilty of helping a German prisoner of war escape from a Canadian prison camp.

According to testimony given by J. Edgar Hoover to a congressional committee in 1946, the FBI during the war investigated 19,587 cases of alleged sabotage. Of these, 2,417 proved to be actual sabotage. Convictions were achieved in 611 of these cases.

An excellent contemporary account of the Nazi saboteurs who were picked up along the East Coast in 1942 is provided by Cyrus Bernstein in "The Saboteur Trial: A Case Study," *George Washington Law Review* 11 (1943):131–90. Three recent books about the FBI deal with espionage activities during the war. In the relevant chapters of Frank J. Donner, *The Age of Surveillance: The Aims and Methods of America's Political Intelligence System* (New York: Alfred A. Knopf, 1980), Athan Theoharis, *Spying on Americans: Political Surveillance from Hoover to the Houston Plan* (Philadelphia: Temple University Press, 1978), and Sanford J. Ungar, *F.B.I.* (Boston: Little, Brown & Co., 1975), the authors point out that the FBI frequently stretched its authority to hunt spies to include American citizens with leftist leanings. Ungar attempts to paint a more balanced picture of the bureau than do Donner and Theoharis.

PAUL L. MURPHY

See also Federal Bureau of Investigation; Hoover, John Edgar

Government agencies, the military, businesses, and private individuals disseminated posters urging vigilance against spies or saboteurs. (National Archives.)

Ethiopia

See Mussolini, Benito; and Italy

Executive Office of the President

See Office of the Presidency

F

Fair Labor Standards Act (1938)

See Cohen, Benjamin Victor; Wages and Hours Legislation

Fala

See Pets

Farm Bureau

See Agriculture

Farm Security Administration

See Agriculture

Farley, James Aloysius
(30 May 1888–9 June 1976)

Postmaster general and Democratic National Committee chairman under Franklin Roosevelt from 1933 to 1940. Born of immigrant Irish parents in Grassy Point, New York, in 1888, Farley began his political career in 1911 as town clerk. He rose during the next seventeen years through various state and party offices to become secretary of the Democratic State Committee in 1928. His outgoing personality and his proven ability as an organizer and campaigner led Roosevelt to select him to assist in his 1928 gubernatorial campaign. Farley helped engineer Roosevelt's narrow victory in 1928, his landslide reelection in 1930, and his nomination and election to the presidency in 1932.

As party chairman and postmaster general after Roosevelt's inauguration in 1933, Farley became one of the president's closest political advisers. His control of patronage in the new administration and his

James Farley, seated to the president's right, shares the happy mood at the Boston Red Sox–Washington Senators opening game of the baseball season at Griffith Stadium, 24 April 1934. (Courtesy FDR Library.)

personal acquaintance with party leaders across the country enabled him to strengthen party loyalty significantly. He was particularly effective in winning state and federal legislative support for the president's program. He worked with party leaders to secure repeal of the Prohibition amendment in 1933, and to defeat the Ludlow Resolution in 1939 to limit the president's power in foreign affairs. One of his most notable achievements was organizing and directing Roosevelt's landslide relection in 1936. Farley's accurate prediction that Roosevelt would carry every state but Maine and Vermont led him to change an old political adage: "As goes Maine, so goes Vermont."

In 1940, Farley resigned as postmaster general and party chairman. Differences between the president and Farley over political matters, Roosevelt's suspicion of Farley's own presidential ambitions, and Farley's opposition to Roosevelt's quest for a third term had led to a deterioration of their relationship during Roosevelt's second term. Following his departure, Farley secured a position with the Coca-Cola Export Corporation in New York, but continued to remain active in state and national politics until his death in New York City in 1976. He is considered one of the shrewdest and most successful campaign managers in American political history.

The most thorough accounts of Farley's life to date are his autobiographical volumes, *Behind the Ballots* (New York: Harcourt, Brace, & Co., 1938), and *Jim Farley's Story* (New York: McGraw-Hill Co., 1948). Scholarly treatments of certain aspects of Farley's career can be found in Gloria A. Newquist, "James A. Farley and the Politics of Victory, 1928–1936" (Ph.D. diss., University of Southern California, 1966); John Syrett, "Roosevelt vs. Farley: The New York Gubernatorial Election of 1942," *New York History* 56 (January 1975):51–81; and "Jim Farley and Carter Glass: Allies against a Third Term," *Prologue* 15 (Summer 1983):89–102.

THOMAS T. SPENCER

See also Democratic Party; Third Term

Fascism

A twentieth-century ideology best known for its dictatorial political methods. The word derives etymologically from the Latin *fasces,* a bundle of rods with protruding ax head carried by classical Roman magistrates as a symbol of office. In modern Italian, however, *fascio* came to denote any group of social or political activists. The first *fascio di combattimento* ("fighting group") was convened by Benito Mussolini in Milan on 23 March 1919. Fascism, then, was an Italian invention, which won worldwide notice on Mussolini's elevation to the premiership in October 1922 and his subsequent proclamation on 3 January 1925 of a one-party fascist dictatorship. Meanwhile, Adolf Hitler, also since 1919, had been constructing a German fascism under the rubric of National Socialism or Nazism. Impressed by Mussolini's swift rise to power, Hitler became his admirer and imitator, although in the end the Nazi leader was to play the major role in shaping *universalfascismo* ("world fascism").

Hitler's appointment as German chancellor on 31 January 1933, followed within weeks by his legal acquisition of absolute executive power, was a tremendous stimulus for universalfascismo. The disorienting effect of the Great Depression and the inability of democratic regimes to fashion effective remedies predisposed many to yearn to follow the German example. Thus, the decade of the thirties became the heyday of a myriad of fascist movements. Save in Rome and Berlin, none gained outright power by their own exertions; yet some participated in ruling coalitions or were later propelled into government by the upheaval of World War II. For instance, in France, while the protofascist Action Française gave way to the authentic fascist "leagues" in the thirties, both elements combined to provide the nucleus of the

collaborationist Vichy regime, 1940–44. In Spain, the Falange was one component of Generalissimo Franco's conservative coalition that emerged victorious from the Spanish civil war, 1936–39. Similarly, the Austrian *Heimwehr* was associated with the authoritarian Fatherland Front regime in Vienna before the Anschluss (1938). The Hungarian Arrow Cross and Rumanian Iron Guard enjoyed brief authority in Hitler's new wartime order. Perhaps the most conspicuous failure was that of Sir Oswald Mosley, whose British Union of Fascists created much sound and fury but signified little politically. Still, whether in or out of office, fascism was a pervading spirit in the era of depression and war.

It arose from the crisis in Western civilization precipitated by the Great War. Even before 1914 in intellectual and artistic circles a revulsion had set in against conventional nineteenth-century materialism. After the war the first fascists catered to this dissatisfaction on a popular level, offering "heroic" in place of "economic man." In this sense, early fascism was an idealistic youth cult in revolt against the values of an older generation. The goal of pristine fascist idealism was social harmony, not surprisingly, since so many fascists came from the fringes of national communities and from that social stratum feeling itself squeezed between big business and big labor. To this end, fascism everywhere aspired to be a mass movement. But if fascism needed the masses' conformity to sustain a cohesive society, it also despised them. The masses were to be led, not consulted; hence fascism stressed hierarchy and authority and sought to secure consensus by constant propaganda and selective terror. Unity at home was to provide the platform for aggrandizement abroad, for fascism was a militant creed. Subscribing to the social Darwinian notion of inevitable struggle among nations, its autarchic economic policies were geared to self-sufficiency in war. The Nazis, of course, assumed not just national but racial conflict, and their ideal society harked back to a premodern, racially homogeneous *Volk* community. This racist ideology, pursued so fanatically to the point of attempted genocide of European Jewry, has led some to place Nazism in a category sui generis.

As social integralists and antimaterialists, fascists and Nazis ranged themselves against the entire modern Left, against classical liberals and Marxian socialists alike. From this antileftist bias all fascist movements entered naturally into alliances with other foes of the Left among the historic ruling classes. In fact, many fascist groups never escaped the embrace of their conservative allies and were absorbed into traditional systems. This was true, for example, in certain "clerico-corporative" regimes where the Catholic church still held sway; it was arguably true in the very birthplace of fascism where the old Italian power structure remained strong enough in 1943 to dismiss Mussolini, having used him for twenty years. On the other hand, it would be quite wrong to see fascism merely as a conservative force. Fascism was the cynosure of the twentieth-century radical Right. It was rightist insofar as it was antiliberal and antisocialist,

Adapted from a novel by Sinclair Lewis, the first American to win the Nobel Prize in literature, It Can't Happen Here *dramatized the rise to power in the United States of a fascist dictator. That a fascist politician could be elected president and turn America into a police state shocked the sensibilities of American audiences (receipts indicated nearly 500,000 people saw the FTP productions).* It Can't Happen Here *opened simultaneously in eighteen cities. The stagings included a Negro, a Spanish-language, and several Yiddish productions. The latter drew newly arrived Jewish refugees from Austria and Germany to the performances. Holding the rifle in this scene from the New York City Yiddish production is Sidney Lumet, who later became director of such films as* Long Day's Journey into Night, The Pawnbroker, *and* Network. *(Courtesy the Library of Congress Federal Theatre Project Collection at George Mason University Library, Fairfax, Virginia.)*

but equally it was radical in its emotive promise to the masses of a new order. Ideologically, fascists had no love for those who, in Hitler's sarcastic phrase, "put von before their name"; given the chance, they intended to replace traditional elites with a new aristocracy of true believers.

These nuances within European fascism were lost on mainstream American opinion. At first, admiration was commonly expressed for Italy's fascist regime which, albeit dictatorial, allegedly made trains run on time and still participated in disarmament conferences. "You're the top, you're Mussolini," ran a Cole Porter hit song. Franklin D. Roosevelt, on becoming president in 1933, mirrored this mood and was pleased to correspond with "that admirable Italian gentleman." There existed at first a vague empathy between the two leaders who, through New Deal and fascist corporativism, respectively, both fought the Great Depression by injecting government into the economic process.

American and Rooseveltian attitudes changed sharply with the Italian-Ethiopian war of 1935–36. Not only did this episode disclose the belligerence at the heart of fascism, but it also led to the Rome-Berlin Axis, which extended Hitler's baleful dominance over *universalfascismo.* This seemed to reactivate Roosevelt's youthful distaste for the German military authoritarianism of 1914, although there was a dawning realization that Nazism was much more than the old *furor teutonicus.* From 1936 Roosevelt's speeches dwelled increasingly on the challenge to the pluralistic society posed by totalitarianism of both the Right and the Left. But fascism/Nazism was clearly presented as the more immediate and greater danger.

In due course, fascism was perceived in North America as a menace coming from within and from without. Predictably, a native U.S. fascism sprang up in rough imitation of the European models. Several fringe groups won some following among the lower middle class in the nadir of the depression and amid a wave of red-baiting. But the peak was passed by 1936, after which the main internal threat was deemed to lie in the susceptibility of the German and Italo-American populations to fascist ideas disseminated by the German-American Bund and *fasci all'estero* ("overseas fasci"). Unquestionably, Roosevelt was concerned about fascism inside the United States; as early as 1934 he ordered an FBI investigation. Yet political considerations, especially for the large and sensitive Italo-American vote, kept him from too public a stance. Pursuit of fascists at home fell to Congress; specifically, the Dies committee of 1938 began as an inquiry into fascist subversion. Similarly, for political reasons, Roosevelt was reluctant to quarrel openly with Huey Long and Father Coughlin, leaving it to his aides to denounce such populist demagogues who might have played the role of American Duce or Fuehrer.

The president responded more vigorously to the external fascist danger. The closer Nazi Germany moved to hegemony over the European continent, the more Roosevelt was convinced that Hitler would soon turn his expansionist attention to the American hemisphere; and he was further convinced that the Nazis possessed the means to pose a direct military threat. Thus, antifascism became an issue of national security. Initially, the neutrality legislation that Roosevelt himself had sponsored restricted him to gestures; he spoke of a quarantine of aggressors and tried to warn the Axis not to count on American isolationism ("We, too, have a stake in world affairs"). With the outbreak of World War II on 3 September 1939, Roosevelt set about to amend and evade the neutrality laws in order to make the United States the famous arsenal of democracy. His evident commitment after the fall of France in 1940 to Britain's salvation and Axis defeat necessitated contingency plans for America's entry into war. The adoption in early 1941 of an Atlantic-first strategy, if not prescribed by the president, reflected the primacy he now accorded the fight against European fascism. Four days after Pearl Harbor, Hitler and Mussolini justified this order of priorities by gratuitously declaring war on the United States.

With Hitler's death on 30 April 1945—less than three weeks after Roosevelt's own—the fascist era ended. Within the triumphant Allied coalition of 1945, Roosevelt's voice had spoken for the cause of liberal democracy—the very obverse of authoritarian, conformist fascism. In the final reckoning, Roosevelt proved a resolute enemy of fascism, and he prevailed.

A seminal if dense work on universalfascismo is E. Nolte, *Three Faces of Fascism: Action Française, Italian Fascism, National Socialism* (New York: Holt, Rinehart & Winston, 1966); it regards fascism as a rejoinder to Marxism and metapolitical denial of transcendence. More straightforward is A. Cassels, *Fascism* (Arlington Heights: Harlan Davison, 1975), which uses modernization theory for its frame of reference. Schools of thought, including the Marxian, are surveyed by R. De Felice, *Interpretations of Fascism* (Cambridge, Mass.: Harvard University Press, 1977). For the impact of European fascism on the United States, see J. P. Diggins, *Mussolini and Fascism: The View from America* (Princeton: Princeton University Press, 1972), and A. Frye, *Nazi Germany and the American Hemisphere* (New Haven: Yale University Press, 1967). A description of native American fascism is contained in A. M. Schlesinger, Jr., *The Age of Roosevelt*, vol. 3 (Boston: Houghton Mifflin Co., 1960). R. Dallek, *Franklin D. Roosevelt and American Foreign Policy, 1932–1945* (New York: Oxford University Press, 1979) is an authoritative account of the subject.

ALAN CASSELS

See also Axis Alliance; Mussolini, Benito, and Italy

Federal Art Project

In August 1935, planners for the newly created Works Progress Administration (WPA) set up special projects for artists, actors, musicians, and writers who could qualify for public welfare. These projects—the Federal Art Project, the Federal Theatre Project,

The Federal Art Project offered unprecedented governmental support and recognition to American artists. Women artists benefited particularly from the FAP's policy of equal opportunity in hiring. Sculptor Lenore Thomas, of the Washington, D.C., arts project, is seen here creating a monumental work from forty tons of limestone for a greenbelt community. (National Archives.)

the Federal Music Project, and the Federal Writers' Project—were designated collectively Federal Project Number One. Being "federal" meant that workers would be directed by individuals mostly responsible to the central administration of the WPA in Washington. The rationale for this arrangement was that people in the arts required special protection from the WPA's state-level bureaucrats, many of whom did not consider activities like painting pictures real work. Asked why the WPA should concern itself with giving work to destitute artists, administrator Harry L. Hopkins retorted, "Hell, they've got to eat just like other people."

Hopkins chose Holger Cahill, a museum curator, as director of the Federal Art Project (FAP). When Cahill received money to begin operations in October 1935, he distributed an operating manual, the first page of which set out the FAP's purposes and the kinds of activities it would undertake:

The primary objective of the project is the employ of artists who are on the relief rolls. . . . Through employment of creative artists, it is hoped to secure for the public outstanding examples of contemporary American art; through art teaching and recreational art activities to create a broader national art consciousness and work out constructive ways of using leisure time; through services in applied art to aid various campaigns of social value; and through research projects to clarify the native background in the arts. The aim of the project will be toward an integration of the arts with the daily life of the community, and an integration of the fine arts and practical arts.

Edward Lanning and his assistants working on the New York City FAP-sponsored Ellis Island mural, "The Role of the Immigrant in the Industrial Development of America." (National Archives.)

Because of peculiarities in the WPA's record keeping, no one knows exactly how many individuals took part in the FAP or exactly how much the project cost. Of approximately 57,000 artists and art teachers counted by the Census Bureau, perhaps 9,000 received help. (At its peak, the FAP employed 5,300; projecting turnover yields the 9,000 figure.) Scholars estimate financial outlays of between $35 million and $43 million.

Artists on relief decorated schools, hospitals, and other public buildings with 2,566 murals and 17,744 pieces of sculpture. Record keepers counted 108,099 pieces off FAP easels and some 240,000 copies of 11,285 original designs in various print media. More than half of the FAP artists did not excel at the traditional fine arts and were assigned to "socially useful" auxiliary projects. These included poster making, photography, recording traditional American designs, craftwork, model making, and teaching. The FAP established more than one hundred community art centers, many of which became permanent. Project

Weathervanes, decoys, ships' figureheads, and other examples of folk art from the entire nation were assembled and researched, and then renderings of them made, for the Federal Art Project's Index of American Design. This collection of artifacts was exhibited in New York City. (National Archives.)

workers completed some twenty thousand renditions of American decorative art that constituted an index of American design. They organized, in 1940 and 1941, two national Art Weeks (to stimulate appreciation and private sales); operated for a time a design laboratory to train commercial artists; and, among other activities, wrote technical bulletins on paint and supplies.

By the middle 1960s experts claimed the market value of art produced by FAP artists far exceeded what all project activities had cost. More important, hundreds of artists—like Jackson Pollock, Willem de Kooning, Jack Levine, and William Gropper—had been able to continue to develop their talents. When the WPA ended in 1943, Americans had not, as Cahill hoped in 1935, integrated art with daily life. But they had made a start. The start was all the more remarkable because it had been made in the context of a federal welfare program.

In 1936 FAP administrators and workers began a book that would be a "report to the nation" and, they hoped, win public support for government patronage. However, when the manuscript was nearly ready for the printer, dramatic cutbacks caused FAP leaders to shelve the work. A generation later, art historian Francis V. O'Connor discovered and edited the manuscript for publication: *Art for the Millions: Essays from the 1930s by Artists and Administrators of the WPA Federal Art Project* (Greenwich, Conn.: New York Graphic Society, 1973). O'Connor also collected and edited the afterthoughts of several project alumni in *The New Deal Arts Projects: An Anthology of Memoirs* (Washington: Smithsonian Institution Press, 1972). Richard D. McKinzie attempted a narrative history in *The New Deal for Artists* (Princeton: Princeton University Press, 1973). For FDR's interest, see William B. Rhoads, "The Artistic Patronage of Franklin D. Roosevelt: Art as Historical Record," *Prologue*, Spring 1983, pp. 5–21. For insight into the work of the artists, see Karal Ann Marling, "A Note on New Deal Iconography: Futurology and the Historical Myth," *Prospects* 4 (1979):421–40. See also William F. McDonald, *Federal Relief Administration and the Arts: The Origins and Administrative History of the Arts Projects of the Works Progress Administration* (Columbus: Ohio State University Press, 1969).

RICHARD D. MCKINZIE

See also Works Progress Administration.

Federal Bureau of Investigation

Franklin D. Roosevelt brought the New Deal to federal police policy just as surely as he brought it to depression era farmers and industrial workers. When the Bureau of Investigation became the Federal Bureau of Investigation (FBI) in 1935, it signified more than a simple name change. The bureau's new nomenclature symbolized the success of the Roosevelt administration's attempt to extend the New Deal to yet another realm considered by some Americans to be the exclusive prerogative of state and local government—namely, crime control. Later, as the United States crept toward war with Hitler and Tojo and

President Roosevelt's concerns about "our security" broadened beyond criminal elements to encompass the activities of communists, native fascists, and other "subversives," the administration again turned to the FBI by encouraging the bureau to develop a domestic intelligence (that is, noncriminal) capability. The bureaucratic and institutional changes that allowed the pursuit of this dual mission, however, also enhanced the FBI's independent status and enabled FBI officials to pursue political goals that were quite different from the liberal ideals of the New Deal.

The movement to nationalize crime control dates from 1908 with the formation of the Bureau of Investigation as the first national police force. Progressive Era lawmakers began to erode states' rights attitudes on crime with the passage in 1910 of the White Slave Traffic (or Mann) Act and in 1919 of the Dyer Act. The first act prohibited the transportation of a woman across a state line for immoral purposes, and the second prohibited interstate transportation of a stolen motor vehicle. Further efforts to expand federal criminal jurisdiction were for the most part frustrated during the new era, as revelations of wartime and postwar abuses by the Bureau of Investigation (including the surveillance of members of Congress) were publicized during congressional investigations of Teapot Dome and other Warren G. Harding administration scandals. The only additional federal criminal legislation came in 1932 following the kidnapping of Charles Lindbergh's infant son (the so-called Lindbergh Law and a companion act).

When Franklin D. Roosevelt moved into the Oval Office, then, the Bureau of Investigation remained a small (266 special agents and 60 accountants) and somewhat obscure division within the Justice Department. The new president, nonetheless, had ambitious plans for the bureau. In response to the well-publicized exploits of John Dillinger, George "Machine Gun" Kelly, Charles "Pretty Boy" Floyd, Bonnie Parker and Clyde Barrow, and dozens of other hoodlums of the early 1930s who took advantage of the limited jurisdiction of state and local police, President Roosevelt sought to mobilize "the strong arm of Government" for a war on crime. This could be accomplished only by bringing "the Federal Government's anti-crime machinery up to date" and making the FBI "as effective an instrumentality of crime detection and punishment as any of the similar agencies of the world."

The Roosevelt administration pursued a "war with the organized forces of crime" on two levels. First, the Justice Department drafted a New Deal crime-control package which Congress passed in mid-1934 without even taking a record vote. Consisting of nine specific statutes, the anticrime legislation dramatically increased FBI jurisdiction (for example, an amendment to the federal bank-robbery statute extended federal jurisdiction to any bank insured by the FDIC) and granted bureau agents full arrest power and the authority to carry any kind of firearm. Second, Attorney General Homer Cummings launched an ambitious public relations campaign on behalf of the federal agency chosen to lead the anticrime crusade—a campaign described privately by White House press secretary Stephen Early as a "plan to publicize and make the G-men heroes."

FBI director J. Edgar Hoover enthusiastically accepted this new responsibility and quickly immersed the bureau in the world of public relations and opinion molding. A separate FBI division, Crime Records, was expanded and charged with promoting the bureau's image and influencing the public's supposedly romantic view of John Dillinger and the other colorful malefactors of the era. Assisted by dozens of Crime Records agents and an imaginative ghostwriter, former Denver newspaperman Courtney Ryley Cooper, the FBI director emerged as one of the most prolific publicists in the country—with sixteen articles detailing the bureau's war on crime appearing under Hoover's signature between 1934 and 1936 in *American* magazine alone. Bureau officials also assisted with the production of at least two comic strips and various Hollywood gangster films and with the marketing of G-man secret rings, pajamas, and toy machine guns. By 1936 the FBI had acquired a formidable image of efficient professionalism—a development attested to by the bureau's appropriation of $6,025,000 for that year (more than double the appropriation when Franklin Roosevelt took office) and the emergence of a bipartisan FBI constituency in the U.S. Congress.

Thereafter, the FBI budget continued to double every four or five years, reaching some $70 million per year during the Harry S Truman era. By 1936 these new resources enabled the bureau to manage yet another mission for the Roosevelt administration. Following a White House meeting with Hoover, President Roosevelt directed the FBI to develop more systematic intelligence about "subversive activities in the United States, particularly Fascism and Communism." Three years later, in the aftermath of the September 1939 Nazi invasion of Poland, the president issued another directive instructing the FBI "to take charge of investigative work in matters relating to espionage, sabotage, and violations of the neutrality regulations."

FBI intelligence reports to the Roosevelt White House, however, were not confined to bona fide threats to the national security. President Roosevelt and several senior White House aides routinely solicited investigations of the administration's foreign policy critics and domestic political adversaries. These reports included political intelligence on the activities of Hamilton Fish, the Republican congressman from New York; isolationist senators Burton K. Wheeler and Gerald P. Nye; and Martin Dies, chairman of the Special House Committee to Investigate Un-American Activities. FBI officials, for their part, invariably serviced specific White House requests and frequently volunteered reports on a wide spectrum of subjects. This willingness to ingratiate themselves with an incumbent president, moreover, was only partly indicative of the scope of FBI officials' political activism. At the same time, the bureau pursued independent political objectives, including support for the efforts of Martin Dies and other congressional conservatives to purge the federal civil service, which often militated against the programs and policies of the Roosevelt administration. FBI officials, indeed, defined *subversion* broadly enough to encompass the New Deal's demands for social and economic reform, in the process compiling dossiers on dozens of prominent New Dealers—including the first lady, Eleanor Roosevelt.

The New Deal did not create the FBI's political activism. Surveillance of domestic dissidents was a routine, if covert, part of the bureau's work throughout the new era. By bringing the New Deal to federal police policy, the Roosevelt administration nevertheless unintentionally provided FBI officials with the resources to pursue their political objectives on an unprecedented scale. And the bureau's public relations machinery, which President Roosevelt had encouraged as part of the crime-control crusade, would later be mobilized almost exclusively, during the cold war era, to promote the domestic communist issue. Although President Roosevelt and FBI director Hoover were in general agreement on the threat posed by crime, they were often at odds regarding the perceived dangers of "subversion." The last thing the president wanted, but what ultimately emerged as a New Deal legacy, was an independent political force more concerned with shaping public opinion and influencing national politics on domestic dissent than with crime control.

In the wake of Watergate-related abuse of power revelations and the addition in 1974 of amendments to the Freedom of Information Act, the past decade has seen the emergence of a significant body of historical literature on the FBI. The best general study is Sanford J. Ungar, *FBI* (Boston: Little, Brown & Co., 1975), a lively journalistic account based heavily on interviews with FBI officials and agents. The bureau's pursuit of depression era gangsters and the emergence of the G-man image is the subject of Richard Gid Powers, *G-Men: Hoover's FBI in American Popular Culture* (Carbondale: Southern Illinois University Press, 1983). For the Roosevelt admininistration's role in promoting the growth of the bureau and expanding its investigative functions, see Kenneth O'Reilly, "A New Deal for the FBI: The Roosevelt Administration, Crime Control, and National Security," *Journal of American History* 69 (December 1982):638–58. Frank J. Donner, *The Age of Surveillance* (New York: Alfred A. Knopf, 1980), and Athan Theoharis, *Spying on Americans* (Philadelphia: Temple University Press, 1978), offer well-documented accounts of FBI political activism. Bureau preoccupation with and attempts to shape public opinion on the domestic communist issue is treated in Kenneth O'Reilly, *Hoover and the Un-Americans: The FBI, HUAC, and the Red Menace* (Philadelphia: Temple University Press, 1983).

KENNETH O'REILLY

See also Cummings, Homer Stillé; Espionage; Hoover, John Edgar; Internment of Japanese-Americans; Isolationism

Federal Communications Commission

Regulatory body established under the 1934 Communications Act to oversee both wired and wireless communication. The Federal Communications Commission (FCC) is made up of seven members, appointed by the president with the advice and consent of the Senate; they serve seven-year terms, with one member chosen by the president to be chair. The FCC replaced the Federal Radio Commission (FRC), established by the 1927 Radio Act.

Passage of the first comprehensive radio legislation in 1927, the Radio Act, had failed to solve the problems facing radio broadcasting. Despite having debated radio regulation since 1921, Congress remained confused about the technical, political, and economic questions involved. Thus, the FRC was established to serve for a year and bring order to the airwaves. Congress then passed legislation in subsequent years to continue the FRC and correct defects in the Radio Act.

By 1933, the need for a new comprehensive radio bill had become apparent. Congress passed such a bill in 1933, only to see it blocked by President Herbert Hoover's pocket veto. The 1927 Radio Act had been written in a series of conferences called by Hoover as secretary of commerce. Proud of his handiwork, Hoover apparently wanted no changes in what he considered his act. Congress had already agreed in 1933 that a new act was necessary both to consolidate and organize the amendments to the 1927 act and to deal with some long ignored issues. Thus, the 1934 Communications Act profited from debate in earlier Congresses, especially in 1933.

The New Deal added to the push for new legislation. Many of the approaches to radio developed through the 1920s fit the spirit of the early New Deal. Congressional actions during the first months of Franklin Roosevelt's administration established agencies that were much like the FRC—vested with large discretionary powers and subject to only narrow judicial review. Congress also moved away from a concern for small business toward attempts to regulate existing combinations, in the same way earlier Congresses had approached the radio industry. A not unimportant consideration, too, was the lesson members of Congress had learned from Roosevelt, who in six fireside chats in 1933 and 1934 made clear the potential political impact of the medium.

In a 1934 message to Congress, Roosevelt proposed a commission charged with the regulation of all forms of communications. Increasingly knowledgeable about the intertwined nature of the industry, Congress had mentioned such a commission as early as 1929. Although observers expressed surprise that the Communications Act, with its grant of large discretionary power to the newly created FCC, passed Congress so easily and with so little debate, the timing and content of the act had facilitated its passage.

The FRC's own bureaucratic momentum had made its inclusion in the regulatory framework practically a foregone conclusion. Moreover, radio's growing use as a political tool and as an adjunct to everyday life made administrative regulation, because of its flexibility, more appealing than prescriptive legislation.

Thus, although encouraged by Roosevelt's request for a commission and by the atmosphere of the early New Deal, Congress had long been moving toward the acceptance of a concentrated radio system regulated by a conventional federal agency.

The only narrative history that examines radio legislation is Philip Rosen's *The Modern Stentor: Radio Broadcasting and the Federal Government, 1920–1934* (Westport, Conn.: Greenwood Press, 1980). Also useful are Edward Sarno, "The National Radio Conferences," *Journal of Broadcasting* 13 (Spring 1969):189–202; C. M. Jansky, "The Contribution of Herbert Hoover to Broadcasting," *Journal of Broadcasting* 1 (Summer 1957):241–49; and Bernard Schwartz, *The Economic Regulation of Business and Industry: A Legislative History of U.S. Regulatory Agencies*, vol. 4 (New York: Chelsea House, 1973), pp. 2373–76.

SUSAN SMULYAN

Federal Deposit Insurance Corporation

Often hailed as the most important banking reform to arise from the New Deal, the Federal Deposit Insurance Corporation (FDIC) provides insurance to depositors in commercial banks. First proposed by Congressman Henry Steagall in 1932 and attached by Senator Vandenberg as an amendment to the Emergency Banking Act of 1933, the insurance plan was designed to prevent runs on bank deposits by increasing the depositor's confidence in the security of savings. However, Roosevelt himself was against the measure, but his opposition weakened after discussions with Jesse Jones and John Nance Garner, both determined insurance supporters. In the end, the FDIC Act was the only major piece of legislation passed during the hundred days that was neither requested nor supported by the White House. The temporary plan created by the 1933 legislation was made permanent by the Banking Act of 1935.

Under the terms of the act, a new federal agency, the Federal Deposit Insurance Corporation, was created which supervised the insurance of deposits in state and national banks. The FDIC provided insurance of deposits up to $2,500 (raised to $5,000 in 1934 and frequently since then). All member banks of the Federal Reserve System were required to purchase the insurance, and nonmember state banks were permitted to acquire coverage upon examination by the FDIC. By June 1934, over 90 percent of the nation's commercial banks had purchased the insurance.

Without doubt, the legislation has been a great success. Since its passage, commercial bank failures have plummeted, as have losses by depositors in the few banks that have failed. It is ironic that this landmark of New Deal economic reform was originally sponsored by a Republican senator against the wishes of FDR himself.

The best discussion of the effects of the passage of the FDIC Act is in Milton Friedman and Anna Jacobson Schwartz's *A Monetary History of the United States, 1867–1960* (Princeton: Princeton University Press, 1963),

pp. 434–42. Arthur Ballantine's article "When All the Banks Closed," *Harvard Business Review* 26 (March 1948):129–43, examines the banking crisis of 1932–33, and "The Deposit Insurance Legislation of 1933," *Political Science Quarterly* 75 (June 1960):181–200, by Carter Golombe, discusses the political and economic consequences of the act's passage.

See also Monetary Policy

Federal Emergency Relief Administration

A federal relief agency established in 1933 to provide cash relief to several million needy families. The Federal Emergency Relief Administration (FERA) also developed thousands of work projects manned by unemployed adults.

Congress passed the Federal Emergency Relief Act creating the FERA on 12 May 1933 as part of the famous hundred days of legislation of the Roosevelt administration. The FERA began officially ten days later when the president administered the oath of office to Harry L. Hopkins, the zestful and dynamic chief administrator of FERA during its entire existence.

Hopkins acted promptly. Before nightfall of his first day in office, he distributed millions of dollars to states in desperate need of funds to feed and clothe sufferers in the Great Depression, which had begun during the Herbert Hoover administration (1929–33).

The FERA staff established three key objectives for providing relief: (1) the provision of an adequate level of relief, (2) an emphasis on work relief for the employable needy, and (3) diversification of work relief so that skills already possessed might be maintained and new skills developed.

Hopkins established four operational divisions: the Division of Research, Statistics and Finance; the Works Division; the Division of Rural Rehabilitation; and the Division of Relations with States. Regional field representatives served as the major means for Hopkins and the Washington staff to secure timely information on conditions in the states and to provide information and interpretation of directives to state relief administrators appointed, usually, by the governor of each state. The majority of the regional field representatives became significant influences in shaping relief. They needed to be politically astute, as well as keen analyzers of economic and social conditions. Eager for even more information than his new bureaucracy could provide, Hopkins benefitted from the vivid reports of roving field observer Lorena Hickok, who toured the country in 1934–35.

Hopkins's own Washington staff consisted of a mixture of former social workers, economists, engineers, and accountants who were usually capable and resourceful, and who, like Hopkins, believed that government could and should actively assist in providing immediate relief to the needy and temporary employment to the unemployed. His staff loved Hopkins' informality, his ability to think *and* do, his driving devotion to the needy.

Most federal emergency relief funds were expended in two ways: first, matching dollar grants, one federal dollar for every three state-supplied dollars, and second, direct grants to states when a governor could prove the state could not provide matching dollars. The direct-grant procedure, which became the dominant method, placed Hopkins in a position to shape types of relief and to place more funds in areas where suffering was the greatest rather than in wealthier states, which could provide matching dollars. Identified need was the primary guideline for distributing funds, despite the establishment of a formula system.

The major goals of President Roosevelt and Hopkins to force states to increase their funds for relief and to improve the monthly level of relief caused sharp conflicts with several state governors. Governors in Ohio and Illinois, for example, claimed that Hopkins was shaping the policy on relief rather than the state. In several states, Hopkins moved in to eliminate political payoffs. Several U.S. senators complained to President Roosevelt that Hopkins was interfering in their states. In most instances, Roosevelt backed Hopkins in these skirmishes.

Although direct cash relief for the unemployable (blind, crippled, elderly, mothers with young children, etc.) continued into 1936, work relief became the focus of operation for the FERA. Construction projects dominated; but a great variety of projects existed by 1935 for teachers, writers, musicians, and doctors. These white-collar projects were controversial and were sharply and constantly criticized. Hopkins counterattacked with dynamic, colorful language, emphasizing that the best work relief recognized the varying skills and interests of the unemployed.

Work relief included projects to construct roads, sewers, bridges, and buildings and to pay the unemployed for processing surplus food and clothing into usable articles for themselves and others on relief. During the years 1934 and 1935, over 500,000 people attended FERA-sponsored literacy classes. FERA medical workers provided over 1 million vaccinations and immunizations, and FERA-employed workers constructed at least 240,000 miles of roads, and 5,000 new public buildings, and laid thousands of miles of sewer lines and storm drainage systems.

Because economic recovery was not strong by the fall of 1934, liberal Democrats and Republicans pressured FDR to undertake additional reforms and recovery measures. Conservatives were caustic in their criticism of the president, while at the same time, radical leaders like Huey P. Long received support from hundreds of thousands of people. Roosevelt continued to be bothered by the heavy dependence on direct relief with no systematic contributions by the states and individuals. In early 1935, therefore, he moved in two major directions. Realizing millions would be unemployed for several years, he launched a long-term work program to be known as the Works Progress Administration. He also supported Secretary of Labor Frances Perkins and several U.S. senators for passage of the Social Security Act which provided for an organized means to finance and to help the unemployable.

The most useful secondary sources pertaining to the FERA are books by Edward A. Williams, *Federal Aid for Relief* (New York: Columbia University Press, 1939) and Searle F. Charles, *Minister of Relief: Harry Hopkins and the Depression* (Syracuse: Syracuse University Press, 1963). For detail data, Dorothy Carothers's *Chronology of the Federal Emergency Administration*, Research Monograph No. 6 (Washington: Government Printing Office, 1937) is very valuable. Lorena Hickok's papers have been published in *One Third of a Nation; Lorena Hickok Reports on the Great Depression*, ed. Richard Lowitt and Maurine Beasley (Urbana: University of Illinois Press, 1983). Valuable insights to Hopkins as an administrator are provided by Henry H. Adams in his biography of Harry Hopkins published by the Putnam Company (1977). Interesting accounts of the political battles of Hopkins for this period are contained in Charles's *Minister of Relief*, and in Robert Sherwood's descriptive book, *Roosevelt and Hopkins: An Intimate History* (New York: Harper and Brothers, 1948). Hopkins presented his own concepts concerning relief as envisioned by him in 1934, in *Spending to Save* (Seattle: University of Washington Press, 1936).

SEARLE F. CHARLES

See also Hopkins, Harry L.

Federal Housing Administration

See Housing and Resettlement; Mortgage Financing

Federal Reserve Board/System

See Banking; Eccles, Marriner Stoddard; Federal Deposit Insurance Corporation; Great Depression; Monetary Policy

Federal Theatre Project

In August 1935, when the Works Progress Administration (WPA) established a work program for actors on welfare, the Federal Theatre Project (FTP), several unprecedented conditions existed. Most important, the American president believed that the arts enriched life, and although it never ranked high among his priorities, he did want to use government to support artistic people, thereby uplifting other Americans. Second, a substantial minority of artistic intellectuals were caught up in the era's "Red romance." More communists of the heart than ideologues, they insisted that government owed the public good art as a "cultural right." Third was the fact that among Roosevelt's most dedicated officials, more than a few hoped their work might bring about "cultural democracy"—the logical sequel, they said, to political and economic democracy. Finally, the depression had made Americans more sensitive to their own uniqueness, even in the arts. Together, these inclinations and

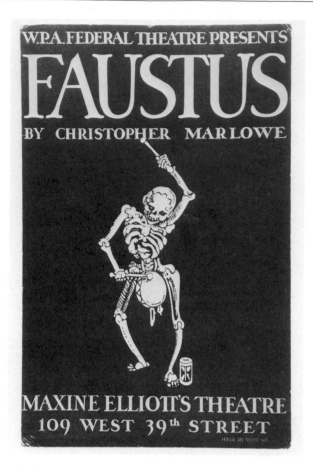

A lively range of entertainment was sponsored by the Federal Theatre Project: children's theater, puppet shows, vaudeville, the circus, revivals of classics, and contemporary plays. The John Houseman–Orson Welles combination that in 1936 had produced an electrifying Macbeth produced in 1937 a dazzling Dr. Faustus, dominated by Orson Welles's vision and energy; he designed the costumes, directed the production, and played the title role of Faustus. (Courtesy the Library of Congress Federal Theatre Project Collection at George Mason University Library, Fairfax, Virginia.)

pressures made possible government work programs for artists of the theatrical guild.

When Hallie Flanagan, the exuberant director of the Vassar College Experimental Theatre, accepted the directorship of the FTP, half the theaters in New York were dark and more than half the actors were unemployed. WPA administrator Harry L. Hopkins had promised help in building a "free, adult, uncensored theater." Within two years, thirteen thousand people in thirty-one states were attempting to achieve the FTP's cultural mission to provide free entertainment for underprivileged groups in recreation centers, settlement houses, and hospitals; and to provide shows through which good theater at low cost would develop new audiences for the art. At its peak, FTP plays entertained (in six languages) a weekly audience of 350,000. In all, the project cost about $46 million. Director Flanagan encouraged plays with a "vital connection" to the immediate problems of people in the audience. One manifestation of this outlook was the Living Newspaper—documentary dramas on is-

sues of the day. The FTP repertoire also included programs ranging from Shakespeare to modern farce, Gilbert and Sullivan, plays for children, folk plays, and the work of living American dramatists.

The FTP was, by far, the most controversial of the schemes to relieve distress in the fine arts and to raise America's cultural consciousness. There were two main reasons. First, a minority among FTP workers were political radicals whose views of America tinged some of the stage productions. Second, America's thespians were too concentrated in New York City, and WPA regulations discouraged their redistribution. As a result, large areas of the country (and numbers of taxpayers) received no services from the project. The requirement that all WPA workers meet state qualifications for welfare, which usually meant a year's residency, prevented actors in New York from migrating to places like North Dakota, Kansas, or Texas where there were too few actors to justify local FTP troupes. There was also the reality that in many rural and conservative minds play acting was the worst perversion of the principle of work relief.

When bipartisan opposition to Roosevelt's programs began to peak among conservative congressmen, the House Committee on Un-American Activities and the House Subcommittee on Appropriations focused on the FTP as one of the New Deal's most

Transformed by director Yasha Frank into movement, music, and commotion, the Italian story of the wooden puppet who wanted to be a real boy enchanted Federal Theatre audiences young and old. Designed unabashedly to entertain children, the plays directed by Frank always contained a "character-building" theme—in Pinocchio's case, sharing his pennies with the poor—and included in the performance participation by the children themselves. (Courtesy the Library of Congress Federal Theatre Project Collection at George Mason University Library, Fairfax, Virginia.)

vulnerable creations. Congressmen combed the records and examined witnesses for (real and imagined) examples of waste, communist activity, and salacious and defaming plays. Few journalists who covered these investigations considered them fair, but the president's political opponents made elimination of the FTP a cause célèbre. "I want the Federal Government to get out of the theatre business," asserted Democrat Clifton Woodrum as he shepherded the annual appropriation bill through Congress in 1939. On the last day of the fiscal year (June 1939), Congress legislated the FTP out of existence.

Hallie Flanagan left a narrative account of her experiences in *Arena: The History of the Federal Theatre* (New York: Duell, Sloane & Pearce, 1940). The standard history is Jane D. Mathews, *The Federal Theatre: 1935–1939: Plays, Relief, and Politics* (Princeton: Princeton University Press, 1967). Mathews also analyzed the motives of fine arts planners in "Arts and the People: The New Deal Quest for a Cultural Democracy," *Journal of American History* 62 (September 1975):316–39. Hundreds of boxes of FTP records were virtually inaccessible from 1939 to 1975, when they were removed from a warehouse and became the nucleus of the Institute on the Federal Theatre Project and New Deal Culture at George Mason University. One early result, filled with personal reminiscences of FTP actors, directors, and technicians, and illustrated with set and costume designs, FTP posters, and photographs of productions, is John O'Connor and Lorraine Brown, eds., *Free, Adult, Uncensored: The Living History of the Federal Theatre Project* (Washington: New Republic Books, 1978). See also William F. McDonald, *Federal Relief Administration and the Arts: The Origins and Administration of the Arts Projects of the Works Progress Administration* (Columbus: Ohio State University Press, 1969) and Marguerite D. Bloxom, comp., *Pickaxe and Pencil: References for the Study of the WPA* (Washington: Library of Congress, 1982).

RICHARD D. MCKINZIE

See also Works Progress Administration.

Federal Writers' Project

The Federal Writer's Project (FWP) was a component of Federal Project Number One, a small subunit of the Works Progress Administration, which gave work relief to artists, actors, musicians, and writers. The FWP was unique among the projects to aid the arts in the sense that writers did more utilitarian work than did WPA artists, actors, and musicians. From the first day of operations on 1 November 1935, FWP director Henry G. Alsberg eschewed poetry, short stories, and novels in favor of nonfiction. Such a course would be less controversial among politicians and the public, and, moreover, FWP was designed as a catch-all for unemployed white-collar workers. At one point FWP payrolls contained about 6,800 names; approximately 10,000 people had assignments during its seven-year life span. Very few among them were creative writers; most were teachers, preachers, newspaper people, lawyers, librarians, physicians, recent college graduates, and people even further removed from creative writing.

Henry Alsberg, a former editorial writer, eventually had people in every state at work on books that would comprise the American Guide Series, a unique state-by-state portrait of the nation. The inspiration had come from Baedeker guidebooks, somewhat dry but factual aids that travelers in Europe had known for decades. FWP officials in Washington instructed writers in each state to craft the books in three parts. Part 1 offered essays on a variety of subjects important to a state—its history, people, the arts, economics, politics, and religion. Part 2 consisted of up-to-date, fact-laced pieces on the state's cities. The last part, which was the longest, directed the reader throughout the state on motor tours. Mile by mile, the guide offered a running commentary on scenery just beyond the windshield. FWP's leadership announced noble but unobtainable goals: to aid business by stimulating travel; to encourage resources conservation by arousing local pride; and to broaden scholarly interests by making available more historical facts.

The research that went into writing the American Guide Series was enormous. Information not used in the state guides spilled onto the pages of about thirty city guides, a score of regional books (like *The Berkshire Hills*), and a few volumes on scenic or historic highways (*The Oregon Trail; U.S. One*). Almost without exception the literary community received the major guides favorably. Skillful direction and editing in the Washington offices kept the books from reading like committee reports. FWP also published some 150 titles in a Life in America Series. The subjects were as diverse as *Who's Who in the Zoo* and *The Armenians in Massachusetts*. Many writers indulged their creative urges outside their thirty-hour week for FWP. One result was *American Stuff*, an anthology of particular interest to readers of a later generation because it contained a piece by the talented young black writer Richard Wright.

Beyond the state guidebooks and the topical Life in America volumes, FWP mainly concerned itself with America's vanishing folklore and the stories of former slaves. John A. Lomax set up the system for collecting folklore; Benjamin A. Botkin replaced him as folklore editor in 1938. In all, FWP took down the reminiscences of more than 2,000 ex-slaves in seventeen states. FWP file cabinets became repositories as well for snippets on the folklore of shooting craps or on wishing wells—whatever the local idiosyncrasy. FWP claimed about 1,200 publications—counting everything from 4-page pamphlets off the mimeograph machines to 1,100-page hardbacks distributed by commercial publishers. The agency sold or gave away 3.5 million copies of books and pamphlets.

Big-city FWP projects faced charges of radicalism and waste in 1939. Congress did not abolish FWP but greatly restricted its scope. In December 1942, when Roosevelt ordered the dissolution of all WPA projects by 30 June 1943, much of the material collected by state FWP projects had yet to be used. Books that were planned but never published included a state fact book series, a recreation series, a crafts series, "America Eats," and volumes on conservation. Although some of the raw materials were brought to Washington, many were improperly stored or destroyed.

Each component of Federal Project Number One is treated in Marguerite D. Bloxom, comp., *Pickaxe and Pencil: References for the Study of the WPA* (Washington: Library of Congress, 1982). See also William F. McDonald, *Federal Relief Administration and the Arts: The Origins and Administrative History of the Arts Projects of the Works Progress Administration* (Columbus: Ohio State University Press, 1969). A sympathetic account by a former project worker is Jerre G. Mangione, *The Dream and the Deal: The Federal Writers' Project, 1935–1943* (Boston: Little, Brown & Co., 1972). Monty N. Penkower, *The Federal Writers' Project: A Study in Government Patronage of the Arts* (Urbana: University of Illinois Press, 1977), is standard literature. FWP interviews with former slaves were published in the early 1970s in George P. Rawick, ed., *The American Slave: A Composite Autobiography,* 19 vols. (Westport, Conn.: Greenwood Publishing Co., 1972–73). For a cautionary note on their use, see John W. Blassingame, "Using the Testimony of Ex-slaves: Approaches and Problems," *Journal of Southern History* 41 (November 1974):473–92.

RICHARD D. MCKINZIE

See also House Committee to Investigate Un-American Activities; Roosevelt, Anna Eleanor; Works Progress Administration

Finances, Personal

A privileged son of a New York patrician family and husband of an heiress, Franklin Roosevelt for the most part lived comfortably even while pursuing some imprudent investments.

The Roosevelt side of the family fortune came from great-great-grandfather Isaac who built the first sugar refinery in New York when it was still a colony. From this lineage FDR acquired a $100,000 estate on which he predictably earned a respectable, but not lavish, $5,000 annually. FDR's maternal grandfather, Warren Delano, left a legacy of Pennsylvania property and mines. Most of what FDR realized from this $700,000 fortune, however, came to him through the largesse of his mother, Sara. Sara, in fact, made it possible for Franklin and Eleanor to live at Hyde Park. She continued to own and maintain the family homestead while they paid only their own household expenses. Eleanor was an heiress who also contributed an annual income of at least $5,000 to the marriage, and FDR's employment, investments, and authorship royalties brought their average prepresidential income to $27,500.

When FDR was twenty-five, he earned a small salary by clerking in the law firm of Carter, Ledyard & Milburn. At twenty-eight, he was elected to the $1,500-a-year post of New York state senator. As assistant secretary of the navy at age thirty-one, he earned $5,000 a year. In post–World War I Washington high society, this base of $15,000 a year proved inadequate for a family of seven. FDR wrote to a friend in 1919, "I am honestly a fit candidate for a receiver," but Sara soon rescued her son from his financial difficulties. By 1920, he had returned to the private sector and in 1921 earned $25,000 as the vice-president of the Fidelity & Deposit Company of Maryland.

Shortly thereafter, Roosevelt was stricken with polio. His recuperation at Warm Springs, Georgia, encouraged him to establish a foundation there to assist other polio victims. During this time away from public office, he became involved in a number of ill-fated investment schemes. Oil refineries, dirigible airships, Argentine herb teas, tidal-power generation, luxury resort chains, and small-denomination bonds captured FDR's fancy in rapid sequence. His ideas were numerous and often risky. Roosevelt's penchant for blue-sky commitments was a subject of comment and some jest at his expense among his broker friends. Even his United European Investors Corporation, which paid off financially, brought him some disrepute, however, "as critics charged that he had made money on the miseries of the German people."

Even though FDR managed several other profitable investments, he was forced to borrow to develop the Warm Springs Foundation. On 29 April 1926, Roosevelt signed a demand note for $201,667.83 and bought the Warm Springs property. This debt represented more than two-thirds of his personal net worth. Sara's concern that Warm Springs would go the way of herb tea proved unwarranted, but he continued to make payments on the note for the rest of his life. A 1927 bequest from his brother James improved FDR's finances considerably. As president, FDR took the unusual step of returning to the Treasury 15 percent of his $75,000 salary in acknowledgment of the country's greater financial plight.

For more information on FDR's finances and investment schemes, see Nathan Miller, *FDR: An Intimate History* (Garden City, N.Y.: Doubleday & Co., 1983), pp. 163, 213–16. In October 1932, just before FDR's election, *Fortune* magazine published the article, "Franklin and Eleanor Roosevelt's Fortune," reprinted in Don Wharton, ed., *The Roosevelt Omnibus* (New York: Alfred A. Knopf, 1934), pp. 136–47.

Fireside Chats

Roosevelt's intermittent national radio reports, usually devoted to a single issue. Broadcast from the White House Diplomatic Reception Room, the fireside chats initiated presidential addresses directed solely to a radio audience. The term—intended to convey their informality—was first applied by Harry C. Butcher of the Columbia Broadcasting System to the second such talk on 7 May 1933.

The fireside chats were Roosevelt's most memorable use of radio, which he employed frequently both as governor of New York and as president, not only to speak directly to a mass audience, but to bypass what he considered newspaper distortions. His voice and delivery—clear, conversational, buoyant—were admirably adapted to the new medium. Roosevelt wrote that he tried to picture himself talking to individuals as he spoke, and John Gunther observed, "He gave the impression . . . of speaking to every listener personally. . . . You could practically feel him physically in the room." The fireside chats often drew thousands of letters, and opponents considered them to be among Roosevelt's most formidable weapons.

Despite their seeming informality, the talks, like other Roosevelt speeches, were prepared painstakingly through many drafts. Their intimate phrasing—use of "we" and "you" and homely references to, for example, a "batting average" or to "pulling the covers over our heads"—resulted from polishing. Still, Roosevelt ad-libbed effectively, as when once he asked for a glass of water (24 July 1933).

Political judgment rather than the calendar set the schedule for the chats. Roosevelt's *Public Papers and Addresses* lists twenty-seven fireside chats, the first on 12 March 1933, the last on 12 June 1944. The average interval was 5½ months; the longest was a little over 16 months (28 April 1935 to 6 September 1936). They averaged about thirty minutes and were most often delivered between 9 and 11 P.M. (eastern time) on Sunday, the night with the largest radio audience.

Topically, the fireside chats fell into three groups: six delivered in the New Deal's first nineteen months, designed to rally the country from the Great Depression; six on various subjects over the next four years; and fifteen from 1939 into 1944 on World War II. Few advocated particular measures; most were reports aimed, Elmer E. Cornwell has said, "at setting events in context . . . and relating the policies of his administration to those events." In addition to the fireside chats of 3 September 1939 and 9 December 1941 on the start of World War II and Pearl Harbor, respectively, others of historical importance included:

12 March 1933: Eight days in office, Roosevelt went on the air to "explain clearly" what government had done during the bank holiday; he was credited with quelling panic.

9 March 1937: Roosevelt attempted unsuccessfully to win support for his ill-fated plan to pack the Supreme Court.

29 December 1940: The arsenal of democracy fireside chat helped to swing American opinion toward support of Britain.

23 February 1942: Roosevelt likened war setbacks to Valley Forge and asked listeners to follow his strategic discussion on world maps. Samuel I. Rosenman considered this "one of the most important and effective" fireside chats.

In the years since Roosevelt, the presidential broadcast from the White House has become commonplace. But only Jimmy Carter has presented a speech called a fireside chat (delivered on television beside a real fireplace). The fireside chats have remained a trademark of Roosevelt and of the age of radio; Cornwell called them "political leadership via the mass media in its most effective and subtle form."

Although some sources estimate there were as many as thirty fireside chats, the figure used here is the total in the *Public Papers and Addresses*, ed. Samuel I. Rosenman (New York: 1938–50), which contains the texts. Sound recordings of four of the chats can be heard on *F.D.R. Speaks* (New York: Washington Records, 1960). Among Roosevelt's associates, those who provide the most information on the fireside chats are Samuel I. Rosenman, *Working with Roosevelt* (New York: Harper & Bros., 1952) and Robert Sherwood, *Roosevelt and Hopkins: An Intimate History* (New York: Harper & Bros., 1948). Valuable background detail can be found in John H. Sharon, "The Fireside Chat," *Franklin D. Roosevelt Collector* 2 (November 1949):3–20. Evaluations include Waldo W. Braden and Ernest Brandenburg, "Roosevelt's Fireside Chats," *Speech Monographs*, November 1955, pp. 290–307; William Stott, *Documentary Expression and Thirties America* (New York: Oxford University Press, 1973); and Elmer E. Cornwell, *Presidential Leadership of Public Opinion* (Bloomington: Indiana University Press, 1966). William E. Leuchtenburg's *In the Shadow of FDR* (Ithaca: Cornell University Press, 1983) discusses the influence of the fireside chats on later presidents.

JAMES R. BOYLAN

See also New Deal

Fiscal Policy

Fiscal policy under Franklin Roosevelt—meaning the taxing and spending actions of government, as distinguished from monetary and regulatory policies—was only marginally successful in peacetime (1933–41). Fiscal policy also aimed at social reform with greater results. But if economic recovery eluded Rooseveltian fiscal policy efforts until wartime, the administration's experimentation paved the way for a more vigorous, informed, and effective fiscal policy in the postwar era.

Franklin Roosevelt began his presidency with orthodox, pre-Keynesian fiscal ideas. In his 1932 presidential campaign, Roosevelt promised to balance the federal budget, which for three years the administration of Herbert Hoover had been unable to do. In 1933, he warned Congress that "too often in recent history liberal governments have been wrecked on the rocks of loose fiscal policy." His desire to balance the budget was based on both economics and politics. Until 1938, Roosevelt believed that a balanced budget was important as a means of fostering the confidence of the public, especially business, in government, thereby encouraging investment and economic recovery. He followed closely the polls which suggested that the vast majority of Americans, even during the 1936 campaign, wished him to balance the budget.

Budget balancing, however, was not easy. New Deal programs were often expensive, so that both financing them and balancing the budget required additional tax revenues. But facing a depressed tax base, Roosevelt and Congress could obtain those tax revenues only by massive increases in tax rates or by the introduction of new, substantial taxes. If Roosevelt and Congress had raised taxes sufficiently to balance the budget in the short run, they might well have made the Great Depression even worse. Roosevelt realized this and accepted some deficit spending as a short-run necessity. He hoped that his tax increases would be adequate to balance the budget once the economy returned to full health. During his first term, Roosevelt asserted in every budget message that the deficits should disappear along with the depression.

Deficits grew from $2.6 billion in 1933 to $4.4 billion in 1936. Judging by these *actual* deficits, the Roosevelt administration's fiscal policy could be interpreted as one of consistent, and increasingly more vigorous, promotion of economic recovery through deficit spending. However, the deficits resulted, in part, from the depressed tax base and were unintended and unwelcome. The New Deal repeatedly raised taxes in an effort to reduce deficits. Is it possible to measure what fiscal policy was *intended* to be during the New Deal?

To separate the effects of policy decisions, as contrasted with the effects of a depresson on the tax base, economists invoke the concept of the full-employment deficit (or surplus) as a measure of fiscal policy. This is the deficit that would be attained if the economy were operating at full employment and producing the greatest possible national income. If this measure changes, it has to be because of changes in policy rather than changes in economic conditions. When applied to fiscal policy during the 1930s, this measure reveals that (1) only about half of the Roosevelt deficits resulted from deliberate policy decisions; (2) in Roosevelt's first term, he and Congress adopted expansionary fiscal policy only in 1933 and 1935; and (3) because of Roosevelt's effort to balance the budget, his fiscal policy was no more expansionary than that of Herbert Hoover between 1929 and 1931.

It appears that Roosevelt could have embraced larger deficits without sacrificing economic recovery. Because he had succeeded in liberating monetary policy from Federal Reserve control and in creating an expansive money supply, he did not run the risk that increased deficits would drive up interest rates to the point of discouraging investment. His reluctance to pursue as active a fiscal policy as circumstances permitted indicates that he and his administration had not chosen to seek salvation in the policy prescriptions of the English economist John Maynard Keynes. In *The Means to Prosperity* (1933), Keynes urged depression governments to undertake as their central activity the stimulation of private investment through the vigorous use of government deficits. Roosevelt paid little attention to Keynes's ideas, even after they met in 1934. Recalling the visit, Keynes remarked that he had "supposed the President was more literate, economically speaking." Roosevelt remembered that Keynes "left a whole rigmarole of figures. He must be a mathematician rather than a political economist."

In 1938, Roosevelt did shift his economic policy toward a Keynesian position. Toward the end of the recession of 1937–38, Roosevelt launched an energetic new spending program that was unaccompanied by significant tax increases. In March 1938, he asked Congress for substantial increases in WPA, Farm Security Administration, Civilian Conservation Corps, public works, and housing expenditures. Conse-quently, the full-employment deficit surged upward in both 1938 and 1939.

The influence of Keynesian ideas on Roosevelt's fiscal policy was only indirect. Of greater importance in explaining Roosevelt's shift was his recognition that conservative opposition to the New Deal had grown too strong for him to seek significant tax increases or to pursue economic recovery through redistributional tax reform. However, as nearly always, Roosevelt learned something from bitter experience. He could not ignore the strong likelihood that restrictive fiscal policy had contributed to the sharp downturn in 1937–38. Consequently, he listened more closely to a group of government officials, scattered across the WPA, the Department of Agriculture, and the Federal Reserve, who pressed Keynesian ideas upon him.

These officials, who included Harry Hopkins, Henry Wallace, and Marriner Eccles, had consistently advocated a recovery policy that would emphasize augmenting consumption through federal deficits. In 1938, they advanced their position with greater force and confidence because they found in some new Keynesian ideas a theoretical justification for the fiscal policies they favored. In Keynes's *General Theory of Employment, Interest, and Money,* which appeared in 1936, they discovered an argument they found compelling: that in a technically advanced economy there would be a *permanent* need for government deficits (or for other measures, such as a massive redistribution of income away from the wealthy) to stimulate consumption and to maintain full employment. There is no evidence that they ever convinced Roosevelt that permanent deficits would be necessary. But, in 1938, he shifted fiscal policy in line with Keynesian prescriptions and used a Keynesian argument to justify what he had done. He explained to Congress that his large increases in expenditures, unaccompanied by tax increases, would add "to the purchasing power of the Nation."

By 1938, the Roosevelt administration had established a clear consensus that the federal government should avoid adopting restrictive fiscal policies (such as the Hoover administration's tax increase of 1932 and Roosevelt's expenditure cuts of 1937) during recession or depression conditions. Moreover, the nation had begun to make a commitment—based on widespread recognition of the power of fiscal policy—to the use of deficit spending as a tool for promoting economic recovery. The public at large grew more accustomed to, if not enthusiastically in favor of, continued deficits to manage economic recovery. It is true that the federal government lacked a clearly defined strategy of spending and deficits; no one was capable of specifying reliable techniques and magnitudes. But, through the medium of the New Deal, the nation had institutionalized the maintenance or extension of spending programs during economic reversals. Most important, key groups, such as commercial farmers and organized labor, had come to expect a positive government response in periods of economic adversity. Even some key businessmen, such as Beardsley Ruml of Macy's, shared this expectation. In effect, they supported programs that would supplement private consumption.

In addition, economic experts in government service were more decisively in favor of deficits than they had been in 1933 or in 1937, and they had begun to discover a rationale for their political position in the work of John Maynard Keynes. Augmenting their ranks during 1939 and 1940 were economists who enthusiastically embraced Keynesian ideas. Some, like Alvin Hansen, were senior economists who used Keynes to order their long-standing belief that economic stagnation was inevitable without permanent deficits or drastic income redistribution. Others, like Paul Samuelson, were weaned on *The General Theory*. These economists staffed agencies such as the Division of Industrial Economics within the Department of Commerce, the Budget Bureau (Fiscal Division) within the Executive Office of the president, and the National Resources Planning Board.

During World War II, the Roosevelt administration shaped fiscal policy according to the objectives of successfully prosecuting the war effort. During the war, preventing inflation rather than curing depression became the major problem. Roosevelt sought to avoid the excessive inflation that great deficits had helped cause between 1917 and 1920.

The pressures for inflation, however, were enormous. Energized by Pearl Harbor, governmental expenditures soared and continued to increase through 1945. These expenditures represented a more massive shift of resources from peacetime to wartime needs than was the case during World War I. The average level of federal expenditures from 1942 through 1945 amounted to roughly half of the national product, more than twice the level during World War I. In addition, the shift of resources was faster and more prolonged. The period of American neutrality, during which adjustment to wartime pressures could take place, was short in contrast with the long period preceding American entry into World War I, and the period of belligerency was much more extended than during World War I. However, the Roosevelt administration was able to take advantage of greater economic slack after Pearl Harbor than the Wilson administration enjoyed in 1917, when the economy was already at full employment, demand was already pressing hard on available supply, and too much money was already chasing too few goods and forcing up prices.

Learning from Wilson's unfortunate experience, Roosevelt sought to raise taxes as much as possible to pay for wartime spending and to prevent consumers from bidding up prices in competition with the government. He succeeded; the federal deficit, after increasing from $6.2 billion in 1941 to $57.4 billion in 1943, held at about the 1943 level for the remainder of the war. Partly as a consequence, prices rose much more slowly (at a measured rate of 4 percent per year) during World War II than during World War I.

Despite the moderation of Roosevelt's wartime fiscal policy, the deficits were far larger than any incurred during the Great Depression. The conjunction of great deficits and dramatic economic expansion converted many Americans to the Keynesian faith. They concluded that great deficits not only had produced the economic expansion of World War II, ending the Great Depression, but also were required for sustained prosperity in peacetime. They argued that only peacetime deficits would avoid a resumption of the Great Depression. Among the converted were a growing number of businessmen who vastly preferred permanent deficits to income redistribution. A consequence of the emerging Keynesian consensus fostered by the New Deal and World War II was congressional passage of the Employment Act of 1946.

This was the first institutionalization of what was believed to have been the implicit fiscal policy of Franklin Roosevelt. The act became the formal vehicle for the reform impact of Roosevelt's fiscal policy. Like Roosevelt's real fiscal policy, the content of the act was limited. The act was vague. It failed to make a guarantee of full employment, it restricted countercyclical actions to only those consistent with other economic objectives, and it avoided a specific definition of appropriate policy. However, the act captured two important elements in Roosevelt's fiscal policy. First, it declared the federal government's central responsibility for managing the level of employment. Second, by creating the Council of Economic Advisers and charging it with the development of an annual published report, the act established that the president and the public should have economic advice that was expert and independent.

Between 1932 and 1946, policymakers had become far more aware of the power of fiscal policy and far more cautious in avoiding actions that could cause depression. Roosevelt had brought the federal government from 1932, when the Hoover administration declared that the prime objective of fiscal policy was to maintain order in capital markets, to 1946, when Congress established the primacy of protecting and creating jobs. The New Deal had replaced property values with human values as the context for setting and evaluating fiscal policy.

We have not had the benefit of a monographic history of Roosevelt's fiscal policy, but there is a moderately large body of literature on its various aspects. The best single source is Herbert Stein, *The Fiscal Revolution in America* (Chicago: University of Chicago, 1969). Stein emphasizes the conservative content of Roosevelt's fiscal ideas and is particularly effective in explicating the varieties of Keynesian analysis. The books most helpful in exploring the full complexity of Roosevelt's fiscal ideas are John Blum, *From the Morgenthau Diaries, Years of Crisis, 1928–1938* (Boston: Houghton Mifflin Co., 1959), and Frank Freidel, *Franklin D. Roosevelt: Launching the New Deal* (Boston: Little, Brown & Co., 1973). In "Fiscal Policies in the 'Thirties: A Reappraisal," *American Economic Review* 46 (December 1956):857–79, E. Cary Brown, using the concept of the full-employment deficit, helps define what fiscal policies Hoover and Roosevelt actually implemented.

W. ELLIOT BROWNLEE

See also Currie, Lauchlin; Eccles, Marriner Stoddard; Great Depression; Henderson, Leon; Monetary Policy; Recession of 1937–38; Regulation, Federal; Taxation; Temporary National Economic Committee

Flynn, Edward Joseph

(22 September 1891–18 August 1953)

The son of well-to-do Irish immigrants, Edward Flynn was born in New York City and educated at parochial schools and then at Fordham University. Flynn was admitted to the New York bar in 1913 and elected as a New York state assemblyman in 1917. A member of Tammany Hall, Flynn rose in the organization to become in 1922 chairman of the Democratic party in the Bronx, a position he held until his death. Unlike other Tammany officials Flynn came from a well-educated, upper-middle-class background and reportedly preferred reading to the usual talk of politics. Flynn wielded the machine's power to help control New York's political future, but always kept his district free from the corruption that plagued Tammany elsewhere in the city. Flynn also campaigned especially hard for Franklin Roosevelt in his race for governor in 1928 and was rewarded with the job of secretary of state, which he held under Governor Roosevelt and his successor, Herbert Lehman. In 1933 Flynn backed the independent mayoral candidacy of Joseph V. McKee in a campaign that drew strength from the regular Democratic candidate and allowed the Republican Fiorello La Guardia, a personal favorite of Roosevelt, to win.

Flynn was a close and consistent supporter of Roosevelt and the New Deal. He introduced Roosevelt to Jim Farley and worked with Farley in the 1932 and 1936 presidential election campaigns. In 1933 President Roosevelt appointed Flynn to be a regional administrator for the National Recovery Administration's public works program and Flynn enjoyed a spot in the inner circle of Roosevelt's political advisers. When Farley refused to support Roosevelt for a third term, Flynn stepped in as national chairman of the Democratic party and engineered Roosevelt's campaign in 1940 and 1944. In 1943 Roosevelt tried to appoint Flynn minister to Australia but withdrew the nomination when the Senate would not confirm the appointment because of Flynn's too close association with Tammany Hall. Always a Roosevelt loyalist, Flynn accompanied the president to Yalta and was in Rome working for better postwar treatment for Catholics inside Soviet Russia when Roosevelt died. Flynn finished his career where it began, in the Bronx, still the machine politician and party loyalist out to prove that big-city bosses need not be corrupt. In his relationship with Roosevelt, Flynn demonstrated how urban machines could, under the right leadership, be compatible with New Deal welfare policies.

The well-educated Flynn wrote an autobiography entitled *You're the Boss* (New York: Viking Press, 1947). Charles Van Devander, *The Big Bosses* (New York: Howell, Soskin, 1944) contains a chapter critical of Flynn's machine politics. A view of Flynn as a well-meaning victim of Roosevelt's selfish and manipulating politics is Lyle W. Dorsett, *Franklin D. Roosevelt and the City Bosses* (Port Washington, N.Y.: Kennikat Press, 1977).

Foreign Economic Policy

Franklin Roosevelt entered office in March 1933 with one overriding mandate: to lift the United States from the most wrenching economic depression it had ever known and return prosperity and material well-being to its citizens. Within his administration, those advocating an international approach to combating the depression looked for leadership to Secretary of State Cordell Hull. Alarmed by the steep drop in the value of American exports since 1929, from $5.24 billion to just $1.61 billion three years later, Hull preached—nagged, some said—the virtues of a multilateral world order of liberalized trade. Roosevelt, on the other hand, initially leaned toward unilateral solutions to the nation's economic woes, and many of the early actions of his administration reflected this nationalistic approach: the abandonment of the gold standard, his inflexibility on the issue of intergovernmental war debts, his undermining of efforts at the London Economic Conference in mid-1933 to devise a new currency stabilization agreement, his acceptance of the mischievous 1934 Johnson Act, which prohibited foreign governments that had defaulted on their war debts from floating loans in the United States.

Gradually, however, those who, like Hull, pushed the view that expanded foreign markets offered the best means for both restoring prosperity and safeguarding peace gained the upper hand within the administration. Early in 1934 Roosevelt created an Export-Import Bank with the authority to extend loans and credits to overseas purchasers of American goods, up to this time the job of private lenders. Several months later, Hull realized one of his lifelong ambitions with congressional passage of the Reciprocal Trade Agreements Act. This measure represented a significant departure from its Republican-sponsored predecessors by reversing the nation's long commitment to protectionism. Although failing to reduce trade restrictions to the degree Hull had hoped and failing as well to lift the depression, the Reciprocal Trade Agreements Act stands today as a watershed in the movement toward international economic cooperation and interdependence.

As it gained further experience, the administration found that it could use economic tools for a variety of political, military, financial, and ideological ends. From time to time the Eximbank made approval of loan requests contingent upon debtors settling their accounts with private American lenders, or rejected these requests altogether if political considerations overrode Washington's desire to foster additional trade. In Latin America credits, development loans, sugar quotas, and commercial agreements replaced old-fashioned military intervention, but proved just as effective in protecting American interests, public and private.

At the same time, the Roosevelt administration recognized a distinction between private and national interests. The expropriation of American property in

Bolivia and Mexico, for instance, drew angry protests from the State Department, but the president instinctively sensed that other objectives—the promotion of friendly relations with Latin America, hemispheric collaboration for security purposes, a more benevolent image among the peoples of the South—limited the responses available to the United States. But even as the administration on occasions subordinated the interests of private groups to a broader conception of the national interest, the entire thrust of its foreign policies looked toward the establishment of an international climate generally favorable to the nation's liberal capitalist economic system, an important fact FDR's conservative critics frequently overlooked.

As the threat of global war drew closer after mid-decade, Washington initially turned to economic policy to defend American interests. The early neutrality acts reflected the conviction that the nation must guard against being drawn into any future conflict, even if it had to forswear the profits economic dealings with the belligerents might bring. Seldom were national policies more misbegotten—or less effective. Following the Italian invasion of Ethiopia, the president called for a "moral embargo" on munitions and petroleum supplies; instead, exports to Italy climbed dramatically. By the end of the decade, Congress had repealed even the prohibition on the sale of arms, and the cash-and-carry provisions of the 1939 neutrality law revisions appeared designed not to protect the United States from the contagion of war but to assist Germany's foes at minimal risk for American business.

The economic sanctions implied in Roosevelt's controversial quarantine speech in October 1937 offered a more promising approach to the problem of global aggression, but the president quickly backed off from committing himself to any specific course of action. In the Far East, credits, silver purchasing agreements, and other financial aid may have encouraged the Chinese in their resistance to Japan but did not noticeably augment the martial prowess of Chiang Kai-shek's forces. It was American economic pressures against Tokyo that proved most effective—though not in the sense Washington intended. The gradual escalation of economic restrictions against Japan convinced the Japanese of implacable American hostility, intensified pressures on Tokyo to move into Indochina and the East Indies, and ultimately pushed the Japanese into a preemptive attack on American naval forces at Pearl Harbor.

In Latin America, economic diplomacy proved a far more potent tool in neutralizing Axis influence. Eximbank credits, development loans, preclusive purchasing agreements, and trade pacts served to counteract the worrisome German presence in the region in the years before Pearl Harbor. Private American concerns, including Pan Am and IT&T, received government assistance to oust German and Italian competitors. Once Washington had entered the war, economic means satisfied both military and nonmilitary objectives. Government-created subsidiaries bought up critical raw materials, thereby denying these to the enemy and tying the producer nations more tightly into Washington's economic sphere, a development with important postwar implications. A similar process occurred during the war years in the Middle East, where both private firms (notably American oil companies) and administration officials worked to enlarge the U.S. presence in the region (though for different reasons).

In other ways as well, World War II saw the employment of economic warfare on a scale never before attained, an effort supervised after mid-1943 by the Foreign Economic Administration (FEA). Headed by Leo Crowley, the FEA administered Lend-Lease, oversaw the procurement of strategic materials for war production and domestic consumption, ran the export controls and preclusive buying programs, directed relief operations, and provided the armed forces with economic intelligence about the Axis nations. Under Lend-Lease alone, the United States supplied $42 billion in goods and services to its military allies, a contribution that, by shoring up British and Soviet might, undoubtedly saved thousands of American lives.

Roosevelt appreciated that the country's vast wealth also gave him leverage in shaping the postwar economic order, but the president often accorded precedence to other objectives. For instance, he gave only sporadic support to Hull's attempts to use Britain's great need for American assistance to break down London's system of imperial preference. In fact, administration policies frequently reflected the assessment that American interests demanded a vigorous Great Britain after the war, and that the United States should help the United Kingdom rebuild itself rather than take advantage of London's distress to push into markets formerly dominated by British traders. Moreover, Roosevelt, believing that military necessity overrode all competing purposes, brushed aside the objections of his State Department and refused to attach conditions of any sort to Russian Lend-Lease. Nor did the promise of American reconstruction aid prevent the Soviets from turning Eastern Europe into a closed sphere.

Nonetheless, the Roosevelt administration inexorably moved toward the creation of a multilateral world economy in which the nation's capitalist system would prosper. The World Bank and the International Monetary Fund, established at Bretton Woods in 1944, were designed to restore a global economic order in which the American economy, the world's strongest by far, would be preeminent. And on balance, Washington policymakers succeeded, for the postwar period saw an unprecedented prosperity in which both the United States and most of its primary allies shared. For this fortuitous development, Rooseveltian economic diplomacy must be accorded a not insignificant share of the credit. As with much else from the Roosevelt years, the administration's foreign economic policies long outlived their progenitor.

Lloyd C. Gardner, *Economic Aspects of New Deal Diplomacy* (Madison: University of Wisconsin Press, 1964) is the standard monograph on the subject. A more balanced account may be found in Robert M. Hathaway, "Economic Diplomacy in a Time of Crisis," in *Economics and World Power: An Assessment of American Diplomacy Since 1789,* ed. William H. Becker and Samuel F. Wells, Jr. (New York: Columbia University Press, 1984). Cordell Hull, *Memoirs,* 2 vols. (New York: Macmillan, 1948) is essential, but somewhat stodgy. Frederick C. Adams, *Economic Diplomacy: The Export-Import Bank and American Foreign Policy, 1934–1939* (Columbia: University of Missouri Press, 1976) highlights an important tool used in the fight to lift the depression. Irvine H. Anderson, Jr., *The Standard-Vacuum Oil Company and United States East Asian Policy, 1933–1941* (Princeton: Princeton University Press, 1975) illustrates the diverse economic considerations behind the coming of the Pacific war.

ROBERT M. HATHAWAY

See also Chiang Kai-shek; Good Neighbor Policy; Hull, Cordell; Isolationism; Japan; Lend-Lease; London Economic Conference; Monetary Policy; Neutrality Acts; Open Door Policy; Recipocal Trade Agreements

Foreign Policy

The policies of the Roosevelt administration vis-à-vis other nations, 1933–45. Stimulated in his formative years by several trips to Europe in the company of his parents, Franklin Roosevelt's interest in goings-on beyond the shores of his native land never weakened. In the years at Groton the future president participated in discussions on international affairs and became persuaded that the United States should assert itself in the world arena. He took unabashed pride in the diplomatic undertakings of his kinsman Theodore Roosevelt during the latter's occupancy of the White House. Convinced that strength on the seas was essential to the exercise of national influence in world affairs, he urged a buildup of American naval power when he became assistant secretary of the navy in 1913. As the Great War was moving to a conclusion in 1918, he became an outspoken supporter of a "general association of nations" and, as the Democratic party's candidate for vice-president in 1920, appealed to the country to sanction American membership in the League of Nations.

Preoccupied after 1921 with the quest to regain use of his withered legs, Roosevelt nonetheless kept in touch with world happenings. He wrote an article for *Asia* magazine entitled "Shall We Trust Japan?" and one for *Foreign Affairs* in which he excoriated the Republican administrations of the 1920s for their management of foreign relations. Alas, when he made his run for the presidency in 1932, he felt compelled to modify his positions in foreign affairs—to put them in rhythm with the isolationist impulses that animated much of the American electorate in that period. For example, he disavowed the League. In truth, he said comparatively little about international relations in the course of the campaign, for like nearly all Americans his great overriding concern at the moment was the national economic crisis.

Temple, New Orleans Times Picayune, *17 May 1933.*
(Courtesy New Orleans Times Picayune.)

In his inaugural address of 4 March 1933, the thirty-second president limited his remarks about foreign policy to a single utterance: in world affairs, he said, he dedicated the United States to a Good Neighbor policy. What did the phrase mean? It probably meant that Roosevelt, his attention riveted on the economic crisis, had no clearly defined policy in the area of foreign affairs. Still, the new administration in Washington could not ignore diplomacy entirely. Delegates to an international conference in Geneva were trying to work out a formula for reducing the level of the world's armaments—at the same time that the new chancellor in Berlin, Adolf Hitler, was renewing his intention to renounce provisions of the Treaty of Versailles (1919) that severely restricted the military strength of Germany. Moreover, a world economic conference would soon convene in London.

Inhibited by the isolationist impulses of the country, Roosevelt declined to make commitments that seemed essential if the disarmament conference were to achieve any success at all. Having concluded that the United States should find its own exit from the Great Depression, he declined to cooperate with the London Economic Conference. Only in the matter of diplomatic undertakings that held out promise of reinforcing the domestic program to achieve economic recovery did the Washington government exercise notable initiative in Roosevelt's first year or so in the White House. It set about to implement what came to be referred to as the Good Neighbor policy in Latin America in some measure in the hope that improved relations with the region would stimulate trade and hence encourage economic recovery. And in late 1933 it worked out an agreement establishing diplomatic relations with the Soviet Union—again in some measure because of a hope that such relations would strengthen the American economy by stimulating commerce. A similar hope prompted the Roosevelt administration to negotiate reciprocal trade treaties after congressional passage of the Trade Agreements Act of 1934.

Meanwhile an organized peace movement that had achieved influence in the 1920s when large numbers of Americans became disillusioned over their country's participation in the Great War in 1917–18 was stepping up its activities. A high moment in the movement's enterprise came to pass in 1934 when pacifists prevailed on the U.S. Senate to adopt a resolution mandating a special investigation of the manufacturers and distributors of armaments, the so-called merchants of death who, it was widely believed, were instrumental in provoking nations to war in the interest of corporate and personal profits. The resultant munitions investigation headed by Senator Gerald P. Nye reinforced what seemed an ever-enlarging national will to peace, whatever the fate of nations beyond the borders of the United States that might fall victim of armed aggression. That enlarging will to peace manifested itself in the demands of uncounted Americans that the Washington government keep the country isolated from new wars that might break out in other parts of the world.

These demands became well-nigh irresistible in 1935–36 when Hitler, in defiance of the Versailles settlement, set about to achieve German rearmament and remilitarized the Rhineland; when Benito Mussolini's Italy invaded Ethiopia; when Hitler and Mussolini forged the Rome-Berlin Axis; when Germany and Japan became veritable allies by signing the Anti-Comintern Pact; when Spain became engulfed in civil war. The structure of peace fashioned at Paris in 1919 was clearly coming apart, and people who were wise and not-so-wise suspected that its collapse would signal the start of a new general war. Accordingly, Congress in 1935–37 passed a succession of neutrality acts, which Americans hoped would enable the United States to remain isolated from such a conflict.

As for the Roosevelt administration, it was swept up in the passions of the moment. The president therefore felt constrained to sign the neutrality legislation and even make utterances that seemed to ring of isolationism. In response to isolationist pressures (and also to pressures by Roman Catholics), he sought to insulate the United States from the Spanish civil war. Still, Roosevelt, Secretary of State Cordell Hull, and other leaders of the administration were not isolationists who could blandly ignore unprovoked attacks on peaceful nations and cling to the notion that changes wrought in the international strategic balance by the machinations of aggressor states would have no important bearing on the life of the American nation. They revealed as much during the debate of 1935 when they pressed (unsuccessfully) for a provision in the neutrality legislation that would permit the president, in the event of war anywhere in the world, to designate the aggressor and impose an embargo on arms shipments to the aggressor while permitting arms shipments to the aggressor's victim.

His attention still fixed on domestic problems, Roosevelt maneuvered as best he could in 1935–37 to counter aggression, notwithstanding the country's rampant isolationism. He urged what he and Hull described as a "moral embargo" against the belligerents in East Africa, that is, a limitation on shipments of nonmilitary commodities to the belligerents which the two American leaders expected would function to the disadvantage of the Italian aggressors. When Japan invaded China in the summer of 1937, the president declined to invoke the Neutrality Act (by declining to proclaim that China and Japan were at war) because of his conviction that if invoked the law would work to the disadvantage of the Chinese. In the autumn of 1937, he issued his famous quarantine proposal. But the proposal failed to strike a chord with isolationist-minded Americans, so his administration declined to pledge cooperative action against aggressors during the Brussels Conference of November 1937 and made a tepid response when Japanese aircraft sank the American gunboat *Panay* on the Yangtze River in China a few weeks later.

The policy of tepidity continued when Hitler seized Austria in March of 1938: the Washington government suspended a commercial treaty with Austria and refused to recognize the Anschluss. When Hitler a few months later pressed Czechoslovakia to cede its Sudeten territory to Germany, the American president appealed to the German dictator to seek a peaceful solution to the Sudeten question—and seemed genuinely relieved when, at Munich in September 1938, the British and French prevailed on the Czechs to accede to the dictator's demands. When the Germans, in defiance of the Munich accord, seized the rest of Czechoslovakia in early 1939, and when Mussolini sent Italian troops to occupy Albania a short time later, the Washington government felt powerless to do anything more than condemn the Axis aggressors and continue to recognize the Czech and Albanian ministers in Washington.

As Europe teetered ever nearer to the precipice of war in the spring of 1939, Roosevelt, instinctively hostile to aggression and persuaded that victory by the Axis in a new European war would be subversive of the interests and values of the United States, sought revision of that part of the neutrality law that mandated an embargo on arms shipments to all belligerents, aggressors, and their victims alike. Clearly he hoped to make American armaments available to the enemies of Germany and Italy in the event that Europe indeed slipped into general hostilities. In the face of a continuing national impulse to isolation, his enterprise came to nothing. Then, in the first days of September 1939, the Second World War finally erupted when Hitler unleashed his Blitzkrieg against Poland, and Britain and France declared war on Germany. Making no effort to conceal his contempt for the German aggressors, Roosevelt determined to provide as much assistance as possible to the British and

French, and hence renewed his appeal that Congress revise the neutrality statute—by repealing the arms embargo provision altogether. After a momentous debate of six weeks, the national legislature complied: it repealed the arms embargo but required that belligerents pay for American arms in cash and carry them away in their own ships.

While Congress was repealing the arms embargo, in November 1939, a new act of aggression jarred the sensibilities of the American people: the Soviet Union, whose infamous pact with Germany in August 1939 had cleared the path for the latter's attack on Poland, sent its forces against Finland. Americans denounced the Soviets and cheered the Finns. But the Roosevelt administration, however much it deplored the Soviet aggression, calculated that the Soviet-German alliance of the previous August was not likely to endure and that in time the Soviets might become allies of the Western democracies in the war against the Germans; hence he adopted a policy of avoiding a break with the Soviet Union over its aggression against Finland.

The Roosevelt administration looked on helplessly in the spring of 1940 when the Germans occupied Denmark and Norway and then overran the Low countries and France. But as German forces advanced toward Paris, the American president made a momentous decision. Turning aside the counsel that the beleaguered British were apt to prove unequal to the task of turning back a German invasion of their home islands, he determined to provide large-scale assistance to Britain and other nations, such as Canada, that remained in the fight against the Axis, notwithstanding the protests of isolationists and the restrictions of the neutrality law. To borrow an expression that he would invoke several months later, he set about to make the United States a great arsenal of democracy. Most dramatically, in September 1940, during his campaign for a third term in the White House, he authorized the transfer of fifty antiquated American destroyers to the British in the so-called destroyer deal. A few months later in early 1941, he prevailed on Congress to enact legislation that would allow him to lend war equipment to belligerents on the condition that they return it when the war was over.

It seemed idiotic, of course, to make costly equipment available to Hitler's enemies and then stand by while Hitler's submarines sent the vessels carrying the equipment to the bottom of the sea. No idiot, Roosevelt in the spring of 1941 ordered a neutrality patrol by American planes and ships in the Western Atlantic—planes and ships that would search out German U-boats and radio their positions to Lend-Lease convoys and British warships. Ostensibly to broaden the neutrality patrol, he next brought Greenland and Iceland into "our sphere of cooperative hemispheric defense" and then dispatched American troops to Iceland. After his shipboard rendezvous with the British prime minister Winston Churchill in Placentia Bay in August 1941, he ordered American warships to escort Lend-Lease convoys as they made their way across the Atlantic; and when the destroyer USS *Greer,* in early September 1941, exchanged shots with a German submarine he directed American naval commanders to "shoot on sight" at Axis submarines and cruisers in the North Atlantic. Following a murderous clash between German ships and the USS *Kearny* in mid-October 1941, he prevailed on Congress to repeal most of the remaining restrictions of the neutrality statute.

Meanwhile, in June 1941, Hitler had launched Operation Barbarossa, the invasion of the Soviet Union. Some Americans thought the United States should stand apart from the Nazi-Soviet confrontation in the hope that the two forces would grind each other to pieces on the plains of Russia. But as they advanced relentlessly toward Moscow in the summer and autumn of 1941, Hitler's armies appeared on the verge of knocking the Soviets from the war. Commanding the vast human and material resources of the European heartland from the Urals to the Atlantic, the Germans in that event might achieve virtual invincibility. In such circumstances, Roosevelt concluded that he had no choice than to offer American support to the Soviets, however despicable their past behavior. So in November 1941 he proclaimed the Soviet Union eligible for Lend-Lease assistance.

It was clear by December of 1941 that the United States was edging almost inexorably toward full participation in the European war. But it was events in the Pacific that eventually propelled the country into the global maelstrom.

As in the matter of German and Italian aggression in Europe, Roosevelt believed that aggression in the Far East, if successful, would be subversive of American interests and ideals. And as in Europe, the policy of the Roosevelt administration in the face of Japan's aggression in China and, at length, in Indochina was to counter it with measures short of full-dress hostilities. So at the same time that it was doing what little was possible to bolster China, the United States cut back on the shipment of scrap metal and aviation gasoline to Japan. When Japan became a full-fledged member of the Axis alliance in the summer of 1940, the Washington government imposed additional restrictions, and when Japanese troops moved into southern Indochina in the summer of 1941, the president froze all Japanese assets in the United States, the most dramatic consequence of which was the termination of shipments of precious oil supplies from the United States to Japan.

Through the late summer and autumn of 1941, the Washington and Tokyo governments sought a negotiated settlement of their differences. But negotiations seemed unpromising at best. The United States was bent on compelling the Japanese to disgorge their imperial conquests in China; the Japanese were bent on disgorging nothing. Concluding that war with the United States was essential if they were to preserve and indeed expand their empire, the Japanese set in motion plans for aerial attacks against American military and naval installations in Hawaii and the Philippines. In response to the actual attacks, the United States on 8 December 1941 declared war on Japan, and after Germany and Italy on 11 December declared war on the United States, the Washington government formally recognized that it was at war with Japan's Axis partners.

Pearl Harbor and the declarations of war inevitably produced a dramatic reorientation of American foreign policy. Whereas in the previous eighteen months the policy of the Washington government had been to assist the victims of Axis aggression and obstruct Axis operations while striving, halfheartedly perhaps, to avoid a full-dress clash of arms with the Axis powers, the policy now was, first and foremost, to assure the achievement of total victory in the war at the earliest possible date and, secondarily, to prepare a foundation for a durable peace in the postwar era. In the interest of an early victory, the Roosevelt administration declined to intercede in behalf of the Jewish population of Europe, which, it had reason to suspect, Hitler had marked for extermination. Arguing with the Nazis over the fate of Jews, it reasoned, might result in prolongation of the war. In the interest of stability and peace in the postwar era, particularly in the East, the administration perpetrated the fiction that Generalissimo Chiang Kai-shek was a wise and effective leader and that China was one of the world's major powers.

In the last analysis, of course, a total and early victory in the war and a stable peace after the war would depend on the ability of the Big Three powers, namely, the United States, Britain, and the Soviet Union—parties of an informal coalition that came to be referred to as the Grand Alliance—to retain their cohesion. Cohesion in turn would depend on the ability of the three powers to maintain trustful and harmonious relations. Trustful and harmonious relations between the United States and Britain were assured; shared values and essentially common purposes in the war guaranteed that there would be no rupture between the great English-speaking nation-states. Relations between them and the Soviet Union, the citadel of world communism, were another matter. The Soviets were unlikely to forget that the Western powers had sought to subvert their revolution in its early years and that up to the time Hitler unleashed Barbarossa had viewed the Soviet state with undisguised contempt. Americans and Britons were not apt to lose sight of the manifest brutality of the Soviet dictatorship or forget that the Soviets had abetted Hitler's aggression in the early stages of the present war—had in fact weighed the prospect of membership in the Axis alliance in those awful months when the British were standing almost alone against the Nazi juggernaut.

Whatever their estimates of the Soviets and their system, leaders in Washington and London believed that a total and early victory in the war—and perhaps any victory at all—would turn on the outcome of the German-Soviet confrontation on the Russian plains. If the Germans prevailed in that confrontation, succeeded in bringing Russia's human and material resource into their empire, and turned the full might of their military mechanism against the Western Allies, the task of arranging the Germans' eventual defeat would become immeasurably more formidable, conceivably impossible. The task would be only slightly less formidable if the Soviets, on expelling the Germans from Mother Russia, negotiated a separate peace with Hitler. Was it realistic to suspect that the Soviets might work out their own settlement with the Germans? American and British leaders thought that it was. The Soviets, after all, had made a separate peace with the Germans in the First World War at Brest-Litovsk in 1918, an act that had made it possible for the Germans to organize offensives on the western front that might have carried them to victory had American forces not arrived in the nick of time. Who was to say that the Soviets might not strike a similar bargain with the Germans in the present war?

Keeping the Soviets in the European war until the Grand Alliance had extracted Germany's unconditional surrender thus became a central object of American policy. But leaders in Washington, unlike those in the Kremlin, were not totally preoccupied with the war against Hitler; while striving to take the measure of the Germans, they also had to contend with the enemy in the Pacific. Another object of American policy, then, was to draw the Soviets into the war against Japan. Omitting atomic weapons from their calculations, leaders of the United States reckoned that Soviet participation in the struggle in the Pacific upon conclusion of the war in Europe would dramatically hasten the termination of the former struggle—and save hundreds of thousands of American lives.

If persuaded that achievement of a total and early victory in both Europe and the Pacific required unflinching cooperation by the Big Three powers, the Washington government was likewise persuaded that achievement of a stable peace would require their continued cooperation in the postwar era. Roosevelt indeed perceived the United States, Britain, the Soviet Union, and China as "four policemen" who, as agents of a new international organization, the United Nations, would guard the peace in the aftermath of the present war. That the United States and Britain—and also China—would cooperate in the postwar period seemed a foregone conclusion. But what of the Soviet Union? Would it cooperate?

Securing and maintaining the trust and good will of the Soviet Union thus became the great overriding imperative of American foreign policy in the course of the Second World War. To that purpose the United States sought to avoid giving offense to the Stalinist dictatorship. Preferring to postpone decisions regarding postwar political and territorial arrangements until the final defeat of the Axis powers, leaders in Washington offered no protest when Stalin made clear his intention to exercise hegemony in Eastern Europe after the war—and declined to put a brake on Soviet ambitions in Eastern Europe by withholding, or threatening to withhold, Lend-Lease assistance from the Soviet Union. Moreover, they acquiesced in Stalin's demands for concessions in the Far East. Leaders of the United States were restrained by the fear that if they took what one might describe as a hard-line approach in their relations with their counterparts in the Kremlin, the Soviets might be tempted to make a separate peace with the Germans, stay clear of the war in the Pacific, and scuttle pledges to cooperate in keeping the peace after the war. If hindsight makes it manifest that the Soviets would never have consented to a separate settlement with the Germans, that Stalin doubtless would have projected the Soviet Union into the war against Japan (to gain spoils in the Far East) without the urging of the United States, and that the dream of Soviet cooperation in the postwar era on terms acceptable to Americans had no chance of fulfillment, the logic on which that fear rested was hard to confute in 1941–45.

In sum, the foreign policy of the Roosevelt administration from 1933 to 1945, resting on careful calculations of political, military, and strategic realities, was essentially a policy of weakness—or, more accurately perhaps, a policy hobbled by the weak bargaining position these realities continually imposed. The national impulse to isolation, which even the magniloquent Roosevelt was powerless to contain, prevented the administration from fashioning responses to the worsening world situation in 1933–39 that might have forestalled the powers of Europe and Asia from sliding toward global war. That same isolationist impulse prevented Roosevelt from placing the full weight of the United States in the balance against aggression in 1939–41—or even making adequate preparations against the possibility that the United States might be drawn into war against the national will. Because of its manifest unpreparedness when the Japanese projected it into the war in December 1941, and because it required two full years to mobilize the country's human and material resource for total war, the United States had little choice than to pursue what amounted to a policy of appeasement vis-à-vis the Soviet Union in the years that followed.

In retrospect, one may argue that Roosevelt, pressing on in spite of isolationist protests, might have done more than he did to prepare the United States for war in 1939–41 and thereby stregthened his hand in foreign policy—vis-à-vis Germany and Japan before December 1941 and vis-à-vis the Soviet Union after December 1941. He might have taken a more realistic view of the chances of securing Soviet cooperation in the postwar era (although it is hard to imagine how such a view might have resulted in more farsighted decisions than those that were made in 1941–45). Compromising the unconditional surrender dogma, he might have made a peace overture to the Japanese after Japan's monstrous defeats in the Marianas Islands in summer of 1944, which in the unlikely event of its acceptance by the Tokyo government could have dramatically shortened the Pacific war, saved uncounted lives, and left Japan as a bulwark against Soviet expansion in Northeast Asia. But whatever the shortcomings of Roosevelt's performance in foreign affairs, whatever the missed opportunities, one must keep in mind that it was his policy of bolstering the British in 1939–41 that probably prevented Hitler from forcing Britain to terms and achieving total dominance in the Eastern Atlantic—that possibly prevented the German tyrant from fulfilling his dream of achieving absolute mastery over the European continent. And it was Roosevelt's policy of cooperation and conciliation that was in no small measure responsible for keeping the Grand Alliance together in 1941–45 and bringing about the destruction of the most formidable mechanisms of death and devastation that the forces of aggression and tyranny had assembled to that time.

Unquestionably, the premier study of the foreign policy of the Roosevelt administration from the time of Roosevelt's inauguration in March 1933 to his death in April 1945 is Robert Dallek, *Franklin D. Roosevelt and American Foreign Policy, 1932–1945* (New York: Oxford University Press, 1979). Resting on prodigious research in source materials, Dallek's volume considers all aspects of foreign policy in the Roosevelt years—and generally takes a favorable view of that policy. A careful study of Roosevelt's often strained relations with isolationists is Wayne S. Cole, *Roosevelt & the Isolationists, 1932–45* (Lincoln: University of Nebraska Press, 1983). Seemingly persuaded that Roosevelt's instincts in matters of foreign policy were superior to those of isolationists, Cole nonetheless makes clear his contempt for the heavy-handed manner in which Roosevelt sometimes countered the isolationists, for example, by intimating that the latter were in some sort of alliance with aggressors. An excellent survey of foreign policy in the Roosevelt years is provided in Julius W. Pratt, *Cordell Hull, 1933–44* (New York: Cooper Square Publishers, 1964), a two-volume contribution to *The American Secretaries of State and Their Diplomacy*. A distinguished scholar of American foreign relations, Pratt tended to be generous in his estimates of Roosevelt-Hull diplomacy. An excellent study of the policy of the Roosevelt administration in the mid-1930s, when the United States was wrestling with the neutrality question, is Robert A. Divine, *The Illusion of Neutrality* (Chicago: University of Chicago Press, 1962). A classic study of American foreign relations in the critical period of 1937–41 is the two-volume work by William L. Langer and S. Everett Gleason, *The Challenge to Isolation, 1937–1940* (New York: Harper, 1952) and *The Undeclared War, 1940–1941* (New York: Harper, 1953). Encyclopedic in scope, the volumes by Langer and Gleason provide more detail than the ordinary reader is apt to feel comfortable with, but for the reader who wishes to probe the intricacies of American policy in 1937–41 they are indispensable. Like other scholars who have labored over the foreign policy of the Roosevelt administration, the authors generally accord Roosevelt high marks as a diplomatist. Equally valuable to the serious student of American policy in the years before the United States became an active belligerent in the Second World War is Herbert Feis, *The Road to Pearl Harbor: The Coming of the War between the United States and Japan* (Princeton: Princeton University Press, 1950). More suitable for the casual reader perhaps are John Edward Wil[t]z, *From Isolation to War, 1931–1941* (New York: Thomas Y. Crowell Co., 1968), and Robert A. Divine, *The Reluctant Belligerent: American Entry into World War II* (New York: Wiley, 1965). The best treatment of American foreign policy in the time of the Second World War is

Herbert Feis, *Roosevelt, Churchill, Stalin: The War They Waged and the Peace They Sought* (Princeton: Princeton University Press, 1957). Detailed and scholarly as are most of Feis's books, this volume offers minimal criticism of Roosevelt's management of foreign policy. Less generous to the president is Robert A. Divine, *Roosevelt and World War II* (Baltimore: Johns Hopkins Press, 1969). Considerable criticism of Roosevelt's diplomacy during the war likewise appears in the provocative volume by the distinguished historian-diplomat George F. Kennan, *Russia and the West under Lenin and Stalin* (Boston: Little, Brown & Co., 1961).

JOHN EDWARD WILZ

See also America First Committee; Atlantic Conference and Charter; Atomic Bomb; Axis Alliance; Berle, Adolf Augustus, Jr.; Biographers and Public Reputation; Brussels Conference; Cairo Conference; Casablanca Conference; Chiang Kai-shek; Churchill, Winston Leonard Spencer; Colonialism; Commander in Chief; Declaration of War; de Gaulle, Charles; Fascism; Foreign Economic Policy; Good Neighbor Policy; Harriman, William Averell; Hitler, Adolf, and Germany; Holocaust; Hopkins, Harry L.; Hull, Cordell; Internationalism and Peace; Isolationism; Japan; Jews; Kennedy, Joseph Patrick; Leahy, William Daniel; Lend-Lease; Lindbergh, Charles Augustus; Lippman, Walter; London Economic Conference; Mussolini, Benito, and Italy; Neutrality Acts; Open Door Policy; Pearl Harbor; Personal Diplomacy; Quarantine Speech; Quebec Conferences; Reciprocal Trade Agreements; Refugees; Spanish Civil War; Stalin, Joseph, and Soviet Union; Stettinius, Edward Reilly, Jr.; Stimson, Henry L.; Teheran Conference; Truman, Harry S; Vandenberg, Arthur Hendrick; Welles, Benjamin Sumner; Willkie, Wendell Lewis; World War II; Yalta; Zionism

---

Forgotten Man

A phrase popularized by Franklin Roosevelt in 1932 in one of his earliest important statements to a national audience of the federal government's responsibility in aiding ordinary citizens in the depression.

The expression "forgotten man" was first used in an 1883 essay by the conservative sociologist William Graham Sumner to describe the ordinary citizen who bears the cost of government excesses. It was adopted by Raymond Moley for a national radio address made by Governor Roosevelt on 7 April 1932 under Democratic National committee auspices. In the speech, designed to present the emerging presidential candidate as having a constructive program for economic reform, Roosevelt called for such federal measures to help the unprivileged as home mortgage assistance and programs to increase the purchasing power of the farmer. These steps, Roosevelt claimed, were akin to the full-scale economic mobilization by the government of 1917. Planning "from the bottom up" was necessary for an emergency that approached war-

time dimensions, whereas President Hoover's "from the top down" aid to corporations ignored the damage done to smaller units of the economy. "These unhappy times," Roosevelt said, "call for the building of plans that rest upon the forgotten, the unorganized but the essential units of economic power, . . . that put their faith once more in the forgotten man at the bottom of the economic pyramid."

Conservative Democrats such as Al Smith immediately condemned the phrase "forgotten man" as demagogic. However, to the public, it quickly lost its primarily economic context and became synonymous with powerless ordinary people, victimized by the forces of the depression and dismissed by a callous Hoover. At first identified, like Sumner's original forgotten man, with the decent middle-class citizen struggling to keep his family afloat, soon the phrase was also applied to those down-and-out people whom only radical measures would help. The expression, and the 7 April speech, firmly identified Roosevelt with progressive economic currents, though without committing him as yet to a definite program of action.

Roosevelt's forgotten man address may be found in Samuel I. Rosenman, ed., *The Public Papers and Addresses of Franklin D. Roosevelt*, vol. 1 (New York: Random House, 1938). The political context of the address is described in Frank Freidel, *Franklin D. Roosevelt: The Triumph* (Boston: Little, Brown & Co., 1956). William Graham Sumner's original use of the phrase "forgotten man" is in Sumner, *What Social Classes Owe to Each Other* (New York: Harper & Bros., 1883); it is analyzed in Donald Fleming's essay "Social Darwinism," in *Paths of American Thought*, ed. Arthur M. Schlesinger, Jr., and Morton White (Boston: Houghton Mifflin Co., 1963). Some idea of how the phrase was used as a popular cliché of the depression can be gathered from Sinclair Lewis's novel of American fascism, *It Can't Happen Here* (1935; reprint, New York: New American Library, 1970).

Forrestal, James Vincent

(15 February 1892–22 May 1949)

Undersecretary of the navy, 1940–44, and secretary of the navy, 1944–47. Born in Matteawan, New York, James Forrestal attended Dartmouth and Princeton. After having succeeded as a bond salesman, Forrestal enlisted in the navy in World War I. He returned to the stock market after the war and, by 1938, had reached the presidency of Dillon, Read and Co. on Wall Street. A self-made millionaire, he nonetheless helped draft some of the provisions for the Securities Exchange Commission.

His liberal credentials led FDR to appoint him in 1940 as an administrative assistant to work on the Pan-American Union. Less than two months later (in August), Forrestal left the White House to fill the newly created office of under secretary of the navy.

Responsible for the enormous task of overseeing the navy's shipbuilding and munitions procurement, Forrestal proved himself an able and tireless administrator. He ultimately emerged victorious from a long-running battle with Adm. Ernest J. King who wanted to bring industrial mobilization under the jurisdiction of the office of the chief of naval operations.

Forrestal worked well with Secretary Frank Knox and followed the older man's lead by visiting war zones (the Marshalls and southern France in 1944; Iwo Jima in February 1945). Upon Knox's death, Forrestal was unanimously confirmed in his place on 18 May 1944.

His new post brought him into closer contact with FDR, and Forrestal quickly showed himself a man of independent views. He argued strongly for a large American role in the postwar world—a world that he believed would be threatened by Soviet domination. From within the cabinet, Forrestal worked to prevent Henry Wallace's renomination as vice-president and rejoiced when Harry Truman supplanted the pro-Soviet spokesman. As early as September 1944, Forrestal warned against the consequences of the Russian domination of Eastern Europe.

Following FDR's death, Forrestal played increasingly the role of the outsider. The only cabinet officer to oppose both the use of the atomic bomb without prior warning and the policy of unconditional surrender, Forrestal flew uninvited to Potsdam to press his views on Truman. A staunch opponent of the unification of the armed forces, he nonetheless loyally served the president as the first secretary of defense from September 1947 to March 1949. Depressed by his inability to persuade Truman to increase military spending and worn out by bureaucratic squabbles, overwork, and family problems, Forrestal suffered a mental breakdown that led to his hospitalization and suicide at Bethesda, Maryland, in 1949.

Forrestal's diaries, edited by Walter Millis (New York: Viking, 1951), are sketchy until May 1945. Two classic works centering on his wartime career are Robert H. Connery, *The Navy and the Industrial Mobilization in World War II* (Princeton: Princeton University Press, 1951) and R. G. Albion and R. H. Connery, *Forrestal and the Navy* (New York: Columbia University Press, 1962).

MALCOLM MUIR, JR.

Four Freedoms Speech

Roosevelt's 6 January 1941 State of the Union message defining his conception of America's role in the world conflict and of the fundamental purposes of American democracy.

January 1941 saw Europe at war and divided between German and Russian spheres of influence; Britain was the only power still holding out against the Nazi onslaught. Japan was engaged in its ruthless war in China and had begun to occupy French Indochina. The United States had managed to stay out of the conflict, but the ongoing revision of neutrality legislation was facilitating the sale of ever-increasing supplies to Britain. Roosevelt, newly elected to a third term as president, was steering a fine course between the country's desire to stay out of war and his own realization that the security of the nation depended on its preparedness for the contingency of going to war.

In his address, FDR outlined the tasks that had to be carried out to prevent the Axis nations from achieving victory and defined the positive goals such a policy would ultimately achieve. A fascist victory would bring not peace but danger to America. "Those who would give up essential liberty to purchase a little temporary safety deserve neither freedom nor safety," he said. The two key proposals of his program as outlined in the speech were the rapid reorientation of America's industrial base to armaments production and the continuing channeling of resources to Britain even if it was no longer possible to expect immediate repayment. (The latter proposal was implemented by congressional passage of Lend-Lease legislation in March 1941.)

The ultimate defeat of the aggressor nations, Roosevelt stressed, would constitute a victory for the democratic principles underlying the American political system. FDR used this speech to clarify his conception of those principles. No less important than the traditional liberal values of freedom of speech and freedom of religion were freedom from want and freedom from fear. Thus he affirmed the obligation of government to provide for economic security and social stability, protecting the individual from the unpredictable jolts and shocks of an advanced industrial economic system. In a few words, he had provided a theoretical framework for New Deal policies.

Aware of the public's fear of direct U.S. involvement in the war, Roosevelt carefully avoided any open statement of intention to intervene in the conflict. Instead, the speech stressed the need to enhance America's capacity to defend itself. Nonetheless, FDR made it clear that America's safety depended on an Allied victory. He held forth the vision of a peaceful world community of democratic nations ultimately emerging from the devastation of war. The principles of political and economic democracy would thus be extended to the far corners of the earth. The combination of pragmatism and idealism characterizing this speech epitomizes Roosevelt's public style.

The text of the speech is to be found in Samuel I. Rosenman, ed., *The Public Papers and Addresses of Franklin D. Roosevelt,* 1940 volume (New York: Macmillan Co., 1941). For foreign policy background, see Robert Dallek, *Franklin D. Roosevelt and American Foreign Policy, 1932–1945* (New York: Oxford University Press, 1979).

Norman Rockwell's depiction of The Four Freedoms *became one of the most popular Office of War Information posters of World War II. (National Archives.)*

*Felix Frank-
furter. Artist:
Eleanor Platt.
(Date unknown.
National Portrait
Gallery, Smith-
sonian
Institution.)*

Frankfurter, Felix

(15 November 1882–22 February 1965)

Professor of law, presidential adviser, and associate justice of the U.S. Supreme Court from 1939 to 1962. Felix Frankfurter was born in Vienna and came to America with his parents in 1894. Educated at the City College of New York and the Harvard Law School, he became an assistant to Henry L. Stimson in the War Department during the Taft administration, joined the faculty of the Harvard Law School in 1914, and remained there until FDR named him to the Supreme Court. During these academic years, however, he also served the Wilson administration during World War I, advised governors Al Smith and Roosevelt, and became involved in several celebrated criminal trials, including those of Tom Mooney and Sacco and Vanzetti.

Frankfurter and Roosevelt first met during World War I, when the latter served as assistant secretary of the navy and Frankfurter headed the War Labor Policies Board. Their personal and political friendship flourished again during the late twenties, when FDR turned to his favorite law professor for advice on public utility regulation in New York and for recommendations about appointments to various state boards and agencies.

"Felix has more ideas per minute than any man of my acquaintance," Roosevelt marveled on one occasion. "He has a brilliant mind but it clicks so fast it makes my head fairly spin. I find him tremendously interesting and stimulating." Many of FDR's other advisers in New York and Washington during the depression also found Frankfurter to be stimulating, as well as ambitious and somewhat ruthless in the pursuit of his goals. They resented his influence with Roosevelt and often accused him of sycophancy, a charge reinforced by his frequent, flattering notes to the president. Raymond Moley described him as the "patriarchal sorcerer" who cast dark spells over the New Deal's young lawyers, many of whom came from the Harvard Law School. The *New York American* compared him to Iago. Hugh Johnson, the first head of the NRA, declared that he was "the most influential single individual in the United States," and William O. Douglas recalled that "people either loved or hated Felix. He was brilliant and able, friendly yet divisive."

During the New Deal years, Frankfurter exercised far less influence than his critics or admirers often believed, but he nonetheless managed to play an important role with respect to personnel and selected policies—above all, securities regulation, tax reform, and public utility regulation. The New Deal, as one historian observed, was fundamentally "a lawyer's deal," and no one was a better judge of legal talent than Felix Frankfurter, who became one of the key recruiters of such expertise for the burgeoning federal bureaucracy. His former students at Harvard, who included Benjamin V. Cohen, Thomas G. "Tommy the Cork" Corcoran, Dean Acheson, David Lilienthal, James Landis, Nathan Margold, and Alger Hiss, secured important posts in the White House, departments of the executive branch, and independent regulatory commissions. Yet Felix's "happy Hot Dogs," a sobriquet attached to these busy, gifted, and reform-minded young lawyers, seldom constituted a monolithic ideological group within the administration.

Frankfurter himself, a longtime intimate of Justice Louis D. Brandeis, had little use for the initial programs of the New Deal in 1933 and 1934 with their broad emphasis upon national planning, the acceptance of big business, and the expansion of federal authority. Like Brandeis, he feared the curse of bigness and hoped to break up concentrations of corporate power, nourish reforms at the state level, and use the federal government's powers of taxation and spending to redistribute wealth and cure the depression. An early disciple of John Maynard Keynes, he attempted without success to convince FDR of the utility of the Englishman's theories about budget deficits, but the president remained deaf to these ideas until the recession of 1937.

Frankfurter's social ideals and legal abilities made a deep impression upon several key reforms of the New Deal, including the Securities Act of 1933, which he helped to write, the Public Utility Holding Company Act of 1935, where he fashioned a compromise for the controversial "death sentence" provisions, and the unemployment compensation provisions of Social Security, where he and Brandeis favored a solution that encouraged considerable state autonomy.

Fearing Frankfurter's opposition, FDR did not inform him about the ill-fated Court-packing legislation until after this bombshell had been dropped in 1937. But out of loyalty to FDR, disgust with the Court's behavior, and a careful calculation of where his own interest lay, Frankfurter did not speak out against the plan and chided friends who did. In 1939, he became Roosevelt's third appointment to the Court, filling the seat once occupied by Oliver Wendell Holmes and Banjamin Cardozo. "Let people see how much I loved Roosevelt," he remarked before his own death, "how much I loved my country, and let them see how great a man Roosevelt really was."

The best single volume on Frankfurter's prejudicial career is Michael E. Parrish's *Felix Frankfurter and His Times: The Reform Years* (New York: Free Press, 1982). His relationship to Brandeis and their joint political activities are traced in Bruce Allen Murphy, *The Brandeis/ Frankfurter Connection: The Secret Political Activities of Two Supreme Court Justices* (New York: Oxford University Press, 1982). The Frankfurter-Roosevelt relationship may be explored through their letters in Max Freedman, ed., *Roosevelt & Frankfurter: Their Correspondence, 1928–1945* (Boston: Little, Brown & Co., 1967).

MICHAEL E. PARRISH

See also Brandeis, Louis Dembitz; Corcoran, Thomas Gardiner; Supreme Court of the United States

Franklin D. Roosevelt Collector

The semiannual publication of the Franklin D. Roosevelt Collectors' Association, which was founded in April 1946. Six volumes of the *Franklin D. Roosevelt Collector* appeared between 1948 and 1955. It featured articles on Roosevelt's early political career, his own interest in book and manuscript collecting, and bibliographies, for example, Jerome K. Wilcox, "Anti-FDR Checklist," *FDR Collector* 7, no. 1 (May 1954):3–19. The journal also frequently highlighted Rooseveltiana collections that ranged from autographs to FDR china.

Franklin D. Roosevelt Library and Museum

Library, manuscript repository, and museum in Hyde Park, New York, which is part of the presidential library system operated by the National Archives and Records Service. The library houses the personal and official papers of Franklin Roosevelt, manuscript collections and oral history transcripts of his family and associates, collections of various New Deal agencies and administrators, photographs and memorabilia pertaining to Roosevelt's personal and political life, and books, pamphlets, and other published material either belonging to Roosevelt or pertaining to his life and career. The museum contains displays of photographs, noteworthy documents and letters, gifts Roosevelt received, selected items from his collection of U.S. naval materials, and other memorabilia.

Roosevelt's interest in selecting a repository for his papers dates from 1935 when he informed Robert D. W. Connor, archivist of the United States, that he felt his papers should be deposited in the National Archives. By 1937, Roosevelt had changed his mind and began planning a separate depository on his family estate in Hyde Park, New York. One year later he further defined his plans and proposed to Connor and presidential adviser Frank C. Walker that his papers be deposited in a repository in Hyde Park that would be financed by private donations but under the control and operation of the archivist of the United States. After obtaining support for his proposal from an advisory group of historians and academicians, Roosevelt announced his plans to the public in December 1938.

Funds for the library's construction were raised by a special committee, headed by Frank Walker, which collected approximately $400,000 from private donations and from various publications, including the early volumes of the thirteen-volume edition of *The Public Papers and Addresses of Franklin D. Roosevelt,* edited by Samuel Rosenman. The publication was as much a testament to Roosevelt's historical consciousness in preserving his public papers as it was to Rosenman who organized the papers and wrote most of the explanatory notes. (Rosenman's own memoir, *Working with Roosevelt,* was originally intended as an introduction to the last four volumes and still serves as an important supplement to the entire series.) Despite some criticism of the editing and selection of documents, reviewers acclaimed the publication as a "source book indispensable to any student of the recent past or of the near future."

Construction of the one-story Dutch colonial library began in September 1939 and was completed in the summer of 1940. Fred Shipman, an experienced professional archivist with the National Archives, was appointed first director, and the building was officially opened to the public on 30 June 1941. During World War II, Roosevelt used the library for a number of purposes, including receptions and radio broadcasts, but its prime function as a center for scholarly research was slow in developing. It was not until 1 May 1946 that the main research room was opened, and even then little important material was available since the president's papers could not be processed until their ownership was legally established by the Surrogates Court of New York. The task was completed by 1950, and approximately 85 percent of the president's papers were then made available to scholars. In view of the relative inaccessibility of other presidential papers at that time, this constituted a considerable archival achievement and an unprecedented boon to historical scholarship.

The processed holdings of the library as of June 1982, consisted of approximately 7,500 linear feet (or 15 million pages) of manuscript material, 109,000 photographs, 700 reels of motion picture film, 42,000 books and pamphlets (including Roosevelt's personal library of 15,000 volumes and pamphlets), 194 rolls of microfilm, 14 oral history transcripts (with an additional 68 transcripts in the Eleanor Roosevelt Oral History Collection), and a large collection of dissertations, government publications, reference materials, and periodicals. While over 99 percent of the manuscript material is available to researchers, a few items are still restricted because of donor requests or security classifications.

The library has undertaken a number of publication projects. The most extensive is the sixteen-volume collection of documents and letters relating to Roosevelt's foreign policy, entitled *Franklin D. Roosevelt and Foreign Affairs.* Edgar Nixon's editing of the two-volume edition of *Franklin D. Roosevelt and Conservation, 1911–1945,* and William Stewart's *The Era of Franklin D. Roosevelt: A Selected Bibliography of Periodical Essay and Dissertation Literature, 1945–1971* are both highly respected. In addition, the library has several collections available for purchase on microfilm, including *The Press Conferences of Franklin D. Roosevelt, 1933–1945* and *The Papers of Henry A. Wallace as Vice President, 1941–1945.*

In 1972 a two-wing addition was added to the library in honor of Eleanor Roosevelt, and the Eleanor Roosevelt Institute for a time provided financial assistance to scholarly researchers and to conferences, symposia, and other activities. More recently those activities have been assumed by the Franklin D. Roosevelt–Four Freedoms Foundation. The library and museum remain one of the more popular and successful of the presidential libraries in the United States, visited extensively by scholars and the public alike.

The best historical treatment of the formation and early years of the library is Donald R. McCoy, "The Beginnings of the Franklin D. Roosevelt Library," *Prologue* 7 (Fall 1975):136–50. Also worthy of consideration is Robert D. W. Connor, "The Franklin D. Roosevelt Library," *American Archivist* 3 (April 1940):81–92, and Waldo Gifford Leland, "The Creation of the Franklin D. Roosevelt Library: A Personal Narrative," *American Archivist* 18 (January 1955):11–29. A listing of the library's manuscript holdings, microfilms, and oral history transcripts through June 1982 is provided in *Historical Materials in the Franklin D. Roosevelt Library* (Hyde Park, N.Y.: Franklin D. Roosevelt Library, 1982).

THOMAS T. SPENCER

See also Biographers and Public Reputation; Hyde Park; Naval Collection

Funeral

See Death of FDR

G

Garner, John Nance

(22 November 1868–7 November 1967)

Vice-president of the United States, 1933–41. John Nance Garner was born in West Texas in 1868 and lived ninety-nine years. He should be remembered as a successful southern politician of the older type; as the man who helped Franklin Roosevelt reach the White House when he released his own state delegation to the New Yorker after three ballots in 1932; as vice-president of the United States from 1933 to 1941; and as one of those many Democrats, most of them southern, who basically disliked and successfully fought to limit the New Deal.

Garner was Roosevelt's rival for a brief time in

John Nance Garner, 1935. Artist: Peggy Bacon. (National Portrait Gallery, Smithsonian Institution.)

1932, one of many men who thought himself at least the equal and probably the superior of the man in the wheelchair from Hyde Park. Comparing the men now, one is struck by Garner's lack of gifts for the role Roosevelt won. The Texan was skimpily educated and parochially knowledgeable only about his Uvalde district and the legislative branch of the federal government. He had no vision for a reconstituted political economy and communicated well only in convivial groups of white male politicians who knew the rules of the game. That he challenged Roosevelt at all in 1932 is a reminder of how thin the ranks of leadership were in the Democratic party on the eve of its test.

But if Garner was not presidential material in spite of his coming so close to the office, he was an important political figure in his own sphere. He was superbly equipped for the southern politics of his day (and probably would have done well in Boston or Chicago or Wyoming). A robust man of ruddy complexion, an easy manner, and considerable intelligence, he read law after very brief formal education. Accepted to the Texas bar, he was successively elected judge (1895), member of the Texas house (1898), and U.S. congressman (1902). In those days, to be elected a congressman from a safe southern district was to receive virtually a life appointment, with increasing power assured by the seniority system. Normally in the minority as a Democrat, Garner like other party leaders was not expected to have legislative ideas or to formulate programs, only to refrain from mistakes and keep his word to other members in the bargaining that was the stuff of existence on Capitol Hill. "His career is based upon the obituary column and the power of inertia," wrote a journalist in 1934. He became minority leader in 1928 and speaker of the House in 1931. He was a national figure, but he had never faced a national or even a state electorate. No program, law, or policy idea was ever associated with his name.

Boosted for the presidency by William Randolph Hearst, Garner made his timely withdrawal in favor of FDR and received his reward. He was not an active vice-president, but none of them ever had been. He once assessed the office as "not worth a pitcher of warm spit." Roosevelt did not often consult Garner, principally because Garner's distaste for the New Deal was well known; like many southern Democrats, he was at heart a Republican. He liked the New Deal very little at the outset, when his legislative help was occasionally useful, and he liked it even less as time went on. He was a "Jeffersonian," which to him meant a small-government Democrat, opposed to the welfare state, labor legislation, and deficit spending. The slight New Deal tilt toward blacks after 1936, along with the Court-packing plan, put Roosevelt's vice-president on the side of the opposition, though Garner played by the rules and did not openly break with the administration.

He was replaced as vice-president in 1940 by Henry A. Wallace, by mutual agreement. Always the entrepreneur, he retired to Texas and continued to build his large fortune in real estate, ranching, and banking. He died in Uvalde in 1967, his career as a mediocre and unimaginative politician who almost became president a reminder of the flaws in the U.S. presidential selection system and also of the distinctive assets of Franklin Roosevelt.

Sketches of Garner appear in the *Encyclopedia of American Biography* (1974) and in Robert Vexler, ed., *Vice Presidents and Cabinet Members* (Dobbs Ferry, N.Y.: Oceana, 1975). An unflattering portrait is John Franklin Carter (The Unofficial Observer), *The New Dealers* (New York: Literary Guild, 1934), which is exceeded in acerbity only by Marquis James, "Poker-Playing, Whiskey-Drinking, Evil Old Man," *Saturday Evening Post*, 9 September 1939. The only biography is very favorable; see Bascom Timmons, *Garner of Texas* (New York: Harper, 1948). A more scholarly account is Michael J. Romano, "The Emergence of John Nance Garner as a Figure in American National Politics, 1924–1941" (Ph.D. diss., St. John's University, 1974).

OTIS L. GRAHAM, JR.

See also Democratic Party; Hearst, William Randolph

Genealogy

Franklin D. Roosevelt was one of the Roosevelt family's most assiduous students of genealogy and often cited his ancestry to deflect political attacks on his loyalty to American institutions. He never exhibited an overwhelming pride of ancestry in private, however, and visitors to Hyde Park were sometimes regaled with hints of skeletons supposedly lurking in the family closet. Waving toward one or another of the family portraits, FDR would refer to this ancestor as "an old drunk" or that one as "a reprobate." And he shocked the Daughters of the American Revolution by reminding them (21 April 1938) that "all of us, and you and I especially, are descended from immigrants and revolutionists."

The family's founding father in America, Claes Martenszen van Rosenvelt (?–1659), arrived in New Amsterdam from Holland sometime before 1648 but little is known of his origins or background. Asked upon one occasion if the family might not originally have been Jewish, FDR replied: "In the dim, distant past, they might have been Jews or Catholics or Protestants. What I am more interested in is whether they were good citizens and believers in God. I hope they were both." One of the few clues to Claes's past is his name which, rendered into English, is Nicholas, son of Martin, of the Rose Field. In those days, Dutchmen took in addition to their baptismal name that of their father and the locality from which they came. The family name indicates that the ancestral home of the Roosevelts was on the island of Tholen at the mouth of the Rhine, where there was once a tract of land known as *het rosen velt*, or the field of roses, and where there lived a Van Rosevelt family which was prominent in the district. The Van Rosevelt family motto, *Qui Plantavit Curabit*—He Who Has Planted Will Preserve—has been adopted by the American Roosevelts.

Claes and his wife Jannetje, thought to be the daughter of an Englishman named Thomas Samuels who had settled in Holland, operated a forty-eight-acre farm, or *bouwerie*, on the slopes of Murray Hill until his death in 1659. Claes and Jannetje had six children, five of whom grew to adulthood. Nicholas (1658–1742), the sole surviving son, was the last common ancestor of Theodore and Franklin Roosevelt. As a young man, Nicholas moved to Esopus in the Hudson River Valley where he did well in the fur trade. Returning to New York City in 1690, he opened a flour mill, bought real estate, and was elected alderman. During this period, the Van disappeared from the family name and the spelling was standardized as Roosevelt.

Nicholas had two sons, Johannes (1689–?), or John, progenitor of the Oyster Bay branch of the family, and Jacobus (1692–1776), or James, founder of the Hyde Park branch. Both were successful businessmen and real estate operators. Isaac (1726–94), the fifth son of Jacobus, was the most renowned member of the family until Theodore Roosevelt became president. Businessman, banker, sugar refiner, politician, and a member through marriage of the Hudson River aristocracy, he is known in the family annals as "The Patriot." Unlike most members of his class, Isaac supported the cause of American independence. He served in the New York Provincial Congress which took over the reins of the state government in 1775, helped finance the Revolution and was a leading supporter of ratification of the U.S. Constitution after independence was won. FDR cited Isaac's services in his application for membership in the Sons of the American Revolution. James Roosevelt, Isaac's older brother, became a captain of militia at the age of sixty-six.

Through a series of "good" marriages into prominent families—the Barclay, De Peyster, Crommelin, Low, Kip, Varick, Schuyler, and Walton clans, among others—the Roosevelts were elevated from the well-to-do commercial class into the aristocracy. Through

HYDE PARK BRANCH

OYSTER BAY BRANCH

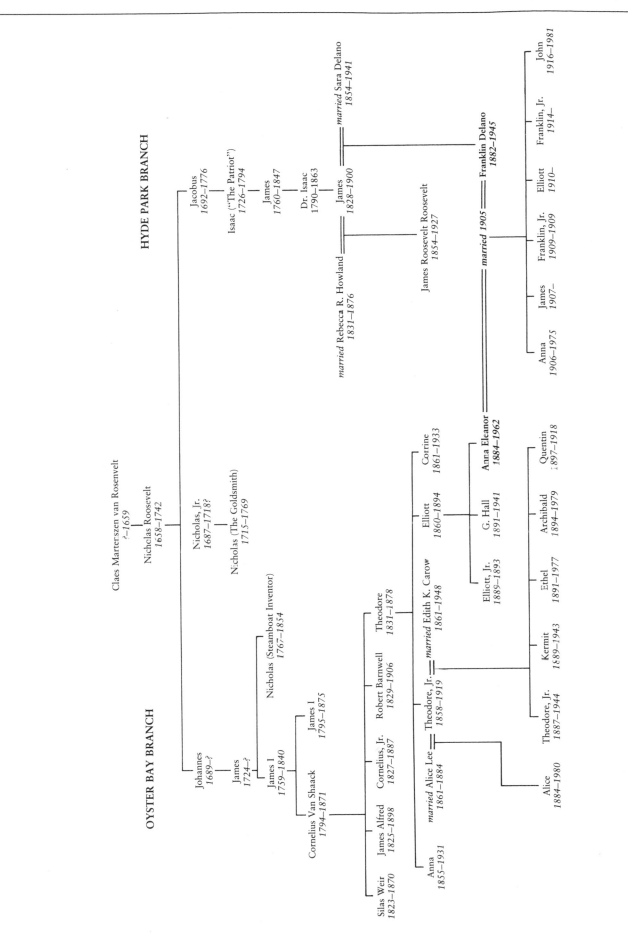

such alliances, FDR wrote in a sophomore history thesis at Harvard, the family stock was "kept virile and abreast of the times" while many of New York's old families lost their dynamism. The percentage of Dutch blood in the President's veins was also reduced. Although aides would say that his "Dutch was up" when he was angry, it has been calculated that FDR was only about 3 percent Dutch.

Isaac Roosevelt's son James (1760–1847) set his branch of the family on the road to Hyde Park. Although he operated the family sugar refinery and expanded its real estate holdings, James preferred country life to commerce. In 1818, he purchased Mount Hope, an estate situated on the east side of the Albany Post Road just above Poughkeepsie. He spent his summers there while his son Isaac (1790–1863) lived at Mount Hope the year round. Isaac studied medicine but did not practice because, it was said, he could not stand the sight of blood. Something of a recluse, he did not marry until he was thirty-seven when he took as his bride Mary Rebecca Aspinwall, a member of one of America's leading merchant families. A year after their marriage, she gave birth to a son, James (1828–1900), who became FDR's father more than a half-century later.

The Oyster Bay branch of the family also had some notable members. Nicholas III (1715–69) was one of colonial America's finest gold- and silversmiths. Nicholas J. (1767–1854) was one of the first engineers in the United States. Largely self-taught, he opened a machine shop in Belleville, New Jersey, that produced the first steam engines made in this country. In 1798, he developed the paddlewheel steamboat—only to see the credit go to Robert Fulton—and took the first steamboat down the Mississippi River to New Orleans. Cornelius Van Shaack (1794–1871) used the hardware and glass business operated by his branch of the family as a springboard to amassing a $13 million fortune in real estate. Hillborne (1849–86), his grandson, pioneered the development of the electric organ and built the finest instruments seen in the United States until that time. John Henry (1800–1863) bequeathed the money to found Roosevelt Hospital in New York City—money earned by playing the stock market after he was afflicted with polio.

James Roosevelt Bayley (1812–77) is one of the most curious sprigs of the Roosevelt family tree. He was the nephew of Mother Elizabeth Ann Bayley Seton, who was canonized by the Catholic church in 1975, and was Catholic archbishop first of Newark and then of Baltimore, the primal see in America. Originally ordained an Episcopal clergyman, James Roosevelt Bayley was disinherited by his grandfather (FDR's great-grandfather) James Roosevelt, when he joined the Catholic priesthood.

C. V. S. Roosevelt had six sons, including Robert Barnwell (1829–1906) and Theodore (1831–78). Vigorous and outspoken, Robert was a reformer who helped drive the Tweed ring from power and was the founder of the American conservation movement. Theodore, active in philanthropic work and a founder of the Metropolitan Museum of Art and the American Museum of Natural History, married Martha Bulloch (1834–84) in 1853. They had four children, Anna (1855–1931), Theodore (1858–1919), who became president of the United States, Corinne (1861–1933), and Elliott (1860–94), the father of Anna Eleanor (1886–1962), who married Franklin Roosevelt in 1905.

James Roosevelt, FDR's father, married Mary Rebecca Howland (1831–76) in 1853. They had one son who was given the distinctive name of James Roosevelt Roosevelt (1854–1927) because his father disliked the appendage "Junior." Four years after the death of his first wife, James married a distant cousin, Sara Delano (1854–1941), who was linked to some of New England's most prominent families. The first of the family in America was a French Huguenot named Philippe de la Noye (b.1602). The Delanos were a seafaring family—whalers, merchant seamen, privateers—and made their home in New Bedford, Massachusetts, and nearby Fairhaven. Franklin Delano Roosevelt, the only child of the union of Sara and James Roosevelt, was born on 30 January 1882 at Springwood, the family estate just south of the village of Hyde Park, New York.

The most recent and most complete history of the Roosevelt family is Nathan Miller, *The Roosevelt Chronicles* (Garden City, N.Y.: Doubleday & Co., 1979). Charles B. Whittelsey, *The Roosevelt Genealogy 1649–1902* (Hartford, Conn.: J. B. Burr & Co., 1902) is outdated and will be replaced by a new genealogy being prepared with the cooperation of all branches of the family under the auspices of the Theodore Roosevelt Association in Oyster Bay, N.Y. For FDR's own account of the family history, see his sophomore thesis, "The Roosevelt Family in New Amsterdam" in the Franklin D. Roosevelt Library, Hyde Park, N.Y. It is based primarily on entries in the family Bible. For the Delano family, see Daniel W. Delano, Jr., *Franklin Roosevelt and the Delano Influence* (Pittsburgh: James W. Nudi Publications, 1946). Alvin P. Johnson, *Franklin D. Roosevelt's Colonial Ancestors* (Boston: Lathrop, Lee & Shepherd Co., 1933) is useful.

NATHAN MILLER

Germany

See Hitler, Adolf, and Germany

G.I. Bill of Rights (1944)

See Veterans

Gold Standard

See London Economic Conference; Monetary Policy

Good Neighbor Policy

Policy of the United States vis-à-vis Latin America in the years of Franklin Roosevelt's presidency. In his inaugural address of 4 March 1933, Roosevelt announced that "in the field of world policy I would dedicate this nation to the policy of the good neighbor." Obviously, the thirty-second president was asserting that neighborliness should animate the relations of the United States with countries and peoples in every part of the globe. But the policy that came to be referred to as the Good Neighbor policy was that which defined the approach of the United States in its dealings with the nation-states of Latin America in the years of the Roosevelt presidency.

By embracing the Good Neighbor policy, the United States signaled an intention to be friendly and respectful in its dealings with neighbors in the hemispheric community. Above all, it would not be meddlesome. That the United States had often been less than neighborly in its behavior toward the states of Latin America was generally conceded. "The Colossus of the North," as Latin Americans sometimes referred to the United States, had compromised the independence of Cuba by compelling the Cubans to accept the Platt Amendment, had engaged in what had been described as "cowboy diplomacy" to secure the Panama Canal Zone, and at various times had dispatched armed forces to the Dominican Republic, Nicaragua, Mexico, and Haiti. The Washington government meanwhile had encouraged and supported the activities of what in the view of great numbers of

Latin Americans were exploitive and even rapacious North American corporations.

What prompted the Good Neighbor policy? Answer: a mixture of self-interest and changing perceptions tinctured with idealism. (It should be noted that some historians, including Calvin Coolidge's biographer Donald R. McCoy, have written that one may discern the origins of the Good Neighbor policy in various initiatives and pronouncements by the Republican administrations of 1921–33, for example, when Coolidge sent Henry L. Stimson to Nicaragua to mediate a civil conflict and when the American ambassador to Mexico, Dwight W. Morrow, another Coolidge appointee, resolved differences with the Mexican government over concessions to U.S. oil companies. But Irwin Gellman, the author of the most recent and best book on the Good Neighbor policy, has argued that the policy had its essential beginnings in the Roosevelt administration.)

The overbearing realities in the world at the time the Good Neighbor policy took shape were the Great Depression, a global economic crisis of unprecedented dimension, and a steady weakening of the structure of international peace fashioned by the victorious powers at the end of the First World War. Determined to chart their country's exit from the depression, leaders of the new administration of Franklin Roosevelt

The Good Neighbor policy in practice: President Roosevelt meeting with President Justo of Argentina rides through *the streets of Buenos Aires in late 1936. (Courtesy FDR Library.)*

groped for ways to stimulate the domestic economy. One way, they believed, was to bring about an increase of trade with Latin America. Alas, achievement of the latter purpose seemed to require that the United States improve its political relations with its neighbors to the south. Conscious of the increasingly dangerous state of the international environment, those same leaders likewise determined to strengthen the strategic position of the United States. That purpose, too, seemed to require improved political relations with Latin America. A requisite for improvement, of course, was to persuade Latin Americans that the North American colossus had recanted its imperious behavior of recent decades and henceforth would conduct itself as a good neighbor.

But considerations other than economic and strategic interests contributed to the formulation of the new policy. Of special moment was a shifting perspective in the minds of North Americans as to what constituted proper international behavior. The shift resulted in no small measure from an abating of the imperial spirit that had animated much of the citizenry in previous decades, particularly in those early years of the twentieth century when Franklin Roosevelt's kinsman Theodore Roosevelt was brandishing his celebrated big stick in Latin America. North Americans, in a word, increasingly recognized that big-stick behavior was inconsistent with the democratic principles on which their republic presumably rested.

Thus foreshadowed by acts and pronouncements of the administrations of presidents Calvin Coolidge and Herbert Hoover, the Good Neighbor policy took on substance at the Pan-American Conference at Montevideo, the capital of Uruguay, in late 1933. Its chief architects were FDR, Secretary of State Cordell Hull, and Assistant Secretary (later Under Secretary) of State Sumner Welles. To the immense satisfaction of Latin Americans, who long had deplored the habit of their powerful neighbor to the north of intervening in Latin American affairs, the United States accepted the central provision of a Convention on the Rights and Duties of States: "No State has the right to intervene in the internal or external affairs of another." Although it attached to the declaration an ambiguous reservation that might be used to justify future interventions, the United States appeared to repudiate what it hitherto had presumed to be its sovereign right to intervene in the affairs of states in the Western Hemisphere whenever it judged the behavior of those states to be irresponsible—a presumed right spelled out in 1904 by Theodore Roosevelt in his famous corollary to the Monroe Doctrine of 1823: "Chronic wrongdoing, or an impotence which results in a general loosening of the ties of civilized society, may in America, as elsewhere, ultimately require intervention by some civilized nation, and in the Western Hemisphere the adherence of the United States to the Monroe Doctrine may force the United States, however reluctantly, in flagrant cases of such wrongdoing or impotence, to the exercise of an international police power." The following year, 1934, the Washington government abrogated the Platt Amend-

ment, dramatically reduced import duties on Cuban sugar, and withdrew the last North American troops from Haiti. In 1936 it negotiated a treaty with Panama (not ratified till 1939) that eliminated some of the inequities of the treaty of 1903 by which the United States had secured control of the Canal Zone.

As the structure of peace in the world continued to weaken—in the aftermath of Italy's invasion of Ethiopia and Germany's renunciation of critical provisions of the Treaty of Versailles—the Good Neighbor policy assumed a new dimension: the Washington government set about to achieve "hemispheric solidarity." To that purpose, in 1936, it arranged a special Inter-American Conference in Buenos Aires "to determine how the maintenance of peace among the American Republics may best be safeguarded." Its enterprise was not without result, for delegates to the conference pledged their governments to cooperation and friendly consultation whenever peace appeared to be threatened. A declaration following a similar conference at Lima in 1938 expressed the determination of the American states "to resist all foreign intervention or activities that may threaten them." In the Declaration of Panama of 1939, the foreign ministers of the American republics established a so-called security zone around the Americas to the south of Canada, and in the Declaration of Havana of 1940, the foreign ministers—to prevent Dutch and French territories in the New World from passing to control of the Axis powers subsequent to Germany's conquest of the Netherlands and France—stated that territory held in the Western Hemisphere by a non-American power might not be transferred to another non-American power.

Following Pearl Harbor, all the Latin American states save Argentina, later described by Secretary Hull as a "bad neighbor," seemed anxious to cooperate in the war against the Axis. In time, all of them (including, in the last months of the war in 1945, Argentina) formally declared war. A Brazilian infantry division fought in Italy, and a Mexican air squadron served in the Pacific. The Cuban navy hunted German submarines in the Gulf of Mexico. In exchange for Lend-Lease assistance, the United States obtained military bases in Brazil, Cuba, Ecuador, and Panama.

At the time the Second World War ended, in the summer of 1945, the architects of the Good Neighbor policy—Roosevelt, Hull, Welles—were all dead or in retirement. The United States, moreover, was preoccupied with tasks that diverted its attention from Latin America: demobilizing its armed forces and reconverting its economy, assisting governments and peoples in the areas of devastation in Europe and the Far East, fashioning a new structure of peace in what was to be a bipolar world, coping with the fearsome power it had unleashed at Hiroshima and Nagasaki. It is small wonder, then, that in the postwar era the Good Neighbor policy became little more than a faded memory.

A useful if somewhat dated summary of the Roosevelt administration's policy toward Latin America is Edward O. Guerrant, *Roosevelt's Good Neighbor Policy*

(Albuquerque: University of New Mexico Press, 1950). Taking the view that the United States' policy of restraint toward Latin America in the 1930s yielded handsome dividends in World War II, Guerrant sees the Good Neighbor policy as highly successful. Bryce Wood's *The Making of the Good Neighbor Policy* (New York: Columbia University Press, 1961) is an analysis of the dealings of the administrations of Hoover and Roosevelt with Cuba, Nicaragua, Bolivia, Mexico, and Venezuela down to 1943. If sometimes vague and repetitious, the book is often provocative. Of larger merit is Donald M. Dozer, *Are We Good Neighbors?: Three Decades of Inter-American Relations, 1930–1960* (Gainesville: University of Florida Press, 1961). A onetime Latin American specialist in the State Department as well as a history scholar, Dozer deals with the harmonizing of relations between the United States and Latin America in the 1930s, inter-American solidarity during World War II, and the deterioration of inter-American relations in the postwar period. He views the policy in the years before 1945 as an achievement of the highest order. Taking the opposite view is David Green in his book *The Containment of Latin America: A History of the Myths and Realities of the Good Neighbor Policy* (Chicago: Quadrangle Books, 1971). The intent of the policy, according to Green, was to advance North American capitalism by encouraging and protecting trade and investments in Latin America. Writing from the New Left perspective, he argues that the policy inhibited Latin America's economic and social development and inadvertently stimulated revolutionary nationalism in the region after World War II. More orthodox in its conclusions is the most recent study of the Good Neighbor policy, Irwin F. Gellman's *Good Neighbor Policy: United States Policies in Latin America, 1933–1945* (Baltimore: Johns Hopkins University Press, 1979), a volume resting on extensive use of manuscript sources and oral history tapes. Finding few antecedents for the policy in the acts and pronouncements of Roosevelt's predecessors, Gellman sees the policy as the handiwork of Roosevelt, Hull, and Welles. Still, he seems inclined to the view that the change in the United States' Latin American policy was less pronounced than it appeared. The United States, he argues, gave up only those advantages in the Western Hemisphere that were manifestly obsolete while retaining those it considered important to its national interest. Accordingly, considerable room remained for the United States to meddle in the affairs of the Latin Americans.

JOHN EDWARD WILZ

See also Daniels, Josephus; Foreign Economic Policy; Foreign Policy; Personal Diplomacy; Welles, Benjamin Sumner

Governor of New York

From the end of World War I through 1928 the contours of New York state politics had been decisively reshaped by the reform leadership of Gov. Alfred E. Smith. Smith had been elected four times as governor of New York and in 1928, during his own quest for the presidency, he successfully prevailed upon Franklin D. Roosevelt to accept a Democratic gubernatorial draft. Roosevelt's two-term tenure (1928–32) as governor reflected the politics both of continuity and of caution. For FDR would extend the substantial progressive Smith legacy while, also, artfully eluding potential threats to his viability as the 1932 Democratic presidential nominee.

Roosevelt at age forty-six was a man who had been out of public life for eight years and yet was a veteran of state and national politics. New York voters in 1928 encountered a self-assured, intuitive, sometimes vague candidate, who exhibited remarkable charm and vitality. Roosevelt's campaign demonstrated masterful sensitivity to the perils of a fractious state politics divided between an upstate Republican Old Guard and New York City's Tammany Hall. Both his formal addresses and especially his extemporaneous remarks revealed a temperamental optimism and activism. Roosevelt's determined disposition—his conviction that state government could be a crucible for forging a new concept of social responsibility that he called an "age of social consciousness"—left no doubt that his executive leadership would provide progressive challenges to the state legislature's reflexive public policy conservatism.

With only a narrow 25,000-vote victory margin and no working legislative majority, Roosevelt still moved quickly to enhance the governor's leverage for fiscal initiatives by fighting for an executive budget. Although the budget innovation had been approved by the voters as a constitutional amendment in 1927, FDR's budget of 28 January 1929 was the first to be submitted to the legislature. Some legislators resisted the constraints the new executive budget placed on its prerogatives and excoriated him for his extravagance and usurpation of power. Since the executive budget empowered the governor to prepare budget estimates and control the actual disposition of funds appropriated by the legislature, it symbolized a fundamental shift of power. Such a new administrative tool was obviously congruent with FDR's own activist conception of the office. When the New York Court of

Governor Roosevelt at ground-breaking ceremonies for Union Island Terminal No. 1, New York City, 30 April 1931. (Courtesy FDR Library.)

Appeals upheld the constitutionality of the executive budget in November of 1929, Roosevelt had won an important first victory over the legislature.

The salient features of FDR's executive leadership were apparent from the outset. There was the rhetorical and programmatic continuity with the Smith administrations; excellent appointments to staff positions and the recruitment of resourceful advisers—especially university professors, trade unionists, and social workers—to a series of investigative commissions; close liaison with Democratic legislators; and effective use of the radio to pressure the state legislature by adeptly simplifying governmental issues for the public and making the appeals for his positions seem enlightened, neighborly, morally humane, and socially responsible.

Roosevelt's initial moves as governor indicated that he would not be a timid timeserver interested only in maneuvering the governership as a convenient way station to the presidency. Nor would he merely complement Al Smith's record. FDR's own outlook and the onset of the Great Depression in 1929 ensured that his governership would be activist.

By any conventional reckoning, FDR's four years as governor of New York placed him in the progressive political tradition. To catalog the public policy victories he wrested from the legislature is to be reminded of the reform agenda shaped during the Progressive Era: increased authority for state agencies, a subordination of patronage to professional administrative appointments, aid for labor unions and farmers, increased support for social service activities, prison reform and the professionalization of the criminal justice system, and increased regulatory supervision of business and corporate practices. More important, however, Roosevelt extended the pre–World War I progressive tradition by espousing a more expansive conception of social and economic reform.

Early in his administration, FDR moved to assist farmers by reducing the contributions of rural counties to state highway construction costs, by having the state assume a greater share of rural education costs, and by supporting the formation of the New York Milk Shed—a cooperative dairy marketing association. He approved tax relief for small farms and, reflecting an enthusiasm for planning, inaugurated studies in land use that convinced him that crop restriction, through the elimination of marginal land, was necessary.

Roosevelt's desire for public development of New York's bountiful water power resources, especially the St. Lawrence River, was at least partly motivated by his conviction that cheaper utility rates were necessary for the welfare of rural upstate counties. Ownership and control of the state's natural water power sites had to be inalienably vested in the people, with a state agency regulating how private companies distributed the power. The Water Power Law of 1930 embodied much of this thinking. FDR then appointed Frank P. Walsh as head of the New York State Power Commission to ensure that it would be a truly independent body. Roosevelt's leadership in the controversial public power conflicts endeared him to many national progressive political leaders. And Frank P. Walsh was himself instrumental in organizing the National Progressive League endorsement of FDR's 1932 presidential campaign.

A similar resoluteness marked his defense of the trade union movement. He selected Frances Perkins to head the Labor Department. Statutes to improve labor's power were endorsed "as matters of an absolute right." Temporary injunctions without a hearing were prohibited in labor disputes; jury trials were mandated for alleged violations of injunctions; an eight-hour law for public workers, and a forty-eight-hour week for women were created; factory inspection laws were strengthened and workmen's compensation laws were broadened to cover disabilities omitted from earlier statutes. And at the 1930 national Governors' Conference in Salt Lake City, FDR became the first governor publicly to champion old-age pensions funded by "contributions from public resources, employers, and the workers themselves." Just as we have come, said Roosevelt, to "workmen's compensation for industrial injury," so also would we be "insuring against old age want." Later, during his second term, FDR would also be in the reform vanguard in advocating unemployment relief.

FDR's 725,000 plurality over his Republican opponent, Charles H. Tuttle, in 1930 was an extraordinary triumph. It was also the first time in the twentieth century that a Democratic candidate for governor surpassed the Republican vote in the fifty-seven counties outside of New York City. Two of his key political strategists, Louis Howe and James Farley, especially savored the electoral mandate. It meant FDR would be a formidable candidate for the 1932 Democratic presidential nomination and that his governership would have to be wary of provocative issues capable of jeopardizing his appeal.

In the 1930 campaign, FDR's deft political artistry was apparent. He straddled the wet/dry polarities on Prohibition by being "damp"—coupling repeal with the provision for local option; he tried to distance himself from "the messy corruption of his party's Manhattan organization" and vetoed, on presumed constitutional grounds, the state legislature's bill for the governor to investigate the administration of New York City. Later, in his second term, when Judge Samuel Seabury's comprehensive assessment of political corruptions made New York City mayor Jimmy Walker an inescapable problem, FDR finally put the mayor in a position where Walker had no recourse but to resign. He removed Thomas M. Farley as sheriff of New York County, but continued to clear patronage appointments through Tammany.

This politics of caution ran concurrently, however, in 1930–32 with an increased assertiveness about government's responsibilities for the social emergency caused by the Great Depression. "There is no question in my mind," wrote FDR in a private letter of May 1930, "that it is time for the country to become fairly radical for a generation. History shows that where this occurs occasionally, nations are saved from revolution." Perhaps the single best example of Roosevelt's belief that social reforms were vital for preserving social stability came in the struggle he led for unemployment relief.

Studies done for FDR by the Joint Committee on Unemployment Relief of the State Board of Welfare and the New York State Charities Aid Association led him to call a special legislative session in August 1931. He urged passage of a $20 million appropriation financed by an increase in personal income taxes. Since the temporary relief would spring from the taxes paid by all during their periods of employment, it would be a responsible solution. Actually, he had already arrived at the conclusion that the aid "must be extended by government not as a matter of charity, but as a matter of social duty." And by 1932 the balanced-budget, pay-as-you-go principle was replaced by borrowing. The FDR who as late as 1930 had assailed President Hoover's public works projects as an unconscionable drain on the Treasury was acceding to new realities. (Roosevelt would reminisce in 1938 that "during the twenties, I in common with most liberals did not at the start visualize the effects of the period, or the drastic changes which were even then necessary for a lasting economy.")

New York's State Unemployment Relief Act (the Wicks Act) of 23 September 1931 was the first state relief measure passed in the United States. It created a new independent agency, the Temporary Emergency Relief Administration (TERA), to aid the jobless. Harry Hopkins, a young social worker from the New York Tuberculosis Public Health Association, became its executive director. By the end of April 1933, after eighteen months of operation, TERA had spent $136,954,952 of state funds. Before Hopkins left for Washington in February 1933, there were 412,882 relief cases being managed by TERA.

One of FDR's particular strengths was "his lucid education of the public" on issues like old-age pensions and unemployment. When he had to confront intractable administrative problems, however, as in the December 1930 banking collapse of the City Trust Company in New York, what Samuel Rosenman called "his general distaste for details—and his inefficiency in dealing with them" led to irresolution and negligence. Felix Frankfurter believed his "limitations" stemmed "from lack of incisive intellect and a kind of optimism that sometimes makes him timid as well as an ambition that leads to compromises."

Bernard Bellush's analysis of FDR's governorship acknowledges that "he did not make the same crusading impact on New York's social, economic and political history that Smith made." Yet his "timing of decisive political acts, his lucid education of the public, his able handling of obstructionist Republic majorities in the State legislature and of a divisive and corrupt Tammany Hall in New York City showed unusual executive ability and political acumen." These achievements coupled with what Basil Rauch described as FDR's "clear and persistent presentation of the liberal argument" represented the enduring significance of his governorship. For in articulating "an integrated philosophy and program of liberalism" Roosevelt gave important clues to the character of his presidency. Moreover in comparing FDR's "legislative goals as Governor with his domestic programs as President," there was, as Bellush has contended, "a striking, logical development."

The standard work on this topic is Bernard Bellush's excellent account in *Franklin D. Roosevelt as Governor of New York* (New York: Columbia University Press, 1955). See, as well, *The Public Papers of [Governor] Franklin D. Roosevelt* (Albany: J. B. Lyon, 1930, 1931, 1937, 1939). Frank Freidel's *FDR: The Ordeal* (Boston: Little, Brown & Co., 1954), pp. 245–69, and his *FDR: The Triumph* (Boston: Little, Brown & Co., 1956) are indispensable. Excellent concise summaries of FDR's governorship can be found in Rexford Guy Tugwell, *The Democratic Roosevelt* (Baltimore: Penguin Books, 1969), pp. 190–209; James T. Patterson's *The New Deal and the States* (Princeton: Princeton University Press, 1969), pp. 26–49; Alfred B. Rollins, *Roosevelt and Howe* (New York: Alfred A. Knopf, 1962), pp. 233–95; and David M. Ellis et al., *A History of New York State* (Ithaca: Cornell University Press, 1967). On the drafting of FDR for the gubernatorial nomination, see Chapter 1 of Ernest K. Lindley, *Franklin D. Roosevelt, A Career in Progressive Democracy* (New York: Bobbs-Merrill, 1931). For a characterization of FDR's temperament and executive style, see Chapter 1 of Raymond Moley's *After Seven Years* (New York: Harper & Row, 1939). On the FDR–Al Smith relationship, see Frances Perkins, *The Roosevelt I Knew* (New York: Harper & Row, 1964), pp. 49–53. An exceptionally useful insight into FDR's political thought can be found in one of his 1928 essays, "Why Bother with the Crippled Child?" reprinted in Robert H. Bremner, ed., *Children and Youth in America: A Documentary History*, vol. 2 (Cambridge, Mass.: Harvard University Press, 1971). Clinton Rossiter's "The Political Philosophy of F. D. Roosevelt: A Challenge to Scholarship," *Review of Politics* 11 (1929):87–95, is also very important. On New York State political corruption, see Herbert Mitgang, *The Man Who Rode the Tiger: The Life and Times of Judge Samuel Seabury* (Philadelphia: Lippincott, 1963), and Raymond Moley's *27 Masters of Politics* (New York: Funk & Wagnalls, 1949), pp. 204–14, for FDR's role in the resignation of Jimmy Walker as mayor of New York City. On the disappointment with FDR on the part of some progressives in 1932, see William Leuchtenberg's remarks on pp. 174–75 of John Garraty, ed., *Interpreting American History: Conversations with American Historians*, vol. 2 (New York: Macmillan, 1970). For Walter Lippmann's reservations about FDR, see his *Interpretations, 1931–32* (New York: Macmillan, 1933), pp. 259–63. For a critique of FDR's leadership on the bank collapse, see Richard Hofstadter's *The American Political Tradition* (New York: Vintage Books, 1948), p. 327, and John T. Flynn, *Country Squire in the White House* (New York: Doubleday, Doran, 1940), pp. 38–47. On FDR and social welfare issues, see Daniel Nelson, *Unemployment Insurance: The American Experience, 1915–1935* (Madison: University of Wisconsin Press, 1969), pp. 162–65; Walter Trattner, *From Poor Law to Welfare State* (New York: Free Press, 1974), pp. 232–34; and Rexford Guy Tugwell, *The Brains Trust* (New York: Viking Press, 1968), pp. 16–19.

FRANK ANNUNZIATA

See also Conservation, Election of 1928; Flynn, Edward Joseph; Hopkins, Harry L.; Howe, Louis; La Guardia, Fiorello; LeHand, Marguerite; Lehman, Herbert Henry; Liberalism and Progressivism; Regulation; Smith, Alfred E.; Tammany Hall

Great Depression

The American economy suffered its most severe and enduring depression from 1929 to 1941. As Franklin Roosevelt took his presidential oath on 4 March 1933, the economy had hit bottom, with the banking system in collapse, 25 percent of the labor force unemployed, and both prices and output about a third below their 1929 levels. The depression was by then unprecedented and worldwide, with over 30 million people unemployed and the international system of trade, capital flows, and finance in disarray.

Economists now define a depression as a failure of aggregate demand (total spending) to keep pace with the gradual expansion of aggregate supply (productive capacity). When producers discover that demand is insufficient, they can either cut their prices (and perhaps their wages and payments for other inputs) or cut their production, laying off workers and idling factories and offices.

Whatever the mix of reduced prices and reduced output, the lower spending translates into lower incomes in wages, rents, dividends, or profits throughout the economy, and these lower incomes mean less capacity to spend (or save) in the next period. This conception of a depression derives from the theory of the British economist, John Maynard Keynes, who published his *General Theory of Employment, Interest and Money* in 1936 in the midst of the depression.

The Keynesian conception came to dominate economic theory and policy by the 1940s, and it has undergone extensive challenges and revisions in the years since. But during the 1930s there were many alternative definitions and explanations that influenced public discussion and policy responses. Most started from the presumption that the market economy would normally maintain itself at the full employment capacity level. Depression, then, could result only from monopolistic rigidities, which blocked prices from balancing supply and demand, or from government interference with market mechanisms, or from speculative "manias," which might cause temporary boom-bust deviations from the normal full employment path. Some critics of the market economy argued that the growth of monopoly power had brought a chronic tendency to maldistribution of income and underconsumption or overproduction. During the 1920s, Wesley C. Mitchell developed the theory of recurring business cycles, which described a periodic ebb and flow (recession—trough—recovery—peak) that would move rhythmically through the economy. Mitchell's theory acknowledged that the economy would periodically experience recessions and greater unemployment; but he also believed that such fluctuations could be made milder through better business forecasting and planning and through cyclically stabilizing public works and monetary policies.

To Herbert Hoover and many business progressives, the economy of the 1920s seemed to have entered a new era of lasting prosperity and progress

A 1930s soup line. (Courtesy FDR Library.)

Unemployment, 1925–1941 (1000s)

YEAR	TOTAL EMPLOYED*	TOTAL UNEMPLOYED	PERCENT
1925	44,192	817	1.8
1926	45,498	464	1.0
1927	45,319	1,620	3.6
1928	46,057	1,857	4.0
1929	47,925	1,429	3.0
1930	46,081	2,896	6.3
1931	42,530	7,037	16.5
1932	38,727	11,385	29.4
1933	38,827	11,842	30.5
1934	41,474	9,761	23.5
1935	42,653	9,092	21.3
1936	44,830	7,386	16.5
1937	46,279	6,403	13.8
1938	43,416	9,796	22.6
1939	44,993	8,786	19.5
1940	46,683	6,995	15.0
1941	51,434	2,699	5.2

*Total labor force = Civilian labor force + Armed forces

Source: U.S. Bureau of the Census, *Historical Statistics of the United States, 1789–1945* (Washington, D.C.: U.S. Government Printing Office, 1952).

built upon technology, scientific management (in both business and government, and in their cooperative planning efforts), high wages, and mass consumption. They had ample evidence of progress. National income in 1929 was 22 percent above its 1923 level; people were buying 3 million new cars each year and millions of radios, refrigerators, and other electrical appliances. The Federal Reserve had helped relieve the recessions of 1924 and 1927, and the unemployment rate was only 3 percent.

They were hopeful too about the stability and progress of the international economy. World War I had brought tremendous destruction to Europe and disrupted the world financial system centered in London. The huge burdens of Allied war debts (mostly owed ultimately to the United States) and German obligations to pay reparations had to be renegotiated after the French occupation of the Ruhr and the German hyperinflation in 1923. But with the Dawes Plan of 1924 refinancing the reparations and with the British pound returning to the gold standard at its prewar value in 1925, the world economy looked more stable.

Imagine the shock and chagrin that Hoover and many others felt when this new era of durable prosperity and international stability descended in just four years into the misery of worldwide depression. Looking back from the perspective of the 1930s, many critics blamed the depression on the economic sins, excesses, and errors of the 1920s. Historians have often portrayed the 1920's prosperity as "artificial" or "unbalanced" or "speculative" as though preparing us for the inevitable tragedy to follow. But the 1920's prosperity was quite authentic and proba-

bly as balanced among industries and classes as other periods of growth before or since. The growth rate was not exceptionally rapid, and there was no inflationary pressure on the prices of goods and services, even in 1929. The prosperity was real; it was just not guaranteed to be perpetual.

Neither was a twelve-year depression inevitable in 1929. There was at least one long-term depressing influence in the declining demand for residential construction owing to immigration restrictions and slower formation of new family units. A surge of housing construction (1923–28) may have oversatisfied that demand and helped bring on recession. A similar temporary saturation of the automobile market and surges of investment in some other industries in the late 1920s probably added to the cyclical vulnerability of the economy, once the recession began.

But what about the speculative boom in the stock market and the great crash of October 1929? Surely that episode must demonstrate the excesses of the 1920s, and the crash must have caused or at least triggered the depression. In fact, one cannot clearly support either popular view. Certainly there are sensational stories about stock manipulations, buying pools, and wildly inflated prices for individual companies. The Standard Statistics Index (of 421 common stocks) did rise 128 percent between 1926 and the peak in September 1929. But recent statistical analysis has shown that about 80 percent of the stocks were not really wildly overvalued in relation to their high current earnings and the prevailing expectations of continued growth. Median price-earning ratios of 20.4 in 1929 are actually comparable to the averages for more recent decades.

A homeless tenant farm family, Oklahoma, 1938. Photographer: Dorothea Lange. (© The City of Oakland, The Oakland Museum, California.)

The $8.5 billion of loans to brokers and dealers to finance their customers' purchases of stocks on margin (partial credit, rather than cash payment) did make the market more vulnerable to a cumulative downswing, as brokers would demand new cash infusions from their customers or force sales in a falling market to cover their loans. When the overall economy experienced a pause in growth in the summer of 1929 and indexes of industrial production began to slide, the stock market grew nervous. After all, if you dropped that prevailing assumption of permanent growth, then stocks were indeed greatly overvalued. After an avalanche of panicky selling, the market, by the end of October, had wiped out nearly $26 billion of paper wealth from its September peak values of $90 billion. The market recovered briefly in early 1930 (up 20 percent from the preceding October) but then resumed its jagged downward course as stock earnings and prices followed the whole economy into deep depression. At their low point in mid-1932, total stock values were only 17 percent of their peak in September 1929.

In any event, the impact of the stock market crash on the national economy was much more limited than popularly believed (then or now). The crash certainly did not start the depression because the economy turned down in June, well ahead of the market peak. It did remove a cheap source of corporate financing, but that did little to reduce real investment in plant and equipment because most of the new issues during the boom had financed mergers and acquisitions rather than real expansion. The losses of stock market wealth might possibly have caused consumers to reduce their early spending by something

less than $1 billion (roughly 1 percent of the GNP). Many observers have suspected that the market crash lowered expectations about future economic growth (as contrasted to future stock market growth) but the evidence for this is weak. President Hoover's belief that the economy was fundamentally sound was widely shared in 1930; at most a brief business cycle recession was expected.

The stock market boom and crash did have some disruptive international impacts. The boom market (1927–29) strongly attracted both American and foreign savings and this reduced our foreign lending, especially to Germany and the less developed nations that depended on exporting raw materials. Of course, after the crash the financial losses and recession prevented the recovery of U.S. foreign lending. The world depression really started with the collapse of raw material prices and with the decline in Germany, but by 1930–31 America felt the reverberations through the sharp decline in our export sales. The passage of the Smoot-Hawley protective tariff in June 1930 and retaliatory tariffs and restrictions from many other countries further depressed international trade and finance. By 1931 the collapse of World War I reparations and debt payments and of international trade and lending brought European banks and treasuries to the moment of crisis. As the crisis spread, Britain and many smaller nations abandoned the gold standard and depreciated their currencies in hopes of promoting their exports and domestic recovery.

The British withdrawal from gold in September 1931 confronted the U.S. Federal Reserve system with the classic dilemma between domestic and international stabilization goals. The Fed had vigorously expanded bank reserves in the last weeks of 1929 to alleviate the liquidity pressure on the New York banks after the crash. It had incrementally lowered its discount rate from 6 percent in 1929 to 1½ percent in May 1931, viewing this as a cheap-money policy to encourage recovery. (Throughout the 1930s the Fed judged the ease of its policy too much by the low discount rates and low nominal interest rates. It failed to notice that price deflation kept real interest rates from falling as much, and that meanwhile banking failures and contractions and Fed inaction were allowing the money supply to shrink by 25 percent between 1929 and 1933.) But now in October 1931, with sterling depreciating, the dollar was under attack and over $700 million of gold left the country within six weeks. To support the dollar and the crumbling international gold standard, the Federal Reserve quickly raised the discount rate from 1½ percent to 3½ percent and allowed the abrupt drainage of $1.1 billion of gold and currency, nearly half of all bank reserves. Even though the Fed, under congressional pressure, later replenished $1 billion of bank reserves through purchases of government securities (spring and summer 1932), the sharp contraction of 1931 certainly drove the financial system toward insolvency and the economy deeper into depression.

The severe monetary restraints of 1931 did not save the dollar or the gold standard for long. By 1933 the damage to American exports and domestic prices from a stable dollar (in a world where other countries were depreciating their currencies) brought overwhelming political pressure for "reflation." In April 1933, Roosevelt accepted legislation that halted the export of gold and allowed the dollar to begin depreciating on private exchange markets. That fall, he tried a naive experiment that attempted to raise commodity prices by raising the dollar price of gold at the U.S. mint. Finally, in February 1934, he restabilized the dollar at $35 per ounce of gold (a 41 percent devaluation vs. gold). Not until 1936 did Britain, France, and the United States establish minimal exchange stabilization agreements; the larger reconstruction of international finance had to wait until after World War II.

The contraction and failure of financial institutions were both effect and cause of the severe depression and its long endurance. Declining incomes meant sharply reduced inflows of savings: household and corporate saving dropped from $7.0 billion to $5.2 billion between 1929 and 1933. Meanwhile declining values on all financial assets (stocks, bonds, mortgages) and defaults on many debts (nearly 40 percent of home mortgages by 1934) pushed banks and savings institutions toward insolvency. Over five thousand banks (20 percent) failed between 1929 and the end of 1932, with the heaviest incidence among smaller independent country banks and those in the most depressed communities. By February 1933, panicky depositors were withdrawing currency and forcing the banks into further contractions, which ended finally in a national banking holiday in the last days of Hoover's term. The banking system had ceased to function, and the lack of credit was strangling the financing of housing or consumer or business investment spending so necessary for recovery.

The greatest failure of monetary policy both before and after 1933 was the failure of the Federal Reserve to expand the money supply by expanding bank reserves through purchase of government bonds. Bank reserves did expand in 1934–36 as a result of gold inflows from Europe (and Treasury purchases of silver), but the Fed took little leadership. Federal Reserve leaders believed credit policy already was easy because the discount rate was low, and they feared that more aggressive monetary expansion would reignite speculation or inflation, creating another 1929 boom-bust episode. This fear of speculation also led the Fed to raise bankers' reserve requirements sharply in 1936–37, which helped to bring on the recession of 1937–38.

A number of legislative measures did improve the health of the financial system even though they did not produce economic recovery. The Reconstruction Finance Corporation, started in 1932 under Hoover and greatly expanded under Roosevelt, made loans to financial institutions (and to railroads and local governments) to rescue them from the threat of bankruptcy. The Home Owners Loan Corporation, Federal Farm Mortgage Corporation, and Federal Housing Administration refinanced and insured mortgages, aiding both the farm and home owners and the financial institutions that held their defaulted mortgages.

The Federal Deposit Insurance Corporation and similar agencies insured deposits and ended the dangers of panicky runs against financial institutions. But dealing with the symptoms and consequences of financial collapse did not increase aggregate spending: higher spending, income, and saving would have done more for financial solvency.

Federal budget policy also did little to stimulate that increased aggregate spending. With federal spending ($2.6 billion in 1929) amounting to only 2.5 percent of GNP, even doubling of expenditures or total abolition of federal taxes would only modestly have increased aggregate demand. As the downturn began in 1929, President Hoover recommended small expansionary budget measures: 1 percent reductions in income tax rates and $200 million of additional public works spending. But as the worsening depression reduced incomes and therefore tax revenues, producing a $1.5 billion deficit by fiscal year 1932, Hoover gave higher priority to budget balancing than to public works. The Revenue Act of 1932 sharply increased income, excise, estate, and gift taxes, but the deepening depression kept revenues down and the budget in red ink. Although publisher William Randolph Hearst, Senator Robert La Follette and others advocated gigantic $5 billion public works programs, Franklin Roosevelt campaigned in 1932 against Hoover's budget deficits, and as president he immediately cut about $450 million from spending on federal employees' salaries and veterans' benefits. It was not an expansionary fiscal inaugural.

The depression had massive but uneven impacts on American society. From its peak of 25 percent (12.8 million people) in 1933, unemployment declined only gradually, never falling below 14 percent until 1941. Hardest hit were youth, minorities, the elderly, and workers in capital goods or consumer durables industries. Where unemployment lasted for only a year or more, it often destroyed not just the family's economic resources but its mental health, gender and parent-child relationships, and career and educational paths for the younger generations. Communities hardest hit by unemployment (e.g., Chicago 40 percent in 1931, Detroit 50 percent in 1933) experienced widespread hunger and suffering and soon ran out of local charitable and governmental resources for relief. The depression sharply squeezed the tax revenues of all communities (but especially those with heaviest unemployment), forcing them to raise tax rates or cut expenditures drastically just as the claims for relief were rising. By the end of 1933, some 1,300 local governments (counties, cities, towns, school districts, etc.) had actually defaulted on their debt obligations. Under such financial pressures, local governments (and states as well) cut back their construction and other spending, thus adding to the unemployment problem far more than they could provide relief for it. Only with the entry of the federal government under the New Deal did the relief programs even begin to respond to the severity of the unemployment. Relief programs reached 4 to 5 million households each month during most years (1933–41), while the Civil Works Administration and its successor, the Works Progress Administration, provided government jobs for 3 to 4 million workers and also helped preserve some of their craft and professional skills, their "human capital." Yet all these relief and job programs still fell far short of producing recovery to full employment.

Farmers, of course, rarely suffered unemployment, but they still suffered severely from the sharp declines in world farm prices (53 percent from 1929 to 1932). With the fixed costs in machinery (whose prices fell little), debts, and taxes, farmers saw their net income fall 70 percent. By early 1933, 45 percent were delinquent on their mortgages, facing the threat of foreclosure. But depreciation of the dollar (which stimulated farm exports) and recovering prices brought partial recovery early, doubling farm incomes between 1932 and 1934. The various New Deal farm programs sought to raise prices by limiting production for the domestic market, while dumping surpluses overseas at lower world market prices. Such supply restrictions also raised food prices to urban consumers and did little to raise aggregate demand toward national recovery.

Money income in manufacturing declined even more sharply from 1929 to 1933 than in agriculture (65.5 percent vs. 55.6 percent decline). But the variation from industry to industry was tremendous, with far greater declines coming in postponable consumer durables and in capital goods. For example, output of shoes fell only 3.4 percent and gasoline 7.5 percent, while automobile production fell 65 percent, furniture 55.6 percent, iron and steel 59.3 percent, and locomotives 86.4 percent. Thousands of companies, especially smaller ones, went out of business entirely. The New Deal's 1933 National Industrial Recovery Act (NIRA) mistakenly blamed the depression on overproduction and destructive competition, and retarded recovery by promoting industry cartels which raised prices and limited investment in new productive facilities. After the Supreme Court declared the NIRA unconstitutional in 1935, special price-fixing and production-limiting laws were passed for the oil and coal industries. Some have argued that revival of other business investment spending was discouraged somewhat by Roosevelt's political rhetoric against "economic royalists" and by such "reforms" as "soak the rich" taxes, the National Labor Relations Act, minimum wages, and the splitting of commercial and investment banking.

Recovery did begin with Roosevelt's inauguration, but it moved slowly and erratically through eight years of continuing hardship and underused human and capital resources. The initial upturn in 1933 partly responded to the optimism generated by Roosevelt's leadership style and the intense hundred days of New Deal legislation (even though much of it was counterproductive for recovery). American exports were aided by the earlier recovery momentum in Britain, Sweden, Japan, and other countries, by the rises in world commodity prices, and by the $4 billion of gold flowing here from Europe in 1934–36. The expansion of money and credit based on those increased gold reserves nourished economic expansion until 1937.

The New Deal embodied several confused and contradictory theories of the causes of depression, and its recovery programs were targeted at specific sectors: agriculture, manufacturing, relief, financial reforms, and so on. There was no coherent macroeconomic budgetary (or monetary) strategy for recovery. The slowly rising budget deficits were more the result of depression (reduced revenues) and of specific responses to programmatic needs rather than of any bold fiscal strategy. Only in 1936 was the federal deficit large enough (given the contraction of state and local budgets) to provide more fiscal stimulus than in 1929, and that was largely the result of a $1.7 billion veterans' bonus law passed over Roosevelt's veto. The attempts to balance the budget (and to raise bank reserve requirements) in 1937 helped bring on the sharp 1937–38 recession, pushing unemployment back up to 19 percent. Only after this tragic setback was FDR persuaded (in April 1938) to adopt a Keynesian program of expanded deficit spending to stimulate aggregate demand. Programs were designed in the Treasury Department for public housing, slum clearance, railroad reconstruction, and other massive public works spending, but these were soon crowded off the budgetary stage by the military spending for World War II. Recovery of private investment spending (housing, nonresidential construction, plant and equipment) still lagged afer 1938, but war-related export demands and expanded government spending led the economy back to full employment capacity production by 1941.

The classic economic history of the 1930s, obsolete in its theoretical analysis but still full of useful information, is Broadus Mitchell, *Depression Decade: From New Era through New Deal, 1929–1941* (New York: Holt, Rinehart & Winston, 1947). John Kenneth Galbraith's *The Great Crash, 1929* (Boston: Houghton Mifflin Co., 1961) has influenced countless historians, but it overdramatizes the impact of the crash and of structural flaws in the economy. The best recent overview for noneconomists is Lester V. Chandler, *America's Greatest Depression, 1929–1941* (New York: Harper & Row, 1970). For international aspects, see Charles P. Kindleberger, *The World in Depression, 1929–1939* (London: Penguin Press, 1973). The evolution of economic theorizing about the depression would begin with Robert Lekachman's readable *The Age of Keynes* (New York: Random House, 1966) and then move to the more technical recent controversies reflected in Karl Brunner, ed., *The Great Depression Revisited* (Boston: Martinus Nijhoff Publishing, 1981).

GEORGE D. GREEN

See also Congress, United States; Federal Emergency Relief Administration; Fiscal Policy; Forgotten Man; Hoover, Herbert Clark; Hundred Days; New Deal; Regulation, Federal; Relief; Taxation; Temporary National Economic Committee

Green, William

(3 March 1873–21 November 1952)

President of the American Federation of Labor (AFL), 1924–52. Born in Coshocton, Ohio, William Green was president of the AFL during the crucial New Deal "revolution" in labor law. Succeeding Samuel Gompers in 1924, the mild-mannered and unassuming Green presided over eight years of stagnation before union growth resumed in 1933. Green was appointed to a number of posts by the Roosevelt administration—he was a member of the Advisory Council of the President's Committee on Economic Security (1934–36), of the Labor Advisory Board of the National Recovery Administration (1933–35), and of the National Labor Board (1933–34)—and played an important role in encouraging the passage of legislation, notably Section 7 of the National Industrial Recovery Act (1933) and the National Labor Relations Act (1935), facilitating the extension of union organizing and collective bargaining.

Green's influence with the White House was, however, limited, a fact early underlined by Roosevelt's appointment of Frances Perkins as secretary of labor despite AFL objections. His claim to represent the interests of all American labor was further eroded when splits within the AFL gave birth to a rival federation—the Congress of Industrial Organizations. The CIO was successful in establishing a close political relationship with the Roosevelt administration, and by the end of the decade Green's overriding concern had become to limit the ambit of federal intervention in the fields of labor relations and labor standards in order to protect vested AFL interests. Never a commanding figure ("I have done a lot of exploring in Bill's mind," John L. Lewis once said of him, "and I give you my word there is nothing there."), Green was overshadowed both within the AFL by the craft union leaders who kept him in office and outside it by the charismatic founder of the CIO, John L. Lewis. He died in Coshocton in 1952.

The only full-length biography of Green available is Max Danish, *William Green, A Pictorial Biography* (New York: Inter-Allied Publications, 1952). Biographical information may also be found in Charles A. Madison, *American Labor Leaders* (New York: Ungar, 1962). Irving Bernstein, in *The Lean Years* (Boston: Houghton Mifflin, 1960) and *Turbulent Years* (Boston: Houghon Mifflin, 1969), discusses Green's performance as president of the AFL in the context of a general history of the labor movement from 1920 to 1940. Green's own *Labor and Democracy* (Princeton: Princeton University Press, 1939) describes his ideology and details his personal reaction to the split in the labor movement that brought the formation of the CIO. His correspondence is available on microfilm at the New York School of Industrial and Labor Relations, Ithaca. Some papers are also included in the microfilm series *The American Federation of Labor Records: The Samuel Gompers Era.*

CHRISTOPHER L. TOMLINS

See also Labor

Greenbelt Towns

See Housing and Resettlement

Groton School

A small boarding school in Groton, Massachusetts, attended by Franklin Roosevelt. It was founded in 1884 by the Reverend Dr. Endicott Peabody and two associates to prepare the sons of wealthy and prominent families for college. Peabody, the headmaster from its founding until his retirement in 1940, modeled the school on English public schools with a program of religious observances, vigorous exercise, and spartan living. Though he ruled the school with an iron hand, the headmaster was an affectionate father figure. Each night after the evening prayer, in a ritual known as the "go by," he and Mrs. Peabody shook the hand of each boy as he marched off to bed. His boys regarded him with awe and competed for his praise. They continued to do so long after they had left the school.

FDR in white turtleneck, center, on the Groton School's second football team, October 1899. (Courtesy FDR Library.)

Franklin Roosevelt entered Groton in 1896 at fourteen years of age. Because his parents had been reluctant to part with him, he entered two years behind the other members of his class. They had already formed friendships, and Franklin always felt somewhat an outsider. Distinction at Groton came through athletics, but Franklin with his slight build and no previous team experience was not an athlete. He did, however, play football on the "second eleven," become manager of the baseball team, and excel in the high kick. Although he did not shine academically, he stood fairly high in his class, mainly because of good grades in French and German which he had studied with his tutors and had spoken abroad. Yet, despite all this, Groton left an indelible mark on him, and the headmaster's influence proved to be one of the most important in his life. It has been said that the only firm requirement Eleanor and Franklin Roosevelt made of their sons was attendance at Groton. Their four sons complied.

Considering Groton's small size (during Peabody's tenure, enrollment never exceeded 200), it has produced an astonishing number of men of high achievement. The alumni roll includes cabinet members, ambassadors and ministers, senators, congressmen, and other prominent figures. Groton today is coeducational. Of its 300 students, about 40 percent are women.

For additional material, see Frank Freidel's *Franklin D. Roosevelt: The Apprenticeship* (Boston: Little, Brown & Co., 1952), Kenneth Davis's *FDR: The Beckoning of Destiny, 1882–1928* (New York: G. P. Putnam's Sons, 1972), and Laura Crowell's "Roosevelt the Grotonian," *Quarterly Journal of Speech* 38 (February 1952):31–36.

See also Education; Peabody, Endicott

Groves, Leslie

(17 August 1896–13 July 1970)

Army officer and engineer, director of the Manhattan Project. Born in Albany, New York, the son of an army chaplain, Leslie Groves grew up at a series of army posts. He attended the University of Washington and Massachusetts Institute of Technology, and graduated from the U.S. Military Academy in 1918. Groves joined the U.S. Army Corps of Engineers and served in a variety of places during the twenties and thirties, including Hawaii and Nicaragua briefly, but mostly in the States. His most impressive prewar achievement was to direct the design and construction of the War Department's new Pentagon Building, which was completed in half its estimated time.

When World War II began, Groves looked forward to an overseas field command. Instead, Chief of Staff George Marshall appointed and President Franklin Roosevelt approved Groves to head the Manhattan Engineering District, a secret project to develop the atomic bomb. At first disappointed, Groves was reassured that this project could win the war, and he plunged into the monumental task. Groves appointed the physicist J. Robert Oppenheimer to direct the scientific work and brought the scientists together in a central laboratory and village at Los Alamos, New Mexico. General Groves, a bulky man known for his well-starched uniforms, contrasted in several ways with the scientists and especially with the gaunt Oppenheimer. Groves was accustomed to military discipline and tried to compartmentalize information in order to ensure secrecy. The scientists, used to the free flow of information, reacted against Groves's security measures and repeatedly violated his censorship directives. General Groves was anxious to develop a bomb in order for it to have a decisive effect in the war and, in contrast to the scientists, never doubted that it should be used as soon as possible. Groves also opposed sharing the development and use of the atomic bomb with the Allies, as Roosevelt wanted to do. British prime minister Winston Churchill complained several times to Roosevelt that Groves refused to share information on the project, and the two leaders agreed on 18 September 1944 that "full collaboration between the United States and the British Government" in developing atomic weapons "for military and commercial uses should continue after the defeat of Japan." Yet Groves resisted Roosevelt's desire to make atomic power a joint venture and later testified that he "did everything to hold back on" cooperation with the British. After the Japanese surrender, Groves worked to keep atomic knowledge under the control of the military until 1947 when the civilian Atomic Energy Commission took charge. The following year he left the army and worked in private industry until 1961 when he retired.

Groves's own story of the Manhattan Project is *Now It Can Be Told* (New York: Harper & Bros., 1962). The scientists' point of view is presented in Robert Jungk, *Brighter Than a Thousand Suns* (New York: Harcourt, Brace & Co., 1956). For a readable overview of the project, see James W. Kunetka, *City of Fire* (Albuquerque: University of New Mexico Press, 1978). A fine history of the tangled decision making concerning the bomb is Walter S. Schoenberger, *Decision of Destiny* (Athens: Ohio University Press, 1969).

H

Hague, Frank

(17 January 1876–1 January 1956)

Political boss of Jersey City. Born in Jersey City to Irish immigrant parents, Frank Hague left public school early and spent his youth in a variety of odd jobs. He won his first public office in 1899 and quickly advanced in the local Democratic party. A slim, healthy-looking man with auburn hair, Hague adopted the civic reform spirit of the Progressive period and in 1913 won a spot on Jersey City's new commission form of government. He effectively used his reform image to gather power and in 1917 was elected mayor, a position he held for thirty years. During that time, he used his considerable organizational talents and his dominating personality to build around himself a powerful political machine that could rival any in the nation for efficiency and control. A mediocre public speaker, Hague maintained power by his personal domination of opponents in private and with an organization that kept a representative in every ward in Jersey City. While opponents dubbed him the "Hitler of Hudson County," he could make good on his boast that "I am the law."

As the dominant Democrat in New Jersey, Hague played a role in national politics during the twenties and thirties. In 1932 he favored Al Smith and led the opposition to Franklin Roosevelt's nomination. He went so far as to claim publicly that Roosevelt, if nominated, could not win in any state east of the Mississippi. After the convention, however, he cast his lot with the winner and delivered New Jersey for Roosevelt. In return for Hague's support, Roosevelt channeled New Jersey's relief and public works programs through the Jersey City boss. The New Deal patronage at least temporarily increased Hague's control, and despite growing public complaints of Hague's ruthlessness, Roosevelt hesitated to break with the man who controlled New Jersey's electoral destiny. In 1941, with Roosevelt's quiet support, New Jersey governor Charles Edison launched a reform campaign against Hague but had only limited success.

Roosevelt, although he disliked Hague personally and politically, did not openly challenge the Hague machine, which continued to deliver votes for Roosevelt in 1940 and 1944. In 1947 Hague resigned and his machine split into factions and never recovered, despite a brief comeback attempt by Hague in 1953.

Richard Connors, *A Cycle of Power* (Metuchen, N.J.: Scarecrow Press, 1971) is the standard biography of Hague. An older but useful diatribe against Hague is Dayton McKean, *The Boss* (Boston: Houghton Mifflin Co., 1940). For a critical view of Roosevelt's relationship with Hague, see Lyle W. Dorsett, *Franklin D. Roosevelt and the City Bosses* (Port Washington, N.Y.: Kennikat Press, 1977).

See also Edison, Charles

Halsey, William Frederick, Jr. ("Bill," "Bull")

(30 October 1882–16 August 1959)

An American naval officer and commander of the U.S. Third Fleet in World War II, William F. Halsey was born in Elizabeth, New Jersey, and graduated from the U.S. Naval Academy in 1904. He began his seagoing career on the 12,500-ton battleship *Missouri*, the "Mizzy."

Halsey and Franklin D. Roosevelt became friends when Halsey was a lieutenant and Roosevelt was assistant secretary of the navy. In the summer of 1913, Halsey, who was commanding a destroyer, picked up the assistant secretary at the latter's summer home on Campobello Island and took him on an inspection tour of naval installations on the Maine coast. On the way back to Campobello, Roosevelt impressed Halsey with his seamanship by piloting the destroyer through a narrow strait. "At this time," said Halsey later, "Mr. Roosevelt was a splendid-looking, vigorous man, full of vitality."

In 1918, not long after the Armistice, Lieutenant Halsey conveyed the assistant secretary and his party

William Frederick Halsey, Jr., 1949. Artist: Albert K. Murray. (National Portrait Gallery, Smithsonian Institution. Gift of the International Business Machines Corp.)

from England across to Belgium. During the Democratic National Convention of 1920, which nominated Roosevelt for vice-president, Halsey was happy to receive the assistant secretary on board his destroyer in San Francisco Bay. Afterward, when they chanced to meet in the street, Roosevelt, referring to a recent scuffle for a banner in the convention hall, said, "Bill, I've just had a fight." Halsey, mindful of Roosevelt's muscular build, asked, "What hospital is he in, Mr. Secretary?"

Nineteen years later, at the conclusion of Fleet Problem XX in the Caribbean, Rear Admiral Halsey, together with other flag officers, called on President Roosevelt on board the cruiser *Houston* to pay his respects. For Halsey, the aristocratic FDR had always been a regal figure. Now, seated, with polio-shrunken legs, unable to rise unassisted, the aging Roosevelt seemed to Halsey more majestic than ever.

In the fall of 1942, during World War II, Vice Admiral Halsey took over a previously disheartened and defeatist South Pacific command, instilled it with courage and the will to victory, and in a three-day struggle, threw the Japanese for the first time on the defensive, assuring the American reconquest of Guadalcanal. President Roosevelt rewarded him by nominating him for four-star admiral, at that time the top professional rank in the navy.

In January 1945, Roosevelt in his State of the Union message before Congress praised Halsey lavishly for discovering the weakness of the enemy in the central Philippines and advising a direct attack on Leyte. Acted upon, Halsey's advice probably shortened the Pacific war by several months.

The old friends met for the last time in March 1945, a month before the president's death. Summoning Halsey to the White House, Roosevelt awarded him a gold star in lieu of a third Distinguished Service Medal. After lunch, the president took the admiral to his upstairs office for a private conversation.

By an odd coincidence, Halsey's last World War II flagship was another battleship *Missouri*, the 45,000-ton "Mighty Mo." On board, he hosted the officers and others who came to sign, and observe the signing of, the instrument of Japanese surrender. In recognition of his achievements and services in World War II, Halsey in December 1945 was promoted to the new top rank of fleet admiral.

Halsey's life and career are recounted in Ralph B. Jordan, *Born to Fight: The Life of Admiral Halsey* (Philadelphia: David McKay, 1946), William F. Halsey and J. Bryan III, *Admiral Halsey's Story* (New York: McGraw Hill, 1947), Benis Frank, *Halsey* (New York: Ballantine Books, 1974), James M. Merrill, *A Sailor's Admiral: A Biography of William F. Halsey* (New York: Thomas Y. Crowell, 1976), and (in preparation) E. B. Potter, *Halsey* (Naval Institute Press).

E. B. POTTER

"Happy Warrior" Speech
See Smith, Alfred E.

Harriman, William Averell
(15 November 1891–)

William Averell Harriman, born in New York City, was educated at the Groton School and Yale, graduating with a B.A. in 1913. Two years later, he became vice-president of the Union Pacific Railroad, after which he busied himself with a number of entrepreneurial activities. Harriman rejected the Republican party in 1928 and strongly supported the presidential ambitions of FDR. At the urging of Harry Hopkins, Harriman entered the Roosevelt administration as a member of the National Recovery Administration (1933–37), becoming a divisional administrator (1934–35). Appointed chairman of the Business Advisory Council (1937–40), he served three months in the Office of Production Management in early 1941 and was named defense expeditor to Great Britain (1941–42).

Regarded as a pivotal person in FDR's foreign affairs organization, Harriman attended the Atlantic Conference in 1941, headed the Harriman-Beaverbrook Lend-Lease mission to the Soviet Union, and returned with Churchill in 1942 to ease Stalin's fears on the absence of a second front. Appointed ambassador to Russia in October 1943, where he remained until March 1946, Harriman was constantly at FDR's side at the conferences at Cairo, Teheran, and Yalta. Averell Harriman developed a clear-eyed and common sense approach to Russian-American relations. His advice to FDR was usually sound, particularly regarding the Russians. Three weeks before his death, the president declared: "Averell is right; we can't do business with Stalin. He has broken every one of the promises he made at Yalta."

After FDR's death, Harriman served President Truman as ambassador to Great Britain (March-

October 1946), as secretary of commerce (1946–48), as U.S. coordinator of the European Recovery Program (1948–50), and as director of the Mutual Security Agency (1951–53). In 1954, he became governor of New York; he tried unsuccessfully for the Democratic presidential nomination in 1952 and 1956, and for reelection as governor in 1958. During the Kennedy years, Harriman served as ambassador-at-large and as assistant secretary of state for far eastern affairs. In 1963, as under secretary of state for political affairs, he negotiated the limited nuclear test ban treaty. He served President Johnson as ambassador-at-large at the Paris peace talks with North Vietnam. Now retired, Mr. Harriman is still perceived by Democrats as an active link with the great era of FDR.

For further information, see W. Averell Harriman and Elie Abel, *Special Envoy to Churchill and Stalin, 1941–1946* (New York: Random House, 1975), George C. Herring, Jr., *Aid to Russia, 1941–1946* (New York: Columbia University Press, 1973), Lee H. Burke, *Ambassador at Large: Diplomat Extraordinary* (The Hague: Nijhoff, 1972), and John Taft, "The Ancient Mariner," *New Republic,* 20–27 April 1977, pp. 18–20.

JOHN C. WALTER

Harvard Crimson ("The Crime")

Undergraduate daily newspaper at Harvard, which Franklin Roosevelt headed during his collegiate days. At Harvard at the turn of the century, as at other Ivy League colleges, athletics and extracurricular activities drew the attention and efforts of ambitious undergraduates far more than scholarship. Barred from athletic recognition by his slightness of build, Roosevelt found an outlet in the intense competition for election to, and preferment on, the editorial board of the *Crimson.* He was elected on the second go-round at the end of his freshman year, largely as a consequence of a journalistic scoop involving a Harvard appearance by his distant cousin President Theodore Roosevelt. In his sophomore year, he was elected secretary, traditionally a sophomore position, and at its conclusion was one of two rising juniors picked as assistant managing editor, or "Crimed," locally. Elec-

W. Averell Harriman, 1935. Artist: Jo Davidson. (National Portrait Gallery, Smithsonian Institution.)

tion as managing editor in the middle of his junior year led automatically to the presidency of "the Crime" in his last year (1903–4). It was young Roosevelt's first political success—and in the Harvard of those days a considerable one. In later years, Roosevelt often amused and annoyed newspapermen by invoking his journalistic "career" on the *Crimson* as common ground with them and a basis on occasion for criticizing their coverage of his presidency. His contemporaries on the Cambridge scene felt that his leadership of the paper was competent but not outstanding, and the editorials for which he was responsible as president were conventional if not stuffy, criticizing poor team spirit on the athletic fields, lagging school spirit in the stands, muddy walks in "the Yard" and the other commonplaces of collegiate journalism through the years. But the significance of FDR's career on the *Crimson* lay less in the substance of the paper than in the skill and tenacity with which he pursued and gained its headship, despite the fact that he was not altogether liked by his contemporaries. He conceded this years later when he remarked, "I must say frankly that I remember my own adventures as an editor rather more clearly than I do my routine work as a student."

FDR's editorship on the *Crimson* is covered in Frank Freidel's *Franklin D. Roosevelt: The Apprenticeship* (Boston: Little, Brown & Co., 1952) and, with more particularity, in an article by Philip M. Boffey in the *Harvard Crimson* of 13 December 1957.

See also Education

Harvard University

See Education

Hassett, William D.

(28 August 1880–29 August 1965)

Correspondence secretary and sometime press secretary to Franklin D. Roosevelt from 1935 to 1945. Hassett was born in Northfield, Vermont, and attended Clark University for two years. He became a reporter, first with the *Burlington Free Press* and later with the Associated Press and United Press in Washington and London and various newspapers including the *Washington Herald,* the *Washington Post,* and the *Philadelphia Public Ledger.* He began his government career in 1933 with the National Recovery Administration and joined the White House staff in 1935 as an assistant to Stephen T. Early, Roosevelt's press secretary. President Roosevelt swore him in as secretary on 19 February 1944. The two men had been friends since Roosevelt's years as assistant secretary of the navy. It was Hassett who called the correspondents into the Little White House at Warm Springs, Georgia, on 12 April 1945 to inform them that the president had died. He remained as secretary

FDR (front row center) with the staff of the Harvard Crimson. *(Courtesy FDR Library.)*

As William Hassett looks on, President Roosevelt signs proclamation for "I Am an American Day," 3 May 1940. (Courtesy FDR Library.)

under President Truman and is credited with drafting replies to 300,000 letters addressed to the presidents.

He retired in 1952, and died of a heart attack at his home in Northfield at the age of eighty-five.

Hassett wrote several articles and books about his White House years, the best known being *Off the Record with FDR* (New Brunswick, N.J.: Rutgers University Press, 1958). His papers are in the Franklin D. Roosevelt and Harry S Truman libraries.

Health

When FDR died in April 1945, many persons alleged he had been in declining health for a long time. In recent years, some writers have embroidered his medical history to make it seem that he had been in declining health since 1937, too sick to carry out fully his presidential functions. The significant point about FDR's health was that he carried on so well for so many years in positions of responsibility that would have taxed the strength of the most vigorous able-bodied person. His physical disability did not impair his work function. The source of all the rumors was FDR's struggle with polio, a dreaded subject about which the public knew little. It was only in the last year and a half of his life that his decline set in, and then there is no proof that it affected his judgment.

The greatest bone of contention is the Yalta Conference, which took place 4–11 February 1945. He chaired all the plenary sessions and worked on a back-breaking schedule for ten to twelve hours a day. He answered mail from the United States during the morning, lunched with Churchill and his military and diplomatic advisers at noon, went into plenary session at four, came out at eight, and attended long dinners at night. He showed no evidence of memory lapses, slurred speech, disorientation, or confusion. He was suffering, however, from unstable blood pressure (pulsus alternans) which forced him to rest until noon on 9–10 February. Averell Harriman, who was present at the Yalta Conference, concluded that a healthier FDR might have held out a little longer against Stalin on the question of Russian hegemony in Eastern Europe, but that it probably would have made little difference since the Russian Army already occupied Poland and was racing toward Berlin. The important points to remember are that FDR's policy toward Russia grew out of his wartime relationship with Stalin and was formulated long before he went to Yalta. Even if the judgments he made at Yalta were not correct—and that is open to debate by historians—those judgments cannot be attributed to his declining health.

Little documentation survives from FDR's early medical history. What is known comes from Sara Delano Roosevelt's diaries and FDR's personal letters. The doctor almost smothered him at birth with an excessive dose of chloroform for his mother. Nevertheless, he survived and weighed ten pounds. He was breast fed for almost one year and was given constant love and attention by his parents and nurses. Being reared on a great country estate, the young FDR was not exposed to the usual childhood illnesses and was vulnerable to infectious disease much later in life. He was plagued by the common cold from infancy to age eighteen, as evidenced by his letters to his parents. This tendency to fall victim to colds and sinus infections persisted for a lifetime. At age seven, he was taken ill with typhoid fever while making a sea voyage to Europe. His parents minimized his illness, and his mother hardly mentioned it in her diaries. FDR learned from such experiences that illness was something to be endured. After he entered Groton at age fourteen, he quickly succumbed to measles, scarlet fever, and various upper and lower respiratory tract infections.

When Roosevelt entered Harvard four years later in 1900, he was comparatively underdeveloped physically, socially, and sexually. He did not possess the muscular strength required for athletic distinction. Although he became a member of the Harvard crew and loved to swim, play golf, and sail, he was never an outstanding athlete. After marriage in March 1905 to his distant cousin, Eleanor, he became ill with hives on a belated honeymoon three months later. Because hives are usually an allergic reaction to sudden stress, FDR's attitude toward sexuality must be considered in this connection. He was brought up in a Victorian home with conservative values. His mother's attitude toward sex held it to be an obligation and duty. When FDR married, he was no less inhibited than Eleanor and no more informed about birth control.

In the next ten years of marriage, his medical history was uneventful, with the exception of a severe case of typhoid fever, which kept him at home during his 1912 campaign for reelection as state senator. During this year, he supported the presidential candidacy of Woodrow Wilson at the Democratic National Convention and in 1913 was appointed assistant secretary of the navy by Wilson. The Roosevelts moved to Washington, quickly settling in with the highest diplomatic and social circles, where Franklin was remembered as gay, amusing, lovable, handsome, athletic, somewhat frivolous, and self-confident. Photographs of him during the navy period show him playing tennis and golf, exercising, sailing, and climbing out of a navy seaplane.

From 1915 to 1921, however, he suffered from a long series of illnesses, operations, and chronic health problems. In July 1915, he was operated upon for an acute attack of appendicitis. In 1916 and 1917, he had several throat infections and in the summer of 1917 had to be hospitalized. In September 1918, he was stricken with double pneumonia while returning from Europe and was taken from ship to the hospital. A month later, he fell ill from influenza, which was raging in epidemic proportions at the end of World War I. In December 1918, he had a tonsillectomy after several years of sore throats. The interplay between FDR's emotional and physical health at this time cannot be ignored, for these were the years when he was struggling with a decision about divorcing Eleanor to marry Lucy Mercer. Before 1921, he had been an ambitious politician with great promise in the Democratic party.

On 10 August 1921, FDR suffered an attack of poliomyelitis, a severe viral infection that resulted in motor paralysis from the waist down. Despite seven years of treatment, including a four-year stay at Warm Springs, Georgia, FDR never again walked without long leg braces, crutches or canes, and an attendant holding his arm and acting as a brace. The medical records indicate that FDR's sexual function was unimpaired. Following polio, a man does not lose sensation and is capable of maintaining erection and ejaculation. After 1918, however, he was physically estranged from Eleanor, and there is no evidence as to whether he resumed a sexual relationship with her or anyone else after the polio attack.

After a seven-year effort to overcome his disability, he accepted the Democratic nomination for governor of New York and won the election. In Albany, he showed he had the stamina to be governor. In 1930, while running for reelection, a group of eminent doctors examined him and pronounced him in excellent health. The same tactic was used in the 1932 presidential campaign.

There was no question about FDR's great vitality and activity up to 1943. Until 1937 his heart and blood pressure were normal. Most of the time he was confined to a wheelchair or was carried. Rumors about his health appeared as early as 1935 in support of reactionary opposition to his policies. He was falsely alleged to have had syphilis and Parkinson's disease, and to have suffered a series of little strokes. Most recently, Goldsmith alleged that he had a dormant melanoma which became malignant in 1944, as evidenced by photographs of removal of a lesion over his left eyebrow prior to the presidential campaign of 1944. None of these rumors or allegations has any basis in medical documentation or fact. Fragmentary medical records at the FDR Library, Hyde Park, New York, show that he registered some systolic elevation of blood pressure in April 1937, but a sporadic reading due to stress cannot be labeled hypertension. Not until 13 November 1940, after election to a third term, did FDR begin to show consistent readings of systolic and diastolic hypertension with significant deviation from the normal. The stress of the war years took its toll, unrelieved by cruises and trips to Warm Springs.

After the Teheran Conference in November 1943, his health rapidly declined. On 27 March 1944, he was examined by a U.S. Navy cardiologist, Dr. Howard G. Bruenn, who treated him for the next twelve months and has written the only authentic medical history of his last year. Bruenn made a diagnosis of hypertension, hypertensive heart disease, cardiac failure, and acute bronchitis. Despite a regimen of restricted low-fat diet, digitalis, weight reduction, and occasional sedation, he died from a massive cerebral hemorrhage one year later on 12 April 1945. An autopsy was not performed.

There is no comprehensive medical history of Franklin D. Roosevelt. The most complete account is found in Richard T. Goldberg, *The Making of Franklin D. Roosevelt: Triumph over Disability* (Cambridge, Mass.: Abt Books, 1981), which makes use of the Dr. Robert Lovett collection on FDR's poliomyelitis and integrates FDR's medical history with his political career and family life. FDR's early health problems are best documented in a series of articles by Noah Fabricant in *Eye, Ear, Nose and Throat Monthly*: "Franklin D. Roosevelt, the Common Cold and American History," 37 (March 1958):179–85, "Franklin D. Roosevelt's Nose and Throat Ailments," 36 (February 1957):103–6, and "Franklin D. Roosevelt's Tonsillectomy and Poliomyelitis," 36 (June 1957):348–49. His mother's diaries and his personal letters housed at the FDR Library, Hyde Park, New York, make references to his health. For his later medical history, the most accurate source is Howard G. Bruenn, "Clinical Notes on the Illness and Death of President Franklin D. Roosevelt," *Annals of Internal Medicine* 72 (April 1970):579–91. Dr. Bruenn treated FDR from 28 March 1944 to 12 April 1945. Jim Bishop, in *FDR's Last Year* (New York: Morrow, 1974), gives a narrative description of Roosevelt's health problems but does not provide medical documentation. Several medical writers have speculated upon the causes of FDR's decline—among them Harry S. Goldsmith, "Unanswered Mysteries in the Death of Franklin D. Roosevelt," *Surgery, Gynecology, and Obstetrics* 149 (December 1979):899–908, and Alvan L. Barach, "Franklin Roosevelt's Illness,"

New York State Journal of Medicine 77 (November 1977):2154–57—but they do not possess or cite the necessary medical records to support their claims.

RICHARD T. GOLDBERG

See also Death of FDR; Polio

Hearst, William Randolph

(29 April 1863–14 August 1951)

Publisher and politician. William Randolph Hearst was the only child of George Hearst, San Francisco's millionaire mining magnate, and Phoebe Apperson Hearst, later a philanthropist and regent of the University of California. Raised in fabulous wealth derived from his father's San Francisco mining empire, William Randolph's early life was sheltered. He attended St. Paul's preparatory school in New Hampshire for two years and then quit and was tutored at home until he left for Harvard University in 1882. There he earned a reputation as a frivolous prankster and was twice expelled. Hearst entered the newspaper business in 1886, when his father reluctantly gave him control of the family-owned *San Francisco Examiner.*

From this start Hearst immediately began to build a newspaper empire and with it, a reputation for yellow journalism—a sensationalist style that sacrificed factual accuracy for popular appeal. After George Hearst died in 1891, William Randolph used his inheritance from his father to expand to New York and compete against Joseph Pulitzer's established newspapers. He raided Pulitzer's best talent and played easy with the facts in order to make his papers popular. Hearst's yellow journalism reached its peak in 1898 during the Spanish-American War, when his papers made emotional appeals against the Spanish in order to encourage prowar sentiment. He reportedly told one of his correspondents in Cuba who saw no fighting, "You furnish the pictures and I'll furnish the war." How much credit or blame for the war may be laid to Hearst is an open question, but he certainly made the public more receptive to President McKinley's war message.

In 1900 Hearst began his own political career as president of the National Association of Democratic Clubs. Two years later he won election to Congress from Manhattan's safely Democratic Eleventh District, but his gala celebration was ruined by the accidental death of twelve spectators at a rowdy Madison Square fireworks display. Hearst's two terms in Congress were marked by a vague but ineffective progressive record in which he earned the respect of neither party. In 1905 he ran unsuccessfully for mayor of New York City and the next year was defeated in a bid for governor of New York. All the while Hearst continued to enlarge his publishing interests. His pro-German stance before and during World War I and his direct conflict with Alfred E. Smith in New York politics finished Hearst's opportunities for public office, but left him in the twenties and thirties as a powerful manipulator of public opinion.

By 1931 Hearst, now an old man hiding away in his mountaintop mansion near San Francisco, became disenchanted with President Hoover's leadership. In Hearst's search for Democratic alternatives, he promoted John Garner of Texas so strongly that the otherwise unknown candidate managed to make the margin of difference between the leading contenders Smith and Franklin Roosevelt. After the third ballot Roosevelt's floor manager Jim Farley began actively to court Hearst in order to swing Garner's votes. Hearst considered Roosevelt the least objectionable of the alternatives and released Garner's votes for Roosevelt, thus playing a key role in Roosevelt's nomination.

Hearst's newspapers initially backed the New Deal, but Hearst broke with the president over New Deal policies favoring a wealth tax, labor unions, and the regulation of business. By 1935 Hearst instructed his newspapers to refer to the New Deal as the "Raw Deal" and continued his drift to the Right with attacks on labor unions and red-baiting of college professors. As World War II approached, Hearst's sympathies with Germany and his fear of Communist Russia placed him in the isolationist camp as a staunch opponent of Roosevelt's internationalist policies.

Meanwhile, the depression severely cut into Hearst's fortune. He was forced to retrench his newspaper organization in order to avoid bankruptcy, and only with the return of prosperity during the war did he regain a substantial part of his publishing network. When Hearst died in 1951, he left to his family the largest newspaper conglomerate in the nation.

Of the many biographies of Hearst, the most balanced is W. A. Swanberg, *Citizen Hearst* (New York: Charles Scribner's Sons, 1961). An informative monograph on Hearst and Roosevelt is Rodney P. Carlisle, *Hearst and the New Deal* (New York: Garland Publishing Co., 1979).

Henderson, Leon

(26 May 1895–)

Economist and administrator. Born in Millville, New Jersey, Leon Henderson received his B.A. in economics from Swarthmore College in 1920. He taught at the Wharton School of Business and the Carnegie Institute from 1921 to 1923. After serving two years as deputy secretary of Pennsylvania, he joined the Russell Sage Foundation, investigating problems of consumer credit and usury.

Henderson came to the New Deal almost by accident. As a delegate to the Emergency Conference of Consumer Organizations in December 1933, he publicly quarreled with National Recovery Administration (NRA) chief Hugh Johnson, whom he correctly felt was unsympathetic to consumer needs. Johnson then offered him a position as special adviser on consumer affairs; in March 1934, Henderson joined the Research and Planning Division of the NRA.

Always concerned with the welfare of the individual citizen, Henderson became a persistent critic of business practices under the NRA, particularly production restrictions and high prices that were often the results of industry-written NRA codes. His price studies revealed the unfairness and inefficiency of the codes at the NRA price hearings of 1935, which helped bring the NRA into disfavor before it was abolished. He was a strong advocate of vigorous and, if necessary, government-enforced competition for recovery. However, he was not necessarily a defender of small businesses, which were more inefficient than large organizations. For Henderson, obstacles to recovery were imperfect competition and monopoly. He shared the "administered-price thesis" which asserted that business combinations in many sectors pegged prices at artificially high levels and impaired the market mechanism. Only the government could restore the dependency of prices on supply and demand. He strongly encouraged the government to study the causes and effects of monopoly, and in 1938 he became executive secretary of the Congressional Temporary National Economic Committee, which investigated monopolistic business practices.

Henderson also favored government spending to compensate for lapses in private investment. Along with Thomas Blaisdell, Marriner Eccles, and Beardsley Ruml, he supported large-scale deficit spending. A series of memos written with Ruml in April 1938 helped convince FDR to resume deficit spending to cope with the recession of 1937. Henderson thus played a significant role in establishing Keynesian economics in America.

FDR appointed him to the Securities and Exchange Commission in 1939, which aroused controversy. Henderson's long record as a loyal New Dealer and servant of the Democratic party (he was consulting economist for the 1936 election) plus his outspoken manner already had made him enemies in business and industry. This enmity worsened when FDR made him head of the Office of Price Administration in April 1941. By 1942 he had authority to regulate and control the production and distribution of retail goods and to prevent unwarranted price increases. Throughout his tenure, Henderson incurred the ire of business as well as the conservative coalition in Congress which objected to his unprecedented powers as well as his tenacious protection of consumers.

After the 1942 elections, Henderson, who was suffering from ill health and overwork, resigned from the government. His successor Chester Bowles noted that he "had courageously and successfully led the fight for a stable economy . . . and in the process brought down upon his head the wrath of every economic group in the country."

There is no biography of Henderson, but his career is charted most fully in Ellis Hawley, *The New Deal and the Problem of Monopoly* (Princeton: Princeton University Press, 1966), an absolutely essential study of New Deal economics. Henderson's contributions to consumer interests are noted in Persia Campbell, *Consumer Representation and the New Deal* (New York: Columbia University Press, 1940); his work on Keynesian economics is discussed in Dean L. May, *From New Deal to New Economics* (New York: Garland, 1981). Henderson in the OPA is treated briefly by Richard Chapman, *Contours of Public Policy, 1939–1945* (New York: Garland, 1981).

See also Temporary National Economic Committee

Hillman, Sidney ("Simcha")
(23 March 1887–10 July 1946)

Sidney Hillman. (National Portrait Gallery, Smithsonian Institution.)

President of the Amalgamated Clothing Workers of America, labor adviser to Roosevelt, and director of the CIO-PAC. Born in Zagare, Russian Lithuania, the intense and loquacious "Simcha" Hillman seemed in his boyhood to be destined for the rabbinate. At age fifteen, however, he abandoned the yeshiva at Kovno for membership in the Jewish socialist *Bund* and shortly thereafter was imprisoned as a labor agitator. Hillman left Russia in 1906 and settled in Chicago; in 1909, he became a garment cutter at Hart, Schaffner and Marx. Over the next five years, he played a major role in the development of unionism among Jewish garment workers in Chicago and New York, and in 1914 he became president of the Amalgamated Clothing Workers (ACW). The outstanding intellect among his generation of labor leaders, Hillman's politics blended efficiency and progressive social programs with disciplined cooperation with employers. He was admired by contemporaries as a "labor statesman" who was creating a new model for American unionism.

During the early New Deal, Hillman took advantage of the opportunities afforded by the passage of the National Industrial Recovery Act (1933) to improve markedly the industrial position of the ACW. Simultaneously, he became a strong supporter of the Roosevelt administration's recovery policies, serving on the National Recovery Administration's Labor Advisory Board (1933–35) and on the National Industrial Recovery Board (1934–35). He was also a member of the National Advisory Board of the National Youth Administration. Within the labor movement, Hillman was identified with the industrial union wing of the AFL, and in 1935 he helped launch the Committee for Industrial Organization (CIO). Two years later, Hillman would mastermind the CIO's drive to organize textile workers, becoming a central figure in the eventually independent Congress of Industrial Organizations (1938–55).

Already by 1936, however, Hillman's main attention was focused on national politics. Committed to entrenching organized labor at the center of the New Deal coalition, Hillman joined fellow CIO leaders John L. Lewis and David Dubinsky and AFL Printing Pressmen president George L. Berry in founding labor's Non-Partisan League (April 1936) to mobilize the labor vote and union money behind Roosevelt's reelection. Acting as league treasurer, Hillman raised $1 million. Administration support for the enactment of fair labor standards legislation (1938), for which Hillman had lobbied hard, brought him even closer to Roosevelt, and by 1940 his consistent efforts to unite the two wings of the labor movement behind the administration had earned him a place of influence within the White House unparalleled among labor leaders. Roosevelt made him labor member of the National Defense Advisory Commission in 1940, and subsequently he became associate director-general of the Office of Production Management (1940–42). Creation of the War Production Board (WPB) early in 1942 signaled a weakening of Hillman's authority, however, and although he remained a labor adviser to the president and head of the WPB's labor division, the reorganization effectively concluded organized labor's direct participation in the top levels of government. Major business figures were to dominate the war mobilization program.

Despite his eclipse, Hillman remained unshaken in his commitment to Roosevelt. In 1943, in the wake of conservative gains in the mid-term elections, he became chairman and director of the CIO's Political Action Committee, overseeing the creation of a national campaign to ensure labor's support for Democratic party candidates in 1944. PAC's strength was demonstrated in May 1944 when it effectively forced Congressman Martin Dies's withdrawal from his Texas primary. Hillman went on to play a pivotal role in the negotiations that placed Harry Truman on the Democratic ticket, a role made famous by Roosevelt's instructions to his aides that they should "clear it [Truman's nomination as vice-president] with Sidney." The victim of recurrent heart attacks since 1942, Hillman died in 1946.

Mathew Josephson's *Sidney Hillman, Statesman of American Labor* (Garden City, N.Y.: Doubleday, 1952), is a comprehensive general biography. For more recent and critical views of the Amalgamated Clothing Workers under Hillman and of Hillman's trade union ideology, see Ronald Radosh, "The Corporate Ideology of American Labor Leaders," *Studies on the Left* 6 (1966); and Steve Fraser, "Dress Rehearsal for the New Deal," in *Working Class America*, ed. Michael H. Frisch and Daniel J. Walkowitz (Urbana: University of Illinois Press, 1983). J. David Greenstone, *Labor in American Politics* (Chicago: Chicago University Press, 1969) discusses the CIO's political role, and Mike Davis, "The Barren Marriage of American Labor and the Democratic Party," *New Left Review* 124 (1980), offers a rather different assessment. Finally, Nelson Lichtenstein, *Labor's War at Home: The CIO in World War Two* (New York: Cambridge University Press, 1983) provides an important analysis of relationships between the CIO and the administration during the war mobilization.

CHRISTOPHER L. TOMLINS

See also Labor

Hirohito

See Japan

Hitler, Adolf, and Germany

When Franklin D. Roosevelt became president in March 1933, Europeans widely feared that Adolf Hitler, chancellor of Germany for less than five weeks,

Germany, too, sought to ease domestic unemployment in the early thirties by implementing large-scale public works programs. Chancellor Adolf Hitler is seen here breaking ground for the Reichsautobahnen, "the world's most perfect speedways—his own creation," 12 February 1933. (National Archives.)

would soon provoke war by his truculent demands that the Western powers rescind the military and political restrictions they had imposed on Germany through the Treaty of Versailles in 1919. Roosevelt's views about modern Germany were deeply ambivalent. He abhorred the Nazis' assault on personal and political liberties, and their chauvinistic propaganda, saber-rattling diplomacy, and overt war preparations. Early in his presidency, he talked privately about boycotts or blockades of Germany and publicly deprecated its "insane rush" to armaments and reversion to the "law of the sword" to gain diplomatic ends.

At the same time Roosevelt, who had spent summers and school days in Germany in the 1890s, also greatly respected traditional German—as distinct from Nazi—culture. He believed German society to be admirably organized, efficient, and productive, a "heavenly city" for American trade, investment, and cultural exchange, as the Weimar Republic had been in the 1920s. Thus in 1933 Roosevelt longed to see a return to "that German sanity of the old type" and spoke favorably about German traditions as opposed to alleged British economic imperialism and French incapacity to govern well. And even after war had begun in Europe in the autumn of 1939, the president wrote approvingly of German "upbringing," "independence of family life," and property-holding traditions, which he contrasted to Russian "brutality."

Throughout the 1930s Roosevelt favored appeasement, that is, the revision of seemingly unfair or outdated treaty restrictions in order that a politically content and economically prosperous Germany might play its proper role in a new post-Versailles Europe. Thus Roosevelt deliberately acquiesced in German rearmament in March 1935 and military reoccupation of the Rhineland in March 1936. Shortly thereafter Roosevelt, spurred by his closest diplomatic adviser, Under Secretary of State Sumner Welles, sought to redress German claims by proposing to summon a world conference to establish universal codes for international relations, trade practices, arms limitation, and peaceful treaty revision. But the president was hesitant, and his extremely cautious secretary of state, Cordell Hull, dissuaded him from acting in 1937. The president renewed his effort in early 1938, but again backed off when British prime minister Neville Chamberlain responded coldly to the conference proposal. Then Hitler further unsettled international politics by purging his most cautious diplomats and military officials and engaging in brutal diplomacy leading to the Anschluss with Austria in March 1938.

Roosevelt deplored Hitler's truculence over Czechoslovakia, but reluctantly encouraged the British and French to accede to German demands through the Munich Conference in September 1938. Thereafter, however, Roosevelt promoted "methods short of war"—rearmament—to resist aggression even while he still hoped vainly for peaceful resolution of German claims against Poland. But when the British and French were forced into war with Germany in September 1939, Roosevelt declared that Americans did not have to be neutral in thought, and after Germany and the Soviet Union partitioned Poland, he insisted that German-Soviet domination from the Rhine to Manchuria threatened American national security.

Nonetheless, Roosevelt sent Under Secretary Welles to Europe in March 1940 to assess even remote prospects for a negotiated settlement that might tempt Hitler or tempt German moderates to depose their chancellor if he proved intransigent. Hitler rejected any serious discussion, however, and Germany's invasion of Western Europe in the spring of 1940 made peace talks unthinkable. Thereafter Roosevelt never spoke publicly of "Germany," only of a "Nazi" state: totalitarian, unappeaseable, and bent on global conquest.

Following Germany's signing of its Tripartite Pact with Italy and Japan in September 1940, Roosevelt declared that no combination of "dictator countries" would halt U.S. aid to those nations who were keeping the "aggressors" from American shores. Then in December 1940 he denounced the "unholy alliance" of Axis powers, and insisted that because the Nazis sought to enslave the world, the United States had to become "the great arsenal of democracy" and provide the British with everything they needed in their battle to preserve "their liberty and our security."

Roosevelt remained unswerving in his commitment to sustain Great Britain against Germany, even if this meant unneutral acts, stretching executive authority beyond fair use, and making misleading statements to rouse public ire. Thus in September 1940 the president provided the British with forty desperately needed over-age destroyers, and by March 1941 persuaded Congress to vote massive Lend-Lease military aid. And Roosevelt extended Lend-Lease to the Russians to contain the Nazi juggernaut after Hitler invaded the Soviet Union in June 1941. The president also approved armed convoys of British ships, publicly exaggerating encounters with German subma-

A United States anti-Nazi propaganda device. (National Archives.)

rines and purporting to have a secret map showing Germany's intention to divide Central and South America into vassal states; he ordered naval commanders virtually to "shoot on sight," which led to undeclared warfare in the Atlantic in the autumn of 1941.

Roosevelt's determination to defeat Nazi Germany was politically and morally responsible, although some historians think that he might better have served his honorable ends and the national interest by direct action that avoided use of questionable tactics. Ironically, however, Hitler precipitated American entry into the conflict by declaring war on the United States after Japan attacked Pearl Harbor on 7 December 1941. Hitler's decision to act just as German armies were bogging down in Russia remains perplexing. Conceivably he believed his own 1930's propaganda that the United States was politically and economically effete and racially corrupt—"half Judaized and the other half Negrified"—and thus militarily inconsequential. Or perhaps his insatiable lust for conquest and the dynamics of National Socialism led him to believe that he had to annihilate the United States in order to fulfill his divine obligation, as he told a cheering Reichstag on 11 December 1941, to lead Germany in the struggle to determine the world's fate for the next thousand years.

Roosevelt's wartime planning was often ambiguous, but he firmly believed that justice, history, and geopolitical considerations demanded that he impose a harsh peace on the German nation and people. Thus, in 1943 he demanded unconditional surrender and postwar Allied occupation of Germany, because he believed that the Germans must know, as they had not in 1918, that they had been defeated and must bear the burden of their responsibility—or guilt—for their "lawless conspiracy." Roosevelt was adamant that Germany rid itself of "Hitler and the Nazis," the "Prussian military clique," and "war-breeding gangs," and he spoke viscerally in private about mass castrations, thin daily diets from army soup kitchens, or following Premier Joseph Stalin's suggestion that they shoot 50,000 "war criminals."

At the Teheran Conference in November 1943, Roosevelt, Stalin, and Prime Minister Winston Churchill agreed in principle that Germany would be divided, or "dismembered," pay large reparations to atone for war damages, and cede portions of eastern Germany to Poland, which would return territory it had taken from the Soviet Union in 1921. Then in September 1944 Roosevelt supported Secretary of the Treasury Henry M. Morgenthau, Jr.'s "Program to Prevent Germany from Starting a World War III," which envisaged dividing Germany into northern and southern states, ceding to France or internationalizing Germany's western coal-industrial areas, dismantling heavy industry, and extracting large reparations from existing German resources. Roosevelt and Churchill approved this program to "convert Germany into a country primarily agricultural and pastoral," but the president retreated after the State and War departments and the British Cabinet argued that the Morgenthau Plan—or "planned chaos"—was too vengeful and that European prosperity depended upon revived German productivity.

Thus at Yalta in February 1945, Roosevelt, Churchill, and Stalin compromised. Dismemberment of Germany was left in abeyance, but that nation would be demilitarized, pay about $20 billion in reparations (with the Russians to get half) from existing resources and future production, and grant "substantial accessions" of territory to Poland, which would return former Russian territory. And France would join the Big Three on the Allied Control Council, which would determine German occupation policy.

Roosevelt's German policy toward the end of the war was neither naive nor purely vindictive. He sought both retributive justice and to respond to the Russians, whose country had been devastated but who now occupied Eastern Germany. Roosevelt hoped that German-Polish territorial transfers would redress the Soviet Union's historical-national security claims; that German reparations would provide the Russians, French, and others with compensation for war losses and security against German war potential; and that the British would resuscitate their economy by taking over Germany's former export trade. Moreover, the president would not have to ask Congress, already reluctant about Lend-Lease appropriations, for huge postwar loans for Europe.

After Yalta the State and War departments pressed Roosevelt to revise his German policy, but his last directive in March 1945—"Joint Chiefs of Staff 1067"—maintained his Yalta policy. Until his death in April 1945, therefore, President Roosevelt sought to have the Germans assume responsibility for "what they have brought upon themselves"; to secure balanced political and economic redress and security—or détente—in the Old World; and to minimize commitment of American troops and dollars to postwar Europe. Unfortunately, however, growing disputes between the United States and the Soviet Union, especially over German reparations and terms for unification, soon led to the political, economic, and military division of Germany that both symbolized and fostered the demise of the Grand Alliance and the rise of the cold war between the superpowers.

Arnold A. Offner, *American Appeasement: United States Foreign Policy and Germany, 1933–1938* (Cambridge, Mass.: Belknap Press, Harvard University Press, 1969) is the most thorough assessment of policy toward Germany. James W. Compton, *The Swastika and the Eagle: Hitler, the United States, and the Origins of World War II* (Boston: Houghton Mifflin, 1967) shows the German chancellor's disdain for America as a factor in the world balance of power. For an account of Morgenthau's proposals, which Roosevelt liked, see John M. Blum, *From the Morgenthau Diaries: Years of War, 1941–1945* (Boston: Houghton Mifflin, 1967). John L. Gaddis, in *The United States and the Origins of the Cold War, 1941–1947* (New York: Columbia University Press, 1972), says that Roosevelt was undecided between "repression" or "rehabilitation," and Diane Clemens, in *Yalta* (New York: Oxford University Press, 1970), insists that the Americans and Russians sought to compromise over Germany. Bruce Kuklick, *American Policy and the Division of Germany: The Clash with Russia over Reparations* (Ithaca, N.Y.: Cornell University Press, 1972) argues that American economic policy helped to spur the cold war division of Germany and Europe.

ARNOLD A. OFFNER

See also Axis Alliance; Fascism; Foreign Policy; Holocaust; World War II

Hobbies

See Education; Naval Collection; Ornithology; Personal Writings; Pets; Photographs; Reading; Sailing; Stamp Collecting

Holcomb, Thomas

(5 August 1879–24 May 1965)

Roosevelt's World War II commandant of the Marine Corps, who shaped his service to meet the test of amphibious combat in the Pacific. Born in New Castle, Delaware, and reared in Washington, D.C., he was a descendant of Revolutionary War naval hero Joshua Barney. His first attempt to enter the Marines—during the Spanish-American War—was rebuffed. "Youngster," the recruiting sergeant told him, "better go home and forget about the Marines—you'd never stand the gaff." Taking a clerk's job with a Baltimore

Thomas Holcomb. (Courtesy FDR Library.)

shipping firm, Holcomb persisted and two years later passed the competitive examination for direct appointment. Not quite twenty-one years of age, he was commissioned a second lieutenant in 1900.

In a service that was half seagoing light infantry and half colonial constabulary, Holcomb won early distinction as a competitive marksman and a Chinese linguist. His appointment in 1907 as a White House aide brought his first meeting with President Theodore Roosevelt's cousin, twenty-six-year-old New York attorney Franklin D. Roosevelt. A long tour in China was followed by marriage to Beatrice Miller Clover, the Washington debutante daughter of a retired admiral. He was sent to France in 1918 and commanded a battalion in the hard fighting at Belleau Wood. His "courage, skill and untiring energy" won him the Croix de Guerre, the Legion d'Honneur, and further meetings with Roosevelt, then touring the front as assistant secretary of the navy.

Thereafter, as the corps sought to develop the amphibious assault tactics essential to war plan Orange (the contingency plan for war with Japan), Holcomb attended both the Naval and Army War colleges. Preparation of this sort helped to secure his promotion to general officer's rank early in 1935. Although far down on the seniority list, he was soon chosen to succeed Maj. Gen. Commandant John H. Russell in the corps' highest office. A personal friend of Roosevelt, Russell had come to see in Tommy Holcomb the best chance for moving the Fleet Marine Force from the planning stages to actual forces, a true amphibious striking arm. As such, by 1940 *Time* magazine could characterize the corps as "the Navy's Professional Fighters"—an elite force whose ranks comprised "a small, well-integrated army" able to mount difficult seaborne assaults.

With the start of World War II, Holcomb participated, as an amphibious warfare expert, in the early strategic planning sessions of the body that would eventually become the Joint Chiefs of Staff. Perhaps the greatest test of the force he had molded came with the assault on coral-ringed Tarawa Atoll in the autumn of 1943. For although the defending Japanese managed to inflict appalling casualties on their attackers, the Marines nevertheless prevailed. As Holcomb expressed it to Roosevelt, this "was our first atoll attack and the sort of operation we have always been planning. If we can take Tarawa, we can take anything."

With the concept now tested and found workable, Holcomb retired at the end of 1943—only to be recalled as a special adviser to Secretary of the Navy Frank Knox. He was also given the four stars of a full general, the first Marine ever to achieve that rank. He served, at the instigation of Edward R. Stettinius, until 1948 as minister to the Union of South Africa. When he died at age eighty-five, it was noted that Holcomb had, twenty-five years before, presided over the final shaping of what British historian J. F. Fuller called "perhaps the most far-reaching tactical innovation" of World War II, the amphibious assault. Between 1936 and 1944, Holcomb served Roosevelt well by ensuring that the Marine Corps was prepared to conduct the assaults needed to conquer the island-bastions guarding the long sea route to Japan.

There is no satisfactory biography of Holcomb, but the *Marine Corps Gazette* 59 (November 1975):31–97, devoted much of its 200th anniversary issue to "Portraits of the Commandants," of which the Holcomb segment is useful. The standard institutional study is Allan R. Millett, *Semper Fidelis: The History of the United States Marine Corps* (New York: Macmillan Co., 1980), and the chapter in Robert W. Love, ed., *The Commandants of the Marine Corps* (Annapolis, Md.: United States Naval Institute, in press) details Holcomb's contributions to the development of that institution from 1936 to 1943. Holcomb's letters and copies of service records are lodged in the General Thomas Holcomb Collection (P.C. 107), Marine Corps Historical Center, Washington Navy Yard. Other materials are contained in the Thomas Holcomb (17th CMC) Biography File, also lodged at the Marine Corps Historical Center.

JOHN W. GORDON

Holmes, Oliver Wendell, Jr.
(8 March 1841–6 March 1935)

Supreme Court justice, 1902–32. Oliver Wendell Holmes, Jr., was born into an aristocratic Boston family in 1841. After attending Harvard from 1857 to 1861, he enlisted and fought in the Civil War until 1864 when he returned to Harvard Law School. Upon graduating, Holmes entered private practice and in 1882 was appointed to the Supreme Judicial Court of Massachusetts. Always a scholar, Holmes's well-reasoned and voluminous opinions attracted the attention of President Theodore Roosevelt, who appointed Holmes to the Supreme Court where he served until 1932.

Throughout his career he was known for his independent thinking, his insistence that the law be flexible to meet the demands of changing times, and his fierce desire for rational legal principles. Two days after his ninety-second birthday, newly elected President Franklin Roosevelt paid Holmes a visit. Roosevelt asked the aged former justice, "We face grave times. What is your advice?" Holmes, the Civil War veteran, replied, "Form your ranks and fight." Later, Holmes gave this evaluation of Roosevelt: "A second-class intellect but a first-class temperament." In 1935 when Holmes died, President Roosevelt eulogized the great legal thinker as one who had "faith in the creative possibilities of the law" and "a capacity to mold ancient principles to present needs."

An early favorable biography of Holmes is Francis Biddle, *Mr. Justice Holmes* (New York: Charles Scribner's Sons, 1942). A more balanced recent treatment is David J. Nordloh, *Oliver Wendell Holmes, Jr.* (Boston: Twayne Publishers, 1980).

Holocaust

The term *Holocaust* refers to the extermination of 6 million Jews by the Nazis during World War II. Although Adolf Hitler and the Germans rightfully de-

Although the genocide of the Jews was not fully known in the U.S. during the war, Hitler's murderous tactics had been reported. This instance of mass execution and deportation of civilians to a concentration camp was decried in an FAP poster by Ben Shahn. (Courtesy FDR Library.)

serve the blame for this slaughter, since the 1960s accusations of willful negligence and malfeasance have been hurled at Pope Pius XII, Winston Churchill, and Franklin D. Roosevelt, among others, for standing by and not using every power at hand to thwart the Nazi massacres. Roosevelt, in particular, has been chastised for failing to mobilize the American Congress to relax immigration laws, for agreeing not to ransom those European Jews who might have been saved, and for refusing to order planes to bomb the railway tracks leading to the gas chambers and crematoriums at camps like Auschwitz, Treblinka, and Buchenwald.

Formal German discrimination against Jews began after Hitler assumed power in 1933. Restrictive legislation, random beatings, and disappearances of Jews punctuated the rest of the decade, and violent and vicious attacks throughout Germany on the night of 9–10 November 1938 (*Kristallnacht*) resulted in the burning of 195 synagogues, the looting of 7,500 Jewish shops, and the destruction of more than 800 others. Before the night was out, more than 20,000 Jews had been arrested and sent to concentration camps. Roosevelt, as aghast at this onslaught as any other rational person, acknowledged that he "could scarcely believe that such things could occur in a twentieth-century civilization." But his shock did not lead to significant American action.

When the luxury liner *St. Louis*, filled with Jews escaping Germany in 1939 and bound for Cuba, reached Havana, the Cuban government informed the passengers that their landing certificates had been invalidated and refused to let them disembark. After fruitless negotiations with Cuban officials, a committee of the passengers wired Roosevelt seeking his assistance. He never responded. Since no other Ameri-

can official would sanction aid, the boat turned around and returned to Europe, which meant probable death for those on board.

Roosevelt justified his inaction on the grounds that severe American immigration legislation tied his hands. But he was also responding to existing anti-Semitism and restrictionist sentiments in the United States. Once this country entered the war, the president, until 1944, shied away from any direct intervention on behalf of European Jews, even though he heard in 1942 of Hitler's plan to wipe them out. Not until confronted by Henry Morgenthau, Jr., his secretary of the treasury, in December 1943 did the president move to thwart Hitler's diabolical actions. Then, in January 1944, Roosevelt established the War Refugee Board and provided it with a mandate to rescue all those people who might still be saved from Hitler's ovens.

No overt criticisms of Roosevelt's inaction occurred during his lifetime. In fact, the first questioning in the United States of the president's politics did not begin until journalist Arthur D. Morse published *While Six Million Died* in 1968; and even Morse focused his indictment on officials in the State Department. Thereafter, historians David S. Wyman and Henry Feingold, among others, underscored the inadequacies of the Roosevelt administration both in dealing with refugees and in not attempting to undermine Hitler's purposes. Direct attacks on Roosevelt from seasoned scholars were rare. But in commenting upon the policies that the State Department followed, Feingold observed that the "President . . . was responsible for the actions of his administration." Robert Dallek, who has written the definitive account of Roosevelt's foreign policy, tried to explain the president's position. Although acknowledging the critics' complaints, Dallek wrote:

Nazi determination to kill as many Jews as possible placed even the most ardent rescue advocates under an insurmountable constraint. The congressional restrictionists, the British, the Arabs, the Latin Americans, the Vatican, the neutrals, the exiled governments, and even the Jews themselves, divided between Zionists and non-Zionists, threw up additional direct and indirect obstacles to effective mass rescue which Roosevelt saw no way to overcome. Yet if mass rescue was out of reach, there were opportunities which Roosevelt would not take to save many thousands of lives; he saw these opportunities as destructive to the war effort. Unwilling to compromise his unconditional-surrender policy toward Germany and jeopardize Soviet confidence in his determination to fight the war to a decisive end, he rejected appeals for rescuing Jews through negotiations with Berlin. And unwilling to risk divisions at home and abroad which he thought might prolong the war, he refused to press the case for greater Jewish immigration to the United States or other parts of the world. In short, the best means he saw for saving the Jews was through the quickest possible end to the fighting—a policy of "rescue through victory."

In the 1970s some anti-Zionist zealots published articles questioning whether the Holocaust had ever occurred. The survivors of the German concentration camps and the soldiers who freed the prisoners from places like Auschwitz, Dachau, Buchenwald, Bergen-Belsen, and Treblinka could not believe that any rational or knowledgeable person could make such an assertion.

Roosevelt's Holocaust policies are detailed in Arthur D. Morse, *While Six Million Died* (New York: Random House, 1968), David S. Wyman, *Paper Walls* (Amherst: University of Massachusetts Press, 1968) and *The Abandonment of the Jews: America and the Holocaust 1941–1945* (New York: Pantheon, 1984), Henry Feingold, *The Politics of Rescue* (New Brunswick, N.J.: Rutgers University Press, 1970), and Robert Dallek, *Franklin D. Roosevelt and American Foreign Policy 1932–1945* (New York: Oxford University Press, 1979). The quote expressing Roosevelt's reaction to *Kristallnacht* is from Morse, p. 240; the quote about Roosevelt being responsible for his administration is from Henry Feingold, *Zion in America* (New York: Hippocrene Books, 1974), p. 288; the quote from Dallek's book is on pp. 447–48.

LEONARD DINNERSTEIN

See also Foreign Policy; Hitler, Adolf, and Germany; Jews; Refugees; Stimson, Henry L.; Zionism

Home Owners Loan Corporation

See Mortgage Financing

Homes

See Campobello; Hyde Park; Shangri-La; Warm Springs

Honors

See Awards; Memorials

Hoover, Herbert Clark

(10 August 1874–20 October 1964)

Roosevelt's opponent in the presidential election of 1932 and one of his most important critics, especially from 1934 to 1941. Born in West Branch, Iowa, Herbert Hoover was educated at Stanford University, graduating with a B.S. degree in 1894. He became president in 1929.

During and for a long time after the New Deal, most historians agreed that Hoover and Franklin D. Roosevelt diverged widely in their beliefs. Hoover's reputation for humanitarianism and engineering accomplishment had come into sharp question by 1932 as the nation's economy slid further into depression. Hoover's coolness toward the Bonus Army, a march on Washington by world war veterans during 1932 for early payment of pensions, turned the public against him. The presidential campaign seemed to accentuate the differences between the two men. Hoover appeared unreceptive both to fresh thinking about the nation's economic problems and even to its suffering. In a famous Madison Square Garden speech on the tariff, he warned that if FDR were elected,

"the grass will grow in streets of a hundred cities, a thousand towns; the weeds will overrun the fields of millions of farms. . . . their churches and schoolhouses will decay." It was an appeal to fear. Roosevelt's warmth and good cheer at that time may not have offered concrete solutions to the country's economic ills, but cheer and warmth were what the public needed and perhaps what the economy psychologically needed. Hoover's sensitivity to criticism kept him from abandoning his own stale ideas about the tariff and the gold standard, and his pride made it hard for him to appreciate Roosevelt's political skill and to cooperate with him during the interregnum between Roosevelt's victory and his ascension to the presidency.

Hoover in his vociferous attacks on the New Deal, after a two-year virtual silence, contributed to the image of him as a reactionary and a heartless friend of wealth. *The Challenge to Liberty* (1934) and the several volumes of *Addresses upon the American Road* (1938-), certainly at first reading, argue for an individualism that seemed largely irrelevant to the needs of a suffering nation.

In 1948 Richard Hofstadter was almost alone in noting in *The American Political Tradition and the Men Who Made It* that Hoover and Roosevelt had been reared on much the same economic and social philosophy. Recent writers have rediscovered Hoover's progressivism, and some now stress the conservative side of Roosevelt. Both men in fact had been young progressive protégés of Woodrow Wilson in the era of World War I: Hoover served as the head of the Commission for Relief of Belgium from 1914 to 1919 and as food administrator in the United States after its entry into the war, as well as director general of the postwar American Relief Administration. Roosevelt, Wilson's assistant secretary of the navy, urged that Hoover be the Democratic presidential candidate in 1920. Hoover as a businessman argued for enlightened policies—for example, toward labor unions. His humanitarianism was not only morally impressive but innovative; he gathered resources and administered their distribution with a skill in organization that also made him a champion of economic collectivity. As secretary of commerce he worked for various goals, among them the standardization of weights and sizes, associated with that side of progressivism that demanded efficiency and expertise. And as president, Hoover tilted slightly to the Left, instituting improved welfare programs for such groups as Indians and prisoners. He relied particularly on the device (which the Left of the 1960s would speak for in other forms) of spontaneous and voluntary communal action. Typical of Hoover were his conferences examining education or child welfare and programs encouraging farm cooperatives.

His floundering from November 1932 to March 1933 makes it easy to overlook what Hoover had in common with Roosevelt. The banking legislation passed in March 1932, for example, was largely drafted by departing members of the Hoover administration. And it is only a quick reading of the anti-Roosevelt *Challenge to Liberty* and the first volume

Herbert Clark Hoover, 1931. Artist: Douglas Chandor. (National Portrait Gallery, Smithsonian Institution.)

of *Addresses upon the American Road* that makes Hoover appear so implacably hostile to public welfare. What preoccupied Hoover, as it has come to preoccupy some liberals and radicals since, was unrestrained growth in federal and presidential power, along with the impersonality of overcentralized administration severed from the community and its voluntary initiatives.

In his private letters, Hoover vented his opinions on New Deal legislation. He wrote of the "tyranny" of the National Recovery Administration (NRA) and noted that its "demagogue" leader, Gen. Hugh Johnson, had the faults of a "typical West Pointer." The NRA codes, he wrote, "are ruinous to [character-building] small business and favor big business," which, he said, was being exempted from prosecution under the Sherman Antitrust Act. The NRA was "Fascistic." So was the Civilian Conservation Corps: "I find that the military officers in one of these camps think they are laying plans for a new military arm of government." The Agricultural Adjustment Administration, too, was "fascist," resembling the agricultural programs of Mussolini and Hitler. It was also a blow at sharecroppers and consumers, and its personnel were "totalitarian liberals." With consistency, however, Hoover termed the end of Prohibition a victory for freedom. And he refused to join the conservative Liberty League ("as to liberty of the Wall Street model, I am not for it"). More astonishing is Hoover's remark to Thomas E. Dewey that he would have signed practically all the New Deal legislation.

Where Hoover and Roosevelt came into conflict had much to do with circumstances and personality. Earlier in the century, it had been Hoover rather than Roosevelt who spoke repeatedly on the national stage for political progressivism, not because he was in fact more progressive than Roosevelt but because he was more prominent.

During the 1932 campaign, Roosevelt called for a cut of 25 percent in the federal budget, which was an understandable position to take when the advantages of massive government spending had not yet revealed themselves. Hoover, the president at the beginning of the depression, was identifiable with that disaster in a way that Roosevelt could not be, and his responses to it, which involved more government relief than the nation had ever before spent, were more halting than Roosevelt's largely because they were the first responses. Roosevelt's personality, along with a feeling for politics that Hoover had never acquired, made everything that he did seem energetic, compassionate, and fresh. Some of the programs later incorporated into the New Deal came too slowly or at the nudging of advisers, and some historians have claimed that the labor movement virtually forced itself on Roosevelt's attention, much as the civil rights movement would later compel the federal government to notice it.

Yet Roosevelt, responding to pressures that would ultimately have moved a reelected Hoover toward more activism, did bring government and the American community more closely and intimately together than had ever been the case before. Hoover

J. Edgar Hoover. (Constant Collection. Courtesy FDR Library.)

was at least partially wrong in his fear of government impersonality. Roosevelt's charm, his energy, his political skills so alien to Hoover tightened the connections still further. In a sense, therefore, Roosevelt was the conservative in that larger meaning of the word that some critics are now recovering, wherein it means something other than the thinking of the Republican Right.

In one particular, Hoover's thought was clearly close to that of much of earlier twentieth-century progressivism than was Roosevelt's. He opposed American entry into World War II until Pearl Harbor, continuing an isolationism that had once bespoken the progressive belief that this country should preserve its own advanced institutions and not risk their ensnarement in the politics of the Old World. Wars, moreover, "breed despotism": one reason he opposed war, he wrote in a letter to a friend, "is the necessity to adopt Fascism to win wars." But twentieth-century internationalism also came out of the progressive tradition, and it was Roosevelt's lot to be president at a time when that strain within progressivism needed to emerge most strongly. During the war, Hoover's Wilsonian strain reasserted itself; he wrote two books that looked forward optimistically, *The Problems of Lasting Peace* (1942) and *The Basis of Lasting Peace* (1945). Hoover outlived his old adversary by nearly twenty years, dying in 1964.

The three major biographies of Hoover are Joan Hoff Wilson, *Herbert Hoover* (Boston: Little, Brown & Co., 1974); David Burner, *Herbert Hoover: A Public Life* (New York: Alfred A. Knopf, 1979); and George Nash, *The Life of Herbert Hoover: The Engineer, 1874–1914* (New York: W. W. Norton, 1983). Nash's book is the first of a planned three volumes. A fourth study of particular interest to students of the New Deal is a two-volume publication on Hoover's postpresidential career: Gary Dean Best, *Herbert Hoover: The Postpresidential Years, 1933–1964* (Stanford, Calif.: Hoover Institution, 1983).

DAVID BURNER

See also Conservatism; Democratic Party; Election of 1928; Elections in the Roosevelt Era; Great Depression; Hundred Days; Interregnum; Liberalism and Progressivism; Relief; Republican Party

Hoover, John Edgar
(1 January 1895–2 May 1972)

J. Edgar Hoover, born the third child of an ordinary Washington family of civil servants, held more power for a longer period of time than any comparable figure in American public life. If a handful of the administrative czars who presided over the various fiefdoms of the federal government's bureaucratic empire have rivaled Hoover's discipline and resourcefulness, none has matched him in staying power. From his appointment to the directorship of the Bureau of Investigation in 1924 to his death in 1972, Hoover led the conservative and virtually unaccountable Federal Bureau of Investigation (FBI) on crusades against the machine-gun-toting gangsters and native fascist saboteurs of the 1930s, the cold war dissidents and Red agents of the 1940s and 1950s, and the antiwar and civil rights activists of the 1960s. Hoover was not simply a bureaucrat but a national hero, a guardian of the cultural order who stood between the "real America" and the anarchy of crime or the totalitarianism of communism. As Hoover's body lay in state in the Capitol rotunda, President Richard M. Nixon eulogized the FBI director as "a legend in his own time. For millions [of Americans] he was a symbol of the values he cherished most: courage, patriotism, dedication to country, and a granite-like honesty and integrity."

For his transformation from obscure bureaucrat to national hero, Hoover owed a debt to the help of Franklin D. Roosevelt and the New Deal. The Roosevelt administration encouraged Hoover's efforts to build a reputation of invincibility for the bureau and did not object to his efforts to construct what became a cult around himself as part of the New Deal program to federalize crime control. By the time President Roosevelt's first term ended, the G-man image had taken root, with Hoover presiding over a thriving federal bureaucracy complete with an aggressive public relations division. From there, Hoover, a one-time indexer at the Library of Congress, expanded his authority through a series of unilateral bureaucratic reforms designed to enhance the FBI's autonomy. These reforms created a hierarchical internal decision-making process while restricting outside access to bureau records—with the use of document destruction procedures, phony paper records, "Do Not File" files, and other separate filing systems to ensure that the most sensitive records would be inaccessible even to the FBI director's ostensible superiors.

In addition to such institutional reforms, Hoover consolidated his authority by performing political tasks at the request of powerful Americans. White House use and abuse of the FBI's domestic intelligence resources, for example, became a more or less regular part of the governing process during the New Deal and World War II eras. In 1941 Vincent Astor, then head of a covert intelligence operation mandated by President Roosevelt and operating out of New York City, forwarded a White House request for such assistance through the FBI's New York office. When later rebuking Astor for not submitting this request directly to FBI headquarters in Washington, Hoover (in a memorandum dated 5 July 1941 in Louis B. Nichols Unserialized Official and Confidential FBI Files, J. Edgar Hoover Building, Washington, D.C.) outlined the correct procedure:

> A thing like that ought not be given directly to our New York Office. As a matter of fact if you'd called me or called Washington in the first instance I would have arranged to put a special on right away; in other words, I would have had somebody probably fly from Washington by plane so that nobody in our New York Office would necessarily know about it. . . . A story like this if it got out by chance would just be terribly embarrassing to the big boss. It's a kind of a case that we usually handle in a little different way.

The FBI's intelligence-gathering resources, public relations machinery, and conscious attempts to accumulate political capital by servicing the needs of every Oval Office occupant from Franklin Roosevelt to Richard Nixon help explain J. Edgar Hoover's remarkable forty-eight-year reign. Hoover's career was a mixture of bureaucratic genius, Madison Avenue wizardry, and tireless pursuit of independent political objectives. The FBI director did not succeed simply because he symbolized values held dear by many Americans and knew how to promote himself, whether as the wise sage of law and order or as anticommunist crusader. He succeeded also because he understood power and was not unduly burdened by legal, constitutional, or moral constraints when in pursuit of the bureau's interest.

Two major biographies of Hoover are currently being prepared. Until they are published, the most complete sources of information on the FBI director will remain Ovid Demaris, *The Director: An Oral Biography of J. Edgar Hoover* (New York: Harper's Magazine Press, 1975) and Ralph de Toledano, *J. Edgar Hoover: The Man in His Time* (New Rochelle, N.Y.: Arlington House, 1973). The memoirs of former bureau personnel should also be consulted. See especially William C. Sullivan with Bill Brown, *The Bureau: My Thirty Years in Hoover's FBI* (New York: Norton, 1979) and the whimsical account of life in the bureau provided by Joseph L. Schott, *No Left Turns* (New York: Praeger, 1975). Frank J. Donner, *The Age of Surveillance* (New York: Alfred A. Knopf, 1980) has written an excellent chapter on Hoover ("The Lengthened Shadow of a Man," pp. 79–125), and Kenneth O'Reilly, *Hoover and the Un-Americans: The FBI, HUAC, and the Red Menace* (Philadelphia: Temple University Press, 1983) explores the FBI director's half-century pursuit of communists and other dissidents.

KENNETH O'REILLY

See also Espionage; Federal Bureau of Investigation

Hopkins, Harry L.
(17 August 1890–29 January 1946)

Hopkins, with his penetrating mind, his knack for knowing President Franklin D. Roosevelt's preferred decisions, his ability to implement them, and his length of close association with Roosevelt was surely the most valuable of FDR's many officials during the years of the Great Depression and World War II.

The American town in a midwestern rural setting, a small liberal arts college, and parents of contrasting personalities and interests forged the character and personality of Harry Hopkins. As he observed later after several years of colorful, eventful service as a top-level administrator in our nation's capitol, when "you grow up in a household with your father and mother and brothers and sisters, go to Sunday School perhaps, to grade school and high school and someway get yourself through college, you are made. That's you." Hopkins carried with him both the devotion to people of his mother and the pranksterism of his father. In addition, stimulating professors in the social and political sciences at Grinnell College in

Harry L. Hopkins. (Constant Collection. Courtesy FDR Library.)

Iowa taught Hopkins that people and institutions had an impact on one another. Hopkins believed government belonged to the people, and the people had both the opportunity and the responsibility to make the relationship work.

Arriving in New York City in 1912, following visits to the Republican and Democratic National conventions and working in a summer camp for deprived youth, Hopkins soon learned firsthand of poverty, starvation, bitterness toward established government, inadequate health care for the needy, and the tensions of racial mixtures. From 1912 into the year 1931, Hopkins's professions were those of social worker (1912–18), Red Cross administrator (1918–21), and director of health agencies (1921–31). Throughout these years he was sincerely interested in the poor, in those suffering from ill-health, and in liberals striving through government to diminish the negative aspects of a capitalistic society. He was instrumental in enlarging the activities of the Tuberculosis Association to encompass the New York Heart Association, the Children's Welfare Federation, the Allied Dental Clinic, and the Associated Out-Patient Clinic. Hopkins was also instrumental in forming a group that developed a means to eliminate silica dust from enclosed excavation projects.

During these years Hopkins was an "ulcerous type"—a chain smoker, a heavy drinker of coffee, restless, pushing to help the unfortunate. He placed response to need first, the securing of funds second. As the number of unemployed increased in the late twenties, Hopkins devoted much time and energy to assisting the unemployed and their families.

In 1928 while struggling to find answers to complex social problems and amid marriage difficulties, Hopkins visited England where he learned more about the life of his favorite poet, Keats, and studied the health and relief agencies of England and life among the low-income population in London's East End. From the depth of these personal struggles came a decision to divorce and remarry.

In 1931 Governor Franklin D. Roosevelt named Harry Hopkins to be head of the New York Temporary Relief Agency. Hopkins met the challenge with zeal, determination, and a philosophy consistent with that of Governor Roosevelt, who stated that government must fulfill the duty of "caring for those of its citizens" who become victims of adverse circumstances so severe "they cannot provide for themselves the basic necessities of life."

Hopkins did not believe the American democratic and capitalistic systems should let people live "in misery" and conditions of "rock-bottom" destitution, or allow hunger among children. America could do better. Every man in the United States, emphasized Hopkins, should "have access to the opportunity to provide for himself and his family a decent and American way of living." President Roosevelt turned to Hopkins in the spring of 1933 to organize public relief on a national scale.

Hopkins was a doer, who sought new ideas and detested red tape. He cared little for the management structure of charts and boxes. Hopkins was sympathetic to the poor, but "hard-boiled," nevertheless, and sarcastic toward many of his critics. He drove himself at his work day after day, with only occasional breaks for a day at the race tracks or an evening with friends. Described by several observers as a "bundle of nervous energy," he responded directly and forcefully to reporter's questions.

Although he was filled with visions and hope for a better America, Hopkins was not a visionary. Rather he was a practical analyzer seeking means to feed, to clothe, to provide health care, to employ. In the later years of his career, Prime Minister Winston Churchill referred to him as "Lord Root of the matter." President Roosevelt soon learned that Hopkins was to be trusted.

During the years 1933–38, Hopkins administered the Federal Emergency Relief Administration, the Civil Works Administration, the Federal Surplus Relief Administration, and the Works Progress Administration, and assisted in the management of aid for transients and the National Youth Administration. These were controversial agencies, and Hopkins had many supporters and active critics. Typical of several colorful exchanges between Hopkins and his critics was the one with the former governor of New York, Al Smith. Smith characterized the Civil Works Administration with these words: "Halfway between a lemon and an orange is a grapefruit" and "Halfway between a public work and a relief work is a civil work." To which Hopkins replied, "If putting 4 million men back to work means going into the grapefruit business, then I'm delighted to be in it."

By 1938 Hopkins's ill-health prevented him from continuing as relief administrator. He suffered intensely from stomach and digestive disorders that were never fully alleviated. He was fatigued and disheartened by the death of his second wife, Barbara Duncan, in 1937. To some extent he had become discouraged by criticism and the failure of the economy to revive. Intellectually and emotionally he sought new adventures and horizons. Roosevelt named him secretary of commerce in December 1938, but his health allowed him to be in his office only a few weeks in nearly a year and a half. It was during 1938–39 that Hopkins let some of his friends and staff support him as a possible presidential candidate in 1940, but he later regretted this activity, recognizing it as a shadow on his career.

Having proved to President Roosevelt that he was "utterly trustworthy," but able to criticize the president in conversation, Hopkins became Roosevelt's man for counsel and assistance with various projects during World War II. In the early years of World War II, Hopkins's office was in the White House, and he and his daughter Diane lived there.

The first major diplomatic task Hopkins performed for FDR was a crucial visit to England in January 1941 at a time when the president wanted more accurate reports on equipment and supplies needed by England. He also determined the appropriateness of a personal meeting between the president and Prime Minister Winston Churchill. Churchill noted that Hopkins "was a crumbling lighthouse [referring to Hopkins's health] from which there shone the beams that lead great fleets to harbours."

In the spring of 1941 Hopkins became the head of Lend-Lease, this nation's gigantic effort to provide supplies and equipment to countries fighting against the Axis powers. He encouraged FDR to be more aggressive and to use more naval power for protecting Lend-Lease goods being shipped across the Atlantic Ocean. Hopkins met frequently with Gen. George C. Marshall to explore the overall war strategy.

Shortly after Germany attacked Russia in June 1941, Hopkins returned to England to pinpoint the type and extent of U.S. military aid that would be needed for an attack against Germany on the European mainland. From England he went to Russia where he learned from Joseph Stalin that if Russia were provided equipment and war supplies, it could probably avoid defeat by Germany. When he returned to America, Hopkins found means to ship war materials to the USSR.

After meeting with Stalin, Hopkins traveled home via England, stopping to brief Churchill on his meeting with Stalin. He returned to American waters on the British battleship *Prince of Wales* so he could be present for the first meeting between President Roosevelt and the prime minister. At this time, some observed that Hopkins was so ill they doubted he would live to make his report to Roosevelt. Hopkins rallied, though, and actively participated in several of the discussions. These activities in the summer of 1941 were some of the most valuable in his entire career.

In 1942 and 1943 Hopkins attended the conferences of the Allied leaders at Cairo, Teheran, and Casablanca. Between these meetings, one of the difficult tasks Roosevelt assigned Hopkins was the cajoling of Madame Chiang Kai-shek, telling her on more than one occasion of the need to postpone aid to China because of the more immediate demands of the European military preparations. At the Teheran meeting, Hopkins pressed Churchill particularly hard, finally forcing the prime minister to support a cross-channel invasion of France in 1944. As Charles Bohlen has stated, Hopkins's role "was paramount" in the military agreements worked out at the 1943 Teheran Conference, and Robert Sherwood wrote that the conference "represented the peak" in Hopkins's career. Shortly after the conference, Hopkins again became seriously ill and was out of action for nearly seven months. It was during this time that he learned that his son Stephen had been killed in military action at Kwajalein. All three of Hopkins's sons served in the military forces in World War II.

Hopkins was not active during the 1944 presidential campaign. His contact with Roosevelt was slight during the fall except for comments in opposition to Secretary of Treasury Henry Morgenthau's postwar plans for Germany. By January 1945, however, Roosevelt needed Hopkins again for a major overseas assignment. Hopkins left for England where he reviewed with British and American military leaders global war plans and general concepts for peace with Germany. Then he met with French officials in France, visited the pope in Rome, and toured American military forces in Italy. By the time he finished these strenuous activities, Hopkins was again quite ill. Nevertheless, he continued on to the Crimea Sea area to participate in the Yalta Conference in February 1945.

Hopkins remained in his own quarters, frequently working with the American staff, during most of the conference except for the major plenary sessions and a few dinner meetings. He assisted Roosevelt in warding off many of the Russian demands by suggesting useful compromises. Hopkins was not a naive negotiator at Yalta, although, contrary to subsequent events, he thought Stalin would keep his word on major agreements. He never doubted, however, that Stalin's overriding concern was to keep Russia in a dominant position in Europe.

Within several days of the Yalta Conference, Hopkins was suffering intense pain and chose to return to America by plane rather than with Roosevelt on the USS *Quincy*. The two men never saw each other again. Hopkins was recuperating at the Mayo Clinic in Rochester, Minnesota, when he learned of Roosevelt's death on 12 April 1945.

Hopkins resigned from his government post in early May 1945 after sharing insights and information with the new president, Harry Truman, but by 23 May he was on his way to Moscow at the request of the president. Shortly after the San Francisco Conference to formulate a new world organization commenced, it seemed doomed to failure: top British and Russian delegates had returned home. Hopkins's tasks were to convince Stalin to adjust Russia's attitudes on Poland, control of Germany, and voting rights in the new peace organization and to ensure

Baer, Roslindale *(Mass.)* News, *c. 1936.*

that Russia would move against Japan. After six meetings with Stalin, Hopkins returned to America, having assisted in the completion of the San Francisco Conference, the seating of a Russian representative on the War Council for Germany, and the calling of the Potsdam Conference of Truman, Stalin, and Churchill.

President Truman awarded Harry Hopkins the Distinguished Service Medal on September 1945. Hopkins hoped to be in England in October 1945 to receive from Oxford University the honorary degree of D.C.L., but he was too ill to travel. He died finally in 1946 of hemochromatosis, the result of an inadequate digestive system.

The most useful secondary resources on Harry L. Hopkins include Robert E. Sherwood, *Roosevelt and Hopkins: An Intimate History* (New York: Harper & Bros., 1948), Searle F. Charles, *Minister of Relief: Harry Hopkins and the Depression* (Syracuse: Syracuse University Press, 1963), and Henry W. Adams, *Harry Hopkins: A Biography* (New York: Putnam Co., 1977). The personal and government-related papers of Harry Hopkins are housed in the Franklin D. Roosevelt Library, Hyde Park, New York.

SEARLE F. CHARLES

See also Atlantic Conference and Charter; Federal Emergency Relief Administration; Relief

House Committee for the Investigation of Un-American Activities

Although not to become infamous until after FDR's death, the Special House Committee for the Investi-

The argument over whether a Federal Theatre Project play, Revolt of the Beavers, *was a typical fairy tale or Marxism veiled as Mother Goose reached the floor of Congress, when the play became prime evidence for the House Un-American Activities Committee in its inquiry into alleged Communist control of the FTP. (Courtesy the Library of Congress Federal Theatre Project Collection at George Mason University Library, Fairfax, Virginia.)*

gation of Un-American Activities (HUAC), under the leadership of Martin Dies of Texas, was a constant thorn in the side of the New Deal. Ironically authorized by the House on 26 May 1938 to investigate profascist organizations in the United States, the committee quickly turned its investigatory spotlight on various left-wing groups. Throughout his seven years as committee chairman, Dies used its power against two groups in American society—leftist political activists and immigrant organizations. Using smear tactics later perfected by Senator McCarthy, Dies announced "investigations" of prominent liberal organizations, accused government officials of "shielding" Communists, and publicly labeled many immigrants "known socialists" after their identification by dubious expert witnesses.

HUAC first attacked the Roosevelt administration in a series of hearings that resulted in the ending of funding for the Federal Writers' Project in the summer of 1938 and the Federal Theatre Project in the summer of 1939. The committee then objected to the failure of Labor Secretary Perkins to deport Harry Bridges, the West Coast labor leader. Dies next led the committee into an investigation of Michigan governor Frank Murphy's handling of the sit-down strikes in automobile plants. HUAC's published conclusions that Murphy, a staunch FDR supporter, had been duped by Communists during the strike contributed to his defeat in the 1938 elections.

With the weakening of Roosevelt's power in Congress after 1938, Dies's attacks on the New Deal increased. Dies, relying on the expertise of J. B. Matthews, a reformed Communist, began to replace full-scale hearings with special sessions, scheduled at a moment's notice and often attended only by Dies, the witness, and the always alerted press. In 1940, HUAC investigated subversive influences in Hollywood, labor unions, and the munitions industry.

The committee's power declined during the war. Its last major investigation was of the internment of Japanese-Americans in California after Pearl Harbor. The committee praised life in the camps as "wonderful," but wondered why some of the inmates had been released.

In 1944 Dies announced he would not seek reelection. Although some politicians hoped that his retirement would ensure the disappearance of the committee, in January of 1945 Mississippi congressman John Rankin succeeded in reestablishing the committee.

The best account of HUAC under Dies is August Raymond Ogden's *The Dies Committee*, 2d ed. (Washington: Catholic University of America Press, 1945). Walter Goodman's *The Committee* (New York: Farrar, Straus & Giroux, 1968) is less scholarly but lively reading. Martin Dies's autobiography, *The Martin Dies Story* (New York: Bookmailer, 1963) is self-serving drivel.

See also Fascism

Housing and Resettlement

The New Deal marked a turning point in the history of moderate- and low-income housing in the United States. The public housing programs of the 1930s, which became a permanent activity under the Wagner Housing Act of 1937, brought the United States into the field of subsidized low-income housing—an area in which the nations of Europe had been active for many years. The New Deal community-building projects, namely the rural resettlement projects and the suburban greenbelt towns, were pioneering efforts that for a short time made the United States a world leader in these areas.

FDR had been a supporter of subsidized public housing as governor of New York and continued to aid housing reformers in formulating a permanent housing program at the federal level. The president and his wife Eleanor took a great personal interest in the suburban and rural community projects, since both of them believed urban life for low-income families was destructive. They thought rural families should be allowed to remain in the country village atmosphere and were willing to support limited experiments in resettling low-income city dwellers in cooperative rural communities. Although the president and his wife drew a great deal of public attention in the 1930s for their endorsement of these back-to-the-land projects, the overwhelming bulk of New Deal funds spent on housing was targeted to urban areas. As governor of the Empire State, FDR had worked with New York City's housing reformers, who were among the leading experts in the world in the area of low-income housing. Many of them played a central role in the development of the federal housing program, and New York's senator Robert F. Wagner was

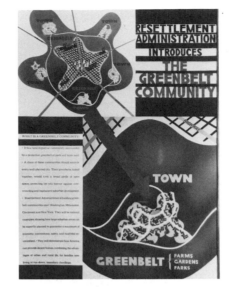

WHAT IS A GREENBELT COMMUNITY?
• It is a rural industrial community, surrounded by a protective greenbelt of park and farm land.
• A chain of these communities should encircle every well-planned city. Their green belts, linked together, would form a broad girdle of open space, protecting the city forever against over-crowding and haphazard suburban development.
• Resettlement Administration is building green-belt communities near Washington, Milwaukee, Cincinnati, and New York. They will be national examples, showing how large suburban areas can be expertly planned to guarantee a maximum of economy, convenience, safety, and healthful environment. They will demonstrate how America can provide decent homes, combining the advantages of urban and rural life, for families now living in run-down, insanitary dwellings.

the man most responsible for the United States Housing Act of 1937.

The housing concerns of the nation received prompt attention from the Roosevelt administration in 1933. In May of that year FDR signed the Emergency Farm Mortgage Act to protect farms and farm homes from foreclosure; the following month he signed the Home Owners Loan Corporation Act to protect urban dwellings. These temporary emergency laws were followed in 1934 by the National Housing Act of 27 June 1934, the landmark piece of legislation in the history of American home financing. The act created the Federal Housing Administration (FHA), which guaranteed home mortgage loans made by savings and loan institutions. It had a major impact on urban home ownership, which expanded from 46 percent in 1930 to 65 percent in 1980. Prior to the FHA law, home ownership was limited largely to the middle and upper classes, but the reduction in down payments from 30 percent to 10 percent and the extension of repayment time from twenty to thirty years now made home ownership feasible for millions of moderate-income Americans. In addition, the written minimum standards code of the FHA, enforced by on-site inspection, ensured purchasers against jerry-built houses—a widespread problem in the construction of moderate-income dwellings.

For those too poor to purchase a home, the New Deal launched a large program of subsidized housing in urban slums. Title II of the National Industrial Recovery Act provided for the construction of public housing in cities with demonstrated needs. Although

Urban housing problems were explored in a volatile play performed by the Federal Theatre Project, One Third of a Nation. *The drama provided careful documentation of the effects of slum life on American families. This play, Eleanor Roosevelt argued, achieved immortality and served a vital role in the "education and growing-up of America."* (Courtesy the Library of Congress Federal Theatre Project Collection at George Mason University Library, Fairfax, Virginia.)

only about 22,000 housing units were built under this program, it sparked thirty-one states to pass housing enabling legislation and galvanized housing leaders throughout the nation to work for a permanent housing act. The Housing Division of the Public Works Administration (PWA) surveyed substandard housing in America's cities and showed that small cities and towns as well as New York's Lower East Side were desperately in need of minimum standard affordable housing for its low-income residents.

The investigations of the PWA Housing Division aroused many public interest groups, particularly organized labor, and the PWA projects brought housing officials together, giving them valuable firsthand experience in the planning and administration of public housing projects. These groups, led by Senator Robert Wagner, pushed through Congress the U.S. Housing Act of 1937 with the support of President Roosevelt. The act provided for federally funded, locally administered housing projects to be built in conjunction with slum clearance programs. By the end of 1940, there were 334 projects completed or under construction involving 118,045 housing units at a cost of slightly over $549 million.

The rural housing and community program of the New Deal was also funded initially out of the National Industrial Recovery Act of 1933, but involved the construction of only about 8,000 housing units in ninety-six rural "communities," ranging in size from 11 to 294 units with over two-thirds under 100 units. The program was begun under the Subsistence Homesteads Division of the Interior Department, was transferred in 1935 to Rexford Tugwell's Resettlement Administration, and was lodged finally in the Farm Security Administration where it remained until the program was liquidated shortly after World War II. Most of the rural communities were completed in 1937 and 1938 just as congressional opponents of the New Deal were solidifying their strength. Consequently, the critical early years of their housing, cooperative farming, and small-scale manufacturing programs were seriously compromised by budget cuts, by highly publicized congressional investiga-

Housing and resettlement programs flourished under several New Deal umbrellas, including the Farm Security Administration. Here a family stands before their new house in Longview Homesteads, an FSA development in Washington, September 1935. (Courtesy FDR Library.)

tions, and finally by World War II itself. While projects like Arthurdale, West Virginia, a particular favorite of Eleanor Roosevelt and Louis Howe, proved extremely expensive and only marginally successful, others such as Jersey Homesteads near Hightstown, New Jersey, fared better. Jersey Homesteads was established by the Resettlement Administration at the behest of a group of idealistic Jewish garment workers from New York City who hoped to build a community supported by mutally owned garment factories and cooperative agricultural enterprises. The factories failed, the cooperative farm struggled to survive, but the community itself was very successful. Changing its name to Roosevelt, New Jersey, after its sale by the federal government in 1945, it survives today as a small, happy, close-knit cooperative community.

Without a doubt, the most striking and successful housing and community experiment of the New Deal was the suburban greenbelt town program of the Resettlement Administration. Three of them were constructed: Greenbelt, Maryland, outside Washington, D.C.; Greenhills, Ohio, outside Cincinnati; and Greendale, Wisconsin, outside Milwaukee. Drawing on the British garden city tradition, but following more closely the planning concepts embodied in the model suburban town of Radburn, New Jersey, the greenbelt towns made the United States, for a brief moment, the world's leading new town planner. Surrounded by a greenbelt of agricultural land (from which they drew their names), the three towns demonstrated the advantages of building complete suburban towns rather than patchwork uncoordinated housing projects. Communitywide preplanning ensured an efficient and attractive land use pattern and allowed the development of neighborhood units, the separation of pedestrian and automobile thoroughfares, and many other features that have become standard elements in all subsequent new towns and larger suburban subdivisons. Although the three projects were criticized by anti–New Dealers for their supposed high cost and "socialistic" features (like cooperative retail stores), they proved to be an outstanding success for their original moderate-income tenants. Federal sale of the towns in 1952–53 allowed their expansion by private builders, and they are thriving, sought-after places of residence at the present time. Housing and planning experts from all over the world still regularly visit them.

It can be seen that the four major New Deal programs in the area of housing and community building were developed separately and that each has fared differently in terms of its influence and the judgment of critics. The rural community program, aimed at the poorest segment of American society in a rapidly declining sector of the national economy, accomplished the least amount of tangible good for the generation of the 1930s, but it provided a vast and unique body of data on rural cooperative living. The greenbelt towns, although they failed to attract sufficient political support to become a permanent federal program, were clearly the most influential and imaginative housing and community projects ever built by the federal government. The low-rent slum-clearance housing program, aimed largely at the nation's established cities and towns, was not as innovative as the community projects, but it alone became a permanent feature of the federal home building effort. In an indirect fashion, the FHA program has improved the housing conditions of low-income urban residents by allowing moderate-income families to move into new (or newer) homes, which in turn opened large numbers of housing units to low-income persons. Thus, although this is not a very socially responsible or economically efficient manner in which to provide low-income housing, the FHA program has, in the absence of a larger direct construction effort, been an important factor in the expansion of the low-income housing supply.

The fundamental contribution of the New Deal to the progress of American housing was to establish in law the principle that the federal government, under its obligation to provide for the general welfare, had a duty "to remedy the . . . acute shortage of decent, safe and sanitary dwellings for families of low income . . . that are injurious to the health, safety, and morals of the citizens of the Nation." These words, from the preamble of the 1937 Wagner Housing Act, continue to express the major goal of the nation's low-income housing policies almost half a century later.

There is no complete history of the New Deal housing and community programs, but Mark I. Gelfand's *A Nation of Cities: The Federal Government and Urban America, 1933–1965* (New York: Oxford University Press, 1975) provides a rather full discussion. The most recent study of the policies of the HOLC and the FHA, focusing on their discriminatory policies rather than their positive contributions, is Kenneth T. Jackson, "Race, Ethnicity, and Real Estate Appraisal: The Home Owners Loan Corporation and the Federal Housing Administration," *Journal of Urban History* 6 (August 1980):419–52. The best brief survey of housing conditions in the 1930s is Edith Elmer Wood, *Slums and Blighted Areas in the United States* (PWA Housing Division Bulletin No. 1, 1936; reprint, College Park, Md.: McGrath Publishing Co., 1969). The standard history of the PWA activities and the background of the U.S. Housing Act of 1937 is Timothy McDonnell, *The Wagner Housing Act* (Chicago: Loyola University Press, 1957). The best study of the rural communities is Paul K. Conkin, *Tomorrow a New World: The New Deal Community Program* (Ithaca, N.Y.: Cornell University Press, 1959); Joseph L. Arnold, *The New Deal in the Suburbs: A History of the Greenbelt Town Program, 1935–1954* (Columbus: Ohio State University Press, 1971) is the standard history of the greenbelt towns. There are numerous studies of federal housing programs in individual cities. One of the best (and certainly the most important since it deals with New York City and with people who came to dominate the federal programs) is Anthony Jackson, *A Place Called Home: A History of Low-Cost Housing in Manhattan* (Cambridge, Mass.: MIT Press, 1976).

JOSEPH L. ARNOLD

See also Mortgage Financing; Public Works Administration; Tugwell, Rexford Guy

Howe, Louis McHenry
(14 January 1871–18 April 1936)

Louis Howe at Democratic campaign headquarters in New York, 1932. (Courtesy FDR Library.)

Louis Howe was Franklin Roosevelt's most important adviser and aide before 1928. He remained a significant principal on Roosevelt's staff until his death near the end of the president's first term. Howe mastered the role of "man behind the scenes." Although he was proud and ambitious, he recognized that he could exercise power and gain public reputation only as an aide to some more charismatic public figure. A plain, unattractive little man, he became indispensable to FDR, because he could never be a threat. Only Harry L. Hopkins, later in the presidency, reached the same level of intimacy with Roosevelt. Ghostwriter, strategist, adviser, and daily companion to Franklin Roosevelt for more than twenty-two years, Howe could say no to his friend, could argue with him strenuously, but could never control him.

Louis Howe was born in Indianapolis in 1871, the child of Edward Porter Howe, a Civil War veteran and journalist, and of Eliza Blake Ray. The elder Howe was chronically unsuccessful in Indiana and later in Saratoga Springs, New York. Louis grew up there, moving freely among the small-town residents and the wealthy, worldy patrons of the Saratoga racing season. After graduation from the local high school, he went to work immediately in his father's print shop and helped write their weekly Democratic newspaper, the *Sun*. He also worked as a stringer for city newspapers during the racing season. He added to both income and political connections after 1906 as a back-up reporter in Albany for the *New York Herald* during the annual legislative sessions. The *Sun* and its print shop were driven out of business by 1900.

Meanwhile, in 1899, Howe had married Grace Hartley, daughter of a substantial Fall River, Massachusetts, family, whom he had met at one of the Saratoga summer hotels. Their first child, Mary, was born in 1900. A son, Hartley Edward, was born in 1911.

Howe was drawn early toward a career in political staff work. He could not make a living as a freelance reporter and was always desperately short of money. His wife spent long periods with her mother back in Massachusetts, as Louis tried to establish a regular career and reliable income. He began to see that what he had learned by watching politicians and businessmen at the racetrack and the state house could be put to work for one of those politicians. Louis was moderately progressive in his views, Democratic by family and habit, but his real passion was getting things done for "his" man. He saw himself as an expert at creating successful politicians.

By 1906 he was on the payroll of Thomas Mott Osborne, an Auburn, New York, mayor who led an anti-Tammany Democratic League and who had gubernatorial ambitions. Louis taught himself his new trade by handling Osborne's political affairs and scrambling to remain on the payroll. Osborne was not easily satisfied, and he dropped Howe in 1909.

But Louis watched with excitement the insurgency the new Hudson Valley senator Franklin D. Roosevelt led in the 1911 session of the general assembly. Louis got his lifetime's opportunity in the fall of 1912, when Roosevelt fell ill during his first campaign for reelection. Eleanor Roosevelt called Louis to come to Hyde Park to run the campaign. He did, and he never really left. When young FDR's support of Woodrow Wilson was rewarded with appointment as assistant secretary of the navy, Louis went along as Roosevelt's chief staff member. He managed FDR's extensive participation in federal patronage for New York, relentlessly manipulating appointments to hurt Tammany and help the Democratic League. He wrote speeches, cultivated Franklin's growing national network, and worked tirelessly on his practical political education. Their effort culminated in the vice-presidential nomination of 1920. Louis managed Roosevelt's personal campaign.

The 1920 defeat left both men with new lives to build. Howe planned a business career. But on 10 August 1921 Roosevelt was struck by polio. Louis tended his friend personally, managed the difficult trip back to New York, and established himself as a member of the Roosevelt household. He persisted in believing that they had a political future. He kept up the correspondence, wrote articles for Roosevelt's signature, inserted his boss into other peoples' decision making, and maintained business ventures for them which made little money but helped build the image of a vigorous, competent, cheerful man, only moderately inhibited by crutches. He also worked on Eleanor's political education.

In 1924, Louis arranged a peace treaty with Tammany, and FDR made a dramatic appearance at Madison Square Garden to nominate Alfred E. Smith for the governorship. In 1928 Roosevelt ran for governor and Smith for president. Roosevelt won, Smith lost, and Howe found himself the key person in one of the nation's most significant political organizations. But he was no longer alone. From 1929 to 1933, he remained in New York City, working on the governor's politics while others handled the state administration. He continued to have unparalleled personal access to Roosevelt, and FDR respected his judgment. But he was now one of many advisers to be balanced off against one another by a boss who was careful to remain the chief. Louis was jealous of Samuel I. Rosenman who drafted speeches and of others who came to advise on water power, prisons, highways, farm policy, economics, and foreign policy. His own views were often uninformed, rigid, and traditional. By 1932 his health was deteriorating rapidly. He had always suffered from asthma, and at the Chicago convention he had to act through intermediaries. Others wrote the acceptance speech. FDR used only the first page of Louis's draft.

In Washington, Howe was established as *the* secretary to the president and lived in the White House. He had few regular responsibilities, but he could get to anything he wanted to touch. He sometimes worked on special projects with Eleanor. The president treated him with affection and respect, but oth-

ers ran the show. After a long hospitalization, he died in 1936. He was buried at Fall River, where there was later erected a smaller but exact replica of the stone beneath which FDR is buried at Hyde Park. Louis was quoted during his last illness as saying, "Franklin's on his own now." In fact, he had been for some time. But for the first twenty years, Howe had been essential to Roosevelt's success.

The principal source of information on Howe is Alfred B. Rollins, Jr., *Roosevelt and Howe* (New York: Alfred A. Knopf, 1962). Also useful is his secretary's memoir, Lela Stiles, *The Man behind Roosevelt: The Story of Louis McHenry Howe* (Cleveland and New York: World Publishing Co., 1954).

ALFRED B. ROLLINS, JR.

See also Roosevelt, Anna Eleanor; Speech Writing; State Senator of New York

HUAC

See House Committee to Investigate Un-American Activities

Hughes, Charles Evans
(11 April 1862–27 August 1948)

Chief justice of the United States during the decade of the Great Depression. Charles Evans Hughes was born in Glens Falls, New York, and educated at Brown University and Columbia University Law School. He served as two-term governor of New York from 1906 to 1910 and as associate justice of the U.S. Supreme Court from 1910 to 1916. In the latter year, as the nominee of the Republican party, he narrowly lost the presidency to Woodrow Wilson. Prior to his appointment as chief justice by President Hoover in 1930, he held the post of secretary of state under Harding and Coolidge.

"We are under a Constitution," Governor Hughes once quipped, "but the Constitution is what the judges say it is." As New York's first progressive governor, he compiled an admirable record of administrative and political reforms that served as a foundation for later governors, including Al Smith and Franklin Roosevelt. But Hughes and FDR came into sharp conflict during the depression era when a majority of the justices on the Supreme Court invalidated many state reform measures and key programs of the New Deal in 1935 and 1936, including the National Industrial Recovery Act, the Railroad Retirement Act, the Agricultural Adjustment Act, and the Guffey Bituminous Coal Act.

Hughes's alignment with the Court's conservatives in 1935–36 surprised many observers. He had displayed considerable toleration for economic experimentation in the early years of the depression when he joined majorities to sustain a drastic state mortgage moratorium law, a price-fixing statute for the milk industry, and the New Deal's monetary reforms. After a flurry of opposition to the New Deal, he again led the Court's liberal wing in 1937, when by narrow majorities the justices upheld the constitutionality of state minimum wage laws as well as the New Deal's National Labor Relations Act and the Social Security Act.

Like many other old progressives from the World War I era, Hughes became alarmed by the leftward drift of the Roosevelt administration in 1935. He feared the growth of a leviathan federal government and the New Deal's attempts to redistribute income from the well-to-do to the poor. Hughes's votes against the administration in 1935 and 1936 were an effort to check these trends by calling into question the New Deal's fidelity to the Constitution. When the electorate gave FDR a stunning victory in the presidential race of 1936, Hughes bowed to political reality and led the constitutional revolution of 1937, which finally took the Supreme Court out of the business of managing the nation's economic system by means of the judicial veto.

In 1937, mobilizing the Court's conservatives such as Justice Van Devanter and its liberals including justices Brandeis and Stone, the chief justice led an effective counterattack against FDR's ill-devised plan to reorganize the judiciary by adding new justices. When the Senate killed the key provisions of the so-called Court-packing scheme, Hughes could claim a major political victory over the president, which left intact the independence of the federal judiciary and the basic structure of judicial review, but now administered by a somewhat chastened Supreme Court. Hughes, who compiled a splendid record on civil liberties and civil rights while on the Court, retired as chief justice in 1941 and died seven years later.

There has not been a modern study of Hughes's judicial career since the publication of Samuel Hendel's *Charles Evans Hughes and the Supreme Court* (New York: Russell & Russell, 1951). A more revealing portrait of him as chief justice may be found in Alpheus T. Mason, *Harlan Fiske Stone: Pillar of the Law* (New York: Viking, 1956), especially pp. 293–464. See also Paul Freund, "Charles Evans Hughes," *Harvard Law Review* 81 (November 1967):16–34.

MICHAEL E. PARRISH

See also Supreme Court of the United States

Hull, Cordell
(2 October 1871–23 July 1955)

When President-elect Roosevelt announced his decision to nominate Sen. Cordell Hull of Tennessee to be secretary of state on 21 February 1933, the news was greeted with little surprise but with widespread approbation. During the 11½ years that Hull remained in that position—longer than any of his predecessors or successors to date—he consistently enjoyed strong public and political approval and support, if not always that of the president and some of his closest associates.

From the time he was elected, FDR seemed determined to be his own secretary of state. His intellect and temperament and his memories of Woodrow Wilson's disconcerting experiences with his first two secretaries of state, William Jennings Bryan and Robert Lansing, probably contributed to Roosevelt's decision, which he adhered to throughout his administration. As a result, Hull's influence on the president, his impact on the shaping and conduct of U.S. foreign policy, and even his personal direction of the department remained distinctly circumscribed. From his first days in office to his last in November 1944, Hull found himself not infrequently secretary of state in name rather than in fact.

From Roosevelt's point of view, on the other hand, Hull's appointment made considerable sense. FDR had known the Tennessean—eleven years his senior—since the days of the Wilson administration, when Hull was a rising young member of the U.S. House of Representatives. Personally, Roosevelt and Hull got on well together; they liked and respected each other. "In pure theory," FDR once wrote Hull, "you and I think alike but every once in a while we have to modify principle to meet disagreeable fact!" Whatever their differences and disagreements, as William L. Langer and S. Everett Gleason have written, "the two men, one daring and pliable, the other circumspect and inflexible, made a good team."

Their Wilsonian experience doubtless weighed heavily on both their minds. Roosevelt and Hull had not forgotten Wilson's tragically unsuccessful struggle to secure Senate approval of the 1919 Paris peace treaties and the League of Nations, and the president, as Frank Freidel has written, believed that "with a prestigious cautious friend like Hull in charge of the State Department, it would not be likely to recur."

Hardly had Roosevelt been elected than he began to display his personal brand of diplomacy. In late 1932, he sent his friend William C. Bullitt on a confidential fact-finding mission to Europe. But it was the World Economic Conference in London in June and July 1933 that foreshadowed the Roosevelt administration's frequently unsettling way of conducting American foreign policy. The president's thoughtless torpedoing of that conference—to which he had dispatched Hull as head of the U.S. delegation and whom he had repeatedly promised his unequivocal support—was not the secretary's first experience with Roosevelt's personal diplomacy nor would it be his last.

This disturbing state of affairs was not long becoming known. Publicly, the secretary accepted it with remarkable grace and equanimity. In private, Hull would sometimes launch into a bitter denunciation of what he called "the White House attitude and treatment of the Department and encroachment in foreign affairs," although Breckenridge Long, the senior assistant secretary of state whose experience in the department went back to the Wilson administration, recorded in his diary that "this is child's play compared with the Lansing situation."

Hull's determination to carry on in the face of such distracting circumstances was not, however, surprising. He had been Roosevelt's most dependable

Cordell Hull, 1945–46, detail of a portrait. Artist: Gregory C. Stapko after Edward M. Murray. (National Portrait Gallery, Smithsonian Institution.)

and effective southern political contact throughout the 1920s. He had been a Roosevelt leader at the Chicago convention that first nominated FDR in July 1932. After March 1933, Hull and Roosevelt were doubtless in general agreement about the main outlines and general principles of U.S. foreign policy. In particular, they shared a determination to keep the country out of any future conflict in Europe and the Pacific if at all possible and lost no opportunity to say so. Hull was more devoted than FDR to the persistent advocacy of certain high principles of international conduct and relations. A faithful Wilsonian, Hull articulated these beliefs in a series of widely noted addresses throughout the 1930s.

Like Wilson a generation earlier, Hull was especially concerned with the reduction of tariffs and other trade barriers, which he believed were an important cause of international conflict, tension, and ultimately war. With Roosevelt's strong support, Hull took a leading role, for instance, in the enactment of reciprocal trade legislation in June 1934. Furthermore, like FDR, Hull paid special and productive attention to the improvement of U.S. relations with Central and Latin America, which helped implement what became known as the Good Neighbor policy.

The rise of international aggression in the 1930s—Japanese, Italian, and German—deeply troubled Hull, but like Roosevelt, he seemed uncertain how to respond to it effectively. Hull was aware, for instance, that the president, the Congress, and public opinion all opposed an activist—that is to say, interventionist—U.S. policy to halt the new international anarchy.

The secretary made no serious effort to challenge the prevailing isolationist tide. He supported Roosevelt's neutrality policy, which had the unintended, if unsurprising, effect of favoring the aggressors. His circumspectly phrased criticism of spreading aggression, moreover, apparently pleased many, including the president, who found himself under mounting attack both from a variety of vociferous isolationists and from a handful of interventionists, including former secretary of state Henry L. Stimson and Prof. William E. Dodd and Claude G. Bowers, his ambassadors to Germany and Spain, respectively. On the other hand, there is no evidence to suggest that Hull's repeated moral exhortations made the slightest impression on the rulers in Tokyo, Rome, and Berlin, who confidently looked forward to continued U.S. nonintervention in world affairs.

One reason for Hull's limited influence on Roosevelt may also have been the secretary's personal style. As Louis B. Wehle, one of the president's old friends, wrote later to FDR, "A moment of boredom was a desperate ordeal. He often preferred to consider foreign relations with . . . others who came to the point quickly, instead of with Cordell Hull who had a rare quality of wisdom but was given to building up his case fact by fact and reason by reason."

The Roosevelt-Hull relationship changed insignificantly, if at all, with the approach of the Second World War. Hull was dismayed, for instance, by the crucial passages of Roosevelt's quarantine speech in Chicago in October 1937, about which he had not been consulted in advance. During the president's ineffectual diplomacy during the 1938 Munich crisis, Hull played no substantial role. Indeed, the late 1930s witnessed the rise of the glacial Sumner Welles, a fellow Harvardian who had attended Roosevelt's wedding as a boy and whom FDR promoted to the number two position in the department—under secretary of state—in a major reorganization in May 1937.

The unsurprising result of Welles's appointment was that, until the under secretary's involuntary resignation in September 1943, Hull found himself bypassed on more than a few occasions. As time went on, Hull strongly objected also to what he called Treasury Secretary Henry Morgenthau, Jr.'s "persistent inclination to try to function as a second Secretary of State"; but such complaints produced no significant improvements in Hull's position. As Henry L. Stimson observed in his diary, the president was not an orderly administrator, and he did nothing to curb the repeated violations of Hull's authority, if indeed Roosevelt was not the source of such intrusions in the first place.

Despite repeated slights—or perhaps because of them—Hull's political prestige and national stature remained unimpaired. In the spring of 1940 before Roosevelt had decided, or indicated his willingness, to run for a third term, there was widespread talk of a Democratic ticket headed by Hull. Indeed, as James MacGregor Burns has pointed out, "On several occasions during 1939 and early 1940 Roosevelt indicated to Hull—without absolutely committing himself—that he hoped that the Secretary would be his successor."

As the United States was drawn steadily closer to war in 1940–41, Hull, in accordance with Roosevelt's instructions, did his best to bring about some kind of honorable diplomatic settlement with Japan. By late November 1941, however, the secretary was compelled to admit defeat and accordingly informed the president and the cabinet.

In Roosevelt's wartime diplomacy, Hull played an even smaller role than he had before 1941. He strongly supported the Wilsonian tone of the Atlantic Charter that Roosevelt and Churchill had agreed on at their Argentia Bay conference in August 1941, and he had been the first to suggest something like the United Nations declaration of Allied political goals, issued during Churchill's first wartime visit to Washington on New Year's Day 1942.

On the other hand, Roosevelt had deliberately not invited Hull to his first meeting with Churchill nor even informed him about it until it was over, nor did the president take the secretary to his subsequent summit conferences with Churchill and Stalin. Explaining his decision not to take Hull to his conference with Churchill at Casablanca in January 1943, Roosevelt told W. Averell Harriman, soon to become U.S. ambassador to the Soviet Union, that Hull was "forceful, stubborn, difficult to handle. He had some rigid ideas and . . . would be a nuisance at the conference." And, indeed, Hull was long and vigorously opposed to the unconditional surrender formula Roosevelt and Churchill agreed on at Casablanca.

Following Adm. William D. Leahy's return from his post as U.S. ambassador to Vichy and his appointment as chief of staff to the commander in chief in July 1942, the handling of sensitive foreign policy issues became even further centralized in the White House. Hull soon felt his remaining power and influence slipping away. A year later, in July 1943, Morgenthau quoted Hull as complaining bitterly: "The President runs foreign affairs. I don't know what's going on. . . . I asked to see the political part of the cables between the President and Churchill, because I have to find out from [British ambassador Lord] Halifax what's going on between the President and Churchill. . . . The President said . . . he would give it to me and, three hours later, I get a message that the President had decided he would not do it. . . . I know the President is running foreign affairs and I know the President will not let me help him any more. . . . Since Pearl Harbor he does not let me help in connection with foreign affairs."

It is not known whether Hull ever seriously considered resignation during his earlier years as secretary of state. In his unusually interesting two-volume memoirs published in 1948, Hull recalled that he left Philadelphia on the eve of the Democratic National Convention there in late June 1936 when "the platform . . . planks on tariff and foreign affairs . . . utterly ignored the suggestions I had submitted." And Hull added: "I protested to the President about these planks, but he gave me no reply of any consequence."

It is known that Hull contemplated resigning shortly after Pearl Harbor, this time over Roosevelt's continued habit of carrying on important negotiations behind the secretary's back. The immediate issue then was Gen. Charles de Gaulle's dramatic seizure of the islands of St. Pierre and Miquelon (just south of Newfoundland), although it should be added that on the whole Hull was even more critical of the Free French leader's egocentric conduct than was the president.

Under the circumstances, it is rather surprising perhaps that the wartime State Department functioned as well as it did. It did so probably because of the important issues on which Hull and Roosevelt continued to see eye to eye. Hull, for instance, strongly agreed with FDR's Wilsonian position on postwar self-determination for colonial territories. Hull also agreed with Roosevelt regarding the postwar importance of China and the significance of economic issues.

Above all, Roosevelt allowed—indeed encouraged—Hull and the State Department to develop their own ideas and plans for a postwar political organization, although the president—doubtless to Hull's considerable dismay—looked forward to a postwar world largely directed by the Big Four policemen, including himself. Recalling the United States' lack of effective postwar preparation and policy in Wilson's time, Hull threw himself into that task with all his remaining energy. It was these efforts—crowned by the conferences at Dumbarton Oaks (August-October 1944) and San Francisco, and the establishment of the United Nations Organization—that earned Hull the Nobel Peace Prize in 1945.

All the same, Hull's participation in wartime top-level diplomacy remained limited, and—like Roosevelt's—his judgment of men and events often proved fallible. In early October 1943, for instance, the frail seventy-two-year-old secretary undertook his first journey by air to attend the Foreign Ministers' Conference in Moscow with Anthony Eden and V. M. Molotov. That strenuous conference—which Hull regarded as one of the outstanding achievements of his career—was crowned by the signing on 30 October 1943 of a Four Nation Declaration calling for the "establishing at the earliest practicable date a general international organization."

Returning home, Hull on 18 November 1943 became the first secretary of state in American history to be invited to address a joint session of Congress. It was not to be a prophetic speech. "As the provisions of the Four-Nation Declaration are carried into effect," Hull remarked, "there will no longer be need for spheres of influence, for alliances, for balance of power, or any other of the special arrangements through which, in the unhappy past, the nations strove to safeguard their security or to promote their interests." Hull went on to say that he had "found in Marshal Stalin a remarkable personality, one of the great statesmen and leaders of his age." (FDR, incidentally, agreed with Hull's assessment of the Foreign Minister's Conference. "Moscow," he wrote to Walter Lippmann, "was a real success.")

During the following year, the hopeful atmosphere and agreements reached at Moscow proved considerably less durable than Hull had optimistically expected. Hull was not unaware of the changing climate of East-West relations, and he became increasingly concerned about growing evidence of Soviet hostility and uncooperativeness.

Like Roosevelt's wartime diplomacy, Hull's performance has not escaped serious criticism. As Dean Acheson, himself a not unsympathetic member of the Hull State Department, observed later, "Only slowly did it dawn upon us that the whole world structure and order that we had inherited from the nineteenth century was gone." On the other hand, it seems rather excessive to contend—as two younger historians, Theodore A. Wilson and Richard D. McKinzie, have done—that "as a sop to Hull . . . FDR assigned him to the supervision of the State Department planning for American participation in wartime and postwar programs. . . . This honor proved illusory, since Hull and his cohorts were permitted only to spin gossamer dreams. . . . This . . . amused FDR, and he ignored the tangle of purposes and the enormous waste it produced."

It is true that the passage of time brought no increase in Hull's effective authority at the department. In January 1943, William Bullitt, FDR's former ambassador to France and the Soviet Union, addressed that subject in a long memorandum to Roosevelt on the state and structure of U.S. foreign policy, present and prospective.

"Hull," Bullitt wrote, "has an old line American wisdom which is so great. . . . Moreover, his prestige in the nation is unique. He is far more trusted than any other member of your administration. . . . But Hull's authority in his own Department has been nibbled at so long by various subordinates. . . . The first step toward getting the same drive into our fight for peace that we now have in our fight for victory is to give Hull orders to dismiss any and every member of his Department or the Foreign Service that he chooses to get rid of and to strengthen his Department in every possible way; and to take on his own shoulders—with responsibility to you alone—the fight for peace. . . . It is not yet too late. It soon will be too late."

Nothing, however, came of these and similar recommendations. Given his other overwhelming wartime responsibilities, FDR was not inclined to expend his limited time and energy to reorganize the State Department, with whose structure, if not operation, he had become reasonably comfortable.

By mid-1944, Hull knew that his rapidly waning physical powers demanded his early retirement. Approaching his seventy-third birthday, Hull found himself utterly exhausted. Breckenridge Long recorded Hull as saying that he was "tired of intrigue . . . tired of being bypassed . . . tired of being relied upon in public and ignored in private."

Roosevelt was well aware of Hull's undiminished political stature. He wanted Hull to deliver some "nonpolitical" foreign policy speeches during the 1944 campaign, but Hull politely ignored him. In any case, FDR wanted Hull to stay on until after the election, and to that the secretary agreed. On 27 November, after visiting Hull at Bethesda Naval Hospital, Roosevelt announced his retirement and the succession of Under Secretary of State Edward R. Stettinius, Jr.

Discussing Hull's retirement at a special news conference, Roosevelt remarked that "as a matter of practical fact, of course" Hull would be "in close touch and do everything that he can possibly do to carry on and carry out the wonderful start that he has made on the United Nations' plan, aiming toward peace during everybody's lifetime at least." Nothing came of Roosevelt's expectation, and less than six months later, the president himself was dead.

In November 1945, Hull was awarded the Nobel Peace Prize, the third U.S. secretary of state—after Elihu Root (1912) and Frank B. Kellogg (1929)—to be so honored.

In quietly active retirement, Hull, with the assistance of several former State Department aides, wrote a two-volume memoir—calm, dispassionate, discreetly revealing, proud of achievement, brief on slights and failures suffered—that appeared to highly favorable reviews in 1948.

Hull died in 1955 after an extended illness. "Cordell Hull," observed the *New York Times*, "will

rank among our great Secretaries of State besides the foremost statesmen of his time. The epic years in which he served this nation would alone have given him eminence. His own qualities—his integrity, courage, steadfastness, human dignity and scope of mind—mark the true measure of his stature."

Cordell Hull told his own story at length in his two-volume *Memoirs* (New York: Macmillan, 1948), a work of lasting interest. Julius W. Pratt's two-volume biography, volumes 12 and 13 of the series *The American Secretaries of State and Their Diplomacy* (New York: Cooper Square, 1964), is a helpful introduction to Hull, his times and his problems. The volumes for 1933–1944 in the State Department's documentary series *Foreign Relations of the United States* (Washington, D.C.: Government Printing Office, 1949–1967) contain some of Hull's most important official papers. There are others to be found in the State Department's *Peace and War—United States Foreign Policy 1931–1941* (Washington, D.C.: Government Printing Office, 1943), and in the seventeen-volume series *Franklin D. Roosevelt and Foreign Affairs*, vols. 1–3, ed. Edgar B. Nixon (Cambridge, Mass.: Belknap Press, Harvard University Press, 1969); vols. 4–16, ed. Donald B. Schewe (New York: Clearwater Publishing Co., 1979). Herbert Feis, *1933—Characters in Crisis* (Boston: Little, Brown, 1966), one of several illuminating volumes by one of Hull's ablest associates, treats some of the Secretary's early problems. Charles A. Beard, *President Roosevelt and the Coming of War, 1941* (New Haven: Yale University Press, 1948) is representative of the bitter isolationist criticism of Hull and Roosevelt and should be compared with William L. Langer and S. Everett Gleason's masterful *The Challenge to Isolation 1937–1940* (New York: Harper, 1952) and *The Undeclared War 1940–1941* (New York: Harper, 1953). Robert Dallek, *Franklin D. Roosevelt and American Foreign Policy 1932–1945* (New York: Oxford University Press, 1979), is a competent introduction to Rooseveltian diplomacy, generally sympathetic to the president, less so to Hull.

FRANCIS L. LOEWENHEIM

See also Foreign Economic Policy; Foreign Policy; Good Neighbor Policy; Reciprocal Trade Agreements

Hundred Days

The hundred days of 1933 began the political and economic New Deal programs of President Franklin D. Roosevelt.

"This nation is asking for action, and action now," declared Roosevelt in his inaugural address on 4 March 1933. Roosevelt matched his bold rhetoric by launching New Deal relief and recovery programs with a remarkable series of fifteen major laws enacted from 9 March to the early hours of 16 June 1933. Dubbed the "hundred days" by newsmen, the name derived from Napoleon's return to power for one hundred days before the Battle of Waterloo in 1815. For Roosevelt, however, it meant that in just over three months his presidency became based on a solid foundation of progressive legislation with a liberal leadership image.

When Roosevelt took office as 32d president, the United States was suffering its worst depression ever,

Breaking the Jam

Enright, New York American, *18 March 1933.*

part of a worldwide calamity. Unemployment averaged 25 percent nationally in a work force of about 50 million. But manufacturing industries had a jobless rate averaging 35 percent, and construction suffered the highest at 75 percent. Economically, the domestic economy was stagnating, and numerous trade barriers reduced the flow of foreign commerce. Socially, statistics indicated the human cost: marriages, births, and deaths were decreasing, while suicides, crime, and insanity were increasing. Psychologically, the great mass of Americans lived in quiet despair.

The inaction seemingly gripping the federal government under President Herbert Hoover's leadership added to the banking crisis of late February and early March 1933. Almost every bank in the nation was closed by 4 March. Over 5,500 banks with assets of $3.4 billion had closed since 1930. Roosevelt's proclamation of 6 March declared a four-day bank holiday.

Roosevelt changed those conditions and that climate of opinion with the soon famous hundred days special session of the 73rd Congress. The new president's leadership provided "action now" and, perhaps more important, hope and inspiration. First, the president requested legislation—planned primarily by holdover Republican officials—to deal with the banking crisis. Congress enacted the Emergency Banking Act in a few hours on 9 March, the first day of the special session. On 10 March, Roosevelt recommended a bill to provide over $4 billion in governmental economies. The harried Congress passed that legislation in just over a week, thus helping FDR keep his 1932 pledge to cut government costs by 25 percent.

By 16 March Roosevelt had decided to keep Congress in session, rather than adjourning. He indicated that decision by recommending passage of the Agricultural Adjustment Act, which finally became

law on 12 May. From his first legislative request on 9 March to approval of the controversial Independent Offices Appropriation Act (containing severe cuts in veterans' compensation) on 16 June, the president led, persuaded, and compelled Congress to pass the most impressive relief and recovery program to date.

Roosevelt's 1933 New Deal was based on the triple-priority programs of the Agricultural Adjustment Administration (AAA) for farm relief, the Economy Act for fiscal prudence, and the National Recovery Administration (NRA) for business and labor recovery. However, the president also approved the Civilian Conservation Corps (31 March) to employ a quarter million young men; the Federal Emergency Relief Administration (12 May) to deal with unemployment and hunger; the Emergency Farm Mortgage Act (12 May) and the Home Owners' Loan Corporation (13 June) to refinance farm and home mortgages, respectively; the Tennessee Valley Authority (18 May) to revive an entire devastated region; the Securities Act (27 May) to provide investors with accurate information about investments; the Railroad Coordination Act (16 June) to induce railroad self-reorganization; and the Glass-Steagall Banking Act (16 June) with its provision for the Federal Deposit Insurance Corporation—which FDR resisted until the end.

Amidst daily headlines in almost every American newspaper describing the potpourri of New Deal bills, Roosevelt deftly captivated public attention. Beginning on 8 March, he held the first of twice-a-week,

Ding Darling, New York Herald Tribune, *9 April 1933. (© I.M.T. Corporation. Reprinted by permission.)*

THE REST OF THE BOYS MIGHT AS WELL GET READY WHILE THERE'S PLENTY OF HOT WATER

informal press conferences, which totaled 30 during the hundred days (almost 1,000 during four of his twelve years in office). The frequent pictures by ubiquitous White House photographers—all carefully arranged by press secretary Steve Early—and Roosevelt's two highly successful "fireside chat" broadcasts (12 March and 7 May) also helped capture the public's interest.

The activist president also conferred endlessly with key policy advisers such as Raymond Moley and Lewis W. Douglas as well as with government officials, senators and representatives, businessmen, and others. In addition, Roosevelt gave numerous public speeches, held talks with representatives of foreign nations, and directed foreign policymaking—which culminated in the World Economic Conference at London.

During those hectic days Roosevelt also turned the White House into a living symbol of positive thinking and cheerfulness. "The truth is that F.D. really loves the appurtenances of the job," adviser Rexford G. Tugwell recorded in his diary on 31 May 1933. That point rapidly became evident to the public, and it helped Roosevelt restore hope and confidence across the nation.

Roosevelt's campaign and inauguration had aroused great expectations. In the hundred days, he satisfied many of his constituents' hopes. But the president's enduring achievements in 1933 were the creation both of public hope and confidence and of a moderately conservative New Deal foundation upon which he could build.

Arthur M. Schlesinger, Jr., *The Coming of the New Deal* (Boston: Houghton Mifflin Co. 1958) was the first detailed analysis of FDR's early New Deal in 1933–34. Schlesinger included significant, colorful material on the hundred days, employing a liberal interpretation of FDR's aims and results. William E. Leuchtenburg, *Franklin D. Roosevelt and the New Deal, 1932–1940* (New York: Harper & Bros., 1963) remains the most balanced account of the entire New Deal era, with a useful chapter on 1933. Frank Freidel, *Franklin D. Roosevelt*, vol. 4, *Launching the New Deal* (Boston: Little, Brown & Co., 1973) is the most complete and judicious discussion of FDR's domestic and foreign policies from November 1932 through July 1933. Covering the same period, James E. Sargent, *Roosevelt and the Hundred Days: Struggle for the Early New Deal* (New York: Garland, 1981) is a recent analysis primarily of FDR's domestic New Deal. Sargent stressed the difficulties the president had with Congress and the contradictions between his liberal image and the moderately conservative substance of New Deal programs.

JAMES E. SARGENT

See also Congress, United States; Great Depression; New Deal; Regulation, Federal

Hyde Park

Town and village in Dutchess County, New York, on the eastern bank of the Hudson River five miles north of Poughkeepsie, where President Franklin D. Roosevelt was born on 30 January 1882 and was buried on 15 April 1945.

Although Hyde Park owes its measure of renown to its association with the Roosevelts, and especially with President Franklin D. Roosevelt, the family's connection with the town was of relatively brief span. Roosevelts had held property and resided elsewhere in Dutchess County from the eighteenth century. But the house in Hyde Park in which Franklin Roosevelt was born in 1882 had been purchased by his father, James Roosevelt, only fifteen years earlier, and upon FDR's death in 1945, it passed into the hands of the National Park Service as a national historic site. Mrs. Eleanor Roosevelt continued to reside in the town, in her place at Val-Kill, until her death in 1962. That ended the Roosevelts' direct association with Hyde Park, and at present no members of the family reside in the town.

The earliest European settlement of the vicinity dates to about 1700. At that time, Jacobus Stoutenburgh, a farmer-merchant of Dutch descent, settled his family in the area. Members of the Stoutenburgh family still reside in Hyde Park today, and for generations the village was known as "Stoutenburgh's." At about the same time, one Peter Fauconnier, personal secretary to the then royal governor of New York, Edward Hyde, Lord Cornbury, was granted the patent for a sizeable estate in the vicinity which he called Hyde Park in gratitude to his patron. When the town was incorporated in 1821, the name of the estate was appropriated for it, somewhat to the discomfiture of the owners. There is no connection with the famous London park of the same name.

In the mid-eighteenth century, Fauconnier's estate passed through marriage into the Bard family of New York City, apart from the Roosevelts the most celebrated inhabitants of the village. Dr. John Bard, the first American educated abroad as a physician, held Hyde Park until his death in 1799, when it passed to his son Dr. Samuel Bard, founder of the College of Physicians and Surgeons in New York City, and ultimately to his grandson William Bard. In 1828 William Bard sold it to a medical colleague, Dr. David Hosack of New York City. The Bards and Hosacks were enthusiastic "improvers" and horticulturists, and through their efforts the estate was developed over the years as an extensive arboretum, one of the first in this country and still the object of praise by silviculturists. The efforts of the Bards and Hosacks were extended and intensified when the estate was purchased in the 1890s by the late Frederick J. Vanderbilt, who also adorned it with a hulking great mansion in the approved beaux arts style of the time. After Vanderbilt's death in 1938, the property was deeded to the U.S. government and is now the Vanderbilt National Historical Site, managed by the National Park Service conjointly with the Home of Franklin D. Roosevelt National Historic Site and the Eleanor Roosevelt National Historic Site at Val-Kill.

Midway between New York City and Albany and overshadowed by its larger neighbor Poughkeepsie, Hyde Park developed only slowly during the nineteenth century. The town, or more properly township, numbered 2,800 individuals at the time of the 1880 census just before Franklin Roosevelt's birth

Aerial view of the Roosevelt estate, Hyde Park, 1932. The formal garden on the right is where both Franklin and Eleanor Roosevelt are buried. In the foreground now stands the Franklin D. Roosevelt Library and Museum.

The museum and the family home are open to the public and contain extensive displays on the life and career of FDR. (Courtesy FDR Library.)

and only about 4,000 persons at the time of the 1940 census. The smaller village of Hyde Park amounted to only a few hundred persons at the time of Roosevelt's birth and about a thousand at the time of his death. The core of this population has remained solidly Dutch through the generations and still is largely so, with a predominance of family names such as Stoutenburgh, Rymph, Teller, and van Wagner which trace back to the town's earliest settlement.

Primarily agricultural in its early years, Hyde Park has undergone two significant transformations during its history. In the mid-nineteenth century, wealthy New Yorkers purchased large blocks of riverfront property and developed a series of opulent estates, somewhat on the English country house model, stretching north from Hyde Park about twenty-five miles into Columbia County, signally transforming thereby the character of the town and the surrounding country. Principal among these newcomers were the Pendleton Rogerses, the Bramans and the Newbolds in Hyde Park itself and the Ogden Millses, the Dinsmoors and the Huntingtons in the village of Staatsburg immediately to the north. The ornate Vanderbilt mansion was the last and most splendiferous

effort along these lines. The great estates provided large-scale employment for the villagers of Hyde Park for a time but left in their wake not a few lingering resentments which even today occasionally roil the otherwise tranquil surface of life in the town.

If the arrival of "the gentry" affected the lives of Hyde Parkers in the nineteenth century, the tremendous growth of the International Business Machines Corporation in nearby Poughkeepsie in the 1950s revolutionized it. From the sleepy rural community of a few hundred souls which FDR knew and loved, Hyde Park was transformed into a bustling and somewhat unkempt dormitory community for IBM and a number of other large industrial enterprises that developed in Poughkeepsie during World War II and after. In the decade of the fifties, the population doubled to 13,000 and almost doubled again by the 1980 census. The old core of largely Dutch families continues in place today but increasingly has been submerged by "outsiders" who bring with them, and to the town's affairs, a different and somewhat cosmopolitan outlook not always appreciated by old Hyde Parkers. This adds a certain spice to local politics, especially school board elections.

In view of President Roosevelt's electoral prowess, his vote-getting record in Hyde Park and Dutchess County is a matter of interest and occasional and sometimes sidelong local comment. In his long political career, FDR contested nine general elections—two for state senator in 1910 and 1912, one for vice-president in 1920, two for governor of New York State, and four for president. He carried Hyde Park in only three of them—the two state senator races and his second run for the governorship in 1930. The closest he otherwise came to carrying Hyde Park was in the 1940 presidential election when he got 48.9 percent of the vote against Wendell Willkie's 50.9 percent. His record in Dutchess County generally was identical, but even more lopsidedly negative. If it leads to reflection about "prophets without honor," it also betokens a certain independence of mind on which Hyde Parkers still pride themselves.

There is no satisfactory history of Hyde Park. Beatrice Fredriksen treats it briefly in a fifty-six-page pamphlet, *Our Local Heritage* (Hyde Park: Hyde Park Historical Association, 1962), and Dr. Henry Noble MacCracken provides details in his *Old Dutchess Forever* (New York: Hastings House, 1956) and *Blithe Dutchess* (New York: Hastings House, 1958). F. Kennon Moody, "FDR and His Neighbors" (Ph. D. diss., State University of New York, 1981) is the most substantial work yet done on that subject, and a Vassar College senior thesis of 1979 by Nancy Fogel, "Change in Hyde Park," based on extensive interviews with elderly Hyde Parkers, is illuminating. Both these works are available in manuscript at the Franklin D. Roosevelt Library. An amusing sketch of Lord Cornbury is provided by Ormonde de Kay, Jr., in "His Most Detestable High Mightiness," *American Heritage* 27, no. 3 (April 1976):60-.

WILLIAM R. EMERSON

I

Ickes, Harold LeClair

(15 March 1874–3 February 1952)

Secretary of interior from March 1933 to February 1946. Harold Ickes was fifty-nine years old, a seasoned and crusty veteran of urban progressive reform, when Franklin D. Roosevelt brought him out of the obscurity of Chicago politics and appointed him to the cabinet. Born on a farm in Blair County, Pennsylvania, Ickes moved to Chicago in 1890 after the death of his mother and emotional rejection from his debt-ridden father, an aberrant Greenbacker and unsuccessful Republican office seeker, who ran a notions store in Altoona.

Ickes graduated from Englewood High School and cum laude from the second class at the University of Chicago in 1897. His collegiate experience in the midst of the depression of 1893 was marred by grinding poverty and personal humiliation because of his inadequate financial and social position. Ickes worked for several years as a reporter for various Chicago newspapers, received a J.D. degree from the University of Chicago Law School in 1907, and practiced law with moderate success in association with Donald R. Richberg.

Beginning with the mayoralty campaign of 1897, Ickes supported independent Republican reform candidates, including Charles E. Merriam in 1911. He established himself as an effective political operative and an astute organizational manager. He was drawn into the Progressive party of 1912 through his association with Chicago settlement workers and his efforts for social justice legislation and good government. He came to the attention of Theodore Roosevelt because of his organizational skills and administrative ability. Ickes remained a leader of the Progressive remnant throughout the 1920s, organizing Progressives for James M. Cox and Franklin D. Roosevelt in 1920 and managing Hiram Johnson's unsuccessful presidential bid in 1924. Although most of his candidates and causes were defeated at the polls and by the

"interests," Ickes had notable confrontations with such public utilities tycoons as Charles T. Yerkes and Samuel Insull, whom he successfully identified as dangerous to democratic government. In the course of these contests, Ickes developed strong positions on the role of electricity in American life and advanced notions of public ownership.

Unable to "progressivise" the Republican party and tired of being a political outsider, Ickes managed the Western Independent Republican Committee for Roosevelt in 1932. His ambitions for political office were advanced by such prominent progressive Republicans as Hiram Johnson and Bronson Cutting, as well as by friendly Democrats. His surprise appointment as secretary of interior was a matter of timing and luck. Although Ickes was unknown to the president-elect, he was impressed by Ickes's record. Roosevelt's election gave the "man with the funny name" power and prestige for the first time in his life. It also provided an unmatched platform for public service.

Harold Ickes brought to the job of interior secretary unsurpassed energy, ego, and administrative virtuosity. Roosevelt recognized and rewarded Ickes's gifts and tolerated his irascible, pugnacious personality because of them. While never a member of Roosevelt's inner circle in the same way as Henry Morgenthau was, Ickes was prominent in legislative discussions, a frequent White House guest for poker, and a reluctant fishing companion for the president. Over time, Ickes was the recipient of greater executive authority from the president than any other cabinet officer.

With the passage of the National Industrial Recovery Act in June 1933, Roosevelt appointed Ickes to two of the most difficult and sensitive recovery positions in government: oil administrator under Section 9-C, and two months later, public works administrator under Title II of the act. Obsessed with a dread that scandal would wreck the administration's recovery program, "Honest Harold" presided fretfully and carefully over the enormous public works budget. Criticized unduly for his care, Ickes nevertheless instituted projects that not only changed the landscape of America but also mitigated the serious economic downturn of 1936–37.

For all his worthwhile public works, "Harold the Holy" was mighty hard to live with. A tyrant within his own department, he once locked the building's doors five minutes after opening time in order to catch late employees. He was suspicious, vengeful, and constantly at odds with others over real or imagined slights and territorial encroachments. At the same time, Ickes constantly raided other departments of their bureaus and functions, and was outraged when his forays were criticized or deflected.

Roosevelt named Ickes chairman of a number of important governmental committees. His direction of the National Resources Planning Board, in its several forms, and the National Power Policy Committee were notable, because Ickes was successful in initiating policies that were often in advance of Roosevelt's and broadened the New Deal's conservation program.

When the war broke out, Ickes's official role was less than he had hoped, but important nonetheless— he was appointed solid fuels administrator as well as petroleum administrator for war. Roosevelt was able to test public opinion by letting his avowedly internationalist secretary recommend controversial policies and take on the controversy that resulted. Ickes made important contributions to energy and power planning for the war. Roosevelt appreciated his services, and kept the grumpy secretary's periodic threats to resign under control and in perspective by countering them with disarming humor.

The president penned the following limerick to Ickes after the latter had been particularly abused by the press for the lack of fuel available on the East Coast as the winter of 1941 approached:

> There was a lady of fashion,
> Who had a terrific passion,
> As she jumped into bed,
> She casually said,
> "Here's one thing that Ickes can't ration."

Ickes also served Roosevelt's need to have within his official family a spokesman for policies with regard to civil liberties and protection of minority rights that the president himself declined to take. Long an advocate of Indian reform and of legislation to improve reservation conditions, Ickes presided over the first integrated government cafeteria, recommended the first black justice for the Virgin Islands, and publicly snubbed the Daughters of the American Revolution by his sponsorship of soprano Marian Anderson. As director of the War Relocation Authority, Ickes adamantly argued for the release of the interned Japanese and warned the president of the consequences of such wholesale civil rights violations.

Sadly, Roosevelt denied Ickes his most sought-after request—that of presiding over a reorganized Department of Conservation, to include the Forest Service transferred from the Department of Agriculture. Although Roosevelt agreed in principle with Ickes's argument that forests belonged in Interior, the political repercussions accompanying such a transfer would have been too great.

The same energies that made Ickes a successful administrator made him an invaluable political supporter for Roosevelt's reelection and an important weapon in the Democratic party arsenal. The owner of one of the most vitriolic pens in Washington, Ickes loved controversy and combat. A master of irony and invective in private correspondence, he was equally formidable in public debate and soon became the most sought after public speaker in the cabinet.

Ickes made critical speeches for Roosevelt in both the 1936 and 1940 campaigns and in 1944 made a staggering number of appearances and speeches. An ardent champion of public ownership of electric power, Ickes delighted in taunting utility magnate Wendell Willkie, whom he castigated as that "simple, barefoot Wall Street lawyer." After Roosevelt was elected to a fourth term, he complimented his self-styled "curmudgeon" on his oratorical efforts, telling him that what was left of the Republican party had complained that he had "a buzz-saw for a Secretary of Interior. I can't say that I blame them and I must say that I like it."

When Roosevelt shocked most of the cabinet in February 1937 with the announcement that he intended to introduce legislation to "reorganize" the Supreme Court, Ickes was one of the very few who applauded the decision and worked to support it. As an administrator of two provisions of the National Industrial Recovery Act whose enforcement efforts had been frustrated by adverse court decisions, Ickes criticized the president only for acting too cautiously to save the liberal legislation of the early New Deal.

Ickes was often critical of Roosevelt's tendency to approach adversaries obliquely. A man given to immediate and often explosive reaction to challenge or criticism, Ickes was an early and ardent interventionist in foreign affairs. He took every available opportunity to push Roosevelt to amend the neutrality legislation and ardently supported Lend-Lease. He met secretly with other liberal New Dealers to devise strategy to push the president toward harsher sanctions against Japan's aggressiveness in the Pacific. While Roosevelt kept to his own mysterious timetable, Ickes's pleas for an oil embargo and his stubborn refusal to sell helium to Germany balanced the overcautious counsels of others surrounding the president.

Ickes also acted as Roosevelt's bellwether for changes in public sentiment toward Germany and the activities of Adolf Hitler. He became the administration's chief antagonist against the isolationist sentiment collected around America's flying hero, Charles A. Lindbergh, and the America First supporters. Although the president privately winced at Ickes's brutal attacks on the aviator, he did not restrain him.

Ickes's long cabinet career and his service to the New Deal involved him most deeply in the issues of conservation, natural resource policy planning, and the shaping of the American environment. Ickes was the perfect instrument to put into effect the presi-

Harold LeClair Ickes, 1933. Artist: S. J. Woolf. (National Portrait Gallery, Smithsonian Institution.)

in Truman's administration. But when Truman persisted in the nomination of California oil executive and former Democratic national treasurer Edwin C. Pauley as under secretary of the navy, the specter of Albert Fall was too much for the man who had spent so long rehabilitating the Department of Interior. Harold Ickes offered Truman his resignation one last time on 13 February 1946 and left his job of thirteen years.

In retirement on a farm in Maryland with his young wife and two small children, he worked on his voluminous memoirs, and wrote a syndicated column which he had long coveted called "Man to Man" for the *New York Post*. Ickes was a frequent contributor to the *New Republic* and was sought after for advice and counsel by a variety of public officials.

Ickes campaigned against Thomas Dewey, the "candidate in sneakers" in 1948, worked for Herbert Lehman's election in New York in 1949, and supported Helen Gahagan Douglas in 1950. Suspicious of Dewey, Richard Nixon, and big business, his liberalism was unshaken, although he admitted that he felt like a "museum piece occasionally dusted off by the Democratic high command."

After a brief respiratory illness, Harold Ickes died at the age of seventy-seven still passionately interested in politics, the environment, and public affairs. More than merely an "old progressive in the New Deal," he was obsessed with fighting for what he considered fundamental liberal causes—most of which he had shared with the president he had served with such energy for so long.

Harold Ickes intended his prolific autobiographical writing to help establish his place in the New Deal. The *Secret Diary of Harold L. Ickes*, 3 vols. (New York: Simon & Schuster, 1953–54) describes his activities and attitudes minutely through 1940. A nearly equal amount of diary material exists in unpublished form to 1952 as part of the massive collection of the Papers of Harold L. Ickes in the Manuscript Division of the Library of Congress, Washington, D.C. Among Ickes's many published works, the best can be discerned in *Fightin' Oil* (New York: Alfred A. Knopf, 1943), *America's House of Lords* (New York: Harcourt, Brace, 1939), and *The New Democracy* (New York: W. W. Norton, 1934). Ickes's administrative activities are equally massive in Record Group 48 and in the Official Files of Secretary of the Interior, Harold L. Ickes, at the National Archives, Washington, D.C. The relationship between secretary and president can be viewed from Ickes's perspective in the series he wrote for the *Saturday Evening Post,* "My Twelve Years with FDR," June-July 1948, and from the president's eyes in Official File 6 and in the papers of other administrative colleagues at the Franklin D. Roosevelt Library, Hyde Park, New York. Linda J. Lear has begun a full-scale biography with *Harold L. Ickes: The Aggressive Progressive, 1874–1933* (New York: Garland Publishing Co., 1981). It is a carefully researched account of Ickes's life and political career to 1933. Her article, "Harold L. Ickes and the Oil Crisis of the First Hundred Days," *Mid-America* (January 1981):3–17, explores Ickes's views on energy and conservation. Some of the important inconsistencies in Ickes's liberalism can be scrutinized in Otis L. Graham, Jr., *An Encore for Reform* (New York: Oxford University

dent's own conservation program. But he embellished it with his unique concern for the efficient use of resources and pioneered in measures promoting aesthetic and ecological preservation. Although he sometimes sided with big interests, he more often opposed them, as he did in the case of the Alcoa monopoly and the promotion of diversified industrial development of the West.

Ickes's petulance, his egomania, his insufferable self-righteousness, his continual marauding of other's territory, the "terror" with which he ran his own department, and the hair shirt he constantly wore were qualities that Roosevelt weighed on the balance of Ickes's ultimate utility to him and to the New Deal. But Roosevelt shrewdly calculated these qualities against Ickes's energy, loyalty, administrative genius, and his capacity to be unfailingly right on the big issues. The president took the correct measure of the quality and integrity of Harold Ickes as a public servant. The "Eeyore" of the cabinet was humored, ignored, cajoled, and despaired over, but always valued, respected, rewarded, and even affectionately regarded.

Ickes remained uncomfortably at his job for little more than a year after Roosevelt's death. His interests in an Anglo-American oil agreement, the crisis of the coal industry and of oil, and particularly policy involving offshore deposits compelled him to remain

Press, 1967), as well as in the well-known studies of Roosevelt and the New Deal by Arthur Schlesinger, Jr., William D. Leuchtenburg, James M. Burns, and Frank Freidel. Wayne S. Cole, *Roosevelt and the Isolationists* (Lincoln: University of Nebraska Press, 1983) provides important insights into Ickes's views and activities as a liberal interventionist. His activities as petroleum administrator for war and as head of the American delegation to the oil conference have been analyzed by Michael B. Stoff, *Oil, War and American Security* (New Haven: Yale University Press, 1980) and Stephen J. Randall, "Harold L. Ickes and U.S. Foreign Petroleum Policy Planning," *Business History Review* (Autumn 1983):367–87. His efforts to develop a long-term power policy are evaluated critically by Philip J. Funigiello, *Toward a National Power Policy* (Pittsburgh: University of Pittsburgh Press, 1973). Clayton R. Koppes, "Environmental Policy and American Liberalism: The Department of Interior, 1933–1953," *Environmental Review* 7 (Spring 1983):17–41, provides new perspectives on Ickes's leadership in environmental matters as secretary of interior.

LINDA J. LEAR

See also Cabinets: Conservation; Indian Policy; Public Works Administration

---

Immigration

See Jews; Niles, David K.; Refugees; Stimson, Henry L.

Inaugurations

The wintry weather prevailing on 4 March 1933 reflected the state of the nation as Chief Justice Hughes administered the oath of office to Franklin D. Roosevelt on the east portico of the Capitol. Banks throughout the nation were closed, unemployment had idled a fourth of the work force, and outgoing President Hoover, having failed to persuade FDR to continue with modest economic reform policies, remained taciturn throughout the ceremony. In his first inaugural address, the president, fully aware of the enormous challenges ahead, asked the nation to place its confidence in his administration. Rephrasing words penned by Thoreau, FDR assured his audience that "the only thing we have to fear is fear itself" and promised that should Congress fail to take measures necessary to relieve "a stricken nation," he would ask for "broad executive powers to wage a war against the emergency."

Although FDR requested simple ceremonies to mark the day, thinking it more in keeping with the times, the Democratic party insisted on celebrating. General MacArthur led a jubilant parade that trooped down Constitution Avenue to the strains of the Franklin Delano Roosevelt March, composed in honor of the occasion by W. H. Woodin. Mrs. Woodrow Wilson served as vice-chairperson on the Committee on Distinguished Guests, which included the surviving members of Wilson's cabinet. An evening concert concluded the day's festivities.

During the next twelve years, the president, as he had promised he might, invoked executive powers many times, but in 1936 the Supreme Court, not Congress, threatened to be his nemesis. Swept into office again, however, by an overwhelming majority, FDR took advantage of his popular mandate and publicly confronted his judicial adversaries as soon as Chief Justice Hughes had administered the oath of office. In his second inaugural address on 20 January 1937, once again delivered under gray skies, the president asserted that "the essential democracy of our nation and the safety of our people depend not on the absence of power, but upon lodging it with those whom the people can change or continue at stated intervals through an honest and free system of elections." FDR also called upon government to "find practical controls over blind economic forces and blindly selfish men" in order to attend to the needs of that one-third of the nation still "ill-housed, ill-clad, ill-nourished." His words signaled to many a shift in the New Deal's emphasis from planning for economic recovery to advancing reform measures that would restructure both the economy and American society. Despite the urging of Democratic leaders, FDR insisted on a modest inaugural ceremony and a short parade, led by General M. Craig; and he forbade an inaugural ball.

FDR pushed the New Deal forward, but by 1939 the threat of foreign war, not domestic economic problems, posed a greater concern. His plurality waning, Roosevelt nonetheless won a third term with a decisive victory over Wendell Willie. Americans trusted the president to bring the country through the crisis of war as he had brought it through the crisis of imminent economic collapse. His inaugural address of 20 January 1941 echoed the themes of his stirring four freedoms speech, delivered before Congress on 6 January. "The democratic aspiration is no mere recent phase in human history," FDR assured his audience. "It is human history."

War tested America's strength during the next four years, and it took its toll on Roosevelt's health as well. With four sons in uniform, he took the oath of office for his fourth term on 20 January 1945 in a simple ceremony staged on the south portico of the White House. No parade enlivened the bleak winter day. "Who is there here to parade?" the president responded to a reporter's query. The Yalta Conference, a mere two weeks away, no doubt occupied FDR's thoughts. In his last inaugural address, he pondered the role of a democratic nation in a global context, and his words echoed those uttered twelve years earlier: "We can gain no lasting peace if we approach it with suspicion and mistrust—or with fear."

The first, second, and fourth inaugurations are movingly described by James MacGregor Burns in his two-volume biography, *Roosevelt: The Lion and the Fox* (New York: Harcourt Brace Jovanovich, 1956) and *Roosevelt: The Soldier of Freedom* (New York: Harcourt Brace, 1970). FDR's inaugural speeches are contained in Samuel I. Rosenman, ed., *The Public Papers and Addresses of Franklin D. Roosevelt*, 13 vols. (New York, 1938–50).

THE INAUGURATION OF FRANKLIN D. ROOSEVELT

AN HEROIC PANORAMA DEPICTING THE HIGH CEREMONY ON THE CAPITOL PLAZA AT WASHINGTON ON MARCH 4TH, 1933

Done Into Full Colour, In The Memorial Manner, By Miguel Covarrubias, Painter Extraordinary and Historiographer to the Court on the Potomac

ENGRAVED IN THIS YEAR OF OUR LORD 1933 AND INCLUDED IN THE MARCH NUMBER OF VANITY FAIR. THE GENTRY'S GAZETTEER OF ARTS AND MANNERS

PUBLISHED AT THE SIGN OF THE GRAYBAR BLDG. (WHICH IS HARD BY ST. BARTHOLOMEW CHURCH MEWS AND OLD TONY'S TAVERN IN THE CITY OF NEW YORK)

1. Franklin Delano Roosevelt, 1882–1945, 32nd president of the U. S.
2. Charles Evans Hughes, 1862–1948, Statesman
3. Anna Eleanor Roosevelt, 1884–1962, First Lady, stateswoman
4. John Nance Garner, 1868–1967, Vice president of the U.S.
5. Herbert Clark Hoover, 1874–1964, 31st president of the U.S.
6. Lou Henry Hoover, 1874–1944, First Lady
7. Charles E. Curtis, 1860–1936, Vice president of the U.S.
8. Alfred Emanuel Smith, 1873–1944, Politician
9. James A. Farley, 1888–1976 Postmaster General
10. Raymond Charles Moley, 1886–1975, Author
11. Louis McHenry Howe, 1871–1936, Journalist, political mentor and secretary to F.D.R. 1913–1930

12. Joseph Taylor Robinson, 1872–1937, Lawyer, Congressman
13. Bernard Mannes Baruch, 1870–1965, Financier
14. Owen D. Young, 1874–1962, Industrialist and monetary expert
15. William Gibbs McAdoo, 1863–1941, Lawyer, businessman, politician
16. Albert Cabell Ritchie, 1876–1936, Lawyer, Maryland public official
17. Claude Augustus Swanson, 1862–1939, Lawyer, statesman

18. Byron Patton Harrison ("Pat Harrison"), 1881–1941, Lawyer, politician
19. Herbert Henry Lehman, 1878–1963, Governor of New York 1933–1942
20. Thomas James Walsh, 1849–1933, Lawyer, statesman
21. John William Davis, 1873–1955, Statesman
22. Carter Glass, 1858–1946, Newspaper publisher, statesman
23. Norman Hezekiah Davis, 1878–1944, Statesman
24. Newton Diehl Baker, 1871–1937, Statesman

25. Henry Lewis Stimson, 1867–1950, Statesman
26. Andrew William Mellon, 1855–1937, Financier, statesman, art patron
27. Ogden Livingston Mills, 1884–1937, Lawyer, New York Legislator
28. John Pierpont Morgan, 1867–1943, Financier
29. Paul Claudel, 1868–1955, French Ambassador
30. Sir Ronald Lindsay, ?–?, British Ambassador
31. Oriental Ambassador
32. Oriental Ambassador
33. Mark Sullivan, 1874–1952, Author
34. Walter Lippmann, 1889–1974, Author
35. Gentlemen of the Press
36. John Joseph Pershing, 1860–1948, World War I general
37. The Forgotten Man
38. The U.S. Navy

The inauguration of Franklin D. Roosevelt, 1933. Artist: Miguel Covarrubias. (National Portrait Gallery, Smithsonian Institution.)

Indian Policy

Major reforms in federal Indian policy were undertaken in the Roosevelt era. Since 1887 the major thrust of federal policy had been to force the integration, or assimilation, of Indians into white society by abolishing their communally owned reservations and forcing them to take individually owned plots of land. This procedure, known as land allotment, made Indian lands subject to sale and taxation and effectively destroyed tribal governments. During the 1920s, the allotment policy came under fire as it became increasingly evident that it was resulting in widespread Indian demoralization and loss of land. FDR was not himself knowledgeable in the field of Indian policy, but he reposed great trust in Secretary of the Interior Harold Ickes and Indian commissioner John Collier, both of whom were critics of the traditional policy. In the first years of the New Deal era, Ickes and Collier were able to secure legislation halting the practice of land allotment and permitting the reformation of Indian societies.

The major goal of the Indian New Deal was to achieve self-determination for Indians, subject only to restraints imposed by the trust responsibility of the federal government. The vehicle for self-determination, the Indian Reorganization Act of 1934 (48 Stat., 984), emerged from Congress severely modified from the original Collier proposal, but it did include the following major provisions: the allotment of tribal lands to individual Indians was ended and the Indian Office was authorized both to consolidate previously allotted land into tribal ownership and to purchase lands for Indians who had none; Indian tribes were empowered to adopt constitutions that would enable them to govern themselves free from bureaucratic meddling and the paternalism of the Indian Office; tribes that incorporated themselves were empowered to purchase, own, manage, operate, and dispose of their property and were to be assisted in achieving economic development through a revolving credit fund of $10 million; Indians were exempted from Civil Service requirements so that they could qualify for positions in the Indian Office previously held almost exclusively by whites; and federal funding for Indian children who sought special vocational, trade school, or college education was authorized. Because of congressional opposition, a federal Court of Indian Affairs with original jurisdiction over Indian tribes who adopted constitutions was dropped, Indians were given the right to reject the Indian Reorganization Act in referenda to be held within two years after its passage, and the Indians of Oklahoma and Alaska were initially exempted from its provisions.

Despite the congressional limitations placed upon Indian self-determination and opposition from a sizable number of assimilated Indians who resisted the revival of tribal governments, 174 Indian tribes and bands approved the Indian Reorganization Act; 78 rejected it. Subsequently, 92 tribes adopted constitu-

tions, and 72 did not; only 71 tribes approved articles of incorporation and thereby qualified for access to the credit loan program. The rejection of the Indian Reorganization Act by many Indians and the failure of others to adopt constitutions and articles of incorporation were severe blows to the Indian New Deal and provided congressional opponents of the legislation with telling arguments for future limitation. Despite these reversals, two permanent reforms were achieved: tribal lands were preserved, free from the threat of division and eventual loss; and the potential for limited Indian self-government, to be achieved mainly after World War II, was guaranteed.

Other policy reforms of the Indian New Deal included the extension of religious freedom to Indians, the repeal of nineteenth-century "espionage" laws which had limited Indian exercise of basic civil liberties, the cancelation of debts against tribal treasuries incurred without Indian approval, and the extension of the Indian Reorganization Act in modified form to the Indians of Oklahoma and Alaska in 1936.

During the Roosevelt years, the Indian Office also participated in a host of programs designed to rehabilitate Indian lands. From the Civilian Conservation Corps and the Public Works Administration, the Indian Office received more than $100 million for soil conservation, irrigation, and road-building projects. From the Resettlement Administration and the Farm Security Administration, over a million acres of submarginal land were obtained for Indians. And from the Federal Emergency Relief Administration and the Works Progress Administration, relief funds were obtained that provided jobs on reservations, assisted in stock reduction programs, and stimulated Indian involvement in traditional arts and crafts. Congressional opposition to these federal programs and the onset of World War II produced severe budget cuts by 1941, thereby crippling the rehabilitation effort.

The story of the Indian New Deal has been told from the administration's point of view in two books by Indian commissioner John Collier: *Indians of the Americas* (New York: W. W. Norton Co., 1947), and *From Every Zenith, a Memoir* (Denver: Sage Books, 1963). More critical accounts have been written by two historians: Kenneth R. Philip, *John Collier's Crusade for Indian Reform* (Tucson: University of Arizona Press, 1977), and Lawrence C. Kelly, *The Assault on Assimilation* (Albuquerque: University of New Mexico Press, 1983).

LAWRENCE C. KELLY

Infantile Paralysis

See Health; Polio; Warm Springs

Inter-American Conference

See Good Neighbor Policy

Internationalism and Peace

It is difficult to characterize Roosevelt's thinking on internationalism or peace because it is impossible to separate his personal views from politics or presidential policies. Robert Dallek, in his thorough study of Roosevelt's foreign policy, hints at the contradictory nature of Roosevelt's thought in two chapter headings: "The Internationalist as Nationalist, 1932–1934" and "The Internationalist as Isolationist, 1935–1938."

Roosevelt's interest in world affairs was always colored by his nationalism and political expediency. He had developed an early cosmopolitan perspective through education, travel, and contacts with Europeans. Then, as assistant secretary of the navy, 1913–20, he came to appreciate Woodrow Wilson's internationalist vision, yet his conversion to Wilsonianism, as embodied in the League of Nations, remained incomplete. He tended to temper his idealism with the practical awareness that while the United States should become more involved in global matters and committed to peace, it should do so only after it first looked after its own interests. Moreover, Roosevelt had no inhibition about using peace slogans, the League issue, or the United Nations as tools to advance his political career or policies.

His support of League membership in 1919–20 helped him gain a place as vice-president on the Democratic ticket in 1920. In the ensuing campaign, he and James M. Cox, the presidential nominee, supported the party's plank favoring League membership, although they personally disagreed with Wilson's insistence on joining without reservations. Roosevelt believed that the country's interests would be better served if it were in the League, even with qualifications. Throughout the 1920s, he held to this moderate position. He served as president of the Woodrow Wilson Foundation during its campaign for an endowment that would honor Wilson's efforts to promote peace, and he often presented his views on contemporary international issues in speeches and

In one of this last meetings before his death, President Franklin D. Roosevelt discusses the establishment of machinery for the preservation of world peace with U.S. delegates to the United Nations Security Conference in April 1945. Standing (left to right) are Rep. Sol Bloom of New York; Virginia Gildersleeve, dean of Barnard College; Tom Connally of Texas; Secretary of State Edward R. Stettinius, Jr.; former governor of Minnesota Harold E. Stassen; Sen. Arthur H. Vandenberg of Michigan; and Rep. Charles A. Eaton of New Jersey. (National Archives.)

articles. He favored some adjustment of war debts and opposed high protective tariffs.

In 1923, he submitted a proposal to the Edward W. Bok Peace Prize Committee. Bok sought "the best practical plan" for U.S. cooperation to achieve and maintain peace, and Roosevelt's essay reflected that perspective. He offered a rationale for the nation to play a responsible role "to eliminate the causes of war" and to confer and assist in containing "the germs of war." He further argued that involvement should come only after constitutional procedures had been followed. The duty for the United States, however, remained clear. It should "confer with other peoples, not in gatherings hastily summoned in time of threatening crisis, but in a continuing permanent society." Roosevelt then presented a constitution for a Society of Nations to replace the League of Nations. Only in this way could U.S. membership be attained. The League's Council would be replaced with an Executive Committee with four permanent members (United States, British Empire, France, and Japan). His modification of Article X deleted the reference to "preserve against external aggression," provided only for respect of territory and political independence rather than their guarantee, and suggested consultation regarding needed action. Nations resorting to war in violation of treaties or pledges would be guilty of "an unfriendly act," and members would then apply economic pressures. If necessary, the Assembly could invite members to contribute to an armed force.

This proposal, although sound from the perspective of concerns of the United States, failed to consider international realities. The League of Nations already existed, and it was unrealistic to think its members would accept a new arrangement based primarily on U.S. interests. His essay is interesting, however, in its contrast with Roosevelt's later views about the need for a police force to maintain peace and for the United States to play a direct role in world affairs.

Given Roosevelt's background and general attachment to cooperation, many internationalists cheered when he announced his presidential candidacy early in 1932. Their joy turned to amazement, however, when early in February he proclaimed that membership in the League was a dead issue, criticized its work, and suggested that even cooperation was no longer desirable. In ensuing months, he reversed his stand on the war debts and even modified his stance against high tariffs. These shifts reflected his philosophy of expediency and his desire to avoid controversial issues that might threaten his candidacy.

Once elected, Roosevelt sought a middle ground between international and national questions. He believed that the United States should play a more important role in the world but concluded that it could be effective only after it achieved internal economic stability. In brief, international problems should be subordinated to domestic ones. That perspective explains his controversial and apparently harmful course toward the World Economic Conference in 1933, his independent action in going off the gold standard, his firmness in insisting on repayment of the war debts, and the unenthusiastic response of the United States

to the Geneva Disarmament Conference, 1932–34. Yet he praised the League, promised to cooperate with it, and maintained cordial relations with ardent American internationalists like Clark M. Eichelberger of the League of Nations Association and Arthur Sweetser, who served on the Secretariat of the League of Nations. They and others could gain Roosevelt's ear, and they kept hoping they could influence his perspective and thus his policies. Their hopeful expressions in letters and memoirs are a testimonial to Roosevelt's ability to charm, because in practice his administration rarely reflected their desires.

The problem of the Permanent Court of International Justice further documents Roosevelt's ambivalent perspective. He had endorsed membership in the World Court throughout the 1920s and after his election promised to again push the issue. Yet domestic issues came first; thus not until late in 1934 did he allow Democratic leaders in the Senate to debate the issue. Even that move may reflect more of a desire to fill the legislative agenda while important domestic bills were being drafted than a commitment to the World Court. Initially it appeared the Senate would act favorably, but an aroused isolationist campaign threatened the outcome. Eleanor Roosevelt campaigned for the treaty in speeches and writings, but her husband remained on the sidelines offering only modest encouragement. He accepted a major qualifying amendment and refused to use his political influence or patronage to force wavering Democratic senators into line. Thus the vote fell seven short of the two-thirds required. While Roosevelt expressed anger over the defeat, the vote apparently convinced him of a growing isolationist mood in the country.

By the mid-thirties, Roosevelt's policies seemed more in full accord with the desires of most citizens to avoid any conflict. Traditional pacifists, who opposed war in principle, joined with isolationists who simply resisted commitments that could lead to armed involvements. Even internationalists, while still favoring League membership, agreed that the collective security concept in Article X should be modified. Thus everyone applauded Roosevelt's famous "I hate war" remark. Although sincere at the time, those words hid Roosevelt's earlier proclivity to rely on arms. Prior to 1920, he had believed in a strong defense establishment, especially a modern navy. As late as 1919, he favored universal military training for males. Yet he had changed his mind on these subjects in the 1920s as he moved toward programs favored by peace leaders. He supported the Five Power Naval Disarmament Treaty of 1922 and naval arms limitation talks during his presidency prior to 1935. He kept military budgets low in the 1930s, approved efforts to control the international trade in arms and endorsed the Nye committee hearings, which disclosed connections among munitions makers, bankers, and war. He withdrew U.S. troops from Haiti in 1934, initiated membership in the International Labor Organization that same year, favored the reciprocal trade treaties promoted by Secretary of State Cordell Hull, and advanced regional cooperation through the Good Neighbor policy. As aggressors became increasingly active, Roosevelt between 1935 and 1938 seemed to rely more and more on moral principles to restrain their behavior. Roosevelt initially accepted the neutrality acts endorsed by peace leaders, isolationists, and many internationalists because they sought to insulate the nation from threatening wars. He differed with peace advocates only in three ways. First, he sought modifications to the neutrality laws that would allow him some flexibility, reserved the right of presidential interpretation, and in the late 1930s, favored revision that allowed the sale of arms on a cash-and-carry basis. Second, he successfully thwarted the drive of peace workers for the Ludlow amendment to the Constitution, which would have required a popular vote prior to a declaration of war. Third, by 1940 he saw the need for a draft. Yet he approached that subject very cautiously because of its political impact.

A special aspect of Roosevelt's world perspective emerged after 1938 when his views toward aggressors corresponded with that of one group of domestic internationalists who favored an interventionist policy on behalf of the democracies. Yet Roosevelt continually tempered his actions, both before the outbreak of war in Europe in September of 1939 and prior to Pearl Harbor, largely in response to a public opposed to involvement in the struggle. He continually reiterated that his policies were designed to keep the United States out of war by providing resources to those countries resisting aggressors.

Roosevelt's thinking about what came to be the United Nations Organization has been fully discussed. It progressed through the Atlantic Charter (1941), the Molotov talks (1942), the Four Power and Moscow declarations (1943), and the conferences at Teheran (1943), Dumbarton Oaks (1944), and Yalta (1945). The documents associated with these events contain significant references to peace, freedom, equality, security, disarmament, and international trusteeships, but these idealistic concepts were overshadowed by Roosevelt's inherent belief that the Big Four, serving as police, should be the backbone of any postwar system. The proposed UN, he declared in 1944, should be given the power to maintain peace even by force.

External events certainly influenced Roosevelt. The popularity of Wendell Willkie's 1943 book, *One World,* the Republican Mackinac Declaration that year, and the emergence of the issue of a postwar union during the presidential campaign of 1944 forced Roosevelt to clarify his views. He appreciated the need for planning but continually worried about commitments to principles that might later be harmful. He walked a tightrope in trying to respond to the Soviet Union's concern for its security, in satisfying Wilsonian-type internationalists and emerging world or regional government advocates within the United States, and in anticipating postwar problems.

The election of 1944 especially challenged his political ability when he sought to reconcile the liberal Wilsonian perspective with his attachment to the Big Four power principle. There is little doubt about his position. He favored an organization built on collective security principles over one based primarily on consultation and mutual collaboration. He seemed oblivious to other options advanced by internationalists, including formulas for federation, the peaceful resolution of conflict, and the strengthening of international justice and law. Such procedural approaches held no attraction for Roosevelt, who saw the need for a system capable of responding to immediate concerns. The United States had a duty not so much to create a workable international organization as it did to police the world through a body to be created. This viewpoint contrasted sharply with the Wilsonian vision of a collective security system in which all shared responsibility. Roosevelt had seen the weakness of that concept and understandably wished to exercise another option.

The most remarkable aspects of Roosevelt's position lay first in the shift it represented from his 1923 Bok Prize ideas and second in the way he was able to cloak his views and persuade American internationalists that he favored a postwar body that would be universal, democratic, and sharing. But Roosevelt was ever the expedient leader both in adjusting to new conditions and in manipulating peace and internationalist leaders.

In sum, it is evident that Roosevelt had no conceptual attachment to the ideology of pacifists. He adapted to their ideas and catered to their positions only to the degree they were politically useful. Likewise, he had little interest in specific aspects of internationalist thought, particularly in the details of working drafts for a postwar organization. His primary concern lay in reconciling major differences among the big powers so that the United Nations would become a reality. That may have been his most significant positive contribution. Yet Roosevelt's political approach, while seemingly realistic at the time, did create problems. Subsequent cold war rivalries have raised doubts about assumptions that the police could cooperate or that they themselves would not need to be policed. The UN has been affected by the veto principle implicit in big-power dominance, while those features of the UN's operation associated with cooperative effort reflected in its many committees, commissions, agencies, and special bodies have become one of its strengths. Such judgments, however, need to be weighed in relation to the complexity of the subject. Workable formulas to maintain peace— whether those of Wilson, Roosevelt, or internationalists or pacifists—all relate to times and circumstances.

Selig Adler, *The Isolationist Impulse: Its Twentieth Century Reaction* (New York: Abelard-Schuman, 1957) deals fully with the pros and cons of involvement in world affairs in the 1930s. Wayne S. Cole, *Roosevelt and the Isolationists, 1932–1945* (Lincoln: University of Nebraska Press, 1983) is one of the best interpretations of a complex subject. Robert A. Divine, in *Second Chance: The Triumph of Internationalism in America during World War II* (New York: Atheneum, 1967), explores Roosevelt in relation to ideas and movements and is generally critical of his role as an internationalist. *Organizing for Peace: A Personal History of the Founding of the United Nations* (New York: Harper & Row, 1977), written by Clark M.

Eichelberger, a key propagandist and organizer, is revealing of Roosevelt's skill in persuading internationalists that he favored their particular aims. Willard Range, *Franklin D. Roosevelt's World Order* (Athens: University of Georgia Press, 1959) examines both the strengths and weaknesses of Roosevelt's thinking on international politics. And Eleanor Roosevelt, in *This I Remember* (New York: Harper & Bros., 1949), presents insights into Roosevelt's early ideas. This book also contains his Bok Prize essay.

WARREN F. KUEHL

See also Congress, United States; Isolationism; Lehman, Herbert Henry; Pacifists and the Peace Movement; Wallace, Henry A.; Welles, Benjamin Sumner; Willkie, Wendell Lewis; Wilson, Thomas Woodrow; World War II

Internment of Japanese-Americans

On 19 February 1942, President Franklin D. Roosevelt signed Executive Order 9066, authorizing military officials to exclude "any or all persons" from areas of the U.S. mainland designated as "military zones." The next month, Congress enacted and Roosevelt signed a law to enforce his order with criminal penalties. By the end of 1942, more than 110,000 Americans of Japanese ancestry—two-thirds of them native-born citizens—had been forced by military order from their West Coast homes into "relocation centers" scattered from the California desert to the swamps of Arkansas. The members of this racial minority spent an average of nine hundred days behind barbed-wire fences before the last internees were released in 1946.

The internment program reflected in part the impact of the long-standing campaign to rid the West Coast of the "Yellow Peril" of Asian immigrants. Building on this racist legacy, fears that Japanese-Americans would aid their "racial brothers" after the

Slated for relocation to an internment camp, a World War I veteran of Japanese ancestry wears his U.S. Navy uniform when he reports to his designated evacuation center, the Wartime Civil Control Administration Center in San Francisco, 6 April 1942. (National Archives.)

Japanese attack on Pearl Harbor were fueled by the press and public officials. Advocates of internment placed the burden of proving their loyalty on the Japanese-Americans, who were portrayed as a potential fifth column of saboteurs and spies. "A patriotic native-born Japanese, if he wants to make his contribution, will submit himself to a concentration camp," one California congressman told his colleagues.

For the public record, Roosevelt's order was designed to protect West Coast military facilities from sabotage and espionage. The shock of the Pearl Harbor attack and reports of Japanese atrocities in the Philippines not only helped create an atmosphere of hysteria on the West Coast but also clearly influenced Roosevelt's decision to accept the internment recommendation of his trusted advisers, led by Secretary of War Henry L. Stimson. The fact that Canada and most Latin American governments adopted similar expulsion measures against residents of Japanese ancestry shows that mass hysteria was widespread and that Roosevelt was not alone in bowing to public pressure for drastic action. Few questions were raised at the time about the exemption of Americans of German and Italian ancestry from the internment orders, although Roosevelt privately told his advisers that political factors had dictated this disparate treatment.

Hidden from the public during the ten-week period between Pearl Harbor and Roosevelt's order was a fierce debate within the government over the need for internment and its legality. Supported by reports from FBI director J. Edgar Hoover that dismissed press and army accounts of sabotage and espionage, Attorney General Francis Biddle resisted the internment campaign. Biddle's doubts were echoed by the Office of Naval Intelligence (ONI), the agency directed by a prewar presidential order to conduct surveillance of the Japanese-American population. ONI officials affirmed the overwhelming loyalty of this group and noted that FBI agents had arrested, within days of the Pearl Harbor attack, every Japanese-American considered to be potentially disloyal or dangerous.

Within the War Department, Assistant Secretary John J. McCloy held the responsibility for a military decision on the fate of Japanese-Americans. Early in February 1942, McCloy ordered Col. Karl R. Bendetsen to prepare a "final recommendation" on the issue for submission to Stimson by Gen. John L. DeWitt, the army's West Coast commander. Even though Bendetsen admitted, ten days before DeWitt's report reached Stimson, that "no one has justified fully the sheer military necessity for such action," DeWitt based his mass evacuation recommendation on the ground that Japanese-Americans were members of an "enemy race" whose loyalty was suspect.

The final showdown in the internment battle took place in Biddle's living room on 17 February 1942. McCloy and Bendetsen confronted two Justice Department lawyers, Edward J. Ennis and James Rowe, who denounced the internment proposal as unconstitutional and unnecessary. McCloy had earlier overridden the qualms expressed by Stimson, who felt that removal on racial grounds would "tear a tremendous hole in our constitutional system." Unknown to Ennis and Rowe when the meeting began, Biddle had spoken with Roosevelt that afternoon and had abandoned his opposition to internment after assurance that the army would relieve the Justice Department in conducting the mass roundup and detention program. With this surrender in hand, McCloy exacted from Biddle an agreement to participate in polishing the executive order placed on Roosevelt's desk two days later.

The forced exodus of Japanese-Americans began in March 1942 with a curfew order and a series of 108 exclusion orders drafted by Bendetsen and signed by DeWitt. In groups of roughly one thousand at a time, citizens and aliens alike were ordered to dispose of their property and report to assembly centers located in fairgrounds and race tracks for eventual transfer to the tar-paper barracks of internment camps that were guarded by armed troops. The residents of these barren camps endured sandstorms, boiling summer heat, and frigid winter cold, imprisoned without any acknowledgment of their constitutional rights. Before the war ended, about one-quarter of the internees were released on parole, after subjection to a loyalty screening and agreement to remain away from their West Coast homes. The supreme irony of the internment program is that more than one thousand young men, whose parents remained behind barbed wire, volunteered for military service and fought with valor in Europe, suffering more casualties and winning more medals for their segregated unit than any other army combat brigade.

It seems surprising in retrospect that only three Japanese-Americans resisted the internment orders and challenged them in the courts. Their choices, however, were limited to confinement behind barbed wire or prison bars. The young men whose test cases reached the Supreme Court differed in background and motivation: Minoru Yasui was a lawyer and reserve army officer who violated the curfew order in Portland, Oregon; Gordon Hirabayashi was a Quaker pacifist and college student in Seattle who broke the curfew and exclusion orders on religious grounds; and Fred Korematsu was a shipyard welder who evaded the exclusion order in San Leandro, California, hoping to escape from the West Coast with his Caucasian girlfriend.

The Supreme Court held in each of these test cases that the war powers granted to the president and Congress by the Constitution outweighed the due process and equal protection claims raised by the Japanese-American challengers. The Court's opinions in the *Hirabayashi* and *Yasui* cases, handed down in June 1943, were unanimous and dealt only with the curfew orders. Eighteen months later, when military victory over Japan seemed certain, the Court upheld the initial detention program in the *Korematsu* case over the sharp dissents of three justices. In granting on the same day a habeas corpus petition brought by a camp resident, the Court reaffirmed its *Korematsu* ruling but held without dissent that Congress had not authorized the continuing detention of Japanese-Americans cleared as loyal by camp officials. Begin-

ning in January 1945, those who had passed the loyalty tests were gradually released from the camps, although several thousand who were considered disloyal remained in detention until after the war ended.

The internment program has continued to evoke emotions on both sides of this contentious issue. Congress responded in 1980 to calls for redress and reparations for the Japanese-Americans by establishing the Commission on Wartime Relocation and Internment of Civilians to review the factors that led to Executive Order 9066 and to examine its consequences. Among those who testified, former Assistant Secretary McCloy defended the internment in part as "retribution" for the Japanese attack on Pearl Harbor. The commission rejected this defense and concluded in its 1983 report that "race prejudice, war hysteria and a failure of political leadership" on the part of Roosevelt and his advisers had resulted in a "grave injustice" to Japanese-Americans.

The commission's findings, along with newly discovered evidence from government files, also prompted legal efforts to erase the criminal records of the wartime defendants. In the first case to be decided, a federal judge vacated Fred Korematsu's conviction in November 1983, holding that the Supreme Court had approved Roosevelt's order and the internment program on the basis of "unsubstantiated facts, distortions and misrepresentations" to the Court by high-ranking government officials. These findings responded to Korematsu's claim that government lawyers had presented tainted evidence to the Supreme Court, a charge backed up by Justice Department records that included complaints by responsible lawyers of "lies" and "intentional falsehoods" in War Department reports submitted to the Court in 1944.

When he signed Executive Order 9066, Franklin Roosevelt set in motion what the American Civil Liberties Union later called "the greatest deprivation of civil liberties by government in this country since slavery." His success in mobilizing the country for ultimate victory in World War II won the admiration, then and now, of most Americans. But the blemish of the internment program cannot be removed from Roosevelt's wartime record.

There is a substantial literature on the internment, virtually all of it condemnatory. The most recent and comprehensive analysis is the official report of the Commission on Wartime Relocation and Internment of Civilians, *Personal Justice Denied* (Washington, D.C.: U.S. Government Printing Office, 1983), based on government records and surprisingly well written for such a document. An older but equally comprehensive work is Jacobus tenBroek et al., *Prejudice, War and the Constitution* (Berkeley: University of California Press, 1954). The War Department's official report on and justification for the internment is the *Final Report: Japanese Evacuation From the West Coast, 1942* (Washington, D.C.: U.S. Government Printing Office, 1943). The first and most critical analysis of the Supreme Court decisions in the internment test cases is Eugene V. Rostow, "The Japanese American Cases—A Disaster," *Yale Law Journal*, June 1945. A full-scale account of the test cases, based on government files, interviews with defendants and lawyers, and the papers of Supreme Court justices, is Peter Irons, *Justice at War: The Story of the Japanese American Internment Cases* (New York: Oxford University Press, 1983).

PETER IRONS

See also Biddle, Francis Beverley; Civil Libertites in Wartime; House Committee to Investigate Un-American Activities; Ickes, Harold LeClair; Stimson, Henry L.; Supreme Court of the United States

Interregnum

Franklin D. Roosevelt overwhelmingly won the 1932 election because of Hoover's failure to overcome the nation's dire economic crisis. Eager for new leadership, Congress had passed the Twentieth Amendment in March, shortening the lame-duck period between the president's election and his inauguration into office by six weeks. Nonetheless, the states did not complete ratification until 23 January 1933, so the country had to wait a full four months to effect a change of leadership. Not wanting Hoover to claim any of his success, not wanting to rescue Hoover from embarrassment, and especially not wanting to risk his program before the political moment was right, Roosevelt also made the country wait to discover the New Deal he had in store.

These four months proved to be among the bleakest of the depression. As food prices fell dramatically, armed and angry farmers defended their property from repossessors. Beggars in record numbers took to the city streets; vagabonds took to the highways; families were separated. Demagogues Huey Long and Father Coughlin captured vast audiences, and the Communist party instigated hunger marches through the streets of Washington. Spending sagged. Banks failed. Congress stuttered. Americans trembled from cold, hunger, and fear.

But leader-to-be FDR seemed unflappable. Behind the scenes he and Raymond Moley busily chose a cabinet from among early Roosevelt supporters and readied the legislative bombardment. They dusted off the questionable Trading with the Enemy Act of 1917 in preparation for an embargo on the exportation of gold and a national bank holiday. They even studied Congress for an appropriate preinauguration chance to push the New Deal, but found none. For all the world could see, however, FDR was carefree, cheerful, and optimistic. An attempt on his life on 15 February 1933 in Miami left Chicago's mayor Anton Cermak mortally wounded and Roosevelt's aides badly shaken, but did not seem to disrupt FDR's own equanimity.

This personal steadiness ultimately did more to promote the country's morale than had all of Hoover's pleas for confidence during the previous three years. Since 1929, Hoover had been claiming that the country's economic structure was fundamentally sound. All that was lacking was enough faith in the system to induce Americans to resume normal economic activity. In a vain attempt to intimidate Roosevelt into

endorsing the Republican policies of a balanced budget and a noninflationary currency, Hoover sent the president-elect a letter, dated 17 February 1933. In this letter, Hoover asserted that morale would rise upon Roosevelt's assurance that he would remain true to these policies. Hoover knew that he was asking nothing less than for Roosevelt to renounce his New Deal before enacting a single element of it. Nonetheless, the lame-duck president was so convinced that traditional policies were the answer to the depression that he called Roosevelt a "madman" for refusing to acquiesce. In his turn, Roosevelt called Hoover's actions "cheeky," and delayed acknowledging the letter.

Roosevelt not only spurned Hoover's interpretation of the crisis but promised privately to call a bank holiday as his first official act. Nothing would repudiate Hoover more flagrantly. A frustrated and perhaps desperate Hoover eschewed the traditional White House dinner for the new first family and instead hosted a tea on 3 March. Rather than offer pleasantries along with the brew, however, Hoover once more tried to persuade Roosevelt to cooperate with him, but Roosevelt would not bend. Not until that night, inauguration eve, after two more telephone calls to FDR, did the White House announce, "There is nothing more we can do."

Throughout the interregnum, Roosevelt remained a model of confidence. To him it was clear that Hoover had failed, and he was eager to get on with his own program, for he himself had no intention of failing. The moment of his inauguration, as he well knew, could represent the return of hope to America. He chose to await that moment to capture for the New Deal the remaining vitality of an enervated country.

All of Roosevelt's biographers explore the mysteries of these four months to some extent. Frank Freidel's *Launching the New Deal* (Boston: Little, Brown & Co., 1973) offers one of the fullest expositions. See also Arthur M. Schlesinger, Jr., *The Crisis of the Old Order* (Boston: Houghton Mifflin Co., 1956) and *The Coming of the New Deal* (Boston: Houghton Mifflin Co., 1958). More recently, Nathan Miller's *FDR: An Intimate History* (Garden City, N.Y.: Doubleday & Co., 1983) contains a succinct and colorful chapter on the period.

SHELLEY BOOKSPAN

See also Assassination Attempt of 1933; Brains Trust; Hoover, Herbert Clark; Raymond Moley; Tugwell, Rexford Guy

Interstate Commerce

Three 1935 U.S. Supreme Court rulings, in which the justices consistently rendered a narrow interpretation of the commerce clause, threatened to undermine the federal government's constitutional authority to legislate the economic reforms of FDR's New Deal administration.

In the "hot oil" case (*Panama Refining Company v. Ryan*, 293 U.S. 388; 7 January 1935), the court held Section 9C of the National Industrial Recovery Act (NIRA) to be an improper delegation of legislative authority to the executive branch. Section 9C gave the president power to prohibit interstate transport of oil in excess of those amounts permitted by state laws in order to regulate production according to general NIRA purposes. According to the Court's majority opinion, this particular section extended to the president powers reserved for Congress inasmuch as the law did not sufficiently guide or adequately limit the president's authority regarding matters of interstate commerce in this instance.

The "hot oil" decision signaled the conservative stance the Court would take on two cases of major importance. On 6 May 1935, the Court, in a split decision, invalidated the Railroad Retirement Act of 1934. Although the principal basis for the decision in *Railroad Retirement Board* v. *Alton Railroad Co.* (295 U.S. 330) rested on the Fifth Amendment, the secondary basis for rejection lay in another narrow interpretation of the commerce clause. With justices Hughes, Cardozo, Stone, and Brandeis dissenting, the majority opinion nonetheless held that there was no relation between pensions and the efficiency or safety of interstate commerce, hence the imposition of a federal pension system constituted an unwarranted extension of the government's power to regulate interstate commerce.

The decision did not stop Congress from passing the Social Security Act, and the Wagner-Crosser Railroad Retirement Act reinstated old-age security benefits for railroad workers. But interstate commerce was the central legal issue in the infamous "sick chicken" case, which aptly described the NRA's blue eagle symbol after the Supreme Court invalidated the NIRA on 27 May. In *A.L.A. Schechter Corporation* v. *U.S.* (295 U.S. 495), the government charged that Schechter Poultry Corporation's open violations of NIRA poultry codes "directly" affected interstate commerce in several ways. The Supreme Court disagreed, and in a unanimous decision, ruled in favor of Schechter on the basis that its operations had only an "indirect" effect upon interstate commerce. In their decision, however, the Court went beyond the merits of the case and ruled that the NIRA, by granting the president power to approve codes and to establish implementing agencies, unconstitutionally extended legislative power to the executive office.

The three crucial 1935 decisions are amply discussed by Carl Brent Swisher in *American Constitutional Development*, 2d ed. (Boston: Houghton Mifflin Co., 1954) and by Basil Rauch in *The History of the New Deal, 1933–1938* (New York: Creative Age Press, 1944). Personal recollections of Robert L. Stern, who coauthored the government's brief in the "hot oil" case, appear in Katie Louchheim, ed., *The Making of the New Deal: The Insiders Speak* (Cambridge, Mass.: Harvard University Press, 1983).

REBECCA CONARD

See also Court-Packing Plan; Hughes, Charles Evans; Supreme Court of the United States

Isolationism

The Roosevelt years marked both a high point and the demise of traditional American isolationism, and President Roosevelt played a central role in those patterns. The terms *isolationism* and *isolationist* have had pejorative connotations since Pearl Harbor. If defined literally, they are misleading. Isolationists did not wish to cut the United States off from the rest of the world, nor did they want to sever trade and credit relations with other parts of the world. They were not pacifists. In the 1930s most leading isolationists were not conservatives; many were to the left of Roosevelt and his New Deal. Furthermore, most isolationists were not pro-Nazi or pro-Axis.

Isolationists were opposed to American intervention in European wars. They also opposed involvement in "entangling alliances" and in the League of Nations. They guarded American sovereignty and freedom of action. They wanted to leave Americans free to determine when, where, how, and whether the United States should involve itself abroad.

Isolationists believed that the United States could defend itself in the Western hemisphere. They opposed military preparations that seemed designed for involvement in foreign wars—particularly in Europe; they supported military preparations for continental defense in the Western hemisphere. Generally they were critical of large naval appropriations, fearing that a big navy would be used to support intervention

Ding Darling, New York Herald Tribune, *13 January 1940. (© I.M.T. Corporation. Reprinted by permission.)*

abroad. They tended to give priority to air power preparations.

Isolationists had faith in the power of example. They believed the United States could more effectively lead the world by building democracy, freedom, and prosperity at home than it could through involvement in foreign wars. They opposed American efforts to police the world or to rebuild the world in an American image. Many feared that involvement in foreign wars would shatter domestic reform programs at home and could destroy the very freedoms they were supposed to defend. They favored restraining the president, the military, big business, and financiers as they operated in foreign affairs.

In the 1930s most Americans were isolationists, but there were variations in different segments of the population. Isolationists were most numerous in the Middle West. They were stronger in the Republican party than in the Democratic party. They were relatively numerous among farmers outside the South and among small businessmen. They were relatively more numerous in rural and small-town America than in great cities and among Irish-Americans, German-Americans, and Italian-Americans. In religious terms they were comparatively numerous among Roman Catholics and Lutherans—though those patterns were due more to the ethnic composition of those denominations than to theology. They were slightly more numerous among women than among men. Those were only tendencies, however, and there were exceptions to every generalization.

Millions of Americans were isolationists during the Roosevelt years, but among the more prominent and influential were William E. Borah of Idaho, Hiram Johnson of California, Burton K. Wheeler of Montana, George W. Norris of Nebraska, Arthur Capper of Kansas, Gerald P. Nye of North Dakota, Henrik Shipstead of Minnesota, Robert M. La Follette, Jr., and Philip La Follette of Wisconsin, Bennett Champ Clark of Missouri, Arthur H. Vandenberg of Michigan, Robert A. Taft of Ohio, and Hamilton Fish of FDR's home district in New York. Most famous and controversial was the aviator Charles A. Lindbergh.

Isolationism reached a high tide during Roosevelt's first term as president, with the adoption of the Johnson Act of 1934, Senate rejection of the World Court in 1935, the Nye investigation of the munitions industries in 1934–36, and enactment of neutrality laws beginning in 1935. Generally, however, domestic issues dominated in early relations between Roosevelt and the isolationists. From 1932 to 1937, FDR actively solicited support from progressives, and most western progressives were isolationists. In planning his New Deal legislative moves, the president consulted closely with such progressive senators as Norris, Wheeler, Johnson, and La Follette—isolationists all. Though isolationist senators Borah and Nye criticized Roosevelt's National Recovery Administration for being too favorable to big business, much of the early New Deal was consistent with the economic nationalism they favored. By the time FDR ran for a second term in 1936, leading isolationists felt no overwhelming need to make an issue of the president's performance on foreign affairs. Most of them supported Roosevelt for reelection, and foreign affairs played no significant role in the outcome.

Roosevelt's second term as president from 1937 to 1941 saw a parting of the ways in his relations with isolationists. Again the patterns were set initially by domestic rather than foreign affairs. The president's Court-packing proposal early in 1937 was the first major wedge driven between him and the isolationists during his second term. Wheeler led the opposition, and most Senate isolationists voted with him to kill the president's proposal. As Roosevelt faced growing opposition on domestic issues, alarming international developments increasingly demanded his attention. He was moving with political currents when he shifted from domestic affairs to foreign affairs during his second term. That refocus required a break between Roosevelt and the isolationists, however, and helped to assure his triumph over them.

In October 1937, Roosevelt's quarantine address troubled isolationists, as did his efforts in January 1938 to block consideration of the Ludlow amendment in the House of Representatives. As the president slowly shaped and began to implement his efforts to aid Axis victims with methods short of war, isolationists were more alarmed than Axis leaders were. From 1937 onward, in episode after episode, foreign crises drove the wedge deeper between Roosevelt and the isolationists. One by one individual isolationists turned away from their earlier cautiously cooperative attitudes toward varied degrees of distrust, alienation, and even hatred of FDR.

Until the middle of 1940, the majority of the public believed it was more important for the United States to stay out of the European war than to ensure the defeat of the Axis. But with Dunkirk, the fall of France, and the Battle of Britain those patterns changed. Most Americans continued to oppose a declaration of war, but by the autumn of 1940 a majority believed it was more important for the United States to assure a British victory over the Axis than to stay out of the war. The president's moves to aid Britain short of war won majority approval. In that sense, FDR had already won his battle against isolationists; from then on isolationists were a minority.

In the summer of 1940, isolationists were still strong enough to get noninterventionist planks in the platforms of both major political parties, but both parties rejected isolationist contenders for their presidential nominations. Roosevelt's reelection to an unprecedented third term prepared the way politically for the final phase of his contest with the isolationists. During his third and fourth terms from 1941 to 1945, Roosevelt skillfully and almost ruthlessly demolished the isolationists.

At a time when 80 percent of the American people continued to oppose a declaration of war, President Roosevelt's aid-short-of-war tactics provided the maximum involvement that Congress and the public seemed willing to approve before Pearl Harbor. The isolationists were unable to defeat any administration aid-short-of-war proposal actually put to a vote in

Congress after the European war began. The patrol system and shoot-on-sight policy in the Atlantic, and the increasing economic squeeze on Japan in the Pacific, encouraged the possibility that developments abroad might cause Congress and the American people to abandon their opposition to a declaration of war (as they did after the Japanese attack on Pearl Harbor).

Roosevelt and his top advisers used guilt-by-association methods to discredit isolationists. That is, they helped build the impression that the isolationists were serving the Nazi cause. Even before Pearl Harbor, patriotic isolationist opponents of Roosevelt's foreign policies were depicted as little better than Nazis. The president authorized wiretaps and FBI probes in contending with opposition. Shortly before Pearl Harbor he urged the attorney general to initiate a grand jury investigation of the America First Committee. Freedom of expression and the right to dissent on foreign policy matters did not rank high in FDR's scale of priorities as he contested with isolationists during his third and fourth terms as president. Isolationists continued their opposition until the Japanese attacked Pearl Harbor, but they were thoroughly discredited even before that attack provided the coup de grace.

With the attack on Pearl Harbor, Senate and House isolationists (save only Jeannette Rankin) joined with their colleagues in voting for war against Japan and then against Germany and Italy. Most of them ceased their noninterventionist activities and pledged support for the war effort.

In 1943 the Fulbright resolution overwhelmingly adopted in the House and the Connally resolution in the Senate were designed to proclaim that Congress would not block American membership in the world organization to be created at the close of World War II. President Roosevelt urged creation of a postwar United Nations partly to make certain that the United States did not return to isolationism as it had after World War I.

One by one isolationists faded from the scene. Borah died early in 1940. Hiram Johnson died the day the United States dropped its atomic bomb on Hiroshima. Isolationists in Congress generally were turned out of office the first time they faced the voters during and after World War II. Roosevelt won his battle against the isolationists as surely as the United States under his leadership had shared in winning the military victory over the Axis power.

Fundamentally American isolationism succumbed to changing circumstances at home and abroad that Roosevelt did not create and did not really control. The declining power of Britain and France, the challenges from the Axis states and later from the Soviet Union, and terrifying modern military capabilities forced the United States to play a larger role in world affairs. At the same time within the United States, urbanization, the decline of rural and small-town America, improved communication facilities, and the spectacular growth of American industrial capacities and capital accumulations compelled the United States to seek broader horizons. Nonetheless, President Roosevelt provided leadership for the destruction of American isolationism. His triumph was so decisive, and isolationism was so thoroughly discredited, that America's later deliberations on alternatives in foreign affairs were narrowed and inhibited to avoid any damaging allegations of "isolationism." With FDR's triumph over the isolationists, there could be no turning back either for the United States or the world.

Information in this article is drawn, in sharply condensed and revised form, from Wayne S. Cole, *Roosevelt and the Isolationists, 1932–45* (Lincoln: University of Nebraska Press, 1983). That book is a detailed, balanced account based on research in more than one hundred manuscript and archival collections. A scholarly study that provides a fair portrait of the isolationists and makes clear the diversity of views among them is Manfred Jonas, *Isolationism in America, 1935–1941* (Ithaca: Cornell University Press, 1966). For scholarly books on individual isolationist leaders, see Wayne S. Cole, *Senator Gerald P. Nye and American Foreign Relations* (Minneapolis: University of Minnesota Press, 1962), Michele Flynn Stenehjem, *An American First: John T. Flynn and the America First Committee* (New Rochelle: Arlington House, 1976), and Wayne S. Cole, *Charles A. Lindbergh and the Battle against American Intervention in World War II* (New York: Harcourt Brace Jovanovich, 1974). The book on Nye emphasizes agrarian bases for isolationism, whereas the book on Flynn looks more closely at urban isolationists. The book on Lindbergh is based on research in the aviator's personal papers. For a scholarly study of the attitudes of old isolationists after World War II during the cold war with the Soviet Union, see Justice D. Doenecke, *Not to the Swift: The Old Isolationists in the Cold War Era* (Lewisburg: Bucknell University Press, 1979). For an exhaustive analytical bibliography on American isolationism, see Justus D. Doenecke, *The Literature of Isolationism: A Guide to Non-Interventionist Scholarship, 1930–1972* (Colorado Springs: Ralph Myles, Publisher, 1972).

WAYNE S. COLE

See also American First Committee; Barnes, Harry Elmer; Beard, Charles A.; Congress, United States; Declaration of War; Foreign Economic Policy; Foreign Policy; Hoover, Herbert Clark; Hull, Cordell; Internationalism and Peace; Johnson, Hugh Samuel; LaFollette, Philip Fox; LaFollette, Robert Marion, Jr.; Lindbergh, Charles Augustus; McCormick, Robert Rutherford; Neutrality Acts; Norris, George William; Pearl Harbor; Reciprocal Trade Agreements; Spanish Civil War; Stalin, Joseph, and the Soviet Union; Vandenberg, Arthur Hendrick; Wheeler, Burton Kendall; Wilson, Thomas Woodrow; World War II

J

Jackson, Robert Houghwout

(13 February 1892–9 October 1954)

Robert H. Jackson. (Constant Collection. Courtesy FDR Library.)

Solicitor general, attorney general, and associate justice of the Supreme Court during the Roosevelt administration. Robert Jackson was born in Spring Creek, Pennsylvania, and studied at the Albany Law School for one year, leaving without a degree. He clerked for Frank Mott, a lawyer in Jamestown, New York, and a major figure in the state's Democratic politics. Jackson was admitted to the bar in November 1913 and became a prominent trial lawyer in upstate New York, where his activity in state politics brought him to FDR's attention.

Appointed general counsel to the Bureau of Internal Revenue in 1934, Jackson attracted notice for his successful prosecution of Andrew Mellon, former secretary of the treasury, for tax evasion. He then moved successively from positions as special counsel to the Department of the Treasury and to the Securities Exchange Commission, to the Department of Justice, where he headed first the Tax and later the Antitrust divisions. After actively supporting the proposal to enlarge the Supreme Court, he became solicitor general in 1938 and attorney general in 1940. While attorney general he drafted an opinion, requested by FDR, that ingeniously defended the legality of the destroyer-base agreement with Great Britain. In June 1941, he was appointed to the Court, filling the seat left open as Harlan Fiske Stone became chief justice. Although a liberal and a nationalist, he did not become a classic New Deal justice in the pattern of Black or Douglas; instead he crafted more moderate opinions.

In 1945 he accepted President Truman's request to become the chief prosecutor at the Nuremburg war crimes trials. Jackson returned to the Court in the fall of 1946, having completed his controversial assignment in Europe, and continued to serve until his death.

The only biography is Eugene C. Gerhart, *America's Advocate: Robert H. Jackson* (Indianapolis: Bobbs-Merrill Co., 1958). Gerhart also wrote an analysis of Jackson's judicial career, which he had left out of the biography; see *Supreme Court Justice Jackson: Lawyer's Judge* (Albany: Q Corporation, 1961). Charles S. Desmond et al., eds. *Mr. Justice Jackson* (New York: Columbia University Press, 1969) contains four lectures by distinguished jurists that comment on different aspects of his career. Glendon Schubert, *Dispassionate Justice* (Indianapolis: Bobbs-Merrill Co., 1969) is a detailed commentary on the important opinions written by Justice Jackson.

See also Supreme Court of the United States

Japan

Few experiences in Franklin D. Roosevelt's presidency were more traumatic than his dealings with Japan. When thinking of his policy toward Japan, one immediately recalls the Pearl Harbor attack and his castigation of it as a dastardly deed that "will live in infamy." Yet it is not altogether clear what his own role was in bringing about the disaster, or what precisely was his idea of a satisfactory relationship with the Japanese empire.

The fact is that Roosevelt's foreign policy was mostly reactive, and until the onset of the Second World War he did not define a consistent approach to Japan or for that matter to any other country. Before becoming president in 1933, he had developed two broad views of Japan which he shared with most American leaders of the time. One was that of Japan as a naval power. This was a theme that had become widely accepted in the United States by the time Roosevelt became assistant secretary of the navy in the Wilson administration in 1913. He had read, among other things, Homer Lea's *Valor of Ignorance*, a 1908 story of an imaginary war between the two countries. During the First World War, naval rivalry across the Pacific became a reality, as the Japanese and American navies increased in size and came to dominate the Pacific while the European powers were preoccupied elsewhere. The second was a product of developments in the 1920s which saw a rapprochement between the two countries, a developing pattern of solid business relations derived from economic interdependence. Japan looked to the United States for capital and technology, and cooperated with it in reducing armaments and maintaining a stable regime in China. The Japanese government on the whole pursued an internationalist policy of "cooperative diplomacy," emphasizing cooperation and consultation with the Western powers in dealing with trade, China, and naval issues.

Beyond his broad images of Japan, Roosevelt does not seem to have developed a particular interest in Japan either as a nation or as a culture. To the extent that he was interested in Asia, he was more drawn to China because of the commercial activities his forebears, the Delanos, had carried on in the nineteenth century.

The situation had changed drastically by 1933. During 1931–33, Japan had established control over Manchuria, breaking away from the framework of American-oriented international cooperation. Under normal circumstances, Roosevelt might have responded to the challenge vigorously in order to preserve that framework. The onset of the depression, however, immobilized American policy, and the new president was compelled to devote his energies to alleviating the domestic economic crisis. In doing so, he was not above ignoring the mechanisms that had been established during the 1920s for maintaining international cooperation: the gold standard, the Open Door, the League of Nations. The result was that during most of the 1930s Roosevelt dealt with Japan, if he did so at all, in an ad hoc fashion, not in terms of a larger framework.

To the extent that there was an overall pattern, it was to refer back to the rudimentary fact of power. Not international cooperation or economic interdependence, but a simple equation on the basis of actual and potential military capabilities became the groundwork for Roosevelt's attitude toward Japan. This simplified matters considerably, as he would cope with American-Japanese relations in terms of changing power realities. For instance, he would make sure that Japan's naval predominance in the western Pacific would not threaten the status quo in the rest of the ocean. He was adamantly opposed to granting Japan naval priority for this reason, and when the latter abrogated the arms limitation agreements and launched an ambitious building program, Roosevelt responded by initiating his own programs for naval construction and fortification. A showdown between two such powers was always a possibility, and he recalled that while he was a student at Harvard a Japanese student had predicted the coming of war in the Pacific. This does not mean, however, that he made specific plans for such a war. At least until 1939, he was anxious to avoid trouble with Japan that could lead to an open conflict. This was because he did not think Japan as yet threatened American security or that the Japanese leaders really wanted war with America.

In this he proved to be ultimately wrong. There was, to be sure, no Japanese blueprint for war with the United States until early 1941, but Japan's top military strategists worked from a logic of relative weakness; because they perceived their country far weaker in resources and armaments than the United States, they argued for striking first and for establishing an Asian sphere of influence to ensure self-sufficiency and reduce economic dependence on America. Such thinking was a product of what they perceived to be the global trend toward autarkies and "pan-regions." They wanted to establish Japan's regional hegemony, which necessitated excluding the United States from Asia and the western Pacific. Prime Minister Tojo Hideki, assuming power in October 1941, accepted these premises and supported war against America in the name of "national survival." It was a decision dictated by considerations of weakness, not strength.

In any event, the disbelief that Japan would seriously contemplate going to war may have reflected Roosevelt's complacency and sense of superiority; even after Pearl Harbor, he continued to believe that the physical and mental characteristics of the Japanese made them inferior to Americans. His suspicion of them, and his view that they were significantly different from white Americans, undoubtedly underlay his approval of the wartime relocation of Japanese-Americans from the West Coast. But this does not quite make him a "racist." After all, he was friendly toward China and the Chinese, whom he regarded as hard-working, heroic, and even "democratic" people. He tended to view Japanese and Chinese as opposites, as two extreme examples of what could happen to non-Western countries. Japan he saw as a country of quick learners and imitators who turned their newly acquired technology against their Western teachers; the Chinese, on the other hand, had been slow to modernize but remained more human, civilized, and friendly toward the West. It was in the latter's interest to encourage Chinese modernization in such a way that it would not turn into another Japan. Roosevelt's image of China has been criticized as naive, but we should realize that it was the exact opposite of his perception of Japan.

During 1939–41, Roosevelt's policy toward Japan became increasingly bound up with the situation in Europe, where the survival of Great Britain was at stake. It is interesting to note that whereas in Europe he was willing to practice realpolitik—for instance, by giving aid to the Soviet Union as soon as the latter was attacked by Germany—in Asia he did not consider the option of making compromises with Japan so as to concentrate on European affairs. He consistently viewed Japanese power as an adversary factor, particularly so after Japan entered into an alliance with Germany in 1940. He had no faith in any agreement with Japan, which he thought would only respond to the language of power. It was imperative to prevent Japanese conquest of China, which would enable that country to expand southward toward Southeast Asia and the western Pacific, the region of rich resources that was vital to Britain. For this reason, President Roosevelt stepped up his aid to China and authorized the imposition of economic sanctions against Japan. One climax came during the summer of 1941 when he approved the freezing of Japanese assets in the United States, reinforced the defense of the Philippines by stationing a large number of fighter planes there, and sent personal emissaries to the wartime Chinese capital of Chungking to assure the Nationalists of continued American support. His attitude toward Japan became even more hardened in proportion as the tides of war on the Russian front and in the Atlantic appeared to turn against the possibility of a quick German victory.

Given such measures, the final showdown could have occasioned no surprise. Roosevelt was, nevertheless, angered by the Japanese attack on Pearl Harbor, as it indicated the failure of his strategy of restraining Japan by military and economic pressures. At the same time, the attack helped him immeasurably by uniting American opinion and making the war acceptable to the entire nation.

Just before Pearl Harbor, the president had sent a personal message to Emperor Hirohito to urge him to preserve the peace in the Pacific. This was less an expression of Roosevelt's confidence in the emperor than another example of his tendency to personalize diplomacy. He had, throughout the 1930s, appealed to world leaders such as Hitler, Mussolini, and Stalin to work hard to maintain world peace. Such appeals had not been heeded, but Roosevelt never gave up the practice, and after war came, he met several times with the leaders of the Allied nations. Regarding Emperor Hirohito, however, he never again referred to him except indirectly, when talking of an unconditional surrender on which he would insist as the only acceptable way of ending the war.

Actually, he gave little thought to Japan during the war beyond ensuring its defeat by whatever means, including atomic bombs. The problem of peace did not interest him, and he let the State Department work out specific policies concerning Japanese affairs after the expected surrender. In the meantime, he authorized the navy to begin making plans for retaining islands in the Pacific for postwar military use. He visualized the United States, predominant in the Pacific, and the Soviet Union, emerging strengthened in northeastern Asia, policing Japan so that the latter would never again menace the peace and security of the area. China he continued to view with favor as a potential power, but he did not think the country would develop as a modern state soon after the war. At least, Asia's future lay more in China's than in Japan's hands, and he was confident that after the Japanese were expelled from all lands they had grabbed after the 1870s, they would accept their fate as a small, weakened country of no real importance.

In all this, he may have seriously miscalculated the nature of U.S.-Japanese relations. A better understanding of Japan, or a greater willingness to listen to the advice of officials knowledgeable about the country, might have given him a more sophisticated way of dealing with Japan, both before and during the war. But he could hardly be blamed for singling out the power factor, for that was what the Japanese themselves were doing. They, too, miscalculated the

degree of economic and cultural ties across the Pacific and sought to entrench Japanese power in Asia and the Pacific. Roosevelt showed the futility of such an ambition, and in this sense he may be viewed as the father of postwar Japan.

The following titles indicate the range of topics that have been studied in connection with Roosevelt and Japan. The best balanced treatment is Robert Dallek, *Franklin D. Roosevelt and American Foreign Policy, 1932–1945* (New York: Oxford University Press, 1979). David Reynolds in *The Creation of the Anglo-American Alliance: A Study in Competitive Cooperation, 1937–1941* (Chapel Hill: University of North Carolina Press, 1982) treats the Japanese question in the larger context of Anglo-American cooperation. Akira Iriye, *Power and Culture: The Japanese-American War, 1941–1945* (Cambridge, Mass.: Harvard University Press, 1981) is a study of wartime American policies toward Japan. The best treatment of Roosevelt's attitudes toward the Japanese is Christopher Thorne, *Allies of a Kind: The United States, Britain, and the War against Japan, 1941–1945* (London: Hamish Hamilton, 1978). Waldo H. Heinrichs, *American Ambassador: Joseph C. Grew and the Development of the United States Diplomatic Tradition* (Boston: Little, Brown & Co., 1966) is an interesting study of the gaps between Roosevelt's and a professional diplomat's perceptions of Japan.

AKIRA IRIYE

See also Atomic Bomb; Axis Alliance; Chiang Kai-shek; Declaration of War; Foreign Economic Policy; Foreign Policy; Open Door Policy; Pearl Harbor; Stimson, Henry L.; World War II

Japanese-Americans

See Civil Liberties in Wartime; Internment of Japanese-Americans

Jews

Franklin Delano Roosevelt enjoyed the support of a majority of America's Jewish population throughout his years as governor of New York and president of the United States. When he died, political analyst Sam Lubell wrote, "No group in the nation felt more homeless politically than the Jews." They saw him as their friend and champion, and a great leader in the fight for social justice. In assessing his career and accomplishments, Jewish publications in 1945 noted that he would "be remembered with gratitude as long as the nation survives" and that he "was the greatest American of our day." There were no suggestions at that time that the Jewish people had any reason to question his accomplishments as president. Such queries arose a generation later when scholars began to reevaluate his position in regard to refugee policy and the Holocaust.

Until Roosevelt became president, the Protestant elite both reigned and ruled in Washington. To be sure, Catholics and Jews had been rewarded with occasional appointments, some of great prominence,

President Franklin D. Roosevelt receives the Zeta Beta Tau fraternity Gottheil medal for distinguished service to Jewry, Washington, D.C., 17 May 1937. (Courtesy FDR Library.)

but essentially the government had been run by Protestant descendents of old-stock Americans. When Roosevelt took office, he set the tone for an administration that recruited people on the basis of their intellectual and administrative talents, not their heritage. As a result, large numbers of Catholics, Jews, and blacks found opportunities to utilize their professional skills. This was especially important because existing prejudice toward these groups barred many of them from private employment. As members of the new administration, Jews attracted attention from other Americans. Historians Thomas Krueger and William Glidden later estimated that although Jews constituted only 3 percent of the American population, they made up 15 percent of the higher civil service and upper-echelon appointments during Roosevelt's presidency. Contemporaries sensed this overrepresentation and bigots decried the so-called Jew Deal and its accomplishments.

In retrospect it is understandable why so many Jews worked with Roosevelt. He came to the presidency with a fundamental belief in the efficacy of federal action to reverse the course of the depression and to restore prosperity. He had few concrete plans to execute, but he listened to suggestions from bright and imaginative people. Throughout his political career he surrounded himself with people of talent, and their ethnic heritage did not affect his evaluation of their work. When governor of New York, he chose Samuel Rosenman as chief associate, and Rosenman remained close to Roosevelt longer than any of his other advisers. As president, he turned to an old friend from Hyde Park, Henry Morgenthau, Jr., and made him secretary of the treasury. Originally more knowledgeable about agricultural problems than urban ones, Roosevelt learned about labor from people like Sidney Hillman and Rose Schneiderman. While in the White House, he told Schneiderman that she taught him everything he knew about trade unionism.

Hillman and Schneiderman reflected the values not only of Jewish laborers but of Judaic thought as well. "In probably no other American subculture," political scientist Lawrence Fuchs has written, "is so high a value placed upon . . . helping of the poor by the rich and the weak by the strong." Jews in general favored more governmental planning and activity to improve the quality of people's lives, and this blended well with the president's thoughts. It is not coincidental, therefore, that Jewish activists found the Roosevelt years in Washington appealing. Abe Fortas, later a U.S. Supreme Court justice, recalled that in the early days of the New Deal one "could see the world and feel it taking form under our hands. It was one of those periods of flux when there was practically no obstacle between thinking up an idea and putting it in effect."

Given Roosevelt's goals and penchant for ideas that evolved into action, it is understandable that men and women of similar views found their way into the administration. And the path was often paved for them by Felix Frankfurter, then on the faculty of Harvard University's Law School. Frankfurter served not only as a close confidant of the president's but as a conduit to governmental employment for the brightest and most socially responsible graduates of Harvard's Law School. His recommendations to the president, as well as to cabinet secretaries Frances Perkins, Harold Ickes, and others, resulted in a proliferation of Jewish appointees to New Deal agencies.

Moreover, because of Frankfurter's influence, Roosevelt brought other Jews into the White House orbit. David Niles of Boston roamed as a behind-the-scenes political emissary, and Ben Cohen, an attorney from Indiana, wrote some of the New Deal's most significant legislation like the Public Utilities Act of 1935 and the wage and hours bill of 1938. Along with Thomas Corcoran, an Irishman from Rhode Island, Cohen served as one of the rallying points for progressive and liberal thought in the White House.

Although Roosevelt pursued goals of social justice that most Jews favored, and although he appointed well-qualified Jews to positions of influence in the government, he never acted with verve on issues of specific concern to the Jewish community. Thus he made little attempt to relax immigration barriers in order to bring more Jewish refugees from Europe to the United States in the 1930s, and during World War II, he did nothing to bomb the gas chambers the Germans were using in their efforts to destroy European Jewry.

But having said this, one must also acknowledge that Roosevelt showed a sensitivity to the needs of minorities in the United States, that he brought many of them into his administration, and that his policies and programs, designed to help all Americans, proved particularly beneficial to those who were most victimized by prejudice in America. Roosevelt also articulated the views previously expressed by those who valued governmental intervention to provide for a more rationally ordered society. Furthermore, he utilized the talents of large numbers of Jews and honored them by making dramatic and symbolic appointments like that of Felix Frankfurter to the U.S. Supreme Court. Values and activities such as these endeared him to the American Jewish community, and its gratitude was reflected in the polling booths. In 1932 Jews voted for Roosevelt over Hoover by a margin of 3½ to 1. By 1940 and 1944, however, pollsters estimated that 90 percent of the Jewish people cast their ballots to reelect the president.

The two fullest accounts of Franklin D. Roosevelt and the Jews are Leonard Dinnerstein, "Jews and the New Deal," *American Jewish History* 72 (June 1983): 461–76, and Shlomo Shafir, "Roosevelt: His Attitude toward American Jews, the Holocaust and Zionism," *Forum* 44 (Spring 1982): 37–52. The former concentrates on the New Deal years, 1933–39; the latter gives equal attention to domestic and foreign affairs. Jerold S. Auerbach, *Unequal Justice: Lawyers and Social Change in Modern America* (New York: Oxford University Press, 1976) has the most detailed information on opportunities available for Jewish attorneys in the federal government while Roosevelt served as president. The best discussion of anti-Semitism during the Roosevelt era is Myron I. Scholnick, "The New Deal and Anti-Semitism in America" (Ph.D. diss., University of Maryland, 1971). The statistics on the Jewish population in the United States and Jews in the upper echelons of the New Deal are from Thomas Krueger and William Glidden, "The New Deal Intellectual Elite," in *The Rich, the Well Born, and the Powerful,* ed. Fred Jaher, (Urbana: University of Illinois Press, 1974), p. 344. The quotes from Samuel Lubell and Lawrence H. Fuchs are from *Future of American Politics* (New York: Harper & Row, 1965), p. 198, and "American Jews and the Presidential Vote," *American Political Science Review* 49 (June 1955):399, respectively. The statistics on Jewish voting are from Scholnick, "The New Deal and Anti-Semitism in America," p. 18, and Fuchs, "American Jews and the Presidential Vote," p. 386.

LEONARD DINNERSTEIN

See also Baruch, Bernard Mannes; Brandeis, Louis Dembitz; Cohen, Benjamin Victor; Democratic Party; Foreign Policy; Hillman, Sidney; Holocaust; Morgenthau, Henry T., Jr.; Moskowitz, Belle Lindner Israels; Niles, David K.; Refugees; Rosenman, Samuel Irving; Stimson, Henry L.; Zionism

---

Johnson, Hugh Samuel

(5 August 1882–15 April 1942)

Army officer, industrialist, public administrator, and journalist, who achieved his greatest prominence as head of the National Recovery Administration (NRA) 1933–34. In that position Johnson helped to shape the industrial code system through which the Roosevelt administration hoped to restore economic prosperity. In the larger debate over New Deal recovery policy, he became an articulate and forceful, if often erratic, spokesman for corporatist planning mechanisms similar to those of World War I.

Born at Fort Scott, Kansas, Johnson grew up on the frontier in Oklahoma, attended Oklahoma Northwestern Teachers College, and became the first Oklahoman to graduate from West Point. After receiving his commission in 1903, he served stints of duty in Texas, California, the Philippines, and Arizona, was

sent to the University of California for legal training, participated in the Pershing expedition to Mexico in pursuit of Pancho Villa, and in 1916 became assistant legal officer for the Bureau of Insular Affairs. He also published during this period a number of boys' adventure books. During World War I he was assigned to the army's General Staff, where he helped develop and implement the selective service system and then, as director of a new Purchase and Supply Branch, organize the institutional network linking the military supply agencies to the War Industries Board. In the later capacity he rose to the rank of brigadier general and formed connections with business leaders that would shape his subsequent career.

In 1919 Johnson resigned from the army and shortly thereafter became general counsel of the Moline Plow Company, a position in which he worked with George Peek to develop an agricultural relief plan that subsequently became the basis for the McNary-Haugen bills. In 1925, when Moline Plow was reorganized as the Moline Implement Company, Johnson became chairman of the board. But the company did not prosper, and in 1927 he took a position as adviser and assistant to Bernard Baruch, the former head of the War Industries Board. In this capacity he helped Baruch with his political activities and particularly with his efforts to promote mobilization and industrial planning. During the 1932 presidential campaign, he became the "Baruch man" in Franklin D. Roosevelt's brains trust. And in 1933, after work-

Hugh S. Johnson. (From the collections of the Harry Ransom Humanities Research Center, the University of Texas at Austin. Artist: Miguel Covarrubias)

ing briefly for the National Transportation Committee, he helped write the National Industrial Recovery Act and was chosen by Roosevelt to administer the code system that was to be developed under Title I of the new law.

Of the leading administrators in the early New Deal, Johnson was one of the most colorful. Ruggedly built, rough in demeanor, and skilled in picturesque and vituperative invective, he projected an image of the tough-minded troubleshooter who could cut through the guff and get things done. Yet "Old Iron Pants" was also a man capable of imaginative theorizing, emotional evangelism, and periodic retreats into rueful self-criticism and maudlin sentimentality. It was a mixture, Baruch thought, that made Johnson a good number-three or number-two man. But as administrator of the NRA, charged with resolving its confusing welter of contradictions and policy conflicts, he became increasingly unstable, swinging from excitement to despair and escapes into alcohol, and demonstrating a striking incapacity to sustain decisions or develop coherent policies. The new code system failed to bring recovery and came under increasing criticism as being monopolistic, undemocratic, and unworkable. Efforts to reestablish its political support were unsuccessful, and in September 1934, Roosevelt eased Johnson out and replaced him with an administrative board. In retrospect he seems to have been a poor choice for the position. But whether anyone could have made the program work under the conditions of the time is doubtful.

Following his departure from the NRA, Johnson wrote his memoirs, served briefly as head of the Works Progress Administration in the state of New York, and began a syndicated column entitled "Hugh Johnson Says." At first Johnson in his column supported Roosevelt and in 1936 urged his reelection. But he early became critical of such New Dealers as Harry Hopkins, Rexford G. Tugwell, and Felix Frankfurter, arguing that the problem with the administration was the "Hop-Tugs" and "happy Hot Dogs" and calling upon Roosevelt to get "back to the New Deal" as originally conceived. After the Court-reform proposal of 1937, he also became increasingly critical of the president himself, charging that he was seeking to establish a dictatorship and was entangling the United States in foreign quarrels that were none of its business. By 1939 Roosevelt and Johnson had broken personally, and in 1940 Johnson worked for the election of Wendell Willkie and helped launch the America First Committee. In retaliation, so Johnson believed, Roosevelt saw to it that his reserve commission would not be renewed and that he would have no role in the rearmament programs that preceded and followed Pearl Harbor.

In histories of the New Deal, Johnson is remembered chiefly for his colorful invective, his personal peccadilloes, and an administrative performance that helped discredit the idea of industrial self-government and revive the antitrust and regulatory traditions. But seen in longer perspective, his public career also reflected the emergence of an American corporatism

and its transmission from the mobilization of 1917 through the associationism of the 1920s to the recovery program of 1933. He was part of a search for a particular kind of federal state, one that would serve not as a director or regulator but as a developer and coordinator of new ordering mechanisms imbedded in an organizational society; and he participated in both the successes and failures of this search. A champion of the early New Deal, he came to see its later phases as recipes for bureaucratic tyranny and social disorder and became in his last years one of Roosevelt's most vociferous critics. He was such when he died of pneumonia in 1942.

The only full-scale biographical study of Johnson is John Kennedy Ohl, *Old Iron Pants: The Career of Hugh S. Johnson* (DeKalb: Northern Illinois University Press, in press). Johnson's memoirs, useful but sometimes misleading, were published under the title *The Blue Eagle from Egg to Earth* (Garden City, N.Y.: Doubleday, Doran, 1935). There are also good character sketches in "Unofficial Observer" (John F. Carter), *The New Dealers* (New York: Literary Guild, 1934) and Arthur M. Schelsinger, Jr., *The Coming of the New Deal* (Boston: Houghton Mifflin Co., 1959). An excellent article on Johnson's role as war manager is John Kennedy Ohl, "General Hugh Johnson and the War Industries Board," *Military Review* 54 (May 1975):35–48.

ELLIS W. HAWLEY

See also National Recovery Administration

Joint Chiefs of Staff

The four-officer body that, with the assistance of its committees, served as the president's principal advisory group on wartime strategy and military policy. At the Arcadia Conference in Washington, December 1941 to January 1942, between President Roosevelt, Prime Minister Winston S. Churchill, and their key diplomatic and military officials, it was decided to establish the Combined Chiefs of Staff to coordinate Anglo-American strategy, logistics, and operations. This agency was made up of the American service chiefs and their British counterparts, with a liaison committee of the latter stationed in Washington and with specialized combined committees as needed. FDR and his service chiefs were impressed by the efficiency of the British Chiefs of Staff Committee, which constituted the military component of the war cabinet's Defense Committee. The U.S. Joint Chiefs of Staff system that evolved in the wake of Arcadia resulted from the necessity to achieve better interservice collaboration after America's entry into World War II and from the need for the American chiefs to work as a team to avert British dominance of Anglo-American strategy making. Roosevelt never validated the system by specific directive or charter; in fact, no statutory basis for the Joint Chiefs existed until the National Security Act of 1947.

The Joint Chiefs' first formal meeting was held on 9 February 1942, the members then being General

George C. Marshall, army chief of staff; Admiral Harold R. Stark, chief of naval operations; and General Henry H. Arnold, commanding general of the Army Air Forces. By mid-summer of 1942 the Joint Chiefs consisted of the four men who would continue in those posts for the remainder of the war: Marshall; Arnold; Admiral Ernest J. King, who in March became chief of naval operations and commander in chief of the U.S. fleet; and Admiral William D. Leahy, whom Roosevelt appointed in July as chief of staff to the president. Marshall and King soon emerged as the dominant members on matters of strategy and logistics, often differing with each other since the former strongly advocated top priority on the defeat of Germany and the latter wanted more resources for the Pacific war. An army officer under Marshall, Arnold played a relatively minor role at first, but as his air units' contributions to the war mounted, his stature in Joint Chiefs' deliberations grew. Leahy served as the main liaison between the service chiefs and FDR and was the informal chairman of the Joint Chiefs.

At the Casablanca Conference of Anglo-American leaders in January 1943, the Joint Chiefs were not well organized and lost almost every round at the Combined Chiefs' sessions on strategy, with the British chiefs well prepared and coordinated in their arguments for further operations in the Mediterranean rather than an early invasion of France. Out of the Casablanca setbacks came a revised American joint committee structure that would prove effective later in countering British strategems for continuing a war of attrition. Eventually the Joint Chiefs had an elaborate system of working groups, among the most important being the Joint Staff Planners, Joint War Plans Committee, Joint Strategic Survey Committee, and Joint Logistics Committee.

Roosevelt, who enjoyed his role as commander in chief and regarded himself as a strategist, developed good rapport with all members of the Joint Chiefs, with perhaps Marshall ranking first in his esteem. But during the first eighteen months or so after Pearl Harbor, he sometimes overruled the Joint Chiefs or did not consult the group when making decisions under the suasion of confidant Harry L. Hopkins or the British prime minister. After about mid-1943, however, the president relied increasingly upon the Joint Chiefs in formulating military strategy and policy, at the same time leaving his war and navy secretaries to administer their internal departmental affairs and to defend their services' needs before Congress. Because of its improved organization and the preponderance of American power in the European and Pacific theaters, the Joint Chiefs by 1944–45 took the lead in Anglo-American strategy making. By a working agreement of March 1942, strategic responsibility had been delegated to the U.S. Joint Chiefs for the Pacific, to the British Chiefs for the Mediterranean and Mideast, and to the Combined Chiefs for the European theater. But during the final two years of the war, the American influence was dominant in virtually all aspects of planning for operations in northwest Europe and in the logistics of the Mediterranean and Mideast theaters, while Pacific

plans and operations continued to be almost exclusively an American sphere of strategic control.

The Joint Chiefs system, though invaluable in rationalizing and centralizing American strategy, command, and logistics, was sometimes criticized at the theater level, because its directives, usually resulting from numerous compromises and revisions in the complex committee process, led to delays in shipments to the theaters and in decisions about operations. Moreover, in the war against Japan, the Joint Chiefs gave little consideration to the strategic interests of "lesser" allies like Australia and China. Also, the U.S. chiefs made little progress in coordinating strategic plans with their Soviet counterparts, with neither group appearing eager to cooperate or compromise. But, although the Joint Chiefs system may have been flawed, its top four officers proved able in coping with complicated problems of global war and in working with the often unpredictable Roosevelt.

Only one of the several offical studies of the wartime Joint Chiefs was published: Grace P. Hayes, *The History of the Joint Chiefs of Staff in World War II: The War against Japan* (Annapolis, Md.: Naval Institute Press, 1982) a solid, comprehensive work completed in 1953. The main documents of the Joint and Combined Chiefs and their committees are in *Records of the Joint Chiefs of Staff, 1942–1945,* 50 microfilm reels (Frederick, Md.: University Publications of America, 1981). Forrest C. Pogue, *George C. Marshall,* 3 vols. (New York: Viking, 1963–73) is a masterful biography of the general to 1945. The other three wartime chiefs wrote memoirs, each of which is a valuable contribution to understanding the World War II body: William D. Leahy, *I Was There: The Personal Story of the Chief of Staff to Presidents Roosevelt and Truman; Based on His Notes and Diaries Made at the Time* (New York: Whittlesey House, 1950) by the JCS chairman; Ernest J. King, with Walter M. Whitehill, *Fleet Admiral King: A Naval Record* (New York: Norton, 1952) by the naval chief; and Henry H. Arnold, *Global Mission* (New York: Harper & Bros., 1949) by the head of the Army Air Forces. An excellent essay on the Joint Chiefs' role, 1942–45, is chapter 7 of Paul Y. Hammond, *Organizing for Defense: The American Military Establishment in the Twentieth Century* (Princeton: Princeton University Press, 1961).

D. CLAYTON JAMES

See also Arnold, Henry Harley; Commander in Chief; Cooke, Charles Maynard, Jr.; King, Ernest J.; Leahy, William Daniel; Marshall, George Catlett; Stark, Harold Raynsford; World War II

Jones, Jesse Holman
(5 April 1874–1 June 1956)

Jesse Holman Jones, banker and czar of the New Deal credit establishment, was born in Robertson County, Tennessee, to William Hasque Jones and Laura Anna Holman. Although the family had farmed for generations, William Jones wanted good educations for his children, so he moved to Dallas, Texas, in 1883, and went to work for his brother's lumber business. In 1886, however, William Jones purchased

Jesse H. Jones. (Constant Collection. Courtesy FDR Library.)

a six-hundred-acre farm on the Kentucky-Tennessee state line. Five years later the family returned to Texas so the children could finish school, and seventeen-year-old Jesse entered Hill's Business College in Dallas. Quickly mastering the curriculum, he graduated a few weeks later, taught at the college for a short time, and then joined his uncle's lumber business. Despite a competitive rivalry between the two men, M. T. Jones could not deny his nephew's business acumen, and Jesse rose quickly in the firm. When his uncle died, Jesse was given management of the estate and the business, and he then amassed a personal fortune in lumber, real estate, construction, and banking in Houston. By 1910, he had become the leading figure in the Houston business community.

Jones inherited his politics from several generations of Democratic farmers, but he was a conservative Democrat and was uncomfortable with the free-silver populism of William Jennings Bryan. In the election of 1896, Jones had finally voted for William McKinley, after a long period of introspection. The decline of farm radicalism ended his brief alienation from the party, and in 1912 he enthusiastically campaigned for Woodrow Wilson. In return, Wilson offered Jones the cabinet position of secretary of commerce, but the Houstonian declined. He headed up the American Red Cross's Military Relief Section during World War I, and then returned to Houston in 1919 and resumed his private business affairs. The next year he married Mary Gibbs. In 1926, they purchased the *Houston Chronicle*, adding the newspaper to a personal financial empire that included the National Bank of Commerce.

During the 1920s, Jones maintained his interest in Democratic politics and became a national symbol of the emerging political and economic power of the Southwest. He labored diligently to raise money for the party's 1924 election debts, served as finance chairman for the Democratic National Committee, and succeeded in bringing the Democratic National Convention to Houston in 1928, where Governor Al Smith of New York received the nomination to oppose Secretary of Commerce Herbert Hoover for the presidency.

Between 1929 and 1932, Jones concentrated on his personal business affairs; the collapse of the stock market and financial pressures on the nation's banking system kept him busy trying to stabilize the Houston economy. By 1931, however, the nation's money markets were in serious financial trouble. Hundreds of banks were failing each month, thousands more were threatened with collapse, and industrial credit was shrinking rapidly. At President Herbert Hoover's request, Congress established the Reconstruction Finance Corporation (RFC) in January 1932. Endowed with up to $2 billion in working capital, the RFC was to make low-interest loans to banks, savings banks, savings and loan associations, credit unions, railroads, and insurance companies. For Hoover, the Great Depression was largely a crisis of confidence, and employment and production would not increase until private bankers were more willing to make business loans. The RFC would restore banker confidence

and stimulate business loans; recovery would then ensue. Because the enabling legislation required a bipartisan RFC board of directors, Hoover turned to Jesse Jones and asked him to fill one of the Democratic spots, and Jones accepted. On the board—which included former vice-president Charles Dawes, Secretary of the Treasury Ogden Mills, and Federal Reserve Board chairman Eugene Meyer—Jones consistently worked to prevent domination by eastern and Wall Street banking houses. Although he wholeheartedly agreed with the economic philosophy justifying the RFC, he felt the corporation had not been aggressive enough in 1932 and early 1933 in extending credit to small banks outside the New York and Chicago financial markets. When Hoover left office in March 1933, the RFC had loaned $2 billion, but the banking system was in a state of collapse.

The first measure of President Franklin D. Roosevelt's New Deal was the Emergency Banking Act permitting the RFC to purchase preferred stock in commercial banks. The new president also asked Jesse Jones to take over the chairmanship of the agency. Both men were concerned about continuing declines in business loans, but with repayment of RFC loans always imminent, they felt bankers were reluctant to increase their lending. By permitting the RFC to invest in bank stock and receive dividends, Roosevelt and Jones felt that private bankers would have more freedom and time to make long-term commitments. By mid-1935, the RFC had purchased $1.3 billion in preferred stock from more than 6,200 commercial banks. But even that did not increase bank credit and stimulate recovery. From a high of more than $38 billion in 1930, commercial bank loans had dropped to little more than $20 billion in 1935, a precipitous decline that Jones and Roosevelt both decried.

Continuing difficulties in the economy increased RFC responsibilities and, in the process, the power Jones wielded in the federal government. President Roosevelt converted the RFC into a major funding agency, the source of money for the Federal Emergency Relief Administration, the Home Owners' Loan Corporation, the Farm Credit Administration, the Regional Agricultural Credit Corporations, the Federal Home Loan Bank Board, the Federal Farm Mortgage Association, the Federal Housing Administration, the Rural Electrification Administration, and the Resettlement Administration. To assist the Tennessee Valley Authority by creating a market for electricity, the RFC established the Electric Farm and Home Authority which financed the sales of small electrical appliances. Roosevelt also had the RFC set up the Disaster Loan Corporation to extend financial assistance to victims of natural disasters. Second, to liquefy bank assets even further, the RFC established and directed the RFC Mortgage Company, the Export-Import Bank, the Commodity Credit Corporation, and the Federal National Mortgage Association. Finally, Roosevelt and Jones succeeded in getting the RFC to make direct business loans as a means of stimulating industrial expansion. When the Reorganization Act of 1939 created the Federal Loan Agency to take control of the RFC, Federal Housing Agency, Home Owners' Loan Corporation, and Export-Import Bank, Roosevelt selected Jones to serve as the new Federal Loan administrator. The next year, after his nomination for a third term, Roosevelt asked Jones to accept the cabinet position of secretary of commerce in his new administration. Jones agreed as long as he could continue to serve as Federal Loan administrator. The president secured the necessary congressional permission, and Senator Robert A. Taft of Ohio, although supporting the move, remarked that "I do not think with the exception of the president of the United States any man in the United States ever enjoyed so much power." By 1940, the RFC had loaned more than $8 billion to thousands of businesses and financial institutions, and had become one of the most powerful government agencies in American history.

Jesse Jones's own position in the New Deal during the 1930s had always been a philosophically tenuous one, for he found himself caught between the views of budget balancers like Secretary of the Treasury Henry Morgenthau, Jr., or former head of the Bureau of the Budget Lewis Douglas, and the compensatory spenders like WPA administrator Harry Hopkins and Federal Reserve chief Marriner Eccles. Jones did not like the idea of incurring huge government deficits every year because he felt they undermined business confidence; at the same time, he had to fight off the attempts of Morgenthau to cut the RFC budget. In Jones's opinion, RFC spending was legitimate because most of the money was repaid to federal coffers and because it encouraged rather than dampened business confidence and the impulse to invest and expand production. Jones won that battle in the fall of 1937 when the president reversed himself and, over Henry Morgenthau's objections, restored the RFC budget when a severe recession developed. Ultimately, the outbreak of World War II in Europe settled the issue of government spending.

The German invasion of France in June 1940 almost immediately transformed the RFC into a war agency. Between 1940 and 1945, Jesse Jones managed an RFC empire of powerful government corporations. The Defense Plant Corporation spent $9.2 billion in constructing 2,300 factories in forty-six states, after which the RFC leased them to private companies. The Defense Supplies Corporation also spent more than $9 billion in procuring and storing scarce and strategic materials. The Metals Reserve Company used approximately $2.7 billion in acquiring and storing such materials as copper, scrap iron, nickel, tungsten, and mercury. The RFC also established a subsidiary—the U.S. Commerical Company—to disrupt the German and Japanese war effort by entering the markets of neutral countries and purchasing any materials the Axis powers needed. It spent more than $2 billion buying such commodities as wolfram, ammonium sulphate, petroleum, and cellulose. The Rubber Reserve Company stockpiled approximately 600,000 tons of crude before the Japa-

nese attack on Pearl Harbor and supervised the government-supported synthetic rubber industry. The RFC's Defense Homes Corporation constructed nearly eleven thousand housing units by 1945. Finally, the War Assets Corporation disposed of surplus property after the war.

Although Jesse Jones remained one of the most powerful people in Washington during World War II, his personal relationship with President Roosevelt had grown increasingly strained. Jones had always found the president politically capricious and too given to bureaucratic manipulation and became especially alienated because of his own administrative infighting with Vice-President Henry A. Wallace, Jr. At Wallace's request in 1941, Roosevelt had created a Board of Economic Warfare, with Wallace at the helm, to procure strategic materials anywhere in the world. Jones, who had long since decided that Henry Wallace was politically ambitious as well as emotionally unreliable, saw the move as an enormous conflict of interest, primarily because the RFC's Defense Supplies Corporation, Metals Reserve Company, and U.S. Commercial Company were already performing that function with specific congressional authorization. The acrimony between the two men surfaced publicly, and Roosevelt eventually handled it by creating a new Office of Economic Warfare under Leo T. Crowley, which essentially stripped Wallace's Board of Economic Warfare of its authority. But in the process, the president had grown distant from both Jones and Wallace. In 1945, after dropping Wallace from the ticket as vice-president, Roosevelt acquiesced to his demands to become secretary of commerce. Jones resigned from the cabinet and from the RFC and returned to Houston in January 1945.

After his resignation, Jones continued to pursue his business interests in Houston. His basic conservatism left him increasingly disturbed with the drift of the Democratic party, particularly the dramatic increases in federal spending and the accumulation of social welfare legislation. Impressed with the experience and political philosophy of Governor Thomas Dewey, Jones bolted the Democratic party in 1948 and endorsed the Republican from New York. He spent the next three years writing his memoirs, *Fifty Billion Dollars,* which were published in 1951. Jones's health became increasingly fragile, and he died in 1956 at the age of eighty-two.

For additional information see Bascom M. Timmons, *Jesse H. Jones: The Man and the Statesman* (New York: Henry Holt & Co., 1956); Jesse H. Jones, *Fifty Billion Dollars: My Thirteen Years with the R.F.C.* (New York: Macmillan, 1951); James S. Olson, *Herbert Hoover and the Reconstruction Finance Corporation, 1931–1933* (Ames: Iowa State University Press, 1977) and "The Reconstruction Finance Corporation, 1932–1940" (Ph.D. diss., State University of New York, Stony Brook, 1972); Gerald T. White, *Billions for Defense: Government Finance by the Defense Plant Corporation During World War II* (University: University of Alabama Press, 1980).

JAMES S. OLSON

K

Kennedy, Joseph Patrick

(6 September 1888–18 November 1969)

Financier; fund raiser and adviser, Roosevelt campaigns of 1932 and 1936; chairman, Securities and Exchange Commission, 1934–35; chairman, Maritime Commission, 1937–38; ambassador to the Court of St. James, 1938–41; father of President John F. Kennedy. Joseph Kennedy was born in East Boston, Massachusetts, son of a second-generation Irish-American saloon keeper, ward boss, and state legislator. He attended parochial school until the eighth grade and then the eminent Boston Latin School before matriculating at Harvard, long viewed by the Irish with suspicion as a Yankee preserve. He was graduated in 1912 with the goal of earning a million dollars before reaching thirty-six.

This goal he achieved easily. Between 1912 and 1932, Kennedy served as a bank examiner and bank president, shipyard manager, financier, and key figure in the merger wave that remade the motion picture industry in the late 1920s. By 1932, Kennedy had

Joseph P. Kennedy. (National Archives.)

amassed a fortune estimated at $6 million and a reputation for financial manipulation and ruthless business dealings.

He first met his fellow Harvard man Franklin Roosevelt in 1917 when, as assistant manager of the Fore River (Mass.) shipyard, he refused to deliver unpaid-for battleships to Argentina that Roosevelt, assistant navy secretary, deemed vital to American security. Roosevelt made good on his threat to send in a detachment of Marines to seize the ships and tow them from the harbor. Kennedy later pronounced him "the hardest trader I'd ever run up against."

In 1932, convinced of Roosevelt's electability, Kennedy raised funds and lobbied friends. At the Democratic National Convention, he urged his friend, the publisher William Randolph Hearst, by telephone to shift his votes to Roosevelt and thereby guarantee his candidate's nomination. Kennedy expected Roosevelt to appoint him secretary of the treasury, but by March 1933, he had received no job offers.

Puzzled and hurt, he fumed and waited until the president appointed him the first chairman of the new Securities and Exchange Commission in June 1934. Roosevelt deflected criticism by some who thought that Kennedy should not be the man to police financial machinations by suggesting that Kennedy knew "the tricks of the trade" and was hence well qualified to eliminate them: "Set a thief to catch a thief," he said. By the time of his resignation in September 1935 to return to private business, Kennedy had won almost universal praise for his leadership in devising and winning acceptance for securities regulation both in Washington and on Wall Street.

Kennedy served as a liaison between the president and sundry elements in business and finance, and the Catholic church, as well as the radio priest Father Charles Coughlin. In 1936, in support of the second term, he organized banquets, made radio speeches, and wrote articles and a book called *I'm for Roosevelt.*

In February 1937, he yielded to Roosevelt's appeals to serve as first chairman of the new Maritime Commission, created by Congress to rescue the flagging U.S. shipping industry. He settled old claims, paved the way for federal subsidies, and completed a report on shipping that gained wide acclaim.

In March 1938, after campaigning strenuously for the job, Kennedy went to London as Roosevelt's ambassador to the Court of St. James, the first Irish Catholic to win the post. The president knew that American aid to Britain in a European war was a possibility and evidently thought that having Kennedy making the arrangements would help to assuage the anti-British isolationist Catholic population of the Northeast. But Kennedy would not serve as a mere instrument of Roosevelt's foreign policy. He quickly grew close to Prime Minister Neville Chamberlain and prodded the president to comply with Chamberlain's policy of appeasing Adolf Hitler that led to the Munich pact of 1938. When war began in Europe in September 1939, Kennedy doubted that Britain could resist the Germans and loudly cautioned Roosevelt to avoid involvement. As the president edged toward U.S. aid through 1940, he further angered Kennedy by circumventing the London embassy. In October 1940, Kennedy threatened to endorse Wendell Willkie on radio and reveal secret collaboration between Washington and London. Only after Roosevelt heard out Kennedy's complaints in Washington on 27 October 1940 did Kennedy agree to endorse a third term in a highly persuasive radio speech.

But by then, their relations were irrevocably damaged. Resigning after the election, Kennedy testified against Lend-Lease aid to Britain. During the Second World War, after Roosevelt refused to appoint him to more than a minor post, Kennedy threatened to campaign against a fourth term and was evidently dissuaded only by a private talk with the president in October 1944, their last meeting.

Still the two men remained allied through their families. James, Elliott, and Franklin Roosevelt, Jr., spoke for John F. Kennedy in 1960 during a campaign in which Kennedy repeatedly hailed their father and his programs as an example of strong presidential leadership. After 1945, Joseph Kennedy multiplied the size of his fortune and quietly aided his sons' political ambitions, but the controversial reputation gained in London barred him from holding major political office again. In December 1961, he suffered a massive stroke that almost completely incapacitated him until his death.

Michael R. Beschloss, *Kennedy and Roosevelt: The Uneasy Alliance* (New York: W. W. Norton & Co., 1980) is a joint biography and history of the relationship between the two men. Joseph P. Kennedy's *I'm for Roosevelt* (New York: Reynal & Hitchcok, 1936) states why conservative businessmen should support Roosevelt's reelection. David E. Koskoff's sprawling *Joseph P. Kennedy: A Life and Times* (Englewood Cliffs, N.J.: Prentice-Hall, 1974) is the most comprehensive life of Kennedy in print, with particular detail on the London years. William E. Leuchtenburg's *In the Shadow of FDR: From Harry Truman to Ronald Reagan* (Ithaca, N.Y.: Cornell University Press, 1983) includes a chapter tracing FDR's influence on John F. Kennedy in part to the early relations between Roosevelt and Joseph Kennedy. Richard J. Whalen's *The Founding Father: The Story of Joseph P. Kennedy* (New York: New American Library, 1964) was

Ernest J. King. (Constant Collection. Courtesy FDR Library.)

the first book-length work on Joseph Kennedy, based primarily on interviews by the author, at that time a writer for *Fortune.*

MICHAEL R. BESCHLOSS

See also Securities and Exchange Commission

Keynesian Economics

See Fiscal Policy; Great Depression; New Deal; Recession of 1937–38; Temporary National Economic Committee

---

King, Ernest J.
(23 November 1878–25 June 1956)

The son of a Scottish railroad foreman, King grew up in the middle-class town of Lorain, Ohio. Intelligent and ambitious, he earned a nomination to the U.S. Naval Academy, saw action as a midshipman during the Spanish-American War, and graduated fourth in his class of 1901.

He served as a junior officer on a gunboat, a cruiser, destroyers, and two battleships, as well as at the academy. Although a gifted commander, he earned a reputation for ruthlessness, hard drinking, and liking the ladies. He set exacting standards for his subordinates, yet broke tradition and reviewed fitness reports with each man. Within the navy, King was not well liked, but most acknowledged his ability and more than a few owed their careers to his training. During World War I, he served as chief of staff to Adm. Henry Mayo, who commanded the Atlantic fleet. Thereafter, King headed the Postgraduate School, commanded a submarine base at New London, Connecticut, and earned a Navy Cross for the heroic salvage of the sunken submarine *S-51.*

He became a naval aviator at the age of forty-nine, commanded the carrier *Lexington;* and succeeded Rear Adm. William Moffett in 1933 as chief of the Bureau of Aeronautics. King helped convince Congress to fund a large increase in naval aircraft production, terminated the airship program, and successfully resisted an attempt by the chief of naval operations (CNO) to control his bureau. As commander of an aircraft battle force, he conducted a spectacular multicarrier task force exercise in 1938. He hoped to become CNO himself, but Roosevelt chose Adm. Harold R. Stark instead.

King sat on the derelict General Board for a year, earning the confidence of Navy Secretary Frank Knox. In the fall of 1940, Stark named King to command the Atlantic neutrality patrol. On 1 February 1941, this force became the Atlantic fleet, and King retained command through the delicate escalation of warfare operations against German U-boats that included the *Reuben James, Greer,* and *Kearney* incidents. He deployed U.S. Marines to Iceland, organized a successful eastern Atlantic convoy system to assist the Royal Navy, and established American naval bases from the North Atlantic to the Caribbean to Brazil.

After the attack on Pearl Harbor, Roosevelt named King commander in chief of the U.S. fleet. In March 1942, Stark resigned and King assumed a second billet as CNO. Of the four Joint Chiefs, King enjoyed the widest experience; he grasped the industrial and technological elements of global war and proved to be a wise strategist. He disliked what he saw as British affectations, tenaciously defended Navy Department interests, and earned a fearful reputation for his temper. On the other hand, he enjoyed Roosevelt's complete confidence and remained aware throughout the conflict that he had to please only one constituent.

To slow the Japanese advance in the spring of 1942, King adopted a strategy of raiding outlying enemy bases and establishing garrisons along the sea line of communications from Hawaii to Australia. The carrier raid against Tokyo in April induced the Japanese to attack Midway Island in June. King concentrated his Pacific fleet, which then ambushed Adm. Isoroku Yamamoto's force and sank four carriers. The mounting scale of Pacific operations caused Army Chief of Staff George C. Marshall to complain about the "suction pump" to the West that violated the basic strategy of Europe first. He was surprised when King readily agreed to a cross-channel invasion of France in 1942 or 1943, and both were angered when the British retracted their support and persuaded the president to mount an invasion of North Africa.

To hold the line in the South Pacific, King ordered a small offensive against Guadalcanal in August. However, Yamamoto foolishly mounted a massive air campaign to defend Japan's base at Rabaul. King seized the chance and surged carrier- and land-based aircraft into the Solomons; within nine months, Japan's air arm was destroyed. This denuded Tokyo's sea control in the central Pacific, where King implemented the major naval stroke that crushed Japan's military power.

After two disastrous months of shipping losses in the eastern Atlantic in 1942, King helped organize a system of escorted convoys that forced the U-boats back into the North Atlantic by the fall and fostered a massive construction program of destroyer escorts that defeated the German submarine offensive the following year.

Throughout 1943, King supported Marshall's demand for a cross-channel operation, but opposed expending resources for the Mediterranean theater. When Roosevelt used Stalin as a lever to force Churchill to agree to Operation Overlord (the invasion of northwestern France), King bypassed the troublesome British naval commander, Admiral Sir Bertram Ramsey, ensuring that American forces on 6 June 1944 would enjoy massive naval gunfire support from a squadron of old battleships and cruisers. He also diverted large numbers of landing craft from the Pacific to further bolster the success of the operation. And he was a prime mover behind the American demand for the seizure of Marseilles, since a major port was needed to support Gen. Dwight D. Eisenhower's front in northwest Europe.

In the Pacific, King consistently strangled Gen. Douglas MacArthur's early operations and then shifted the balance of strategic weight into the central Pacific. From the invasion of the Gilberts to the fall of the Marianas, King helped orchestrate the defeat of Japanese sea power within a span of eight months. At Yalta, however, in January 1945, King argued that Soviet belligerency would be necessary to defeat Japan, but he changed his views after the conclusion of the Okinawa campaign. Although he believed that a base on the Chinese coast would be required for the invasion of Honshu, he agreed to invade Kyushu to intensify the blockade and bombing of the home islands. When the atomic bomb became available, however, King was among those who encouraged President Harry S Truman to use it to end the carnage that was forecast if Americans invaded Honshu.

Relieved as CNO by Fleet Adm. Chester Nimitz in December 1945, King opposed unification of the armed forces before Congress in 1947, wrote his memoirs with the assistance of Walter Muir Whitehill, and spent his last years shuffling between naval hospitals in Bethesda and Newport. When he died in 1956, his body lay in state under the Capitol dome and was laid to rest in the cemetery at his beloved Naval Academy.

King emerged from the war, in the opinion of some, as one of the great military commanders of the century. Few officers enjoyed his breadth of command experience, and few admirals matched his intellectual powers. He lacked the restraint of a statesman, but his ability to integrate tactics, production, manning, and politics into cohesive strategies made him a war leader of the first rank.

Walter Muir Whitehill assisted King in completing his memoirs, *Fleet Admiral King* (New York: Norton, 1952). The best chapters deal with King's prewar career. Thomas Buell's *Master of Sea Power* (Boston: Little, Brown, 1979) has been the only complete biography to date. Very well-written, this work stresses King's intense professionalism. A slightly angular approach is adopted in "Ernest J. King," in *The Chiefs of Naval Operations,* ed. Robert William Love, Jr. (Annapolis, Md.: Naval Institute Press, 1980), and a more synthetic analysis may be found in "Fighting a Global War," in Kenneth J. Hagan, ed., *In Peace and War: Interpretations of American Naval History, 1775–1978* (Westport, Conn.: Greenwood, 1978). An almost complete bibliography of secondary sources on King's life may be found in Buell, *Master of Sea Power,* and additional primary sources may be found in the notes for Chapter 9 of *Chiefs of Naval Operatons.* Dean C. Allard, et al., eds., *U.S. Naval History Sources in the United States* (Washington, D.C.: U.S. Government Printing Office, 1979) lists the location of King's personal and official papers.

ROBERT WILLIAM LOVE, JR.

See also Cooke, Charles Maynard, Jr.; Joint Chiefs of Staff; Knox, William Franklin

Frank Knox. (Constant Collection. Courtesy FDR Library.)

Knox, William Franklin

(1 January 1874–28 April 1944)

Republican vice-presidential candidate, 1936, and secretary of the navy, 1940–44. Frank Knox, who was born in Boston, left school in 1898 to join the Rough Riders. An ardent admirer of Teddy Roosevelt, Knox adopted many of Roosevelt's vigorous mannerisms and his passion for physical fitness. Knox became a successful newspaperman and backed the Bull Moose campaign in 1912.

In 1917, he enlisted as a private at the age of forty-three and ended his service as a colonel in the reserves. Resuming his newspaper career, he became general manager of the Hearst papers and then editor of the *Chicago Daily News* in 1931. A voice of moderate, internationalist Republicanism, Colonel Knox sought his party's presidential nomination in 1936 but had to settle for the second spot.

In December 1939, FDR, to Knox's surprise, asked him to take over the Navy Department. The president was determined to avoid Wilson's mistake of shunning the Republicans. Knox initially refused the appointment, but then accepted it during the crisis month of June 1940. Top Republicans denounced Knox (and Stimson) as traitors, but the Senate confirmed both men on 10 July.

For a man with no naval experience whatsoever, Knox immediately showed himself to be a diligent student and an important force. He visited the fleet, boarded as many ship types as possible, flew in the navy's planes, and dove in a submarine. With an eye for able subordinates, he brought into his department Adlai Stevenson and James Forrestal. He also earmarked Chester Nimitz and Ernest J. King for top commands.

His most significant impact on policy came before Pearl Harbor. After only a month in office, he worked out with Lord Lothian many of the details of the destroyers-for-bases deal. Knox also often led the administration in publicly advocating stronger measures against the Axis. In June 1941, for instance, he spoke openly for escorting Lend-Lease convoys with U.S. warships—a suggestion that led to isolationist demands for his impeachment. Knox broke the news to FDR of the Pearl Harbor attack and left on 9 December for Hawaii. He concluded that both services had been unready and called for a full investigation. Knox then replaced Kimmel with Nimitz and Stark with King.

From this point, Knox played a lesser role. FDR preferred to work directly with King and saw Knox only rarely. Knox did not have access on a daily basis to the sensitive and pivotal naval discussions in the Map Room, possibly because of his outspoken nature. Of the major wartime conferences, Knox attended only Quadrant (Quebec, August 1943) and that only briefly. He did visit the war zones at Guadalcanal (and was under air attack there) in January 1943 and at Naples in September of that year. Perhaps the secretary's most important wartime effort was to oppose successfully King's plans to reorganize the navy by putting procurement in the office of the chief of naval operations. Knox died suddenly in Washington, D.C., in 1944. His services were honored with flags flown at half-mast by the British, Canadian, and United States navies.

Unfortunately, there is no biography of Frank Knox. His career, however, is examined in detail by George H. Lobdell in *American Secretaries of the Navy*, vol. 2, ed. Paolo Coletta (Annapolis: Naval Institute Press, 1980). Ernest J. King offers his view of Knox in *Fleet Admiral King: A Naval Record* (New York: Norton, 1952). See also Robert Albion, *Makers of Naval Policy, 1798–1947* (Annapolis: Naval Institute Press, 1980).

MALCOLM MUIR, JR.

See also Stimson, Henry L.

L

Labor

The rise of a powerful trade union movement was the most important social phenomenon of the Roosevelt era. In the twelve years that followed Franklin Roosevelt's inauguration, union ranks grew fivefold, from less than 3 to 14 million. By 1945 the proportion of all nonfarm wage earners in labor organizations exceeded 30 percent, a density greater than at any other time in American history and more than triple the ratio of the early depression years. But size alone does not account for the significance of the new union movement, for three additional qualities made it central to the political and economic history of the New Deal. First twentieth-century unions would no longer be confined primarily to a thin stratum of skilled craftsmen, for in the 1930s and 1940s the union movement finally organized the nation's basic productive infrastructure: the heavily capitalized, mass-production industries like steel, automobiles, rubber, and electrical products, which then stood at the core of the American economy.

Second, the new unions, and especially those organized by the Congress of Industrial Organizations

CHILD-LABOR STANDARDS FOR THE NATION'S CHILDREN

No Child Under 16 Years of Age Should Leave School for Gainful Employment

School Is Their Full-Time Job

A basic 16-year minimum age, applying to industrial work at any time and to agricultural work during periods of required school attendance, is the standard set by the child-labor provisions of the Fair Labor Standards Act, administered by the Children's Bureau, which apply to producers of goods for shipment in interstate commerce.

Children working for their parents in agriculture or other occupations except manufacturing and mining are exempt from these provisions.

U. S. DEPARTMENT OF LABOR
CHILDREN'S BUREAU

Dealing with labor strikes, Injunction Granted *met Federal Theatre Project director Hallie Flanagan's criterion that FTP plays must have a "vital connection" to the immediate problems of people in the audience. (Courtesy the Library of Congress Federal Theatre Project Collection at George Mason University Libary, Fairfax, Virginia.)*

(CIO), recruited for the first time millions of first- and second-generation immigrants who had heretofore existed on the margins of American political and social life. These immigrants, largely from south and east Europe, represented about half of the working class; their mobilization into a well-organized trade union movement gave them a sense of representation and citizenship both within the workplace itself and within the larger American polity. Finally, the union movement of the 1930s and 1940s proved important because it played a key role in the realignment of

227

American politics. By giving so much of the working class an institutional voice, the union movement provided one of the main political bulwarks of the Roosevelt Democratic party and became part of the social bedrock in which the New Deal welfare state was anchored. Moreover, many unions in the mass-production industries were organized with the aid of a corps of politically alert radicals whose influence helped shift both the union movement and the liberal community to the left.

When Franklin Roosevelt became president in March 1933, the Great Depression had already reduced American trade unions to their lowest ebb in more than a generation: unemployment stood at one in three for urban wage earners; real wages were 20 percent lower than in 1929; the American Federation of Labor (AFL), which in 1919 had boasted more than 5 million members, now enrolled less than 3 million. Although radicals of communist or socialist persuasion had organized a series of unemployment demonstrations and rent strikes in the early 1930s, most American workers confronted the insecurity of the Great Depression in a decidedly unrebellious mood: work stoppages declined in 1930 and 1931 even as wages were cut and working conditions made more onerous. When unemployed, many workers blamed only themselves for their plight.

Much changed in the eighteen months that followed Roosevelt's inauguration. The president's personal attitude toward the union movement proved one of merely vague sympathy, but his administration nevertheless presided over a remarkable legitimization of the union idea in 1933 and 1934. Section 7a of the newly enacted National Industrial Recovery Act, the linchpin of the New Deal recovery program, declared that "employees shall have the right to organize and bargain collectively through representatives of their own choosing."

Although the administrative implementation of this sentiment would prove both difficult and time

Strikes in the news made an impression on all segments of the public. A student in the FAP-sponsored Harlem Community Art Center painted this impression of CIO pickets. (National Archives.)

consuming, its assertion in the spring of 1933 had an electrifying social and political effect throughout much of industrial America. During the early years of the depression, the authority and prestige of business leadership had steadily eroded; now the government seemed to be endorsing trade unionism itself as part of the recovery program. "The President wants you to join a union," declared one United Mine Workers' organizing leaflet. Hundreds of thousands of newly hopeful workers breathed life into established unions in coal and clothing, filled hastily chartered AFL "federal" locals in the auto, rubber, and electrical industries, and created an independent rank-and-file movement in the steel industry. The most spectacular manifestation of this new spirit came during the spring and summer of 1934 in Minneapolis, Toledo, and San Francisco, where ideologically committed radicals led thousands of workers in quasi-military confrontations with employers and local government authorities.

For the most part this remarkable burst of rank-and-file militancy did not survive long into 1935. The basic problem was that no legal or institutional framework existed that might accommodate these new workers, whose episodic militancy could not alone sustain permanent trade union organization. As business became more hostile to the National Recovery Administration (NRA) experiment, Section 7a became more and more of an administrative dead letter. Hundreds of union locals in heavy industry collapsed after their demands for recognition were taken up and then unrecognizably diluted by NRA labor boards. Meanwhile many employers, like Chrysler and U.S. Steel, set up company unions, which management claimed fulfilled the Section 7a mandate. But an even greater problem lay withiin the ranks of organized labor itself. Most leaders of the half-century-old AFL were craft unionists, often of Protestant northern European extraction, who feared that the effort to organize the mass-production workers would end in either failure or bitter jurisdictional conflict within the AFL. They mistrusted these immigrant workers and their sometimes radical local leaders,

Violence erupting between police and striking truckers in Minneapolis in 1934. (Courtesy FDR Library.)

whom one AFL leader judged to be the "rubbish at labor's door."

Not all union leaders agreed; certainly not John L. Lewis, the burly, sonorous president of the United Mine Workers (UMW). The essential difference between Lewis and AFL president William Green did not center on the frequently debated issue of craft versus industrial unionism, which Lewis endorsed as the proper form of organization for workers in the mass-production industries. Rather, it arose over the issue of whether the AFL leadership would seize the unparalleled organizing opportunities of the mid-1930s, evident not only in the growing insurgency from below but by the recent enactment of the Wagner Act, which for the first time established a permanent government agency, the National Labor Relations Board, designed to curb unfair labor practices by employers and encourage independent trade unions. By the fall of 1935 Lewis and a few like-minded colleagues, notably Sidney Hillman of the Amalgamated Clothing Workers, concluded that any mass organizing effort would have to take place under the banner of a new Committee for Industrial Organization outside the old AFL framework. Although this split in labor's ranks did not become permanent until 1937, it was neatly symbolized during the AFL's October 1935 convention when John L. Lewis sent the conservative carpenters' union leader, "Big Bill" Hutchinson, sprawling across the floor with a celebrated right punch to the latter's six-foot-four-inch frame.

The success of the CIO campaign in 1936 and 1937 rested on its ability to tap the energy of thousands of grass-roots activists while at the same time providing the national coordination and leadership that enabled the new unions to confront such multiplant corporations as U.S. Steel and General Motors. Because of their exceptional ability as mass organizers, Lewis hired scores of communists and socialists and backed their efforts with several hundred thousand dollars from the UMW treasury. The CIO drive was also closely linked with Roosevelt's 1936 reelection campaign. Lewis broke new ground by providing the national Democratic party with an unprecedentedly large half-million-dollar contribution; and on the local level the Roosevelt landslide seemed as much a repudiation of the old industrial order as a defeat of the Republican candidate. In sharp contrast to virtually every other labor upsurge during the last half century, the CIO held at least the friendly neutrality of the federal government during the most crucial phase of its organizing work.

The breakthrough in the CIO campaign came during a dramatic six-week strike at General Motors Corporation in the winter of 1937. Success at GM had a dual basis: first the determination of hundreds of radically led auto workers to maintain an occupation, or sit-down strike, at several of GM's key production facilities in Flint, Michigan; and second, the reluctance of key political figures, including Frank Murphy, the newly elected Democratic governor of Michigan, and President Roosevelt himself, to use the police power of the state to evict the strikers before a negotiated settlement had been reached. The mid-February victory of the United Automobile Workers (UAW) touched off a wave of sit-down strikes, not only among blue collar workers in heavy industry, but among department store clerks, office workers, and utility service employees. At least a million and a half workers joined trade unions in the first half of 1937, most in the CIO-dominated automobile, steel, rubber, packinghouse, and electrical product industries, but many also in the AFL-organized trades, especially construction and trucking.

CIO unionism had a profound impact on the daily life of millions of ordinary workers. Although the new unions negotiated for higher wages and lobbied for much needed social legislation, they had their greatest impact in the factory itself where dramatic changes might take place in the power relationship between the worker and the boss. Shop stewards often aggressively represented heretofore inarticulate immigrant workers in their daily battle against the petty dictatorship of foreman and plant manager. The grievance procedures and seniority systems instituted by the new unions established a rough system of industrial jurisprudence, which for the first time brought something of the orderliness and predictability of civil society to the shop floor of the privately managed factory. This working-class empowerment soon had its impact in the community as well: in many company-dominated towns throughout the East and Midwest, old-line Republican officials were either defeated or forced to share political power with ethnic Democrats allied with the union movement.

Although its prospects seemed boundless, CIO momentum was soon checked by a combination of forces that stalemated the industrial union advance for almost four years. The radicalism of many CIO activists, the sit-down-strike tactic, and the union assault on management's shop floor prerogatives, helped frighten and mobilize conservative forces in the business community and the national political arena. During a strike against Bethlehem, Republic, and other "Little Steel" companies, management-sponsored vigilante groups often fought the CIO, while the Democratic governors of Ohio and Pennsylvania deployed National Guard troops against the work stoppages. Ten strikers were killed by police at the infamous Memorial Day massacre outside a Republic Steel plant near Chicago. CIO efforts to unionize a million workers in the southern textile industry also proved frustrating, as state and local officials in that region backed mill-owner opposition to the union threat. Since President Roosevelt's alliance with the new industrial unions had always been one of calculated convenience, he did not hesitate to distance himself from CIO militancy if it proved embarrassing, as when he declared a "plague" on the houses of both labor and management in the violence-filled Little Steel conflict.

The CIO organizing drive was also slowed by the sharp recession of 1937–38. Steel, auto, and rubber production declined by more than 50 percent, generating widespread layoffs which sapped both union finances and worker spirit in these mass-production industries. At the same time, many of the trade unions affiliated with the AFL underwent a remarkable rejuvenation during the latter years of the Great Depression. Even in its most dynamic moments, the CIO never exceeded the AFL in size. The older labor federation was a more broadly based institution with tens of thousands of local unions spread across almost every town and city. In the late 1930s the AFL grew steadily: employers often preferred the more moderate AFL to the seemingly radical CIO, and AFL trade unions like the Teamsters, the Machinists, and the Carpenters did not hesitate to sign sweetheart contracts on this basis. Some AFL leaders also cooperated with antilabor congressional conservatives to make the National Labor Relations Board less useful to unions with an industrial structure.

But the AFL also incorporated much of the CIO's basic outlook in its own decentralized and increasingly flexible organizing strategy. The Machinists and the Boilermakers transformed many of their affiliated locals into industrial unions so as to compete directly with the CIO for the allegiance of unskilled workers. The Teamsters organized long-distance truck drivers, using the innovative tactics pioneered by a group of Teamster Trotskyists centered in the Upper Midwest. The International Brotherhood of Electrical Workers began to organize some of the many thousand semiskilled utility workers whom they had once spurned. AFL unions in such service trades as hotel, restaurant, and retail sales all grew rapidly in the social environment engendered by the late New Deal. By 1940 the AFL had enrolled almost 5 million workers, about twice the number in the CIO.

Beginning with the defense mobilization of 1940, American unions again entered an era of rapid growth. The CIO completed the organization of basic industry, including the unionization of such bitter holdouts as Ford and Bethlehem Steel. The AFL monopolized the booming defense construction industry and competed successfully with the CIO in the rapidly expanding aircraft and shipbuilding facilities of the West Coast. During the war more than 5 million new workers would be recruited by organized labor, including hundreds of thousands of white women and blacks who flocked to war plant jobs in northern and western defense manufacturing centers.

The war era political context, however, differed markedly from that of the depression years of union growth. The Roosevelt administration demanded social peace and full production on the home front, and the president soon made clear that work stoppages considered disruptive of the defense effort, like the UAW's strike at North American Aviation in June 1941, would be crushed by use of army troops. Most union leaders supported Roosevelt's foreign and domestic policies, and few dissented from the need for a union no-strike pledge, which they offered the government in the immediate aftermath of the Pearl Harbor attack. Counseled by the CIO's Sidney Hillman, then serving as a prominent official in the administration's mobilization apparatus, Roosevelt established a powerful, tripartite War Labor Board to set wage scales and adjudicate labor-management conflicts.

The board soon promulgated a far-reaching policy that allowed wages to rise only 15 percent above prewar levels (the Little Steel formula), but that simultaneously assured the unions of the automatic enrollment of the many thousands of raw factory recruits who became employed in the war plants where the unions held or secured bargaining rights. This "maintenance-of-membership" policy had a broad impact on the trade union movement, especially its industrial union wing, for while it forged close ties between the government and union officialdom and assured their organizations of ever increasing membership and dues income, it also served to bureaucratically distance the leadership from the union rank and file.

The rigidities of the war economy and the power of the War Labor Board did not sit well with all unionists. UMW's Lewis, who had relinquished his CIO presidency to the steel union leader, Philip Murray, because of his opposition to Roosevelt's third term, led 600,000 miners out on strike in a 1943 effort to break the government's wage ceiling. Lewis's bold, confrontational gambit was widely denounced in Congress and the press, and it helped advance the antilabor mood that was to culminate in the postwar enactment of the Taft-Hartley Act. But the coal strikes also helped inspire a growing volume of wildcat work stoppages, centered chiefly in the auto, rubber, and shipbuilding industries, by workers who sought to defend the shop floor they had won in the 1930s. Although this movement did not crack the no-strike pledge nor break labor's political alliance with Roosevelt, it did set the stage for the massive postwar strike wave that began in late 1945.

THIS RUINED EUROPE

DISUNITY

MANAGEMENT   LABOR

NEVER LET IT HAPPEN OVER HERE

During the war the CIO, through its new Political Action Committee, had established strong institutional links between the Democratic party and the industrial union wing of the labor movement. And under War Labor Board tutelage, collective bargaining had become increasingly routine, so that few business or government leaders contemplated the kind of assault upon the unions that had followed the end of World War I. Although the union movement was still divided and the political climate was becoming noticeably more conservative, American labor had become an important if still junior voice in the process that shaped the national political economy at the end of the Roosevelt era.

For more information on labor during the Roosevelt era, see the following: Irving Bernstein, *Turbulent Years: A History of the American Worker, 1933–1941* (Boston: Houghton Mifflin Co., 1970); David Brody, *Workers in Industrial America* (New York: Oxford University Press, 1980); Bert Cochran, *Labor and Communism: The Conflict That Shaped the Unions* (Princeton: Princeton University Press, 1977); Nelson Lichtenstein, *Labor's War at Home: The CIO in World War II* (New York: Cambridge University Press, 1982); Melvyn Dubofsky and Warren Van Tine, *John L. Lewis: A Biography* (New York: Times Books, 1977); Christopher L. Tomlins, "AFL Unions in the 1930s: Their Performance in Historical Perspective," *Journal of American History* 65 (March 1979):1021–42; and Mike Davis, "The Barren Marriage of American Labour and the Democratic Party," *New Left Review* 124 (November-December 1980):43–84.

NELSON LICHTENSTEIN

See also Biddle, Francis Beverley; Civilian Conservation Corps; Dubinsky, David; Green, William; Hillman, Sidney; House Committee to Investigate Un-American Activities; Lewis, John Llewellyn; National Labor Relations Board; Perkins, Frances; Randolph, Asa Philip; Wages and Hours Legislation; Wagner, Robert Ferdinand

La Follette, Philip Fox

(8 May 1897–18 August 1965)

Governor of Wisconsin. The son of "Fighting Bob" La Follette, Sr., Philip received an education in Progressive politics as part of his family life. He attended the University of Wisconsin where he earned his law degree in 1922. His venture into politics began with his father's third-party presidential bid in 1924 and his brother, Bob, Jr.'s, successful Senate campaign in 1925. An aggressive man who read widely, ate rapidly, and talked hurriedly, Phil La Follette won election as Wisconsin's governor in 1930, but was unable to convince a divided legislature to enact most of his reform plans. Defeated for reelection in 1932, La Follette quit the Republican party and ran successfully for governor in 1934 as head of the Wisconsin Progressive party. His legislative package for 1935 included an ambitious jobs program which, in a series of meetings in Washington, he had persuaded the Roosevelt administration to support. The whole plan fell through, however, when the Wisconsin legislature again refused to pass the governor's legislation.

Through 1938 La Follette continued to forge an uneasy alliance with the New Deal. Although he criticized the New Deal for not going far enough in its reforms, he still supported Roosevelt, especially after the flurry of New Deal reforms in mid-1935. In the 1936 election La Follette urged Progressives to support Roosevelt as the best choice for "all liberal-minded people." The following year La Follette vigorously backed Roosevelt's Supreme Court reorganization proposal and pushed through the Wisconsin legislature a comprehensive reform plan sometimes referred to as the "Little New Deal." Roosevelt viewed La Follette as a key ally on the Left, and the two men enjoyed a friendly relationship during La Follette's visits to the White House and Hyde Park.

La Follette's influence declined after 1938 when he turned away from Roosevelt and tried to shape a national third party under his own leadership. His National Progressives of America, which was to be a left-leaning alternative to the major parties, alienated most liberals who remained loyal to Roosevelt and quickly faded. With the approach of World War II, he joined the isolationist America First Committee, although he remained uneasy with its right-wing orientation. Once the war began, he volunteered and served in the Pacific under Gen. Douglas MacArthur, whom he promoted for president in 1944 and 1948. La Follette's turncoat image among liberals was strengthened when he and his brother disbanded the Progressive party after the war and returned to the Republican fold. La Follette, never again elected to office, ended his career as a lawyer in Wisconsin. His later career should not obscure his earlier success in staking out for Progressives an interesting position to the Left of, yet still supporting, Franklin Roosevelt.

A skillful argument for the essential continuity of La Follette's career is made by John E. Miller in *Governor Philip F. La Follette: The Wisconsin Progressive and the New Deal* (Columbia: University of Missouri Press, 1982). Phil tells his own story in *Adventure in Politics*, ed. Donald Young (New York: Holt, Rinehart & Winston, 1970).

See also Election of 1934; Liberalism and Progressivism

La Follette, Robert Marion, Jr.

(6 February 1895–24 February 1953)

Republican-Progressive U.S. senator from Wisconsin, 1925–47. The son of a renowned Wisconsin governor and U.S. senator, "Young Bob" attended the University of Wisconsin from 1913 to 1915 and served from 1919 to 1925 as his father's secretary. Upon his father's death in 1925, he was elected to fill the Senate vacancy.

During the Hoover era, La Follette introduced legislation for a massive public works program and direct relief to the unemployed. Although backing President Roosevelt's first and second New Deal programs, he favored much bolder spending for public works projects and sharply raising taxes on high personal income, inheritances, and corporations. From 1936 to 1940, he chaired the widely publicized Civil Liberties Committee, which exposed numerous employer antiunion tactics. A vocal critic of Roosevelt's foreign policies, he helped direct isolationist senators who were resisting American assistance to the anti-Hitler coalition. He backed the neutrality acts of the 1930s, fought their modification, and protested the Lend-Lease Act. La Follette, whose influence diminished after 1941, supported Roosevelt's World War II programs after Japan attacked Pearl Harbor. Although favoring American membership in the United Nations, he feared that Roosevelt planned to overextend American postwar world leadership. The La Follette-Monroney Reorganization Act of 1946 increased congressional staff assistance and streamlined the committee system. After losing the 1946 primary to Republican Joseph McCarthy, he remained in Washington as a business consultant, foreign aid adviser, and philanthropic fund administrator. In 1953, an increasingly moody, depression-prone La Follette committed suicide.

For additional information see the La Follette Family Papers, Manuscripts Division, Library of Congress, Washington, D.C.; Patrick J. Maney, *"Young Bob" La Follette: A Biography of Robert M. La Follette, Jr., 1895–1953* (Columbia: University of Missouri Press, 1978); Edward N. Doan, *The La Follettes and the Wisconsin Idea* (New York: Rinehart, 1947); Roger T. Johnson, *Robert M. La Follette, Jr., and the Decline of the Progressive Party in Wisconsin* (Madison: University of Wisconsin, 1964); Jerold S. Auerbach, *Labor and Liberty: The La Follette Committee and the New Deal* (Indianapolis: Bobbs-Merrill, 1966); Alan Edmond Kent, "Portrait in Isolationism: The La Follettes and Foreign Policy" (Ph.D. diss., University of Wisconsin, 1956); Theodore Rosenof, "The Ideology of Senator Robert M. La Follette, Jr." (M.A. thesis; University of Wisconsin, 1966); Charles H. Backstrom, "The Progressive Party of Wisconsin, 1934–1946" (Ph.D. diss., University of Wisconsin, 1956); *Current Biography*, 1944, pp. 368–72; *Dictionary of American Biography*, Supplement Five, pp. 403–4.

DAVID L. PORTER

La Guardia, Fiorello

(11 December 1882–20 September 1947)

Congressman and mayor of New York. Fiorello La Guardia was born in New York to an Italian and formerly Catholic father and a Jewish mother, educated at a series of western army posts, and grew to adulthood at his mother's home in Trieste, Austria. Returning to New York in 1906, he worked his way through New York University Law School and began to practice law in 1910. An idealist committed to social justice, La Guardia, who spoke several European languages, worked closely with labor and immigrant groups on Manhattan's Lower East Side before entering electoral politics as a Republican in 1915. The "Little Flower" (the English translation of *Fiorello*), a short fat man, became a colorful yet issue-oriented

Fiorello La Guardia. Artist: S. J. Woolf. (Date unknown. National Portrait Gallery, Smithsonian Institution.)

campaigner ready to take on Tammany Hall or to challenge his own Republican party. Elected to Congress in 1916, he took a leave in 1917 to fight in Europe as a pilot, where he met Assistant Secretary of the Navy Franklin Roosevelt. Returning to Congress in 1922, La Guardia established a reform record and a maverick image by bolting his own party to join Robert La Follette's Progressive campaign.

La Guardia and Roosevelt's political careers paralleled each other's in several ways; they were both rising stars in New York politics who shared personal and political views but whose parties forced them to oppose each other. Thus La Guardia's 1929 campaign for mayor of New York City suffered from, and perhaps lost because of, Governor Roosevelt's refusal to investigate Tammany Hall. In the 1932 election the Republican La Guardia lost and the Democrat Roosevelt won. In the lame-duck Congress that year, Roosevelt chose La Guardia—his biographer calls him a "New Dealer before the New Deal"—to introduce Roosevelt's first legislation. The next year the Little Flower was elected mayor of New York City and embarked on twelve years of cooperation with Roosevelt's administration. New Deal recovery plans made federal funds available for a variety of La Guardia's projects, including slum clearance, neighborhood projects such as schools, parks, and roads, reform of the relief system, and an airport in Queens, later named after him.

Despite party differences, La Guardia campaigned vigorously for Roosevelt's reelection, and in return Roosevelt tacitly supported La Guardia against his Democratic opponents. With the approach of World War II, La Guardia hoped for an appointment from Roosevelt as secretary of war, but was disappointed when he received the title of director of civil defense. His third term as mayor was less productive than the first two, and La Guardia left City Hall for retirement in 1945. The close cooperation between La Guardia's program and the New Deal is perhaps the best example of the mutually supportive relationship that developed between Roosevelt and a few of the more liberal city bosses.

The best accounts of La Guardia's early years are Arthur Mann, *La Guardia, a Fighter against His Times: 1882–1933* (Philadelphia: J. B. Lippincott, 1959) and *La Guardia Comes to Power: 1933* (Philadelphia: J. B. Lippincott, 1965). See Charles Garrett, *The La Guardia Years: Machine and Reform Politics in New York City* (New Brunswick, N.J.: Rutgers University Press, 1961) and August Heckscher, *When La Guardia Was Mayor: New York's Legendary Years* (New York: W. W. Norton & Co., 1978) for a complete account of La Guardia and Roosevelt during the New Deal.

Lame Duck Amendment (1932)

See Interregnum; Norris, George William

Landon, Alfred Mossman

(9 September 1887–)

Governor of Kansas, 1933–37, and Republican nominee for president, 1936. Alfred M. Landon was born in Pennsylvania and raised in Ohio. After his father, John, joined the Kansas Natural Gas Company in 1904, young Landon entered the University of Kansas, graduating in 1908 with a law degree. Instead of practicing law, he soon became an independent oil producer. Landon remained in this business throughout his life, although after 1936 he also pursued other commercial interests.

Thanks to his father's participation in insurgent Republican politics, the son also became active in politics early in his career. He was a county chairman for the Progressive party in 1914; secretary to Governor Henry J. Allen in 1922; and a lieutenant in William Allen White's independent gubernatorial campaign against the Ku Klux Klan in 1924. Landon became the Republican state committee chairman in 1928, though he lost this post in 1930 in a factional fight. He recaptured political prestige in 1931 by leading a campaign against monopoly and for conservation in the depression-stricken oil industry. In 1932 he won the Republican gubernatorial nomination, appealing effectively for party unity. The odds for election seemed against Landon, though, for the Democrats controlled the governship and were favored to sweep the nation. Nevertheless he ran an energetic campaign against Governor Harry Woodring and a colorful independent candidate, John R. Brinkley. In a heated contest, Landon won the governorship by a scant plurality of votes.

Like other American officials in 1933, Landon was sorely beset by the problems of the Great Depression. He advocated economy and efficiency in government, proclaiming that one "cannot get something for nothing." He sponsored laws and administrative actions that led to tax reform, governmental reorganization, more effective regulation of banks, insurance companies, and utilities, protection of farmers from foreclosures, and reform of local finances. Under his

leadership, Kansas secured some $300 million in federal funds—proportionately more than most Plains states—to combat economic hardship. This mirrored his ability to work effectively with the Franklin D. Roosevelt administration on a variety of programs. Landon was a particularly strong backer of the New Deal's conservation, farm, and unemployment relief efforts. Reflecting his own area of expertise, he worked closely with President Roosevelt and Interior Secretary Harold L. Ickes in developing programs to deal with distress in the oil industry.

Landon was easily reelected in 1934, the only Republican governor who won that year. As a result of his unique position, he was soon considered a national leader of his party. Landon-for-president clubs were even being organized by early 1935. Indeed each passing month brought new tidings of interest in him as a presidential candidate. The reason was plain. As a consequence of overwhelming Democratic election victories in 1932 and 1934, there were relatively few Republican governors, senators, and representatives. Of these officials, Landon was alone not only in having a successful record and no connection with Herbert Hoover's generally discredited presidency but also in occupying the middle ground between Republican conservatives and insurgents. There were other Republicans who sought their party's presidential nomination. But remaining moderate on the issues and effectively using his limited campaign resources, Landon was able to win the Republican nomination in June 1936

Alfred Mossman Landon, 1936. Artist: Vera Dvornikoff. (National Portrait Gallery, Smithsonian Institution. Gift of Tassia Peters.)

He led a divided party into the 1936 presidential race. Some Republicans supported Roosevelt, while many others took positions to the right of their party's standard-bearer, ferociously attacking the New Deal. Some Democratic leaders endorsed Landon, including former presidential nominees Alfred E. Smith and John W. Davis, but they brought little popular support to the Kansas governor. In a vigorous and well-financed campaign, Landon sought to sound a moderate note, in contrast to what he believed was Roosevelt's increasing immoderation. The governor championed the family farm and conservation. Moreover, he vowed to give a fair deal to organized labor and the needy. He proposed aid programs for tenant farmers and fairer though effective regulation of big business. Appealing to minorities, Landon forthrightly denounced racial prejudice and religious bigotry. He pledged to seek international cooperation on issues of peace and world trade. What he emphasized, though, was his dedication to efficient administration and a balanced budget. Charging that the New Deal had not brought recovery to America, Landon declared that a well-administered and soundly financed government could promote the rapid expansion of business and jobs.

At the height of the New Deal, the cards were stacked against Landon. He had neither the record, the personality, the patronage, nor the organization to match Roosevelt. He was at his best when dealing with issues like conservation on which the president was equally strong. The Kansan's campaign was on the whole a gallant one. And it served to keep the Republican party a viable, if far from victorious, opposition. Roosevelt polled 27,752,869 votes to Landon's 16,674,665 and 523 electoral votes to 8. The two nominees said many highly critical things about each other during the 1936 contest, but neither of them often crossed the line of fair play as far as the other was concerned. Whenever they met afterward—and when Landon was in Washington Roosevelt always invited him to the White House—they got along cordially.

Landon was a trenchant critic of administration policies during Roosevelt's second term. Yet all was not disagreement, as the Kansan supported the president on the *Panay* issue in 1937, the Ludlow resolution in 1938, and often on defense measures before 1941. Roosevelt appointed Landon vice-chairman of the American delegation to the Lima Inter-American Conference of 1938. He also considered him for secretary of war in 1940 (which Landon scotched by demanding that Roosevelt refuse nomination for a third term). The two men increasingly divided on foreign policy by 1941 as Landon concluded that Roosevelt was trying to maneuver the United States into World War II. Yet their cordial personal relationship endured during the war, despite their often sharp policy differences.

Although Landon faded as a political force outside Kansas as the years passed, he frequently addressed national and world issues. Indeed, without holding party or public office, he was able to speak out independently, thereby gaining a reputation as an elder statesman by the late 1950s. Landon was, however, often enough in the main-line Republican fold to be an honored member of his party. As he was before and during Franklin D. Roosevelt's presidency, he remained ever after—a man one could disagree with on public issues, yet a person one could respect for his decency and integrity. Certainly, Landon had done his part in keeping Republicanism up with the times, calling the opposition to account, and reminding his fellow citizens that there was more than one way to view affairs of state.

The standard biography of Landon is Donald R. McCoy, *Landon of Kansas* (Lincoln: University of Nebraska Press, 1966). Frederick Palmer wrote a serviceable campaign biography, *This Man Landon* (New York: Dodd, Mead, 1936). Francis W. Schruben's *Kansas in Turmoil, 1930–1936* (Columbia: University of Missouri Press, 1969) is an excellent account of state economic and political events that involved Landon. The presidential politics of 1936 are covered admirably in Arthur M. Schlesinger, Jr., *The Age of Roosevelt*, vol. 3, *The Politics of Upheaval, 1935–1936* (Boston: Houghton Mifflin Co., 1960), and William E. Leuchtenburg, "Election of 1936," in *History of American Presidential Elections, 1789–1968*, ed. Arthur M. Schlesinger, Jr., and Fred L. Israel (New York: Chelsea House, 1971), 3:2809–49. A good introduction to Landon's work as titular head of his party is George H. Mayer, "Alf M. Landon, as Leader of the Republican Opposition, 1937–1940," *Kansas Historical Quarterly* 32 (Autumn 1966):325–33. Alfred M. Landon, *America at the Crossroads* (Port Washington, N.Y.: Kennikat Press, 1971) contains a selection of his public statements in 1935

and 1936. The voluminous personal papers of Alfred M. Landon are located in the Kansas State Historical Society, Topeka, Kansas.

DONALD R. MCCOY

See also Elections; Republican Party

Latin America

See Good Neighbor Policy; Welles, Benjamin Sumner

Law Practice

Roosevelt entered Columbia Law School in the fall of 1904. Although he earned only average grades and failed two courses, he passed the New York Bar before the end of his third year in 1907; he never received an LL.B. He went to work in the same year for the New York City law firm of Carter, Ledyard, and Milburn as an unpaid law clerk, a position obtained through family connections. Although Carter, Ledyard, and Milburn handled antitrust suits for clients like Standard Oil of New Jersey and the American Tobacco Company, Roosevelt was not much involved in such cases. During his three years with the firm, however, he worked his way up to its municipal court and admiralty divisions.

After his election to the New York State Senate in 1910, Roosevelt abandoned law for the next decade in order to concentrate on building a career in politics. Even when he reentered the profession after losing the 1920 election as Democratic vice-presidential nominee, Roosevelt combined his practice of law with various business ventures. In 1920, he established a partnership known as Emmet, Marvin, and Roosevelt, a firm specializing in estates and wills, and in the same year, he also accepted a position as vice-president with Fidelity and Deposit Company of Maryland. Never very active in the law firm, Roosevelt left it in 1924 to form a new partnership with Basil O'Connor, a 1915 graduate of Harvard Law School. Roosevelt and O'Connor specialized in corporate law, maintaining offices at 120 Broadway in the heart of Wall Street. Roosevelt remained in partnership with O'Connor until 1933, when he resigned after his inauguration as president.

Records concerning Roosevelt's law practice are contained in Group 14 of the FDR Library. The documentary record, however, is not extensive, and biographers have been unable to treat these years of Roosevelt's career in any great depth. See, for example, Arthur M. Schlesinger, Jr., *The Crisis of the Old Order, 1919–1933* (Boston: Houghton Mifflin Co., 1957), James MacGregor Burns, *The Lion and the Fox* (New York: Harcourt Brace Jovanovich, 1956), and the multivolume work by Frank Freidel, *Franklin D. Roosevelt* (Boston: Little, Brown & Co., 1952–56). Sparse documentary evidence did not, however, prevent Antony C. Sutton from employing a guilt-by-association analysis of Roosevelt's legal and business career during the 1920s; see his *Wall Street and FDR* (New Rochelle, N.Y.: Arlington House Publishers,

1975). Sutton is critical of biographers who have, in his opinion, neglected to examine closely the political ramifications of FDR's Wall Street connections.

See also O'Connor, Basil

League of Nations

See Internationalism and Peace; Wilson, Thomas Woodrow

Leahy, William Daniel

(6 May 1875–20 July 1959)

Admiral of the fleet, chief of staff to the commander in chief, and principal military assistant to President Roosevelt during most of World War II. Adm. William Leahy, who served as the main conduit of information and counsel between the president and the Joint Chiefs of Staff, played a vital role in the coordination of political purpose and military strategy during wartime. After Roosevelt's death, Leahy similarly served President Truman until his final retirement in 1949.

Leahy was born in Hampton, Iowa, the son of a lawyer. On graduation in 1893 from Ashland School in Wisconsin, he sought appointment to West Point; but because no place was available, he entered the Naval Academy instead, graduating in the middle of the class of 1897. His acquaintance with Franklin Roosevelt dated to 1913 when Roosevelt was assistant secretary of the navy and Leahy was serving in the key position of detail officer in the Bureau of Navigation. The bureau at that time controlled all naval appointments and necessarily involved Leahy closely with Roosevelt and his superior, Josephus Daniels. His command of the USS *Dolphin,* the Navy Department yacht, in 1915–16 deepened their relationship since Roosevelt used it often, and each grew to admire the other's knowledge of the sea.

Both afloat and ashore Leahy's naval career during the interwar years was a distinguished one. He was one of the few men ever to serve as chief of both the crucial navy administrative offices, the Bureau of Ordnance and the Bureau of Navigation. After commanding minesweepers, destroyers, and cruisers, he was made rear admiral in 1935 as commander of the battleships of the navy's battle force and full admiral in 1936 as overall commander of battle force. He capped his career as chief of naval operations in 1937–39, laying the groundwork for the tremendous expansion of the navy in World War II. On his mandatory retirement at age sixty-four in 1939, President Roosevelt personally awarded him the Distinguished Service Medal and prophetically remarked, "Bill, if we have a war, you are going to be right back here helping me to run it."

This came to pass on 18 July 1942 when Roosevelt announced Leahy's appointment to the new and unprecedented position of chief of staff to the commander in chief, by constitutional provision a power of the presidency. Prior to that appointment, however, Roosevelt in November 1940 had given Leahy the equally delicate and even more controversial assignment of U.S. ambassador to Vichy France, a post he held for eighteen critical months. Roosevelt's policy of maintaining friendly relations with Vichy was much criticized at the time but has since come to be seen as a wise and prudent one fully justified by results. His choice of Admiral Leahy to implement it was a master stroke. Leahy's high military background, his character, and his personality provided him with unique access to an influence with the aging Marshal Petain, and he succeeded in restraining accommodation between France and Nazi Germany during a desperate period of the war when control of the French fleet was a vital issue no less for a neutral American than for a beleaguered Great Britain. Moreover, the penetration of French Northwest Africa by American intelligence operatives under cover of administering our food relief program there was the cornerstone of future military successes in that theater and in the Mediterranean generally. The return to power of Pierre Laval in spring 1942 along with the growing senility of the marshal largely ended Leahy's usefulness in Vichy, and he was withdrawn in May of that year, much saddened by the sudden death of his wife earlier that winter. But his mission to Vichy at a critical phase of the war can now be seen as not the least of his many services to his country.

His greatest service by far was that as chief of staff to the president from July 1942 onwards. The title was a misnomer, for apart from a few personal assistants Leahy never had a military staff per se nor did the president, save in the military departments themselves. Roosevelt, never given to precision in such matters, carefully left Leahy's duties and responsibilities vague; when questioned about them on announcing Leahy's appointment, he nonchalantly responded that he would be "doing an awful lot of legwork, and indexing work, and summarizing work." That, as far as is known, was the only charter Leahy ever got.

It hardly does justice to the situation as it existed in summer 1942 and as it developed. Beset by disasters to ourselves and our Allies around the world, the strategic views of the newly constituted Joint Chiefs of Staff (JCS), Gen. George C. Marshall, Adm. Ernest King, and Gen. Henry ("Hap") Arnold, had drifted apart from those of their service peers, of the British, and most important, of the president himself. General Marshall, concerned about this drift and about poor liaison with the White House generally, proposed that Leahy be named chairman of the Joint Chiefs. Roosevelt, always jealous of his power as commander in chief, demurred, postponing decision on the matter for weeks. In the end Leahy was appointed—but not as chairman. At the first JCS meeting he attended, on 30 July 1942, he simply took the chair by default, by prior informal arrangement with Marshall and by right of seniority. Nobody ever questioned the arrangement (although the redoubtable Admiral King

William D. Leahy. Artist: Bernard Godwin. (Courtesy FDR Library.)

initially and understandably had doubts about it), and it continued satisfactorily for the rest of the war and into the Truman administration.

There was no precedent in American history for the structure for higher direction of the war that evolved in the ensuing months. Prior to World War II the army and navy had had little experience of joint planning or operations, and their relations, never easy, were complicated by the emergence of the air arm to (effectively) coequal status in American strategic counsels. There was not one theater of war but many—seven or eight major ones at the height of the war, literally spread all around the globe. Relations with the Allies and direction of the vast and intricate processes of industrial mobilization and munitions allocations worldwide further complicated the problems facing Roosevelt and his military chieftains. By war's end the Joint Chiefs' machinery for dealing with them comprised scores of major military planners and hundreds of lesser ones. It evolved gradually, with no particular design or plan, more often than not in direct response to specific needs or problems of the moment. If it must be said that, like Topsy, it "just grew," it can also with complete justice be said that in the greatest war in history the JCS cannot be charged with responsibility for a major strategic mistake or miscalculation.

Leahy's contributions to this process were many, but two were preeminent. First, as a military leader of wide experience and cool and balanced judgment, and of great skill in bureaucratic manuever, he was never the proponent of any particular strategic viewpoint but served rather as an impartial arbiter among viewpoints and their sometimes heated advocates. In dealing with the American Joint Chiefs and with their British counterparts, this fact and his reputation for rocklike integrity were of immense value. Of equal value was his close and trusting relationship with President Roosevelt. He was the first of Roosevelt's staff to see him every morning, on occasion while he was still shaving; he was at his side during all his wartime travels; and he knew his thoughts and desires better than anyone, other perhaps than Harry Hopkins. He was thus in a position to provide the Joint Chiefs with invaluable counsel as to the president's thinking on strategic and political issues and, equally, to gain the president's ear for their thinking when need arose.

It must not be thought that Leahy was without opinions and served merely as a transmission belt for those of others. On the contrary, he held strong views on numbers of issues and contended strongly for them before the Joint Chiefs and with the president. Best known was his negative evaluation of the atomic bomb: "it is a lot of hooey, the thing will not work and I speak as an ordnance expert." His suspicion of General de Gaulle and the Free French movement and his gloomy view of the prospects of postwar France undoubtedly influenced Roosevelt's hard line in both these connections. Less influential with Roosevelt, but much more so with President Truman, were his ingrained anti-Communist views and his visceral distrust of the Russians. Indeed it was General Mar-

shall's feeling that in the war's closing stages Leahy was so involved with political matters that he was much less helpful to the Joint Chiefs than earlier. Leahy's major role, however, was as a coordinator rather than an originator of strategy, and his key contribution was to serve as a bridge between policy and strategy, between the White House and the Pentagon. It was a role he continued to play with increased scope and influence during President Truman's first administration until his retirement in 1949 at the age of seventy-four.

Leahy lived on for ten years more in a quiet, almost reclusive retirement. His last great cause was a national campaign to save and restore the frigate *Constellation* of War of 1812 fame. In view of Leahy's great seniority, it is interesting to note that he was the last of the World War II Joint Chiefs to die, Arnold, King, and Marshall all having preceded him.

There is no definitive biography of Admiral Leahy. His memoir, *I Was There* (New York: McGraw-Hill, 1950), was based on a personal diary Leahy kept during the war; it is useful but lacks depth. The diary is with Leahy's papers at the Library of Congress; other Leahy materials are at the Wisconsin Historical Society in Madison. Prof. John Major has contributed a sketch of Leahy's tenure as chief of naval operations in Robert W. Love, Jr., ed., *The Chiefs of Naval Operations* (Annapolis: Naval Institute Press, 1980). For his early years, see Gerald Thomas, "Admiral Leahy and America's Imperial Years" (Ph.D. diss., Yale University, 1973). Col. Paul L. Miles, Jr., of the West Point history department is currently at work on a full-scale scholarly biography.

See also Joint Chiefs of Staff

Legacy of the New Deal

See Biographers and Public Reputation; Conservation; Liberalism and Progressivism; New Deal; Office of the Presidency; Regulation, Federal Relief

---

LeHand, Marguerite ("Missy")
(13 September 1898–31 July 1944)

At a time when executive secretary was the highest practical career ambition of most American women, Marguerite LeHand (the Roosevelt children named her "Missy") was the first secretary of the United States. At a time when executive secretaries were often in practice or at least in theory "office wives," she was that, too.

Born in Potsdam, New York, at the end of the nineteenth century, LeHand grew up in Somerville, Massachusetts. She graduated from high school in 1917 and held a number of clerical and secretarial jobs with a paper company, a picture store, a tire company. In 1920, she went to work for the Democratic National Headquarters, and after the party's defeat, which included his own, FDR hired her.

The president with secretaries Missy LeHand, Marvin McIntyre, and Grace Tully (left to right) at Hyde Park, 4 November 1938. (Courtesy FDR Library.)

LeHand was, therefore, working for Roosevelt at the time he suffered the polio attack in 1921. In the course of his hopeful searches for a cure and recovery of the use of his legs, he discovered the run-down spa at Warm Springs, Georgia. FDR invested considerable amounts of his limited capital to refurbish the area, for he sincerely believed in its recuperative powers. Mrs. Roosevelt disliked Warm Springs and sought every excuse to avoid accompanying her husband on his numerous trips south. As a result, Missy LeHand became housekeeper-hostess-secretary there. Mrs. Roosevelt was undoubtedly ambivalent about this arrangement—grateful to be relieved of going, resentful of another woman's performance of wifely duties.

When Roosevelt became governor of New York, a similar division of labor between the women occurred in Albany. LeHand lived in the executive mansion. Mrs. Roosevelt continued to teach at the Todhunter School in New York City and was absent from the state capital most weekdays. At Hyde Park, she already occupied her own cottage with close friends. By the late 1920s, gossip surfaced about the relationship between FDR and LeHand, and the speculation continued after Roosevelt's election to the presidency. Like Louis Howe, Missy LeHand lived in the White House where, among her many duties, she met her boss with or without the company of his male secretaries as he had breakfast in bed, read the morning papers, and prepared for the day's schedule.

In the White House, LeHand, along with her other duties, continued to serve as hostess when Eleanor was absent. A possible conflict was pushed aside when Mrs. Roosevelt volunteered to do substantive work by handling some of her husband's correspondence. In a reply that was more a rebuke, FDR reminded her that Missy might consider it interference. LeHand's responsibilities extended beyond correspondence, much of which she answered herself. She held power of attorney and managed Roosevelt's accounts, actually paying his bills by check. Her opinion on numerous matters of state was sought and valued. Like other members of his staff, she was treated like family and often dined with them formally and informally. When groups of advisers gathered around the radio to hear election returns, she joined them as "one of the boys." She was always in attendance at FDR's afternoon cocktail hours.

Like other members of both the Roosevelts' staffs, LeHand was devoted and hard-working to the point of self-denial. She rarely took an afternoon off, let alone a vacation. Whatever resentment Eleanor Roosevelt may have harbored, in her treatment of LeHand she behaved like a helpful friend and supportive relative. She accompanied Missy to her mother's funeral, brought the gifts and attended the weddings of Missy's nieces, and according to one source, even bought Missy's clothes.

After twenty-one years of loyal service, LeHand in 1941 suffered a debilitating stroke. After several months of hospitalization, she continued her convalescence in Warm Springs and then at home in Massachusetts. She never fully recovered her speech or her ability to work unaided. Inactivity added to the difficulties of illness until her death in July 1944.

The nature of her relationship to FDR remains speculative. He paid all her hospital bills, and though she predeceased him, his will stipulated that her medical expenses be covered from income from the estate. When she died, however, it was Eleanor who attended the funeral in North Cambridge, Massachusetts, presided over by Bishop Richard J. Cushing. James Farley, Felix Frankfurter, and Joseph P. Kennedy were among the mourners.

LeHand's prominence in the Roosevelt administration can be gauged by the response of *New York Times* columnist Arthur Krock. She was part of the original group that had passed from the scene who, like Howe, were influential, devoted, and wise. War and political missteps marked the contemporary scene, according to Krock, and the absence of LeHand was one measure of the "spiritual decline" of the administration. For Americans who have become accustomed to evaluating Eleanor Roosevelt as the nation's and the president's conscience, it is interesting to read Krock's reference to LeHand as FDR's acknowledged conscience. The two women staked out claims to separate domains of great influence. At the time of her death, contemporaries thought it unlikely that Missy LeHand would become a mere historical footnote.

LOIS SCHARF

LeHand's early years as well as her role in the Roosevelt administration are described in the *New York Times* obituary of 1 August 1944. The editorial page of the same issue carried Arthur Krock's column. Joseph Lash refers to the divided domains and ambivalent relationship of Mrs. Roosevelt and Miss LeHand in *Eleanor and Franklin* (New York: W. W. Norton, 1971). Lash transcribes an interview with chauffeur and close friend, Earl Miller, which reveals the convolutions of the ER-LeHand-Miller-FDR relationships in *Love, Eleanor: Eleanor Roosevelt and Her Friends* (Garden City, N.Y.: Doubleday and Co., 1982). Grace Tully writes sympathetically of her friend and coworker in *FDR: My Boss* (New York: Charles Scribner's Sons, 1949).

Lehman, Herbert Henry
(28 March 1878–5 December 1963)

Investment banker, New York governor, U.S. senator, and director of the United Nations Relief and Rehabilitation Administration. Herbert Lehman was born in New York City to wealthy German-Jewish parents. His father was a cotton merchant with a progressive outlook on politics. Herbert, a handsome, stocky man who was both energetic and personable, graduated from Williams College in 1899 and began working for cotton manufacturer J. Spencer Turner Company. He rose to vice-president before joining his brother, Arthur, at Lehman Brothers, by then an important investment banking firm. Along with his growing career, Lehman devoted much time to public service activities, including the Henry Street Settlement, a relief organization in New York's slums. At the onset of World War I, he helped the Joint Distribution Committee, a charitable agency for Jews in Europe and Palestine.

With U.S. entry into World War I, Lehman began his public career as a textile-procurement specialist in the Navy Department, where he met and became friends with Franklin Roosevelt. Lehman rose to the rank of colonel before leaving the Navy in 1919. During the twenties, Lehman worked for Alfred E. Smith, and in 1928 he became the finance chairman for the Democratic National Committee. That same year Democratic leaders convinced Roosevelt to run for governor of New York. Roosevelt, still recovering from his bout with polio, was a reluctant candidate but agreed to run when Lehman consented to run as lieutenant governor and to assume the duties of governor while Roosevelt was away on recuperative vacations. Both Democrats were elected narrowly in what was a strong Republican year, and for two terms Lehman was a very active lieutenant governor, so much so that Roosevelt once called him "my good right arm."

Their working friendship continued in 1932 when Roosevelt moved on to Washington and Lehman began the first of four terms as governor of New York. Elected by a large majority, Lehman supervised an ambitious "Little New Deal" that combined reform with fiscal conservatism. Under his administration, New York's state treasury went from deficit to surplus and he pushed through the legislature some (but not all) of his public utility regulation and labor reforms. His record of appointments was nonpartisan, which enhanced his reputation in a state sometimes dominated by machine politics. Lehman's only close election came in 1938 when he ran against Thomas E. Dewey, who Lehman feared would roll back the liberal gains of the previous decade. Throughout the New Deal period, with the single exception of a private disagreement over Roosevelt' Supreme Court reorganization plan of 1937, Lehman remained a close friend and valuable ally of the president. Lehman and his wife, Edith, were frequent guests at the White House and formed a congenial foursome with the president and Eleanor Roosevelt,

(*Courtesy FDR Library.*)

who later referred to the Lehmans as "among our oldest and best friends."

A strong internationalist, Lehman began working on international relief operations out of the State Department in 1942 and in 1943 became the director of the United Nations Relief and Rehabilitation Administration (UNRRA). UNRRA, more than anything else, was a much-lauded creation of Roosevelt and Lehman, which arose out of their concern over international suffering. After Roosevelt's death, however, Lehman grew tired of his solitary crusade. When President Truman appointed Herbert Hoover to survey food needs in Europe, Lehman feared that his international approach to relief would give way to Hoover's more nationalistic outlook, and he resigned in frustration.

The still-active Lehman did not retire from politics, however, and in 1946 he ran for the U.S. Senate in his only unsuccessful election. Three years later at the age of seventy-one, Lehman defeated John Foster Dulles in a special election to fill the Senate seat vacated by New York's Robert F. Wagner. Lehman served until 1957 through some difficult years for liberals in the Senate. Although he sponsored no major legislation, he was noted as an early and angry opponent of Senator Joe McCarthy and as an advocate of immigration reform. When he retired in 1957, he was one of the last visible links to the old New Deal years. Even after his eightieth birthday he did not slow his vigorous pace, and in 1959 he launched, together with Eleanor Roosevelt, a campaign to rid New York City of Tammany Hall's machine politics. He died in New York City one day before he was to receive the Presidential Medal of Freedom.

A thorough biography of Lehman is Allan Nevins, *Herbert H. Lehman and His Era* (New York: Charles Scribner's Sons, 1963).

Lemke, William ("Liberty Bell")
(13 August 1878–30 May 1950)

Union party presidential candidate, 1936. William Lemke was born to a prosperous, immigrant North Dakota farm family and was educated on a mixture of prairie populism and formal training at Georgetown and then Yale Law School where he graduated in 1905. After an aborted land deal in Mexico, he plunged in 1916 into the third-party politics of North Dakota's Nonpartisan League and was elected to Congress in 1932.

Before the North Dakota presidential primary of that year, Lemke met Roosevelt at Hyde Park and agreed to campaign for Roosevelt in return for what he thought was Roosevelt's support for his farm program. When Roosevelt's congressional leaders fought several of Lemke's farm bankruptcy relief measures, Lemke felt betrayed by Roosevelt and became the standard-bearer for the Union party's bitter campaign against Roosevelt in 1936. Lemke fit the image of a hick, often clad in an ill-fitting gray suit, dusty black shoes, blue work shirt, and colorful galluses, with a bald, freckled head and frequently unshaven face. But he reminded his listeners, "My coat may be wrinkled, but my record is not." During the campaign, Union party backer Father Coughlin dubbed him "Liberty Bell" Lemke, but the nickname backfired as detractors joked that the bell too was cracked. Despite a fast-paced campaign, Lemke collected a disappointing 882,479 votes and damaged his personal reputation by association with the anti-Semitic fringe of the Union party. Although he never regained his former prestige, he continued to work in Congress for his farm policies until his death in 1950.

A critical treatment of Lemke is found in David H. Bennett, *Demagogues in the Depression* (New Brunswick, N.J.: Rutgers University Press, 1969). Edward C. Blackorby, *Prairie Rebel: The Public Life of William Lemke* (Lincoln: University of Nebraska Press, 1963) takes a more sympathetic view.

See also Coughlin, Charles Edward; Union Party

Lend-Lease

A skillfully devised mode of wartime aid to America's allies, Lend-Lease was originally conceived by the Roosevelt administration to assist in the British war effort against Nazism without breaking any domestic or international law. Its apparent legality and popularity caused Congress to approve the measure overwhelmingly on 11 March 1941.

The immediate trigger for the Lend-Lease idea was Prime Minister Churchill's letter of early December to President Roosevelt stating that by June 1941, Britain would no longer be able to pay for American arms and supplies. Churchill ended by expressing his belief in FDR's ability to solve the impending crisis. The heart of the crisis lay in the Johnson Debt-Default Act of 1934, which forbade the United States from trading with any warring nation except on cash terms. As a response to debt defaults by a number of nations after World War I, this law was still too new and popular for the administration to ask for its repeal.

Since the president and the large majority of his closest advisers believed the prime minister's statements, a novel approach had to be found to aid the British. After a week of rumination, the president announced on 17 December his desire to aid the British through loan and lease arrangement. In an inspired analogy, he likened the loan-lease concept to the loan of a garden hose to a neighbor whose house was on fire, thereby implying the protection of one's own home. So favorably received was the loan-lease concept that the president made it the central theme of his 29 December fireside chat, adding the warning that aid to Britain then would serve as insurance against Americans living in the future "at the point of a gun." But, FDR warned, the United States had to become not only a giver of aid, but "the great arsenal of democracy." The next day, Treasury lawyers began drafting the Lend-Lease bill to give the president broad discretionary powers to "sell, transfer title to, exchange, lease, lend or otherwise dispose of" articles to any country the president had decided was vital to U.S. security. Congress would control the appropriation of funds, but the repayment schedule would be left to the president's discretion.

Presented to Congress on 10 January, the bill, fortuitously numbered H.R. 1776, proved popular. Although attacked severely by the American hero Charles A. Lindbergh, the historian Charles Beard, and the America First Committee, the bill passed by a vote of 250–165 on 8 February. In the Senate, the opposition seemed stronger, particularly because of the influence of Republican Gerald P. Nye and Democrat Burton K. Wheeler who argued that the president's policies would result in "every fourth American boy being plowed under." This view did not prevail, and on 9 March, the Senate voted 60–31 for Lend-Lease with the original articles virtually intact. On 11 March, Roosevelt signed it into law.

Since the original and primary purpose of the act was to provide aid to Britain, and so certain was President Roosevelt that the bill would pass, as early as 18 February he announced that by the end of the month, W. Averell Harriman would leave for Great Britain to expedite American aid. FDR's confidence was not misplaced, for within thirteen days of the enabling legislation, the Congress appropriated the $7 billion he requested. Initially, Harry Hopkins ran the

The Lend-Lease plan aroused strong passions in the American populace. A faction of the opposition, the Mother's Crusade against Lend-Lease, demonstrates before the Capitol in 1940. (UPI/Bettmann Archive.)

Lend-Lease program, but in August 1941, Edward R. Stettinius, Jr., assumed Hopkins's role and was appointed administrator in October, when the Office of Lend-Lease Administration was established.

Lend-Lease assisted at least thirty-eight countries before the war's end. Great Britain received the largest share, but historians are not agreed on the total figure which varies from $13.5 to $20 billion. After the German attack on Russia, the president decided that the Russians qualified for aid. Estimates of their receipts vary from $9.1 to $10 billion. France and French Northwest Africa also received approximately $3.5 billion aid, and China and India $2.2 billion each. Although there is no firm consensus of the total Lend-Lease expenditure, it is generally agreed that aid approximated $48 billion. Reverse Lend-Lease, repayment in kind, approximated $8 billion, the bulk of this coming from France and the British Empire. Most Lend-Lease debts were canceled after the war, except for civilian goods on hand or supplies ordered and forwarded. For this the British eventually paid $650 million and the French $750 million. Russian debt, however, posed a problem. Assessed at $10 billion, the Russians refused both to pay and to return a number of ships and charged the United States with ingratitude. After long negotiations, the debt figure was finally settled at $722 million during the Nixon-Brezhnev Moscow summit talks in 1972, the final payment to be made in 2001.

For President Roosevelt, the passage of Lend-Lease was a major victory. It signaled to his domestic detractors that despite his lowered majority in the elections of 1940, he was still a most popular president, fully supported by the Congress. The Lend-Lease debate clearly demonstrated the willingness of the American people to give the president even greater powers to protect them from involvement in war, although many of his opponents saw the president's aim as the opposite. There exists, at present, no evidence that the president intended anything but aid to the Allies, and the program proved to be very

popular to the war's end. Lend-Lease is considered today to be one of FDR's most inspired ideas, the precursor to the foreign aid program of the post–World War II era.

Edward Stettinius, Jr.'s *Lend-Lease: Weapon for Victory* (New York: Macmillan Co., 1944) is the earliest work on Lend-Lease and provides an excellent view of the administration of the program. Warren Kimball's *The Most Unsordid Act: Lend-Lease, 1939–1941* (Baltimore: Johns Hopkins Press, 1969) is a comprehensive treatment of the precursors of Lend-Lease, the politics of its passage. The most rigorous work on Lend-Lease to Russia is George C. Herring, Jr.'s *Aid to Russia, 1941–1946* (New York: Columbia University Press, 1973), as is James J. Dougherty's *The Politics of Wartime Aid* (Westport, Conn.: Greenwood Press, 1978) in its treatment of Lend-Lease aid to France and French Northwest Africa between 1940–46. A cogent and insightful contemporary response to the Lend-Lease debate is the *New Republic* editorial commentary on the bill, "The Battle of 1776," *New Republic*, 20 January 1941; pp. 69–70, in which nearly all the bothersome questions were raised and positively dispatched with care.

JOHN C. WALTER

See also Churchill, Winston Leonard Spencer; Cohen, Benjamin Victor; Currie, Lauchlin; Foreign Economic Policy; Foreign Policy; Good Neighbor Policy; Hopkins, Harry L.; Neutrality Acts; Stalin, Joseph and the Soviet Union; Stettinius, Edward Reilly, Jr.; World War II

Lewis, John Llewellyn
(12 February 1880–11 June 1969)

President of the United Mine Workers of America (UMW), founder of the Committee for Industrial Organization, and first president of the Congress of Industrial Organizations. Born near Lucas, Iowa, John L. Lewis was to become the preeminent labor leader of his age. A beetle-browed giant, whose fondness for Biblical allusion reflected his immigrant Welsh coal-mining background, Lewis's formal education was completed at the seventh grade, and he spent the rest of his youth and early adulthood in the mines, first in Lucas and then, for several years, as a migratory mine worker in the western states. Lewis eventually returned to Lucas, and in 1907 was elected president of the UMW local union. In 1909 he moved to Illinois where he became president of the UMW local in Panama (1909) and Illinois UMW lobbyist (1910–11). Appointed an American Federation of Labor (AFL) general field agent in 1911, Lewis returned to the UMW in 1917 as statistician and, shortly after, vice-president. He became UMW president in 1920.

For thirteen years, Lewis presided over a union in turmoil. Throughout the 1920s, the bituminous coal industry was wracked by overcapacity, and the union lost over 80 percent of its membership as collective bargaining structures collapsed in the face of pressure for wage reductions. Lewis's plans to create a fully centralized and administratively hierarchical union compounded the decline by provoking factional conflict, and the depression finished the job. Like Sidney Hillman and David Dubinsky, however, the charismatic and opportunistic Lewis brilliantly turned Section 7 of the National Industrial Recovery Act into a virtual presidential injunction to organize unions, and within three months the UMW had reenrolled some 92 percent of the nation's coal miners.

With the UMW restored to its traditional strength, Lewis's attention shifted to the fortunes of the wider labor movement. Winning election to the AFL Executive Council in 1934, Lewis pressed throughout 1935 for the extension of organizing efforts to the steel, automobile, and other mass production industries. The AFL's failure to act culminated in the creation of the Committee for Industrial Organization (CIO) late in 1935, and over the next two years, Lewis led the CIO in a series of organizing campaigns, financed largely by the UMW, that brought industrial unionism to the centers of American manufacturing industry. Suspended and eventually expelled by the AFL for dual unionism, the CIO formed an independent federation (the Congress of Industrial Organizations) in 1938. Inevitably, Lewis was chosen as its first president.

Lewis's relations with the Roosevelt administration were initially extremely close. Once a preacher of laissez-faire, Lewis had been convinced by the UMW's experiences during the 1920s that only government action could bring collective bargaining and permanent stability to unorganized industries. Consequently, the UMW became closely involved in the preparation of the National Industrial Recovery Act and helped to ensure the inclusion of Section 7 in the legislation. Lewis went on to become a member of the National Recovery Administration's Labor Advisory Board (1933–35) and was also appointed to the National Labor Board (1933–34) and the National Industrial Recovery Board (1934–35). In 1935 he helped secure administration backing for the National Labor Relations Act, and also—by threatening a general miners' strike—the Guffey-Snyder Coal Stabilization bill. In 1936 he helped create labor's Non-Partisan League and, although a lifetime Republican, committed half a million dollars of UMW money to Roosevelt's reelection.

During Roosevelt's second term, however, the close relationship quickly soured. By attempting to remain neutral during the CIO's General Motors and Little Steel strikes (January and May–June 1937), Roosevelt indicated that he did not feel beholden to Lewis for his reelection. Lewis, in turn, grandiloquently condemned Roosevelt's "betrayal" of his labor supporters (September 1937). "It ill behooves one who has supped at labor's table . . . to curse with equal fervor and fine impartiality both labor and its adversaries when they become locked in deadly embrace," he declaimed. The next two years brought repeated clashes over foreign policy issues, over AFL-CIO unity (ardently desired by the administration), over the government's unwillingness to abrogate contracts with employers violating labor laws, and over the prospect that Roosevelt would seek a third term. Early in 1940, Lewis suggested that his opposi-

tion could be assuaged, and Roosevelt's reelection assured, if he were made the Democrats' vice-presidential nominee. Rebuffed, Lewis accused the administration of having "made depression and unemployment a chronic fact in American life." During the spring and summer, he toyed with the possibility of becoming a presidential candidate himself at the head of a Farmer-Labor party, or alternatively, of endorsing Herbert Hoover for the Republican nomination. Finally, in a national radio broadcast to an estimated audience of 30 million on 25 October 1940, Lewis delivered a slashing personal attack on Roosevelt, exhorted union labor to vote for Wendell Willkie, and added that he would treat the return of Roosevelt as a vote of no confidence in his own leadership of the CIO.

Roosevelt's 1940 victory was duly followed by Lewis's resignation from the CIO presidency. Two years later, he took the UMW out of the CIO altogether and from then on concentrated on the affairs of the union. Highly successful wartime strikes won the union important wage increases but also brought government seizure of the mines (1943) and threats to draft strikers, and made passage of the War Labor Disputes Act (1943) a certainty. In the postwar period, miners' strikes again brought seizure (1946) and alienated public opinion, and again smoothed the path for regulatory legislation (Labor-Management Relations Act, 1947). Lewis's position within the UMW nevertheless remained secure, and he retained the presidency until retirement in 1960. He died in Washington, D.C., in 1969.

The definitive biography of Lewis is Melvyn Dubofsky and Warren Van Tine, *John L. Lewis* (New York: Quadrangle, 1977). Less reliable and bordering on hagiography is Saul Alinsky, *John L. Lewis* (New York: Putnam, 1949). On Lewis and the CIO in the 1930s, see Irving Bernstein, *Turbulent Years* (Boston: Houghton Mifflin, 1969). On Lewis and Roosevelt, see C. K. McFarland, *Roosevelt, Lewis and the New Deal, 1933–1940* (Fort Worth: Texas Christian University Press, 1970). Aspects of the 1940 election are discussed in Hugh Ross, "John L. Lewis and the Election of 1940," *Labor History* 17, no. 2 (1976). Lewis's early commitment to laissez-faire is illustrated in his book, *The Miners Fight for American Standards* (1925).

CHRISTOPHER L. TOMLINS

See also Labor

John L. Lewis, 1937. Artist: S. J. Woolf. (National Portrait Gallery, Smithsonian Institution.)

Liberalism and Progressivism

When the New Deal came into existence, the United States was caught in a time lag as well as a depression. By 1932 the Western world was far along in what sociologist Karl Polanyi aptly termed the "Great Transformation." A surge of nationalism and industrial development during the late nineteenth century had created rival concentrations of power that finally exploded in World War I. The aftermath of that struggle saw great changes in governing forms. Revolutionary response to chaos gave rise to authoritar-

Jerry Doyle, New York Post, *4 March 1935. Political developments of the day were perceived as the changing products of a changing "Liberalism Company" in this period cartoon.*

ian states in Russia, Japan, Turkey, and Italy. More democratic nations, such as Britain, France, and the Scandinavian countries, developed policies that comparably shifted the emphasis of their liberalism from individual autonomy toward the welfare state.

In the United States, however, the reverse of that collectivist trend occurred. Affluence and recoil from war led to the ascendancy of conservative leaders who deferred to the resistance of business to regulation and so ended a period of progressive reform that had briefly involved the United States in the Great Transformation before World War I.

The end of the Progressive Era left socially conscious Americans with a dilemma. Not only was the nation out of phase with other Western nations but its reformers also faced imperfect choices at home. Pre–World War I progressivism had been fully located within the political mainstream and so could be patriotically traditional and strive for substantial change at the same time. Progressives sought to unify these two stances by presenting their reforms as the use of modern means to restore old values enshrined within the constitutional system. Campaigns for Prohibition, restrictions on child labor, laws against prostitution, and the use of the schools to inculate "Americanism" were prominent ways of honoring ethical traditions. So, too, on the regressive side, were enthusiasm for eugenics and willingness to exclude minorities from a full share of the benefits of American life. Other progressive reforms, in contrast, sought to guide modernism toward further innovation. That was true of the scientific management

movement for industrial efficiency, progressive education, and support for modern art and literature.

In the twenties, such coherence from within a loyal consensus was undermined by conservative control, and so reformers had to either curtail their hopes drastically or break with the establishment. Those who chose to maintain their allegiance tended to side with the idea put forward most vigorously by Herbert Hoover that carefully conceived patterns of voluntary association between business and government could lead to a new era of progress and prosperity. The progressives who took part had to hope that their reform aims would be met by the diffusion of wealth and wisdom from the leaders of free enterprise to the rest of society, and in that they were mostly dissappointed.

Unaffiliated progressives tended to react to the pressures of the times by becoming more cynical and bolder. As witnesses to the contradiction between rhetoric about trickle-down beneficence and the threadbare state of workers, farmers, and the dependent, they were moved to frame strong measures with scant regard for the practical politics of the moment. Specialization also inclined them in that direction. In step with modern organization, reformers divided into segments, each concentrating on a particular avenue of change—whether social insurance, psychological case work, scientific management, progressive education strategies to outlaw war, plans for resource conservation, or various forms of radicalism, Marxist and other. The situation pushed reformers toward the liberal or radical Left in accord with the way alienation and specialization naturally press concepts and designs toward the limits of their possibilities.

In 1924 the Progressive party—a radicalized remnant of the prewar third-party vehicle of Theodore Roosevelt's New Nationalism—gathered a large number of activists behind a program of collectivist reform that drew from prewar ideas for national planning and social welfare programs of the sort being developed in Europe. After the failure of the party to score well in the national election, some of its survivors traveled to Russia to witness that most spectacular and comprehensive example of collectivism. They returned filled with enthusiasm for rational planning and found a number of undertakings in motion that could claim their support. Public policy research organizations, for example, led by the Brookings Institution and the National Bureau of Economic Research, were gathering the data of economic life into a general understanding of social institutions and the business cycle. Out in the countryside, agents of the Department of Agriculture extension service were preaching scientific farming and cooperation. In the interests of conserving natural resources and America's folk heritage, regional projects, like the analysis of resources in New York State by the Regional Planning Association of America and the survey of southern regions by Howard Odum and coworkers at the University of North Carolina, were gaining understanding of how to coordinate public policy on the basis of distinctive local assets and needs. And, in a comparable celebration of differences, advocates of cultural pluralism were helping direct sympathy toward the rights and problems of minorities. To lend these movements legitimacy, a new concept of legal realism had arisen which contended that, since court decisions were predicated more on the psychology of judges and the press of current events than by precedent or jurisprudence, it followed that the law should be guided by a sense of the deepest needs of the public rather than by legal doctrine that one realist derided as "robeism."

Because the New Deal had that seedbed of ideas and zeal to draw upon, it was able to produce a mass of legislation in the astonishing speed that characterized the first hundred days. New Deal programs reflected both the progressive heritage and the specialized and skeptical experience of the twenties. Problems were dealt with in piecemeal fashion, as suited the relativist approach of the twenties. Substance as well as style linked the two eras. Regional and resource planning provided the basis for the Tennessee Valley Administration and the National Resources Planning Board. Advances in scientific management and farming, along with mobilization for World War I, shaped the National Recovery Administration and the Agricultural Adjustment Administration. From the long debate over European social insurance came the impetus for Social Security. And the legal realist revolt paved the way for eventual Court acceptance of New Deal intervention into the economy through taxing and regulation.

These linked developments indicated that traditional progressivism, rooted in middle-class values, adherence to capitalist free enterprise, and belief in sacrosanct constitutional tenets, had given way at the center of American reform to a new liberalism characterized by relativism and a willingness to experiment within the limits of political expedience. The major emphasis of reform thus shifted from social betterment to economic security; and during the course of the thirties several of the older progressive concerns were phased out. The "noble experiment" of Prohibition was repealed; religious activism moved left; racist and ethnic discrimination became taboo; old ideas of class and status respectability were scorned in the wake of the crash that discredited the plutocrats; and social order came to be thought of mainly in collectivist rather than individualist terms. It followed that many old progressives criticized the New Deal for what seemed unprincipled violations of individual freedom, states' rights, property holdings, and economic common sense. Some of these disaffected progressives joined the conservative opposition, as was prominently the case with Roosevelt's own political mentor, Al Smith, who became a charter member of the Liberty League.

By the end of the thirties, New Deal liberalism had taken the shape of a coalition of economic and ethnic interest groups centered within the large cities. In Senator Robert Wagner of New York, the immigrant son of a janitor who began by selling newspapers on a city street corner, the New Deal had the perfect representative figure to set the pace. Wagner galvanized support in Congress for Social Security, low-cost housing, an antilynching bill, and most important, the astonishingly far-reaching act that bore his name, which guaranteed collective bargaining rights.

The broadening effect of coalition politics extended beyond the urban working class to include all those to whom the favored New Deal image of the common man applied. That folkish ideal especially fitted the small farmer, even as it produced egalitarian rhetoric and artists' conceptions of such stock types as the burly factory worker, the striving victim of prejudice against minorities, and the small businessperson contending against the big interests. That liberal imagery was enhanced by the need to confront the worldwide menace of fascism, a menace that made the common man the embodiment of beleaguered democratic civilization as well as New Deal reform. And with the several New Deal appointments to the Supreme Court, the Bill of Rights was for the first time extensively interpreted to give broad legal sanction to free speech, laws against discrimination, and religious freedom—all with the effect of protecting the common man.

The crystallizing of the new liberalism into that New Deal coalition pattern was never completed, however. Conservative reaction against the welfare state halted the momentum of New Deal reform by the end of the thirties. And before any resolution of the struggle could occur on either New Deal or conservative grounds, World War II intruded. It followed that the exigencies of wartime mobilization, not plans to strengthen the executive and break up concentrations of economic royalists, brought the recovery the New Deal had sought.

On that basis, the new liberalism entered the era of postwar affluence in an ambivalent state. Politically, the New Deal coalition remained dominant; economically, the ideal of a cooperative commonwealth gave way to a revival of the free enterprise individualism Herbert Hoover continued to defend against the New Deal. Evolution toward a centralized welfare state hesitated at the point where several particular reforms and self-interest groups confronted a society that refused to fashion them into a governing whole.

Critics have divided in their response to the legacy of New Deal liberalism in ways that indicate some persistent life in the old argument over the New Nationalism of Theodore Roosevelt and the New Freedom of Woodrow Wilson. To some critics the New Deal wielded excessive central power; others contend that the New Deal was too cautiously wedded to obsolete notions of individualism to gain control over oligarchic forces. But the experience of the thirties did propel the argument well beyond the stage of 1912. A welfare state of some sort, whether centrally directed or democratically decentralized, has become the joint ideal of reformers. What remains unattained is a liberal consensus to match the progressive consensus that held before World War I. The piecemeal activism of the New Deal never achieved its ideal of the cooperative commonwealth; and the new liberalism, for all its many-sided influence, never evolved into an intellectually and pragmatically coherent whole.

The most thorough account of the formation of the New Deal out of the welter of previous ideas and practices is contained in the three volumes of Arthur M. Schlesinger, Jr.'s study of *The Age of Roosevelt: The Crisis of the Old Order* (Boston: Houghton, Mifflin, 1957) describes the failure of progressive and radical, as well as conservative, approaches to solve the depression; and the succeeding volumes, *The Coming of the New Deal* (1959) and *The Politics of Upheaval* (1960), chart the reformist path of the Roosevelt administration. Schlesinger's argument that the New Deal was truly new, as well as desperately necessary in the wake of discredited alternatives, follows the earlier and highly influential contention by Richard Hofstadter in *The Age of Reform* (New York: Alfred A. Knopf, 1955) that the New Deal was a sharp departure from past reform. Helping to solidify that view of New Deal distinctiveness are three preeminent works that appeared at roughly the same time: James MacGregor Burns, *Roosevelt: The Lion and the Fox* (New York: Harcourt Brace Jovanovich, 1956), a political scientist's analysis of shrewd presidential leadership; Rexford G. Tugwell, *The Democratic Roosevelt* (Garden City, N.Y.: Doubleday, 1957), an account from inside experience by Roosevelt's chief brains truster; and William E. Leuchtenburg, *Franklin D. Roosevelt and the New Deal* (New York: Harper, 1963), a tour de force that draws an enormous range of sources into the best single-volume account of the subject. The differences between New Dealers and older progressives are quantitatively explored in Otis L. Graham, Jr., *An Encore for Reform* (New York: Oxford University Press, 1967). Steven Kesselman, *The Modernization of American Reform* (New York: Garland, 1979), extends the analysis of differences into an evaluation of how the legacy of New Deal reform helped create yet another variety of "postmodern" reform in the 1960s. A more despairing, yet comparable, appraisal of how New Deal relativism led to the fragmentation of politics into selfish interest groups is given in Theodore J. Lowi, *The End of Liberalism* (New York: W. W. Norton & Co., 1979). On the other side of the divide, the progressivism of the early twentieth century has been looked upon alternately as a source of egalitarian reform and of moralistic regimentation for the benefit of a corporate elite. The former view informs Eric Goldman, *Rendezvous with Destiny* (New York: Vintage, 1955), which gave recent interest in the history of progressivism its greatest impetus; and the latter view was spurred by Samuel Hays, *The Response to Industrialism* (Chicago: University of Chicago Press, 1957) and, in a more radical vein, by Gabriel Kolko, *The Triumph of Conservatism* (New York: Free Press, 1963) and Christopher Lasch, *The New Radicalism in America* (New York: Alfred A. Knopf, 1965). A recent work by Robert Crunden, *Ministers of Reform* (New York: Basic Books, 1983), comports with the current stress on subjective factors in human social development by arguing that progressivism was more importantly a cultural than a political movement. The New Deal has not received comparable attention as a cultural movement; but a suggestion of the fruits of such an approach is given in T. V. Smith, "The New Deal as a Cultural Phenomenon," in *Ideological Differences and World Order*, ed. F. S. C. Northrop (New York: Macmillan, 1949).

R. ALAN LAWSON

See also Biographers and Public Reputation; Brandeis, Louis Dembitz; Conservation; Douglas, William Orville; Election of 1910; Election of 1920; Frankfurter, Felix; Good Neighbor Policy; Hoover, Herbert Clark; Hundred Days; Ickes, Harold LeClair; LaFollette, Philip Fox; LaFollette, Robert Marion, Jr.; Long, Huey Pierce; New Deal; Pinchot, Gifford; Planning; Rayburn, Samuel Taliaferro; Regulation, Federal; Roosevelt, Theodore; Sinclair, Upton; Smith, Alfred E.; Taxation; Townsend, Francis E. M.D.; Wagner, Robert Ferdinand; Wallace, Henry A.; Welles, Benjamin Sumner; Williams, Aubrey Willis; Wilson, Thomas Woodrow

Liberty League

See American Liberty League

Liberty Ships

See Maritime Commission

Lilienthal, David E.

(8 July 1899–15 January 1981)

Appointed to the board of the Tennessee Valley Authority (TVA) by President Roosevelt in 1933, David E. Lilienthal served until 1945 and for the last four years was its chairman. He had been a member of the Wisconsin Public Service Commission and a labor lawyer in Chicago. Born in Morton, Illinois, he was a graduate of DePauw University and Harvard Law School.

His achievements at TVA included developing the program of electrical power for the valley, conducting the legal defense of TVA against challenges from private utilities, popularizing the TVA idea to the nation, and guiding TVA into support of war production in World War II. Lilienthal and his fellow board member, H. A. Morgan, were critical of TVA chairman A. E. Morgan's conception of TVA as a social planning and demonstration agency for the development of subsistence farming, cottage industries, and exemplary models of electric power distribution. Morgan wished to compromise with the private utilities by demarcating separate and competing areas of service so that TVA might demonstrate its superiority. Lilienthal believed that the utility companies wished to destroy TVA, through court challenges, and that the new authority must dominate power services in the valley to survive. He was also opposed to Morgan's ideas of social planning.

The Lilienthal view prevailed, as the right of TVA to exist and distribute power was upheld by the courts. In 1939 Lilienthal arranged the TVA purchase of the properties of the Commonwealth and Southern Corporation. He developed innovative contracts for the purchase and distribution of TVA power by municipal distributors. But TVA became more of a power company and less of an agency for regional planning.

Roosevelt valued both A. E. Morgan and Lilienthal, telling the latter in 1936 that both must stay at TVA with Morgan as planner and Lilienthal as fighter against the power companies. Both were needed he said, to keep the idea of public authorities alive. FDR did not choose between the two men until Morgan forced his hand in 1938 by making public charges against his two colleagues. Roosevelt then called the three board members to the White House and invited Morgan to repeat his charges. When he refused to do so, the president fired him and coached Lilienthal for the subsequent congressional hearings.

FDR appreciated Lilienthal's political contribution to the New Deal and the 1936 election through his fight against the utilities. Lilienthal consciously used this fight as a means of building public support for TVA. When Roosevelt switched from being "Dr. New Deal" to "Dr. Win the War," Lilienthal moved TVA in the same direction by developing capacities for war production, the most dramatic of which was the provision of power to the atomic energy installation at Oak Ridge, Tennessee. Lilienthal successfully resisted the efforts of Secretary of the Interior Harold Ickes to sweep TVA under his administrative umbrella by popularizing TVA decentralized administration as "grass-roots democracy" in his 1944 book, *TVA Democracy on the March*. Lilienthal felt that FDR had lost interest in the TVA ideal and resolved to keep it alive by influencing public opinion. Roosevelt had been temporizing in the fight between Ickes and Lilienthal, but after reading Lilienthal's book, the president used the ideas in a speech and praised the book to its author. President Truman reappointed Lilienthal as chairman in 1945, saying that he wished to carry on Roosevelt's policies. Later that year, Lilienthal became chairman of the Atomic Energy Commission, serving until 1950. His subsequent career was devoted to the leadership of a private overseas economic development firm. He died in 1981.

The best study of the contrast between Lilienthal's and A. E. Morgan's conceptions of TVA is Thomas K. McCraw, *Morgan vs. Lilienthal: The Feud within the TVA* (Chicago: Loyola University Press, 1970). McCraw has also told the story of the development of the TVA power programs in *TVA and the Power Fight: 1933–1939* (Philadelphia: Lippincott & Co., 1971). Lilienthal's diaries describe primarily the war years and his chairmanship and contain interesting snapshots of FDR: *The Journals of David E. Lilienthal: The TVA Years, 1939–1945* (New York: Harper & Row, 1964). For a portrait of Lilienthal's leadership that compares him to the other TVA chairmen, see Erwin C. Hargrove, "The Task of Leadership: The Board Chairman," in *TVA, Fifty Years of Grass-roots Bureaucracy,* ed. Erwin C. Hargrove and Paul K. Conkin (Urbana and Chicago: University of Illinois Press, 1984).

ERWIN C. HARGROVE

See also Morgan, Arthur Ernest; Tennessee Valley Authority

Lindbergh, Charles Augustus
(4 February 1902–26 August 1974)

Noted aviator and the most prominent opponent of American entry into World War II. Born in Detroit, Lindbergh grew up the son of an isolationist congressman near the town of Little Falls, Minnesota. In 1920, he entered the University of Wisconsin, only to leave two years later to become a barnstormer, air force captain, and airmail pilot. Lindbergh achieved worldwide fame on 20 May 1927, when he flew nonstop from New York to Paris in a tiny single-engine monoplane, *The Spirit of St. Louis*. In 1930, he married Anne Spencer Morrow, daughter of a prominent banker and diplomat. Two years later, in one of the most publicized crimes of the century, their son Charles was kidnapped and murdered. During the 1930s, though he had become independently wealthy, he served as technical adviser for Pan-American Airways and Trans-Continental & Western Air Transport. From 1935 to 1939, the Lindberghs lived in Europe, during which time Lindbergh reported on German air power for American military intelligence.

Although Lindbergh condemned the anti-Semitism of the Nazis, he maintained in the late thirties that war between Germany and the Western powers would be fratricidal, particularly with Russia in the wings. When war broke out in 1939, Lindbergh called for noninvolvement and a Continental defense. He never publicly endorsed an Allied victory and, in August 1940, hinted at American-German cooperation. On 10 April 1941, he agreed to become a member of the America First Committee (AFC) and thereafter was its most popular spokesman. By asserting in September 1941 that "the Jews" (whose persecution he did condemn) were among the groups most active in pressing the United States to enter the war, Lindbergh dealt the AFC and himself a staggering blow.

Berryman, Washington Star, 2 May 1941. (*Copyright* Washington Post. *Reprinted by permission of the D.C. Public Library.*)

Lindbergh never voted for Roosevelt, as he claimed he could not trust him. Early in 1934, he publicly criticized Postmaster General James A. Farley's cancelation of private airmail contracts. Appointed in 1931 to the National Advisory Committee for Aeronautics, he continued to serve under Roosevelt, though he resigned in December 1939 on the grounds that the committee was a waste of time. During his only meeting with Roosevelt, held on 20 August 1939, conversation was limited to pleasantries. On 15 September 1939, Lindbergh recorded in his diary that the administration was trying to buy his silence by offering him a new cabinet post, that of secretary of air. Soon Lindbergh concluded that Roosevelt would "sacrifice this country in war if it were to his personal interests."

In his speeches of 1939 and 1940, Lindbergh did not mention the president by name. Only on 29 May 1941 did Lindbergh refer to Roosevelt directly. He accused the president of advocating "world domination" by maintaining "it is our business to control the wars of Europe and Asia" and to "dominate islands lying off the African coast." Lindbergh called for "new policies" and "a new leadership," though he soon said that he sought change only by constitutional methods. By October, Lindbergh was accusing the administration of treating Congress the way the Nazi regime had treated the Reichstag.

The White House helped arrange replies to Lindbergh's speeches by prominent interventionists. After Secretary of the Interior Harold Ickes had repeatedly accused Lindbergh of Nazi sympathies, Lindbergh protested in an open letter to Roosevelt on 16 July 1941. He denied that he had ties to any foreign government, claimed that he had not communicated with anyone in Germany or Italy since 1939, offered to open his files for the president's investigation, and said he would answer any questions concerning his activities the president might have. Roosevelt did not respond.

Roosevelt had strong opinions about the aviator. As early as 20 May 1940, he confided to Treasury Secretary Henry Morgenthau, Jr., that he was "absolutely certain that Lindbergh is a Nazi." Lindbergh's most recent speech, Roosevelt wrote privately the next day, could have been "written by Goebbels himself." In May 1941, letters to the White House endorsing Lindbergh's opposition to the use of American convoy escorts were forwarded to the Secret Service. Moreover, Lindbergh became an object of FBI surveillance.

On 25 April 1941, Roosevelt publicly compared Lindbergh to Clement L. Vallandigham, the leading Civil War Copperhead. In a letter to the president that was released to the press, Lindbergh resigned his commission, saying that his loyalty, character, and motives had been questioned. Privately he confided to his diary that if he took such an insult, "more, and worse, will probably be forthcoming."

Once the Japanese attacked Pearl Harbor, Lindbergh called for national unity and support of the war effort. Rebuffed by the administration in his attempts to serve in the U.S. Army Air Force or with private aviation firms, he first worked in a civilian capacity as consultant to the Ford Motor Company. In 1944, although a civilian, he flew some fifty combat missions in the Pacific, gathering data for United Aircraft to improve the design of fighter airplanes. During the postwar years, he was a consultant to the Department of Defense and a director of Pan American World Airways. In 1954 President Eisenhower made him a brigadier general in the Air Force Reserve. In the later years of his life, he was active in the preservation of wildlife throughout the world.

There is no first-rate biography of Lindbergh. Definitive on its topic is Wayne S. Cole, *Charles A. Lindbergh and the Battle against American Intervention in World War II* (New York and London: Harcourt Brace Jovanovich, 1974). Detailed firsthand accounts include *The Wartime Journals of Charles A. Lindbergh* (New York: Harcourt Brace Jovanovitch, 1970), Anne Morrow Lindbergh, *The Flower and the Nettle: Diaries and Letters, 1936–1939* (New York and London: Harcourt Brace Jovanovich, 1976), and Anne Morrow Lindbergh, *War Within and Without, 1939–1944* (New York: Harcourt Brace Jovanovich, 1980). Raymond H. Fredette, in "Lindbergh and Munich: A Myth Revived," *Missouri Historical Society Bulletin* 33 (April 1977):197–202, denies that Lindbergh influenced British policy at Munich. For a critique of the Lindbergh diaries, see Justus D. Doenecke, "A New Look at the Lone Eagle," *Historical Aviation Album* 14 (September 1975): 279–81.

JUSTUS D. DOENECKE

See also America First Committee; Isolationism

Lippmann, Walter

(23 September 1889–14 December 1974) Columnist, editor, author. Born in New York City, of German-Jewish ancestry, Walter Lippmann grew up enjoying the privileges attendant upon even moderate wealth in the late Victorian era. As a Harvard student he discovered Fabian socialism and founded the Harvard Socialist Club; yet even his early articles reveal an elitist distrust of the masses. Lippmann's romance with socialism barely survived a brief foray into practical politics; disillusioned by his experiences as an aide to the socialist mayor of Schenectady, he retired to the Maine woods to write his first book.

His warnings in *A Preface to Politics* (1913) against the tyranny of popular majorities dismayed his Greenwich Village circle; the years—and the First World War—widened this rift into an ideological gulf. Lippmann abandoned socialism for the New Nationalism and Herbert Croly's *New Republic,* and outlined his reformulated, liberal political philosophy in *Drift and Mastery* (1914). The outbreak of war in Europe forced Lippmann to survey the international scene, and in foreign affairs he found his métier.

Lippmann moved swiftly from vague pacifism to support of an official neutrality that was actually pro-Ally; he soon decided that entry into the war was both necessary and inevitable. Hoping to make war palatable to liberals, he advanced the concept of an

Atlantic community upon which America's security depended.

When war came Lippmann headed for Washington. There he served briefly with FDR on an interagency military wage commission; it was the first meeting between the two men. In 1917 Lippmann was tapped to work in the secret inquiry team that formulated Wilson's Fourteen Points. Unhappy with the peace treaty negotiated in Paris, Lippmann turned against Wilson. His idealism severely shaken, he ruminated on the nature of democracy; *Public Opinion* (1922) questioned the competence of the average citizen to make informed political judgments. Paradoxically, the book's publication coincided with Lippmann's move from the *New Republic* to newspaper journalism, a shift that marked a professional commitment to educating a wider audience.

Not content with commenting on political affairs, Lippmann assiduously cultivated those who controlled policy and occasionally functioned as an unofficial diplomat. As his national prestige mounted, his liberalism grew more conservative. Although he supported Al Smith for president—and FDR for governor of New York—in 1928, he admired Herbert Hoover. As the depression deepened, however, he came to believe that the country needed a new man, if not new policies, in the White House.

Franklin Roosevelt was not the man Lippmann would have chosen for this hour of crisis. In his widely read and politically potent syndicated column, "Today and Tomorrow," he charged that FDR was "a pleasant man who, without any important qualifications for the office, would very much like to be President." Lippmann attempted to undermine FDR's bid for the nomination, but saddled with a choice between Hoover and FDR, he voted Democratic.

Lippmann's mistrust of the masses made him favor the concentration of authority during an emergency. He urged FDR to exercise dictatorial powers and applauded the aggressive legislative program of the first hundred days. As a convert to Keynesian economics, Lippmann approved of abandoning the gold standard and praised FDR for refusing to cooperate in international currency stabilization. By early 1934, however, he was warning against unlimited government intervention in the economy. He continued to support the first New Deal and actively promoted it among his Wall Street friends. But as fascism spread in Europe and support grew for a collection of extremists in America, he became fearful of endorsing measures that threatened to change fundamentally America's political structures. For him, the second New Deal went too far; in 1936 Lippmann reluctantly supported Alf Landon. And when FDR unveiled his Court-packing plan, Lippmann launched an all-out attack. The bitterness of the Court battle soured Lippmann on FDR. He never repudiated the New Deal legislation to which he had given his approval, but *The Good Society* (1937) laid bare his ambivalence toward Roosevelt. It would take world war to effect a rapprochement.

As late as the election of 1940, Lippmann remained unhappy with FDR. Initially he supported Wendell Willkie's candidacy and finally refused to take sides at all. After the election, as FDR's foreign policy moved the United States inexorably toward war, Lippmann found little to quarrel with in the president's decisions. He applauded the Lend-Lease bill (which he had helped draft) and even came round to FDR's view that Japanese imperialism must be opposed. After the declaration of war, Lippmann supported internment of Japanese-Americans and generally approved of the conduct of the war, although he faulted the administration for its tardy support of Charles de Gaulle.

On the vital issue of postwar policy, Lippmann parted company with those, including FDR, who hoped for a world government that would secure peace and freedom. He scoffed at the Dumbarton Oaks plan for a United Nations; instead, he reiterated in *United States War Aims* (1944) the call he had made in *United States Foreign Policy* (1943) for alliances and spheres of influence based on a realistic assessment of military strength and national interests. But since Governor Dewey was, in his opinion, even less competent to conduct foreign affairs, Lippmann supported FDR for a fourth term. Only after FDR's virtuoso performance at Yalta did Lippmann finally admit him to his pantheon of personal heroes. (Lippmann never recognized the ironic discrepancy between the forceful men he most admired—Theodore Roosevelt, Winston Churchill, de Gaulle, and FDR—and the "disinterested man" he celebrated in *A Preface to Morals* [1939].)

Through the postwar years, Lippmann battled to persuade the Western Allies to agree to a realistic accommodation with the Soviet Union, although in the fifties he frequently employed the confrontational language that characterized cold war diplomacy. During the Kennedy and Johnson administrations, Lippmann at last achieved the insider status he had long sought as an adviser on foreign affairs. His adamant opposition to the commitment of ground forces in Vietnam led, however, to a final and bitter break with Johnson in 1965. The geopolitical realism that made him oppose the war reflected the same pragmatism that had governed his political judgments from the first New Deal forward and had finally won from him a tribute to FDR's international power brokerage.

Lippmann's personal papers and other archival materials are in the Walter Lippmann Collection at Yale University. Ronald Steel's massive *Walter Lippman and the American Century* (Boston: Little, Brown & Co., 1980) is the definitive biography. Steel's bibliographical notes provide an exceedingly useful guide to critical studies on Lippmann, although he curiously omits any reference to Larry L. Adams's analysis of Lippmann as a social and political theorist in *Walter Lippmann* (Boston: Twayne, 1977).

PATRICIA R. HILL

Literary Digest Poll

See Opinion Polls

London Economic Conference

In order to devise strategems to overcome the international depression, the London Economic Conference (sometimes referred to as the World Economic Conference) convened in London between 12 June and 28 July 1933. Before leaving the White House, Herbert Hoover had agreed to send an American delegation to the conference, but Roosevelt was less enthusiastic about its prospects to solve economic problems and had postponed it for several months. Roosevelt and Rexford Tugwell and Raymond Moley, members of the president's brains trust, believed that domestic economic recovery and reform was a prerequisite to international financial cooperation. In an attempt to promote a successful conference, European statesmen had visited Washington and had discussed the forthcoming meetings' agenda with Roosevelt. All expressed the view that currency stabilization should receive foremost consideration at the conference.

Roosevelt selected Secretary of State Cordell Hull to chair the American delegation, with James M. Cox, Key Pittman, Samuel McReynolds, James Couzens, and Ralph W. Morrison joining him. The president instructed them to try to reach agreement with the conference participants in a number of general areas encompassing tariff reductions, the cessation of foreign exchange and artificial trade restrictions, the development of monetary and fiscal policies for strengthening national economies and improving prices, the creation of a fair and long-lasting international monetary standard, and the control of the production and distribution of certain commodities.

At the outset of the conference, the gold-bloc European nations, led by France, proposed an immediate agreement on currency stabilization, which required that the countries that had abandoned the gold standard, including the United States and England, would return to it. The American delegation balked at the suggestion, insisting that its purchasing power, not its gold content, needed stabilizing. On its part, the United States proposed to enact a general 10 percent tariff reduction.

Hull worked out a tentative stabilization accord for the dollar, the franc, and the pound. American newspapers printed articles predicting imminent currency stabilization, causing negative reactions among both a segment of the general public and American markets. It was against this background that Roosevelt decided to reject the London proposal. In a statement on 3 July often referred to as the "bombshell message" that destroyed the conference, Roosevelt argued that "the sound internal economic system of a nation is a far greater factor in its well being than the price of its currency in changing terms of the currencies of other nations." A skeptical Roosevelt believed the protected rate for the dollar put America in an unfavorable economic position; he also objected because the policy to stabilize the dollar would not give him freedom to pursue domestic price-raising programs.

The gold-bloc delegates now thought the conference was a "pure waste of time." Their position was that each nation should either stay on or return to the gold standard, whereas Roosevelt believed that each nation must first put its own house in order through internal adjustment; the subsequent impasse was inevitable.

The conference met for another three weeks, but little international cooperation was achieved. The American delegation refused to discuss settlement of the war debts, although Senator Pittman got an agreement that pledged U.S. support of the silver market. Secretary of State Hull has been given credit for doing the best he could, given the lack of support not only from the president and the Congress but also from other members of the American delegation. The conference, therefore, adjourned on 27 July 1933 with no important accomplishments.

Robert Dallek, *Franklin D. Roosevelt and American Foreign Policy, 1932–1945* (New York: Oxford University Press, 1979) provides detailed information and analysis on the London Economic Conference. More general coverage is contained in Elliot A. Rosen, *Hoover, Roosevelt and the Brains Trust: From Depression to New Deal* (New York: Columbia University Press, 1977). See also Arthur M. Schlesinger, Jr., *The Coming of the New Deal* (Boston: Houghton Mifflin Co., 1958) and Raymond Moley, *After Seven Years* (New York: Harper & Bros., 1939).

See also Cox, James Middleton; Foreign Economic Policy; Foreign Policy; Hull, Cordell; Moley, Raymond

Long, Huey Pierce

(30 August 1893–10 September 1935)

Governor of Louisiana, U.S. senator, dissident leader and Roosevelt antagonist during the first years of the New Deal. Huey Long was a product of the relatively poor hill country of northern Louisiana (although his own family was reasonably prosperous); and it was the disaffected, vaguely populist sentiments of that region that shaped much of his political career. Largely self-educated and a successful lawyer, he served for eight years as a member of the Louisiana Public Service Commission and in 1928 was elected governor as the champion of the common people against the Old Guard, the oil interests, and the planter elite.

Long's record of accomplishment as governor was a relatively conventional progressive one by national standards (although not by the standards of Louisiana, where the conservative oligarchy had frustrated most reform efforts for decades). Long oversaw a massive road-building and public works program; he funded improvements in public health and public education; he achieved a modest reform of the tax codes and a modest restriction of corporate power in the state. But Long's methods were neither conventional nor modest, for he created a political machine whose powers within Louisiana were almost certainly without precedent in American history. Long concentrated virtually all state power—executive power, legislative power, even judicial power—in his own hands and won national renown as the "dictator of Louisi-

Huey P. Long. (Courtesy FDR Library.)

ana" or (within the state itself) as the "Kingfish." When in 1932 he resigned the governorship to assume a seat in the U.S. Senate to which he had won election two years earlier, he chose a compliant ally to succeed him in the statehouse and continued thereafter to control Louisiana politics as completely as he had while serving as its chief executive.

During his first months in the Senate, Long established himself as a harsh critic of the conservative policies of the Hoover administration and as a tireless advocate of redistribution of wealth—the only solution, he insisted, to the economic crisis of the Great Depression. In the spring of 1932, at the urging of several Senate progressives (most notably George Norris), he endorsed Franklin Roosevelt's candidacy for president; and he worked strenuously and effectively for Roosevelt both at the Democratic convention and in the general election campaign that followed.

By the fall of 1933, however, Long's fragile alliance with Roosevelt had dissolved, a victim of policy differences, disputes over patronage, and Long's own thinly concealed ambitions for the presidency. From that point on, Long worked to establish independent political power and to lay the groundwork for his own bid for national power in 1936 or 1940. In particular, he created his own national political organization, the Share Our Wealth Society, and promoted his own economic program, the Share Our Wealth Plan. The plan called for steeply graduated, confiscatory income and inheritance taxes to scale down large fortunes and the redistribution of the surplus wealth thus collected to the citizenry at large. Every American family would be guaranteed a "homestead" of $5,000 and an annual income of $2,500. Share Our Wealth clubs proliferated rapidly in 1934 and 1935,

at first largely in the South, but by mid-1935 in many other regions as well. Speculation was growing that Long planned to make the organization the basis of a third party, from which he would challenge Roosevelt for the presidency in 1936. Long's open flirtations with other popular dissident leaders (among them Father Charles E. Coughlin of Detroit and old-age pension crusader Francis Townsend) added fuel to that speculation. So did Long's frequent national broadcasts over the NBC radio network, his national speaking tours, and his increasingly frequent and strident attacks on the New Deal for its failure to work for wealth redistribution.

Roosevelt regarded Long with contempt and alarm and once called him "one of the two most dangerous men in America" (the other was Douglas MacArthur). After the break in 1933, the administration attempted, unsuccessfully, to undermine Long's power in Louisiana by denying him patronage and by launching investigations of alleged tax fraud within the Long organization. By mid-1935, however, Democratic politicians throughout the country were warning the president that the Long movement was making inroads into the New Deal coalition; and a privately conducted public opinion poll the same year revealed that Long would receive as much as 10 percent of the popular vote as a third-party candidate. When Roosevelt began in 1935 to promote the vigorous new legislative program that became known as the second New Deal (and which included a new revenue bill denounced by its critics as the "soak the rich tax"), there was considerable speculation that part of his motive was to undercut Long's popular appeal.

But Long's popularity had not, by 1935, reached the point where it posed a genuine threat to Roosevelt. Supporters of Long had not yet had to choose between him and the president, and there was considerable evidence that many of those supporters admired both men simultaneously and that if forced to choose they were as likely to choose Roosevelt as Long. Long's organization was flimsy and decentralized, a dubious basis for an effective third party, and his incipient alliances with other dissidents were troubled by personal rivalries and ideological divisions. In any case, Long had no opportunity to demonstrate his national political potential. In September 1935, he returned to Louisiana to supervise a special session of the state legislature. While walking down a corridor in the state capitol in Baton Rouge, he was fatally shot by a young physician, Carl Austin Weiss, who was immediately gunned down by Long's bodyguards and whose motives were never clearly established. After Long's death, his national organization collapsed and disappeared almost immediately, and what remained of his political machine in Louisiana quickly made its peace with the Roosevelt administration.

Long himself was the author of two books: *Every Man a King* (New Orleans: National Book Co., 1933), an autobiography, and *My First Days in the White House* (Harrisburg, Pa.: Telegraph Press, 1935), a fanciful account of a Long presidency. The fullest biographical treatment is T. Harry Williams, *Huey Long* (New York: Alfred A. Knopf, 1969). Allan P. Sindler, *Huey Long's Louisiana* (Baton Rouge: Louisiana University Press, 1956) examines Long's impact on the politics of his own state. Alan Brinkley, *Voices of Protest: Huey Long, Father Coughlin, and the Great Depression* (New York: Alfred A. Knopf, 1982) examines his national impact.

ALAN BRINKLEY

See also Democratic Party; New Deal; Union Party

Longworth, Alice Roosevelt
(12 February 1884–20 February 1980)

Fifth cousin of Franklin D. Roosevelt, first cousin of Eleanor Roosevelt. Directly related to two presidents—her father, Theodore Roosevelt, and her cousin, Franklin D. Roosevelt—Alice Roosevelt Longworth was born in New York City in 1884 when her father was a member of the New York State Assembly. Her mother, Alice Hathaway Lee, died from Bright's disease two days after her birth. For the next three years she was brought up by her aunt, Anna "Bamie" or "Bye" Roosevelt. In 1887 after Theodore Roosevelt's remarriage to Edith Kermit Carow, Alice went to live at Sagamore Hill, the rambling Roosevelt homestead at Oyster Bay on Long Island, where her

childhood soon was shared with four half brothers and a half sister. Her attendance at formal school totaled less than a year, and she was chiefly tutored at home. She became a remarkable self-educated woman largely because of two things: her association with highly literate people in the family circle and her voracious capacity for reading on an unusually wide range of topics. Until her death she almost always concluded her day by reading until dawn.

When her father succeeded McKinley to the presidency in 1901, Alice was seventeen. Later she would recall the time: "I was the daughter of an enormously popular President, and the first girl in the White House since Nellie Grant, and I looked upon the world as my oyster." It was not long before "Princess Alice," as she was being called, began to break social customs and set new ones in Washington. She smoked in public, bet on horse races, used rouge, traveled without a companion, and drove a motor car. While the president might become enraged by some of her antics, he was never ashamed of his daughter. Once chided by critics he did say, however, that he could look after the country or look after Alice, but no man was capable of both. Some of her friends feared that she would never find a man to put up with her headstrong individuality. At family gatherings and Oyster Bay socials, she was often matched

Alice Roosevelt (center row, second from left) and Franklin D. Roosevelt (front row, far right) at a relative's wedding, 1904. (Courtesy of Joanna Sturm.)

with her distant cousin from upstate, Franklin Delano Roosevelt, and indeed the two did make a handsome couple. In 1905 after a trip to the Orient, however, she announced her engagement to Representative Nicholas Longworth, a dapper young Republican congressman from Ohio.

Alice Longworth was a political ally of both her father and her husband, but in 1913, her alliance with her husband was tested when she worked for her father's Bull Moose presidential ticket while Representative Longworth remained loyal to the regular Republicans. Both men were defeated, but Longworth was returned to the House the following year and remained there until his death in 1931, having been speaker since 1925.

Although she herself never held any political office, Alice Longworth was a woman who was really absorbed in politics. Her political intrigue and awareness of issues charmed and fascinated presidents and political leaders for nearly eight decades. Her political differences with her cousin, President Franklin D. Roosevelt, were well known, and her criticisms of his New Deal policies and "alphabet agencies" were quite vociferous. She once commented that under the New Deal, Miss Columbia had become the girlfriend of the whirling dervish! Nonetheless as "family" Alice continued to be invited to White House affairs, and she continued graciously to accept the invitations. Alice Roosevelt Longworth was a true symbol of Washington. Her biographer says of her: "Alice burst upon the American people, and soon after the rest of the world, like a rocket at night on the Fourth of July; she zoomed high, she was clearly seen, but unlike a rocket, the sparks she left behind never completely disappeared." Mrs. Longworth died in 1980 of bronchial pneumonia at her Washington home. She was ninety-six.

Alice Longworth wrote an autobiography, *Crowded Hours, Reminiscences of Alice Roosevelt Longworth* (New York: Charles Scribner's Sons, 1933). For a full-scale biography, see Howard Teichmann, *Alice: The Life and Times of Alice Roosevelt Longworth* (Englewood Cliffs, N.J.: Prentice-Hall, 1979). An interesting, well-illustrated volume is Michael Teague, *Mrs. L.: Conversations with Alice Roosevelt Longworth* (New York: Doubleday, 1981).

Lynch Laws

See National Association for Advancement of Colored People; Negroes

M

MacArthur, Douglas

(26 January 1880–5 April 1964)

Army chief of staff and Pacific theater commander. Douglas MacArthur was born at Little Rock, Arkansas, the son of a distinguished general. A West Point graduate of 1903, he rose to brigadier general in 1918 as an outstanding combat leader in World War I. After service in the 1920s as West Point superintendent, corps area commander, and Philippine department head, he became the army chief of staff in 1930.

MacArthur and Roosevelt became acquainted in 1916–17 while they were in the War and Navy departments. When Roosevelt became president, he re-

Douglas MacArthur, 1930. Unidentified photographer.
(National Portrait Gallery, Smithsonian Institution.)

tained MacArthur as chief of staff until late 1935. Now a four-star general, MacArthur oversaw the founding and administration of the Civilian Conservation Corps, one of the most efficient relief programs of the New Deal. From autumn 1935 until mid-1941, he was military adviser to the Philippine Commonwealth. With U.S.-Japanese relations deteriorating, Roosevelt federalized the Philippine army and chose MacArthur to command U.S. army forces in the Far East in July 1941.

Upon the outbreak of war that December, MacArthur led a gallant defense of the Philippines, concentrating his forces on the Bataan peninsula and Corregidor Island where they prevented the Japanese from using valuable Manila Bay. On Roosevelt's orders, he left Corregidor in March 1942 and went to Australia where he took command of Allied ground, sea, and air forces in the new Southwest Pacific theater. Late that summer he launched a counteroffensive in New Guinea, driving the enemy out of Papua by early 1943.

In a large number of well-planned amphibious assaults in 1943–44, MacArthur's American and Australian units conquered the rest of New Guinea, the Admiralties, western New Britain, and Morotai. During these campaigns, he often complained to his military superiors and sometimes to Roosevelt about his need for more men and matériel and for better support from the Pacific fleet. He frankly, if futilely, challenged the strategic priorities of Roosevelt and the Joint Chiefs, asserting that operations against Japan were being neglected in favor of the war in Europe and that his Southwest Pacific offensive was being deprived of logistic means in order to strengthen the advance in Admiral Chester W. Nimitz's Central Pacific theater.

Some conservative Republicans tried to get MacArthur nominated for the presidency in 1944. The movement was unsuccessful, but it pointed up a considerable degree of right-wing dissatisfaction with Roosevelt's conduct of the war. Probably for political as well as strategic reasons, Roosevelt journeyed to Pearl Harbor in July 1944 to discuss future offensive alternatives in the Pacific with MacArthur and Nimitz. No final decision was made at the conference, but the president strongly endorsed the Joint Chiefs' later approval of MacArthur's plan to reconquer Luzon and the dropping of a proposal by naval leaders to bypass the Philippines and assault Formosa. At Pearl Harbor, FDR had been impressed by MacArthur's arguments, and he continued to hold the general's judgments and command abilities in high esteem. Largely on the impetus of Roosevelt, MacArthur was promoted to the five-star rank of general of the army in late 1944 and the next spring was named commander of all American army forces in the Pacific.

Both MacArthur and Roosevelt were masters of role playing, and when together, they seemed to relish maneuvering in a game of appearances. From 1933 onward, they differed often, sometimes angrily, on various military matters, but basically they respected each other. As President Harry S Truman did, Roosevelt probably would have chosen MacArthur as supreme allied commander over the occupation of Japan.

MacArthur headed the United Nations forces during the first ten months of the Korean War, but he was relieved in April 1951 after a long controversy with Truman. He served as board chairman of Remington Rand, 1952–55, and of Sperry Rand Corporation, 1955–64.

Douglas MacArthur, *Reminiscences* (New York: McGraw-Hill, 1964) is disappointing, written when he was in his eighties and seriously ill. The Southwest Pacific war is covered extensively in Charles A. Willoughby, ed., *Reports of General MacArthur*, 4 vols., (Washington: Department of the Army, 1966), but the work is uncritical on MacArthur. A useful collection is Vorin E. Whan, Jr., ed., *A Soldier Speaks: Public Papers and Speeches of General of the Army Douglas MacArthur* (New York: Praeger, 1965). Louis Morton, *Strategy and Command: The First Two Years* (Washington: Department of the Army, 1969), a volume in the army's Pacific War Series, gives perspective on MacArthur's leadership. A recent provocative study of the man and the commander is Carol M. Petillo, *Douglas MacArthur: The Philippine Years* (Bloomington: Indiana University Press, 1981). The most comprehensive work on his career to 1945 is D. Clayton James, *The Years of MacArthur*, 2 vols. (Boston: Houghton Mifflin Co., 1970–75).

D. CLAYTON JAMES

McCormick, Robert Rutherford ("Bertie," "Colonel")

(30 July 1880–1 April 1955)

Publisher and editor of the *Chicago Tribune* and one of the most vehement conservative and isolationist opponents of Franklin Roosevelt. Robert R. McCormick was born in Chicago in 1880. His family background and education were similar to the East Coast elite that he so resented. His father was a distinguished diplomat who served as ambassador to several European countries and his mother was the daughter of the publisher of the *Chicago Tribune*.

McCormick was educated briefly in England and then at Groton where one of his younger classmates was Franklin Roosevelt. He went on to Yale, graduating in the class of 1903.

After a brief career in politics as a progressive republican, McCormick became publisher of the *Chicago Tribune*, his public voice for the next forty years. The *Tribune* opposed American involvement in World War I, but after the declaration of war, McCormick served with distinction in the army, achieving the rank of colonel. After the war he returned to his isolationist beliefs; the Colonel wanted no involvement with the League of Nations or concessions on Allied war debts. His hatred of the British Empire was rivaled only by his abhorrence of the Soviet Union and communism. On domestic affairs McCormick was a strong opponent of government spending, Prohibition, and Wall Street.

Although the *Tribune* did not endorse Roosevelt in 1932, the Colonel told one of his editors to "treat Roosevelt nicely in your editorials. I want that boy that I went to school with at Groton to know I wish him well in his career." However, the honeymoon ended quickly. The Colonel contended in June 1933 that NRA licensing was a threat to the freedom of the press. Roosevelt dismissed the charge with a wisecrack, telling a correspondent, "Bert McCormick . . . is seeing things under the bed." McCormick then angrily denounced the NRA as "fascistic" and "revolutionary." With the exception of the Securities and Exchange Commission, which regulated the accursed Wall Street, the Colonel opposed all New Deal domestic programs and "socialistic" spending. In one political cartoon, he linked FDR with Hitler, Stalin, and Mussolini as the Four Horsemen of the Apocalypse. He never forgave FDR's decision to recognize the Soviet Union, believing that it stimulated labor unrest in America. The Colonel's support for Landon was manifest on the front page of the *Tribune*, while news of FDR's campaign was buried in the back pages. Ironically enough, the *Tribune* was one of the few papers FDR read daily. "He wanted to know the worst being said about him," remembered one aide.

During FDR's second term, McCormick's *Tribune* became the leading isolationist journal. The Colonel advocated appeasement of German claims in Central Europe and Japanese conquests in China. After Roosevelt's quarantine speech, the Colonel called the president "the most warlike head of government in any government today at peace." Opposition like this strengthened FDR's caution in his approach to international involvements. After the outbreak of war, the *Tribune* renounced its earlier support for American naval rearmament and universal military service; Lend-Lease was a "dictator bill," it editorialized, and the draft, "a threat to peace." Unlike most other isolationists, the Colonel refused to support *any* assistance for England. He saw no threat to the United States from a Nazi conquest of the British Isles. McCormick feared that a war led by Roosevelt would destroy the "American way of life" and usher in communism. Only three days before Pearl

Harbor, the *Tribune* infuriated the administration by publishing a secret War Department strategic plan which anticipated American entry into the war. Although the Colonel supported the war after the Japanese attack, the *Tribune* frequently ran afoul of government censorship during the war years.

For a man who despised "Perfidious Albion," McCormick looked the proper English gentleman. Six feet, four inches in height, trim, mustached, and perfectly tailored, McCormick's leisure activities were polo and hunt riding. His campaigns for modified spelling reform, new Fourth of July traditions, and the return of the horse to the farm contributed to his reputation for eccentricity. A paternalistic employer, the Colonel also considered himself an expert on military strategy. He was sincerely convinced of the virtue and patriotism of his beliefs and the lack of either of these qualities in his opponents.

McCormick remained the voice of conservative isolationism after the war, backing Dewey in 1948 and Taft in 1952. The picture of a smiling Truman holding an early edition of the *Tribune* announcing Dewey's "election" is one of the most famous in the annals of American politics. McCormick died in 1955.

There is no scholarly biography of McCormick. Joseph Gies, *The Colonel of Chicago* (New York: E. P. Dutton, 1979) is the most recent popular and very sympathetic account. Frank C. Waldrop, *McCormick of Chicago: An Unconventional Portrait of a Controversial Figure* (Englewood Cliffs, N.J.: Prentice-Hall, 1966) is anecdotal and entertaining. It should be supplemented by the straightforward Jerome E. Edwards, *The Foreign Policy of Colonel McCormick's Tribune, 1929–1941* (Reno: University of Nevada Press, 1971) and Walter Trohan, *Political Animals: Memoirs of a Sentimental Cynic* (Garden City, N.Y.: Doubleday, 1975). The short sketch in Maxine Block, ed., *Current Biography, 1942* (New York: H. W. Wilson Co., 1942), pp. 545–48, is scathing, but a good balance to the above works.

See also Isolationism

McIntire, Ross T.

(11 August 1889–December 1959)

Personal physician to Franklin D. Roosevelt from 1935 to 1945. Ross T. McIntire, who was born in Salem, Oregon, received his medical degree from Willamette University (now the University of Oregon) in 1912 and began practicing in his hometown. He served in the U.S. Navy Medical Corps during World War I and, following the war, decided to stay in the navy, practicing at naval hospitals and aboard the hospital ship *Relief* and pursuing graduate studies in ophthalmology and otolaryngology. When Roosevelt was seeking a personal physician, Admiral Cary Grayson, who had been President Woodrow Wilson's physician, recommended McIntire. During the last decade of the president's life, McIntire saw more of Roosevelt than anyone except Mrs. Roosevelt.

Following Roosevelt's death, he was criticized by some for having been overly optimistic about the president's health and by others of deliberately deceiving the American public for political reasons. In his book *White House Physician*, McIntire defended his 1944 judgment that Roosevelt was in excellent condition for a man his age. He received support in 1970, when Howard Bruenn, the navy cardiologist who attended Roosevelt during his last year, wrote that the president was not too ill to perform his duties. The cerebral hemorrhage that felled Roosevelt could not have been predicted.

In addition to being Roosevelt's doctor, McIntire was also surgeon general of the navy and chief of the Bureau of Medicine and Surgery, having been appointed to both positions by the president in 1938. He was promoted to vice admiral in 1944. As surgeon general, he effectively supervised the great expansion of the medical department during World War II. After leaving the navy in 1947, he organized the American Red Cross blood program. From 1947 to 1954, he was chairman of the President's Committee for Employment of the Physically Handicapped. He spent his last years as executive director of the International College of Surgeons. He died in Chicago at age seventy.

McIntire wrote of his experiences in *White House Physician* (New York: G. P. Putnam's Sons, 1946). The Ross T. McIntire Papers are in the Roosevelt Library. There is a brief biography of McIntire by William J. Stewart in the *Dictionary of American Biography*, Supplement 6 (New York: Charles Scribner's Sons, 1980), pp. 413–14.

McIntyre, Marvin Hunter ("Mac")

(27 November 1878–13 December 1943)

Assistant secretary and, after 1937, secretary to the president from 1933 until his death. With Louis Howe, Steve Early, and "Missy" LeHand, "Mac" McIntyre was one of the key insiders, the so-called Cufflinks Gang, who first served Franklin Roosevelt in his vice-presidential campaign in 1920 and then formed the core of his White House staff after his election in 1932. A Kentuckian by birth, McIntyre like Howe and Early had a newspaper background and first made Roosevelt's acquaintance when he took over the Navy Department's press relations in 1917. In 1920 he handled publicity for the vice-presidential race and did so again in 1932. His service on the staff of the *Army and Navy Journal* from 1920 to 1932 gave him a wide familiarity with Washington and military circles, which served him and his employer well during the White House years. Until 1939 he was in charge of political appointments, insofar as anybody was; afterwards ill health greatly reduced his contributions, but he continued to handle confidential matters for the president until his death in 1943. Somewhat conservative and distinctly southern in outlook, McIntyre had very sensitive political antennae but was little interested in policy matters. His loyalty was unquestioned but went to Roosevelt personally rather than to the New Deal, some of which seemed to bemuse him. He displayed to the fullest the "passion for anonymity" that Roosevelt sought in his political family.

Mahan, Alfred Thayer
(27 September 1840–1 December 1914)

The son of Dennis Hart Mahan, the distinguished military teacher, Mahan grew up at West Point amidst a life of scholarship and military commitment. He graduated from the U.S. Naval Academy in 1859, served with the South Atlantic and Western Gulf Blockade Squadrons, and slowly moved up the promotion ladder during the Gilded Age. An exceptional officer, Mahan preferred to research and write, and came to dislike sea duty.

Rear Adm. Stephen B. Luce founded the Naval War College in 1884, but he soon received a squadron command. Two scholars rejected his offer to relieve him at Newport, but Mahan gladly accepted. He served two tours as president: from 1886 to 1889 and from 1892 to 1893. During this first tour, he prepared a series of lectures using the rise of English sea control to demonstrate the importance of maritime warfare to littoral powers; these essays plus a critical preface were published in 1890 as *The Influence of Sea Power upon History*. A best-seller in Britain and then in America, this single work established Mahan as a strategist and historian of the first rank. Among his students, he counted Theodore Roosevelt, Henry Cabot Lodge, and a large cast of Progressive statesmen. During the Spanish-American War, Mahan headed the Strategy Board; in retirement, he served as Roosevelt's naval adviser, and as a delegate to the first Hague Peace Conference; he was also a member of several official commissions. He wrote another dozen important books and hundreds of articles on foreign policy and naval affairs prior to his passing in 1914.

Mahan espoused economic determinism, tempered by factors of geography, politics, and culture. He argued that command of the sea earned a littoral state control of the key lines of communications and that modern economies depended on international trade to survive. Tactically, he maintained that concentration rather than dispersion usually achieved victory and denounced the historical American strategies of commerce raiding and coastal defense.

Mahan was a devout Anglican, and his theological work demonstrated profound reflections on that communion. Often miscast as an imperialist, he opposed noncontiguous annexations except for naval bases to serve as coaling stations for the battle fleet. Although he recognized the material benefits that the West could bring to Africa, Asia, and Araby, he concluded that the primary goal of modern civilization was not exploitation but conversion to the Eucharist.

Mahan's influence on Franklin Roosevelt is difficult to underestimate. They met and corresponded, and Roosevelt kept well-read copies of Mahan's works in his library. He frequently quoted Mahan with great precision. And, despite his disdain for doctrine, Roosevelt adhered to Mahanian principles throughout the Second World War.

Of several biographies, the best is Robert Seager II, *Alfred Thayer Mahan* (Annapolis, Md.: Naval Institute Press, 1979). Seager and Doris McGuire edited *The Papers of Alfred Thayer Mahan*, 3 vols. (Annapolis, Md.: Naval Institute Press, 1975). Harold and Margaret Sprout in *The Rise of American Naval Power* (Princeton: Princeton University Press, 1936) based their critique of American naval policy on Mahanian principles. However, they argued incorrectly that Mahan never considered tridimensional warfare. The New Left treated Mahan as a typical imperialist and capitalist, and Peter Karsten propounded this warped thesis in his delightful and well-researched study of *The Naval Aristocracy* (New York: Free Press, 1972). A more scholarly synthesis by Ronald Spector may be found in Kenneth J. Hagan, ed., *In Peace and War* (Westport, Conn.: Greenwood Press, 1977), ch. 9. The classical interpretation of Mahan's influence on Franklin Roosevelt's strategy in World War II is Russell Weigley, *The American Way of War* (New York: Macmillan, 1967). The most useful list of Mahan's works may be found in Paolo Coletta, ed., *American Naval History: A Bibliography* (Annapolis, Md.: Naval Institute Press, 1978). Coletta provides Library of Congress numbers for each entry.

ROBERT WILLIAM LOVE, JR.

Manchuria
See Open Door Policy; World War II

Manhattan Project
See Atomic Bomb; Groves, Leslie

March on Washington
See Randolph, Asa Philip; War Effort on the Home Front

Marine Corps
See Holcomb, Thomas

Maritime Commission

In 1935, President Roosevelt, still concerned with stimulating economic recovery, pressed Congress to authorize direct federal subsidies to private shipbuilding companies in order to provide jobs for seamen, shipbuilders, and suppliers of the maritime industry and, at the same time, to modernize and maintain an adequate U.S. merchant marine. After fifteen months of debate over whether the government should subsidize private industry, Congress passed the Merchant Marine Act in June 1936. The act established a five-member Maritime Commission empowered (1) to

THE RUNT!

THERE DOESN'T SEEM TO BE ANY "M's" IN THAT ALPHABET!

Gale, Los Angeles Times. *(Copyright 1933, Los Angeles Times. Reprinted by permission.)*

grant construction subsidies to American shipyards in order to offset the difference between lower foreign and higher U.S. labor and materials costs, and (2) to grant operating subsidies to U.S. shipping companies so as to maintain American service along essential trade routes, provided a company had a plan for replacing old ships with modern ones.

The commission, first under the chairmanship of Joseph P. Kennedy (1936–February 1938) and then Adm. Emory S. "Jerry" Land (1938–46), an old friend of FDR's, assumed a leading role in rebuilding the nation's merchant marine. Its initial goal of delivering fifty new ships per year, a bold move in 1936, seems insignificant compared to its enormous wartime accomplishments. With the outbreak of World War II, the commission assumed greater importance: its mission was to see that U.S. shipyards "build merchant ships faster than they were being sunk."

Between 1939 and 1945, 5,777 merchant and military vessels were delivered under commission contracts. These included about 2,700 Liberty Ships, the large-capacity emergency cargo ships that became famous as the workhorses of the war. The "ugly" ducklings," as FDR called them, escorted Lend-Lease ships across the Atlantic and later transported men and matériel to every theater of the war. They also helped transform shipbuilding from a heavy industry based on highly skilled labor to one based on discrete tasks and assembly-line techniques. The wartime emergency demanded both increased and standardized production. During the peak production years of 1944 and 1945, over 640,000 people were employed in shipyards across the nation. Blacks and women, especially, were recruited to fill these new jobs. Women constituted 10 to 20 percent of the work force in most yards, a major, albeit temporary, advancement in the labor force. The Andrews sisters celebrated

"Rosie the Riveter" in song, and Norman Rockwell immortalized her in a cover painting for the *Saturday Evening Post.*

"Rosie," however, was more likely to be a welder than a riveter. Increased production required not only a massive labor force, but standardized production as well. Thus, the commission instigated the process of breaking down highly skilled jobs into their component tasks, which new workers could learn with a few weeks training rather than a three-to-four-year apprenticeship. The commission also made the crucial decision to replace riveting with welding wherever possible in ship construction. These techniques made possible record production, which, in the case of the Liberty Ships, was further enhanced by uniform design and specifications. By November 1942, Liberty Ship production was standardized to the point that the Richmond, California, shipyard built the *Robert E. Peary* in only four days, fifteen hours.

The standard reference for the U.S. Maritime Commission during the New Deal is Frederic C. Lane et al., *Ships for Victory: A History of Shipbuilding under the U.S. Maritime Commission in World War II* (Baltimore: Johns Hopkins University Press, 1951), from which the quote is taken. Additional information on the Liberty Ships is contained in John Gorley Bunker, *Liberty Ships: The Ugly Ducklings of World War II* (Annapolis: Naval Institute Press, 1972).

REBECCA CONARD

See also Kennedy, Joseph Patrick; War Effort on the Home Front; War Mobilization

Marriage and Family

As husband and wife, Eleanor and Franklin seemed to exemplify the ideal of the twentieth-century, sharing, companionate marriage. Mrs. Roosevelt's public activities were new phenomena on the national scene and were strongly condemned, even ridiculed, in some quarters, but she supposedly was substituting for the physically limited president. Few Americans who admired the public partnership and presumed a firm foundation of private affection guessed the circumstances that had actually led husband and wife down separate, if complementary, paths. Americans of the depression decade would not have tolerated a president who had threatened the breakup of his family with an extramarital affair nor a First Lady whose emotional comfort and political education came primarily from an accomplished group of women with whom she often shared residence. Finally, there were the children—all five of whom were adults by the time their parents occupied the White House, whose record of marriages and divorces staggered the national imagination even as it tested their parents' patience and understanding.

Yet for all the complexities of their interpersonal relationships, the Roosevelts presented the public with combined images of strength, courage, and meaningful activity. The president became the ulti-

Mr. and Mrs. Franklin D. Roosevelt in Coronado, Calif., 2 October 1934. (Harold A. Taylor.)

Family. *Mother and Daughter: The Letters of Eleanor and Anna Roosevelt,* ed. Bernard Asbell (New York: Coward, 1982) reveals Mrs. Roosevelt's views on matters both personal and in the public interest. *FDR: A Centenary Remembrance* (New York: Viking Press, 1982) contains reminiscences of family member Joseph Alsop. Sons James and Elliott Roosevelt each wrote a number of books and articles about their parents and their own life as children of the president.

See also Campobello; Death of FDR; Hyde Park; Longworth, Alice Roosevelt; Roosevelt, Anna Eleanor; Roosevelt, Anna Eleanor (daughter); Roosevelt, Elliott; Roosevelt, Franklin, Jr.; Roosevelt, James (father); Roosevelt, James (son); Roosevelt, James Roosevelt; Roosevelt, John Aspinwall; Roosevelt, Sara Delano; Roosevelt, Theodore; Rutherfurd, Lucy Page Mercer

mate father figure to a disoriented nation. And the White House during the FDR administrations, at least until the war years, was an open and comfortable place where political leaders, trusted aides, close friends, and Mrs. Roosevelt's perennial "waifs" shared terrible food, stimulating conversation, and a relaxed sense of visiting the American people's home at the invitation of a gracious and unpretentious First Family.

Several books about or by members of the Roosevelt family provide glimpses of their life as the nation's First

Marshall, George Catlett

(31 December 1880–16 October 1959)

Chief of staff of the U.S. Army including army air forces) under Roosevelt from 1 September 1939 until Roosevelt's death and then under Truman until 20 November 1945. Born in Uniontown, Pennsylvania, George C. Marshall graduated from Virginia Military Academy in 1901 and was commissioned a second lieutenant in the infantry in 1902. In a career covering the first half of the twentieth century, Marshall

The president with thirteen of his grandchildren on inauguration day, 20 January 1945. The president holds David Boynton Roosevelt (left) and Franklin D. Roosevelt III. Others are, front row (left to right): Christopher Roosevelt, Ann Sturgis Roosevelt, John Roosevelt Boettiger, Elliott Roosevelt, Jr., and Sara Delano Roosevelt (extreme right, seated). Second row: Curtis [Boettiger] Roosevelt, Haven Clark Roosevelt, and Kate Roosevelt (partially behind Sara D. Roosevelt). Third row: Anna Eleanor Boettiger, William Donner Roosevelt, and Ruth Chandler Roosevelt. (U.S. Navy Photo)

George Catlett Marshall, 1949. Artist: Thomas Edgar Stephens. (National Portrait Gallery, Smithsonian Institution. Gift of Ailsa Mellon Bruce.)

served almost forty-five years as an army officer, ending as a five-star general; headed a mission to China from December 1945 to January 1947; served as secretary of state, 1947–49; was head of the American Red Cross, 1949–50; and acted as secretary of defense, 1950–51. He received the Nobel Peace Prize in 1953.

Marshall's first tour of duty was in the Philippines. Returning in 1903 to the United States, he did company duty in the Oklahoma Territory and Texas. From 1906 to 1908 he attended army schools at Fort Leavenworth, Kansas, and was an instructor there from 1908 to 1910. He served again in the Philippines, 1913–16. Among the first American soldiers to go to France in 1917, he served a year as training officer and chief of operations of the First Division and during the final campaigns of the war was operations officer, First Army. For the next five years he was General John J. Pershing's chief aide in Europe and in the War Department. His career between the wars was marked by the three years' duty in China and five years as assistant commandant in charge of instruction, Infantry School, Fort Benning, Georgia. He served afterward with field units, charged with Civilian Conservation Corps duties, and with the Illinois National Guard. Called in 1938 to Washington as chief of the War Plans Division, he soon afterward became deputy chief of staff. In the spring of 1939, President Roosevelt nominated him for the post of chief of staff of the army. After serving two months as acting chief of staff, he became head of the army the day Hitler invaded Poland.

Relations between Marshall and FDR were formal and distant in the first years of his duty because Marshall felt that Roosevelt, formerly assistant secretary of navy favored the navy over the army. But they became more cordial after the United States entered the war. Roosevelt was impressed by Marshall's close working relationships with members of Congress and his commitment to civilian control in military decisions.

Marshall accompanied Roosevelt to all the important wartime conferences and represented him in several other conferences abroad. As a strong supporter of Roosevelt's Europe first strategy and the cross-channel invasion concept, Marshall was a forceful advocate in Allied councils. In the fall of 1943 at Quebec, Roosevelt indicated to Churchill that he wanted Marshall to lead the Allied forces in the invasion of Europe. He held to this course until the meeting at Cairo in 1943, when he asked Marshall what future command he preferred. Marshall said that his wishes should not be considered. Roosevelt then said that he could not sleep at night with Marshall out of the country and named Eisenhower as supreme commander.

Roosevelt gave Marshall increasing freedom of action as the war in Europe neared its close. Upon the president's death, Mrs. Roosevelt asked Marshall to arrange the details of the funeral.

Marshall's early reserve toward Roosevelt changed to admiration, for in times of adversity, the president gave full support to the chief of staff. Marshall noted particularly that at the most difficult times during the fighting in the Ardennes, Roosevelt asked no questions but left the handling of the critical situation to Marshall. Their smooth-working collaboration was an important element in the ultimate victory of the Allies.

Marshall's career through the end of the war in Europe is most thoroughly covered in the authorized biography, Forrest C. Pogue's three volumes, *Marshall, Education of a General; Ordeal and Hope;* and *Organizer of Victory* (New York: Viking Press, 1964, 1966, 1973). Volume 4 is in the hands of the publisher and will appear in 1985. The volumes are based on extensive interviews with Marshall and on his papers. The first of six volumes containing his selected papers issued by the Marshall Foundation has been published (Baltimore: Johns Hopkins Press, 1982).

FORREST C. POGUE

See also Eisenhower, Dwight David; Joint Chiefs of Staff

Memorials

By the time of his death on 12 April 1945, FDR had been president for twelve years. For many Americans, he was a beloved symbol of sensitive leadership. Even for those not so taken with the Roosevelt charm, he was a symbol of stability, an American institution. Indeed, he was a world institution, and the encomia honoring him issued from all parts of the globe.

France's Charles de Gaulle called FDR's death "a terrible loss . . . for all of humankind." Joseph Stalin offered a lengthy eulogy after a night of seclusion, and Chiang Kai-shek, Nationalist Chinese leader, also required a period of solitude. The Canadians and the English were particularly saddened. In 1946, the Historic Sites and Monuments Board of Canada erected a plaque in FDR's honor on Campobello Island and, as late as 1962, named the new bridge linking the island to Maine the Roosevelt International Bridge. Winston Churchill said he had "lost a dear and cherished friendship . . . forged in the fire of war," and the royal court observed a week-long period of mourning. Afterwards, England's Pilgrims Association commissioned sculptor Sir William Reid Dick to create a statue for an FDR memorial in Grosvenor Square. Over Churchill's objections, Dick depicted FDR as a standing figure, albeit with a cane and cape. Eleanor Roosevelt delighted in this vibrant portrayal when she attended the unveiling in 1948.

Plaques and statues of FDR soon began to grace many a park and landmark in the United States, also. Countless schools, highways, and bridges bore his name after 1945. A number of entrepreneurs sought to capitalize on the Roosevelt mystique by offering such commercial memorabilia as FDR photographs, trays, plates, and record albums. "The Voice of FDR," a 1952 Decca album, offered the buyer a chance to hear the great radio star again, even though the narrator's commentary nearly obscured the famous voice.

Special editions of journals and magazines included a memorial issue of the *Harvard Alumni Bulletin* 40, no. 14 (28 April 1945), published two weeks after FDR's death. Books such as Donald Day's *Franklin D. Roosevelt's Own Story: Told in His Own Words from His Private and Public Papers* (Boston: Little, Brown & Co., 1951) were unabashed tributes to Roosevelt. Frank Kingdon's *As FDR Said: A Treasury of His Speeches, Conversations, and Writings* (New York: Duell, Sloan & Pearce, 1950) and Maxwell Meyersohn and Adele Archer's *Wit and Wisdom of Franklin D. Roosevelt* (Boston: Beacon Press, 1950) helped create as well as preserve Roosevelt's image and secure his place in America's memory.

After his death, several official acts of the U.S. government authorized Roosevelt's portrait on various staples of American life: his likeness distinguishes the fifty-dollar savings bond; Roosevelt stamps are standard, not one-time issues; and his profile is engraved on the dime. FDR has in this way attained the distinction of his predecessors, George Washington and Abraham Lincoln, of being recognizable to Americans of all generations.

For a critical discussion of the many publications following FDR's death, see Edgar Eugene Robinson, *The Roosevelt Leadership, 1933–1945* (Philadelphia: J. B. Lippincott, 1955), especially pt. 2. William S. White's *Majesty and Mischief: A Mixed Tribute to F.D.R.* (New York: McGraw-Hill, 1961) is a *New York Times* correspondent's recollections and research on the aftermath of 12 April 1945. Eleanor Roosevelt in *On My Own* (New York: Harper & Bros. 1958) discusses her attempts and those of others to keep the FDR spirit alive.

See also Campobello; Hyde Park; Portraits; Roosevelt Dime; Roosevelt Stamps

---

Mercer, Lucy

See Death of FDR; Rutherfurd, Lucy Page Mercer

Minimum Wage

See Supreme Court of the United States; Wages and Hours Legislation

---

Modern Presidency

See Biographers and Public Reputation; Commander in Chief; Congress, United States; Early, Stephen Tyree; Office of the Presidency

---

Moley, Raymond

(27 September 1886–18 February 1975)

Franklin D. Roosevelt's principal economic adviser in the formulation of the New Deal program. Born in Berea, Ohio, educated at Baldwin-Wallace College (B.A., 1906), he was in his youth an admirer of William Jennings Bryan's and Henry George's critiques

Raymond Moley at the wheel. (Courtesy FDR Library.)

of the special interests that dominated our society, as well as of Cleveland mayor Tom Johnson's administrative progressivism. During his mature years, Moley perceived himself as being in their mold, a product of the Middle West and its small-town populist-progressive tradition.

Moley began as a secondary teacher and superintendent of schools in the village of Olmsted Falls, near Cleveland; his long-range goal was the practice of law and involvement in politics. A three-year bout with tuberculosis (1909–11) led to a shift from legal studies to political science. On his return from New Mexico and Colorado where he took "the cure," he earned an M. A. (1913) at Oberlin College while teaching at Cleveland's West High School. Eager for a position at the college level, Moley enrolled for the Ph.D. (1918) at Columbia University and secured an appointment in the Hanna Department of Political Science at Western Reserve University. His imagination and reform instincts were fired by Charles A. Beard, who guided his doctoral dissertation on the reorganization of state government under the Progressive influence. The dissertation was published under the auspices of the Bureau of Municipal Research.

The choice of a dissertation subject in the area of public administration led to Moley's employment (1919–23) as director of the Cleveland Foundation. The nation's first community trust, the foundation served as a force for business-sponsored civic reform and also as a conduit for local philanthropy into changing community needs. It followed business practices: collection and analysis of data, alliance with the social sciences, and presentation of expert findings to the community for implementation. One of the foundation's projects, the Cleveland Crime Survey, which reflected a major concern in the 1920s, afforded Moley national attention, and served as a model for other communities and states.

It led to collaboration with Dean Roscoe Pound and Prof. Felix Frankfurter of the Harvard Law School, to appointment as an associate professor at Barnard College and Columbia University in 1923; and to publication of two major works, *Politics and Criminal Prosecution* (1928) and *Our Criminal Courts* (1930). Service on the Illinois, Missouri, and New York state crime commissions (his New York appointment was made during the Smith governorship in 1927) brought Moley into contact with Louis M. Howe, then a member of the National Crime Commission, and led to authorship of a speech in 1928, for FDR's initial gubernatorial campaign, on the administration of justice. During Roosevelt's governorship, Moley, now professor of public law at Columbia, won further notice as research director for Judge Samuel Seabury's investigation of New York City's magistrate's courts.

When it became apparent that Roosevelt would be the Democratic party's presidential nominee in 1932, Moley offered his services at a luncheon on 8 January of that year in the governor's mansion at Albany. Judge Seabury's third investigation led Roosevelt early in 1932 to decide on removal of New York County's Sheriff Thomas M. ("Tin Box") Farley. Moley drafted the removal statement, which insisted on a public official's accountability for major sources of income during his term of office. With the pressures of the campaign approaching and the candidate's need to address the economic issues raised by the Great Depression, Samuel I. Rosenman, the governor's counsel, suggested to Roosevelt, in late March 1932, the creation of an informal group of academic advisers. His demonstrated ability both to harness men and ideas and to compose prose free of academic jargon led to Moley's being chosen to head the brains trust. Rexford Guy Tugwell was recruited for his knowledge of agriculture and Adolf A. Berle, Jr., for his expertise in finance and corporate aggregation. Moley, Tugwell, and Berle, all of the Columbia University faculty, educated Roosevelt on the issues of depression causation and requisite governmental responses during the 1932 campaign, shaping in the process the New Deal program.

The initial Moley-Roosevelt collaboration, a radio address delivered on 7 April 1932, the forgotten man speech, focused on rural poverty and the collapse of commodity prices as the root cause of the depression. With farmers unable to sell at prices above cost and thereby unable to consume the product of industry, Roosevelt proclaimed, the nation's factories, financial institutions, and labor force had ultimately been sucked under as well. Roosevelt had adopted underconsumption theory and in the process rejected Herbert Hoover's trickle-down approach to the nation's economic needs.

Moley's lengthy economic memorandum of 19 May 1932 introduced the "New Deal" phrase into our political lexicon. He proposed a major political realignment that would reorient a conservative Democratic party, then dominated by the Du Ponts of Delaware and conservative legislators, toward progressivism and the nation's lower classes. The memorandum outlined the essential components of Roosevelt's campaign as well as of his early presidential programs: the institution of a massive federal public works–relief program and its funding by an emergency budget, relegating budget balance to normal federal functions; heavier taxation of income, inheritances, and corporate "surpluses" (accumulated in the twenties for speculation and tax avoidance); regulation of utilities holding companies, securities issuance, and exchanges; banking reform, including separation of commercial and investment banking; recognition of the Soviet Union; and achievement of internal recovery through the restoration of wages and commodities prices in a climate of altered price relationships. Roosevelt had come to most of these positions himself in his years as governor or before, and he found Moley's views compatible and his speech-drafting skills useful.

The forgotten man speech represented only the beginning of an important political collaboration. At St. Paul, Minnesota, in April, Roosevelt described a "concert of interests," or the economic interdependence of our society's components. Roosevelt's acceptance of the "New Deal" phrase put Moley's stamp on the era. At Topeka, Kansas, on 14 September 1932, relying on memoranda submitted by Tugwell, M. L. Wilson, Henry Wallace, and Henry I. Harriman, Roosevelt proposed the elimination of "the shadow of peasantry." And at the Commonwealth Club in San Francisco on 23 September, relying on a Berle memorandum, Moley and Roosevelt offered the creation of a new economic constitutional order, foreshadowing the federal government's enlarged role in our economy.

During the 1932–33 interregnum, the New Deal program fashioned by Roosevelt and the brains trust came under attack from two sources. Conservative internationalists of both parties—including Herbert Hoover's secretary of state, Henry L. Stimson, and the Democratic diplomat, Norman Davis, who had served Republican presidents since Wilson—pressed the president-elect for a shift to international priorities. These included a United States-led debts reparations settlement, an issue that would have strained Roosevelt's relationship with a nationalistic Congress and jeopardized his domestic program, along with stronger leadership in the Geneva disarmament talks and in tariff reduction and currency stabilization. Moley pressed for intranationalism with its emphasis on domestic priorities. Internal adjustment of wage and commodities price levels required for a time insulation of our economy from a world market beset by currency and trade warfare. Moley served as Roosevelt's principal adviser at two conferences with Hoover and Treasury Secretary Ogdon L. Mills, intended to commit the incoming administration to debts reduction, a balanced budget, and adherence to the gold standard. Swayed for a time by Stimson and Davis, Roosevelt finally resolved to stay the course outlined by his adviser during the 1932 campaign. During the winter months, Moley served also as Roosevelt's major aide in the recruitment of a cabinet, and they completed their drafting of the first inaugural address, a process begun during the campaign.

Roosevelt's designation of Moley as assistant secretary of state derived from several purposes: Louis Howe's objection to the presence of another adviser in the White House; proximity of the Old State Department building to the White House; and the freedom of the office from statutory duties. Likely, too, Moley could serve as a check on Cordell Hull and Herbert Feis, the department's economic adviser, who favored lowered tariffs and generally the international route to recovery. Taciturn, tough, intolerant of second-raters, Moley proved a valuable asset to the new administration in the bank crisis, in the forging of relations with congressional leaders who respected his ability, and in helping to shape major legislation of the hundred days.

The State Department appointment and a growing association with conservative opponents of the New Deal program, among them Bernard M. Baruch, proved the brains truster's undoing. Moley held his colleagues at State in open contempt as "cookie pushers" and questioned Cordell Hull's faith in tariff reduction as a viable depression cure. No longer the internationalist he had been in the 1920s and more attuned to views of Hiram Johnson than Hull, Moley warned publicly that the World Economic and Monetary Conference scheduled for London in the early summer of 1933 would prove barren. When the conference threatened to come apart on the issue of currency stabilization, which both Moley and Roosevelt opposed for fear that it would abort a nascent recovery, the president's principal economic adviser was dispatched to London. Following Roosevelt's instructions, Moley attempted to keep the conference going by negotiation of a vague agreement for future monetary stabilization, whereupon Roosevelt telegraphed his famous "bombshell message." For all practical purposes, it appeared that the president had repudiated his closest adviser, and with Cordell Hull's insistence upon his return on Moley's dismissal, Roosevelt complied by shifting him to the Justice Department.

Moley departed public service in September 1933 to assume the editorship of *Today* magazine, initially a New Deal organ. As an occasional speech writer, his relationship with Roosevelt deteriorated and finally ended after their collaboration on the president's 1936 acceptance speech. Gradually, like many old-time Progressives, Moley drifted to the business community in his associations and opposed the Court-packing plans and later Roosevelt's inclination toward intervention in Europe. Though he continued to teach a course at Columbia until 1953, his principal occupation became that of editor of *Newsweek*, when it merged with *Today*.

Publication of *After Seven Years* in 1939 marked an open break with the New Deal, which Moley believed had moved from reform and regulation toward an antibusiness atomistic philosophy molded by Thomas G. ("Tommy the Cork") Corcoran. In his later years, Moley befriended Herbert Hoover and insisted that many critical New Deal programs originated in the Hoover administration. An avowed conservative, he became allied with the Taft-Bricker-Goldwater wing of the Republican party and promoted Richard Nixon's political career. A major participant in the origin of the New Deal had, in fact, become one of the most bitter and consistent critics of the Rooseveltian legacy.

Moley authored three memoirs. *After Seven Years* (New York and London: Harper & Bros., 1939), though critical of Roosevelt's antibusiness stance and unconsciously reflective of Moley's own growing conservativism, remains an invaluable source on the origins of the New Deal. Raymond Moley, with the assistance of Elliot A. Rosen, *The First New Deal* (New York: Harcourt, Brace & World, 1966) is a detailed examination, based largely on Moley's papers, of the Hoover-Roosevelt interregnum; international economic relations, including the World Monetary and Economic Conference held at London in 1933; and the hundred days legislation. The composition of Roosevelt's first inaugural and the selection of his original cabinet are also examined in detail. Formative intellectual influences, his early life and education, and early professional career are recalled in Raymond Moley, *Realities and Illusions, 1886–1931: The Autobiography of Raymond Moley* ed. Frank Freidel (New York and London: Garland Publishing, 1980). Moley's papers are located in the Hoover Institution, Stanford, California.

ELLIOT A. ROSEN

See also Brains Trust

Monetary Policy

Franklin D. Roosevelt established presidential leadership over regulation of the size of the money supply (currency plus deposits in banks)—regulation that is known as monetary policy. By so doing, he reduced the power of the Federal Reserve System over monetary policy and gave that policy a more activist purpose than Federal Reserve leadership had provided. Whereas the Federal Reserve's main objective had been to protect the international gold standard, Roosevelt manipulated the money supply primarily to promote economic expansion within the United States. Roosevelt's monetary policy may have played a crucial role in the economic recovery that ensued in 1933 and remained rapid throughout most of the period between 1933 and 1945.

In 1933, Roosevelt committed his administration to a program of monetary expansion. As early as January, he informed the press that "we may be forced to an inflation of our currency." By April, he became convinced, relying on advice from Raymond Moley, economist George F. Warren of Cornell University, and Secretary of the Treasury Henry Morgenthau, Jr., that an expansive money supply would promote economic recovery. A liberal monetary policy, he believed, would bring about the inflation of prices and thereby stimulate demand for goods and services.

Roosevelt had an unusual opportunity to establish a broad consensus behind an expansive monetary policy. During the early 1930s, almost all economists, in varying degrees, believed in the ability of the money supply to shape the business cycle. Further, the seriousness of the depression created a curious political alliance favoring an inflated money supply. Some bankers, including investment banker J. Pierpont Morgan and Frank A. Vanderlip, president of the National City Bank of New York, formed one element in the alliance. The other key element was comprised of rural Democrats who were steeped in populist traditions and was well represented in Congress by senators like Elmer Thomas of Oklahoma.

Bankers, other businessmen, and leaders of farm groups joined forces in early 1933 by forming the Committee of the Nation to Rebuild Prices and Purchasing Power, headed by James H. Rand, Jr., of Remington Rand. Neopopulists, however, wanted more than monetary expansion; they demanded banking reforms as well. Even this demand did not disrupt the consensus. In the crisis of the Great Depression, bankers were willing to submit to significant reforms as an alternative far preferable to revolution, and some believed that reforms were, in fact, necessary to ensure that an expansive monetary policy would succeed. On the one hand, Roosevelt could satisfy inflationists by promoting a massive expansion of the money supply and by attacking the concentration of financial power in Wall Street. On the other hand, Roosevelt could gratify bankers by protecting them from radical assaults, by ensuring banking stability, and by enabling the banking system to meet internal demands for currency, thus permitting economic recovery to go forward.

The New Deal began to promote monetary expansion indirectly, with banking reform designed to augment public confidence in the banking system. In 1933, the bank holiday, the Emergency Banking Act, and the Banking Act of 1933 (creating the Federal Deposit Insurance Corporation) made the nation's depositors once more willing to put their funds in the custody of banks. With increased deposits, banks were able to expand their loan activities and, in effect, enlarge the nation's supply of money.

Also in 1933, Roosevelt pressured the Federal Reserve into adopting a permissive stance toward a more expansive monetary policy. Roosevelt did not want the Federal Reserve to exercise monetary leadership, for he did not yet trust the Federal Reserve, which had retained its legal autonomy. Disciplined by banking reform, the Federal Reserve might implement Roosevelt's policies in 1933 but later might undertake an independent course of action. Roosevelt wanted the Federal Reserve to remain neutral, stand aside, and allow the administration and Congress to set monetary policy.

In the winter of 1933, recovery progressed only sluggishly and inflationist forces in Congress became more vocal. In response, Roosevelt took an initiative that, in the context of a reformed banking system and a passive Federal Reserve, produced swift monetary expansion. In November, he announced a new gold policy, declaring that he sought "continuous control" over the nation's currency; he was moving, he said, "toward a managed currency," under the control of the presidency. His policy was to exercise an option that Congress had given him, in legislation drafted by Elmer Thomas and supported by Roosevelt, to reduce the gold content of the dollar by as much as 50 percent. Each day through January, over his morning eggs, he authorized purchases of gold that kept the U.S. price of gold, in terms of dollars, higher than the price abroad.

The new prices, pegged at artificially high levels, provided a bonanza for foreigners holding gold and for world gold production. Consequently, both gold production and the importation of gold into the United States soared. People or corporations who acquired gold (by, for example, exporting goods to Europe or digging it up in South Africa) took it to the Federal Reserve Bank in New York and received the premium price offered in the United States. They received a check for that gold. (The check represented brand new Federal Reserve notes and when a holder deposited the check in a bank, those notes enlarged the total deposits held by the banking system.) The Federal Reserve Bank, in turn, would turn the gold over to the Treasury, which would place it in Fort Knox and pay the Federal Reserve for it with money called gold certificates.

Subsequently, the Gold Reserve Act of 1934 made the devaluation of the dollar official by fixing a buying and selling price for gold of $35 an ounce rather than the $21 an ounce adhered to formerly. The act first called in all domestically held gold at $21 an ounce to prevent its holders from reaping enormous windfalls; thereafter, the federal government would pay $35 an ounce for all gold offered to it. (Selling gold would be more limited, however, in that the federal government would sell gold only for foreign payments and would prevent the domestic circulation of gold.)

Between early 1934 and the end of 1940, the stock of gold in Fort Knox more than tripled. Correspondingly, deposits of Federal Reserve notes paid out for gold imports underwent a large increase, enabling banks to increase their reserve holdings and thus expand their loan activities while still maintaining reserves in excess of legal requirements.

The sharp devaluation of the dollar enlarged the nation's gold stock, which in turn expanded deposits of Federal Reserve notes and thus initiated the powerful money-creating mechanism of multiple-deposit expansion. Roosevelt's domination of the Federal Reserve was central to his strategy. If he had allowed the Federal Reserve System to act independently, and if it had operated upon the assumptions that had governed its policy during the period between 1929 and 1933, it would have taken action to offset the large influx of gold and thus restrict the money supply.

The strong inflow of gold produced dramatic monetary expansion; from April 1933 through March 1937 it forced an expansion of the stock of money at the extremely rapid rate of almost 11 percent per year. This monetary expansion apparently played a major role in the nation's economic recovery between 1933 and 1937. Wealthy people and institutions, especially banks, found that they had more money than they needed and, at the same time, became convinced that prices were going to go up. Hence, they began to spend dollars, which seemed likely to depreciate in value. That spending stimulated demands for goods and services; idled manufacturers resumed production and hired workers; and those workers tended to spend their new earnings.

Between 1933 and 1937, the rate of increase in national product (the total value of goods and services produced) was an astounding 12 percent per year. The nation has never had another four-year period with such a rapid growth of real product and income, and the fifty-month period of recovery was the longest period of peacetime expansion until the 1960s. Perhaps monetary policy was most responsible.

In mid-1937, the Roosevelt administration concluded that the expansion had become too rapid and that inflation threatened. In response, Roosevelt's secretary of the treasury allowed the Federal Reserve Board to offset the inward flow of gold. The sharp, restrictive shift in monetary policy that the Reserve subsequently undertook contributed to the severe recession of 1937–38. Roosevelt emerged from the economic crisis with an even greater appreciation of the power of monetary policy and a greater determination to maintain presidential control over monetary policy. Quickly, and successfully, he directed the Federal Reserve to encourage the inward flow of gold.

Whatever success Roosevelt's expansive monetary policy enjoyed at home was not matched abroad. In fact, his monetary policy impeded international recovery. His reliance on the inward flow of gold made trade under the gold standard virtually impossible, for better or worse.

In 1933, at the outset of Roosevelt's administration, the international economic system was in chaos. Most important, the gold standard had ceased to function. Britain had abandoned it in 1931, and by 1932, twenty-four countries had suspended the gold standard and seventeen others had rendered it inoperative. Consequently, in 1933, the world had no orderly system for adjusting the values of international currencies; unstable exchange rates meant an even more acute restriction of international trade. Debt defaults, higher tariffs, and abandonment of gold fed international distrust which, in turn, stifled the flow of international capital, especially from the United States, and accelerated the dissolution of international economic order.

Roosevelt, nonetheless, took no significant action to restore monetary stability abroad. He was primarily responsible for scuttling the London Economic Conference in 1933, which tried to develop new rules and procedures to revive the gold standard and international trade. Moreover, he modified the gold standard in 1933 and 1934 knowing full well that this would handicap a return to the gold standard and would make economic recovery elsewhere in the world more difficult.

The Roosevelt administration certainly did not bear sole blame for the breakdown of the world monetary and trading system. The administrations of Warren G. Harding and Calvin Coolidge created the inherently unstable monetary system that collapsed in 1931. Even if the United States had pursued more internationalist monetary policies, it is by no means clear that the rest of the world would have responded cooperatively. Even before the international economic crisis of 1931–33, each nation had bound itself to limiting concepts of national self-interest. And then, by 1933, the extreme international economic debacle was beyond the control of any single trading nation, including even the United States. Roosevelt believed, perhaps correctly, that the health of the world's trading nations required a prosperous American economy and that to reestablish American prosperity it was necessary to weaken, temporarily, American ties with the international economy.

Between 1934 and the spring of 1941 (with the exception of the 1937–38 recession), Roosevelt's monetary policy caused foreign gold to flow continuously into American banks. Under normal circumstances, either a rapid depreciation of the dollar or a marked increase in American prices would have resulted, closing the gap between the United States and world prices for gold. However, at the same time that the United States offered a high dollar price for gold, wealthy Europeans demanded to exchange their European assets for dollars. Germans, including Jews, who feared Hitler's rise to power and other Europeans who believed their assets threatened by the outbreak of war sought to convert their European assets to dollars held in the secure haven of the United States. They traded their European capital for gold and then transformed their gold into dollars deposited in American banks.

When the European war broke out in 1939, the flow of European gold to the United States became especially intense. At first, the Roosevelt administration, welcoming the further stimulus to monetary expansion, did nothing to offset the flow. Moreover, the Johnson Act of 1934 forbade loans to nations that had defaulted on their World War I debts and thus required the Allied nations to pay cash (dollars purchased with gold) for war goods. Between May 1940 and March 1941, the Allies, primarily Great Britain, purchased over $2 billion worth of war matériel.

By 1941, however, the flow of gold to American shores threatened the very existence of the Anglo-American trading world. During the winter of 1940–41, Britain seemed likely to be drained of dollars and gold. Financially depleted, it could not offer effective resistance to Germany. Consequently, the Roosevelt administration began, for the first time, to assert international priorities in determining monetary policy. During March of 1941, the Roosevelt administration adopted its Lend-Lease program, under which the United States paid for much of the war supplies used by the Allies. (During the course of the war, the United States spent some $50 billion under the program, without any intention of ever receiving payment in cash.) In April of 1941, the flow of gold into the United States stopped.

After America entered the war, Roosevelt continued to emphasize the nation's global economic responsibilities. He led Allied planning for the postwar monetary order. The culmination was the United Nations conference held at Bretton Woods, New Hampshire, in 1944. Its explicit goal was to find monetary mechanisms that would surmount the narrow economic and political nationalism that had become endemic during the 1930s. Roosevelt welcomed the delegates by declaring that "commerce is the life blood of a free society," and that "we must see to it that the arteries which carry that blood stream are not clogged again, as they have been in the past, by artificial barriers created through senseless economic rivalries."

To the gold standard system of the 1920s, the Bretton Woods conference added a major reform: the creation of a powerful supranational agency, the International Monetary Fund (IMF). The fund was to be a central currency pool on which member national banks had limited borrowing rights to meet temporary deficits in their international accounts. Thus, the IMF's central objective was to spare any nation the necessity of running persistent, large deficits in its balance-of-payments account, thereby staving off restrictions on the international movements of currency, preventing currency devaluations, and protecting international trade.

The assumption of international responsibilities and the related acceptance of a cessation of major gold flows into the nation's banks meant that the Roosevelt administration had to seek new means of sustaining monetary expansion at home. In particular, the administration had to use informal pressure to push the Federal Reserve Board into a more activist monetary policy. During World War II, Treasury sought support for the deficit financing it undertook on behalf of the war effort. The Federal Reserve, mindful of presidential power over appointments to the board and of congressional ability to restructure the system, cooperated fully.

The Federal Reserve's support of U.S. securities was direct. In addition to enlarging the money supply and easing credit to finance bond purchases, the Federal Reserve itself bought government securities; it protected the prices of government securities by guaranteeing to buy whatever amounts were necessary to keep their prices from falling. Federal Reserve protection automatically transformed the Treasury's issues of new securities into an equivalent amount of new money; in effect, the Federal Reserve let the Treasury control the quantity of money in circulation.

By the end of his administration, Roosevelt had established the central mechanisms of postwar monetary management: internationally, a reformed gold standard, and domestically, a central bank—the Federal Reserve System—that was legally independent but in practice worked within the framework of policies set by the president and the Department of the Treasury. Thus, in addition to playing a major role in reviving the monetary system of the 1920s, Roosevelt had significantly enhanced presidential management of the money supply. The Roosevelt administration did not define exactly what monetary policies the federal government should follow in the future. This was understandable since Treasury officials, bankers, and economists rarely reached any agreement among themselves as to the specific content of monetary policy. And the economists, increasingly influenced by Keynesian analysis in the late 1930s, began to deemphasize the power of money and to ignore it in developing their policy prescriptions. But Roosevelt estab-

lished and clarified presidential responsibility for making certain that, at the very least, monetary policy avoided drastic turns that could produce depression conditions. As late as 1984, under Roosevelt's system of presidential management of monetary policy, the nation had escaped an economic disaster on the scale of that which had occurred between 1929 and 1933.

The most thorough and analytical study of the content and effects of monetary policy during the Roosevelt era is found in Milton Friedman and Anna J. Schwartz, *A Monetary History of the United States, 1867–1960* (Princeton: Princeton University Press, 1963). During the 1970s and 1980s, their argument that monetary policy shaped the course of depression and recovery won a growing number of supporters across the political spectrum. The one significant dissent is that of Peter Temin, who, in *Did Monetary Forces Cause the Great Depression?* (New York: W. W. Norton & Co., 1976), attempted to revive the Keynesian argument that monetary policy was ineffective during the depths of the Great Depression. We lack a monograph carefully detailing what Roosevelt and his administration believed they were doing in setting monetary policy, but parts of that story can be found in John Morton Blum, *From the Morgenthau Diaries, Years of Crisis, 1929–38* (Boston: Houghton Mifflin Co., 1959), Frank Freidel, *Franklin D. Roosevelt: Launching the New Deal* (Boston: Little, Brown & Co., 1973), and Herbert Stein, *The Fiscal Revolution in America* (Chicago: University of Chicago Press, 1969).

W. ELLIOT BROWNLEE

See also Banking; Fiscal Policy; Foreign Economic Policy; Great Depression; New Deal; Recession of 1937–38; Supreme Court of the United States; Taxation

Morgan, Arthur Ernest ("A. E.")
(20 June 1878–15 November 1975)

Engineer, educator, first chairman of the board of the Tennessee Valley Authority. Although A. E. Morgan was not formally educated beyond high school, his diaries indicate a disciplined mind influenced by Christian perfectionism and later secular utopianism. Entering the relatively new field of wetlands drainage, Morgan achieved national recognition as an engineer in 1913 when Dayton, Ohio, selected him to build the Miami Conservancy, then the most advanced flood prevention sytem in the country. His reformist roles included national committeeman of the League to Enforce Peace, founder of Moraine Park School in Dayton, first president of the Progressive Education Association, and charter member of the American Eugenics Society.

In 1921, Morgan accepted the presidency of failing Antioch College in Yellow Springs, Ohio, with the aim of making it an ideal community based on his moral principles. Despite internal bickering over his paternalism and continuing economic problems, Antioch built a reputation as a leader in educational reform. In April 1933, Roosevelt offered him the chairmanship of the Tennessee Valley Authority (TVA), which was signed into law on 18 May. Morgan understood that the president desired a broad experiment in social and economic planning. They shared a common vision of TVA as far more than a government agency for the production of electricity and fertilizer. Roosevelt encouraged Morgan to use the TVA as a laboratory for testing economic and community development, and Morgan added his own ideas on education and moral reform. As chairman of the board with nine-year term, Morgan recommended Harcourt A. Morgan ("H. A.," no relation) for the six-year-term and David E. Lilienthal for three years.

As general manager and chief engineer, Morgan acted on his own in hiring staff and planning prior to the arrival of the other two directors. Morgan began implementing his expansive definition of the authority, and many of his ideas found expression in the model town of Norris, Tennessee. His fellow directors preferred a more narrow view, and Morgan's numerous speeches and writings brought him early criticism, both internal and external to TVA. He was especially vulnerable when he suggested a "moral code" for TVA employees, when he appeared, in an offhand comment, to recommend a local monetary system for the valley, and when he consistently refused to make political appointments. Lilienthal felt that Morgan was a moral dogmatist and visionary who threatened the public power mission of the TVA. Within months of the organization of the board, he and H. A. Morgan moved to limit A. E.'s authority.

A bitter split followed, and after his 1936 failure in opposing Lilienthal's reappointment A. E. became increasingly despondent. In early 1938, he publicly accused Lilienthal of conspiracy and corruption. On 11 March 1938, Roosevelt called an unprecedented White House hearing to allow Morgan to substantiate his charges. Morgan adamantly refused to participate, and Roosevelt dismissed him on 22 March 1938. In a subsequent congressional investigation, Morgan produced no material evidence of malfeasance by Lilienthal or other TVA officials. His exit ended the concept of TVA as an agency for social and economic experimentation and development.

Morgan thereafter returned to Yellow Springs where he remained until his death.

Morgan was a prolific writer, the most important of his books being *Edward Bellamy* (New York: Columbia University Press, 1944) and *Nowhere Was Somewhere: How History Makes Utopias and How Utopias Make History* (Chapel Hill: University of North Carolina Press, 1946). He never produced a traditional autobiography, but he did summarize his philosophy in *Search for Purpose* (Yellow Springs, Ohio: Antioch Press, 1955). No comprehensive biography of Morgan exists, but the board conflict is admirably covered in Thomas K. McCraw, *Morgan vs. Lilienthal: The Feud within the T.V.A.* (Chicago: Loyola University Press, 1970). Morgan's papers are located at Antioch College.

ROY TALBERT, JR.

See also Lilienthal, David E.; Tennessee Valley Authority

Morgenthau, Henry T., Jr.
(11 May 1891–6 February 1967)

Henry Morgenthau, Jr., was a close friend and neighbor of FDR. That friendship led to his appointment as chairman of the New York State Agricultural Advisory Commission and commissioner of conservation during Roosevelt's two terms as governor (1928–33). As president, FDR appointed Morgenthau chairman of the Federal Farm Board and governor of its successor, the Farm Credit Administration (March-November 1933), acting secretary of treasury (November 1933-January 1934), and secretary of treasury (January 1934-July 1945). Three months after Roosevelt's death, Morgenthau resigned as secretary of the treasury and retired from public life.

Morgenthau was born into a wealthy New York City family, which was dominated by a confident, assertive father of German-Jewish ancestry. Both his father and his mother, Josephine Sykes Morgenthau, were heavily involved in social welfare concerns and Democratic party politics. As the son, he bore a particularly heavy burden of parental, especially paternal, expectations. Yet the path to his adult career was marked by hesitancy and indirection. He began college preparation at Phillips Exeter in 1904, but he did not do well and left after two years. In 1909 he was admitted to Cornell, but after three semesters decided to try his hand at other ventures.

In 1911, at the age of twenty, Morgenthau went to Texas to convalesce from typhoid fever. Upon returning home the next year, he announced to his father that he had decided to become a farmer, a gesture that clearly expressed the strength of his desire to begin an independent life. After a brief return to Cornell as an agriculture major, he purchased several hundred acres close to home in Dutchess County, New York. Overseeing the smallest details of his extensive enterprise with indefatigable energy, he developed a reputation as a progressive, successful farmer. In 1922 he began publishing the *American Agriculturalist,* which soon became a leading farmers' journal in New York State.

Morgenthau met Franklin D. Roosevelt in 1915. Sharing a common interest in building rural strength in the Democratic party to counter New York City control, the two men developed an enduring friendship. In 1928 when Roosevelt was elected governor of New York, he appointed Morgenthau chairman of the New York State Agricultural Advisory Commission, and at the beginning of his second term, he named him state conservation commissioner. After that appointment, Morgenthau's wife, Elinor (whom he had married in 1916), sent Roosevelt a remarkably insightful letter. "Henry always goes about his work with a real feeling of consecration," she wrote, "but the fact that he is working under you and for you, fills him with . . . enthusiasm. . . . The part which pleases me the most is that while you are moving on in your work . . . it gives Henry a chance to grow, so that your friendship can continue to be cemented by

Henry T. Morgenthau, Jr., 1938. Artist: Joseph Margualies. (National Portrait Gallery, Smithsonian Institution.)

a community of interest as well as by the deep affection with which he holds you."

When Roosevelt was elected to the presidency, Morgenthau hoped to be appointed secretary of agriculture. His disappointment at being passed over did not prevent him, however, from enthusiastically accepting his assignment as head of the Federal Farm Board. He served successfully in this capacity until 13 November 1933 when the president asked him to become acting secretary of the treasury to replace the ailing William Woodin. When it became clear in January that Woodin would not be able to return to his duties, Morgenthau was made secretary. He served in the position longer than any but Andrew Mellon.

Morgenthau's service in Washington was marked by controversy over his capacities for high public office as well as over particular policy questions in which he figured prominently, especially the gold-buying policy of early 1934, the drive to balance the budget during the recession of 1937, and his plan for dealing with Germany at the end of World War II. Many observers considered Morgenthau a man with little grasp of the complicated problems of managing government finances. However, the secretary was by no means the obsequious bumbler that such accounts seem to suggest. Transcripts of Treasury staff meetings make it clear that when surrounded by trusted friends and subordinates the secretary frequently presented his views with sound, determined arguments, parried effectively when challenged, and launched vigorous counterattacks against those opposing his views. His unimpressive manner on other occasions seems to have been in large measure the result of deep-seated lack of confidence in his own abilities.

Roosevelt's confidence in him was based upon a clearer reading than others had of Morgenthau's skills, plus a full awareness of the latter's loyalty, essential good judgment, and sensitivity to human suffering and humane values. Moreover, Roosevelt was appreciative of Morgenthau's strong commitment to efficiency in government and his scrupulous honesty. Sharing absolute trust in each other's friendship and loyalty, the two met often and discussed critical questions with candor.

Morgenthau was still with the Farm Credit Administration when, influenced partly by Cornell agricultural economists George F. Warren and Frank A. Pearson, he joined others in encouraging Roosevelt to devalue the dollar by raising the dollar price of gold. Faced with falling prices and an outflow of gold, the president gradually raised the price from $20.67 an ounce to $35.00 an ounce between 25 October 1933 and 31 January 1934. The action was highly controversial and failed to accomplish its aims, but it did free the president from monetary restraints inhibiting an expansionist economic policy.

It was Morgenthau's firm conviction that balanced federal budgets were the hallmark of efficient, honest government. Early in 1937 with recovery under way, he concluded that the time had come to deliver on the president's oft-repeated promise to balance the budget. When in the fall a sharp recession struck, the secretary continued to urge a balanced budget, now not as a fruit but as an instrument of recovery. When Roosevelt announced a renewed spending program in April 1938, Morgenthau threatened to resign; this surely marked the low point of his public career. FDR's rejection of his friend's efforts to impose his own symbol of integrity and coherence upon the administration in the form of a balanced budget left enduring scars. Years later Morgenthau told his biographer, John Morton Blum, that "a balanced budget had never been tried and might have worked."

As the war began to command the president's full attention, Morgenthau involved the Treasury in several key issues. He opposed the indiscriminate incarceration of Japanese-Americans in early 1942. In 1943–44 he played a major role in publicizing Hitler's extermination program against Jews in Europe and helped establish the War Refugee Board as a government agency capable of effective action in the matter.

In the wake of a flood of shocking reports from Nazi Germany, he directed preparation of the "Morgenthau plan" for dealing with Germany after the war. Completed on 4 September 1944, Morgenthau's plan called for the complete demilitarization of Germany, to be accomplished through dismantling armaments and heavy industrial plants; granting key territories, such as East Prussia, the Saar, and Silesia, to neighboring states; and internationalizing the Ruhr basin. The remainder of Germany was to be divided into two agrarian states. Morgenthau envisioned a wide range of programs that would control the content of education, publication, and broadcasting until the wartime populace had passed from the scene. However, the central aims of his plan were greatly attenuated or abandoned as other policymakers concluded that a strong postwar Germany was necessary for stability in Europe.

For three months after Roosevelt's death, Morgenthau worked somewhat uneasily with Truman, who was cool toward the Morgenthau plan. Finally, amidst rumors that the president was considering asking him to step down, Morgenthau on 5 July 1945 tendered his resignation. In his letter he mentioned an understanding he and Roosevelt had had that "when he was through we would go back to Dutchess County together." Though without his friend and mentor, Morgenthau returned to his farm in 1945 and led a quiet, uneventful life as a gentleman farmer until his death at Poughkeepsie in 1967.

The principal studies of Morgenthau are John Morton Blum, *From the Morgenthau Diaries,* 3 vols. (Boston: Houghton Mifflin Co., 1959–67), and *Roosevelt and Morgenthau: A Revision and Condensation of From the Morgenthau Diaries* (Boston: Houghton Mifflin Co., 1970). These draw primarily from the more than eight hundred bound volumes of minutes, memos, and other materials from Morgenthau's office. Blum's work is indispensable to an understanding of Morgenthau and to the New Deal generally. The gold-buying policies of 1933–34 are explored thoughtfully in Elmus Wicker, "Roosevelt's 1933 Monetary Experiment," *Journal of American History* 57 (1970):864–79. The secretary's role in the recession crisis of 1937–38 is detailed in Dean L. May, *From New Deal to New Economics: The American*

Liberal Response to the Recession of 1937 (New York: Garland Publishing, 1981). The Morgenthau plan is carefully examined in J. K. Sowden, *The German Question 1945–1973* (New York: St. Martin's Press, 1975). Morgenthau's involvement in Jewish relief is discussed and evaluated in Noam Monty Penkower, "Jewish Organizations and the Creation of the U.S. War Refugee Board," *Annals of the American Academy of Political and Social Science* 450 (1980):122–39.

DEAN L. MAY

See also Hitler, Adolf, and Germany; Holocaust; Monetary Policy; Quebec Conferences; Taxation

Mortgage Financing

The principal aims of FDR's New Deal mortgage financing programs were to revitalize the building industry, rectify a nationwide housing shortage, and make the dream of single-family home ownership accessible to middle-class, white Americans. In 1934, the country registered 93,000 housing starts, or one-tenth the 937,000 housing starts recorded in 1925. Prior to government participation in the mortgage market, private lenders typically required a 35 percent down payment, high interest rates, and rapid repayment of nonamortized mortgages. The latter meant that the entire principal came due after seven

to ten years of interest payments. After the crash of 1929, few Americans could meet those stringent mortgage requirements, and as a result, families doubled up and the building industry tumbled down. This situation is what Roosevelt looked at in 1937 when he still saw "one-third of the nation ill-housed."

The housing crisis was serious enough that the Hoover administration established the Federal Home Loan Banks through which to channel public mortgage money to private lenders. The Roosevelt administration, however, aggressively pursued the undergirding of the mortgage market. The Home Owners Loan Corporation (HOLC), established during the crucial hundred days of 1933, was eventually to have insured or purchased 20 percent of the nation's nonfarm dwellings. During its first three years, HOLC spent more than $3 billion refinancing more than 1 million homes. Distressed home owners thus avoided losing their homes as well as their hold on the American dream. The Federal Savings and Loan Insurance Corporation, established as part of the 1934 National Housing Act, spent $275 million to insure the mortgages that federally chartered savings and loan associations made. Under the law's provisions, these associations reformed housing finance by inaugurating the long-term amortized loan that eliminated the frightening balloon payment due at the end of the loan period.

The National Housing Act also created the Fed-

Estimated Number of Nonfarm Home Mortgages, 1925–1945 ($000,000s)

YEAR	TOTAL	SAVINGS AND LOANS ASS'NS	LIFE INSURANCE COMPANIES	MUTUAL SAVINGS BANKS	COMM'L BANKS	HOLC
1925	4,763	1,620	400	863	760	—
1926	5,321	1,824	465	809	943	—
1927	5,733	1,895	500	834	1,144	—
1928	5,778	1,932	525	915	1,156	—
1929	5,088	1,791	525	612	1,040	—
1930	3,536	1,262	400	484	670	—
1931	2,175	892	169	350	364	—
1932	1,092	543	54	150	170	—
1933	865	414	10	99	110	132
1934	3,070	451	16	80	110	2,263
1935	2,011	564	77	80	264	583
1936	2,158	755	140	100	430	128
1937	2,499	897	232	120	500	27
1938	2,455	798	242	105	560	81
1939	2,873	986	274	112	610	151
1940	3,290	1,200	324	133	689	143
1941	3,810	1,379	371	171	798	63
1942	3,155	1,051	374	130	606	40
1943	3,183	1,184	272	120	515	54
1944	3,830	1,454	300	140	601	31
1945	4,701	1,913	209	184	840	4

Source: U.S. Bureau of the Census, *Historical Statistics of the United States, 1789–1945* (Washington, D.C.: U.S. Government Printing Office, 1952).

eral Housing Administration (FHA), the Roosevelt administration's most direct means of intervention into housing finance. The FHA allowed Americans of modest means access to a mortgage by offering their creditors insurance against default. From 1935 to 1939, the FHA insured 400,000 housing units, or 23.4 percent of the total number of units financed during that period. During the next five-year period, that percentage increased to 45.4, or 806,000 units. Since the FHA played such an important role in housing finance, it inevitably influenced housing and settlement policies. The suburban single-family home was the FHA's operative ideal, and FHA insurance for an older, urban home mortgage was elusive. Its lending policies encouraged flight from the city. Racial segregation was also an early FHA ideal since homogeneous neighborhoods seemed the most stable. Until the Supreme Court in 1948 declared restrictive covenants unconstitutional, the FHA actually encouraged neighborhoods to prohibit blacks. James A. Moffett, the first head of FHA and John A. Fahey, head of HOLC, were advocates of private housing and opposed much of the New Deal's post-1937 public housing efforts. The work of their agencies during the Roosevelt administration successfully expanded the housing market to include middle- and lower-middle-class whites and contributed to such postwar trends as suburbanization and the idealization of the nuclear family.

For a survey history of housing in America, including problems of finance, see Gwendolyn Wright, *Building the Dream: A Social History of Housing in America* (Cambridge, Mass.: MIT Press, 1983). In *Politics and the Housing Crisis Since 1930* (New York: Universe Books, 1973), Nathaniel S. Keith provides a discussion of mortgage policy from FDR through Nixon. A government report, National Commission on Urban Problems, *Building the American City* (Washington, D.C.: U.S. Government Printing Office, 1968), is a detailed study of U.S. housing policy since the New Deal.

SHELLEY BOOKSPAN

See also Housing and Resettlement

Moskowitz, Belle Lindner Israels

(5 October 1877–2 January 1933)

Political adviser to Al Smith. Born into an immigrant Jewish family in New York City, Belle Lindner (later Moskowitz) was educated at Horace Mann School and then Teacher's College. She plunged into the work of helping settle the masses of European immigrants arriving in New York City at the turn of the century and became first a prominent social worker and then a labor manager for a women's garment manufacturers' association. Along the way, she uncovered sexual abuses in the management of dance halls, helped pass reform legislation, and worked for better housing and neighborhood improvements.

In 1918, she was drawn to the reform gubernatorial candidate Alfred E. Smith. Almost immediately she became a close adviser and confidante to the gov-

ernor and impressed him with her shrewd political judgments. She masterminded the idea for a Reconstruction Commission to reorganize New York's state government and held so much sway with Smith that some political opponents complained that he was dominated by Moskowitz. She directed publicity for all of Smith's campaigns but was never herself conspicuous. As Smith's adviser, she pushed for the social causes dear to her and yearned to elect Smith to the presidency as "the Savior of Tolerance."

After Smith's defeat in the 1928 presidential election, he tried to place Moskowitz in the new Roosevelt administration of New York. Despite several pleas from Smith, Roosevelt did not offer Moskowitz a position, perhaps because Eleanor Roosevelt advised her husband to avoid this woman who might dominate his decisions and perhaps because of a natural reluctance to include in his inner circle a person with known strong loyalties to another politician. Moskowitz was disheartened by the rejection and spent her final years as a publicity consultant in New York City.

Although no biography of Belle Moskowitz exists, a fertile source of information on her career is Matthew and Hannah Josephson, *Al Smith: Hero of the Cities* (Boston: Houghton Mifflin Co., 1969).

Murphy, Charles Francis

(20 June 1858–25 April 1924)

Tammany Hall political boss. Charles Murphy, the son of Irish immigrants, was born and raised in Manhattan's East Side. After a brief formal education, he moved through a series of jobs and then opened the first of several saloons. He used his neighborhood connections and his organizational skills to work for the Tammany machine and was elected leader of his district in 1892. Six years later, he was appointed dock commissioner, his only salaried political office. In 1902 Murphy emerged as the leader of Tammany Hall and maintained that position until his death twenty-two years later. These years coincided with the Progressive Era, and Murphy worked to bring about a more respectable "New Tammany." He brought to power several young Progressives, including Alfred E. Smith and Robert F. Wagner, who later proved to be important national figures. He tolerated only "honest graft" and insisted that the police and the courts be kept free from machine politics. A quiet man who stayed out of the public eye, Murphy nevertheless helped to elect several mayors and was one of Tammany's more powerful leaders.

Murphy did not content himself with leadership of New York City only, but tried to extend his power to the state Democratic party and so ran afoul of the young Franklin Roosevelt. In 1911 State Senator Roosevelt led the opposition to Murphy's choice for a new U.S. senator from New York. This ten-week struggle embittered Murphy and Roosevelt and resulted in a compromise with both sides claiming victory. As a leader of the genteel reformers from up-

Franklin D. Roosevelt with Charles F. Murphy in New York on the Fourth of July, 1917. (Courtesy FDR Library.)

state, Roosevelt steadfastly opposed Murphy's brand of city machine politics. It came as a surprise, then, when Murphy consented to support the Roosevelt vice-presidential nomination in 1920, partly no doubt to remove him from the New York Democratic slate. In giving Roosevelt national exposure, Murphy unwittingly advanced the career of his longtime political opponent. Four years later, Murphy died, leaving behind him a more powerful and more respected Tammany organization than he found.

Nancy Joan Weiss, *Charles Francis Murphy, 1858–1924: Respectability and Responsibility in Tammany Politics* (Northampton, Mass.: Smith College, 1968) is a sympathetic biography. The first two volumes of Frank Freidel's *Franklin D. Roosevelt* (Boston: Little, Brown & Co., 1952, 1954) detail Murphy's relationship with Roosevelt.

See also Tammany Hall

Murphy, Francis William (Frank)

(13 April 1893–19 July 1949)

Governor general of the Philippines, 1933–36, governor of Michigan, 1937–38, attorney general, 1939–40, associate justice of the Supreme Court, 1940–49. Born in a Michigan farm town, Frank Murphy entered the University of Michigan in 1908 and completed his law degree in 1914. After serving abroad in the First World War as a U.S. Army officer in 1918, he studied law at Lincoln's Inn, London, and Trinity College, Dublin, in 1919. Returning to Michigan bent on a political career, Murphy ran for Congress in 1920, but was defeated. In 1923 he was elected to the Detroit Recorder's Court.

He gained national attention in 1926 for his handling of a celebrated criminal trial of a man named Sweet. Murphy sympathized with lawyer Clarence Darrow and his client, a black gynecologist accused of a murder that took place when a group of whites violently protested his move into a white neighborhood. Murphy successfully ran for mayor of Detroit in 1930 and quickly became a spokesman for those mayors who refused to end social services to their growing ranks of unemployed despite dwindling ur-

ban revenues. Roosevelt courted Murphy at the beginning of the 1932 campaign, and Murphy became one of Roosevelt's earliest prominent supporters.

Roosevelt rewarded Murphy with an appointment as governor general of the Philippines, then in the first stages of decolonization. Murphy convinced nationalists to include written guarantees of New Deal economic rights in their country's new constitution even though such rights had yet to be made law in the United States. At Roosevelt's request, Murphy returned and ran for governor of Michigan in 1936. He won and became a controversial governor. He refused to stop the sit-down strikes of auto workers in 1937. Although he successfully mediated that dispute, auto manufacturers believed that Murphy had forced them to give up too much. He ran for reelection in 1938 and lost.

Roosevelt immediately made Murphy attorney general. While in the cabinet, he proposed that William O. Douglas be nominated to the Supreme Court. In 1940, amidst political controversy over which government agencies should handle internal security investigations, Murphy himself was appointed to the Court. Believing he had been kicked upstairs, Murphy requested other cabinet appointments right up to Roosevelt's death, but was always refused.

On the Supreme Court, Murphy gained a reputation as an uncompromising liberal idealist. He often voted with the minority, and yet his opinions are still cited. Norman Thomas wrote of one of them (in the case of the internment of Japanese-Americans during the Second World War), "If America is to continue to grow as a democracy, I believe your dissenting opinion will live as one of that democracy's greatest documents." Murphy delivered his last opinion three weeks before his death.

Two volumes of Sidney Fine's definitive biography have been published, *Frank Murphy: The Detroit Years* (Ann Arbor: University of Michigan Press, 1975) and *Frank Murphy: The New Deal Years* (Chicago: University of Chicago Press, 1979). J. Woodward Howard's *Mr. Justice Murphy: A Political Biography* (Princeton: Princeton University Press, 1968) is the best study of Murphy on the Supreme Court. Its early chapters also cover Murphy's political career, the focus of Richard D. Lunt's shorter *The High Ministry of Government: The Political Career of Frank Murphy* (Detroit: Wayne State University Press, 1965).

CRAIG MURPHY

Francis William Murphy, 1941. Artist: Oskar Stoessel. (National Portrait Gallery, Smithsonian Institution.)

See also Civil Liberties in Wartime; House Committee to Investigate Un-American Activities; Labor; Supreme Court of the United States

---

Mussolini, Benito, and Italy

In an interview with Benito Mussolini in 1933, biographer Emil Ludwig asked the Italian premier why he enjoyed great popularity with Americans who disliked dictatorship. Mussolini retorted that Roosevelt himself was a "dictator." In a critique of Roosevelt's *Looking Forward,* he concluded that the New Deal,

Benito Mussolini (arms crossed, center) and members of the Italian Parliament. (National Archives.)

although "boldly interventionist," didn't get to the root of the problem. Mussolini later argued that if Roosevelt wanted the New Deal to be effective, he would have to muzzle the press.

Roosevelt no more understood Mussolini or Italian facism than Mussolini comprehended Roosevelt or American democracy. While Roosevelt disliked Hitler and Nazism from the first, his attitude and policy to Mussolini and Italy evolved more slowly and cautiously. Secretary of Labor Frances Perkins suggested that "a man like Mussolini was a puzzle to him."

In later recalling his impressions of Mussolini before the election of 1932, Roosevelt remembered that he had viewed fascism as a "phenomenon somewhat parallel to the Communist experiment in Russia," but noted that Mussolini still followed at that time a semblance of parliamentary government. "Having restored order and morals he would, of his own accord," Roosevelt had hoped, "work toward a restoration of democratic process." Yet like most Americans in the twenties, his image of the Italian leader was blurred. As Democrats were considering their attitude on the sensitive Italian war debt problem, Roosevelt prophetically argued that "we cannot, for instance, contend against the settlement on the mere ground that we do not like Mussolini the Dictator or that the proposed Morgan loan may be used by the Dictator to finance another war."

From his inauguration in 1933 to the Ethiopian war two years later, Roosevelt on several occasions expressed sympathy and regard for Mussolini. In private letters, he confessed that he was impressed by Mussolini's accomplishments in restoring Italy and preventing European trouble and specifically characterized Mussolini as "that admirable Italian gentleman." Nevertheless, Roosevelt did not appreciate the frequent comparisons between the New Deal and the Corporate State or the reference to himself as the American Mussolini. The beginning of the Italo-Ethiopian conflict in 1935 made foreign policy more significant and brought Roosevelt to a more serious and critical consideration of Mussolini.

For several years prior to 1935, Mussolini had been planning the conquest of Ethiopia. As war clouds gathered during the spring and summer, Roosevelt appealed directly to Mussolini to take the high road and agree to arbitration while Congress debated neutrality legislation designed to isolate the United States from foreign wars. Furious over the idea of an Italian attack on Ethiopia, Roosevelt sought discretion in applying neutrality laws in order to punish Italy and to demonstrate this American intention to Germany and to Japan. But fearing the power of isolationists in Congress and in public opinion and realizing that the discretionary feature would not benefit Ethiopia which couldn't buy much anyway, Roosevelt acquiesced in the mandatory embargo.

When the war finally broke out in October 1935 with the long expected Italian invasion, Interior Secretary Ickes recorded in his diary after a cabinet meeting that he had "not met anyone whose sympathy in this situation is not with Ethiopia." Harry Hopkins remarked that Roosevelt "scanned the news dispatches and everything favorable to Ethiopia brought a loud 'good.'" With Roosevelt's private approval, the League of Nations immediately and unanimously condemned Italy for its act of aggression against a League member. Roosevelt applied the mandatory embargo quickly because it would penalize Italy more than Ethiopia.

In November 1935, the League declared an arms and credit embargo on Italy, a ban on imports from Italy, and a partial ban on exports to Italy. The vital omission was oil which Italy badly needed and of which the United States produced half of the world's supply. American exporters could supply all Italian needs should the League extend oil sanctions to Italy. It was Britain and France, however, that sabotaged League efforts to halt Mussolini; their Hoare-Laval plan of December 1935 offered cynically to partition Ethiopia in the hope of mollifying Mussolini. Roosevelt viewed the Anglo-French proposal as "outrageous" and as only further disillusioning Americans about Europe and the League. "What a commentary on world ethics these past weeks have been!"

In his State of the Union address of 3 January 1936, the president castigated autocratic rulers in Europe and Asia who believed "in the law of the sword" or in their having been "chosen to fulfill a mission." With the 1935 neutrality legislation about to expire, Roosevelt again sought a discretionary option. The issue remained oil because American supplies were reaching Italy at three times the normal rate, the League was still procrastinating about the oil embargo to see what the United States would do, and Britain and France were blaming America for the inability of imposing the oil embargo they did not want. Even the modest administration bill to limit raw material exports to prewar levels was denounced by isolationists and by organized Italian-American groups, who correctly saw this as an attempt by Roosevelt to cooperate with the League against Mussolini and Italy. Faced by these domestic pressures, Roosevelt agreed to an extension of the 1935 law, fearing that with further debate Congress might enact even more mandatory measures.

The president, nevertheless, continued to press his so-called moral embargo to dissuade American exporters from trading with Italy in important raw materials. Public opinion supported Roosevelt's position on moral suasion, but it was increasingly ineffective and meaningless as the League procrastinated and Italian troops advanced southward to the capture of Addis Ababa in May 1936. The fear and weakness of European leaders was the primary factor in seeking to appease Mussolini, but American inability to act definitively on restraining oil exports to Italy allowed Britain and France to avoid an action they feared would antagonize Mussolini.

Roosevelt adamantly refused to recognize the Italian conquest of Ethiopia. He would not allow Ambassador Phillips to resign since the credentials of a new ambassador would have to recognize the Italian position in Ethiopia. "I can't do that at any cost," he said. With reference to the British decision to do so, Roosevelt commented caustically that "the police chief who dealt with gangsters would remain heroic only so long as the gangsters failed to attack."

Despite the proclamation of the Rome-Berlin Axis in October 1936, Mussolini's active support of Franco in the Spanish Civil War, and Italy's invasion of Albania in April 1939, Roosevelt repeatedly sought to make direct and personal contact with the Italian leader in hopes of preventing a total alliance with Hitler. After the Italian invasion of Albania, Roosevelt publicly appealed to both Hitler and Mussolini to give assurance of peaceful intentions to thirty-one neighbors. Mussolini offered no formal reply but dismissed it as a "Messiah-like message" from a man with "creeping paralysis."

Roosevelt pointedly informed the new Italian ambassador in 1939 that American aid as well as sympathy would go to the victims of aggression in a European war and that Mussolini could play a significant role in preventing that war and gaining concessions at the conference table. But if the Italian premier continued to cooperate with Hitler, he would simply become another of the German leader's victims. By diplomatic efforts, by offering trade conces-

sions, by personal pleas, and by thinly veiled warnings, Roosevelt had sought to dissuade Mussolini from the path he had followed since the Ethiopian war.

Mussolini's invasion of France in June 1940 constituted the final straw and Roosevelt publicly condemned the Italian ruler: "The hand that held the dagger has struck it into the back of its neighbor." Sumner Welles urged Roosevelt to omit this condemnation in order not to jeopardize relations with Italy, but Roosevelt in his anger reinserted it before delivering the speech. The effort to keep Italy from maintaining the Axis alliance had failed, and the usual admonitions not to antagonize the Italian-American voters no longer restrained Roosevelt from making clear his real feelings about Mussolini. Four days after Pearl Harbor, Mussolini and Hitler declared war on the United States in fulfillment of the Tripartite Pact with Japan.

After the decision to initiate an Italian front in 1943 and the consequent fall of Mussolini in July, Roosevelt and Churchill disagreed strongly over Italian peace terms and the post-Mussolini regime. Roosevelt insisted on a totally new Italian government—liberal and democratic without fascist or monarchist elements. "We will permit no vestige of Fascism to remain." Even in the middle of the war, the ideal of a democratic and liberal postwar world was very much in Roosevelt's mind. His hands had been restrained during the thirties by domestic political and economic considerations, and he had been unable to check or dissuade Mussolini from his disastrous course. But the United States would be in a better position now to cooperate with the new Italy in the coming postwar world.

Robert Dallek, *Franklin D. Roosevelt and American Foreign Policy, 1932–1945* (New York: Oxford University Press, 1979) is a thorough study of American foreign policy during the Roosevelt years. For the broader picture of the American response, both private and governmental, to Mussolini and Italy, see John P. Diggins, *Mussolini and Fascism: The View from America* (Princeton: Princeton University Press, 1972). A specific case study of Italian-American relations is Brice Harris, Jr., *The United States and the Italo-Ethiopian Crisis* (Stanford: Stanford University Press, 1964).

BRICE HARRIS, JR.

See also Axis Alliance; Fascism; Foreign Policy

N

National Association for the Advancement of Colored People

A leading organization advocating the rights of black Americans. During the Roosevelt years, the National Association for the Advancement of Colored People (NAACP) fought vigorously for several basic reforms, all designed to protect the rights of black Americans. The major issues the association worked on included eradication of the poll tax and white primaries, integration in education and in New Deal programs, and an antilynching bill. Roosevelt did not generally support the association's efforts. He felt that pressing for such measures would endanger congressional support for the most important New Deal programs. Eleanor Roosevelt and Harold Ickes (a one-time president of the Chicago chapter of the NAACP) were much more supportive of the organization's efforts.

The NAACP's battle for an antilynching bill was perhaps its most publicized work in the 1930s. The bill was a response to the large number of lynchings, mostly of blacks, and the inability or indifference of local and state authorities to prosecute those involved in them. In 1930, for example, there were twenty-one lynchings. In fifteen of the cases, no indictment was handed down. In the other six cases, there were a total of forty-nine indictments, but only four of the defendants were ultimately convicted. In November 1933, the association's legal council drafted an antilynching bill and presented it to the next session of the Senate. Senators Edward Costigan of Colorado and Robert Wagner of New York cosponsored the bill and in March 1934, the Senate Judiciary Committee recommended its passage with only minor amendments. The NAACP, pressing for passage of the legislation, presented a petition to Roosevelt in December 1934, signed by prominent public figures supporting it. Among the signers were nine governors or ex-governors; 27 mayors; 58 bishops and churchmen; 54 college presidents and professors; and 109 lawyers, editors, writers, and jurists. In the midst of the antilynching bill discussion, Claude Neal, a black Floridian, was lynched on 26 October. His murder was predicted by many people across the country; several newspapers printed stories of the anticipated lynching even before it occurred. The NAACP asked the Justice Department to intervene because of the inability or unwillingness of the local and state authorities to prosecute the case effectively, but the governor denied jurisdiction in the matter. The effort for a federal antilynching bill ultimately failed in Congress, perhaps in part because of the president's unwillingness to make the bill a piece of must legislation. After the president declined to push vigorously for the bill, the association placed more emphasis on publicizing the lynching problem; the intensity of the campaign increased even as the number of lynchings declined in the late 1930s.

The NAACP also supported legal challenges to the separate-but-equal institutions that had existed since the 1896 Supreme Court decision in *Plessy* v. *Ferguson*. In 1934 the organization supported Donald Murray, a graduate of Amherst, in his efforts to get into the University of Maryland Law School. Thurgood Marshall, arguing the case for the NAACP, demonstrated that the university's unwillingness to admit Murray constituted a violation of the separate-but-equal provisions of the law because there was no comparable law school for blacks. When the case was won, the university admitted Murray, a less expensive option than opening a law school for blacks. Similarly, the NAACP filed five suits between 1936 and 1938 to demand equal pay for black teachers. Again, the organization's efforts were successful. Perhaps the most important case the NAACP worked for in the 1930s was *Missouri ex rel. Gaines* v. *Canada* (1938). In this instance, the organization's case for Gaines won him the right to be admitted to the law school at the University of Missouri. One scholar commenting on this case has noted that the NAACP "went out of its way to stress that, although it had not asked the Court to overrule *Plessy* (believing the time not quite ready for that yet), a majority of justices agreed to reevaluate the basic meaning of 'separate but equal.' " These legal victories also strengthened the NAACP;

each triumph demonstrated the importance of the organization.

The NAACP supported A. Philip Randolph, the leader of the Brotherhood of Sleeping Car Porters and Maids, in his efforts for a march on Washington to protest government discrimination in defense industries. The march, scheduled for 1 July 1941, was designed to protest the occupational discrimination endemic in these industries. At the time, according to a 1941 report of the U.S. Employment Service, only thirteen blacks were among eight thousand new employees added to the payroll in aviation plants. In spite of this situation, Roosevelt sent for Randolph and Walter White, then executive secretary of the NAACP and urged them to stop the plans for the march. Finding the black leadership unyielding, Roosevelt issued Executive Order 8802, abolishing discrimination in the defense industries and establishing the Fair Employment Practices Committee. The march was subsequently canceled.

The NAACP marshaled a great deal of support for its efforts to secure the basic rights of black Americans. In 1941, a year of rapid growth for the organization, the membership topped 100,000. The association's work was generally not supported by FDR, who although perhaps recognizing the plight of the most forgotten of humans, felt that advocacy of black rights would endanger other pieces of legislation he thought were more important. Ultimately, despite the efforts of the NAACP, little substantive civil rights legislation was adopted during Roosevelt's tenure.

For more information, see Harvard Sitkoff, *A New Deal for Blacks: The Emergence of Civil Rights as a National Issue*, vol. 1, *The Depression Decade* (New York: Oxford University Press, 1978); Nancy J. Weiss, *Farewell to the Party of Lincoln: Black Politics in the Age of FDR* (Princeton: Princeton University Press, 1983); Robert L. Zangrando, "The Efforts of the National Association for the Advancement of Colored People to Secure Passage of a Federal Anti-lynching Law, 1920–1940," (Ph.D. diss., University of Pennsylvania, 1963); and Langston Hughes, *Fight for Freedom: The Story of the N.A.A.C.P.* (New York: W. W. Norton & Co., 1962). For a contemporary account, see Robert L. Jack, *History of the National Association for the Advancement of Colored People* (Boston: Meador Publishing Co., 1943). Any historical analysis of the NAACP must confront the issue of the president's lack of support for its programs. This is examined forcefully by Barton Bernstein, ed., "The Conservative Achievements of Liberal Reform," in *Toward New Past: Dissenting Essays in American History* (New York: Vintage Books, 1969), p. 279.

National Association of Manufacturers

An organization of representatives from individual businesses promoting manufacturing interests through public relations, legislative lobbying, and formation of business policy. Founded in 1895, the National Association of Manufacturers (NAM) concentrated on opposing and eliminating labor unions in any form. It was the principal supporter of the "open shop"

movement of the 1920s and spoke for business in opposing any protective or ameliorative labor legislation. The depression, however, brought a crisis to the NAM; membership declined from 5,350 to 1,500 businesses. Furthermore, loss of the prestige the public image of business had enjoyed in the 1920s put the organization in a defensive position when FDR was elected. Business was to blame for the depression, it was commonly thought. The NAM was almost alone in feeling that this perception was unfair and unjustified. As an NAM publication said, "At 1:08 P.M. on March 4, 1933, the New Deal began. Business overnight came under attack."

Despite this defensiveness, initial response to the New Deal was ambivalent. FDR's encouragement of industrial self-government under the proposed National Recovery Administration (NRA) evoked enthusiasm from the NAM, and it was deeply interested in and involved with the drafting of the National Industrial Recovery Act (NIRA). It had long advocated a loosening of antitrust regulations to encourage centralization, planning, and curbs on competition; the NIRA provided the NAM an opportunity to help secure these goals as well as to gain cartel privileges for joint production and price planning in large industries. New NAM president James Emery, in addition to embarking on an extensive public relations drive, sought to turn the leadership of the association over to representatives of large and wealthy industries, such as steel production, that had previously exercised little influence in the NAM.

The Senate passage of Hugo Black's wages and hours bill galvanized the NAM. Seeking to defeat government regulation of wages and hours as well as to secure control by business of competition within industries, the NAM began intensive lobbying against the Black bill throughout April 1933. Assistant Secretary of Commerce John Dickinson, who drafted the original NIRA bill with Senator Robert Wagner, shared NAM goals. Meeting constantly with congressmen and cabinet officials, NAM representatives promised dramatic reemployment levels if the Black bill were defeated and antitrust relaxation were substituted instead. A business committee led by Emery met constantly with FDR's committee which was drafting the final NIRA bill. The NAM primarily objected to the bill's Section 7(a), which guaranteed the rights of labor to bargain collectively and represented a challenge to the NAM-sponsored idea of the company union. Despite this opposition Section 7(a) remained.

Once the NRA came into being, NAM opposition to Roosevelt's policies and the New Deal organizations grew, despite Hugh Johnson's and the president's efforts at business conciliation. The NAM fought most of the New Deal in its publications, speeches, and press releases. Of thirty-eight major pieces of legislation from 1933–41, the NAM supported only seven that represented either direct subsidies to business (such as loan guarantees or allocations) or indirect aid, such as reductions in capital gains taxes. With the Liberty League, with which it shared many members, the NAM remained the strongest center of business-dominated opposition to organized labor in the 1930s and the strongest opponents of the New Deal's large-scale government intervention in the economy.

There is no history of the NAM, although some historians have noted its significance. Ellis Hawley, *The New Deal and the Problem of Monopoly* (Princeton: Princeton University Press, 1966) shows the nature of business opposition to FDR's policies. Robert Himmelberg, *The Origins of the National Recovery Administration* (New York: Fordham University Press, 1976) thoughtfully reviews the NAM's role in the evolution of the NRA with an extensive analysis of the drafting of the bill. Richard Tedlow, *Keeping the Corporate Image* (Greenwich, Conn.: JAI Press, 1979) details the public relations efforts of the NAM during the 1930s with its emphasis on harmony between management and labor. And Alfred S. Cleveland, "NAM: Spokesman for Industry?" *Harvard Business Review* 26, no. 3 (May 1948):353–71, presents a hostile view of NAM opposition to the New Deal.

See also Business

National Industrial Recovery Act

A major piece of national economic legislation passed during the hundred days in 1933 and in effect until held unconstitutional in May 1935. Under the National Industrial Recovery Act (NIRA), the president was authorized to establish an industrial code system and a temporary public works program that, working together, were supposed to restore economic prosperity. As implemented, the law failed to achieve most of its avowed objectives and has come to be regarded as one of the New Deal's major mistakes.

Although some historians have depicted the NIRA as an innovative response to an unprecedented crisis, the roots of the legislation can be traced back to the system of industrial self-government sponsored by the War Industries Board and other national agencies during World War I. After the war there was agitation for a similar peacetime system, and after 1929 such an approach was urged as a way to deal with depression conditions. With governmental backing, it was argued, organized industries could devise and implement regulatory codes that would end destructive competition, stimulate new spending, and put idle men and resources back to work.

In 1931 Gerard Swope, president of the General Electric Company, set forth a plan for establishing such a code system, and by early 1933 similar schemes were being advocated by a variety of groups, including the U.S. Chamber of Commerce, the National Civic Federation, key figures in Roosevelt's brains trust, and the leaders of trade associations and labor unions in particularly depressed industries. The idea was one with which Roosevelt himself was sympathetic, partly because of his war experience and involvement in the associational activities of the 1920s. Thus during the hundred days it became the central idea of his industrial recovery program.

Several competing groups were involved in the writing of the law, one centering in the Commerce Department, another attached to the office of Senator Robert Wagner, and a third congregating around Gen. Hugh Johnson, a former member of the War Industries Board and a close associate of its former chairman, Bernard Baruch. By 17 May a compromise draft had emerged, and with minor changes this became the measure that the president signed into law on 16 June. At its core were provisions suspending the antitrust laws for two years and authorizing the formulation of industrial codes governing trade, pricing, and labor practices, such codes to have the force of law when approved by the president. In addition, the act contained Section 7(a) guaranteeing labor's right to organize and bargain collectively, Title II authorizing an expenditure of $3.3 billion for public works, and provisions under which the president could impose codes, control imports, regulate interstate oil shipments, and license particular industries should these things become necessary. As enacted, it did not contain the governmental financial incentives for new investment and reemployment that had appeared in some early drafts.

To administer the law, Roosevelt created the National Recovery Administration under Hugh Johnson and the Public Works Administration headed by Harold Ickes, a division of authority that made coordination of the code and works programs difficult. In all, 541 codes were eventually approved. But in operation they tended to foster restrictive cartelization rather than reemployment and new growth. They were also bitterly criticized by labor leaders who saw them as thwarting genuine unionization, by small-business and consumer spokespersons concerned about the growth of "monopoly," and by political leftists who saw in them an incipient "corporate state." In the face of such criticism, the system was in an almost constant state of turmoil and reorganization.

In early 1935 Roosevelt recommended that the law be extended in a modified form. But efforts to do this came to an end on 27 May, when the Supreme Court, in the case of *Schechter* v. *United States,* held that the code system involved both an unconstitutional delegation of legislative power and an unconstitutional attempt to expand the federal power to regulate interstate commerce. The ill-fated attempt at recovery through corporative planning mechanisms had failed not only its economic and political tests but its legal ones as well, and these failures helped clear the way for other kinds of recovery programs.

The best work on developments leading to the law is Robert F. Himmelberg, *The Origins of the National Recovery Administration* (New York: Fordham University Press, 1976). On its implementation, see Ellis W. Hawley, *The New Deal and the Problem of Monopoly* (Princeton: Princeton University Press, 1966), Bernard Bellush, *The Failure of the NRA* (New York: Norton, 1975), Irving Bernstein, *The New Deal Collective Bargaining Policy* (Berkeley: University of California Press, 1950), and Leverett S. Lyon et al., *The National Recovery Administration* (Washington: Brookings Institution, 1935). A good account of developments leading to the *Schechter* decision can be found in Peter H. Irons, *The New Deal Lawyers* (Princeton: Princeton University Press, 1982).

ELLIS W. HAWLEY

See also Housing and Resettlement; Ickes, Harold LeClair; Johnson, Hugh Samuel; Labor; Lewis, John Llewellyn; New Deal; Wagner, Robert Ferdinand

National Labor Relations Board

The National Labor Relations Board (NLRB) was an independent, quasi-judicial government agency, which played a key role in advancing the fortunes of the trade union movement and reshaping the character of labor-management relations. An administratively weak NLRB had existed as part of the National Recovery Administration in 1934, but a permanent labor board came into being only with the passage of the Wagner Act in May 1935. Given rather tepid support by President Roosevelt but pushed through Congress by Sen. Robert Wagner, the National Labor Relations Act proved one of the New Deal's most dramatic, and even radical, legislative initiatives. Eschewing both repression and arbitration, the act sought to advance industrial peace by encouraging the formation of strong, independent unions capable of bargaining with employers. Hence a generation of unionists would soon declare that the Wagner Act was organized labor's "Magna Carta."

The statute established a National Labor Relations Board authorized to determine bargaining unit jurisdictions, hold elections, and certify as the legally binding representative of the workers those unions that received a majority vote. The law curbed much employer antiunion activity by declaring a whole series of coercive management practices to be illegal, and it gave the new unions a legal standing that helped shield them from direct employer assault. The three-member NLRB asserted the duty of an employer to bargain with a properly certified union, but, of course, it did not compel managers to meet union demands or even sign a contract.

The NLRB was bitterly attacked by employers, and until its constitutionality was affirmed by the Supreme Court in the 1937 *Jones & Laughlin Steel* case, its influence was limited. Thereafter, the board became much more active, sympathetic to union organizing efforts in general and supportive of the Congress of Industrial Organization's (CIO) brand of unionism in particular. The first three board members, J. Warren Madden, Donald Wakefield Smith, and Edwin S. Smith, were all prolabor liberals, and the NLRB secretary, Nathan Witt, was close to the Communist party. Because of its innovative and exciting work, the growing NLRB staff became a mecca for liberal New Dealers and radical lawyers.

By 1939 the board had come under sharp attack, both from traditionally antilabor conservatives in Congress and from the American Federation of Labor (AFL), which considered the board to be pro-CIO. Fearful that these forces might weaken the Wagner Act itself, Secretary of Labor Frances Perkins convinced President Roosevelt to appoint first William Leiserson and then Harry A. Millis to the board. These men, both with broad mediation experience, were friendlier toward the AFL's point of view and hostile to NLRB radicalism.

The NLRB's new majority forced Witt and many of his staff to resign in 1940. On the crucial issue of unit jurisdiction, they stressed the importance of stability and respect for the history of the collective bargaining relationship; hence, they tended to defend the claims of an older craft unit against those of a newer factorywide union. Where industrial unions were found to be appropriate, Leiserson and Millis reversed an earlier board policy ordering multiplant unions and instead mandated elections on a plant-by-plant basis. They also narrowed somewhat the employer duty to bargain and allowed strike-breaking replacement employees to vote in representation elections following a stoppage over chiefly economic issues.

During World War II President Roosevelt's appointments to the NLRB were increasingly conservative, but the board ceased to play as central a role in shaping U.S. labor relations as it had in the late 1930s. A powerful National War Labor Board, empowered to arbitrate disputes and dictate wages, temporarily usurped many NLRB functions, while the NLRB found itself swamped with a new duty: conducting strike votes under the 1943 War Labor Disputes Act. The NLRB's eclipse ended after the war with the renewal of intense debate over government labor policy. Despite chairman Paul Herzog's effort to accommodate the board's business critics, the 1947 Taft-Hartley Act killed the New Deal–era NLRB and replaced it with a new, five-member board whose mandate was of far less value to labor than that of its predecessor.

For more information, see James A. Gross, *The Making of the National Labor Relations Board: A Study in Economics, Politics and the Law, 1933–1937* (Albany: State University of New York Press, 1974) and *The Reshaping of the National Labor Relations Board: National Labor Policy in Transition, 1937–1947* (Albany: State University of New York Press, 1981). Also see Fred Witney, *Wartime Experiences of the National Labor Relations Board, 1941–1945* (Urbana: University of Illinois Press, 1949).

NELSON LICHTENSTEIN

See also Biddle, Francis Beverley; Labor; Wagner, Robert Ferdinand

National Recovery Administration

A federal agency created under the National Industrial Recovery Act of 16 June 1933 and abolished on 1 January 1936, following litigation in which the law's major provisions were held unconstitutional. The purpose of the National Recovery Administration (NRA) was to establish and administer a system of industrial codes, which through appropriate controls over pricing, production, trade practices, and labor relations in codified industries was supposed to check the contraction of the national economy and bring recovery from the Great Depression.

The development making the NRA possible was the national economic crisis of 1933, a crisis that by March of that year had left the nation with over 13 million unemployed, about half of its industrial plant idle, and its financial system paralyzed. But the form the agency took is best understood in the light of developments reaching back to the system of industrial self-government utilized by the federal war agencies during World War I. After the war there was agitation for a similar peacetime system, agitation that persisted through the 1920s and gained new strength with the coming of the depression. If organized industries were assisted in developing instruments of responsible self-government, it was argued, they could stabilize their markets and reemploy the jobless. And with this argument a number of the early New Dealers, themselves former war administrators or veterans of the agitation against "destructive competition," were in sympathy.

Pressed to experiment with national recovery planning, they turned to the kind of planning that had seemed to work in another crisis, readily enlisting the support of a president who had been involved in the earlier endeavor. The result was the legislation under which the NRA was established. As enacted, it suspended the antitrust laws for two years and authorized industrial organizations to formulate codes that could secure the fair competitive behavior and

(Courtesy FDR Library.)

enlightened labor practices thought necessary to restore economic prosperity. When approved by the president, such codes would have the force of law, and in cases where no approvable code was forthcoming the president might devise and impose one.

To head the agency, Roosevelt chose General Hugh S. Johnson, a former member of the War Industries Board. Under Johnson's leadership, the NRA set out to identify codification with national patriotism, all patriots being urged to boycott businesses operating without the NRA's official Blue Eagle emblem. At first industrial groups tended to hold back, hoping to benefit from revived markets without shouldering new social obligations. But as good patriots, most employers signed a president's reemployment agreement committing them to minimum labor standards; having signed this, most became anxious to secure similar rules against price cutting, overproduction, and unethical trade practices. Although code making often generated heated controversies, it moved ahead rapidly after July of 1933, and by the end of the year Johnson had most of the major industries under codes.

In all, some 541 industrial codes were eventually written and approved, each combining controls over business practices with a required section guaranteeing labor's right to organize and bargain collectively (Section 7a of the enabling act). Once in operation, the system did result in reduced competition and enhanced business and labor organization. Trade associations underwent new growth, not only in membership, but also in areas organized and resources committed to their activities; in the labor sector, there was growth both of independent unionism and of company unions established in efforts to retain managerial control. But such organizational developments failed to bring economic recovery. On the contrary, codification is generally thought to have contributed to a further downturn in late 1933, and by early 1934 the new codes were becoming the subject of mounting criticism. They were charged now with fostering "monopoly," preventing genuine unionization, creating a "corporate state," and establishing "government control" rather than self-government.

Such criticism became particularly pronounced in the spring and summer of 1934, manifesting itself in a series of price hearings, in congressional debates and press coverage, and in the reports of a National Recovery Review Board headed by Clarence Darrow. It also strengthened dissident groups within the administrative structure, particularly the Research and Planning Division, the Consumer Advisory Board, and the National Labor Board, all of which began challenging Johnson's industrial orientation and calling for changes in code content and enforcement. But what it produced in the way of policy changes and code revision tended to be minimal. Although there were moves toward exempting small businessmen and reducing the power entrusted to trade associations, the defenders of the original code structure were generally successful in shunting aside the attacks on anticompetitive regulations, company unions, and administrative syndicalism.

As criticism continued and internal quarrels intensified, Johnson became increasingly unstable, behaving in ways that eventually led Roosevelt to put through a major reorganization of the agency. In September 1934 Johnson was replaced by a National Industrial Recovery Board, headed initially by S. Clay Williams and later by Donald Richberg. In late 1934 and early 1935, further efforts were made to revise the codes in ways that would reduce their "monopolistic" aspects, prevent further abuses by code authorities, and strengthen their labor provisions. In addition, a new National Labor Relations Board (NLRB), created in June 1934, tried to formulate and enforce rules under which genuine unions would become labor's officially recognized bargaining agents. But again, the results tended toward stalemate and deadlock rather than effecting any major changes in the system and its orientation. In the places that counted, particularly the NLRB and the White House, the code administrators and their business constituencies retained enough power to block the revisionists, although not enough to make the system work for the purposes they had intended. For almost all concerned, the experience became an increasingly frustrating and disillusioning one.

In early 1935, as the date for the expiration of the National Industrial Recovery Act approached, Roosevelt recommended that it be extended in a somewhat modified form. But by this time the NRA system had few friends left, and in Congress there was much reluctance to carry out the president's recommendations. In the hearings, particularly those conducted by the Senate Finance Committee, the "sins" of the agency were again highlighted, and in mid-May the Senate adopted a resolution under which the agency would be stripped of most of its regulatory power and extended only until April 1936. The House of Representatives was less hostile, but the chances of translating this into legislation seemed slim. There was by late May a growing likelihood that a deadlock between competing extension measures might block any legislation at all.

As it turned out, however, Congress never got to decide the matter. On 27 May 1935, in the case of *Schechter* v. *United States*, the Supreme Court held that the code system involved both an unconstitutional delegation of legislative power and an unconstitutional attempt to expand the federal power to regulate interstate commerce. The decision meant that the code rules no longer had the force of law. It also meant that none of the extension measures under consideration could pass a constitutional test, and the result was the substitution of extension legislation that gave the agency a few more months of life but left it little to do beyond studying its past operations. During its last days, the NRA under the direction of James O'Neill functioned primarily as a study agency, correlating the industrial data it had gathered and producing histories and analyses of the code experience. It attempted also to develop voluntary codes, but its efforts to do this failed to produce anything upon which the interested industries and the antitrust authorities could agree. Although a number of conferences were held, all proprosals for government-approved business agreements were eventually withdrawn or rejected.

Historians have generally regarded the NRA's code system as one of the New Deal's greatest failures and most egregious mistakes. The underlying economic theory, they argue, was badly flawed, and in operation the system tended to hamper recovery, foster restrictive cartelization, and create obstacles to effective forms of public regulation. Some, however, have credited the program with giving an initial psychological lift to the nation's depressed spirits, helping to improve business ethics, putting an end to child labor, and paving the way for mass unionization. Others have attributed its failure less to the planning mechanisms than to the lack of coordination between them and the public spending programs. And still others have seen it as an American forerunner of the corporative planning toward which advanced capitalist economies have subsequently moved. Parts of it, moreover, were resurrected in the post-Schechter period. "Little NRAs" were established through special legislation in a number of natural resource, transportation, and service industries, and the labor provisions required of NRA codes were, in strengthened form, incorporated in the National Labor Relations Act of 1935.

The best work on the coming of the NRA is Robert F. Himmelberg, *The Origins of the National Recovery Administration* (New York: Fordham University Press, 1976). For discussions of the agency in operation, see Ellis W. Hawley, *The New Deal and the Problem of Monopoly* (Princeton: Princeton University Press, 1966); Bernard Bellush, *The Failure of the NRA* (New York: Norton, 1975); Leverett S. Lyon et al., *The National Recovery Administration* (Washington: Brookings Institution, 1935); and Michael M. Weinstein, *Recovery and Redistribution under the NIRA* (New York: North-Holland Publishing Co., 1980). For the view that it foreshadowed the direction in which modern capitalist planning would eventually move, see Andrew Shonfield, *Modern Capitalism* (New York: Oxford University Press, 1965).

ELLIS W. HAWLEY

See also Biddle, Francis Beverley; Consumerism; Harriman, William Averell; Henderson, Leon; Johnson, Hugh Samuel; Perkins, Frances

National Resources Planning Board

The closest the United States has come to having a national planning agency was during the administration of Franklin Roosevelt. In 1933, the Public Works Administration (PWA) was created to relieve unemployment through the construction of socially valuable public works. It quickly became apparent that few preplanned projects were available and that no method of evaluating proposals had been worked out. To help him get the much needed relief under way, Harold Ickes, the PWA administrator, created the National Planning Board (NPB) to establish evaluation criteria and advise him on project selection. The members of the board were Frederick A. Delano, Charles P. Merriam, and Wesley C. Mitchell (succeeded by George Yantes), and the staff was headed by Charles W. Eliot II.

The NPB performed this function, but the board members became increasingly aware of the lack of information necessary for the wise use of the nation's resources. Accordingly, the NPB recommended that a permanent, broadly based planning agency be established. President Roosevelt agreed and in 1934 established the National Resources Board (NRB) as an independent cabinet committee responsible directly to him. The NRB expanded its activities well beyond those of its predecessor. Because it was an independent agency, it was able to establish study committees representing many government agencies and private interests, thus tapping the talents and knowledge of the best experts in the country. The NRB produced important reports on the use of water and land resources, but its most important contribution was its final report, which was the first national inventory of the country's resources and their associated problems.

In 1935 the NRB lost its legislative authority when the Supreme Court invalidated the National Industrial Recovery Act. The president, however, desirous of continuing the agency, reconstituted it as the National Resources Committee (NRC) under the authority of the Emergency Relief Appropriations Act. In 1939, the NRC was specifically excluded from the act, and again Roosevelt saved the agency. Using the power given him under the Reorganization Act of 1939, he consolidated the NRC and the moribund Federal Employment Stabilization Board into the National Resources Planning Board (NRPB) and placed it in the Executive Office of the President.

The NRPB continued to expand its areas of interest. From a limited perspective of improving natural resources use, the NRPB moved to a primary concern for the human condition. Such interests took the agency into the area of social policy and the controversies surrounding it. By the late 1930s the NRPB was undertaking studies and issuing reports concerned exclusively with social and economic issues.

When the Second World War began, the NRPB found that an increasing amount of its work was committed to the war effort. The board made valuable contributions to more effective resource use, improved industrial location, and the relief of urban congestion. The role of the NRPB was limited largely, however, to furnishing data and expert advice. As the war agencies gained experience, they relied more on their own staffs and less on the NRPB.

Beginning in 1940, the NRPB began to examine the problems of reconversion and the postwar period. It expected serious dislocations and in a series of pamphlets urged the use of countercyclical spending to prevent a boom-and-bust economy. The acceptance of Keynesian economics earned for the NRPB the enmity of traditionalists.

In March 1943, the two most famous and provocative reports of the NRPB appeared: *Post-War Plan and Program* and *Security, Work, and Relief Policies*. The reports included discussions of natural resources, but of far more importance were the sections on health, education, welfare, and economic policy. The board was endorsing a smooth and, if necessary, regulated conversion, a more equitable distribution of income, government responsibility for full employment, and countercyclical economic policies. All eventually became government policy, but at the time they provoked bitter criticism.

Almost at the same time that the controversy over the postwar reports was raging, the NRPB was engaged in a losing fight for its life. The board had had appropriations difficulties since it lost its legislative authorization in 1939, and by 1943 other issues had surfaced. One was that the NRPB was only duplicating the functions of other agencies. Roosevelt pointed out that the coordinating function of the board actually prevented duplication, but to no avail. Congress seemed most eager to end planning by the executive branch. Planning, especially the overall control made possible by a central planning agency, tended to make the president more effective, and Congress was already unhappy with the secondary role it had played since 1933. The NRPB was only one of several agencies ended in 1943 in a broad conservative effort to cut back on the New Deal.

Although there has been no central planning agency since the NRPB, some of its functions have been taken over by the Council of Economic Advisers, the Office of Management and Budget, and private research organizations.

Those interested in a more detailed account should consult Marion Clawson, *New Deal Planning: The NRPB* (Baltimore: Johns Hopkins University Press, 1981) or Philip W. Warken, *A History of the National Resources Planning Board, 1933–1943* (New York: Garland Publishing, 1979). The records of the NRPB are held by the National Archives and constitute Record Group 187.

PHILIP W. WARKEN

See also Conservation; New Deal; Office of the Presidency; Planning; Rural Electrification Administration; Tennessee Valley Authority

National Union for Social Justice

See Coughlin, Charles Edward; New Deal

National Youth Administration

"I have moments of real terror," remarked Mrs. Eleanor Roosevelt in May 1934, "when I think we might be losing this generation." There was good reason for her fear, for the question of unemployed and unemployable young people was a crucial concern in depression America. Though the statistics on youth unemployment are incomplete, those that do exist point to the conclusion that nearly 30 percent of Americans between sixteen and twenty-four years of age who were in the labor market were totally unemployed. Youth were among the cruelest casualties of economic collapse. The country was in danger of producing a whole generation of misfits, unskilled and untrained, lacking in self-esteem, incapable of becoming the productive adults upon whom recovery would depend.

The Roosevelt administration moved swiftly to combat the problem. Within weeks of its taking office, the Civilian Conservation Corps (CCC) had been established, and thousands of young men were already working in the woods. The accomplishments of the CCC were genuinely impressive, and it soon became enormously popular. But it was not an adequate answer to the problems of young people in depression America. It catered to the most desperate cases only and was in any event an all-male enterprise. There was a need for a much more wide-ranging youth program, one based in the home community, one that would impart skills of permanent value, one that would employ young women as well as men. The National Youth Administration (NYA) was an attempt to meet this need.

Created on 26 June 1935 by executive order as part of the new Works Progress Administration (WPA), the NYA had its origins in a number of existing federal programs. One was a plan by the Federal Emergency Relief Administration (FERA) to enable needy college students to stay in school; a second was a FERA transient scheme; a third was administration efforts to stimulate vocational training. The NYA coordinated these existing schemes, but it also expanded them beyond recognition.

There were always two divisions in the NYA. One involved student work. College and high school students, mainly from relief families, were to be given grants in return for work to enable them to stay in school, grants, it was hoped, that would bridge the gap between the students' own resources and what was needed to keep studying. The intent was twofold—to develop the talents of young people as fully as possible and to keep them out of the swollen labor market.

The second function was the more difficult one of providing assistance for those young people who were no longer in school but were out of work. The NYA needed to give them both relief and job training of permanent value. Consequently, programs had to be developed that were of relevance both to the individual and his or her community.

To head the new agency, Roosevelt selected Aubrey Williams, the WPA's deputy director, a southerner, a former social worker, and an outspoken liberal, who was already closely identified with the New Deal's left wing. Williams had no desire to run a tightly centralized agency, believing that the the NYA would succeed only if local supervisors and directors were given the widest possible latitude in program development, assisted by an advisory council of local citizens. He perceived the job of the national office, therefore, as being little more than to set the broadest policy guidelines, leaving state and local officials to fill in the details.

The student work program was relatively easy to get going. By early 1937, more than 400,000 young people were receiving assistance, and the monthly number rarely dropped below 300,000 thereafter. By the time the program was terminated in 1943, more than 2 million young people had received assistance. The educational institutions ran the scheme themselves; it was the responsibility of the college president or school principal to see that the money was equitably distributed, that NYA regulations were complied with, and that the students performed some work around the campus in return. Student work was the most popular component of the NYA's program. It worked well from its inception and caused Williams and his officers very few worries indeed.

More difficult to develop was the program for out-of-school youth. Given the need to get as many youth working as possible, plus the importance of creating community goodwill, the first projects tended to involve high-labor, low-capital-outlay content. By the beginnning of 1936, youths all over the nation were developing parks and other recreation areas, cleaning up public buildings, and performing similar tasks. No doubt this approach was of benefit to communities, but it scarcely gave the enrollees the training they needed to find jobs at the end of the emergency.

In any event, the approach was abandoned by 1937 in favor of a policy that only projects involving a substantial degree of training were to be approved. The emphasis on acquiring skills, then, had been firmly established. Other developments had occurred, too, that helped give the NYA a more solid look. The NYA had begun to establish residence centers in order to accommodate youth from rural counties for whom community-based programs were not appropriate. It had developed its own job placement offices. And, in keeping with Williams's commitment to the cause of racial justice in America, it had developed a special Negro program, headed by the redoubtable black educator, Mary McLeod Bethune. It was one of the very few New Deal agencies to concern itself particularly with the problems of America's most disadvantaged group.

In 1939 Williams began to shift the emphasis of the agency toward training youth for defense industry work, and this trend was accelerated once World War II broke out. From mid-1940, its nondefense functions were progressively shed until by 1942 it was involved solely in the war effort. The NYA introduced its enrollees to machines, gave them basic shop training, and then poured them into the nation's industrial plants. It combed the country looking for young people to train; it transported them to areas of labor shortage, found them jobs, and acclimatized them before letting them go. It was particularly concerned to bring black and female enrollees into the industrial mainstream. The enthusiastic testimony of thousands of businessmen from all over the nation was compelling evidence of its importance to the general defense effort.

Yet the agency was abolished in 1943, despite President Roosevelt's attempts to save it, a victim of the drive to prune federal expenditures to the bone by eliminating all agencies not considered vital to the war effort. Its accomplishments had been numerous.

It had enabled millions of young Americans to complete an education that would otherwise have been denied them, it gave millions more vocational training of lasting value, it was a vital contributor to the nation's defense effort, it allowed minority groups to participate in some approximation to need, and it provided community amenities of permanent value. Of the many New Deal agencies, it is one of the best examples of what can be accomplished when enlightened, committed people, if only for a short time, receive a measure of public support.

There is no standard history of the NYA. Still the best detailed discussion of its early history and accomplishments is Ernest K. Lindley and Betty Lindley, *A New Deal for Youth: The Story of the National Youth Administration* (New York: Viking, 1938). Other useful contemporary discussion can be found in Paul B. Jacobson, "Youth at Work," *Bulletin of the National Association of Secondary School Principals* 25 no. 99 (May 1941), and in the NYA's *Final Report* (Washington: U.S. Government Printing Office, 1944). The most recent evaluation of its activities can be found in John A. Salmond's biography of Aubrey Williams, *A Southern Rebel, the Life and Times of Aubrey Willis Williams, 1890–1965* (Chapel Hill: University of North Carolona Press, 1983). There is also useful material in George P. Rawick "The New Deal and Youth" (Ph.D. diss., University of Wisconsin, 1957).

JOHN SALMOND

See also Bethune, Mary McLeod; Hopkins, Harry L.; Relief; Roosevelt, Anna Eleanor; Williams, Aubrey Willis

---

Native Americans

See Indian Policy

Naval Collection

Though best remembered as a stamp collector, Franklin Roosevelt was above all a serious collector of materials on the history of the American navy. He began the collection in his youth and added to it throughout his life, even during the busy presidential years. At his death it contained more than 1,000 prints and paintings, 2,500 books, and hundreds of pamphlets, documents, letters, log books, ship models, and miscellaneous memorabilia.

He collected most actively during his years as assistant secretary of the navy (1913–20) and the agonizing years he spent recuperating from polio (1921–28). Of this latter period, he once said that he owed his life to his hobbies. In those years of enforced leisure, he cataloged his books, writing out in long hand some nine hundred catalog cards, and started to write a biography of John Paul Jones, whose career had long fascinated him. Unfortunately for posterity, he lost interest in the project, and only a few pages in long hand on ruled paper remain.

Roosevelt was well known to dealers who sent him items on approval and lists and catalogs from which he ordered. He went to auctions before the at-

Model boats were a lifelong interest of FDR, seen here with sons James (left) and Elliott (right) on board the Vireo, *27 July 1920. (Courtesy FDR Library.)*

tack of polio, but when he could no longer do so his secretary, Louis McHenry Howe, went in his stead, armed with catalogs that FDR had marked with a system of one to four check marks and the price Howe should bid. Howe's instructions were: "On single check marks don't go over bid." The more check marks, the more FDR wanted the item and permitted Howe a certain leeway in bidding. A frugal man, FDR was a conservative buyer. He bought many of the books, pamphlets, and documents for less than a dollar and paid as little as ten cents for letters from unknown sailors. But he would not haggle over price when a truly unique item came his way. The most celebrated part of the collection consists of 1,200 prints and paintings of ships, actions, and naval officers, ranging from items of great rarity or artistic merit to illustrations cut from eighteenth- and nineteenth-century publications. FDR's favorites were "eyewitness" drawings because, though often naive, he believed them historically accurate. His concern was history, not technique. Outstanding among such works is a scrapbook of watercolors by William H. Meyers, a gunner aboard the USS *Dale* during the California operations in the war with Mexico. FDR paid $900 for the scrapbook, the most he ever paid for an item in the collection.

He bought few prints after 1939 because, as he plaintively wrote a dealer, "I have no more wall space." Naval prints covered the walls of his Hyde Park and New York City houses and his private quarters in the White House. When the Franklin D. Roosevelt Library opened in 1941, he transferred a large part of the collection there, and at his death the library—and the American people—was bequeathed the rest, except for some eighty prints which hang in his Hyde Park house as they did in his lifetime. Although an entire gallery in the FDR Library is devoted to the collection, only a fraction can be displayed at one time. But items are often loaned to other museums, and the entire collection is open to research.

The papers of Franklin D. Roosevelt in the Franklin D. Roosevelt Library, Hyde Park, New York, contain extensive correspondence, lists and catalogs, bills and receipts from antiquarians, dealers, and others dealing with FDR's collection of naval materials. *The Old Navy, 1776–1860* (Washington, 1962) is a catalog of an exhibit of prints and watercolors from the naval collection of Franklin D. Roosevelt. *Exhibition of paintings, prints and models of ships . . . lent by the President of the United States* (Washington: Corcoran Gallery of Art, 1936). Two articles about the collection include John F. Kennedy, "The Strength and Style of Our Navy Tradition," *Life*, 10 August 1962, pp. 79–84, and William J. Stewart and Cheryl C. Pollard, "Franklin D. Roosevelt, Collector," *Prologue: The Journal of the National Archives* (Winter 1969).

See also Sailing

Nazism

See Fascism; Hitler, Adolf, and Germany; Holocaust

Negroes

No ethnic group anticipated the inauguration of Franklin Delano Roosevelt with less hope for a new deal than Afro-Americans; and none had less leverage on the president-elect. Despite an unemployment rate hovering around 50 percent, over two-thirds of the Negroes voting in 1932 went Republican, an even higher proportion than had voted for Herbert Hoover in 1928. The Democrats, for most blacks, remained the party that had opposed emancipation and reconstruction and still defended racial discrimination, disfranchisement, segregation, and white supremacy. Roosevelt, in addition, had never done anything to champion the Negroes' cause. Indeed, his political career had been a model of deference to the white South on racial issues. His need to work harmoniously with a largely white southern-controlled Congress and a white southern-staffed federal bureaucracy clearly augured for a continuation of racial neglect. Powerful party traditions of states' rights and decentralization further undermined the hopefulness of Negroes. Those who would administer the relief and recovery projects at the local level would likely be the very planters and politicians, industrialists and union leaders, who stood to gain the most by maintaining the oppression of blacks. The powerlessness of blacks in a political system dispensing assistance on the basis of the strength of the groups demanding it also dampened the expectations of the largely poor and unorganized black community. And the very ubiquity of the worst depression in American history made it even more unlikely that Roosevelt would act to remedy the plight of blacks. Hard times defined his mandate. None of his advisers considered jeopardizing economic reconstruction for some racial reform that would surely arouse a storm of political opposition.

The consequences of these conditions, reflecting three centuries of Negro poverty and powerlessness, were starkly revealed in the initial New Deal treatment of Afro-Americans. The indifference, if not racial hostility, of the National Recovery Administration (NRA) quickly earned it the black epithet "Negro Run Around." Heavily weighted in favor of large-scale, modernized business enterprises and unionized workers, the NRA codes forced many disadvantaged black entrepreneurs to close shop and permitted either lower wage scales for unorganized Negroes or the displacement of black workers by white employees. The Agricultural Adjustment Administration (AAA) practically invited discrimination by allowing white large landowners to dominate the county committees. The nearly 400,000 Negro sharecroppers and more than 300,000 black tenant farmers almost never received the proportionate share of

Black playwrights, actors, and technicians found an opportunity to practice and develop their craft in the Federal Theatre Project's sixteen Negro units. The productions ranged from adaptations of classics like Macbeth, The Mikado, *and* Lysistrata, *to African dance, minstrel shows, and vaudeville, to new works written for the FTP by both black and white playwrights. The* Big White Fog *of racism was of particular concern to black playwright Theodore Ward. Juxtaposing Garveyism, black capitalism, and socialism in the play as alternatives open to black Americans, the play won acclaim for the Chicago Negro Unit and praise from Langston Hughes, who called it "the greatest, most encompassing play on Negro life that has ever been written." (Courtesy the Library of Congress Federal Theatre Project Collection at George Mason University Library, Fairfax, Virginia.)*

The CCC offered young black men jobs and training, but within the segregated structure of the era. Two off-duty enrollees in a Yanceyville, North Carolina, CCC unit relax in the camp recreation center. (National Archives.)

crop reduction payments they were entitled to, and the AAA acquiesced in the wholesale eviction of tenants whose labor was no longer needed.

The latitude given local authorities similarly resulted in much discrimination and segregation in the Civilian Conservation Corps (CCC). Not until 1936 did the number of Negroes reach 10 percent of the total enrollment. Black enrollees always remained below the percentage of unemployed young Negroes in the nation; and they were largely confined to segregated CCC units and kept out of the training programs that could lead to their advancement. Those who had traditionally oppressed southern blacks also controlled the local administration of the Tennessee Valley Authority, and they too succeeded in maintaining living and working conditions that adhered to the customs of racial exclusion, discrimination, and segregation. The New Deal's early capitulation to racial prejudice was also manifest in the refusal to admit Negroes in the subsistence homestead program, the encouragement of residential segregation by the Federal Housing Administration, and the toleration of discrimination by state and local officials in the selection and payment of relief recipients for the Federal Emergency Relief Administration and the Civil Works Administration.

After 1934, however, counterforces gradually pushed Roosevelt and the New Deal toward a more equitable treatment of Negroes. Most important, a host of racial advancement and protest organizations campaigned for Negro rights on a scale, and with an intensity, unknown in previous decades. Simultaneously, a marked upsurge in the number of Negroes who registered and voted, especially in the states richest in electoral votes, developed a relatively sizable and volatile bloc that national politicians could no longer ignore. In addition, the radical Left and the labor movement, intellectuals and southern liberals, all for their own reasons, began to campaign for racial

justice and equality and to demand racial reforms in the New Deal. Their efforts were augmented by the pressure for racial change within the Roosevelt administration emanating from people sympathetic to the Negro's cause such as Will Alexander, Harry Hopkins, Harold Ickes, Aubrey Williams, and particularly, Eleanor Roosevelt.

President Roosevelt could neither ignore the growing force for Negro rights nor disregard the strength of those arrayed against any change in the racial status quo. He did what he could in ways that would not cost him much politically. Always the fox and never the lion on racial issues, Roosevelt nevertheless took steps to ensure Negroes a far fairer and fuller share of New Deal benefits after 1934 and began to act in ways that had the unintended consequence of laying the groundwork for the second Reconstruction. Largely because of the efforts of the Farm Security Administration, the National Youth Administration, the Public Works Administration, the United States Housing Administration, and the Works Progress Administration, the disparities between white and black in matters of employment, income, education, housing, and health narrowed significantly in the 1930s.

The New Deal also altered the participation of Negroes in government work. The number of blacks in federal jobs tripled during the thirties, more than doubling the proportion of Negro government employees in 1930. Moreover, the Roosevelt administration began to desegregate work facilities in federal agencies and departments, an unprecedented action, and to hire thousands of Negroes for managerial and professional positions. The president further broke prevailing customs of racial prejudice by appointing more than a hundred blacks to administrative posts in the New Deal. Those in Washington were popularly referred to as the Black Cabinet or the Black Brain Trust, and although they did not accomplish the transformation of the New Deal into a crusade for civil rights, they did succeed in making the federal government far more aware of black needs and in prodding other government officials to speak out for greater federal assistance to Negroes.

Additionally, Roosevelt's appointments to the Supreme Court championed the rights of minorities and formulated new constitutional guarantees to protect civil rights. With the exception of James Byrnes, Roosevelt's eight appointees played a key role in dismantling a century of law discriminating against blacks. Their decisions in the late 1930s and 1940s severely circumscribed the permissibility of private discrimination, left blacks less and less at the mercy of states' rights, and signaled the demise of the legality of the separate-but-equal doctrine.

Tentatively yet increasingly, Roosevelt also became more egalitarian in his gestures and rhetoric. By his well-publicized invitations to blacks to visit him in the White House, his conferences with civil rights leaders, his appearances before Negro audiences, and especially, his association with the campaigns for antilynching and anti–poll tax legislation, the president helped educate and inspire others. Two southern filibusters killed the chances for a federal act to prevent lynching, but lynchings did decline from a high of twenty-eight in 1933 to two in 1939. The pressure for federal legislation, moreover, persuaded several southern states to enact measures against both lynchings and the poll tax. As the head of his party, Roosevelt also charted a new racial course for the Democrats. In 1936, for the first time, the national party accredited Negroes as convention delegates; invited black reporters into the regular press box; selected Negroes to deliver an invocation, a welcome address, and a seconding speech for Roosevelt's nomination; and abolished the century-old rule, utilized by the white South as a veto, that required the Democratic nominee to win two-thirds of the delegates' votes in order to obtain the nomination. In 1940, Roosevelt insisted that the Democrats include a specific Negro plank in the party platform pledging to end racial discrimination in all government services and benefits. Such actions and the substantial assistance accorded Negroes by the New Deal led a majority of blacks to desert the Republican party for the first time in history in 1934; and in 1936 and 1940 more than two-thirds of the Negro vote went to Roosevelt.

"It is true that the millennium in race relations did not arrive under Roosevelt," the NAACP summed up the record. "But cynics and scoffers to the contrary, the great body of Negro citizens made progress." That swelled hope in the formerly disheartened. A belief that "we are on our way" took root in the Negro community. Despite the continuity of racism staining the New Deal, the beginnings of change helped transform despair and discouragement into a new Negro hopefulness that a better world could soon and surely be achieved.

Harvard Sitkoff, *A New Deal for Blacks: The Emergence of Civil Rights as a National Issue* (New York: Oxford University Press, 1978) fully develops the themes outlined in this article. The racial views of key New Dealers are well analyzed by John B. Kirby, *Black Americans in the Roosevelt Era, Liberalism and Race* (Knoxville: University of Tennessee Press, 1980) and Morton Sosna, *In Search of the Silent South: Southern Liberals and the Race Issue* (New York: Columbia University Press, 1977). See Nancy J. Weiss, *Farewell to the Party of Lincoln, Black Politics in the Age of FDR* (Princeton: Princeton University Press, 1983) for an explanation of the dramatic shift in Negro voting in the 1930s, and Raymond Wolters, *Negroes and the Great Depression: The Problem of Economic Recovery* (Westport, Conn.: Greenwood Publishing Corp., 1970) for an analysis of the ways in which Negroes were affected by and responded to the New Deal. The indispensable classic is Gunnar Myrdal, *An American Dilemma: The Negro Problem and Modern Democracy* (New York: Harper & Bros., 1944).

HARVARD SITKOFF

See also Bethune, Mary McLeod; Biddle, Francis Beverley; Black Cabinet; Democratic Party; Elections in the Roosevelt Era; National Association for the Advancement of Colored People; National Youth Administration; New Deal; Randolph, Asa Philip; Roosevelt, Anna Eleanor; South, The; Supreme Court of the United States; War Effort on the Home Front

Neutrality Acts

The neutrality acts were a series of laws, passed piecemeal by Congress from 1935 to 1939, designed to prevent U.S. involvement in a nonhemispheric war. Characteristic features of the legislation included: a ban on loans and credits to belligerents; a mandatory embargo on direct or indirect shipments of arms or munitions; presidential discretion to require payment and transfer of title before exporting any articles whatsoever to a belligerent; the prohibition of American citizens traveling on ships of belligerents; and the prohibition of the arming of American merchant vessels. The controversies concerning American entry in World War I were much on Congress's mind as it passed this legislation, which marked the high tide of American isolationism. Not only was the United States abandoning its traditional doctrine of neutrality; it was failing to distinguish between "aggressor" and "victim" nations.

The first major piece of neutrality legislation was the Johnson Act. Although it was never technically part of the neutrality laws of 1935–39, it had strong neutrality overtones. In its original form, the bill introduced by isolationist senator Hiram Johnson (Rep.-Calif.) prohibited private loans to governments in default of obligations to the U.S. government or its citizens. The Senate passed the bill on 14 January 1934 in the wake of France's third consecutive default and Britain's offering $460 million in full settlement of her $8 billion debt. Roosevelt insisted upon limiting the scope of the bill to debts owed to the United States government, as he considered the matter of money owed to private parties too difficult to administer. Once Johnson agreed to the restriction, albeit reluctantly, Roosevelt quietly backed the bill. In its revised form, it passed the Senate on 2 February and the House on 4 April, and was signed by the president on 13 April. The bill never succeeded in its goal: to press the nations owing debts contracted during World War I into equitable settlements with the United States. It gave no consideration to nations making partial payments, and of the debtor nations, only Finland made further payment.

On 19 March 1935, President Roosevelt asked the Senate's Special Committee Investigating the Munitions Industry chaired by Senator Gerald P. Nye (Rep.-N.D.) to prepare neutrality legislation. The president by no means shared the isolationist sentiments of most of the committee members. However, he could well have wanted to prod the State Department, which he believed was procrastinating in drafting neutrality legislation, and to divert the committee into less controversial channels. The committee itself introduced no bill, but its staff did much work behind the scenes.

On 21 August after much parliamentary jockeying and intensive arguments, the Senate passed a neutrality bill without a record vote. Introduced by Foreign Relations Committee chairman Key Pittman (Dem.-Nev.), the bill contained a mandatory arms embargo, but gave the president power to define "implements of war" and to say when the embargo should go into effect. In addition, the president had the option of prohibiting American vessels from carrying war materials to belligerents and of withholding protection from Americans traveling on belligerent ships. The bill established a munitions control board to regulate American arms shipments. Two days later, the House quickly, unanimously, and without a record vote passed a similar bill, though the House bill set a six-month limit to the embargo. Within a day, the Senate voted 72 to 2 to concur in the House deadline, with 15 senators not voting.

On 31 August Roosevelt signed the first neutrality bill, though he warned that "the inflexible provisions might drag us into war instead of keeping us out." Yet the president appreciated the six-month deadline and the flexibility concerning timing and scope of certain restrictions. He did not want to jeopardize pending domestic legislation like the Guffey-Snyder Coal Act over foreign policy matter. In addition, he thought that the bill would probably injure Italy—on the verge of invading Ethiopia—far more than it would injure her victim.

When in October 1935, Mussolini invaded Ethiopia, Roosevelt banned the sale of munitions to either side while hoping that a "moral embargo" would keep American raw materials from being sent abroad. Yet he soon found that oil shipments to the invading power, Italy, suddenly and drastically rose.

On 29 February 1936, Roosevelt signed a second neutrality bill, one that extended the existing law fourteen months. Introduced by Senator Elbert D. Thomas (Dem.-Utah), it continued travel restrictions, made it mandatory for the president to extend the arms embargo to states entering a war in progress, and added a prohibition on loans to belligerents. The House adopted it on 17 February by a vote of 353 to 27; the Senate ratified it the next day by voice vote.

Though the bill imposed more restrictions upon a president already opposed to mandatory legislation, Roosevelt signed it without comment. He feared that a fight would risk further stripping of presidential power, produce debate that could only comfort Mussolini, and risk votes in the impending presidential race.

During the 1936 campaign, Roosevelt called the neutrality legislation "new weapons" to preserve American peace, though he asked for a discretionary neutrality policy. When in July 1936, the Spanish civil war broke out, Roosevelt first called for a moral embargo and then sponsored a nondiscriminatory arms embargo. The embargo act passed the Senate 81 to 0 and the House 404 to 1; on 8 January 1937, it was signed by the president. For months Roosevelt blocked efforts to repeal it, though in January 1939 he said that the embargo had been a great mistake.

On 1 May 1937, Roosevelt signed the third neutrality bill. Like the previous ones, it retained the ban on arms sales, loans, credit, and travel on belligerent ships whenever the president found that a foreign or civil war endangered the United States. In addition, it

banned all arming of merchant ships trading with belligerents, and forebade such ships from carrying munitions. The president had discretionary authority to put the sale of nonembargoed goods on a cash-and-carry basis, with title on all such exports transferred before the goods left the United States. He also had discretionary authority to prohibit armed belligerent ships from using American ports. Although most provisions were "permanent," the cash-and-carry proviso could expire in two years. Pittman introduced the main provisions in the Senate, which passed them on 3 March by 63 to 6. On 18 March the House passed a neutrality bill, introduced by Sam D. McReynolds (Dem.-Tenn.), 376 to 12. It was similar to the Pittman bill but made the transfer-of-title clause a matter of presidential discretion. On 28 April the conference report compromised in favor of the discretionary House resolution, which was then approved by both House and Senate.

Roosevelt, in the midst of a bitter struggle over the Supreme Court, had no desire for additional conflict and signed the bill without protest. By remaining aloof from debate while quietly backing the House's flexible provisions, he was able to maintain discretionary authority in levying trade restrictions. He also used his limited freedom to advantage in the undeclared Sino-Japanese war that began on 13 July 1937. While operating within the letter of the law, he could permit American munitions trade with China.

On 4 January 1939, Roosevelt told Congress that the neutrality legislation "may actually give aid to an aggressor and deny it to a victim." Yet efforts to repeal the arms embargo could not even reach the Senate floor, and the termination of the cash-and-carry provision on 1 May permitted American vessels to transport arms directly to belligerents. Congressman Sol Bloom (Dem.-N.Y.), chairman of the House Foreign Affairs Committee, introduced an administration bill to permit more presidential discretion, but on the House floor John M. Vorys (Rep.-Ohio) reinserted the arms embargo. On 30 June the House passed the Bloom bill, with the Vorys amendment, 214 to 173. But as the Senate had not acted, most of the 1937 law was still in effect.

Only on 4 November 1939 did Roosevelt sign a fourth neutrality act, one that combined the cash-and-carry provision with repeal of the arms embargo. Aside from giving the president latitude in proclaiming combat zones, the bill retained the stringency of the 1937 law. It passed the Senate on 27 October by a vote of 63 to 30 and the House on 2 November by 243 to 181. Roosevelt had taken advantage of the change in public sentiment to skillfully work behind the scenes, and in the process he won the support of many conservative Democrats.

On 17 November 1941, Roosevelt signed a bill authorizing the arming of American merchant vessels and permitting them to carry cargo into belligerent ports. Passed by the Senate on 7 November (50 to 37) and the House on 13 November (212 to 94), the bill permitted Americans ships to cross the Atlantic, enter a war zone under siege of German submarines, and travel to British ports. Yet, in remnant form, the 1937 neutrality act remained law until Pearl Harbor.

In the definitive work on the neutrality acts, Robert A. Divine, *The Illusion of Neutrality* (Chicago: University of Chicago Press, 1962), places the main responsibility for the acts upon public opinion, but finds Roosevelt usually failing to exert strong leadership. Wayne S. Cole, *Roosevelt and the Isolationists, 1932–45* (Lincoln: University of Nebraska Press, 1983) stresses the role of the Nye committee and Roosevelt's domestic priorities, while John E. Wiltz, "The Nye Committee Revisited," *Historian* 23 (February 1961):211–33, sees the committee as a minor factor. For Pittman's ambivalent role, see Cole, "Senator Key Pittman and American Neutrality Policies, 1933–1940," *Mississippi Valley Historical Review* 46 (March 1960):644–62, and Fred L. Israel, *Nevada's Key Pittman* (Lincoln: University of Nebraska Press, 1963). Stuart L. Weiss, "American Foreign Policy and Presidential Power: The Neutrality Act of 1935," *Journal of Politics* 23 (August 1968):672–95, claimed that Roosevelt could have avoided the restrictions of the 1935 act had he taken initiative two years earlier.

JUSTUS D. DOENECKE

See also Foreign Economic Policy; Foreign Policy; Internationalism and Peace; Isolationism; Lend-lease; World War II

New Deal

"A New Deal for the American people"—it was a phrase written for Franklin Roosevelt's acceptance speech before the Democratic National Convention in 1932, and it quickly caught on as a label for the changes he would make in a depression-stricken America. The elements of that New Deal were vaguely sketched during the 1932 campaign against Hoover, but Roosevelt straddled many issues and projected a very general set of ideas, some of them contradictory. It is clear only in retrospect that Roosevelt as president intended to blend his exposure to the conservation movement, Theodore Roosevelt's Nationalism, Woodrow Wilson's New Freedom, and wartime planning into a dynamic program of internal reform to heal America in the thirties.

The basic outlines of the New Deal were in his mind in 1932, as his brains trust helped him sharpen the ideas he brought to that year. But political and economic circumstances were to shape the New Deal's contours from the very first. He was inaugurated on a cold March Saturday when the entire national banking system was paralyzed. Events handed Roosevelt a profound crisis, and the national yearning for decisive leadership opened a way for unprecedented reform measures if the new president could seize the moment. Cautious for a week or two in which he spoke of budget cuts and retrenchment, Roosevelt in mid-March held Congress in session and launched a program that would lead in a hectic hundred days to fifteen major laws. This would be the

HE NEVER WAS MUCH GOOD AT THE GAME OF "FOLLOW THE LEADER"

Copyright, 1933, New York Tribune Inc.

New York Herald Tribune. (© I.M.T.Corporation. Reprinted by permission.)

opening of the longer season of reform (1933–38) that was the New Deal era.

The first hundred days had a revolutionary appearance, as a normally obstructive Congress yielded the initiative to a confident president who seemed fully in charge of the pace and direction of legislation. From the Roosevelt White House came program proposals, backed by legislative drafts from White House or congressional allies. The administration wanted major new programs in industrial and agricultural planning, a regional authority in the Tennessee Valley, broad relief measures, banking reform. As historians later reconstructed the events of those days, Congress and pressure groups were not passive responders but active initiators, often more radically inclined than the president himself. FDR and his advisers did not originate everything that was suggested and did not completely control final outcomes.

But contemporaries found it an unforgettably exciting time, and the universal impression was of a buoyant president in charge of the swirl of events. From the White House came a stream of ideas, and in press conferences and two fireside chats, Roosevelt calmly explained the evolving New Deal: "All of the proposals and all of the legislation since the fourth day of March," he said as the hundred days closed, "have not been just a collection of haphazard schemes, but rather the orderly component parts of a connected and logical whole." It was not quite true, but the unifying element was Roosevelt, presiding over, even if he did not entirely control, events.

Most historians discern a large pattern in the five years of the New Deal and trace that pattern to Roosevelt's broad sense of strategy. He wished to do three things at once, and the strategic issue was how to formulate and blend them. They were: unemployment or poverty relief, economic recovery, and economic and social reform. Relief is usually mentioned first among the three New Deal goals because it was the most immediately urgent in a nation with one-quarter of the labor force unemployed, a nation living at half the material output of four years earlier. Roosevelt had concluded that assistance to the destitute must now become not just a private or local government assignment but a federal project, too. But if relief was first in urgency, it was not the New Deal's primary objective in the longer view of things. The primary objective was both recovery and reform together! Roosevelt wanted a revived economy, which would shrink or eliminate the need for relief and restore health to the entire society. He was also determined to pursue reform of an economic and social structure so flawed that the prosperous 1920s ended in a crash and worldwide depression.

It has seemed to many historians that Roosevelt placed recovery a bit ahead of reform between 1933 and 1935, and then reversed the apparent priority (while still wanting both together) from 1935 to the end of the New Deal, usually dated 1938. These apparent patterns have been called the first (1933–35) and second (1935–38) New Deals. Recently a third New Deal has been discerned, in which FDR by 1937 had discovered and proposed the far-reaching *governmental* as well as *economic* reforms the New Deal required if it were to be fully realized. Thus the five-year burst of change over which Franklin Roosevelt presided should be seen as a government pursuit of aid to the impoverished, a revived economy, a reformed political economy. Roosevelt's ranking of these, and his evolving sense of how they should be institutionalized, gave the New Deal its progressive pattern from the first to the third stage. Yet even these patterns of overall strategy in pursuing three goals at once were sufficiently blurred in the hectic legislative-administrative history of the New Deal that some historians still question their validity.

New Deal strategic direction remains a matter of dispute because FDR was satisfied with a very broad and loosely defined sense of direction and both permitted and encouraged contradictory lines of policy at all times. The first phase of the New Deal sprang into life during the hundred days of spring, 1933. It combined unemployment relief, banking and securities reform, the audacious regional development experiment embodied in the Tennessee Valley Authority, the legalization of beer, and sectoral planning in industry and agriculture. These were many policy directions at once, but the central idea of the early New Deal was national planning for economic recovery. The planning idea was relatively new to American policy discussion, but in the emergency atmosphere of 1933 it held strong appeal for elements of the business community and, more important, for Franklin Roosevelt and others in his councils who recalled the successful wartime mobilization of 1917–18.

At the center of New Deal planning was the National Recovery Administration (NRA), a hastily designed experiment in government-business-labor cooperation. Yet to FDR, factories could not prosper if farming remained in depression. Agricultural recovery to the New Dealers required the creation of institutions through which America's scattered farmers could collectively control their output and thus their profit margins, and it was embodied in the Agricultural Adjustment Administration (AAA). The first New Deal built its hopes on these experiments in forms of planning that retained capitalist incentives and were run by the producers themselves. Roosevelt had spoken of "a concert of all interests," of cooperation between capital and labor, as in wartime. Thus planning would not be imposed, but would be built upon voluntarism. The New Deal also planned for regional development in the Tennessee Valley and primed the pump by spending on public works projects and relief. The projects were grouped mainly under the Public Works Administration (PWA) headed by Harold Ickes; relief spending was administered through the Federal Emergency Relief Administration (FERA) headed by Harry Hopkins.

Would all this bring recovery? Roosevelt appeared supremely confident that the broad direction was correct and that, like a quarterback, he could try another play if tactics needed to be changed. The strategy was recovery through producer-oriented planning, government becoming the helpful ally of businessmen and businessmen-farmers. Direct assaults upon business were kept to a minimum so as not to spoil the cooperative spirit that had been established or was hoped for. Federal relief of unemployment and poverty was offered in innovative ways, but it was not allowed to grow to match the needs of all the unemployed, lest surging deficits threaten the confidence of investors. A central thread in the early New Deal was the effort to provide investors with psychological and institutional supports for private-sector expansion.

The first legislative outburst took three months— or exactly one hundred days. During the rest of 1933 and 1934, Roosevelt was busy with administrative decisions, fireside chats, and press conferences to explain the sprawling new programs to the public. He acted as head cheerleader, radiating confidence and encouraging the mass parades launched by the NRA to generate support for its industrial codes. To New Deal programs he thus added the maximum amount of positive thinking; the New Deal would combine structural innovation with optimistic psychology. Restless by nature and uncertain that his new programs combined with official optimism would bring recovery soon enough, Roosevelt also in 1933–34 added monetary expansion. He did not leave this to the Federal Reserve, but participated personally in several experiments in gold and silver purchases after taking the nation off the gold standard in 1933.

Washington, formerly a sleepy southern town,

New Deal Acronyms

AAA—Agricultural Adjustment Administration 1933
BCLB—Bituminous Coal Labor Board 1935
BOB—Bureau of Budget 1939
CAA—Civil Aeronautics Authority 1938
CCC—Civilian Conservation Corps 1933
CCC—Commodity Credit Corporation 1933
CWA—Civil Works Administration 1933
FCA—Farm Credit Administration 1933
FCC—Federal Communications Commission 1934
FCIC—Federal Crop Insurance Corporation 1938
FDIC—Federal Deposit Insurance Corporation 1933
FERA—Federal Emergency Relief Agency 1933
FFMC—Federal Farm Mortgage Corporation 1934
FHA—Federal Housing Administration 1934
FLA—Federal Loan Agency 1939
FSA—Farm Security Administration 1937
FSA—Federal Security Agency 1939
FTC—Federal Trade Commission 1914
FWA—Federal Works Agency 1939
HOLC—Home Owners Loan Corporation 1933
MLB—Maritime Labor Board 1938
NBCC—National Bituminous Coal Commission 1935
NLB—National Labor Board 1933
NLRB—National Labor Relations Board 1934–35

NRAB—National Railroad Adjustment Board 1934
NRA—National Recovery Administration 1933
NRB—National Resources Board 1934
NRC—National Resources Committee 1935
NRPB—National Resources Planning Board 1939
NYA—National Youth Administration 1935
PWA—Public Works Administration 1933
RA—Resettlement Administration 1935
REA—Rural Electrification Administration 1935
RFC—Reconstruction Finance Corporation 1932
RRB—Railroad Retirement Board 1935
SCS—Soil Conservation Service 1935
SEC—Securities and Exchange Commission 1934
SSB—Social Security Board 1935
TNEC—Temporary National Economic Committee 1938
TVA—Tennessee Valley Authority 1933
USEP—United States Employment Service 1933
USHA—United States Housing Authority 1937
USMC—United States Maritime Commission 1936
WPA—Works Progress Administration 1935 (name changed in 1939 to Works Projects Administration)

---

was electric with activity and confidence, as the New Deal drew into federal service a motley crew of young lawyers, social workers, social scientists from the universities, and business executives. They worked late and feverishly at agency building and administration. As the writer Edmund Wilson commented:

For a graduate of the school of New York liberalism, it is Old Home Week today in Washington. Everywhere in the streets and offices you run into old acquaintances: the editors and writers of the liberal press, the "progressive" young instructors from the colleges, the intelligent foundation workers, the practical idealists of settlement houses, the radicals who . . . conceive that there may just be a chance of turning the old order inside out.

The public responded enthusiastically to the New Deal and its confident impresario from Hyde Park. The Democratic party gained seats in both houses of Congress in the November 1934 elections, the first and only time the presidential party had not lost ground in its first electoral test. But the economy did not respond as hoped. The GNP moved upward from $56 billion in 1933 to $65 billion in 1934 and $72

billion in 1935, but in the second year of the New Deal over 10 million workers were still unemployed. Angry voices were heard, criticizing the administration for caution and ineffectiveness. The industrial labor force surged with militancy in 1934, expressed in a wave of strikes and factory violence along with a rapid increase in union membership.

The year 1935 was marked by what historian James M. Burns called "thunder on the Left," a wave of protest against the New Deal's slow progress toward recovery and its reluctance to confront business power and redistribute income and wealth. Millions responded to Louisiana's senator Huey Long, whose Share Our Wealth program promised to bring a decent life to average citizens through redistribution of large fortunes; to Father Charles Coughlin, the "radio priest" of Royal Oak, Michigan, whose National Union for Social Justice burgeoned as he criticized bankers, capitalism, and the caution of the New Deal; and to Dr. Francis Townsend, the Long Beach, California, physician who mobilized millions of elderly Americans behind a promise of government pensions.

These leaders of mass movements for social change ran only a little ahead of other ambitious pol-

C. Klessig, Sheboygan *(Wis.)* Press, *c. 1934. (Courtesy* Sheboygan Press.*)*

iticians who sensed that Roosevelt's New Deal was failing. Some were to FDR's left—socialists like Norman Thomas and Upton Sinclair, progressives such as Robert and Philip La Follette of Wisconsin. There was also in 1934–35 a "thunder on the Right,"—attacks upon the New Deal by businessmen, former president Hoover, and the new American Liberty League, an organization funded by large capitalists and conservatives to argue that the New Deal threatened liberty. The year 1935 presented Roosevelt with a still depressed economy and swelling numbers of politicians eager to replace him. In the face of that political challenge, he altered and energized the New Deal, proving that in a political fight he had no peers.

The first evidence of a change came in the annual message of January 1935, when FDR spoke of unfinished business, including public works and a comprehensive social security program. In April, Congress agreed to spend $4.8 billion for a new relief and public works package until turning unemployables back to the states. The sheer size of the appropriation suggested a strong commitment to the casualties of the depression. A comprehensive social insurance proposal had been sent to Congress in January, but for months Roosevelt exerted little pressure for its passage and held back on tax reform and permanent labor legislation. Then on 27 May the Supreme Court by a 9–0 vote invalidated the NRA, centerpiece of the early New Deal.

Roosevelt was furious, denounced the Court for a horse-and-buggy interpretation of the government's capacity to regulate the modern economy, and then energetically backed a broad range of reforms: Social Security, progressive tax reform, an attack upon public utility holding companies, and compulsory collective bargaining as envisioned in a bill by Senator Rob-

ert Wagner. The New Deal had entered its second phase. The "concert of all interests," cooperate-with-business rhetoric of NRA days gave way to a denunciation of entrenched interests, big business, and the wealthy. The New Deal was now more clearly than ever identified with the working class and the disadvantaged, as it challenged the existing distribution of income and business power.

The measures of 1935 (Social Security with old-age pensions and unemployment insurance, tax reform, dissolution of utility holding companies, and the Wagner National Labor Relations Act plus an undistributed profits tax passed in 1936) were more modest in impact and more conservative in design than was implied by the language of the president and his increasingly vocal conservative critics. The tax measure raised little income from the wealthy or corporations; Social Security was financed by a regressive tax and excluded millions who worked in agriculture and domestic service; and compulsory collective bargaining in time was seen even by employers as a measure contributing to labor-management industrial stability, leaving untouched the basic prerogatives of management.

But these were major steps even if hedged with compromise. Accompanied by administration rhetoric more radical than the eventual social impact of the extended reform agenda of 1935, the second New Deal had a decisive political effect. Franklin Roosevelt had firmly regained the leadership of the many elements in society who were pressing for governmental action against the depression. Opposition within the Democratic party vanished, and when FDR ran for a second term against the GOP's Alfred M. Landon, he not only buried the Republicans under a forty-six-state landslide but steamrollered the Socialists and obliterated the third (Union) party effort mounted by a coalition of Townsend, Coughlin, and the followers of Huey Long (who had been assassinated in Louisiana in September 1935). Roosevelt had reshaped American politics, grafting together with his New Deal a coalition of urban workers, farmers, ethnic and racial minorities, and intellectuals that would give the Democratic party majority status until well into the 1970s.

The election of 1936 appeared to give Roosevelt an irresistible mandate to complete the New Deal in his second term. He had not, as usual, been very clear about what remained to be done, but informed people knew how much remained on the agenda of the president and the reformers who identified with him. Recovery was not complete, and he privately thought it would not be lasting without a revival of NRA-style planning in some form. The New Deal still did not contain wages and hours legislation, a permanent program of rural resettlement, expansion of TVA to other river valleys, and a reorganized executive branch to allow more effective presidential government. Moreover, Roosevelt privately chafed at the Democratic party's conservatism, thinking the New Deal safe in the long run only if his own party could be realigned to attract all liberal voters. Thus, there was much unfinished business for the second term, and historians have recently suggested that the core of his efforts for 1937–38 was a coherent strategy for national planning under a permanent planning board. This might be called the third New Deal, a fusion under planning of the industrial self-government of 1933–34 and the attacks upon wealth and monopoly of 1935–36.

This final drive toward a completed New Deal opened with the ringing words of the second inaugural speech, declaring how far the New Deal had yet to go: "I see one-third of a nation ill-housed, ill-clad, ill-nourished," Roosevelt announced. Far-reaching proposals for change would be sent to Congress in 1937—but before February was out, Roosevelt had jeopardized it all with a serious political mistake. Instead of moving first on the rest of the unfinished agenda, he decided to move against the Supreme Court, nine men who had blocked so much of the program of a popular and reelected president. The Court had indeed decimated the New Deal as president and Congress had fashioned it, killing NRA and the first AAA (in 1936), and showing signs of an intention to invalidate TVA, Social Security, and the Wagner act. Roosevelt rejected more cautious approaches to this problem, such as constitutional amendments to narrow judicial review, and startled the country in February 1937 with a plan to enlarge the Court from nine to fifteen judges when any of the original nine reached the age of seventy and declined to retire. It was a subterfuge quickly called "Court packing" (New Deal loyalists liked to call it "Court unpacking," since seven of the nine judges of his first term had been appointed by Republican presidents), and conservative opponents of the New Deal were able to depict FDR as an enemy of the Constitution and the balance of powers.

At last the conservative opponents of the New Deal had an issue that might cut into FDR's support. Then, just weeks after the Court proposal, Roosevelt asked Congress for a broad reorganization of the executive branch, which would give the president effective control of all departments and agencies along with a planning board. Republicans could now attempt to rally some Democrats to oppose the administration on the principled grounds of resistance to executive power. This argument somewhat strengthened congressional opposition to FDR's second-term programs, but more decisive was a swing in the business cycle. In the autumn of 1937 came a sharp downturn in key economic indicators.

The president who had claimed credit for more than four years of continuous economic improvement was now saddled with a recession—with unemployment statistics moving in the wrong direction. By the end of 1937, the Court-packing plan and reorganization proposal were snarled in bipartisan objection. A conservative coalition of Democrats and Republicans had come together in Congress to halt the New Deal.

In 1938, Roosevelt was able to sign the Fair Labor Standards Act, abolishing child labor in a few industries and extending federal wage and hour regulation to parts of the economy. But the congressional struggle had been exhausting. Not until 1939 would Congress pass a weak reorganization bill, denying FDR effective control of executive agencies and rejecting a permanent planning board. The New Deal's legislative creation was at an end.

How should the New Deal be appraised? It had critics on the Right and the Left in those days, and it still does. In the 1930s and 1940s, the conservative critics claimed that government intervention in the economy and society had gone too far, impairing the market mechanism, encouraging dependence upon government among a formerly self-reliant people and concentrating too much power in Washington in general and in the White House in particular. These arguments were rejected by a majority of the American electorate during Roosevelt's lifetime and have not been reflected in the mainstream of historical scholarship.

There were also critics on the Left, who argued that the New Deal saved a capitalist system that had manifestly failed, that it achieved only minor reforms when more sweeping change was possible. They pointed out that recovery did not come until wartime, that inequalities of income were not noticeably narrowed, that regulatory agencies were soon captured by the industries they regulated, that relief of poverty was stingy and limited. These arguments, as well, were rejected by a majority of the electorate and by most historians, though a significant minority of historians has kept such a perspective alive and influential.

The popularity of the New Deal was tested and affirmed at the polls at least twice—when Roosevelt ran for reelection in 1936 and again in 1940. A massive flow of White House mail reflected the public's basic approval of what FDR was attempting, as did the contemporary polls. The New Deal, of course, was the product of many minds and pressures apart from Roosevelt. Brains trust professors, agricultural

"And the rocket's red glare, and bombs bursting in air, gave proof through the night that our flag was still there!"

Berryman, Washington Star, *c. 1935–36. (Copyright* Washington Post. *Reprinted by permission of the D.C. Public Library.)*

experts, politicians with useful or popular ideas such as senators Robert Wagner, George Norris, and Robert La Follette—these and many others contributed ideas and impulses to the New Deal. But President Roosevelt and the New Deal became fused in the public mind, for he was the leader at the center of it all. Both Roosevelt and his New Deal commanded majority enthusiasm; those who disliked the one were sure to dislike the other.

The New Deal's constituent parts, when considered separately, elicited varying reactions. Some programs were almost universally applauded—the CCC, for example, or federal deposit insurance. TVA was widely popular, as was Social Security and the farm program. The WPA, according to polls, was most frequently named as the most popular single New Deal program, but also as the most unpopular! Much of the New Deal was unknown to most of the public or too complex for public opinion to grasp: the work of the National Resources Planning Board, for example, or reform of transportation regulation or the control of domestic oil production and pricing.

But the New Deal was always understood to be greater than the sum of its parts, to be a change in the overall American system. At the close of the thirties, politics was inextricably meshed with economics in a new system of regulated and (to use a term in recent vogue) "safety-netted" capitalism. And the new system was certainly a vast change from what had gone before. The foundations of the welfare and regulatory state were solidly in place; the government had accepted responsibility for economic management and had made progress in learning that art; strengthened the presidency; brought organized labor into the industrial system in a new bargaining position; insured the elderly against loss of all income; altered the party system; and changed the agenda of American politics by demonstrating the positive uses of government in preserving the nation's soil and forests, developing its river systems, and employing some of its idle manpower.

These changes gave America a new political economy—a different mesh of the public and the private, government and capitalism. It was not revolutionary, for the post–New Deal system was still capitalism on its economic side and still a parliamentary republic on its political side. Other nations, most notably Germany, did not come through the 1930s with its basic arrangements unchanged. But if the United States remained a capitalist democracy, after the New Deal it was nonetheless one with vastly changed arrangements of power and responsibility. Thus the appropriateness of historian William Leuchtenburg's description of the New Deal as a "half-way revolution."

In the year of Franklin Roosevelt's centennial—1982—President Ronald Reagan raised the interesting question of FDR's real intentions. An unabashed Roosevelt fan, Reagan expressed the view that FDR had not meant the New Deal to be permanent, but had intended to restore the free-market economy of the Coolidge era as soon as the emergency was over! That such a comment could be made suggests an appalling ignorance of Roosevelt's basic intentions. And

the question of those intentions is an important one. The vision behind the New Deal was Franklin Roosevelt's, drawn together from many sources and communicated brilliantly to his contemporaries—and is now apparently in danger of being lost. It was a vision of a reformed America, not a mere restoration of a social and economic order whose weak foundations shattered in 1929.

We may best glimpse it through Roosevelt's own words, from the introduction to the first volume of his collected papers and addresses:

> There were inconsistencies of methods ... inconsistencies born of insufficient knowledge. There were inconsistencies springing from the need of experimentation. But through them all, I trust that there also will be found a consistency and continuity of broad purpose.
>
> Consistently I have sought to maintain a comprehensive and efficient functioning of the representative form of democratic government in its modern sense. Consistently I have sought through that form of government to help our people to gain a larger social justice.

To these goals should be added a third preoccupation of the New Deal, which he expressed in the 1933 inaugural address: "We aim at the assurance of a rounded, permanent national life."

How did the New Deal pursue social justice? That term, in FDR's parlance, meant a broader chance that was to be realized through a governmental helping hand extended to those without inherited advantage, those who were blocked from full lives by the accidents of class, race, or geography. This was the purpose behind the enlargement of the number of those groups who were the beneficiaries of government. Historian Arthur M. Schlesinger, Jr., has called the government of the 1920s and earlier "single-interest" government as contrasted to the many constituencies to which the New Deal attempted to respond—labor, farmers, the aged, the unemployed (though it did less for groups suffering from deepseated, mainly noneconomic disadvantage, such as blacks and women). A dominant idea in the discourse of New Dealers was that of balance, by which liberals meant a more equitable relationship among social groups, arranged by government. By social justice, Roosevelt meant a fairer chance, which the marketplace offered in theory but not in practice.

The goal of "a comprehensive and efficient functioning of the representative form of democratic government" pointed the New Deal toward its political agenda: not only more government programs for more groups in difficulty, but realigned parties, invigoration of the presidency and executive branch, a stimulus to regionalism. Across the New Deal there was a stress upon enlarged participation—farmers voting through AAA referenda on matters formerly out of their reach, workers voting on unionization and through unions on the terms of working life, government programs and careers newly open to formerly excluded or underrepresented groups such as Jews, women, and blacks.

And the words "a rounded, permanent national life" expressed FDR's desire for a stronger sense of community mutuality and obligation, man to man and man to Land, which were in his view the only basis of a lasting security. A European historian, Torbjorn Sirevag, looking back on the New Deal after thirty years, noted that its stress on cooperation rested on Roosevelt's central idea, that of interdependence. "This" Sirevag wrote, "was probably the most central concept of the New Deal, at least in terms of frequency. . . . It approached obsession." In December 1932 following his election, Roosevelt, when writing a draft of an article entitled "A New Deal in the White House," had used the word *interdependence* three times by page 7. In the competitive world of laissez-faire, he thought, people had exploited one another and the riches of nature. He intended the New Deal as an occasion for moral exhortation and institutional reforms, building from the recognition of interdependence toward the broadest set of changes one could imagine within a capitalist framework: an end to environment-damaging habits, a planned balance among social groups.

Whatever the adequacy of this vision, or of Roosevelt's leadership in attaining it, he was forced to admit that the New Deal as finally constructed fell short of its fulfillment.

While American government after the New Deal responded to more groups and addressed more social problems than ever before, it did not do so with full equity. Business interests that were well organized benefited greatly from government regulation, subsidies such as RFC loans, and the general boost to economic activity; large farmers benefited from New Deal farm programs more than did small farmers or tenants; black Americans participated in government work and relief programs, but not at the level of their economic need and not on equal terms with whites. FDR had promised to come to the aid of "the forgotten man" in a 1932 speech, and the New Deal had moved in that direction. But it did not bring full economic recovery, and it left millions in poverty and outside the structures of government aid. As for the New Deal's energetic pursuit of natural resource protection and planning, the great advances of the 1930s not only fell short of the hopes of conservationists but were swamped by the economic boom that came after World War II. In the end, the New Deal's economic achievements were less than its political ones, and its tangible attainments were less sweeping than an intangible one—the revival of hope in America's fundamental system and leadership in a decade in which several modern societies were abandoning representative democracy for the expediency of dictatorship.

In private, FDR mixed the satisfaction of achievement with disappointment that the New Deal system had not come closer to his intentions. But he often acknowledged its flaws as democracy's price. Obstacles could not be simply overpowered, as in closed societies; like the sailor he was, Roosevelt had been forced to tack toward harbor but had not yet made it by the time war intervened. Historians refer to the developments of 1933–38 as "the New Deal," but Roosevelt in 1944 and 1945 was talking with friends about how much of the New Deal was yet undone. After the war, he said, there must be renewed efforts to achieve resource and public works planning, more river valley authorities, perhaps even a third, liberal party. In the meantime, shortcomings should be noted in the spirit of a remark he made in 1936, so often quoted:

> The immortal Dante tells us that divine justice weighs the sins of the coldblooded and the sins of the warmhearted in different scales. Better the occasional faults of a government that lives in a spirit of charity than the constant omissions of a government frozen in the idea of its own indifference.

Intending to lead the nation closer to the New Deal after the war, Roosevelt died in Georgia as spring pushed up the eastern seaboard. He had more than once said that a democratic people could address and remedy errors of omission and commission through experimentation in the future. For half a century and more, that experimentation would take place within the framework laid down by the New Deal.

Perhaps the earliest historical treatment of the New Deal was Basil Rauch, *The History Of The New Deal, 1933–1938* (New York: Creative Age, 1944), a book that established the concept of two New Deals. Rauch's favorable interpretation was reflected in the major biographies to follow, those by Schlesinger, Burns, and Freidel. The only scholarly effort at a conservative critique of the New Deal remains Edgar E. Robinson's *The Roosevelt Leadership, 1933–1945* (Philadelphia: Lippincott, 1955). Strong reappraisals of the New Deal from scholars emphasizing the gap between New Deal promise and performance came from Barton J. Bernstein, ed., "The New Deal: The Conservative Achievements of Liberal Reform," in *Towards A New Past* (New York: Random House, 1967) and Paul Conkin, *The New Deal,* 2d ed. (Arlington Heights, Ill.: Harlan Davidson, 1975). William E. Leuchtenburg's *Franklin D. Roosevelt And The New Deal, 1933–1940* (New York: Harper & Row, 1963) is widely considered the most balanced account, sound in scholarship and engagingly presented. For a review of the literature on the New Deal, see Otis L. Graham, Jr., ed., *The New Deal* (Boston: Little, Brown, 1973). In John Braeman et al., *The New Deal,* 2 vols. (Columbus: Ohio State University Press, 1975), one finds a treasury of essays on the New Deal at both national and local levels. The broad patterns of New Deal economic ideology and recovery efforts are superbly sketched in Ellis Hawley, *The New Deal And The Problem of Monopoly* (Princeton: Princeton University Press, 1966). Barry D. Karl's *The Uneasy State* (Chicago: University of Chicago Press, 1983) discerns a third New Deal. For a fascinating effort at comparative history, see John A. Garraty, "The New Deal, National Socialism, and the Great Depression," *American Historical Review* 78 (1973):907–14.

OTIS L. GRAHAM, JR.

See also Biographers and Public Reputation; Brains Trust; Congress, United States; Conservatism; Court-Packing Plan; Democratic Party; Great Depression; Hundred Days; Interregnum; La Guardia, Fiorello; Fiscal Policy; Labor; Liberalism and Progressivism; Long, Huey Pierce; Monetary Policy; Office of the Presidency; Planning; "Purge" of 1938; Rayburn,

Samuel Taliaferro; Regulation, Federal; Relief; Reorganization Act of 1939; Supreme Court of the United States; Women and the New Deal; Taxation

New Left Critique

See Biographers and Public Reputation; Conservatism

New Republic

See Lippmann, Walter; Thomas, Norman Mattoon

New Towns

See Housing and Resettlement

News Media

Franklin Roosevelt's success in handling the contemporary news media is one index of his extraordinary political skill. In the crucial early months of his presidency, he adroitly used the radio, the press, and the newsreels to convey a message of reassurance and hope. His first radio broadcast, on the financial crisis, revealed his gift for simple, logical analysis, his ability to use homely metaphors to explain a complex subject like banking so that, as Will Rogers quipped, even the bankers could understand it. The rich, vibrant voice, the easy cadences of his speech, his capacity for making people believe that he was talking to them personally—all these hallmarks of the Roosevelt style were on display.

At critical times during his presidency he used these fireside chats to signal important policy initiatives and rally support, and the easy intimacy of such appeals was normally proof against the hail of editorial criticism those initiatives sometimes provoked. One classic example of the Roosevelt technique was his explanation of that momentous foreign policy decision known as Lend-Lease, which he cast in terms of allowing one's neighbor whose house was on fire to borrow the hose without first requiring him to pay for it. So relaxed were his radio broadcasts that one contemporary remarked that Roosevelt sounded as though he were holding the microphone in one hand and roasting chestnuts with the other. So persuasive was he that veteran columnist Mark Sullivan speculated that if Roosevelt were to recite the Polish alphabet it would be accepted as an eloquent plea for disarmament. Before the newsreel cameras, too, he was a near faultless performer, effectively dramatizing his

A presidential press conference, Washington, D.C., 25 August 1939. (Courtesy FDR Library.)

actions and pronouncements and easily communicating an aura of vitality and strength.

But to maintain support for his programs, Roosevelt needed to be in continuous communication with the public, and to achieve this, he wooed and won the Washington press. His first presidential press conference has become part of his legend. Reporters accustomed to being suspected as spies suddenly found themselves welcomed as friends. He hoped, the new president told them, that his regular meetings with them could be the kind of delightful family gatherings he had enjoyed with the reporters at Albany. He called them by their first names and took them into his confidence; some matters would have to be kept "just between us boys and girls," Roosevelt would say.

The contrast with former presidents could hardly have been greater. Hoover's gloom had deepened with the depression until, sullen and vindictive, he had dried up as a news source. Before him, Calvin Coolidge had defeated the correspondents' attempts to learn his views by insisting that their questions be submitted in writing before the press conferences and then shuffling awkward ones to the bottom of the pile. He was also an inveterate twaddler and would spin out interminable folksy tales and reminiscences to fill up the available time. But Roosevelt was friendly and forthcoming, meeting the reporters' questions directly with good-natured, informative replies. Experienced reporters admired his news sense, his knack of timing releases so that they achieved maximum impact, and his ability to give them information in a form suitable for incorporation in their dispatches, a quality greatly prized during the early New Deal when the pace of events was frantic. Columnist Heywood Broun went so far as to call Franklin Roosevelt the best newspaperman ever to have been president of the United States. Coolidge and Hoover had been dull, but Roosevelt's vivid, exciting personality made wonderful copy.

By and large, Roosevelt continued to meet reporters twice a week for the entire period of his presidency (for a total of 997 press conferences), and the relationship between them remained uncommonly productive. The correspondents' regular contacts meant a continual supply of "live" news and an opportunity to gain early insights into presidential thinking. Roosevelt, too, gained much from these meetings. Their very frequency meant that he could make an immediate comment on big news stories as soon as they broke, which helped portray him as the focus of national activity. The general run of press conference questions allowed him to gauge public opinion. Such was his skill, moreover, that he could create sufficient dramatic news to dominate the front pages of the nation's newspapers, leaving hostile press owners, such as William Randolph Hearst, Robert McCormick, and Cissy and Joseph Patterson, to protest through their editorial columns, which, as Roosevelt knew, few people read. And because his routine contacts with the press were so pleasant, they often presented his policies in a favorable light. Photogra-

phers never showed him in awkward positions, alighting from cars, being carried up steps. Cartoonists gave a generally sturdy appearance to a president whose legs were no thicker than a man's wrist.

Underlying Roosevelt's confident handling of the media was his clear perception of what their role in a democratic system ought to be. He saw the presidency as a great clearinghouse of information and ideas, which he must collect from the people, sift, refine, and communicate to them again, thereby completing the vital informational circuit on which democracy depended. The media could help, but must not obstruct this process. About the radio and the moving pictures Roosevelt had few qualms: through both he could talk directly to the people. But the press was different, since reporters, in the employ of conservative publishers tied to business advertisers, often "interpreted" his remarks or slanted their dispatches against his administration. (Reporters' and editors' heated denials of such charges produced some of the bitterest clashes between Roosevelt and the Washington correspondents.) Roosevelt's hatred of "interpretation"—that is, versions of events other than his own—erupted most violently in his denunciations of newspaper columnists, who presumed regularly and authoritatively to comment on national affairs. How could columnists or, for that matter, reporters or editors hope to approach his own profound understanding of national and world events, since his sources of information were infinitely superior to theirs and since he possessed a "sixth sense" enabling him to understand what the American people were thinking?

Such assumptions and attitudes made Roosevelt a baffling opponent for sections of the media, but they did not reduce the effectiveness of a man whose virtuosity in this area of presidential politics was, and is likely to remain, unsurpassed.

Leo Rosten's *The Washington Correspondents* (New York: Harcourt, Brace, 1937), an account of Roosevelt's initial impact on reporters, will never be bettered. James E. Pollard's *The Presidents and the Press* (New York: Macmillan Co., 1947) carries Rosten's account through to 1945, though without the benefit of *The Complete Presidential Press Conferences of Franklin D. Roosevelt*, 25 vols. (New York: Da Capo Press, 1972). Graham J. White's *FDR and the Press* (Chicago: University of Chicago Press, 1979) examines Roosevelt's relations with owners as well as reporters, evaluates press treatment of his administration, and interprets his attitudes within the wider context of his beliefs about the presidency. Several of Roosevelt's fireside chats are included in Samuel I. Rosenman, ed., *The Public Papers and Addresses of Franklin D. Roosevelt*, 5 vols. (New York: Random House, 1938).

GRAHAM J. WHITE

See also Death of FDR; Early, Stephen Tyree; Fireside Chats; Hassett, William D.; Hearst, William Randolph; Lippmann, Walter; McCormick, Robert Rutherford; Office of the Censorship; Office of the Presidency; Office of War Information; Opinion Polls; Pegler, Westbrook; Photographs; Speech Writing

Niebuhr, Reinhold

(21 June 1892–1 June 1971)

Christian theologian and political thinker. A minister's son born in Wright City, Missouri, Reinhold Niebuhr grew up in the Protestant church. He studied at Elmhurst College in Illinois, then at Eden Theological Seminary in St. Louis, and finally at Yale University where he received his degree in 1914. Ordained as a minister the following year, he accepted the pastorate of Bethel Church in Detroit. In the city of Henry Ford, Niebuhr saw the abuses of capitalism and identified himself and his religion with the struggles of the working class. In 1928 he left Detroit to become a professor at Union Theological Seminary in New York. There he joined the Socialist party and became the nation's leading spokesman for a radical Christianity dedicated to social justice.

During the next two decades, Niebuhr's political views, especially in relation to Franklin Roosevelt and liberalism, went through great change. In the 1932 election, Niebuhr denounced both parties as instruments of the ruling class, and in 1935 together with several cohorts, he founded *Radical Religion,* a journal of politics and society from a Marxist Christian perspective. In the 1936 election Niebuhr again disdained both major parties in favor of Norman Thomas's Socialist party. During Roosevelt's second term, however, the growing threat of European fascism and a greater appreciation for the liberal gains of the New Deal raised Niebuhr's estimation of the president, and Niebuhr drifted away from Marxist doctrine. His break from the Socialist party came in 1940 when he publicly supported Roosevelt's reelection because he believed Roosevelt's war preparedness was necessary and he now viewed FDR to be the only protection from domestic reaction. During the war, Niebuhr's admiration for Roosevelt's pragmatic politics grew, and after Roosevelt's death Niebuhr became the champion of a philosophy of Christian realism with Franklin Roosevelt as his model. Niebuhr, still not content with either major political party, helped to form in 1948 the Americans for Democratic Action, which he viewed as an organization for advancing Roosevelt's practical liberalism at home and opposing the spread of communism abroad. During his long life, Niebuhr wrote many works on theology and politics and was well-known as a major twentieth-century philosopher and the leading exponent of Christian realism in politics.

Niebuhr's own writings are too numerous to list. Two worthwhile political biographies of Niebuhr are Paul Merkley, *Reinhold Niebuhr: A Political Account* (Montreal: McGill-Queen's University Press, 1975) and Ronald H. Stone, *Reinhold Niebuhr: Prophet to Politicians* (Nashville: Abingdon Press, 1972).

See also Thomas, Norman Mattoon

Niles, David K.

(23 November 1892?–28 September 1952)

Perhaps no key White House adviser to Franklin Roosevelt is less well known than David K. Niles. Friend and associate of Louis D. Brandeis, Felix Frankfurter, and Harry Hopkins (one journalist called him "Harry Hopkins' Harry Hopkins"), Niles functioned in a wide array of activities for the president between 1935 and 1945. Although officially detailed to Harry Hopkins, first as federal emergency relief administrator in Massachusetts, later as Works Progress Administration (WPA) assistant, and then, in 1938, as aid to the secretary of commerce, Niles roamed in and out of the White House on numerous assignments from the president. He did not receive an official appointment as special administrative assistant to the president, however, until 1942. Chiefly concerned with civil rights, immigration, and welfare, he also marshaled political support for the president, collected major campaign contributions, and served as a political liaison with party functionaries.

His closeness to Brandeis, Frankfurter, and Hopkins resulted in his involvement with the most sensitive aspects of Roosevelt's policies. Moreoover, the president's respect for him allowed him to work sometimes in tandem with Frankfurter, and other times by himself, honeycombing the government with his own protégés. Niles, who played an important part in every Democratic presidential convention from 1928 through 1952, was a leader in the third-term "draft Roosevelt" movement, and was an almost daily political adviser and consultant during the 1940 and 1944 election campaigns, exerted an influence upon government far in excess of what his official titles might suggest. Writing in 1983, Abram L. Sachar of Brandeis University, wondered "how a man with such impact on White House policy could have remained so obscure."

Born in Baltrementz, a Polish part of Russia, to Ascher and Sophie Neyhus, the young David grew up in the slums of North Boston. He attended the Boston Latin School but limited finances prevented him from going on to college. Before he matured his parents changed the family name to Niles. As a young man, he worked in Filene's department store in Boston and then associated himself with David Coleman of the Ford Hall Forum, which sponsored free lectures on political subjects. Beginning in 1924, when Niles campaigned for Robert La Follette on the Progressive ticket for the presidency, he always managed to make his presence felt in the political arena. In 1928 he rallied independent voters for Al Smith, and in 1932 he did the same for Franklin D. Roosevelt. His efforts were then rewarded with an appointment as assistant to Harry Hopkins in distributing relief in Massachusetts, and in 1935 he joined his boss in Washington. Even before Niles started working with the WPA, Harold Ickes noted the Bostonian's presence during important political and legislative discussions with Roosevelt.

In the White House, Niles's varied assignments included dealing with politicos, collecting an alleged $500,000 campaign contribution from United Mine Workers' president John L. Lewis in 1936, working with Sidney Hillman and other labor leaders, dispersing federal patronage (he distributed 100,000 census jobs in 1940), and serving as a generally useful factotum for the president. Niles, whom FDR once described as having a "passion for anonymity," was so secretive about his work, however, that he avoided contact with the media, and contemporaries rarely saw his name in print.

After Roosevelt's death, Niles remained with Harry S Truman as adviser on minority affairs. As had Roosevelt, Truman used him on many assignments that never received widespread publicity, such as relations with the Jewish community on issues affecting Palestine and the displaced persons.

Niles retired as special administrative assistant in 1951 and died of cancer in 1952. In its obituary, the *New York Times* observed, "Facts always have been in short supply for those seeking to talk or write about David K. Niles, a man who lingered in and just out of the limelight for a quarter of a century."

The literature on David Niles is thin, and the few sources extant differ on the date of his birth. Abram Sachar, who has possession of the Niles Mss., wrote in *The Redemption of the Unwanted* (New York: St. Martin's, 1983) that he was born in 1890; George Q. Flynn, on the other hand, in the biographical sketch of Niles in the *Dictionary of American Biography* supp. five, 1951–55, ed. John A. Garraty (New York: Charles Scribner's Sons, 1977), cites the year as 1892. Aside from these references, the only other thoughtful analysis of Niles is in Alfred Steinberg, "Mr. Truman's Mystery Man," *Saturday Evening Post* 222 (24 December 1949):24, 69–70. (The Harry Hopkins quote is from Steinberg.) The *New York Times's* obituary of Niles was published on 29 September 1952.

LEONARD DINNERSTEIN

See also Jews

Nimitz, Chester William

(24 February 1885–20 February 1966)

An American naval officer, commander in chief in World War II of the Pacific fleet and Pacific Ocean areas, Chester W. Nimitz was born in Fredericksburg, Texas, and graduated from the U.S. Naval Academy in 1905.

Appointed chief of the Bureau of Navigation in 1939, Rear Admiral Nimitz advised President Roosevelt on the selection of officers for top navy posts. In early 1941 the president offered him command of the Pacific fleet. Nimitz begged off, not wanting to be jumped over the heads of his many seniors. In December, however, after the Japanese raid on Pearl Harbor, the president ordered him to take command, and Nimitz did so on the last day of 1941.

In March 1944, Admiral Nimitz, in Washington for a conference, joined admirals Ernest J. King and William D. Leahy at the White House to discuss new strategic decisions with President Roosevelt and get his approval. The following July, directly after being nominated for a fourth presidential term, Roosevelt, accompanied by Leahy, visited Pearl Harbor, ostensibly to discuss strategy with Nimitz and General Douglas MacArthur, but more probably to display himself before the electorate in his role as commander in chief of U.S. armed forces.

In March 1945, five weeks before the president's death, Nimitz lunched and discussed strategy at the White House with Roosevelt and Secretary of the Navy James Forrestal. On 2 September 1945, on board the battleship *Missouri,* wearing the five stars of a fleet admiral, he signed the instrument of Japanese surrender as representative of the United States. After the war, he served a term as chief of naval operations.

See Edwin P. Hoyt, *How They Won the War in the Pacific: Nimitz and His Admirals* (New York: Weybright & Talley, 1970), E. B. Potter, *Nimitz* (Annapolis, Md.: Naval Institute Press, 1976), and Frank A. Driskill and Dede W. Casad, *Chester W. Nimitz: Admiral of the Hills* (Austin, Texas: Eakin Press, 1983).

E. B. POTTER

Nisei

See Internment of Japanese Americans

Non-Partisan League

See Dubinsky, David; Hillman, Sidney; Lewis, John Llewellyn

Norris, George William

(11 July 1861–2 September 1944)

Congressman (1903–13) and senator (1913–43) from Nebraska. George W. Norris was born on a farm in Sandusky County, Ohio, educated at Baldwin University (now Baldwin Wallace College) in Ohio in 1877–78 and Northern Indiana Normal School and Business Institute (now Valparaiso University) where in 1883 he received the LL.B. degree. He first came to national attention as a congressman in 1910 when he sparked the insurgent revolt against the power of the speaker, Joseph G. Cannon, and again as a senator when in 1917 as one of the "little group of willful men" he opposed America's entrance into the First World War. During the 1920s, he became an outspoken advocate of farm relief, the rights of labor, efficient use of the nation's natural resources, and the direct election of presidents. Following the death of Robert M. La Follette in 1925, Norris emerged as the outstanding progressive in the Congress.

George William Norris, 1942. Artist: Jo Davidson. (National Portrait Gallery, Smithsonian Institution. Gift of Mr. and Mrs. James Louis Robertson and John P. Robertson.)

Franklin D. Roosevelt's election in 1932 dramatically helped change George W. Norris's senatorial career. Alienated from the Republican administrations in the 1920s, he became during the New Deal years an influential and venerable figure whose advice and presence were welcome as never before in the White House. Both men were attracted to each other and were compatible in the views they espoused and the causes they championed. Roosevelt benefited from Norris's support and Norris saw some of his dreams come true during Roosevelt's presidency.

As early as December 1930, when asked to name a Democrat who might appeal to western progressives and Republicans, Norris named Franklin D. Roosevelt. In March 1932, at a conference of progressives, Norris said that the "country needs another Roosevelt." He previously had turned down a request to consider leading a third-party campaign in 1932 for the same reason. And according to Huey Long, Norris influenced his decision to have the Louisiana delegation endorse Roosevelt at the Chicago convention.

Once the Democratic convention nominated Roosevelt, Norris, the first of the progressive Republicans to endorse the New York governor, announced that he would also speak in his behalf. In addition, he served as chairman of the National Progressive League for Roosevelt. Norris campaigned for Roosevelt, beginning in Philadelphia on 17 October 1932 and ending in Los Angeles on the Saturday before the election.

Roosevelt in turn reciprocated. After Norris introduced the candidate before an enthusiastic crowd in his hometown of McCook, Roosevelt in a remarkable tribute, something he never extended to another living person, said, "I honor myself in honoring you," and noted Norris's integrity, unselfishness, courage, and consistency, concluding with the statement that "he stands forth as the very perfect gentle knight of American progressive ideals."

In January 1933 the president-elect invited Norris to accompany him on an inspection tour of Muscle Shoals. And a month before his inauguration, Roosevelt, at Warm Springs, Georgia, outlined for newspaper reporters a proposal calling for the development of the entire Tennessee River watershed. He called, in effect, for the realization of George W. Norris's dream for public ownership and operation of the federal facilities at Muscle Shoals, involving the multiple-purpose development of the river valley.

Introduced in the Senate by Norris on the first day of the Seventy-third Congress, the measure creating the Tennessee Valley Authority was signed by Roosevelt on 18 May. After five previous failures beginning in April 1922, Norris had succeeded in introducing a Muscle Shoals measure that became law. The measure Roosevelt signed was the only bill enacted during the first hundred days of the New Deal that was not immediately and directly related to the grave economic crisis engulfing the nation.

Throughout the rest of his tenure, Norris enjoyed presidential endorsement for most of the measures he introduced, though in not every instance, such as Norris' call for further regional authorities, was Roosevelt's support translated into congressional approval. In turn, Norris endorsed most of the New Deal. He reluctantly supported the president's proposal for expanding membership on the Supreme Court, endorsed most of Roosevelt's appointees, shifted his views on foreign policy from that of reluctant isolationist to a reluctant internationalist, and favored Roosevelt's reelection in 1936, 1940, and 1944. When he disagreed, he usually blamed or criticized someone else in the administration: Postmaster General and Democratic National Committee chairman James A. Farley for blatant patronage and lack of interest in furthering civil service, and Secretary of the Interior Harold L. Ickes for seeking to absorb TVA into his department and for opposition to the creation of a Columbia Valley Authority.

In turn, Norris rarely went over the head of a government official to appeal directly to the president. He did this only to get Public Works Authority officials to release funds for the further construction of the Tri-County project, a broad-based multiple-purpose TVA-like project in Nebraska. In each instance, Norris's appeal resulted in a prompt and favorable response.

Seeking a fifth term in the Senate in 1936, Norris ran for reelection as an independent candidate, dropping his affiliation with the Republican party and endorsing the New Deal and the president. Roosevelt in his reelection bid in October campaigned in Omaha, endorsing Norris as "one of the major prophets of America" whose candidacy "transcends state and party lines." Roosevelt's reelection projected Norris to the forefront of national attention.

Before returning to Washington for the inauguration ceremonies, Norris was on hand for the convening of the first session of the Nebraska unicameral legislature whose creation he championed in 1934, when he stumped the state endorsing the amendment creating it. Roosevelt was the first president to be inducted into office under the terms of the Twentieth Amendment, introduced by Norris in the Congress in the 1920s and ratified in 1933. It changed the date of inauguration from 4 March to 20 January and in the process eliminated the lame-duck session of Congress. The president had invited Senator and Mrs. Norris to sit near him when he reviewed the inaugural parade from the stands in front of the White House. Norris was the guest of honor of the inaugural committee and participated in the numerous social activities surrounding the event.

In 1940, with animosity to the president and his policies becoming increasingly evident in the nation, Norris played a significant role in Roosevelt's bid for a third term. Once again he helped organize a committee, this time called the National Committee of Independent Voters for Roosevelt and Wallace. He served as honorary chairman but devoted his major effort to campaigning for the president, first by delivering a radio address on a nationwide hookup on 15 October. Shortly thereafter, he left Washington to tour the Pacific Coast states championing the cause of public power and lambasting the Republican candidate, Wendell Willkie, former chief executive officer of a large public utility holding company opposed to TVA.

In his last years as a member of the Senate, Norris was distressed at the bitterness of the opposition to Roosevelt and the New Deal increasingly evident in the Congress. He nevertheless continued his support of the administration as the nation prepared for and then became involved in World War II. And he played a role in bringing to the president's attention the necessity of locating war plants in mid-America, a plea to which Roosevelt favorably responded.

Roosevelt, unable to leave Washington during Norris's campaign for reelection in 1942, endorsed him by repeating the remarks he uttered during the 1936 campaign, and after Norris's defeat, the president suggested several jobs in government. Norris turned them all down and returned to his home in McCook, where he finally accepted a post as special consultant to the State Department to advise on matters pertaining to the peace.

In 1944, unable to accept an active position in Roosevelt's campaign for reelection, Norris served as honorary chairman of the National Citizens Political Action Committee and announced his support of the president. On 28 August 1944, he suffered a cerebral hemorrhage. He never fully regained consciousness. Roosevelt, upon learning of Norris's illness, immediately sent a get-well telegram. Mrs. Norris read it to him and reported that "a pressure of his fingers and a smile told me he knew he had a message from his President." Norris died shortly thereafter.

Richard Lowitt, *George W. Norris: The Triumph of a Progressive, 1933–1944* (Urbana: University of Ilinois Press, 1978) is a soundly researched volume that carefully examines Norris's career during the era of Franklin D. Roosevelt. George W. Norris, *Fighting Liberal* (New York: MacMillan Co., 1945) was written by Norris after his return to McCook largely from memory with the assistance of James E. Lawrence, editor of the *Lincoln Star* and his campaign manager in 1936 and 1942. It was completed shortly before Norris's death. The paperback edition (New York: Collier Books, 1961) contains an excellent introductory essay by Arthur M. Schlesinger, Jr., delineating the liberalism of George W. Norris. David E. Lilienthal, *The Journals of David E. Lilienthal: The TVA Years, 1939–1945* (New York: Harper & Row, 1964) provides interesting insights pertaining to Norris's continuing concern with TVA. James C. Olson, *History of Nebraska* (Lincoln: University of Nebraska Press, 1966) contains chapters that examine the state in the twentieth century and are an excellent introduction to the issues concerning Norris with regard to his home state.

RICHARD LOWITT

See also Conservation; Liberalism and Progressivism; Tennessee Valley Authority

Nye (Gerald P.) Committee

See Isolationism

O

O'Connor, Daniel Basil ("Doc")

(8 January 1892–9 March 1972)

Roosevelt's law partner and president of the National Foundation for Infantile Paralysis–March of Dimes drive against poliomyelitis. Born in Taunton, Massachusetts, in relatively humble circumstances, Basil O'Connor (he dropped the Daniel when he moved to New York and found the telephone book crowded with hundreds of "D. O'Connors") rose by dint of uncommon sagacity and untiring drive to become one of the great philanthropists of American history, responsible for raising the millions of dollars that in the 1950s and 1960s led to the conquest of poliomyelitis. He first met Roosevelt during the 1920 campaign and in 1925 formed the law partnership of Roosevelt and

Basil O'Connor meeting with FDR at Warm Springs. (J. T. Holloway, Atlanta, Ga.)

O'Connor, which was dissolved in 1933 when FDR became president.

Meanwhile, interested in his partner's infirmity and his efforts to regain the use of his legs, O'Connor assisted him in incorporating the Georgia Warm Springs Foundation in 1927, of which he became treasurer and then president. Their efforts went into high gear in the 1930s when Roosevelt was president. The annual Birthday Balls on January 30 and the nationwide March of Dimes campaign were "Doc" O'Connor's inspirations, but the key to his success in fund raising was a centralized organization, run on near-military lines, with state and local chapters directing a large corps of volunteer solicitors in unceasing efforts.

O'Connor also dominated the research and rehabilitation studies supported by this largesse. When the Salk vaccine showed promise in the early 1950s, O'Connor spurned professional recommendations that it be given a ten-year field test and instead ordered a crash one-year testing program on a million children. When results proved positive, he provided funds to immunize 9 million children, starting in 1955. Five years later, Dr. Albert B. Sabin's parallel research efforts produced his live-virus oral vaccine, and the conquest of polio was complete. Few men in history can have seen their endeavors so completely and triumphantly requited. When they were commenced in the 1930s, polio claimed about forty thousand victims each year; recently the annual toll has been about thirty.

In 1944 Roosevelt, anticipating heavy postwar reconstruction and rehabilitation needs, asked O'Connor to assume the chairmanship of the American Red Cross. When he completed those duties in 1949, President Trumen conferred the Legion of Merit on him. In later years O'Connor directed the National Foundation's efforts toward research on arthritis and congenital birth defects. He was preparing for a meeting of the organization's scientific advisory committee in Phoenix in March 1972 when at age eighty he suddenly died of a heart ailment complicated by pneumonia.

A scrappy bantamweight Irishman, "one generation removed from servitude," as he once put it, O'Connor was a key member of Roosevelt's inner circle of confidential advisers, although he never held any formal appointment apart from his position at the Red Cross. One irony befell their long association. "Doc's" elder brother, Rep. John J. O'Connor, a Tammany congressman from Brooklyn and chairman of the powerful House Rules Committee, proved to be the lone casualty of Roosevelt's otherwise disastrous "purge" of conservative Democrats in 1938. Despite the brothers' closeness, this circumstance seemed never to becloud "Doc" O'Connor's relationship with Roosevelt.

O'Connor's papers are at the Roosevelt Library at Hyde Park.

See also Law Practice; Polio

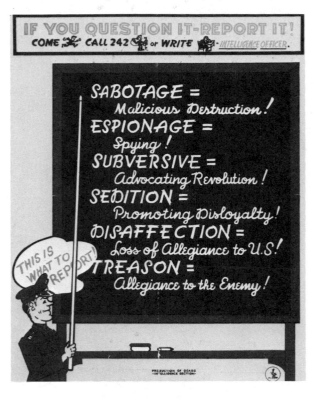

Office of Censorship

The Office of Censorship was established by Executive Order 8985 two weeks after Pearl Harbor in December 1941 under authority given to the president by the first War Powers Act. Byron Price, the fifty-year-old executive news director of Associated Press, was appointed by Roosevelt as director of the office. The president also appointed an eight-person Censorship Policy Board, consisting of the postmaster general, the librarian of Congress, and six other high government officials, to advise the director.

The purpose of the office was to carry out the provisions of the War Powers Act, which gave the government absolute discretion in the censorship of all communications with foreign governments. To this end, the office issued a series of codes of wartime practices for the press, broadcasters, the postal department, and cable and telegraph communications.

Both Price and the president were determined to avoid the excesses of censorship that had occurred during World War I under George Creel's Committee on Public Information. Price frequently said publicly that he abhorred censorship but believed that it was necessary in wartime in order to keep certain information from the enemy. Price described the duties of censors as stopping "any information which the enemy would like to have . . . [about] defense matters, shipping data, weather conditions, and details of war production." Censorship of such information was to be at point of origin rather than prior to publication. Price wrote: "Censorship of the dissemination of public information must hold unceasingly, day in and day out, to the single purpose of keeping dangerous information from the enemy. Editorial opinions and criticisms never can be brought under government restraint, and ought not to be, so long as our present form of government endures."

The emphasis was on voluntary cooperation. Radio scripts, for example, could be submitted for review, but this was not required, and very few scripts were actually submitted. There were, however, strict guidelines in the code for broadcasters as to what could and could not go over the air. The code stated that man-on-the-street interviews, special music requests, and audience-participation quiz programs should be curtailed because enemy agents could use them to send prearranged coded messages.

Mail leaving and coming into the country at border locations was watched carefully. Letters found "unacceptable" were either suppressed or delayed until it was determined they were no longer dangerous. Occasionally, sentences or paragraphs were cut away with scissors, and then the expurgated letter was allowed to be sent.

One duty of the Office of Censorship was to keep a watch on carrier pigeons. As Price explained, "There are literally millions of carrier pigeons in the United States, and many of them are almost unbelievably clever in their operations. We must be certain that they are not used to carry messages from enemy agents in the United States to associates outside the country."

There were inevitable complaints about censorship. At the time of the German breakthrough to Belgium and Luxembourg in December 1944, many newspaper writers complained that too much information was suppressed. Price defended the secrecy on the grounds that it was necessary to prevent the enemy from knowing the nature of the proposed Allied counterattack. The governor of Alaska, Ernest Gruening, frequently complained that censorship delayed a great deal of mail to servicemen stationed there and that certain items were snipped out of his copies of *Newsweek* magazine.

The office was financed in its early days by a $7.5 million allocation from the Emergency Fund for the President. In the subsequent years of its existence, Congress appropriated $26.5 million in 1943, $29.6 million in 1944, and $29.7 million in 1945.

The Office of Censorship went out of business on a directive from President Truman in August 1945 and was formally abolished by executive order in November. The mail and other printed matter the office had collected were given to the Library of Congress and the National Archives.

Most of the general literature on censorship ignores wartime activity, except that which occurred in World War I. A good description of the activities of the Office of Censorship related to broadcasting can be found in Erik Barnouw, *The Golden Web: A History of Broadcasting in the United States, Volume II, 1933–1953* (New York: Oxford University Press, 1968). Clinton Rossiter, in *Constitutional Dictatorship: Crisis Government in the Modern Democracies* (New York: Harcourt, Brace & World, 1948), discusses the Office of Censorship in his chapter on the Second World War. The best available source for the office's operations is *A Report on the Office of Censorship* (Washington, D.C.: U.S. Government Printing Office, 1945). For Byron Price's views, see his articles, "Governmental Censorship in War-Time," in the *American Political Science Review* 36 (1942):837–49, and "The Censor Defends the Censorship," in the *New York Times Magazine,* 11 February 1945, pp. 11+.

PAUL L. MURPHY

Office of Price Administration

See Henderson, Leon; War Mobilization

Office of Production Management

See Hillman, Sidney; War Mobilization; War Production Board

Office of Scientific Research and Development

The Office of Scientific Research and Development (OSRD) was the administrative organization that coordinated the invention and production of new weapons during World War II. It was initiated by civilian scientists who believed that the development of new weapons was too important to be left to the military. Organized by Executive Order 8807 in June 1941, it altered the relationship between weapons and tactics, between the military and industry, between science and war. It was the experiential foundation upon which the military-industrial-scientific complex was built during the cold war.

OSRD reversed the process of weapons acquisition. In all previous wars scientists had stood by, ready to respond to military requests on the assumption that the armed services would know what they needed. But the men who convinced Roosevelt to establish OSRD argued that the military commanders did not know enough about the state of modern sci-

ence to ask for the weapons they needed. Scientists who were made familiar with the military situation would be in a better position to recommend research and development strategies than military officers who might have a passing familiarity with science.

When OSRD was created, it superceded and absorbed the National Defense Research Committee (NDRC), which had been organized for the same purposes in June 1940. But the NDRC alone did not have sufficient independence to carry out the tasks its members considered essential: to expedite procurement and to coordinate its research with research being carried on by armed services and the National Advisory Committee for Aeronautics.

The founding fathers of the NDRC and OSRD were academic, foundation, and industrial executives. Vannevar Bush, the most influential member of the group, an electrical engineer trained at Tufts University and the Massachusetts Institute of Technology (MIT), was president of the Carnegie Institution of Washington, D.C. He served as the first chairman of the NDRC and thereafter as the director of OSRD. James B. Conant, a chemist, who was president of Harvard University, took over as chairman of NDRC and served as Bush's deputy throughout the war. Frank B. Jewett, an electrical engineer, whose influence in Washington was important in obtaining President Roosevelt's support for these new, powerful science-dominated organizations, was president of the National Academy of Sciences and president of the Bell Telephone Laboratories. Prof. Richard C. Tolman of the California Institute of Technology, a physicist, served as vice-chairman of NDRC. On the list of members of NDRC, reconstituted as the advisory committee of OSRD, were Karl T. Compton, the president of MIT, the commissioner of patents, and an array of high-ranking military personnel representing the army and navy.

The research and development work sponsored and supervised by the various divisions of OSRD/NDRC covered the spectrum of war gadgetry from the atomic bomb to insecticides. The organization dealt with the problems of antisubmarine, amphibious, land, sea, and air warfare. It developed navigation devices, radar, radar countermeasures, rockets, proximity fuses, and flamethrowers. It initiated basic research on antimalarial drugs, blood, blood substitutes, penicillin, and rodenticides. It invented a new medical field—aviation medicine—and a new area of strategic studies—operations research. It was, in a word, a revolutionary organization whose legacy was best expressed by Irwin Stewart, when he wrote in August 1947 in the epilogue of his official history of OSRD:

> The action of the 80th Congress in creating the Department of National Defense should simplify the coordination of research for military purposes. The Research and Development Board of the new Department, with its committees and panels, provides a means for introducing civilian scientists into military planning. There seems reason to hope that the experiences of OSRD may thus be of continuing benefit to the country

in its preparation for an eventuality which we all hope may never transpire.

A concise and readable account of the results of OSRD's labors (the weapons, the gadgets, and the bomb) can be found in James Phinney Baxter, III, *Scientists against Time* (Boston: Little, Brown & Co., 1946). An administrative history of OSRD is also available: Irvin G. Stewart, *Organizing Scientific Research for War* Salem, N.Y.: Ayer, 1980). However, to understand the ideas that inspired the organization and that created the foundation for its postwar legacy, it is necessary to read Vannevar Bush, *Science the Endless Frontier* (Salem, N.Y.: Ayer, 1980).

MARTIN J. SHERWIN

See also Atomic Bomb; War Mobilization

Office of the Presidency

When Franklin D. Roosevelt died in 1945, the modern presidency had been firmly established. In the Roosevelt years, the White House became the focus and vital center of national government. Roosevelt expanded the White House staff, created the Executive Office of the President, and transformed the presidency from an umpire and administrative officer to initiator of policy leadership and spokesman for the national interest. Since his presidency, Congress has routinely expected presidents to present an agenda of policy proposals for its consideration.

Did the transformation of the presidency come about because of the crises Roosevelt confronted or because of his style and character? The answer is both. The presidency expanded because of the devastating challenge to the economic system and the threats to national security posed by Hitler and the Japanese attack on Pearl Harbor. "War is the mother of executive aggrandizement," James Madison once said; during the Second World War, the American presidency became an enduringly powerful institution. Together the crises of depression and war called for unprecedented and sustained national political leadership and governmental activity. Plainly, however, Roosevelt's spirited enthusiasm, his understanding of the office and its promise, and his skilled use of the presidency as both a moral and political pulpit contributed to the evolution of the modern presidency.

Franklin Roosevelt came to the White House well prepared to be an active president and a strong national leader. He had impressive administrative and political experience. He had been editor of the *Crimson* at Harvard and had cut his political teeth as a reformist New York state senator. For over seven years, he was assistant secretary of the navy in the Woodrow Wilson administration. He ran as his party's nominee for the vice-presidency in 1920 and served two successful terms as governor of New York.

As assistant secretary of the navy (1913–20), FDR functioned as the number two executive in the navy and worked closely with the White House. Like his cousin Theodore, Franklin Roosevelt was a strong advocate of a "big navy." Even before the First World War broke out, he devoted himself to strength-

FDR's Use of Presidential Powers, 1933–1945

DATE	SELECTED PROCLAMATIONS AND EXECUTIVE ORDERS	VETOES	PARDONS
1933			
9 March	declared bank holiday; embargoed gold and silver shipments		
27 March	abolished Federal Farm Board		
16 June		amendment to Federal Farm Loan Act	
10 August	directed federal contractors to conform to NRA codes		
29 August	modified embargo on gold exports and sales		
18 October	established Commodity Credit Corporation		
23 October	revised NRA retail code		
21 December	ordered Treasury to buy all U.S. silver at 64.5 cents per ounce		
24 December			1,500 World War I violators of Selective Service Act
30 December	relinquished federal control of state banks not members of federal reserve		
1934			
31 January	value of dollar fixed at 59.06 cents		
2 February	export/import bank established		
27 February	NRA board of review established		
1 March		relief bill	
5 March	excluded from federal contracts businesses not complying with NRA codes		
28 May	prohibited sale of arms and munitions to Bolivia and Paraguay		
29 June	prohibited shipment of arms to Cuba		
30 June	abolished NRA board of review		
9 August	recalled all silver to mints within 90 days		

FDR's Use of Presidential Powers, 1933–1945

DATE	SELECTED PROCLAMATIONS AND EXECUTIVE ORDERS	VETOES	PARDONS
10 August	waived import duties on hay and other forage		
24 August	announced reciprocal tariff treaty with Cuba		
1935			
8 February	withdrew public lands from use		
1 May	established Resettlement Administration		
11 May	established Rural Electrification Administration		
22 May		soldier's bonus	
7 June	established National Resources Committee		
26 June	established National Youth Administration		
5 October	imposed embargo on arms to Italy and Ethiopia		
6 October	warned citizens against travel on Italian or Ethiopian ships		
1936			
21 February	placed Kure Island under Navy Dept. control		
20 July	placed postmasters under civil service		
1937			
14 September	prohibited transport of war materials to China and Japan in government-owned merchant ships		
1939			
1 April	ended embargo on sales of arms to Spain		
5 September	announced U.S. neutrality		
5 September	prohibited export of arms to belligerents		
8 September	announced limited national emergency		
18 October	restricted foreign submarines from U.S. waters		

ening the navy and to instituting administrative efficiency in its operations. Once the United States entered the war, Roosevelt played an even more important administrative role and gained firsthand wartime leadership experience. He was in an excellent position to observe the mobilization of the government and the expansion of executive power and leadership in the war years.

As governor of the nation's then largest state (1929–33), Roosevelt surprised many people by demonstrating himself to be a determined and capable chief executive and a shrewd politician. He reached out to voters in person during frequent visits around the state and appealed for public support through informal radio talks, the forerunners of his White House fireside chats. He championed reform measures and successfully wrestled some of his legislative programs from a Republican-controlled legislature. More important, Roosevelt viewed the office of governor as an opportunity to provide vigorous personal, programmatic, and political leadership. His predecessor, Al Smith, had reorganized the office and left it one of the nation's strongest: Roosevelt made the governor's powers stronger yet.

FDR's gubernatorial administration was in some ways a prelude to the New Deal. Governor Roosevelt recruited able policy advisers, appointed commissions to respond to problems, exercised control over the budget, and pushed for labor, health, and relief legislation. In short, he refused to accept a narrow definition of his role as governor; in this he was following in Smith's footsteps. In Albany Governor Roosevelt was convinced government had a responsibility to compensate for the incapacities of individuals and to remedy deficiencies in the economic system. After some hesitation, he was ready to experiment vigorously with programs to combat the depression. "In these programs," writes Frank Freidel, Roosevelt "was not only establishing himself as a most resourceful governor, but was also directly challenging President Hoover."

Herbert Hoover may have had a genius for entrepreneurial success in the business world and nobody doubted his effectiveness as secretary of commerce, but he was not well suited to the presidency. He disliked politics and he disliked the office's demands for symbolic leadership and dramatization. "This is not a showman's job," he declared. "I will not step out of character." The result was that he often seemed indifferent or uncaring. Hoover was a man of enormous integrity, and he worked extremely hard as president. But he displayed little flare, little passion, little compassion. He was a worrier and a pessimist. In the end he said, "This office is a compound hell." Although finally he realized that government had to respond to the depression, his response was timid, grudging, and late.

In the 1932 election, Roosevelt deftly campaigned on Hoover's left *and* right. He did not win because of any bold conception of the office of the presidency; probably any Democratic candidate could have defeated Hoover in the gloomy atmosphere of 1932. But where Hoover was cold, austere, remote, and doctrinaire, Roosevelt was warm, personal, charming, and uncommonly self-confident. He may have lacked depth, but he had breadth. He liked politics, loved people, and yearned to be in the center of things. He accepted the inevitability of change and seemed to have no fear of the future. He was confident of his own strength and ability to lead, to manage, and to succeed. He was ready to use the power of government to deal with the crisis of the Great Depression.

From his first day in office, Roosevelt began to change the presidency. He forcefully directed his enlarged staff of full- and part-time workers to reach out for new ideas, prepare legislation, enlist political support, and mobilize popular opinion. "This Nation asks for action, and action now," Roosevelt proclaimed at his 4 March 1933 inauguration. When he called Congress into special session five days later, Congress immediately passed an Emergency Banking Act and Roosevelt signed the bill the same day; the whole process took less than eight hours. The important point is that the bill was prepared and offered under presidential auspices. The Republicans joined in calling for strong presidential leadership in the great economic crisis. Roosevelt provided that leadership then and later.

So the hundred days of action began. In the next three months Congress and the nation witnessed a barrage of new ideas and experimental programs. The first days of the New Deal were permeated by the mood of emergency. It was natural for FDR to look back to the last great national emergency—the First World War. He wanted broad executive power, Roosevelt said, "to wage a war against the emergency as great as the power that would be given me if we were in fact invaded by a foreign foe." The war against the depression was waged with the devices of the Wilson war years—the expansion of executive power and the creation of a series of powerful executive agencies. Many New Deal agencies resembled the executive agencies created by Wilson in the First World War— the Agricultural Adjustment Administration resembled the Food Administration, the National Recovery Administration resembled the War Industries Board, and the Tennessee Valley Authority resembled the Emergency Fleet Corporation and the U.S. Grain Corporation, which were the first U.S. government corporations. These great national agencies, born of war and depression and later revived and nurtured in the Second World War, left a powerful and enduring mark on the nature of the American presidency.

During the hundred days of 1933, Roosevelt sent fifteen messages to Congress, delivered ten major addresses, guided at least fifteen significant laws to enactment, launched his fireside chats, held press conferences, and conducted endless cabinet and advisory group meetings. It was the most concentrated period of legislative activity in American history; it was also the most intense period of presidential influence in the legislative process. Roosevelt's energy and initiatives dazzled the nation and gave it hope in a time of despair.

Roosevelt in this first year and even through his

FDR's Use of Presidential Powers, 1933–1945

DATE	SELECTED PROCLAMATIONS AND EXECUTIVE ORDERS	VETOES	PARDONS
10 December	extended $10 million credit to Finland for purchase of U.S. supplies		
1940			
6 April		bill requiring deportation of alien drug addicts	
10 April	prohibited transactions in Norwegian and Danish credits and assets		
11 May	announced neutrality in war between Germany and the Netherlands, Belgium, and Luxembourg		
11 May	prohibited transactions in Dutch, Belgian, and Luxembourg credits and assets		
10 June	announced neutrality in war between Italy and France and Great Britain		
2 July	prohibited export of war materials except by State Dept. license		
26 September	limited export of scrap iron and steel		
15 November	announced neutrality in war between Italy and Greece		
20 December	established Office of Production Management		
1941			
19 March	established National Defense Mediation Board		
7 April	formed United Service Organizations for National Defense		
5 May	increased production of heavy bomber aircraft		
27 May	announced unlimited national emergency		

FDR's Use of Presidential Powers, 1933–1945

DATE	SELECTED PROCLAMATIONS AND EXECUTIVE ORDERS	VETOES	PARDONS
9 June	ordered army to seize Inglewood, Calif., aviation plant after wildcat strike		
14 June	prohibited transactions in U.S. credits and assets by Germany and Italy		
16 June	ordered State Dept. to close German and Italian consulates in U.S.		
7 July	blacklisted 1,800 Latin American firms and individuals for aiding Germany and Italy		
26 July	nationalized Philippine armed forces for duration of emergency		
26 July	prohibited transactions in U.S. credits and assets by China and Japan		
9 August	established Economic Defense Board		
24 October	established Office of Facts and Figures		
28 October	established Lend-Lease Administration		
18 December	appointed commission to investigate Pearl Harbor attack		
18 December	established Office of Defense Transportation		
19 December	established Office of Censorship		
28 December	pledged support to the Philippines		
1942			
12 January	established National War Labor Board		
16 January	established War Production Board		
7 February	established War Shipping Administration		

first term was so caught up with the exigencies of the economic crisis that he was less concerned with the theory and structure of government than with getting laws passed and starting new programs. His inclination was to create new agencies, deliberately bypassing older departments in the process. Roosevelt wanted fast results, new blood, and flexibility. The result was creativity, activity, and a measure of chaos; he presided imperturbably over a turbulent Washington scene. Rexford Guy Tugwell, a member of the original brains trust, called it "a renaissance spring," a "time of rebirth after a dark age." If Hoover's presidency had lacked motion in the face of crisis, Roosevelt's lacked coherence and direction. But as dozens of new agencies were created, more and more governmental leaders looked to Roosevelt and the White House for guidance and leadership.

When Roosevelt entered the office, he was aware that the physical arrangements and tools for presidential planning and coordination were inadequate. He had insufficient assistance; departments and agencies needed to be strengthened. But the emergencies facing the country were so urgent they had to be met with the means at hand; only later could he turn to improving the management capabilities of the office of the presidency and the executive branch.

Roosevelt changed the size and added to the responsibilities of the White House staff. Hoover had had only two professional-level personal assistants, although legislation at the end of his term provided for more. Roosevelt used all the aides he was entitled to and appointed other advisers to posts in assorted departments. Thus members of the early brains trust received departmental appointments—Raymond Moley as assistant secretary of state and Rexford Guy Tugwell as assistant secretary of agriculture. In fact, many officials in the cabinet or subcabinet departmental positions served as White House aides.

President Roosevelt's style was sometimes referred to as "administration by conversation." He had a tremendous capacity for detail and a hunger for reliable information. Knowledge provided the basis for action. He relished chatting with advisers and administrators and spent several hours a day engrossed in conversations with small groups of aides or cabinet officers plotting his next initiative or trying to compromise some administrative dispute. No other president had ever brought such a galaxy of talent to Washington. Many were persons of independent stature, not mere functionaries who lived only by virtue of presidential favor. Roosevelt drew on them as individuals, but he seldom turned to the cabinet or any other group for collective decisions. His was the deciding mind and voice. "Our Cabinet meetings are pleasant affairs" wrote Secretary of Interior Harold Ickes, "but we only skim the surface of things on routine matters."

Although FDR liked to make his own decisions, he was always experimenting—with his staff, with emergency councils, with planning boards, and with countless other makeshift administrative arrangements. Invariably small teams from FDR's advisory network were charged with drafting new proposals and seeing that plans were translated into programs, action, and results. Roosevelt liked to keep all the reins in his own hands, but his administrative style was seldom tidy or easily understood. He relished giving different people overlapping assignments and letting them compete both for governmental resources and his continued support. His favorite technique, Arthur Schlesinger, Jr., wrote "was to keep grants of authority incomplete, jurisdictions uncertain, charters overlapping." The result was a competitive theory of administration. No other method "could so reliably insure that in a large bureaucracy filled with ambitious men eager for power the decisions, and the power to make them, would remain with the President."

To mold national opinion and political support for his programs, Roosevelt began the modern use of the news media, particularly the relatively new medium of radio. He held an unprecedented number of press conferences (over seven hundred in his first two terms) to cultivate support and to derive information about opinion in the nation. In his hands, the press conferences were institutionalized as a forum in which the president placed himself before the nation (like the prime minister's question period in the House of Commons). In his famous fireside radio addresses, he entered the living rooms of ordinary Americans. His was the first prime-time media presidency. Roosevelt demonstrated that a skilled president can exercise enormous personal influence through national press and radio.

Yet the leadership of a government could not be altogether a personal matter. The longer Roosevelt was in office, the more he realized there had to be some means beyond a president's personal style to integrate policy planning and bring coherence to its execution. Roosevelt began to rely more on the Bureau of the Budget (which was still located in the Treasury Department) as a device for centralized program and policy coordination. His need for coordination was also partly met with the creation of an Executive Council in the summer of 1933. When it failed to live up to his expectations, he turned to yet another coordinating body, the National Emergency Council. For a short while, it enabled Roosevelt to gain some control over the sprawling recovery agencies and to coordinate legislative proposals from diverse points of origin within the government. Centralized clearance of this kind became essential to FDR as a means to preserve his initiative and defend his authority.

Some of the early New Deal programs, such as the Tennessee Valley Authority and the Agricultural Adjustment and National Recovery administrations, incorporated tentative elements of national planning. But Roosevelt's more liberal advisers kept searching for stronger instruments of social and economic control, and a National Resources Planning Board was established. However, planned social intervention in land use and agricultural and population distribution turned out to be more difficult than anticipated. FDR's planning boards provided neither immediate and practical economic plans nor overall policy coordination. Although Roosevelt was not a committed

FDR's Use of Presidential Powers, 1933–1945

DATE	SELECTED PROCLAMATIONS AND EXECUTIVE ORDERS	VETOES	PARDONS
9 February		bill to provide for registration of certain foreign propaganda agencies	
24 February	established National Housing Agency		
28 February	reorganized War Dept.		
11 March	established Office of Alien Property Custodian		
12 March	reorganized Navy Dept.		
18 March	established War Relocation Authority		
18 April	established War Manpower Commission		
13 June	established Office of War Information		
13 June	military order established Office of Strategic Services		
2 July	military order established military commission to try eight captured German saboteurs		
17 September	provided for coordination of rubber program		
2 December	established Petroleum Administration for War		
5 December	centralized war food policies under Agriculture Dept.		
1943			
5 February	established interdepartmental committee to consider cases of subversive activities by federal employees		
9 February	established 48-hour work week in war plants		
19 April	established Solid Fuels Administration for War		

FDR's Use of Presidential Powers, 1933–1945

DATE	SELECTED PROCLAMATIONS AND EXECUTIVE ORDERS	VETOES	PARDONS
1 May	ordered secretary of interior to seize coal mines		
27 May	established Office of War Mobilization		
27 May	banned war contractors from racial discrimination		
15 July	established Office of Economic Warfare		
25 September	established Foreign Economic Administration		
1 November	again ordered secretary of interior to seize coal mines		
27 December	ordered U.S. Army to seize railroads		
1944			
22 January	established War Refugee Board		
3 October	expanded OWM to Office of War Mobilization and Reconversion		

Keynesian (he was committed to no single theory or program), in his second term he relied more on government influence over taxing and spending than on planning controls to restore production and employment. Thus, he pointed the way to increased presidential direction of the national economy through diverse fiscal and monetary measures. The realization of institutionalized national economic influence awaited the Employment Act of 1946 and the establishment of the President's Council of Economic Advisors.

In 1936, Roosevelt established the President's Committee on Administrative Management. This group's report recommended the consolidation of agencies, the establishment of an economic staff in the White House, and the development of ways to enhance the president's control over career civil servants. The committee also urged the strengthening of the presidency by the addition of six senior administrative assistants, a clearinghouse planning agency, and other centralizing and streamlining reforms.

President Roosevelt realized reorganization was a key to governmental effectiveness. When he sent his first reorganization plan to Congress, he said, "This Plan is concerned with the practical necessity of reducing the number of agencies which report directly to the President and also of giving the President assistance in dealing with the entire Executive Branch by modern administrative management." Congress delayed and eventually watered down his plans, but a Reorganization Act did go into effect on 1 July 1939. A presidential executive order a few weeks later implemented the act and established the Executive Office of the President.

Although the establishment of the office was not widely noticed at the time, it confirmed the growing importance of the White House staff, the need for policy review groups at that level, and the reality that presidents would become more important in national economic and domestic policy planning. It provided for an expanded staff, for the shifting of the Budget Bureau to the Executive Office, for a National Resources Planning Board, for a liaison office for personnel management, and for an office of government reports.

The creation of the Executive Office of the President signaled that FDR wanted to place major reliance upon top-level coordination of the executive branch from his own office rather than decentralizing responsibilities to cabinet officers. The cabinet was to be subordinate, as individuals and as a body, to overall administrative leadership from the White House. FDR believed that the presidency itself had to be strengthened if the nation was to meet its present and future tests.

As Roosevelt concluded these reorganization efforts, he was forced to devote increased attention to strengthening the country's defense preparedness. The war in Europe nourished and enlarged the presidency even more than had the Great Depression. Indeed, it is often noted that it was during the Second World War that the modern presidency was created. Congress delegated sweeping powers to the president; the consequence was an enduring erosion of legislative authority. The necessities of war forced the greatest changes; for example, the war brought the application of Keynesian deficit financing on a scale never possible as domestic policy during the New Deal.

Roosevelt took an unprecedented role in the conduct of the war and in war diplomacy, even greater than had those active and able wartime presidents, Lincoln and Wilson.

Although Cordell Hull was an influential secretary of state, important matters were sent to the White House. From time to time, Roosevelt bypassed established State Department authorities and procedures. For example, he used Harry Hopkins as a personal emissary in dealing with Stalin, and the ultimate decisions on war strategy and the future of the postwar world were not made by foreign ministers and professional diplomats but by the chiefs of state themselves. The cordial personal cooperative relationship between Roosevelt and Churchill was a landmark in the establishment of chief executive control of diplomatic affairs. The great wartime conferences of Roosevelt, Churchill, and Stalin set the pattern for presidential summit diplomacy in subsequent years.

Commander in Chief Roosevelt created a variety of advisory and coordinating units to help prepare for

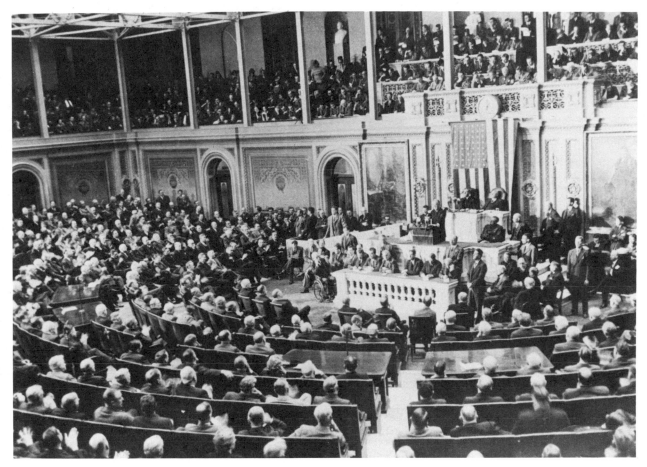

President Roosevelt addressing a joint session of Congress in 1942. (Courtesy FDR Library.)

and wage war. Among these were the National Defense Advisory Commission, the Office of Scientific Research and Development, the Office of Price Administration, the Office of War Information, the Office of War Mobilization, the War Manpower Commission, and the War Production Board. Roosevelt administered the war partly through the Joint Chiefs of Staff and partly through key personal advisers, such as Harry Hopkins and James F. Byrnes. But he insisted on being involved in everything himself, as he had in dealing with economic recovery in the 1930s.

Roosevelt's penchant for overlapping assignments and ad hoc agencies again led to administrative problems. Yet he managed to guide an array of able civilian and military leaders to victory. Doubtless his genius in recruiting talented aides and lieutenants compensated for his unique, sometimes unpredictable, improvisational administrative behavior. Still, his style often infuriated his subordinates. Many thought him unduly devious and manipulative; some thought him careless. James MacGregor Burns suggests that textbook administrative doctrines were not usually relevant to Roosevelt's needs in the crisis atmosphere of war. Roosevelt's problem, Burns wrote, "was less one of *management* than of dramatizing goals, enunciating principles, lifting hopes, pointing out dangers, raising expectations, mobilizing popular energies, recruiting gifted aides and administrators, harmonizing disputants, protecting administrative morale."

The war years again demonstrated Roosevelt's ambivalence about long-range planning. He often talked about the importance of planning but he preferred piecemeal, incremental policies and he distrusted allowing the cabinet or the Office of War Mobilization to serve as a collective agency for unified planning and decision making. Nor would he allow the Bureau of the Budget to realize its potential.

Still, the seeds of an institutionalized, more powerful presidency were planted during the Second World War. The national government entered new areas—for example, as a catalyst for scientific research and development. It would only be a few years before the Bureau of the Budget would become a vital staff agency, indispensable to activist presidents. And it was all but inevitable that a Council of Economic Advisers (1946) and a National Security Council (1947) would facilitate further White House influence over the national economy and foreign policy.

Critics of the Roosevelt conception and use of the presidency sometimes see in FDR's methods the beginning of the "imperial presidency." Roosevelt's ill-conceived Court-packing scheme, his secret diplomacy, his undisputed authority as commander in chief, his executive orders calling for the relocation of Japanese-Americans, and his denunciation of the U.S.

Senate for obstructing administration measures in the wartime period all added to an exalted and, some would say, an unhealthy conception of presidential power. Then too his sometimes ruthless, manipulative administrative and political style irritated friends as well as critics.

Of course, assessments of the Roosevelt presidency vary according to viewpoint and time period. In conservative eyes, Roosevelt was sometimes dictatorial and diminished liberty and self-reliance. "The effort to crossbreed some features of Fascism and Socialism with our American free system speedily developed in the Roosevelt administration," Herbert Hoover wrote. From the viewpoint of the Left, the Roosevelt presidency was often indecisive and inept; it saved capitalism without undertaking fundamental and enduring reforms. Moreover, the doctrine of emergency, the use of First World War administrative models in the early New Deal, and the expansion of executive power in the war against Hitler and Japan ushered in the military-industrial state.

Roosevelt's defenders retort that his presidency must be assessed in the context of what was needed and what was possible in tough and extraordinary times. Those unique times demanded bold, experimental, and sometimes brash leadership. The development of the presidency in Roosevelt's hands reflected developments in Western society, in the private as well as the public sectors—the rise of large-scale organization, specialization, and centralization of power. Roosevelt's presidency was responsive to previously neglected social needs. "If private endeavor fails to provide for willing hands and relief for the unfortunate," he said, "those suffering hardship from no fault of their own have a right to call upon the government for aid; and a government worthy of its name must make fitting response." Presidents afterwards would never dare to turn their backs on human suffering and stand by while impersonal market forces punished the nation. In the hands of an overpowering and unprincipled person, such a presidency might become "imperial." In the hands of a wise and prudent leader, Roosevelt-style presidency was a power for national well-being and world peace.

Franklin Roosevelt sought to be a great president, not a great administrator, and the distinction was important to him. "In his administrative methods he was usually concerned most of all," writes A. J. Wann, "not with whether they were neat and orderly, or whether they were especially efficient or in conformity with a logically designed, elaborate plan, but with the questions of whether they worked or not, and what effect they might have upon the over-all performance of his presidential obligations."

Americans have always been a pragmatic people, shaping their ideas and acts according to changing circumstances. In the age of Franklin Roosevelt, the presidency became frankly pragmatic. Although subsequent presidents have been committed to certain points of view and programs, none has been as rigid as Hoover and all have functioned in the shadow of FDR's pragmatism.

The presidents who came after Roosevelt have

Growth of Federal Expenditures and Civilian Employees

	EXPENDITURES (IN BILLIONS)	EMPLOYEES
1933	$ 4.6	603,587
1939	8.8	953,891
1941	13.2	1,437,682
1945	98.3	3,816,310

Source: Bureau of the Census, *Historical Statistics of the United States: Colonial Times to 1970* (Washington, D.C.: U.S. Government Printing Office, 1975), 2:1102, 1114.

been hard pressed to fill the large office he created. Since FDR, the American public has expected presidential initiative, presidential action, and presidential leadership. Presidents are supposed to symbolize the nation's promise, summon the nation's strength, and articulate the hopes and wants of common people. After FDR, America's presidents were inescapably world leaders. The great collaboration between Roosevelt and Churchill and the summit conferences of the Allied leaders set an enduring precedent. People now expect the president to play a personal role in resolving foreign policy problems. Few of our problems, however, have demanded the scope of leadership Roosevelt exercised. In a sense, FDR's performance may be paradoxically responsible for some of the disillusionment and cynicism people exhibit toward politics and politicians. Roosevelt's crisis leadership raised expectations for the presidency beyond the capacities of many of those who followed.

Franklin Roosevelt's contributions to the evolution, enlargement, and vitalization of the presidency were as great and probably greater than any president since George Washington. If Washington had set the all-important initial precedents for presidential conduct, Roosevelt created resources and vivified informal powers that would allow the presidency to flourish and survive in the modern world.

The presidency had been transformed from a mere enforcer and implementer of the will of Congress to a central leadership agency—planning, prodding, and lobbying for solutions to national and international problems. More than ever, it became the place where the national interest is hammered out. The presidency serves, usually, as a counterweight to parochialism, sectionalism, isolationism, and narrow self-interest.

Roosevelt's virtuoso performance permanently redefined the presidency as a central leadership post for nation and world. What the presidency is at any particular point in time of course depends in important measure on who is president—but Roosevelt's performance and use of the office is the standard we now have in mind when we recruit, nominate, and elect people to that office. "The presidency is not merely an administrative office," said Roosevelt. "That is the least of it. It is more than an engineering job, efficient or inefficient. It is pre-eminently a place of moral leadership." After Roosevelt we necessarily have a presidency-centered national government. Harvard Law Professor Laurence Tribe put it well:

"We are, and must remain, a society led by three equal branches, with one permanently 'more equal' than the others: as the Supreme Court and Congress are preeminent in constitutional theory, so the President is preeminent in constitutional fact."

Three standard works on the evolution of the modern presidency are Thomas E. Cronin, *The State of the Presidency,* 2d ed. (Boston: Little, Brown, 1980); Richard Neustadt, *Presidential Power* (New York: Wiley, 1960); and Arthur Schlesinger, Jr., *The Imperial Presidency* (Boston: Houghton, Mifflin, 1973). Important works on FDR's administrative style and reorganization efforts are Patrick Anderson, *The Presidents' Men* (Garden City, N.Y.: Doubleday, 1968); Barry D. Karl, *Executive Reorganization and Reform in the New Deal: The Genesis of Administrative Management, 1900–1939* (Cambridge, Mass.: Harvard University Press, 1963); Richard Polenberg, *Reorganizing Roosevelt's Government: The Controversy Over Executive Reorganization, 1936–1939* (Cambridge, Mass.: Harvard University Press, 1966); and A. J. Wann, *The President As Chief Administrator: A Study of Franklin D. Roosevelt* (Washington, D.C.: Public Affairs Press, 1968). Polenberg's *War and Society* (Philadelphia: Lippincott, 1972) is useful for the impact of the Second World War on the national government. Two books that discuss planning in the Roosevelt period are Marion Clawson, *New Deal Planning: The National Resources Planning Board* (Baltimore: Johns Hopkins University Press, 1981) and Otis L. Graham, *Toward a Planned Society: From Roosevelt to Nixon* (New York: Oxford University Press, 1976). Rexford Guy Tugwell's *The Democratic Roosevelt,* (New York: Harper & Row, 1957); *The Brains Trust* (New York: Viking, 1968); and *The Enlargement of the Presidency* (Garden City, N.Y.: Doubleday, 1960) are among the best of a number of insightful works by former Roosevelt aides that illuminate transformations of his presidential years.

THOMAS E. CRONIN
WILLIAM R. HOCHMAN

See also Biographers and Public Reputation; Commander in Chief; Congress, United States; New Deal; Supreme Court of the United States

Office of War Information

The Office of War Information (OWI) was established on 13 June 1942, when Franklin Roosevelt signed Executive Order 9182 which created the national information agency. Roosevelt feared the possibility of another Creel Committee (a World War I committee on war information criticized for encouraging a postwar red scare through an over-zealous wartime propaganda role) and resisted pressure to create a strong, powerful morale or propaganda agency. Instead, OWI was a consolidation of several prewar agencies—Office of Government Reports, Office of Facts and Figures (OFF), Division of Information in the Office of Emergency Management (OEM), and the Foreign Information Service. Elmer Davis, the popular journalist and radio newsman from Indiana, was named director.

OWI was divided into two branches—Domestic and Overseas. The Domestic Branch, headed until

January 1943 by Archibald MacLeish and then by Gardner Cowles, Jr., was embroiled in controversy from the start. Staffed by New Deal liberals from OFF such as Henry Pringle and Arthur Schlesinger, Jr., the Domestic Branch under MacLeish believed that OWI should educate the American people on the major issues of the war and the necessity of an American involvement in a postwar world. Through pamphlets like *Divide and Conquer* and *The Thousand Million,* OWI stressed the evils of fascism, World War II as a war of conflicting ideologies, and the concept of a United Nations. The propaganda agency naturally gave emphasis to FDR as a leader of a free and democratic people and to the accomplishments of the New Deal. This direction caused congressional conservatives to protest that OWI was trying to influence American voters.

When OWI released *The Negroes and the War,* domestic criticism of the agency increased. The publication satisfied no one. To southern conservatives, the publication preached racial equality; Republicans protested the emphasis given to FDR and the New Deal for black progress; and blacks resented the "fight or else" message.

The Domestic Branch was also active in Hollywood. Lowell Mellett, director of the Bureau of Motion Pictures, urged the film industry to portray an idealized, homogeneous America united in support of the war effort. That the industry produced government propaganda shorts is well known. But as Elmer Davis observed, "The easiest way to inject a propaganda idea into most people's minds is to let it go in through the medium of an entertainment picture." In three years OWI officials altered more than five hundred films to conform with American policy.

Using films, radio programs, posters, and publications, OWI projected to a domestic audience that American middle-class values were the utopia of the present. Symbolic of those values was the president and his New Deal programs, which were to be extended to all segments of American society as well as to a larger world. The war, rather than slowing down the New Deal, would accelerate and expand it to a greater audience. But there was disagreement over this approach within OWI, which resulted in Mac-Leish resigning in January and Pringle and the writers walking out in April 1943. When Congress slashed the Domestic Branch budget in June 1943, it merely confirmed OWI's lessening role in domestic affairs. FDR, uneasy from the beginning over OWI's role, gave no support to Davis or the agency.

The Overseas Branch of OWI, headed by Robert Sherwood, directed its messages toward foreign audiences and was less controversial. Yet *Victory* magazine, produced for foreign readers, was branded as "FDR re-election literature." Sherwood advocated that America's best propaganda was a "strategy of truth." But the truth was elusive. When the agency branded Italian king Victor Emmanuel III a "moronic little king," it may have been close to the truth, but it ran counter to current policy. FDR said it should not have happened, and Sherwood was forced to label it a "regrettable slip."

OWI, always viewed as a temporary agency, was eliminated on 31 August 1945. In three years, it had spent more than $125 million, but had failed to convince Congress, the press, or the American people that a propaganda agency was necessary—especially one that took an active role in domestic affairs.

The most complete study of OWI to date is Allan M. Winkler's *The Politics of Propaganda: The Office of War Information 1942–1945* (New Haven: Yale University Press, 1978). Winkler believes the greatest success for OWI was in the military theaters of war. The Domestic Branch and the question of propaganda in a democracy, however, are not covered in detail. Richard Dyer MacCann. *The People's Films: A Political History of United States Government Motion Pictures* (New York: Hastings House, 1973) contains an excellent chapter on the documentary film produced by OWI. Clayton R. Koppes and Gregory D. Black, in "What to Show the World: The Office of War Information and Hollywood, 1942–1945," *Journal of American History* 64 (1977):87–105, detail the relationship between OWI and the Hollywood film industry in producing entertainment films that supported OWI's view of America, the United Nations, and the enemy. David Lloyd Jones, "The U.S. Office of War Information and American Public Opinion during World War II, 1939–1945" (Ph.D. diss., State University of New York at Binghamton, 1976) is the most detailed study available on the domestic activities of OWI.

Office of War Mobilization

See Byrnes, James Francis; War Production Board; World War II

Old Age Pensions

See New Deal; Social Security; Townsend, Francis E., M.D.

Old Age Revolving Pensions, Ltd.

See Townsend, Francis E., M.D.

Open Door Policy

Long-standing U.S. policy guaranteeing the territorial and administrative integrity of, and equal commercial opportunity in, China. In two notes of 1899 and 1900, Secretary of State John Hay unilaterally demanded that the European powers recognize the right of all nations to equal commercial opportunity in China. The notes were addressed not to the Chinese government but to the imperialist powers England, France, Germany, and Russia. Led by the British, these powers had established spheres of influence in China in the 1890s and resented American interference in the carving up of the Middle Kingdom. Hay cloaked the notes in moralistic terms: the United States wished only to help China maintain her independence. But actually he wanted to secure a part of the Chinese trade for the United States. Although traditionalist interpretations have maintained that the United States wanted to secure the "territorial and administrative integrity" of China, revisionist historians such as William A. Williams see the Open Door as part of America's drive for overseas markets and an "informal empire."

In 1922 the Nine Power Treaty of the Washington Naval Conference made the Open Door policy a point of international law and formally denied special privileges in China to any nation. But in 1931 Japan occupied Manchuria and thus began to challenge the international order of the 1920s in Asia. President Hoover's secretary of state, Henry L. Stimson, refused to recognize the new Japanese puppet state Manchukuo, the Japanese name for Manchuria (1932). Yet despite this blatant challenge to the Open Door and to the post–World War I collective security system, America did not help the Chinese combat Japanese aggression.

Despite the fact that Roosevelt personally sympathized with China—his family had once engaged in the China trade—he did not continue Stimson's rhetorical belligerence when he became president. Early in his first term, Roosevelt initiated a new naval buildup, which was partly directed against Japan. But he hesitated to change his predecessors' Far Eastern policy for three basic reasons: (1) the important economic ties with Japan had priority over the challenge to the Open Door; (2) the American military was not prepared for an all-out conflict with Japan; and (3) Chinese domestic politics were so faction-ridden and divided between Chiang Kai-shek's Nationalists and Mao Tse-tung's Communists that American help did not seem warranted. For most of the 1930s, Roosevelt left Far Eastern policy in the hands of the State Department. Secretary of State Cordell Hull sent occasional notes of mild protest to Tokyo; but he dared not alienate the Japanese completely. The principal expert in the State Department, Stanley K. Hornbeck, however, strongly advocated the traditional Open Door in China.

In 1937 the Sino-Japanese War finally erupted in northern China. Hegemony over China was part of the new order—the "Greater East Asia Co-Prosperity Sphere"—that the expansionist Japanese military secretly planned for the Far East. This represented a clear challenge to Great Britain, the United States, and the other Pacific powers, in particular to the Open Door in China. Facing the Japanese onslaught, Chiang Kai-shek was more than ever certain of American support. In view of the strong isolationist sentiment in America, however, Roosevelt decided to act cautiously while exerting increasing pressure for Japanese withdrawal. In 1939 he abrogated the 1911 trade agreement with Japan in order to open the way for economic sanctions. By 1940, when the Japanese threat to Southeast Asia and the American Pacific interests was fully comprehended, American public opinion turned anti-Japanese. After Japan concluded the Tripartite Pact with Hitler Germany and Fascist Italy in September 1940, Roosevelt was able to act more firmly. He embargoed important war materials such as scrap metals and gasoline. But the Japanese continued their drive for hegemony over China, and in late 1941 America severed her diplomatic relations with Tokyo. Thus America's historic commitment to an Open Door in China, even though it was somewhat muffled by Rooseveltian caution, came into play as one of the major causes of the U.S.-Japanese conflict, which finally erupted into open warfare at Pearl Harbor.

After Pearl Harbor Roosevelt gave strong financial and military support to Chiang to stem the Japanese tide in China. But internal dissension frustrated Roosevelt's and, later, Truman's efforts to reopen the door in China. In 1949 Mao's Communist victory shut and locked it for the United States and the West.

For a quick introduction, see Richard W. Van Alstyne, "The Open Door Policy," in *Encyclopedia of American Foreign Policy,* ed. Alexander De Conde, vol. 2 (New York: Scribner's, 1978); in the same volume, see also William Appleman Williams, "Open Door Interpretations." John King Fairbank's *The United States & China* is the classic treatment of the flip-flopping relationship (Cambridge, Mass.: Harvard University Press, 1982). Equally useful for Japan is Charles E. Neu, *The Troubled Encounter: The United States and Japan* (Malabar, Fla.: Krieger, 1981); for a general view, see James C. Thomson, Jr., Peter W. Stanley, and John Curtis Perry, *Sentimental Imperialists: The American Experience in East Asia* (New York: Harper Colophon, 1981); and for an incisive treatment, see Dorothy Borg and Shumpei Okamoto, eds., *Pearl Harbor as History: Japanese American Relations, 1931–1941* (New York: Columbia University Press, 1973).

See also Foreign Economic Policy; Foreign Policy

Opinion Polls

Public opinion polls matured during Roosevelt's administration. In 1932 all the polls agreed that Roosevelt would win by a large majority. The polls, although far from being an exact science, gave Roosevelt such confidence that he campaigned in October in the safely Democratic South rather than expending his energies to swing disputed states. By the 1936 election, the message of the polls was anything but uniform. The *Literary Digest,* which had called every election right since 1920, coming within 1 percent of the actual margin in 1932, predicted a landslide for Alf Landon, Roosevelt's Republican rival, and saw FDR strong only in the South and Southwest. Other straw polls, notably that of the *Cleveland News,* agreed on a Landon victory. In contrast, the new polls of George Gallup, Archibald Crossley, and Elmo Roper all forecast that Roosevelt would win by a large margin, as did Roosevelt's campaign manager and private poll taker Jim Farley. The election results confirmed Farley's private poll and the newer "scientific" measures of public opinion and discredited the *Literary Digest's* method of taking straw polls. Because it relied on large mailings to voters gathered from lists of automobile owners and telephone directories, the *Literary Digest* did not account for Democratic strength among the lower classes who had neither phones nor automobiles.

The future of polling belonged not to this old style of sample voting but to the new breed of pollsters who based their predictions on smaller numbers derived from more representative samples. George Gallup, the apostle of the new method, followed his success in 1936 with an accurate call of both the 1938 congressional elections and the 1940 presidential race. The growing credibility of these scientific polls caused some to worry that the polls might damage the integrity of the election process by creating for the candidates and the electorate the illusion of strength or weakness. Some Roosevelt supporters grumbled that Gallup, who was thought to have Republican sympathies, consistently underestimated Roosevelt's strength. Roosevelt himself worried in 1940 that Gallup might exaggerate Republican Wendell Willkie's gains late in the campaign and so give a false impression of a tighter race than in fact existed. But Gallup proved these fears wrong by predicting accurately Roosevelt's victories in 1940 and 1944, thus giving the public a greater measure of confidence in the new polls. For his part Roosevelt still preferred the private polls taken by his own staff. Hadley Cantril had replaced Farley as Roosevelt's chief sampler of public opinion; the results remained both accurate and useful to the president. Yet Roosevelt grew increasingly uncomfortable with the power of public polls not only to measure opinion but to shape it. In achieving the status of a science, public opinion polls became a participant in as well as an observer of the electoral process and contributed to the decline of party loyalty and the growing influence of the media in shaping voter behavior.

The best single source on the 1936 election is William E. Leuchtenberg, "Election of 1936," in *History of American Presidential Elections*, ed. Arthur M. Schlesinger, Jr. (New York: McGraw-Hill Book Co., 1971). Michael Wheeler, *Lies, Damn Lies, and Statistics* (New York: Liveright, 1976) is a lively yet critical story of the growth of polling. Of the biographies of Roosevelt, James MacGregor Burns, *Roosevelt: The Lion and the Fox* (New York: Harcourt, Brace, & World, 1956) pays special attention to Roosevelt's handling of public opinion.

Ornithology

Franklin Roosevelt was about seven years old when he became interested in watching and collecting birds. His parents had taken him with them on their annual trip abroad. In Pau, a city of southwestern France, Franklin met "dear old Mr. Foljambe" who took the boy on long walks, introduced him to bird-watching and bird listening, told him all about his collection of mounted birds at home in England, and invited him with Sara and James to visit him there. Although his parents had other plans, they did visit England, and Franklin went by himself to view the collection: "I'd go anywhere alone to see those birds," he said.

FDR's bird collection. (Courtesy FDR Library.)

By the time he reached his eleventh birthday, he knew very well what he wanted: a gun and a bird collection. His father agreed to provide him with the gun, a small-caliber rifle, on condition that he limit himself to one pair of each variety of bird found in the Hudson River valley, that he not shoot a nesting pair nor any bird during the mating season, and that he learn to prepare, stuff, and mount the birds himself. James taught his son how to shoot and how to handle a gun without endangering himself or others and encouraged the boy in his new interest.

Franklin became a very good shot, and the bird collection grew to include an oriole, a heron, a robin, a woodpecker, a hawk, and a winter wren. His mother tells the story about the last named: Franklin came in one day and said that he'd come to fetch his gun. There was a winter wren perched on a tree, which he wanted for his collection. Mrs. Roosevelt doubted that the bird would still be there when Franklin got back to it and said so. But the boy was confident that the wren would wait. And wait it did, for Franklin returned to the house with the bird in his hand. Preparing and stuffing the small creatures Franklin found unexpectedly unpleasant, but he slowly overcame his distaste until he felt competent in the task. Then, with the consent of his parents, he turned the chore over to a professional.

His collection grew in two years' time to over three hundred specimens, all housed in cabinets or on shelves at Springwood. In the first year of his collecting, he wrote an essay on his hobby, "Birds of the Hudson River Valley," and read it to assembled members of the family. His grandfather, Warren Delano, was so impressed that he presented Franklin with a life membership in the Museum of Natural History in New York. While at Groton he was concerned that his collection be protected and wrote to his mother in 1897, "I hope you will seal up my birds before the babies come to stay with you or else I should be afraid of the consequences." Franklin added specimens from time to time throughout his life: a hawk, a black guillemot, a bittern. And even when he was president, he drove into the woods of Springwood on an occasional early morning to enjoy listening to a chorus of hundreds of swamp birds. His interest in birds remained a lifelong hobby.

For more information, see Finis Farr, *FDR* (New Rochelle, N.Y.: Arlington House, 1972); Frank Freidel, *Franklin D. Roosevelt: The Apprenticeship* (Boston: Little, Brown & Co., 1952); Rita Halle Kleeman, *Gracious Lady: The Life of Sara Delano Roosevelt* (New York and London: D. Appleton-Century Co., 1935); Ernest K. Lindley, *Franklin D. Roosevelt: A Career in Progressive Democracy* (New York: Blue Ribbon Books, 1931); Research Collection, *Roosevelt Family Papers* (Hyde Park, N.Y.: FDR Library and Museum); and Mrs. James Roosevelt as told to Isabel Leighton and Gabrielle Forbush, *My Boy Franklin* (New York: Ray Long & Richard R. Smith, 1933).

P

Pacifism and the Peace Movement

Like Woodrow Wilson and Lyndon Johnson, Franklin Roosevelt was constrained in the formulation of foreign policy by organized public pressure and by the internal contradictions of his own goals. Public debate was initiated by peace advocates in the thirties, and the administration largely maneuvered in their wake, adapting to international exigencies and to the shifting role of pacifists in the American peace movement.

Peace advocates constituted a loose coalition of disparate organizations. There were two broad groupings of them, both with roots in World War I. Most internationalists had supported that war in the interest of creating a new international order. Roosevelt himself had been attracted to that view. In the twenties internationalists were divided over alternative strategies for peace—the League of Nations, the World Court, or the outlawry of war—and their division itself was a factor in the politics of foreign policymaking. Although they worked through several organizations, their strongest base lay in the League of Nations Association closely related to the Carnegie Endowment for International Peace, and the Foreign Policy Association.

A strong nucleus of progressives, however, had organized in opposition to World War I. Opponents of war on principle, they were pacifists; but they differed from traditional, nonresistant pacifists in that they were politically active and had a distinctly international outlook. During and after the war, these pacifists formed organizations that would play a significant role in public debate: the Fellowship of Reconciliation (1915), the American Friends Service Committee (1917), the Women's International League for Peace and Freedom (1919), and the National Council for Prevention of War (1921).

Japanese aggression in Manchuria (1931) pulled pacifist and nonpacifist internationalists into a tenuous alignment on behalf of sanctions under the aegis of the League of Nations. In succeeding years they co-

Two stirring and commercially successful plays of the mid-1930s dramatized and bitterly denounced the impact of war: Irwin Shaw's Bury the Dead *and Paul Green's* Johnny Johnson. *The latter, originally performed in New York by the Group Theatre under the direction of Lee Strasberg, was later successfully staged on both coasts by local units of the Federal Theatre Project. (Courtesy the Library of Congress Federal Theatre Project Collection at George Mason University Library, Fairfax, Virginia.)*

operated also to support disarmament (specifically at the World Disarmament Conference of 1933) and a liberal, internationalist policy for the world economy (notably at the London Economic Conference of 1933). They were frustrated by what they perceived to be the intransigence of national interests, and their disappointment was aggravated by the defeat of proposals for U.S. participation in the World Court.

Pacifists especially helped prepare the public for the revision of neutrality legislation in the mid-thirties. Throughout the twenties antiwar poetry and fiction and revisonist history had reshaped American attitudes. Social evangelist Kirby Page had popularized revisionism and tied it to his pacifist point of view, and his books were widely circulated among church and YMCA workers. Pacifists shifted the positions of

Boston Post, *17 May 1933*.

major church bodies on the war question, and their journals regularly imbued international issues with moral dimensions. Moreover, pacifist organizations used specific issues to mobilize public opinion. The Women's International League obtained thousands of signatures to petitions for disarmament, which it presented successively to presidents Hoover and Roosevelt. The Fellowship of Reconciliation challenged ROTC in education. The American Friends Service Committee developed programs of popular education on the community level. Challenging defense budgets, the National Council for Prevention of War put together an extensive network of contacts in civic and church associations and in labor, farmer, and youth groups, sent news releases to some 2,500 newspapers, created a legislative reference service, and effectively lobbied Congress. It gained access to national leaders and helped initiate the Nye committee's investigation of the munitions industry, providing staff support and materials and popularizing the committee's disclosures.

Writing in 1942, a prominent friendly critic, F. Ernest Johnson, wrote of the pacifists, "The influence of the spoken and written word, unsupported by vested interest of any kind, has perhaps never been so strikingly demonstrated." He added that skepticism of war had been purveyed by leaders who were intelligent, liberal, and socially conscious. He might have added that they were internationalists. In the early years of the Roosevelt administration, they aligned with nonpacifists in a common search for attaining international order without risking war. Roosevelt himself supported these twin goals, so that he was faced with a well-organized movement whose political force and values he respected. The consequence of this alignment was the neutrality legislation of 1935.

Strict neutrality attracted some pacifists because it offered a way to keep the United States isolated from European wars of national interest. It appealed also to nonpacifists insofar as it could be used to prevent interference through economic and political sanctions against aggressor states, which ran the risk of involving the nation in warfare. After a good deal of wavering, the administration accepted strict neutrality with whatever presidential discretion it could salvage.

Crisis mounted in Europe, notably in Italy's invasion of Ethiopia and in the Spanish civil war. The two wings of the peace movement formed stronger links. Nonpacifist internationalists, with initiatives from Newton Baker, Norman Davis, Senator James Pope, and nominally, President Nicholas Murray Butler of Columbia University, sought to swerve the antiwar public toward international cooperation, especially in economic measures. They proposed to work through James T. Shotwell and Clark Eichelberger of the League of Nations Association in the National Peace Conference, which had pacifist support, and they secured nonpacifist Walter Van Kirk as its leader. They also won modest funding from the Carnegie endowment.

Pacifist organizations met this initiative by cooperating fully, but with a much stronger emphasis on neutrality. Indeed, they reorganized the National Peace Conference in order to secure parity in it, obtained large-scale and independent funding, and took real control of a half-million-dollar Emergency Peace Campaign in 1936–37. Under the leadership of Ray Newton and Clarence Pickett of the American Friends Service Committee, Frederick Libby of the National Council for Prevention of War, Mildred Scott Olmstead of the Women's International League, John Nevin Sayre of the Fellowship of Reconciliation, and the independent Kirby Page and Devere Allen, they brought all their resources to bear in a public movement that increasingly stressed neutrality under the theme, "No Foreign War." In effect, they formed a political base for the "small but highly effective neutrality bloc in Congress," which Robert Divine has credited with primary responsibility for strict neutrality legislation. Public response was strong, not least from young people who circulated the famous Oxford Pledge to withhold support of a foreign war, a program that originated in England. The National Council went beyond neutrality legislation to provide much time and support for the Ludlow amendment for a public referendum on war, and it was largely responsible for bringing the resolution to the floor of the House in December 1937, where it was narrowly defeated by all the resources Roosevelt could muster.

Even before the Emergency Peace Campaign had run its course, nonpacifists had begun to build a countermovement that supported ever more explicit collective security measures. They focused on opposition to the Ludlow amendment and on support of revision of neutrality legislation to permit the president to authorize trade with allies while applying sanctions against aggressor nations. A National Committee for Concerted Peace Efforts was created under Clark Eichelberger, and this ended the loose coalition of pacifists and nonpacifist internationalists. Subsequently, advocates of collective security were self-consciously active, forming a series of groups that culminated in the Committee to Defend America by Aiding the Allies. Sometimes they acted as spokesmen for the administration, as in the cause of neutrality revision in 1939; but often they pressed Roosevelt to give more forthright support to the democratic nations, as when they initiated an exchange of destroyers for bases with Britain in 1940.

The terms of the national debate over neutrality were cast by the increasingly defensive position of the Allies in Europe. By September 1939 there was no longer any hope that another world war could be avoided, and the issue narrowed to the question of U.S. involvement. Accordingly, the peace movement narrowed to a neutralist coalition of pacifists and socialists who found themselves uncomfortably aligned with isolationists organized in the America First Committee. As war became more likely, religious pacifist groups gave ever more priority to achieving legislative provisions for conscientious objectors to military service and spent less energy on political action. So intense was the neutrality debate of 1940–41 and so vociferous were the isolationists, however, that Roosevelt probably overemphasized the strength of the coalition. Certainly he grouped them together as opponents.

Well before Pearl Harbor, the opposition waned, and the administration achieved a strong base of public support. The division among peace advocates was instrumental in shifting public opinion, and it coincided with Roosevelt's own clarification of purpose.

In retrospect, the neutrality controversy can be understood only with reference to the peace movement that preceded and underlay it, for that movement had both broad access to the public and the respect of the president who shared its twin goals of international order and the avoidance of war. Similarly, isolationism must be interpreted with reference to the internationalist peace movement whose division in 1937–38 made possible a national realignment on foreign policy. The peace movement that constrained Roosevelt's foreign policy was highly organized but inherently divided. The president's policy followed from this fact, as he supported the collective security wing and followed its lead in proportion to the clarity and dominance of its position.

In *Roosevelt and World War II* (Baltimore: Johns Hopkins University Press, 1969), Robert Divine interprets both Roosevelt's early support for the League of Nations in relation to his subsequent disillusionment with it and his attachment to the notion of an active national role in the world in terms of his drift from collective security in the twenties and early thirties. Charles DeBenedetti, *Origins of the American Peace Movement, 1915–1929* (Milwood, N.Y.: KTO Press, 1978) supplants previous accounts of the movement. The full history of the peace movement is recounted in Merle Curti's classic *Peace or War: The American Struggle* (New York: W. W. Norton, 1936), DeBenedetti's *The Peace Reform in American History* (Bloomington: Indiana University Press, 1980), and Charles Chatfield's introduction to *Peace Movements in America* (New York: Schocken, 1973). The basis for the alliance of pacifist and nonpacifist internationalists is dealt with in Robert Divine, *The Illusion of Neutrality* (Chicago: University of Chicago Press, 1962), James T. Shotwell, *The Autobiography of James T. Shotwell* (New York: Bobbs-Merrill, 1961), and Clark M. Eichelberger, *Organizing for Peace: A Personal History of the Founding of the United Nations* (New York: Harper & Row, 1977). The work of the Women's International League is surveyed in Gertrude Bussey and Margaret Tims, *Women's International League for Peace and Freedom, 1915–1965* (London: George Allen & Unwin, 1965) and is reflected in Mercedes Randall's biography of Emily Green Balch, *Improper Bostonian* (New York: Wayne, 1964). The work of the Friends Service Committee is recalled in the autobiography of Clarence E. Pickett, *For More Than Bread* (Boston: Little, Brown & Co., 1953), and that of the National Council for Prevention of War in autobiographies by Frederick J. Libby, *To End War* (Nyack, N.Y.: Fellowship, 1969) and Dorothy Detzer, *Appointment on the Hill* (New York: Henry Holt, 1948). For the contribution of the National Council to the Senate munitions investigation, see John Edward Wiltz, *In Search of Peace: The Senate Munitions Inquiry, 1934–36* (Baton Rouge: Louisiana State University Press, 1963) and Allan Kuusisto, "The Influence of the National Council for Prevention of War on United States Foreign Policy, 1935–39" (Ph.D. diss., Harvard University, 1950). Robert Divine reinterprets what some regarded as Roosevelt's indecision or deviousness as a product of both his realism in the face of public pressure and his struggle to sort out the priorities of peace and world order in *Roosevelt in World War II, The Illusion of Neutrality* and *The Reluctant Belligerent* (New York: John Wiley & Sons, 1965). Pacifist efforts are described in relation to the peace movement and foreign policy issues in Selig Adler, *The Isolationist Impulse: Its Twentieth Century Reaction* (New York: Abelard-Schuman, 1957), Robert Osgood, *Ideals and Self-Interest in America's Foreign Relations* (Chicago: University of Chicago Press, 1957), and Robert Ferrell, "The Peace Movement," in *Isolation and Security*, ed. Alexander DeConde (Durham: Duke University Press, 1957). For the story of the war referendum campaign and the role of the National Council for Prevention of War in it, see Ernest C. Bolt in *Ballots before Bullets: The War Referendum Approach to Peace in America, 1914–1941* (Charlottesville: University Press of Virginia, 1977). The role of Norman Thomas and of pacifists is discussed in Bernard Johnpoll, *Pacifist's Progress: Norman Thomas and the Decline of American Socialism* (New York: Quandrangle, 1970), but the author underestimates the internationalism of pacifists and the political analysis of Thomas and is weak on organizational history. These elements are covered in Charles Chatfield's *For Peace and Justice: Pacifism in America, 1914–1941* (Knoxville: University of Tennessee Press, 1971), which interprets the origin and development of modern, reform-oriented pacifism in relation to social and foreign policy issues of the interwar years.

E. CHARLES CHATFIELD

See also Internationalism and Peace; Thomas, Norman Mattoon

Peabody, Endicott

(30 May 1857–17 November 1944)

Founder and longtime headmaster of the Groton School, Groton, Massachusetts, a small boarding school attended by Franklin Roosevelt. Endicott Peabody was born in Salem, Massachusetts, in 1857 and was educated at Cambridge University in England and the Episcopal Theological School in Massachusetts. After a brief period of service at Arizona's First Episcopal Church in Tombstone, he returned to Massachusetts and was ordained in 1884. In that same year the Reverend Dr. Peabody and two associates opened the Groton School and for the next fifty-six years he was its headmaster. In 1885 he married Fanny Peabody, his first cousin.

Peabody was a remarkable individual whose single-minded mission was to instill in his students "manly Christian character." To this end he modeled Groton on English public schools, especially Rugby, with a program of religious observance, vigorous exercise, and spartan living. He taught his students that service to mankind, especially public service, was the noblest career. The headmaster's influence on Franklin Roosevelt was considerable. The president would say in later years, "As long as I live, the influence of Dr. and Mrs. Peabody means and will mean more to me than that of any other people next to my father and mother." Until his death his relationship to the Roosevelt family was close. He officiated at the wedding of Franklin and Eleanor as well as those of their children; he also taught the Roosevelt sons and participated in FDR's inaugural church services in Washington.

For a full-length biography, see Frank D. Ashburn's *Peabody of Groton* (New York: Coward, 1944). Laura Crowell's "Roosevelt the Grotonian," *Quarterly Journal of Speech* 38 (February 1952):31–36, is of interest.

See also Education; Groton School

Pearl Harbor

On 7 December 1941 Japanese planes attacked the American fleet based at Pearl Harbor, inflicting one of the worst military defeats in the nation's history. The Pearl Harbor attack ended years of mounting diplomatic tension between the United States and Japan, rallied the American people behind war in the Pacific, and spawned a search for explanations that would continue long after the end of World War II.

Throughout 1941 President Franklin D. Roosevelt and his advisers were preoccupied with the war in Europe and wished to avoid a showdown with Japan, but public and congressional opinion pushed them toward a firmer stand, as did their conviction that Japan would not, in the end, challenge America's superior power. They engaged in a diplomacy of deterrence, hoping that American military and economic moves would force Japan's leaders to curb their expansionist vision and accept American terms for a settlement of the East Asian crisis. The more the two governments talked, however, the larger the gap between them appeared, and leaders on both sides of the Pacific lost their faith in the possibility of a peaceful solution. On 24 July 1941, when Japanese forces marched into southern Indochina, completing their occupation of that colony, the Roosevelt administration responded by freezing Japanese assets, in effect cutting off trade between the two nations.

While the embargo was only the culmination of American economic restrictions, it deepened the American-Japanese crisis by ending all oil shipments to Japan. That nation's leaders now faced a dilemma. With oil supplies dwindling, they must either accept American demands or strike deep into Southeast Asia and the Pacific against American, British, and Dutch possessions. In the second half of 1941, Japan's leaders continued talks with the United States while laying the groundwork for a vast Pacific war. Navy and army planners decided on a complex, coordinated offensive that included assaults on Malaya, the Philippines, the Netherlands East Indies, and key islands in the Pacific. If successful, they calculated that Japan would win a huge empire in Asia and acquire the bases and resources necessary to repulse an American counterattack.

The idea of an attack on Pearl Harbor originated with Adm. Isoroku Yamamoto, the brilliant commander in chief of the navy's combined fleet. Yamamoto recognized America's superior industrial power and doubted that Japan could win a long war with the United States. If it must come, however, he wanted to paralyze America's Pacific fleet for at least six months, thereby protecting the flank of Japanese convoys moving toward Southeast Asia and providing crucial time for the consolidation of Japan's new empire. Rejecting the defensive thinking of most naval leaders, he urged a bold offensive strategy that would cripple American naval power in the Pacific.

Yamamoto's daring gamble ran into determined opposition in the Naval General Staff, where senior officers feared the detection of the task force and worried about a host of unresolved technical problems, such as refueling at sea and the development of torpedoes that would be effective in the shallow waters of Pearl Harbor. The force of Yamamoto's personality, however, combined with a series of technical breakthroughs, carried the day, and on 26 November the fleet left Japan, prepared to attack Pearl Harbor unless a last-minute diplomatic settlement kept the peace.

The task force that steamed slowly through the northern Pacific toward the Hawaiian Islands was a formidable armada of thirty ships, including six aircraft carriers, two battleships, two heavy cruisers, one light cruiser, eleven destroyers, and eight supporting vessels. Its officers had engaged in meticulous planning, imposed exhaustive training on their men, and taken extraordinary precautions to avoid detection. It was a long, tense voyage through empty, quiet seas, until early on the morning of 7 December the carriers swung into the wind about 220 miles north of Oahu and launched 350 planes that were to carry out the

The Pearl Harbor Naval Air Station after the Japanese attack, 7 December 1941. (National Archives.)

attack in two waves. As the fighters and bombers neared Oahu, the cloud cover parted and Japanese pilots saw much of the American Pacific fleet anchored in the blue-green waters of Pearl Harbor. At 7:53 A.M. the flight leader cried out "Tora! Tora! Tora!" ("Tiger! Tiger! Tiger!"), the code word indicating that the surprise had been complete.

In the years prior to the outbreak of the Pacific war, Pearl Harbor had become the nation's most heavily fortified overseas base, with a ground force of 25,000 men to defend it from invasion, a sizable air force of fighters and bombers, and elaborate tank farms, dry docks, and other facilities for the support of the fleet. On 10 April 1940 the Pacific fleet arrived in Hawaiian waters for maneuvers, and Roosevelt decided to keep it there as a signal to Japan of American power in the Pacific. Beneath the impressive appearances, however, the defending forces suffered from many weaknesses. Everywhere the American military establishment was in the process of transition, suffering from shortages of matériel and trained men, as well as from lingering peacetime inadequacies in its organizational structure. Hawaii was no exception. Many planes were obsolete or lacking spare parts, the early-warning radar network was only becoming operational, and the paucity of long-range patrol planes made 360-degree reconnaissance possible for only

short periods; moreover, by the summer of 1941 the Pacific fleet had been so weakened by transfers to the Atlantic that it was incapable of sustained offensive operations.

Nevertheless, American commanders in Hawaii had ample forces to repel a surprise attack if only they had possessed more imagination in using them. Adm. Husband E. Kimmel and Lieut. Gen. Walter C. Short doubted that Japan would strike at Pearl Harbor, especially from the air. As tension grew in the last months of 1941, Kimmel's mind remained fixed on offensive operations, and he allowed most of his ships to move in predictable patterns, returning to base every weekend. Short was concerned with resisting an invasion of the islands, not with protecting the fleet. Thus on 27 November 1941, when Washington warned of the imminence of war and ordered a high state of alert, Kimmel and Short misunderstood. Kimmel did not insist on aerial reconnaissance to the north of Hawaii, while Short alerted his forces against sabotage from a Japanese fifth column, in effect lessening their readiness to defend against a Japanese air attack.

Washington had not, to be sure, shared with either commander the information on Japanese intentions gleaned from Operation Magic, the breaking of Japan's top secret diplomatic code, but it is unlikely

Leo Hirshfeld, New York Daily News, 22 August 1944. Rumors circulated periodically that the president had had advance knowledge of the attack on Pearl Harbor. (Copyright 1944 New York News Inc. Reprinted by permission.)

that this information would have altered their behavior. Even with the benefit of Magic intercepts, Roosevelt and his associates reasoned that Japan, if it dared to assault any American possession, would probably choose the Philippines, and they sent warnings to Hawaii that were full of ambiguity. And the confusion in Washington was so great that no top official checked to be certain that the Hawaiian commanders had properly interpreted the final alert messages.

Despite all these mistakes, the defenders of Hawaii might have had nearly an hour's warning had they been more alert. At 7:02 A.M. the Opana Mobile Radar Station picked up the incoming fleet of Japanese planes, and one minute later the USS *Ward* detected an enemy submarine off the entrance to Pearl Harbor and quickly sank it. Neither signal, however, was interpreted correctly. The radar operators believed the planes were American, while officers at the naval command center discounted the destroyer's report. It took the noise of the explosions to convince Americans that the fleet was under attack. At 7:58 A.M. radiomen clicked out the famous message: "AIR RAID, PEARL HARBOR. THIS IS NOT DRILL!" Little defense was possible, since antiaircraft batteries were unmanned and planes were crowded closely together to prevent sabotage. When the first and second waves of Japanese planes finally departed, having lost only twenty-nine aircraft, great clouds of black smoke billowed upward from the sinking ships in the harbor.

Eight battleships, three light cruisers, three destroyers, and four auxiliary craft were either sunk, capsized, or heavily damaged, while nearly two hundred planes were lost. Worst of all, 2,403 men died and 1,178 were wounded. The American defenders were stunned and outraged, convinced that the Japanese would follow up their initial attack with further air raids and an amphibious landing. The army prepared to meet Japanese troops on the beaches, while the navy searched in vain for the enemy's task force. Neither found any release from the humiliation inflicted on them.

For the United States, Pearl Harbor was a disaster rather than a catastrophe. The Japanese had crippled the American fleet, but had missed the three American carriers stationed in the Pacific. The *Saratoga* was on the West Coast for repairs, *Enterprise* near Wake Island, *Lexington* heading toward Midway. Nor had they bombed vital repair facilities and oil storage tanks. Some officers with the Japanese task force urged its commander, Adm. Chuichi Nagumo, to linger while another wave of planes finished the job and found the American carriers. But Nagumo, fearing for the safety of his own carriers and grateful for his extraordinary good fortune, interpreted his mission narrowly and quickly turned his vessels back toward Japan.

Whatever its short-run military gains, the surprise attack was a political miscalculation, for it enraged the American people, uniting them behind a massive war effort against both Japan and Germany. Roosevelt's task of political leadership was greatly simplified, and he and his advisers were relieved that war had finally come. Once the details filtered in, however, they were appalled by the extent of the loss and of American unreadiness. As Secretary of the Treasury Henry Morgenthau, Jr., remarked, "They will never be able to explain it."

Beginning with the Roberts Commission in December 1941, one study followed another, culminating in the creation in September 1945 of the Joint Congressional Committee on the Investigation of the Pearl Harbor Attack. Political opponents of the Roosevelt administration pointed to lapses in Washington, while the president and his advisers shifted most of the blame to Kimmel and Short, who were relieved of their commands and reprimanded for errors of judgment. Gradually the search for scapegoats gave way to a search for a deeper understanding of how the disaster occurred, one that has continued to our own day. Pearl Harbor remains an event of extraordinary fascination, a symbol of how badly two governments can misperceive the policies and intentions of each other.

Charles A. Beard's *President Roosevelt and the Coming of the War, 1941: A Study in Appearances and Realities* (New Haven, Conn.: Yale University Press, 1948) is the classic revisionist work, contending that Roosevelt maneuvered the nation into war, while Husband E. Kimmel's *Admiral Kimmel's Story* (Chicago: Henry Regnery Co., 1955), is an attempt by an important participant to exonerate himself. Our understanding of the Pearl Harbor disaster is greatly deepened by Roberta

Wohlstetter's *Pearl Harbor: Warning and Decision* (Stanford, Calif.: Stanford University Press, 1962), a penetrating study of organizational failure. More recently, Gordon W. Prange's *At Dawn We Slept: The Untold Story of Pearl Harbor* (New York: McGraw-Hill Book Co., 1981) adds much fresh detail, especially on the Japanese side, and Martin V. Melosi's *The Shadow of Pearl Harbor: Political Controversy over the Suprise Attack, 1941–1946* (College Station: Texas A&M University Press, 1977) traces the domestic political repercussions.

CHARLES E. NEU

See also Declaration of War; Foreign Policy; Japan; Open Door Policy; World War II

Peek, George Nelson

(19 November 1873–17 December 1943)

First administrator of the Agricultural Adjustment Administration (AAA), later special adviser to Roosevelt on foreign trade. Peek, born in Polo, Illinois, graduated from Oregon High School in 1891 and attended Northwestern University during the 1891–92 academic year. After leaving school, he worked for the John Deere Plow Company in Omaha. Peek received national attention with his appointment to the War Industries Board (WIB) in December 1917. When Bernard Baruch was appointed chairman of the WIB in March 1918, he recognized Peek's talents and made him the commissioner of finished products, responsible for the coordination of American industry with civilian and military needs. When depression hit the farm industry in the 1920s, Peek rose to prominence among agricultural reformers. His major contribution, outlined in his pamphlet *Equality for Agriculture* in 1921, was the idea that government should purchase the surplus production of American farmers and sell this produce abroad, while American farmers would pay the government an equalization fee for the commodities sold abroad. Peek's ideas for eradicating the surplus, and thus allowing domestic food prices to rise, were a major part of the Agricultural Adjustment Act of March 1933.

Henry Wallace was instrumental in bringing Peek to Roosevelt's attention. But when Wallace was secretary of agriculture and Peek the administrator of the Agricultural Adjustment Administration (AAA), they disagreed constantly. Wallace felt that the AAA's provisions for acreage controls were essential, but Peek found such controls objectionable. Peek resigned from the AAA in December 1933 at Roosevelt's request, but the president appointed him a special adviser on foreign trade because he recognized Peek's abilities and wanted to keep him from criticizing the AAA. But Peek resigned this position in November 1935 and proceeded at once to attack the Roosevelt administration. He became an ardent isolationist and a member of the America First movement. After the attack on Pearl Harbor, Peek supported the war effort but worked to limit postwar cooperation with other nations.

Peek's views changed little from 1923 to 1943.

Although his relationship with Roosevelt certainly changed from 1932 to 1943, this was due largely to Peek's attachment to the concept of farm parity without acreage controls. He was unable to realize that changes in farming—better tools, animals, and plants and increased use of fertilizer—greatly increased the amount of farm production and that responsible farm reform must somehow incorporate these changes. Policies advocating only price supports, through government purchase of surplus produce, simply did not address the major problem of American agriculture in the 1930s—overproduction.

The most thorough source of information on Peek is Gilbert C. Fite, *George N. Peek and the Fight for Farm Parity* (Norman: University of Oklahoma Press, 1954). This biography contains a great deal of material on the development of Peek's thought from his years in agricultural industry through the 1920s when Peek was at perhaps his most creative point. For a contemporary view of the AAA, see Edwin G. Nourse, Joseph S. Davis, and John D. Black, *Three Years of the Agricultural Adjustment Administration* (Washington: Brookings Institution, 1937).

See also Agricultural Adjustment Administration; Reciprocal Trade Agreements

---

Pegler, Westbrook

(2 August 1894–24 June 1969)

Newspaper columnist. The son of a Minnesota reporter, Westbrook Pegler early on became enchanted with the newspaper business. After college at Loyola Academy in Chicago, he went to work as a reporter and covered World War I for the United Press from 1916–18. After the war, he became a sports writer until 1932 when the *Chicago Tribune* sent him to Washington. There Pegler's political column, entitled "Fair Enough," became syndicated in 112 newspapers and reached nearly 6 million readers.

Pegler's popularity owed much to his caustic style and his biting attacks on fascism, labor unions, the New Deal, and the Roosevelt family. He denounced members of the family for, he claimed, their use of the Roosevelt name to receive special favors such as government jobs; he also feuded briefly with Eleanor Roosevelt when she started her own newspaper column. Initially he had been impressed by Roosevelt and wrote in 1934, "Never have I encountered a subject of this type who lays it on the line as Mr. Roosevelt does. . . . For the first time in my life in this business I find myself squabbling for a chance to carry the champion's water bucket." This trust gave way, however, and he opposed the New Deal as a governmental encroachment on individual rights. He attacked James Farley, Harold Ickes, and others in the administration as well as such diverse personalities as Huey Long, Father Coughlin, and Upton Sinclair.

In 1941 Pegler's exposure of crime in a Chicago labor union won him the Pulitzer Prize, but by then the appeal of his vitriolic diatribes (one contemporary called Pegler "one of the most consistently resentful men in the country") was fading. In 1944, when many regarded him as the "stuck whistle of journalism," Pegler joined the Hearst newspaper chain where his conservative views and colorful style were more welcome.

A sympathetic portrait of Pegler written by a contemporary is Jack Alexander, "He's Against," in *Post Biographies of Famous Journalists*, ed. John E. Drewry (New York: Random House, 1942). Edwin Emery and Michael Emery, *The Press and America* (Englewood Cliffs, N.J.: Prentice-Hall, 1978) includes a brief retrospective view of Pegler. Graham J. White, *FDR and the Press* (Chicago: University of Chicago Press, 1979) provides an interesting overview of the topic with sketchy information on Pegler.

Francis Perkins. (Courtesy FDR Library.)

Pendergast, Thomas J.
(22 July 1872–26 January 1945)

Kansas City political boss. Thomas Pendergast was born in St. Joseph, Missouri, to a large Catholic family. He attended local parochial schools and followed his older brother Jim into the Democratic politics of Kansas City's ethnic wards. A short, heavy-set man with a round face and a large mustache, he was once dismissed as a "thick-skulled, heavy-jowled oaf." Yet Tom soon surpassed his older brother in organizing a political machine around the saloons in Kansas City's low-income areas. With neither party dominant locally, Pendergast expanded his control over the Kansas City area and became the only politician in Missouri able to control a large bloc of votes. He provided jobs for the poor and contracts and tax deductions to friendly businessmen, and resorted to ballot-box fraud and bribery when persuasion failed, all the while amassing a comfortable personal fortune.

Pendergast crossed paths with Roosevelt at the 1932 Democratic National Convention in Chicago. While appearing to support the candidacy of Missouri's senator James A. Reed, Pendergast subtly lent his strength to help nominate Roosevelt. In return, Roosevelt gave Pendergast control over many New Deal relief programs in Missouri. Funds for the Civil Works Administration and, in 1935, the Works Progress Administration were funneled into Missouri through Pendergast's hands, allowing him to gain even more power in the state. At the height of his power in 1934, the Missouri boss helped elect Harry S Truman to the Senate.

Pendergast's power began to fade when a federal district attorney, embittered by the experience of his brother with the Pendergast machine, initiated a federal investigation into the machine's illegal voting practices. When antimachine publicity helped elect a political rival in 1938, the Roosevelt administration withdrew favor from Pendergast, and the machine, without New Deal patronage to dispense, collapsed. In 1939, Pendergast was sentenced to fifteen months in prison for income tax evasion, and he died six years later. His machine, which Roosevelt first enhanced and then destroyed, has never been revived.

Although there is no general biography of Pendergast, his public life is described well in Lyle W. Dorsett, *The Pendergast Machine* (New York: Oxford University Press, 1968). An older and still worthwhile social history is William M. Reddig, *Tom's Town* (Philadelphia: J. B. Lippincott Co., 1947). Lyle W. Dorsett, *Franklin D. Roosevelt and the City Bosses* (Port Washington, N.Y.: Kennikat Press, 1977) contains an interesting chapter on Pendergast and Roosevelt.

Perkins, Frances
(10 April 1882–14 May 1965)

Secretary of labor from 1933 to 1945. Although Frances Perkins is often remembered as America's first woman cabinet member, her role in promoting the social and labor legislation that laid the foundation for the modern welfare state was just as important.

Frances Perkins grew up in Massachusetts and graduated from Mount Holyoke College in 1902. Her participation in Progressive Era reform movements such as woman suffrage, her work in settlement houses, and her early efforts to legislate better conditions for America's working people deeply affected the course of her career. Of crucial importance to her developing social philosophy was her role on the commission set up to investigate New York factory conditions in the wake of the fire at the Triangle shirtwaist factory, which killed 146 female garment workers in 1911. Perkins's association with this commission confirmed her commitment to legislative solutions for social problems. "I'd much rather get a law than organize a union," she later said. This orientation would fundamentally affect her priorities as secretary of labor.

One of Perkins's colleagues on the Triangle investigating commission was Alfred E. Smith. When Smith was elected governor of New York in 1918, he gave Frances Perkins her start in government service by appointing her to the New York State Industrial Board, a first for women. In 1928 Governor-elect Franklin Roosevelt promoted Perkins to the post of industrial commissioner, and in 1933 he asked her to serve as his secretary of labor.

Franklin Roosevelt has received much credit for his dramatic decision to appoint the first woman to the cabinet, but his doing so was never a foregone conclusion. The post usually went to a labor leader, and Perkins had no such ties. Although many attributed the selection of Frances Perkins to Eleanor Roosevelt's intercession, Mary ("Molly") Dewson orchestrated nationwide support for the nomination and convinced Perkins to take the job. Roosevelt was sympathetic, but still delayed a decision until just several days before the inauguration. Ironically, the last member of the cabinet chosen was one of only two (along with Harold Ickes) to stay throughout the entire Roosevelt administration.

Frances Perkins was a rather reluctant symbol of the new roles women were playing in public life. She did not consider herself a feminist (she opposed the Equal Rights Amendment), but nevertheless she quietly supported women's causes in Washington. She kept a deliberately low profile, dressing conservatively in black dresses and the ever-present tricorn hat and filling her speeches with facts and figures rather than emotional oratory. At heart, she was a deeply religious woman with a strong sense of privacy. Unfortunately, this earned her the reputation of being uncooperative with the press; reporters never glimpsed the Frances Perkins who enchanted her close friends and associates with her warmth and spontaneous wit.

Perkins saw her mandate as secretary of labor more in terms of promoting the general welfare of American workers than encouraging the growth of the decade's labor movement. She built the Labor Department into a smoothly functioning bureaucracy. Her first act was to reform the corrupt Immigration and Naturalization Service; she then expanded the Bureau of Labor Statistics and created the Division of Labor Standards. Among the talented people she brought to Washington were Arthur Altmeyer, Isador Lubin, Clara Beyer, Mary LaDame, and Charles Wyzanski. Perkins also stimulated state labor departments and engineered American entry into the International Labor Organization. She did not ignore the labor movement, however, and after a period of initial doubt, labor leaders realized that Madam Secretary was an important ally for their rapidly developing movement.

Frances Perkins deserves special credit for her central role in drafting some of the New Deal's most important labor legislation. She was active in the code-drafting process of the National Recovery Administration (NRA), especially the codes for the steel and coal industries; when NRA guidelines protecting labor standards were ruled unconstitutional, she worked for passage of the 1938 Fair Labor Standards Act, which made permanent many of the NRA's gains. Even more significant was Perkins's central role in drafting the 1935 Social Security Act, one of the New Deal's most lasting accomplishments. She took on this task at President Roosevelt's personal insistence.

One reason for Perkins's effectiveness in the New Deal lay in the support she received from the president. Frances Perkins asserted emphatically that FDR had never once let her down. She and Roosevelt had a strong working relationship that dated back to their days in New York; he felt at ease delegating responsibility to talented women like Perkins, and he respected her commitment to improving working conditions through legislation. When she tried to resign in 1940 and 1944, he would not hear of it.

Like the New Deal, Frances Perkins found herself under attack during Roosevelt's second term. In 1939 she faced possible impeachment by the House of Representatives for her refusal to deport Harry Bridges, an official of a West Coast longshoreman's union accused of being a Communist. Although nothing came of this vendetta, it probably contributed to the low profile that Perkins maintained during the war years. She did not seek a powerful wartime administrative role, but concentrated instead on preserving the gains in labor standards won during the 1930s. After Roosevelt's death, Perkins took on a new assignment from President Truman—that of serving on the Civil Service Commission. When the Republicans returned to power in 1952, Perkins left government service for a fulfilling career as a lecturer and speaker, maintaining an affiliation with the Cornell School of Industrial and Labor Relations.

In 1946, Frances Perkins published *The Roosevelt I Knew,* an autobiograhical account of her participation in the New Deal. One of the first books to come out after his death, Perkins's portrait captures the elusive Roosevelt personality. She called FDR the most complicated human being she had ever met, but her ability to make him come alive in *The Roosevelt I Knew* is testimony to the close relationship she enjoyed with President Roosevelt throughout the New Deal.

In addition to Frances Perkins, *The Roosevelt I Knew* (New York: Viking, 1946), see George Martin's sympathetic treatment of her in *Madam Secretary: Frances Perkins* (Boston: Houghton Mifflin Co., 1976). Charles H. Trout supplies a concise biographical sketch in Barbara Sicherman and Carol Hurd Green, eds., *Notable American Women: The Modern Period* (Cambridge: Harvard University Press, 1980), pp. 535–39. For general background on labor in the 1930s, see Irving Bernstein, *Turbulent Years: A History of the American Worker, 1933–1941* (Boston: Houghton Mifflin Co., 1970). The Oral History Collection of Columbia University holds five thousand transcribed pages of interviews done with Perkins in the 1950s, which document her central role in the period's labor and welfare developments.

SUSAN WARE

See also Cabinets; Labor; New Deal; Relief; Women and the New Deal

Personal Diplomacy

Franklin Roosevelt's efforts, particularly during World War II, to shape world events by dealing directly (usually in face-to-face encounters, by personal correspondence, and through special envoys) with other heads of state or heads of government.

Among the occupants of the White House, FDR was certainly not the first personal diplomatist, that is, a president who—at times (but not always) maneuvering with minimal guidance or restraint by the State Department—invokes his own personality and prestige to influence world leaders and thereby determine the course of international affairs. After all, his kinsman, Theodore Roosevelt, virtually dictated the Treaty of Portsmouth which settled the Russo-Japanese War in 1905, and President Woodrow Wilson in 1919 gave himself over to what remains as the most strenuous exercise in personal diplomacy in the American experience when he headed the Washington

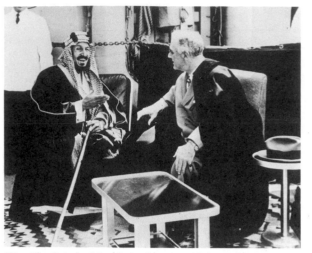

King Ibn Saʻud of Saudi Arabia, one of three monarchs (Haile Selassie of Ethiopia and King Farouk of Egypt were the others) who met with President Roosevelt as he sailed back to the States after the Yalta Conference. (International News Photo.)

Muhammad Reza Shah Pahlevi, shah of Iran, meeting with President Roosevelt during the Teheran Conference, 28 November–1 December 1943. (National Archives.)

Emperor Haile Selassie of Ethiopia and President Roosevelt confer aboard a U.S. cruiser at anchor in Egypt's Great Bitter Lake, February 1945. (U.S. Army Signal Corps.)

government's delegation to the Paris Peace Conference following World War I. But the second President Roosevelt stands unchallenged as the White House's most inveterate practitioner of personal diplomacy. A mere mentioning of the term personal diplomacy is apt to produce in the mind of one's auditor a succession of images of FDR: the thirty-second president exuding high humor while exchanging views with Great Britain's inestimable Winston Churchill aboard a man-o-war in Placentia Bay, entreating with Generalissimo Chiang Kai-shek in the shadows of Egypt's pyramids, looking wan and haggard while seated between Churchill and the Soviet dictator Joseph Stalin at Yalta.

That Roosevelt became a practitioner of personal diplomacy, particularly in the time of the Second World War, is understandable. Endowed (or perhaps burdened) with an outsized ego, FDR was not temperamentally suited to the role of staying in the background and leaving to underlings the task of conducting high-level negotiations with representatives of other governments, the more so when the very future of civilization seemed in the balance. Like a proverbial front-line general, in a word, he felt compelled (if one may invoke a tired expression) to be where the action was. Fully cognizant of his own personal magnetism, he also was serenely confident of his ability to reach the hearts and minds of those who entered his nimbus.

Still, it seems fair to say that considerations that transcended a large ego helped to turn Roosevelt to personal diplomacy. Like other presidents of the present century, he came to view the State Department as a creaky bureaucracy that was often immobilized by red tape. He calculated that by asserting his own personality in diplomatic affairs he could cut through the red tape and achieve results that were beyond the capacity of the harried men at State. Roosevelt doubtless reckoned, moreover, that as the head of a state of unprecedented military and economic power, and as one of the most admired men in the world, he was invested with assets he could exploit with telling effect in personal exchanges with other world leaders.

Preoccupied with home affairs, to wit, the task of moving the United States out of the Great Depression, Roosevelt made no large effort to bring his charismatic personality to bear in foreign affairs in the first years of his presidency. But then, in late 1936, in the face of increasing evidence that Europe was edging toward a new general war, he boarded the cruiser USS *Indianapolis* and made a leisurely voyage to South America to address the opening session of a special inter-American conference aimed at promoting "hemispheric solidarity" in the event the war indeed broke out on the other side of the Atlantic. Styling himself "a traveling salesman of peace," he met tumultuous receptions in Rio de Janeiro, Buenos Aires, and Montevideo, kindled the emotions of delegates to the inter-American conference, and seemed to succeed in his purpose of encouraging cooperation by the states of the Western hemisphere.

Twenty-eight months later, in spring of 1939, as Europe moved ever closer to war, Roosevelt elected to try his hand anew as a personal diplomatist. He dispatched an extraordinary public message to Berlin and Rome asking the dictators Adolf Hitler and Benito Mussolini for assurance that they would not order attacks on any of thirty-one specified countries for ten years. Heaping scorn on the American president, both of the dictators turned aside his appeal.

Less than five months later, the Germans precipitated the Second World War (to borrow a Churchillian phrase) by unleashing a torrent of fire and steel against Poland. Still, it was not until the accession of Churchill to the leadership of Great Britain as prime minister, in spring of 1940, when the Low Countries and France were falling under Hitler's control, that Roosevelt became an earnest practitioner of personal diplomacy. With the new prime minister, whom he had previously encountered only once (at a dinner in London in 1918), Roosevelt found instant rapport, and before long the two leaders were exchanging personal letters and notes at a rate of several per week. If they sometimes disagreed sharply, for example, over Britain's relations with subject peoples of its empire, and if Churchill came to feel that Roosevelt was slighting Britain in his quest to maintain cordial relations with the Soviet Union, the personal bond between the two men nevertheless remained intact to the time of Roosevelt's death near the end of the war.

In the course of the war, Roosevelt—whose enterprise in truth transcended personal diplomacy, and who by assuming traditional functions of the secretary of state became the veritable architect of American foreign policy—dealt at a personal level with other leaders of world renown. Gen. Charles de Gaulle, Chiang Kai-shek, and, most important, Marshal Joseph Stalin. He exchanged written communications with all three men. He communicated with Chiang and Stalin through personal emissaries (in the case of Stalin, for example, through his trusted aide Harry Hopkins). And, of course, he had face-to-face encounters with all three: with de Gaulle at Casablanca in early 1943 and in Washington in the summer of 1944; with Chiang at Cairo in the autumn of 1943; and with Stalin at Teheran in the autumn of 1943 and at Yalta in early 1945.

In these encounters, the president had opportunities to bring his fabled charm to the service of diplomacy. The results were not always encouraging. The meeting with de Gaulle at Casablanca was strained and essentially unproductive. Nor did the two men find much common ground when they met in Washington, notwithstanding public displays of cordiality. Try as he might, Roosevelt was unable to establish easy rapport with Chiang at Cairo. In the first plenary meetings at Teheran, he found Stalin stiff and unsmiling. At length, Roosevelt—by making fun of Churchill—succeeded in making Stalin laugh, whereupon he addressed the Soviet tyrant as "Uncle Joe." Sixteen months later at Yalta, the Soviet leader bristled when Roosevelt told him that in their private conversations he and Churchill referred to him as "Uncle Joe," and then thawed out and became a most agreeable host to his Anglo-American visitors. But at neither Teheran nor Yalta did he permit good fellowship to weaken his determination to press what he perceived to be the interests of the Soviet Union.

During his presidency, notably in the time of the Second World War, Roosevelt also had personal encounters of a diplomatic nature with lesser known national leaders. At Cairo in late 1943, for example, during his return from the Teheran Conference, he and Churchill tried over a three-day period to persuade President Ismet Inönü of Turkey to take his country into the war against Germany. The effort came to nothing, in part because the Americans and British, gathering forces for their much-discussed invasion of Hitler's Fortress Europe by way of the English Channel, were in no position to meet Inönü's demands for military assistance.

More interesting—and, in retrospect, substantially more important—was Roosevelt's meeting with King Ibn Saʿud of Saudi Arabia in early 1945 during a stopover on his return to the United States from the Yalta Conference. The meeting took place aboard the cruiser USS *Quincy* which was resting at anchor in the Great Bitter Lake at the southern end of the Suez Canal.

Transported from Jiddah aboard the destroyer USS *Murphy,* the king, arrayed in traditional Arab garb, arrived for the meeting while seated in a great gilt armchair that stood magnificently on the *Murphy*'s main deck. Guarding the royal presence were barefooted soldiers wielding drawn sabers. The focal point of the king's discussions with the president was the Zionist dream of establishing a Jewish state in Palestine. Calling attention to the suffering of Jews under Hitler, Roosevelt expressed the hope that Arabs would acquiesce in the settlement of ten thousand Jewish refugees in the latter country. Ibn Saʿud replied that he saw no reason why Arabs should be called upon to atone for the sins of Hitler. His argument found a mark with the president, hitherto a supporter of the Zionist dream, and to the consternation of Zionists in the United States he told Congress shortly after his return to Washington: "Of the problems of Arabia I learned more about the whole problem, the Moslem problem, the Jewish problem, by talking with Ibn Saʿud for five minutes that I could have learned in an exchange of two or three dozen letters."

Did Roosevelt's ventures in personal diplomacy yield important returns that were beyond the reach of conventional diplomacy? Probably they did not. One, of course, is tempted to cite the wartime unity between Britain and the United States—a unity that appeared to derive from the president's personal relationship with Churchill—as a glittering achievement of personal diplomacy. But it is clear in retrospect that the common purpose of overcoming the Axis conquerors was the cement that bound the great English-speaking democracies in the course of the Second World War, not the respect and affection that Roosevelt and Churchill obviously felt for each other. That Churchill was capable of resisting the blandishments of the American president when British imperial interests were in the balance demonstrates that in the last analysis he was moved by realpolitik rather than his fondness for Roosevelt. Clearly the personality of Roosevelt made no overpowering impression on de Gaulle or Stalin. De Gaulle manifestly disliked the American president, and both he and the Soviet dictator pressed what they perceived to be the interests of their nations to the limits that circumstances permitted, irrespective of the wishes of the American chief of state. Like Churchill, they were animated by realpolitik, hence cooperated with Roosevelt and his government only to the extent that it appeared in their interest to do so. As noted, such leaders of lesser international reputation as President Inönü of Turkey and King Ibn Sa'ud were likewise not inclined to allow the fabled Rooseveltian charm to beguile them into taking actions or making promises that contravened their principles or the apparent interests of their nations. Nor does it appear probable that a venture in personal diplomacy that Roosevelt refused to take—and for which refusal he later came under heavy criticism—would have dramatically altered the course of events, to wit, a meeting between Roosevelt and the Japanese prime minister, Prince Fumimaro Konoye, that the Tokyo government sought to arrange in August-September 1941.

Did Roosevelt's ventures in personal diplomacy, as latter-day critics have argued, result in mistakes that turned out to be disadvantageous or even disastrous from the perspective of the United States and its friends? More to the point, did Roosevelt airily make concessions, particularly to Stalin, that hardheaded professional diplomats, negotiating in conventional fashion, would have avoided? The answer is no. Critics of Roosevelt have failed to demonstrate that he made a single concession of any substance that had not received careful scrutiny by professionals of the State Department—or indeed made a single concession that military and political realities did not appear to warrant. One may argue that in the time of the Roosevelt presidency the United States made serious mistakes in its foreign relations. But such errors as may have been made, it seems fair to say, were not a result of Roosevelt's personal diplomacy.

Personal diplomacy, as such, remains one of many aspects of the Roosevelt presidency that has not been the subject of a scholarly monograph or even a first-rate article. The individual seeking enlightenment on Roosevelt as a personal diplomatist, therefore, must examine a variety of books and essays. A good place to begin is Robert Dallek's fine book, *Franklin D. Roosevelt and American Foreign Policy, 1932–1945* (New York: Oxford University Press, 1979). The Dallek volume relates Roosevelt's personal dealings with other heads of state and government throughout his presidency—and accords Roosevelt high marks as a personal diplomatist. For the period of the Second World War, when Roosevelt's career as a personal diplomatist reached its apogee, one ought to consult Herbert Feis's masterful volume entitled *Churchill, Roosevelt, Stalin: The War They Waged and the Peace They Sought* (Princeton: Princeton University Press, 1957). Like Dallek, Feis generally took a favorable view of Roosevelt's diplomatic endeavors, as did James MacGregor Burns in *Roosevelt: The Soldier of Freedom* (New York: Harcourt Brace Jovanovich, 1970). More critical is the

slender volume by Robert A. Divine, *Roosevelt and World War II* (Baltimore: Johns Hopkins Press, 1969). For Roosevelt's relationship with Churchill, one ought to consult Francis L. Loewenheim, Harold D. Langley, and Manfred Jonas, eds., *Roosevelt and Churchill: Their Secret Wartime Correspondence* (New York: Saturday Review Press/E. P. Dutton & Co., 1975), and also the volumes in Churchill's autobiographical *The Second World War* (Boston: Houghton Mifflin Co., 1948–53). For his dealings with Stalin, particularly at the Yalta meeting, one might examine the laudatory volume by Edward R. Stettinius, Jr., *Roosevelt and the Russians: The Yalta Conference* (Garden City, N.Y.: Doubleday, 1949). For dealings with de Gaulle, see *The War Memoirs of Charles de Gaulle* (New York: Simon & Schuster, 1960), and David Schoenbrun, *The Three Lives of Charles de Gaulle* (New York: Atheneum, 1966). The meeting between Roosevelt and Ibn Sa'ud is graphically sketched in Charles E. Bohlen, *Witness to History, 1929–1969* (New York: W. W. Norton & Co., 1973).

JOHN EDWARD WILZ

See also Atlantic Conference and Charter; Atomic Bomb; Byrnes, James Francis; Cabinets; Cairo Conference; Casablanca Conference; Chiang Kai-shek; Churchill, Winston Leonard Spencer; Commander in Chief; de Gaulle, Charles; Daniels, Josephus; Foreign Policy; Good Neighbor Policy; Hopkins, Harry L.; Hull, Cordell; Internationalism and Peace; Japan; Joint Chiefs of Staff; Office of the Presidency; Quebec Conferences; Stalin, Joseph and the Soviet Union; Teheran Conference; World War II; Yalta Conference; Zionism

Personal Writings

A prolific and accomplished letter writer, Franklin Roosevelt produced a large corpus of personal correspondence, most of which has been carefully preserved. His penchant for saving was cultivated by his mother who retained even his earliest scribblings, some of which were published in Elliott Roosevelt's collection of his father's personal correspondence. Notably absent are Franklin's courtship letters which Eleanor apparently burned in 1937. On occasion correspondence with particular individuals—Winston Churchill and Felix Frankfurter, for example—was so extensive as to warrant separate publication. Most Roosevelt letters remain unpublished, however, and are deposited with the Roosevelt Library in Hyde Park.

Writing fascinated him almost as much as politics. During the twenties, he tried his hand at books on the navy, a biography of John Paul Jones, and a U.S. history. Roosevelt lacked the temperament for sustained literary efforts, however, and none of these projects reached fruition. Those books that did appear under his imprimatur, *Looking Forward* (1933) and *On Our Way* (1934), were compilations of articles and speeches he had published or delivered previously. A frequent contributor to magazines and an occasional newspaper columnist until his election as governor, he depicted himself as a journalist by avocation and delighted in reminding newspapermen that he had once edited the *Harvard Crimson*. It was not until after he was appointed assistant secretary of the navy, however, that his journalistic contributions appeared with any regularity. Most such efforts ("What the Navy Can Do for Your Boy," *Ladies' Home Journal*, June 1917, and "On Your Own Heads," *Scribner's*, April 1917, are random illustrations) were conceived to generate public support for current programs. Yet some retain considerable interest as harbingers of FDR's subsequent thought. An early advocate of universal military training, he opined that "if every boy of eighteen years of age were to give a year of his life to the nation, the advantage would be at least as much with him as with the country." Other judgments underwent considerable modification. Noting in the *North American* (October 1915) that "the submarine has come to stay," he predicted its principal role would be as "part of the protection to and attacking power of a battleship fleet."

As assistant secretary, Roosevelt's responsibilities included overseeing contingency plans for war with Japan, and his sustained interest in Japanese-American relations is evident from subsequent articles. In a July 1925 article for *Asia* magazine, he explored the "mutual distrust that has undoubtedly been characteristic of Japan and the United States." Roosevelt concluded that since the Philippines were virtually indefensible against Japanese attack and the U.S. Pacific coast impregnable to Japanese invasion, "war would be a futile gesture attended by no sufficiently compensating results." At the root of his expectations for more amiable relations were recent demonstrations by the Japanese government that it "desire[d] to prove to the world that suspicions of the past are no longer justified." Nonetheless, Japanese integration remained a conspicuous issue. Americans, Roosevelt wrote, "honestly believe . . . that the mingling of white with oriental blood on an extensive scale is harmful to our future citizenship." Americans objected to both "non-assimilable immigrants as citizens" and "extensive proprietorship of land without citizenship." Roosevelt's accord with these sentiments is apparent from guest columns he wrote contemporaneously for the *Macon* (Georgia) *Daily Telegraph*.

Throughout the 1920s, a major share of FDR's personal correspondence and journalistic essays was directed toward harmonizing Democratic party politics and heralding the party's virtues. He portrayed the Republican party as the instrument of the moneyed class "wholly lacking in understanding or in fear of the rights of . . . the poor, the uneducated, the average human being." Roosevelt used the occasion of his 1925 review of Claude Bowers's *Jefferson and Hamilton* to dignify these views with historical perspective. A year previous, in letters to Democratic leaders, he had written of Jeffersonian and Hamiltonian ideals so as to "apply their fundamental differences to present-day policies of our two great parties." It made him "boil inwardly" when "smug writers" denied that "the forces hostile to the control of government by the people . . . could still be a

threat." Alexander Hamilton, whom "we honor because of his master stroke for sound money," was nonetheless a "convinced opponent of popular government." Jefferson we honor not only as "the savior of the deeper ideals of the Revolution, but also [as] the man with human feelings, the consummate politician." Jefferson's "conception of a democratic republic came true," but Roosevelt divined that the "same contending forces" that had struggled for supremacy at the birth of the republic were again mobilizing. Hamiltons we have today. "Is there," he pondered "a Jefferson on the horizon?"

Roosevelt's eloquence and ceaseless politicking blended to enhance his reputation as a national party spokesman, and on the eve of the 1928 presidential campaign he articulated "A Democratic View" of foreign policy for the July issue of *Foreign Affairs*. Unless, Roosevelt wrote, the United States took the "deliberate position" that it owes "nothing to the rest of mankind and dare[s] nothing for the opinion of others so long as our seacoasts are impregnable and our pocketbooks are filled," American policy, or lack of policy, over the past nine years "must be counted on the debt side of the ledger." "[T]he outside world almost unanimously views us with less good will today than at any previous period." Accepting as fact that a majority of American voters opposed membership in the League of Nations, his prescription nevertheless included greater cooperation and "definite official help than we have hitherto accorded," especially in "those proceedings which bear on the general good of mankind." Single-handed intervention must give way to collective action. Other nations were as jealous of their sovereignty as we were of ours, and it was "only right that we should respect a similar feeling among other nations."

Shortly after the *Foreign Affairs* article appeared, Roosevelt won election as governor of New York State, continuing as governor or president until his death. While the volume of his personal correspondence continued almost unabated, the demands of high public office restricted his journalistic contributions to very occasional items. The thirteen-volume *Public Papers and Addresses of Franklin D. Roosevelt* is a partial exception. In 1937, the president, in collaboration with Samuel Rosenman, his longtime aide and principal speech writer, began a multivolume edition of his speeches and public papers since 1928. Although private letters and memoranda were not included, there were extensive forewords, prefaces, and explanatory notes either signed by or ascribed to the president. For the first nine volumes, which carried through 1940 and were published before Roosevelt's death, these notes constitute the closest we have to a Roosevelt autobiography. Some critics regard them as "possibly the most valuable part of the whole collection." Rosenman completed the final four volumes after Roosevelt's death, and the explanatory notes that accompany these volumes are not attributed to the president.

A simulated memoir for the years 1932 through 1941, *The F.D.R. Memoirs* written by Bernard Asbell, was published in 1973. Asbell "was in no way connected with F.D.R.—either with his public career or personal life," and conceived the project after the publication of the Truman and Eisenhower memoirs. An engaging biography written in the first person, it makes generous use of Roosevelt's personal writings.

Commentators on Roosevelt frequently stress the importance of his writings as a guide to his actions. It was Samuel Rosenman's firm belief, and one shared by others, that "more than any other president—perhaps more than any other political figure in history—Franklin D. Roosevelt used the spoken and written word to exercise leadership and carry out policies."

For personal correspondence, see Elliott Roosevelt, ed., *F.D.R., His Personal Letters*, 4 vols. (New York: Duell, 1947–50). *Roosevelt and Frankfurter: Their Correspondence 1928–45*, annotated by Max Freedman (Boston: Little, Brown & Co., 1967) and Warren F. Kimball, ed., *Churchill and Roosevelt, the Complete Correspondence*, 3 vols. (Princeton: Princeton University Press, 1984) attest to Roosevelt's long-term and wide-ranging correspondence with particular individuals. FDR's newspaper columns were edited by Donald Scott Carmichael, *FDR Columnist* (Chicago: Pellegrini & Cudahy, 1947). Roosevelt wrote they proved "that no one can write a column on public affairs once a day or twice a week." "Is There a Jefferson on the Horizon?" the review of Claude Bowers originally published in the 3 December 1925 *New York Evening World,* was reprinted in the *American Mercury* (September 1945). *The Public Papers and Addresses of Franklin D. Roosevelt, 1928–45*, 13 vols., were edited by Samuel I. Rosenman and published between 1938 and 1950 by Random House, Macmillan Co., and Harper & Bros. successively. Also see Bernard Asbell, *The F.D.R. Memoirs* (New York: Doubleday & Co., 1973).

SAMUEL B. HAND

FDR and Budgie on donkey back, 1889. (Courtesy FDR Library.)

Fala. (Courtesy FDR Library.)

Pets

At Springwood, as at all the country homes in the Hudson River Valley, there were always dogs and ponies from which Franklin derived much affection and companionship. His mother wrote in mid-November of his first year that "baby tries to imitate Budgy and the cats." Budgy, a Spitz, was the first of the many dogs Franklin loved and kept near him all his life. His parents taught him responsibility for their care when he was five: he was allowed to accept a red setter named Marksman as a gift from his uncle Warren Delano with the understanding that he alone would be responsible for the puppy's feeding and watering and care. He carried out his duties not only for Marksman but for the Welsh pony, Debby, he acquired, for succeeding Texan three-quarter horses, and for the many dogs that followed Marksman. Franklin handled his pony and horses well and became a fine horseman. He enjoyed immensely his rides alone along the winding paths at Springwood, and those with his parents on tours of the estate and later with his wife and children, until his disabling illness made it impossible for him to continue this pastime.

The first of the Scotch terriers was Duffy, purchased in Scotland while Eleanor and Franklin were on their honeymoon. The last of the Scotties, and the best known, was Fala, one of the president's favorites. Franklin's cousin, Margaret Suckley, a dog breeder, gave him the puppy in 1940; his full name was Murray the Outlaw of Fala Hill. Fala joined the president in Washington and rarely thereafter left him; he went with FDR to Hyde Park, to Warm Springs, and on board cruisers at sea. He slept in a special chair in the president's bedroom, received tidbits from the table, and generally was well loved and loving. During the presidential campaign of 1944, Roosevelt answered an attack by the Republican party with his famous Fala speech. Fala had been left behind accidentally on one of the Aleutian Islands while accompanying Roosevelt on a sea trip, and the story was spread that the president had sent a destroyer back for him at a cost to the taxpayers of millions of dollars. Roosevelt in his speech wryly defended the Scotty, saying that he, Roosevelt, expected such criticism aimed at himself and that his family expected critical assaults, but that the Scotty had not been the same since the charge was made: "His Scotch soul was furious." Fala was at Warm Springs when Franklin Roosevelt died in April 1945 and followed the funeral cortege from the Little White House in the family car.

For more information, see Olin Dows, *Franklin Roosevelt at Hyde Park* (New York: American Artists Group, 1949); Richard Harrity and Ralph G. Martin, *The Human Side of F.D.R.* (New York: Duell, Sloan & Pearce, 1960); William D. Hassett, *Off the Record with F.D.R.: 1942–1945* (New Brunswick, N.J.: Rutgers University Press, 1958); Rita Halle Kleeman, *Gracious Lady: The Life of Sara Delano Roosevelt* (New York and London: D. Appleton-Century Co., 1935); and Elliott Roosevelt, ed., *F.D.R.: His Personal Letters, 1905–1928* (New York: Duell, Sloan & Pearce, 1948).

Photographs

The first photograph of Franklin Delano Roosevelt was taken on the day of his christening, seven weeks after his birth on 30 January 1882. From then on family albums and newspapers and magazines display pictures of him taken by his parents, wife, and children, by himself, or by news photographers. He is shown on his donkey with Budgy, his dog; in a tree crow's nest playing at naval battle; with his pony, Debby, in the Springwood stable; and lying on the floor sorting or pasting stamps.

When he was fourteen, he was himself bitten by the camera bug. Given a tripod-mounted Kodak with one of the first self-timers, Franklin developed a lively interest in photography, taking pictures of his parents at home and abroad, of his grandfather and cousins at Algonac, and of himself and his friends at Groton and Harvard. In a shared darkroom using paper and chemicals sent to him by his mother, he developed the plates and printed them himself.

After his marriage to Eleanor Roosevelt and a stint as a lawyer, Franklin entered politics. Then began that "strange and electrical communion between Roosevelt and a lens." Photographers were eager to catch his informality and photogenic features. There were photos of him campaigning for state senator, visiting navy yards and bases as assistant secretary of

A cheerful FDR stands alone at Groton in June of 1932. The seemingly artless pose was carefully engineered, with the car door giving him the support usually provided by crutches, a lectern, or someone's arm. (Courtesy FDR Library.)

Franklin D. Roosevelt, boy photographer, at the Delano family homestead, Fairhaven, Massachusetts, in the autumn of 1897. (Courtesy FDR Library.)

the navy, and accepting the nomination for the vice-presidency. Between 1921 and 1923 his polio attack kept him out of the public eye, although family portraits picture him sunbathing in Palm Beach and fishing at Warm Springs. Then, though he had to wear leg braces and lean for support on crutches or some willing arm to stand, he nevertheless returned to politics and the years of his governorship and the presidency.

It became customary for both still and newsreel photographers to accompany Roosevelt on his trips to Hyde Park, Warm Springs, the Pacific, the Panama Canal, and Europe. One of the cameramen became a favorite because of his exceptional skill. FDR always asked for this press photographer, Sammy Schulman, and singled him out at press conferences. During the 1932 campaign for the presidency on the train going to Columbus, the president asked Sammy to tell him everything about the business of photography. They talked, Schulman wrote, until Roosevelt was satisfied that he knew enough: "why certain poses were better than others; why so many shots were made of the same subject . . . ; how the stuff was developed." And it was Schulman who later taught the president how to use a speed graphic, for which Roosevelt was grateful.

As a shrewd campaigner and politician, the president recognized the value of a strong and vital image and cooperated within reason with photographers' requests for stills, movies, or sound pictures, stipulating only that "he was never to be photographed in pain or discomfort—otherwise, anything went." Because of his "courage to strive despite his handicap," most news photographers and picture editors voluntarily censored their shots, destroying unsuitable plates. However, there were official limitations laid down by Stephen Early, the president's press secretary, and later by the Secret Service, to protect Roosevelt's safety or privacy: photographers were limited as to how close they might approach the president; they were to "use their cameras on tripods"; their pictures were to be "taken simultaneously at a time when the President indicated that he was ready"; and candid cameras were "barred from the White House." These rules controlled the photographic image Roosevelt wished to project: a vigorous, jaunty, active president engaged in the many activities of his office, waving to the crowds, smiling his infectious smile—"the most photographed man in the world during his lifetime."

For more information, see Joseph Alsop, *FDR, 1882–1945: A Centenary Remembrance* (New York: Viking Press, 1982); Kenneth S. Davis, *FDR: The Beckoning of Destiny, 1882–1928, A History* (New York: G. P. Putnam's Sons, 1972); Olin Dows, *Franklin Roosevelt at Hyde Park* (New York: American Artists Group 1949); Compton Mackenzie, *Mr. Roosevelt* (New York: E. P. Dutton & Co., 1944); William McKinley Moore, "FDR's Image: A Study in Pictorial Symbols" (Ph.D. diss., University of Wisconsin, Madison, 1946); Research Collection, *Roosevelt Family Papers* (Hyde Park, N.Y.: FDR Library and Museum); William L. Rivers, *The Opinionmakers* (Boston: Beacon Press, 1965); Sammy Schulman, *"Where's Sammy?"* ed. Robert Considine (New York: Random House, 1943); and Betty Houchin Winfield, "F.D.R.'s Pictorial Image, Rules and Boundaries," *Journalism History* 5, no. 4 (Winter 1978–79):110–14, 136.

See also News Media; Portraits

Pinchot, Gifford

(11 August 1865–4 October 1946)

Forester, conservationist, and governor of Pennsylvania. Born in Simsbury, Connecticut, to wealthy New York parents, Gifford Pinchot was raised in an upper-class social atmosphere that combined European influences with an invigorating combination of American culture and politics. Educated in private schools, Pinchot graduated from Yale in 1889 and pursued his interests in forestry at the French National Forestry School, where he became captivated with the idea of public management of forest resources. He began his

A pensive Gifford Pinchot with FDR during the Governors' Conference at French Lick Springs Hotel, 2 June 1931. (Courtesy of the French Lick Springs Hotel.)

career in 1892 by applying the principles of scientific forestry to the Biltmore estate of George W. Vanderbilt in North Carolina. For the following six years, Pinchot consulted on numerous forestry projects, traveled the country extensively, and advocated public management of forests along utilitarian principles.

In 1898, Pinchot began his public career as chief of the small federal Division of Forestry. He set to work putting his principles into practice and soon established a respected following of professional foresters. This reputation for professionalism, together with support from President Theodore Roosevelt, allowed Pinchot to transfer the nation's forest reserves from the Interior Department to the Agriculture Department under the care of an expanded Forest Service with himself as chief forester. From this position, he expanded his influence among Roosevelt's inner circle to become a leading figure in the fight for progressive conservation. The tall, hardy man with a handlle-bar mustache was an appropriate colleague for the boisterous Roosevelt, and Pinchot was a central personality in many of Roosevelt's conservation projects, including the Inland Waterways Commission and the White House Conference on the Conservation of Natural Resources in 1908. Pinchot remained in office under Roosevelt's successor, William Howard Taft, until a bitter dispute with Taft's secretary of the interior, Richard A. Ballinger, forced Pinchot to resign.

Pinchot returned to public office in 1920 as Pennsylvania's forestry commissioner and won as the Republican party's nominee for governor in 1922. He used this office to continue his progressive agenda of governmental reorganization and tighter control of state utilities. After an unsuccessful try at the Senate in 1926, he was again elected governor in 1930 and forged a curious relationship with the New Deal. Pinchot publicly criticized President Herbert Hoover's handling of the depression and refused to endorse Hoover as his own party's nominee in 1932. Privately he preferred Franklin Roosevelt, a distant cousin of his political mentor and a candidate who shared Pinchot's own conservation and reform impulses.

Pinchot had helped the young Franklin Roosevelt draft a conservation bill for the New York legislature in 1912, and immediately after the election, he again offered his help to the new president. Although Pinchot helped to place his friend Harold Ickes as secretary of the interior, this friendship later soured when Ickes unsuccessfully tried to transfer the Forest Service to Interior. Pinchot's support for Roosevelt was marred only by the 1934 elections when Pinchot criticized the Pennsylvania Democratic ticket which Roosevelt favored. Similar interests in conservation overcame this rift due to party differences, and Pinchot campaigned for Roosevelt in his last three elections. A regular correspondent with President Roosevelt, Pinchot caught Roosevelt's interest with a proposal for a postwar international conference on conservation, but the president died before the idea could be implemented. One year later, Pinchot, a white-haired man of eighty-one, died of leukemia in a New York hospital.

Pinchot tells his own story, including his version of the Pinchot-Ballinger controversy, in *Breaking New Ground* (New York: Harcourt, Brace, & Co., 1947). M. Nelson McGeary, *Gifford Pinchot: Forester-Politician* (Princeton: Princeton University Press, 1960) is a fine general biography. Pinchot's relationship to Roosevelt and the New Deal is detailed in James A. Kehl and Samuel J. Astorino, "A Bull Moose Responds to the New Deal: Pennsylvania's Gifford Pinchot," *Pennsylvania Magazine of History and Biography* 88 (January 1964):37–51.

See also Conservation; Liberalism and Progressivism

Planning

The substance and practice of economic, social, environmental, and strategic planning constituted a creative and critical political and intellectual experience during the administration of Franklin Delano Roosevelt. The planners were a major component of the New Deal's talent, and since FDR himself occupied the position of number one planner as well as principal brains truster, planning set the stage for some of the most dramatic chapters of New Deal history. Moreover, planning remains one of the New Deal's more promising, yet most controversial, legacies to the present day.

Transcending but incorporating the usual forms of material planning, New Deal planning was conceived broadly to be economic, social, and political in content, and it became increasingly regional, national, and international in scope. Planning was defined by New Dealers as (1) pre-vision of emerging developments and future trends (2) systematically portrayed and accurately analyzed (3) in terms of facts pertinent to the problem areas concerned and the policies proposed, and (4) productive of plans continually adjusted by experience and corrected through feedback, (5) all of which was to be finalized through wide interest representation by means of thorough democratic participation. In a society suffering from a depressed economy, New Deal planning was expected to go to the roots of socioeconomic crisis and to formulate mature and responsible policies.

In characteristically empirical style, Roosevelt told how he arrived at his own conception of planning and how planning became one of his "pet children." In December 1931, while serving his final year as governor of New York, Roosevelt addressed a blue-ribbon audience in New York City, which was celebrating publication of the *Regional Plan of New York and Its Environs,* produced under the chairmanship of New York banker-businessman Frederic Delano. Nostalgically, he recalled "the days . . . nearly twenty years ago when my uncle, Mr. Delano, first talked to me about planning for the City of Chicago. (In 1911, Chicago had a faulty government but a superb city plan—the world-renowned Daniel Burnham Plan of 1907—and Delano, then a railroad executive headquartered in Chicago, had gotten deeply involved as a devoted civic leader and concerned city planner in the Burnham Plan's execution.) I think that from that very moment I have been interested in not the mere planning of a single city but in the larger aspects of planning. It is the way of the future, not a science but a new understanding of problems that affect not merely bricks and mortar, subways and streets; planning that affects also the economic and social life of a community, then of a county, then of a state; perhaps the day is not far distant when planning will become a part of the national policy of this country."

This was not the first time Roosevelt captivated audiences with stories about his "original" discovery of planning as a basic building block of his New Deal. The reasons he and his biographers offer for his proclivity toward planning are many: boyhood and early manhood chores at the family Hyde Park estate on farming and forestry matters with their recurring seasonal demands for planning ahead; the pervasive impact from his youth of the progressive conservation movement as an earlier expression of planning in American history spearheaded by his cousin, President Theodore Roosevelt; his military planning and administrative duties as assistant secretary of the navy during World War I; his business experience as president of the American Construction Council, when he tried to teach the nation's builders how to plan their work so as to smooth out the booms and busts in their business cycle; and his vigorous efforts as New York legislator and governor at planning the state's agricultural and industrial recovery, welfare and relief programs, as well as its hydroelectric development, including the St. Lawrence River Basin.

Not all of Roosevelt's associates considered him to be a planning prodigy. Brains truster Raymond

Moley was to caustically observe of the New Deal: "To look upon these policies as the result of a unique plan was to believe that the accumulation of stuffed snakes, baseball pictures, school flags, old tennis shoes, carpenter's tools, geometry books, and chemistry sets in a boy's bedroom could have been put there by an interior decorator." Similarly, Roosevelt's secretary of labor, Frances Perkins, also doubted the existence of any "New Deal plan," but she applauded the humaneness and timeliness of Roosevelt's programs. Perkins concluded: "The New Deal was not a plan. Most of the programs arose out of the emergency. But there was no central unified plan. The New Deal grew out of these emerging and necessary actions. The intellectual and spiritual climate was Roosevelt's general attitude that the people mattered. The action was not projected from a central pattern, but the people mattered."

Although Perkins was right in insisting that the New Deal lacked a unified plan, and to that extent Moley was correct in criticizing Rooseveltian planning, both failed to credit adequately New Deal planning as the first systematic and comprehensive American commitment to deliberative policymaking and effective program formulation.

Not all Roosevelt's efforts in the realm of planning proved fruitful and some were rank failures. Most prominent among these was his National Industrial Recovery Administration (NIRA), held unconstitutional by the Supreme Court. Demolished with NIRA was FDR's full-employment plan, which the New Deal never did achieve until wartime.

The achieved and lasting New Deal plans include: nationalization of public welfare, notably social security; federally insured home mortgage and other governmentally guaranteed popular credit programs; banking and other financial regulatory reforms, including the Securities and Exchange Commission (SEC) and Federal Deposit Insurance Corporation (FDIC); farm income parity through planned production under the Agricultural Adjustment Administration (AAA); urban labor's amelioration through job programs and National Labor Relations Board (NLRB) functions; public works planning; Tennessee Valley Authority (TVA) and other regional and resource development programs such as Civilian Conservation Corps (CCC); defense production planning including wartime wage-and-price control; and Keynesian fiscal planning of government budgets and public debts which, after a half century of unrelenting criticism and attempted dismantling, persists as a viable New Deal legacy.

Although a few such plans had been cursorily conceived by progressives in the 1910s and reformers in the 1920s, and Roosevelt had attained some at the state level as New York's governor from 1928 to 1932, the New Deal's comprehensive planning agenda dates from Roosevelt's brains trusting in the election year of 1932. Upon entering the White House in March 1933, he had to adapt his planning to the immediate economic crisis and evolving political scene. This explains the origin of his partially improvised,

yet seriously planned, roster of congressional enactments during the hundred days.

Then New Deal planning embarked on its own organizational career. The National Planning Board, first placed in the Public Works Administration (PWA), became an intercabinet agency entitled National Resources Board and then National Resources Committee, and finally elevated to the Executive Office of the President as National Resources Planning Board (NRPB). Like the New Deal itself, the NRPB had been born in crisis and was constantly embroiled in dispute, and it was abolished in 1943 following an animated congressional debate that reflected the board's controversial rather than ineffectual record. Yet the NRPB was no sooner abolished than its major planning responsibilities were reassumed by other agencies, both New Deal and post–New Deal like the council of economic advisors.

The decisive feature of the New Deal's planning apparatus was not structural; rather, it was the planning personnel—its quality and character. Not since the country's formative constitutional era were so many American minds available for such devoted and creative public service. By the midpoint of the New Deal in 1939, some one thousand generalist and specialist policy and program planners and formulators, many of potential brains-trust capacity, were at work at various levels of governmental responsibility: (1) in the major New Deal agencies, principally the NRPB itself; (2) in the most planning-minded bureaus in the established federal departments—Treasury, War, Commerce, Interior, Agriculture, and Labor; (3) in the legislative branch, the New Deal's senators and congressmen and their growing committee staffs; and (4) on the NRPB's roster of planning consultants outside of Washington. This consisted largely of professional planners working for the NRPB's network of regional and river basin committees, of planning-oriented academics, and of experienced state and city planners. In fact, the city-planning profession was originally the major source of recruitment for New Deal planners. It had during the twenties enjoyed the blessings of the city-planning- and urban-housing-minded U.S. secretary of commerce, Herbert Hoover. Then under the New Deal in the early thirties, rich supplementary stimuli for planners emerged in newer fields ranging from economic and fiscal planning to welfare and social planning.

The New Deal planning hierarchy included not only a president but two vice-presidents who had cut their political eye teeth on the planning function— Henry Wallace as an Iowa rural planner, Harry Truman as a Missouri county planner. Both burgeoned during the New Deal—Wallace as agricultural planner, Truman as watchdog over military production planning. But the main repository of New Deal planning experience remained the extraordinary personnel of the NRPB, working under its benign chairman, "Uncle Fred" Delano. FDR's habit of sending official communications from the White House to the planning board addressed to "Dear Uncle Fred" infuriated the Republican opposition, but it delighted the inveterate New Deal planners who admired "Uncle Fred" and his provocative writings, such as "What about the Year 2000?" However, the board's driving intellect was its vice-chairman, University of Chicago professor Charles Merriam, eminent leader of the country's political science profession. An active Chicago politician since pre–World War I progressive days, Merriam became a policy scientist and planner early in the New Deal era. He was thoroughly versed in comparative socioeconomic theory and contemporary fiscal and economic practice, and he fruitfully applied this knowledge base to NRPB activities. Flanking Merriam and Delano as the board's third member was Columbia University professor Wesley Mitchell, foremost authority on the American business cycle, which was then the main bugaboo of the nation's economy. Valuable economic and fiscal planning skills were contributed by the NRPB's advisers from the realm of business, Henry Dennison, president of the Dennison Manufacturing company, and Beardsley Ruml, treasurer of Macy's.

The NRPB had at its disposal, moreover, Professor Alvin Hansen, Harvard's most recently converted Keynesian economist, and also its more home-grown NRPB-type planners such as Nobel Prize–winning economist Wassily Leontief. Harvard's Charles Eliot headed NRPB'S entire staff. Columbia contributed such economists as John Maurice Clark, Thomas Blaisdell, Gardiner Means, Adolf Berle, and Social Security planner Eveline Burns. Also utilized were the talents of the University of Chicago's employment planner Paul Douglas, Treasury planner Jacob Viner, resources planner Gilbert White, urbanism planner Louis Wirth, and technology planner William Ogburn. In compiling any NRPB roster, there is the danger of ignoring several inventive junior staffers who fashioned the fiscal formulas and concocted the economic plans for which the NRPB was credited but sometimes condemned: Martin Krost, income-increasing federal expenditures; Oscar Altman, savings-induced investment; Paul Samuelson, full-employment stabilization; John Kenneth Galbraith, public works planning; and Milton Friedman, the consumption, or demand-side, function.

The intimate narratives of the New Deal planners themselves are revealing. Thus, NRPB's postwar planner Luther Gulick has recalled his wartime assignment of elaborating Roosevelt's and Churchill's four freedoms into a United Nations draft Bill of Rights and, simultaneously, into an upgraded New Deal version of the American Bill of Rights. Gulick included everything from "the right to work" to "the right to rest, recreation, and adventure"; nor did he hesitate to insert in between "the right to live in a system of free enterprise, free from compulsory labor, irresponsible private power, arbitrary public authority, and unregulated monopolies."

Recounting a similar NRPB assignment, economic and social planner Floyd Reeves described White House clearance of his plans for postwar demobilization, including his recommendations for what was to become the GI Bill of Rights. After a day devoted to strategic planning concerning the battle of Europe, FDR spent the night shift with Reeves checking every word of his historic report.

Such thoroughgoing socioeconomic plans were to be revived in the late 1960s. Vice-president Hubert Humphrey, who had absorbed every one of the elaborate NRPB reports, resumed the campaign for full-employment planning under a reorganized Council of Economic Advisers, and his understudy, Walter Mondale, advocated a Council of Social Advisers. Yet, in the continuing politics of American planning, Humphrey's unanswered query persists: "Can the 'plain people' of America with the aid of socially-minded experts and leaders build up, planfully and peacefully, a new economic and political equilibrium?"

For more information concerning New Deal planning, see: Marion Clawson, *New Deal Planning: The National Resources Planning Board* (Baltimore and London: Johns Hopkins University Press, 1981); Otis L. Graham, Jr., *Toward a Planned Society: From Roosevelt to Nixon* (New York: Oxford University Press, 1976); David E. Wilson, *The National Planning Idea in United States Public Policy* (Boulder: Westview Press, 1980); George Galloway and Associates, *Planning for America* (New York: Henry Holt and Co., 1941); Albert Lepawsky, "Style and Substance in Contemporary Planning: The American New Deal's National Resources Planning Board as a Model," *Plan Canada* 18, nos. 3–4 (September-December 1978):153–87; Lewis L. Lorwin, *Time for Planning: A Social-Economic Theory and Program for the Twentieth Century* (New York and London: Harper & Bros., 1945); Findlay Mackenzie, ed., *Planned Society, Yesterday, Today, and Tomorrow* (New York: Prentice-Hall, 1937); John D. Millett, *The Process and Organization of Government Planning* (New York: Columbia University Press, 1947); George Soule, *Planning U.S.A.* (New York: Viking Press, 1967); Barbara Wootton, *Plan or No Plan* (New York: Farrar & Rinehart, 1935); U.S. Federal Emergency Administration of Public Works, *National Planning Board, Final Report, 1933–1934* (Washington, D.C.: U.S. Government Printing Office, 1934); and Ferdinand Zweig, *The Planning of Free Societies* (London: Secker & Warburg, 1942). Relevant discussions may also be found in individual issues of the journal of the National Economic and Social Planning Association, *Plan Age*, 1, no. 1A (December 1934) to 6, nos. 9–10 (November-December 1940).

ALBERT LEPAWSKY

See also Agricultural Adjustment Administration; Agriculture; Business; Conservation; Fiscal Policy; Great Depression; Housing and Resettlement; Ickes, Harold LeClair; Liberalism and Progressivism; Monetary Policy; National Resources Planning Board; New Deal; Office of the Presidency; Regulation, Federal; Reorganization Act of 1939; Taxation; Tugwell, Rexford Guy; War Mobilization

Polio

Forty years after FDR's death, every event in his career has been subjected to the most intense scrutiny. But the central characteristic that marked FDR the man—his severe physical disability—has been minimized. From 10 August 1921 to 12 April 1945, every day of his life had to be structured around his disability. How disabled FDR was and how he coped with his physical disability was concealed during his lifetime.

In August 1921, FDR was summering on Campobello Island, New Brunswick, Canada. After returning from Washington and New York, he took his family sailing on 10 August and on the way home spotted on a nearby island a forest fire, which he and his sons fought. When he returned to his cottage, he felt a chill and went to bed. The next morning he found that his left leg dragged and was too weak to sustain his weight. By nightfall, his temperature had risen to 102 degrees, and he had considerable pain in his legs and back. FDR had not become exposed to polio at Campobello, since the incubation period for the virus varies from three to thirty-five days. He may have contracted the disease during the summer in Washington or at a Boy Scout outing in New York. After initial misdiagnosis by the local family doctor, FDR's uncle Fred Delano consulted Dr. Samuel Levine at the Harvard Infantile Paralysis Commission, who, in turn, diagnosed the illness as poliomyelitis. They reached Dr. Robert Lovett, the foremost specialist on infantile paralysis (as polio was then called), and shortly Lovett was on his way to Campobello.

Lovett found FDR paralyzed from the waist down and running a moderate fever in the range of 100 degrees; there was some involvement of his facial muscles, and his back muscles were so weak he could

A rare photograph of FDR in a wheelchair shows him with his grandniece Ruthie Bie and Fala at Hilltop Cottage, Hyde Park, February 1941. (Courtesy of Margaret Suckley.)

not be brought to a sitting position without assistance. In September, Roosevelt was moved to New York by train and was treated at Presbyterian Hospital by a Harvard classmate, Dr. George Draper. At the end of October, he was sent home to his New York City town house. Despite the treatment by Lovett and Draper, he had lost all muscular function below the level of the waist, and by the end of October he was just able to sit up with assistance. Arrangements were made for nurse therapist Kathleen Lake to visit him regularly for muscle training in his home. These exercises were painful, exhausting, and stressful for both the patient and his family.

His polio placed an enormous burden on the family. His wife, Eleanor, and his political adviser, Louis Howe, supported his desire to stay in politics after the polio attack. His mother, Sara, was supportive of his efforts toward rehabilitation, but she also needed to care for and control him. FDR became the center of a titanic struggle in the Roosevelt household. In June 1922, he left for medical treatment and care of his braces in Boston, and when he returned the tension in the house had subsided. FDR's own determination to overcome his disability, characterized by a strong, simple, religious faith, carried him through this crisis.

After two years he learned to adapt to his disability, and he made frequent visits to his New York office. He kept up his political correspondence, almost from the beginning of his illness, with the skillful assistance of Louis Howe. On 28 May 1923, he made his last visit to Dr. Lovett. Although he had learned to handle leg braces and crutches, there was no restoration of muscles that had long since atrophied. Roosevelt never again could walk unassisted.

FDR never accepted the full limitations of his disability. Every search for a cure was another postponement of the realization that he was permanently paralyzed. His reaction to disability was affirmative and life sustaining. He invented devices that gave him greater mobility and access to the ordinary activities of life. He even invented a contraption that permitted him to swing out from the forward davit of his houseboat and be lowered into the water for swimming. For political purposes he concealed the disability as best he could. Although in the Roosevelt household he rarely mentioned his handicap, he was capable of exposing his disability with minimal self-consciousness. He was a cooperative, determined, uncomplaining patient, but he went his own way when the doctor told him no further progress could be made.

In the fall of 1924, he went to Warm Springs, Georgia, more in desperation than in hope of positive recovery. Swimming in the pools every day provided him with an illusion of cure. The water gave him a sense of buoyancy, as he no longer had to push against gravity. The regular swimming developed his arms, chest, and torso to the point where he could compete successfully with able-bodied swimmers. He learned to "walk" with canes while leaning on the strong right arm of his therapist, and he learned to rise from his chair while grabbing on to the strong shoulders of an attendant. Walking with canes was a cosmetic improvement over walking with crutches.

In 1928, after four years at Warm Springs, FDR had to decide whether to forgo any further improvement in order to resume a political career. The inner struggle he resolved at this time resulted in his running for the governorship of New York in the fall of 1928.

For the next seventeen years, FDR dominated the American political landscape. Those who observed him at close hand in the governorship and the presidency were inspired. Here was a disabled man who decided to remain in public life. The handicap erased whatever distance existed between FDR, the product of Groton and Harvard, and the average voter. Did the disability change his political beliefs? FDR's liberalism evolved gradually over many years. His correspondence with fellow polio sufferers broadened his sympathies with the underprivileged. His intimate contact with the rural South at Warm Springs gave him firsthand knowledge of rural poverty. His fight against polio, culminating in the March of Dimes, gave him an understanding of the nation's health problems. His polio enhanced his liberalism; it did not cause it.

In the presidency the disability did not hamper him in the performance of his public duties. Most of the time he was carried up steps where his wheelchair was not easily maneuvered. On airplanes a special ramp and lift were built so that he could be wheeled onto the ramp and into the plane. He was naturally buoyant and optimistic. These characteristics, when combined with his considerable charm and magnetic smile, deflected attention from his wasted legs. There was a gentleman's agreement among reporters not to photograph his useless legs or to show him in a physically helpless position.

Polio steeled FDR to the hardships of a political career. He may have become president even if he hadn't contracted polio, but with the disability he became more compassionate, made more widespread contacts, concentrated on his priorities, and learned to bide his time before making a crucial decision. Polio tested and sharpened FDR's basic character. Having emerged from this struggle with courage and optimism, he learned to endure and master the great political crises of his career.

How Roosevelt reacted to his polio is one of the great myths of American history. His early biographers underestimated the acute reactive depression following the polio attack. They quoted from the cheerful letters put out by Louis Howe and made it seem that FDR made a rapid, almost superhuman recovery. See, for example, Ernest Lindley, *Franklin D. Roosevelt, A Career in Progressive Democracy* (Indianapolis: Bobbs Merrill, 1931). Even the standard biographies—such as James MacGregor Burns, *Roosevelt: The Lion and the Fox* (New York: Harcourt Brace, 1956) and Frank Freidel, *Franklin D. Roosevelt: The Ordeal* (Boston: Little, Brown & Co., 1954)—have underestimated the lasting impact of FDR's disability on his political career and have given it superficial treatment. The most comprehensive history of FDR's polio attack, his psychological reaction, and the meaning of the disability for his political career and life-style can be found in

Richard T. Goldberg's *The Making of Franklin D. Roosevelt: Triumph over Disability* (Cambridge, Mass.: Abt Books, 1981). Goldberg's book makes use of the Dr. Robert Lovett collection; Lovett treated FDR for polio from 1921 to 1923. Two books that treat FDR's stay at Warm Springs are Turnley Walker's *Roosevelt and the Warm Springs Story* (New York: A. A. Wyn, 1953) and Theo Lippman's *The Squire of Warm Springs* (New York: Playboy Press, 1977). Lippman's book is especially useful in describing the political atmosphere of Georgia in the twenties and thirties. For a standard medical textbook on poliomyelitis before the Salk and Sabin vaccines, see *Poliomyelitis* (Geneva: World Health Organization, 1955).

RICHARD T. GOLDBERG

See also Health; O'Connor, Basil Daniel; Warm Springs

Political Philosophy

See Conservation; Education; Governor of New York; Internationalism and Peace; New Deal; Office of the Presidency; Planning; Prohibition; State Senator; Wilson, Thomas Woodrow

Portraits

Numerous portraits were made of Franklin Roosevelt, and although many are well crafted, there are relatively few good likenesses. Artists found him a difficult subject whose mobile features never remained in repose long enough for them to capture the expression they sought. To add to the problem he granted few sittings per se after he became president; instead artists were permitted to observe him as he worked. Given these circumstances, the artist might glimpse the expression he wanted, but it would rarely be sustained. S. J. Woolf once described the difficulty of portraying FDR. "He is a sympathetic sitter who always expresses great interest in the progress of a drawing. But he is rarely quiet and, to make matters harder, his expression constantly changes. . . . I cannot remember any other sitter whose face seemed to vary so much as his, or so often or so quickly."

Beginning in his youth a number of early portraits exist. While a Groton student he was painted by Charles Stuart Forbes (oil, 1897, in Roosevelt home, Hyde Park). When he was elected to the New York State Senate, a life-size seated bronze commissioned by his mother was executed by Prince Paul Troubetskoy (bronze, 1911–12, in Roosevelt home; plaster, in FDR Library, Hyde Park, on loan to the National Portrait Gallery). To mark their tenth wedding anniversary, miniatures of Franklin and Eleanor were painted by Claude Newell (oil, 1915, FDR Library). A portrait drawing by Joseph Cummings Chase dates from FDR's service as assistant secretary of the navy (crayon, 1918, National Portrait Gallery).

When Roosevelt resumed his political career after he had contracted polio, he sat for Prince Pierre Troubetskoy, brother of the sculptor (oil, 1927, owned by Elliott Roosevelt). Shortly after he was elected governor of New York in 1928, S. J. Woolf

Franklin D. Roosevelt, 1896. Artist: Charles Stuart Forbes. (Courtesy FDR Library.)

Franklin D. Roosevelt, 1945. Artist: Douglas Chandor.
(National Portrait Gallery, Smithsonian Institution.)

made drawings of both Roosevelt and his wife. In the ensuing years, Woolf periodically made drawings of FDR that were published as birthday portraits in the *New York Times;* some of them were also issued as separate lithographs. Other portraits from the governorship period are those by DeWitt M. Lockman (oil, 1930, New York Historical Society); Charles E. Ruttan (oil, 1930, location unknown); Jacob H. Perskie (oil, 1932, Executive Chamber, New York State Capitol); and a life-size bust by Prince Serge Yourievitch (bronze, 1930, FDR Library, on loan to the New York State Capitol).

When FDR won the presidential nomination in 1932, Perskie was commissioned to do the official campaign portrait. His charcoal drawing, widely reproduced on posters and buttons, is one of the best known likenesses of FDR. Once he became president, FDR was deluged with requests for sittings. The few who were permitted to work in the Executive Office were usually artists who were known to him or his associates. Shortly after the election, Sara Roosevelt asked Ellen Emmet Rand, longtime family friend, to do her son's portrait. President Roosevelt did not like the finished work, but it remained a favorite with his mother (oil, 1932, Roosevelt home). Mrs. Rand's second portrait of FDR, which he much admired, hung for many years in the White House until President Truman, who disliked it, gave it to the Roosevelt family (oil, 1934, FDR Library). Granted several sessions at the White House, the sculptor Jo Davidson produced a portrait bust that has been widely reproduced in miniature. A favorite of the president and his family, Mrs. Roosevelt kept the No. 1 casting in her White House study, eventually giving it to her

daughter, Anna Halsted (bronze, 1934, FDR Library). FDR subsequently chose Davidson as sculptor of the 1941 and 1945 inaugural medals.

In 1935, the English artist Frank Salisbury was commissioned by the New York Genealogical and Biographical Society to paint the president. The result was so successful that the artist made at least four copies of his original including one ordered by President Truman for the White House. Truman was undaunted by criticism for American artists that the commission had gone to an Englishman (oil, 1935, White House, FDR Library, New York Genealogical and Biographical Society, English-Speaking Union, London, Commonwealth National Library, Canberra, Australia). Salisbury's portrait is widely known through collotype prints produced by the New York Graphic Society. Roosevelt thought it the best portrait of himself and presented inscribed copies of the print to family and friends.

Among others who did portraits of President Roosevelt were Douglas Chandor (oil, 1935, State Capitol, Austin, Texas), and a study intended for a portrait of FDR, Churchill, and Stalin at Yalta (oil, 1945, National Portrait Gallery); David Immerman, from photographs (oil, 1940, FDR Library); Armando Drechsler, commissioned by President Avila Camacho of Mexico (oil, 1941, FDR Library); Oskar Stoessel,—one of Mrs. Roosevelt's favorite likenesses—(dry point, 1939), Nos. 1 and 2 in FDR Library); Irena Wiley (watercolor and gouache, 1944, FDR Library); and A. M. Gerassimov, a Russian artist who sketched FDR at the Teheran Conference (oil, 1943, FDR Library.)

The most famous portrait is undoubtedly the "Unfinished Portrait" on which Madame Elizabeth Shoumatoff was working in the Little White House at Warm Springs, Georgia, when the president suffered a fatal cerebral hemorrhage. The poignant circumstances surrounding the painting, plus its extensive reproduction, have made the portrait a very popular one (watercolor, 1945, Little White House, Warm Springs, Georgia).

There are several good posthumous portraits from photographs: Stanislav Rembski (oil, 1945, FDR Library); Alfred Jonniaux, commissioned by Basil O'Connor, FDR's longtime friend (oil, 1958, Roosevelt Room, White House); and Sir William Reid Dick's heroic standing bronze erected in 1948 in Grosvenor Square, London (sculptor's model, bronze, FDR Library). No comprehensive study has been made thus far of the Roosevelt portraits.

See also Memorials; Roosevelt Dime; Roosevelt Stamps

Presidential Papers

See Franklin D. Roosevelt Library; Personal Writings

Press

See News Media

Propaganda

See Office of War Information

Prohibition

The Eighteenth Amendment to the Constitution outlawing alcoholic beverages. The cause of Prohibition was encountered by Franklin Roosevelt throughout his early political career. In 1910, when Prohibition was an important crusade, Roosevelt avoided taking a direct stand by supporting local option in his campaign for the New York State Assembly. In 1920, the year the Eighteenth Amendment became law, the Democrats nominated Roosevelt for vice-president in part because his image as a moderate dry would balance the ticket with the wet James M. Cox. Three years later, Roosevelt reluctantly advised New York governor Alfred E. Smith to support the state's Prohibition enforcement law in order to avoid alienating dry sentiment. In 1928, Roosevelt consented to run for governor of New York, encouraged by Smith and his prominent adviser John J. Raskob, both leaders of the anti-Prohibitionists. Yet Roosevelt, both in his campaign and as governor, avoided the issue as much as possible, much to the chagrin of Smith and Raskob. Although he addressed the issue only when he had to, Roosevelt suggested at the 1929 Governors' Conference that states be given the task of enforcing Prohibition. The next year, in the midst of a reelection campaign, he came out in favor of giving states the right to choose to sell liquor through state agencies. In the face of growing public opinion against Prohibition, Roosevelt employed this states' preference stance in order to avoid losing either the wet or the dry faction.

As he prepared for his first run at the presidency, the arguments against Prohibition were mounting. Instead of cleansing the nation's morality and politics, Prohibition had brought bootleggers, gangland violence, and widespread disrespect for the law. The economic inefficiencies and loss of tax revenues became unacceptable during the depression. Raskob, meanwhile, began a behind-the-scenes campaign to put the national Democratic party on record in favor of the repeal of Prohibition. Roosevelt, the leading candidate for the party's presidential nomination, feared that a strong wet stand by the Democrats would lose votes in the South and West, and for a time he successfully resisted Raskob's initiatives.

Prohibition was a major issue at the 1932 Democratic National Convention, much to the consternation of Roosevelt who thought the delegates should concentrate on the economic and social problems of the depression. John Dewey observed, "Here we are in the midst of the greatest crisis since the Civil War and the only thing the two national parties seem to want to debate is booze." Roosevelt's forces tried to prevent the convention from adopting a strong repeal plank, but the pressure was overwhelming. Raskob introduced a resolution for repeal, hoping to drive a wedge in the Roosevelt forces and thus clear the way for his favorite, Al Smith. When it became clear that Roosevelt's reluctance on this single issue was hurting his chances for nomination, he dropped his opposition and so removed the basis for an anti-Roosevelt coalition. During the fall campaign, the fact that Roosevelt seldom mentioned his party's anti-Prohibition commitment did not alter his party's wet image, just as Herbert Hoover could not reverse the Republican party's dry image. The 1932 election, for the first time, offered the voters a clear choice on the repeal of Prohibition.

The election results were as decisive for repeal as for the Democrats. In early 1933, the lame-duck Congress passed and sent to the states the Twenty-first Amendment repealing the Eighteenth. While the constitutional amendment made its way through the state legislatures, President Roosevelt during his second week of office asked Congress to amend the Volstead Act to allow the sale of 3.2 percent beer. Congress quickly complied, and on 7 April 1933, the first legal beer was delivered to the White House as a celebrating crowd watched. Later that year, the required number of states passed the Twenty-first amendment, and the president declared the end of Prohibition. Ironically, Franklin Roosevelt, who for most of his political life had dodged the issue except when it was forced upon him, received much of the credit for ending what most Americans considered to be a tragic mistake.

The forces behind the decline of Prohibition are detailed in David E. Kyvig, *Repealing National Prohibition* (Chicago: University of Chicago Press, 1979). Of the many general treatments of Prohibition, a fine summary is Sean Dennis Cashman, *Prohibition: The Lie of the Land* (New York: Free Press, 1981).

TIMOTHY LEHMAN

The candidates' stand on repeal of Prohibition is dramatized on their 1932 campaign license plate. (Courtesy FDR Library.)

See also Election of 1928; Farley, James Aloysius

Public Housing

Public Papers and Addresses

Public Utility Holding Company Act

Publications

Public Works Administration

The Federal Emergency Administration of Public Works, commonly known as the Public Works Administration (PWA), was a direct work relief agency established by Title II of the National Industrial Recovery Act on June 16, 1933. The legislation allocated $3.3 billion to provide jobs, stimulate business activity, and increase purchasing power through the construction of permanent and socially useful public works.

From July 1933 to March 1939, the PWA financed construction of 34,508 federal and nonfederal projects at a cost of over $6 billion. Public works of every description (lighthouse beacons, municipal sewage systems, hospitals, dams, battleships, and bridges)

(Courtesy FDR Library.)

were undertaken in all but three counties of the United States. The PWA allocated $1.8 billion directly to other federal agencies. For nonfederal projects, PWA made grants of 30 percent of the cost of labor and materials to states, municipalities, and other public bodies. The remaining 70 percent of a project's cost had to be secured by bonds. Congress intended that these projects would be self-liquidating with repayment out of various user fees.

During its first two years, PWA organization was marked by extreme centralization in Washington. The Emergency Relief Appropriation Act of 1935 extended its life, facilitated administrative decentralization to regional rather than state offices, and increased the outright grant to 45 percent of total project cost. The Public Works Administration Appropriation Act of 1938 inaugurated the final phase of the Roosevelt administration's work relief program with an appropriation of $965 million for projects completed by June 1940.

Between 1933 and 1938, the total volume of new construction in the nation more than doubled, but it represented only 60 percent of predepression levels. Approximately 1.2 million men received on-site employment at a cost per man-hour ranging from 88¢ to $1.12. Under PWA procedures, between two and four months were required to review projects and award contracts. Actual construction was normally delayed for another month or two following the award of a contract. When the PWA ceased to exist in June 1941, it was clear that the effect of public works funds on business and employment was insufficient to maintain predepression levels or to do more than stimulate industrial activity. In the opinion of many critics, however, public works had been discredited as a recovery instrument, not because of any inherent weakness in policy, but because President Roosevelt and PWA administrator, Interior Secretary Harold L. Ickes, had never really tried it.

Franklin Roosevelt's commitment to direct work relief was consistently limited. He supported the idea of a program of useful public works when it was first suggested by Secretary of Labor Frances Perkins, whose department drafted an early bill for his consideration. Additional cabinet support came from Ickes, James Farley, and Henry Wallace. But Roosevelt still hoped to balance the budget. Hence he was reluctant to embark on a massive spending program of public works that would jeopardize that goal. He was encouraged in this conservative fiscal policy by Budget Director Lewis W. Douglas and later by Treasury Secretary Henry Morgenthau who feared that public works appropriations would worsen the financial crisis and lead to a permanent program of federally funded work relief. The president finally supported the creation of PWA with a reduced appropriation because he hoped it would stimulate employment as well as reform the face of America. Public works legislation underscored a fundamental conflict in Roosevelt's thinking about economic and social planning that was never fully resolved.

As witness to his reluctance to spend large sums

for public works, Roosevelt appointed as administrator of PWA the one official least inclined to spend quickly and most sympathetic to the idea of using public works as an instrument of conservation and reform. After a month of temporary administration under former Federal Stabilization Board official Donald Sawyer and a cabinet-level board chaired by Harold Ickes, Roosevelt named Ickes permanent administrator on 8 July 1933. Ickes remained at the head of the agency throughout its existence.

Ickes's administration of PWA was, and is, a topic of controversy. Bureaucratically suspicious and honest to the point of self-righteousness, Ickes understood the essential conflicts in Roosevelt's thinking and the divergent purposes to which the president had charged the program. He also shared Roosevelt's desire to avoid spending too rapidly and to construct only useful projects. Ickes was less concerned about a balanced budget and "pump-priming" than he was to use PWA funds to aid his conservation policies and to avoid political scandal. Ever sensitive to the politics of spending the largest peacetime allocation of public funds, Ickes was an ambitious administrator who used his position to benefit his own department. Ickes was not insensitive to the problem of unemployment, but he was more concerned with the public benefits to be accrued through projects expanding public power and public housing. Although delay, caution, and tedious bureaucratic process hampered PWA efforts, Ickes's administration was remarkable for its efficiency, its lack of partisan favoritism, the amount of business activity that was generated, and the number and quality of durable additions to the national estate that resulted from the purposefully inadequate appropriation. He pioneered in establishing a program requiring the development of enormous staff expertise and intergovernmental cooperation on an unprecedented scale. At the time, however, Ickes's critics saw only that an emergency agency was being run on the principles of a "good, sound bond house."

The effectiveness of a federal public works program as a recovery measure was neither proven nor disproven by the New Deal experiment. Although PWA failed to alter unemployment or business investment patterns significantly in its six years, its achievements were more impressive than its failures. For all its red tape, PWA created the mechanism for direct funding between federal and local governments and thereby established important precedents for decades of federal programs.

PWA's Housing Division initiated the first federal housing program and became the model for subsequent housing legislation. With the vast power and reclamation projects, especially those constructed in the West, PWA altered the public utility industry, made the federal government the largest producer of power, proved the validity of public power, and literally created the heavy construction industry. PWA significantly advanced conservation of the nation's natural resources and brought conservation into the public dialogue. Finally, while the permanence and quality of PWA projects are still visible today, the

FDR with cane (center) visits the Boulder Dam (later the Hoover Dam), 30 September 1935. (Courtesy FDR Library.)

vast experience in policy planning, administration, and public financing, although less apparent, nevertheless changed the processes of American governance as much, if not more so.

The most important primary source for evaluating the accomplishments of PWA is *America Builds: The Record of PWA* (Washington, D.C.: U.S. Government Printing Office, 1939). A critical evaluation of administrative procedures is given by Jack F. Isakoff, "The Public Works Administration," *Illinois Studies in the Social Sciences* 23 (1938):5–161. As a young government economist, J. K. Galbraith produced a more balanced estimate for the National Resources Planning Board, *The Economic Effects of the Federal Public Works Expenditures, 1933–1938* (Washington, D.C.: U.S. Government Printing Office, 1940). Record Group 135, Records of the PWA, National Archives, Washington, D.C., contains a vast collection of data showing how the agency worked. Roosevelt's shifting objectives for the public works program can be traced in his official statements compiled by Samuel Rosenman in *The Public Papers and Addresses of Franklin D. Roosevelt*, vols. 2–3 (New York: Random House, 1938) and in more detail in the President's Official File 466-B of the Papers of Franklin D. Roosevelt, Franklin D. Roosevelt Library, Hyde Park, New York. Ickes's highs and lows as PWA administrator are best exhibited in *The Secret Diary of Harold L. Ickes*, vols. 1–2 (New York; Simon & Schuster, 1954), and in Boxes 248–255 of the Papers of Harold L. Ickes, Manuscript Division, Library of Congress, Washington, D.C. His official account of PWA is *Back to Work* (New York: MacMillan Co., 1935). Frances Perkins, *The Roosevelt I Knew* (New York: Viking Press, 1946) and Raymond Moley, *The First New Deal* (New York: Harcourt, Brace & World, 1966) are valuable for their estimates of PWA accomplishments. William D. Reeves,

"The Politics of Public Works, 1933–1935" (Ph.D. diss., Tulane University, 1968) and his later article, "PWA and Competitive Administration in the New Deal," *Journal of American History* 60 (September 1973):357–73 provide insight into the failure of PWA as a recovery measure.

LINDA J. LEAR

See also Conservation; Housing and Resettlement; Ickes, Harold LeClair; National Industrial Recovery Act; Relief

"Purge" of 1938

In the 1938 primaries, Franklin Roosevelt sought party realignment along ideological lines by advocating the defeat of certain conservative Democrats in Congress through the electoral process. Roosevelt, who in 1936 had won a second presidential term by a landslide and helped Democrats enhance their overwhelming congressional majorities, urged the legislative branch in January 1937 to adopt more liberal New Deal programs for underprivileged, "ill-housed, ill-clad, ill-nourished" Americans. During the Seventy-fifth Congress, however, a conservative Democratic minority aligned with Republicans to prevent Roosevelt from fulfilling his more liberal programs. The conservative coalition, which protested the expansion of federal and executive power, rejected Roosevelt's Supreme Court reorganization plan and stalled other New Deal reform measures.

Roosevelt found these conservative tactics undemocratic and intolerable. In a June 1938 fireside chat, he publicly announced his intentions to campaign for liberals in selected Democratic congressional primaries and inform the American people which candidates supported his New Deal programs. Roosevelt, who stressed that the Seventy-fifth Congress had not fulfilled his party's "uncompromisingly liberal" 1936 platform, pictured the primaries and elections as ideological contests between pro–New Deal liberals and anti–New Deal conservatives. As Democratic party leader, Roosevelt stated, "I feel that I have every right to speak in those few instances where there may be a clear issue between candidates for a Democratic nomination involving those principles, or involving a clear misuse of my name."

Roosevelt's realignment strategy faced several problems. Besides beginning his party realignment effort belatedly, the president left unclear what he meant by a conservative and what specific tactics he would employ. Administration aides Tom Corcoran, Harold Ickes, and Harry Hopkins favored Roosevelt's strategy, whereas other advisers dissented. Newspapers invidiously accused Roosevelt of attempting to "purge" Democratic party conservatives. Roosevelt did not plan his strategy well, employing a variety of tactics as he zigzagged by train across the nation. The president did not intervene in primaries involving conservatives Bennett Champ Clark of Missouri, Augustine Lonergan of Connecticut, Alva Adams of Colorado, and Pat McCarran of Nevada, all of whom won party renomination.

Several Roosevelt-backed liberal Democratic candidates registered primary victories. Before Roosevelt's June fireside chat, incumbent New Deal senators Lister Hill of Alabama and Claude Pepper of Florida had defeated conservative challengers. Roosevelt enthusiastically endorsed Senate majority leader Alben Barkley of Kentucky, who in August easily defeated conservative governor "Happy" Chandler. Barkley's victory prevented the majority leader post from going to the more conservative "Pat" Harrison of Mississippi. Other Roosevelt-supported primary winners included senators Hattie Caraway of Arkansas, Robert Bulkley of Ohio, and Elmer Thomas of Oklahoma, and Representative Lyndon Johnson of Texas. Roosevelt aides campaigned against New York representative John O'Connor, helping defeat in September the anti–New Deal House Rules Committee chairman.

Roosevelt's party realignment efforts, though, suffered major setbacks in middle western and southern Senate primaries. In Iowa the Roosevelt administration campaigned for liberal congressman Otha Wearin against incumbent Guy Gillette, who had opposed the president's Court plan. Gillette, wholeheartedly endorsed by the state party organization, in June handily defeated Wearin. The Indiana Democratic party organization, to Roosevelt's dismay, could not find a more liberal candidate to challenge anti–New Deal incumbent Frederick Van Nuys. Roosevelt intervened most directly in southern primaries, where he supported lesser known liberal Democrats against veteran conservatives Walter George of Georgia, "Cotton Ed" Smith of South Carolina, and Millard Tydings of Maryland. At a Barnesville, Georgia, Democratic meeting, Roosevelt in August endorsed youthful attorney Lawrence Camp against George. The victorious George, however, nearly doubled Camp's total in a three-way primary. In Greenville, South Carolina, Roosevelt backed Governor Olin Johnston against aging veteran Agriculture Committee chairman Smith. A states' rights segregationist,

Berryman, Washington Star, *1 June 1938. (Copyright* Washington Post. *Reprinted by permission of the D.C. Public Library.)*

Smith won the primary partly because of Roosevelt's intervention. In September the president stumped Maryland two days for liberal representative David Lewis and opposed the renomination of anti–New Dealer Tydings, who easily won the primary. In the House, liberal Maury Maverick of Texas was unseated and conservative House Rules Committee member Howard Smith of Virginia handily won renomination.

Although making an understandable, commendable effort to realign political parties along ideological lines, Roosevelt launched his strategy too late to be effective. The president did not plan well, he varied his tactics too much from state to state, and he relied too heavily on often divided state party organizations. The more provincial American electorate, which disapproved of interference by federal officials in state politics, prevented Roosevelt from realigning political parties ideologically. Although the primaries intensified the liberal-conservative split within Roosevelt's party, the Democrats in November still controlled over two-thirds of the Senate and held a comfortable majority in the House. Most conservative Democrats won reelection, while the Republicans gained eight Senate and eighty-one House seats. Congress continued blocking New Deal legislation, but soon shifted its attention to foreign policy issues.

For additional information see John M. Allswang, *The New Deal and American Politics* (New York: John Wiley & Sons, 1978); James MacGregor Burns, *Roosevelt: The Lion and the Fox* (New York: Harcourt Brace Jovanovich, 1956); John E. Hopper, "The Purge: Franklin D. Roosevelt and the 1938 Democratic Nominations," (Ph.D. diss., University of Chicago, 1966); V. O. Key, ed., *Southern Politics in State and Nation* (New York: Alfred A. Knopf, 1949); William E. Leuchtenburg, *Franklin D. Roosevelt and the New Deal, 1932–1940* (New York: Harper & Row, 1963); James T. Patterson, *Congressional Conservatism and the New Deal* (Lexington: University of Kentucky Press, 1967); James T. Patterson, "The Failure of Party Realignment in the South, 1937–1939," *Journal of Politics* 27 (August 1965):602–17; Milton Plesur, "The Republican Comeback of 1938," *Review of Politics* 24 (October 1962):525–62; Richard Polenberg, "Franklin Roosevelt and the Purge of John O'Connor: The Impact of Urban Change on Political Parties," *New York History* 49 (1968); Richard Polenberg, *Reorganizing Roosevelt's Government 1936–1939* (Cambridge, Mass.: Harvard University Press, 1966); Charles M. Price and Joseph Boskin, "The Roosevelt Purge: A Reappraisal," *Journal of Politics* 28 (1966); J. B. Shannon, "Presidential Politics in the South," *Journal of Politics* 1 (August 1939):278–300; Luther H. Ziegler, Jr., "Senator Walter George's 1938 Campaign," *Georgia Historical Quarterly* 43 (1959):333–52.

DAVID L. PORTER

See also Congress, United States; Corcoran, Thomas Gardiner; Democratic Party; Election of 1938; New Deal; South, The

Q

Quarantine Speech

President Franklin Roosevelt's address in Chicago on 5 October 1937 ambiguously proposing broader American involvement in international affairs. In response to the ongoing Spanish Civil War, improvement in the relations between Nazi Germany and fascist Italy, and most of all the clashes between Japanese and Chinese troops beginning in July, Roosevelt decided to make a major public statement on foreign policy in the nation's isolationist heartland.

Characteristically, he used a metaphor to compare the increase in international lawlessness to the spread of a communicable illness: "When an epidemic of physical disease starts to spread, the community approves and joins in a quarantine of the patients in order to protect the health of the community against the spread of disease." FDR offered no definite measures against the offending nations, however, stating only that "America actively engages in the search for peace." The 1937 Neutrality Act, the "Roosevelt recession," and legislative battles over such domestic issues as the Court-packing plan and executive reorganization constrained bold presidential foreign policy initiatives.

Although even some isolationists applauded the speech, the general reaction in the United States was mixed. Abroad, the speech encouraged Britain and France to call for American leadership against Japan. Roosevelt, however, agreed only to participation in a conference on the Sino-Japanese War in Brussels, his only real follow-through on the speech. This absence of reinforcing action indicates that the quarantine speech was more a statement of a need for a new foreign policy than a major departure in foreign policy itself.

The best recent source, reviewing all relevant literature, is Robert Dallek's *Franklin D. Roosevelt and American Foreign Policy, 1932–1945* (New York: Oxford University Press, 1979). William L. Langer and S. Everett Gleason tend to overestimate the importance of the speech in their classic *Challenge to Isolation: The World Crisis of 1937–1940 and American Foreign Policy* (New York: Harper & Bros., 1952). Two valuable articles are Dorothy Borg, "Notes on Roosevelt's 'Quarantine Speech,' " *Political Science Quarterly* 72 (September 1957):405–33, and Travis Beal Jacobs, "Roosevelt's Quarantine Speech," *Historian* 24 (August 1962):483–502, which establish that the speech was not read by all isolatonists as a statement favoring greater American involvement in foreign conflicts.

See also Foreign Policy; World War II

Quebec Conferences

Two wartime conferences between Franklin Roosevelt and Winston Churchill, significant for the planning of both wartime strategy and postwar policies. The first Quebec Conference, code named Quadrant, was held 17–24 August 1943. The most important topics concerned future operations in the Mediterranean following the successful invasion of Sicily, and Operation Overlord, the invasion of France from the British Isles. The conference took place amid rumors of the impending surrender of Italy. Mussolini had been deposed of 25 July, and the Badoglio government had put out peace feelers though Spain and Portugal. Roosevelt had wanted Eisenhower to insist on simple unconditional surrender with an implied promise of more favorable treatment later. At Quebec, Churchill and Eden persuaded FDR to accept a longer document, which tied surrender to long-term political arrangements and granted a measure of recognition to the Badoglio government. The Allied invasion and surrender of Italy followed shortly after the conference.

Arguments about Italy were overshadowed by the central dispute between American and British planners about the importance of Mediterranean operations. The Americans, especially Chief of Staff General George Marshall and Secretary of War Henry Stimson, urged FDR before the conference to hold to the view that Italian operations were limited and nothing should detract from the planning of a cross-channel invasion. Churchill considered a more

FDR and Churchill and their chiefs of staff pose on the terrace of the Citadel during their conference in Quebec, *11–16 September 1944. (Courtesy FDR Library.)*

extensive Italian campaign to be a way both to weaken the Axis and to exert Western political influence against the Soviet Union in Southern Europe and the Balkans. Though FDR was not totally unsympathetic to this goal, he felt he could not justify a greater commitment to such operations on political grounds alone. Roosevelt extracted a renewed commitment from Churchill to undertake Operation Overlord with the deadline set for 1 May 1944.

FDR and Churchill could not reach agreement on a joint position toward de Gaulle and the Free French Committee of National Liberation. Roosevelt deeply disliked de Gaulle for personal and political reasons, seeing in him an arrogant military dictator and a powerful opponent to FDR's own postwar plans for decolonization and arms control. Both FDR and Secretary of State Hull refused to approve any statement that used the word *recognition* in regard to the Free French Committee. Churchill and Eden were more sympathetic toward granting some measure of

recognition. The American and the British resolved the dispute by issuing separate statements.

The conference also considered the question of cooperation in atomic energy research. At the Trident Conference in May 1943, Churchill had informally obtained FDR's agreement to resume collaboration between the two powers on atomic energy. At Quebec, they reached a formal agreement that also stipulated that neither would communicate any information about atomic development to third parties, namely the Soviet Union, without the other's consent. A year later, at the next Quebec Conference, they strengthened this understanding and specifically excluded the Russians from any share in the control of atomic energy.

The second Quebec Conference, code named Octagon, was held 11–16 September 1944. It took place in an atmosphere of military triumph following D day and the expectation that the collapse of German resistance was imminent. The central problems of the conference were postwar policy toward Germany and postwar economic assistance to Britain. During the month before the conference, a bitter debate had raged within the Roosevelt administration on the proper treatment of Germany. Henry Morgenthau, secretary of the treasury, argued that German industry should be eliminated and the country transformed into an agricultural state. Opposing him was Secretary of War Stimson, who contended that such policy would be disastrous to Europe's economy. FDR leaned toward Morgenthau's ideas and was convinced that "the German people as a whole must have it driven home to them that the whole nation has been engaged in a lawless conspiracy against the decencies of modern civilization." FDR also saw in the plan a way to further cooperation with the Soviet Union and to strengthen Britain. At Quebec, Morgenthau presented his plan to Churchill, whose first reaction was to fear that a radical deindustrialization policy would render Germany bankrupt, which would force the Allies to support her. He told Morgenthau that he refused to "chain himself to a dead German." However, the treasury secretary went on to argue that the elimination of German industry would help the British take over former German markets. Churchill, who needed Morgenthau's support to acquire a continuation of Lend-Lease, grew more interested. Lord Cherwell, the British paymaster general, sympathized with Morgenthau's ideas and sought to convince Churchill of the economic advantages of gaining Germany's export trade. Churchill warmed to the idea, even contributing the word *pastoral* to the final wording of the directive. The Morgenthau plan and the continuation of Lend-Lease after the war were agreed to, as well as the area of each country's zone of oc-

cupation in Germany. FDR, who had stubbornly resisted taking control of the southwest area of Germany, now conceded. The British were given responsibility for northwest industrial Germany. FDR had not only gained British approval of the Morgenthau plan but saddled them with its implementation.

The Morgenthau plan leaked to the press only shortly after the end of the conference. The hostile reaction of public opinion, as well as Thomas E. Dewey's charge that it had strengthened German resolve, led FDR to wish he had never heard of the proposal.

The diplomatic records of the conferences are available in the two volumes of the State Department's *Foreign Relations of the United States* series, *Conferences at Washington and Quebec, 1943* (Washington, D.C., 1970) and *The Conference at Quebec, 1944* (Washington, D.C., 1972). The excellent study by Robert Dallek, *Franklin D. Roosevelt and American Foreign Policy, 1932–1945* (New York: Oxford University Press, 1979) provides a good account of both conferences. Winston Churchill's memoirs, *The Second World War: Closing the Ring* (Boston: Houghton Mifflin Co., 1951) and *Triumph and Tragedy* (Boston: Houghton Mifflin Co., 1953) are splendid reading, but must be used with caution. On atomic policy, see the fine revisionist study by Martin Sherwin, *A World Destroyed: The Atomic Bomb and the Grand Alliance* (New York: Alfred A. Knopf, 1975). James MacGregor Burns, *Roosevelt: The Soldier of Freedom* (New York: Harcourt Brace Jovanovich, 1970) is also a good account.

See also Churchill, Winston Leonard Spencer; de Gaulle, Charles; Foreign Policy; Lend-Lease; Morgenthau, Henry T., Jr.; Mussolini, Benito, and Italy; Personal Diplomacy; World War II

R

Racism

See Civil Liberties in Wartime; Coughlin, Charles Edward; Hitler, Adolf, and Germany; Holocaust; Indian Policy; Internment of Japanese-Americans; Japan; Jews; Negroes; Refugees; Zionism

Radicalism

See Communism; Coughlin, Charles Edward; Labor; Lemke, William; Long, Huey Pierce; National Labor Relations Board; Negroes; New Deal; Sinclair, Upton; Socialism; Thomas, Norman Mattoon; Townsend, Francis E., M.D.; Union Party

Radio

See Federal Communications Commission; Fireside Chats; News Media

Randolph, Asa Philip

(15 April 1889–16 May 1979)

President of the Brotherhood of Sleeping Car Porters and leader of the March on Washington movement. One of the most important black leaders of the twentieth century, Asa Philip Randolph was born in Crescent City, Florida. Completing high school in Jacksonville, Randolph moved to New York City in 1911 where he held several casual jobs while studying at City College and lecturing part time at the Rand School. In 1917 he helped found the *Messenger*, an

Asa Philip Randolph, 1945. Artist: Betsy Graves Reyneau. (National Portrait Gallery, Smithsonian Institution. Gift of the Harmon Foundation.)

independent radical journal for blacks, and began agitating for union organization among black workers. A handsome and commanding figure with an actor's diction, Randolph became organizer and president of the Brotherhood of Sleeping Car Porters in 1925. The Brotherhood was consistently obstructed by company unionism, the impotence of railway labor legislation, and the racism prevalent among other railroad unions and federal administrators. Although Randolph's leadership helped it survive, it was not until after the coming of the New Deal, and in particular the passage of the Amended Railway Labor Act (1934) outlawing company unionism and company discrimination against members of bona fide trade unions, that the brotherhood was able to achieve stability and, eventually, recognition in the shape of a contract with the Pullman Company.

The brotherhood's success made Randolph preeminent among contemporary black leaders, and he broadened his sights to launch a general critique of discriminatory practices against blacks within the labor movement and in government. In 1940, these efforts became focused on the achievement of equality of employment opportunity for blacks in the rapid expansion of defense production. Randolph sought administration support for the inclusion of antidiscrimination clauses in all defense contracts negotiated by the Office of Production Management and for an end to segregation in the armed forces. A meeting with Roosevelt in September 1940 failed to result in administration backing, and considerable tension developed subsequently between the White House and black leaders when administration spokesman Stephen Early represented them as agreeing to the continuation of segregation in the armed forces.

Randolph turned from negotiating with the administration to mass protest, and between January and June 1941 he concentrated on building the march on Washington movement, aimed at organizing a mass demonstration to take place on 1 July in the nation's capital to demand jobs for blacks in defense industries. Randolph's efforts resulted, two weeks before the scheduled date of the demonstration, in a further round of negotiations with the administration. On 25 June Roosevelt issued Executive Order 8802 embracing a posture of nondiscrimination in government employment and defense industries and creating a temporary Fair Employment Practices Committee (FEPC) to investigate complaints. Randolph called off the march, but the march on Washington movement continued in existence until the late 1940s as a mass lobby for a permanent FEPC and an end to military segregation. Randolph became cochairman of the National Council for a Permanent FEPC and founder of the League for Nonviolent Civil Disobedience against Military Segregation. In 1963, he was to play a leading role in the organization of that year's march on Washington. Randolph retired from union activities in 1968, after serving since 1955 as a vice-president and member of the Executive Council of the AFL-CIO.

Randolph's life and activities are described by Jervis Anderson in *A. Philip Randolph: A Biographical Portrait* (New York: Harcourt Brace Jovanovich, 1972). See also Manning Marable, "A. Philip Randolph and the Foundations of Black American Socialism," *Radical America* 14 (1980). On his early career with the brotherhood, see William H. Harris, *Keeping the Faith* (Urbana: University of Illinois Press, 1977). Herbert Garfinkel, *When Negroes March* (Glencoe, Ill.: Free Press, 1959) analyzes the March on Washington movement; Nancy J. Weiss, *Farewell to the Party of Lincoln: Blacks for FDR* (Princeton: Princeton University Press, 1983) is the most recent account of black Americans and the New Deal.

CHRISTOPHER L. TOMLINS

See also Labor; National Association for the Advancement of Colored People; Negroes; Tape Recordings

Rationing
See War Effort on the Home Front

Rayburn, Samuel Taliaferro
(6 January 1882–16 November 1961)

Sam Rayburn and Franklin Delano Roosevelt had much in common. Both were born in January 1882, and both devoted their lives to politics without ever finding it a stale pursuit. Both started as economic conservatives, but a strong desire to combat the Great Depression and reform the economy changed their stance.

Young Sam was raised on a hardscrabble forty-acre farm near Bonham in east Texas. He attended East Texas Normal College and at twenty-four years of age took up state politics. His early idol was the fiery populist congressman Joe Bailey, and the populist credo with its distaste for the heavy monopolistic hand of banks, utilities, and railroads was a continuing influence on his later legislative leadership.

After several terms in the state legislature, Rayburn was elected Democratic congressman from the Fourth Texas District in 1912 and attended Woodrow Wilson's first inaugural. He was reelected twenty-four times thereafter and became speaker of the House of Representatives for five terms, thereby establishing a record for serving both as a representative and as speaker longer than any other man in American history.

Although he disagreed with some New Deal policies, especially labor relations, he had an abiding faith in Roosevelt's leadership and was invaluable in guiding through Congress such early proposals as Social Security and the acts establishing the Agricultural Adjustment Administration and the Tennessee Valley Authority. He personally dictated some of the details of the Truth in Securities Act of 1933 and played a major role in passing the Securities Exchange Act of

1934. His populist feelings about the utilities came to the fore in 1935 in his sponsorship of the public utility holding company bill and the Wheeler-Rayburn bill. In spite of what has been called the biggest lobbying effort ever seen in Congress, Rayburn's tireless efforts were instrumental in passing the two bills that virtually destroyed the powerful "empty" holding companies, which had long been milking the operating companies and consumers and defrauding investors with watered stocks and bonds.

Rayburn felt that he must support his friend and mentor, John Nance Garner of Texas, for the presidential nomination in 1940. However, after Roosevelt won the nomination, he had Rayburn's full support and loyalty. Their years of working together evoked his sincere characterization of Roosevelt as "the greatest humanitarian to occupy the White House in fifty years" (i.e., since Woodrow Wilson).

In 1941, all of Rayburn's talents as "the greatest compromiser since Henry Clay" were called upon to extend the Selective Service Act. He had personally convinced several strong opponents to change their vote and support the bill. When the vote came, it was 203 for and 202 against. Rayburn immediately gaveled down all moves to reconsider the bill, thereby preventing the army from being blocked from expansion a few months before Pearl Harbor.

The office from which Rayburn worked his congressional strategies was referred to as "Rayburn's board of education," where young congressmen were instructed in the finer points of House procedures. Here he and his cronies followed the Garner tradition of "striking a blow for liberty," which translated as frequent libations of bourbon and branch water.

In later years, Rayburn became absorbed in the architectural designing and erection of several new congressional structures. Among the more notable was the remodeling of the Capitol Building itself. He is more remembered for his work in planning, funding, and helping to design a huge new structure to furnish badly needed office space for his beloved House of Representatives. This became, after his death in 1961, the new Rayburn Office Building.

The newest work on Rayburn, Anthony Champagne, *Congressman Sam Rayburn* (New Brunswick, N.J.: Rutgers University Press, 1984), emphasizes relations between the congressman and his constituents of the Fourth District. Common concern and a genuine neighborliness were the ties and the basis for his political longevity. Dwight C. Dorough, *Mr. Sam* (New York: Random House, 1962) is an authorized biography by a fellow Texan with reminiscences about Mr. Sam, his unique political style, and the folks back home. Lengthy, but readable, Alfred Steinberg, in *Sam Rayburn: A Biography* (New York: Hawthorn, 1975) focuses on Rayburn's relations with eight presidents and his congressional colleagues and on the important legislation he sponsored.

RALPH F. DE BEDTS

See also New Deal

Reading

There is widely varying testimony by those who knew Franklin Roosevelt well as to how much he read and how deeply.

His mother often read aloud to him when he was young, much of it sentimental fiction possibly more interesting to her than to him—and she said that as a boy he was a voracious reader who devoured books at amazing speed. By her own account, she once found him sitting up in bed with the huge Webster's Unabridged Dictionary propped open against his knees. He was reading it, he told her, because "there are lots of words I don't understand" and claimed to be "almost half way through." Others who knew him as a boy testify that, stimulated by his hobbies of stamp and bird collecting, by his interest in his seafaring maternal Delano ancestors, and by his hero worship of his distant cousin Theodore Roosevelt, he had acquired through wide reading when in his teens a remarkable amount of information about geography, naval history, military history, political history, and natural history. From all accounts, he took relatively little interest in fiction or poetry, though *St. Nicholas* was his favorite childhood magazine; but in his early teens he read, among other historical works, Francis Parkman's *Montcalm and Wolfe,* Alfred Thayer Mahan's *Influence of Sea Power upon History,* Theodore Roosevelt's *Naval War of 1812,* and

Books cannot be killed by fire.

People die, but books never die. No man and no force can put thought in a concentration camp forever. No man and no force can take from the world the books that embody man's eternal fight against tyranny. In this war, we know, books are weapons. *Franklin D. Roosevelt*

BOOKS ARE WEAPONS IN THE WAR OF IDEAS

Respect for books as well as the force of FDR's liberal convictions emanated from this World War II anti-Nazi poster. (Courtesy FDR Library.)

TR's four-volume *Winning of the West.* By the time of his departure for Groton, his favorite periodicals were the *Illustrated London News, Survey Graphic,* and *Scientific American,* the latter of which was considerably less "scientific" in its contents than it is today.

At Groton and Harvard, of course, he read on class assignment the standard classics of English, American, and French literature, and continued his reading of history and biography, especially biographies of political figures. In the 1920s, after his attack of polio and before he returned fully to public life, he devoted much time to books. According to Frances Perkins, he read at this time "political history, political memoirs, books of travel," including Doughty's *Arabia Deserta* and Younghusband's "brilliant story of the hazardous penetration into Tibet." He was, she says "an avid atlas reader" and had "an amazing amount of information about the heights of mountains and the depths of oceans, the rivers and their sources and the plains they watered."

Yet he gave no sign, then or later, in his public speeches or published writings, that he ever read so much as a page of Marx, Freud, Spengler, Ortega y Gasset, Lenin, Dewey, Bergson, Whitehead, Veblen, Russell, Parrington, Beard, the Webbs, Keynes, or Henry Adams (though his wife had given him the *Education* for Christmas in 1919)—all of whom had a major impact upon the intellectual life of America in those years. There is no evidence either that he read such contemporary best-selling popularizers of ideas as Will Durant, H. G. Wells, or Sir James Jeans, or such popularizers of economics as Stuart Chase or William Z. Ripley (though he had taken one of Ripley's courses at Harvard).

When he reviewed Claude G. Bowers's *Jefferson and Hamilton* for the *New York World* in late 1925 at the age of forty-two, he revealed a truly astonishing lack of elementary historical ideas and of intellectual sophistication for a man of his interests, experience, and educational advantages. He had evidently read with understanding no earlier historical work dealing with the conflict of philosophies between Jefferson and Hamilton, a conflict fundamental to any understanding of American history as process from the early years of the Republic into the twentieth century. Reading Bowers's "thrilling" book, he wrote, "I felt like saying 'at last.'" He had a "breathless feeling as I lay down this book . . . a picture of escape after escape which this nation passed through in those first ten years; a picture of what might have been if the Republic had been finally organized as Alexander Hamilton sought." He was also "breathless" with "wonder if, a century and a quarter later, the same contending forces are not again mobilizing."

By that time he had become an avid reader of detective stories, an interest he shared with his close friend and associate Louis Howe. After 1928, when he was elected governor of New York, detective stories seem to have constituted virtually the whole of his book reading save for that required by his job. Ed Flynn, who was as intimate an associate of his between 1928 and 1945 as any man, with the exception of Howe and Harry Hopkins, wrote that he "never saw him read a book" or even "read a magazine unless a particular portion was called to his attention." Raymond Moley, Rexford Tugwell, and many others who were for a time close to him commented that he seldom, if ever, read a serious book all the way through during the years they were associated with him.

"He liked to read for fun," observed Jonathan Daniels in an essay on FDR's reading habits. But Roosevelt retained all his life his early capacity to absorb the line of argument and significant detail from anything he read, and in an amazingly short time. In the presidential years, when he was required daily to absorb vast reams of reports and letters on a wide range of topics, this facility for quick apperception of the essential meaning and data contained in what he read served him well.

On the evidence, then, Franklin Roosevelt was notably aural rather than visual in gathering ideas and general information; throughout his life, he learned far more from listening to talk than he did from reading. Significant in this regard is a remark he once made to Frances Perkins: "I like to read aloud—I would almost rather read to somebody than read to myself."

Much of the literature about Roosevelt and books has to do with his book collecting. He began to collect Americana while he was his club's librarian at Harvard; soon he concentrated on naval history and within a few years had acquired at little cost a very fine collection, one of the best in the country, of naval books, manuscripts, pamphlets, articles, and prints. Accounts of his reading, by those who knew him personally, are given in Frances Perkins, *The Roosevelt I Knew* (New York: Viking, 1946) and Eleanor Roosevelt, *This I Remember* (New York: Harper, 1949). Rita Halle Kleeman, *Gracious Lady: The Life of Sara Delano Roosevelt* (New York: Appleton-Century, 1935), based on personal interviews with Roosevelt's mother, gives information on Roosevelt's experience of books as a boy. Jonathan Daniels wrote the essay on Roosevelt's reading in *Three Presidents and Their Books,* ed. Robert B. Downs (Urbana: University of Illinois Press, 1955).

KENNETH S. DAVIS

Recession of 1937–38

The recession of 1937–38 was the major break in the recovery the American economy made from the depths of the Great Depression. Between 1933 and 1937, the economy expanded rapidly. Given the severity of conditions in 1933, however, the rapid recovery was insufficient to restore full employment by 1937. In September of that year, at the peak of the 1933–37 recovery, about 14 percent of the labor force (over 7 million people) remained unemployed.

In September 1937, production and income once again began to slide. The economic decline continued until June 1938 and was among the most severe in American history. Industrial production declined by 33 percent; national income declined by 13 percent; wages fell 35 percent; and manufacturing employment fell 23 percent. The nation seemed close to returning to 1933 conditions, and during the winter, starvation once again threatened. In Cleveland, families fought over spoiled produce dumped in the streets, and thousands on the relief rolls went through the first week of the year without food. In Chicago, people on relief nearly tripled in the first five months of 1938; in Detroit, Works Progress Administration rolls increased nearly 500 percent between October 1937 and May 1938.

The cause of the recession was primarily bad policy. In the fall of 1937, the Roosevelt administration, convinced that recovery was taking place so rapidly that inflation was likely to ensue, allowed the Federal Reserve Board to restrict monetary expansion. At the same time, the administration attempted to balance the budget. Roosevelt sought not only to cool the economy but to avoid the high costs of financing deficits that were unavoidable with the Federal Reserve tightening the supply of money and exerting an upward pressure on the interest rate. Even the administration's staunchest defender of deficit spending, Marriner Eccles, advocated balancing the budget for these reasons.

By March 1938, 4 million people had lost their jobs, steel production had declined by two-thirds, and the stock market had begun to decline again. Roosevelt knew that he had to take decisive action. In April, he asked Congress and the Federal Reserve to join him in a massive program of spending and lending. They responded quickly, and by June, nine months after the recession began, the recovery was well under way once again.

The recession of 1937–38 had a decisive effect on the nation's policies of economic stabilization. It strengthened conservative opposition to the New Deal, and business representatives convinced a growing number of middle-class Americans that the New Deal initiatives since 1935 had caused the recession. Roosevelt took the measure of this opposition. And he was now acutely aware of the sensitivity of the economy to fiscal and monetary policies. Consequently, he moved away from active efforts to seek economic justice through a restructuring of society, he stressed his commitment to economic recovery, and he turned toward deficit spending and monetary expansion as the best means of achieving recovery.

Elaborating the economic dimensions of the recession is Kenneth D. Roose, *The Economics of Recession and Revival, An Interpretation of 1937–38* (New Haven: Yale University Press, 1954). For additional information see Milton Friedman and Anna J. Schwartz, *A Monetary History of the United States, 1867–1960* (Princeton: Princeton University Press, 1963); Peter Temin, *Did Monetary Forces Cause the Great Depression?* (New York: W. W. Norton & Co., 1976); John Morton Blum, *From the Morgenthau Diaries, Years of Crisis, 1929–38* (Boston: Houghton Mifflin Co., 1959); and Herbert Stein, *The Fiscal Revolution in America* (Chicago: University of Chicago Press, 1969).

W. ELLIOT BROWNLEE

See also Fiscal Policy; Monetary Policy; Taxation

Reciprocal Trade Agreements

After World War I, in a wave of isolationism and protectionism, Republicans instituted a series of tariffs higher than any before or since in U.S. history. Even after the crash of 1929, when economic crisis demanded a change in economic policy, the isolationists responded by withdrawing further from a cooperative world economy. Afraid of becoming vulnerable to international events beyond American control, they erected trade barriers that in fact impeded economic recovery. The Hawley-Smoot Tariff of 1930 was such a barrier and, initially, a target for Roosevelt during his first presidential campaign.

In principle an advocate of internationalism, Roosevelt attacked Hawley-Smoot as the reason for the retaliatory high duties on American goods abroad and a major culprit in dulling the domestic economy. Even though the wisdom of a free-trade, or most-favored-nation, policy seemed evident to Roosevelt and his supporters, the quest for tariff reform proved unpopular, and its implementation produced considerable rancor within FDR's administration. In order to secure passage of other legislation that he considered more urgent, particularly the National Industrial Recovery Act, Roosevelt delayed action until after the London Economic Conference failed to halt the growth of trade restrictions. Even then he appointed an Interdepartmental Advisory Board on Reciprocal Treaties to gather ample evidence in favor of tariff reform before sending a bill to Congress.

The Reciprocal Trade Act of 1934, presented for Roosevelt's signature on 7 June, enabled the executive to negotiate bilateral trade agreements on a country-by-country basis. At first, some observers thought that Roosevelt might entrust these negotiations to his foreign policy adviser, George N. Peek. Peek had been the first head of the Agricultural Adjustment Administration and was a confirmed protectionist. Secretary of State Cordell Hull, however, received this authority on 29 June. Long a congressman and internationalist, Hull had argued for years against protective tariffs as "immoral and dishonest." Hull managed to negotiate twenty-two reciprocal trade agreements by the end of 1940 in spite of considerable opposition from various interest groups as well as the prominent New Deal figure, Raymond Moley, who believed that FDR's social programs required American self-sufficiency. Hull considered the Canadian agreement, ratified in 1936, a model of free-trade ideals because its Article I was the mutual, unconditional, most-favored-nation clause central to his internationalist philosophy.

Even though the Canadian agreement angered farmers not accustomed to competitive pricing of foreign products and in spite of the secretary of state's internationalist rhetoric, Hull's negotiations in general "chiefly served American rather than world economic interests." As the administration's chief diplomat as well as negotiator of reciprocal trade agreements, Hull adopted some of the "practicality" of Peek which Roosevelt so admired; Hull in many cases exploited the existing high tariffs to gain bargaining leverage by which the United States more than doubled its export-to-import ratio (excluding gold and silver) by 1940. New Deal trade reform broke the protectionist barrier, but under FDR's pragmatic direction, it was not as international as Hull, in theory, had wanted it to be.

For more about these agreements and the controversies about them within and outside the FDR administration, see Robert Dallek, *Franklin D. Roosevelt and American Foreign Policy, 1932–1945* (New York: Oxford University Press, 1979); Henry J. Tasca, *The Reciprocal Trade Policy of the United States* (New York: Russell & Russell, 1967); and *The Memoirs of Cordell Hull* (New York: Macmillan Co., 1948).

See also Foreign Economic Policy; Foreign Policy; Hull, Cordell; Isolationism; London Economic Conference; Peace and Internationalism; Peek, George Nelson

Reconstruction Finance Corporation

See Banking; Corcoran, Thomas Gardiner; Hoover, Herbert Clark; Jones, Jesse Holman; War Mobilization

Reed, Stanley Forman

(31 December 1884–3 April 1980)

Solicitor general, 1935–38, Supreme Court justice, 1938–57. Born in Minerva, Kentucky, Stanley Reed earned two bachelor's degrees before entering law school. After graduating from Columbia University Law School, he returned to Kentucky to establish a legal practice and there entered Democratic politics. His expertise in legal matters surrounding tobacco production brought him to the attention of Herbert Hoover during the late twenties. Hoover first appointed Reed counsel to the Federal Farm Board but in 1932 named him general counsel to the Reconstruction Finance Corporation. Reed continued to serve in the latter position during the first years of the Roosevelt administration.

In 1935, FDR drafted Reed to provide the legal basis for taking the country off the gold standard. As a special assistant to the attorney general, Reed argued and won the *Gold Clause Cases*, 294 U.S. 240 (1935), before the Supreme Court. In March of 1935, Roosevelt named Reed solicitor general. Facing an antagonistic bench increasingly suspicious of New Deal measures, Reed argued, and lost, cases that invalidated the National Industrial Recovery Act, the Agricultural Adjustment Act, and the president's removal of a member of the Federal Trade Commission.

With the retirement of Justice Sutherland in 1938, Roosevelt chose Reed as his second appointment to the Supreme Court. On the Court, Reed exhibited a moderate judicial temperament, usually vot-

Stanley Forman Reed. Artist: Oskar Stoessel. (Date unknown. National Portrait Gallery, Smithsonian Institution.)

ing to uphold federal regulatory authority. Although in the postwar years Reed joined in voiding segregation statutes, during the conflict he concurred in the removal of American citizens of Japanese descent from coastal areas. The justice retired from the Court in 1957 and died in 1980.

The best biography of Reed is by C. Herman Pritchett in *The Justices of the United States Supreme Court, 1789–1969*, ed. Leon Friedman and Fred Israel (New York: Chelsea House, 1969), pp. 2373–98. A critical study of Reed and his views on the issue of religious freedom is *Justice Reed and the First Amendment* by William F. O'Brien (Washington: Georgetown University Press, 1958). For a description of Reed's work as solicitor general, the best introduction is Paul Murphy, *The Constitution in Crisis Times* (New York: Harper & Row, 1971).

See also Supreme Court of the United States

Refugees

Franklin Roosevelt's refugee policy is never offered as one of his outstanding accomplishments. Characterized more by caution than boldness, the president's actions failed to provide any significant assistance to those (mainly Jews) fleeing Germany and other European countries during his tenure in the White House. The president may have been restricted to a considerable extent by existing immigration statutes and consular rigidity in interpreting the laws. Yet he exacerbated the refugees' plight in 1940 by appointing Breckinridge Long assistant secretary of state in charge of twenty-three of the department's forty-two divisions, including the bureau that issued visas. Congressman Emanuel Celler later described Long as the person "least sympathetic to refugees in all the State Department."

Immigration and refugee policy became an issue in the United States after Adolf Hitler assumed power in Germany in 1933. Until that time, the Immigration Act of 1924, which restricted the numbers of foreigners eligible for admission to the country, dictated the nation's policy in that area. In 1930, because of the severity of the economic depression, President Herbert Hoover ordered the State Department, whose Consular Division issued entry visas to applicants, to be quite strict in enforcing restrictions against persons "likely to become a public charge." Roosevelt never rescinded that order but did instruct consulars to act humanely and give the most favorable treatment that the law permitted. The Visa Division's personnel, however, usually applied the severest interpretations possible when Jewish refugees sought permits. This reflected not only State Department but existing national prejudices as well.

The German dictator wanted to rid his country of its Jews and until 1941 encouraged emigration. But the Western nations put up barriers restricting the admission of Jews, and no world leader sought their entry to his country. In March 1938, President Roosevelt proposed a major conference to discuss aiding refugees, and the United States invited twenty-nine nations to meet that summer in Evian-les-Bains, France. But nothing of value resulted from the meeting. The nations did establish an Intergovernmental Committee on Refugees which proved woefully inadequate and accomplished little before its demise after World War II.

In the United States, on the other hand, Senator Robert F. Wagner and Congresswoman Edith N. Rogers introduced a measure in 1939 to bring twenty thousand German refugee children to this country. The president failed to support the proposal, patriotic groups like the American Legion and the Daughters of the American Revolution opposed it (a spokeswoman for the Ladies of the Grand Army of the Republic feared that Congress might just "admit twenty thousand German-Jewish children"), and the bill never saw the light of day. The next year, however, legislation to bring English children to the United States sailed through Congress without any opposition.

During the war, with Breckinridge Long calling the tune, State Department officials became more severe in interpreting their responsibilities and fewer European applicants received visas. The early years of Roosevelt's tenure in office, 1933–36, saw only about 17,500 Jews enter the country. Historians Richard Breitman and Alan Kraut, in a work not yet published, argue that the State Department then became more lenient in granting visas, and existing figures support their conclusion. During the next four years, approximately 135,000 Jews arrived in the United States with highs of 43,450 and 39,945 in fiscal years (ending 30 June) 1939 and 1940, respectively. But after Long assumed authority and the impact of his policies took effect, the approximate number of Jews reaching this country fell to 23,737 in 1941, 10,608 in 1942, 4,705 in 1943, and 2,400 in 1944. Roosevelt told Long that he was in complete agreement with excluding prospective immigrants about whom doubts existed.

It is impossible to ascertain even an approximate number of refugees before World War II because Jews had difficulty getting visas for any country; therefore there was no record of how many wanted to leave Germany. Had other nations, including the United States, been more hospitable to newcomers, it is likely that the exodus from Germany, Poland, and other European nations might have approached 300,000 to 500,000 Jews and Gentiles. Before World War II, President Roosevelt unsuccessfully tried to find homes for refugees in other lands, and in 1940 he appointed Henry Field, a Chicago archaeologist and anthropologist, to devise a scheme for handling an anticipated 10 to 20 million displaced persons after the war (the "M" project). In 1942 Roosevelt queried congressional leaders about relaxing immigration restrictions but quickly retreated when they told him that their colleagues would not do so. The next year, the president allowed American participation in the Bermuda Conference on refugees but no solutions or new policies emerged.

Political pressures to do something for refugees forced Roosevelt's hand in 1944. Stirrings in the U.S. Senate, thoughts about the upcoming presidential election in November, and the report of Secretary of the Treasury Henry Morgenthau, Jr., documenting American acquiescence in the murder of millions of European Jews resulted in the establishment of the War Refugee Board. Created by executive order in January 1944, the War Refugee Board had a presidential mandate to save those Europeans who might still be rescued from annihilation by the Germans. In the spring, the president opened up a "free port" in the military barracks at Fort Ontario, Oswego, New York. The free port, which began receiving people in August 1944, permitted 987 refugees, then mostly in Italy and North Africa, to spend the rest of the war in safety before their intended repatriation afterwards. (In December 1945, President Harry S Truman allowed the people to leave the fort and enter the United States as immigrants.)

When Roosevelt died in April 1945, no new plans for dealing with refugees or immigrants existed. Neither the country nor the Congress wanted to welcome more foreigners, especially Jewish ones, to our shores.

The most readable and detailed analyses of Roosevelt's refugee policies appear in David S. Wyman, *Paper Walls* (Amherst: University of Massachusetts Press, 1968) and Henry L. Feingold, *The Politics of Rescue* (New Brunswick: Rutgers University Press, 1970). Additional tidbits may be garnered from Robert Dallek, *Franklin D. Roosevelt and American Foreign Policy, 1932–1945* (New York: Oxford University Press, 1979). Emanuel Celler's comment is from Leonard Dinnerstein, *America and the Survivors of the Holocaust* (New York: Columbia University Press, 1982), p. 3. The quote from the spokeswoman for the Ladies of the Grand Army of the Republic comes from Wyman, *Paper Walls*, p. 85; the statistics about Jewish immigrants to the country in the 1930s and 1940s come from Leonard Dinnerstein and David M. Reimers, *Ethnic Americans*, 2d ed. (New York: Harper & Row, 1982), p. 164.

LEONARD DINNERSTEIN

See also Jews; Stimson, Henry L.; Zionism

Regulation, Federal

To many Americans, a mention of FDR conjures up visions of increased government economic regulation in the United States, both during the New Deal as well as during the Second World War. Yet such an expansion was not simply the product of Roosevelt's handiwork. When he assumed the burdens of the presidency in 1933, a well-established comprehensive pattern of federal economic regulation was already in place. It provided a foundation upon which he would leave his own imprint in ensuing years.

That pattern of regulation had evolved over a period of more than two centuries. As a supremely pragmatic and practical people, Americans had developed it in response to specific problems within a framework of their political ideology and values. They conceived of government as the people's servant, not their master, in stark contrast to European experiences. The task of government was to promote

Ding Darling, New York Herald Tribune, 15 May 1933.
(© I.M.T. Corporation. Reprinted by permission.)

and regulate economic activities of individuals engaged in developing their own and the nation's economic potentials. Sometimes this required promotional activities such as the payment of bounties; at other times it necessitated public ownership and operation as in the building of roads and canals; more often than not it required regulation to provide a favorable economic environment for farmers, merchants, entrepreneurs, or bankers. During most of the nineteenth century, the thrust of government activities tended to be promotional; but with the expansion of industry after 1870 the regulatory functions of the federal government became increasingly prominent.

FDR grew to manhood during the early years of the twentieth century when the rise of big business spawned such new problems as the decline of agriculture, corporate concentration and monopoly, and the exploitation of labor. The response of many Progressive reformers such as Theodore Roosevelt to these issues was to advocate increased government regulation, at the federal as well as state and local levels.

Even in his formative years, FDR was acutely sensitive to major political currents of his day. As a young legislator in the New York State Senate (1911–13), he made a name for himself by strongly endorsing a wide range of Progressive reforms. When he moved to Washington in 1913 to serve as assistant secretary of the navy, he became intimately involved with increased federal regulation in wartime, particularly with U.S. Navy shipyards directly under his su-

pervision. That he absorbed these experiences was well reflected not only in his policy statements as the Democratic party's vice-presidential candidate in 1920, but in his actions as governor of New York (1928–32) where he extended state regulation in many spheres including agriculture, business, labor, relief, and natural resource conservation.

By the time he became president, therefore, FDR had already gained considerable firsthand experience with government regulation. Much of that experience he incorporated in the New Deal. To cope with economic stagnation and mass unemployment, FDR relied not only on his own personal experiences but also on the established traditions of government regulation, particularly as expanded by Theodore Roosevelt in his New Nationalism and Woodrow Wilson in the New Freedom.

In the midst of the unprecedented economic crisis of 1933 when 15 million were unemployed, FDR fell back on his wartime experiences. He told Congress that he expected "to wage a war against the crisis as if we were in fact invaded by a foreign foe." In likening the Great Depression to war, the president also prescribed relevant remedies. He advocated the reestablishment of many World War I agencies or their likeness. The National Recovery Administration, which was to mobilize business, was modeled on the War Industries Board; the Agricultural Adjustment Administration adopted some of the policies of the U.S. Food Administration; the National Labor Board mediated labor disputes, following the example of the National War Labor Board; and the expanded lending activities of the Reconstruction Finance Corpora-

Like many "living newspapers" produced by the FTP, Triple A Plowed Under informed the audience in a vivid documentary presentation of the size, nature, and origin of a social problem, and then called for a specific action to solve it. In several instances, the recommended action was government regulation. Triple A itself examined the Soil Conservation Act; Injunction Granted, The Guffey Act, the NRA, the Labor Relations Act, and the Minimum Wage Law; Power, public ownership of utilities; and One Third of a Nation, creation of Federal housing. (Courtesy the Library of Congress Federal Theatre Project Collection at George Mason University Library, Fairfax, Virginia.)

tion were based on the experience of the War Finance Corporation. Many of the individuals whom FDR called to Washington to staff these New Deal agencies, such as Director Hugh Johnson of the National Recovery Administration, had played important roles in the World War I mobilization program. FDR's emergency measures hardly solved the main problems of unemployment and economic stagnation. But they staved off a possible collapse of the American economic system and revived the waning hopes of millions of Americans who had lost faith in themselves, their leaders, and the prevailing economic system.

Once the immediate crisis of 1933 had been surmounted, FDR turned his attention to the long-range problems of economic recovery. As he and his advisers viewed the issues before them, one major remedy for the weaknesses in the nation's economic structure was the extention of federal regulation. Many reform measures between 1933 and 1939 were conceived and implemented with this assumption. The Securities Act of 1933 and the Securities and Exchange Act of 1934 brought federal regulation into the world of stock markets and security trading; the Banking Acts of 1933 and 1935 expanded the powers of the Federal Reserve Board, along with instituting federal insurance of bank deposits. Both the Tennessee Valley Authority measure and the Holding Company Act of 1935 subjected public utilities to government competition and to detailed regulation governing their organization, finances, and mode of operation. Federal regulation was also extended to the nation's broadcasters with creation of the Federal Communications Commission and to the transportation system as the Interstate Commerce Commission now regulated trucking, the U.S. Maritime Commission, shipping, and the Civil Aeronautics Board, air carriers. The Robinson-Patman Act of 1937 greatly extended federal regulation over business practices at the same time that FDR embarked on a vigorous antitrust campaign. Supplanting the Pure Food Act of 1906, the Wheeler-Lea Act of 1939 introduced more stringent restriction of foods, drugs and cosmetics.

Viewed in its entirety, the New Deal's extension of federal regulation was designed to save American capitalism. Critics charged, however, that it centralized government authority in a manner pointing toward totalitarian regimes in Italy, Germany, and the Soviet Union. FDR himself steadfastly maintained that he hoped to rescue American democracy rather than to destroy it. Extension of federal regulation was only a means to preserve the American system whereby abuses or shortcomings of private enterprise could be remedied to protect the public interest.

American entrance into World War II further extended the scope of federal regulation. Instead of recovery, the president's goal now was to secure maximum production in pursuit of total victory. With that objective, FDR created scores of new agencies, often with overlapping functions. To mobilize the economy, he established the War Production Board and the Office of War Mobilization to allocate resources and supplies. The Office of Price Administration supervised rationing and price controls; scores of new

agencies extended federal controls in particular industries such as the Petroleum Administration for War, the Rubber Reserves Corporation, the Defense Plants Corporation, and the Smaller War Plants Corporation. Few areas of the economy remained untouched by wartime federal regulation. Although peace ended the life of many emergency agencies, some continued to function in the postwar era.

Despite obvious differences in federal regulation in depression and war, certain continuities in the pattern of public policies was evident. The two major crises of depression and war which FDR confronted led him to undertake a vast expansion of governmental powers. He greatly extended the role of the president in steering the nation's economic course. In stark contrast to his predecessors, FDR took an active part in formulating and administering economic policies, first, as he phrased it, as Dr. New Deal, and then, as Dr. Win the War. Although he received advice from the brains trust in the New Deal and from professional economists in the war, he took it upon himself to educate the American public about this new function of the presidency.

If the White House was a focal point of expanded federal regulation, it was only one aspect of the vast expansion of government's involvement with the economy during the Roosevelt Era. Between 1933 and 1945, Congress and the Supreme Court joined the president in institutionalizing a great extension of federal regulation. This included the proliferation of fiscal policies and the expanded regulation of agriculture, business, labor, and social welfare. Almost implicitly, between 1933 and 1945, the federal government was assuming primary responsibility for maintaining economic stability and growth, a responsibility that Congress made explicit in the Employment Act of 1946.

An inescapable consequence of these shifting attitudes about the theory and practice of federal regulation was a significant growth of the bureaucracy. Both the New Deal and World War II mobilization programs spawned scores of new agencies with hundreds of thousands of new civil servants. This, too, was one of the legacies FDR left behind.

During his presidency, the American people encountered two of the most serious crises in their history. In coping with the Great Depression and World War II, FDR not only provided daring leadership but also reflected a broad consensus that the extension of federal regulation constituted a powerful tool for ensuring national survival.

One of the best contemporary accounts of federal regulation during the New Deal in its historical context is Leverett S. Lyon et al., *Government and Economic Life: Development and Current Issues of American Public Policy,* 2 vols. (Washington: Brookings Institution, 1939–40). FDR's role in shaping regulatory policies is perceptively analyzed by one of his former associates, Rexford Tugwell, in *FDR: Architect of an Era* (New York: Macmillan Co., 1967), and by Ellis W. Hawley, *The New Deal and the Problem of Monopoly* (Princeton: Princeton University Press, 1966) who stresses business regulation. Bruce Catton, *The War Lords of Washington* (New York:

Harcourt, Brace, 1948) provides a shrewd and rather critical assessment of FDR's wartime regulatory policies, and Eliot Janeway, *The Struggle for Survival* (New Haven: Yale University Press, 1951) offers a general survey of wartime organization and domestic policies. A more recent and rather favorable appraisal of FDR's war regulation is in Richard Polenberg, *War and Society* (Philadelphia: Lippincott, 1972). On the impact of New Deal regulation on American life during the Roosevelt era and the succeeding three decades, see Otis L. Graham, Jr., *Toward a Planned Society: From Roosevelt to Nixon* (New York: Oxford University Press, 1976).

GERALD D. NASH

See also Agriculture; Banking; Business; Fiscal Policy; Hundred Days; Liberalism and Progressivism; Monetary Policy; New Deal; Planning; Taxation; War Mobilization

Relief

Relief was a term used in the realm of social and political organizations to describe giving of cash, goods, and work by public and private agencies to the needy. The needy are those in our society who cannot provide for themselves an adequate health level and job stability. It is estimated that at least 18 million Americans were in need of food, medical care, clothing, and employment in the spring of 1933. This tremendous number of individuals in desperate economic straits forced a pronounced change within the United States in providing relief to the needy.

In the agricultural society of early America, local and county governments provided "outdoor" relief whereby the care of "paupers" was farmed out to bidders by contracts. The able-bodied were required to work. The unemployable needy received goods and food, not money. In the nineteenth century, industrialism, combined with major economic depressions every twenty to twenty-five years, plus natural disasters having more impact with a denser population, caused many state governments to establish agencies and funding to provide relief. The number of county poor farms, almshouses, and state institutions for the insane, blind, and crippled increased considerably.

Private charity efforts varied with economic conditions and within regions of our nation. In times of major regional catastrophes and major nationwide economic depressions, private charity proved to be increasingly inadequate. By the late 1920s, public tax dollars provided approximately 70 percent of relief in our fifteen major cities.

President Herbert Hoover (1929–33) involved the federal government in encouraging state, local, and private funding for the increasing number of needy and unemployed. He supported federal funds for construction projects to stimulate employment. Hoover enlisted leading American businesspersons and organizations to raise more funds and to organize more effectively relief to the needy. Even though economic conditions deteriorated drastically, President Hoover steadfastly refused to use federal dollars to provide food, clothing, work, or cash directly to the needy or unemployed.

In the early days of his governorship of New York, (1929–33) Franklin D. Roosevelt, like Herbert Hoover, did not wish to involve the state or federal government more extensively in providing relief. However, finding state- and federal-financed public works, local government, and private relief efforts inadequate to meet the crisis, Roosevelt's basic humane philosophy and pragmatic approach toward governing allowed him to respond to the cry of the needy and the evidence of that need provided by leading social workers and mayors of the larger New York cities.

Roosevelt stated in an address to a special session of the New York State Assembly on 28 August 1931:

One of the duties of the State is that of caring for those of its citizens who find themselves the victims of such adverse circumstances as makes them unable to obtain even the necessities for mere existence without the aid of others. . . . To these unfortunate citizens, aid must be extended by Government, not as a matter of charity, but as a matter of social duty.

In August 1931, Governor Roosevelt requested the New York State Assembly to appropriate $20 million to assist the needy and unemployed. By the end of 1931, his hopes to keep state aid to the needy financed from regular tax resources ended, and he requested $30 million in a bond issue to help finance relief. In both instances, the State Assembly and the voters responded positively.

By the spring of 1932, recognizing the vastness of unemployment and its negative impact on families and the failure of private and public relief efforts and employment activities to meet the crises, Roosevelt stated to the graduating students of Oglethorpe University:

The country needs, . . . the country demands, bold, persistent experimentation. It is common sense to take a method and try it; if it fails, admit it frankly and try another. But, above all, try something.

By November 1931, Governor Roosevelt had established the Temporary Emergency Relief Administration (TERA) to coordinate and direct relief to the needy in New York State. Harry L. Hopkins, reared and formally educated in Iowa, who had previously worked eighteen years as a social worker in the New York City area, soon became the most dynamic spokesman for the needy among state officials. First as the deputy administrator of the TERA, and then as its chief administrator, Hopkins brought to Roosevelt imagination, conviction, perception, devotion, and the actions of a doer. State government relief efforts for the needy in New York improved and expanded under the leadership of Hopkins.

In May 1933, President Franklin D. Roosevelt selected Hopkins to be the chief administrator for the various federal relief agencies of the New Deal. Hopkins now had a tremendous opportunity, and he improved and expanded state government relief efforts effectively. He did not believe that "society owes every man a living," but that certainly "every man" should have "the opportunity to provide for himself and his family a decent and American way of living."

At least 18 million Americans needed public or private relief in the spring of 1933, and the number did not change perceptibly by the end of the year 1935. Social workers, economists, and heads of relief agencies have amply recorded that at least one-fourth, if not one-third, of our nation's 120 million people were ill-fed, ill-clothed, and lacking in adequate shelter by the fall of 1933. Did the New Deal federal relief programs meet the full needs of these people? Certainly not. Franklin D. Roosevelt and Harry Hopkins sought only to alleviate the worst conditions and suffering. As noted earlier, Roosevelt's humaneness caused him to act to encourage and ensure the continuation of faith in our government. He held fast, however, to his firm conviction that the federal government should get out of the relief business as soon as possible. A resurgent private economy providing employment for all employable people was to him the only satisfactory means to diminish the number of needy.

The Roosevelt administration initiated three major relief programs, plus several minor ones during the years 1933–37. The Federal Emergency Relief Administration (FERA; May 1933) provided direct cash relief to the needy through grants to the states. Initially, states were required to match three dollars to one federal dollar for 50 percent of federal relief dollars. By 1934, direct cash grants to states on a nonmatching basis dominated so that less wealthy states could more adequately serve the needy. During the last half of the FERA's existence, its officials stressed work projects for the employable unemployed.

To prevent another winter as catastrophic as 1932–33, the Civil Works Administration (CWA; October 1933) employed, at one point, as many as 4 million Americans. Localities financed 10 percent of the nearly $1 billion spent. Schools, roads, sewer lines, and small airports were built and repaired. Both the CWA and the FERA aided operations of local schools, employing, at one point, fifty thousand school teachers.

The Works Progress Administration (WPA) became the most extensive work relief agency of the Roosevelt administration. Headed by the creative, perceptive, and dedicated Hopkins, it provided work for at least 5 million individuals between the fall of 1935 and December 1938. Most workers came from the public relief roles. Many types of work projects existed as a means to recognize the great variety of skills possessed by the unemployed and, in the years 1937–41, to develop additional skills. WPA workers were encouraged to take part-time private employment to supplement their meager WPA wages which were often limited by bad weather conditions. The WPA staff encouraged movement to privately financed employment. As expected, those remaining on WPA rolls the longest were the less skilled and the older workers.

Concurrent with the FERA, the CWA, and the WPA were several lesser known relief and work relief agencies. These included the Federal Surplus Relief

Unemployed men registering for benefits. Photographer: Dorothea Lange. (Courtesy FDR Library.)

Corporation, which was established to buy, process, and distribute surplus food to the needy (forerunner of the food-stamp program of recent years); the Transient Relief Division of the FERA, which provided relief to over 300,000 transients monthly during most of the winter of 1934–35; and the Rural Rehabilitation Division of FERA, which aided in relocating unsuccessful farmers, as well as assisting farmers on reasonably productive farmland. Later the National Youth Administration (NYA) provided employment for thousands of needy high school and college students. Separate from the relief agencies headed by Hopkins was the popular Civilian Conservation Corps, which during the years 1934–39 provided employment to thousands of young men, who worked to improve our national parks and forests.

The American taxpayers paid out over $11 million for the federal relief programs of the 1930s. A major value of the relief programs was their contribution to convincing millions of Americans that government could respond to *their* needs. The improvement in national morale, the maintenance and improvement of workers' skills, and the preservation of faith in democracy carried a value vastly beyond that of the goods produced, the medical care provided, and the projects completed.

Feeling that our society would henceforth always have hundreds of thousands of unemployable adults and needy children, Franklin D. Roosevelt, encouraged by Secretary of Labor Frances Perkins and Harry Hopkins, established a Social Security system. The Social Security Act of 1935 initiated a program that continues today (with modifications and changes) for old-age assistance payments, unemployment insurance, and economic aid for the crippled, the blind, and dependent mothers and children.

World War II caused only a temporary interruption in federal and state relief efforts. Many Americans viewed the GI bill financial support programs for college education as a version of the NYA. Improved employment levels during and after World War II allowed the nation to review and refine legislation pertaining to various categories of the needy; however, the Roosevelt-Hopkins-Perkins belief that government had an obligation to assist the needy continued.

The Roosevelt-Hopkins-Perkins legacy lives on in America. Roosevelt's conviction that government should respond; Perkins's and Hopkins's belief that unemployables should have food, clothing, shelter, and medical care sufficient to keep them healthy; and Hopkins teaching Americans that though the unemployed may lack money, they do not lack character or the willingness to work or the ability to adjust to community life if provided a chance to be employed— all this continues to shape the giving of relief in our nation.

Josephine C. Brown, *Public Relief, 1929–1939* (New York: Henry Holt & Co., 1940) provides useful, informative insight on public and private relief in the United States prior to 1929. See also Herbert C. Hoover, *Memoirs*, vol. 3 (New York: Macmillan, 1952). The most interesting brief account of the interacting Harry Hopkins and Franklin D. Roosevelt relationship for the years 1931–1938 is in Robert Sherwood's *Roosevelt and Hopkins: An Intimate History* (New York: Harper and Bros., 1948). The best single volume on relief during the 1930s is Searle F. Charles's, *Ministry of Relief: Harry Hopkins and the Depression* (Syracuse: Syracuse University Press, 1962). Donald S. Howard provides the most detailed account of the Works Progress Administration in the *The WPA and Federal Relief Policy* (New York: Russell Sage Foundation, 1943). A work of considerable value is *The Administration of Federal Work Relief* (Chicago: Public Administration Service, 1941) by A. W. Macmahon, J. D. Willett, and Gladys Ogden. For more recent developments stemming from the New Deal years see Eveline M. Burns, *The American Social Security System* (Boston: Houghton Mifflin, 1949) and Jules H. Berman, "Public Assistance," *Encyclopedia of Social Work*, vol. 2. Valuable also is Lewis Meriam's *Relief* and *Social Security* (Washington, D.C.: The Brookings Institution, 1946).

SEARLE F. CHARLES

See also Civil Works Administration; Civilian Conservation Corps; Federal Art Project; Federal Emergency Relief Administration; Federal Theatre Project; Federal Writers Project; Governor of New York; Great Depression; Hopkins, Harry L.; Hundred Days; National Youth Administration; National Resources Planning Board; New Deal; Perkins, Frances; Public Works Administration; Rural Electrification Administration; Social Security; Taxation; Women and the New Deal; Works Progress Administration

Religion

Franklin Roosevelt did not appear to the general public to be a particularly religious man. He revealed virtually nothing of his inner life, his emotional or spiritual life—and certainly he made no more than a conventional display of piety. The prayer at the end of his first inaugural address seemed more a ceremon-

The Roosevelt family Bible (open to page 1 of the New Testament). (Courtesy FDR Library.)

ial gesture than a deeply felt expression of faith. Earlier that morning he had attended a worship service in St. John's Church, a service arranged by himself and attended by the Roosevelt family, cabinet member families, and a few invited guests. The service, conducted by Rev. Endicott Peabody, rector of Groton and headmaster of Groton school, was simple, austere, impersonal, with organ music and selections from the Book of Common Prayer. The Reverend Dr. Peabody prayed, "O Lord . . . most heartily we beseech Thee . . . to behold and bless Thy servant, Franklin, chosen to be President of the United States." Roosevelt remained in private silent prayer, face cupped in his hands, for a half-minute or so after the rector's loud "amen."

Thereafter, he only rarely attended Sunday morning services in St. Thomas's where he had been junior vestryman during World War I and where, as he complained to Frances Perkins, "a couple of pews way down front in the middle aisle" had been reserved for him, set off by "a red silk cord and tassels." He said: "I can do almost anything in the 'Goldfish Bowl' of the President's life, but I'll be hanged if I can say my prayers in it. . . . By the time I have gotten into that pew and settled down with everybody looking at me, I don't feel like saying my prayers." He was profoundly reticent about such matters.

Yet, on the night of 2 March 1933 as he rode a B & O train from New York to Washington for the first inaugural, he summoned Jim Farley to his stateroom and talked to Farley, a devout Catholic, not about the many problems whose solution would become his responsibility in two days' time, but of his faith in God. More important than any plan for resolving the crisis was a great people's religious faith, he said; ultimately the salvation of America depended on the American people's active belief in divine providence, their seeking and accepting divine guidance. According to Rexford G. Tugwell, he "always, when new undertakings were before him, . . . asked all his colleagues in it to accompany him if they would in asking for divine blessing upon what they were about to do." It was clear to such close associates as Tugwell, Perkins, and, of course, his wife that the sustenance of his patient good humor in the face of irritations and frustrations that would have exasperated many men—the main source of his remarkable serenity and cheerfulness under pressure—was his religious faith.

In form, his religion was Anglican. The Bible upon which his hand rested as he took the presidential oath of office was a large seventeenth-century Dutch Bible that had been in the Roosevelt family for at least seven generations. His father had been baptized in the Dutch Reform church, but by the time Franklin was born, he had for a long time been warden and vestryman of Hyde Park's St. James Episcopal Church. It was in the chapel of that church that the infant Franklin, at seven weeks of age, was christened on 20 March 1883. Ever after, as boy, youth, and man, he attended church services as an English gentleman in a genteel environment that discouraged religious enthusiasms, or any show of intense feeling, as ill-bred.

"He found . . . Anglicism . . . satisfactory" because it "required of him no testimony, no embarrassing externalizations of his inner torments and resolutions," Tugwell wrote. "It was simply there, the atmosphere and ceremonial of an institution in which divinity was present but not demanding. If it seems peculiar that Franklin had no adult doubts, no doctrinal difficulties, and only a serene faith that nothing could disturb, that is because the philosophy of religion was not his metier." With this Frances Perkins agreed. "He had little, if any, intellectual or theological understanding of the doctrinal basis of the major religions," she wrote, because he had little interest in "philosophical concepts." She went on to tell of remarking to Eleanor, "Franklin is really a very simple Christian." Eleanor, after a pause and with a significant look, replied, "Yes, a *very simple* Christian." Eleanor herself spoke of once pressing him (too hard) to say whether he was convinced, really intellectually convinced, that Christian doctrine was true. He replied: "I never really thought much about it. I think it is just as well not to think about things like that too much." What his heart accepted should not be questioned or too closely examined by his mind.

What his heart accepted was, on the evidence, a remarkably plain, matter-of-fact Christianity. He believed in an all-wise, all-powerful, wholly good, and infinitely loving God the Father, and in Jesus Christ as Son of God. He believed that history is a working out of God's will and that therefore it inevitably works toward ultimately beneficent ends. He believed himself to be chosen a special agent of God, and that God worked through him and was therefore ultimately responsible for his acts (he was thus to a considerable degree absolved of *personal* responsibility). It was his duty to pay close attention to the signs and cues God gave him in the form of pressures and opportunities and then to follow these to the best of his ability. As Eleanor Roosevelt put it: "He felt that human beings were given tasks to perform and with these tasks the ability and strength to put them through. He could pray for help and guidance and have faith in his own judgment, [thereby informed by divine will] as a result."

The most authoritative accounts of Roosevelt's religious life by those who personally knew him are Eleanor Roosevelt's *This I Remember* (New York: Appleton-Century, 1949), Frances Perkins's *The Roosevelt I Knew* (New York: Viking, 1946), and Rexford G. Tugwell's *The Democratic Roosevelt* (Garden City, N.Y.: Doubleday, 1957), the latter being especially valuable for one who seeks for causal relations between Roosevelt's deepest beliefs and his public actions. These relations are extensively explored in Kenneth S. Davis, *F.D.R.: The Beckoning of Destiny, 1882–1928* (New York: Putnam, 1971).

KENNETH S. DAVIS

St. James Church, Hyde Park. (Sid Light.)

Reorganization Act of 1939

The federal law of 3 April 1939 enabling the president to establish the modern White House staff in the form of the Executive Office of the President. The 1939 act was the last major New Deal measure before the Second World War and marked the transition from depression reform to war mobilization. The final bill represented a significant shift in power from Congress to the presidency, even as the severe restrictions the legislature imposed upon Roosevelt's bold initial reorganization proposals contributed to the decline of New Deal reform.

Two major sources provided the impetus for the reform of presidential executive organization. From the Progressive period came a tradition of improved management in municipal government, particularly the city manager movement, and in state government, including reorganizations of New York State's administration by Al Smith and Roosevelt himself. More

T. *Brown*, New York Herald Tribune, *1937.* (© *I.H.T. Corporation. Reprinted by permission.*)

immediately, the ad hoc group of alphabet agencies created during the hundred days and the burst of legislation in 1935 required rationalization into a structured welfare state.

Although Roosevelt artfully employed informal and duplicative management techniques, by early 1936 he felt the need for a more ordered system of presidential administration. In March he appointed Louis D. Brownlow, Charles E. Merriam, and Luther Gulick, all experienced in progressive local administration, to the President's Committee on Administrative Management. The position of both Roosevelt and the members of the committee differed markedly from that of previous advocates of executive reform in that they perceived reorganization less as an economy measure than as a device for improved bureaucratic control.

The committee's report, which Roosevelt received shortly after the 1936 election, recommended that the presidency be strengthened in five ways. First, the president should have six executive assistants to lighten his personal work load. Second, the civil service system, which had proved ineffectual in handling the increase in personnel wrought by the burgeoning of New Deal agencies, was to be revamped. Third, the Treasury Department's Budget Bureau, a consistent opponent of New Deal spending, was to be brought under the president's direct control. Fourth, the structure of the federal government should be altered through the addition of two new cabinet posts by executive order; further, the independent regulatory commissions, which endangered the separation of powers by functioning in the penumbra between

the executive and the judiciary, must be brought under the control of the departments. Fifth, the capstone of the reorganization was to be the transformation of the advisory National Resources Board into a vigorous statutory National Resources Planning Board to engage in continuous central planning and program coordination. This latter was intended to be instrumental in implementing a program of seven regional authorities along the lines of the Tennessee Valley Authority which FDR submitted to Congress a few months after sending the Committee on Administrative Management's proposals to the Hill in January 1937.

Unfortunately for Roosevelt, the reorganization bill was introduced into an exceptionally hostile legislative environment. Before action could be taken on executive reorganization, Roosevelt put forward his ill-fated plan to enlarge the Supreme Court. Taken together, the court plan and executive reorganization seemed to demonstrate to many that Roosevelt intended to establish some kind of dictatorship; the rise of fascism in Europe and Japan reinforced fears of constitutional overturn. Unlike such earlier reforms as the Agricultural Adjustment Administration or Social Security, executive reorganization had no natural constituency to create a base of support, and the bill failed in 1937. Resistance in Congress centered on Democratic senator Harry Byrd, who insisted on adhering to strict fiscal conceptions of reorganization. Within the federal bureaucracy, Harold Ickes, Henry Wallace, and Frances Perkins defended their bailiwicks against presidential encroachment. Outside of Washington the major opposition came from the National Committee to Uphold Constitutional Government, spearheaded by the Gannett press.

Reorganization remained stalled in 1938 as well. Although the Senate passed a bill in March, bungled management of House leaders halted passage there. With the "Roosevelt recession" reaching its severest stage in April, Roosevelt's popularity and prestige sank to its lowest point. Business leaders, eager to curb FDR's perquisites, argued that reorganization legislation would erode business confidence and impede recovery. Such groups as northwestern progressives and big-city Democrats, which had supported the New Deal in the past, broke with Roosevelt over executive reorganization; a vote against the bill in Congress registered popular dissatisfaction with the president without endangering any obvious benefits.

Roosevelt rebounded quickly, announced a new economic policy to combat recession, and planned a new reorganization bill for the next session of Congress. The mild bill finally presented in 1939 contrasted markedly with FDR's bold proposals of 1937 and eliminated the earlier provisions regarding the creation of new departments, the independent regulatory agencies, and civil service that Congress found objectionable. The president was given the power to reorganize, not by executive order, but through the submission to Congress of reorganizing plans. In addition, he received the authority to appoint six administrative assistants. The easy passage of the bill confirmed its emasculation.

Still, Roosevelt used Congress's limited grant of reorganizing power skillfully. He submitted his first reorganization plan to Congress on 25 April, and it passed easily. Constrained from establishing two new cabinet departments, FDR set up the Federal Security Agency and the Public Works Agency as surrogates. The first plan also united the White House Office, the Bureau of the Budget, and a National Resources Planning Board with limited functions into the Executive Office of the President, which was formally created on 28 September. Roosevelt also used his powers under the Reorganization Act to institute an Office of Emergency Management crucial for military preparedness.

The reorganization powers defined under the 1939 Reorganization Act remain substantially those of the presidency to this day and certainly increased the efficiency and power of the office. Yet relative to what Roosevelt sought to attain—nothing less than a "third New Deal" composed of the Committee on Administrative Management's original proposal including a strong National Resources Planning Board to supervise seven regional planning systems—his achievement appears quite limited. Congress, even after Roosevelt's stunning electoral success in 1936, retained and perhaps even enhanced its capacity seriously to alter, at times beyond recognition, the national domestic program of the chief executive to suit the local interests of which it is the expression.

The two major works on the 1939 Reorganization Act complement one another. Barry D. Karl's *Executive Reorganization and Reform in the New Deal: The Genesis of Administrative Management, 1900–1939* (Cambridge, Mass.: Harvard University Press, 1963) is largely an intellectual history and emphasizes continuities between Progressivism and the 1939 act; Richard Polenberg's *Reorganizing Roosevelt's Government: The Controversy over Executive Reorganization 1936–1939* (Cambridge, Mass.: Harvard University Press, 1966) stresses the need for rationalization after the reforms of the early New Deal. Karl's recent *The Uneasy State: The United States from 1915 to 1945* (Chicago: University of Chicago Press, 1983) revises some of his earlier conclusions and is vital for understanding the late New Deal milieu of the 1939 act; his "Executive Reorganization and Presidential Power," *Supreme Court Review* 1977:1–37, provides the long-term context.

CHARLES SCHILKE

See also New Deal; Office of the Presidency; Planning

Republican Party

Dazed by the severity of the depression, confused by the breadth and implications of New Deal legislation, frustrated by a president politically adroit and electorally attractive, and wracked by internecine struggles, the Republican party during the Roosevelt years barely survived in the political process. Yet, because of its historical connection to power coupled with its symbolic connection to national values and patterns that had meaning to millions, the Grand Old Party

Cecil Jensen, Manchester *(N.H.)* Union, *19 August 1935.*
(Union Leader, Manchester, N.H.)

not only survived but recovered much of its power in the decades following the New Deal.

Few could have predicted its eclipse from power in the 1920s. Assuming the presidency in 1928, Herbert Hoover, the third successive Republican and the most promising, optimistically proclaimed the end of poverty and the ongoing march of prosperity in the United States. His grandiose expectations were echoed by the Republican campaign slogans, "A Chicken in Every Pot" and "Two Cars in Every Garage." Four short years later, however, running for reelection, Hoover faced certain defeat and fearfully argued that the contest was more than between two men, it was between two philosophies of government.

During those years, the Great Depression, beginning immediately after Hoover assumed office, quickly deepened into the most traumatic domestic event since the Civil War. Not only was the Republican party swept out of power in 1932, but it also became the minority party in Congress and suffered decline on local and state levels as well. The depression and New Deal program shaped national politics for the next four decades and deeply affected the character and program of the Republicans.

Not many were prepared either politically or psychologically for their rapid descent, and party leaders reacted with contradictory feelings and proposals. The party's history partly explains the confusions that beset it during the New Deal period. Emerging from a strong minority position in the 1850s, the GOP rode to power in a time of racial strife and swift economic changes. With the election of Abraham Lincoln, it gained control of the federal government and from 1860 to 1932 remained the dominant party in the political structure, although neither party was able to totally control all the levels of government in the latter decades of the nineteenth century. Only two Democratic presidents, Grover Cleveland and Woodrow Wilson who share sixteen years between them, sat in the White House during those years. The Republican grip on Congress and the judiciary was equally impressive. Over a span of seventy-two years, the Republicans controlled the Senate for sixty-two and the House for forty-six years, totally dominating both branches between 1861 and 1875, 1897 and 1911, and 1921 and 1931. As a consequence, the Republican experience was one of lordship. As a minority or out-party, it had very little training or sensitivity.

When relieved of majority status, most office-holding Republicans found it difficult to alter roles. Many felt that the change was but a temporary lapse in their situations and eagerly awaited a shift among the voting public. Their optimism was exceeded by a long drought brought about by three factors: a permanent alteration in the electorate, the character of the depression and its affect on the role of government, and the personality and policies of Franklin D. Roosevelt.

That the party was headed toward decline even before the depression was evident in the demographic changes. Throughout the 1910s and 1920s, as Samuel Lubell wrote in *The Future of American Politics* the GOP "labored on the wrong side of the birth rate." Millions of Eastern European immigrants, displaced African-American farmers, and rural white laborers had migrated into the cities of the country seeking work and motivated by middle-class expectations. The GOP, however, had failed to develop programs to match their needs and ignored the rapid decline in their share of the urban vote. From a high of over a million and a half plurality in twelve of the largest cities in 1920, the party suffered a reversal only eight years later. So swift was the shift that the Democratic party registered a congressional plurality of 38,000 in those same cities in 1928, and for the next three decades, the Republicans were unable to recapture the urban vote.

A further difficulty was the party's inability to identify with the changing ethnic, racial, and religious character of American society and with those groups who had migrated into the urban area. The majority of congressional Republicans grew up in stable, small communities of middle- and upper-income Protestant families whose ancestry had antedated the Civil War. Unfamiliar with urban and minority life-styles and distanced from the harshness of the depression, many Republicans understandably expressed their hostility toward Roosevelt and New Deal social welfare programs in emotionally laden, exaggerated terms. All cries in Congress and elsewhere by Republicans equating New Deal legislation with socialist, communist, statist, and fascist ideologies misinterpreted the complexity of the depression and the reality of urban existence.

Furthermore, internally the party was unable to reconcile a factionalism that had resulted in stagnation at the local and state levels. During the 1920s Republicans were irreconcilably split along conservative and progressive lines. Midwestern and northeastern conservatives who had taken over control of the party after the election of Warren G. Harding had done little to develop programs to attract new voters. So certain of continuing victories were party elders that they courted voters from safe island districts rather than begin the arduous task of building in the cities and other changing areas. The GOP had even neglected farmers and blacks, two traditional allies, with the consequence that both bolted to the Democrats in the 1930s. Farmers would eventually return to the party in the late 1930s, but blacks became a permanent group within the Democratic coalition.

Republican training as an opposition party began instantly in the first hundred days of the New Deal. The furious onslaught of Democratic legislation rendered constructive opposition impossible, and party factionalism regarding the New Deal approach reflected its noncohesiveness. Throughout Roosevelt's first term, the party was divided between domestic progressives who selectively supported certain welfare measures and those who almost totally disassociated themselves from the New Deal and excoriated Roosevelt and his policies. Election results in 1934 proved that Roosevelt's direct governmental philosophy was extremely popular—for the first time since the Civil War the incumbent party actually gained congressional seats in midterm.

In an attempt to counter Roosevelt, an antagonistic conservative element joined with the American Liberty League, a group of extremely wealthy corporate lawyers and directors, members of old-line families, and others of power, which reaffirmed the traditional values of individualism, private enterprise, and laissez-faire. The league would saddle the Republicans with a heavy burden in the national elections in 1936.

In selecting its presidential candidate, the party once again turned to a midwestern figure, Governor Alfred M. Landon of Kansas. A congenial man with politically progressive credentials—he had actually supported many New Deal objectives but strenuously objected to its methods—Landon was thought to combine various features that would strengthen the regular constituencies while attracting newer elements to the party. A purview of the platform demonstrated party divisions regarding the New Deal. Condemned were unemployment insurance, old-age annuities, and collective bargaining and stressed was a balanced budget. Otherwise, the platform mirrored Roosevelt's legislation program. Clearly, a shift toward the New Deal philosophy was partly underway.

Virtually no one was prepared for the landslide. The 523 to 8 electoral margin was the largest in political history since 1820. Roosevelt captured every state but Maine and Vermont. Even Kansas went

Democratic to the embarrassment of the Republican candidate. Congressionally the party fared as well: the next Congress had but seventeen Republican senators and eighty-nine representatives, its smallest delegation in the party's history. Most of the House seats belonged to easterners who had emerged from the campaign in better shape than their midwestern counterparts. In 1932, in cities of more than 100,000, the Democrats captured ninety-nine as opposed to fifteen for the Republicans; four years later the trend reached its apex as Republicans won only two. The *New Yorker* magazine inquired whether the Republicans were going to move their headquarters to the Smithsonian Institution.

Just as it appeared that Roosevelt would overwhelm the Republicans in his second term, he committed a serious political blunder. Frustrated by Supreme Court decisions that had rendered several significant measures unconstitutional, Roosevelt made a dramatic attempt to enlarge the Court from nine to fifteen members. The legislation was immediately attacked in many quarters as a devious attempt to pack the Court. Party leaders decided to undermine Roosevelt by remaining totally silent during the debate in Congress and in the country and allow the Democrats to battle among themselves. Not only did the strategy work but the damage to the Democratic liberal wing was considerable. The Court fight coalesced different factions of both parties who had opposed aspects of the New Deal. Southern Democrats joined with the majority of Republicans in an alliance that would wreak havoc with liberal legislation in the last two years of Roosevelt's second administration and would influence similar legislation for the next several decades.

A united Republican organization confronted the 1938 elections with significant results and indicated that a Republican revival was underway in the industrial East. The election produced several new attractive figures, such as Thomas E. Dewey of New York, Robert A. Taft of Ohio, and Henry Cabot Lodge, Jr., of Massachusetts, who represented different Republican approaches around which the party could launch forays into the newer middle classes.

Yet, it was a renegade Democrat who captured the nomination in 1940. Another midwesterner, Wendell Willkie, a highly successful Indiana corporate lawyer and president, attractive and personable, who combined a domestic conservatism with an international outlook, suddenly emerged as the standard-bearer. The party's platform was significantly different than it had been in the first years of the New Deal. In 1934, the party had bitterly opposed those policies; in the presidential election, it had accepted the majority of its legislation; and several years later, it had successfully wielded together the warring factions. In 1940, however, the party was confronted by several major obstacles. The Roosevelt coalition had established itself as the majority party. The party was still divided between those who opposed New Deal reforms and government action and those who had accepted the permanency of social welfare legislation,

and the war in Europe had split their ranks. A majority of Republicans in Congress supported a unilateral, isolationist position and had adamantly opposed Roosevelt on his foreign policy, whereas a minority, including Willkie, had been favorable to it.

Again, the Republicans went down to defeat. Despite its handicaps, however, the party had demonstrated a stronger following than it had at any time since Hoover's loss. In addition to its traditional support from the upper Midwest, a substantial number of farmers had returned to the fold. But the division between the city and country remained constant. Cincinnati was the only city with a population of over 400,000 that went Republican.

Foreign policy issues and the war emerged as the overriding concerns after 1940. The GOP argued over how to best criticize Roosevelt's policies while appearing to be not overtly damaging to the war effort, an untenable position at best. War actions favor an incumbent president, and Republicans found it difficult to mount a substantial attack on Roosevelt. Nevertheless, the nomination of Governor Thomas E. Dewey of New York signaled the emergence of the liberal, international faction of the party that would control it for the next several decades. At the same time, their defeat further suggested that it would take an unusual turn of events before they could hope to regain power on the national level.

In essence, the Republican descent into a minority status was due not to economics alone but to their myopic view of changing conditions. The Republicans had failed to perceive the transformation of the middle classes, a change related to the massive shift from an agrarian to an industrial society which in turn required highly specialized professional and managerial groups. Even before the depression, second- and third-generation urban inhabitants were developing these skills, which the New Deal would utilize once the Democrats came to power. In this connection, they had failed to take into account the fears and aspirations of rising minority groups who were eager for their place in the new middle classes. Equally, they were unwilling to recognize that Roosevelt's popularity was due to the representation he gave to these ethnic and racial groups. Moreover, they had refused to accept that direct governmental response in aiding citizens and stabilizing the chaotic economic situation was an inevitable aspect of a highly urban, industrial society. Hence, they had to travel the road of reevaluation and reassessment and wait for a major shift in the electorate, or a magnetic presidential candidate, and/or a turn of historic events before they could reassert political domination.

Several broad histories provide perspectives on the Republican party during the 1930s and 1940s. The fullest work is George H. Mayer's *The Republican Party, 1854–1966*, 2d ed. (New York: Oxford University Press, 1967). An earlier book, spritely written but thin for the New Deal period, is Malcolm Moos, *The Republicans* (New York: Random House, 1956). Still one of the best studies on the history and character of the political party system is Wilfred Binkley, *American Political Parties: Their Natural*

History, 4th ed. (New York: Alfred A. Knopf, 1962). Tracing the changing ethnic, economic, and sectional aspects affecting the party in the decade following the New Deal is Louis Harris, *Is There a Republican Majority?* (New York: Harper & Bros., 1954). Excellent biographies of Republican presidential candidates are Donald Bruce Johnson, *The Republican Party and Wendell Willkie* (Urbana: University of Illinois Press, 1960) and Richard Norton Smith, *Thomas E. Dewey and His Times* (New York: Simon & Schuster, 1982).

JOSEPH BOSKIN

See also American Liberty League; Biographers and Public Reputation; Congress, United States; Conservatism; Dewey, Thomas E.; Election of 1928; Election of 1942; Elections in the Roosevelt Era; Hoover, Herbert Clark; Landon, Alfred Mossman; Negroes; Stimson, Henry L.; Willkie, Wendell Lewis

---

Resettlement Administration

See Agriculture; Housing and Resettlement; Tugwell, Rexford Guy

---

Revenue Acts

See Taxation

Roosevelt, Alice

See Longworth, Alice Roosevelt

Eleanor Roosevelt, 1935. Artist: Samuel Johnson Woolf. (National Portrait Gallery, Smithsonian Institution.)

Roosevelt, Anna Eleanor

(11 October 1886–7 November 1962)

Eleanor Roosevelt was a humanistic reformer and consummate politician—a complex figure full of contradictions and paradoxes. A pragmatist, she was prepared to strive for social betterment step by step and to compromise under the dictates of the political reality; an idealist, she was uncompromising in her insistence that the basic principles of democracy and social justice be protected. She became a symbol of American democracy and social justice in her lifetime.

As first lady Eleanor Roosevelt broke precedent in the breadth of her reform activities, but she nevertheless fit into the various contexts of the American reform tradition from which she had emerged. Her omnipresence and involvement in many different causes bewildered her contemporaries and left even her supporters with the feeling that there was no coherent pattern to her activities. There was, however, an underlying coherence: her activities as a social reformer and politician converged around her commitment to social humanitarian ideals and her conviction that the state and federal governments must take an active role in achieving these goals. These commitments emanated from her apprenticeship in the social

reform movements from the Progressive Era to the New Deal.

Eleanor Roosevelt underwent an important transition in her own life from Lady Bountiful in the noblesse oblige tradition to dedicated social reformer. Coming of age at the beginning of the century, a period characterized by historians as the age of reform, she was part of a transitional generation of nonprofessional women reformers, who for a variety of personal and historic reasons transcended or escaped traditional domestic roles, participated in various social or political movements, and emerged as major leaders. In her own case, this transition took on a greater magnitude both because of the special opportunities for power her role of First Lady afforded her and because of the forcefulness of her personality.

Born in New York City in 1886, she was the daughter of Elliott Roosevelt, younger brother of Theodore, and of Anna Ludlow Hall, a descendant of the Livingstons. The oldest of three children, Eleanor was caught between a loving, carefree father and a critical, demanding mother, who was often subject to depressions. Her mother died when Eleanor was eight years old, and her father died a few months later. Eleanor and her two younger brothers were sent to the home of her grandmother, Mrs. Valentine Hall. Shortly thereafter the older of her two brothers died. Eleanor and her younger brother were raised by their stern grandmother in the austere Victorian atmosphere of upper-class society in New York City and Oyster Bay.

Throughout her childhood Eleanor felt lonely and rejected. Her mother had made her painfully aware of her homeliness, and her grandmother deprived her of the carefree pleasures of childhood. Her only consolation was her love for her father, which assumed dimensions of fantasy: "He dominated my life as long as he lived and was the love of my life for many years after he died."

The most important formative influence in Eleanor's early life was her exposure to Mlle. Souvestre, the French mistress of Allenwood, a finishing school in England to which Eleanor was sent along with other society daughters. Under Mlle. Souvestre's personal tutelage Eleanor discovered joy as well as intellectual growth. "I had been a solemn little girl," she wrote. "My years in England had given me my first real taste of being carefree and irresponsible." At the same time Mlle. Souvestre developed her intellectual life, her ability for critical thinking, and her sensitivity to social issues. She gave new direction to the Victorian sense of duty that Eleanor's grandmother had instilled in her, teaching her that "the underdog was always to be championed."

Upon her return to New York at the age of eighteen, Eleanor had difficulty living the social life of her class, feeling both inadequate and bored in an environment "where you accepted invitations to dine and to dance with the right people," and "conformed to the conventional pattern." Under pressure from her grandmother, she made her debut, but retreated to her room during her own coming-out party.

Escaping the life of leisure of young women of her class, she began to embark on her initial social welfare activities. She joined the Junior League and taught dancing at Rivington Street Settlement and visited needy children in slum dwellings. She also began to work for the Consumers League, where she investigated working conditions in garment factories and department stores. She had already been exposed to the poverty of the slums of New York earlier in her childhood, when she was sent to deliver gifts to the poor. "In that society," she said, "you were kind to the poor, you did not neglect your philanthropical duties in whatever community you lived, you assisted the hospitals and did something for the needy."

During her coming-out period in New York society, Eleanor grew to know, and enjoy the company of, her distant cousin Franklin Roosevelt. She appreciated Franklin's social ease, ambition, and good humor, and he respected her discipline and genuine concern for the welfare of others. After keeping their engagement secret for a year and despite Sara Delano Roosevelt's attempts to prevent their marriage, Franklin and Eleanor married on 17 March 1905. They remained in New York where Franklin studied law at Columbia University.

Eleanor's insecurities and sense of inadequacy in her traditional role as housewife and society lady were intensified by the continuing domination of the young family by Franklin's mother. Sara Roosevelt so controlled the couple's household and daily lives that Eleanor was not the real mistress in her own home, even after she began bearing children. Six children arrived in the years 1906 to 1916, one girl and five boys. (The third child died in infancy.) Sara Roosevelt interfered with the child rearing to the point where Eleanor felt that "Franklin's children were more my mother-in-law's children than they were mine." Gradually, however, Eleanor developed in herself the power to resist. "Perhaps," she wrote later, "it was having two such personalities as my husband and his mother; I had to develop willy-nilly into an individual myself."

The first opportunity for at least a temporarily independent existence for Eleanor and for her training in politics to begin came when Franklin was elected to the New York State Senate. Living in Albany away from her mother-in-law, Eleanor conscientiously devoted herself to the duties of a politician's wife, and her home was turned into the headquarters of insurgent Democrats. "So I took an interest in politics," she related, "but I don't know whether I enjoyed it." She further developed her political skills during Franklin's service as assistant secretary of the navy and began to weave her way through Washington's political society.

World War I presented an important stepping-stone in Eleanor's development as a reformer. Her work for the Red Cross exposed her to the sufferings of the wounded soldiers as well as to the depressing conditions of hospitals and mental institutions. Her efforts on behalf of the Red Cross and her advocacy of hospital reform increased her confidence in her own executive ability.

At this point in her life, Eleanor's relationship with Franklin was characterized by mutual respect and personal need, but the combined difficulties of caring for her family, contending with her mother-in-law, and playing the part of a promising politician's wife consumed her energies. When in 1918 she discovered her husband's affair with her social secretary, Lucy Mercer, she at first considered herself a failure as a woman, but soon came to realize that her personal fulfillment could not depend on Franklin or anyone but herself. From this time on, Eleanor continued to develop her political partnership with Franklin, but the marital relationship was gone. Although her loneliness, disappointment, and loss of intimacy was channeled into social reform and political activity, the personal wound festered till the end of her life.

When polio struck Franklin in 1920, Eleanor was still "fitting into the pattern of a fairly conventional social matron." But a major turning point in her career came after her husband's recovery, when under Louis Howe's prodding and her own desire for public activity, Eleanor embarked on more systematic political and social reform activities. By this time Mrs. Roosevelt had demonstrated her sensitivity to human suffering, her indignation over poverty, and her readiness to serve, but she still lacked intellectual commitment and political experience and was not fully distanced from her earlier view of politics as a "sinister affair." She was motivated, however, by a desire to maintain her husband's connections with politics despite his inability to walk.

Thus, her main apprenticeship as a reformer occurred in the 1920s, a period when the Progressive reform movement had ebbed. Although she was a niece of Theodore Roosevelt, she had been hardly touched by the high tide of progressivism. Some progressive programs continued, however, during this decade. Groups like the National Consumers League, the Settlement House movement, and the newly organized League of Women Voters persisted in their struggle, despite the defeatist atmosphere of conservatism,

Eleanor and Franklin at Hyde Park in 1906. (Courtesy FDR Library.)

"normalcy," and surface prosperity. Gaining new vigor and a sense of mission from the granting of suffrage to women, some of these organizations became more professionally oriented and produced a new generation of professional social workers and reformers. Harry Hopkins and Frances Perkins, for example, were to become major architects and administrators of the New Deal's relief and reform programs. When these individuals joined the Roosevelt administration, they helped bridge progressive reform with the New Deal.

Eleanor's training began through her work with various local organizations; eventually she progressed to the national level. She started work with the Women's City Club of New York and the League of Women Voters, whose members taught her how to compile and analyze legislation. Through Louis Howe's tutelage and her work with the New York Women's Democratic Committee, as well as the New York State and National Democratic committees, she learned the political realities and the mechanisms by which reform could be achieved. Settlement work focused her attention on the complexity of urban problems and on the interrelationships among poor housing, poverty, crime, and disease. And from the National Consumers League, she learned the value of investigation and the exposé as first steps toward reform. The conception of the reformer as investigator and educator, which this experience gave her, emerged later as a central feature of her reform work.

Mrs. Roosevelt became familiar too with the women's trade unions, formed a commitment to the rights of labor, and adopted a definition of a living wage that included—in addition to food, housing, and clothing—such considerations as education, recreation, and provision for emergency needs. This was the beginning of her lifelong support of the Women's Trade Union League and of fair labor standards.

It is significant for an understanding of her development as a reformer to note that Eleanor Roosevelt was close to forty when she started to work with these groups. Her involvement came after she had raised her family and had found fulfillment along conventional lines.

All during this period, Louis Howe was working with her, grooming her for political activities, training her in public speaking, and fostering her confidence and public posture. Interested primarily in Eleanor's development as an instrument for Franklin's political career, Howe tutored her in the intricacies of political campaigning. He insisted in 1921 that if Franklin was to return to politics, Eleanor would have to keep his name alive among New York politicians, and he pushed her to join the Women's Division of the State Democratic Committee. She was especially active during Al Smith's campaign for the governorship of New York, acting as intermediary between her husband and the candidate. She brought home guests who represented a variety of interests, and politics became a common topic of conversation at the Roosevelt dinner table.

Eleanor exceeded Louis Howe's expectations.

The tireless Mrs. Roosevelt visiting wounded veterans. (Courtesy FDR Library.)

She embarked on political activity in her own right, for by this time she was convinced that politics was the handmaiden of reform. Becoming an activist, moreover, was her response to the new rights and responsibilities extended to women in the Nineteenth Amendment.

The culmination of these political activities came in the presidential campaign of 1928. Though Franklin was now a candidate for the governorship of New York, Eleanor worked once again for Al Smith, the presidential candidate, not her husband. She was in charge of administrative work under Belle Moskowitz, Smith's campaign manager. As chairman of the Women's Committee for Al Smith, Eleanor was the living spirit of the campaign. Recognizing the organizational ability of Mary W. (Molly) Dewson, she asked her to serve on the Democratic Committee in St. Louis, and soon Dewson extended her activities nationwide.

Looking at Mrs. Roosevelt's four years as First Lady of New York, it would be difficult to predict her emergence later in the White House, but there were some indications of what was to come. Determined to preserve the independent activities she had undertaken in the 1920s, she organized a rigorous working schedule in order to combine them with her formal duties at the executive mansion in Albany. She taught at the Todhunter School in New York City—a progressive school for wealthy girls—which she directed in partnership with Nancy Cook and Marion Dickerman. While in the city she continued to give time to various volunteer organizations. In addition, she administered a furniture factory she had founded with Cook and Dickerman near the Val-Kill Brook at Hyde Park. The factory reproduced early American furniture and provided employment for destitute people in the vicinity.

Her contributions to New York in those years included her work with the Women's Division of the Democratic Committee. Insisting that voters' interest in politics must be kept alive year round, she traveled to remote villages in upstate New York, met with farm women, discussed their problems, and helped Molly Dewson organize those districts. When in 1930 Franklin Roosevelt was reelected, upstate New York voted for a Democratic governor for the first time in history. Jim Farley credited the work of Mrs. Roosevelt and her associates with this victory.

In some respects the time in Albany was a rehearsal for the White House period. Eleanor remarked that those years "cast their shadow before them." She developed friendships with Harry Hopkins, a relief and welfare commissioner in New York; Frances Perkins in the New York State Labor Department; Dr. Thomas Parran, commissioner of public health; and Henry Morgenthau, Jr., conservation commissioner. Thus she laid the foundation for close cooperation with them in Washington. Most important was her training as Franklin's "legs and ears." Traveling in a glass-bottomed boat on the waterways of New York, Eleanor accompanied him on his inspection trips to state hospitals, homes for the aged, and prisons. Eleanor acquired from Franklin the skills of thorough inspection and discriminating appraisal. When convinced once that she had run a thorough investigation, she reported her findings on a mental institution to Franklin. But he criticized her for her superficiality: "Did you bother to lift a pot cover on the stove to check whether the contents corresponded with the menu?" He taught her to pay attention to every detail.

While she was still a pupil, learning from her husband, Louis Howe, Democratic politicians, and active women friends, such as Lillian Wald, founder of the Henry Street Settlement, Mary Simkhovitch, head worker at the Greenwich House, Florence Kelley, founder and president of the National Consumers League, and Rose Schneiderman, president of the New York branch of the Women's Trade Union League, she resolved to maintain her independence. "In my early married years the pattern of my life had been largely my mother-in-law's pattern. Later, it was the children and Franklin who made the pattern. When the last child went to boarding school, I began to want to do things on my own, to use my own mind and abilities for my own aims." It was at this crucial stage of self-realization that she became the First Lady of the land.

Following Franklin Roosevelt's election in the depths of the Great Depression in 1932, Eleanor Roosevelt, somewhat bewildered by the tasks ahead, began to marshal her ideas in preparation for the new challenge. She did not yet have a systematically formulated ideology. There were, however, several consistent patterns in her thought. She transcended the conviction of her class and generation that poverty was a manifestation of personal failure, adopting the progressive view that it was a social problem, a result of inequality and maldistribution of economic resources. The shock of the Great Depression had an important transforming effect on her social thinking. She had seen misery and poverty before, but had always assumed that the system itself was sound; slums, crime, poverty, and labor problems were blotches that could be removed through the dedication of social workers and suitable legislation. The depression forced her to the realization that something was wrong in the system itself, and she began to question basic assumptions of America's society and culture.

She came to see economic security as the indispensable pillar of democracy. She defined economic security as the level "below which no one is permitted to fall, and keeping a fairly stable balance between that level and the cost of living." Her definition included the right of a laborer to a useful and remunerative job, of a farmer to a fair return for his produce, of a businessman to protection from unfair competition, of every family to a decent home, and of every person to adequate care, proper education, and provision for old age. The Great Depression taught her that equality of opportunity meant more than an "honest broker" government; it meant extending aid to underprivileged groups and establishing a social and economic system that would guarantee their individual rights. The government had to undertake the positive role of furthering social justice and ensuring minimum economic security.

When Eleanor Roosevelt arrived in the White House in 1933, she viewed her role at first as that of auxiliary to her husband, but she also started to work independently for the causes she deemed important. Seizing upon the power inherent in the position of First Lady, she developed it into a unique instrument in the service of social reform. Unbound by an official administrative position, she could speak out without the considerations that restricted the president. Her numerous speeches and press conferences fulfilled a dual purpose: on the one hand, she popularized the New Deal's activities and image; on the other, she criticized the New Deal's limitations and pushed for more radical measures and further reform. She often floated the president's own plans for legislation, testing public opinion.

As First Lady, Mrs. Roosevelt created for herself new responsibilities. In the complex administrative machinery of government relief, she occupied a unique role of intermediary between the average person and the government. People in trouble, encouraged by her invitation to write about their problems, would call for help, and she would contact the proper agencies to handle their grievances. She developed the practice of forwarding letters requesting help to the national Democratic committeewoman in the state from which the letters came, and the committeewoman would refer the case to the appropriate relief agency. The fact that the First Lady was accessible and watchful had a profound effect on the administration of relief. Moreover, she brought with her to the White House her network of women reformers, social workers, and politicians. Many of these people received appointments either in Washington or in state relief agencies. Thus, the First Lady had access to a nationwide group of women who investigated local conditions and the administration of relief and reported to her directly.

As New Deal relief agencies were taking shape, Eleanor Roosevelt was concerned that the New Deal should not overlook the needy groups who had been habitually ignored, especially single women, youth, blacks, and sharecroppers. She sought a rational administration of work relief, with a view to the needs of communities and an emphasis on productive employment rather than busywork. Special consideration was to be given to using the skills and experience of professionals.

During the first year of Roosevelt's administration, Eleanor began to serve as a clearinghouse for proposals for relief programs for women, and in collaboration with Harry Hopkins, she called a White House Conference on the Emergency Needs of Women. By December 1933 the Federal Emergency Relief Administration and the Civil Works Administration were employing 100,000 women, and Hopkins was planning to employ 300,000 more.

More than any other agency, however, the National Youth Administration (NYA) was Mrs. Roosevelt's creation. Given conditions in Italy and Germany, she was concerned that the depression might turn a whole generation against democracy. Her involvement in the establishment of the NYA also expressed her conviction that relief should be combined with lasting reform. Following a plan she had formulated with Harry Hopkins, Mrs. Roosevelt urged the president to establish the NYA, and it was created by executive order on 26 June 1935. It was to be administered under the Works Progress Administration (WPA) and was to employ high school and university students so that they could continue their studies. Mrs. Roosevelt was constantly on the alert to see that its services were extended to previously overlooked groups: the homeless, transients, and black youth, while she worked toward making the agency permanent.

From 1936 until 1940 she formed alliances with the American Youth Congress and the American Student Union, both democratic socialist groups advocating extensive extensive social welfare programs. Some youthful activists in these organizations became political liabilities when they followed the Communist line and denounced the European war as imperialistic after the Nazi-Soviet non-aggression pact of 1939. Eleanor Roosevelt, however, defended the youths' right to dissent.

The breadth of her concerns, particularly her commitments to American culture and to the democratization of the arts, were expressed in her support of the WPA's arts and writers' projects. She looked upon these projects as the cultural counterpart of soil conservation and reforestation—the preservation of national resources. She saw in them an opportunity to rediscover common people to manifest an interest in their welfare, their lives and their culture.

Eleanor Roosevelt was the first figure connected with the White House since Lincoln to take an uncompromising public stand on the needs of blacks and on civil rights. She maintained her personal and semiofficial stand even when she risked antagonizing

political support for the president. The rights of blacks emerged as one of her major causes. She advocated fighting discrimination long before the race riots of the 1940s brutally awakened many Americans to the problem and long before civil rights had become a central reform issue. Though the New Deal did not take the initiative in legislative reforms aimed at racial equality, it did provide blacks with an opportunity to benefit from the general improvement of social and economic conditions. Throughout Franklin Roosevelt's presidency, Mrs. Roosevelt tried always to use the New Deal's framework of employment opportunities, proper housing, education, and medical care to improve the condition of blacks. Soon after her arrival in Washington in 1933, she started her campaign for the liquidation of the alley dwellings in Washington, most of which were inhabited by blacks. Her most consistent effort was her dogged watch over the implementation of relief programs to ensure that blacks were not overlooked or discriminated against. "It is a question of the right to work," she said, "and the right to work should know no color lines."

Mrs. Roosevelt fought segregation and discrimination by setting a personal example, anticipating much of the activism of the civil rights movement of the 1960s. In 1938, while attending the Southern Conference of Human Welfare in Birmingham, Alabama, she saw delegates seated in two separate rows according to color. She took a seat on the side marked "Colored" and refused to move to the "White" side. When police threatened to break up the meeting, she reluctantly took her chair to the platform facing the audience, but placed it closer to the blacks' side. Her most dramatic act of protest, however, occurred in 1939 when the Daughters of the American Revolution refused to allow Marian Anderson, the black contralto, to perform in Constitution Hall. Mrs. Roosevelt resigned her membership and offered the White House grounds for the concert.

Her commitment was expressed in her determination to fight for civil rights through legislation. In 1934 she supported Walter White, secretary of the National Association for the Advancement of Colored People (NAACP), in his effort to achieve the president's sponsorship of antilynching legislation. She took a stand on this issue against political prudence. Unlike his wife, FDR and his advisers feared they would lose southern white support if the president pushed the bill; here Franklin drew the line and refused Eleanor's repeated urgings to pressure Congress. "I . . . remember wanting to get all-out support for the anti-lynching bill and removal of the poll tax, but though Franklin was in favor of both measures, they never became 'must' legislation. When I would protest, he would simply say, 'First things come first, and I can't alienate certain voters I need for measures that are more important at the moment by pushing any measures that would entail a fight.' "

Although she probably antagonized southern Democrats, Mrs. Roosevelt was instrumental in rallying black support for the New Deal. Her psychological influence was as significant as her practical intervention. Her presence and support in the White House gave both black leaders and the rank and file the feeling that they had a friend there.

Eleanor Roosevelt carried her vigilance over the New Deal's reform measures and the other causes she supported into the war effort after the United States' entry into World War II. She used the war as an opportunity to drive home the interrelationship between national defense and domestic reform. Viewing the war as a test of democracy, she tried to protect the reforms already achieved and to use the war effort as a lever to press for further social advances. She worked along two lines: mobilization of public support for the defense effort and vigilance for democracy at home.

The war added new forcefulness to her arguments in support of black equality. She pressed for fair employment in defense industries, and through her intervention with the president and her negotiations with the NAACP leadership, she helped bring about an executive order banning discrimination based on race, color, or national origin in industries holding government contracts for war production and in training for jobs in industries. The presidential order, issued on 25 June, 1941, set up the President's Committee on Fair Employment Practices. Similarly, she devised mechanisms for the protection of 2.3 million women employed in war industries. One of her great concerns was that the rights of labor not be compromised in the name of national defense.

In May 1940, when Congress threatened to cut the Works Progress Administration budget, Mrs. Roosevelt helped mobilize public opinion in its support. In similar ways she defended the Civilian Conservation Corps and the NYA. She also used her position to advocate reform of welfare agencies to protect the school lunch program, and to launch housing reform. In 1940, after a tour of federal institutions in Washington, D.C., she broke precedent by being the first president's wife to testify before a congressional committee. Her testimony drew attention to the "shocking and depressing conditions" of a home for the aged, and in another appearance, she stimulated public concern for the plight of migrant workers, especially farmers who had been uprooted from their homes.

In September 1941 Mrs. Roosevelt took on her only official government job during her husband's presidency—that of deputy director of the Office of Civilian Defense. She later referred to this as "an unfortunate episode." Inefficiency and blunders, some her own, doomed the office from its inception. When she finally resigned in February 1942, her activities in this area had not helped the presidency's image in the war effort.

Following her husband's death, Mrs. Roosevelt lost her unique power position and her role of ombudsman. She remained active, however, in the public arena and continued as a private citizen to defend the New Deal's reform tradition. Moreover, she launched a new career in international politics. During her White House years, Eleanor Roosevelt had been both the New Deal's advocate and its inside critic; now she idealized it and made its principles the yardstick of all government policies.

Her reform agenda in the postwar years was consistent with her program in the 1930s, but her stance in domestic issues was more radical. Her ideas had changed, and she became even more outspoken, since she was no longer bound by her position as First Lady. In the area of civil rights, her goals and emphasis changed during the Truman era. She now unequivocally demanded desegregation in housing, education, and other public facilities, looking upon this as the most important goal. For the first time she recognized the issues concerning blacks as a race problem; earlier she had considered it mainly in the context of social justice. Discrimination had ceased to be merely a domestic problem; now it was international. She began to lobby President Harry S Truman about injustice and discrimination, both at home and abroad.

Fittingly, then, Truman appointed her a U.S. delegate to the newly formed United Nations. There she lobbied for the United Nation's 1948 Universal Declaration of Human Rights and served as one of its major architects. Although an advocate of world peace who wished to contain nuclear politics, she supported the U.S. role in the developing cold war as she grew to distrust the Soviet UN delegates. Galvanized as well by the Holocaust and a postwar visit to a Nazi concentration camp, she became a vocal advocate for the new Jewish nation of Israel.

In the last decades of her life, Mrs. Roosevelt continued increasingly to view American society from a world perspective and identified with the world community. Like other idealistic progressive reformers, she wanted to see democracy and social justice prevail in the world. But unlike Woodrow Wilson and other progressive idealists, she did not believe in the imposition of American ideals abroad. In her work with the UN Human Rights Commission, she realized the strength of the potential influence of developing nations and the importance of the impact of diverse economic conditions and cultural traditions on international relations. Her world experience fostered her commitment to pluralism, both at home and abroad.

In the 1950s and 1960s, Eleanor Roosevelt remained a powerful figure in politics. Through her daily newspaper column, "My Day," begun in 1936, she stayed in the public eye. As she aged, her matriarchal status and her insistence on universal human rights made her a national heroine. She continued to champion black civil rights, and she spoke out against McCarthyism. In 1952 and 1956, she campaigned vigorously for her friend, presidential candidate Adlai Stevenson. Although she initially disapproved of John Kennedy's 1960 candidacy (instead of Stevenson), she was later appointed by Kennedy to head the President's Commission on the Status of Women.

Declining health prevented Eleanor Roosevelt from fully participating in the commission's work, and thus she lost the opportunity to tie together her sometimes contradictory views on women's rights.

Earlier, when asked to support the suffrage movement, she had refused, even as her husband endorsed it in his campaign of 1912. From the 1920s on, she had, like many social reformers, opposed an equal rights amendment, fearing the loss of protective labor laws for women. Although Mrs. Roosevelt reversed her opinion in the early 1940s as unions gained bargaining power for workers, she retained enough mixed feelings to stop short of vigorous public endorsement of an amendment.

It is impossible to place Eleanor Roosevelt's reform thought into a particular mold because it was so flexible. On one level, she can best be understood within the pattern of New Deal thought. She was pragmatic, adaptable, willing to experiment, and committed to social justice rather than to dogmatic ideology. Because she was not burdened with the necessity for political decision, she was less compromising on principle than the president and New Deal politicians could afford to be. She adopted causes as they arose, but was ahead of her times on many reform issues.

Eleanor Roosevelt gave new meaning to the role of First Lady by channeling the power and influence it offered into serving the causes she upheld. She destroyed the "pastel and mauve traditions" surrounding women in the White House. Her activities were not those of a model housewife and mother. Even the White House social functions ceased to be exclusive affairs for a few worthy socialites. Delegations of blacks, sharecroppers, and lobster men from Maine walked through her living quarters. The First Lady projected the image not of serene domesticity but of hectic travel, disorganized activities, and busybody occupations. She toured the nation, leading solitary crusades and exposing conditions her opponents would have liked to ignore. One woman made the typical accusation: "Instead of tearing around the country, I think you should stay at home and personally see that the White House is clean. I soiled my white gloves yesterday morning on the stair-railing. It is disgraceful."

What was worse, the marital instability of the Roosevelt children furnished the press with subjects for vicious attacks. The self-righteous blamed Mrs. Roosevelt's "outside interests" for her children's problems, and they insisted she had no right to preach to the nation if she could not educate her own children. From the moment she entered the White House, she was criticized for her professional work and especially for her pursuit of occupations that seemed "undignified" for a First Lady: writing articles for pay, making broadcasts, and even appearing in paid commercials. Although she periodically announced that she divided all her income between the Friends' Service Committee and the Women's Trade Union League, Rep. Hamilton Fish of New York frequently accused her of tax evasion.

In her statements, Mrs. Roosevelt often appeared as an uncomprising idealist, but in her work within the administration and later in political affairs and the UN, she revealed her skill in practical politics and her understanding of the subtle exercise of power and influence. One must remember, however, that Mrs. Roosevelt was not completely free of partisanship. Her reform ideals transcended party lines, but her life with FDR wed her to the Democratic party. In the post–White House years she continued to look at the party as one of the tools of reform.

The major value of Eleanor Roosevelt's statements lay not in their new solutions but in her persistent emphasis on human rights and social justice at a time when the complexity of economic and social problems bred despair and disillusionment. She personified social responsibility, constant vigilance, and dedication on the part of the government. She became a voice of reform, its daily agent, its fighter and laborer, and a source of strength to leaders and movements. Her speeches, articles, daily column, and travels served as counterparts of the president's fireside chats in popularizing the New Deal. She rallied support in a way politicians would not have been able to, because she did not consciously solicit votes. In this respect she was a "political force" rather than a "politician."

Beyond her direct and indirect influence, Eleanor Roosevelt has survived as a symbol in the realm of American and international politics and reform. Her achievements remain an inspiration to fighters for equality, social justice, civil rights, and civil liberties in the United States and abroad. The courageous position she took on behalf of unpopular issues, particularly on the rights of blacks, helped inspire black leaders to continue fighting for their cause. To women she provided a model of a woman who had transcended the limitations of her class and of the role dictated by her times. Far more effectively than any other First Lady in history, Eleanor Roosevelt provided a model of activism in politics and in social reform, first for the United States and later for women who were struggling for equality in other parts of the world. The most powerful and convincing aspect of this model was her insistence that she carried out her responsibilities first as a citizen and then as First Lady. What she did on a large scale, she maintained, others could do more modestly through vigilance and civic dedication.

The voluminous Eleanor Roosevelt Papers in the Roosevelt Library in Hyde Park, New York, contain her correspondence and drafts of her writings and speeches. Her published writings include a syndicated column "My Day" from 30 December 1935 to 11 September 1962, as well as numerous articles in the popular press. Eleanor Roosevelt's autobiographical writings include *This Is My Story* (New York: Harper & Bros., 1937), *This I Remember* (New York: Harper & Bros., 1949), *On My Own* (New York: Harper & Bros., 1958), *It's Up to the Women* (New York: Frederick A. Stoves, 1933), *Ladies of Courage* (New York: Putnam, 1954), *Tomorrow Is Now* (New York: Harper & Row, 1963), *The Moral Basis of*

Democracy (New York: Howell, Saskin & Co., 1940), and *This Troubled World* (New York: H. C. Kinsey & Co., 1938). An analysis of Eleanor Roosevelt's emergence and role as a reformer is contained in Tamara Hareven's *Eleanor Roosevelt: An American Conscience* (Chicago: Quadrangle, 1968). Biographies of Eleanor Roosevelt include Joseph Lash, *Eleanor and Franklin* (New York: W. W. Norton & Co., 1971) and *Eleanor: The Years Alone* (New York: W. W. Norton & Co., 1972), and Lash has edited her personal letters in a volume entitled *Love, Eleanor: Eleanor Roosevelt and Friends* (New York: Doubleday & Co., 1982). A valuable recent reexamination by several scholars of Eleanor Roosevelt's beliefs and achievements is Joan Hoff-Wilson and Marjorie Lightman, eds., *Without Precedent: The Life and Career of Eleanor Roosevelt* (Bloomington: Indiana University Press, 1984) in which portions of this essay have appeared.

TAMARA HAREVEN

See also Campobello; Death of FDR; Federal Writers' Project; Franklin D. Roosevelt Library; Genealogy; Health; Hyde Park; LeHand, Marguerite; Marriage and Family; National Youth Administration; Negroes; Polio; Roosevelt, Sara Delano; Rutherfurd, Lucy Page Mercer; Wallace, Henry A.; Women and the New Deal

Roosevelt, Anna Eleanor (daughter)
(3 May 1906–1 December 1975)

Firstborn child and only daughter of Franklin and Eleanor Roosevelt. Anna Roosevelt was born in New York City and educated at Miss Chapin's finishing school in New York. She chose not to pursue a university education and, in 1926, married Curtis B. Dall, a New York stockbroker. The couple had two children: Anna, born in 1927, and Curtis Roosevelt, born in 1930. After her first marriage ended in divorce, she married John Boettiger, a newspaper correspondent, in 1935. Boettiger adopted the two children by her previous marriage, and another child, John Roosevelt, was born to this union in 1939.

Shortly after Anna married Boettiger, he accepted a position as publisher of the *Post-Intelligencer,* a Hearst-owned newspaper in Seattle. She made her home there until early 1944, when, at FDR's invitation, she moved into the White House. At the time, Boettiger was overseas on a military-government assignment; and FDR, whose long-time secretary and confidante, Marguerite ("Missy") LeHand had taken ill and died, wished to have her nearby.

As the only daughter in the family, Anna, or "Sis," as she was called, enjoyed an especially close relationship with her father. She remained in the White House until FDR's death, one of the companions and confidantes who surrounded the president in the last year of his life. She assisted Grace Tully by assuming many of the duties formerly carried out by Missy LeHand and frequently acted as the president's

Anna with her parents at Warm Springs, en route to the cottage from the railroad station, 24 October 1932. (Courtesy FDR Library.)

assistant by meeting with scheduled visitors. She also acted as the White House hostess during Eleanor's absences, and she shielded her mother from the knowledge that Lucy Mercer Rutherfurd was an occasional dinner guest. At FDR's request, Anna, rather than Eleanor, accompanied him to the Yalta Conference in January-February 1945.

Her second marriage ended in divorce in 1949, and in 1952, she married Dr. James A. Halsted at Malibu, California.

Joseph Lash's book, *Eleanor and Franklin* (New York: W. W. Norton & Co., 1971) remains one of the best sources of information on the Roosevelt family in general and on Anna's relationship with FDR as well. Eleanor Roosevelt includes guarded references to Anna's presence in the White House during 1944–45 in her memoir, *This I Remember* (New York: Harper & Bros., 1949). Passing but insightful references are also contained in James MacGregor Burns, *Roosevelt: The Soldier of Freedom* (New York: Harcourt Brace Jovanovich, 1970). A great deal of information on Anna may be found in *Mother and Daughter: The Letters of Anna and Eleanor Roosevelt,* ed. Bernard Asbell (New York: Coward, McCann, & Geohaghan, 1982).

Roosevelt, Elliott
(23 September 1910-)

Second surviving son of Franklin and Eleanor Roosevelt. Although Elliott Roosevelt ultimately became the most controversial of the Roosevelt children, his childhood and adolescence were not marked by any

Elliott (right) *and FDR, Jr.* (left), *with their father at the Cairo Conference.*

particularly unusual occurrences. Some of his siblings thought that Elliott was spoiled, but his father Franklin showed very little concern when "Bunny" as he liked to call him, fell into a pile of smoldering ashes at the age of eleven. When the time came, Elliott went to Groton, like his father and his brothers, and assisted his father at the 1928 Democratic National Convention, just as his elder brother James had done in 1924. He also sailed to Europe on the *Aquitania* with Franklin in 1929 to visit the ailing Sara Roosevelt and found that his father was an even better flirt than he was, as both men competed for the attention of the attractive women on the ship (including a twenty-year-old Sheilah Graham).

Elliott surprised the family, however, by declining to go to college at Harvard, suggesting that perhaps Princeton would be a better school for him. Ultimately, he went to neither and held a series of disparate and undistinguished jobs in 1931 and 1932. To the surprise of his family, he suddenly married in 1932 and moved to Texas where he eventually settled into a career in communications. His relations with his family, especially his father, were already strained in the early 1930s and became even worse once Franklin became president. The press followed Elliott's movements very carefully and critically, including his first divorce and second marriage which came in rapid succession in 1933. His employment in that same year as manager of the Hearst radio chain also caused journalists to allege that he had obtained professional advancement on the strength of his family name alone.

Franklin's feelings about Elliott changed, however, when the younger man arrived in the Oval Office in uniform in 1940; the president was very proud of his son's enlistment and visited him in training camp. After he became a reconnaissance pilot in the North Atlantic, Elliott and his younger brother Frank served special duty at their father's side at the Atlantic Charter meetings with Churchill in August of 1941. Once America entered the war, the president asked his sons to serve as his aides again on such oc-

casions as the Casablanca meetings of January 1943 and the Cairo-Teheran Conference of November 1944. Elliott Roosevelt went on to compile an outstanding war record in the AAF. After service on flying status in North Africa and the Mediterranean he returned to England in 1944 in command of a joint photo reconnaissance wing that played a crucial and demanding role in D Day operations. He ended the war as a brigadier general; despite ill-founded charges of favoritism, this rank was justly earned in a particularly hazardous line of duty. After his father's death, Elliott chronicled his experiences on these occasions in *As He Saw It* (New York: Duell, 1946), which called for a rededication in the 1950s to President Roosevelt's dream of global peace.

Elliott Roosevelt's first marriage, to Elizabeth Donner, produced one child, William Donner, born in 1932. The second marriage, to Ruth Googins, produced three children: Ruth Chandler, born in 1934; Elliott, Jr., born in 1936; and David Boynton, born in 1942. Subsequent marriages to Faye Emerson in 1944 and to Minnewa Bell in 1951 ended in divorce. He then married Patricia Whitehead in 1960, and adopted her five children.

Besides *As He Saw It,* Elliott published two books about his family, *An Untold Story: The Roosevelts of Hyde Park* (New York: G. P. Putnam's Sons, 1973) and *A Rendezvous with Destiny: The Roosevelts of the White House* (New York: G. P. Putnam's Sons, 1975), both cowritten with James Brough. Both volumes were issued in rebuttal to the writers that Elliott saw as "idolators" of his mother, including Joseph Lash, whose *Eleanor and Franklin* (New York: W. W. Norton & Co., 1971) provides a fascinating contrast to Roosevelt and Brough's happier picture of the lives of the family. Although Lash's subsequent *Eleanor: The Years Alone* (New York: W. W. Norton & Co., 1972) touches on Elliott's later years, a more detailed albeit questionable source is *I Love a Roosevelt* (Garden City, N.Y.: Doubleday, 1967), a memoir by Patricia Peabody Roosevelt, Elliott's fifth wife.

Roosevelt, Franklin Delano, Jr.
(17 August 1914-)

Fifth-born child of Franklin and Eleanor Roosevelt. Franklin, Jr., was born at Campobello Island, the Roosevelt's summer home. Following family custom, he graduated from Groton and Harvard (A.B. 1937), where he distinguished himself both in scholarship and athletics. He earned an LL.B. from the University of Virginia in 1940.

Franklin, Jr., formed close relationships with both of his parents; within the family he was known as "Brother" or "Brud." He chose to study law after FDR's suggestion that a few years' practice in a law firm would be good preparation for politics, and he was the first son to hold elected political office. Following his graduation from the University of Virginia, he worked on FDR's reelection campaign throughout the summer and fall of 1940, coordinating youth activities of the Democratic National Committee as well as those of various Roosevelt college clubs.

He also entered law practice in New York in 1940, but his stay was short; in March 1941 he accepted active duty with the U.S. Navy. Before he was discharged in October 1945, he rose to the rank of lieutenant commander and earned several awards, including the Purple Heart and a Silver Star. After the war, he returned to law practice in New York, joining the firm of Poletti, Diamond, Rabin, Freidin, and Mackay in November 1945; one year later he became a partner in the firm.

He also embarked on his political career after the war, serving as chairman of housing activities for the American Veterans Committee (1945–47); as national vice-chairman of Americans for Democratic Action (1947), a nonpartisan organization of noncommunist liberals; and as vice-chairman of the President's Civil Rights Commission (1949) under Truman. In 1949 he was elected to represent New York's Twentieth Congressional District in the House, and he served as a member of the Eighty-first through the Eighty-third Congresses. He later served as under secretary of commerce during the Kennedy and Johnson administrations (1962–65) and as chairman of the Equal Opportunity Commission under Lyndon Johnson (1965–66). His political philosophy echoed that of his parents, and throughout his political career he championed such causes as public housing, fair employment practices, and civil rights.

He married Ethel du Pont in 1937; the couple had two children: Franklin Delano III, born in 1939, and Christopher du Pont, born in 1940. Following their divorce in 1949, he married Suzanne Perrin in the same year; two daughters, Nancy Suzanne and Laura D., were born in 1952 and 1959, respectively. The second marriage also ended in divorce, and in 1970, he married Felicia Warburg Sarnoff. The marriage ended in divorce, and in 1976 he married Patricia Oakes. One child, John Alexander, was born of that union in 1977. In 1983, after that marriage ended in divorce, he married Linda Weicker.

References to Franklin, Jr., during his youth are contained in Joseph P. Lash, *Eleanor and Franklin* (New York: W. W. Norton, 1971). *Current Biography* (1950), pp. 501–3, contains a useful summary, gleaned from various periodical articles, of his career activities during the late 1930s and 1940s.

Roosevelt, James

(16 July 1828–8 December 1900)

Father of the president. James Roosevelt was born into a wealthy and respectable Knickerbocker family at Mount Hope, his grandfather's estate just north of Poughkeepsie, New York. He was brought up right across the Albany Post Road at Rosedale, the home of his father, Dr. Isaac Roosevelt, a reclusive and querulous physician who had retired to the country rather than practice because he could not abide human suffering. James was tutored at home as a small boy, then educated at private schools in Poughkeepsie and at Lee, Massachusetts, before attending the University of New York and Union College, from which he was graduated in 1847.

FDR on his father's shoulders, June 1883.

He was a high-spirited youth, chastised in college for having joined a fraternity that met in a saloon, and he may have spent a month or so as a red-shirted volunteer in Giuseppe Garibaldi's peasant army while on a grand tour of Europe in 1849. He won his law degree from Harvard in 1850, entered business, and then married his cousin Rebecca Howland in 1853. They had a son, James Roosevelt Roosevelt, in 1854 and purchased the Hyde Park estate they named Springwood in 1867. Thereafter, he confined his restlessness to frequent travel abroad, fox hunting, the raising and racing of fine trotting horses and other

James Roosevelt at Algomac, 13 July 1889. (Courtesy FDR Library.)

FDR with his father at Groton, Mass., April 1899. (Courtesy FDR Library.)

traditional pursuits of the English country gentlemen after whom he patterned himself. He was always serious about business, but never obsessed by it; he did best with the railroads of which he was a director, less well with coal mines and a scheme to cut a canal across Nicaragua. But his obligations to his family and community always came first; he became town supervisor, served tirelessly on the local school board, directed local charities, and acted as vestryman and sometime senior warden at St. James Church.

Rebecca Roosevelt died in 1876, and on 7 October 1880 he married Sara Delano Roosevelt. He was fifty-six; she was twenty-three. Because he was so much older than his formidable wife and because he had always an air of inviolable dignity—only his immediate family felt comfortable calling him anything less formal than "Mr. James"—he was once thought to have been a remote grandfatherly figure to his son. But in fact for the first seven years of Franklin's life, his father was his constant, vigorous companion. The two were "such a gay pair," Sara Roosevelt remembered, sledding and riding and sailing and laughing together. FDR went with him in his private car when he inspected his railroad lines, was introduced to his prominent friends on both sides of the Atlantic, watched as servants and Hyde Park townspeople alike deferred to him. Mr. James inculcated in his son his own love of trees and the land, his serene Episcopalianism, his sturdy sense of a wealthy citizen's duty toward those less fortunate than he, his scorn for those interested only in getting rich. His political legacy is less certain: he was a conservative before he was a Democrat. His friend Grover Cleveland was his political hero; civil service reform, small government, the obliteration of Tammany and the gold standard were his issues; and when the Democrats strayed too far from them, as he believed they had in 1896 and 1900, he happily turned to the Republicans. But he was intensely interested in politics, contributed generously to campaigns, and was always proud both that he had often been asked to run for office and that, as a gentleman, he had refused.

Mr. James suffered the first of a long series of debilitating heart attacks in 1891, but he lived nine more years as his wife's "beloved invalid," continuing to take a keen, loving interest in everything his son said and did. Franklin was eighteen and a Harvard freshman when his father died at New York in 1900.

Sara Roosevelt idolized her husband and could think of no higher goal for her son than that he grow to be just like him—"straight and honorable, just and kind." And Franklin clearly identified closely with his father's memory, even as president he continued to absorb himself in Hyde Park affairs, served in his father's old post as senior vestryman of St. James, and every day of his adult life wore his father's bloodstone ring on the little finger of his left hand.

James Roosevelt has received comparatively little attention from his son's biographers. The most thorough treatment of his life and influence on FDR is to be found in Kenneth S. Davis, *FDR: The Beckoning of Destiny* (New York: G. P. Putnam's Sons, 1971) and Geoffrey C. Ward's *Before the Trumpet: Young Franklin Roosevelt, 1882–1905* (New York: Harper & Row, 1985).

GEOFFREY C. WARD

See also Campobello; Genealogy; Hyde Park; Roosevelt, Sara Delano

Roosevelt, James (son)

(23 December 1907-)

Second-born child and eldest son of Franklin and Eleanor Roosevelt. James Roosevelt was born in New York City, and following family tradition, he was educated at Groton and Harvard (A.B. 1930). After graduating from Harvard, he entered the insurance business and in 1935 cofounded Roosevelt and Sargent, Inc., an insurance partnership located in Boston.

Jimmy, as FDR always called him, played an active role in his father's political career, serving as FDR's campaign manager in Massachusetts in 1932 and, during 1933, as the president's unofficial aide. He also accompanied FDR as official aide to the Inter-American Conference in Buenos Aires in 1936. The next year he resigned as president of Roosevelt and Sargent to join the White House staff. He served until mid-1938 as a presidential assistant, an appointment made amid a climate of hostility from the press and Congress. In October 1937, FDR placed him in charge of coordinating over twenty federal agencies. Members of Congress, however, were wary of the close father-son association, and critics accused James of exploiting his political connections for gain in his outside business interests. This congressional friction and difficulties with other White House aides prompted him to resign his post in late 1938, at which time he

James Roosevelt (far right) on Makin Island, 17 August 1943. (Courtesy FDR Library.)

joined Samuel Goldwyn Productions as a film executive. In 1940, he became president of his own film company, Globe Productions.

He entered active service with the U.S. Marines in November 1940. He was first assigned to serve as a military observer in the Middle and Far East; later he served as a military adviser to William J. Donovan, coordinator of information. After the attack on Pearl Harbor, he chose combat duty and was awarded both the Navy Cross and the Silver Star.

After his release from the Marines in 1945, he rejoined Roosevelt and Sargent as executive vice-president, establishing a West Coast office in 1946. He also reentered politics, serving as chairman of the California State Democratic Central Committee in 1946 and as a Democratic national committeeman from 1948 to 1952. He unsuccessfully challenged Republican Earl Warren for the California governorship in 1950, but in 1955 he was elected to the House of Representatives from the Twenty-sixth Congressional District. After he left the House in 1967, he returned to California to continue his career as a business consultant.

James has written three books about the Roosevelt family: *Affectionately, F.D.R.* (1959), *My Parents* (1976), and *A Family Matter* (1980). The last, written with Sam Toperoff, is a novelistic account of 1944–45 events in which James and FDR conspired to share U.S. information on the atomic bomb with the Soviet Union as a way of ensuring Soviet cooperation in establishing the United Nations.

His four marriages produced six children. In 1930, he married Betsey Cushing, and the couple had two daughters: Sara Delano, born in 1932, and Kate, born in 1936. Following a divorce in 1940, he married Romelle Schneider the next year. Three children were born of this union: James, Jr., 1945; Michael Anthony, 1946; and Anna Eleanor, 1948. The second marriage also ended in divorce, and in 1956, he married Gladys Irene Owens; they adopted a son, Hall Delano, born in 1957. Following a third divorce in 1969, he married Mary Lena Winskill, and another child, Rebecca Mary, was born in 1971.

Succinct information on James's career is contained in *Current Biography* (1950, pp. 503–6) and in *Who's Who in America*, 42d ed., 1982–83. James MacGregor Burns includes very brief, but nonetheless useful, comments on his role as a presidential assistant in *Roosevelt: The Lion and the Fox* (New York: Harcourt Brace Jovanovich, 1956).

Roosevelt, James Roosevelt ("Rosy")

(27 March 1854–7 May 1927)

James Roosevelt Roosevelt was born in New York City, the only child of James Roosevelt and his first wife Rebecca B. Howland. His father was vice-president of the Delaware and Hudson Railroad and a respected businessman in railroad finances and operations; his mother was from an old and prominent Dutchess County family. To avoid the use of "Junior" which his father detested, he was named James Roosevelt Roosevelt, but throughout most of his life he was known simply as "Rosy." A handsome young man and bright as well, Rosy graduated from Columbia with honors in 1877. He gave up the pursuit of law the following year when he married Helen Schermerhorn Astor, daughter of William Astor and *the* Mrs. Astor of New York City's high society where he was considered quite a dashing young blood.

For his monetary support of the Democratic party, President Grover Cleveland named him secretary to the American embassy in Vienna. During Cleveland's second administration, he was rewarded with a similar position in London after making a contribution of $10,000. While serving at this post, his wife died, leaving him with the care of his son, James, Jr. ("Taddy"), and his daughter, Helen. His cousin

James Roosevelt Roosevelt at the reins of the Westchester-Middletown coach, New York, 1886. (Courtesy FDR Library.)

Anna "Bamie" Roosevelt, Theodore Roosevelt's sister, came to London to help him in this family crisis and acted as the embassy's unofficial hostess. Roosevelt distinguished himself in the diplomatic service by helping to bring about an amicable solution to the Venezuela boundary dispute, which had strained relations between the United States and Great Britain.

Upon his return to America, Rosy was content to devote himself to the public, professional, philanthropic, religious, and cultural life of the city and state of New York. He was active in the affairs of the Astor estate, was a trustee of the Fulton Trust Company, and director of the United Railroads of New Jersey Company. He served the parochial interests of St. James Episcopal Church in Hyde Park, was a trustee of the Cathedral of St. John the Divine in New York City, and was one of its most generous donors. He rendered service and funds to the work of St. Francis Hospital in New York City and donated more than a quarter of a million dollars to a hospital of the same name in Poughkeepsie, New York. During World War I, he maintained an office in the Poughkeepsie Post Office Building and devoted his time and energies to the sale of liberty bonds and war savings stamps.

In 1914 Rosy married his longtime companion, Elizabeth Riley. Plagued by chronic asthma and bronchitis in his later years, he sought the milder winters of Arizona and later Bermuda. Here in April of 1927 his condition worsened, and he returned to his Hyde Park home, Red House, where he died at the age of seventy-three. Several weeks after his death, FDR wrote to Auntie Bye about him, "In so many [more] ways than I had realized, I depended on his companionship and on his judgment." Rosy's largesse and assistance to his half-brother continued even after death. His legacy of $100,000 to FDR provided him with the financial windfall he needed to purchase Warm Springs.

For additional information concerning Rosy, see the *New York Times*, 7 May 1927; "In Memoriam," *Yearbook* of the Holland Society, 1928–29; *FDR: His Personal Letters*, ed. Elliott Roosevelt, vols. 1 and 2 (New York: Duell, Sloan & Pearce, 1947–48); and Joseph P. Lash, *Eleanor and Franklin* (New York: W. W. Norton & Co., 1971).

See also Roosevelt, James; Roosevelt, Sara Delano

Roosevelt, John Aspinwall

(13 March 1916–27 April 1981)

Sixth and last child of Franklin and Eleanor Roosevelt. John was born in Washington, D.C., and, like all the Roosevelt sons, was educated at Groton (1934) and Harvard (A.B. 1938). He, as well as Franklin, Jr., spent their teenage years in the White House, and both enjoyed a closer relationship with their mother than did the older children.

Following his graduation from Harvard, John worked at Filene's Department Store in Boston. In 1941, he entered active duty with the U.S. Navy to

John Roosevelt (behind his father, to the right) at the dedication of the head of Jefferson by Gutzon Borglum at Mount Rushmore, South Dakota, 30 August 1936. (UPI/ Bettmann Archive.)

serve in World War II; he was discharged in 1946 with the rank of lieutenant commander. After the war, he was active in several business and financial concerns on the West Coast. In 1967, he joined Bache and Company, spending the rest of his business career with the firm. In December 1980, a few months before his death, he retired as senior vice-president and a director of Bache, Halsey, Stuart, Shields, and Company.

John was the only Roosevelt son not to seek elective public office, and, in 1952, he switched his political affiliation to the Republican party in order to support Eisenhower during his campaign for the presidency. While continuing to support other Republican politicians, he concentrated his own energies on his business career. He was also involved in several philanthropic endeavors, serving as a fund raiser for the National Foundation for Infantile Paralysis, founded by his father; as an executive committee member for the Greater New York Council of the Boy Scouts of America; and as a trustee of the State University of New York.

In 1938, he married Anne Lindsay Clark, and the couple had four children: Haven, born in 1942; Anne Sturgis, born in 1942; Sara Delano, born in 1946 (d. 1960); and Joan Lindsay, born in 1952. The marriage ended in divorce in 1965, and in the same year, he married Irene Boyd McAlpin.

Various references to John during his childhood and the early White House years are contained in Joseph P. Lash, *Eleanor and Franklin* (New York: W. W. Norton & Co., 1971). A brief, but full, account of his career is contained in his *New York Times* obituary, 28 April 1981, Sec. B18, p. 1.

REBECCA CONARD

Roosevelt, Sara Delano

(21 September 1855–7 September 1941)

Mother of the president. Sara Delano Roosevelt was born at Algonac, the big walled estate her father, Warren Delano, had created for his large family on a bluff above the Hudson River just north of Newburgh, New York. He was a forceful, dominating patriarch—an implacable Republican millionaire who had twice made a fortune from the tea and opium trade with China—and she and her three brothers and three sisters were all raised to revere him. All her life, she would focus her love and enormous energy on caring for a man—first her father, then her husband, and finally and most faithfully, her son.

She was educated at home—at Algonac and in Hong Kong where her family moved while her father earned his second fortune (1862–65)—except for brief attendance at a school for young ladies in Dresden, Germany in 1867. Tall, lovely, and conscious always that she came from an illustrious family, she seems to have intimidated most of the young suitors who came to call, and her engagement at twenty-six to James Roosevelt, a widower and business associate

Sara and James Roosevelt at St. Blasien, Germany, in 1896. The photographer was fourteen-year-old Franklin D. Roosevelt. (Courtesy FDR Library.)

of her father exactly twice her age, startled her friends. She married him nonetheless on 7 October 1880 and moved with him to Hyde Park where their twenty years together seem to have been idyllic.

She nearly died from an overdose of chloroform administered to her while giving birth to Franklin on 30 January 1882 and was evidently advised not to have any more children. Perhaps partly for that reason, she threw herself into his raising with astonishing singleness of purpose. Few boys have received more maternal devotion—or had to grow up under more intense scrutiny. He had nurses and governesses, but none was ever allowed to come between her and her "darling Franklin": she read aloud to him by the hour, screened his playmates, supervised his play, even oversaw his baths at least till he had reached the age of eight. She saw to it, too, that all the patrician qualities her father had bred into her were developed in him, too: stoicism, good manners, noblesse oblige, a refusal even to recognize unpleasantness, and above all a serene sense that he could succeed at anything to which he put his hand. And, unwittingly, she taught him the creative uses of indirection. As her son, he learned early that the best technique for getting his own way was often to do one thing while chattering pleasantly about something else, to seem to lean one way while actually going another.

James Roosevelt's long illness brought mother and son still closer together in a loving conspiracy to keep from him anything that might make him worry. She was forty-six when he died in 1900, with a long empty widowhood ahead of her. She filled it with unswerving devotion to her son. Her husband's will had expressed the wish that Franklin "be under the influence of his mother," and he was. She moved to Boston to be near him while he attended Harvard, traveled with him to Europe, offered advice as to which young ladies he might most suitably entertain, and when he announced suddenly in 1904 that he wished to marry his cousin Eleanor Roosevelt, she worked hard to dissuade him—not because she disapproved

Sara Delano Roosevelt. (Courtesy FDR Library.)

of his choice, she said later, but because he was too young at twenty-one to consider marriage. After he insisted on marrying anyway the following year, she worked still harder to maintain her hold on him. She built and furnished two homes in New York so that she could live right next door, purchased for his growing family a cottage adjoining hers at Campobello, hired and fired nurses for her grandchildren, and so indulged the children as to undercut even the possibility of consistent parental discipline. Eleanor Roosevelt at first seemed sometimes to welcome her interest—she was motherless herself, unsure of her own abilities as a mother, and eager for love and attention—but as her independence asserted itself, she came bitterly to resent it. Hyde Park was always her mother-in-law's home and FDR's only secondarily. "It was never my home," Eleanor Roosevelt once said, and her husband's inability ever to decide to which of the two strong women in his life he owed his primary allegiance made his marriage far more difficult than it might otherwise have been.

His mother took a dire view of politics when he first considered running for office. (His father had after all always refused to run when asked, and politics inevitably forced one into contact with alarming sorts of people.) But she was fiercely proud of his subsequent triumphs at the polls and was never surprised by them: "Nothing my son does ever surprises me," she once said. And she loyally defended him against those among her wealthy friends who thought he had betrayed his class.

Roosevelt's critics sometimes charged that he was a malleable "mama's boy," but it should be pointed out that in every crucial question on which his mother is known to have opposed him—his marriage, his decision to enter politics, his more difficult

decision to return to it after he was crippled—he did what he wanted, regardless. When it really mattered, his will was more than a match for hers.

Sara Delano Roosevelt spent her last years living quietly at Hyde Park and Campobello, making an occasional trip to England and the Continent and reminding the president of the United States from time to time to wear his rubbers when it rained and not to forget his thank-you notes at Christmas. She died at Springwood in 1941. Rummaging through the house a few days later, FDR came upon a box she had kept containing a handful of snippets of his baby curls. He began to weep and asked to be left alone. No one on his staff could remember ever seeing him cry before.

Sara Delano Roosevelt is the subject of the biography *Gracious Lady* (New York: D. Appleton-Century, 1935), published during her lifetime by Rita Halle Kleeman. It is filled with useful anecdotal material—Kleeman was her friend as well as her biographer—but it is relentlessly admiring. *My Boy Franklin,* "as told by Mrs. James Roosevelt to Isabel Leighton and Gabrielle Forbush" (New York: Ray Long & Richard R. Smith, 1933) is also rich in anecdotes about life at Hyde Park and abroad during FDR's early years, but it must be consulted with caution. Mrs. Roosevelt found magazine serialization of its early chapters embarrassing and refused to cooperate during the writing of the final ones; Louis Howe and FDR himself helped fill the gap. Careful reading between the lines of Eleanor Roosevelt's voluminous autobiographical writings offers an acid portrait of the mother-in-law she found so intrusive. For somewhat different assessments, see Kenneth S. Davis, *FDR: The Beckoning of Destiny* (New York: G. P. Putnam's Sons, 1971), the series of shrewd "background memorandums" in Bernard Asbell, *The FDR Memoirs* (Garden City, N.Y.: Doubleday & Co., 1973), and Geoffrey C. Ward's *Before the Trumpet: Young Franklin Roosevelt, 1882–1905* (New York: Harper & Row, 1985).

GEOFFREY C. WARD

See also Campobello; Genealogy; Health; Hyde Park; Roosevelt, Anna Eleanor; Roosevelt, James

Sara D. Roosevelt and her son reading congratulations on his reelection as president, 4 November 1936. (Courtesy FDR Library.)

Roosevelt, Theodore

(27 October 1858–6 January 1919)

Twenty-sixth president of the United States and fifth cousin of FDR. While still a junior clerk in the Wall Street law firm of Carter, Ledyard, and Milburn in 1907, Franklin Roosevelt outlined his plans for the future. The law would not hold him long, he told his colleagues; he would enter politics and hoped eventually to become president. He intended first to get himself elected to the New York assembly, then win appointment as assistant secretary of the navy, and finally become governor. "Anyone who is governor of New York," he explained, "has a chance to be president with any luck." The heady sequence of political triumphs to which twenty-five-year-old FDR looked with such apparent confidence had, with one or two modifications, already been marked out by his fifth

Theodore Roosevelt, 1907. Unidentified photographer.
(National Portrait Gallery, Smithsonian Institution.)

cousin, Theodore Roosevelt, whose dramatic career FDR had followed with awe and admiration since he was a small boy.

TR was born in New York and educated at Harvard; he entered the New York assembly as a Republican reformer at twenty-three in 1882, delivering his maiden speech just six days before FDR was born. Both James Roosevelt and his eldest son, James Roosevelt Roosevelt, had dabbled in politics and diplomacy, but always drew back from actually running for office on the grounds that elective office was no place for gentlemen. TR showed, in Sara Roosevelt's words, that a member of the family might "go into politics but not *be* a politician." The Hyde Park and Oyster Bay clans were then close: Elliott Roosevelt, TR's luckless younger brother and the father of Eleanor Roosevelt, was FDR's godfather. Franklin visited Sagamore Hill as a boy, doing his best to keep up as TR led his tireless brood up and down a sand dune; the contrast with his own ailing father must have been vivid. Theodore Roosevelt was a hero to Endicott Peabody as well, and his exploits as colonel of the Rough Riders in Cuba and his election as governor of New York both took place during FDR's years at Groton. Each event made him and his schoolmates "wild with excitement," he said, and delighted his parents as well: Mr. James deserted the Democrats to rally Hyde Park for Franklin's "noble kinsman" in 1898. When Franklin left Groton two years later, he wore pince nez carefully patterned after those the colonel wore up Kettle Hill, and when he got to Harvard he joined the Republican Club so that he could campaign for his cousin. At his wedding in 1905, TR was on hand to give his favorite niece away.

Theodore Roosevelt also indirectly made possible FDR's successful entry into politics; it was TR's Progressive followers who so split the New York GOP in 1910 that even an untried Democrat whose only known asset was his familiar last name could win a state senate seat in the normally Republican Twenty-sixth District. (Ironically, TR's Republicanism may also have helped ensure that when FDR did go into politics, he went in as a Democrat; TR had four Republican sons, any one of whom then stood a better chance of inheriting his mantle than an obscure upstate cousin; only as a Democrat could Franklin hope to rise very high.)

FDR's admiration for TR sometimes took the form of open emulation: his early public persona seems almost consciously to have been modeled after TR's—he bared his teeth, displayed enormous energy and swagger, even threatened fisticuffs with one opponent during his battle against the nomination of William F. ("Blue-Eyed Billy") Sheehan for the U.S. Senate, and when in exchange for his support for Woodrow Wilson in the presidential campaign of 1912 he was offered his cousin's old post of assistant secretary of the navy, he replied, "I'd like it bully well!" It took him some years to develop his own more subtle kind of leadership, and as late as the mid-1920s he seems still to have wanted to follow paths blazed by his cousin. TR had been a skilled and astonishingly prolific writer; FDR was not. Yet at least twice he set out to write ambitious books—a biography of John Paul Jones, a history of the United States—clearly inspired by works by Theodore Roosevelt. Neither project got very far.

TR always liked his younger cousin—"I am so fond of that boy, I'd be shot for him," he once told a proud Sara Roosevelt—and so at least surface amity prevailed between Hyde Park and Oyster Bay until his death in 1919. Thereafter, TR's sons felt free to denounce FDR as, among other things, "a maverick who does not have the brand of our family." This open disaffection distressed FDR and Eleanor Roosevelt, but it never altered his veneration for Theodore Roosevelt's memory; "He was the greatest man I ever knew," he said.

Elements of TR's New Nationalism undergirded the New Deal; progressives lured into politics by the first Roosevelt—Harold Ickes, Frank Knox, and Francis Biddle among them—played important roles in the administrations of the second. Their styles of presidential leadership were very different, but the two Roosevelts shared many strengths: a sense of stewardship of the American land; an unfeigned love for people and politics, and an ability to rally able men and women to their cause; unbounded optimism and self-confidence; impatience with the drab notion that the mere making of money should be enough to satisfy any man or any nation; above all, an unabashed delight in the great power of their office to do good.

A serious work on the impact of Theodore Roosevelt upon the personality and politics of his younger cousin has yet to be written, although all of FDR's biographers touch upon it in passing. The final chapter of John Milton Cooper, Jr., *The Warrior and the Priest: Woodrow Wilson and Theodore Roosevelt* (Cambridge, Mass.: Belknap Press, Harvard University Press, 1983) at least suggests what might someday be done.

GEOFFREY C. WARD

See also Conservation; Genealogy; Liberalism and Progressivism

Roosevelt Coalition

See Democratic Party; Elections in the Roosevelt Era; Labor

Roosevelt Dime

First put in circulation in January 1946, the Roosevelt dime was a fitting tribute to FDR, who had founded the March of Dimes to combat polio. The initial design by the U.S. Mint's chief engraver John R. Sinnock was rejected by the Commission of Fine Arts because the profile of the late president needed "more dignity." He submitted several models before the commission gave its approval. The portrait was based on a bronze plaque of Roosevelt done by the black artist Selma Burke for the Recorder of Deeds Building in Washington, D.C. Sinnock's initials (J.S.), however, appear on the forward edge of the portrait. When the dime was issued, rumors spread that the initials stood for Joseph Stalin, and indicated the alleged influence of the Soviet Union over postwar America. The mint was forced to make an official denial.

For the background of the Roosevelt dime, see Don Taxany, *The U.S. Mint and Coinage* (New York: Arco Publishing Co., 1966). See Ted Schwarz, *A History of United States Coinage* (San Diego and New York: A. S. Barnes & Co., 1980) for a discussion of Selma Burke's role in the design.

See also Memorials; Portraits; Roosevelt Stamps

Roosevelt Library

See Franklin D. Roosevelt Library

Roosevelt Stamps

An avid philatelist, Roosevelt personally approved sketches and proofs of the over two hundred stamps issued during his administration. Given his interest, it was natural that Roosevelt stamps would become a favorite among collectors. Although planned before his death, the United Nations Conference on International Organization Commemorative (San Francisco, 25 April 1945) is considered the first stamp to honor the late president. The four stamps of the Roosevelt Memorial Series were issued between July 1945 and January 1946. Each has a portrait of Roosevelt in an oval on the left and scenes of Hyde Park (one-cent; green), the Little White House at Warm Springs, Georgia (two-cent; red), the White House (three-cent; purple), and a globe with the words, "Freedom of Speech and Religion, From Want and Fear" (five-cent; blue).

A Roosevelt stamp was part of the Prominent American Series, the regular postage between 1965 and 1975; the portrait was based on a photograph

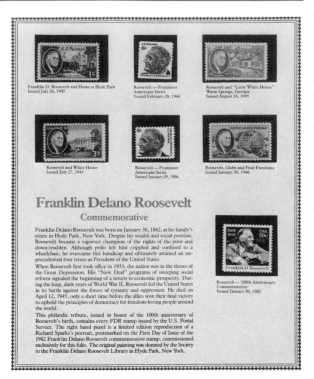

A centennial commemorative stamp booklet issued 30 January 1982. (Courtesy FDR Library.)

taken at the signing of the Atlantic Charter in 1941. The six-cent sheet was issued on 2 January 1966 and the coil and booklet formats on 28 December 1967. The vertical coil version was slightly redesigned for better use in dispensing machines (28 February 1968).

Founded in 1963, the Franklin D. Roosevelt Philatelic Society brings together collectors of Roosevelt stamps and other Rooseveltiana. The society promotes additional commemoratives honoring both Franklin and Eleanor Roosevelt, publishes a bimonthly newsletter (*Fireside Chats*), and issues a check list of Roosevelt stamps.

For more information on Roosevelt stamps, see Fred Reinfeld, *Commemorative Stamps of the U.S.A.* (New York: Thomas Y. Crowell Co., 1956) and U.S. Postal Service, *Postage Stamps of the United States* (Washington: U.S. Postal Service, 1979).

See also Memorials; Portraits; Roosevelt Dime

Roper, Daniel Calhoun
(1 April 1867–11 April 1943)

Secretary of commerce (1933–38). Born in Marlboro County, South Carolina, Daniel Calhoun Roper graduated from Trinity College (Duke University) in 1888 and received his law degree from Washington's National University in 1901. Roper was first assistant postmaster general (1913–16) and then commissioner of internal revenue (1917–20) in the Wilson administration. Active in Democratic party politics, he was the floor manager for his close friend William Gibbs McAdoo at the 1924 Democratic National Convention. Although an early supporter of Roosevelt, his appointment to the Commerce post was probably a gesture to the MacAdoo wing of the party. Roper believed that the principal function of the department was "to promote the legitimate interests of business large and small." To accomplish this, he established the Business Advisory Council to inform Congress and the administration of the attitudes of the business community. Roper also chaired the cabinet committee that supervised the National Recovery Administration and worked on other early New Deal programs. He resigned on 23 December 1938 but briefly served as temporary U.S. minister to Canada in 1939. Roper died in 1943.

The best source of Roper's political career is his autobiography, *Fifty Years of Public Life* (Durham, N.C.: Duke University Press, 1941). The background of his appointment is briefly described in Raymond Moley, *The First New Deal* (New York: Harcourt Brace Jovanovich, 1966).

Rosenman, Samuel Irving

(13 February 1896–24 June 1973)

Jurist and presidential adviser. Samuel Rosenman was born in San Antonio, Texas, the youngest child of Russian-Jewish immigrants who subsequently migrated to New York City. Sam attended Manhattan public schools and graduated from Columbia College, Phi Beta Kappa and summa cum laude in 1915. In 1917, after completing his second year at Columbia Law School, he enlisted as a private in the army and was discharged in August 1919 as a first lieutenant. Receiving his LL.B. shortly after his discharge, he was admitted to the New York Bar in 1920 and sought election to the New York State Assembly the following year. After gaining the support of Tammany Hall district leader James "Jimmy" Hines, Rosenman unseated the Republican incumbent and won successive annual reelections through 1925. In later years, he took special pride in his support of Robert Moses's park system and Margaret Sanger's controversial efforts for dissemination of birth control information; while assemblyman his most publicized activities involved rent-control legislation. Having gained the attention of the state Democratic leadership, he won appointment in 1926 as a legislative bill drafting commissioner.

In that capacity he came into closer association with Governor Alfred E. Smith. When in 1928 Smith won the Democratic presidential nomination, Rosenman eagerly anticipated national campaign assignments; instead he was "loaned" by the Smith forces to New York gubernatorial candidate Franklin Roosevelt. Rosenman had never met Roosevelt:

> Despite [Roosevelt's] reputation, I did not know the full extent of his liberalism. . . . Indeed I was a bit afraid after the work I had done on some of Smith's programs, Roosevelt would be a letdown for me and

all Smith liberals. I knew Roosevelt's family and cultural background: and I was skeptical.

Within days of their meeting Roosevelt converted Rosenman into an enthusiastic aide by channeling his detailed knowledge of state issues into FDR campaign speeches. Upon hearing the applause that followed their first collaboration, Rosenman was "more uplifted than the speaker." He continued to ghost Roosevelt speeches until the president's death and never quite lost the excitement of that first occasion.

With FDR's election, Rosenman was appointed governor's counsel and was tied closely to Roosevelt's political fortunes and administrative routine. Their personal relationship was further cemented during the final year of Rosenman's counselship when he resided in the executive mansion. Less harmonious relations with Louis Howe, the preeminent Roosevelt adviser and another executive mansion boarder, were among the reasons Rosenman later gave for choosing to remain in New York rather than plan for a 1933 Washington appointment.

Roosevelt reluctantly acceded to Rosenman's preferences by appointing him to the New York Supreme Court. Though FDR likened the appointment to "cutting off my right hand" because it denied him Rosenman's further assistance, judicial tenure did not deter Rosenman from political activity. The judge's most celebrated contributions to the 1932 presidential campaign were to recruit and serve as liaison for the brains trust and to author the peroration for FDR's acceptance speech. This speech added "New Deal" to the political lexicon. The judge was also the only individual, apart from Roosevelt's immediate family, to accompany the nominee on his flight from Albany to the Democratic National Convention site.

Samuel I. Rosenman. (Courtesy FDR Library.)

Just prior to the 1932 election, Rosenman was dealt a personal setback when Tammany retaliated against his loyalty to Roosevelt during the Tammany scandals by denying him nomination to a full judicial term. Rejecting Roosevelt's suggestion that he reconsider his decision to remain in New York, Rosenman engaged in a lucrative law practice until July 1933, when newly elected New York governor Herbert Lehman reappointed him to the court. Later that same year, Rosenman won election to a full term.

Occasional White House visits, coupled with the intelligence that Roosevelt had bestowed the sobriquet "Sammy the Rose" upon him, kept the judge a newsworthy item. Until 1936, however, his extrajudicial activities were most frequently on behalf of the Lehman administration. In that year, Roosevelt, preparing for his reelection campaign, reinstated Rosenman as principal speech writer. For the next seven years, the judge shuttled between judicial and presidential assignments, a routine that belied his reputation for avoiding physical exertion. In 1937, he participated in the ill-fated Court reorganization plan and began compiling the thirteen-volume *Public Papers and Addresses of Franklin D. Roosevelt, 1928–1945*. By 1939, his assignments were broadened to include war mobilization and government reorganization projects. Projecting an unruffled demeanor, he was nonetheless beset by overwork and nervous strain and, in early 1943, temporarily lost the sight in one eye. Advised to reduce his work load, he resigned from the bench to accept appointment to the specially created post of special counsel to the president.

Tenure as counsel was spiced with special assignments on postwar economic planning and war criminal trials. The former assignment precipitated bitter jurisdictional disputes with James F. Byrnes and strengthened Rosenman's determination to leave Washington as soon as possible after the war. In January 1945, prior to formal announcement of Rosenman's imminent departure, Roosevelt named him to head an economic mission to Western Europe. Temporarily recalled to assist Roosevelt in the preparation of his Yalta report, Rosenman was in London when he learned of the president's death. Retaining a fierce loyalty to FDR throughout his life, Rosenman later wrote that Roosevelt "did not seek to impose respect toward himself on visitors, friends, or servants; like all natural born leaders, he seemed to command respect and affection unconsciously."

Persuaded by Harry Truman to remain as counsel, Rosenman used his credentials as an FDR confidante to coax Truman toward a domestic program that he believed to be "on the path of New Deal thinking." In 1946, citing financial need, Rosenman returned to New York City. Building a substantial law practice, he never lost his enthusiasm for politics, was closely involved with the establishment of the state of Israel, and continued to advise presidents and governors until his death.

Rosenman's career with Roosevelt is chronicled in the judge's memoir *Working with Roosevelt* (New York: Harper & Bros., 1952). His ultimate conclusions on the Roosevelt presidency can be gleaned from *Presidential Style: Some Giants and a Pygmy in the White House* (New York: Harper & Row, 1976), which he was preparing with his wife, Dorothy Rosenman, at the time of his death and which Dorothy completed. The thirteen-volume *Public Papers and Addresses of Franklin D. Roosevelt* appeared under the imprint of three publishers: Random House in 1938, Macmillan Co., 1941, and Harper & Bros., 1950. For a discussion of the impact of the *Public Papers*, see Samuel B. Hand, "Rosenman, Thucydides, and the New Deal," *Journal of American History* 55 (September 1968):334–48. Hand, *Counsel and Advise* (New York: Garland Publishing, 1979) is a full-length biography.

SAMUEL B. HAND

See also Franklin D. Roosevelt Library; Speechwriting; Zionism

Rural Electrification Administration

With the establishment of the Rural Electrification Administration (REA) in 1935, the New Deal initiated the first steps toward bringing the age of electricity to rural America. Prior to that time farmers enjoyed few of the advantages that electricity had brought to urban residents. In 1933 it was estimated that nine out of ten farm energy sources were gasoline

Fetching water from the pump in Wilder, Tennessee. The pump was the sole water supply for all the houses pictured. (Courtesy FDR Library.)

engines, hand labor, and animal power, with kerosene lanterns used for light. This same proportion of families also had no running water or indoor bathrooms; they brought water from streams or pumped it from nearby wells, bathed and washed laundry out of doors, and heated their homes by stove.

Although electricity in rural areas would transform farm life, private power companies were reluctant to extend lines into the countryside because of the high cost. During the 1920s alternative solutions were suggested, most notably cooperatives, which had been launched with success in Europe, Canada, and a few midwestern states. But cooperative associations often suffered from poor management and leadership, from attacks levied by electric companies, and from inadequate technical and financial experience. Thus, it became evident that extending electric service to farmers either by private companies or by cooperatives created problems of such magnitude that only some well-conceived plan with public support would make rural electrification a reality. Such a proposal was put forth by Morris Cooke.

Cooke, member of a wealthy Philadelphia family, was an engineer and dedicated to Frederick Taylor's principle of scientific management. Believing that the benefits of public power should be shared by all rather than just a privileged few, Cooke had made a reputation for himself as an advocate of rural electricity, first with Governor Gifford Pinchot in Pennsylvania and later as a member of Gov. Franklin D. Roosevelt's New York Power Authority. After President Hoover refused to consider Cooke's plan for full-scale regulation and comprehensive development of energy resources among private companies and state and federal agencies, Cooke supported Roosevelt for the presidency. In 1932 he renewed his power suggestions to the president-elect, noting that given the economic conditions brought about by the depression, rural electrification might then be accomplished.

For the next several years Cooke and Roosevelt, along with Harold Ickes and Harry Hopkins in the executive branch and George Norris of Nebraska in the Senate, explored ways in which rural electrification might be accomplished. Norris, in particular, was a valuable ally, for he had always been one of the prime supporters of cheap electricity for the farmer. These efforts within the administration, the successful completion of an experimental cooperative in public electrification by the Tennessee Valley Authority, and pressure from several states for federal funds to complete their power programs all contributed to the creation of the REA in May 1935, with Cooke as its first administrator.

Because the REA was part of the New Deal's relief programs, the agency had to provide 25 percent of its funds for labor and derive 90 percent of its labor from relief rolls. Unable to operate under this formula, Cooke convinced Roosevelt, Hopkins, and Ickes to make the REA primarily a lending agency.

After the administration adopted that policy, Cooke found private power companies still unwilling to accept low-cost government money to participate in a full-scale rural electrification program. Frustrated by the companies' rebuffs, Cooke turned to nonprofit cooperatives established by the farmers themselves. In view of those developments, Senator Norris recognized that the REA should be removed from the relief program and given a separate identity of its own. Accordingly, Norris and Sam Rayburn of Texas cosponsored legislation in Congress. Backed by REA supporters such as Congressman John Rankin of Mississippi, the measure that established the principle of preference for nonprofit agencies for REA loans became law on 20 May 1936.

In May 1937, John M. Carmody, Cooke's deputy, became administrator of the REA. Like Cooke, he believed in the cooperative solution. Under his leadership the agency encouraged farmers without electric power to form themselves into cooperatives and acquire with low-interest REA loans the necessary generating and distributing facilities. In this way these cooperatives were able to extend power lines into rural areas not served by private companies. Where adequate electric generating power already existed through private companies, the REA cooperatives were to buy their power at wholesale rates and distribute it to their members.

In 1939, the REA was placed under the Department of Agriculture, and Harry Slattery, a veteran conservationist, became its administrator. Despite a considerable amount of bureaucratic and policy disputes, the REA continued progress toward rural electrification. By 1941, 40 percent of farms had electric power; ten years later the number had increased to 90 percent. All this was made possible because rivalries between power companies and the REA had ended by the early 1950s. Industrial and population growth forced companies to cooperate with the REA; with increased appropriations from Congress, the REA's influence was felt throughout the entire power industry. By the 1960s, only the most remote and marginal farms did not have electricity, and the REA could be said to have accomplished its mission of the electrification of rural America.

The coming of electricity to rural America was one of the most important social and economic changes to occur during the New Deal era. Although the REA did not restore the rural way of life as some of its supporters had hoped, it did bring about massive changes to both farming and the rural home. Running water, refrigeration, the radio, and better sanitation enabled farm families to experience many of the same comforts of life to which urban dwellers had long been accustomed. Electricity also improved farm technology and school and community life; it ended the toil and drudgery of farm life and lifted the spirits of farm families. Economically it helped stimulate factory payrolls and individual earnings, while providing increased employment in the construction, maintenance, and operation of transmission lines.

For providing electricity at low rates to rural America, the REA successfully achieved the objectives set for it by the New Deal, and it became one of the landmarks of the Roosevelt era.

The most recent and complete study of the REA is D. Clayton Brown, *Electricity for Rural America: The Fight for the REA* (Westport, Conn.: Greenwood Press, 1980). Also vaulable for its summary is Arthur M. Schlesinger, Jr., *The Politics of Upheaval* (Boston: Houghton Mifflin Co., 1960). Richard Lowitt, *George W. Norris, The Persistence of a Progressive, 1913–1933* (Urbana: University of Illinois Press, 1971) and *George W. Norris, The Triumph of a Progressive, 1933–1945* (Urbana: University of Illinois Press, 1978) discuss Norris's efforts on behalf of rural power. More general are Philip Funigiello, *Toward a National Power Policy: The New Deal and the Electrical Industry* (Pittsburgh: University of Pittsburgh Press, 1973) and Richard S. Kirkendall, *Social Scientists and Farm Politics in the Age of Roosevelt* (Columbia: University of Missouri Press, 1966). Several articles provide specific treatment of New Deal power proposals, among them Jean Christie, "The Mississippi Valley Committee: Conservation and Planning in the New Deal," *Historian* 32 (May 1970):449–69. For Morris Cooke's own views, see "The Early Days of the Rural Electrification Idea, 1914–1936," *American Political Science Review* 42 (June 1948):431–47; and for an overall assessment of the REA, see H. S. Person, "The Rural

Water at hand in the kitchen of an electrified home in the TVA town of Norris. The REA brought the benefits of running water to thousands of rural homes throughout the South. (Courtesy FDR Library.)

Electrification Administration in Perspective," *Agricultural History* 24 (April 1950):70–89.

JOHN MULDOWNY

See also Agriculture; Cohen, Benjamin Victor; Conservation; New Deal; Norris, George William; Relief; Tennessee Valley Authority

---

Russia

See Stalin, Joseph, and the Soviet Union

Lucy Mercer about the time she was a member of Mrs. Roosevelt's staff. (Courtesy FDR Library.)

Rutherfurd, Lucy Page Mercer
(26 April 1891–31 July 1948)

Lucy Mercer was born to a well-connected Maryland Catholic family. Her father, Carroll Mercer, traced his roots to two distinguished colonial families, each of whom has left its mark on the map of the state—Carrollton and Mercerburg. Financially comfortable, the Marine Corps officer married a Virginia belle. The young couple had two daughters, squandered considerable money, and separated. Mrs. Mercer was left to support her daughters.

In 1913, Lucy Mercer arrived in Washington, where she sought employment as a social secretary in order to support herself. Although forced by economic straits to work, she was nevertheless welcome in Washington's social swirl. She was attractive, charming, and pedigreed, which were qualities that counted for a great deal in the nation's capital.

She became part-time secretary for Eleanor Roosevelt soon after the couple's move to Washington. In that capacity, Mercer met the assistant secretary of the navy. Mercer and FDR saw much of each other socially as well. Mercer was often a welcome guest at Washington dinner parties when a lovely young woman was needed, and she filled that role at the Roosevelts' table as well. While Mrs. Roosevelt vacationed at Campobello with the children during the summer of 1916, romance bloomed between Lucy Mercer and Franklin Roosevelt. Alice Roosevelt, daughter of Cousin Teddy, seemed to have encouraged the couple by inviting them to tea and dinner. Eleanor may well have suspected the course the relationship had taken. The following summer, she left for Campobello after considerable hesitation on her part and much encouragement on Franklin's.

During World War I, Roosevelt traveled to Europe in his capacity as naval assistant secretary. He returned in September 1918 with a serious case of pneumonia. While his wife handled his correspondence, she discovered letters Mercer had written to him. Mrs. Roosevelt confronted her husband with a firmly stated choice: she would divorce him or they could maintain the semblance of marriage for the sake of the children, provided he never saw Lucy Mercer again.

Sara Delano Roosevelt, the future president's mother, issued her own ultimatum. She controlled the modest Roosevelt fortune and guarded the patrician family name. If her son was determined to leave his wife and five children for another woman, she informed him that no funds would be dispensed in his direction any longer. For a thirty-six-year-old man who had settled on a political career, loss of income and reputation presented serious threats. Still, according to family accounts, FDR would have forsaken everything for Lucy Mercer.

She, on the other hand, was a devout Catholic, who could not and would not marry a divorced man. Soon after the Roosevelts' confrontation, she wed the older, wealthy, and widowed Winthrop Rutherfurd. The bride became a devoted wife and lovingly raised her husband's orphaned children. She had one daughter of her own. There may have been a few letters and casual encounters after that, but the affair had ended.

In 1941, Lucy accompanied her ailing husband to Washington for medical treatment. A mutual friend arranged for a White House meeting, but Rutherfurd declined to go. Soon afterward, her husband died. Roosevelt wrote a condolence note, Mrs. Rutherfurd replied, and the two began to see each other occasionally. Once, he stopped at her New Jersey home on one of his secret wartime trips; she visited him once at Bernard Baruch's plantation in South Carolina, where Roosevelt spent a month in 1944; she often dined at the White House with Anna Roosevelt Boettiger serving as hostess when Eleanor Roosevelt was away on her many travels; Grace Tully casually refers to Mrs. Rutherfurd's comings and goings in the Oval Office. The meetings were frequent, considering the heavy schedule of the wartime president.

Lucy Rutherfurd came to see FDR and brought her friend, the painter Mme. Elizabeth Shoumatoff, to Warm Springs in April 1945. There, while posing for a portrait, the president suffered the cerebral hemorrhage that caused his death. Lucy Mercer Rutherfurd's name was not included in the list of those who had been with the president when he died, but one of FDR's cousins who was there informed Mrs. Roosevelt of her presence when Eleanor arrived at Warm Springs. Most family and staff were aware of the resumed relationship between FDR and Rutherfurd, but Eleanor apparently suspected nothing. Her bitterness is difficult to measure, especially in light of her own daughter's apparent complicity.

This complex triangle of broken hearts and family scandal of more than a quarter-century duration represented much more than a subject for gossip. It was undoubtedly a watershed in the lives of both Eleanor and Franklin and determined the character of their marriage after 1918. For Mrs. Roosevelt, it signified a cruel rejection that seemed to replicate so much prior unhappiness in her life. From that time, she set out deliberately to carve a role for herself, to create a public persona, to establish personal autonomy. Her efforts were so intense and the results so successful that Eleanor Roosevelt became the most re-nowned, respected, and loved woman of her time.

The impact of failed romance was no less great on FDR. Prior to the Mercer affair, he had gained much recognition as a handsome, fun-loving social butterfly and political lightweight. Members of his social circle attribute the committed and serious politician who emerged after World War I as much to the crushing disappointment of a lost love as to the sobering effects of crippling polio.

The marriage survived, but not mutual love and trust. At best, there was affection and common commitments to social and political policies. Letters from daughter Anna to her mother indicate that Franklin made overtures toward an emotional truce, but that Eleanor never forgave. Instead, they carried on their public lives on separate planes, although Eleanor Roosevelt's public concerns and activities often coincided with her husband's political roles and needs. To many Americans, they represented a unique example of public partnership and private compatibility. But the perception and the reality must account for the influence of Lucy Mercer.

After the president's death, Mercer lived at one of her husband's estates in Aiken, South Carolina. In a response to a letter Anna Roosevelt Boettiger wrote her shortly after FDR's death, Mercer barely disguised the depth of her feeling for Roosevelt. She died a little more than three years later in July 1948. Americans were unaware of the Mercer affair until the publication of *Washington Quadrille: The Dance Beside the Documents* twenty years later. Jonathan Daniels, former FDR aide, Virginia publisher, and son of Josephus Daniels, wrote explicitly about the relationship, and knowledge of the affair entered the public domain.

Joseph Lash describes the Mercer affair in *Eleanor and Franklin* (New York: W. W. Norton & Co., 1971) but gives even greater weight to its effect on Mrs. Roosevelt in *Love, Eleanor: Eleanor Roosevelt and Her Friends* (Garden City, N.Y.: Doubleday & Co., 1982). In his fond memorial to the president, *FDR: A Centenary Remembrance* (New York: Random House, 1982), journalist and relative Joseph Alsop tells the family version of the relationship and assesses the impact on Franklin. Bernard Asbell interviewed Anna Roosevelt about her father and Rutherfurd and printed the letter Rutherfurd wrote to her after FDR's death in *Mother and Daughter: The Letters of Eleanor and Anna Roosevelt* (New York: Coward, McCann & Geoghagan, 1982). The story, guarded by knowing family and friends, became public knowledge with the publication of *Washington Quadrille: The Dance Beside the Documents* by Jonathan Daniels (New York: Doubleday & Co., 1968).

LOIS SCHARF

See also Death of FDR; Roosevelt, Anna Eleanor

Rutledge, Wiley Blount, Jr.
(20 July 1894–10 September 1949)

Wiley B. Rutledge, Jr. (Courtesy FDR Library.)

Supreme Court Justice, 1943–49. Born in Cloveport, Kentucky, the son of a Baptist minister, Wiley Rutledge attended various small colleges before graduating from the University of Wisconsin in 1914. After receiving a law degree from the University of Colorado in 1922, he practiced law for two years before returning to the university as a professor of law. He later served as dean of the Washington University Law School from 1930 to 1935, and then as dean of the University of Iowa College of Law till 1939.

Rutledge was an early supporter of Franklin Roosevelt. He repeatedly spoke out against the 1930's decisions of the Supreme Court that invalidated many New Deal measures. But Rutledge thought it was his support of Roosevelt's Court-packing plan that brought the law professor to the president's attention and resulted in his appointment to the District of Columbia Court of Appeals in 1939.

As an appellate judge, Rutledge relied on a broad interpretation of the general welfare clause of the Constitution to consistently uphold New Deal economic regulation. But his circuit career was cut short by Roosevelt's nominating him to the Supreme Court on 11 January 1943 to succeed Jimmy Byrnes. In making the nomination, FDR publicly stressed Rutledge's academic and judicial record, but privately the president noted that the new justice's western roots would give balance to the previously all-eastern Court.

While on the Supreme Court, Rutledge regularly sided with the liberal faction of Black, Douglas, and Murphy. Rutledge's most famous opinion came in the appeal of Japanese general Tamoyuji Yamashita, who had been tried and convicted in a military court for war crimes allegedly committed by troops under his command. Dissenting from the Court's affirmation of the conviction, Rutledge damned the army's conduct of the trial and its reliance on extraordinarily suspect evidence. Rutledge served for three more years on the Court before his life was ended by a stroke in 1949.

The best biography of Rutledge is the article on him by Fred L. Israel in *The Justices of the Supreme Court of the United States, 1789–1969*, ed. Leon Friedman and Fred Israel (New York: Chelsea House Publishers, 1969), pp. 2593–2613. More personal glimpses of the justice may be found in *Justice Rutledge and the Bright Constellation* by Fowler V. Harper (New York: Bobbs-Merrill Company, 1965), although the book is somewhat loosely edited. Two law review articles, published shortly after Rutledge's death, assess his impact on the issue of civil liberties. They are Landon G. Rockwell's "Justice Rutledge and Civil Liberties," *Yale Law Journal* 59 (December 1949):27–59, and Howard Mann's "Rutledge and Civil Liberties," *Indiana Law Journal* 25 (Summer 1950):532–59.

See also Court-Packing Plan; Supreme Court of the United States

S

Sailing

Franklin Delano Roosevelt always was interested in ships, in sailing, and in tales of the sea. When he was five years old, Franklin enclosed in his second letter to his mother a couple of pen-and-ink sketches of sailboats. Sara Roosevelt had begun early to fascinate her son with thrilling stories of the seafaring Delanos and of her own four-month sea voyage on board the *Surprise,* when as a little girl she accompanied her family to join Warren Delano who was engaged in the China tea trade in Hong Kong. She also gave Franklin a copy of Admiral Mahan's *The Influence of Sea Power,* which he read as he grew older. Grandfather Delano, who inherited his great affection for the sea from his own father, told his grandson exciting tales of the Delano whaling ships and of his adventures as shipowner and captain on American clipper ships sailing in the early nineteenth century to the Orient.

Franklin's father, James, taught him how to handle the *Half-Moon,* their sailboat, on trips up the

FDR sailing the Amberjack II, *from Marion, Mass., to Campobello, 16–29 June 1933. The crew included his four sons. (Courtesy FDR Library.)*

Hudson, along the New England coast, and in the dangerous waters of the Bay of Fundy near the Roosevelts' home on Campobello Island off Maine and Canada. The boy became a skilled sailor, frequently cruising from New York to Halifax even in the worst kind of rough weather, and he had his own twenty-one-foot knockabout, the *New Moon,* at the age of sixteen.

Franklin's love of the sea led him to learn how to make toy boats and sailing models and even a crow's nest in a hemlock tree at Springwood, which served him and his boyhood friends as a lookout post for scanning the Hudson for pirates. The craft later helped him to pass otherwise solitary hours during his convalescence from polio. Franklin designed models of sailing ships and navy cruisers and destroyers and built them out of balsa wood. This pastime he continued through the years, sailing miniature ships and schooners on the Hudson in competition with his children and various friends, beating "all my rivals . . . because of the lightness of my hulls compared with theirs."

Six-year-old Franklin and a playmate take the wheel of the Half Moon *off Campobello, 1888. (Courtesy FDR Library.)*

At Harvard, Franklin started a collection of books having to do with American naval history. This interest expanded to include not only books but manuscripts, pamphlets, and articles, and his collection grew to several thousand. He also began to acquire naval prints, mostly by Currier and Ives, engravings, and paintings as well as ship models and keepsakes, which he displayed in every home he ever occupied, including the White House.

As president, Roosevelt, despite his physical handicap, sailed whenever and wherever he could: afternoons and weekends aboard the *Sequoia* on the Potomac, the James, and rivers off Chesapeake Bay; and on longer trips of several days on the *Amberjack II* along the New England coast, when he acted as skipper most of the time. "I love to be on the water," he said. "All my life I have loved ships and have been a student of the Navy."

For more information, see Olin Dows, *Franklin Roosevelt at Hyde Park* (New York: American Artists Group, 1949); Frank Freidel, *Franklin D. Roosevelt: The Apprenticeship* (Boston: Little, Brown & Co., 1952); Frank Freidel, *Franklin D. Roosevelt: Launching the New Deal* (Boston: Little, Brown & Co., 1973) and *Franklin D. Roosevelt: The Ordeal* (Boston: Little, Brown & Co., 1954); Compton Mackenzie, *Mr. Roosevelt* (New York: E. P. Dutton & Co., 1944); Nathan Miller, *FDR: An Intimate History* (Garden City, N.Y.: Doubleday & Co., 1983); Research Collection, *Roosevelt Family Papers* (Hyde Park, N.Y.: FDR Library and Museum); and Mrs. James Roosevelt as told to Isabel Leighton and Gabrielle Forbush, *My Boy Franklin* (New York: Ray Long & Richard R. Smith, 1933).

See also Mahan, Alfred Thayer

Securities and Exchange Commission

Probably the closest bond between Rooseveltian ideals and a long-lasting reform was the Securities and Exchange Commission (SEC), set up to exercise control over the stock exchanges for the protection of investors. As with many other social and economic reforms, the United States had lagged behind European nations in legislating strict standards to protect those of its citizens who brought their funds into the marketplace.

The high-flying decade of the 1920s had revealed the need for control over the frequently unethical or outright fraudulent activities of the New York Stock Exchange, which accounted for as much as 90 percent of all U.S. securities transactions. Despite the insistence of its president, Richard Whitney (who soon after was sent to Sing Sing for mishandling a client's funds), that the market was an utterly impersonal reflection of supply and demand, Congress and others could glimpse the manipulations by exchange members who rigged secret stock pools, offered bonds that lacked any substantial backing, and scandalously sold short in "bear raids."

Franklin Roosevelt, who as governor of New

Volume of Sales on New York Stock Exchange, 1925–1945 (in millions of shares)

YEAR	VOLUME OF SALES
1925	454
1926	451
1927	577
1928	920
1929	1125
1930	810
1931	577
1932	425
1933	655
1934	324
1935	382
1936	496
1937	409
1938	297
1939	262
1940	208
1941	171
1942	126
1943	279
1944	263
1945	378

Source: U.S. Bureau of the Census, *Historical Statistics of the United States, 1789–1945* (Washington, D.C.: U.S. Government Printing Office, 1949).

York had frequently denounced the frauds in securities sales, now gave strong support and presidential leadership to the regulatory legislation emerging in the wake of congressional hearings. Despite frantic lobbying by many members of the business and financial community of the nation, Roosevelt's pressure and a reform-minded Congress quickly passed the Securities Act of 1933 and the Securities and Exchange Act of 1934 (which formed the SEC). To these was added legislation such as the Federal Bankruptcy Act of 1939 and the Investment Companies and Investment Advisers Act of 1940. Thus, finally, securities and bond frauds were legally outlawed; corporate officers had to make full disclosures and take responsibility for their claims in issuing stocks or bonds; the accounting profession had to abide by a single uniform standard; and all investment dealers and advisers had to be registered and conform to stringent requirements. All exchanges, whether for securities or commodities, were closely monitored by the SEC to ensure compliance.

The commission itself consisted of five members appointed by the president for staggered five-year terms, with no more than three from the same political party. The president named the chairman, which usually meant that the regulatory philosophy favored by the president would predominate. Much of the effectiveness of the first body came from the leadership

A Shotgun Marriage.

Richmond Times Dispatch, *May 1934.*

of its chairman, Joseph P. Kennedy. A millionaire several times over, Kennedy was a Roosevelt supporter "before Chicago." One of his fortunes had been made on Wall Street, and he thus had an insider's knowledge of the Stock Exchange. He quickly demonstrated that the SEC meant business by cracking down on a number of questionable securities dealers. Subsequent chairmen, such as James M. Landis and William O. Douglas, continued the tough supervisory role. Joe Kennedy—although initially feared by many New Dealers because of his Wall Street connections—actually embodied the New Deal philosophy that capitalism must be saved in spite of its self-destructive excesses.

Although the advent of strict regulation first brought threats, for example, that the huge New York Stock Exchange would be moved to the more favorable business climate of Montreal, the atmosphere quickly changed on the part of the larger and more influential brokerage houses. They, and the general financial community, realized that the restoration of public confidence brought about by the SEC's publicized crackdown on malefactors was of enormous benefit to them. And during the New Deal and later years, no other regulatory agency drew such praise—grudging, at first—for its fairness and its widely acknowledged efficiency. Many considered the formation of the SEC to be the longest step toward the necessary social control of American finance.

Ralph F. de Bedts, *The New Deal's S.E.C.: The Formative Years* (New York: Columbia University Press, 1964) traces the political birth and early years of the SEC and its successes, emphasizing its political and philosophical connections with the New Deal. Charles W. Lamden, *The Securities and Exchange Commission* (New York: Arno, 1978) is a dissertation on economics subtitled, *A Case Study in the Use of Accounting as an Instrument of Public Policy.* Robert Sobel, *Inside Wall Street* (New York: Norton, 1977) is a popularized and chatty account of brokerage firms as well as the SEC.

RALPH F. DE BEDTS

See also Business; Cohen, Benjamin Victor; Corcoran, Thomas Gardiner; Douglas, William Orville; Frankfurter, Felix; Henderson, Leon; Kennedy, Joseph Patrick; Regulation, Federal

Selective Service Act

Bill supported by Roosevelt and passed by Congress in 1940 providing for a military draft. In 1940 the U.S. Army was not prepared to provide for the nation's defense. When war broke out in Europe in August of 1939, the United States had a total of 188,000 troops. President Roosevelt responded to the German invasion of Poland by declaring a national emergency and asking for 17,000 additional troops, far less than the 280,000 for which the army had plans. In May 1940 Roosevelt increased this number; one month later Congress appropriated funds to allow the army to grow to its statutory limit of 280,000, still less than the War Plans Division of the Army General Staff thought necessary for war preparedness. All these enlistments were volunteers. The nation had never had a peacetime draft, and President Roosevelt and the War Department thought that Congress and the country would not accept one. They hesitated to make such a politically volatile proposal. The long and deep resistance to compulsory military service in the United States meant that providing for the manpower needs of the army before the actual event of war would not be easy.

The idea of a draft came not from the War Department but from the Military Traning Camp Association, the formal name for the members of the Plattsburg Movement, as the veterans of the special military training held in 1915 in that town were called. These business and professional men celebrated their twenty-fifth anniversary at a meeting at the Harvard Club on 8 May 1940. Talk quickly turned to the impending crisis in Europe and the members became excited about the possibility raised by chairman Grenville Clark of a compulsory military service bill in Congress. The members included some wealthy and influential persons, among them Henry L. Stimson and Robert P. Patterson, so the cause had some political weight. At first the War Department resisted the idea because it was afraid to antagonize congressional and public support. President Roosevelt also initially refused to back the bill publicly for fear that if it were defeated it would show a lack of resolve to the world and so dishearten the Allies and encourage the Axis powers. No doubt he was also reluctant to risk supporting a politically controversial idea as he was preparing to campaign for his third term.

Gradually, however, support built for the Selective Training and Service Act. Leadership at the War Department changed in 1940, and the new secretary, Henry Stimson, secured Roosevelt's support for the act before he agreed to take office. On 2 August 1940, Roosevelt publicly announced that he backed the legislation. He recognized that it might be a "political disaster" but thought that he would be "derelict in his duty" if he did not support it, as he wrote one senator. Republican presidential candidate Wendell Willkie also proclaimed his support for the measure, so the act was not an issue in the presidential campaign. Congressional opposition persisted, however, with New York isolationist Hamilton Fish calling the act a "conspiracy" for war. But the isolationists were not strong enough to stop the bill, and on 14 September Congress passed the Selective Training and Service Act. Two days later, Roosevelt signed the law, and the mobilization of the U.S. Army began.

The terms of the act provided for the registration of all males between the ages of twenty-one and thirty-six. The president could call a maximum of 900,000 draftees who would serve for one year of active duty and ten years in the reserves. The act created the Selective Service System as an independent agency subject to the president. Local draft boards were to select men without regard to race, but could defer some men in specialized instances. In a ceremony on 29 October, Roosevelt delivered a speech and Secretary of War Stimson drew the first number for the lottery system. The first draftees entered the army in November, and by June 1941 there were 629,000 draftees in an army of 1.25 million.

By the summer of 1941 the Selective Service System faced an anticipated problem. Many of the original draftees had nearly served their one-year term, but the army feared that to release these men would risk the deterioration of troop preparedness even as the European crisis continued. On the other hand, there was much political pressure in Congress to abide by the original terms of the act. Roosevelt wanted to amend the law to extend the length of service for the duration of the emergency, but forced to compromise with Congress, he settled for a seventeen-month extension. Even so, the Selective Service Extension Act of 1941 passed the House of Representatives by only one vote and threw a scare into the bill's supporters. Advocates of compulsory military service were spared any more close votes after the Japanese attack on Pearl Harbor made the draft no longer a peacetime proposition.

A view of events sympathetic to the needs of the military is James A. Huston, "Selective Service in the World War II," *Current History* 54 (June 1968):345–50. Albert A. Blum, *Drafted or Deferred: Practices Past and Present* (Ann Arbor: University of Michigan Press, 1967) provides an overview of the draft and manpower problems during the war.

See also Stimson, Henry L.; War Mobilization; World War II

Senate, United States

See Congress, United States

Shangri-La

Recreational camp near Thurmont, Maryland, about 15 miles north of Frederick City, used during World War II by President Roosevelt as a country retreat; now known as Camp David. With America's entry in World War II, President Roosevelt's favored recreational cruises on the presidential yacht *Potomac* in Chesapeake waters became inadvisable, and his aides cast about for alternative means of escape from Washington's stultifying summer climate. Secretary Ickes's staff at the Department of the Interior recommended one of the department's experimental recreational demonstration areas in the Catoctin Mountains of northern Maryland. Roosevelt visited the area on 22 April 1942 and selected Camp No. 3 for development.

In about two months, National Park Service employees developed the camp for President Roosevelt's use and built a simple rustic cottage of his design, containing four bedrooms, two baths, a living room, pantry, kitchen, and screened dining porch. Staff were accommodated in similar smaller cottages elsewhere on the site and in some cases under canvas. The budget for the entire project was $18,650. Roosevelt first used the camp on 3–7 July 1942 and visited it at almost monthly intervals for the remainder of his presidency.

The name was taken from the popular escapist novel *Lost Horizon* by the English author James Hilton. In April 1942 when American warplanes under Lt. Col. James H. Doolittle carried out a surprise raid on Tokyo, Roosevelt at a press conference jocularly stated that they came from "our new secret base at Shangri-La," the imaginary Tibetan mountain fastness in Hilton's novel. He later appropriated the name for his mountain hideaway, the location of which was kept secret for wartime security reasons.

President Eisenhower developed the camp so extensively that it now bears little resemblance to the simple installation of Roosevelt's day. Eisenhower renamed it for his grandson David Eisenhower.

A scrapbook on the selection and development of Shangri-La, with copious photographs, plans, and renderings, was compiled at the time by the Interior Department and is deposited at the Roosevelt Library at Hyde Park.

Share Our Wealth Plan

See Long, Huey Pierce

Shelterbelt

See Conservation

Sherwood, Robert Emmet

(4 April 1896–14 November 1955)

Speech writer for FDR and propagandist as director, Overseas Division, Office of War Information, 1942–44. Robert E. Sherwood was born in New Rochelle, New York. Educated at Milton Academy and Harvard, he was an undistinguished student who left Harvard in 1917 to enlist in the Canadian Expeditionary Force (having been rejected by the U.S. Army). Gassed and wounded in France, he returned to the United States disillusioned and determined to oppose future wars.

His war experience convinced him that as an artist he must remain outside politics, yet the reality of the rise of fascism moved Sherwood to political activity and eventually into the Roosevelt administration. Sherwood won his first Pulitzer Prize in 1936 for his antiwar play, *Idiot's Delight.* Yet by 1937 his pacifism had begun to wane. "It's astonishing," he wrote in his diary, "I'm ready to cheer newsreels of the U.S. Navy steaming out of Pearl Harbor to go trounce the Japs." The Nazi-Soviet pact and the Russian attack on Finland persuaded him that intellectuals needed to use words as a weapon against fascism. In *There Shall Be No Night* (Pulitzer Prize, 1941) Sherwood presented a powerful argument that men, however much they might dislike violence, had to stand and fight against aggression.

After Sherwood joined William Allen White's Committee to Defend America in May 1940, he was drawn into the Roosevelt administration in August of the same year by Harry Hopkins and Judge Samuel Rosenman to work as a speech writer for the president. His evolution from dramatist to propagandist was a natural progression of his commitment. In Sherwood's view, all information "should be considered as though it were a continuous speech by the President." Sherwood took great delight in working with FDR and in hearing his words spoken by a man he greatly admired. To Sherwood, writing for FDR was theater of the highest order.

In June 1942, Sherwood joined the Office of War Information (OWI) as director of the Overseas Division. While his talents were well used as a speech writer for the president, his tenure in OWI was less gratifying. He advocated a strategy of truth for overseas propaganda and developed an effective shortwave broadcasting network that evolved into the Voice of America. Fiercely independent and proud of his personal working relationship with FDR, Sherwood fought with his peers and superiors. After a public battle with OWI director Elmer Davis, Sherwood resigned from OWI in September 1944 and once again worked as a speech writer for FDR's reelection. The victory in 1944 was satisfying, but FDR's sudden death in 1945 ended his official political involvement.

Sherwood tried, but failed, to regain his stature as a playwright in the postwar world, although he did win an Academy Award in 1946 for his screenplay *The Best Years of Our Lives.* Sherwood's ultimate tribute to F.D.R. came with the publication of *Roosevelt and Hopkins* in 1948. The book brought Sherwood his fourth and perhaps most satisfying Pulitzer Prize. At the age of fifty-nine, he died in New York in 1955.

For pertinent writings by Robert Sherwood, see "The Power of Truth," *Vital Speeches,* 1 November 1942, pp. 61–62; "He Was a Great Political Genius," *New Republic,* 15 April 1946; and *Roosevelt and Hopkins: An Intimate History* (New York: Harper & Bros., 1948). For more information on Sherwood himself, see John Mason Brown, *The Ordeal of a Playwright: Robert E. Sherwood and the Challenge of War* (New York: Harper & Row, 1968) and *The Worlds of Robert E. Sherwood: Mirror to His Times, 1896–1939* (New York: Harper & Row, 1965); and Walter J. Meserve, *Robert E. Sherwood: Reluctant Moralist* (New York: Pegasus, 1970).

GREGORY D. BLACK

See also Office of War Information

Sick Chicken Decision

See Interstate Commerce

Sinclair, Upton

(20 September 1878–25 November 1968)

Writer and radical activist whose 1934 campaign for governor of California made him one of the most widely known utopian reformers of the depression. Upton Beall Sinclair, Jr., was born in Baltimore to genteel but impoverished parents. He began writing novels while in college, but his best-selling fictionalized indictment of Chicago meat packers, *The Jungle* (1906), launched him on a new career as a spokesman for radical causes. At first associated with the Socialist party, which had commissioned *The Jungle,* Sinclair became increasingly independent in his views.

He had achieved an international reputation as a forthright if eccentric social commentator when in 1933 he was persuaded to seek the next year's Democratic nomination for governor of California, where he had lived since 1915. His "End Poverty in California" (EPIC) program, compellingly set forth in a pamphlet called *I, Governor of California,* attracted most attention for its demand that idle farmland and factories be turned over to self-sustaining cooperatives of the unemployed. Sinclair's pamphlets and a massive grass-roots effort won him the Democratic nomination in August 1934 over three other contenders. His chances of election improved further when the state's Democratic regulars made a truce with EPIC forces and especially after President Roosevelt was favorably impressed by Sinclair after a meeting at Hyde Park in September. However, vicious and well-orchestrated attacks on Sinclair's radical reputation by Republicans and business interests persuaded Roosevelt's forces to abandon EPIC as a lost cause. Sinclair lost to Republican governor Merriam in the November 1934 election by 250,000 votes.

THE DETROIT FREE PRESS

'Jimandupton,' the Democratic Zebra

OH, UPTON!

HALF SOCIALIST AND HALF TAMMANY

SOCIALIST SINCLAIR

BOSS "CALL ME JIM" FARLEY

Orr, Detroit Free Press, *c. 1935.*

Nonetheless, the EPIC movement had attracted nationwide sympathy and left a strong liberal Democratic presence in California. Sinclair returned to his writing, which he continued almost up to his death at age ninety in 1968.

The most useful account of Sinclair and EPIC can be found in Arthur M. Schlesinger, Jr., *The Politics of Upheaval* (Boston: Houghton Mifflin Co., 1960). Greg Mitchell, "Summer of '34," *Working Papers* (November-December 1982):28–36, and (January-February 1983):18–27, gives an idea of how EPIC operated at the local level. Sinclair's own statement of his aims and impression of the campaign may be found in Upton Sinclair, *I, Governor of California* (Los Angeles, 1933) and *I, Candidate for Governor and How I Got Licked* (Pasadena: The author, 1935). See also Sinclair's *Autobiography* (New York: Harcourt, Brace, 1962). A succinct account of Sinclair's lengthy literary and political career is Jon A. Yoder, *Upton Sinclair* (New York: Frederick Ungar, 1975).

See also Democratic Party; Election of 1934

Smith, Alfred E.

(30 December 1873–4 October 1944)

Governor of New York and 1928 presidential candidate of the Democratic party. The leading Democratic politician of a Republican era, Alfred E. Smith successfully contested four of five gubernatorial elections before gaining the presidential nomination in 1928. His subsequent career, however, was marked by defeat in a bitterly fought campaign, estrangement from

Roosevelt, his successor in Albany, a failed renomination bid, and ultimately Smith's repudiation of his party's leadership and policies.

The realities of Al Smith's heritage belied several of the stereotypes that arose during his public career. Hailed as the hero of the nation's "new immigrant," Al Smith's American roots stretched back beyond the middle of the nineteenth century. Despite benefiting politically from his humble origins, Smith experienced a fairly comfortable childhood in the Lower East Side neighborhood of New York City where his forebears had lived for two generations. Excoriated as an advocate of lax morality, Smith was a fiercely respectable homebody who dissented from Victorian values only on the matter of Prohibition, which he viewed as an affront to the cultural heritage of his fellow Catholics.

The death of his father followed by the illness of his mother caused Al Smith to abandon school for employment at the age of fourteen. Within four years, he was earning the relatively munificent sum of $15 per week as clerk for a firm dealing in wholesale fish. Later he would joke of having earned a degree from FFM—the Fulton Fish Market. But politics and the theater were the true passions of a young man who craved public acclaim. An accomplished amateur actor, he also lent his oratorical skills to the service of Tammany Hall.

In 1895, at the age of twenty-one, Smith found his service rewarded with a post in the municipal court system summoning citizens to jury duty. For nearly a decade, however, Smith failed to realize his ambition to seek public office. Not until 1903 did he receive the call from Tammany that he would be nominated for State Assembly.

Assemblyman Smith proved to be an effective debater, an adroit legislative craftsman, a fanatical worker, and a Tammany loyalist untainted by corruption. These qualities rapidly propelled him to the majority leadership of the State Assembly, a post that landed him the vice-chairmanship of the commission investigating factory conditions in the wake of the Triangle Shirtwaist Company fire of 1911. Service on the investigating commission was a turning point in Smith's career. It sensitized him to the plight of working-class people and to the political value of serving their needs through state action rather than through simple intervention by a political machine.

In 1915, Smith quit the assembly in favor of the post of sheriff of New York County with its lucrative fees. Three years later he gained the first of his four terms as governor, losing only in the Harding landslide of 1920. As governor, Smith earned a national reputation as a progressive concerned both with social welfare and efficiency in government.

During a protracted struggle that lasted through his tenure in Albany, Smith reorganized the agencies of government and gained adoption of an executive budget that transferred fiscal initiative from the legislature to the governor. While Al Smith sought to restrain taxation and curb wasteful spending, he simultaneously pioneered an expansion of public projects through the expedient of state bond financing. The

Alfred E. Smith, 28 February 1928. Artist: S. J. Woolf. (National Portrait Gallery, Smithsonian Institution.)

governor tried and failed to gain a state housing bank and public power legislation, but succeeded in winning expanded workmen's compensation laws, mothers' pensions, and laws regulating work by women and children.

At the Democratic National Convention of 1924—which was deeply divided over the symbolic issue of denouncing the Ku Klux Klan—Smith mustered enough support from the northern urban wing of the party to hold the southern favorite William Gibbs McAdoo below the two-thirds vote necessary for nomination. It was at this convention that Franklin D. Roosevelt, in his speech placing the governor's name in nomination, first dubbed Al Smith "the Happy Warrior of the political battlefield." After a numbing 103 ballots and the withdrawal of both principal contenders, the convention settled on dark-horse candidate John W. Davis. Four years later, Smith gained the nomination with relative ease, only to lose decisively in an election marked by sectarian attacks on his Catholicism.

While Al Smith lost his home state of New York, gubernatorial nominee Franklin D. Roosevelt squeaked by with a plurality of 25,564 votes. Ironically, Roosevelt would likely not have prevailed without anti-Semitic votes cast against his Jewish opponent Albert Ottinger.

Al Smith, the now unhappy warrior, soon found himself to be an elder statesman without much honor in either state or nation. Although Governor Roosevelt acknowledged Smith's influence on his plans for New York State, he neither consulted with his predecessor nor appointed Smith cronies to state office. Undue association with Smith and his coterie could only impede FDR's efforts to bolster his own reputation.

In national politics, Smith increasingly became identified as the captive of a few northern businessmen, dominated by financial wizard John J. Raskob, Smith's choice to manage his 1928 campaign. Party leaders, moreover, were convinced that Smith's religion was a continuing liability. Ironically, the better the Democratic prospects for victory in 1932, the less likely the renomination of Al Smith. Ultimately, he was able only to stand first among the several contenders that temporarily impeded FDR's path to the nomination.

Although Smith begrudgingly campaigned for the Democratic ticket in 1932, his regard for FDR had long since become tinged with feelings of bitterness and betrayal. Increasingly he found himself at odds with New Deal policies as well. Pressed forward by the businessmen who were now Smith's closest associates, he became the leading light of the Liberty League, formed in 1934 as an outlet for conservative criticism of the New Deal and FDR. Once the staunchest of Democrats, Al Smith supported Alf Landon for president in 1936 and Wendell Willkie in 1940.

Al Smith's brand of progressivism foreshadowed elements of the New Deal. Yet his break with FDR was not entirely an aberration founded on personal disappointment. Smith and many like-minded progressives combined humanitarian impulse and concern for efficiency with a suspicion of government interference in business and a distrust of high taxes and redistributive spending. The Happy Warrior of American politics was neither an ideologically consistent conservative nor the uncredited architect of New Deal reform.

Matthew and Hannah Josephson, *Al Smith: Hero of the Cities* (Boston: Houghton Mifflin Co., 1969) draws heavily on the papers of Frances Perkins in tracing the political career of the Happy Warrior. Like other biographies, it is handicapped both by a lack of Smith papers and by a limited canvass of other manuscript material. Richard O'Connor, *The First Hurrah: A Biography of Alfred E. Smith* (New York: G. P. Putnam's Sons, 1970) is the only other recent biography of Al Smith. It covers essentially the same ground as the Josephsons' and relies mainly on secondary sources. Paula Eldot, *Governor Alfred E. Smith: The Politician as Reformer* (New York: Garland Publishing Co., 1983) is a thorough, competent, and largely celebratory account of Smith's tenure as governor of New York State. It argues that Smith's innovations established the crucial precedents for FDR's policymaking as both governor and president. Samuel B. Hand, in "Al Smith, Franklin D. Roosevelt, and the New Deal: Some Comments on Perspective," *Historian* (1965):366–81, discusses Smith's apostacy during the New Deal, arguing that his break with FDR is best explained not by personal disappointment but by Smith's consistently conservative approach to economic policy.

ALLAN J. LICHTMAN

See also American Liberty League; Catholics; Democratic Party; Election of 1928; Elections in the Roosevelt Era; Governor of New York; Liberalism and Progressivism; Perkins, Frances; Prohibition; Tammany Hall

Socialism

Socialism in the age of FDR was expressed in many parts of American life—in novels, essays, splinter political movements such as that of novelist Upton Sinclair in his EPIC campaign in California in 1934. But essentially the history of socialism in those years was that of the Socialist Party of American (SPA). The party had been shattered on the rock of schism in 1919, the result being a debilitated organization and rival communist parties. Only in the late 1920s, when Norman Thomas came onto center stage, did the party begin a slow climb back. A Presbyterian minister in earlier days and a follower of Walter Rauschenbusch, Thomas was a convert to the social gospel, to Christian pacifism during the war, and gradually to socialism. Thus, he came to the party through the ministry and not, like Eugene Debs earlier, out of the working class. As a college graduate, he appealed to intellectuals, again unlike Debs whose largest constituency was in the labor movement.

By 1929 and the great crash, Thomas was surrogate for socialism in America, and he steered the SPA through the so-called Red Decade. Evoking a fervid optimism and confidence for radicals, this decade would convince them that the public was now ready for their ideas and for their challenge to the citadels of power. For SP'ers, the economic downturn confirmed their own diagnosis of the capitalist system. The fact of a revived party spirit and a growing rank and file was further proof. By the early 1930s, the party had a larger membership than at any time since 1923 and no longer seemed comatose, though it still lacked the optimism and youthful energy of the prewar decade.

For all his charisma, however, Thomas could not hold things together, as the tendency of American radicalism to fracture repeated itself. The SPA's composition assured as much. Its mix of pacifists, older Jewish trade unionists (the dominant Old Guard element), and youthful militants was highly volatile. Beginning in 1931, the youthful left wing, composed mostly of those unscarred by earlier factionalism, challenged the leadership of Morris Hillquit and the Old Guard. These "romantic leftists," in Reinhold Niebuhr's pejorative term, were more militant than those who, by virtue of age, occupied senior leadership positions in the party. They had, Hillquit observed, "the natural impetuosity of recent converts"; their "fundamental differences of view," he acknowledged, took the form of open sympathy toward the USSR, criticism of the party's parliamentary tactics, and demands for greater union activities and, after 1938, for a united front with Communists on a number of issues. Leaning in their direction and distrusting his own generation, Thomas nonetheless sought to modify this sweeping endorsement of Russian Communism, while Old Guardists, like *New Leader* editor James Oneal opposed it and went down to defeat. In 1933, the death of Hillquit, the ablest of the Old Guard, ignited a power struggle between the two warring factions, which flared out of control at the 1934 party national convention in Detroit.

The left-wing delegates pressed a declaration of principles that pledged support of Russia, proposed to meet "any international war . . . by mass resistance," and argued for a nonparliamentary route to power—that is, for conforming to "basic revolutionary principles"—always the specter haunting Old Guard socialists. It was, after all, the hateful prospect raised by Communists who, the Old Guard claimed, rejected peaceful, ballot-box, reformist means. Thomas, while fearing that revolutionary politics could lead only to the hermeticism of a sect—"the Party would sign its own death warrant by such a declaration"— was nonetheless troubled by the Old Guard's social pathology. "It is thoroughly unhealthy," he wrote Hillquit as early as 1926, "that the one issue on which a great many of our comrades tend to arouse themselves, the one thing that brings into their eyes the old light of battle, is their hatred of communism." Thomas carried the day in Detroit, and the impassioned pleas of Old Guard New York socialist leader Louis Waldman against the 1934 declaration as "anarchistic, illegal and communist" were rebuffed by the large majority of delegates.

The conflict, rather than abating, simply heated up. It became more bitter, more uncompromising; and thus it paralleled comparable divisions in all radical groups, which were also crippled by discord, contradictions, and doctrinal rigidity. Matters were exacerbated by the entry, in growing numbers, of youthful radicals out of colleges and theological seminaries. These socialist novitiates equated the Kingdom of God with socialism, believed it attainable in their lifetime, and embraced militant tactics and programs. Hence they were hardly the safe social democrats desired by the Old Guard. In May 1938, New York's Old Guard, the key right-wing group, bolted the party, with Waldman acting as the Pied Piper. Following him were New York's leading socialist trade unionists, major socialist institutions like the Rand School, and the Pennsylvania state majority led by the influential Reading leadership. Bridgeport's socialists, including Jasper McLevy, as well as factions in the Indiana and Oregon state organizations also joined the parade. They left a weakened party to Thomas, the militants, and the rank-and-file loyalists, a total of about twelve thousand, little more than half the 1934 total.

The party had thus divided along lines not very different from those apparent at the 1901 founding convention—namely, generational, tactical, and ideological—and the struggle for power emerged out of them. Possibly doctrinal conflict had primacy. But the need to protect their bureaucratic turf in part precipitated the Old Guard reaction to the younger antagonists. Further, for those involved, the 1934 contest was laced with their belief that capitalism was doomed. The depression had been a tocsin. Buoyed by the possibility of an immediate social eruption, they thought their decisions would directly affect the course of history.

Paradoxically, however, the SPA remained loyal to its reformist vision, "immediatist" demands, and parliamentarian orientation; and it entered the political lists in 1936, as it had in 1932, with a program of meliorative reform within the capitalist system. As such, the party gave oblique testimony to its ongoing theoretical poverty. Indeed, with the possible exception of Lewis Corey, not one major or original theoretician emerged during the depression decade.

The 1936 election returns reflected a modest resurgence in socialist fortunes, but internal divisions remained to plague the SPA. Moreover, the admission of splinter-group Communists—the Trotskyite, Lovestoneite, and Gitlow factions—sharpened the struggle for control of the party and its local units. Even the militants did not speak with a single voice. Some of them were eager to work with the American Labor party (ALP), a New York State–based third party founded in 1936 by garment unionists and Old Guard socialists—with the CPA in the same unlikely political bed—who wished to support Roosevelt but not on the Democratic party ticket. But others, adherents to revolutionary socialism, formed a new group, Clarity. It included Trotskyites, drummed out of communist ranks in 1928, as well as other expelled CP'ers—the followers of Lovestone, Gitlow, or Zam— all of them past masters of Byzantine politics and hairsplitting doctrinal debate, which they had refined to a sharp theological edge. With such recruits, Bernard Johnpoll concluded, it would be impossible for the Socialist party to remain cohesive and effective.

Most Trotskyites did not join Clarity, though sharing its suspicions of the ALP, its hostility to reformist politics, and its concern with the Lovestoneite charge that the SPA was a mass reformist party that blocked revolutionary tactics. But they and Clarity socialists were at odds over some critical issues, such as Trotskyite allegiance to the Fourth International, the publication of their own journal, and their refusal to follow official party policy—the initial condition for their admission into party ranks. And it would eventually be the Clarity bloc, collaborating with the militants, that successfully pressed the party's purge of Trotskyites in 1937.

The SPA majority, heirs of the once-messianic organization that sought the "truly human" promised land, had become accommodationist. The trend toward immediatist and collaborationist practices had been linear and long term, with some fitful exceptions. After all, there was the growing menace of fascism and Nazi anti-Semitism, and Roosevelt's stated aversion to fascist aggression was appealing. Furthermore, however humane in their long-range intentions, socialists had long cooperated with those seeking a shorter work week, old-age insurance, federal and state unemployment compensation, and public works for the needy, that is, endorsing immediate demands that had nothing whatever to do with making socialism versus communism a public issue. Official party dicta, to be sure, arraigned the New Deal, arguing that it could offer no more than minor palliatives for a sick society. It was, so the charge went, "a capitalist scheme," a harbinger of imperialism. Roosevelt's program, Thomas claimed, simply adopted some of the "immediatist" demands of the party platform. That Thomas noted this angrily is significant, since Roosevelt produced frustration and, according to John Laslett, "vast ideological confusion" for socialists, indeed for all radicals. Not only did the New Deal program, however inadequate, preempt much of their domestic program, it became a lodestar for many trade union leaders and for workers generally, as well as for Old Guard socialists, who viewed the reformist administration as an important step forward, preparing the way for socialism. That Roosevelt's program was dedicated to reviving capitalism seemed, for American labor, an unimportant observation. His provisions for Social Security, collective bargaining, and raising wage and living standards were what counted. Understandably, then, the party attracted meager labor support in the 1930s, even in traditionally radical voting blocs, like steel and garment workers, or coal miners, with virtually all of them flocking to the Democratic standard-bearer. Thus the SPA's hallowed doctrinal reliance upon the working class was decisively undermined and, it should be noted, by labor itself. This suggests that not even a united party would have much altered the national scene, that not even economic deprivation roused the exploited and revolutionized consciousness, and that, we may speculate, the system's capacity for accommodation, the identification of communism and socialism in the popular mind, the high degree of mobility, were in the end decisive.

The party's dilemma was clear enough. It had campaigned for immediate reforms, and these were now embodied in New Deal statutes. Small wonder, then, that Roosevelt's administration had massive labor support. SPA leadership might claim that the National Recovery Administration did not offer "permanent protection against the evils of capitalism" attack the "broad and undefined powers" the statute gave to the executive office," and prophesy that "fascism will be the next step." The Civilian Conservation Corps might be dismissed for its "proposed labor camps." And the entire New Deal program might be viewed as a "capitalist" scheme to "fool" the workers. But the hungry laborers, poverty-stricken farmers, and unemployed youth were not convinced.

Small wonder, then, that Thomas would be frustrated, that defections to the Democratic party rolls, especially at voting time, would be significant, and that the swing toward Roosevelt by 1938 was plain, even to the most astigmatic socialists. By this election year, Thomas's vote had slipped under 200,000, plummeting in every city and state, and it was only a portent of worse things to come. By 1938, SPA membership had dropped to 7,000, a third of the 1934 total; and it was reduced to 2,000 by 1941. Thomas, in sum, was partly right in explaining the 1936 results: "What cut the ground pretty completely out from under us was this. It was Roosevelt in a word." What he neglected to state was equally apparent: that the Socialist party no longer offered a genuine alternative and deserved what happened to it in the 1930s.

For his part, Roosevelt, pragmatist and opportunist that he was, would reform capitalism, not destroy it. Inspired by the noblesse oblige of the Hudson River landed gentry in which he was reared and raised in an atmosphere pervaded by progressivism, which drenched his years at Groton, Harvard, and Albany, Roosevelt absorbed its lessons of social and economic amelioration, of the positive state, as well as its retention of the system of private enterprise and private profit. He would improve the system's operations, while accepting its basic economic premises. Hence, while willing to accept socialist votes and even adopting an occasional socialist proposal like unemployment compensation, his sotto voce dismissal of socialist premises and doctrines was understandable.

There is no large and comprehensive study of the failure of American socialism. At least none provides a major overview of radicalism in the twentieth century, and none deals with the Socialist party and the New Deal. Relevant chapters and sections, however, may be found in most standard works on socialism, such as Daniel Bell's *Marxian Socialism in the United States* (Princeton: Princeton University Press, 1967), which was originally published in Donald D. Egbert and Stow Person's two-volume *Socialism and American Life* (Princeton: Princeton University Press, 1952) under the title, "The Background and Development of Marxian Socialism in the United States." Chapters 11 and 12 are especially useful for those interested in party policies and actions in the 1930s. David Shannon's *The Socialist Party of America* (New York: Macmillan, 1955) is a conventional, carefully detailed, informative account of the party's history, with chapters 9 and 10, on the SPA in the New Deal years being most useful. Frank Warren's *An Alternative Vision: The Socialist Party in the 1930s* (Bloomington: Indiana University Press, 1974) should be consulted. In the course of defending party tactics, he disagrees with Bell and others who have characterized Norman Thomas as "utopian," "impractical," or "doctrinaire." Thomas, he argues, was a realist who steered a correct course in insisting upon the struggle for union democracy and industrial unionism. The vignette of Max Schachtman, in Rita Simon, ed., *As We Saw the Thirties* (Urbana: University of Illinois Press, 1967) is helpful on the Trotskyites and the Socialist party. So, too, are the relevant chapters in Constance Myers's *The Prophet's Army: Trotsky in America, 1928–1941* (Westport, Conn.: Greenwood Press, 1977). And William Seyler's detailed account of party organization, divisions, and tactics, "The Rise and Decline of the Socialist Party of the United States" (Ph.D. diss., Duke University, 1952), is a valuable study for those interested in the party's internal difficulties in the 1930s. Martin Diamond's "The Problems of the SP after World War One," in John Laslett and Seymour Lipset, eds., *Failure of a Dream?* (Garden City, N.Y.: Doubleday, 1974) is also illuminating on the SP in the depression decade. Finally, for a discussion of the Popular Front, with incidental comments on the Socialist party, chapter 5 of James Weinstein's *Ambiguous Legacy* (New York: New Viewpoints, 1975) is useful.

MILTON CANTOR

See also Niebuhr, Reinhold; Thomas, Norman Mattoon

Social Security

By the time Franklin Roosevelt was elected president, most Americans recognized that the vicissitudes of late life, which perennially had caused individual woes, were fast becoming a societal problem. Only 3 percent of the population was over sixty-five in 1870. Sixty years later, the proportion of older Americans had nearly doubled. As the aged's numbers increased, their economic situation deteriorated. About 70 percent of all elderly men were gainfully employed in 1870, largely as farmers. By 1930, only 33.1 percent of all men and 8.1 percent of all women over sixty-five were in the labor force. Age discrimination in the marketplace and other social institutions was rampant. Private and public resources to deal with old-age dependency were minimal. Only 15 percent of the labor force was covered by pension plans, and only eighteen states had enacted old-age assistance laws, providing on the average a dollar a day to beneficiaries who satisfied strict residency requirements and means tests.

The Great Depression had a devastating impact on the elderly. Unemployment among older workers, estimated at 30 percent, exceeded the national average. Bankrupt corporations and savings institutions lacked the money to pay the elderly the funds upon which they had counted. Families and charities bemoaned the aged's plight, but found the burden of caring for them unbearable. In this context, Americans demanded a novel solution to the financial difficulties of growing old. But it proved to be one thing to demand that Washington do something and quite another to enact legislation that would satisfy the needs of different age groups and various segments of the population.

Millions of frustrated older people rallied to support Dr. Francis E. Townsend's scheme to give everyone over sixty $200 a month on the conditions that they quit working and spend each month's pension within thirty days. Although the "experts" dismissed the Townsend plan as a utopian panacea, few underestimated the need to defuse public clamor. The American Federation of Labor, reversing its earlier stance, called for federal intervention. Senator Clarence Dill and Congressman William Connery offered several bills in the Seventy-third Congress to establish a system of old-age relief at the state level partially underwritten by federal revenues. In February 1934, Senator Robert Wagner and Congressman David J. Lewis introduced a bill designed to accelerate states' efforts to enact unemployment insurance laws. Some wanted the United States to provide universal pensions as many Scandinavian countries did. Others thought that the nation should institute a contributory insurance system for wage earners, as Germany, Austria, and France had done. Still others thought that states should take greater initiative in this area.

Franklin Delano Roosevelt was the first incumbent president to advocate legislation offering some protection against old-age dependency and promoting unemployment insurance. "If, as our Constitution tells us, our Federal Government was established, among other things, 'to promote the general welfare,' " Roosevelt declared on 8 June 1934, "it is our plain duty to provide for that security upon which welfare depends." The president envisioned a program national in scope, with the states and the federal government sharing responsibility for its financing and administration. A prototype was the progressive New York State old-age assistance law enacted in 1930 (while FDR was governor), which required relief to all needy residents over sixty-five and provided that the state share with localities the cost of the pension. Even so, the president realized that any bill faced serious philosophical, political, economic, and constitutional obstacles. Indeed, he had chosen not to act until the economy had begun to recover and until the first round of public agitation and congressional debate had identified the salient issues and put major options into sharper focus.

On 29 June 1934, Roosevelt through Executive Order 6757 created the Committee on Economic Security, chaired by Secretary of Labor Frances Perkins and consisting of Secretary of the Treasury Henry Morgenthau, Attorney General Homer Cummings, Secretary of Agriculture Henry A. Wallace, and Harry L. Hopkins, the Federal Emergency Relief administrator. At the same time, an Advisory Council, including such distinguished figures as William Green, Mary Dewson, University of North Carolina president Frank P. Graham, *Survey* editor Paul Kellogg, General Electric president Gerald Swope, and the National Catholic Welfare Conference's Mgsr. John A. Ryan, was created. Ultimately, eight other advisory subcommittees were established. Edwin Witte, a professor of economics at the University of Wisconsin, served as executive director, supervising the work of government bureaucrats, academic consultants, actuaries, and attorneys.

Roosevelt received recommendations from the Committee on Economic Security on 15 January 1935 and two days later transmitted them to Congress. The House Ways and Means Committee held hearings from 21 January to 12 February and then spent two months reworking the language and order of legislative particulars; it also changed the title of the bill from the Economic Security Act to the Social Security Act. On 19 April, the House approved the measure by a 371–33 margin. The Senate, after amending the House bill, endorsed its version by a 77–6 vote on 19 June. A conference committee struggled for nearly two months to reconcile differences; its report was accepted in the House on 8 August and a day later in the Senate. President Roosevelt signed Social Security into law on 14 August 1935.

The omnibus measure delicately balanced contradictory principles and a mixture of traditional and experimental approaches. Congress initially appropriated $49,750,000 to establish a federal-state program of old-age assistance (OAA) under Title I. To reduce the incidence of dependency in the future (and thereby reduce the cost of OAA from an estimated $1.3 billion to $500 million by 1980), an old-age insurance scheme (Title II) was instituted. At first, only 60 percent of the labor force, mainly employees in commerce and industry, were expected to pay a tax on the first $3,000 of covered wages. Older Americans were not the only potential beneficiaries under Social Security. An unemployment insurance program was created, and other titles allocated grants-in-aid to states to provide funds for dependent mothers and children, the blind, and public health services.

The constitutionality of this federally sponsored "general welfare" package was immediately challenged. In two separate decisions on 24 May 1937, however, the Supreme Court upheld the right of Congress to address problems that were "plainly national in area and dimensions." The Court's action facilitated efforts to expand the Social Security system. Amendments passed in 1939 authorized supplemental benefits for dependents of retired workers and for their survivors in case of death. Although many supported further liberalizations, such as those proposed in the Wagner-Murray-Dingell bill (1943), no expansion took place; Congress postponed scheduled increases in benefits and tax rates. Winning the war took precedence over everything else.

In his 1944 State of the Union address, however, President Roosevelt promulgated a majestic "second Bill of Rights," based on his earlier promises and reports of the now defunct National Resources Planning Board. FDR itemized eight "rights," including access to adequate medical care and the means sufficient to enjoy a comfortable old age: "All of these rights spell security . . . to new goals of happiness and well-being." At the time of his death, however, it was not clear how many citizens shared FDR's belief that the federal government should assume primary responsibility for ensuring this new basis of individual and national security.

The Social Security Board's *Social Security in America* (Washington, D.C.: U.S. Government Printing Office, 1937) provides detailed summaries of staff reports to the Committee on Economic Security (1934–35). J. Douglas Brown offers a succinct summary of *The Genesis of Social Security in America* (Princeton: Princeton University, Industrial Relations Section, 1969), and Edwin Witte's *The Development of the Social Security Act* (Madison: University of Wisconsin Press, 1962) makes accessible the executive director's confidential memorandum tracing the legislative history of the original bill. Martha Derthick's prize-winning *Policymaking for Social Security* (Washington, D.C.: Brookings Institution, 1979) traces the history of Social Security through the mid-1970s, and Carolyn Weaver develops a conservative critique in *The Crisis in Social Security: Economic and Political Origins* (Durham, N.C.: Duke University Press Policy Studies, 1982). More than 2,500 books, articles, public documents, and technical reports have been conveniently annotated in U.S., Department of Health and Human Services, *Basic Readings in Social Security* (Washington, D.C.: U.S. Government Printing Office, 1981).

W. ANDREW ACHENBAUM

See also Dewson, Mary W.; New Deal; Perkins, Frances; Relief; Taxation; Townsend, Francis E., M.D.

Soil Conservation Service

See Agricultural Adjustment Administration; Conservation; Tugwell, Rexford Guy

South, The

Franklin Roosevelt was not a southerner, but, in biographer Frank Freidel's words, he knew the South "uncommonly well, loved it, and aspired to bring it a richer, more noble future." He had a second home in Georgia from a time soon after he arrived in October 1924 at Warm Springs, where the buoyant mineral waters flowing at nearly 90 degrees helped him exercise leg muscles damaged by the effects of polio. There, in 1927, he established the Georgia Warm Springs Foundation, a nonprofit corporation that developed the springs as a health spa. In 1932 he completed the cottage that soon became known as the Little White House.

He mingled on friendly terms with the region's politicians and the people around Warm Springs. He developed nearby timber lands and demonstrated diversified agriculture and cattle breeding to neighboring farmers. His Georgia experience, Roosevelt often said, had important effects on his thinking. High electric bills at Warm Springs, for instance, set him on the path to the Tennessee Valley Authority. Poor schools and other problems in the area convinced him that the region's greatest challenge was poverty, the source of countless deficiencies. In 1931, after a con-

Berryman, Washington Star, *18 July 1938.*

ference on regionalism in Charlottesville, Virginia, he talked informally about the South's needs for land planning, agricultural resettlement, factory-farm living, increased milk production, and other problems.

Southern leaders enlisted in his presidential campaign from the start, and when the Democratic National Convention met in late June 1932, Roosevelt had the votes of every southern delegation except three that backed favorite sons. Among them, only John Nance Garner had a chance to become a serious candidate, but he finally threw his support to Roosevelt and accepted the vice-presidential nomination. In the New Deal administration, as in Woodrow Wilson's, many southerners held high office and dominated congressional chairmanships by virtue of their seniority, and Roosevelt's cordial relations with them stood him in good stead on Capitol Hill.

In the bustle of the hundred days in 1933, congressional leaders had limited influence on policy, but Roosevelt relied heavily on the parliamentary expertise of southern leaders. Southern influence was especially apparent in farm policy. Acreage limitations, price-support loans, marketing quotas, soil conservation—all were ideas that had gestated in southern farmer movements. The Federal Deposit Insurance Corporation was set up largely at the insistence of Congressman Henry Steagall of Alabama. On occasion, radical pressures from southerners would move Roosevelt: when Elmer Thomas of Oklahoma pushed inflation, when Hugo Black of Alabama precipitated the National Industrial Recovery Act in response to his proposed thirty-hour day, or when Huey Long inadvertently provided an impetus for the "soak-the-rich" tax and the Social Security Act as measures to undercut Long's Share Our Wealth plan.

Roosevelt's New Deal affected the South in a number of ways. The agricultural programs broke the old cycles of cotton culture and opened the way for new crops and pasturelands. These, plus the work of the Soil Conservation Service, changed the very ap-

pearance of exhausted lands scarred by erosion. Southern industry, given over largely to consumer nondurables, weathered the depression better than other regions. By 1936 a new expansion was under way with the encouragement of growing public programs of industrial growth. Under the Wagner National Labor Relations Act, a labor movement finally emerged in the region, still weak but at last something more than a vehicle for sporadic revolt.

Seeds of the later civil rights movement were planted in the Roosevelt years. In 1930 the National Association for the Advancement of Colored People began laying plans for a legal assault on segregation. Roosevelt never gave a high priority to the affairs of blacks, but he tolerated people in his administration who did. By 1936 there was a Black Cabinet of some thirty to forty advisers in government departments and agencies. Eleanor Roosevelt by word and deed signaled concern about discrimination and acted as White House intermediary for black leaders. On the grounds that the depression (and later, World War II) took priority, Roosevelt declined to endorse a federal antilynching bill, but in 1941, facing a black march on Washington movement, he issued Executive Order 8802, which set up the Committee on Fair Employment Practices (FEPC) to promote nondiscrimination in defense industries. Black voters during the 1930s moved in growing numbers to the Democratic party. It was the most seismic and enduring change in the political landscape during that decade.

For the South the New Deal era was a time of unusually active intellectual, as well as social and political, ferment. It was the time of the Vanderbilt Agrarians and the Chapel Hill Regionalists, who offered new visions of the regional identity, a period during which the Southern Renaissance in literature reached maturity. A great body of social and economic analyses and an extensive literature of social exploration and descriptive journalism appeared. But the discussion of southern problems had a way of slipping back into the timeworn channels of sectionalism.

Roosevelt increasingly acquired political enemies on a geographic basis. Nearly every New Deal program inadvertently triggered sectional opposition. The crop limitations antagonized the cotton trade, which thrived on quantity; the recovery program annoyed industrialists with codes and labor standards; relief policies raised questions of regional wage differentials. The roots of rebellion lay in what one political scientist labeled the "county-seat elites," and one newsman called "a certain type, the small-town rich man." For such people the New Deal jeopardized a power that rested on the control of property, labor, credit, and local government. Relief projects reduced dependency; labor standards raised wages; farm programs upset landlord-tenant relationships; government credit bypassed bankers; new federal programs skirted county commissioners and even state agencies.

The trends became more ominous to the power structure in 1935 during the second hundred days, when the emphasis swung from recovery to reform with such measures as the Works Progress Administration, Social Security, the Wagner Act, the "soak-the-rich" tax, and later the Farm Tenant Act and the Housing Act of 1937 and the Fair Labor Standards Act of 1938. "Northernization" of the congressional Democrats after overwhelming victories increased the tensions. In 1936 the Democratic convention eliminated the two-thirds rule for nominations, thereby removing the South's veto power, and seated black delegates. South Carolina's senator "Cotton Ed" Smith took one look at a black minister who rose to pronounce the invocation and walked out of the convention.

Abortive anti-Roosevelt electoral slates in 1936 got few votes but proved harbingers of things to come. An effective opposition did not coalesce until Roosevelt provoked a constitutional crisis in 1937 with his Court-packing proposal. Roosevelt later claimed that he lost the battle but won the war. The Senate blocked his bill, but the Court changed its interpretation on several important points, and a vacancy gave Roosevelt the chance to name his first appointee, Hugo Black of Alabama. But his pyrrhic victory divided his party. For the first time southern congressmen, previously inhibited by Roosevelt's popularity, found an issue on which they could openly take the field against him.

Even while the Court bill pended, southern rebellions erupted on other issues: against sit-down strikes and against relief spending. Criticism mounted over regionally discriminatory freight rates, which antedated the New Deal. Southern Democrats became uneasy bedfellows with organized labor and blacks in the New Deal coalition, and some of them drifted toward a countercoalition with conservative Republicans. By 1937 a conservative bloc, if unorganized and mutable, had appeared. And it held the New Dealers to a virtual stalemate.

The New Deal, however, sparked another kind of regional rebellion. Southern New Dealers developed a different vision of the future: an extension into the South of the liberal-labor-black coalition to which the New Deal had given rise in the North. This required an increase in the voting of low-income groups, and it anticipated that low-income voters would see that their self-interest lay in such a coalition. The prerequisite to a liberal coalition, therefore, was repeal of the poll tax, but efforts to that end met with stubborn resistance until much later.

In 1938 a group of southerners in federal service in Washington drafted a *Report on Economic Conditions in the South*, sponsored by the National Emergency Council. The sixty-four-page document amounted to a summary of existing analyses of the South's "colonial" economy. "The paradox of the South is that while it is blessed by Nature with immense wealth, its people as a whole are the poorest in the country," the report declared. "Lacking industries of its own, the South has been forced to trade the richness of its soil, its minerals and forests, and the labor of its people for goods manufactured elsewhere." The report placed Roosevelt squarely behind the critique of the South's colonial status and implied his support for regional development. Roosevelt, moreover, linked it directly to his effort to purge conservative southern senators in the 1938 primaries. "It is my conviction," the president said when the report went out, "that the South presents right now, in 1938, the Nation's Number 1 economic problem." That catchphrase proved easy to misconstrue as another purblind stereotype of the benighted South. During the campaigns of the summer, the import of Roosevelt's commitment to regional development was lost, as was his effort to harness sectional feeling to the New Deal cause.

For the bulk of southern leaders drifted more and more into the old sectionalism. A rising wind of black aspirations fanned the flames of racist reaction, and politicians exploited the issue. A gathering storm of wartime discontent with Negro demands, price controls, labor shortages, rationing, and a hundred other petty vexations reinforced the prevailing winds of conservatism. In 1942 the congressional elections registered a national swing against the New Deal, and so did the southern primaries. With southern Democrats in open revolt, the next Congress undid much of the New Deal.

Nevertheless, southern congressmen provided the bedrock of support for Roosevelt's foreign policies throughout World War II. During the war several southerners in Congress stood forth as leading champions of international cooperation: Claude Pepper, Lister Hill, William Fulbright, and above all, Tom Connally. And if the opinion polls are to be credited, Roosevelt held the support of the mass of southerners until his death at the Little White House in Warm Springs on 12 April 1945.

A short book by Roosevelt's biographer focuses on his southern connections: Frank Freidel, *F.D.R.. and the South* (Baton Rouge: Louisiana State University Press, 1965). The fullest general coverage of the South during the New Deal years is in George B. Tindall, *The Emergence of the New South, 1913–1945* (Baton Rouge: Louisiana State University Press, 1967). The best travel account of the New Deal years gives some of the flavor of the times: Jonathan Daniels, *A Southerner Discovers the South* (New York: Macmillan Co., 1938). James T. Patterson, *Congressional Conservatism and the New Deal* (Lexington: University of Kentucky Press, 1967) chronicles and analyzes the conservative revolt, and Katherine Du Pre Lumpkin, *The South in Progress* (New York: International Publishers, 1940) evokes the southern white liberalism of the time. Effective coverage of black-white relationships may be found in John B. Kirby, *Black Americans in the Roosevelt Era: Liberalism and Race* (Knoxville: University of Tennessee Press, 1979).

GEORGE B. TINDALL

See also Black Cabinet; Democratic Party; Election of 1928; Elections in the Roosevelt Era; Garner, John Nance; Long, Huey Pierce; Negroes; "Purge" of 1938; Two-Thirds Rule

South America

See Good Neighbor Policy; Welles, Benjamin Sumner

Soviet Union

See Stalin, Joseph, and the Soviet Union

Spanish Civil War

During the night of 17 July 1936, North African detachments of the Spanish army rebelled against the republic that had been established five years earlier and that had been governed since the spring of 1936 by a coalition of socialists and liberals (with tacit support from the powerful anarchist movement). The attempted coup turned into a civil war. Although General Francisco Franco, who quickly emerged as the leader of the rebellion, condemned the Popular Front government as a Communist conspiracy, the Communists were at that point an unimportant factor in Spanish politics.

British prime minister Stanley Baldwin, leading a Conservative government that dreaded Stalin more than it feared Hitler, took the lead in the formation of an international London-based Non-Intervention Committee in September 1936. Under pressure from the British, French prime minister Leon Blum set aside his socialist sympathies for the Madrid government and reluctantly closed the border between France and Spain. Although the United States never joined the Non-Intervention Committee, Secretary of State Cordell Hull's tendency to look to London for guidance combined with the intense mood of isolationism that prevailed in the United States after World War I and Washington's policy meshed perfectly with London's. Since the Neutrality Act of February 1936 did not cover civil wars, the administration's first public response was to proclaim a "moral embargo" on 7 August 1936. Americans were asked not to sell armaments to either side. When arms merchant Robert Cuse defied the adminstration's wishes and prepared to ship weapons to the beleaguered government in Madrid, Roosevelt consulted with Acting Secretary of State R. Walton Moore and hurriedly appealed to Congress for emergency legislation. A joint resolution, making it "unlawful to export arms, ammunition, or implements of war from any place in the United States . . . to Spain," was rushed through a nearly unanimous House and Senate on 8 January 1937. The vote was 404–1 and 81–0. Farmer-laborite John Bernard of Minnesota was the lone dissenter. Some months later, the Neutrality Act of 1937 gave Roosevelt discretionary power to continue the originally mandatory embargo imposed by the joint resolution, which he did on the day he signed the new act (1 May).

As the overnight rebellion turned into a three-year war, fascist Italy and Nazi Germany generously supplied General Franco with modern weapons and with an army of "volunteers" whose exploits were front-page news in Berlin and Rome even as Hitler and Mussolini hypocritically assured the Non-Inter-vention Committee of their punctilious cooperation.

The Soviet Union, also denying its involvement in the conflict, supported the republic with weapons and organized a series of International Brigades, which eventually included about two thousand American volunteers who defied the neutrality legislation and fought as the Lincoln Battalion of the XVth International Brigade. The Russians insisted as the price of their support that social revolution in Spain be deferred, and they ousted anarchists and left-wing socialists from positions of political or military influence. By the end of the war, the Communist party had become the controlling force in Madrid.

Roosevelt and his advisers watched the course of events with dismay and concluded that the American embargo had been a hasty mistake. Public opinion was strongly Loyalist (i.e., pro-Republican). Committees of artists, writers, college presidents, Protestant ministers, union leaders, lawyers, and others held pro-Republican pageants and rallies, wrote open letters to newspapers, and published pamphlets appealing for an end to the embargo. Pro-Republican novels, poems, films, ballets, songs, and paintings further intensified the emotional pressure on the Roosevelt administration.

By the middle of 1938, some isolationist leaders in the Senate began to condemn the embargo as the opposite of true neutrality because it allowed Hitler and Mussolini a free hand in Spain while leaving the Republicans no place to turn except to the Soviet Union. On 2 May 1938, Senator Gerald P. Nye of North Dakota offered Senate Joint Resolution 88, calling for repeal of the embargo, but Hull remained convinced of the correctness of his course and obtained Roosevelt's permission to write to Key Pittman of Nevada, chairman of the Foreign Relations Committee, urging that Nye's motion be tabled, which it was.

Contrary to widespread opinion at the time (and even subsequently), religious affiliation was, in the controversy over American policy, a far more important determinant of attitudes than economic status. Indeed, the embargo controversy threatened to turn into a "holy war" in which Protestants, Jews, and nonbelievers, arguing that the issue was one of fascism versus constitutional democracy, were pitted against the hierarchy of the Roman Catholic church, which was almost unanimous in seeing the Spanish war as a contest between Communism and Catholicism. Petitions and appeals proliferated; passions intensified. Depending as he did upon Catholic support for his third-term bid in 1940, but not realizing that a significant portion of the Catholic population was actually sympathetic to the Republic, Roosevelt reluctantly decided not to ask for repeal of the embargo. When he candidly admitted his reasons to House Majority Leader Samuel Rayburn of Texas, Secretary of the Interior Ickes exploded: "This [is] the cat that was actually in the bag, and it is the mangiest, scabbiest cat ever." Ickes's comment suggests the emotionalism of the debate. As the war entered its final winter, Nye repeated his appeal for lifting the embargo on 25 January 1939. The cabinet met on 27

January and debated the embargo at length, Roosevelt now admitted that the embargo had been a grave mistake, but one too politically costly to correct.

The war ended with the surrender of the Republicans on 1 April 1939. The United States recognized the fascist regime on the following day, but American policy during and after the Spanish war continued to be a matter of passionate controversy for another generation.

The best single history of the Spanish civil war is still probably Gabriel Jackson's *The Spanish Republic and the Civil War* (Princeton: Princeton University Press, 1965). There is no study that deals exclusively with Roosevelt and the war, but there is extensive discussion of American policy in F. Jay Taylor's *The United States and the Spanish Civil War* (New York: Bookman, 1956) and in Richard P. Traina, *American Diplomacy and the Spanish Civil War* (Bloomington: Indiana University Press, 1968). A wider study of public attitudes can be found in Allen Guttmann, *The Wound in the Heart: America and the Spanish Civil War* (New York: Free Press–Macmillan Co., 1962).

ALLEN GUTTMANN

See also Fascism; Foreign Policy; Internationalism and Peace; Isolationism; Mussolini, Benito, and Italy; Neutrality Acts

Speeches

See Economic Royalists; Fireside Chats; Forgotten Man; Four Freedoms Speech; Inaugurations; Quarantine Speech; Speech Writing

Speech Writing

Franklin Roosevelt's speeches were team efforts. The manuscript always belonged to Roosevelt and bore his stamp, but it might have been touched by a score of draftsmen. Except for the most perfunctory efforts, FDR did not use ghosted drafts. He merged and mastered the various versions to the point where they became an expression of his own thinking. The writers furnished the raw materials and helped him think. Roosevelt used the speech-writing process to help him decide what indeed he believed about the particular issues involved. There were frequently policy formulation sessions from which speeches developed as one of the essential by-products. Samuel I. Rosenman, Roosevelt's chief speech writer from 1928 through 1945, learned at once that his job was partly to catalyze Roosevelt's thinking on issue after issue. Under his prodding, hunches and notions became finally positions and commitments. And ways were devised for teaching the public to see things as Roosevelt did. FDR had always known that guiding public opinion was the chief challenge of the politician. His own early instincts were sound, but his method evolved slowly.

In his first campaign in 1910 for the New York State Senate, Roosevelt spoke spontaneously. When he used notes, they were sketchy. The 1912 campaign for reelection was conducted by a former newsman, Louis McHenry Howe, while Roosevelt lay ill. From that time until 1928, Howe wrote most of the prepared speeches. The two men's close daily collaboration has made it often impossible to separate their notions or their language.

By the 1928 campaign, Samuel I. Rosenman had joined Roosevelt as speech writer. Despite other duties as a New York State Supreme Court judge, he remained at the core of FDR's speech-writing efforts for the rest of the president's life. These speeches, increasingly planned for radio, were designed to reach people in their homes. They were his device for reaching over the shoulders of the political bosses. During campaigns, Rosenman and others would ride the train or in the auto cavalcade, drafting with Roosevelt the words he would use hours or even minutes later.

Between campaigns the process was more predictable. During the governorship, Rosenman would come to Albany once a week for sessions that might last far into the night. Raymond E. Moley and other members of the brains trust often provided policy drafts. The multiple advice and the rivalries and jealousies gave Roosevelt the two things a chairbound but fast-moving governor most needed—thorough analyses and firm control. As he said, they all had to "come back to Papa."

In the White House, the process for preparing a major speech became standardized. The president's secretary, Grace Tully, would collect proposals. Sometimes Roosevelt dictated language as ideas came to him. Major drafters who might be preparing entire manuscripts of their own included such figures as Thomas Corcoran, Benjamin Cohen, Hugh Johnson, Rexford Tugwell, and Raymond E. Moley. Harry Hopkins became a frequent contributor. During the war years, Robert Sherwood and William Hassett spent a substantial part of their time in speech writing. Rosenman remained the head of the team, with some interruptions, such as the period of 1932 and early 1933 during which Raymond Moley was the leader.

As the crucial day approached, the writing team would move into the cabinet room, perhaps working through multiple drafts before the sessions with the president began. These were often in the evening—the president perhaps lying on a couch, moving through a manuscript already pockmarked with his own notes. He would dictate changes to Tully and discuss major policy and stylistic issues, frequently working out compromises among conflicting advisers. Sometimes he insisted on an entirely new start. At least once—in the basic agricultural speech for the 1932 campaign—he airily directed that conflicting ideas be "woven together."

Roosevelt's speech writing set important presidential precedents. But he never allowed others to control either his words or his delivery. There were no ready-made speeches of any importance, no radio or speech coaches. His resonant voice and precise enunciation became trademarks of his style. The prose, to which he personallly put the final touches, was consistently dignified and graceful in tone, clear and effective in substance.

The most important source is Samuel I. Rosenman, *Working with Roosevelt* (New York: Harper & Bros., 1952). Also very useful is Samuel Hand, *Counsel and Advise: A Political Biography of Samuel I. Rosenman* (New York: Garland Publishing Co., 1979).

ALFRED B. ROLLINS, JR.

See also Berle, Adolf Augustus; Cohen, Benjamin Victor; Corcoran, Thomas Gardiner; Howe, Louis McHenry; Moley, Raymond; Rosenman, Samuel Irving; Sherwood, Robert Emmet; Tugwell, Rexford Guy; Tully, Grace

---

Stalin, Joseph, and the Soviet Union

Franklin Roosevelt, unlike his immediate predecessor, came to the presidency largely unburdened by strong ideological views concerning the Soviet Union and its Communist government. As a ranking official in the Wilson administration, he seems to have evinced little curiosity about the momentous events in Russia that brought the Bolsheviks to power. Never one to accord ideology much weight, he tended to regard the Soviet Union not as the seat of global revolution but much as any other nation-state, possessed by the same fears and ambitions as Europe's other leading countries. This refusal to allow the rhetoric of Marxist messianism to alarm him unduly remained a cen-

This charcoal drawing of Stalin by B. Karpov was a personal gift to Roosevelt from the Soviet premier. The inscription in Stalin's handwriting expressed gratitude to the American president for the opening of a second front. (Courtesy FDR Library.)

tral characteristic of Roosevelt's approach toward the Soviet Union and shaped his policies in foreign affairs throughout twelve years of turmoil.

Roosevelt entered office determined to reestablish the diplomatic relationship with the Soviets that Woodrow Wilson had severed at the time of the Bolshevik revolution. Sixteen years of denying the legitimacy of Moscow's Communist dictatorship had accomplished little, and normalization of ties seemed a logical move to the pragmatic FDR. Some of his advisers hoped that renewed political contacts might open up new markets for American goods, but Roosevelt apparently viewed restoration of relations more in its political context. The knowledge that Washington and Moscow were once more speaking to each other, he reasoned, would inevitably give pause to Japanese militarists advocating further expansion on the Asian mainland and might force greater circumspection on Hitler as well.

In the face of virulent State Department suspicions of Soviet purposes, Roosevelt personally handled the negotiations with Foreign Minister Maxim Litvinov leading to the reestablishment of relations. The agreement they hammered out in November 1933 was riddled with ambiguity, but for the president the act of resuming diplomatic intercourse rendered such considerations inconsequential. Perhaps such nonchalance was unfortunate. Following a brief euphoria after the exchange of ambassadors, controversy over the actual meaning of the Roosevelt-Litvinov agreement quickly soured relations once more. Mutual incomprehension and a general incompatibility between the objectives of the two nations pushed this deterioration along. Roosevelt's first ambassador to Moscow, William C. Bullitt, departed for his new post a longtime supporter of close Soviet-American ties. Two years of firsthand familiarity with his Russian hosts, however, left him disillusioned and bitterly anti-Soviet.

Soviet-American ties remained abysmal throughout the remainder of the decade. Although each side displayed periodic interest in collaborative efforts to restrain German and Japanese aggression, neither was able to persuade the other of its suitability as a partner. In the United States, Roosevelt, unwilling to risk alienating domestic allies by embarking upon strategies smacking of internationalism, was perhaps overly mindful of the isolationist sentiment prevalent among his fellow citizens. Continuing irritation at the Soviet Union's alleged failure to live up to the debt repayment clauses of the Roosevelt-Litvinov agreement and Moscow's refusal to moderate Comintern propaganda against the United States created further impediments to cooperative relations. Of course, the long-standing American distaste for communism remained strong in Congress and among segments of the public, and the spectacle of purges and show trials in the USSR during the 1930s only strengthened this antipathy. Finally, influential elements within the Washington defense and foreign policy bureaucracy, notably in the State and Navy departments, maintained a vigilant eye lest Soviet blandishments about common action seduce the president.

News of the 23 August 1939 Nazi-Soviet pact profoundly jolted administration officials, while Stalin's opportunistic advance into eastern Poland several weeks later convinced many Americans, if not the president, that no essential differences separated fascist Germany and communist Russia. Equally disturbing was Moscow's invasion of tiny Finland later that fall. Americans who equated fiscal responsibility with moral virtue—and there were millions of them—remembered that of all the World War I debtors, only Finland had maintained its repayments throughout the depression-ridden thirties. The tenacious resistance against their giant neighbor offered by the Finns won more admirers, and sentiment abounded in the winter of 1939–40 for the United States to repudiate its traditional noninterventionism in order to aid the brave Finnish nation.

Soviet behavior outraged Roosevelt equally, but the president remained conscious of the need to avoid pushing Moscow and Berlin more tightly into each other's arms. A fundamental cautiousness marked his response to Soviet aggressions. He went so far as to proclaim a "moral embargo" on aircraft sales to the Soviet Union and ordered the Treasury to block Soviet purchases of selected strategic materials, but he carefully refrained from closing the door completely to eventual collaboration against Germany and Japan. By mid-1940, he had sanctioned State Department conversations with the Soviet ambassador once more exploring the possibilities of elevating Soviet-American ties to a more acceptable plane. Early the following year he authorized State to warn Moscow of the impending German attack. Most significant of all, he refused to allow Congress, as it debated his proposal to provide goods to any nation whose defense the president deemed vital to American security, to amend the legislation in ways that would have specifically excluded the Soviet Union from eligibility for assistance. The Lend-Lease Act that finally emerged from these deliberations was to form one of the cornerstones of the Grand Alliance that eventually overthrew the Axis powers.

Hitler's 22 June 1941 invasion of the Soviet Union dramatically transformed the entire character of the relationship linking Washington and Moscow. Many commentators wrote off Moscow's ability to withstand the brutal efficiency of the Wehrmacht, but Roosevelt instinctively sensed that Hitler had this time overreached himself. Firsthand reports from presidential emissary Harry Hopkins reinforced this belief. Two days after the German attack, FDR authorized emergency assistance to Moscow, while quietly maneuvering behind the scenes to build up congressional support for Lend-Lease aid for the hard-pressed Soviets. By the end of October 1941, he was ready to 'move openly, and the first Lend-Lease shipments to Moscow were soon on their way. Over the next 3 1/2 years, the United States would furnish the Soviets with $11 billion of Lend-Lease assistance, an investment repaid many times over in fewer American casualties.

On 1 January 1942 the Declaration of the United Nations was signed and the Grand Alliance was born. But the partnership thereby created between Soviet Russia and the democratic West was never an easy one, and Moscow frequently complained of an Anglo-American consortium that deliberately excluded the USSR. Of the various controversies that rocked the alliance, none proved more disruptive than the second-front issue. Continually reminded by the Soviets that they alone were engaging German soldiers in battle, Roosevelt in May 1942 unwisely promised Foreign Minister V. M. Molotov a second European front by the end of the year. Opposition from Winston Churchill and logistical difficulties made fulfillment of this pledge impossible; indeed, the Soviets did not receive substantial relief in the form of a cross-channel attack until mid-1944. By this time, Stalin's suspicion that his partners sought Moscow's destruction along with Berlin's had received ample confirmation, though such a conclusion was incorrect.

The fear that Stalin might negotiate a separate peace with Germany constantly dogged Roosevelt, who rightly recognized that without Soviet might, Hitler could not be defeated. It had been, in part, this concern that had prompted his rash promise to Molotov of a 1942 second front. The policy of unconditional surrender announced by Roosevelt and Churchill at Casablanca in January 1943 was also designed to reassure Stalin of their intentions and head off pressures on the Soviet leader to open talks with the Germans. Ironically, Stalin seems to have harbored similar fears, professing to see in Western actions the machinations of an untrustworthy ally. Soviet accusations in early April 1945 of a secret Anglo-American understanding with the German armies in Italy produced the most heated exchange of messages between Roosevelt and Stalin of the entire war.

Soviet ambitions in Eastern Europe also troubled the wartime alliance. Roosevelt recognized that the United States was powerless to reverse Moscow's swallowing of the Baltic states and therefore chose not to contest it. He deliberately postponed confronting other Soviet territorial claims, reasoning that such disruptive issues would only divert attention from the immediate task of defeating the Axis. This assessment was surely correct; yet, by deferring these matters until such time as the Red Army physically occupied most of what Moscow desired, the president in effect ensured that the controversies would be settled on Soviet terms. Roosevelt sought to reassure Stalin that he need have no anxieties about Soviet postwar security. At the same time he urged the Russian leader to moderate his ambitions and give lip service at least to the principles of the Atlantic Charter, most notably with the Yalta Declaration on Liberated Europe. Significantly, he refused to sanction military strategies aimed more at thwarting Soviet expansion than at defeating the enemy. But not even this policy of accommodation could paper over the chasm between American and Soviet purposes. Disputes over the future of Poland came to symbolize the differences rending the Grand Alliance. No issue received more high-level consideration or proved less susceptible of solution. Poland ultimately demonstrated the limitations on FDR's abilities to persuade his wartime partner to accept a Rooseveltian view of the postwar order.

Undergirding the president's handling of his Soviet ally lay the belief that through personal diplomacy, he could establish a relationship of mutual trust with the Soviet dictator and thereby win Stalin's cooperation in creating a stable postwar world designed largely along American lines. He hoped that showing Stalin that Washington sympathized with Moscow's legitimate security needs would solve the problem of Soviet expansion. His refusal to demand political concessions from the Soviets in exchange for American Lend-Lease assistance comprised another part of this campaign to convince the Kremlin of American good faith. So, too, did his occasional suggestions to Stalin that Churchill be excluded from certain of their dealings.

Stalin and Roosevelt conferred face to face on two occasions—at Teheran in 1943 and again at Yalta early in 1945. Both meetings reinforced the president's faith in the efficacy of personal diplomacy. The Soviet dictator, cruel and bloodthirsty though he was, could also be an entertaining companion and genial host, and FDR grew to enjoy his company. The president "was very much taken with Stalin," Interior Secretary Harold Ickes reported after Teheran. "He likes Stalin because he is open and frank." Extensive correspondence throughout the war years—some of it sharply worded—and the subsequent conference in the Crimea failed to lessen Roosevelt's conviction that his own obvious sincerity and good intentions could overcome Soviet suspicions and lay the groundwork for a lasting peace based on Big Power cooperation.

Parrish, Chicago Tribune, *26 March 1944.*

Historians today generally agree that FDR failed to see just how expansive the Soviet definition of security would be. Certainly he neglected to prepare the American people for the extent to which Moscow would dominate Eastern Europe after the war. Even so, it is not easy to propose alternative policies Roosevelt might have followed to avert Soviet hegemony in the region. The fact that the Soviets were absorbing huge losses at a time when American casualties were light or nonexistent severely restricted Washington's ability to press Moscow for more acceptable behavior. U.S. inability to deliver all the supplies promised the beleaguered Soviets further limited American leverage in bargaining with the Kremlin. The universal assessment that Moscow's help would be highly desirable in the war against Japan added another constraining factor. Finally, Washington's entire vision of a suitable postwar order depended upon Big Power comity within the framework of an international peacekeeping organization. To have jeopardized the hope of postwar collaboration by too adversarial a stance toward Soviet desires would have sacrificed these plans long before experience proved them wanting.

Roosevelt's final months produced heightened expectations for the future of the wartime alliance, followed by renewed squabbles and mutual recriminations. Roosevelt left the Big Three meeting at Yalta in February 1945 believing he had secured a workable if not fully satisfactory agreement on Poland, a promise of Soviet cooperation in the postwar security organization, and a firm pledge from Moscow to enter the war against Japan shortly after the defeat of Germany. Within weeks this optimism evaporated, as the prospect of imminent victory lessened the need for suppressing disagreement. Soviet actions in Poland and Rumania, barely veiled accusations of Western duplicity, and a general obtuseness and obstructionism on Moscow's part led a number of administration officials to question whether Soviet-American collaboration could survive the coming of peace. Roosevelt's last cable to Churchill, however, minimized these frictions and reverted to the president's characteristic buoyancy.

Critics would subsequently charge Roosevelt with naiveté for thinking he could induce Stalin to join with the Americans and the British in building a postwar order based upon international cooperation and self-restraint. In truth, no one in a position of authority in the Western democracies, including Churchill, realized the full extent of Soviet ambitions—Stalin probably had no clear plans himself. Moreover, the decision to keep the secret of the atom from the Soviets—to create, with the British, a smaller coterie within the alliance—reflects a pragmatism and a sense of realpolitik that belies the notion of naiveté. Roosevelt misled the American people—and himself—as to what to expect for the postwar period. Perhaps this was even necessary in order to maintain public support for the sacrifices global warfare demanded. Out of these dashed expectations flowed the cold war. Yet, forced into partnership with a suspicious ally representing a repellent ideology, Roosevelt had succeeded, by the time of his death, in accomplishing his primary objectives. The uneasy, often unnatural relationship binding Washington and Moscow together had smashed Hitlerism, while Japan's doom was equally certain.

Robert Dallek, *Franklin D. Roosevelt and American Foreign Policy, 1932–1945* (New York: Oxford University Press, 1979) provides, for this subject as for most foreign policy topics, the starting point for an understanding of Roosevelt's diplomacy. Orville H. Bullitt, ed., *For the President: Personal and Secret: Correspondence between Franklin D. Roosevelt and William C. Bullitt* (Boston: Houghton Mifflin Co., 1972) illustrates the process by which the hopes surrounding the resumption of diplomatic ties in 1933 speedily gave way to disillusionment. *Foreign Relations of the United States* (Washington: U.S. Government Printing Office, various dates), the documentary series published by the Department of State, is absolutely essential for anyone interested in the Roosevelt years; supplementary volumes focus on Teheran, Yalta, and some of the other wartime summit meetings. For the war years, John L. Gaddis, *The United States and the Origins of the Cold War, 1941–1947* (New York: Columbia University Press, 1972) remains one of the most satisfying treatments of this much-studied controversy. Contrasting views may be examined in George C. Herring, Jr., *Aid to Russia, 1941–1946: Strategy, Politics, the Origins of the Cold War* (New York: Columbia University Press, 1973) and the New Left account by Gabriel Kolko, *The Politics of War: The World and United States Foreign Policy, 1943–1945* (New York: Random House, 1968). Soviet diplomacy during the Great Patriotic War is ably presented in Vojtech Mastny, *Russia's Road to the Cold War: Diplomacy, Warfare, and the Politics of Communism, 1941–1945* (New York: Columbia University Press, 1979).

ROBERT M. HATHAWAY

See also Atlantic Conference and Charter; Atomic Bomb; Casablanca Conference; Churchill, Winston Leonard Spencer; Communism; Foreign Policy; Harriman, William Averell; Hull, Cordell; Internationalism and Peace; Isolationism; Lend-Lease; Personal Diplomacy; Teheran Conference; World War II; Yalta Conference

Stamp Collecting

Stamp collecting was one of Franklin Delano Roosevelt's major hobbies. It began with his mother's album started in 1866 or 1867 during her early years on the island of Macao, west of Hong Kong. In her twenties, Sara relinquished the collection, turning it over to her younger brother, Frederic, who became a serious philatelist. It was not until about 1891 that young Franklin, probably influenced by his mother's early enthusiasm, became interested in the study of postage and imprinted stamps. As with each of his hobbies, Franklin devoted time and careful attention in sorting out and pasting the stamps into albums. His uncle Frederic, convinced that Franklin's interest was serious, gave the boy his valuable collection.

The president looking at his stamp collection, Hyde Park, 1936. (Courtesy FDR Library.)

That became the solid base for Franklin's lifelong pastime from which he gained a wide knowledge of geography, history, and world affairs. At Groton he added little to his collection, but at Harvard he resumed collecting, and his interest never flagged thereafter. He pored over his stamps when he was kept indoors because of his illness. Later, as governor, when a visitor failed to keep an appointment or during long, tedious telephone conversations, he sorted stamps with his free hand. From a general collection, he began to specialize in stamps from Hong Kong and those from the Americas.

After he became president, Roosevelt asked the assistant secretary of state, Wilbur J. Carr, to send him interesting foreign stamps, and he also had Postmaster General James A. Farley send him first sheets of new issues, always paying for them. The general public, aware of his interest, overwhelmed him with gifts or exchange requests. When these fitted into his specialties, he happily accepted and in a few cases was able to reciprocate. FDR preferred to collect stamps in pairs or blocks of four and varieties showing differences in shade or postmark. As his official duties became more burdensome, the president could not spend much time with his collection. But the forty-odd volumes of about twenty thousand stamps, representing special countries or groups of countries, provided some hours of relaxation, which he spent "examining the stamps through a magnifying glass, picking them up with tweezers, and attaching them by gummed hinges to the pages of his albums."

He often expressed his fondness for stamps and for collecting them, saying that "the best thing about stamp collecting as a pursuit is that the enthusiasm which it arouses in youth increases as the years pass, and it dispels boredom, enlarges our vision, broadens our knowledge of geography and in innumerable ways enriches life and adds to its joy." On 12 April 1945, Roosevelt, at Warm Springs, gave "his last official directive. It was to tell Frank Walker [postmaster general] that he approved his proposal that the President on 25 April buy from the postmaster of San

Francisco one of the new issue stamps commemorating the opening of the United Nations Conference, to be put on the market that day." The president's collection was sold at auction after his death for $230,000.

For more information, see Kenneth S. Davis, *FDR: The Beckoning of Destiny, 1882–1928, A History* (New York: G. P. Putnam's Sons, 1972); Olin Dows, *Franklin Roosevelt at Hyde Park* (New York: American Artists Group, 1949); Finis Farr, *FDR* (New Rochelle, N.Y.: Arlington House, 1972); Frank Freidel, *Franklin D. Roosevelt: Launching the New Deal* (Boston: Little, Brown & Co., 1973); William D. Hassett, *Off the Record with F.D.R.: 1942–1945* (New Brunswick, N.J.: Rutgers University Press, 1958); Emil Ludwig, *Roosevelt: A Study in Fortune and Power,* trans. Maurice Samuel (New York: Viking Press, 1937); and FDR personal papers, Research Collection, FDR Library and Museum, Hyde Park, N.Y.

Stark, Harold Raynsford

(12 November 1880–20 August 1972)

Admiral, U.S. Navy; chief of naval operations, 1 August 1939–26 March 1942. Harold R. Stark was born in Wilkes Barre, Pennsylvania, and was a member of the class of 1903 at the U.S. Naval Academy (where he was nicknamed "Betty"). He met FDR in 1914 when he was commanding the destroyer *Patterson* and refused to turn over the conn to Roosevelt, then assistant secretary of the navy. Thereafter, Stark held the respect and friendship of the man who as president in 1939 approved his appointment as chief of naval operations (CNO).

Stark's career was well balanced. He commanded destroyers, cruisers, and battleships. He was on the staff of Adm. William S. Sims in London during World War I, attended the Naval War College in the 1920s, and served as aide to secretaries of the navy Charles F. Adams and Claude A. Swanson between 1930 and 1934, gaining important administrative and political experience. Promoted to rear admiral in 1934, Stark became chief of the Bureau of Ordnance (1934–37).

The Second World War began a month after Stark assumed his duties as CNO. Full American involvement remained two years distant, so that Stark's main impact on Roosevelt's policies involved preparation and planning for war.

World War I convinced Stark of the need for preparedness, and he kept one step ahead of Congress and FDR when it came to naval increases. In June 1940, with FDR's approval, Stark drafted and defended a naval appropriations bill before Carl Vinson's House Naval Affairs Committee. The ships that would win the war and make the United States the world's preeminent naval power were built under the Two Ocean Navy Act.

Stark oversaw the reassessment of strategic planning, identifying Germany rather than Japan as the main threat to American security. He recommended a new strategic emphasis in his Plan D ("Dog") memorandum of November 1940, the basis of the Europe first policy. At Stark's prompting, staff discussions were begun with the British in early 1941, which led to the ABC-1 agreement and the formation of the combined chiefs of staff.

In general agreement with FDR on the broad outlines of American policy, Stark viewed the oil embargo and the shift of the Pacific fleet from the West Coast to Hawaii as provocative rather than deterrent acts. Nevertheless, he saw to the expansion of the support facilities that would make Pearl Harbor the major American base for the Pacific war.

As CNO, Stark laid the groundwork for victory. Unfortunately, his tenure was marred by the Pearl Harbor debacle and the ensuing investigation. Stripped of his operational responsibilities by the appointment of Adm. Ernest J. King as commander in chief, U.S. fleet, Stark chose to end the division of command, and his resignation was accepted at a 7 March 1942 meeting with FDR.

Stark went on to London as commander, U.S. Naval Forces Europe, serving also as a contact between FDR and European political and military leaders. He retired in April 1946 and during his remaining twenty-six years refused to be drawn into public debate concerning his career.

Stark has not been the subject of a full biography. A good biographical sketch by B. Mitchell Simpson III appears in Robert William Love, Jr., ed., *The Chiefs of Naval Operations* (Annapolis: Naval Institute Press, 1980). Works in which Stark figures prominently include Maurice Matloff and Edwin M. Snell, *Strategic Planning for Coalition Warfare, 1941–1942* (Washington, D.C.: Office of the Center for Military History, 1953); volumes 1 and 3 of Samuel Eliot Morison, *History of United States Naval Operations in World War II,* 15 vols. (Boston: Little, Brown & Co., 1947–62); and Tracy B. Kittredge, "U.S.–British Naval Cooperation, 1940–1945," an unpublished Navy Department monograph held by the Naval Historical Center, Washington, D.C.

MICHAEL PALMER

See also Joint Chiefs of Staff

State Senator of New York

Franklin D. Roosevelt launched his career in the New York State Senate in January 1911. Over the next two years, he would be accorded several opportunities to establish—and to expand—his reputation as a spokesman for independent progressivism among Democrats.

FDR's first opportunity came shortly after his arrival in Albany. The issue was the election of a U.S. senator to replace the retiring incumbent, Republican Chauncey M. Depew. Since New York State did not yet follow the direct election method, the naming of Depew's successor fell to the legislature, where the Democrats held the majority. By the time the Tammany-controlled senate and assembly leadership convened a party caucus in mid-January to choose their candidate, two contenders had emerged: Brook-

Franklin D. Roosevelt in the New York State Senate, Albany. (Courtesy FDR Library.)

lyn independent Edward M. Shepard, who had won the endorsement of Thomas Mott Osborne's Democratic League, and William F. ("Blue-eyed Billy") Sheehan, a regular then residing in Manhattan who boasted the support of Tammany Hall. Naturally enough, Roosevelt joined up with the league and some two dozen other legislators, mostly upstate antimachine men like himself, and quickly transformed the contest into a battle against the dictates of Charlie Murphy bossism. In the face of Tammany's great strength, the insurgents, as they were known, devised the strategy of bolting the party caucus held on 16 January (thus freeing themselves from the unit rule that bound those who attended), voting for Shepard's candidacy in the legislature, and thereby denying Sheehan the requisite 101 votes for election. The strategy worked beautifully, and for the next 2½ months Roosevelt and his colleagues held the regular Democrats at bay. As informal chairman of the group, FDR was able to dominate the spotlight in Albany. Though inexperienced in public relations, he effectively dispensed information to eager newspaper reporters and generally supervised propaganda for the independents. He became the "Galahad of the insurgency," was sought out for special interviews, and was the subject of character sketches for numerous newspapers and magazines. Finally, on 29 March, the contending forces reached a compromise, and Judge James O'Gorman, a progressive-oriented Tammanyite, was named U.S. senator. Some contemporaries

argued that the O'Gorman selection amounted to a capitulation by the insurgents. If so, however, it made little difference to Franklin Roosevelt's career. Overnight he had established himself as a major voice for antimachine progressivism in the state and had become a coleader of Osborne's Democratic League.

The remainder of FDR's tenure in the senate was hardly as dramatic as the first few months. He made an attempt after the senatorial battle to hold the legislative insurgents together, but to no avail. The independents were divided among themselves, and many, chastened by recriminations from the party leadership, simply buckled under constant organization pressure. Roosevelt, however, did go on record in the days ahead on a host of progressive measures, particularly in the areas of political and governmental reform.

He sponsored a resolution urging New York's congressional delegation to approve a proposed amendment to the U.S. Constitution on the direct election of senators. He favored a primary bill that extended direct nominations to statewide offices, but this measure went beyond what the leadership of both political parties would accept. Roosevelt then reluctantly voted for legislation that only modestly altered the traditional nominations system. On labor and social reforms, FDR, coming from an essentially rural district, was less enthusiastic but basically supportive of his party's endeavors in this direction. He played no role in the activities of the Factory Investigating Commission (FIC), which was set up by Tammany leaders Alfred E. Smith and Robert F. Wagner in the wake of the tragic Triangle Shirtwaist Company fire of 25 March 1911. But he did join his Democratic colleagues in voting for most of the FIC bills that were presented to the legislature while he was in Albany. In 1912 and 1913, he helped pass a measure limiting the work week to fifty-four hours for women and children, cosponsored a "one day's rest in seven" bill, which the legislature finally enacted after his departure, and declared in favor of a workmen's compensation bill championed by the New York State Federation of Labor, which won for him the federation's warm endorsement as "one of labor's best friends in Albany."

Above all, Roosevelt dedicated himself in 1911–13 to the cause of conservation. As chairman of the Forest, Fish, and Game Committee of the senate, he dealt not only with routine legislative matters but also with key issues involving conservation and preservation. He pushed for several major aspects of former governor Hughes's program, including public development of hydroelectric sites, equitable distribution of state-generated power, and public control of water resources in state parks. Although he was generally unsuccessful in this ambitious undertaking, he did win legislation extending reforestation and the recodification of fish and game laws. By and large, FDR in these years remained an outspoken advocate of Gifford Pinchot's conservation principles and even brought Pinchot to Albany on one occasion to plug a measure dealing with the preservation of timberlands.

Much of Roosevelt's time and energy in 1912 was devoted to presidential politics. An early supporter of the candidacy of Woodrow Wilson, FDR helped Thomas Mott Osborne rejuvenate the foundering Democratic League, an organization seeking to advance the Wilson cause in New York City and upstate. Roosevelt assumed special responsibility for the league's work in the interior regions. He and Osborne were unsuccessful, however, in generating much support for the antimachine New Jersey governor, largely because they were contiually outmaneuvered by the more powerful regular organizations determined to block a candidacy they considered dangerous to their interests.

For the remainder of the summer and fall, FDR was forced to concentrate on his own reelection to the senate, and in typically pragmatic fashion he made amends with the Democratic regulars. He was fortunate in that the newly formed Progressive party ran a candidate in his district, thus dividing the Republican vote. But Roosevelt also had the misfortune of suffering an attack of typhoid fever just as he was about to begin his campaign in September. At this juncture he hired the gnome-like, wizened newspaperman, Louis McHenry Howe, who had earlier worked for Osborne, to run his campaign. Howe did a masterful job of advertising Roosevelt as a friend of the farmer and a courageous fighter of the bosses. The result was that FDR won reelection with a plurality of 1,631 votes over his nearest rival, John Southard. His victory was again part of a statewide sweep for the Democratic party, though his own vote total, as in 1910, surpassed that of the rest of the ticket, including Wilson, in the Twenty-sixth Senatorial District.

Roosevelt served only a few months of his second term in the New York senate. Considered for several posts in the new Wilson administration in Washington because of his early support for the New Jersey governor, he was finally offered the position of assistant secretary of the navy by Josephus Daniels. FDR gleefully accepted the nod and left Albany for the nation's capital in March 1913, now boasting a solid reputation as an independent progressive and a pragmatic politician. He also took Louis Howe with him as his secretary.

The most thorough treatment of Roosevelt's career in the New York State Senate can be found in Frank Freidel, *Franklin D. Roosevelt: The Apprenticeship* (Boston: Little, Brown & Co., 1952), and Alfred B. Rollins, Jr., *Roosevelt and Howe* (New York: Alfred A. Knopf, 1962). Roosevelt's labor record is analyzed in Rollins, "Franklin Roosevelt's Introduction to Labor," *Labor History* 3 (Winter 1962):3–18. Both the Franklin D. Roosevelt Papers (Hyde Park, New York) and the Thomas Mott Osborne Papers (Syracuse University Library) provide valuable factual information on the politics of 1912 as well as on FDR's senatorial career.

ROBERT F. WESSER

See also Conservation; Election of 1910; Howe, Louis McHenry; Tammany Hall

Stettinius, Edward Reilly, Jr.
(22 October 1900–31 October 1949)

Edward R. Stettinius, Jr. (Constant Collection. Courtesy FDR Library.)

Industrialist, New Deal adviser, and secretary of state in the last Roosevelt administration. Born in 1900, Stettinius attended the Pomfret School and the University of Virginia. After demonstrating little academic promise, he entered a business career, first with General Motors and in the 1930s with U.S. Steel, where at age thirty-seven he became chairman of the board (1938).

He first came to Roosevelt's attention as a man with a social conscience and an innovative mind in business. Roosevelt appointed him to the Industrial Advisory Board to act as liaison with the National Recovery Administration (1933). He developed a warm friendship with Harry Hopkins and became known as one of his "tame millionaires." In 1939 Roosevelt appointed Stettinius chairman of the War Resources Board. The following year Stettinius left U.S. Steel for Washington. In the Advisory Council of National Defense (1940), and then as director of priorities in the Office of Production Management (1941), the silver-haired corporate leader helped direct industry to prepare for the imminent war.

In the summer of 1941, Roosevelt appointed Stettinius head of the Lend-Lease Administration, one of the most important wartime jobs in Washington. Stettinius's skill as an organizer and his good public and congressional relations made Lend-Lease a critical "weapon for victory." In September 1943, these qualities propelled Stettinius on as an under secretary to the State Department, which was in low repute at the time. In two huge reorganization plans, Stettinius adapted State to the new vast tasks of long-term policy planning for the postwar world.

After Secretary Hull's resignation, Stettinius became secretary of state. Roosevelt continued to make the important foreign policy decisions himself, however, and he selected Stettinius because he expected that he would loyally implement his decisions. In these last critical months of the war, Stettinius's main contribution lay in the organization of the United Nations. He chaired the Dumbarton Oaks Conference (1944), maneuvered the controversial veto question through the Yalta meeting (February 1945), and succeeded in reassuring the Latin American nations about the new organization in Mexico City (March 1945). President Truman placed the founding of the United Nations high on his priority list. Therefore, he kept Stettinius in office for the duration of the San Francisco Conference (May-June 1945), whose success Stettinius, the great conciliator among conflicting points of view, helped ensure. Since Truman preferred to have the experienced Henry Stimson in the State Department, he accepted Stettinius's resignation in July 1945. After his death in 1949, UN Secretary General Trygve Lie characterized his achievement: "The name of Edward R. Stettinius, Jr., will live in history as one of the great architects of the United Nations."

For a quick introduction, see Walter Johnson, "Edward R. Stettinius, Jr.," in *An Uncertain Tradition*, ed. Norman A. Graebner (New York: McGraw-Hill, 1961) and Richard Walker in *The American Secretaries of State and Their Diplomacy*, ed. Robert H. Ferrell and Samuel Flagg Bemis, vol. 14 (New York: Cooper Square, 1956). For his role in Lend-Lease, see George C. Herring, Jr., *Aid to Russia, 1941–1946* (New York: Columbia University Press, 1973). *The Diaries of Edward R. Stettinius, Jr., 1943–1946*, ed. Thomas M. Campbell and George C. Herring, Jr. (New York: New Viewpoints, 1975) is a valuable source. Stettinius wrote two books: *Lend-Lease: Weapon for Victory* (1940) and *Roosevelt and the Russians: The Yalta Conference* (Garden City, N.Y.: Doubleday, 1945), on which he collaborated with Walter Johnson.

See also Foreign Policy; Lend-Lease

Joseph W. Stilwell. (Courtesy FDR Library.)

Stilwell, Joseph Warren
(19 March 1883–12 October 1946)

Commander, China-Burma-India theater, 1942–44. Known affectionately to his troops and the public as "Vinegar Joe," Gen. Joseph Stilwell commanded American forces in the China-Burma-India theater for nearly three years. A constant thorn in the side of Chinese Nationalist leader Chiang Kai-shek, he was recalled after Roosevelt bowed to his ally's complaints and threats regarding the controversial general. In subsequent years, Stilwell became a martyr for those Americans who questioned FDR's close wartime alliance with Nationalist China.

As a young officer, Stilwell first visited China in 1911. He returned as a military attaché during the late 1930s where he witnessed the brutal Japanese assault and grew disgusted with the corruption and brutality of the Nationalist, or Kuomintang, regime. He spoke Chinese and traveled widely through the countryside during these years. After the Pearl Harbor attack, when China and the United States became formal allies, Roosevelt accepted Gen. George C. Marshall's advice that he appoint Stilwell both American commander in the China-Burma-India theater and a special adviser to Chiang.

The president and the general had little rapport at their first or subsequent meetings. This reflected both personality differences as well as disagreements over China's role in the Grand Alliance. Stilwell wanted to concentrate on remaking the Chinese army into an effective force against Japan. Roosevelt lavished aid and praise on Chiang, he frequently explained, because China, with its vast population, would be "very useful twenty-five years hence, even though China cannot contribute much military or naval support for the moment." Stilwell faced constant frustrations in his effort to remold the Kuomintang armies, since Chiang preferred to sit back and hoard American aid for his upcoming war against the Chinese Communists. Dismissing Chiang with the epithet "Peanut," Stilwell described him as the ruler of a feudal government "based on fear and favor in the hands of an ignorant and stubborn man." The more

assistance Roosevelt approved, the more furious Stilwell grew with both the president and Chiang, increasingly dismissing the latter as a "grasping, bigoted, ungrateful little rattlesnake."

For three years Stilwell and Chiang continued to snipe at each other over the proper military strategy. Eventually Chiang sponsored a rival American general, Claire Chennault, who promised to defeat the Japanese in China with American air power. Chennault particularly pleased the Chinese leader by his promise not to interfere with Chiang's personal control over the distribution of American aid. Impressed with Chennault's promises and good relations with the Kuomintang leadership, FDR approved an air strategy during 1943 and early 1944. However, as Stilwell predicted, the Japanese retaliated by overrunning Chennault's undefended air bases. By the summer of 1944, China nearly collapsed under the pressure of a renewed Japanese offensive, despite the vast quantities of aid already delivered.

Beginning in July 1944, Roosevelt began to follow Stilwell's advice that Chiang be threatened with a cutoff in aid unless he placed the American commander at the head of his armies. The president also dispatched a small survey group (the Dixie Mission) to the Communist capital at Yenan, both to explore cooperation with Mao's guerrillas and to scare the Kuomintang into behaving better. Hoping to soothe Chiang's hurt feelings, Roosevelt sent a new intermediary to China, Patrick J. Hurley. A former secretary of war under Herbert Hoover, Hurley knew little about China but saw his mission as the chance to alter world history. He quickly allied himself with Chiang Kai-shek and accused Stilwell of being crude, unreliable, and possibly disloyal. In fact, Stilwell's admiration for the Chinese Communists was based on their spirited campaign against the Japanese and their growing popularity among the Chinese peasantry. In any case, when confronted with an ultimatum from Chiang that he might quit the war, Roosevelt, who was facing a fourth-term election in a week, decided to remove Stilwell from his command in October 1944.

After his recall, Stilwell sat out the last nine months of the war in relatively minor posts. During 1946 his health deteriorated quickly. Shortly before dying, he visited President Harry Truman to recount his wartime frustrations and pled with FDR's successor to terminate American involvement on behalf of the Nationalists in the Chinese Civil War.

For more information on Stilwell, see Barbara W. Tuchman, *Stilwell and the American Experience in China, 1911–1945* (New York: Macmillan, 1971); Michael Schaller, *The U.S. Crusade in China, 1938–1945* (New York: Columbia University Press, 1979); and Theodore H. White, ed., *The Stilwell Papers* (New York: W. Sloan Associates, 1948).

MICHAEL SCHALLER

See also Chennault, Claire Lee; Chiang Kai-shek; World War II

Stimson, Henry L.

(21 September 1867–20 October 1950)

Henry L. Stimson was an elder statesman of seventy-three when President Roosevelt nominated him to be secretary of war on 20 June 1940. He had served as secretary of state in the Hoover administration (1929–33) and as secretary of war under William Howard Taft (1911–13). Stimson thus became the first person in twentieth-century American history to hold the same cabinet position twice.

Roosevelt and Stimson had known each other since the early days of the century. Both native New Yorkers, their political paths had first crossed in 1910, when Stimson, then forty-three, ran unsuccessfully for governor on the Republican ticket and FDR, twenty-eight, was narrowly elected state senator as a Democrat from his district.

A youthful friend and admirer of Theodore Roosevelt, Stimson was an early proponent of national preparedness before the United States entered the First World War. An artillery officer in Europe in 1917–18, Stimson was often critical of President Wilson's defense and foreign policies. But unlike most anti-Wilsonians, Stimson regretted the country's repudiation of its international responsibilities and the semi-isolationism of the early postwar years.

Stimson, busy with a prosperous law practice in New York City, was politically inactive during the Harding era. Then in April 1927 President Coolidge appointed him special representative to strife-torn Nicaragua. Stimson's skilled personal diplomacy brought at least a temporary end to that country's violent civil war, restored a measure of orderly government, and provided for reasonably fair elections supervised by the United States, whose military forces, stationed there (most recently) since May 1926, were finally withdrawn in January 1933. In December 1927, Coolidge appointed Stimson governor-general of the Philippines, a post he filled until President-elect Hoover invited him to become secretary of state.

Recognizing the prevailing isolationist temper in the country, Stimson never forgot the overriding meaning of 1917. Like it or not, the global futures of the Atlantic democracies were inextricably linked. To Stimson's regret, this sentiment was not widely shared in leading government or private circles in London or Paris. When Stimson, amidst the deepening world depression, sought to unite the League of Nations powers behind an effective policy of nonrecognition of Japanese aggression and expansion in Manchuria, he met with only limited success.

Often uncomfortable and frustrated by what he considered Hoover's excessively pacifist outlook, Stimson nevertheless during the 1932–33 interrregnum was asked by Hoover to handle a number of difficult transition problems with the president-elect. It was a task Stimson undertook with remarkable skill. At their second meeting at the White House, on 19 January 1932, Roosevelt is said to have remarked,

"We are getting so that we do pretty good teamwork, don't we?"

Roosevelt never forgot those dramatic days, and the two men remained in touch. A serious misunderstanding early in FDR's first term clouded their personal relations for a time. But with the Republican party hopelessly isolationist in the darkening thirties, Stimson looked increasingly to Roosevelt for a new kind of international direction. When dining at the White House and in a series of personal letters and public statements, Stimson called on the president for the leadership only he could provide.

Although critical of many of Roosevelt's New Deal policies, especially his 1937 Supreme Court proposals, Stimson strongly supported FDR's new foreign economic policy, especially his reciprocal trade program. But where Hull, Stimson's successor whom he liked and admired, believed that the key to international peace was economic recovery and cooperation, Stimson believed that it lay in diplomatic and military preparedness. The difference between Hull and Stimson could not have been lost on FDR, who doubtless viewed Stimson's efforts with a mixture of appreciation and uneasiness.

On 15 November 1937—five weeks after Roosevelt's famous quarantine speech, which Stimson warmly endorsed—Stimson sent the president a long letter summing up his thoughts on the current world crisis and setting forth some of the considerations that were to guide him in the following years.

As Stimson saw it, there was an inescapable need for presidential leadership. The "influence of the American nation and its President for leadership, moral and material," Stimson wrote, "are great beyond any computation in the modern international world; . . . this leadership should be exercised not only with a view to the present aspects of problems but for their long distant solution and fruition."

After Munich, Prague, and the Nazi-Soviet pact, the European and world situation steadily worsened, and when war broke out in September 1939, Roosevelt entertained thoughts of some kind of bipartisan government. In December 1939, he corresponded with Col. Frank Knox, publisher of the *Chicago Daily News* and 1936 Republican vice-presidential candidate. "If there should develop," Roosevelt wrote, "a real crisis such as . . . a German-Russian victory . . . it would be necessary to put aside in large part strictly old-fashioned party government, and the people would understand such a situation."

By early June 1940—with France and possibly Great Britain facing almost certain defeat—Roosevelt knew that the time for action had arrived. On 19 June the president telephoned Stimson at his New York law office and invited him to join the cabinet as secretary of war; Knox was to be secretary of the navy. Stimson accepted.

The White House announcement the following day, on the eve of the Republican National Convention in Philadelphia, created a sensation and stunned the G.O.P. Conservative Republicans, in particular, were infuriated by Roosevelt's coup. Stimson, said the

Taft-family-owned *Cincinnati Times-Star,* "who has earned for himself a reputation as one of the greatest war shouters . . . is about as representative of Republican thought throughout the nation as . . . Earl Browder [the Communist party leader]."

Stimson experienced an acrimonious hearing before the Senate Military Affairs Committee, where he was interrogated by such leading isolationists as Arthur H. Vandenberg of Michigan and Robert A. Taft of Ohio, son of the former president whom Stimson had once served in the same position. The questioning left Stimson unapologetic. For years he had been in the forefront of the battle to halt the spread of aggression; he was not about to disavow that record now. As he told his hostile interlocuters, "If you go on reading from my past statements, you make me feel like Winston Churchill for having been right so often." On 9 July Stimson was confirmed by the Senate by a vote of 56 to 28, and the next day, Knox was approved by a vote of 66 to 16.

"It is impossible to exaggerate," Robert Sherwood, Harry Hopkins's biographer, wrote later, "the extent to which Stimson and Knox strengthened Roosevelt's hand in dealing with the immediate problems of 1940 and the longer-range problems of aid to Britain and the building up of our armed forces, as well as in the eventual fighting of the war." And, Sherwood added, "of the two men, Stimson bore appreciably heavier responsibilities because of the President's predilection for the Navy."

Stimson, not surprisingly, found the War Department materially and administratively in grave disrepair, "a situation," he wrote, "that is perfectly horrible." All the same, Stimson urged Roosevelt to press ahead with a massive defense program, including the enactment of Selective Service, the country's first peacetime draft law, which FDR was reluctant to support for fear of possible political repercussions. Time and again Stimson told Roosevelt, in so many words, that "if he would lead, the country would follow."

Similarly, in foreign affairs, Cordell Hull, doubtless scarred by his Wilsonian experience, tended to hold back and wait for public opinion to lead, but Stimson made no secret of his activism. For instance, he strongly supported the controversial destroyers-bases exchange that Churchill considered essential to Britain's survival. In answer to some of FDR's remaining doubts, Stimson declared that the exchange was "an exercise of the traditional power of the Executive in foreign affairs."

Stimson followed a similar strong line in Pacific affairs. Japan, he wrote in a memorandum in October 1940, "has historically shown that when the United States indicates by clear language that she intends to carry out a clear and affirmative policy in the Far East, Japan will yield to that policy even though it conflicts with her own Asiatic policy and conceived interests."

Thus Stimson believed that the time had come to draw the line against further German and Japanese aggression. He strongly supported FDR's innovative Lend-Lease policy and other new defense measures virtually unthinkable only a few months before. In early 1941, long before Roosevelt was prepared to do so, Stimson urged the president to use the U.S. Navy to help convoy supplies to Great Britain. No admirer of Stalin and the Soviet government, to which he had refused to extend diplomatic recognition when he was secretary of state, Stimson was one of Roosevelt's few top advisers to support the president's policy of giving all possible military assistance to the Soviet Union following Hitler's attack in June 1941.

Above all, Stimson was convinced that the crucial problem was and remained presidential leadership, FDR's willingness and readiness to lead the country. It was a theme to which Stimson returned over and over during the war years. On 22 April 1941, for instance, Stimson spoke to Roosevelt about "the necessity of his taking the lead and that without a lead on his part it was useless to expect the people would voluntarily take the initiative in letting him know whether or not they would follow him if he did take the lead." In his memoirs, Stimson emphasized that "*the essential difference between Stimson and the President was in the value they set on candor as a political weapon.* And as Stimson himself fully recognized, it was a good deal easier to advocate his policy as Secretary of War, than to carry it out, as President."

Stimson wrote later that "the impasse into which America had thought herself in 1941 might have continued indefinitely if that had been the will of the Axis," and if that had happened, "the President would have had to shoulder a large part of the blame." To Stimson's relief, Hitler and the Japanese did for Roosevelt what the president could not do for himself.

In the Pacific, Stimson supported a series of increasingly stringent economic measures against Japan. These included an embargo on oil and gasoline sales, a ban on steel and scrap iron purchases, and a freeze on Japanese credits in the United States, all of which Roosevelt imposed, one by one, in 1940–41.

During the war as before, Stimson and Roosevelt did not always see eye to eye on important military, foreign, or domestic issues. Stimson, for instance, strongly supported the Europe-First strategy that Roosevelt and Churchill had agreed on in 1941–42. On the other hand, Stimson long opposed the idea of an initial North African–Mediterranean campaign in 1942–43, an operation that Stimson regarded as a dangerous strategic diversion from the cross-channel attack he wanted launched in 1942 or 1943 at the latest.

Stimson, a moderately conservative Republican, believed that the war was no time for "politics as usual." He vigorously objected to the activities of some of Roosevelt's younger and more liberal aides and to their subtle, or not so subtle, efforts to use the war as an opportunity to advance some of their ideological or political objectives. As Stimson's authorized biographer put it: "In his desire to prepare the body and spirit of the country in a time of danger . . . [Stimson] was not much concerned by the thought that some of the New Deal social gains would have to be set aside for a season." Social needs, including racial issues, would have to wait their turn.

Stimson's overriding concern with how best to win the war led him occasionally to be angered by some of Mrs. Roosevelt's activities, and he made no secret of his feelings. Not unmindful of the need for improved living conditions and more combat opportunities for black servicemen, Stimson nevertheless denounced what he called "Mrs. Roosevelt's intrusive and impulsive folly" in attempting to meliorate military segregation and discrimination.

Stimson's direction of his department was unprecedented. As his biographer Elting E. Morison has written, he established "a harmony of civil and military interests within the War Department that is without other example in the direction of an American armed force in time of war." Stimson's stature, moreover, was such that the growing White House staff, including Fleet Adm. William D. Leahy, its military head, interposed no barrier to Stimson's access to the president, with whom the secretary remained on close and mutually respectful terms.

On the other hand, it must be noted that Stimson long regarded Roosevelt to be a poor administrator and filled his diary with painful examples of FDR's shortcomings. Stimson thought Roosevelt too much the ideologue and diplomatic amateur, often too clever for his own good and the national interest. "I doubt," Stimson wrote in September 1940, "whether we shall ever be able to hold him to any very systematic relations, because that is rather entirely antithetic to his nature and temperament." Two-thirds of his problems, Stimson reflected in November 1941, stemmed from "the topsy-turvy, upside-down system of poor administration [by] which Mr. Roosevelt runs the government." Pearl Harbor brought no change for the better. The president, Stimson wrote in March 1943, "is the poorest administrator I have ever worked under in respect to the orderly procedure and routine of his performance. He is not a good chooser of men and he does not know how to use them in coordination."

Not all of Stimson's decisions were universally approved, then or later. Following Pearl Harbor, in early 1942, Stimson supported the forced resettlement of about sixty thousand Japanese-Americans, deemed a potential security hazard on the West Coast. Stimson agreed to the move reluctantly. It would, he said, "make a tremendous hole in our constitutional system," and he sent his deputy, Assistant Secretary of War John J. McCloy, to try to ensure that the movement was made "with all humanity possible." In December 1944, the government action was formally sustained by the U.S. Supreme Court. More recently, however, the relocation decision has been much criticized.

As regards the unspeakable fate of the Jews and other persecuted minorities in Hitler's Europe, Stimson's humanitarian considerations clashed with his legalistic concerns, and the latter prevailed, although he was an old friend of Surpeme Court justice Felix Frankfurter—who had strongly urged his appointment on Roosevelt—and of leading exiles like former German chancellor Heinrich Brüning. Still, in Stimson's mind, as in Hull's, the millions of Jews and others facing almost certain death had no special priority in American policy. For reasons never fully spelled out, Stimson—or McCloy—supported the War Department's repeated refusal to consider the bombing of some of Hitler's extermination camps. "The positive solution to this problem," wrote McCloy, "is the earliest possible victory over Germany."

Stimson similarly objected to admitting a substantial number of refugee Jews and others to the United States. As late as March 1944, he recorded his opposition to Roosevelt's throwing "open internment camps in the United States for those refugees. . . . I think he ought to consult Congress because I fear that Congress will feel that it is the opening wedge to a violation of our immigration laws."

From his first year in office, Stimson was closely involved with the development of the atomic bomb and was Roosevelt's and Truman's principal civilian adviser on the project. He was convinced that the weapon should be built as speedily as possible. In October 1942, he told Maj. Gen. Leslie R. Groves, the officer in charge of the Manhattan Project, that it was his mission "to produce [the bomb] at the earliest possible date so as to bring the war to a conclusion." Once it was ready for use in the summer of 1945, Stimson supported its deployment against Japan, although he sought to limit casualties as much as possible.

Indeed, his last year in office was overshadowed by the bomb and its implications, which increasingly filled him with apprehension. In March 1945—after

Henry Stimson drawing some of the first capsules in the National Lottery for Selective Service registrants, Washington, D.C., 29 October 1940. Pictured are (left to right) FDR, Edwin Watson, Henry Stimson and C. R. Morris. (Courtesy FDR Library.)

discussing the subject with Roosevelt for the last time—Stimson wrote in his diary that his decision about the bomb was "by far the most searching and important thing that I had to do since I have been in the office of the Secretary of War because [it touches] matters which are deeper even than the principles of present government."

Stimson sought to make every reasonable effort to reach a lasting postwar accommodation with the Soviet Union, but there were limits to his readiness to share atomic information with the Russians. In December 1944, he told Roosevelt that he "knew [the Russians] were spying on our work but that they had not yet gotten any real knowledge of it," and he advised FDR against sharing production secrets of the bomb "until we [are] sure to get a real *quid pro quo* for our frankness." In his diary, he added, "[Roosevelt] said he thought he agreed with me."

When after Yalta Stimson returned to the subject with Roosevelt, he suggested that the United States might expect the liberalization of the Soviet domestic system in return for information on the bomb. At the time of Roosevelt's death, the subject remained open. But at the last cabinet meeting Stimson attended, in September 1945, he still argued for the greatest possible U.S. openness in atomic matters.

Although not unaware of the president's physical decline, Stimson was shocked by the news of Roosevelt's sudden death. In a personal letter to Mrs. Roosevelt, he wrote that Roosevelt had been "an ideal Commander in Chief. His vision of the broad problems of the strategy of the war was sound and accurate, and his relations to his military advisers and commanders were admirably correct. In the execution of their duties he gave them freedom, backed them up, and held them responsible. In all these particulars he seems to me to have been our greatest war President. And his courage and cheeriness in times of great emergency won for him the loyalty and affection of all who served under him."

"Lastly and most important," he went on, "his vision and interpretations of the mission of our country to help establish a rule of freedom and justice in this world raised a standard which put the United States in the unique position of world leadership which she now holds."

Unlike most of Roosevelt's cabinet, Stimson was willing to stay on under FDR's successor, for whom he soon developed a high regard and who reciprocated Stimson's trust and support. Stimson thus became the first person in American history to serve in the cabinets of four presidents. He remained in office until his seventy-eighth birthday on 21 September 1945. "I had long known Henry L. Stimson to be a great American and statesman," Truman wrote in his memoirs, and added that his retirement ended "one of the most distinguished careers of public service to this nation."

Henry L. Stimson published a number of interesting and important volumes of his own—*American Policy in Nicaragua* (New York: Scribners, 1927), *Democracy and Nationalism in Europe* (Princeton: Princeton University Press, 1934), and *The Far Eastern Crisis* (New York:

Harlan Fiske Stone, c. 1941–43. Artist: Oskar Stoessel. (National Portrait Gallery, Smithsonian Institution. Gift of David E. Finley.)

Harper, 1936). In active, if short-lived, retirement, he published (with McGeorge Bundy) *On Active Service in Peace and War* (New York: Harper, 1948). Stimson's article "The Decision to Use the Atomic Bomb" (*Harper's,* February 1947), remains a piece of lasting significance. Biographical accounts of Stimson vary in quality. Elting E. Morison's authorized account, *Turmoil and Tradition* (Boston: Houghton Mifflin, 1960), is thoughtfully reflective rather than adequately detailed. Richard N. Current, *Secretary Stimson* (New Brunswick, N.J.: Rutgers University Press, 1954), is unrelievedly—and wholly one-sidedly—critical. Stimson's background as secretary of state in the Hoover administration is treated sympathetically by Robert H. Ferrell in volume 11 of *The American Secretaries of State and Their Diplomacy* (New York: Cooper Square, 1963), and more critically in Armin Rappaport, *Henry L. Stimson and Japan, 1931–1933* (Chicago: University of Chicago Press, 1963). Stimson's diary has been edited for publication by Francis L. Loewenheim and Harold D. Langley, *The Politics of Integrity—The Personal Diary of Henry L. Stimson, 1929–1945* (New York: McGraw-Hill, in press).

FRANCIS L. LOEWENHEIM

See also Internment of Japanese-Americans; Selective Service Act

Stock Market

See Great Depression; Securities and Exchange Commission

Stone, Harlan Fiske

(11 October 1872–22 April 1946)

Supreme Court justice, 1925–41, chief justice, 1941–46. Born in New Hampshire, Stone graduated from Columbia University Law School in 1898. By 1924 he was dean of his alma mater. Calvin Coolidge appointed Stone attorney general in 1924 and the next year named him to the Supreme Court. Roosevelt, ignoring Stone's Republican background and conservative views, raised him to the chief justice's position in 1941, partly to refute the charge that his previous judicial appointments had been made on purely political grounds.

While on the Court, Stone consistently found himself in dissent, first arguing against the anti–New Deal justices of the 1930s' Court and later against the Roosevelt appointees (Black, Douglas, Rutledge, and Murphy) during the 1940s. Stone's judicial philosophy was marked by self-restraint, and he cautioned against invalidation of New Deal legislation on the grounds that such judicial action threatened legislative independence. But his judicial self-restraint was not total, and he insisted throughout his career on the Court's duty to consider the merits of statutory interpretations advanced by regulatory agencies.

Stone's greatest contribution to American constitutional law may have been his famous fourth footnote to his opinion in *United States* v. *Carolene Products Co.*, 304 U.S. 144 (1938). There Stone suggested that legislation that tends to restrict political processes and institutions protected by the Bill of Rights should be subject to a more exacting level of judicial scrutiny. This idea of "preferred freedoms" was frequently used by the Warren Court to vindicate individual rights threatened by government action. Ironically, Stone soon disassociated himself from this doctrine, and by 1946 he was bitterly dissenting in cases where it was used. While presiding over the Court in 1946, Stone was stricken by a cerebral hemorrhage. He died later that evening, mourned by the nation.

The best life of Stone is Alpheus Mason's *Harlan Fiske Stone* (New York: Viking Press, 1956). S. J. Konefsky, *Chief Justice Stone and the Supreme Court* (New York: Macmillan Co., 1945) is a scholarly analysis of Stone's legal opinions. Stone's own *Law and Its Administration* (New York: Columbia University Press, 1915) reveals the thought behind his belief in judicial self-restraint.

See also Supreme Court of the United States

Strikes

See Labor

Supreme Court of the United States

The highest judicial tribunal of the federal government, composed of one chief justice and eight associate justices; charged with the responsibility of interpreting the Constitution of the United States.

Beginning in the landmark cases of *Marbury* v. *Madison,* 1 Cranch 137 (1803) and *Fletcher* v. *Peck,* 6 Cranch 87 (1810), the Supreme Court laid claim to the power of judicial review over the actions of the coordinate branches of the federal government and those of the individual states as well. "It is, emphatically, the province and duty of the judicial department," wrote Chief Justice John Marshall in the *Marbury* case, "to say what the law is." With respect to acts of Congress, the Court used its power of nullification sparingly in the years after 1803, overturning only one other federal statute before the Civil War in the notorious *Dred Scott* decision of 1857.

The Supreme Court was not timid, however, about invalidating state laws that conflicted with federal statutes or with the constitutional provision granting Congress authority to regulate commerce among the states. "I do not think the United Staes would come to an end if we lost our power to declare an Act of Congress void," declared Justice Oliver Wendell Holmes at the end of the nineteenth century. "I do think the United States would be imperilled if we could not make that declaration as to the laws of the several states."

The decades after Appomattox were dominated by increased social and economic tensions in response to the growth of industry, the maturation of the business corporation, efforts by workers to form labor unions, and protests by farmers against low commodity prices and monopolies. In the midst of these issues, the Supreme Court assumed a much larger role in drawing the boundaries between the power of government to regulate economic affairs in the public interest and the right of individuals to remain free from state intervention.

One group of justices, strongly influenced by the

Members of the Supreme Court of the late Hoover–early Roosevelt administrations with Attorney General Mitchell and Solicitor General Thacher. Pictured are (left to right) Attorney General Mitchell; Justices Cardoza, Stone, Sutherland, Van Devanter, Hughes, Brandeis, Butler, and Roberts; and Solicitor General Thatcher. Missing from the group is Justice McReynolds. (UPI/Bettmann Archive.)

Important Supreme Court Decisions Affecting New Deal Legislation

CASE	VOTE	BASIS FOR DECISION
"Hot Oil," 1935	8–1	Invalidated Section 9(c) of NIRA: improper delegation of legislative power to executive
"Gold Cases," 1935	5–4	Upheld Congressional Joint Resolution of 5 June 1933: private contracts may not limit power of Congress to regulate currency
Schechter, 1935	9–0	Invalidated NIRA: improper delegation of legislative power and improper regulation of intrastate business
Farm Mortgage Moratorium, 1935	9–0	Invalidated Farm Mortgage Foreclosure Act of 1934: confiscated property without due compensation
Humphrey's Executor v. *United States,* 1935	9–0	Held that presidential powers did not include the power to remove a commissioner not working in the executive department
Butler, 1936	6–3	Invalidated Agricultural Adjustment Act of 1933: processing tax for regulating agricultural production not within purview of welfare clause
Ashwander v. *TVA,* 1936	8–1	Upheld the Tennessee Valley Act of 1933: production and sale of power incidental to national defense and navigation a legitimate exercise of federal power
Carter Coal Co., 1936	6–3	Invalidated the Guffey-Snyder Bituminous Coal Stabilization Act of 1935: law violated general welfare and due process clauses
Farm Mortgage Moratorium of 1935, 1937	9–0	Upheld new Frazier-Lemke Farm Mortgage Act: Congress had power to establish uniform bankruptcy laws
Wagner Labor Relations Act Cases, 1937	5–4	Upheld the National Labor Relations Act of 1935: used the interstate commerce clause to maintain right of employees to organize unions
Social Security Act Cases, 1937	7–2 5–4	Upheld the Social Security Act of 1935: federal tax for old-age pensions is a valid exercise of power to tax for general welfare
United States v. *Darby Lumber Co.,* 1941	9–0	Upheld the Fair Labor Standards Act of 1938: Congress may use interstate commerce clause to set workplace standards

Sources: Philip Dorf, *Visualized American History* (New York: Oxford Book Co., 1958), p. 226; also, Basil Rauch, *History of the New Deal,* 1933–1938 (New York: Creative Age Press, 1944) and Carl Brent Swisher, *American Constitutional Development* (Boston: Houghton Mifflin Co., 1954).

old Jacksonian legacy of entrepreneurial individualism, equality, and states' rights, adopted both an expansive reading of the Fourteenth Amendment's due process clause and a narrow interpretation of the interstate commerce and taxation provisions of the Constitution in order to restrict the scope of both state and federal intervention into the sphere of private economic decision making. These justices, for example, denied to the states the authority to regulate most private business firms, except those "affected with a public interest" such as railroads and other public utilities. They prevented adoption of a federal income tax until passage of a constitutional amendment in 1913, vetoed state laws that attempted to limit working hours, and frustrated the efforts of the federal government to prosecute manufacturing monopolies.

Another group of justices, heirs to the Radical Republican tradition of moral reform and positive government, remained far more receptive to governmental efforts at economic manipulation and redistribution. Their constitutional doctrines sustained state regulation of working conditions for certain categories of workers, especially women, allowed Congress to prohibit the use of interstate commerce for many deleterious purposes, and encouraged the use of taxation for regulatory as well as revenue purposes. By the time the nation entered the worst economic depression in its history during the 1930s, the Supreme Court possessed considerable doctrinal flexibility. By invoking prior decisions that limited governmental control over the economy, it could resist change. On the other hand, if it so desired, the Court might accommodate reforms by looking to those precedents that had sustained government intervention in the past.

President Herbert Hoover left Franklin Roosevelt with the most liberal Court in a generation when he filled three vacancies between 1929 and 1932 with a new chief justice, Charles Evans Hughes, and two associate justices, Benjamin N. Cardozo, the most distinguished state jurist in the country, and Owen Roberts, a moderate Pennsylvania Republican, who had gained favor with many progressives for his role in the prosecution of the Teapot Dome criminals. Although twenty-six senators voted against Hughes's appointment because of his Wall Street connections, many observers predicted that the new chief justice would lead the Court in a progressive direction, basing their judgment on his prior record as a member of the Court between 1910 and 1916.

The Hughes Court initially fulfilled these liberal expectations with a series of decisions in 1934 that indicated a generous conception of governmental power to cope with the economic crisis. Hughes himself wrote the Court's opinion in *Home Building & Loan Assn.* v. *Blaisdell*, 290 U.S. 398 (1934), wherein five of the justices upheld a state mortgage moratorium law against objections that it violated private rights of contract. He joined Justice Roberts's opinion in *Nebbia* v. *New York*, 291 U.S. 502 (1934), which swept away over a half century of precedent that limited the states' authority to fix prices. He again wrote for a narrow majority that sustained the New Deal's monetary policies. This last decision, taking the country off the gold standard, led Justice McReynolds to remark: "This is Nero at his worst. The Constitution is gone."

The Court's honeymoon with the New Deal ended abruptly in 1935, when the fragile five-man majority in *Nebbia* and *Blaisdell* began to splinter apart with the initial defection of Justice Roberts. Then, on "Black Monday," 27 May 1935, the Court toppled two important New Deal laws, the controversial National Industrial Recovery Act (NIRA) and the Frazier-Lemke Farm Relief Act. In addition, they sharply curtailed Roosevelt's authority to remove members of the independent regulatory commissions without specific approval from Congress. Although even the Court's liberals (Stone, Brandeis, and Cardozo) joined in portions of the decision invalidating the NIRA, Roosevelt compared their behavior to that of the justices in the *Dred Scott* case and condemned them for adopting "the horse-and-buggy definition of interstate commerce."

The chief justice himself joined the anti–New Deal coalition in earnest during the 1936 term of the Court, when he endorsed Roberts's opinion that doomed the Agricultural Adjustment Administration and concurred in the majority's mutilation of the Guffey Bituminous Coal Act. In addition, he authored an ingenious opinion in *Ashwander* v. *Tennessee Valley Authority*, 297 U.S. 288 (1936), which encouraged dissenting stockholders to sue corporate officers who did not oppose New Deal programs. Viewing the wreckage in the summer of 1936, Felix Frankfurter was moved to denounce the Court's "unreason and

Supreme Court Justices during FDR's Administration

Term of Service

1911–1937	Willis Van Devanter, Wyoming
1914–1941	James C. McReynolds, Tennessee
1916–1939	Louis D. Brandeis, Massachusetts
1922–1938	George Sutherland, Utah
1922–1939	Pierce Butler, Minnesota
1925–1946	Harlan F. Stone, New York (Chief Justice, 1941–1946)
1930–1941	Charles Evans Hughes, New York (Chief Justice, 1930–1941)
1930–1945	Owen J. Roberts, Pennsylvania
1932–1938	Benjamin N. Cardoza, New York
1937–1971	Hugo L. Black, Alabama
1938–1957	Stanley Reed, Kentucky
1939–1962	Felix Frankfurter, Massachusetts
1939–1975	William O. Douglas, Connecticut
1940–1949	Frank Murphy, Michigan
1941–1942	James F. Byrnes, South Carolina
1941–1954	Robert H. Jackson, New York
1943–1949	Wiley B. Rutledge, Iowa

folly" for erecting constitutional barriers to both state and federal action against the depression. "This fateful term is over," he told Justice Stone, "but its ghosts will walk for many a day."

Six months later, however, in the aftermath of FDR's crushing reelection victory and his legislative plan to reorganize the federal judiciary by adding new justices when those over the age of seventy did not retire, the Court reversed gears once again. The old pre-1935 majority, led by Hughes and Roberts, upheld a state minimum wage law almost identical to one vetoed in June by the Court, and they also sustained the New Deal's major labor reform in the landmark case of *National Labor Relations Board* v. *Jones & Laughlin Steel Corp.*, 301 U.S. 1 (1937). The chief justice wrote both opinions, the first one laying to rest the old doctrine of "liberty of contract," and the second one giving Congress broad authority to regulate labor-management conflicts that affected interstate commerce.

Various explanations have been put forth to explain the Court's sudden shift in 1937. Hughes justified his behavior by casting blame upon the New Deal's lawyers, who, he complained, drafted vague, unconstitutional statutes that deserved legal burial. This thesis has some credibility with respect to the fate of the NIRA, but none at all when one reflects upon the care with which very good lawyers wrote the Agricultural Adjustment Act and the Guffey Coal Act.

Other scholars have suggested that Hughes cast his vote with Roberts and the four conservatives (Butler, Van Devanter, Sutherland, and McReynolds) in order to avoid close 5–4 decisions that damaged the Court's reputation for constitutional sagacity. But this hypothesis does not explain why Hughes found 5–4 decisions in favor of the New Deal any less injurious to the Court's reputation in 1937.

A more plausible explanation may be that Hughes looked upon many of the New Deal programs and some of those on the state level as too radical, in terms of both their constitutional implications and their consequences for redistributing social and economic power. By overturning various New Deal measures in 1936, he hoped to portray Roosevelt and his advisers as dangerous subversives who deserved repudiation at the polls. But FDR's landslide victory frustrated this strategy and left Hughes with few alternatives but capitulation to the popular will. The chief justice, who had not opposed state minimum wage laws and who remained flexible on interstate commerce issues, was not required to modify his views significantly in order to lead the constitutional revolution of 1937. Justice Roberts, who had been more dogmatically conservative, could not explain his "shift in time that saved nine" except on the basis of political expediency.

The Hughes Court's confrontation with Roosevelt and the New Deal has tended to overshadow other aspects of the justices' work during the decade. This Court, however, blazed important new trails in the protection of civil liberties and civil rights. In cases such as *Stromberg* v. *California,* 283 U.S. 359 (1931) and *DeJonge* v. *Oregon,* 299 U.S. 353 (1937), Hughes authored distinguished opinions that significantly enlarged the scope of First Amendment rights protected against state abridgement. The justices also drove another nail into the coffin of "separate but equal" with their decision in *Missouri ex rel. Gaines* v. *Canada,* 305 U.S. 337 (1938), which ruled that a state's refusal to provide legal education to a qualified Negro constituted a denial of equal protection. The Hughes Court also broadened the reach of habeas corpus to attack constitutionally defective state trials and greatly expanded the in forma pauperis docket, which permitted indigent defendants to challenge their convictions.

By 1943, the Hughes Court of the depression decade had become "the Roosevelt Court" of the World War II era as retirements and deaths permitted FDR to make more appointments than any other chief executive since George Washington. Roosevelt named as associate justices eight loyal New Dealers—Hugo Black, Stanley Reed, Felix Frankfurter, William O. Douglas, Frank Murphy, James F. Byrnes, Robert Jackson, and Wiley Rutledge. Upon Hughes's retirement in 1941, he elevated Harlan Stone, a liberal Republican, to the chief justiceship. Despite their common New Deal credentials, however, Roosevelt's justices displayed as much conflict as their predecessors during the previous decade.

Under Chief Justice Stone the Court did not return to the discredited judicial activism of the past with respect to economic issues. Instead, the justices regularly bowed to the will of the legislature in this area and sustained very extensive federal powers over the economy. In the landmark case of *Wickard* v. *Filburn,* 317 U.S. 111 (1942), for example, a unanimous Court upheld the authority of the Department of Agriculture to limit the amount of wheat a farmer might grow even for immediate home consumption.

No such consensus characterized the justices' views on cases that touched civil liberties and civil rights. One faction, led by Stone, Black, Douglas, and Murphy, believed that the Court had a special mission to protect preferred freedoms, including speech, press, and the right to vote, from legislative violation and to defend "discrete and insular minorities" from the tyranny of the majority. Another faction, usually led by Justice Frankfurter, believed that the Court should display the same degree of judicial restraint in this area as when passing upon purely economic regulations. By 1945, in cases involving freedom of speech and the mandatory flag salute, a majority of the justices had repudiated the Frankfurter approach in favor of Stone's preferred freedoms concept.

With one glaring exception, the Stone Court compiled a strong civil liberties record during the period of the Second World War. In *Cramer* v. *United States,* 325 U.S. 1 (1945), they imposed strict conditions upon the federal government for all treason prosecutions, and they quashed the government's principal espionage indictment in *Hartzel* v. *United States,* 324 U.S. 213 (1944). The exception concerned resident Japanese, citizens and aliens, whom the federal government forced into relocation camps in 1942. With only three dissenters, the Court placed the stamp of constitutional approval upon the worst violation of civil liberties in the nation's history.

The best survey of the Court's activities in the Roosevelt era is still Alfred H. Kelly and Winfred A. Harbison, *The American Constitution,* 6th ed. (New York: W. W. Norton & Co., 1982), pp. 682–802. A brief, cogent analysis may be found in Paul L. Murphy, *The Constitution in Crisis Times, 1918–1969* (New York: Harper & Row, 1972). On the Hughes Court specifically, see Michael E. Parrish, "The Hughes Court, the Great Depression, and the Historians," *Historian* 40 (February 1978):286–308. On the Court under Chief Justice Stone, see C. Herman Pritchett, *The Roosevelt Court: A Study in Judicial Politics and Values, 1937–1947* (New York: Viking Press, 1948) and Alpheus T. Mason, *Harlan Fiske Stone: Pillar of the Law* (New York: Viking Press, 1956).

MICHAEL E. PARRISH

See also Agricultural Adjustment Administration; Black, Hugo Lafayette; Brandeis, Louis Dembitz; Byrnes, James Frances; Civil Liberties in Wartime; Court-Packing Plan; Douglas, William Orville; Frankfurter, Felix; Holmes, Oliver Wendell, Jr.; Hughes, Charles Evans; Internment of Japanese-Americans; Interstate Commerce; Jackson, Robert Houghwout; Monetary Policy; Murphy, Francis William; National Industrial Recovery Act; Negroes; New Deal; Office of the Presidency; Reed, Stanley Forman; Rutledge, Wiley Blount, Jr.; Wages and Hours Legislation

Swanson, Claude Augustus

(31 March 1862–7 July 1939)

Secretary of the navy, 1933–39. Born in the old Confederacy at Swansonville, Virginia (near Danville),

Claude Swanson graduated from Randolph-Macon in 1885 and received his law degree from the University of Virginia in 1886. Soon entering politics, Swanson served as congressman (1893–1906), governor of Virginia (1906–10), and senator (1910–33).

With his frock coat and winged collar, Swanson seemed a gentlemanly anachronism in the twentieth century, but his seat on the Senate Committee on Naval Affairs and his strong espousal of a navy "second-to-none" brought him into contact with FDR during World War I.

Aged and ill in 1933, Swanson looked out of place in the New Deal cabinet. But his appointment as secretary of the navy opened a Senate seat for Governor Harry Byrd, and his poor health allowed FDR to deal directly with the Navy Department.

Swanson did push Congress, with modest success, to fund navy complements to their authorized level, but for much of 1934, he was bedridden with high blood pressure and thus played little part in fighting for the pivotal Vinson-Trammel Act. Again, in 1936, Swanson was sidelined for six months with a broken rib, and FDR became personally involved in drafting the plans for the *North Carolina* class of battleships.

In 1937, Swanson, who was deeply suspicious of Japan, proposed strengthening Pearl Harbor and turning Guam into a major base, but Congress rebuffed these proposals. Swanson proved more successful in forestalling the navy's desire for a general staff. By rejecting, with FDR's approval, three such requests, Swanson kept in place the machinery for tight civilian control.

Swanson's health declined to such a degree in 1938 that he had to be carried into cabinet meetings. In April 1939, FDR remarked to Josephus Daniels, "Swanson is too sick a man to do much, but I haven't the heart to let him go. . . . You know, I am my own secretary of the navy." Three months later, Swanson died at Rapidan Camp in the Blue Ridge Mountains near Criglersville, Virginia.

The most recent and extensive look at Swanson's career is provided by Allison Saville in *American Secretaries of the Navy,* vol. 2, ed. Paolo Coletta (Annapolis: Naval Institute Press, 1980). Harold L. Ickes in *The Secret Diary* (New York: Simon & Schuster, 1953) offers some observations on Swanson's health problems.

MALCOLM MUIR, JR.

T

Tammany Hall

New York City's Democratic political organization, which had long dominated city politics and carried a reputation for corruption and bossism. Franklin Roosevelt began his public career as a vigorous opponent of Tammany Hall. In 1911 the New York legislature had the task of electing a U.S. senator, this being before senators were directly elected. Of the possible candidates, Tammany boss Charles F. Murphy chose Billy "Blue-eyed" Sheehan, who Roosevelt was convinced was not the best candidate. Moreover, Roosevelt objected to the power of Tammany over the Democratic caucus and hence over the election. Roosevelt joined and soon became the informal leader of a group of insurgent Democrats who withheld support from Sheehan and so stalemated the legislature. Roosevelt felt that "the Democratic party is on trial, and having been given control of the government chiefly through up-State votes, cannot afford to surrender its control to the organization in New York City." Murphy brought various means of pressure to bear on members of the group, including attacking their personal character and their strength with the voters, but the stubborn insurgents held on from January until late March.

As pressure mounted and the group wearied, they finally agreed to a compromise, Judge James A. O'Gorman, who was at least as much a Tammany man as Sheehan. Despite the fact that Roosevelt claimed victory from the situation, observers at the time agreed that Roosevelt and his band had been outmaneuvered. Yet the episode brought Roosevelt favorable national publicity as a valiant crusader for progressive politics, and with the passing of time the memory of a man sticking to his principles grew stronger than that of his defeat at the hands of Tammany.

As the decade progressed, Roosevelt's attitude toward the New York City organization changed. In 1912 he organized a short-lived "Empire State Democracy" to counter Tammany's power but was again outwitted by Murphy. Two years later Roosevelt announced his candidacy for the senate in a bid to wrest control of the party away from Tammany. In his only serious electoral defeat, Roosevelt lost badly in the primary to James Gerard, Tammany's choice, who in turn lost to the Republican. Roosevelt had learned that he could not win statewide office without support from Tammany. He was also impressed with some of the social legislation sponsored by Tammany in New York and with a few of the progressive members of the machine, notably Alfred E. Smith and Robert F. Wagner. On the Fourth of July, 1917, the truce became official when Roosevelt spoke at Tammany headquarters in New York City and was photographed with Murphy. This more tolerant relationship paid off for Roosevelt in 1920 when Democratic presidential nominee James M. Cox of Ohio selected Roosevelt as his running mate. Cox had checked first with Murphy who admitted to not liking Roosevelt but agreed nevertheless to approve his nomination.

In his campaign for the presidency, Roosevelt forged an uneasy working relationship with Tammany. In 1931 public opinion forced New York governor Roosevelt to take a stand against the corruption in the Tammany machine. FDR walked a tightrope, not wanting the nation to perceive him as a friend of corruption, yet also not wanting to alienate Tammany and risk a divided party. He remained aloof from Judge Samuel Seabury's investigations until August of 1932 when he had secured the Democratic presidential nomination. Then he led a series of hearings at Albany, New York, inquiring into the administration of Tammany-backed New York City Mayor Jimmy Walker, who was accused of corrupt practices. After several days of sharp questioning, Walker resigned and thus relieved Roosevelt of having to choose between appearing to be soft on corruption or straining his tenuous relationship with Tammany. Roosevelt entered the fall campaign of 1932 with his clean-government image intact and with the support of Tammany. In his troubled relationship with Tammany Hall, Roosevelt set the pattern for other interactions with urban political machines. Although his

414

reform inclination was to oppose bossism, many times Roosevelt found it politically necessary to work with rather than against the big-city bosses.

The best source on Roosevelt's early career is Frank Freidel, *Franklin D. Roosevelt*, vol. 1–3 (Boston: Little, Brown & Co., 1952, 1954, 1956). Much of Roosevelt's relationship with Tammany is also included in less detail in James MacGregor Burns, *Roosevelt: The Lion and the Fox* (New York: Harcourt, Brace & World, 1956).

See also Governor of New York; Murphy, Charles Francis; State Senator of New York; Smith, Alfred E.; Wagner, Robert Ferdinand; Walker, James John

---

Tape Recordings

A collection of sound recordings of FDR's conversations with aides and visitors to the Oval Office, made in the fall of 1940, known as "The FDR Tapes." In early February 1939, FDR had been deeply angered at being misquoted on the issue of American neutrality in reports of his conference with the Senate Military Affairs Committee. Henry M. Kannee, the president's stenographer, and Steve Early, his press secretary, soon after discussed with FDR means of keeping accurate mechanical transcriptions of future conversations in the Oval Office so as to prevent further misquotes and distortions. Kannee, in consultation with inventor Harry Payne, designed a continuous film recording machine, based on the principles of the film sound track. The machine was built by RCA as a gift to FDR and was presented to the president in June 1940; it was installed in the White House basement beneath the Oval Office.

Only a few tapings were made of FDR's conversations, however, and they vary greatly in subjects and participants. Some of the tapes reveal FDR's manner of dominating conversation, as well as his shrewd approach to problems. A conversation of 4 October 1940 with House Speaker Sam Rayburn and House Floor Leader John McCormick shows FDR's concern with maintaining neutrality with Japan while continuing arms sales to Axis enemies. "I'll say [to Japan]: I'm terribly sorry. We do not consider ourselves [chuckle] a belligerent. . . . Now all we can say to you is that, of course, if you act on that assumption—that we're a belligerent—and make any form of attack on us, *we're going to defend our own*—we're going to defend our *own*—and nothing further." Other conversations reveal FDR as a shrewd Democratic party tactician planning the 1940 campaign, sympathetically discussing segregation in the armed forces with A. Philip Randolph of the Brotherhood of Sleeping Car Porters, and planning strategies to combat hostile press reports.

FDR immediately placed Kannee in charge of the machine when it was installed, and thereafter he apparently had little to do with its use. There was no apparent pattern to the types of conversations recorded. They were clearly not meant for entrapment; FDR dominates every conversation and his listeners have difficulty getting a word in. Taping did not continue past the autumn of 1940. Despite his desire to maintain accurate records of statements, FDR was very uncomfortable with the notion of mechanical recording or even extensive note taking of private conversations. As Arthur Schlesinger points out, FDR greatly opposed the publication of the transcriptions of the Big Four conferences of 1919. "Four people cannot be conversationally frank with each other if somebody is taking down notes for future publication. I feel very strongly about this." That reservation, coupled with the extremely poor sound quality of the tapes, may explain why they were abandoned as suddenly and secretly as they were begun.

R. J. C. Butow, the historian who "discovered," transcribed, and analyzed the tapes at the FDR Library, has written an account of their history. This account, along with a brief commentary by Arthur M. Schlesinger, Jr., may be found in R. J. C. Butow, "The FDR Tapes," *American Heritage* 32, no. 2 (February–March 1984): 8–23.

Tariff Reform

See Reciprocal Trade Agreements

Taxation

The highest priority of Franklin D. Roosevelt's tax policies was the raising of revenues for new programs, but Roosevelt made a determined, although largely unsuccessful, effort to shift the tax burden to the wealthiest individuals and corporations.

During the Roosevelt years, the tax revenues of the federal government massively increased from $1.9 billion in 1933 (about 3 percent of gross national product) to $44.1 billion in 1945 (about 21 percent of gross national product). Increasing these revenues was a continuing priority of Roosevelt's. During most of the New Deal, he sought balanced budgets, and during World War II, he sought to mitigate inflation through high taxes. He valued taxes more for their ability to fund new programs than for their capacity to redistribute income and wealth, although both were his goals. During the New Deal, he would support even regressive taxation if he believed that it was necessary to the political success of a new program he desired. During World War II, Roosevelt cooperated with Congress in the introduction of income taxation directed more at wages and salaries than at profits and rents.

Roosevelt, however, wanted taxes that would not only raise revenues but also enhance economic justice. He preferred to finance the New Deal and World War II with taxes that took large shares of the income of the largest corporations and wealthiest individuals. When he could do so without jeopardizing his spending programs, he always tried to increase the progressivity of the tax system.

In the early New Deal, Roosevelt moved cautiously in creating a more redistributional tax system.

He wished to conserve his political resources to pursue other reforms, and he and his secretary of the treasury, Henry Morgenthau, Jr., required time to rebuild, after the sixteen years of Republican leadership, a Treasury staff capable of the technically difficult work of devising new progressive taxes that would be effective in raising revenue. Consequently, until 1935, when Congress and Roosevelt increased taxes, they did not make them significantly more progressive. The National Industrial Recovery Act (NIRA) provided only a small tax (0.1 percent) on corporate capital stock; the NIRA's more substantial excess-profits tax was designed only to induce compliance with the modest capital-stock tax. Roosevelt supported the Agricultural Adjustment Act's food-processing taxes, which, like sales taxes, were passed on to urban consumers. The Revenue Act of 1934, the major budget-balancing effort of that year, only slightly increased the progressivity of income, estate, and gift taxation. And in 1935, Roosevelt advocated employee payroll taxes to help finance Social Security. He believed that such taxes were necessary, despite their regressivity, to prevent conservative counterattacks that might demolish Social Security. Roosevelt pointed out that "we put those payroll contributions there so as to give the contributors a legal, moral, and political right to collect their pensions and their unemployment benefits." He explained that "with those taxes in there, no damn politician can ever scrap my social security program."

In June of 1935, Roosevelt launched tax reform. In a message to Congress, he called for a graduated tax on corporations to check the growth of monopoly, a tax on the dividends that holding companies received from corporations they controlled, surtaxes that would raise the maximum income tax rate on individuals from 63 to 79 percent, and a tax on inheritances (to be imposed in addition to federal estate taxation). Budget balancing was less important than reducing the concentration of wealth and income. In his message, Roosevelt declared that accumulations of wealth meant "great and undesirable concentration of control in relatively few individuals over the employment and welfare of many, many others." Later, Roosevelt explained that his purpose was "not to destroy wealth, but to create broader range of opportunity, to restrain the growth of unwholesome and sterile accumulations and to lay the burdens of Government where they can best be carried." Thus, Roosevelt justified his tax reform program in terms of both its inherent equity and its ability to liberate the energies of individuals and small corporations, thereby advancing recovery.

These purposes put Roosevelt squarely in the tradition of redistributional taxation that had carried forward the single-tax movement, tariff reform, and the wartime income tax program of the Wilson administration. For Roosevelt, however, tax reform had an objective that was specific to the 1930s: promoting recovery from the Great Depression through the energizing of individual enterprise. To some extent Roosevelt's enthusiasm for tax reform was a response to the growing "thunder on the Left," particularly Huey Long's Share Our Wealth movement, and to calls from western progressives like George Norris, Robert La Follette, Jr., Hiram Johnson, and William Borah for sharply graduated income, inheritance, and estate taxes. But, more important, Roosevelt, like Woodrow Wilson before him, was personally devoted to *both* balanced budgets and redistributional taxation. By appointing Morgenthau in 1934, he deliberately selected a secretary of the treasury who shared his beliefs on taxation and who, Roosevelt expected, would bring redistributional taxation to the fore and strive for balanced budgets.

Congress gave Roosevelt only some of what he wanted in the Revenue Act of 1935. Congress set the new rates lower than Roosevelt desired and did not enact the inheritance tax. Moreover, the act raised little new revenue. But Congress increased estate taxes and approved the rest of Roosevelt's proposals. Roosevelt and Supreme Court justice Louis Brandeis, like other champions of a more competitive economy, viewed the act as the entering wedge of crucial social change.

After the decisive tax reform victory in 1935, Roosevelt thought that he would not have to request any new taxes until after the presidential election of 1936. However, in early 1936, the Supreme Court's invalidation of the Agricultural Adjustment Act's processing tax and Congress' override of Roosevelt's veto of the bonus threatened a substantial increase in the federal deficit. In response, Roosevelt asked Congress to pass a revenue-raising measure that he expected to have even more redistributional significance than the Revenue Act of 1935: an undistributed profits tax. He proposed to eliminate the existing taxes on corporate income, capital stock, and excess profits and to place a tax only on the profits that corporations did not distribute to their stockholders. The tax would be graduated according to the proportion of profits that were undistributed. Morgenthau believed that the tax would fight both tax avoidance and the concentration of corporate power. He was convinced that corporations deliberately retained profits to avoid the taxation of dividends under the individual income tax. And he believed that large corporations used undistributed surpluses to achieve an unfair advantage in competing with small firms for new capital. The tax would provide a powerful incentive for corporations to distribute their profits to their shareholders. Those shareholders, in turn, would generate large revenues by paying high surtaxes.

The undistributed profits tax encountered trouble in Congress, but did include a modest graduated tax on the undistributed profits of corporations. Even after watering down, however, the Revenue Act of 1936 was probably the most dramatic closing of a tax loophole ever to be undertaken in an election year.

Roosevelt followed the Revenue Act of 1936 with a campaign to make the "present tax structure evasion-proof." He was concerned about the loss of revenues from the increasingly clever discovery of loopholes and genuinely outraged by wealthy individuals who used the loopholes. He threatened to go on the radio and "name names." Following explicit testimony by Morgenthau, Congess passed the Revenue Act of 1937, which increased taxation of personal holding companies, limited deductions for incorporated yachts and country estates, restricted deductions for artificial losses from sales or exchanges of property, reduced tax incentives for the creation of multiple trusts, and eliminated favors for nonresident taxpayers.

The Revenue Act of 1937 was the high-water mark of New Deal tax reform. In 1938, Roosevelt was prepared to take tax reform even further. He wished to increase, and to make more progressive, the undistributed profits tax, establish a graduated tax on capital gains, and tax the income from federal, state, and local bonds. However, the tax reform of 1935–37, more than any other aspect of the New Deal, had stimulated business hostility to Roosevelt. Business was eager to counterattack. Roosevelt's unsuccessful Court fight, which had strengthened congressional opposition to the New Deal, and the recession of 1937–38, which made Congress more receptive to business pleading, presented the opportunity.

Led by Bernard Baruch and Joseph P. Kennedy, business opponents of New Deal tax reform charged that Roosevelt's taxes, particularly the undistributed profits tax, had caused the recession by discouraging investment. Some professional economists and even members of the administration, including Harry Hopkins, agreed. Worried about receiving blame for the recession in a congressional election year, conservative Democrats in Congress broke with the president and supported the business argument that tax cuts were necessary to restore business confidence. They pushed through Congress a measure that reduced to insignificance the tax on undistributed profits and discarded the graduated corporate income tax. Roosevelt, respecting the strength of the opposition, decided not to veto the unpalatable bill. Instead, he allowed the Revenue Act of 1938 to become law without his signature and denounced the act as the "abandonment of a important principle of American taxation."

In 1939, Congress formally closed out New Deal tax reform by eliminating altogether the undistributed profits tax. Facing a Congress now consistently hostile to tax reform, Roosevelt emphasized antitrust action as his means of combating the concentration of corporate power and concentrated upon deficit spending and monetary expansion to promote economic recovery.

The revenue acts of 1935, 1936, and 1937 did not revolutionize the distribution of wealth or dramatically increase economic opportunities. The acts reduced only modestly the incomes received by the nation's richest families and had virtually no effect on their wealth holdings. The acts left the corporate structure intact. However, their failure was not the responsibility of the New Deal. Roosevelt's tax reform program was the most progressively redistributional since Woodrow Wilson's wartime tax program. And the revenue acts of 1935–37 were almost certainly as redistributional as any that could have been passed during those years. By 1937, economic recovery had advanced far enough to undermine the sup-

port for redistributional taxation that existed among professionals, small businesspersons, the more prosperous farmers, and skilled workers. Then the recession of 1937–38 intervened, allowing conservatives to confirm growing middle-class fears that the structural reforms instituted by the New Deal had gone too far and now threatened economic expansion. The wealthiest corporations and individuals regained the upper hand in setting tax policy and held their power through World War II.

The war proved to be more important than the New Deal in shaping the modern tax system. The wartime crisis brought enormous increases in the government's need for resources. The Roosevelt administration acquired those revenues through borrowing and through the initiation of a "mass-based" income tax, placing the tax upon wages and salaries, rather than profits and rents. To produce a more predictable flow of revenue and to reduce taxpayer resistance to the new taxes on wages and salaries, Roosevelt and Congress introduced withholding of income taxes. The new system worked. With the number of income tax–paying individuals growing from 3.9 million in 1939 to 42.6 million in 1945 and with national income increasing rapidly during the same period, federal income tax collections grew astonishingly. They had increased from $747 million in 1933 to $2.2 billion in 1933 but accounted for a lesser share of federal tax revenues (42 percent) in 1939 than in 1933 (46 percent). By 1945, federal income tax collections grew to $35.1 billion and accounted for 80 percent of federal tax revenues.

Roosevelt faced enormous expenditures for a mobilization of unprecedented capital intensity, and he wished to avoid the kind of economically and politically disastrous inflation that had raged during World War I. Consequently, he favored massive tax increases, but would have preferred to finance the war with taxes that bore heavily on business and upper-income groups. His problem was that congressional opposition to such taxes had grown even more potent. If he fought for them, he risked suffering a humiliating defeat, as he did in 1944, when Congress, for the first time in its history, overrode a presidential veto of a revenue act. Consequently, Roosevelt usually deferred to congressional leadership.

Congress was able to impose a revenue system that was both highly productive of revenue and extremely favorable to business because of the wide popularity of the war effort. In contrast to World War I mobilization, it was not necessary to leverage the support of the Left for the war by enacting a highly redistributional tax system. The World War II tax system, despite its highly regressive features, was not a major political liability to the Democratic party.

Once in place, the revenue system created during World War II had a longevity that the revenue system of World War I had lacked. The withholding and generous deductions contributed to that longevity by reducing the pain of taxpaying. So did the fear of a renewed depression that led to public tolerance of taxation favorable to business. But perhaps most important was the New Deal's reinforcement of the legitimacy of the income tax—a legitimacy that extended even to the income tax of World War II. Ironically, the New Deal program of tax reform assisted the World War II income tax to survive with almost no major revisions into the 1980s.

We have no history of taxation during the Roosevelt era, and must rely on scattered sources. The best place to obtain an understanding of Roosevelt's personal approach to taxation is John Morton Blum, *From the Morgenthau Diaries, Years of Crisis, 1928–1938* (Boston: Houghton Mifflin Co., 1959). The best summary of the content of New Deal tax legislation is found in Sidney Ratner, *American Taxation, Its History as a Social Force in Democracy* (New York: W. W. Norton & Co., 1942). Clarifying the relationship of Roosevelt's tax policies to the rest of the New Deal are Ellis Hawley, *The New Deal and the Problem of Monopoly* (Princeton: Princeton University Press, 1966) and Herbert Stein, *The Fiscal Revolution in America* (Chicago: University of Chicago Press, 1969). Hawley explores New Deal interest in using taxation to attack concentrations of economic power, and Stein discusses the extent and significance of business hostility to New Deal tax policies.

W. ELLIOT BROWNLEE

See also Court-Packing Plan; Fiscal Policy; Monetary Policy; Recession of 1937–38

Teheran Conference

First meeting of the Big Three, President Franklin D. Roosevelt, British prime minister Winston S. Churchill, and Soviet premier Joseph Stalin, 28 November to 1 December 1943 (code name Eureka). Roosevelt was accompanied by Harry Hopkins, W. Averell Harriman, Chief of Staff Admiral William Leahy, and Charles Bohlen. Churchill had with him Foreign Minister Anthony Eden and General Hastings Ismay. Roosevelt had pressed for Cairo as the site of the talks, but Stalin had insisted on Teheran, claiming the need to maintain secure communications with his armed forces.

Teheran lay just south of the Elbenz Mountains, which cut the Persian capital off from the Caspian Sea. Roosevelt had planned to stay at the American legation, but reports of a planned assassination plot by Nazi agents against the Big Three led him to accept Stalin's offer to stay at the Soviet Embassy. Churchill stayed at the United Kingdom legation, which with the Soviet embassy made up one large compound.

The major result of the Teheran Conference was the decision to mount the cross-channel invasion of Europe (Overlord) in May 1944 in conjunction with an invasion of southern France (Anvil) and a Russian drive from the East. Stalin also restated his promise to enter the war against Japan once Germany was defeated. The Overlord decision was Roosevelt's major consideration at the conference. Besides resolving the long-standing tensions among the Allies over Stalin's persistent push for a second front, the decision on Overlord also served to deflect Churchill's pressures for military operations in the Balkans and the eastern

Mediterranean in 1944. Partly in concession to Churchill's interests, the Big Three did agree to try to persuade Turkey to enter the war against Hitler.

Roosevelt came to the meeting hoping also to establish a close rapport with Stalin and to address important political issues concerning the postwar settlement in Europe. In his efforts to create a good personal relationship with the Soviet leader, Roosevelt resorted to joining Stalin in taunting Churchill. At a dinner the second night, Stalin began needling Churchill that England wanted a "soft" peace for Germany; Stalin for his part thought fifty thousand German officers should be liquidated. Seeing how this aroused Churchill, Roosevelt joined in on Stalin's side. Then, at a private meeting of the Big Three on the fourth day of the conference, Roosevelt began teasing Churchill about his disposition, his cigars, and his habits in order to break down Stalin's reserve. Roosevelt felt by the end of the conference that he had established a good relationship with the Soviet premier.

In discussions on the political issues surrounding the postwar settlement, Roosevelt achieved mixed results. He attempted to convince Stalin of the desirability of the American president's "Four Policemen" plan and his hopes for a postwar international organization to keep the peace and maintain global security. Stalin was dubious about the scheme, but did give a general acceptance to a world scope for the proposed organization. In discussions about Russia's intentions in the Baltic states and Poland, Roosevelt also had to worry about U.S. public opinion in the 1944 presidential campaign. Russian annexations in these areas could alienate important ethnic blocs of American voters. Roosevelt acknowledged Russia's historic ties to the Baltic states, but stressed the need to take note of the importance U.S. public opinion gave to self-determination. Roosevelt also agreed to Russian plans to redefine Poland's borders to meet Soviet security concerns, but took pains to impress Stalin with American interest in the future independence of Poland. The issue of Poland's borders and legitimate government would continue to be a central concern at the Yalta Conference in 1945 and would serve as a major point of contention in the early cold war. Finally, on the issue of postwar plans for Germany, Stalin continued to press for a punitive settlement. The details of the division of Germany were deferred to the European Advisory Commission established by the Moscow foreign ministers' meeting in October 1943.

Besides the strictly diplomatic plenary sessions, there were more ceremonial gatherings such as Churchill's presentation to Stalin of the Sword of Stalingrad, given by King George to the "steel-hearted citizens" of that beleaguered city, and the banquet given to celebrate Churchill's sixty-ninth birthday. Such expressions of Allied solidarity, as well as the decisions on Overlord and Anvil and Stalin's pledge to enter the war against Japan would support the judgment that the Teheran Conference was the high-water mark of Big Three agreement. The decision to defer facing the knottier political problems of the postwar settlement indicated, however, that there were underlying tensions that would trouble the Grand Coalition in the future.

The best and most recent account of Roosevelt's wartime diplomacy and the Teheran Conference can be found in Robert Dallek, *Franklin D. Roosevelt and American Foreign Policy, 1932–1945* (New York: Oxford University Press, 1979). More personal details can be found in James MacGregor Burns, *Roosevelt: The Soldier of Freedom, 1940–1945* (New York: Harcourt Brace Jovanovich, 1970). The conference is treated in the context of the developing cold war in John Lewis Gaddis, *The United States and the Origins of the Cold War, 1941–1947* (New York: Columbia University Press, 1972). Older, but still useful, is Herbert Feis's magisterial account in *Churchill, Roosevelt, Stalin: The War They Waged and the Peace They Sought* (Princeton: Princeton University Press, 1957).

See also Cairo Conferences; Churchill, Winston Leonard Spencer; Foreign Policy; Hitler, Adolf, and Germany; Hopkins, Harry L.; Personal Diplomacy; Stalin, Joseph, and the Soviet Union; World War II

Temporary National Economic Committee

Headed by Wyoming senator Joseph C. O'Mahoney, the Temporary National Economic Committee (TNEC), held formal hearings from 1 December 1938 to 11 March 1941 to review persistent problems of the American economy in the wake of the Great Depression, especially the effects of monopoly. The committee called 552 witnesses, their testimony and deliberations filling thirty-seven volumes of printed material. The investigation turned out to be in part a showcase for Keynesian economics, publicizing economic theories whose policy implications the experience with the recession of 1937 had seemed to confirm. Yet the range of testimony was so broad and diverse that few recommendations emerged with sufficient clarity to be enacted into law.

Though there had been suggestions for a broad official inquiry into America's economic problems since at least 1935, coming especially from Leon Henderson, an aide to Harry Hopkins, the TNEC was primarily a product of the recession of 1937. The recession, beginning in October and November of 1937, threatened the New Deal as no other event could have done, for it suggested that Roosevelt had failed in his most essential self-proclaimed task—building a sustained recovery. It precipitated a long winter of soul-searching among New Dealers, the most common complaint being that the New Deal had no program—no consistent philosophy that could inform its response to economic stagnation.

The crisis evoked a plethora of proposals, including Henry Morgenthau's urging of a rigorous drive to balance the budget, suggestions from the Treasury and elsewhere that monopolies were impeding recovery, and Harry Hopkins's and Marriner Eccles's insistent advocacy of a spending program. When, in April

1938, the president decided to renew spending, many, himself included, saw the decision as a pragmatic one, not based in the kind of program or philosophy the New Deal needed. Thus, on 29 April, two weeks after announcing his spending proposal, the president sent a message to Congress in which he recommended "a thorough study of the concentration of economic power in American industry," which might help lead to a coherent New Deal program.

Senator O'Mahoney, noting the absence of reference to congressional involvement in the proposal, was quick to take up the cause, introducing a resolution on 5 May for a study to be carried out by four members of Congress and three representatives of the administration. As Congress debated the resolution, the commitee was expanded to twelve members, with equal representation from both camps. It was also broadened in focus, charged to examine not only economic concentration but also "the effect of the existing, tax, patent, and other government policies upon competition, price levels, unemployment, profits, and consumption." Leon Henderson, executive secretary to the TNEC, concluded that the fundamental question was "why have we not had full employment and full utilization of our magnificent resources?" In other words, there was hardly any aspect of the functioning of America's economic system that was not to fall under the committee's purview. By 14 June 1938, the bill creating the committee had passed both houses of Congress and on 16 June the president signed it.

The committee was dominated by men who had spoken out in favor of an antimonopoly investigation in the past, though by December 1938 it could by no means be said that they were uniform in their thinking on economic questions. Appointed by Vice-president John Nance Garner, presiding officer of the Senate, were O'Mahoney to be chairman, William King of Utah, and William E. Borah of Idaho. Both King and Borah were later replaced—King, by James Mead of New York, when King was not reelected in 1940, and Borah, by Wallace H. White of Maine, after Borah's death in January 1940. The speaker of the House, John H. Bankhead, appointed Hatton W. Sumners of Texas, who became TNEC vice-chairman, Carroll Reece of Tennessee, and Edward C. Eicher of Iowa. Eicher, who retired from Congress in January 1939, was replaced by Clyde Williams of Missouri after attending only a few meetings. One Republican was appointed from each house, a policy maintained in replacement as well, with senators Borah and White and Representative Reece representing the minority party. Only O'Mahoney, Eicher, and Mead were strong New Dealers.

The president appointed Thurman Arnold from the Justice Department, Herman Oliphant from the Treasury, Isadore Lubin from the Department of Labor, William O. Douglas from the Securities and Exchange Commission, Garland Ferguson from the Federal Trade Commission, and Richard Patterson from the Commerce Department. There were some alternates and eventual replacements for several of these, such as Jerome N. Frank and Sumner Pike. However, the most persistent and important work in conducting the investigations was done by O'Mahoney, Henderson, and Lubin.

Three main perspectives on how best to deal with a stagnant economy are evident in the views of the committee and their witnesses. One group accepted trusts and monopolies as inevitable and perhaps desirable for large sectors of the economy. They favored regulation of industry through government-sponsored negotiations and agreements in a manner reminiscent of the National Recovery Administration. Others felt that monopolistic setting of prices and wages had created bottlenecks of underconsumption which were inhibiting recovery. They urged government action in breaking up trusts and monopolies, the resultant competition to render direct regulation largely unnecessary. A third group felt the government could have great economic impact without the burden of regulation through appropriate taxing and spending measures—a compensatory fiscal policy.

This latter group was rapidly gaining influence in Washington for three reasons. The economy was clearly rebounding by the time the committee first met in December, which most attributed to the president's spending program of that April. A group of Harvard and Tufts economists provided that summer a rationale for spending in a book that translated Keynes's *General Theory of Employment, Interest, and Money* (1936) into layman's language and placed it in the setting of New Deal America. Their *Economic Program for American Democracy* (1938) seemed to give spending a legitimacy and academic sanction it had hitherto lacked, making it a viable part of an overall program based on Keynesian ideas. And finally, several economists, most notably Harvard's Alvin Hansen, and Lauchlin Currie of the Federal Reserve Board research staff, had become converts to Keynesian economics. Their testimony before the TNEC was highly influential and presaged a subsequent placement of Keynesians in key government positions, with Richard V. Gilbert heading the Commerce Department's Division of Industrial Economics, Gerald Colm appointed to the Fiscal Division of the Executive Office of the President, and Alvin Hansen officially advising both the Federal Reserve and the National Resources Planning boards.

The dissemination of ideas recommending a compensatory fiscal policy, though an unintended consequence of the hearings, was perhaps the TNEC's most important legacy. Corporate announcements of price cuts in the beryllium, steel, and building materials industries seem to have been indirectly a result of the hearings. And Thurman Arnold began a vigorous program against monopoly from his base in the Antitrust Division of the Justice Department, which, though independent of the TNEC, gained legitimacy from the fact the hearings were in session.

O'Mahoney, however, determined to keep the deliberations evenhanded, welcomed testimony from all parties. The mass and variety of recommendations thus defied summary and offered no consensus useful in policy formulation. Most committee members and witnesses were of the same opinion at the end of the hearings as they had been at the beginning. Five

TNEC proposals to alter patent law in the direction of providing more ready public access to inventions were enacted by Congress and became law. Beyond that, the seventeen thousand pages of testimony stand as a compendium of the economic ideas economists, publicists, businesspeople, politicians, and corporate attorneys held in the late 1930s—a useful body of historical documentation, but not an important informant of subsequent policy. The play given to Keynesian economics early in the hearings had already helped provide the philosophy or program New Dealers were seeking, and as attentions turned to the war effort, the summary report seemed largely irrelevant.

The standard study of the TNEC, David Lynch's *The Concentration of Economic Power* (New York: Columbia University Press, 1946) has so thoroughly covered the subject as to intimidate subsequent researchers. All general studies of the New Deal have a few lines on the TNEC, mostly drawn from Lynch. Ellis Hawley offers a helpful interpretive chapter in his *The New Deal and the Problem of Monopoly: A Study in Economic Ambivalence* (Princeton: Princeton University Press, 1966). Herbert Stein points out the role of the committee in disseminating Keynesian economic thought in his *The Fiscal Revolution in America* (Chicago: University of Chicago Press, 1969). The policy concerns of Roosevelt and his chief aides that led to the TNEC hearings are discussed in Dean L. May, *From New Deal to New Economics: The American Liberal Response to the Recession of 1937* (New York: Garland Publishing, 1981).

DEAN L. MAY

See also Henderson, Leon

Tennessee Valley Authority

In May 1933, when President Franklin D. Roosevelt signed the Tennessee Valley Authority (TVA) into existence, he concluded a debate that had opened in the Progressive Era over public versus private development of natural resources. Much of that debate had evolved in the 1880s as awareness grew of the potential for hydroelectric generation and the need to preserve and develop natural resources for the common good. The Tennessee River, the focus of this attention, was a worthy subject. Running through seven states (with its tributaries), the river cut through some of the most disadvantaged areas of the South. Although it offered great potential for riverine transportation, the Tennessee was rendered unnavigable in the middle of its course to the Mississippi—at a rapids called Muscle Shoals.

The earliest federal involvement in the area had come in the nineteenth century with a series of bills to enhance navigation around the shoals, but several aspects of American history would intervene to make Muscle Shoals more than a navigational problem. For one, there was the potential of hydroelectric power; with that possibility came a host of other issues, some explosive: public power versus the corporate utilities; the government versus business magnates, and the use (or misuse) of natural resources. Moreover, with the advent of World War I came Woodrow Wilson's National Defense Act of 1916 and its commitment to use

Flood destruction, Tennessee Valley. (Courtesy FDR Library.)

hydroelectrically produced nitrates at Muscle Shoals to avoid dependence on Chilean nitrates. The Tennessee River and Muscle Shoals thereupon emerged as a focus of national interest, for the issue of nitrate fertilizer was an object of singular concern to the South with its nutrient-starved soil. Consequently, the area and the controversy surrounding it became the nation's classroom in the matter of conservation and public ownership.

The debates over Muscle Shoals and the Tennessee River involved some major figures and issues in American conservation history: Gifford Pinchot's drive for multipurpose river development; Theodore Roosevelt's Inland Waterways Commission (1907), his Conservation Congress (1909), and his National Conservation Commission Report (1909) on resource protection and development of watersheds, which historians feel contains the basic principles undergirding the TVA; Woodrow Wilson's National Defense Act of 1916 and, subsequently, the construction of Wilson Dam; Henry Ford's Muscle Shoals purchase offer and the fervor of land speculation surrounding that "Little Detroit"; Sen. George Norris's comprehensive legislation for the development of the river; and much more.

Six bills proposed by Senator Norris for the development of the Tennessee came to grief through vetoes in the Republican administrations of Calvin Coolidge and Herbert Hoover, for the ideological representatives of private capital resisted public administration of natural resources. The onset of the depression, however, made their position vulnerable. The acute loss of confidence in American financiers and financial institutions led to the assertion of a new mood in the country, and Americans now looked with favor on federal intervention in the public interest. Thus, probably any Democratic president in 1932 would have reinstated the idea of some type of federal development of the Tennessee River.

Franklin D. Roosevelt, however, by virtue of his background, was particularly suited to restore the project. His experience with the St. Lawrence Commission and the New York Power Authority had prepared him for combat with the private utilities, and he had always been strongly interested in the conservation efforts of Theodore Roosevelt, Gifford Pinchot, and New York governor Alfred Smith, who employed the planning talents of Benton McKaye of the U.S. Forest Service and Clarence Stein, a progressive city planner. When he himself was governor of New York, Roosevelt was committed to programs of afforestation, reforestation, withdrawal of submarginal land, and rural community development. In short, he shared with Norris a dislike of private utilities and a commitment to watershed multipurpose development. Added to this was his commitment to planning and a belief in broad socioeconomic reform.

On 10 April 1933, when Roosevelt submitted

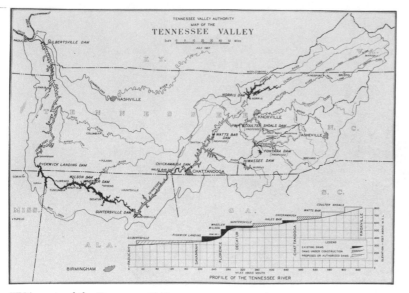

TVA map of the Tennessee Valley. (Courtesy FDR Library.)

TVA legislation to Congress, his accompanying message said:

> It is clear that the Muscle Shoals development is but a small part of the potential public usefulness of the entire Tennessee River. Such use, if envisioned in its entirety, transcends mere power development: it enters the wide fields of flood control, soil erosion, afforestation, elimination from agricultural use of marginal lands, and distribution and diversification of industry. In short, this power development of war days leads logically to national planning for a complete river watershed involving many States and the future lives and welfare of millions. It touches and gives life to all forms of human concerns. . . . Many hard lessons have taught us the human waste that results from lack of planning. Here and there a few wise cities and counties have looked ahead and planned. But our Nation has "just grown." It is time to extend planning to a wider field, in this instance comprehending in one great project many States directly concerned with the basin of one of our greatest rivers.

The Tennessee Valley Authority was to be a radical departure in American politics. It represented to many, in its earlier stages, a challenge to state sovereignty. Its transmission lines, like its rivers, made it clear, as Barry Karl noted, "that the old political boundaries were no longer realistic dividing lines." State barriers, it seemed, would yield to the promise of economic planning, a new departure in American government. But, in the long run, tradition and politics made it inevitable that the vision of Roosevelt would not become fully realized.

Roosevelt chose Arthur E. Morgan to lead the fledgling agency as chairman of its board of directors. Morgan, a progressive with strong anticapitalistic, utopian, and communitarian impulses, wanted the agency to reflect the social reform latent in Roosevelt's vision of TVA. But his idealism was dampened by the pragmatism of the two other directors, H. A. Morgan and David Lilienthal. The former saw Arthur Morgan's plans for afforestation, reforestation, population removal, retirement of submarginal land, co-

operatives, and other ventures as wildly experimental and idealistic as well as inimical to the interests of the small capitalist farmer. Lilienthal, meanwhile, was deeply involved in defending TVA against the encroachments of private utilities, who challenged the authority three times on constitutional grounds. Stockholders of the Alabama Power Company brought the first suit, the *Ashwander* case, in 1934.

By 1935 the breach was complete between Arthur Morgan's idealism and the pragmatism of Lilienthal and H. A. Morgan. Arthur Morgan threatened to resign if Lilienthal remained on the board, but although Roosevelt appeared to agree, he needed the support of Lilienthal's patrons, the La Follettes, in the election of 1936, and he renewed Lilienthal's appointment. The split in the board of directors, now a Washington scandal, broadened in 1937 when Arthur Morgan openly derided Lilienthal's power policies in journals like the *New Republic* and the *Atlantic Monthly*. Thus Roosevelt was forced into a confrontation with Arthur Morgan, who refused to substantiate in person his vague accusations against Lilienthal. In March 1938, FDR removed Arthur E. Morgan from the board of directors for his "contumacious" behavior. The friction on the board led to a congressional investigation of TVA, which, though it had been feared by New Dealers, ended by exonerating the agency of Arthur Morgan's charges.

Although Roosevelt had breathed life into the TVA, its history symbolized the New Deal's problems. Arthur Morgan represented the president's idealism and his desire to plan for the common good. But H. A. Morgan and Lilienthal represented the realities of American political and economic life, which Roosevelt, the consummate politician, was well aware of. Without an overarching planning structure and the necessary power to effect it, the TVA, like many New Deal agencies, became enmeshed in the net of traditional American politics. At the end of World War II, TVA became merely a power-producing agency, when its general regional planning mission was formally rejected. As much as anything, TVA reflected the ambiguity of New Deal planning.

The best background for the TVA is found in Preston Hubbard, *Origins of the TVA: The Muscle Shoals Controversy, 1920–1932* (Nashville: Vanderbilt University Press, 1961). Norris's role in TVA is placed in the context of his political career in Richard Lowitt's excellent *George W. Norris: The Persistence of a Progressive, 1913–1933* (Urbana: University of Illinois Press, 1971). For information on Lilienthal, see his *Journals*, vol. 1, *The TVA Years: 1939–1945* (New York: Harper, 1965) and the self-congratulatory *TVA: Democracy on the March* (New York: Harper, 1953). A. E. Morgan tells his own story in a somewhat disjointed and discursive manner in *The Making of TVA* (Buffalo, N.Y.: Prometheus Books, 1974). The Morgan-Lilienthal disagreement is best covered in two superb books by Thomas K. McCraw, *Morgan versus Lilienthal: A Feud within the TVA* (Chicago: Loyola University Press, 1970) and *TVA and the Power Fight: 1933–1939* (Philadelphia: Lippencott, 1971). Wilmon Droze has provided an exemplary programmatic investigation of TVA's navigation policy in *High Dams and Slack Waters: TVA Rebuilds a River* (Baton Rouge:

Louisiana State University Press, 1965). The best examination of TVA's changing ideological structure is still Phillip Selznick's *TVA and the Grass Roots: A Study in the Sociology of Formal Organization* (New York: Harper, 1966), which is the cornerstone of contemporary revisionist views on TVA. For a good survey of the latter, see Erwin Hargrove and Paul K. Conkin, eds., *Fifty Years of Grass Roots Bureaucracy* (Urbana: University of Illinois Press, 1984). A recent case study of TVA's early program is Michael J. McDonald and John Muldowny, *TVA and the Dispossessed: The Resettlement of Population in the Norris Dam Area* (Knoxville: University of Tennessee Press, 1982). The most eloquent and broad contextual background for TVA can be found in Barry D. Karl, *The Uneasy State* (Chicago: University of Chicago Press, 1983).

MICHAEL J. MCDONALD

See also Conservation; Hundred Days; Lilienthal, David E.; Negroes; New Deal; Norris, George William; Rural Electrification Administration; Willkie, Wendell Lewis

Third Term

Roosevelt's decision to break tradition and accept his party's nomination for a first-ever third-term presidency. Soon after the election of 1936 questions arose as to who would become the next president. A tradition since the days of George Washington and Thomas Jefferson held that presidents should not remain in office longer than two terms. Whether Roosevelt would abide by this rule was not certain. Conservative and liberal elements struggled for control of the Democratic party in the elections of 1938 and in behind-the-scenes maneuverings in preparation for the 1940 election.

Roosevelt himself promoted several candidates, but none was able to establish the stature of a worthy successor. Robert Jackson, Harry Hopkins, Harold Ickes, Cordell Hull, and Paul McNutt were all groomed by the president to take over his office, but all proved imperfect for reasons personal and political. Meanwhile, conservative Democrats rallied around the lead of the vice-president, John Nance Garner of Texas, and the postmaster general and presidential aide, Jim Farley. Secretary of the Interior Harold Ickes countered by launching a campaign on behalf of Roosevelt that united the New Deal wing of the party and ensured that a majority of the nominating convention delegates would support Roosevelt or at least a worthy liberal successor. The Roosevelt forces, working in his name, succeeded despite the fact that Roosevelt himself refused to campaign and offered no public help, although he did cooperate privately with the nomination effort. With the failure in turn of each available liberal successor, a third term for Roosevelt seemed the best way for the Democratic party to continue its New Deal leanings.

The events in Europe of 1940 greatly enhanced Roosevelt's third-term prospects. The phony war, or "sitzkrieg," in Europe gave way to the German lightning conquest of France in May of 1940, and suddenly the situation became more ominous. With Hitler's Lutfwaffe daily besieging England, public opinion in the United States rallied around the president. The crisis in Europe pointed up the need for a stable leadership in the United States and made the idea of a third term for Roosevelt more acceptable to many Americans.

For his part, Roosevelt remained deliberately vague as to his intentions. He maintained a silence calculated to keep his options open and dropped only hints that he wished to retire to manage his Hyde Park estate, tend to his beloved trees, enjoy the role of elder statesman, organize his personal papers, and write his own history of the New Deal. Most of his family including Eleanor encouraged him not to run, and his declining health also spoke for retirement. Yet Roosevelt wanted to protect the social gains of the New Deal and had ambitions for a role in world affairs. At an uncomfortable meeting on 7 July with Jim Farley, Roosevelt discussed his plans with his adviser and potential opponent. Roosevelt told Farley, "Jim, I don't want to run and I'm going to tell the convention so." Farley replied, "If you make it specific, the convention will not nominate you." But Roosevelt refused to state that he would not run under any circumstances, and Farley interpreted this to mean that Roosevelt had already decided to go for a third term. Historians and contemporaries alike disagree on when Roosevelt decided to run, but it is clear that he wanted to be nominated by an overwhelming margin, in effect to be called to an irresistible duty to his party and his country.

Anti–third term campaign buttons. (Courtesy FDR Library.)

When the convention opened in Chicago, Roosevelt spurned the advice of most of his advisers and stayed away. He thought his presence would ruin the effect of the overwhelming acclamation he thought he needed in order to overcome the tradition against a third term. Roosevelt sent a personal message to the convention, announcing that he had "no wish to be a candidate again" and that "all of the delegates to this convention are free to vote for any candidate." After a moment of stunned silence, the convention members roared back "We want Roosevelt" and began an hour-long celebration. This seemingly spontaneous acclamation was in fact carefully orchestrated by Roosevelt's campaign managers to make his candidacy for a third term appear irresistible. After this, the actual balloting in which Roosevelt won 910 votes to 72 for Farley, his closest challenger, was anticlimactic. Roosevelt waited to accept the nomination until he had pushed through his choice for vice-president, Henry Wallace, who, Roosevelt thought, was necessary to ensure a liberal ticket.

Opponents of Roosevelt charged that a third term gave Roosevelt "dictatorial" powers and tried to make this a campaign issue. Roosevelt, however, decisively defeated Republican Wendell Willkie in the election, although his margin of victory was smaller than in his previous two presidential races. In a belated slap at Roosevelt, foes guaranteed that his would be the only third-term presidency by passing in 1951 the Twenty-second Amendment to the Constitution, which prohibits presidents from serving for more than two terms.

A fine history of the 1940 election is Herbert S. Parmet and Marie B. Hecht, *Never Again: A President Runs for a Third Term* (New York: Macmillan Co., 1968). Bernard F. Donahoe, *Private Plans and Public Dangers* (Notre Dame, Ind.: University of Notre Dame Press, 1965) concentrates on the forces leading to Roosevelt's third-term decision.

See also Corcoran, Thomas Gardiner; Wallace, Henry A.

Norman Mattoon Thomas, 1948. Artist: Miriam Troop. (National Portrait Gallery, Smithsonian Institution.)

Thomas, Norman Mattoon

(20 November 1884–20 December 1968)

The American Socialist party and Norman Thomas were virtually synonymous for forty years—1928 to 1968. This was true during the early and middle 1930s, when Thomas was a militant radical, as well as during the 1920s and the period from 1945 until his death in 1968, when he was a moderate reformer. Thomas's overall position varied during different periods of his career. From the late 1930s until 1941, Thomas was interested primarily in keeping America out of the Second World War; later he was opposed to any prolongation of the war, no matter what the long-term cost. During all this time, he was a Christian socialist and pacifist.

Born in the parsonage of the Presbyterian Church of Marion, Ohio, Thomas was the son and grandson of ministers. His father was minister of the church where Norman was born; his paternal grandfather was a Welsh-born circuit-riding preacher in northeastern Pennsylvania, and his maternal grandfather, the Reverend Stephen Mattoon, whose Irish-Scot-Huguenot ancestors settled in upstate New York during the seventeenth century, served as a Presbyterian missionary to Thailand and later as president of the black college that would become Johnson C. Smith University in North Carolina.

Thomas himself was educated at Bucknell University (for one year), Princeton University, from which he earned his bachelor of arts degree in 1905, and Union Theological Seminary, from which he was graduated in 1910, the year he was ordained. That year he also married Frances Violet Stewart.

After several temporary church appointments, he was named pastor of the American Parish among Immigrants and the East Harlem Parish of the National Board of Missions of the Presbyterian church. The parish—for both comprised only one parish—was as much a settlement house as a church. It was located in one of the poorer sections of New York City, populated primarily by immigrants from eastern and southern Europe. His observation of the poverty among the immigrant residents of the area plus his readings in the literature of the Social Gospel movement in the Protestant churches convinced Thomas to become a socialist.

The outbreak of the war in Europe strengthened Thomas's convictions and led him into an active role in the socialist and antiwar movements. He wrote two books during the period between the outbreak of the war in Europe in 1914 and America's entry into the war in 1917. The first, *The Church and the City,* was a Christian socialist analysis of the role of the church in an urban setting. The second, *The Christian Patriot,* was an antiwar plea. In 1916 Thomas joined the pacifist Fellowship of Reconciliation and helped found the National Union against Militarism and the American Civil Liberties Union.

With the American entry into the war, Thomas's pacifism made his position in the church untenable, and he resigned from the parish in 1918. At this point he moved into the political arena, editing the Christian socialist *World Tomorrow;* working for Morris Hillquit in the latter's Socialist antiwar campaign for mayor of New York in November 1917, and joining the Socialist party, although he still disagreed with some of its Marxist rhetoric.

Almost as soon as he joined the party Thomas became one of its leaders. Oratory was a major attribute of Socialist leadership, and Thomas was an excellent speaker who had been trained in the classic circuit-rider tradition. Moreover, he was an intellectual clergyman in a party that cherished learned and altruistic spokesmen. He was named an executive director of the League for Industrial Democracy, an associate editor of the *Nation* and editor of the short-lived prolabor daily *New York Leader.* In 1924 he was nominated as the Socialist candidate for governor in the ticket headed by Robert La Follette. During all this period, Thomas remained an agitator for social reform, particularly relief from unemployment and the vicissitudes of old age.

In 1928, Thomas was nominated as the Socialist candidate for president. His platform read like an outline for Franklin D. Roosevelt's New Deal that was enacted some five years later. In the election, Thomas polled less than 270,000 of almost 40 million votes, but he became nationally known. Frances Perkins recalled in her book *The Roosevelt I Knew* that FDR was interested in the reform component of Thomas's platform, which was to resemble his later New Deal legislation—unemployment and old age insurance, minimum wage laws, the Tennessee Valley Authority, control of speculation, and the right of labor to collective bargaining.

It is true that Roosevelt had been a progressive Democrat during most of his political career and that he had supported virtually all reform legislation during his term in the New York State Senate. But it was only after he had read Thomas's 1928 reform planks that he fully developed the philosophy for what was to become the New Deal.

In 1929, Thomas became active in municipal reform in New York City, polling 175,000 votes as the anti-Tammany Socialist candidate for mayor and winning the support of the conservative Citizens Union, the *New York Telegram,* and such disparate civic leaders as Rabbi Stephen S. Wise, Professor John Dewey, and columnist Heywood Broun. It was during this campaign that Thomas first became acquainted with New York's governor Roosevelt, for Thomas was the leader in the drive that forced Tammany's corrupt mayor James J. Walker from office.

In 1932 Thomas was again the Socialist candidate for president. In this election, when he opposed Franklin D. Roosevelt and Herbert Hoover, Thomas polled almost 885,000 votes; but the total was disappointing to Socialists who had expected several million votes, since this was in the middle of the nation's worst economic crisis. Thomas would later concede that Roosevelt had stolen his thunder.

During the early years of the New Deal, Thomas vehemently opposed the Roosevelt program. His vehemence and the Marxian rhetoric that he then used caused severe disagreements in his party, which split in 1936. Thomas, who was again the Socialist candidate against Roosevelt, polled 187,572 votes that year—only .4 percent of the total cast. Most Socialists, especially labor union men, had by then left the party and supported Roosevelt's reelection. The Socialist party splintered and began a steady decline that year. Asked in the 1950s to explain the party's demise, Thomas replied, "It was Roosevelt, in a word."

Between 1936 and 1939, Thomas tried to persuade the party to abandon electoral activities and even indicated that he might support Roosevelt in 1940. But the outbreak of war in Europe plus Roosevelt's inability to improve the impoverished condition of southern tenant farmers, particularly in eastern Arkansas, prevented Thomas from making the shift. Moreover, Thomas was an active isolationist during the period between the outbreak of the war in Europe and Pearl Harbor and Roosevelt was an interventionist.

After Pearl Harbor, Thomas was a critic of some of America's actions. He was particularly incensed at the evacuation of Japanese-Americans from their California homes and the atomic bombing of Hiroshima and Nagasaki. He also warned Americans of the danger of an alliance with Stalin's Soviet regime.

After the war, Thomas again proposed that the Socialist party forgo electoral activity. But the party—for the first and last time—rejected his proposal. In his last book, *Democratic Socialism: A New Appraisal* (1953), Thomas formally abandoned classical socialism with its rigid commitment to total nationalization of all means of production and distribution. He favored, instead, a mixed economy committed to social welfare under a democratic state.

Thomas had always considered himself a friendly critic of Roosevelt and the New Deal; he also looked upon FDR as a political rival. Both men agreed with Roosevelt's 1940 comment in a letter to Thomas: "I am a damned sight better politician than you."

Thomas remained an active Socialist until he was seriously injured in a taxicab accident in New York in 1966. He formally retired in January 1968 and died that December.

There are six biographical studies of Norman Thomas. Only two of them are serious; the others are either hagiographic or demonographic. Bernard K. Johnpoll, *Pacifist's Progress: Norman Thomas and the Demise of American Socialism* (New York: Quadrangle, 1970) is a critical analysis of Thomas as a Socialist politician. W. A. Swanberg, *Norman Thomas: The Last Idealist* (New York: Charles Scribner's Sons, 1976) is a well-written, well-researched biography. Thomas himself wrote more than fifty books and pamphlets of which eight are significant: *America's Way Out* (1931) expresses his pre–New Deal views; *The Choice before Us* (1934) examines the New Deal from a Socialist perspective; *Socialism on the Defensive* (1938) is his most pessimistic work, written at a low point for world socialism; *We Have a Future* (1941) is a strong antiwar statement; *What Is Our Destiny?* (1944) proposes a prescription for the postwar period; *Appeal to the Nations* (1947) is a plea for a world without conflict; *A Socialist's Faith* (1951) is a reaffirmation of Thomas's belief that a better world is possible; and *Democratic Socialism: A New Appraisal* (1953) is (despite its small size) a major statement of nondogmatic democratic socialism, probably Thomas's most important single work.

BERNARD K. JOHNPOLL

See also Socialism

Townsend, Francis E., M.D.

(13 January 1867–1 September 1960)

Retired physician whose Townsend Plan for a national system of old-age pensions made him the leader of one of the most popular mass movements of the depression. Francis Everett Townsend, who was born in rural Illinois, worked as a farm laborer and a schoolteacher before earning a medical degree at the age of thirty-six. He practiced medicine in the Black Hills of South Dakota from 1903 to 1919 when, with his family, he moved to Long Beach, California, for his health. Townsend speculated in real estate and practiced intermittently until 1930. In that year he was appointed a Los Angeles County health officer. The suffering of the indigent county charges he treated—many of them elderly persons ruined in the crash—horrified Townsend. In the fall of 1933, after discontinuation of the county health program for which he worked, Townsend published a preliminary version of his pension plan as a letter to a Long Beach newspaper and began organizing local senior citizens to petition Congress to make his plan a national law. These petitions were eventually signed by 90 percent of Long Beach's voters and established Townsend's political power in California. In January 1934, Townsend founded Old Age Revolving Pensions, Limited, with his former real estate partner Robert E. Clements.

Townsend's pension plan, as eventually refined, called for all persons over sixty to retire from work and to receive from the federal government a monthly pension of $200 on condition that it be spent in its entirety. This plan, Townsend claimed, would open the job market to the young unemployed, increase total cash flow in the economy through the retirees' spending, and give the elderly both security and a sense of participation in the economy. The pension would be financed through a tax on all exchange transactions. For the nation's growing number of elderly citizens, the plan addressed the demographic changes—longer life expectancy due to better health conditions, and less support from children—that made them outlive their financial security. To the public at large, the Townsend Plan was simply a straightforward solution for the suffering of the helpless. Townsend's own personality and rhetoric—a mix of kindly frontier integrity, calm optimism, and a highly traditional vision of a democracy of citizen activists—increased the movement's attractiveness. Among the elderly, who were offered not only security but a sense of dignity and solidarity by the move-

ment, "Townsendism" reached a near-religious pitch of devotion. The pension movement's transformation into a national crusade was especially rapid after Townsend clubs, local branches of the national organization, were started in August 1934. By October 1935, the date of the first national Townsend convention in Chicago, there were more than 4,500 clubs. By spring 1936, the Townsend movement had between 2 million and 3.5 million paying members.

Townsend achieved his greatest popularity in late 1935 and early 1936. The Roosevelt administration's support for the Social Security Act of 1935 was to some degree influenced by Townsendite pressure for a national pension, as was congressional passage of the bill; nonetheless, widespread dissatisfaction with the act kept enthusiasm for Townsend's own pension scheme high. At the same time, the Townsend Plan's political difficulties were mounting. Congressional Democrats, both annoyed by Townsend's anti–New Deal statements and afraid his conservative populism might become demogoguery, launched increasingly hostile investigations. The May 1936 Bell committee hearings humiliatingly revealed Townsend's ignorant suspicion of all politics and economics, including those of his own plan. His subsequent involvement with Gerald L. K. Smith's and Father Charles Coughlin's unsuccessful Union party (despite Townsend's increasing aloofness from the party before the 1936 election) and financial scandals surrounding his partner Clements further embarrassed Townsend and reduced his movement's prestige. In April 1938, Townsend was belatedly sentenced to jail for contempt of Congress as a consequence of his Bell committee performance, but was immediately pardoned by President Roosevelt.

After 1937, Townsendism became a marginal force in national politics, but Townsend continued to propagandize for his plan in the West until his death in Los Angeles in 1960, at the age of ninety-three.

The fullest introduction to Townsend and the Townsend Plan can be found in David H. Bennett, *Demagogues in the Depression: American Radicals and the Union Party, 1932–1936* (New Brunswick, N.J.: Rutgers University Press, 1969). However, as a discussion of mass movements of the depression, this work has been superseded to an extent by Alan Brinkley, *Voices of Protest: Huey Long, Father Coughlin and the Great Depression* (New York: Alfred A. Knopf, 1982). Townsendism as a political force is exhaustively treated in Abraham Holtzman, *The Townsend Movement: A Study in Old Age Pressure Politics* (New York: Bookman, 1963). Townsend's autobiography, *New Horizons* (Chicago: J. L. Stewart, 1943) is more appealing than informative. His original letters to the *Long Beach Press-Telegram* containing the first statement of the Townsend Plan have been reprinted in *Southern California Quarterly* 52, no. 4 (1970):365–82.

See also Democratic Party; New Deal; Social Security; Union Party

Trade Union Movement

See Labor; National Recovery Administration; Socialism

Truman, Harry S

(8 May 1884–26 December 1972)

Vice-president during Franklin D. Roosevelt's fourth term, president after Roosevelt's death in April 1945.

"Who the hell is Harry Truman?" asked Roosevelt's military adviser, William D. Leahy, when he heard that the Missouri senator had been tabbed as the Democratic vice-presidential nominee in 1944. Truman scarcely deserved such sarcasm, for in his unassuming, efficient way, he had already achieved considerable success as a national leader. In many ways his career was rather unconventional. Born in Lamar, Missouri, he had farmed for a time and served with distinction in the army during World War I, and then had gone bankrupt in a short-lived haberdashery business venture. Truman never attended college; yet his range of knowledge, largely acquired through extensive reading, was impressive. Although support by a corrupt political machine smoothed the way for his early political victories, Truman managed to escape any personal taint of wrongdoing.

After compiling a solid record as an elected county official, Truman won a Senate seat in the 1934 Democratic landslide. An enthusiastic supporter of New Deal programs, he quickly became identified

Campaign poster, 1944. (Courtesy FDR Library.)

as a Roosevelt loyalist. He surprised many pundits who regarded him as a political lightweight by welding together a coalition of labor, Negroes, and farmers and winning reelection in 1940. Shortly after, he became chair of the Senate Select Committee to Investigate the National Defense Program. The hardworking Truman committee, as it became known, concentrated on contractor selection, benefits, and performance; the types of contracts awarded and their geographic distribution; the use of small business; and the effect of contract awards on organized labor. The committee gained credit for saving the taxpayers $15 billion and an enviable reputation as a model for congressional investigative committees. Despite Truman's firm determination not to use the committee as a vehicle for political glory, his capable leadership brought him a measure of fame.

Though the fact was not publicized, Roosevelt's health by 1944 was failing rapidly, and a great many Democratic party leaders privately doubted that he could live four more years. Nevertheless, they believed that he could handily win reelection and that at the head of the ticket he would sweep other Democratic candidates into office. It was also obvious that the selection of the vice-presidential nominee was particularly important. The incumbent, Henry A. Wallace, was popular with Democratic liberals but strongly opposed by the party's moderates and conservatives. To retain the controversial Wallace, Roosevelt decided, would require more energy and persuasiveness than he was willing to commit. Though emphasizing that he still personally supported Wallace, FDR agreed to accept a new running mate. James F. Byrnes, a South Carolinian with a long and varied political background, received the chief executive's blessing for the job. But labor and Negro leaders in the party immediately vetoed the southerner, and Roosevelt was as unwilling to fight for Byrnes as for Wallace. The president then suggested Judge William O. Douglas or Truman. Support for Douglas was nil, but Truman had few enemies and was the second choice of many Wallace backers. The Missouri senator did not seek the position and actively supported his old friend Byrnes. Nevertheless, he grudgingly yielded to FDR's plea not to split the party and accepted the nomination.

Preoccupied with military and diplomatic concerns, Roosevelt left the heavy campaign work to Truman. The president appreciated his running mate's energetic efforts in winning reelection, but he did not take Truman into his confidence. Truman met rarely with the chief executive and remained unaware of critical national policies and decisions. He did not know until after he became president, for example, that the United States was developing an atomic bomb or what secret agreements Roosevelt had made at the Yalta Conference.

Once Truman became president, many Americans found the contrast between the patrician FDR and the new chief executive difficult to accept. Truman's personal style made him especially suspect at first to ardent New Deal liberals. Bespectacled, with graying hair and a toothy grin, Truman was physically unimposing. His appearance, combined with his harsh Missouri accent and his lack of formal education, made him seem rather ordinary, and in truth, Truman liked to be identified with the common people. Spunky and willing to make hard decisions, he took pride in projecting a no-nonsense, practical approach to problems. During his almost eight years in the White House, Truman continued and actually expanded the social-economic programs of his predecessor. Historians disagree, however, about whether Truman, as the cold war developed, significantly changed Roosevelt's policies in dealing with America's former ally, the Soviet Union.

No fully satisfactory biography of Truman exists, but Margaret Truman's *Harry S. Truman* (New York: William Morrow, 1973) is a readable and interesting account of her father's life. Truman's *Memoirs* (Garden City, N.Y.: Doubleday & Co., 1955) remain valuable. The literature on the Truman presidency is already large, especially on foreign policy. See Herbert Feis, *From Trust to Terror* (New York: W. W. Norton & Co., 1970); Richard M. Freeland, *The Truman Doctrine and the Origins of McCarthyism* (New York: Alfred A. Knopf, 1970); and Alonzo Hamby, *Beyond the New Deal* (New York: Columbia University Press, 1973).

JIM F. HEATH

See also Atomic Bomb; Death of FDR; Democratic Party; Elections in the Roosevelt Era; Hopkins, Harry L.; Pendergast, Thomas J.

Tugwell, Rexford Guy

(10 July 1891–21 July 1979)

Rexford Guy Tugwell was born in Sinclairville, New York, to Charles Henry and Dessie (Rexford) Tugwell. In 1904, his family moved seventy-five miles northward to Wilson, New York, north of Buffalo on the southern shore of Lake Ontario, where his father soon became a moderately well-to-do orchard farmer and canner.

In 1911, Tugwell was graduated from Masten Park High School in Buffalo and entered the Wharton School of Finance and Commerce of the University of Pennsylvania. He received his B.S. in 1915 and was an instructor in economics at Pennsylvania for two years, earning his master's degree in 1917. He was assistant professor of marketing at the University of Washington, 1917–18; business manager of the American University Union in Paris, 1918; and assistant manager of the Niagara Preserving Corporation, his father's firm, 1919. In the years 1920–32, Tugwell taught economics at Columbia University. He received his Ph.D. from Pennsylvania in 1922 and was promoted to full professor at Columbia in 1931.

In the 1920s and early 1930s, Tugwell evidenced interest in both agriculture and industry. He published several articles on the farm problem and made his knowledge of agriculture available to two would-be presidents, Governor Frank Lowden of Illinois and

Rexford Tugwell, in white, speaking with a Colorado farmer during the 1936 Great Plains Drought Area Committee tour. (Courtesy FDR Library.)

Alfred E. Smith. He prepared a lengthy memorandum for Smith, but did not meet him in 1928.

In early 1932, Tugwell was recruited into the original brains trust by his Columbia colleague, Raymond Moley. Moley hoped that Tugwell's knowledge of agriculture would be especially useful to candidate Roosevelt, as indeed it was to be. For Tugwell was among that small but growing group of farm policy experts who had moved beyond the unworkable "overseas dumping" proposal embodied in the McNary-Haugen legislation of the 1920s. He understood that some form of production control was necessary in agriculture and in 1931 had met the brilliant agricultural expert M. L. Wilson who had worked out a domestic allotment scheme for voluntary acreage restriction among farmers organized for that purpose by the government. Tugwell brought Wilson's ideas into the Roosevelt camp, and they became the core of the Agricultural Adjustment Act of early 1933.

But Tugwell's importance to Roosevelt and the New Deal went far beyond agriculture. Tugwell's mind was broad ranging; he had absorbed and reformulated the Institutionalist economics as expressed by Charles Van Hise, Simon Paten, John R. Commons, and Wesley Mitchell. To the Institutionalists, the idealized world of market capitalism had long since been destroyed by the large corporation, unions, professional and trade associations, monopoly and oligopoly, and government regulation. In such a world, intervention by the state was required to achieve balanced production and mass consumption. His many articles and three books of pre–New Deal years—*Industry's Coming of Age* (1927), *Mr. Hoover's Economic Policies* (1932), and *The Industrial Discipline and the Governmental Arts* (1933)—marked him as a literate, committed theorist of a socially managed economy, an exponent of the New Nationalism side of progressivism.

Roosevelt did not like all the potential advisers Ray Moley brought up to Hyde Park in early 1932, but he was immediately taken by the witty, iconoclastic, and confident Rex Tugwell. Roosevelt had a thirst for innovative ideas, and Tugwell presented these in a comprehensive planning philosophy descended from the New Nationalist outlook that FDR had always found attractive. Tugwell at once became a vital member of the brains trust triumvirate—the other Columbia professors were Ray Moley and law professor Adolf Berle—and supplied FDR through the campaign with drafts of speeches, ideas, and introductions to other experts in varied areas.

Following the election, Roosevelt asked him to make the transition from adviser to administrator. With some misgivings, Tugwell became an assistant secretary of agriculture. (There was no White House staff of any consequence in 1933 to which advisers like Tugwell or Moley could be appointed.) From that post Tugwell influenced both departmental and large policies, maintaining a close interest not only in the design of the farm program but also in the National Recovery Administration (NRA), conservation, food and drug regulation, Social Security, and national planning. In many talks with Roosevelt, he gave a boost to some programs, advisers, and plans and discouraged others, playing a central role in the push and pull of ideas around the president. In his years within the New Deal (Tugwell left the government at the end of 1936), he never lost Roosevelt's confidence and involved himself energetically in a broad and unpredictable range of issues.

He was, by every account, an unusually confident person, sure of the basic soundness of his analysis of the larger crisis and of his own administrative abilities. To men of insecure ego or sharply divergent outlook, his confidence often seemed like arrogance. Brilliantly articulate in person and on paper, Tugwell had the rare gift of incisive comment on complex problems. He was never windy or boring, as professors were universally expected to be. Roosevelt, a man of complete and imperturbable self-confidence, liked the Columbia professor's powerful and integrated social outlook, his flexibility and innovative turn of mind within his larger view, his aggressive appetite for bold departures.

By the spring of 1934, Tugwell had become a controversial figure and a prime target for the opposition press, especially because of his connection with a pure food and drug bill introduced in 1933 and vigorously opposed by certain manufacturing and advertising interests. In June 1934, Tugwell was promoted to the new post of under secretary of agriculture after a clamorous hearing.

In 1933 and 1934, Tugwell devoted considerable time to departmental affairs, including the reorganization of old-line bureaus, particularly the Forestry Service, in order to increase efficiency, preserve research activities in the face of Budget Director Lewis Douglas's efforts to reduce them, and promote conservation. He encouraged Hugh H. Bennett, head of the Soil Erosion Service, which was transferred from Interior to Agriculture in 1935 as the Soil Conservation Service; and during the drought of 1936, he traveled to "every center of our vast organization to see

that everything possible was done." Tugwell also served on ad hoc boards or committees in the fields of public works, industrial recovery, economic security, farm tenancy, drought relief, housing, and commercial policy and was appointed to the Surplus Relief Corporation.

In a major battle in the Agricultural Adjustment Administration (AAA) in 1935, Tugwell was on the losing side. He stood with those who wanted a share of AAA benefit payments for tenants and sharecroppers as well as owner-farmers. Chester C. Davis, AAA administrator, dismissed the leaders of the group that deplored the co-optation of the AAA—the domination of the regulators by those who were supposedly being regulated in the public interest. Tugwell concluded that if anything were to be done to assist tenants, sharecroppers, and small subsistence farmers, a new agency would have to be created. On 1 May 1935, by executive order, the president established the Resettlement Administration (RA) and appointed Tugwell head.

In the mid-1930s, there were 650,000 farm families on 100 million acres of submarginal land. The RA's Land Utilization Division (LUD) intended to "retire" this land after purchases from voluntary sellers and turn it to nonagricultural uses, but in the end LUD retired only about 9 million acres. The Rural Resettlement Division assisted the sellers in establishing themselves on new land. It also administered a number of subsistence homestead projects, some inherited from other agencies. Tugwell, however, did not agree with the back-to-the-land enthusiasts who envisioned the settlement of many urban as well as rural folk in communities combining subsistence farming with self-help cooperatives and outside employment. The construction by the RA's Suburban Resettlement Division of three garden, or greenbelt, cities as demonstrations of future possibilities in city development was the most publicized RA activity, but the Rehabilitation Division accounted for most of the RA's outlay of funds under its program of loans to small farmers.

Whether with reference to agriculture, industry, regions, or the entire society, Tugwell was a planner. His writings and his administrative career were a joint search for the mechanisms for coordinated social intervention to ensure the benefits of the efficient use of American technology. In *The Industrial Discipline and the Governmental Arts,* Tugwell had offered a proposal for centralized direction of capital investment by means of a hierarchical organization of intra- and interindustry planning boards. This sketch of business self-government under government supervision bore some resemblance to the NRA, but neither this nor any subsequent structure for New Deal planning fully satisfied Tugwell. His role in writing the recovery bill was peripheral, and he watched the NRA experiment with growing unhappiness. "Operational wholeness; . . . that was the central, the original meaning of NRA," he wrote, lamenting that the machinery for central coordination had been too weak to curb the desires of organized business groups to use NRA planning as a chance to restrict production and maintain profits. The New Deal veered away from holistic planning after 1935 and moved toward the antitrust, antibusiness New Freedom thrust of the second New Deal which Tugwell scornfully called "atomistic progressivism." Increasingly the target of denunciation in the media and among New Deal critics as "Rex the Red," Tugwell kept a low profile through the election year of 1936 and resigned in the next year. His relationship with Roosevelt remained cordial to the end.

After leaving Washington, Tugwell was vice-president of the American Molasses Company, 1937; chairman of the New York City Planning Commission, 1938–40; chancellor of the University of Puerto Rico, 1941; governor of Puerto Rico, 1941–46; professor of political science at the University of Chicago, 1946–57; and senior fellow, then associate, of the Center for the Study of Democratic Institutions, 1964–79.

He continued to write on a broad number of themes—planning, the U.S. Constitution, and Franklin D. Roosevelt. The latter was his chief subject; Tugwell wrote a prize-winning biography of Roosevelt in 1957, *The Democratic Roosevelt,* and several other books of combined history and memoir in which he reflected upon the career of Roosevelt and the meaning of the New Deal. In a distinguished series of articles published in the late 1940s and early 1950s, Tugwell was critical of the New Deal's missed opportunities for more thoroughgoing change. Much of the New Deal had been "planting shrubbery on the shoulders of a volcano," he wrote, and he tended to lay a good deal of the blame upon FDR's unwillingness to leave the older New Freedom progressivism behind and embrace the planning necessities taught by the New Nationalism. As the years went by, Tugwell softened this judgment, concluding that Roosevelt had been substantially blocked by conservative politicians and judges and that on the whole he had made brilliant use of the small openings for institutional change that the depression had given him. Concluding that full employment and social justice would continue to elude presidents, Tugwell devoted his energies in the 1960s to a proposed revision of the U.S. Constitution (1967) which would regionalize the country and establish a fourth, planning branch. In all, Tugwell wrote thirty-three books, among them a three-volume autobiography, completed in 1982 by the posthumous publication of *To the Lesser Heights of Morningside.*

Rex Tugwell died in Santa Barbara in 1979.

Among Tugwell's many books, indispensable are *The Democratic Roosevelt* (Garden City, N.Y.: Doubleday & Co., 1957), outstanding on FDR's childhood; *The Brains Trust* (New York: Viking, 1967); and *In Search of Roosevelt* (Cambridge, Mass.: Harvard University Press, 1972), a collection of articles evaluating Roosevelt and the New Deal. Bernard Sternsher, *Rexford Tugwell and the New Deal* (New Brunswick, N.J.: Rutgers University Press, 1964) provides an exegesis of Tugwell's thought and a detailed account of his career in Washington. On Tugwell's economic ideas, see Allan G. Gruchy, *Modern Economic Thought: The American Contribution* (New York: Prentice-Hall, 1947); Steven Kesselman, *The Modernization of American Reform: Structures and Perceptions* (New York: Garland Publishing Co., 1980); and Otis L. Graham, Jr., Epilogue to *To the Lesser Heights of Morningside* by Rexford G. Tugwell (Philadelphia: University of Pennsylvania Press, 1982).

BERNARD STERNSHER
OTIS L. GRAHAM, JR.

See also Brains Trust; Consumerism; Housing and Resettlement; Planning

Tully, Grace
(9 August 1900–15 June 1984)

Among the women who staffed FDR's office, Marguerite ("Missy") LeHand was called "the Queen." Grace Tully was, in her words, "Number two girl." LeHand's stroke, which she suffered in mid-1941, resulted in Tully's elevation to the top secretarial position.

Born in Bayonne, New Jersey, Tully was a young girl when her father died. Her mother raised three daughters and a son amid financial difficulty, but much affection. Tully was educated at parochial and convent schools and then a secretarial school run by the Sisters of Charity. Before graduating, she went to work for Bishop (later Cardinal) Patrick Hayes, finishing her stenographic studies at night classes.

After ten years in the employ of the church, Tully searched for and found new work and excitement with the Democratic National Committee. She was assigned to help Eleanor Roosevelt who was already organizing support for the 1928 presidential nominee, Alfred Smith. When FDR was nominated for the New York governorship, Louis Howe co-opted Tully's services for the Roosevelt campaign, and she moved fully into the FDR orbit. In her own estimation, she had achieved "the ultimate in secretarial aspiration."

Tully performed the dictation and typing chores that Missy LeHand shunned. By the time the Roosevelt team made its final move to Washington, the division of labor was well established and agreeable to both women. Additional staff performed lesser clerical chores. There was one break in the pattern. For about one year, following the first inauguration until early 1934, Tully battled tuberculosis in various sanatoria. She was absent, therefore, during the hectic and heady early months of the administration.

Upon her return, the secretarial routine was quickly reestablished. Tully arrived at work at 10:00 and quickly scanned the already-opened incoming mail for items of particular importance. After a greeting and sometimes a lengthier conversation, she did the typing from the previous day's dictation. Late afternoon was the time FDR handled the mail Tully brought him, dictated his replies, asked her to compose occasional responses, or referred letters to appropriate individuals or agencies for clarification and answers. Tully kept careful track of the referrals and return.

Taking dictation in preparation for fireside chats and major speeches were among her essential duties. Speeches were cooperative efforts among aides, speech writers, Tully, and the president, but according to Tully, FDR always put his own distinctive mark on what was to be said and how. Speeches were usually last-minute undertakings that involved several drafts. On those occasions when rewriting exceeded four or five versions, the work day, which usually ended at seven in the evening, was extended to midnight or beyond. After typing the triple-spaced reading copy, Tully became the self-appointed guardian of the original copy, saving it for posterity.

Like LeHand and other close aides and advisers, Tully often dined with the Roosevelt family, attended social events at the White House, and traveled on campaign trips and to Hyde Park, Warm Springs, and conventions. There was no doubt that both Roosevelts expected and received hard work, loyalty, and significant doses of self-sacrifice from their staffs. Nor was there any doubt that the staffs perceived themselves as members of two distinct households. When Tully was identified in a newspaper photograph as Mrs. Roosevelt's secretary, the first lady was quick to note that the error would cause Tully great displeasure. And Eleanor did not attend the late afternoon cocktail hours at which FDR prepared old-fashioneds and martinis with great relish for his secretaries and aides. In the early years of the administration, this ritual was supplemented by the "children's hour," shakedown sessions during which administrative problems and procedures were discussed.

The name for the staff sessions is revealing and indicates the manner in which FDR envisioned his "official family" and his role within it. In her memoir published four years after the president's death, Tully recreated countless conversations with her boss in which he referred to her not by name but as "child." Grace Tully was twenty-eight years old when she began working for Roosevelt; she was forty-five at the time of his death, but was still called "child."

Tully was present at Warm Springs in April 1945 when FDR died. In her doting memoir, she presented an affectionate view of the president, positive evaluations of his campaigns and programs, and a complimentary compendium of New Deal personalities. The family, including the domineering Sara Delano Roosevelt, are described with affection. Only political opponents roused her Irish ire. She was also as discreet as she was devoted. She ignored the family tensions of which she was certainly aware. She wrote of Mme. Shoumatoff who was painting the portrait of FDR when he was fatally stricken and casually mentioned that the artist had been commissioned by Mrs. Winthrop Rutherfurd. In an interview thirty years later, she acknowledged the comings and goings of Rutherfurd in and out of the Oval Office past her desk during the war years.

Following the president's death, Tully maintained the Washington apartment she shared with her mother, who was as ardent an FDR supporter as her daughter. She spent her remaining working years on Capitol Hill as secretary for both Senator Lyndon Johnson and Senator Mike Mansfield.

Grace Tully receives much less attention than Missy LeHand in histories of the New Deal and biographies of Franklin and Eleanor Roosevelt. Her memoir, *F.D.R.: My Boss* (New York: Charles Scribner's Sons, 1949) is a loving tribute to the president but offers some insight into her own secretarial role and workings of the Roosevelt White House. Justice William O. Douglas described her possession of much good sense and Irish wit in the foreword he wrote to her book, and the *New York Times* interview printed 3 August 1980 on the occasion of an eightieth birthday party given for her by Thomas Corcoran indicates that time did not diminish these attributes.

LOIS SCHARF

Two-Thirds Rule

Democratic party rule that required a two-thirds vote for the party's presidential nomination. During Franklin Roosevelt's first run for the presidency in 1932, the Democratic party required for its nomination not a simple majority but a two-thirds vote. This one-hundred-year-old rule gave reason for Roosevelt's opponents to hope for a deadlocked convention and a compromise candidate. The candidacies of Al Smith and of numerous native sons left Roosevelt with a majority of votes but still about one hundred votes shy of the necessary two-thirds. At a preconvention strategy conference at Hyde Park, Roosevelt and his advisers decided that, since the rule could be revoked by a simple majority vote, the Roosevelt forces should first move to repeal the rule, and then the majority of delegates already committed could nominate FDR. The danger was that this tactic would appear as a weakness in the Roosevelt campaign, or worse, as an unfair attempt to circumvent the normal process.

When the convention began, a group of Roosevelt's supporters took the issue out of his hands. At a meeting of sixty-five Roosevelt backers, Louisiana's senator Huey Long sponsored a resolution to abolish the two-thirds rule. Jim Farley, Roosevelt's campaign manager, tried to control the Louisiana Kingfish, but Long's oratory persuaded the meeting to pass the resolution. Once Roosevelt's plans were out in the open, the opposition had time to coalesce. Some southern delegates who otherwise supported Roosevelt opposed the rule change because the rule had long given them near veto power over the nomination. Roosevelt's opponents charged that he was immorally changing the rules in the middle of the game and made this a rallying cry around which to unite the otherwise disparate anti-Roosevelt interests. Fearing a defeat that could ruin his candidacy, Roosevelt backed down from the rule change, announcing that he still opposed it but would not challenge it since "the issue was not raised until after the delegates to the convention had been selected, and I decline to permit either myself or my friends to be open to the accusation of poor sportsmanship or to use methods which could be called, even falsely, those of a steam roller."

Roosevelt's defeat on this strategic matter lent strength to the opposition and nearly cost him the nomination. Four years later at the next Democratic convention, Roosevelt, now firmly in control, quietly had the two-thirds rule revoked. The elimination of the rule meant that southerners no longer had a veto over the party's presidential nomination and proved important in determining the emerging configuration of the Democratic party.

Frank Freidel, *Franklin D. Roosevelt, The Triumph* (Boston: Little, Brown & Co., 1956) covers Roosevelt's maneuverings at the 1932 convention. Ralph M. Goodman, *Search for Consensus: The Story of the Democratic Party* (Philadelphia: Temple University Press, 1979) examines the importance of the two-thirds rule in shaping the party's presidential politics.

See also Elections in the Roosevelt Era; Negroes

U

Unconditional Surrender

See Casablanca Conference; Foreign Policy; Hitler, Adolf, and Germany; Japan; World War II

Unemployment

See Civil Works Administration; Civilian Conservation Corps; Federal Art Project; Federal Emergency Relief Administration; Federal Theatre Project; Federal Writers Project; Great Depression; National Resources Planning Board; National Youth Administration; Negroes; New Deal; Public Works Administration; Recession of 1937–38; Relief; Rural Electrification Administration; Social Security; Veterans; War Effort on the Home Front; Women and the New Deal; Works Progress Administration

Union Party

Third-party challenge to Roosevelt in the 1936 election. The Union party was born out of frustration with the shortcomings of the New Deal. In 1935 the persistence of the depression and Roosevelt's reluctance to push ahead with further reforms made the time seem ripe for a third-party challenge from the Left of the major parties. Roosevelt's leadership faltered while the radical trend of the 1934 elections and the popularity of protest movements such as Huey Long's Share Our Wealth plan demonstrated the formidable potential for a new progressive party. Roosevelt's insistence on an all-class alliance in spite of business's criticism of the New Deal left many progressives dismayed with Roosevelt and ready to look for new leadership.

Yet by the next year much of the third-party sentiment had dissipated. Roosevelt pushed through Congress a second hundred days of reform legislation in mid-1935 to reemerge as the leader of liberal forces. In September of 1935, Huey Long was assas-

sinated and the protest movements lost their most dynamic leader. What remained was a loose collection of dissenting movements without a forceful leader and with their potential following among progressive leaders and disaffected voters already heading for the Roosevelt reform banner. In June 1936, Father Charles E. Coughlin, Detroit's demagogic "radio priest," announced the creation of a "third force" which would command the attention of 25 million voters. Three days later William "Liberty Bell" Lemke, a congressman from North Dakota who felt betrayed by Roosevelt's opposition to his farm policies, announced his candidacy for president and promised a party convention in July. Reporters joked that the convention had already occurred in a phone booth with Coughlin on the other end of the line. The two were joined by Dr. Francis Townsend, the leader of an old-age pension organization based in California. Finally, from the remnants of Huey Long's Share Our Wealth movement came Gerald L. K. Smith, who was snubbed by Louisiana politicians and brought nothing except his crowd-stirring abilities as an orator.

Although the Union party at first appeared to be a potentially powerful new force in the election, it soon became apparent that internal dissension and lack of a mass organization made the party's strength illusory. At a national Townsendite convention in July, the delegates cheered for and against Roosevelt as the Union party leaders struggled to arouse the lagging interest in the party. Father Coughlin, trying to outdo the rabble-rousing oratory of Gerald Smith, pulled off his coat and clerical collar and denounced Roosevelt as a "betrayer and liar." What had promised to be a "love feast" degenerated into an exercise in confusion. In August at Coughlin's National Union for Social Justice convention, the ruptures in the party widened further. Coughlin prevented Smith and Townsend from speaking and claimed, "As I was instrumental in removing Herbert Hoover from the White House, so help me God, I will be instrumental in taking a Communist from the Chair once occupied by Washington." But the Union party platform offered only an amorphous collection of contradictory statements, not satisfying any of the different constituencies. Worse, although Townsend pledged his personal support to the party, his organization was in no way ready to follow his lead.

Although nominally opposed to both major parties, the Union party focused its attack on Roosevelt. Townsend called the two parties "left and right wings of the same bird of prey, the banker," but the Union party speakers reserved their most powerful invectives for attacks on Roosevelt from both the Left and the Right. Lemke charged that if Roosevelt was not a Communist himself, then "Communist leaders have laid their cuckoo eggs in his Democratic nest." The most reckless anti-Roosevelt vendetta came from Coughlin, who called Roosevelt a "scab President" who was "surrounded by red and pink communists" including "Rexie Tugwell, hand-shaker of Russia" and "plow-me-down Wallace." Coughlin also blamed "the ventriloquists of Wall Street" and promised to rid the State Department of internationalists and establish a "real American department." Coughlin could so easily attack Roosevelt from both the Left and the Right because he believed the New Deal to be "a broken down Colossus straddling the harbor of Rhodes, its left leg standing on ancient capitalism and its right mired in the red mud of communism."

Despite a fast-paced campaign involving nearly every state but the deep South, the Union party was not able to deliver on its promise to be a decisive third force. Both major parties refused to acknowledge the Union party as a serious challenge and Socialist Norman Thomas summarized the attitude of the established Left by denouncing the new party as "two and a half rival messiahs plus one ambitious politician plus some neo-populists plus a platform that reminds me of the early efforts of Hitler." The liberal *Nation* opined that "there is nothing so damaging to a panacea as another panacea on the same platform." By late October the party was in shambles. Smith had been purged for his advocacy of a fascist army "to save the U.S.A. from the internationalists," and Coughlin had been rebuked by his ecclesiastical superiors for his rhetorical excesses.

Townsend at the last minute announced that "Roosevelt is our sworn enemy" and urged his supporters to vote for either Lemke or Republican candidate Landon. Lemke himself was forced to spend the last days of the campaign in North Dakota, battling to salvage his seat in Congress. It was no surprise, then, when the Union party polled only 892,000 votes, less than 2 percent of the total and a lower proportion of votes than other recent protest candidates such as Norman Thomas in 1932 had received.

Coughlin, who had promised at least 9 million votes, retired from radio broadcasting, tearfully admitting that the Union party was "thoroughly discredited" and allowing that "President Roosevelt can be a dictator if he wants to." Only Lemke tried to keep the struggling party afloat, but gave up by 1939 with his national headquarters in debt and the party's shell of a local organization infiltrated by disreputable fringe elements, including the National Socialist party in Illinois. As an attempt to transform the protest movement of the mid-thirties into effective opposition to Roosevelt, the Union party had been a complete failure.

David H. Bennett, *Demagogues in the Depression* (New Brunswick, N.J.: Rutgers University Press, 1969) gives a critical view of the Union party. A recent, more sympathetic interpretation of the forces at work is Alan Brinkley, *Voices of Protest* (New York: Alfred A. Knopf, 1982). An excellent short treatment is David O. Powell, "The Union Party of 1936: Campaign Tactics and Issues," *Mid-America* 46 (April 1964):126–41.

TIMOTHY LEHMAN

See also Coughlin, Charles Edward; Lemke, William; Townsend, Francis G., M.D.

Unions

See Dubinksy, David; Green, William; Hillman, Sidney; Labor; Lewis, John Llewellyn; National Recovery Administration; Perkins, Frances; Randolph, Asa Philip

United Automobile Workers

See Labor

United Mine Workers

See Labor; Lewis, John Llewellyn

United Nations

See Cohen, Benjamin Victor; Hull, Cordell; Internationalism and Peace; Lehman, Herbert Henry; Roosevelt, Anna Eleanor; Stettinius, Edward Reilly, Jr.; Vandenberg, Arthur Hendrick; Welles, Benjamin Sumner; Yalta Conference

V

Val-Kill

See Hyde Park; Roosevelt, Anna Eleanor

Vandenberg, Arthur Hendrick

(22 March 1884–18 April 1951)

Republican U.S. senator from Michigan, 1928–51. Arthur Vandenberg was born in Grand Rapids, Michigan, and attended the University of Michigan Law School for one year. In 1902, he joined the staff of the *Grand Rapids Herald* and gained considerable influence in state Republican politics from 1906 to 1928 as its editor. He was appointed to the U.S. Senate in 1928 to fill a vacancy and supported most early New Deal measures except the National Industrial Recovery Act and the Agricultural Adjustment Act. After becoming Senate minority leader in 1935, he opposed most second New Deal measures. Vandenberg, who advocated a balanced budget and reduced taxation, feared Roosevelt had usurped congressional power. A conservative coalition leader, Vandenberg criticized the National Labor Relations Act, Roosevelt's Supreme Court proposal, and the Fair Labor Standards Act.

Vandenberg, a staunch Foreign Relations Committee isolationist, led Republican resistance to Roosevelt's internationalist policies. Besides backing the Nye Committee hearings, he favored the Neutrality Acts of the 1930s, opposed their modification, and protested the Lend-Lease Act. After American entry into World War II, however, he supported the president's defense measures and helped develop a bipartisan foreign policy among President Roosevelt, the State Department, and congressional leaders.

Vandenberg helped write the Connally resolution for American membership in the future United Nations subject to Senate ratification as a treaty. During the fall of 1943, he codrafted a Republican party statement endorsing American membership in the United Nations on the Connally resolution terms. In 1944 he urged Republican presidential candidate Thomas Dewey to avoid foreign policy issues in the campaign. Before the Senate in January 1945, Vandenberg advocated cooperation and candor between Roosevelt and the Senate toward creation of the United Nations. Roosevelt, impressed with Vandenberg's cordial speech and bipartisan gestures, appointed the Michigan Republican as an American delegate to the San Francisco Conference drafting the UN Charter.

Memories of Woodrow Wilson inspired the Roosevelt-Vandenberg rapprochement. Vandenberg had opposed President Wilson until American entry into World War I. Vandenberg thereafter backed Wilson's conduct of the war and urged Senate ratification of the Treaty of Versailles and American entrance into the League of Nations with appropriate reservations. The chief Republican foreign policy spokesman after January 1945, he believed that Soviet Communism threatened American security and urged an aggressive, bipartisan foreign policy in response. Besides helping secure Senate ratification of the UN Charter, he served as an American delegate to the first and second UN General Assemblies. Subsequently, he ardently backed the Truman Doctrine, Marshall Plan, North Atlantic Treaty Organization, and other containment policies.

For additional information see the Arthur Vandenberg Papers, Michigan Historical Collection, University of Michigan, Ann Arbor; C. David Tompkins, *Senator Arthur H. Vandenberg: The Evolution of a Modern Republican, 1884–1945* (East Lansing: Michigan State University Press, 1970); Arthur H. Vandenberg, Jr., and Joe A. Morris, eds., *The Private Papers of Senator Vandenberg* (Boston: Houghton Mifflin Co., 1952); Aurie N. Dunlap, "The Political Career of Arthur H. Vandenberg" (Ph.D. diss., Columbia University, 1956); Newell S. Moore, "The Rise of Senator Arthur H. Vandenberg in American Foreign Affairs" (Ph.D. Diss., George Peabody College, 1954); *Current Biography* (1940) pp. 821–23; *Current Biography* (1948) pp. 637–41; *Dictionary of American Biography*, Suppl. 5 pp. 702–4.

DAVID L. PORTER

Veterans

Beneficiaries of the Roosevelt-sponsored GI Bill of Rights passed during World War II. The Roosevelt government's generous treatment of World War II veterans emerged out of a historical backdrop of hostility between veterans' groups and the government. Throughout the twenties and thirties, veterans of World War I, led by the American Legion, pressed the government for the compensation they thought they deserved. Servicemen argued that their greater sacrifices in lost time and wages entitled them to "adjusted compensation," or a bonus payment. The government responded from the fiscal conservatism of the time that it could not afford to run a deficit simply to meet the demands of a special class of citizens. The coming of the depression heightened the arguments on both sides, and clamor for a bonus reached a peak in July 1932, when twenty thousand "bonus marchers" descended on Washington to demand payment from the government. President Herbert Hoover ordered the marchers disbanded, but Gen. Douglas MacArthur carried the orders too far as he used troops and tanks to disperse the marchers and then set fire to their temporary shacks. This rough treatment increased the public perception of Hoover as insensitive to peoples' needs during the depression and sealed his electoral defeat.

The new president Franklin Roosevelt was no more sympathetic to veterans' demands. During his first week in office, Roosevelt sponsored a budget-balancing economy measure that reduced pension payments. He explained, "Too often in recent history liberal governments have been wrecked on the rocks of loose fiscal policy." In October 1933, he took the offensive as he told an American Legion conference that, in light of the widespread poverty and unemployment of the depression, "no person, because he wore a uniform, must thereafter be placed in a special class of beneficiaries over and above all other citizens." Roosevelt believed that veterans' demands constituted an unwarranted raid on the federal treasury by a special interest group which jeopardized his efforts to bring an end to the depression. The veterans had more success with Congress, which in 1935 passed over Roosevelt's veto a bill restoring the pensions cut two years earlier. Even in defeat, Roosevelt showed his determination by reading his veto message to Congress in person, declaring again that to give special treatment to veterans impeded the general recovery and weakened the federal budget. The following year, Congress yielded to election-year pressures and passed legislation providing bonus payments to veterans. Again Roosevelt vetoed the bill but this time quietly and in full recognition that Congress would override. By the end of the decade, the veterans' groups had achieved most of their goals while the Roosevelt administration believed more than ever that veterans constituted a narrow special interest group.

The mutual hostility that had developed between veterans' organizations and the Roosevelt administra-

Brooklyn (N.Y.) Eagle, *19 September 1932.*

tion seemed less important by the middle of World War II, as Roosevelt began to think not only about winning the war but about the peace that would follow. Memories of the depression remained strong in the minds of many Americans, and there was widespread fear that the postwar demobilization would bring a return to massive unemployment and economic hardship.

Concerned about the postwar economy, Roosevelt first sought the advice of his planners. In 1942 the National Resources Planning Board sponsored a Post-War Manpower Conference which planned for economic priorities in the demobilization process. A second and overlapping set of recommendations came from the Armed Forces Committee on Post-War Educational Opportunities for Service Personnel chaired by Brig. Gen. Frederick G. Osborn. Together these two reports formed the basis for later legislation and convinced President Roosevelt to publicly endorse the concept of special treatment for veterans. In a fireside chat on 28 July 1943, Roosevelt revealed that "among many other things we are, today, laying plans for the return to civilian life of our gallant men and women in the armed services. They must not be demobilized into an environment of inflation and unemployment, to a place on the bread line or on a corner selling apples." The president urged Congress to provide for veterans the education, unemployment, disability, and pension benefits as suggested by the National Resources Planning Board and the Osborn Committee reports. The proposal received broad-based support; liberals saw it as an extension of New Deal social ideals to at least one group of society, while conservatives felt obligated to provide for the "soldier boys."

Roosevelt did not send a specific legislative package to Capitol Hill, and it took nearly six months for the legislators to agree on one. The American Legion presented a bill in January of 1944 that formed the basis for what passed three months later as the "GI Bill of Rights." The law provided veterans with an array of privileges, including occupational guidance, preference in hiring for many jobs and monthly allowances while looking, full tuition and expenses for any education from elementary through graduate school, and subsidized loans for veterans to invest in small businesses, farms, or homes. The GI Bill was later amended to include medical care for the disabled and an expanded number of veterans' hospitals. In short, veterans were given the social benefits desired by most citizens. At the insistence of veterans' organizations, the management of the new program was lodged in a single agency, the Veterans' Administration. By all measures, the program succeeded magnificently. By 1955 over 50 percent of all World War II veterans in civilian life had enjoyed the benefits of the GI Bill. The plans laid by Roosevelt's advisers bore fruit in the most successful reentry of soldiers into civilian life of any war in U.S. history.

A thorough monograph on the topic is Davis R. B. Ross, *Preparing for Ulysses: Politics and Veterans During World War II* (New York: Columbia University Press, 1969).

See also National Resources Planning Board

Vice-President

See Garner, John Nance; Truman, Harry S; Wallace, Henry A.

Vichy France

See de Gaulle, Charles; Eisenhower, Dwight David; Leahy, William Daniel

Voice of America

See Sherwood, Robert Emmet

Voting Analyses and Statistics

See Election of 1928; Elections

W

Wages and Hours Legislation

The first general attempt by the federal government to establish wage minimums and hour maximums collapsed when the U.S. Supreme Court in 1935 struck down on constitutional grounds the National Recovery Administration experiment in the *Schechter* poultry decision and the Guffey Coal Act, which had set a minimum wage for coal miners.

The issue of federal wages and hours legislation was debated in the 1936 campaign, with the Republicans taking the position that the decision should be left to the states (where the Court, however, had ruled such laws to be unconstitutional). The Democrats promised to enact national legislation, and Roosevelt himself pledged action. The president believed that wages and hours legislation was necessary to arrest the further downward spiral of wages.

Despite Roosevelt's landslide victory at the polls, New Dealers moved cautiously to enact legislation concerning wages and hours. Senator Hugo Black and Congressman William P. Connery introduced a bill in May 1937. Predictably, the proposed legislation encountered stiff opposition, particularly from southern Democrats and Republicans who hoped to preserve the differential that allowed them to pay lower wages than other sections of the country. Nor did organized labor wholeheartedly endorse the proposed law, with American Federation of Labor leaders Bill Hutcheson and William Green saying no to the proposal.

By the time Congress convened in January 1938, little progress had been made, and Roosevelt once again recommended that a federal law "to end starvation wages and intolerable hours" be approved. Within six months, Congress had secured passage of the Fair Labor Standards Act, sometimes referred to as the Wage and Hour Act. The president signed the bill on 25 June 1938. "That's that," a relieved Roosevelt sighed. The law proved to be the last reform measure of the New Deal.

The Fair Labor Standards Act established a minimum wage of twenty-five cents an hour for covered employees. This increased in a series of steps to a forty-cent minimum wage seven years after the law's enactment. While the new law did not limit the number of hours employees could work, it did stipulate payment at the rate of 1½ times the regular rate for overtime work, the standard work week at the time being forty-four hours. After two years, the average work week was forty hours. The 1938 measure also prohibited the employment of children under age sixteen in most occupations and age eighteen in more hazardous jobs.

Still, in order to garner support for the law, compromises had to be made. Some industries were not covered. Retail and service employees were totally exempted from the regulations, as were local transportation personnel, people in the fishing or agricultural industries, and seasonal employees. And the issue of wage differentials was left to the Department of Labor, which administered the law. So many exemptions had been included in the legislation that one congressman prepared a sarcastic addendum with reference to Secretary of Labor Frances Perkins saying, "Within ninety days after appointment of the Administrator, she shall report to Congress whether anyone is subject to this bill." Nevertheless, within a short time, the wages of approximately 300,000 persons were raised and the work weeks of some 1.3 million people were shortened.

Commonly, New Deal legislation faced legal challenges, and the 1938 act was no different. In 1941, in the case concerning Darby Lumber Company, the Supreme Court unanimously approved the federal wages and hours legislation. With occasional increases in the minimum wage rate, the law still governs America's workers.

The definitive account of labor in the New Deal era is Irving Bernstein, *Turbulent Years: A History of the American Worker, 1933–1941* (Boston: Houghton Mifflin Co., 1970). General accounts detailing the attempts to set wage minimums and hour maximums include John G. Rayback, *A History of American Labor* (New York: Macmillan Co., 1966), John H. Leek, *Government and Labor in the United States* (New York: Rinehart & Co.,

1952), and William E. Leuchtenburg, *Franklin D. Roosevelt and the New Deal* (New York: Harper & Row, 1963).

GREGORY KING

See also New Deal; Perkins, Frances; Supreme Court of the United States

Wagner, Robert Ferdinand
(8 June 1877–4 May 1953)

Senator from New York and author of landmark New Deal legislation. Robert F. Wagner was born in Nastatten, Germany. His family emigrated to the United States in 1886, settling in the Yorkville section of Manhattan. He graduated from the City College of New York in 1898 and New York Law School in 1900. In 1904 he was elected to the state assembly with the support of the local affiliate of Tammany Hall, and in 1908 he was elected to the state senate. In 1911, at the age of only thirty-three, he was made president pro-tem of the senate, as Charles Francis Murphy, chief of Tammany, tried to stave off an anti-Tammany revolt among progressive Democratic senators.

The calamitous fire in 1911 at New York's Triangle Shirtwaist Factory prompted Wagner and his house counterpart, Alfred E. Smith, to sponsor the creation of a commission to investigate factory conditions throughout the state. Both Wagner and Smith served on the commission along with prominent business leaders, philanthropists, and trade unionists. During the four years of its existence, the commission served as the major vehicle for the largely successful efforts to alter industrial working conditions in New York. This effort created important legal and political precedents for the landmark labor and social welfare legislation that Wagner championed during the New Deal.

In 1918, Wagner was elected to the New York Supreme Court, and in 1926, he entered the U.S. Senate. He convinced the Republican-controlled Senate in 1930 to pass bills dealing with unemployment and public works, and his proposal for using public works to fight recession became law the next year. In 1932 he authored the first federal relief law and the largest public works bill to date. Wagner's ability to achieve such extraordinary influence as a minority member was due to his method of operation. Unlike other progressives, he did not act as a gadfly criticizing the conservative bent of the upper chamber at every opportunity. Rather, he marshaled his speaking opportunities and used them exclusively in support of the particular bills he had crafted. Thus he developed the reputation of a craftsman and a specialist, one who knew more about labor conditions and labor economics than any other senator. To preserve this reputation, he relied heavily upon the advice of trained professionals. To mobilize support for his bills, he enlisted the aid of a wide network of interested labor and philanthropic organizations.

After Al Smith's defeat in 1928, Wagner joined the ranks of those promoting FDR for president, but when Smith decided to seek the office again in 1932, Wagner, in deference to his close personal friendship with Smith, refrained from any further public participation in the FDR cause. During the New Deal, Wagner enjoyed a close working relationship with FDR, although his personal relationship was not as close as it had been with Smith.

After FDR's election, Wagner became deeply involved in the complex process of conflict and negotiations that took place during the formulation of the National Industrial Recovery Act (NIRA). He aligned himself with the planning faction, which was seeking to end cutthroat competition by enabling industries to better coordinate their activities. Wagner favored relaxing the antitrust laws, which he felt only served to keep small businessmen from making common cause to defend themselves against aggression committed by big business. His greatest victory was in resisting intense pressure from the National Association of Manufacturers to weaken the guarantee of free collective bargaining contained in Section 7(a) of the NIRA.

Robert F. Wagner. (Constant Collection. Courtesy FDR Library.)

FDR appointed Wagner to chair the National Recovery Administration Labor Board to adjudicate dispute arising under Section 7(a). The board's lack of clear-cut jurisdictional and enforcement powers severely limited its usefulness. Therefore, Wagner, in March of 1934, introduced legislation providing for a National Labor Board which would be empowered to engage in mediation and arbitration, certify bargaining agents, and act against unfair labor practices committed by employers. In view of the highly controversial nature of the bill, FDR chose to press his Senate allies not to stage a full-scale debate over the question prior to the 1934 election. Wagner acceded to this request.

With the election safely past, Wagner's strong sense of party loyalty no longer inhibited him from waging a strong battle for labor legislation. In February of 1935, he introduced a bill that contained important changes from the 1934 version. These revisions served the purpose of emphasizing the central function of the board as a high court of labor management relations enforcing labor's rights rather than an administrative means for settling labor disputes. The clear purpose of the legislation was to ensure that the federal government would have the tools to fulfill its responsibility to guarantee the right of free and effective collective bargaining. This right was central to Wagner's vision of a powerful and responsible labor movement capable of protecting its members from encroachments on their liberties perpetrated by either the state or the corporate sphere.

FDR's position on the Wagner bill remained steadfastly neutral. Wagner overcame this difficulty by capitalizing on a temporary prolabor shift in public opinion brought about by the wave of worker unrest that crested in 1935. He used his tactical skill to force the Senate to take quick action, avoiding protracted debate that would enable labor's enemies to stall until the tide ebbed. On 16 May 1935, the Wagner bill passed the Senate by the overwhelming margin of 63–12 after only two days of debate. FDR no longer considered it politically prudent to remain neutral, and on 24 May 1935 he endorsed the bill. It passed the House of Representatives a month later and was signed into law as the National Labor Relations Act on 5 July 1935.

As a senator from the president's home state, Wagner faced special pressure to support FDR; nonetheless he chose to demonstrate his independence of the president on two important occasions. His experience as a judge made him reluctant to tamper with judicial independence, so he remained neutral throughout the entire Court-packing debate. He opposed FDR's administrative reorganization plan for fear that it would permit his cherished National Labor Relations Board to be swallowed up within the Department of Labor.

In addition to labor, Wagner's other great legislative concerns were health, housing, civil rights, and economic planning. He led the unsuccessful congressional battle for antilynching legislation, and in 1937 his public housing bill was passed by Congress. As chairman of the Banking and Currency Committee, he played a key role in securing passage of the Employment Act of 1946. The scope of his concerns mirrored those of the liberal wing of the Democratic party of which he was the chief Senate spokesman. Along with senators Norris and La Follette, he served as the modern prototype of the "national" Senator more recently exemplified by Hubert Humphrey, Henry Jackson, and Edward Kennedy. Senator Wagner retired from the Senate in 1949.

The outstanding source for Wagner is J. Joseph Huthmacher's magisterial biography *Senator Robert Wagner and the Rise of Urban Liberalism* (New York: Atheneum, 1968). It is richly detailed in regard to all aspects of his life and work. However, Huthmacher so closely identifies with Wagner's political perspective that no criticism is offered. A good short sketch of his life and accomplishments is contained in "Robert Wagner," by John C. O'Brien, in *The American Politician*, ed. J. T. Salter (Chapel Hill: University of North Carolina Press, 1938). There is no other significant scholarly writing about Wagner. Those who find Huthmacher to be insufficient with regard to a particular topic must look for information regarding that topic, for example, the National Labor Relations Act.

MARC LANDY

See also Housing and Resettlement; Labor; National Labor Relations Board; Social Security; Tammany Hall

Walker, Frank Comerford
(30 May 1886–13 September 1959)

Democratic party treasurer and national chairman, New Deal administrator, postmaster general, and presidential adviser. Frank Walker was born at Plymouth, Pennsylvania, of second-generation Irish-American parents. In 1890, the family moved to Butte, Montana, where Walker was educated in the Roman Catholic parochial school system. He attended Gonzaga University, Spokane, Washington, and earned an LL.B. from Notre Dame University School of Law in 1909.

Returning to Butte to practice law, Walker was appointed deputy county prosecuting attorney. He was elected to the Montana House of Representatives and served as chairman of the Judiciary Committee in the thirteenth legislative session from January to March 1913. His political hero was the progressive Montanan, Senator Thomas J. Walsh.

Not satisfied with his income, Walker moved to New York City in 1924 to become legal counsel for his uncle, Michael E. Comerford, whose moving picture theater chain eventually made Walker wealthy. This enabled him to become active again in politics. Through Eddie Dowling, a Broadway actor and producer, Walker met Henry Morgenthau, Sr., who took Walker in as a member of the "For Roosevelt Before Chicago" group supporting FDR's presidential nomination. Walker was appointed treasurer of the Democratic party in 1932, helped in fund raising for 1936, and was treasurer of the Franklin D. Roosevelt Library fund.

In July 1933, FDR appointed Walker executive secretary of the Executive Council, which attempted to coordinate the alphabet agencies. Walker's responsibility was to prepare the agenda and circulate reports for government departments. Disappointed with the council's failure, FDR created a streamlined replica named the National Emergency Council with Walker as its executive director. This cast him in 1935 between Harry Hopkins and Harold Ickes in the controversy over use of Federal Emergency Relief funds. Because of the illness of his uncle and the death of his cousin, Walker left the administration in December 1935 to oversee his business interests.

Walker's major contributions to the Roosevelt presidency came when he was chosen to succeed Postmaster General James A. Farley in 1940 and Democratic National Chairman Edward J. Flynn in 1943. Walker extended the mails to 12 million armed service personnel, served as chairman of the War Censorship Board, and organized the party for the 1944 election campaign. Through his efforts, the regular Democratic and farm-labor factions were unified in Minnesota. He was also a key member of the conservative group who convinced FDR to dump Vice-President Wallace.

After Roosevelt's death, Walker resigned to return to his business, but was appointed by President Truman to the delegation of the London organizational meeting of the United Nations in 1946. His career reflected the rise of Roman Catholics to political prominence and the influence of wealthy and conservative men around Roosevelt.

Frank C. Walker. (Constant Collection. Courtesy FDR Library.)

There are no biographies of Walker, although one is in process by Dean Kohlhoff. His papers (135 shelf feet) are in the archives at the University of Notre Dame. Scholarly work on Walker includes Paul L. Simon, "Frank Walker, New Dealer" (Ph.D. diss., University of Notre Dame, 1965) and "Frank Walker: Coordinator of the New Deal, 1933–1935," *Hudson Review* 2 (1969):75–90.

DEAN KOHLHOFF

See also Franklin D. Roosevelt Library

Walker, James John

(19 June 1881–18 November 1946)

Mayor of New York City, 1925–32. Jimmy Walker was born to Irish Catholic parents in New York's Greenwich Village, a neighborhood dominated by Tammany Hall. Pushed by his father first into education and then into politics, Jimmy reluctantly attended New York Law School and began a political career as a Tammany district captain, but not until he had spent ten years as a songwriter in New York's Tin Pan Alley. His preference for show business over politics affected his political career, where he was known more for his showboat personality than his hard work. A slim figure given to colorful double-breasted suits and stylish hats, he preferred the spontaneity of legislative debate to the tedium of drafting bills. After working his way up in the Tammany machine, he was elected in 1909 to the state legislature, where he served for sixteen years as a legislator known more for his vote-getting ability and party loyalty than for legislative initiatives.

In 1925 Walker became Tammany's choice for mayor of New York City, and he brought the Jazz

FDR and Jimmy Walker, c. 1932. (Courtesy FDR Library.)

Age style to city politics. His tenure was not without accomplishment, notably the creation of a Department of Sanitation and several transportation improvements. He was better known, however, for attending baseball games and nightclubs, taking extended vacations, and flaunting his extramarital affair with an attractive actress. In the midst of this flamboyant administration, an official investigation headed by Judge Samuel Seabury exposed various instances of graft, incompetence, and bribery in Walker's management of City Hall. The investigation led in 1932 to an inquiry by Governor Franklin Roosevelt into Walker's administration. Roosevelt, a presidential candidate, was harsh in questioning Walker but was hesitant to remove Walker from office because he hoped for Tammany's support at election time. Walker solved Roosevelt's dilemma by resigning on 1 September 1932. He then spent a few years in Europe before returning to hold several minor political posts in city government. Shortly before his death, Walker renounced his glamorous life and announced that he had found true happiness in fundamental Catholicism.

A fine biography of Walker is George Walsh, *Gentleman Jimmy Walker* (New York: Praeger Publishers, 1974). An earlier biography is Gene Fowler, *Beau James: The Life and Times of Jimmy Walker* (New York: Viking, 1949).

Wallace, Henry A.

(7 October 1888–18 November 1965)

Served FDR as secretary of agriculture (1933–40), vice-president (1941–45) and secretary of commerce (1945). Born on an Iowa farm, Henry A. Wallace spent most of his early years in Ames and Des Moines. He graduated from Iowa State College in 1910 and went to work for the family paper, *Wallaces' Farmer*, which his grandfather, "Uncle Henry" Wallace, served as first editor. The family had considerable prestige in farm circles—Uncle Henry was a member of Theodore Roosevelt's Country Life Commission, and Wallace's father, Henry C., after a term as editor of *Wallaces' Farmer*, became secretary of agriculture, serving in the Harding-Coolidge administrations from 1921 to 1924 and leaving the editorial responsibilities to his oldest son. As a farm editor, a major participant in the battle for "Equality for Agriculture," and a leader in the development of hybrid corn, the third Henry Wallace added to the family's reputation.

Wallace's prestige in farm circles—his reputation as a man of ideas and action—plus his role in politics recommended him to Franklin Roosevelt as secretary of agriculture in the new administration. He had broken with the Republican party over farm relief and the high protective tariff and thrown his articulate support to Democrats, first Al Smith in 1928 and then Franklin Roosevelt in 1932. And Iowa farmers followed his lead in the latter year, breaking with their Republican tradition to vote for FDR in large numbers.

Henry Wallace with FDR in Washington, D.C., 9 March 1942. (Courtesy FDR Library.)

A many-sided and controversial man, Wallace became the champion of a broad program of reform at home and cooperation abroad. He was an idealist and an intellectual, but he was also a hardheaded administrator and politician. Influenced by political and economic "realities" as well as lofty ideals, he was not inflexible.

When he took on his new responsibilities in 1933, Wallace was a traditionalist as well as a modernizer. He had plans for change in agriculture that envisioned new, larger roles for government. But ideas about new activities for Washington or better breeds of corn did not monopolize his thinking. His mind was influenced also by the agrarian tradition that ran back to Thomas Jefferson and beyond—a tradition that exalted the family farm and insisted upon the fundamental importance of farming and rural life. Influenced by that tradition, Wallace feared the total industrialization and urbanization of the United States and advocated changes in policy and other areas that would build a rich rural civilization and hold a large population on the land.

In his first years in Washington, Wallace was interested mainly in agriculture—and in the more substantial commercial farmers. A very active, innovative, and constructive secretary, he shaped a complex set of programs designed chiefly to make the farm business profitable once again.

As time passed, Wallace became much more than an advocate of the nation's commercial farmers. He developed a cautious concern for the rural poor, made a bolder effort to reform land-use practices, and became a champion of greater purchasing power in the cities. His emergence as a broad-gauged liberal concerned about industrial workers and full employment in the cities as well as rural people was so striking that some of his former allies became very critical of him, convinced that he had deserted the farmer for other groups. Other people, however, came to see him as a man of presidential quality and pushed him forward as Roosevelt's successor.

Roosevelt found Wallace even more attractive than before and, after deciding to run for a third term, selected him for the vice-presidency in 1940. From the president's point of view, Wallace had major assets. He had admirable intellectual and moral qualities and seemed to be growing as a politician; he agreed with the president on both foreign and domestic issues; he had built strength among liberals and labor in the cities to complement his support in the farm areas; and he seemed capable of being a worthy successor, should fate remove FDR from office.

To get the nomination for Wallace, however, FDR had to threaten to decline the nomination for the presidency. Discontented Democrats protested against dictation and insisted that Wallace was a poor choice. They complained that he had been a Republican until only a few years before, that he did not have a wide following, even in the Corn Belt, that he was too idealistic and not a good politician, and that he would not balance the ticket. His nomination would mean that it would be composed of two New Dealers, two internationalists. As such arguments were made, Roosevelt carried his threat to the point of preparing a statement declining the nomination. The party, the statement explained, had not made "overwhelmingly clear its stand in favor of social progress and liberalism" and had not shaken off "all shackles of control fastened upon it by the forces of conservatism, reaction and appeasement."

To calm the storm, Eleanor Roosevelt addressed the convention. She believed, she later explained, that "if Franklin felt that the strain of a third term might be too much for any man and that Mr. Wallace was the man to carry on best in times such as we are facing, he was entitled to his help," and she tried "to persuade the delegations . . . to sink all personal interests in the interests of the country and to make them realize the potential dangers in the situation we were facing." The Roosevelt pressure forced the delegates to accept Wallace.

As vice-president, his outlook continued to expand. He became more interested in international affairs and became a leading spokesman for American liberalism, building a large following among New Dealers. He championed "the Century of the Common Man" and insisted that the war should lead to the revival of reform at home, the weakening and eventual destruction of the imperial systems abroad, the granting of independence and self-rule to all peoples, the elevation of standards of living throughout the world, the destruction of trade restrictions, and the establishment of an international organization with its own military force to govern relations among nations.

Although many liberals, including Eleanor Roosevelt, came to see Wallace as the logical successor to FDR, many other Democrats feared the man and his ideas and worked with considerable success to persuade the president not to choose Wallace as his running mate in 1944. FDR concluded that to obtain Wallace's renomination he would need to fight as he had in 1940, but he was now unwilling to make such a fight, apparently because of fear of its impact on the party and his own chances in November. His desire to win then so as to finish the war and influence the postwar world was very strong. He did not wish to weaken his chances by alienating members of his own party. So he gave Wallace only a restrained endorsement, writing to the delegates that if he were one of them he would vote for Wallace but that he did "not wish to appear in any way to be dictating to the convention." He indicated his willingness to run with others, writing that he would be "glad" to run with Senator Harry S Truman or Justice William O. Douglas and believed that either "would bring real strength to the ticket." Wallace brushed aside suggestions that he withdraw, battled for renomination, and demonstrated considerable strength, but the delegates selected Truman.

After Roosevelt's death, Wallace saw himself both as the person who should have succeeded FDR and as the chief proponent of his views. He became the most prominent critic on the Left of Truman's "get tough" and "containment" policies, as well as the leading proponent of a full-employment economy and a foe of racial discrimination. Convinced that the United States and Russia must cooperate and that all nations must trade with one another, he blamed the new foreign policies on the influence of an economic and military elite, labeled the policies imperialistic, and insisted they were leading toward atomic war. His critique also stressed the domestic consequences of international conflict, especially the frustration of reform, and called for reliance on the United Nations for the management of international matters.

Convinced that Communists and liberals must work together, Wallace joined with Communists and some liberals in an unsuccessful third-party venture in 1948. Foes portrayed him as a tool of Moscow, and he received only a small vote, in spite of his very strenuous campaign.

Playing little part in politics, Wallace devoted much of the last seventeen years of his life to scientific experiments on his New York farm.

An old book, Russell Lord, *The Wallaces of Iowa* (Boston: Houghton Mifflin Co., 1947), remains useful. Edward L. and Frederick H. Schapsmeier provide a more thorough account in *Henry A. Wallace of Iowa: The Agrarian Years, 1910–1940* (Ames: Iowa State University Press, 1968) and *Prophet in Politics: Henry A. Wallace and the War Years, 1940–1965* (Ames: Iowa State University Press, 1970), but they did not have access to the Wallace papers. J. Samuel Walker did explore those sources for *Henry A. Wallace and American Foreign Policy* (Westport, Conn.: Greenwood Press, 1976), but much remains to be done with this fascinating and significant person. For recent efforts to explore some of the issues, see Richard S. Kirkendall et al., "Henry A. Wallace and Iowa Agriculture," *Annals of Iowa* (October 1983).

RICHARD S. KIRKENDALL

See also Agricultural Adjustment Administration; Agriculture; Democratic Party; Jones, Jesse Holman; Third Term

Walsh, Thomas James
(12 June 1859–2 March 1933)

Roosevelt's choice as his first attorney general, Thomas J. Walsh was born in Two Rivers, Wisconsin, and received a law degree from the University of Wisconsin in 1884. He practiced law in the Dakota Territory for six years and then moved to Helena, Montana, where he was primarily involved in mining litigation. Elected to the Senate in 1913, he was responsible for the farm organization and union exemptions in the Clayton Anti-Trust Act and led the fight to confirm Louis D. Brandeis to the Supreme Court. The high point of Walsh's Senate career was his investigation of the leasing of the naval oil reserves in California and Wyoming that exposed the Teapot Dome scandal. He was the permanent chairman of the 1932 Democratic National Convention and actively campaigned for Roosevelt in the West.

Roosevelt always wanted Walsh to head the Justice Department, but Walsh was reluctant to leave the Senate. Finally agreeing, he opposed the possible appointment of Felix Frankfurter to the solicitor general post. Raymond Moley recalled in *After Seven Years* that Walsh didn't want someone in the job "who would lose cases in the grand manner." Walsh eventually agreed to serve as attorney general but died on 2 March 1933 on his way to the inauguration.

Josephine O'Keane's *Thomas J. Walsh: A Senator from Montana* (Francestown, N.H.: Marshall Jones Co., 1955) is a sound but undocumented biography. Walsh's role in the campaign and his views on the Justice Department are briefly described in Raymond Moley, *After Seven Years* (New York: Harper & Bros., 1939).

War Bonds
See War Effort on the Home Front

War Effort on the Home Front

World War II dramatically altered American life. The conflict influenced the pace and often diverted the direction of changes underway before the war began. Some—such as the trend toward the greater concentration of power in the federal government, the expansion of executive authority at the expense of Congress, the unparalleled stimulation of technology, and the wartime strains on civil liberties evidenced by the forced relocation of 110,000 Japanese-Americans—were readily apparent. Others—for example, the heightened expectations of full equality among black Americans, the permanent trend toward more secrecy in government, and new arrangements in the complex business-labor-government triangle—were less quickly recognized.

Japan's sneak attack on Pearl Harbor unified the

World War II posters urged patriotic consumers to economize voluntarily and to refrain from buying around the rationing system. (Courtesy FDR Library.)

United States and powered a desire for revenge. The "Jap Hunting License" issued by the Yellow Cab Company in Laramie, Wyoming, was not untypical of the national reaction. Americans gloried in their new military heroes; worked with the Office of Civilian Defense as air raid wardens, auxiliary police, or nurses' aides; planted victory gardens on vacant lots; and contributed overshoes and old tires to scrap rubber drives. With few exceptions, church groups and college youth who had earlier voiced pacifist feelings rallied to the flag. Public opinion surveys revealed a strong expectation of ultimate victory, friendship for the nation's allies, and a willingness to sacrifice. Pride in having a member of one's family serving in the armed forces merged with the constant worry of receiving—as did the families of 291,000 servicemen killed in battle—a dreaded telegram from the War or Navy Department that began "I regret to inform you . . ." Keeping the people unusually well informed about the conflict helped morale greatly. Although at times censors emasculated servicemen's letters, a policy of cooperation between government and the news media, which voluntarily censored itself, worked well.

Federal authorities, recognizing that all work and no play dulled enthusiasm for the war effort, allowed entertainment and recreational activities to continue, though on a subdued level. Professional sports teams, orchestras, and theaters continued, using performers over or under the draft age or physically unfit for military service. The motion picture industry continued

to produce westerns and musicals, but specialized in war movies like *Commandos Strike at Dawn.* Entertainment celebrities contributed to the war effort in many ways. In one marathon radio broadcast, singer Kate Smith convinced listeners to buy an amazing $39 million in war bonds. But show business stars also helped by taking people's minds off more serious matters. The army magazine *Yank* reported at one point that the number one controversy raging back home was "over whether Bing Crosby or Frank Sinatra is the better crooner."

Government spending for war ended the Great Depression, created plentiful jobs, and boosted public confidence about the future. The unemployment rate dropped from 17.2 percent in 1939 to a low of 1.2 percent in 1944. Personal income more than doubled from $72.8 billion in 1939 to $165.3 billion in 1944. Even farming, the segment of the economy whose depression had begun the earliest, regained its economic health. Despite the war boom, pockets of poverty persisted, and in 1943 perhaps as many as 10 million family units remained below the $1,675 per year that was the recognized minimum subsistence level. But thanks largely to unusually high tax rates, there was greater redistribution of income during the war years than during any period of the century.

With critical raw materials needed to make implements for war, the government halted the production of nonessential civilian goods such as refrigerators, tennis balls, and new cars in early 1942. As a result, American consumers had considerably fewer outlets for their surging incomes and saved over $100 billion during the war years. Rationing, started in 1942 for ten commodities and subsequently expanded to many others, helped greatly to ensure equitable distribution of the scarce civilian items that were

don't feed
black market greed

PAY NO MORE THAN CEILING PRICES

available. Rationing was also indispensable for making the price controls that were established as a check on inflation effective. Some 5,600 rationing boards dispensed the books, stamps, and tokens needed to obtain limited quantities of gasoline, sugar, coffee, red meat, and shoes. Rationing helped to foster a sense of shared sacrifice, though those with spare cash, a willingness to pay more than fixed prices, and the conscience to break the law could obtain rationed goods through the black market, a rampant criminal activity that continued throughout the war.

Twenty-seven million Americans, pursuing better jobs or serving in the armed forces, moved during the conflict. The farm population declined 17 percent, yet those remaining produced record quantities of crops. The longtime westward movement continued, with California gaining the most new inhabitants. A prewar metropolis, Los Angeles, grew even larger as people poured in to work in defense facilities, especially aircraft plants. And a sleepy farm village, Seneca, Illinois, became a bustling factory town when a landing craft construction firm located there. Localities with swollen populations faced sharply increased demands for recreational facilities, utilities, schools, hospitals, and especially housing. Even if funds for such needs could be found, the necessary building materials were often unavailable. Not surprisingly, older residents often resented newcomers, particularly if the new arrivals failed to abide by the accepted customs of their new homes.

Race relations in wartime boom towns were particularly ugly. During the war, black Americans obtained broader employment opportunities, better pay for their labor, and improved prestige in the armed services. But in truth all gains were grudgingly won. The job market in defense plants opened up only after blacks threatened a mass march on Washington. Roosevelt headed off the protest by issuing an executive order establishing a modestly effective Fair Employment Practices Commission. But despite mild federal pressure, real progress in many industries came only gradually. The exodus of southern blacks increased rapidly, once war mobilization began. In crowded northern cities with housing shortages, black ghettoes overflowed into white residential areas. Such a situation in Detroit during June 1943 sparked a violent race riot that halted only after the president ordered in six thousand army troops. Despite the daily humiliations and indignities heaped upon them, most blacks, including a million serving in all branches of the military, supported the war effort loyally. Nevertheless, the sparks kindled in the forties were instrumental in producing the civil rights fires of the sixties.

The war's impact on the American family was striking. The withdrawal of young men in large numbers from civilian life disrupted normal social patterns and helped foster a liberalized sexual code. The combination of husbands away in the service and wives working outside the home intensified the trend toward a companionship family structure, which stressed interpersonal relationships, increased equality of the sexes, and democratic procedures in contrast to the traditional institutional family, which was authoritarian in nature with the father functioning as an autocrat. Women showed that they could manage family affairs with skill, and although only a small number served in the military, the number in the civilian work force increased by over 4 million. "Rosie the Riveter" was more than a song; the women demonstrated convincingly that they could perform so-called masculine jobs.

The marriage rate, stimulated by short wartime romances, the new prosperity, and weakened social controls, rose dramatically between 1939 and 1942 (from 10.7 per 1,000 to 13.2), declined slightly, and then soared to a record level (16.4) in 1946. Unfortunately, the increase in the rate of divorces was also high (from 1.9 per 1,000 in 1939 to 4.3 in 1946). The number of births per thousand also climbed dramatically, peaking in 1947. American children, compared to those in Europe, were physically untouched by the conflict, but emotionally the absence of fathers in the service and mothers working brought new experiences and traumas. Child care centers helped, when available, but "latchkey" children—youngsters left alone at home—became common. Among older children, juvenile deliquency increased sharply.

The educational system declined in overall quality as older students left school in large numbers to take jobs and the armed services called thousands of teachers to duty. Academic studies suffered, although concentrated efforts were made to teach youth the meaning and values of democracy. The military, realizing the worth of education, deferred college students in fields deemed vital to the national interest and sent thousands of personnel to universities for intensive courses in special subjects.

Although there are many fine studies that deal with specific aspects of the home front, three excellent surveys of domestic America during the conflict are especially valuable: Richard Polenberg, *War and Society* (Philadelphia: J. B. Lippincott Co., 1972), John Morton Blum, *V Was for Victory* (New York: Harcourt Brace Jovanovich, 1976), and Geoffrey Perrett, *Days of Sadness, Years of Triumph* (New York: Coward, McCann & Geoghegan, 1973).

JIM F. HEATH

See also Agricultural Adjustment Administration; Civil Liberties in Wartime; Election of 1942; Fiscal Policy; Ickes, Harold LeClair; Internment of Japanese-Americans; Jones, Jesse Holman; Maritime Commission; Office of Censorship; Office of War Information; Randolph, Asa Philip; Taxation; War Mobilization; War Production Board

War Mobilization

As a belated entrant into the Second World War and geographically removed from the actual fighting, the United States mobilized its manpower and its economy less fully than any other major belligerent. Even so, the extent of the American war effort was far greater than in any previous foreign conflict.

American manpower was the nation's primary resource factor in waging the global struggle, but the proper allocation of men and women probably constituted the government's worst administrative record. Fortunately, the nation's work force was the best educated and most innovative in the world. In addition, organized labor entered the conflict with improving morale, thanks to the success enjoyed by trade unions in the late 1930s. Over 16 million men and women served at one time or another in the armed forces, including 10 million draftees. Initially, only men between twenty-one and thirty-five registered for Selective Service, with those called serving for twelve months. Once the United States entered the war, Congress extended the tenure of duty to the duration plus six months and amended the law to require all men between twenty and forty-four to register for war service and men forty-four to sixty-four to register for potential labor service. In actuality, however, the drafting of men over thirty-eight was quickly abandoned, but in November 1942 the draft age was lowered to eighteen. Only a relative handful of men—approximately 42,500—claimed to be conscientious objectors. Mainly members of the Quaker, Mennonite, and Brethren faiths, most agreed to serve the military as noncombatants and received no punishment. Among those who refused to put on any uniform at all, slightly under 12,000 accepted assignment to civilian public service camps and 5,500 went to jail.

With so many Americans in uniform, the manpower barrel was virtually emptied. Even with the addition of millions of housewives, older children, and elderly citizens to the work force, unemployment by 1944 dropped to 1.2 percent, the lowest rate in modern times. With employers competing for scarce labor, pay rates escalated. Between 1940 and 1944, average weekly wage earnings for manufacturing production workers rose from $24.96 to $45.70. Offers of higher pay enticed employees to skip from one job to another. To keep skilled craftsmen working at essential war projects, the government appealed to their patriotism or, if they were of military age, threatened to draft them if they left their jobs. Eventually, the difficulty in keeping critical workers on vital jobs prompted mobilization officials to propose a National Service Act, modeled after the British law, authorizing the conscription and assignment of civilian employees as needed. Reluctant at first to ask for such a drastic enfringement on personal freedom, President Roosevelt concluded in January 1944 that some type of national service legislation was necessary. The House passed such a bill, but with victory on the horizon the Senate withheld approval.

Mobilizing industry for defense and subsequently for war was no less frustrating and controversial than mobilizing manpower, and it was even more complex. Shortly before World War II began, Roosevelt appointed a blue-ribbon War Resources Board to review the War Department's Industrial Mobilization Plan. The board's findings raised disturbing questions about America's defensive capabilities; yet the board recommended against concentrating authority in any new federal superagency. An official history of industrial mobilization guardedly described FDR's response: "The President determined for the time being to avoid bold assertions of his prerogative in the field of national defense but to maintain direction of the limited preparations deemed advisable."

Hitler's savage blitzkrieg against Western Europe in the spring of 1940 prodded Roosevelt to ask Congress for special appropriations of $1.1 billion to initiate a major rearmament program. The president stunned many Americans by setting a production goal of fifty thousand airplanes per year, a figure that seemed impossibly large at the time. Although he still declined to establish a comprehensive mobilization agency, he acknowledged the need for civilian expertise. Consequently, he appointed a National Defense Advisory Commission, composed of prominent persons with experience in various fields, to advise, though not direct, the defense program. By the end of the year, the worsening international situation generated strong demands for even more vigorous efforts to rearm. Finally, in January 1941, Roosevelt created a specific mobilization organization, the Office of Production Management (OPM).

Under the leadership of the new agency, defense production began slowly to shift out of low gear, but the overall state of American preparation remained depressing. Some draftees drilled with broomsticks for lack of rifles and drove trucks labeled "tank" during field maneuvers. The Roosevelt administration's policy of trying to superimpose defense needs upon the production of civilian goods grew especially controversial. But not until mid-1941 did shortages of

War Agencies and Their Heads

BEW—Board of Economic Warfare, Henry A. Wallace, 1942

FEPC—Fair Employment Practice Committee, Mark Ethridge, 1941

FIS—Foreign Information Service, Robert Sherwood

NDMB—National Defense Mediation Board, William H. Davis, 1941

NDRC—National Defense Research Committee, Vannevar Bush, 1940

NHA—National Housing Agency, 1942

NWLB—National War Labor Board, William H. Davis, 1942 (formerly NDMB)

OAPC—Office of Alien Property Custodian, 1942

OC—Office of Censorship, Byron Price, 1941

OCD—Office of Civilian Defense, Fiorello La Guardia, 1942; James M. Landis

OCIA—Office of Coordinator of Inter-American Affairs, Nelson A. Rockefeller, 1941

ODT—Office of Defense Transportation, 1941

OEM—Office of Emergency Management, 1942

OES—Office of Economic Stabilization, James F. Byrnes, 1942

OEW—Office of Economic Warfare, Leo T. Crowley, 1943

OFF—Office of Facts and Figures, Archibald MacLeish

OFRR—Office of Foreign Relief and Rehabilitation, 1942

OLLA—Office of Lend-Lease Administration, Harry Hopkins, 1941

OPA—Office of Price Administration, Leon Henderson, 1942; Prentiss M. Brown, January 1943; Chester Bowles, October 1943; Paul A. Porter, 1946

OPCW—Office of Petroleum Coordinator for War, Harold L. Ickes, 1941

OPM—Office of Production Management, William S. Knudsen, 1940

OSRD—Office of Scientific Research and Development, Vannevar Bush, 1941

OSS—Office of Strategic Services, William J. Donovan, 1942

OWI—Office of War Information, Elmer Davis, 1942

OWM—Office of War Mobilization, James F. Byrnes, 1943

OWMR—Office of War Mobilization and Reconversion, James F. Byrnes, 1944

PAW—Petroleum Administrator for War, Harold L. Ickes, 1942

PJBD—Permanent Joint Board on Defense, 1940

RA—Rubber Administration, William M. Jeffers, 1942

SFAW—Solid Fuels Administrator for War, Harold L. Ickes, 1943

SPAB—Supply Priorities and Allocation Board, 1941

SPARS—*Semper Paratus* Always Ready Service, 1942

SWPC—Smaller War Plants Corporation, 1942

WFA—War Food Administration, 1942

WMC—War Manpower Commission, Paul V. McNutt, 1942

WAACS—Women's Auxiliary Army Corps, 1942

WAVES—Women Appointed for Voluntary Emergency Service, 1942

WAFS—Women's Auxiliary Ferrying Squadron, 1942

WLB—War Labor Board, Elmer Davis, 1941

WPB—War Production Board, Donald M. Nelson, 1942

WRB—War Refugee Board, John Pehle, 1944

WRC—War Relocation Authority, Milton Eisenhower, 1942

WRMC—Women's Reserve of the Marine Corps, 1942

WSA—War Shipping Administration, Emory S. Land, 1942

---

steel, copper, and other critical raw materials force Washington to reconsider its guns *and* butter strategy and begin to curtail seriously the manufacture of civilian products.

Actually, during the defense buildup, many businesses were reluctant to switch from civilian to military production. Relations between big business and the Roosevelt administration—openly hostile during the later New Deal years—were still strained. Even more important, companies worried that defense work could cause a permanent loss of market share to competitors. A firm making 15 percent of all bicy-

cles sold each year might never regain its customers if it converted to producing rifles. Executives of major industrial corporations also remembered clearly that during the depression their companies had operated at well below maximum capacity. Fear that investing in new facilities might leave them with unneeded or even unusable plants and machinery was gradually eased by very favorable financial arrangements made available through such federal agencies as the Defense Plant Corporation.

Faced with a swelling torrent of complaints about the laggard pace of rearmament in the frustrat-

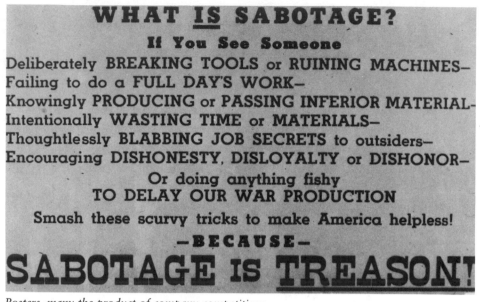

Posters, many the product of company competitions,
stressed war production needs to workers in both agriculture and industry. (Courtesy FDR Library.)

ing weeks after Pearl Harbor, Roosevelt resorted to one of his favorite tactics—administrative reorganization. In January 1942, he created the War Production Board (WPB) with much greater authority to mobilize production than the OPM. To run the new agency, the president tapped Donald M. Nelson, a former Sears marketing executive who had served with distinction in the OPM. Roosevelt's choice won enthusiastic congressional approval. But the order establishing the WPB stopped considerably short of a full delegation of power over mobilization to Nelson. FDR actually followed his customary habit of dividing responsibility and authority, splitting vital mobilization duties among a crazy-quilt pattern of new emergency agencies and old departments. The War Manpower Commission, the Petroleum Administration, the Office of Price Administration, the Rubber Reserve Company, the War Shipping Board, the Office of Scientific Research and Development, and the Office of Defense Transportation—to name but a few—exercised command in vital areas of industrial mobilization. The result was fierce bureaucratic infighting and divided and overlapping authority.

The president deliberately chose this seemingly confusing method of operation. He gambled on the vitality of the American economy to accomplish the necessary production goals, despite the inherent inefficiency in the system he created. Reasoning that only the chief executive was accountable to all the voters, Roosevelt rejected the advice of those like Bernard Baruch who urged him to concentrate authority in an industrial czar and refused to delegate full power over mobilization to any one person. Ironically, he opted

for a form of decentralization at the same time that more power than ever before was being concentrated in the hands of the federal government.

The WPB neither operated plants nor awarded contracts, private industry handling the former, the armed services and other government agencies the latter. Nevertheless, through its control of resource scheduling, Nelson's organization was the key to optimum production. The board's initial efforts to allocate scarce raw materials were pathetically ineffective. But in the fall of 1942, a former investment banker, Ferdinand Eberstadt, devised the Controlled Materials Plan which broke the raw materials logjam. The CMP was simple but spectacularly successful: the WPB allotted available quantities of copper, steel, and aluminum to government user agencies who in turn distributed the materials to the producing contractors.

Bickering between the civilians who directed the WPB and military leaders over policy decisions persisted throughout the war. Army and navy officials wanted more control over production, and they frequently disagreed with decisions by the WPB to continue production of nonmilitary goods deemed vital for civilian morale. The military at times, particularly in the early stages of conversion, also pushed for production totals that WPB staffers knew were economically unrealistic. As Nelson later wrote, "Sometimes the Army doesn't seem to know the difference between its enemies and its friends."

Debate over the role played by big business executives working for the WPB was equally fractious. Critics sharply challenged the use of dollar-a-year men, high-salaried executives from large corporations who drew their regular pay from their civilian employers while working for the government. The executives argued that such arrangements were necessary, because they could not possibly meet financial commitments made previously on the salaries paid by government. Many congressmen, however, wondered if key officials in the WPB were able to divorce themselves completely from looking out for the interests of their company or their industry. Especially in the gloomy months following Pearl Harbor, complaints were common that some in the WPB were delaying the maximum conversion of private industry to war production in order to protect profitable civilian markets. Nelson, arguing that the WPB simply had to have such experienced executives, was able to convince hostile legislators to permit the continued use of the businessmen. Despite stinging criticism from Thurman Arnold, head of the Antitrust Division, Congress, at the urgent request of the WPB and the armed services, also agreed to exempt from prosecution companies violating the antitrust laws if the illegal actions were certified by government officials as essential to the war effort.

Although the army and navy strongly preferred to deal with the more sophisticated and knowledgeable large companies, many congressmen were greatly sympathetic to the plight of small manufacturers. But despite considerable political pressure, the Roosevelt administration never effectively utilized small business. Although economists disagree about whether big business actually tightened its grip on the American economy during the war, major producers unquestionably captured the lion's share of federal contracts. Perhaps most significant of all, major corporations and the federal government began to appreciate the mutual benefits of close cooperation. When Nelson proposed in early 1944 to allow small firms to reconvert gradually from military to civilian production, the military and big business combined to block the plan, the former because it feared that a premature cut in the output of vital war supplies might jeopardize the final push for victory, the latter because it sensed a threat to its prewar domination of civilian markets.

The United States spent, according to a congressional report issued in 1970, $288 billion to fight the Second World War. When estimated expenditures for veterans' benefits and interest payments on war loans are added, the total cost of the conflict exceeds $660 billion, a startling figure when contrasted with the $9 billion annual federal budget in 1940. By the end of the war, the budget had climbed to just under $100 billion, while the public debt had grown from $49 billion in 1941 to $258.7 billion in 1945.

Just how to pay for the war stimulated sharp debate. Ultimately, taxes contributed over 40 percent of the total cost, with tax rates reaching their all-time highs for both individuals and corporations. The practice of withholding personal income taxes from wages began in 1943, and the number of persons paying income taxes rose from less than 4 million in 1939 to over 40 million by mid-war. Nevertheless, many economists at the time and later argued that even higher tax levels were reasonable and feasible. Yet when Roosevelt asked Congress for another tax increase in 1944, the legislators, mindful of their constituents' fears that peace would bring a return to depression, gave the president only a fraction of what he had requested. Washington officials sought to obtain the balance of funds needed to fund the war effort by borrowing from nonbanking sources. But though individuals and institutions purchased nearly $100 billion worth of war bonds, borrowing of this nature proved insufficient. The Federal Reserve System and commercial banks made up the difference by buying—at pegged low interest rates—government securities, a practice that sharply increased the money supply and contributed to inflationary pressures.

The long depression of the 1930s had dulled America's fear of inflation and delayed vigorous action to head off the wage-price spiral that began even before Pearl Harbor. Not until January 1942 did Congress give the Office of Price Administration authority to set maximum prices. Even then, until late in the year, the politically powerful farm bloc succeeded in exempting agricultural product prices from control until they reached a substantially higher level. The tide in the battle against inflation turned during the spring of 1943 after Roosevelt arbitrarily rolled back prices on key commodities and seized idle coal mines to break a miners' strike for higher wages. Al-

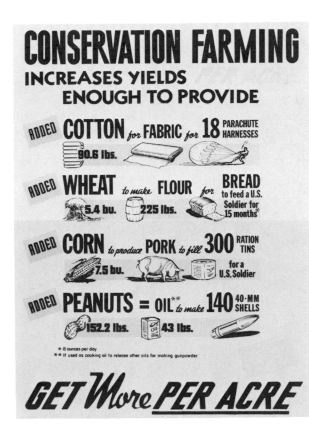

CONSERVATION FARMING
INCREASES YIELDS
ENOUGH TO PROVIDE

ADDED COTTON *for* FABRIC *for* 18 PARACHUTE HARNESSES
90.6 lbs.

ADDED WHEAT *to make* FLOUR *for* BREAD to feed a U.S. Soldier for 15 months*
5.4 bu.   225 lbs.

ADDED CORN *to produce* PORK *to fill* 300 RATION TINS for a U.S. Soldier
7.5 bu.

ADDED PEANUTS = OIL** *to make* 140 40-MM SHELLS
152.2 lbs.   43 lbs.

* 8 ounces per day
** If used as cooking oil to release other oils for making gunpowder

GET More PER ACRE

though between 1940 and 1945 the consumer price index climbed over 28 percent, less than 2 percent occurred after the president's decisive action.

The speed with which the United States mobilized for war after the Japanese attack testified to the latent strenghth of the American economy. In less than two years—by November 1943—the production of war goods, measured by their total dollar volume, had peaked. This remarkable accomplishment came only after a myriad of problems were solved. For example, when the war began, the United States made virtually no synthetic rubber and possessed limited stockpiles of natural rubber. Since the Japanese quickly occupied the rubber-growing areas of the world, the shortage of the substance threatened to cripple the war effort. But thanks to a crash program American companies produced over 800,000 tons of synthetic rubber by 1944. Other statistics were equally impressive. The index of manufacturing more than doubled. Aluminum production increased by over six times. Between 1939 and the end of the war, the aircraft industry made 275,000 planes. In 1941, the first Liberty-class cargoship required 244 days to build; by mid-1943, the time was down to a mere 41 days. It is perhaps a cliché, but as the journalists of the war years liked to write, the United States, the Allies' arsenal of democracy, did indeed achieve a miracle of production.

An important dimension of the production miracle was that wartime mobilization both provided a powerful stimulus to and benefited from an amazing array of scientific and technological innovations produced by a talented corps of researchers. The discovery or advanced development of radar, rockets, jet aircraft, and penicillin contributed invaluable assistance to winning the global struggle. Dramatic as such items were, however, their significance pales when compared to the unleashing of nuclear power and to the intimate relationship between the scientific-technological establishment and the federal government that emerged from World War II.

Favorable to the government's efforts to mobilize for World War II are Donald M. Nelson, *Arsenal of Democracy: The Story of American War Production* (New York: Harcourt, Brace, 1946) and James W. Fessler et al., *Industrial Mobilization for War, History of the War Production Board and Predecessor Agencies, 1940–45,* vol. 1 (Washington D. C.: U.S. Government Printing Office, 1947). More critical are Eliot Janeway, *The Struggle for Survival: A Chronicle of Economic Mobilization* (New Haven: Yale University Press, 1951) and Bruce Catton, *The War Lords of Washington* (New York: Harcourt, Brace, 1948). Richard Polenberg's *War and Society* (Philadelphia: J. B. Lippincott Co., 1972) is a balanced and perceptive study.

JIM F. HEATH

See also Cooke, Charles Maynard; Douglas, Lewis Williams; Hillman, Sidney; Labor; Maritime Commission; Randolph, Asa Philip; Regulation, Federal; Taxation; Selective Service Act; War Effort on the Home Front; War Production Board

Warm Springs

During FDR's presidency, Americans came to know Warm Springs, Georgia, as the site of the Little White House; but when Roosevelt first visited there in 1924 seeking to recover from the paralysis inflicted by polio, Warm Springs was little more than a dilapidated resort built around mineral springs. New York banker George Foster Peabody, who had acquired ownership of the resort, suggested that his friend try the springs; and Roosevelt was delighted to find that he could walk when immersed in its buoyant waters. During the next few years, he spent considerable time there, building his muscles to the point where he could walk with braces and two canes.

Although Roosevelt never attained the complete recovery he dreamed of, Warm Springs became a symbol of hope to which he committed unusual devotion. In 1926, over Eleanor's objections, he purchased the resort from Peabody to convert it into a hydrotherapeutic center for the treatment of polio victims. A year later, he established a nonprofit organization, the Georgia Warm Springs Foundation. Roosevelt personally invested almost $200,000 in the foundation, which acquired the property and 1,200 surrounding acres of mountain farmland. When he was in residence, Roosevelt took on the role of unofficial physiotherapist. Dr. LeRoy W. Hubbard, a New York orthopedic surgeon, and physiotherapist Helena T. Mahoney provided constant medical attention for patients, of which there were sixty-one in 1927, the foundation's first year in operation. In 1928, Mr. and Mrs. Edsel Ford donated $25,000 to enclose the mineral springs with glass, thereby making year-round therapy possible.

Roosevelt's New York governorship began and his presidency abruptly ended at the cottage he built at Warm Springs. In the spring of 1928, he debated whether to accept the proffered Democratic party nomination for governor, agreeing to run only after John J. Raskob, vice-president of General Motors and Du Pont, consented to assume the foundation's finan-

FDR fishing at Warm Springs, May 1930. (Courtesy FDR Library.)

FDR *in the driver's seat with Missy LeHand to his right; Grace Tully and Gus Gennerich are in the back seat.*

Warm Springs, 22 November 1935. (Reprinted from the Saturday Evening Post. © *The Curtis Publishing Co.)*

cial responsibilities. During his four years as governor, Roosevelt spent March, April, and several weeks each fall at Warm Springs, a routine he maintained to a certain degree throughout his years in the White House. Warm Springs provided FDR an opportunity to explore the political as well as the human aspects of the rural South. He took a genuine interest in the crop and livestock problems faced by the tenants who tilled the Warm Springs farmland and, in so doing, learned much about the broader economic and conservation problems facing the South.

During the course of FDR's tenure in the White House, the cottage at Warm Springs, however, became less the place he went to continue his recovery and more the remote retreat where he relaxed while carrying on the unrelenting responsibilities of public office. As president, FDR looked forward to the comradeship of friends at Warm Springs whenever he could steal time away from the capital, although his

close White House associates always accompanied him to tend the necessary affairs of state. In late March 1945, FDR left Washington, D.C., for what would be his last visit to the Little White House. Following a tiring trip abroad to confer with Churchill and Stalin at Yalta, the president needed the restorative powers of Warm Springs more than ever. As always, Warm Springs fulfilled its promise; FDR enjoyed two weeks basking in the Georgia sun, surrounded by old and dear friends, before his death there on 12 April.

FDR's biographers and others who have written personal accounts of his presidency invariably include mention of Warm Springs. The story of Roosevelt deliberating whether to accept the nomination for governor of New York, for instance, is recounted by Arthur M. Schlesinger, Jr., in *The Crisis of the Old Order* (Boston: Houghton Mifflin Co., 1956), and Joseph Lash includes many details regarding Roosevelt and the genesis of the Warm Springs Foundation in *Eleanor and Franklin* (New York: W. W. Norton, 1971). Turnley Walker presents a more complete account of the Roosevelt connection in *Roosevelt and the Warm Springs Story* (New York: A. A. Wyn, 1953). Frank Freidel analyzes the political influence of Warm Springs in *F.D.R. and the South* (Baton Rouge: Louisiana State University Press, 1965).

See also Death of FDR; Finances, Personal; Polio; Roosevelt, James Roosevelt; South, The

War Production Board

Established by Executive Order 9024 on 16 January 1942, the War Production Board (WPB) had direct responsibility for mobilizing the nation's wartime economy. In contrast to its predecessors, the Office of Production Management (January 1941–January 1942) and the Supply Priorities and Allocations Board (August 1941–January 1942), broad authority over all aspects of production and procurement was vested in the chairman, Donald M. Nelson. But Nelson had a more limited conception of his role. He agreed, for example, to leave military procurement under the armed services and did not oppose the creation of the independent War Manpower Commission. These decisions often created overlapping jurisdictions and became sources of conflict.

As the conversion of the economy gained momentum, the WPB faced the critical problem of allocating scarce raw materials. After a period of trial and error, it adopted the Controlled Materials Plan in November 1942 that divided the available supplies of aluminum, copper, and steel among various agencies, which then made allocations to their prime contractors. The position of the WPB deteriorated during 1943. Despite the earlier accommodation, disputes between the services and the WPB over the military supply program became acute in early 1943 and almost led to Bernard Baruch replacing Nelson. In addition, Congress criticized the WPB's failure to exercise all the power originally granted it. The creation of the Office of War Mobilization (OWM) in May 1943 reflected a further dilution of the board's influence. Under Director James F. Byrnes, the OWM assumed many of its policymaking functions and became the arbiter of the disagreements within the war agencies.

A major dispute with the military over the pace of reconversion led to Nelson's resignation in September 1944. He was replaced by Julius A. Krug, who had held numerous posts in the WPB. Reconversion was shelved until the spring of 1945. Spot authorization for the resumption of civilian production was announced in April, and the orders prohibiting civilian use of critical materials were rescinded soon after the German surrender on 8 May 1945. The WPB was abolished on 4 October 1945.

The evolution of the WPB's program and policies is treated in great detail in Civilian Production Administration, *Industrial Mobilization for War: History of the War Production Board and Predecessor Agencies* (Washington, D.C.: U.S. Government Printing Office, 1947). Nelson defends his tenure as chairman in *Arsenal of Democracy: The Story of American War Production* (New York: Harcourt, Brace & Co., 1946). A contemporary account is John Lord O'Brian and Manly Fleischmann, "The War Production Board: Administrative Policies and Procedures," *George Washington Law Review* 13, no. 1 (December 1944):1–60. Richard Polenberg's *War and Society: The United States, 1941–1945* (Philadelphia: J. P. Lippincott Co., 1972) also discusses the work and controversy of the WPB.

PAUL SOIFER

See also Hillman, Sidney; War Effort on the Home Front; War Mobilization

War Relocation Authority
See Ickes, Harold LeClair; Internment of Japanese-Americans

Watson, Edwin Martin ("Pa")
(10 December 1883–20 February 1945)
Military aide to President Roosevelt throughout his presidency and from 1939 secretary to the president as well. A Virginian by ancestry and residence, Watson was born in Eufaula, Alabama. He graduated from the West Point Military Academy in 1908, where he excelled as a tackle in football and acquired the nickname "Pa" to distinguish him from another burly Watson on the squad who was known as "Ma." After distinguished service as an artillery battalion commander in France in 1918, he was made chief of the military section of President Wilson's personal staff at the Versailles Conference and thereafter held routine military assignments until his appointment as military aide to Roosevelt on 1 June 1933.

Major General Watson's great personal charm and his considerable gifts as raconteur endeared him to Roosevelt and he became a fixture in a position that ordinarily was rotated among rising army officers. When ill health forced James Roosevelt to retire as his father's secretary in 1939, Watson was named his successor and served thereafter in his unusual dual role. On Roosevelt's staff, function was not differentiated as in recent presidencies, but Watson, without the title, effectively served as appointments secretary and was a zealous if amiable guardian of the president's time and strength. In a staff of uncommon closeness and stability, no one was closer to Roosevelt. His death from a stroke aboard the cruiser *Quincy* returning from the Yalta Conference in 1945 saddened Roosevelt like no other personal loss during his presidency and was felt by associates to have cast a pall over his brief later days.

Watson's papers are in the Alderman Library of the University of Virginia.

Edwin M. Watson. (Constant Collection. Courtesy FDR Library.)

Welfare

See Relief

Welfare State

See Liberalism and Progressivism; New Deal; Perkins, Frances

Welles, Benjamin Sumner

(14 October 1892–24 September 1961)

Assistant secretary and under secretary of state, ambassador to Cuba under Franklin D. Roosevelt, as well as personal friend and adviser to Roosevelt. Sumner Welles was born in New York City, the son of Benjamin Welles and Frances Swan Welles, and a grand-nephew of Charles Sumner, the Massachusetts abolitionist senator. Educated at Groton and Harvard, Welles entered the Foreign Service in 1915, in part because of influence of a family friend, Assistant Secretary of the Navy Franklin D. Roosevelt. After a brief tour of service in Tokyo, he was assigned to Buenos Aires, beginning many years of professional and personal interest in Latin American affairs. Tall, handsome, dignified, and intelligent, Welles rose quickly to become acting chief of the Division of Latin American Affairs in the State Department. Feeling that Latin American affairs were a neglected area deserving greater attention, he worked to improve the image of the United States in the region, especially by reducing America's military presence there. He was able to put these concerns into practice in the Dominican Republic through his work to end its U.S. military government and establish an independent government in 1924. Leaving the diplomatic service in 1925, Welles continued to pursue his interest in the region, writing *Naboth's Vineyard: The Dominican Republic, 1844–1924* (1928). This book was partly responsible for Roosevelt naming Welles his principal adviser on Latin American affairs in 1933.

As assistant secretary of state in 1933, Welles is credited with originating the "Good Neighbor" phrase to describe U.S. policy toward Latin America. A serious test of that policy came with the disorders in Cuba in 1933. Roosevelt named Welles ambassador to the island in April, and he immediately became involved in the complicated politics that preceded the rise of Fulgencio Batista. At one point, Welles pressed for the introduction of U.S. troops under the provisions of the Platt Amendment, but was countered by Roosevelt and Secretary of State Cordell Hull. (In 1934 Welles negotiated a new treaty with the Batista government that abrogated the Platt Amendment.) His involvement with Latin American affairs continued as war grew nearer in Europe. He played an important role in the Buenos Aires Inter-American Conference in 1936 and the Rio de Janeiro Conference in

Summer Welles (in front of the crucifix) in procession at memorial service for Sara Delano Roosevelt, St. Paul's Church, Mt. Vernon, N.Y., 6 December 1941. (Metropolitan Photo Service, New York City.)

1942 which aimed at coordinating inter-American diplomacy toward Hitler.

As tensions increased in Europe, Welles continued to be an important adviser to Roosevelt, who named him under secretary of state in 1937 against the wishes of Hull who resented the close relationship between the president and Welles. In 1937, Welles almost convinced the president to call a meeting of foreign ambassadors to discuss the prospects for averting war in Europe, but Hull's opposition led Roosevelt to shelve the plan. In August 1941, Welles accompanied Roosevelt to his first meeting with Churchill, which occurred at sea off Argentia, Newfoundland, and was involved with the drafting of the Atlantic Charter which emerged from the conference. Welles also headed up a special State Department committee charged with developing plans for a postwar international organization. These plans, later modified, became the basis for the United Nations.

The tensions between Hull and Welles grew as the secretary of state increasingly worried that the close relationship between Welles and the president undermined his authority and influence. In August 1943, these concerns were augmented by unsubstantiated rumors of homosexual activities on Welles's part. Hull finally insisted to Roosevelt that Welles be dismissed or Hull would resign. Despite his personal distress at the decision, Roosevelt agreed and asked for Welles's resignation. This act pained Roosevelt doubly, for in addition to his personal loss, he knew that Welles's departure would deprive the government of possibly its most eloquent spokesman for the liberal, Wilsonian vision of a postwar world based on internationalist principles.

Welles spent the years after retiring in writing

and commenting on diplomatic affairs. A series of books, including *The Time for Decision* (1944) and *Seven Decisions That Shaped History* (1950), provided a combination of memoirs and analysis of U.S. diplomacy, wherein Welles's commitment to a liberal, universalist conception of world order was clearly stated. Welles was married three times and had two sons. He died in 1961 at Bernardsville, New Jersey.

The basic information about Welles's life and career can be found in the entry on Welles by William M. Franklin in the *Dictionary of American Biography*, Supp. 7, ed. John A. Garraty (New York: Charles Scribner's Sons, 1981) and in his *New York Times* obituary, 25 September 1961. The best recent work for understanding Roosevelt's diplomacy and Welles's role therein is Robert Dallek, *Franklin D. Roosevelt and American Foreign Policy, 1932–1945* (New York: Oxford University Press, 1979). Additional details can be found in Joseph P. Lash, *Roosevelt and Churchill, 1939–1941* (New York: W. W. Norton & Co., 1976).

See also Good Neighbor Policy; Hitler, Adolf, and Germany; Hull, Cordell

Wheeler, Burton Kendall

(27 February 1882–7 January 1975)

Democratic U.S. senator from Montana, 1923–47. The youngest of ten children of a Quaker shoemaker, Burton K. Wheeler was born in Hudson, Massachusetts. He received a law degree in 1910 from the University of Michigan and practiced law in Butte, Montana. After serving in the state House of Representatives and as district attorney for Montana, Wheeler in 1922 was elected to the U.S. Senate. Besides being Senate prosecutor in the Teapot Dome scandals, he was the Progressive party vice-presidential candidate in 1924.

During President Roosevelt's first term, Wheeler backed most New Deal legislation and directed the floor battle for the Public Utility Holding Company Act of 1935. In 1937 Wheeler protested Roosevelt's plan to enlarge the U.S. Supreme Court as an unconstitutional attempt to seize power. Roosevelt personally sought to dissuade Wheeler, who helped rally conservative Democrats to bury the president's proposal. Wheeler battled the president's internationalist policies until the Japanese attacked Pearl Harbor. A powerful, sharp-tongued orator, Wheeler in 1941 spoke at numerous America First Committee rallies opposing American aid to the anti-Hitler coalition. In January 1941, Wheeler infuriated Roosevelt by denouncing the Lend-Lease Act as "the New Deal's Triple A foreign policy, it will plow under every fourth American boy."

An adept legislative infighter, he usually criticized government programs rather than initiating or building them. Wheeler declined dramatically in influence during World War II and lost the 1946 Democratic primary. After leaving the U.S. Senate, he practiced corporate law in Washington, D.C.

For additional information see Burton K. Wheeler, *Yankee from the West* (Garden City, N.Y.: Doubleday & Co., 1962); Richard T. Ruetten, "Burton K. Wheeler of Montana: A Progressive between the Wars," (Ph.D. diss., University of Oregon, 1961); *New York Times*, 8 January 1975; *Current Biography*, 1940, pp. 857–60; Joseph Alsop and Turner Catledge, *The 168 Days* (Garden City, N.Y.: Doubleday & Co., 1938); Wayne S. Cole, *America First: The Battle against Intervention, 1940–1941* (Madison: University of Wisconsin Press, 1953); Wayne S. Cole, *Roosevelt & the Isolationists, 1932–45* (Lincoln: University of Nebraska Press, 1983).

DAVID L. PORTER

White House

See Currie, Lauchlin; Early, Stephen Tyree; Forrestal, James Vincent; Hassett, William D.; Hoover, John Edgar; Hopkins, Harry L.; Howe, Louis McHenry; LeHand, Marguerite; McIntyre, Marvin Hunter; National Resources Planning Board; Niles, David K.; Office of the Presidency; Reorganization Act of 1939; Roosevelt, James (son); Tully, Grace; Watson, Edwin Martin

Wickard, Claude Raymond

(23 February 1893–2 April 1967)

Secretary of agriculture, 1940–45. Born on a farm near Camden, Indiana, Claude R. Wickard took over the family farm after graduating from Purdue University in 1915. Wickard was elected to the Indiana State Senate in 1932, but resigned the office to work for the Agricultural Adjustment Administration in 1933. He rose quickly through the bureaucracy, serving as head of the Corn and Hog Section (1935), director of the North Central Division (1936), and under secretary of agriculture (1939). Franklin Roosevelt named him secretary of agriculture on 5 September 1940 after Henry Wallace was nominated for vice-president.

Wickard pressed for increased agricultural production at higher price levels to meet both civilian and Lend-Lease demands and believed that the department should have control over farm prices in spite of the creation of the Office of Price Administration. He reduced the number of agencies reporting directly to the secretary to allow him more time to participate in the war effort and set up state and county war boards as part of the mobilization of the nation's agricultural resources. He resigned on 2 June 1945, but was quickly appointed head of the Rural Electrification Administration (1945–53) by President Truman. Wickard died in 1967.

Dean Albertson's *Roosevelt's Farmer: Claude R. Wickard and the New Deal* (New York: Columbia University Press, 1961) is a study of New Deal agricultural policy based on interviews with Wickard and Wallace in the Columbia University Oral History Collection. Walter W. Wilcox, *The*

Farmer in the Second World War (Ames: Iowa State College Press, 1947) is also useful.

See also Agriculture

Williams, Aubrey Willis

(23 August 1890–3 March 1965)

Deputy Federal Emergency Relief Administration and Works Progress Administration administrator under Harry Hopkins and, later, administrator of the National Youth Administration. Aubrey Williams was born in Alabama into a family ruined economically and spiritually by the Civil War. Forced to leave school at seven, he worked in various jobs in Birmingham until he was twenty-one, when he was at last able to gain some formal education at Maryville College in Tennessee. By this time he had already developed the strain of social activism that was to remain with him throughout his life.

After Maryville, he briefly attended the University of Cincinnati before going to work with the YMCA on the battlefields of Europe during World War I. Later he fought with the French Foreign Legion and, after 1917, with the U.S. Army. Remaining in France after the Armistice, he gained a degree at the University of Bordeaux before returning to Cincinnati to complete the training in social work the war had interrupted.

In 1922, Williams became executive secretary of the Wisconsin Conference of Social Work, a privately funded social agency based in Madison, and there he was to remain for ten years. His skills as an administrator eventually brought him to the attention of Frank Bane of the American Public Welfare Association, who in the dying days of the Hoover administration, arranged for a temporary appointment to the Reconstruction Finance Corporation (RFC). His task there was to organize the effective disbursement of RFC relief loans in the southern and western states.

He performed this difficult job with distinction. Thus, when Roosevelt entered office and the relief and welfare functions of the federal government were expanded, he was brought to Washington, initially as southwest regional director for the Federal Emergency Relief Administration, but soon as Hopkins's trusted deputy, counselor, and friend. Indeed, because of his superior's increasingly lengthy absences from Washington, first because of illness and then because of other political duties, Williams was in effective control of the day-to-day operations of the Works Progress Administration (WPA) for long periods of time. This gave him considerable influence in New Deal circles, as did his growing friendship with Mrs. Roosevelt.

As an administrator, Williams was tough, resourceful, and outspoken. A committed liberal and a champion of civil rights for blacks, he used his power wherever possible to further such ends and was recognized as one of the leaders of the New Deal's liberal wing. As such, he made powerful enemies, who in 1938 were able to prevent his becoming head of the WPA when Hopkins became secretary of commerce. Instead he became full-time administrator of the National Youth Administration (NYA), an agency he had headed on a part-time basis since its creation in 1935.

As NYA administrator, Williams made the agency both a provider of vocational training and employment opportunity for the nation's disadvantaged youth and a crucial adjunct to American's defense effort. It lasted until 1943, when it was dismantled during a drive to eliminate all federal projects not deemed essential to the war effort. Despite President Roosevelt's express wish that he remain in federal employment, Williams left public service and was never to return to it. In 1945, FDR nominated him to head the Rural Electrification Administration, but the Senate, influenced by southerners who abhorred his racial views and conservatives who distrusted his liberal political perspectives, refused confirmation.

Williams returned to Montgomery, Alabama, there to edit Marshall Field's *Southern Farmer*, which he turned into the region's leading magazine of liberal opinion. Throughout the 1950s, he continued his advocacy of civil rights and civil liberties, especially as a member of the Southern conference for Human Welfare, as president of its offshoot, the Southern Conference Education Fund, and finally, as president of the National Committee to Abolish the House Un-American Activities Committee. As such, he often came under attack from the dominant right-wing forces of the time and was himself investigated in 1954 by the Senate Subcommittee on Internal Security. His last years, then, were lonely and embattled ones. In 1963, his magazine having failed, he moved back to Washington, where he died of stomach cancer two years later.

There is only one biography of Williams, by John Salmond, *A Southern Rebel, The Life and Times of Aubrey Willis Williams, 1890–1965* (Chapel Hill: University of North Carolina Press, 1983).

JOHN A. SALMOND

See also Negroes

Willkie, Wendell Lewis

(18 February 1892–8 October 1944)

Roosevelt's Republican opponent in the 1940 presidential election. Wendell L. Willkie was born in Elwood, Indiana, and graduated from Indiana University in 1913. After a brief experience as a high school history teacher in Coffeyville, Kansas, he entered the University Law School, from which he received his law degree in 1916. He then entered his father's law office, but when the United States entered World War I in April 1917, he volunteered for military service. His regiment got to France but did not see action.

Wendell Lewis Willkie. Photographer: Samuel Johnson Woolf. (Date unknown. National Portrait Gallery, Smithsonian Institution.)

On his return, he took a job in the legal department of the Firestone Tire & Rubber Company in Akron, Ohio, but soon joined a private firm. During the next nine years, he became one of Akron's leading citizens, but evidently found no time for politics except on two occasions. In 1924, he went as a delegate to the Democratic National Convention to fight for two resolutions: endorsement of the League of Nations and condemnation of the Ku Klux Klan. Both were defeated; but in local politics, the following year, he led a successful fight against a Klan attempt to gain control of the Akron school board.

In 1929, Willkie went to New York as counsel to the Commonwealth & Southern Corporation, a recently formed public utilities holding company with assets of more than $1 billion, and in 1933, he became president and chief executive officer. In this position, he first gained national attention through his conflict with the New Deal over the Tennessee Valley Authority (TVA), which became a direct competitor of a Commonwealth & Southern subsidiary, the Tennessee Electric Power Company (TEPCO). He lost bitter battles in Congress and the Supreme Court, but in the end he gained what was widely regarded as a victory by selling TEPCO to TVA and local municipalities for $78 million.

Willkie's winning of the 1940 Republican presidential nomination was a unique achievement. Until 1938 he had been a registered Democrat; he had never held public office; he had no powerful political supporters; and he began his serious campaign only a few weeks before the convention. But the delegates were overwhelmed by his immense popular—and vocal—support.

His dramatic victory was due partly to his personal character and partly to the international situation. He won admirers, in the first place, by his candor, his vigor, his optimism, and his obvious liking for people. Of his two chief opponents, on the other hand, Senator Robert A. Taft of Ohio was perceived as cold and aloof, while crime-busting Manhattan district attorney Thomas E. Dewey seemed to many persons to be lacking in forthrightness on controversial issues.

The most urgent issue, as Hitler's armies rolled across Belgium and the Netherlands and, a few days before the Republican convention, forced the surrender of France, was the U.S. role in the conflict. On this issue, Taft was firmly for nonintervention and Dewey hedged. Only Willkie argued, with passion and eloquence, for all-out aid, short of war, to the Allies—and, finally, to Britain alone. This stand was shared by a majority of Americans, and it won him the nomination.

In the election, however, it was outweighed by the Republican party's unbroken record of isolationism; and this, together with the popular belief that the Republicans were responsible for the depression, made Roosevelt's victory inevitable. A furious campaign by Willkie gained him the largest popular vote achieved by any Republican before Eisenhower in 1952, but he lost in the electoral college 449 to 82.

Willkie's greatest contribution to his country was his support, after the election, of Roosevelt's foreign policy, as America moved inevitably toward total involvement in World War II. His tour of England, with Roosevelt's approval, in early 1941 at the height of the great night bombings by Hitler's Luftwaffe, became a symbol of America's sympathy and support; and he followed it by exerting his tremendous popular influence in favor of the Lend-Lease program to supply economic and military aid to Britain. This won him the permanent friendship of Roosevelt and the permanent hatred of the Republican isolationists.

During the remainder of 1941 Willkie sought to prepare the United States, physically and morally, for participation in the war. In the intense struggle between the interventionists and the isolationists—the Fight for Freedom Committee and the America First Committee—Willkie was the former group's most effective crusader. And after Pearl Harbor, his was a leading voice in urging total national commitment to the war effort.

His most dramatic undertaking during the war was his 1942 tour as Roosevelt's emissary, to the Middle East, Russia, and China to make clear to the world the United States' determination to defeat the Axis and to spread the hope of a new world after the war in which there would be equality of opportunity for all peoples.

The grounds of this hope were memorably stated in Willkie's sensationally popular book *One World*, which sold millions of copies. The last two years of his life were devoted to a passionate crusade for the creation of an instrument—an international organization whose authority would transcend narrow national interests—to make this vision a reality. Equally intense was dedication to the allied goal—implicit in the concept of "one world"—of racial equality within the United States.

In pursuit of these goals, he again sought the Republican presidential nomination in 1944, but withdrew after a crushing defeat in the Wisconsin primary.

At this point, Roosevelt approached him with a proposal that after the election they join forces in a realignment of political parties, uniting liberals of both major parties against the Republican Old Guard and the Democratic Southern Bourbons. Willkie was receptive, but preferred not to discuss it until after the election. A month before the election, however, on 8 October, he died of a massive heart attack.

Willkie's achievements immediately before and during the war were largely intangible and seem now to be forgotten, but their effect on the course of U.S. history was strong and enduring.

Ellsworth Barnard, *Wendell Willkie: Fighter for Freedom* (Marquette: Northern Michigan University Press, 1966) is a full-scale, fully documented biography of Willkie. Joseph Barnes, *Wendell Willkie* (New York: Simon & Schuster, 1952) is an account by a personal friend, undocumented but scrupulously accurate, of Willkie's public career. Another biography, Mary Earhart Dillon, *Wendell Willkie* (Philadelphia: Lippincott, 1952) is essentially political and is undocumented and not always reliable. A romanticized account of Willkie's boyhood, Alden Hatch, *Young Willkie* (New York: Harcourt, Brace, 1944) is faithful in spirit if not always in fact. Donald B. Johnson, *The Republican Party and Wendell Willkie* (Champaign: University of Illinois Press, 1960) painstakingly studies the topic stated in the title; it is accurate and fully documented. A campaign biography, Herman O. Makey, *Wendell Willkie of Elwood* (Elwood, Ind.: National Book Co., 1940) offers useful information about Elwood and the Willkie family. Two important collections of unpublished Willkie material are in the Franklin D. Roosevelt Library, Hyde Park, New York, and the Lilly Library, Indiana University, Bloomington.

ELLSWORTH BARNARD

See also Democratic Party; Elections in the Roosevelt Era; Republican Party

Wilson, Thomas Woodrow
(28 December 1856–3 February 1924)

The only president under whom Franklin D. Roosevelt served and, with Theodore Roosevelt, one of the two greatest influences and models for his political career. Woodrow Wilson was born in Staunton, Virginia, the son of a Presbyterian minister, and grew up in Georgia and South Carolina. After graduation from Princeton in 1879, he briefly studied and practiced law before beginning an academic career which included graduate study and a Ph.D. at the Johns Hopkins University, teaching at Bryn Mawr College, Wesleyan University, and Princeton, and the presidency of Princeton from 1902 to 1910. During his academic years, Wilson distinguished himself as a leading student of American politics and government, a widely regarded lecturer, and finally a renowned and increasingly controversial educational reformer. Capitalizing on the prestige and notoriety of his Princeton presidency, he entered politics in 1910 to win the governorship of New Jersey. Two years later, he was elected president; narrowly reelected in 1916, he served two full terms. In 1919, Wilson suffered a crippling stroke, which left him an invalid during the last year and a half of his presidency. He died less than three years after leaving office.

Inasmuch as Wilson and twenty-eight-year-old Franklin Roosevelt emerged on the political scene at the same time, as successful Democratic candidates in normally Republican northeastern states, it was natural for the young New Yorker, newly elected to the New York State Senate, to be attracted to the older man who had just been elected governor of neighboring New Jersey. Even more attractive to Roosevelt were Wilson's social and educational credentials as a former professor and president of Princeton. That background immediately elevated Wilson to national leadership among the Democrats, who sought a fresh face after four successive presidential defeats and an image that was more respectable and fashionable than the outlander aura cast by William Jennings Bryan and his southern and western cohorts. Roosevelt first met Wilson in 1911, and he became an en-

Woodrow Wilson, 1919. Photographer: Lucien Swift Kirtland. (National Portrait Gallery, Smithsonian Institution.)

ergetic and enthusiastic, though not notably important, supporter of the governor's drive for the presidential nomination. In the fall election of 1912, Roosevelt loyally backed Wilson even though that meant opposing the rival candidacy of his distant kinsman, sometime patron, and wife's uncle, Theodore Roosevelt. As both a reward for his support and a recognition of his politically attractive last name, Franklin Roosevelt received an appointment in 1913 in the Wilson administration as assistant secretary of the navy—the same post Theodore had held under William McKinley sixteen years earlier.

The next seven years found the young Roosevelt, in the words of one of his biographers, "in Professor Wilson's school of public administration." The Wilson administration gave him a political education that was at once formative, inspiring, and trying. The work of the Navy Department and high-level party dealings transformed Roosevelt into a thoroughgoing political professional. Wilson's feats first in passing spectacular programs of reform legislation and later in advancing plans for a new world order provided a lasting inspiration that later guided Roosevelt's own presidency. "I wonder if you realize how often I think of our old Chief when I go about my daily tasks," he told Wilson's former secretary at the height of the hundred days in 1933. "Perhaps what we are doing now will go a little way towards the fulfillment of his ideals."

Another significant impact of the Wilson years lay in breaking down Roosevelt's provincialism as an upper-class, ivy league–educated northeasterner. Initially, he sneered at and ridiculed behind his back his immediate superior, Secretary of the Navy Josephus Daniels, a Bryanite newspaper editor from North Carolina, and he leaked damaging information to such opposition leaders as Theodore Roosevelt and Senator Henry Cabot Lodge. Gradually, however, Roosevelt grew to respect Daniels and his wing of the Democratic party, thereby gaining a set of political contacts that later proved invaluable in his own pursuit and exercise of the presidency.

Certainly the most trying and possibly the most important impact that Wilson made on Roosevelt stemmed not from his successes but from his greatest failure. The president's unavailing effort to gain American membership in the League of Nations in 1919 scarred the younger man even more than most Democrats. After running as the party's unsuccessful vice-presidential candidate in 1920 as a fervent Wilson loyalist, Roosevelt remained his devoted admirer and revered his memory, praising him many times during the next twenty-five years. "Let us feel that in every thing we do there still lives with us," he avowed to the Democratic National Convention at the outset of the 1932 campaign, ". . . the great indomitable, unquenchable, progressive soul of our Commander-in-Chief, Woodrow Wilson."

Yet when he became president, Roosevelt wrought much less of a Wilsonian restoration in personnel, ideas, and spirit than many had expected. Privately, he regarded his predecessor as an object lesson in the perils of too high ideals and excessive expectations from the public. In 1935, Roosevelt explained his attitude toward both of his great political models this way: "Theodore Roosevelt lacked Woodrow Wilson's appeal to the fundamental and failed to stir, as Wilson did, the truly profound moral and social convictions. Wilson, on the other hand, failed where Theodore Roosevelt succeeded in stirring people to enthusiasm over specific individual events, even though those specific events may have been superficial in comparison with the fundamentals."

Lessons drawn from Wilson's experience affected Roosevelt most deeply in his foreign policies, particularly during World War II. "As you doubtless know," he confided to a friend in September 1939, "I did not wholly like President Wilson's war set-up," and his military and diplomatic practices frequently departed from Wilson's precedents. Roosevelt's caution about arousing unrealistic expectations after the United States entered the war and his deviousness in not divulging his objectives before intervention equally reflected resolves to avoid what he perceived as Wilson's mistakes. Still, Roosevelt did not wholly avoid echoes of Wilsonian idealism in his designs for a new American role in world affairs, particularly in the four freedoms declaration and Atlantic Charter in 1941 and in the establishment of the United Nations.

Roosevelt acknowledged his debt in May 1941 when he called Wilson "a statesman who, when other men sought revenge and material gain, strove to bring nearer the day which should see the emancipation of conscience from power and the substitution of freedom for force in the government of the world."

In the end, as a shaper of Franklin Roosevelt's political views and character, Woodrow Wilson ranked second to Theodore Roosevelt, but as a model of presidential success and, possibly still more, of failure, he exerted the profoundest of all political influences on him.

All biographies of Roosevelt recount his service in the Wilson administration. A clear detailed account is in Frank Freidel, *Franklin D. Roosevelt: The Apprenticeship* (Boston: Little, Brown & Co., 1952). The most insightful view of his experience is the part-history, part-memoir by the son of Josephus Daniels who himself became Roosevelt's last press secretary, Jonathan Daniels, *The End of Innocence* (Philadelphia: J. B. Lippincott, 1954). His most direct statement about Wilson and Theodore Roosevelt as presidential models is in Roosevelt to Ray Stannard Baker, 20 March 1935, in Elliott Roosevelt, ed., *F.D.R.: His Personal Letters, 1928–1945* (New York: Duell, Sloan & Pearce, 1950), 1:467. For accounts of his use of Wilson as a negative object lesson in foreign affairs, see Robert E. Sherwood, *Roosevelt and Hopkins: An Intimate History* (New York: Harper & Bros., 1948) and Robert A. Divine, *Roosevelt and World War II* (Baltimore: Johns Hopkins University Press, 1969). Roosevelt's fulfillment of Wilsonian and Theodore Roosveltian political legacies is discussed in John Milton Cooper, Jr., *The Warrior and the Priest: Woodrow Wilson and Theodore Roosevelt* (Cambridge, Mass.: Harvard University Press, 1983).

JOHN MILTON COOPER, JR.

See also Democratic Party; Liberalism and Progressivism

Withholding Tax

See Taxation

Women and the New Deal

The New Deal represented an exciting period for women in public life. During Roosevelt's four terms, women were appointed to high government positions in precedent-breaking numbers; many of these appointments, such as Frances Perkins as the secretary of labor, were firsts for their sex. Women served the New Deal as ministers to foreign countries, as heads of New Deal agencies, and as political advisers; women played especially large roles in the New Deal's relief programs. Like male New Dealers, many of these women look back on the 1930s as the most rewarding period of their entire careers.

Women's progress in the New Deal was facilitated by several factors. The depression posed such a fundamental challenge to the American political sys-

Knott, Dallas Morning News, *22 November 1933.*

tem that the federal government was forced to respond in broad and innovative ways: this experimental climate worked to the benefit of women. Just as important to women's success was the fortuitous election of Franklin Roosevelt to the presidency, for along with Franklin came Eleanor, one of the greatest two-for-one deals in American political history. Eleanor Roosevelt was a true friend to women in Washington. She gave women administrators free publicity at her press conferences, offered them the White House for their meetings, and most important, gave them access to the president. Politician Molly Dewson recalled, "When I wanted help on some definite point, Mrs. Roosevelt gave me the opportunity to sit by the President at dinner and the matter was settled before we finished our soup." Lorena Hickok, roving reporter for Harry Hopkins's Federal Emergency Relief Administration, was not the only woman who later found out that her reports to Eleanor had ended up as FDR's bedtime reading matter at night.

Franklin Roosevelt deserves major credit for women's progress in the New Deal. Roosevelt felt at ease in entrusting major policy responsibilities to women, many of whom he met through Eleanor. Superb politician that he was, he also recognized the need to reward women for their expanding roles in the Democratic party. There were limits, however, to his "feminism"—he appointed Florence Allen to the circuit court of appeals in 1934, but balked at elevating her to the Supreme Court. Had he anticipated that Norway would be drawn into World War II, he

probably would not have nominated Daisy Harriman as minister to Norway in 1937. And no woman was ever part of his brains trust. Yet at a time when most men distrusted or ignored women in public life, Franklin Roosevelt functioned more as women's advocate than women's nemesis.

The most outstanding characteristic of women's participation in the New Deal was the existence of a network of professional contact and personal friendship that linked the women in top New Deal positions. Led by Molly Dewson, Eleanor Roosevelt, and Frances Perkins, the women pooled their talents to influence New Deal policy in two major areas: Democratic party politics and social welfare legislation. In politics, Molly Dewson built the Women's Division into a vital part of the Democratic National Committee through extensive grass-roots organization and won recognition for women through patronage and larger roles in the party hierarchy. In the field of social welfare, women played key roles in the development of the National Recovery Administration (NRA), the Social Security Act, the Fair Labor Standards Act, and the relief policies of the Works Progress Administration (WPA). At every level of the New Deal bureaucracy, women played important, if often unheralded roles.

Although the New Deal opened up exciting opportunities for women in the Roosevelt administration, its record on helping ordinary women is mixed. To be sure, women benefited from the New Deal's relief programs: NRA codes covered more than 4 million women workers, and the WPA offered assistance to 405,000 women at its peak. Yet women's coverage was less extensive than men's and was often hindered by sexist assumptions. One-quarter of NRA codes allowed lower minimum wages for women than men in the same jobs, and the WPA lumped women in sew-

New Deal labor legislation improved both men's and women's expectations of fair practices in the workplace. Here a wage-and-hour division inspector hands checks to women for back wages and overtime owed to them by their employer, a shade-pull manufacturer. (Copyright New York News Inc. Reprinted by permission.)

ing rooms and canning projects and then paid them wages that were less than half of what men received on construction projects. Certain New Deal programs like the popular Civilian Conservation Corps excluded women altogether, leading critics to ask where was the "she-she-she"? Social Security programs slighted women who did not work outside the home and left large areas of women's employment like domestic service totally outside their scope. In this respect, women's experiences on relief parallel broader New Deal patterns: those who were helped never forgot the experience, but many never received their due. In the long run, women probably benefited more from the establishment of the modern welfare state, which guaranteed basic economic rights to all Americans, than from efforts to single them out as a sex.

The successful 1936 election campaign marked the peak of women's participation in the New Deal. In the second term, progress stalled as social welfare programs where women administrators were concentrated faced cutbacks from a hostile Congress. In politics as well, women lost their momentum: women were so securely ensconced in the Democratic coalition that it was easy to take them for granted. Women's roles underwent further changes as the country's attention shifted from depression to war. Women continued to be tapped for high government positions throughout the war years, but they found fewer opportunities in politics and government than they had in the heyday of the early New Deal. The Roosevelt years remain, however, a shining example of a time when women were taken seriously in public life. The reasons for this breakthrough lie in the unprecedented conditions caused by the depression, the opportunities created by the Democrats' return to power, and the unflagging support of women like Eleanor Roosevelt and Molly Dewson. Franklin D. Roosevelt himself, and the policies his administration supported, played no small part in fostering these expanded roles for women in public life.

For an introduction to this subject, see Susan Ware, *Beyond Suffrage: Women in the New Deal* (Cambridge, Mass.: Harvard University Press, 1981). A more critical view of New Deal programs as they affected women is found in Lois Scharf, *To Work and to Wed: Female Employment, Feminism and the Great Depression* (Westport, Conn.: Greenwood Press, 1980). Joseph P. Lash, *Eleanor and Franklin* (New York: W. W. Norton & Co., 1971) and *Love, Eleanor: Eleanor Roosevelt and Her Friends* (Garden City, N.Y.: Doubleday, 1982) contain information on women's activities in the 1930s and 1940s. For general background on women in the Roosevelt years, see Susan Ware, *Holding Their Own: American Women in the 1930s* (Boston: Twayne, 1982) and Susan M. Hartmann, *The Home Front and Beyond: American Women in the 1940s* (Boston: Twayne, 1982).

SUSAN WARE

See also Bethune, Mary McLeod; Dewson, Mary W.; LeHand, Marguerite; New Deal; Perkins, Frances; Roosevelt, Anna Eleanor; Tully, Grace; War Effort on the Home Front

Rosie the Riveter, Jenny on the Job, and other "model" women war workers were popular images of the several million women who joined the labor force during World War II. (Courtesy FDR Library.)

Woodin, William Hartman
(27 May 1868–3 May 1934)

Industrialist and secretary of treasury. William H. Woodin was born at Berwick, Pennsylvania, and was educated at the Woodbridge School in New York City and the School of Mines at Columbia University. He went into his family's business in the production of iron as a molder and cleaner of castings. Woodin started his own company and eventually rose to serve as president of the American Car and Foundry Company and chairman of the board of the American Locomotive Company.

A lifelong Republican, Woodin was a personal friend of Franklin Roosevelt and a trustee of the Warm Springs Foundation. He was active in the Business Men for Roosevelt Committee and made sizable contributions to the Democratic party campaign chest.

Woodin quickly became one of Roosevelt's advisers following the 1932 election and was named secretary of the treasury in 1933, after Senator Carter Glass had declined the position. With his business experience and as former director of the Federal Reserve Bank of New York, Woodin helped to restore for the new administration the confidence of bankers at a time when the nation's banking system teetered on the brink of collapse.

Woodin was committed to carrying out the president's experimental economic and monetary policies; his optimistic and buoyant personality was crucially important to the success of the programs. Traditionally, it was believed that William Woodin deserved most of the credit for the promulgation of the emergency banking legislation prepared in the first days of the administration, but more recently Raymond Moley and Hoover carryovers have also been recognized for their roles in the banking reforms.

Some members of Congress demanded Woodin's resignation after an investigation by the Senate Banking Committee indicated that he was a preferred customer of J. P. Morgan and Company, but Roosevelt continued to support his secretary of treasury. With his health failing, Woodin submitted his resignation on 31 October 1933, but FDR did not accept it, granting him a leave of absence instead. In November, Woodin released a statement declaring his faith in the New Deal and his loyalty to Roosevelt. His health continued to decline, and Roosevelt accepted his resignation in December. Henry Morgenthau, Jr., took over as secretary of treasury.

A contemporary perspective on William Woodin's role in the first one hundred days is contained in Raymond Moley, *After Seven Years* (New York: Harper & Bros., 1939). Both Helen M. Burns, *The American Banking Community and New Deal Banking Reforms, 1933–1935* (Westport, Conn.: Greenwood Press, 1974) and Susan E. Kennedy, *The Banking Crisis of 1933* (Lexington: University Press of Kentucky, 1973) discuss Woodin's efforts to draft the emergency banking legislation as Roosevelt's new secretary of treasury.

Woodring, Harry Hines

(31 May 1890–9 September 1967)

Secretary of war, 1936–40. Harry H. Woodring was born in Elk City, Kansas. He attended local public schools and completed a one-year course in business and commerce at Lebanon University. A successful banker, Woodring acquired controlling interest in the First National Bank of Neodesha, Kansas, where he had once been the cashier. He retired briefly in 1929, but ran successfully for governor of Kansas in the following year. Woodring was named assistant secretary of war by Roosevelt in 1933 and was responsible for procurement matters. He became secretary of war ad interim on the death of George Dern and was officially appointed to the top post a month later on 25 September 1936.

During his tenure, Woodring sought increased appropriations for personnel and equipment to improve the army's readiness. At the same time, however, he firmly believed the department had to observe strictly the neutrality legislation. His position led to an open and bitter feud over policy between himself and Assistant Secretary of War Louis Johnson that demoralized and weakened the department. Woodring became increasingly isolated within the

administration, and Roosevelt turned to the State and Treasury departments for defense planning as war in Europe grew near. He was not a member of the president's Liaison Committee, which was established in December 1939 to facilitate the flow of aid to Great Britain; Treasury Secretary Henry Morgenthau, Jr., played the key role here. Woodring still continued to oppose providing the Allies with American planes and surplus military supplies in light of the state of the nation's own preparedness.

Although Roosevelt had tolerated these objections to his policies for some time, the president finally asked for Woodring's resignation on 19 June 1940. Woodring took this opportunity to reiterate his belief that the United States should not get involved in a European war. He was defeated in his bid for another term as governor of Kansas in 1946 and failed to get the Democratic gubernatorial nomination a decade later. Woodring died in 1967.

Keith D. McFarland's *Harry H. Woodring: A Political Biography* (Lawrence: University Press of Kansas, 1975) is a revisionist study that stresses Woodring's contributions to American rearmament.

See also Cabinets

Work Projects Administration

See Works Progress Administration

Works Progress Administration

In the spring of 1935, despite two years of unprecedented emergency measures and federal spending to prime the economic pump, about 20 percent of the nation's labor force remained unemployed. President Roosevelt felt obliged to devise yet another scheme, as he put it, to "preserve not only the bodies of the unemployed from destruction, but also their self-respect, their self-confidence and courage and determination." Some of the president's closest advisers urged him to resolve the problem by initiating massive, federally financed construction projects with an emphasis on durability, efficiency, and obtaining the greatest value for the taxpayers' dollars. Others, notably Harry L. Hopkins, favored a relief program that could be more quickly initiated, that promised a larger percentage of each dollar to laborers, and that preserved or developed skills among people outside the building trades. Roosevelt eventually sided with the latter position. When he asked Congress for money to support a new independent agency that would employ people on the relief (welfare) rolls, he laid out six guiding principles:

1. The projects should be useful.
2. Projects should be of a nature that a considerable portion of the money spent would go into wages for labor.

3. Projects that promised ultimate return to the federal treasury of a considerable portion of the costs would be sought.

4. Funds allotted for each project should be actually and promptly spent and not held over until later years.

5. In all cases, projects should be of a character to give employment to those on the relief rolls.

6. Projects would be allocated to localities or relief areas in relation to the number of workers on relief rolls in those areas.

Roosevelt created the Works Progress Administration (WPA) by executive order on 6 May 1935. Harry L. Hopkins served as its administrator and guiding spirit until December 1938 when he resigned to become secretary of commerce. Because of the political need to give state governments a say in the op-

erations of the program, the WPA was organizationally complex; and the details of its structure and the centers of influence changed a number of times during its eight-year history. Central offices in Washington and administrations in each state possessed dual authority over the projects and the people who did the work. State administrations dominated the hiring, firing, and supervision of workers, and the designing of projects. The national offices insisted on a direct line of technical instructions to projects in the field.

Except for six "federal" projects operated by the WPA in Washington, work projects began as proposals at the local level by some public agency, which would sponsor the work and contribute a portion of the cost. Cities in need of improved facilities and services were most active. Although contributions of local sponsors fluctuated according to time and place, they averaged about 22 percent of all project costs. About three-fourths of the projects involved construc-

"Leaning on a Shovel"
(Lyrics by John LaTouche; music by Lee Wainer.)

We're not plain every day boys,
Oh, no, not we.
We are the leisurely playboys
Of industry,
Those famous little WPA boys

Of Franklin D.
The Republicans insist we're gay deceivers.
Their anger is so terrific,
While the other workers slave away like beavers
They say we're merely—soporific.
So tonight you can detect us
As we're seen in the GOP prospectus—:

Here we stand asleep all day
While F.D. shooes the flies away
We just wake up to get our pay
What for? For leaning on a shovel!

In the forest the CCC
Is also snoozing peacefully,
Cause only Hoover can make a tree
While we keep leaning on a shovel!

When you look at things today
Like Boulder Dam and TVA
And all those playgrounds where kids can play
We did it—by leaning on a shovel!

We didn't lift a finger
To build the parks
That you see in every city.
At home we always linger
And read Karl Marx
If you don't believe us—ask the Dies Committee.

Miles of roads and highways, too,
And schools and buildings bright and new—
Although it may seem odd to you
We did it—by leaning on a shovel!

You politicians voting against our crew,
Can't you see folks getting wiser?
You ought to be a 'toting a shovel, too,
The way you shovel up the same old fertilizer.
Let the papers have their say,
Let the elephant snore and the donkey bray,
If we can get things done this way—
Hurray for leaning on a shovel!

"Leaning on a Shovel," the WPA–Federal Theatre Project's attempt to poke fun and at the same time answer the critics of the WPA, the CCC, the TVA, and FDR himself seems healthy and imaginative in retrospect. But at the time, Sing for Your Supper, *the show from which it came, was severely criticized before the House Committee to Investigate Un-American Activities. Ironically, "The Ballad of Uncle Sam" survived the show as "Ballad for Americans." (Courtesy the Library of Congress Federal Theatre Project Collection at George Mason University Library, Fairfax, Virginia.)*

tion. Before it ended in 1943, WPA workers had improved 572,000 miles or rural roads and repaired 85,000 public buildings. They built 78,000 new bridges and viaducts and laid 67,000 miles of city streets and 24,000 miles of sidewalks. They brought into being 8,000 parks, 350 airports, and 40,000 buildings, not to mention a vast miscellany of sewage systems, water systems, and riverbank reinforcements.

In keeping with Roosevelt's purpose—maintaining morale and preventing the atrophy of skills—the WPA also carried out a bewildering variety of nonconstruction projects. There were WPA projects to stuff mattresses, can peaches, survey property boundaries, seal mines, tend children, write books in Braille, count cattle, paint murals, stitch winter coats, and inventory housing—more activities than can be cataloged neatly. Still, WPA's resources never permitted the employment of more than one-third of the people who needed jobs.

Roughly 90 percent of the WPA's employees were certified as needy. Their pay scale depended on skill classification (unskilled, intermediate, skilled, or professional) and geography (highest in the Northeast; lowest in the rural South). Unskilled workers averaged about $60 a month, and professionals a little over $100. Roosevelt doled out money to the WPA according to his perception of prospects for employment in the private sector and the money available from Congress. His alternating optimism and pessi-

mism caused the number of WPA jobs to fluctuate frequently. The 3,019,000 jobless Americans who received WPA assistance in February 1936 dwindled in number to 1,454,000 in September 1937; then, by November 1938, the number of recipients rose to 3,330,000 and trailed off erratically until the program ended in 1943. The "average" WPA worker remained with WPA slightly more than a year. There was an understanding—largely unspoken— between Congress and the WPA organization that relief should not be more appealing than employment in the private sector.

In 1938 and 1939 a powerful coalition of Republicans and conservative Democrats in Congress attacked many New Deal programs. The House Committee on Un-American Activities, the Senate Special Committee to Investigate Campaign Expenditures and Use of Government Funds, and the House Subcommittee on Appropriations subjected the WPA to intense scrutiny. The Senate committee concluded that there had been in several states, and in many forms, unjustifiable political activity. The Un-American Activities Committee singled out WPA actors and writers (particularly in New York City) as spectacularly "un-American." The appropriations subcommittee, charging waste, inefficiency, and radicalism, set in motion a law that eliminated theater, cut back funds for other projects, and required all workers to sign a loyalty oath. On 1 July 1939, Roosevelt placed the WPA under the jurisdiction of the Federal Works

A Brooklyn hospital nursery brightened by a WPA effort. The murals on the walls were painted by artists from the local WPA–Federal Art Project. (Courtesy FDR Library.)

Agency as part of a reorganization plan and changed its name to the Work Projects Administration to stress tangible achievements rather than welfare. Francis C. Harrington and then Philip B. Fleming administered the WPA under the new name.

Whatever the truth of the charges against it, the WPA injected more than $10 billion into an ailing economy and provided needy Americans with 13,686,000 person-years of employment. With the advent of World War II, the need for the WPA ended and on 4 December 1941, Roosevelt ordered all projects phased out by 30 June 1943. The WPA, he said, had served America well, and had "earned its honorable discharge."

In the early 1980s bibliographers at the Library of Congress perceived a growing curiosity about the WPA. They responded with Marguerite D. Bloxom, comp., *Pickaxe and Pencil: References for the Study of the WPA* (Washington, D.C.: Library of Congress, 1982). The volume cites popular and scholary articles, books, and doctoral dissertations. No single work stands out as an overview of the WPA. Hopkins explained the agency from his own perspective in *Spending to Save: The Complete Story of Relief Policy* (New York: W. W. Norton, 1936). Policy and administrative issues are best covered in a lengthy volume by Donald S. Howard, *The WPA and Federal Relief Policy* (New York: Russell Sage Foundation, 1943). Searle F. Charles has treated fairly WPA administrator Harry L. Hopkins in *Minister of Relief: Harry Hopkins and the Depression* (Syracuse: Syracuse University Press, 1963). A perceptive analysis of the WPA's problems is William W. Bremer, "Along the 'American Way': The New Deal's Work Relief Program for the Unemployed," *Journal of American History* 62 (December 1975):636–52. For statistics on unemployment during Roosevelt's administration, see U.S. Dept. of Commerce, *Historical Statistics of the U.S.* (Washington, D.C.: U.S. Government Printing Office, 1960).

RICHARD D. MC KINZIE

See also Federal Art Project; Federal Theatre Project; Federal Writers Project; Hopkins, Harry L.; House Committee to Investigate Un-American Activities; Relief; Roosevelt, Anna Eleanor; Williams, Aubrey Willis

World Court

See Internationalism and Peace

World Disarmament Conference

See Internationalism and Peace

World War II

Franklin D. Roosevelt's presidential leadership role in preparing the United States for World War II, guiding the nation's wartime military strategy in conjunction with Churchill and Stalin, and looking beyond the war to a new world order to be policed by great powers illustrates Roosevelt's complex character and provides ample opportunity for controversy among historians.

The German invasion of Poland on 1 September 1939 marked the beginning of World War II, but the historical process moving the world toward a general war began much earlier. Underscoring the League of Nations' inability to deal with aggression and pointing to a growing imbalance of power in Europe and the Far East was a series of aggressive acts beginning 18 September 1931 with the Japanese move against Manchuria and followed by Italy's invasion of Ethiopia 2 October 1935, Japanese aggression against China 7 July 1937, and Hitler's seizure of Austria (the Anschluss) 12 March 1938. The unsuccessful effort to appease Hitler at Munich on 29–30 September 1938 and the resultant German occupation of the Sudetenland 1 October 1938 and dismemberment of Czechoslovakia in March 1939 signaled both the need to use force to stop aggression and the inevitability of war. World War II was the eventual result of the international community's failure to deal effectively with aggressor states. The conspicuous absence of the isolationist United States at the League of Nations and the U.S. failure to exert influence internationally commensurate with its power also contributed to the coming of World War II.

President Franklin Roosevelt was keenly aware that aggression in Europe and the Far East represented a growing threat to American security. He also recognized the strength of isolationist sentiment in the United States and the limitations on policy that such sentiment posed. Roosevelt thus moved meticulously to prepare the American public for war, while sys-

WAR or PEACE – September, 1939

Forces of aggression

If United Nations had been united then...

Active Army & trained reserves   16,300,000   34,815,850

Tanks   7,900   9,160

First line planes   9,800   13,175

Warships – all types   620   1,154

DATA·OWI·   Drawn for OWI

tematically improving American defense readiness. He gradually increased assistance and commitments to the British, although voicing a desire to keep the United States out of war. Roosevelt's propensity for secrecy and his indirect style of action complicated efforts to interpret his intentions as he prepared America for the coming of war.

Roosevelt signaled the need to depart from isolationism in his quarantine speech in Chicago 5 October 1937. He maintained that with "the very foundations of civilization . . . seriously threatened . . . peace-loving nations must make a concerted effort" to join in a "quarantine" to stop the epidemic of war and lawlessness. He warned that "there is no escape through mere isolation or neutrality." The negative public reaction to the speech confirmed the strong isolationist influence and suggested extreme care was necessary to move the nation toward war. When the Czech crisis loomed in the fall of 1938, Roosevelt urged restraint and negotiation, but refrained from direct American involvement. In November he quietly issued an order that American industry must prepare to produce ten thousand combat aircraft annually. Roosevelt emphasized the need to strengthen American defenses in his annual message to Congress 4 January 1939. His concern for maintaining domestic unity, which he asserted was an essential element of defense, was apparent in his caution in avoiding dramatic moves that might precipitate war and prove divisive domestically.

The president responded to Germany's invasion of Poland and the outbreak of World War II by warning America in a fireside chat on 3 September 1939. He charged that "when peace has been broken anywhere, the peace of all countries everywhere is in danger." He refused still to make any overt move toward war, however, and announced that the United States would "remain a neutral nation" and that there would be "no black-out of peace." He issued a formal proclamation of neutrality on 5 September 1939 and declared a limited national emergency three days later. In an effort to bolster France and Britain, Roosevelt urged Congress on 21 September to remove the arms embargo provisions of the neutrality law and allow cash-and-carry trade, while reemphasizing his desire to keep the United States out of war. The law repealing the arms embargo provisions was approved on 4 November 1939.

The German blitzkrieg through Belgium and Holland into France in the spring of 1940 led Roosevelt to call for a massive defense buildup, including raising plant capacity for aircraft to fifty thousand annually. At the University of Virginia on 10 June 1940, he called for all-out assistance to Britain and France over the protests of his military advisers. Roosevelt's decision on 3 September 1940 to transfer fifty destroyers to the British for eight bases, made in the name of hemispheric defense, not because of urgent British need, illustrates his careful attention to political considerations. During his campaign for reelection in 1940, Roosevelt promised once again he would keep the United States out of foreign wars. After the

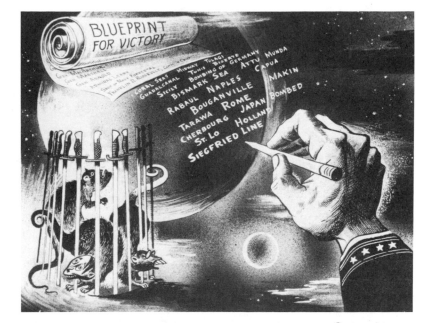

Cartoonist: Henry Sternberg. (Courtesy FDR Library.)

election, however, he took more definitive steps to assist the British by pushing Lend-Lease aid. In a fireside chat on 29 December 1940, he called for the United States to become "the great arsenal of democracy."

At Roosevelt's initiative, American military officials held secret talks with the British 29 January to 27 March 1941. They agreed that should war come with Germany and Japan, Germany had to be defeated first. Roosevelt's preparations for war continued with a proclamation of an unlimited national emergency on 27 May 1941 and the freezing of assets of numerous European states on 14 June. In response to Japan's expansion into Indochina, Roosevelt froze Japanese assets and placed an embargo on oil to Japan. He indicated that he had previously refrained from such an embargo because he feared it would precipitate Japanese aggression. He wanted to concentrate his attention on the Atlantic and avoid a showdown with the Japanese in the Pacific. Roosevelt secretly met with Churchill at Placentia Bay, Newfoundland 9–12 August 1941 and drew up the Atlantic Charter, which provided the first glimpse of America's war aims and envisioned "the establishment of a wider and permanent system of general security."

By the fall of 1941 the United States was essentially engaged in an undeclared war with Germany. Roosevelt, however, continued to walk a tightrope between isolationists and interventionists, as indicated by his vacillation on the issue of convoying British ships. This ended 4 September 1941 when the American destroyer *Greer* was fired upon by a German submarine. Roosevelt seized on the incident as German aggression. On 11 September 1941, in a worldwide radio address, Roosevelt labeled the Germans "rattlesnakes" and called on American warships to shoot-on-sight as necessary for American defense.

Japan, denied U.S. oil while seeking to expand in Southeast Asia, attacked the American fleet at Pearl

Harbor 7 December 1941. The United States declared war on Japan the next day. Germany and Italy, signatories of a tripartite defense pact with Japan (27 September 1940), declared war on the United States on 11 December 1941. The United States responded with a declaration of war the same day.

American industry was primed and ready to build the world's most powerful military machine, notwithstanding some initial administrative difficulties. The Selective Training and Service Act of 16 September 1940 had set America's first peacetime draft in motion. War plans had already been coordinated with the British. Ironically, Roosevelt had approved funding for atomic bomb research on 6 December 1941, the day before the Japanese attack.

President Roosevelt, as commander in chief, dominated wartime military strategy. He payed close attention to the war plans of his military advisers, but did not hesitate to overrule their decisions. He was also active diplomatically, meeting with Allied leaders throughout the war until his death. His proclivity for secrecy tended to obscure his motivations in his dealings with Stalin and Churchill. He was sensitive to the political realities of the day and especially to the role of power.

The thrust of Allied strategy was to defeat Hitler first. Early American success in the Pacific encouraged the United States to hedge on their Europe-first policy. Having broken the Japanese fleet code, U.S. naval forces were victorious in the Battle of Midway in early June 1942, thus stopping Japanese expansion. Roosevelt's decision to launch offensives in the Pacific under Admiral Nimitz and General MacArthur did not significantly change his emphasis on Europe, but did serve to delay any early move across the English Channel.

Intent on committing ground forces in Europe in 1942, Roosevelt overruled his military advisers and opted for the British plan to invade North Africa (Torch). Operation Torch began 8 November 1942. The Allied successes in late 1942 and early 1943 in North Africa and the Soviet counterattack at Stalingrad put the Axis powers on the defensive.

Roosevelt met with Churchill at Casablanca 14–23 January 1943 to shape Allied strategy. There he announced a policy of seeking unconditional surrender. (The policy has been lauded for strengthening the moral commitment to victory, but also criticized for probably lengthening the war and enabling the Soviets to consolidate their power in Eastern Europe.) At the Trident Conference in Washington, D.C., Roosevelt and Churchill agreed on 1 May 1944 as the target date for the cross-channel invasion of Europe (Overlord). The date for Operation Overlord was re-affirmed at the Quadrant Conference in Quebec 14–24 August 1943. A Chinese representative joined Churchill and Roosevelt in Quebec, but Stalin did not attend as hoped, although he was pushing for the Allies to open a second front in Europe and had made some overtures to the Allies, including promising to disband the Comintern.

Roosevelt, Churchill, and Stalin met at Teheran 28 November–1 December 1943. Roosevelt, believing that Soviet cooperation was necessary for the establishment of a peaceful world order, sought to befriend Stalin at the conference, and afterwards, relations appeared to be improving. Roosevelt had broached the idea of a new international organization with "four policemen" to enforce the peace, and the response was positive. Stalin was promised a second front and agreed to enter the war against Japan after Hitler was defeated. Stalin's offer of Soviet participation in the Far East against Japan lessened China's significance and led to Roosevelt's withdrawal from his promise to assist Chiang Kai-shek.

On 6 June 1944, D day, the Allied forces successfully landed on the northern coast of France and began their thrust at the heart of Germany. Allied successes and Germany's impending defeat set the stage for the Yalta Conference, 4–9 February 1945, and Roosevelt's last meeting with Churchill and Stalin.

At Yalta the Big Three sought to resolve questions on Poland and the occupation of Germany, as well as clarify the Soviet role against Japan and the nature of the future United Nations Organization. The resulting territorial settlements in Eastern Europe and the Far Eastern accords led to accusations that Roosevelt had "caved in to the Russians." The strength and location of the Soviet ground forces, however, suggest that Roosevelt and Churchill could not realistically have expected to exert great influence on Stalin as victory approached.

Following the Yalta Conference, Roosevelt was looking forward to the San Francisco Conference with great anticipation. Having had an American proposal on great-power voting approved at Yalta, Roosevelt had high hopes for the formation of the United Nations. He died, however, on 12 April 1945, twelve days before the conference opened in San Francisco.

The war in Europe ended the next month when Germany signed an unconditional surrender. V-E Day was declared 8 May 1945. The war in the Far East did not end until atomic bombs, which were dropped on Hiroshima on 6 August 1945 and on Nagasaki on 9 August, brought the Japanese unconditional surrender on 14 August. (The Soviet Union had formally entered the war against Japan on 9 August.) V-J Day was declared 15 August 1945.

The costs of the war are difficult to assess. Estimates suggest as many as 50 million lives were lost, with Soviet dead numbering 18 to 21 million, Germany, about 6 million, Japan, about 2 million, Italy, about 400,000, and the United States, possibly as many as 320,000 lives. Estimates of British war dead vary greatly and range as high as over 460,000. The French lost more than 375,000, and the number of Jews killed is placed at about 6 million.

The war had a far-reaching impact on American society. Roosevelt's careful attention to national unity and his early preparations to mobilize the civilian population for war production set the stage for a total war effort and the emergence of a strong, unified America. His efforts to centralize planning were enmeshed in an administrative jungle early in the war, but later impressive successes were realized. Congressional legislation extending the authority of the Office of War Mobilization in 1943 resolved many bureaucratic squabbles, and the war years saw an expansion of government in general. Individual rights suffered, especially with the internment of Japanese-Americans, but the status of blacks was fundamentally altered as equal rights were pushed. Family situations changed as more women entered the work force. Numerous economic restrictions were placed on the American populace, but despite rationing, shortages, and ceilings on salaries, the standard of living increased. The war brought a major increase in the power of the Office of the President and a relative decline in congressional power, especially in foreign affairs. Party politics, to Roosevelt's irritation, were not set aside despite calls for a bipartisan response to war demands.

World War II ushered in the nuclear era, decolonization, the cold war, and a new American prominence on the world scene. President Roosevelt was a principal architect of the new America and the new world order.

The voluminous literature on President Roosevelt and World War II is sharply divided between those critical of Roosevelt and U.S. entry into the war and those supportive of his actions. Charles A. Beard's *President Roosevelt and the Coming of the War, 1941* (New Haven: Yale University Press, 1948) is the prime example of revisionist writing critical of Roosevelt and illustrates the harsh isolationist response to America's role in World War II. Charles C. Tansill's *Back Door to War: The Roosevelt Foreign Policy, 1933–1941* (Chicago: Henry Regnery, 1952) is another revisionist classic that questions Roosevelt's motivations and suggests that Japan was "maneuvered into firing the first shot at Pearl Harbor." Robert Sherwood, on the other hand, explains Roosevelt's policy in a positive light and is generally critical of isolationist influence in *Roosevelt and Hopkins: An Intimate History*, rev. ed. (New York: Harper & Row, 1950). Robert A. Divine contrasts Roosevelt's roles as an early isolationist, an interventionist, a realist, and a pragmatist in *Roosevelt and World War II* (Baltimore: John Hopkins Press, 1969). Divine focuses upon Roosevelt's vision of a new international organization and approach toward the Soviet Union. James MacGregor

Burns underscores the complexity of Roosevelt's character as he critically assesses the political and diplomatic affairs of World War II in *Roosevelt: The Soldier of Freedom* (New York: Harcourt Brace Jovanovich, 1970). Burns also offers substantial insights into the situation on the home front during the war. In a more recent work, Robert Dallek questions whether Roosevelt's attention to domestic concerns limited his international influence in *Franklin D. Roosevelt and American Foreign Policy, 1932–1945* (New York: Oxford University Press, 1979). Dallek's work represents a comprehensive diplomatic history, with an emphasis on World War II.

CHARLES G. MAC DONALD

See also Agricultural Adjustment Administration; America First Committee; Atlantic Conference and Charter; Atomic Bomb; Axis Alliance; Brussels Conference; Byrnes, James Francis; Cairo Conference; Casablanca Conference; Chennault, Claire Lee; Chiang Kai-shek; Churchill, Winston Leonard Spencer; Civil Liberties in Wartime; Colonialism; Commander in Chief; Congress, United States; Cooke, Charles Maynard; Declaration of War; de Gaulle, Charles; Eisenhower, Dwight David; Fascism; Foreign Economic Policy; Foreign Policy; Good Neighbor Policy; Groves, Leslie; Halsey, William Frederick; Hitler, Adolf, and Germany; Holcomb, Thomas; Holocaust; Hull, Cordell; Internationalism and Peace; Internment of Japanese-Americans; Isolationism; Japan; Joint Chiefs of Staff; King, Ernest J.; Leahy, William Daniel; Lend-Lease; MacArthur, Douglas; Marshall, George Catlett; Maritime Commission; Mussolini, Benito, and Italy; Neutrality Acts; Nimitz, Chester William; Office of Censorship; Office of War Information; Open Door Policy; Pacifism and the Peace Movement; Pearl Harbor; Personal Diplomacy; Quarantine Speech; Quebec Conferences; Refugees; Selective Service Act; Spanish Civil War; Stalin, Joseph, and the Soviet Union; Stark, Harold Raynsford; Stettinius, Edward Reilly, Jr.; Stilwell, Joseph Warren; Stimson, Henry L.; Swanson, Claude Augustus; Teheran Conference; Veterans; War Effort on the Home Front; War Mobilization; War Production Board; Yalta Conference; Zionism

Y-Z

Yalta Conference

On 4 February 1945, the last of the wartime conferences of the leaders of the Grand Alliance opened at the Black Sea resort of Yalta in the Soviet Crimea. "Ten years of research could not have unearthed a worse place to meet," a gloomy Winston Churchill told Harry Hopkins eleven days before. Lice, bedbugs, and typhus bacilli bit and terrified Churchill, FDR, Joseph Stalin, and their staffs who had assembled to mold the postwar world. Over the next eight days, the Big Three grappled with the treatment of Germany, the political map of Poland and Eastern Europe, the future of Japanese-occupied East Asia, and the structure of the new United Nations organization.

The issue of how to treat defeated Germany led to recriminations between Roosevelt and Churchill. The British leader was appalled when FDR expressed the hope that Stalin "would again propose a toast to the execution of 50,000 German officers." Churchill's distress at FDR's vindictiveness eased, however, once the Americans accepted Britain's suggestion that the France of Charles de Gaulle receive an occupation zone in Germany. Stalin voiced no objection, as long as the French territory came from lands previously awarded to the two Western Allies. The Soviets expressed more concern about securing reparations. The three leaders fixed no final figure, but they agreed in principle that the Soviets would receive half of Germany's payments. The precise amount would be decided at a later conference, but all accepted $20 billion as a working number.

Discussions of the future of Poland and Eastern Europe provoked more disagreement. Aware that 6 or 7 million Polish-Americans felt strongly that their ancestral land should become independent inside large borders, FDR encouraged Stalin to loosen the grip of the Red Army and the pro-Soviet, Communist-dominated government established at Lublin. At the same time the president knew the limits of his influence with the Soviets. The appearance of Big Three

amity was more important than the impossible dream of a genuinely independent Poland. They adopted a vague statement guaranteeing that the British and American ambassadors in Warsaw would keep their governments "informed about the situation in Poland." Adm. William Leahy remarked, "Mr. President, this is so elastic that the Russians can stretch it all the way from Yalta to Washington without ever technically breaking it." To which Roosevelt replied, "I know it. But it's the best I can do for Poland at this time."

The conference offered even less specific guarantees regarding the future of the remainder of Eastern Europe. The Big Three spent little time discussing a general Declaration on Liberation Europe in which they committed themselves to assist the nations occupied by the Nazis to form democratic governments through free elections.

The military situation in the Far East affected the talks. Roosevelt's major concern was to make certain that the Soviet Union would enter the war against Japan. Stalin agreed to send his forces against Japan two or three months after the final surrender of Germany. In return, Roosevelt and Churchill acknowledged Soviet interests in the Far East. The Kuriles Islands and the southern half of Sakalin Island, taken by Japan from Russia in 1905, would revert to Soviet control. A Soviet-dominated regime would remain in Outer Mongolia. The Western leaders agreed that twenty-five Soviet divisions would enter Manchuria, and the Manchurian railroads would be run by the Soviet Union. For his part, Stalin intimated that he would acknowledge Chiang Kai-shek as the leader of the Chinese government and press the Chinese Communists to enter a coalition with Chiang.

Roosevelt took the lead in discussing the new world security organization, the United Nations (UN). Secretary of State Edward Stettinius outlined plans for voting in the security council of the UN. Each of the five permanent members would have the right to veto resolutions, but they could not by themselves block council consideration of issues. Stettinius argued that the American public insisted upon "a fair

The Big Three—Churchill, Roosevelt, and Stalin—at Yalta, February 1945. (Courtesy FDR Library.)

hearing for all members of the organization, large and small." To gain Soviet assent for permitting the council to discuss questions affecting Russia, the president acceded to Stalin's request for two additional seats in the General Assembly for the Soviet Republics of the Ukraine and Beylorussia. "This is not so good," Roosevelt mourned, but the advantage of Soviet support for the UN overcame his qualms.

After the conference adjourned on 12 February, Hopkins reported a mood of "supreme exultation" on the part of the American delegation. "We really believed in our hearts that this was the dawn of the new day we had all been praying for." Others were not so certain, and Yalta became in memory the most controversial summit conference in history.

During the cold war, many Republican politicians excoriated Roosevelt and every American who took part in the negotiations for yielding too much to Stalin. Sen. Joseph McCarthy charged that the agreements were treasonous and unjustly permitted Communist dominance of Eastern Europe and China. Sen. John Bricker introduced a constitutional amendment outlawing executive agreements like Yalta. In 1955, the State Department published the papers of the Yalta Conference early both to discredit the Democrats and to suggest that their critics had gone too far.

Recent scholarship directly refutes the reckless charges of the Yalta critics. Athan Theoharis characterizes the "spirit of Yalta" as one of "guarded cooperation and trust." He decries McCarthy and other critics for judging Yalta in "simplistic monolithic terms of black and white." He notes that in the cold war years "a rigidity in thought, an intolerance toward ideas and dissent, and a belief in the omnipotence and altruism of U.S. power emerged." Roosevelt's political adversaries chose to forget the very real need to preserve the fragile coalition in the midst of World War II. They overlooked the desire of the Joint Chiefs of Staff to ensure Soviet participation in the war against Japan, and they ignored the dominant position of the Red Army in Eastern Europe in early 1945. Historian Diane Shaver Clemens provides the most balanced view of Yalta. All participants got something from the conference. It was "a diplomatic encounter in which all sides, not without misgivings and harsh words, struggled to achieve their aims, . . . an encounter in which they prized agreement by traditional negotiations as preferable to unilateral action which might undermine international stability."

The standard scholarly study of the conference is Diane Shaver Clemens's *Yalta* (New York: Oxford University Press, 1970). She uses techniques of bargaining theory to demonstrate that all three powers altered their positions in the interests of reaching an agreement. Robert Dallek's *Franklin D. Roosevelt and American Foreign Policy, 1932–1945* (New York: Oxford University Press, 1979) contains a good summary based upon up-to-date research. It supersedes Herbert Feis's earlier summaries in *The China Tangle* (Princeton: Princeton University Press, 1953) or *Churchill, Roosevelt, Stalin: The War They Waged and the Peace They Sought* (Princeton: Princeton University Press, 1957). Athan Theoharis presents the fullest account of Yalta's effects upon American memory in *The Yalta Myths: An Issue in U.S. Politics, 1945–1955* (Columbia: University of Missouri Press, 1970). Mark Elliott raises disturbing questions about the human costs of the agreements in *Pawns of Yalta: Soviet Refugees and America's Role in Their Repatriation* (Champaign: University of Illinois Press, 1982).

ROBERT D. SCHULZINGER

See also Byrnes, James Francis; Churchill, Winston Leonard Spencer; Foreign Policy; Health; Hitler, Adolf, and Germany; Hopkins, Harry L.; Personal Diplomacy; Stalin, Joseph, and the Soviet Union; World War II; Zionism

Youth and the New Deal

See Bethune, Mary McLeod; Civilian Conservation Corps; National Youth Administration; New Deal; Williams, Aubrey Willis

Zangara, Joseph (Giuseppe)

See Assassination Attempt of 1933

Zionism

Zionism is a political movement that arose at the end of the nineteenth century with the goal of ending anti-Semitism by securing a politically guaranteed homeland for the Jewish people in Palestine. In November 1917 during the First World War, the British, in order to gain support for their war efforts, issued the Balfour Declaration, promising to establish a Jewish homeland in Palestine after the war. At the San Remo Conference in 1920, the League of Nations awarded Great Britain a mandate over Palestine and incorporated the Balfour pledge as part of the charge. Throughout the 1920s, thousands of Jewish settlers poured into Palestine and, under the sponsorship of the World Zionist Organization, began to make the barren wastelands prosper. In the 1930s, however, a growing Arab nationalism led Great Britain to renege on the Balfour Declaration, cutting off continued immigration at the same time that the rise of Hitler threatened Jewish existence in Europe.

American Zionists, led by Stephen S. Wise, Abba Hillel Silver, Julian W. Mack, and behind the scenes, Louis D. Brandeis, for the most part considered Franklin Roosevelt a friend to their cause. They recognized that an American president had limited power over Palestinian affairs, but they constantly urged him to use his influence with the British to keep the gates of Palestine open for Jewish refugees fleeing fascism. At least one time, in 1936, he did intervene and managed to delay a British plan to severely restrict further Jewish immigration into the Holy Land. Such gestures, as well as his repeated statements, both public and private, of support for the Zionist program, as well as his appointments of numerous Jews to important governmental positions in the New Deal, won Roosevelt overwhelming political support in the American Jewish community. In 1936, 1940, and 1944, he carried many Jewish precincts by better than a 90 percent margin.

During the war years, especially after news reached America of the genocide of European Jewry, the Zionists found themselves in a frustrating position. They constantly importuned Roosevelt to force the British to open Palestine for refugees fleeing Hitler's "final solution," only to be told that nothing could be done that might impede the war against Hitler. At the Bermuda Refugee Conference in 1943, as at the earlier Evian-les-Bains Conference in 1938, the United States agreed to British insistence that Palestine not even be on the agenda as a possible haven. Moreover, despite Roosevelt's continued expressions of good will toward Zionism, the Middle East section of the State Department adopted the Arabist view of the British Foreign Office, which viewed Palestine as part of an Arab-dominated, although British-controlled, sphere of influence.

With the opening of private papers as well as State Department records, the earlier interpretation of Roosevelt as a friend of Zionism has undergone considerable reinterpretation. Many Zionists, led by Silver, had begun to question the president's sincerity even before the war ended. It now appears that even while assuring American Zionist leaders of his support, Roosevelt secretly gave similar promises of support to British and Arab leaders that nothing be done without their consent in implementing any Zionist plans for a Jewish homeland in Palestine. When Roosevelt went to Yalta in 1945, he returned via Cairo where he met with the Arab chieftain Ibn Sa'ud, who impressed the chief executive with his hostility toward Zionism. In his report to Congress on 1 March 1945, Roosevelt declared that he had learned more about the "Moslem problem, the Jewish problem, by talking with Ibn Sa'ud for five minutes" than he had ever known before. Although Roosevelt evidently believed that he would be able to solve the Middle East dilemma after the war through personal diplomacy, his death cut short that option.

There have been numerous articles and books detailing the Roosevelt relationship with the American Jewish community in general and with Zionism in particular. Much of the debate revolves around Roosevelt's handling of the refugee crisis, and the most bitter attack is by Saul S. Friedman, *No Haven for the Oppressed* (Detroit: Wayne State University Press, 1973); much more balanced is Henry L. Feingold, *The Politics of Rescue* (New Brunswick, N.J.: Rutgers University Press, 1970), which brilliantly explores the bureaucratic dynamics involved. A still useful article, one of the first to exploit the State Department material, is Selig Adler "Franklin D. Roosevelt and Zionism—The Wartime Record," *Judaism* 21 (1972):265–76. The State Department role, upon which Roosevelt heavily relied, is explicated in Phillip J. Baram, *The Department of State in the Middle East, 1919–1945* (Philadelphia: University of Pennsylvania Press, 1978). A useful synthesis may be found in Melvin I. Urofsky, *American Zionism from Herzl to the Holocaust* (Garden City, N.Y.: Doubleday, 1975), ch. 10, and *We Are One!* (Garden City, N.Y.: Doubleday, 1978), chs. 1, 2.

MELVIN I. UROFSKY

See also Brandeis, Louis Dembitz; Cohen, Benjamin Victor; Personal Diplomacy

Franklin D. Roosevelt's first inaugural medal by Paul Manship, 1933. (Courtesy FDR Library.)

Franklin D. Roosevelt's fourth inaugural medal by Jo Davidson, 1945. (Courtesy FDR Library.)

INDEX

Also by John Updike

POETRY

THE CARPENTERED HEN *(1958)*

TELEPHONE POLES *(1963)*

SHORT STORIES

THE SAME DOOR *(1959)*

PIGEON FEATHERS *(1962)*

OLINGER STORIES: *A Selection (1964)*

THE MUSIC SCHOOL *(1966)*

NOVELS

THE POORHOUSE FAIR *(1959)*

RABBIT, RUN *(1960)*

THE CENTAUR *(1963)*

OF THE FARM *(1965)*

ESSAYS

ASSORTED PROSE *(1965)*

COUPLES

John Updike

COUPLES

Alfred A. Knopf   New York

1968

THIS IS A BORZOI BOOK
PUBLISHED BY ALFRED A. KNOPF, INC.

FIRST EDITION
SECOND PRINTING, MARCH 1968
© *Copyright 1968 by John Updike*

TO MARY

There is a tendency in the average citizen, even if he has a high standing in his profession, to consider the decisions relating to the life of the society to which he belongs as a matter of fate on which he has no influence —like the Roman subjects all over the world in the period of the Roman empire, a mood favorable for the resurgence of religion but unfavorable for the preservation of a living democracy.

—PAUL TILLICH,
The Future of Religions

We love the flesh: its taste, its tones,
Its charnel odor, breathed through Death's jaws. . . .
Are we to blame if your fragile bones
Should crack beneath our heavy, gentle paws?

—ALEXANDER BLOK,
"The Scythians"

Chapters

COUPLES

i. *Welcome to Tarbox*

"WHAT did you make of the new couple?"

The Hanemas, Piet and Angela, were undressing. Their bed-chamber was a low-ceilinged colonial room whose woodwork was painted the shade of off-white commercially called eggshell. A spring midnight pressed on the cold windows.

"Oh," Angela answered vaguely, "they seemed young." She was a fair soft brown-haired woman, thirty-four, going heavy in her haunches and waist yet with a girl's fine hard ankles and a girl's tentative questing way of moving, as if the pure air were loosely packed with obstructing cloths. Age had touched only the softened line of her jaw and her hands, their stringy backs and reddened fingertips.

"How young, exactly?"

"Oh, I don't know. He's thirty trying to be forty. She's younger. Twenty-eight? Twenty-nine? Are you thinking of taking a census?"

He grudgingly laughed. Piet had red hair and a close-set body; no taller than Angela, he was denser. His flattish Dutch features, inherited, were pricked from underneath by an acquired American something—a guilty humorous greed, a wordless question.

His wife's languid unexpectedness, a diffident freshness born of aristocratic self-possession, still fascinated him. He thought of himself as coarse and saw her as fine, so fair and fine her every gesture seemed transparently informed by a graciousness and honesty beyond him. When he had met her, Angela Hamilton, she had been a young woman past first bloom, her radiance growing lazy, with an affecting slow mannerism of looking away, the side of her neck bared, an inexplicably unscarred beauty playing at schoolteaching and living with her parents in Nun's Bay, and he had been laboring for her father, in partnership with an army friend, one of their first jobs, constructing a pergola in view of the ocean and the great chocolate-dark rock that suggested, from a slightly other angle, a female profile and the folds of a wimple. There had been a cliff, an ample green lawn, and bushes trimmed to the flatness of tables. In the house there had been many clocks, grandfather's and ship's clocks, clocks finished in ormolu or black lacquer, fine-spun clocks in silver cases, with four balls as pendulum. Their courtship passed as something instantly forgotten, like an enchantment, or a mistake. Time came unstuck. All the clocks hurried their ticking, hurried them past doubts, around sharp corners and knobbed walnut newels. Her father, a wise-smiling man in a tailored gray suit, failed to disapprove. She had been one of those daughters so favored that spinsterhood alone might dare to claim her. Fertility at all costs. He threw business his son-in-law's way. The Hanemas' first child, a daughter, was born nine months after the wedding night. Nine years later Piet still felt, with Angela, a superior power seeking through her to employ him. He spoke as if in self-defense: "I was just wondering at what stage they are. He seemed rather brittle and detached."

"You're hoping they're at our stage?"

Her cool thin tone, assumed at the moment when he had believed their intimacy, in this well-lit safe room encircled by the April dark, to be gathering poignant force enough to vault them over their inhibitions, angered him. He felt like a fool. He said, "That's right. The seventh circle of bliss."

"Is that what we're in?" She sounded, remotely, ready to believe it.

They each stood before a closet door, on opposite sides of an unused fireplace framed in pine paneling and plaster painted azure. The house was a graceful eighteenth-century farmhouse of eight rooms. A barn and a good square yard and a high lilac hedge came with the property. The previous owners, who had had adolescent boys, had attached a basketball hoop to one side of the barn and laid down a small asphalt court. At another corner of the two acres stood an arc of woods tangent to a neighboring orchard. Beyond this was a dairy farm. Seven miles further along the road, an unseen presence, was the town of Nun's Bay; and twenty miles more, to the north, Boston. Piet was by profession a builder, in love with snug right-angled things, and he had grown to love this house, its rectangular low rooms, its baseboards and chair rails molded and beaded by hand, the slender mullions of the windows whose older panes were flecked with oblong bubbles and tinged with lavender, the swept worn brick of the fireplace hearths like entryways into a sooty upward core of time, the attic he had lined with silver insulation paper so it seemed now a vaulted jewel box or an Aladdin's cave, the solid freshly poured basement that had been a cellar floored with dirt when they had moved in five years ago. He loved how this house welcomed into itself in every season lemony flecked rhomboids of sun whose slow sliding revolved it with the day, like the cabin of a ship on a curving course. All houses, all things that enclosed, pleased Piet, but his modest Dutch sense of how much of the world he was permitted to mark off and hold was precisely satisfied by this flat lot two hundred feet back from the road, a mile from the center of town, four miles distant from the sea.

Angela, descended from piratical New Bedford whaling captains, wanted a property with a view of the Atlantic. She had mourned when the new couple in town, the Whitmans, had bought, through the agency of Gallagher & Hanema, Real Estate and Contracting, a house she had coveted, the old Robinson place, a jerrybuilt summer house in need of total repair. It had a huge view of the salt marshes and a wind exposure that would defy all insulation. She and Piet had gone over it several times in the winter past. It had been built as a one-story cottage around 1900. In the early twenties it had been jacked up on posts and a new first floor built under it, with a long screened porch that darkened the living room. Then new owners had added a servants' wing whose level differed by two steps from the main structure. Piet showed Angela the shabby carpentry, the crumbling gypsum wallboard, the corroded iron plumbing, the antique wiring with its brittle rubber insulation, the rattling sashes chewed by animals and rain. A skylight in the main bedroom leaked. The only heat came from a single round register in the living-room floor, above a manually fed coal furnace in an unwalled clay hole. A full cellar would have to be excavated. Solid interior walls and a complete heating system were essential. The roof must be replaced. Gutters, sashes. Ceilings. The kitchen was quaint, useless; servants had run it, summers only, making lobster salads. On the two windward sides the cedar shingles had been warped and whitened and blown away. Forty thousand the asking price, and twelve more immediately, minimum. It was too much to ask him to take on. Standing at the broad slate sink contemplating the winter view of ditch-traversed marsh and the brambled islands of hawthorn and alder and the steel-blue channel beyond and the rim of dunes white as salt and above all the honed edge of ocean, Angela at last agreed. It was too much.

Now, thinking of this house from whose purchase he had escaped and from whose sale he had realized a partner's share of profit, Piet conservatively rejoiced in the house he had held. He felt its lightly supporting symmetry all around him. He pictured his two round-faced daughters asleep in its shelter. He gloated upon the sight of his wife's body, her fine ripeness.

Having unclasped her party pearls, Angela pulled her dress, the black décolleté knit, over her head. Its soft wool caught in her hairpins. As she struggled, lamplight struck zigzag fire from her slip and static electricity made its nylon adhere to her flank. The slip lifted, exposing stocking-tops and garters. Without her head she was all full form, sweet, solid.

Pricked by love, he accused her: "You're not happy with me."

She disentangled the bunched cloth and obliquely faced him. The lamplight, from a bureau lamp with a pleated linen shade, cut shadows into the line of her jaw. She was aging. A year ago, she would have denied the accusation. "How can I be," she asked, "when you flirt with every woman in sight?"

"In sight? Do I?"

"Of course you do. You know you do. Big or little, old or young, you eat them up. Even the yellow ones, Bernadette Ong. Even poor little soused Bea Guerin, who has enough troubles."

"You seemed happy enough, conferring all night with Freddy Thorne."

"Piet, we can't keep going to parties back to back. I come home feeling dirty. I hate it, this way we live."

"You'd rather we went belly to belly? Tell me"—he had stripped to his waist, and she shied from that shieldlike breadth of taut bare skin with its cruciform blazon of amber hair—"what do you and Freddy find to talk about for hours on end? You huddle in the corner like children playing jacks." He took a step forward, his eyes narrowed and pink, party-chafed. She resisted the urge to step backwards, knowing that this threatening mood of his was supposed to end in sex, was a plea.

Instead she reached under her slip to unfasten her garters. The gesture, so vulnerable, disarmed him; Piet halted before the fireplace, his bare feet chilled by the hearth's smooth bricks.

"He's a jerk," she said carelessly, of Freddy Thorne. Her voice was lowered by the pressure of her chin against her chest; the downward reaching of her arms gathered her breasts to a dark crease. "But he talks about things that interest women. Food. Psychology. Children's teeth."

"What does he say psychological?"

"He was talking tonight about what we all see in each other."

"Who?"

"You know. Us. The couples."

"What Freddy Thorne sees in me is a free drink. What he sees in you is a gorgeous fat ass."

She deflected the compliment. "He thinks we're a circle. A magic circle of heads to keep the night out. He told me he gets frightened if he doesn't see us over a weekend. He thinks we've made a church of each other."

"That's because he doesn't go to a real church."

"Well Piet, you're the only one who does. Not counting the Catholics." The Catholics they knew socially were the Gallaghers and Bernadette Ong. The Constantines had lapsed.

"It's the source," Piet said, "of my amazing virility. A stiffening sense of sin." And in his chalkstripe suit pants he abruptly dove forward, planted his weight on his splayed raw-knuckled hands, and stood upside down. His tensed toes reached for the tip of his conical shadow on the ceiling; the veins in his throat and forearms bulged. Angela looked away. She had seen this too often before. He neatly flipped back to his feet; his wife's silence embarrassed him. "Christ be praised," he said, and clapped, applauding himself.

"Shh. You'll wake the children."

"Why the hell shouldn't I, they're always waking me, the little bloodsuckers." He went down on his knees and toddled to the edge of the bed. "Dadda, Dadda, wake up-up, Dadda. The Sunnay paper's here, guess what? Jackie Kenneny's having a *ba*by!"

"You're so cruel," Angela said, continuing her careful undressing, parting vague obstacles with her hands. She opened her closet door so that from her husband's angle her body was hidden. Her voice floated free: "Another thing Freddy thinks, he thinks the children are suffering because of it."

"Because of what?"

"Our social life."

"Well I have to have a social life if you won't give me a sex life."

"If you think *that* approach is the way to a lady's heart, you have a lot to learn." He hated her tone; it reminded him of the years before him, when she had instructed children.

He asked her, "Why shouldn't children suffer? They're supposed to suffer. How else can they learn to be good?" For he felt that if only in the matter of suffering he knew more than she, and that without him she would raise their daughters as she had been raised, to live in a world that didn't exist.

She was determined to answer him seriously, until her patience dulled his pricking mood. "That's positive suffering," she said. "What we give them is neglect so subtle they don't even notice it.

We aren't abusive, we're just evasive. For instance, Frankie Appleby is a bright child, but he's just going to waste, he's just Jonathan little-Smith's punching bag because their parents are always together."

"Hell. Half the reason we all live in this silly hick town is for the sake of the children."

"But we're the ones who have the fun. The children just get yanked along. They didn't enjoy all those skiing trips last winter, standing in the T-bar line shivering and miserable. The girls wanted all winter to go some Sunday to a museum, a nice warm museum with stuffed birds in it, but we wouldn't take them because we would have had to go as a family and our friends might do something exciting or ghastly without us. Irene Saltz finally took them, bless her, or they'd never have gone. I like Irene; she's the only one of us who has somehow kept her freedom. Her freedom from crap."

"How much did you drink tonight?"

"It's just that Freddy didn't let me talk enough."

"He's a jerk," Pict said and, suffocated by an obscure sense of exclusion, seeking to obtain at least the negotiable asset of a firm rejection, he hopped across the hearth-bricks worn like a passageway in Delft and sharply kicked shut Angela's closet door, nearly striking her. She was naked.

He too was naked. Piet's hands, feet, head, and genitals were those of a larger man, as if his maker, seeing that the cooling body had been left too small, had injected a final surge of plasma which at these extremities had ponderously clotted. Physically he held himself, his tool-toughened palms curved and his acrobat's back a bit bent, as if conscious of a potent burden.

Angela had flinched and now froze, one arm protecting her breasts. A luminous polleny pallor, the shadow of last summer's bathing suit, set off her surprisingly luxuriant pudenda. The slack forward cant of her belly remembered her pregnancies. Her thick-thighed legs were varicose. But her tipped arms seemed, simple and symmetrical, a maiden's; her white feet were high-arched and neither little toe touched the floor. Her throat, wrists, and triangular bush appeared the pivots for some undeniable effort of flight, but like Eve on a portal she crouched in shame, stone. She held rigid. Her blue irises cupped light catlike, shallowly. Her skin breathed hate. He did not dare touch her, though her fairness gathered so close dried his tongue. Their bodies hung upon them as clothes too gaudy. Piet felt the fireplace draft on his ankles and became sensitive to the night beyond her hunched shoulders, an extensiveness pressed tight against the bubbled old panes and the frail mullions, a blackness charged with the ache of first growth and the suspended skeletons of Virgo and Leo and Gemini.

She said, "Bully."

He said, "You're lovely."

"That's too bad. I'm going to put on my nightie."

Sighing, immersed in a clamor of light and paint, the Hanemas dressed and crept to bed, exhausted.

As always after a party Piet was slow to go to sleep. There had not been many parties for him as a child and now they left him overexcited, tumescent. He touched his own self to make himself sleepy. Quickly his wife was dead weight beside him. She claimed she never dreamed. Pityingly he put his hand beneath the cotton nightie transparent to his touch and massaged the massive blandness of her warm back, hoping to stir in the depths of her sleep an eddy, a fluid fable she could tell herself and in the morning remember. She would be a valley and he a sandstorm. He would be a gentle lion bathing in her river. He could not believe she never dreamed. How could one not dream? He always dreamed. He dreamed last night he was an old minister making calls. Walking in the country, he crossed a superhighway and waited a long time on the median strip. Waiting, he looked down into a rural valley where small houses smoked from their chimneys. He must make his calls there. He crossed the rest of the road and was relieved when a policeman pulled up on a motorcycle and, speaking German, arrested him.

The party had been given by the Applebys in honor of the new couple, the what, the Whitmans. Frank had known Ted, or Dan, at Exeter, or Harvard. Exeter, Harvard: it was to Piet like looking up at the greenhouse panes spattered with whitewash to dull the sun. He shut out the greenhouse. He did not wish to remember the greenhouse. It was a cliff.

Stiffly his fingers tired of trying to give his wife a dream: a baby on the river of herself, Moses in the Nile morning found snagged in the rustling papyrus, Egyptian handmaids, willowy flanks, single lotus, easy access. Sex part of nature before Christ. *Bully*. Bitch. Taking up three-quarters of the bed as if duty done. Mouthbreathing with slack lips. Words in and out. Virgins pregnant through the ear. Talk to me psychologee. He touched in preference again himself. Waxen. Wilted camellia petals. In his youth an ivory rod at will. At the thought of a cleft or in class a shaft of sun laid on his thigh: stand to recite: *breathes there a man with soul so dead*. The whole class tittering at him bent over. The girl at the desk next wore lineny blouses so sheer her bra straps peeped and so short-sleeved that her armpits. Showed, shaved. Vojt. Annabelle Vojt. One man, one Vojt. Easy Dutch ways. Married a poultry farmer from outside Grand Rapids. Wonderful tip of her tongue, agile, squarish. Once after a dance French-kissed him parked by the quarry and he shot off behind his fly. Intenser then, the duct narrower, greater velocity. Not his girl but her underpants satiny, distant peaty odor, rustle of crinoline, formal dance. Quick as a wink, her dark tongue saucy under his. His body flashed the news nerve to nerve. Stiff in an instant. Touch. A waxworks petal laid out pillowed in sensitive frizz: wake up. Liquor. Evil dulling stuff. Lazes the blood, saps muscle tone. He turned over, bunched the pillow, lay flat and straight, trying to align himself with an invisible grain, the grain of the world, fate. Relax. Picture the party.

Twisting. Bald Freddy Thorne with a glinting moist smirk put on the record. Chubby. *Huooff: cummawn naioh evvribuddi less* Twist! Therapy, to make them look awful. They were growing old and awful in each other's homes. Only Carol had it of the women, the points of her pelvis making tidy figure eights, hands aloof like gentle knives, weight switching foot to foot, a silent clicking, stocking feet, narrow, hungry, her scrawny kind of high-school beauty, more his social level, the motion, coolly neat, feet forgotten, eyelids elegantly all but shuttered, making a presumed mist of Frank Appleby bouncing opposite, no logic in his hips, teeth outcurved braying, gums bared, brown breath, unpleasant spray. Everybody twisted. Little-Smith's black snickering feet. Georgene's chin set determinedly as if on second serve. Angela, too soft, rather swayed. Gallagher a jerking marionette. John Ong watched sober, silent, smiling, smoking. Turning to Piet he made high friendly noises that seemed in the din all vowels; Piet knew the Korean was worth more than them all together in a jiggling jouncing bunch but he could never understand what he said: *Who never to himself has said.* Bernadette came up, broad flat lady in two dimensions, half-Japanese, the other half Catholic, from Baltimore, and asked Piet, *Twist?* In the crowded shaking room, the Applebys' children's playroom, muraled in pink ducks, Bernadette kept bumping him, whacking him with her silken flatnesses, crucifix hopping in the shallow space between her breasts, thighs, wrists, bumping him, the yellow peril. *Whoofwheeieu. Wow.* Better a foxtrot. Making fools of themselves, working off steam, it's getting too suburban in here. The windows had been painted shut. Walls of books.

Piet felt, brave small Dutch boy, a danger hanging tidal above his friends, in this town where he had been taken in because Angela had been a Hamilton. The men had stopped having careers and the women had stopped having babies. Liquor and love were left. Bea Guerin, as they danced to Connie Francis, her drunken limpness dragging on his side so his leg and neck ached, her steamy breasts smearing his shirt, seemed to have asked why he didn't want to fuck her. He wasn't sure she had said it, it sounded like something in Dutch, *fokker, in de fuik lopen,* drifting to him from his parents as they talked between themselves in the back room of the greenhouse. Little Piet, Amerikander, couldn't understand. But he loved being there with them, in the overheated warmth, watching his father's broad stained thumbs packing moss, his mother's pallid needling fingers wrapping pots in foil and stabbing in the green price spindles. Once more with the eyes of a child Piet saw the spools of paper ribbon, the boxes holding colored grits and pebbles for the tiny potted tableaux of

cactuses and violets and china houses and animal figurines with
spots of reflection on their noses, the drawerful of stacked gift
cards saying in raised silver HANEMA, his name, himself, restraining constellated in its letters all his fate, *me, a man, amen ah.*
Beside the backroom office where Mama did up pots and Papa
paid his bills were the icy dewy doors where cut roses and
carnations being dyed and lovely iris and gladioli leaned, refriger-
ated, dead. Piet tensed and changed position and erased the greenhouse with the party.

The new couple. They looked precious to themselves, self-
cherished, like gladioli. Cambridge transplants, tall and choice.
Newcomers annoyed Piet. Soil here not that rich, crowding.
Ted? Ken. Quick grin yet a sullen languor, a less than ironical
interest in being right. Something in science, not mathematics like
Ong or miniaturization like Saltz. Biochemistry. Papa had distrusted inorganic fertilizer, trucked chicken dung from poultry
farms: *this is my own, my native land.* She was called oddly Foxy,
a maiden name? Fairfox, Virginia? A southern flavor to her. Tall,
oak and honey hair, a constant blush like windburn or fever. She
seemed internally distressed and had spent two long intervals in
the bathroom upstairs. Descending the second time she had revealed her stocking-tops to Piet, reclining acrobatically below.
Tawny ashy rims in an upward bell of shadow. She had seen him
peek and stared him down. Such amber eyes. Eyes the brown of
brushed fur backed by gold.

Bea. What did you say? I must be deaf.

Sweet Piet, you heard. I must be very drunk. Forgive me.

You're dancing divinely.

*Don't poke fun. I know I can't matter to you, you have
Georgene, and I can't compare. She's marvelous. She plays such
marvelous tennis.*

That's very flattering. You really think I'm seeing Georgene?

It's all right, singingly, gazing into a blurred distance, *don't
bother to deny it, but Piet—Piet?*

Yes? I'm here. You haven't changed partners.

*You poke fun of me. That's mean, that's not worthy of you,
Piet. Piet?*

Hello again.

I'd be kind to you. And someday you're going to need some-body to be kind to you because—now don't get cross—you're surrounded by unkind people.

For instance who? Poor Angela?

You're cross. I feel it in your body you're cross.

No, he said, and stood apart from her, so her dragging was no longer upon his body, and she sagged, then pulled herself erect, blinking, injured, as he went on, *it happens every time I try to be nice to a drunk. I wind up getting insulted.*

Oh!—it was a breathless cry as if she had been struck. *And I meant to be so kind.*

Whitewash wore away after two or three rains, but after the war the chemical companies came up with a compound that lasted pretty well until winter. In winter there could not be too much light. The Michigan snows piled in strata around the glass walls and within the greenhouse there was a lullaby sound of dripping and a rasping purring in the pipes rusted to the color of dirt as they snaked along the dirt floor flecked with tiny clover. A child cried out in her sleep. As if being strangled in a dream. From the voice he guessed it had been Nancy. She, who could tie her shoes at the age of three, had lately, now five, begun to suck her thumb and talk about dying. *I will never grow up and I will never ever in my whole life die.* Ruth, her sister, nine last November, hated to hear her. *Yes you will die everybody will die including trees.* Piet wondered if he should go to Nancy's room but the cry was not repeated. Into the vacuum of his listening flowed a rhythmic squeaking insistent as breathing. A needle working in the night. For her birthday he had given Ruth a hamster; the little animal, sack-shaped and russet, slept all day and ran in its exercise wheel all night. Piet vowed to oil the wheel but mean-while tried to time his breathing with its beat. Too fast; his heart raced, seemed to bulge like a knapsack as into it was abruptly stuffed two thoughts that in the perspective of the night loomed as dreadful: soon he must begin building ranch houses on Indian Hill, and Angela wanted no more children. He would never have a son. *Eek, ik, eeik, ik, eeek.* Relax. Tomorrow is Sunday.

A truck passed on the road and his ears followed it, focused on its vanishing point. As a child he had soothed himself with the sensation of things passing in the night, automobiles and trains, their furry growling sounds approaching and holding fast on a momentary plateau and then receding, leaving him ignored and untouched, passing on to Chicago or Detroit, Kalamazoo or Battle Creek or the other way to the snow, stitched with animal tracks, of the northern peninsula that only boats could reach. A bridge had since been built. He had pictured himself as Superman, with a chest of steel the flanged wheels of the engines could not dent, passing over him. The retreating whistles of those flatland trains had seemed drawn with a pencil sharpened so fine that in reality it broke. No such thing in nature as a point, or a perfect circle, or infinitude, or a hereafter. The truck had vanished. But must be, must. Must. Is somewhere.

Traffic this late in this corner of New England, between Plymouth and Quincy, between Nun's Bay and Lacetown, was sparse, and he waited a long stretch for the next truck to come lull him. Angela stirred, sluggishly avoiding some obstacle to the onflow of her sleep, a dream wanting to be born, and he remembered the last time they had made love, over a week ago, in another season, winter. Though he had skated patiently waiting for her skin to quicken from beneath she had finally despaired of having a climax and asked him simply to take her and be done. Released, she had turned away, and in looping his arm around her chest his fingers brushed an unexpected sad solidity.

Angel, your nipples are hard.

So?

You're excited and could have come too.

I don't think so. It just means I'm chilly.

Let me make you come. With my mouth.

No. I'm all wet down there.

But it's me, it's my wetness.

I want to go to sleep.

But it's so sad, that you liked my making love to you after all.

I don't see that it's that sad. We'll all be here another night.

He lay on his back like a town suspended from a steeple. He felt delicate on his face a draft from somewhere in his snug house,

a loose storm window, a tear in the attic foil, a murderer easing
open a door. He rolled over on his stomach and the greenhouse
washed over him. The tables like great wooden trays, the flowers
budding and blooming and dropping their petals and not being
bought. As a child he had mourned the unbought flowers, be-
seeching the even gray greenhouse light with their hopeful corol-
las and tepid perfume. He surveyed the party for a woman to
bring home and picked Bea Guerin. *Dear Bea, of course I want
to fuck you, how could I not, with your steamy little body so
tired and small and kind. Just about all lilies, aren't you? Now
spread your legs. Easy does it. Ah.* The moisture and light within
the greenhouse had been so constant and strong that even weeds
grew; even when bright snow was heaped against the glass walls
like a sliced cross section in a school book, clover from nowhere
flourished around the legs of the tables and by the rusty pipes,
and the dirt floor bore a mossy patina and was steeped in an odor
incomparably quiet and settled and profound. He saw them, his
father and mother, *vader en moeder,* moving gently in this receding polyhedral heart of light carved from dank nature, their
bodies transparent, and his mind came to a cliff—a slip, then a
skidding downward plunge. Left fist clenched upon himself, he
groped in his mind for the party, but it was no longer there.

God help me, help me, get me out of this. *Eek ik, eeik ik.* Dear
God put me to sleep. Amen.

A golden rooster turned high above Tarbox. The Congregational Church, a Greek temple with a cupola and spire, shared a
ledgy rise, once common pasturage, with a baseball backstop and
a cast-iron band pavilion used only on Memorial Day, when it
sheltered shouted prayers, and in the Christmas season, when it
became a crêche. Three edifices had succeeded the first meeting-
house, a thatched fort, and the last, renovated in 1896 and 1939,
lifted well over one hundred feet into the air a gilded weathercock that had been salvaged from the previous church and thus
dated from colonial times. Its eye was a copper English penny.
Deposed once each generation by hurricanes, lightning, or re-

pairs, it was always, much bent and welded, restored. It turned in the wind and flashed in the sun and served as a landmark to fishermen in Massachusetts Bay. Children in the town grew up with the sense that the bird was God. That is, if God were physically present in Tarbox, it was in the form of this unreachable weathercock visible from everywhere. And if its penny could see, it saw everything, spread below it like a living map. The central square mile of Tarbox contained a hosiery mill converted to the manufacture of plastic toys, three dozen stores, several acres of parking lot, and hundreds of small-yarded homes. The homes were mixed: the surviving seventeenth-century salt-boxes the original Kimballs and Sewells and Tarboxes and Cogswells had set along the wobbly pasture lanes, quaintly named for the virtues, that radiated from the green; the peeling Federalist cubes with widow's-walks; the gingerbread mansions attesting to the decades of textile prosperity; the tight brick alleys plotted to house the millworkers imported from Poland; the middle-class pre-Depression domiciles with stubby porches and narrow chimneys and composition sidings the colors of mustard and parsley and graphite and wine; the new developments like even pastel teeth eating the woods of faraway Indian Hill. Beyond, there was a veiny weave of roads, an arrowing disused railroad track, a river whose water was fresh above the yellow waterfall at the factory and saline below it, a golf course studded with bean-shapes of sand, some stubborn farms and checkerboard orchards, a glinting dairy barn on the Nun's Bay Road, a field containing slowly moving specks that were galloping horses, level breadths of salt marsh broken by islands and inlets, and, its curved horizon marred, on days as clear as today, by the violet smudge that was the tip of Cape Cod, the eastward sea. Casting the penny of its gaze straight down, the cock could have observed, in dizzying perspective, the dotlike heads of church-goers congregating and, hurrying up the gray path, the red head of Piet Hanema, a latecomer.

The interior of the church was white. Alabaster effects had been skillfully mimicked in wood. Graceful round vaults culminated in a hung plaster ceiling. A balcony with Doric fluting vertically scoring the parapet jutted as if weightless along the sides of the sanctuary and from under the painted Victorian organ in the rear. The joinery of the old box pews was still admirable. Piet seldom entered the church without reflecting that the carpenters who had built it were dead and that none of their quality had been born to replace them. He took his accustomed place in a left back pew, and latched the paneled door, and was alone with a frayed grape-colored pew cushion—a fund drive to replace these worn-out cushions had only half succeeded—and a pair of powder-blue Pilgrim hymnals and a hideous walnut communion-glass rack screwed to the old pine in obedience to a bequest. Piet always sat alone. His friends did not go to church. He adjusted the cushion and selected the less tattered of the two hymnals. The organist, a mauve-haired spinster from Lacetown, rummaged through a Bach prelude. The first hymn was number 195: "All Hail the Power." Piet stood and sang. His voice, timid and off-key, now and then touched his own ears. ". . . on this terrestrial ball . . . let angels prostrate fall . . . and crown him, Lorhord of all . . ." On command, Piet sat and prayed. Prayer was an unsteady state of mind for him. When it worked, he seemed, for intermittent moments, to be in the farthest corner of a deep burrow, a small endearing hairy animal curled up as if to hibernate. In this condition he felt close to a massive warm secret, like the heart of lava at the earth's core. His existence for a second seemed to evade decay. But church was too exciting, too full of light and music, for prayer to take place, and his mind slid from the words being intoned, and skimmed across several pieces of property that concerned him, and grazed the faces and limbs of women he knew, and darted from the image of his daughters to the memory of his parents, so unjustly and continuingly dead.

They had died together, his mother within minutes and his father at the hospital three hours later, in a highway accident the week before the Christmas of 1949, at dusk. They had been driving home to Grand Rapids from a Grange meeting. There was an almost straight stretch of Route 21 that was often icy. The river flowed near it. It had begun to snow. A Lincoln skidded head-on into them; the driver, a boy from Ionia, survived with lacerations. From the position of the automobiles it was not clear who had skidded, but Piet, who knew how his father drove, as ploddingly as he potted geraniums, one mile after the other, did not doubt that it had been the boy's fault. And yet—the dusk was confusing, his father was aging; perhaps, in an instant without perspective on that deceptive flat land, at the apparition of on-rushing headlights, the wheels for a moment slithering, the old man had panicked. Could there have been, in that placid good gardener, with his even false teeth and heavy step and pallid stubby lashes, a fatal reserve of unreason that had burst forth and destroyed two blameless lives? All those accumulated budgets, and hoarded hopes, and seeds patiently brought to fruition? Piet pictured shattered glass strewn across the road and saw snow continue to descend, sparkling in the policemen's whirling lights. He had been a sophomore at Michigan State, studying toward an architect's certificate, and felt unable to continue, on borrowed money and the world's sufferance. There was a shuddering in his head he could not eliminate. He let his brother Johan—Joop—cheaply buy his share of the greenhouses and let himself be drafted. Since this accident, the world wore a slippery surface for Piet; he stood on the skin of things in the posture of a man testing newly formed ice, his head cocked for the warning crack, his spine curved to make himself light.

". . . and we lift our hearts in petition for those who have died, who in the ripening of time have pierced the beyond . . ." Piet bent his thought toward the hope of his parents' immortality, saw them dim and small among clouds, in their workaday greenhouse clothes, and realized that if they were preserved it was as strangers to him, blind to him, more than an ocean removed from the earthly concerns of which he had—infant, child, boy, and beginning man—been but one. *Kijk, daar is je vader. Pas op, Piet, die hond bijt. Naa kum, it makes colder out. Be polite, and don't go with girls you'd be ashamed to marry.* From the odd fact of their deaths his praying mind flicked to the odd certainty of his own, which the white well-joined wood and the lucent tall window beside him airily seemed to deny.

Piet had been raised in a sterner church, the Dutch Reformed, amid varnished oak and dour stained glass where shepherds were paralyzed in webs of lead. He had joined this sister church, a milder daughter of Calvin, as a compromise with Angela, who believed nothing. Piet wondered what barred him from the ranks of those many blessed who believed nothing. Courage, he supposed. His nerve had cracked when his parents died. To break with a faith requires a moment of courage, and courage is a kind of margin within us, and after his parents' swift death Piet had no margin. He lived tight against his skin, and his flattish face wore a look of tension. Also, his European sense of order insisted that he place his children in Christendom. Now his daughter Ruth, with his own flat alert face and her mother's stately unconscious body, sang in the children's choir. At the sight of her submissively moving her lips his blood shouted *Lord* and his death leaned above him like a perfectly clear plate of glass.

The children's choir's singing, an unsteady theft of melody while the organ went on tiptoe, ceased. In silence the ushers continued their collection of rustles and coughs. Attendance was high today, Palm Sunday. Piet held his face forward, smiling, so that his daughter would see him when, as he foresaw, she searched the congregation. She saw him and smiled, blushed and studied her robed knees. Whereas with Nancy his manhood had the power to frighten, with Ruth it could merely embarrass. The ushers marched up the scarlet carpet, out of step. Crossing a bridge. Vibration. The minister extended his angel-wing arms wide to receive them. The golden plates were stacked. The hymn: "We Are Climbing Jacob's Ladder." Amid Yankees trying to sing like slaves, Piet nearly wept, knowing the Dutch Reformed would never have stooped to this Christian attempt. "Sinner, do you love your Jesus?" Abolitionism. Children of light. "Every rung goes higher, higher . . ." Two of the four ushers sidled into the pew in front of Piet and one of them had satyr's ears, the holes tamped with wiry hair. The back of his neck crisscrossed, pock-marked by time. Minutes. Meteors. Bombarding us. The sermon commenced.

Reverend Horace Pedrick was a skeletal ignorant man of sixty.

His delusions centered about money. He had never himself had enough. A poor boy from a Maine fishing family, he had entered the ministry after two business bankruptcies brought about by his extreme caution and fear of poverty. Too timid and old to acquire a city church, worn out with five-year-stints in skimping New England towns, he imagined his flock to be composed of "practical men," businessmen whose operations had the scope and harshness of natural processes. In the pulpit, his white hair standing erect as the water on it dried, he held himself braced against imagined mockery, and his sermons, with contortions that now and then bent his body double, sought to transpose the desiccated forms of Christianity into financial terms. "The man Jesus"—one of his favorite phrases—"the man Jesus does not ask us to play a long shot. He does not come to us and say, 'Here is a stock fo speculation. Buy at eight-and-one-eighth, and in the Prom' Land you can sell at one hundred.' No, he offers us *t security*, four-and-a-half per cent compounded every Now I realize I am speaking to hard-headed men, *t* whose decisions are far-ranging in the unsentimer yond this sanctuary . . ."

Piet wondered if the hair sprouting from *t'* him were trimmed. A cut-bush look: an el He fingered his own nostrils and the through him; he fought a sneeze. H*e* cross and wondered if Freddy Tho* Jesus was crucified on an X-shape* falsify because of the immod* groin. Not much made of H*i* all? Not likely, Arab boy* sodomy, part of natur in Africa right in th* how fucking clear lucent air vault* feared Fredd* him yet had p*i* hostage, spread X-* head with cross-etche*

under Piet's gaze rotated and the ear orifice became a round
brown eye. In Pedrick's sermon the palms spread across Jesus's
path had become greenbacks and the theft of the colt a troubled
disquisition on property rights. Pedrick struggled and was not
reconciled. How blithe was God, how carefree: this unexpected
implication encouraged Piet to live. "And so, gentlemen, there *is*
something above money, believe it or not: a power which treats
wealth lightly, which accepts an expensive bottle of ointment and
scorns the cost, which dares to overturn the counting tables of
respectable bankers and businessmen like yourselves. May we be
granted today the light to welcome this power with hosannahs
into our hearts. Amen."

They sang "Lift Up Your Heads, Ye Mighty Gates" and sat for
prayer. Prayer and masturbation had so long been mingled in
Piet's habits that in hearing the benediction he pictured his mistress naked, a reflected sun pooled between her breasts, her prim
chin set, her slightly bulging green eyes gazing, cleared. Erotic
warmth infused Piet's greetings as he edged down the aisle,
through a china-shop clutter of nodding old ladies, into the nar-
thex redolent of damp paper, past Pedrick's clinging horny hand-
shake, into the open.

At the door Piet was given a palm frond by a combed child in
rduroy shorts.

Waiting for his daughter to emerge, he leaned by a warm white
r, the frond in his left hand, a Lark in the right. Outside the
uary, the day was surpassingly sentimental: a thin scent of
nd sap, lacy shadows, leafless trees, the clapboarded houses
the rocky green basking chalkily. The metal pavilion,
green, sharpened the gay look of a stage set. The sky
ue, layer on layer. Overhead, held motionless against the
feet tucked up like parallel staples, a gull hung outlined
that thickened at the wingtips. Each pebble, tuft,
d erosion gully in the mud by the church porch had
its precise noon shadow. Piet had been raised to
but in a decade he had grown to love this land.
vantage. Gallagher liked to say they didn't sell
views. As he gazed downhill toward the business

district, whose apex was formed where Divinity Street met Charity Street at Cogswell's Drug Store and made a right-angled turn up the hill, Piet's vision was touched by a piece of white that by some unconscious chime compelled focus. Who? He knew he knew. The figure, moving with averted veiled head, moved with a bride's floating stiffness. The color white was strange this early in the year, when nothing had budded but the silver maples. Perhaps like Piet she came from a part of the country where spring arrives earlier. She carried a black hymnal in a long glove and the pink of her face was high in tone, as if she were blushing. He knew. The new woman. Whitman. Evidently she was an Episcopalian. St. Stephen's Episcopal Church, unsteepled fieldstone, sat lower down the hill. Walking swiftly, Mrs. Whitman walked to a black MG parked at the foot of the green, far from her church. Perhaps like Piet she habitually came late. A subtle scorn. Thinking herself unseen, she entered her car with violent grace, hitching her skirt and sinking backwards into the seat and slamming the door in one motion. The punky sound of the slam carried to Piet a moment after the vivid sight. The distant motor revved. The MG's weight surged onto its outside tires and she rounded the island of rocks downhill from the green and headed out of town toward her house on the marshes. The women Piet knew mostly drove station wagons. Angela drove a Peugeot. He tipped back his head to view again the zenith. The motionless gull was gone. The blue fire above, layer on layer of swallowed starlight, was halved by a dissolving jet trail. He closed his eyes and imagined sap rising in blurred deltas about him. A wash of ashes. A chalky warmth. A nice bridal taste. Shyly, fearing to wake him, his elder daughter's touch came into the palm of his hanging hand, the hand holding the frond welcoming Jesus to Jerusalem.

After what seemed to Foxy far too long a cocktail time, while the men discussed their stocks and their skiing and the new proposal to revive the dead train service by means of a town contract with the MBTA, and Ken who drove to B.U. in his MG sat looking fastidious and bored, with an ankle on his knee, pondering the intricacies of his shoelaces as if a code could be construed there, Bea Guerin as hostess hesitantly invited them to dinner: "Dinner. Please come. Bring your drinks if you like, but there's wine." The Guerins lived in an old saltbox on Prudence Street, the timbers and main fireplace dating at least from 1680. The house had been so expensively and minutely restored it had for Foxy the apprehensive rawness of a new home; Foxy empathized with childless couples who conspire to baby the furniture.

Rising and setting down their drinks, the company moved to the dining room through a low varnished hallway where on a mock cobbler's bench their coats and hats huddled like a heap of the uninvited. It was Foxy's impression that this set of couples—the Guerins, the Applebys, the Smiths, whom everybody called the little-Smiths, and the Thornes—comprised the "nicer" half of the little society that was seeking to enclose her and Ken. To put herself at ease she had drunk far too much. Under the mechanical urging of her inflexibly frowning host she had accepted two martinis and then, with such stupid false girlishness, a third; feeling a squirm of nausea, she had gone to the kitchen seeking a dilution of vermouth and had whispered her secret to her hostess, a drunken girlish thing to do that would have outraged Ken, yet the kind of thing she felt was desired of her in this company. In a breathy rush Bea Guerin had said, laying a quick tremulous hand on Foxy's forearm, *How wonderful of you.* Though up to this moment Bea had seemed vulnerable to Foxy, defensively whimsical and tipsy, wearing a slightly too naked red velvet Empire dress with a floppy bow below the bosom that Foxy would have immediately snipped, she became now the distinctly older woman, expertly slapping the martini down the sink, retaining the lemon peel with a finger, replacing the gin with dry vermouth. *Don't even pretend to drink if you don't want to. The oven is funny, we had it put in a fireplace and the wind down the chimney keeps blowing out the pilot light, that's why the lamb isn't doing and everything is so late.* It appealed to Foxy that Bea, though Roger was so rich his money was a kind of joke to the others, so rich he apparently barely pretended to work and went in to Boston mostly to have lunch and play squash, was her own cook, and so indifferent at it. Janet Appleby had told her that one of the things they and their friends *loved* about Tarbox was that there were no country clubs or servants; it's so *much* more luxurious to live *simply*. Bea opened the oven door and gingerly peeked in and shut it in a kind of playful fright. The flesh of her upper arm bore a purplish oval blue that might have been a bruise. When she laughed an endearing gap showed between her front teeth. *My dear, you're wonderful, I'm so envious. So envious.* Now the touch of her hand was wet, from handling the drink. Foxy left the kitchen feeling still unsettled.

April was her second month of pregnancy and she had hoped the primordial queasiness would ebb. It offended her, these sensations of demur and rebuke from within. She had long wanted to be pregnant and, having resented her husband's prudent postponement, his endless education, now wondered, at the age of twenty-eight, if the body of a younger woman would have felt less strain. She had imagined it would be like a flower's unresisted swelling, a crocus pushing through snow.

Candlelight rendered unsteady a long table covered by an embroidered cloth. Foxy held herself at attention; her stomach had lifted as if she were in flight above this steaming miniature city of china and goblets and silver flickering with orange points. Namecards in a neat round hand had been arranged. Roger Guerin seated her with a faintly excessive firmness and precision. She wanted to be handled driftingly and felt instead that a long time ago, in an incident that was admittedly not her fault but for which she was nevertheless held to account, she had offended Roger and made his touch hostile. The cloud of the consommé's warmth enveloped her face and revived her poise. In the liquid a slice of lemon lay at fetal peace. Foxy waited instinctively for grace. Instead there was the tacit refusal that has evolved, a brief bump of silence they all held their breaths through. Then Bea's serene spoon tapped into the soup, the spell was broken, dinner began.

Roger on her right asked Foxy, "Your new house, the Robinson place. Are you happy in it?" Swarthy, his fingernails long and buffed, her host seemed older than his age; his dark knitting eyebrows made constant demands upon the rest of his face. His mouth was the smallest man's mouth she had ever seen, a snail's foot of a mouth.

She answered, "Quite. It's been primitive, and probably very good for us."

The man on her left, the bald dentist Thorne, said, "Primitive? Explain what you mean."

The soup was good, clear yet strong, with a garnish of parsley and a distant horizon of sherry: she wanted to enjoy it, it was lately so rare that she enjoyed food. She said, "I mean primitive. It's an old summer house. It's cold. We've bought some electric heaters for our bedroom and the kitchen but all they really do is roast your ankles. You should see us hop around in the morning; it's like a folk dance. I'm so glad we have no children at this point." The table had fallen silent, listening. She had said more than she had intended. Blushing, she bent her face to the shallow amber depths where the lemon slice like an embryo swayed.

"I understand," Freddy Thorne persisted, "the word 'primitive.' I meant explain why you thought it was good for you."

"Oh, I think any hardship is good for the character. Don't you?"

"Define 'character.' "

"Define 'define.' " She had construed his Socratic nagging as a ploy, a method he had developed with women, to lead them out. After each utterance, there was a fishy inward motion of his lips as if to demonstrate how to take the bait. No teeth showed in his mouth. It waited, a fraction open, for her to come into it. As a mouth, it was neither male nor female, and not quite infantile. His nose was insignificant. His eyes were lost behind concave spectacle lenses that brimmed with tremulous candlelight. His hair once might have been brown, or sandy, but had become a colorless fuzz, an encircling shadow, above his ears; like all bald heads his had a shine that seemed boastful. So repulsive, Freddy assumed the easy intrusiveness of a very attractive man.

Overhearing her rebuff, the man across the table, Smith, said, "Give it to him, girl," adding as if to clarify: "*Le donnez-lui.*" It was evidently a habit, a linguistic tic.

Roger Guerin broke in. Foxy sensed his desire, in this presuming group, to administer a minimal code of manners. He asked her, "Have you hired a contractor yet?"

"No. The only one we know at all is the man who's the partner of the man who sold us the place. Pi-et . . . ?"

"Piet Hanema," the Smith woman called from beyond Freddy Thorne, leaning forward so she could be seen. She was a petite tense brunette with a severe central parting and mobile earrings whose flicker communicated across her face. "Rhymes with sweet."

"With indiscreet," Freddy Thorne said.

Foxy asked, "You all know him?"

The entire table fully laughed.

"He's the biggest neurotic in town," Freddy Thorne explained. "He's an orphan because of a car accident ten years or so ago and he goes around pinching everybody's fanny because he's still arrested. For God's sake, don't hire him. He'll take forever and charge you a fortune. Or rather his shyster partner Gallagher will."

"Freddy," said his wife, who sat across from Foxy. She was a healthy-looking short woman with a firm freckled chin and narrow Donatello nose.

"Freddy, I don't think you're being quite fair," Frank Appleby called from the end of the table, beyond Marcia little-Smith. His large teeth and gums were bared when he talked, and there was a salival spray that sparkled in candlelight. His head was florid and his eyes often bloodshot. He had big well-shaped hands. Foxy liked him, reading an intended kindness into his jokes. "I thought at the last town meeting that the fire chief was voted the most neurotic. If you had another candidate you should have spoken up." Frank explained to Foxy, "His name is Buzz Kappiotis and he's one of these local Greeks whose uncles own the town. His wife runs the Supreme Laundry and she's pretty supreme herself, she's even fatter than Janet." His wife stuck out her tongue at him. "He has a pathological fear of exceeding the speed limit and screams whenever the ladder truck goes around a corner."

Harold little-Smith, whose uptilted nose showed a shiny double inquisitive tip, said, "Also he's afraid of heights, heat, water, and dogs *L'eau et les chiens.*"

Appleby continued, "The only way you can get your house insured in this town is to give Liberty Mutual even odds."

Little-Smith added, "Whenever the alarm goes off, the kids in town all rush to the spot with marshmallows and popcorn."

Roger Guerin said to Foxy, "It is true, the rates in town are the highest in Plymouth County. But we have so many old wooden houses."

"Yours is beautifully restored," Foxy told him.

"We find it inhibiting as far as furniture goes. Actually, Piet Hanema was the contractor."

Seated between Ken and little-Smith, Janet Appleby, a powdered plump vexed face with charcoal lids and valentine lips, cried, "And that alarm!" Leaning toward Foxy in explanation, she dipped the tops of her breasts creamily into the light. "You can't hear it down on the marsh, but we live just across the river and it's the absolutely worst noise I ever heard anything civic make. The children in town call it the Dying Cow."

"We've become slaves to auctions," Roger Guerin was continuing. From the square shape of his head Foxy guessed he was Swiss rather than French in ancestry.

Her side was nudged and Freddy Thorne told her, "Roger thinks auctions are like Monopoly games. All over New Hampshire and Rhode Island they know him as the Mad Bidder from Tarbox. Highboys, lowboys, bus boys. He's crazy for commodes."

"Freddy exaggerates," Roger said.

"He's very discriminating," Bea called from her end of the table.

"That's not what I'm told they call it," Harold little-Smith was saying to Janet.

"What are you told, dear?" Janet responded.

Harold dipped his fingers into his water goblet and flicked them at her face; three or four drops, each holding a spark of reflection, appeared on her naked shoulders. *"Femme méchante,"* he said.

Frank Appleby intervened, telling Ken and Foxy, "The phrase the children use when the alarm goes would translate into decent language as, 'The Deity is releasing gas.'"

Marcia said, "The children bring home scandalous jokes from school. The other day Jonathan came and told me, 'Mother, the governor has two cities in Massachusetts named after him. One is Peabody. What's the other?' "

"Marblehead," Janet said. "Frankie thought that was the funniest thing he'd ever heard."

Bea Guerin and the silent wife of Freddy Thorne rose and took the soup plates away. Foxy had only half-finished. Mrs. Thorne politely hesitated. Foxy rested her spoon and put her hands in her lap. The soup vanished. Oh thank you. Circling the table, Bea said singingly, "My favorite townsperson is the old lady with the *National Geographics.*"

Little-Smith, aware that Ken had not spoken a word, turned to him politely; fierily illuminated, the tip of his nose suggested something diabolical, a cleft foot. "Did Frank tell me you were a geographer, or was it geologist?"

"Biochemist," Ken said.

"He should meet Ben Saltz," Janet said.

"The fate worse than death," Freddy said, "if you don't mind my being anti-Semitic."

Foxy asked the candlelit air, *"National Geographics?"*

"She has them all," the little-Smith woman said, leaning not toward Foxy but toward Ken across the table. From Foxy's angle she was in profile, her lower lip saucily retracted and her earring twittering beside her jaw like a tiny machine. Ken abruptly laughed. His laugh was a boy's, sudden and high and disproportionate. In private with her, he rarely laughed.

Encouraged, the others went on. The old lady was the very last of the actual Tarboxes, and she lived in one or two rooms of a big Victorian shell on Divinity Street toward the fire station, crammed in among the shops, diagonally across from the post office and Freddy's office, and her father, who had owned the hosiery mill that now makes plastic ducks for bath tubs, and teething rings, had been a charter subscriber. They were neatly stacked along the walls, twelve issues every year, since 1888.

"The town engineer," Frank Appleby pronounced, "calculates that with the arrival of the issue of November 1984, she will be crushed to death."

"Like a character in Poe," little-Smith said, and determinedly addressed his wife. "Marcia, which? *Not* 'The Pit and the Pendulum.' "

"Harold, you're confused by 'The House of Usher,' " she told him.

"*Non, non,* tu *es confuse,*" he said, and Foxy felt that but for the table between them they would have clawed each other. "There *is* a story, of walls squeezing in."

Janet said, "It happens on television all the time," and went on in general, "What *can* we do about our children watching? Frankie's becoming an absolute zombie."

Frank Appleby said, "It's called 'The Day the Walls Squeezed In.' As told to Jim Bishop."

Ken added, "By I. M. Flat, a survivor in two dimensions," and laughed so hard a candle flame wavered.

Marcia said, "Speaking of television, you know what I just read? By the year 1990 they're going to have one in every room, so everybody can be watched. The article said"—she faltered, then swiftly proceeded—"nobody could commit adultery." An angel passed overhead.

"My God," Frank said. "They'll undermine the institution of marriage."

The laughter, Foxy supposed, was cathartic.

Freddy Thorne murmured to her, "Your husband is quite witty. He's not such a stick as I thought. I. M. Flat in two dimensions. I like it."

Harold little-Smith was not amused. He turned the conversation outward, saying, "Say. Wasn't that a shocker about the *Thresher?*"

"What shocked you about it?" Freddy asked, with that slippery thrusting undertone. So it wasn't just women he used it on.

"I think it's shocking," little-Smith iterated, "that in so-called peacetime we send a hundred young men to be crushed at the bottom of the sea."

Freddy said, "They enlisted. We've all been through it, Harry boy. We took our chances honeymooning with Uncle, and so did they. *Che sarà sarà,* as Dodo Day so shrewdly puts it."

Janet asked Harold, "Why 'so-called'?"

Harold snapped, "We'll be at war with China in five years. We're at war with her now. Kennedy'll up the stakes in Laos just enough to keep the economy humming. What we need in Laos is another Diem."

Janet said, "Harold, that's reactionary shit. I get enough of that from Frank."

Roger Guerin said to Foxy, "Don't take them too seriously. There's nothing romantic or eccentric about Tarbox. The Puritans tried to make it a port but they got silted in. Like everything in New England, it's passé, only more so."

"Roger," Janet protested, "that's a rotten thing for you to be telling this child, what with our lovely churches and old houses and marshes and absolutely grand beach. I think we're the prettiest unself*con*scious town in America." She did not acknowledge that, as she was speaking, Harold little-Smith was blotting, with the tip of his index finger, each of the water drops he had flicked onto her shoulders.

Frank Appleby bellowed, "Do you two want a towel?"

A leg of lamb and a bowl of vegetables were brought in. The host stood and carved. His hands with their long polished nails could have posed for a cookbook diagram: the opening wedge, the lateral cut along the lurking bone, the vertical slices precise as petals, two to a plate. The plates were passed the length of the table to Bea, who added spring peas and baby potatoes and mint jelly. Plain country fare, Foxy thought; she and Ken had lived six years in Cambridge, a region of complicated casseroles and Hungarian goulashes and garlicky salads and mock duck and sautéed sweetbreads. Among these less sophisticated eaters Foxy felt she could be, herself, a delicacy, a princess. Frank Appleby was given two bottles to uncork, local-liquor-store Bordeaux, and went around the table twice, pouring once for the ladies, and then for the men. In Cambridge the Chianti was passed from hand to hand without ceremony.

Freddy Thorne proposed a toast. "For our gallant boys in the *Thresher.*"

"Freddy, that ghoulish!" Marcia little-Smith cried.

"Freddy, really," Janet said.

Freddy shrugged and said, "It came from the heart. Take it or leave it. *Mea culpa, mea culpa.*"

Foxy saw that he was used to rejection; he savored it, as if a dark diagnosis had been confirmed. Further she sensed that his being despised served as a unifying purpose for the others, gave them a common identity, as the couples that tolerated Freddy Thorne. Foxy glanced curiously at Thorne's wife. Sensing Foxy's perusal, she glanced up. Her eyes were a startling pale green, slightly protruding, drilled with pupils like the eyes of Roman portrait busts. Foxy thought she must be made of something very hard, not to show a scar from her marriage.

"Freddy, I don't think you meant it at all," Janet went on, "not at all. You're delighted it was them and not you."

"You bet. You too. We're all survivors. A dwindling band of survivors. I took my chances. I did my time for God and Uncle."

"You sat at a steel desk reading Japanese pornography," Harold told him.

Freddy looked astonished, his shapeless mouth inbent. "Didn't everybody? We've all heard often enough about you and your geishas. Poor little underfed girls, for a pack of cigarettes and half of a Hershey bar."

His wife's bottle-green eyes gazed at the man as if he belonged to someone else.

"You wonder what they think," Freddy went on, swimming, trying not to drown in their contempt, his black mouth lifted. "The goddam gauges start spinning, the fucking pipes begin to break, and—what? Mother? The flag? Jesu Cristo? The last piece of ass you had?"

A contemptuous silence welled from the men.

"What I found so touching," Bea Guerin haltingly sang, "was the way the tender—is that what it is?—"

"Submarine tender, yes," her husband said.

"—the way the tender was called *Skylark*. And how all morning it called and circled, in the sea that from underneath must look like a sky, circling and calling, and nobody answered. Poor *Skylark*."

Frank Appleby stood. "Too much of water hast thou, poor Ophelia. I propose a toast, to the new couple, the Whitmans."

"Hear," Roger Guerin said, scowling.

"May you long support our tax rolls, whose rate is high and whose benefits are nil."

"Hear, hear." It was little-Smith. "*Écoutez.*"

"Thank you," Foxy said, blushing and feeling a fresh wave of rebuke rising within her. She quickly put down her fork. The lamb was underdone.

Little-Smith tried again with Ken. "What do you do, as a biochemist?"

"I do different things. I think about photosynthesis. I used to slice up starfish extremely thin, to study their metabolism."

Janet Appleby leaned forward again, tipping the creamy tops of her breasts into the warm light, and asked, "And then do they survive, in two dimensions?" Through a lucid curling wave of nausea Foxy saw that her husband was being flirted with.

Ken laughed eagerly. "No, they die. That's the trouble with my field. Life hates being analyzed."

Bea asked, "Is the chemistry very complex?"

"Very. Incredibly. If a clever theologian ever got hold of how complex it is, they'd make us all believe in God again."

Ousted by Bea, Janet turned to them all. "Speaking of that," she said, "what does this old Pope John keep bothering us about? He acts as if we all voted him in."

"I like him," Harold said. "*Je l'adore.*"

Marcia told him, "But you like Khrushchev too."

"I like old men. They can be wonderful bastards because they have nothing to lose. The only people who can be themselves are babies and old bastards."

"Well," Janet said, "I tried to read this *Pacem in Terris* and it's as dull as something from the UN."

"Hey Roger," Freddy called across Foxy, his breath meaty, "how do you like the way U Whosie has bopped Tshombe in the Congo? Takes a nigger to beat a nigger."

"I think it's *lovely*," Bea said emphatically to Ken, touching his sleeve, "that it's so complex. I don't want to be understood."

Ken said, "Luckily, the processes are pretty much the same throughout the kingdom of life. A piece of yeast and you, for example, break down glucose into pyruvic acid by exactly the same eight transformations." This was an aspect of him that Foxy rarely saw any more, the young man who could say "the kingdom of life." Who did he think was king?

Bea said, "Oh dear. Some days I *do* feel moldy."

Freddy persisted, though Roger's tiny mouth had tightened in response. "The trouble with Hammarskjöld," he said, "he was too much like you and me, Roger. Nice guys."

Marcia little-Smith called to her husband, "Darling, who isn't letting you be a wonderful old bastard? Terrible me?"

"Actually, Hass," Frank Appleby said, "I see you as our local Bertrand Russell."

"I put him more as a Schweitzer type," Freddy Thorne said.

"You bastards, I mean it." The tip of his nose lifted under persecution like the flowery nose of a mole. "Look at Kennedy. There's somebody inside that robot trying to get out, but it doesn't dare because he's too young. He'd be crucified."

Janet Appleby said, "*Let's* talk news. We always talk people. I've been reading the newspaper while Frank reads Shakespeare. *Why* is Egypt merging with those other Arabs? Don't they know they have Israel in between? It's as bad as us and Alaska."

"I love you, Janet," Bea called, across Ken. "You think like I do."

"Those countries aren't countries," Harold said. "They're just branches of Standard Oil. *L'huile étendarde.*"

"Tell us some more Shakespeare, Frank," Freddy said.

"We have laughed," Frank said, "to see the sails conceive, and grow big-bellied with the wanton wind. *Midsummer Night's Dream.* Isn't that a grand image? I've been holding it in my mind for days. Grow big-bellied with the wanton wind." He stood and poured more wine around. Foxy put her hand over the mouth of her glass.

Freddy Thorne leaned close to her and said, "You don't have much of an appetite. Tummy trouble?"

"Seriously," Roger Guerin said on her other side, "I'd have no hesitation about calling Hanema and at least getting an estimate. He does very solid work. He's one of the few contractors left, for instance, who puts up honest plaster walls. And his job for us, though it took forever, was really very loving. Restoration is probably his forte."

Bea added, "He's a dear little old-fashioned kind of man."

"You'll be so-orry," Freddy Thorne said.

Frank Appleby called, "And you can get him to build a dike for you so Ken can farm the marsh. There's a fortune to be made in salt hay. It's used to mulch artichokes."

Foxy turned to her tormentor. "Why don't you like him?" She had abruptly remembered who Hanema was. At Frank's party, a short red-haired man clownishly lying at the foot of the stairs had looked up her dress.

"I *do* like him," Freddy Thorne told her. "I love him. I love him like a brother."

"And he you," little-Smith said quickly.

Thorne said, "To tell the truth, I feel homosexually attracted to him."

"Freddy," Thorne's wife said in a level voice hardly intended to be heard.

"He has a lovely wife," Roger said.

"She *is* lovely," Bea Guerin called. "So serene. I envy the wonderful way she *moves*. Don't you, Georgene?"

"Angela's really a robot," Frank Appleby said, "with Jack Kennedy inside her, trying to get out."

"I don't know," Georgene Thorne said, "that she's so perfect. I don't think she gives Piet very much."

"She gives him social aplomb," Harold said.

Freddy said, "I bet she even gives him a bang now and then. She's human. Hell, everybody's human. That's my theory."

Foxy asked him, "What does he do neurotic?"

"You heard Roger describe the way he builds. He's anally neat. Also, he goes to church."

"But *I* go to church. I wouldn't be without it."

"Frank," Freddy called, "I think I've found the fourth." Foxy guessed he meant that she was the fourth most neurotic person in town, behind the fire chief, the Dutch contractor, and the lady doomed to be crushed by magazines.

Foxy came from Maryland and partook of the aggressiveness of southern women. "You *must* tell me what you mean by 'neurotic.' "

Thorne smiled. His sickly mouth by candlelight invited her to come in. "You haven't told me what you mean by 'character.' "

"Perhaps," Foxy said, scornfully bright, "we mean the same thing." She disliked this man, she had never in her memory met a man she disliked more, and she tried to elicit, from the confusion within her body, a clear expression of this.

He leaned against her and whispered, "Eat some of Bea's lamb, just to be polite, even if it is raw." Then he turned from her, as if snubbing a petitioner, and lit Marcia's cigarette. As he did so, his thigh deliberately slid against Foxy's. She was startled, amused, disgusted. This fool imagined he had made a conquest. She felt in him, and then dreaded, a desire to intrude upon, to figure in, her fate. His thigh increased its pressure and in the lulling dull light she experienced an escapist craving for sleep. She glanced about for rescue. Her host, his eyebrows knitted tyrannically above the bridge of his nose, was concentrating on carving more lamb. Across the table her husband, the father of her need for sleep, was laughing between Bea Guerin and Janet Appleby. The daggery shadow in the cleft between Janet's lush breasts changed shape as her hands darted in emphasis of unheard sentences. More wine was poured. Foxy nodded, in assent to a question she thought had been asked her, and snapped her head upright in fear of having dropped asleep. Her thigh was nudged again. No one would speak to her. Roger Guerin was murmuring, administering some sort of consolation, to Georgene Thorne. Ken's high hard laugh rang out, and his face, usually so ascetic, looked pasty and unreal, as if struck by a searchlight. He was having a good time; she was hours from bed.

As they drove home, the night revived her. The fresh air was cool and the sky like a great wave collapsing was crested with stars. Their headlights picked up mailboxes, hedgerows, crusts of dry snow in a ditch. Ken's MG swayed with each turn of the winding beach road. He asked her, "Are you dead?"

"I'm all right now. I wasn't sure I could get through it when we were at the table."

"It *was* pretty ghastly."

"They seemed so excited by each other."

"Funny people." As if guilty, he added, "Poor Fox, sitting there yawning with her big belly."

"Was I too stupid? I told Bea."

"For God's sake, why?"

"I wanted a pretend martini. Are you ashamed of my being pregnant?"

"No, but why broadcast it? It'll show soon enough."

"She won't tell anybody."

"It doesn't matter."

How little, Foxy thought, *does matter to you.* The trees by the roadside fell away, and rushed back in clumps, having revealed in the gaps cold stretches of moonlit marsh. The mailboxes grew fewer. Fewer houselights showed. Foxy tightened around her her coat, a fur-lined gabardine cut in imitation of a Russian general's greatcoat. She foresaw their cold home with its flimsy walls and senile furnace. She said, "We *must* get a contractor. Should we ask this man Hanema to give us an estimate?"

"Thorne says he's a fanny-pincher."

"That's called projection."

"Janet told me he almost bought the house himself. His wife apparently wanted the view."

Janet, is it?

Foxy said, "Did you notice the antagonism between Frank and the little-Smith man?"

"Aren't they both in stocks somehow? Maybe they're competing."

"Ken, you're so work-oriented. I felt it had to do with s-e-x."

"With Janet?"

"Well, she was certainly trying to make some point with her bosom."

He giggled. *Stop it,* she thought, *it isn't you.* "Two points," he said.

"I knew you'd say that," she said.

There was a rise in the road, cratered by frost heaves, from which the sea was first visible. She saw that moonlight lived on the water, silver, steady, sliding with the motion of their car, yet holding furious myriad oscillations, like, she supposed, matter itself. Ken worked down there, where the protons swung from molecule to molecule and elements interlocked in long spiral ladders. A glimpse of dunes: bleached bones. The car sank into a dip. There were four such rises and falls between the deserted, boarded-up ice-cream stand and their driveway. They lived near the end of the road, an outpost in winter. Foxy abruptly craved the lightness, the freedom, of summer.

Ken said, "Your friend Thorne had a very low opinion of Hanema."

"He is *not* my friend. He is an odious man and I don't understand why everybody likes him so much."

"He's a dentist. Everybody needs a dentist. Janet told me he wanted to be a psychiatrist but flunked medical school."

"He's awful, all clammy and cozy and I kept feeling he wanted to get his hands inside me. I cut him short and he thought I was making a pass. He played kneesies with me."

"But he sat beside you."

"Sideways kneesies."

"I suppose it can be done."

"I think his poor opinion should be counted as a plus."

Ken said nothing.

Foxy went on, "Roger Guerin said he was a good contractor. He did their house. With their money they could have afforded anybody."

"Let's think about it. I'd rather get somebody nobody knows. I don't want us to get too involved in this little nest out here."

"I thought one of the reasons we moved was so our friendships wouldn't be so much at the mercy of your professional acquaintance."

"Say that again?"

"You know what I said. I didn't have any friends of my own, just chemical wives."

"Fox, that's what we all are. Chemicals." He knew she didn't believe that, why did he say it? When would he let her out of school?

A mailbox rammed by a snowplow leaned vacantly on the moonlight. The box belonged to summer people and would not be righted for months. Foxy wrapped her greatcoat tighter around her and in the same motion wrapped her body, her own self, around the small sour trouble brewing in her womb, this alien life furtively exploiting her own. She felt ugly and used. She said, "You really *liked* those women, didn't you, with their push-me-up bras and their get-me-out-of-this giggles?" The women they had known in Cambridge had tended to be plain Quaker girls placidly wed to rising grinds, or else women armored in a repellent brilliance of their own, untouchable gypsy beauties with fiery views on Cuban sovereignty and German guilt. Foxy sighed as if in resignation. "Well, they say a man gets his first mistress when his wife becomes pregnant."

He looked over at her too surprised to speak, and she realized that he was incapable of betraying her, and marveled at her own disappointment. She puzzled herself; she had never been in their marriage more dependent upon him, or with more cause for gratitude. Yet a chemistry of unrest had arisen within her body, and she resented his separation from it. For she had always felt and felt now in him a fastidious, unlapsing accountability that shirked the guilt she obscurely felt belonged to life; and thus he left her with a double share.

He said at last, "What are you suggesting? We were invited. We went. We might as well enjoy it. I have nothing against mediocre people, provided I don't have to teach them anything."

Ken was thirty-two. They had met when he was a graduate student instructing in Biology 10 and she was a Radcliffe senior in need of a science credit. Since her sophomore year Foxy had been in love with a fine-arts major, a bearish Jewish boy from Detroit. He had since become a sculptor whose large welded assemblages of junk metal were occasionally pictured in magazines. There had been a clangor about him even then, a snuffly explosive air of self-parody, with his wiglike mop of hair, combed straight forward, and a nose so hooked its tip appeared to point at his lower lip. The curves of his face had been compressed around a certain contemptuousness. His tongue could quickly uncoil. *Eat me up, little shiksa, I'm a dirty old man. I sneeze black snot. I pop my piles with a prophylactic toothbrush.* He scorned any sign of fear from her. He taught her to blow. His prick enormous in her mouth, she felt her love of him as a billowing and gentle tearing of veils inside her. Before he took her up she had felt pale, tall, stiff, cold, unusable. His back was hairy and humpily muscular across the shoulder blades and thickly sown, as if by a curse, with moles.

With a tact more crushing than brute forbidding her parents gradually made her love grotesque and untenable. She did not know how they did it: it was as if her parents and Peter communicated through her, without her knowing what was being said, until the *No* came from both sides, and met beneath her ribs. That schoolgirl ache, and all those cigarettes. Her senior year at Radcliffe, it had snowed and snowed; she remembered the twittering of the bicycles pushed on the paths, the song of unbuckled galoshes, the damp scarf around her neck, the fluttering of crystals, meek as thoughts, at the tall serene windows of the Fogg. She remembered the bleached light that had filled her room each morning before she awoke to the soreness in her chest.

Ken appeared, was taller than she, wanted her, was acceptable and was accepted on all sides; similarly, nagging mathematical problems abruptly crack open. Foxy could find no fault with him, and this challenged her, touched off her stubborn defiant streak. She felt between his handsomeness and intelligence a contradiction that might develop into the convoluted humor of her Jew. Ken looked like a rich boy and worked like a poor one. From Farmington, he was the only son of a Hartford lawyer who never lost a case. Foxy came to imagine his birth as cool and painless, without a tear or outcry. Nothing puzzled him. There were unknowns but no mysteries. After her own degrading miscalculation—for this was what her first romance must have been, it ended in such a flurry of misery—Foxy sought shelter in Ken's weatherproof rightness. She accepted gratefully his simple superiority to other people. He was better-looking, better-thinking, a better machine. He was fallible only if he took her, on the basis of the cool poise her tallness had demanded, for another of the same breed.

She was, Elizabeth Fox from Bethesda, known to herself in terms of suppressed warmth. Applaudingly her adolescent heart had watched itself tug toward stray animals, lost children, forsaken heroines, and toward the bandaged wounded perambulating around the newly built hospital, with its ugly tall rows of windows like zipped zippers. They had moved from east Washington in the spring of 1941, as the hospital was being built. Her father was a career navy man, a lieutenant commander with some knowledge of engineering and an exaggerated sense of lineage. One of his grandfathers had been a Virginia soldier; the other, a New Jersey parson. He felt himself to be a gentleman and told Foxy, when she came to him at the age of twelve inspired to be a nurse, that she was too intelligent, that she would someday go to college. At Radcliffe, looking back, she supposed that her sense of deflected tenderness dated from her father's long absences during World War II; the accident of global war had deprived her of the filial transition to heterosexual relationships free of slavishness, of the expiatory humiliations she goaded Peter to inflict. Now, herself married, milder and less mathematical in her self-analyses, she wondered if the sadness, the something broken and uncompleted in her upbringing, was not older than the war and belonged to the Depression, whose shadowy air of magnificent impotence, of trolley cars and sinusitis, still haunted the official mausoleums of Washington when she visited her mother. Perhaps the trouble had merely been that her mother, though shrewd and once pretty, had not been a gentlewoman, but a Maryland grocer's daughter.

Foxy had no sooner married than her parents had gotten divorced. Her father, his thirty years of service expired, far from retiring, took a lucrative advisory job to the shipbuilding industry, and moved to San Diego. Her mother, as if defiantly showing that she too could navigate in the waters of prosperity, remarried: a wealthy Georgetown widower, a Mr. Roth, who owned a chain of coin-operated laundromats, mostly in Negro neighborhoods. Foxy's mother now made herself up carefully, put on a girdle even to go shopping, kept a poodle, smoked red-tipped filtered cigarettes, was known to their friends as "Connie," and always spoke of her husband as "Roth."

The couple Foxy's parents had been had vanished. The narrow shuttered frame house on Rosedale Street. The unused front porch. The tan shades always drawn against the heat. The electric fan in the kitchen swinging its slow head back and forth like an imbecile scolding in monotone. The staticky Philco conveying Lowell Thomas. The V-mail spurting through the thrilled slot. The once-a-week Negro woman, called Gracelyn, whose apron pockets smelled of orange peels and Tootsie Rolls. Veronica their jittery spayed terrier who was succeeded by Merle, a slavering black-tongued Chow. The parched flowerless shrubbery where Elizabeth would grub for bottlecaps and "clues," the long newspaper-colored ice-cream evenings, the red-checked oilcloth on the kitchen table worn bare at two settings, the way her mother would sit nights at this table, after the news, before putting her daughter to bed, smoking a Chesterfield and smoothing with a jerky automatic motion the skin beneath her staring eyes: these images had vanished everywhere but in Foxy's heart. She went to church to salvage something. Episcopalianism—its rolling baritone hymns to the sea, its pews sparkling with the officers' shoulder-braid—had belonged to the gallant club of Daddy's friends, headed by caped Mr. Roosevelt, that fought and won the war.

She was graduated and married in June of 1956.

Every marriage is a hedged bet. Foxy entered hers expecting that, whatever fate held for them, there were certain kinds of abuse it would never occur to her husband to inflict. He was beyond them, as most American men are beyond eye-gouging and evisceration. She had been right. He had proved not so much gentle as too fastidious to be cruel. She had no just complaints: only the unjust one that the delay while she waited barren for Ken to complete his doctorate had been long. Four intended years of post-graduate work had been stretched into five by the agonies of his dissertation; two more were spent in a post-doctoral fellowship granted by the U.S. Public Health Service; and then Ken squandered another as an instructor in the vicinity of the same magnetic Harvard gods, whose very names Foxy had come to hate. For her, there had been jobs, little research assistantships amid Flemish prints or Mesozoic fern fossils in comfortable dusty Harvard basements, a receptionist's desk at University Hall, an involvement in a tutoring project for mentally disturbed children that had led her to consider and then to run from a career in social work, some random graduate courses, a stab at a master's degree, two terms of life-drawing in Boston, vacations, even flirtations: but nothing fruitful. Seven years is long, counted in months paid for with a punctual tax of blood, in weeks whose pleasure is never free of the belittling apparatus of contraception, longer than a war. She had wanted to bear Ken a child, to brew his excellence in her warmth. This seemed the best gift she could offer him, since she grew to know that there was something of herself she withheld. A child, a binding of their chemistries, would be an honest pledge of her admiration and trust and would remove them for good from the plane where the sufficiency of these feelings could be doubted. Now this gift was permitted. Ken was an assistant professor at the university across the river, where the department of biochemistry was more permeable to rapid advancement. Their reasons for happiness were as sweeping as the view from their new house.

The house had been Ken's choice. She had thought they should live closer to Boston, in Lexington perhaps, among people like themselves. Tarbox was an outer limit, an hour's drive, and yet he, who must do the commuting, seized the house as if all his life he had been waiting for a prospect as vacant and pure as these marshes, those bony far dunes, that rim of sea. Perhaps, Foxy guessed, it was a matter of scale: his microscopic work needed the relief of such a vastness. And it had helped that he and the real-estate man Gallagher had liked each other. Though she had raised all the reasonable objections, Foxy had been pleased to see him, after the long tame stasis of student existence, emerge to

want something new, physical, real. That he had within him even
the mild strangeness needed to insist on an out-of-the-way impractical house seemed (as if there had been a question of despair)
hopeful.

The house tonight was cold, stored with stale chill. Cotton,
their cat, padded loudly toward them from the dark living room
and, stiff from sleep, stretched. He was a heavy-footed caramel
tom that in years of being their only pet had acquired something
of a dog's companionableness and something of a baby's conceit.
Courteously he bowed before them, his tail an interrogation
mark, his front claws planted in the braided rag rug the Robinsons had abandoned in the hall. Cotton pulled his claws free with
a dainty unsticking noise and purred in anticipation of Foxy's
picking him up. She held him, his throaty motor running, beneath her chin and like a child wished herself magically inside
his pelt.

Ken switched on a light in the living room. The bare walls
leaped into being, the exposed studs, the intervals of varnish, the
crumbling gypsum wallboard, the framed souvenirs of old summers—fan-shaped shell collections and dried arrays of littoral
botany—that the Robinsons had left. They had never met them
but Foxy saw them as a large sloppy family, full of pranks and
nicknames for each other and hobbies, the mother watercoloring
(her work was tacked all around upstairs), the older boys sailing
in the marsh, the girl moonily collecting records and being teased,
the younger boy and the father systematically combing the shore
for classifiable examples of life. The room smelled as if summer
had been sealed in and yet had leaked out. The French windows
giving onto a side garden of roses and peonies were boarded. The
shutters were locked over the windows that would have looked
onto the porch and the marsh. The sharp-edged Cambridge furniture, half Door Store and half Design Research, looked scattered
and sparse; the room was a good size and of a good square shape.
It had possibilities. It needed white paint and walls and light and
love and style. She said, "We *must* start doing things."

Ken felt the floor register with his hand. "The furnace is dead
again."

"Leave it to morning. No warmth gets upstairs anyway."

"I don't like being outsmarted. I'm going to learn how to bank this bastard."

"I'm more worried about dying in my sleep of coal gas."

"No chance of that in this sieve."

"Ken, please call Hanema."

"You call him."

"You're the man of the house."

"I'm not sure he's the right man."

"You like Gallagher."

"They're not twins, they're partners."

"Then find somebody else."

"If you want him, you call him."

"Well I just might."

"Go ahead. Fine." He went to the door that led down into the narrow hole that did for a basement. The register began to clank and release a poisonous smell. Foxy carried Cotton into the kitchen, plugged in the electric heater, and poured two bowls of milk. One she set on the floor for the cat; the other she broke Saltines into, for herself. Cotton sniffed, disdained the offering, and interrogatively mewed. Foxy ignored him and ate greedily with a soup spoon. Crackers and milk had been a childhood treat between news and bedtime; her craving for it had come over her like a sudden release from fever, a gust of health. While the glow of the heater and the begging friction of fur alternated on her legs, she spread butter thickly on spongy white bread, tearing it, overweighting it, three pieces one after the other, too ravenous to bother with toast, compulsive as a drunk. Her fingertips gleamed with butter.

Washing them, she leaned on her slate sink and gazed from the window. The tide was high; moonlight displayed a silver saturation overflowing the linear grid of ditches. Against the sheen was silhouetted a little houseless island of brambles. In the distance, along the far arm of Tarbox Bay, the lights of another town, whose name she had not yet learned, spangled the horizon. A revolving searchlight rhythmically stroked the plane of ocean. Its beam struck her face at uneven intervals. She counted: five, two, five, two. A double beam. Seconds slipping, gone; five, two. She hastily turned and rolled up the cellophane breadwrapper; a voluminous sadness had been carved for her out of the night. It was after midnight. Today was Easter. She must get up for church.

Ken returned from the furnace and laughed at the traces of her hunger—the gouged butter, the clawed crumbs, the empty bowl.

She said, "Yes, and it's the cheap bread I feel starved for, not Pepperidge Farm. That old-fashioned rubbery kind with all the chemicals."

"Calcium propionate," he said. "Our child will be an agglutinated monster."

"Did you mean it, I should call this Dutchman?"

"Why not? See what he says. He must know the house, if his wife wanted it."

But she heard doubt in his even voice and changed the subject. "You know what bothered me about those people tonight?"

"They were Republicans."

"Don't be silly, I couldn't care less. No what bothered me was they wanted us to love them. They weren't lovable, but that's what they wanted."

He laughed. Why should his laugh grate so? "Maybe that's what *you* wanted," he told her.

They went to bed up a staircase scarred and crayoned by children they had never seen. Foxy assumed that, with the revival of her appetite, she would enjoy a great animal draught of sleep. Ken kissed her shoulder in token of the love they should not in this month make, turned his back, and quickly went still. His breathing was inaudible and he never moved. The stillness of his body established a tension she could not quite sink through, like a needle on the skin of water. Downstairs, Cotton's heavy feet padding back and forth unsatisfied seemed to make the whole house tremble. The moon, so bright it had no face, was framed by the skylight and for an hour of insomnia burned in the center of her forehead like a jewel.

Monday morning: in-and-out. A powdery blue sky the color of a hymnal. Sunshine broken into code by puffs and schooners of cumulus. The Thornes' sunporch—the tarpaper deck-roof of their garage, sheltered from the wind by feathery tall larches, entered by sliding glass doors from the bedroom—cupped warmth. Every year Georgene had the start of a tan before anyone else. Today she looked already freckled, austere and forbidding in her health.

She had spread her plaid blanket in the corner where she had tacked reflecting sheets of aluminum broiling foil to the balustrade. Piet took off his suède apricot windbreaker and sank down. The sun, tepid and breezy to a standing man, burned the skin of his broad face and dyed his retinas red. "Bliss," he said.

She resumed her place on the blanket and her forearm touched his: the touch felt like a fine grade of sandpaper with a little warm sting of friction left. She was in only underwear. He got up on his elbow and kissed her belly, flat and soft and hot, and remembered his mother's ironing board and how she would have him lay his earaches on its comforting heat; he put his ear against Georgene's belly and overheard a secret squirm of digestion. Still attentive to the sun, she fingered his hair and fumblingly measured his shoulders. She said, "You have too many clothes on."

His voice came out plucking and beggarly. "Baby, I don't have time. I should be over on Indian Hill. We're clearing out trees." He listened for the rasp and spurt of his power saws; the hill was a mile away.

"Please stay a minute. Don't come just to tease me."

"I can't make love. I don't tease. I came to say hello and that I missed you all weekend. We weren't at the same parties. The Gallaghers had us over with the Ongs. Very dreary."

"We talked about you at the Guerins Saturday night. It made me feel quite lovesick." She sat up and began to unbutton his shirt. Her lower lip bent in beneath her tongue. Angela made the same mouth doing up snowsuits. All women, so solemn in their small tasks, it tickled him, it moved him in a surge, seeing suddenly the whole world sliding forward on this female unsmilingness about things physical—unbuttoning, ironing, sunbathing, cooking, lovemaking. The world sewn together by such tasks. He let her fumble and kissed the gauzy sideburn, visible only in sun, in front of her ear. Even here a freckle had found itself. Seed. Among thorns. Fallen. She opened the wings of his shirt and tried to push the cloth back from his shoulders, an exertion bringing against him her bra modestly swollen and the tender wishbone blankness above. The angle of her neck seemed meek. He peeled his shirt off, and his undershirt: weightless as water spiders, reflected motes from the aluminum foil skated the white skin and amber hair of his chest.

Piet pulled Georgene into the purple shadow his shoulders cast. Her flesh gentle in her underthings possessed a boyish boniness not like Angela's elusive abundance. Touch Angela, she vanished. Touch Georgene, she was there. This simplicity at times made their love feel incestuous to Piet, a connection too direct. Her forbearance enlarged, he suspected, what was already weak and overextended in him. All love is a betrayal, in that it flatters life. The loveless man is best armed. A jealous God. She opened wide her mouth and drew his tongue into a shapeless wet space; fluttering melted into a forgetful encompassing; he felt lost and pulled back, alarmed. Her lips looked blurred and torn. The green of her eyes was deepened by his shadow. He asked her, "What was said?"

Gazing beyond him, she groped. "The Whitmans were wondering—she's with chi-yuld, by the way—the Whitmans were wondering if you should be the contractor for their house. Frank said you were awful, and Roger said you were great."

"Appleby talked me down? That son of a bitch, what have I done to him? I've never slept with Janet."

"Maybe it was Smitty, I forget. It was just one remark, a joke, really."

Her face was guarded in repose, her chin set and the corners of her mouth downdrawn, with such a studied sadness. The shadows of the larch boughs shuffled across them. He guessed it had been her husband and changed the subject. "That tall cool blonde with the pink face is pregnant?"

"She told Bea in the kitchen. I must say, she did seem rude. Freddy was being a puppy dog for her and she froze over the soup. She's from the South. Aren't those women afraid of being raped?"

"I watched her drive away from church a Sunday ago. She burned rubber. There's something cooking in that lady."

"It's called a fetus." Her chin went firm, crinkled. She added, "I don't think as a couple they'll swing. Freddy thinks *he's* a stick. I sat right across the table from *her*, and I must say, her big brown eyes never stopped moving. She didn't miss a thing. It was insulting. Freddy was being his usual self and I could see her wondering what to make of *me*."

"None of us know what to make of you."

Pretending to be offended yet truly offended, Piet felt, by his interest in the Whitman woman, Georgene drew herself from his arms and stretched out again on the blanket. Giving the sun his turn: whore. The reflecting foil decorated her face with parabolic dabs and nebulae and spurts: solar jism. Piet jealously shucked his shoes and socks and trousers, leaving his underpants, Paisley drawers. He was a secret dandy. He lay down beside her and when she turned to face him reached around and undid her bra, explaining, "Twins," meaning they should both be dressed alike, in only underpants.

Her breasts were smaller than Angela's, with sunken paler nipples, and, uncovered, seemed to cry for protection. He brought his chest against hers for covering and they lay together beneath the whispering trees, Hansel and Gretel abandoned. Shed needles from the larches had collected in streaks and puddles on the tarpaper and formed rusty ochre drifts along the wooden balustrade and the grooved aluminum base of the sliding glass doors. Piet stroke the uninterrupted curve of her back, his thumb tracing her spine from the knucklelike bones at the nape of her neck to the strangely prominent coccyx. Georgene had the good start of a tail. She was more bone than Angela. Her presence pressing against him seemed so natural and sisterly he failed to lift, whereas even Angela's foot on his instep was enough, and he wondered, half-crushed beneath the span of sky and treetops and birdsong, which he truly loved.

Before their affair, he had ignored Georgene. She had been hidden from him by his contempt for her husband. His, and Angela's, dislike of Freddy Thorne had been immediate, though in their first years in Tarbox the Thornes as a couple had rather courted them. The Hanemas in response had been so rude as to refuse several invitations without an excuse or even a reply. They had not felt much in need of friends then. Piet, not yet consciously unhappy with Angela, had dimly dreamed of making love to other women, to Janet or to stately gypsy-haired Terry Gallagher, as one conjures up fantasies to induce sleep. But two summers ago the Ongs built their tennis court and they saw more of Georgene; and when, a summer ago, Piet's dreams without his volition began to transpose themselves into reality, and unbeknownst to himself he had turned from Angela and become an open question, it was Georgene, in a passing touch at a party, in the apparently unplanned sharing of a car to and from tennis, who attempted an answer, who was there. She said she had been waiting for him for years.

"What else?" he asked.

"What else what?" Behind the sunstruck mask of her face her senses had been attending to his hand.

"What else with you? How's Whitney's cold?"

"Poor little Whit. He had a fever yesterday but I sent him off to school in case you decided to come."

"You shouldn't have done that."

"He'll be all right. Everybody has a spring cold."

"You don't."

She carried forward the note of contention. "Piet, what did you mean, a minute ago, when I told you Frank criticized you, you said you had never slept with Janet?"

"I never have. It's been years since I wanted to."

"But do you think—stop your hand for a second, you're beginning just to tickle—that's why Freddy doesn't like you? I lied, you know. It was Freddy who told the Whitmans you were a bad contractor."

"Of course. The jerk."

"You shouldn't hate him."

"It keeps me young."

"But do you think he *does* know, about us? Freddy."

Her curiosity insulted him; he wanted her to dismiss Freddy

utterly. He said, "Not as a fact. But maybe by osmosis? Bea Guerin implied to me the other night that everybody knows."

"Did you admit it?"

"Of course not. What's the matter? *Does* he know?"

Her face was hushed. A thin bit of light lay balanced across one eyelid, trembling; a stir of wind was rippling the sheets of foil, creating excited miniature thunder. She said carefully, "He tells me I must have somebody else because I don't want him as much as I used to. He feels threatened. And if he had to write up a list of who it might be, I guess you'd be at the top. But for some reason he doesn't draw the conclusion. Maybe he knows and thinks he's saving it to use later."

This frightened him, altered the tone of his body. She felt this and opened her eyes; their Coke-bottle green was flecked with wilt. Her pupils in the sun were as small as the core of a pencil.

He asked her, "Is it time to break off?"

When challenged, Georgene, the daughter of a Philadelphia banker, would affect a playful immigrant accent, part shopgirl, part vamp. "Dunt be zilly, fella," she said, and sharply inched upward and pressed her pelvis against his, so that through his cotton he felt her silk. She held him as if captive. Her smooth arms were strong; she could beat him at tennis, for a set. He wrestled against her hold and in the struggle her breasts were freed, swung bulbous above him, then spilled flat when, knees on thighs and hands on wrists, he pinned her on her back. Tarpaper. Her glistening skin gazed. Wounded by winning, he bowed his head and with suppliant lips took a nipple, faintly salt and sour, in. Suddenly she felt to be all circles, circles that could be parted to yield more circles. Birds chirped beyond the rainbow rim of the circular wet tangency holding him secure. Her hand, feathery, established another tangency, located his core. If her touch could be believed, his balls were all velvet, his phallus sheer silver.

Politely he asked, "Do we have on too many clothes?"

The politeness was real. Lacking marriage or any contract, they had evolved between them a code of mutual consideration. Their adultery was divided precisely in half. By daring to mention their breaking up, by rebuking her with this possibility, Piet had asked

Georgene to cross the line. Now it was her turn to ask, and his to cross. She said, "What about those trees on Indian Hill?"

"They can fall without me," he said. The sun was baking a musty cidery smell from the drift of needles near his face, by the blanket's edge. The tarpaper scintillated. Good quality: Ruberoid Rolled Roofing, mineralized, $4.25 a roll in 1960. He had laid this deck. He added, "I'm not sure you can."

"Oh I'm not so fallen," Georgene said, and quickly sat up, and, kneeling, flauntingly stretched her arms to the corners of the sky. She possessed, this conscientious clubwoman and firm mother, a lovely unexpected gift. Her sexuality was guileless. As formed by the first years of her marriage with Freddy, it had the directness of eating, the ease of running. Her insides were innocent. She had never had an affair before and, though Piet did not understand the virtue she felt in him, he doubted that she would ever take another lover. She had no love of guilt. In the beginning, deciding upon adultery with her, Piet had prepared himself for terrible sensations of remorse, as a diver in midair anticipates the under-water rush and roar. Instead, the first time—it was September: apples in the kitchen, children off at school, except for Judy, who was asleep—Georgene led him lightly by one finger upstairs to her bed. They deftly undressed, she him, he her. When he wor-ried about contraception, she laughed. Didn't Angela use Enovid yet? *Welcome*, she said, *to the post-pill paradise*, a lighthearted blasphemy that immensely relieved him. With Angela the act of love had become overlaid with memories of his clumsiness and her failure to tolerate clumsiness, with the need for tact and her irritation with the pleadingness implicit in tact, her equal disdain of his pajama-clad courting and his naked rage, his helpless trans-parence and her opaque disenchantment. Georgene in twenty minutes stripped away these laminations of cross-purpose and showed him something primal. Now she kneeled under the sun and Piet rose to be with her and with extreme care, as if setting the wafery last cogwheels of a watch into place, kissed the glossy point of her left shoulder bone, and then of her right. She was double everywhere but in her mouths. All things double. Without duality, entropy. The universe God's mirror.

She said, "You're in my sun."

"It's too soon to have a tan." Politely: "Would you like to go inside?"

The sliding glass door led off the sun deck through a playroom into their big bedroom, a room adorned with Chinese lanterns and African masks and carved animal horns from several countries. Their house, a gambrel-roof late-Victorian, with gingerbread eaves and brackets, scrolling lightning rods, undulate shingling, zinc spouting, and a roof of rose slates in graduated ranks, was furnished in a style of cheerful bastardy—hulking black Spanish chests, Chippendale highboys veneered in contrasting fruitwoods flaking bit by bit, nondescript slab-and-tube modern, souvenir-shop colonial, Hitchcock chairs with missing rungs, *art nouveau* rockers, Japanese prints, giant corduroy pillows, Philippine carpets woven of rush rosettes. Unbreakable as a brothel, it was a good house for a party. Through his illicit morning visits Piet came to know these rooms in another light, as rooms children lived in and left littered with breakfast crumbs as they fled down the driveway to the school bus, the *Globe* still spread open to the funnies on the floor. Gradually the furniture—the antic lamps, the staring masks—learned to greet him, the sometimes man of the house. Proprietorially he would lie on the Thornes' king-size double bed, his bare toes not touching the footboard, while Georgene had her preparatory shower. Curiously he would finger and skim through Thorne's bedside shelf—Henry Miller in tattered Paris editions, Sigmund Freud in Modern Library, *Our Lady of the Flowers* and *Memoirs of a Woman of Pleasure* fresh from Grove Press, inspirational psychology by the Menningers, a dove-gray handbook on hypnosis, *Psychopathia Sexualis* in textbook format, a delicately tinted and stiff-paged album smuggled from Kyoto, the poems of Sappho as published by Peter Pauper, the unexpurgated Arabian Nights in two boxed volumes, works by Theodor Reik and Wilhelm Reich, various tawdry paperbacks. Then Georgene would come in steaming from the bathroom, a purple towel turbaned around her head.

She surprised him by answering, "Let's make it outdoors for a change."

Piet felt he was still being chastised. "Won't we embarrass God?"

"Haven't you heard, God's a woman? Nothing embarrasses Her." She pulled the elastic of his underpants toward her, eased it down and around. Her gaze became complacent. A cloud passingly blotted the sun. Sensing and fearing a witness, Piet looked upward and was awed as if by something inexplicable by the unperturbed onward motion of the fleet of bluebellied clouds, ships with a single destination. The little eclipsing cloud burned gold in its tendrilous masts and stern. A cannon discharge of iridescence, and it passed. Passed on safely above him. Sun was renewed in bold shafts on the cracked April earth, the sodden autumnal leaves, the new shoots coral in the birches and mustard on the larch boughs, the dropped needles drying, the tarpaper, their discarded clothes. Between the frilled holes her underpants wore a tender honey stain. Between her breasts the sweat was scintillant and salt. He encircled her, fingered and licked her willing slipping tips, the pip within the slit, wisps. Sun and spittle set a cloudy froth on her pubic hair: Piet pictured a kitten learning to drink milk from a saucer. He hurried, seeking her forgiveness, for his love of her, on the verge of discharge, had taken a shadow, had become regretful, foregone. He parted her straight thighs and took her with the simplicity she allowed. A lip of resistance, then an easeful deepness, a slipping by steps. His widening entry slowly startled her eyes. For fear of finding her surrendered face plain, he closed his lids. The whispering of boughs filtered upon them. Distant saws rasped. The breeze teased his squeezing buttocks; he was bothered by hearing birds behind him, Thorne's hired choir, spying.

"Oh, sweet. Oh so sweet," Georgene said. Piet dared peek and saw her rapt lids veined with broken purple and a small saliva bubble welling at one corner of her lips. He suffered a dizzying impression of waste. Though thudding, his heart went mournful. He bit her shoulder, smooth as an orange in sun, and traveled along a muffled parabola whose red warm walls she was and at whose end she also waited. Her face snapped sideways; drenched feathers pulled his tip; oh. So good a girl, to be there for him, no matter how he fumbled, to find her way by herself. In her strange space he leaped, and leaped again. She said, "Oh."

Lavender she lay in his shadow, the corners of her lips flecked. Politely Piet asked her, "Swing?"

"Dollink. Dunt esk."

"I was sort of poor. I'm not used to this outdoor living."

Georgene shrugged under him. Her throat and shoulders were slick. A speck of black construction dust, granular tar from his hair, adhered to her cheek. "You were you. I love you. I love you inside me."

Piet wanted to weep, to drop fat tears onto her deflated breasts. "Did I feel big enough?"

She laughed, displaying perfect teeth, a dentist's wife. "No," she said. "You felt shrimpy." Seeing him ready, in his dilated suspended state, to believe it, she explained solemnly, "You hurt me, you know. I ache afterwards."

"Do I? Do you? How lovely. How lovely of you to say. But you should complain."

"It's in a good cause. Now get off me. Go to Indian Hill."

Discarded beside her, he felt as weak and privileged as a child. Plucking needs agitated his fingers, his mouth. He asked at her side, "What did Freddy say about me that was mean?"

"He said you were expensive and slow."

"Well. I suppose that could be true."

He began dressing. The birds' chirping had become a clock's ticking. Like butter on a bright sill her nakedness was going rancid. She lay as she must often lie, accepting the sun entirely. The bathing-suit boundaries were not distinct on her body, as on Angela's. Her kitten-chin glutinous with jism. The plaid blanket had been rumpled and pulled from under her head, and some larch needles adhered to her hair, black mixed with gray. Because of this young turning of her hair she kept it feather-cut short.

"Baby," he said, to fill up the whispering silence surrounding his dressing, "I don't care about Freddy. I don't want the Whitmans' job. Cut into these old houses you never know what you'll find. Gallagher thinks we've wasted too much time restoring old heaps for our friends and the friends of our friends. He wants three new ranch houses on Indian Hill by fall. The war babies are growing up. That's where the money is."

"Money," she said. "You're beginning to sound like the rest of them."

"Well," he told her. "I can't be a virgin forever. Corruption had to come even to me."

He was dressed. The cool air drew tight around his shoulders and he put on his apricot windbreaker. With the manners that rarely lapsed between them, she escorted him from her house. He admired and yet was slightly scandalized that she could walk so easily, naked, through doors, past her children's toys, her husband's books, down stairs, under a shelf of cleansing agents, into her polished kitchen, to the side door. This side of the house, where the firewood was stacked and a single great elm cast down a gentle net of shade, had about it something rural and mild unlike the barbaric bulk of the house. Here not a brick or stone walk but a path worn through grass, now muddy, led around the corner of the garage, where Piet had hidden his pick-up truck, a dusty olive Chevrolet on whose tailgate a child had written WASH ME. Georgene, barefoot, did not step down from the threshold but leaned silent and smiling in the open doorway, leaving framed in Piet's mind a complex impression: of a domestic animal, of a fucked woman, of a mocking boy, of farewell.

Next Sunday, a little past noon, when Foxy had just returned from church and with a sigh had dropped her veiled hat onto the gate-legged table where the telephone sat, it impudently rang. She knew the voice: Piet Hanema. She had been thinking of calling him all week and therefore was prepared, though they had never really spoken, to recognize his voice, more hesitant and respectful than that of the other local men, with a flattish blurred midwestern intonation. He asked to speak to Ken. She went into the kitchen and deliberately didn't listen, because she wanted to.

All week she had been unable against Ken's silent resistance to call the contractor, and now her hands trembled as if guiltily. She poured herself a glass of dry vermouth. Really, church was getting to be, as the weather grew finer, a sacrifice. Magnolia buds swollen by heat leaned in the space of air revealed by the tilted ventilation pane of commemorative stained glass, birds sang in the little late-Victorian cemetery between the church and the river, the sermon dragged, the pews cracked restlessly. Ken came back from the phone saying, "He asked me to play basketball at two o'clock at his place."

Basketball was the one sport Ken had ever cared about; he had played for Exeter and for his Harvard house, which he had told her as a confession, it had been so unfashionable to do. Foxy said, "How funny."

"Apparently he has a basket on his barn wall, with a little asphalt court. He said in the spring, between skiing and tennis, some of the men like to play. They need me to make six, for three on a side."

"Did you say you would?"

"I thought you wanted to go for a walk on the beach."

"We can do that any time. I could walk by myself."

"Don't be a martyr. What is that, dry vermouth?"

"Yes. I developed a taste for it at the Guerins'."

"And then don't forget we have Ned and Gretchen tonight."

"They won't get here until after eight, you know how arrogant Cambridge people are. Call him back and tell him you'll play, it'll do you good."

Ken confessed, "Well, I left it that I might show up."

Foxy laughed, delighted at having been deceived. "Well if you told him yes why are you being so sneaky about it?"

"I shouldn't leave you here alone all afternoon."

Because you're pregnant, the implication was. His oppressive concern betrayed him. They had gone childless too long; he feared this change and added weight. Foxy made herself light, showed herself gay. "Can't I come along and watch? I thought this was a wives' town."

Foxy was the only wife who came to basketball, and Angela Hanema came out of the house to keep her company. The day was agreeable for being outdoors; nothing in the other woman's manner asked for an apology. The two together carried a bench, a weathered moist settee with a spindle-rung back, from beside the barn to a spot on the gravel driveway where simultaneously they could see the men play, have the sun on their faces, and keep an eye on the many children running and hiding in the big square yard and the lacy screen of budding woods beyond.

Foxy asked, "Whose children are all these?"

"Two are ours, two girls. You can see one of them standing by the birdbath sucking her thumb. That's Nancy."

"Is thumb-sucking bad?" It was a question probably naïve, another mother wouldn't have asked it, but Foxy was curious and felt she could hardly embarrass herself with Angela, who seemed so graceful and serenely humorous.

"It's not aesthetic," she said. "She didn't do it as an infant, it just started last winter. She's worried about death. I don't know where she gets it from. Piet insists on taking them to Sunday school and maybe they talk about it there."

"I suppose they feel they should."

"I suppose. The other children you see—the happy loud ones belong to our neighbors who run the dairy farm and the rest came with their proud daddies."

"I don't know all the daddies. I see Harold—why is it *little-*Smith?"

"It's one of those jokes that nobody knows how to get rid of. There were some other Smiths in town once, but they've long left."

"And that big imposing one is our real-estate man."

"Matt Gallagher. My husband's partner. The bouncy one with red hair is my husband."

Foxy thought, how funny that he is. She said, "He was at the Applebys' party for us."

"We all were. The one with the beard and grinning is Ben Saltz. S-a-l-t-z. I think it's been shortened from something."

"He looks very diabolical," Foxy said.

"Not to me. I think the effect is supposed to be rakish but it comes out Amish. It's to cover up pockmarks; when we first moved to town it was bushier but now he cuts it square. It's misleading, because he's a terribly kind, uxorious man. Irene is the moving spirit behind the League and the Fair Housing group and whatever else does good in town. Ben works in one of those plants along 128 that look as though they make ice cream."

"I thought that was a Chinaman."

"Korean. That's John Ong. He's not here. The only things he plays are chess and very poor tennis. His chess is quite good, though, Freddy Thorne tells me. He's a nuclear physicist who works in MIT. *At* MIT? Actually, I think he works *under* MIT, in a huge underground workshop you need a password to get into."

Foxy asked, "With a cyclotron?"

Angela said, "I forget your husband's a scientist too. I have no idea. Neither he nor Ben can ever talk about their work because it's all for the government. It makes everybody else feel terribly excluded. I think a little tiny switch in something that missed the moon was Ben's idea. He miniaturizes. He once showed us some radios that were like fingernails."

"At the party, I tried to talk to—who, Ong?—you all have such funny names."

"But aren't all names funny until you get used to them? Think of Shakespeare and Churchill. Think of Pillsbury."

"Anyway I tried to talk and couldn't understand a word."

"I know. His consonants are not what you expect. He was some kind of booty in the Korean War; I can't believe he defected, he doesn't seem to have that kind of opinion. He was very big with them I guess; for a while he taught at Johns Hopkins and met Bernadette in Baltimore. If they ever dropped an H-bomb on Tarbox it would be because of him. Like the Watertown arsenal. But you're right. He's not sexy."

Her tone implied a disdain of sex mixed with the equanimous recognition that others might chose to steer by it. Studying the other woman's lips, pale in the sunlight, composed around the premeditation of a smile, Foxy felt as if she, Foxy, were looking up toward a luxurious detached realm where observations and impressions drifted nodding by one another like strolling aristocrats. Every marriage tends to consist of an aristocrat and a peasant. Of a teacher and a learner. Foxy, though by more than an inch the taller, felt beneath Angela, as a student, at once sheltered and challenged. Discovering herself blushing, she hastily asked, "Who's the quick one with the ghostly eyes?"

"I guess they are ghostly. I've always thought of them as steely but that's wrong. His name is Eddie Constantine. He's an airline pilot. They just moved a year or so ago into a grim big house on the green. The tall teen-ager who looks like the Apollo Belvedere is a neighbor's boy he brought along in case there weren't six. Piet didn't know if your husband would come or not."

"Oh. Ken has made the sides uneven?"

"Not at all, they're delighted to have another player. Basketball isn't very popular, you can't do it with women. He's very good. Your husband."

Foxy watched. The neighbor boy, graceful even ill at ease, was standing aside while the six grown men panted and heaved, ducked and dribbled. They looked clumsy, crowded on the little piece of asphalt whose edges fell off into mud softened and stamped by sneaker footprints. Ken and Gallagher were the tallest and she saw Ken, whose movements had a certain nice economy she had not seen displayed for years, lift the ball to the level of his forehead and push it off. It swirled around the rim and flew away, missing. This pleased her: why? He had looked so confident, his whole nicely poised body had expressed the confidence, that it would go in. Constantine seized the rebound and dribbled down low, protecting the ball with an outward elbow. Foxy felt he had been raised in a city. His eyes in their ghostly transparence suggested photographic paper now silver, now black, now clear, depending upon in what they were dipped. His sharp features flushed, little-Smith kept slapping his feet as if to create confusion. He had none of the instinctive moves and Foxy wondered why he played. Saltz, whom she was prepared to adore, moved on the fringes cautiously, stooped and smiling as if to admit he was in a boys' game. His backside was broad and instead of sneakers he wore black laced shoes, such as peek from beneath a priest's robe. As she watched, Hanema, abruptly fierce, stole the ball from

Constantine, braving his elbow, pushed past Ken in a way that must be illegal, hipped and hopped and shot. When the ball went in he jumped for a joke on Gallagher's back. The Irishman, his jaws so wide his face was pentagonal, sheepishly carried his partner on a jog once around the asphalt.

"Discontinuous," Saltz was protesting.

"And you fouled the new guy," Constantine said. "You are an unscrupulous bastard."

Their voices were adolescently shrill. "All right crybabies, I won't play," Hanema said, and waved the waiting boy into his place. "Shall I call Thorne to come and make four on a side?"

Nobody answered; play had already resumed. Hanema draped a sweater around his neck and came and stood above the watching pair of women. Foxy could not study his face, a circular purple shadow against the sun. A male scent, sweat, flowed from him. His grainy courtly voice asked his wife, "Shall I call Thorne or do you want to? He's your friend."

Angela answered, "It's rude to call him this late, he'll wonder why you didn't call him sooner." Her voice, lifted toward the man, sounded diminished to Foxy, frightened.

He said, "You can't be rude to Thorne. If rudeness bothered him he'd have left town long ago. Anyway everybody knows on Sundays he has a five-martini lunch and couldn't have come earlier."

"Call him then," Angela said. "And say hello to Foxy."

"Pardon me. How are *you*, Mrs. Whitman?"

"Well, thank you, Mr. Hanema." She was determined not to be frightened also, and felt that she was not.

Sun rimmed his skull with rainbow filaments. He remained an upright shadow in front of her, emanating heat, but his voice altered, checked by something in hers. "It's very endearing," he said, and repeated, "en*dear*ing of you to come and be an audience. We need an audience." And his sudden explosion of energy, his bumping of Ken, his leap to Gallagher's back, were lit in retrospect by the fact of her watching. He had done it for her to see.

"You *all* seem very energetic," Foxy said. "I'm impressed."

He asked her, "Would you like to play?"

"I think not," she answered, wondering if he knew that she was pregnant, remembering him looking up her skirt, and guessing that he did. He would make it his business to know.

"In that case I better call Thorne," he said, and went into his house.

Angela, her casual manner restored, told Foxy, "Women sometimes do play. Janet and Georgene are actually not too bad. At least they look to me as if they know what they're doing."

Foxy said, "Field hockey is my only game."

"What position did you play? I was center halfback."

"You played? I was right inner, usually. Sometimes wing."

"It's a lovely game," Angela said. "It was the one time in my life when I enjoyed being aggressive. It's what men must have a lot of the time." There was a flow and an authority in the drifting way she spoke that led Foxy to agree, to nod eagerly, as the sun drifted lower into a salmon overcast. Keeping their pale faces lifted to the pale light, they talked, these two, of hockey ("What I liked about halfback," Angela said, "was you were both offensive and defensive and yet nobody could blame you for anything."); of sports in general ("It's so good," Foxy said, "to see Ken playing at anything. I think being with students all the time makes you unnecessarily old. I felt ancient in Cambridge."); of Ken's profession ("He never talks to me about his work any more," Foxy said. "It used to be starfish and that was sort of fun, we went to Woods Hole one summer; but now it's more to do with chlorophyll and all the breakthroughs recently have been in other fields, DNA and whatnot."); of Piet's house ("He likes it," Angela said, "because everything is square. I loved the house you have now. So many things could be done with it, and the way it floats above the marsh! Piet was worried about mosquitoes. Here we have these terrible horseflies from the dairy. He's from inland, you know. I think the sea intimidates him. He likes to skate but isn't much of a swimmer. He thinks the sea is wasteful. I think *I* prefer things to be somewhat formless. Piet likes them finished."); and of the children who now and then emerged from the woods and brought them a wound, a complaint, a gift:

"Why, Franklin, thank you! What do you think it can be?"

"A coughball," the boy said. "From an owl or a hawk." The boy was eight or nine, intelligent but slow to form, and thin-skinned. The coughball lay in Angela's hand, smaller than a golf ball, a tidy dry accretion visibly holding small curved bones.

"It's beautiful in its way," Angela said. "What would you like me to do with it?"

"Keep it for me until they take me home. Don't let Ruthie have it. She says it's hers because it's her woods but I want to start a collection and I saw it *first* even though she did pick it up." Making this long statement brought the child close to tears.

Angela said, "Frankie, go tell Ruth to come see me." He blinked and turned and ran.

Foxy said, "Isn't that Frankie Appleby? But Frank himself isn't here."

"Harold brought him. He's friends with their Jonathan."

"I thought the Smith boy was years older."

"He is, but of course they're thrown together."

Of course?

Three children returned from the woods—four, counting little Nancy Hanema, who hung back near the birdbath and, thumb in mouth, fanned her fingers as if to hide her face from Foxy's gaze.

Ruth was a solid tall round-faced girl. Her body jerked and stamped with indignant energy. "Mother, he says he saw it *first* but he didn't see it at all until *I* picked it up. Then he said it was *his* because he saw it *first.*"

The taller boy, with a clever flickering expression, said, "That's the truth, Mrs. Hanema. Old Franklin Fink here grabs everything."

Young Appleby, without preamble, broke into sobs. "I don't," he said, and would have said more, but his throat stuck shut.

"Boo hoo, Finkie," the Smith boy said.

"Mother," Ruth said, stamping her foot on the gravel to retrieve Angela's attention. "Last *summer* we found a bird's nest and *Frankie* said it was *his* for a *collection* and grabbed it out of my hand and it all came apart and fell into *nothing,* all because of *him!*" She flounced so hard her straight hair fanned in space.

Jonathan little-Smith said, "Lookie, Finkie's crying again. Boo hoo, oh dear, goodness gracious me oh my oh."

With a guttural whimper the younger boy attacked his friend with rotating fists. Jonathan laughed; his arm snaked out and flipped the frantic red face aside; he contemptuously pushed. Angela rose and parted them, and Foxy thought how graceful yet solid she looked, and imagined her as a hockey player standing abstracted yet impenetrable in the center of the limed field, in blue bloomers. Her body in turning showed a trace of the process that makes middle-aged women, with their thickened torsos and thinned legs, appear to be engaged in a balancing act.

"Now Jonathan," Angela said, holding each boy's hand equally, "Frankie wants to start a collection. Do you want to have a collection too?"

"No I don't give a fart about some old bird's throw-up. It's Ruthie he stole from."

"Ruthie is here all the time and I *know* she can find another in the woods. I want you all to help her. There's an owl hoots every night in that woods and if you find his tree I bet you'll find lots more coughballs. You help too, Nancy."

The child had approached closer. "Mouse died," she said, not removing her thumb.

"Yes," Ruth said, wheeling, her hair lifting winglike, "and if you don't watch out this enormous owl will come and eat you and your thumb will be sticking out from an enormous coughball with eyes on it!"

"Ruth!" Angela called, too late. Ruth had run back to the woods, her long legs flinging beneath her flying skirt. The boys, united by need for pursuit, followed. Nancy came to her mother's lap and was absent-mindedly caressed. "You have all this," Angela said to Foxy, "to look forward to."

Her pregnancy, then, was common knowledge. She discovered she didn't mind. She said, "I'll be glad when it's at that stage. I feel horrible half the time, and useless the rest."

"Later," Angela said, "it's splendid. You're so right with the world. Then this little package arrives, and it's utterly dependent, with these very clear sharp needs that you can *sat*isfy! You have everything it wants. I loved having babies. But then you have to raise them." The eyes of the child half lying in her lap listened wide open. Her lips around her thumb made a secret, moist noise.

"You're very good with children," Foxy told her.

"I like to teach," Angela said. "It's easier than learning."

With a splashing sound of gravel, a yellow convertible, top down, came into the driveway and stopped not a yard from their bench. The Thorne man was driving; his pink head poked from the metal shell like the flesh of a mollusc. Standing in the back seat were a sickly-looking boy who resembled him and a younger girl, six or so, whose green eyes slightly bulged. Foxy was jarred by the readiness with which Angela rose to greet them. After an hour of sharing a bench and the sun with her, she was jealous. Angela introduced the children: "Whitney and Martha Thorne, say hello to Mrs. Whitman."

"I know you," the boy told her. "You moved in down the road from us into the spook house." His face was pale and his nostrils and ears seemed inflamed. Possibly he had a fever. His sister was definitely fat. She found herself touched by these children and, lifting her eyes to their father, even by him.

"Is it a spook house?" she asked.

"He means," Angela intervened, "because it stood empty so long. The children can see it from the beach."

"All shuttered up," Whitney said, "with smoke coming out of the chimneys."

"The kid hallucinates," his father said. "He chews peyote for breakfast."

Whitney defended himself. "Iggy Kappiotis said he and some guys snuck up on the porch one time and heard voices inside."

"Just a little innocent teen-age fucking," Freddy Thorne said, squinting at the sallow spring sun. By daylight his amorphous softness was less menacing, more pitiable. He wore a fuzzy claret sports shirt with an acid-green foulard and hightop all-weather boots such as children with weak ankles wear.

"Hey, big Freddy," Harold little-Smith called from the basket-ball court. The thumping and huffing had suspended.

"It's Bob Cousy!" Hanema called from the porch.

"Looks more like Goose Tatum to me," said Gallagher. "You

can always tell by de whites ob dare eyes."

"What whites?" Hanema asked. He hurried over and, taking Thorne by the elbow, announced, "This man is living gin."

"Those are not official sneakers," Ben Saltz protested.

"Those are Frankenstein shoes," Eddie Constantine said. He went mock-rigid and tottered the few steps needed to bump into Thorne's chest. He sniffed Thorne's breath, clutched his own throat, and screamed, "Aagh! The fumes! The fumes!"

Thorne smiled and wiped his mouth. "I'll just watch," he said. "You don't need me, you got plenty of people. Why did you call?"

"We *do* need you," Hanema insisted, handling the man's elbow again and seeming to exult in his relative shortness. "Four on a side. You guard me. You belong to Matt, Eddie, and Ben."

"Thanks a holy arse-licking bunch," Constantine said.

"How many points are you spotting us?" Gallagher asked.

"None," Hanema said. "Freddy will be all right. He's an asset. He's loose. Take a practice shot, Freddy." He slammed the ball off the asphalt into Thorne's stomach. "See how loose he is?"

From the stiff-fingered way Thorne handled the ball Foxy saw he was nothing of an athlete; he was so waddly, so flat-footed, she averted her eyes from the sight.

Beside her, Angela said, "I suppose the house may have been broken into by a few young couples. They have so few places to go."

"What were the people like who owned it before?"

"The Robinsons. We hardly knew them. They only used it summers and weekends. A middle-aged couple with pots of children who suddenly got divorced. I used to see her downtown with binoculars around her neck. Quite a handsome woman with hair in a bun and windburn in tweeds. He was an ugly little man with a huge voice, always threatening to sue the town if they widened the road to the beach. But Bernadette Ong, who knew them, says it was *he* who wanted the divorce. Evidently he played the cello and she the violin and they got into a string quartet with some people from Duxbury. They never did a thing for the house."

Foxy blurted, "Would your husband be willing to look at the house for us? And give us an estimate or some notion as to where to begin?"

Angela gazed toward the woods, a linear maze where children's bodies were concealed. "Matt," she said carefully, "wants Piet to concentrate on building new houses."

"Perhaps he could recommend another contractor then. We must make a beginning. Ken seems to like the house as it is but when winter comes it will be impossible."

"Of course it will." The curtness startled Foxy. Gazing toward the trees, Angela went on hesitatingly, as if her choice of words were distracted by a flowering of things unseen. "Your husband—perhaps he and Piet could talk. Not today after basketball. Everybody stays for beer."

"No, fine. We must hurry back, we have some friends coming from Cambridge."

Thus a gentle rift was established between them. The two faced differently, Angela toward the woods full of children and Foxy toward the men's game. Four on a side was too many. The court, now deep in the shadow of the barn, was crowded and Thorne, with his protrusive rear and confused motions, was in everyone's way. Hanema had the ball. Persistently bumped by Thorne in his attempts to dribble amid a clamor of shouts, he passed the ball on the bounce to the Constantines' neighbor's boy; in the same stride he hooked one foot around Thorne's ankle and by a backwards stab of his weight caused the bigger man to fall down. Thorne fell in stages, thrusting out an arm, then rolling face down on the muddy asphalt, his hand under him.

Play stopped. Foxy and Angela ran to the men. Hanema had kneeled to Thorne. The others made a hushed circle around them. Smearily smiling, his claret shirt muddy, Thorne sat up and showed them a trembling hand whose whitened little finger stuck out askew. "Dislocated," he said in a voice from which pain had squeezed all elasticity.

Hanema, kneeling, blurted, "Jesus Freddy, I'm sorry. This is terrible. Sue me."

"It's happened before," Thorne said. He took the injured hand in his good one and grimaced and pulled. A snap softer than a twig breaking, more like a pod popping, shocked the silent circle. Freddy rose and held his hand, the little finger now aligned, before his chest as something tender and disgraced that must not be touched. He asked Angela, "Do you have surgical tape and anything for a splint—a tongue depressor, a popsicle stick? Even a spoon would do."

Rising with him, Hanema asked, "Freddy, will you be able to work?"

Thorne smirked down at the other's anxious face. He was feeling his edge enlarge, Foxy felt; she thought only women used their own pain as a weapon. "Oh," he said, "after a month or so. I can't go into somebody's mouth wearing a plaster cast, can I?"

"Sue me," Hanema said. His face was a strange stretched mixture of freckles and pallor, of the heat of battle and contrition. The other players had divided equally into two sympathizing rings. Freddy Thorne, holding his hand before him, led Angela and Constantine and the neighbor boy and Saltz into the house, in triumph. Yet Foxy's impression remained that he had been, in the minute before exploitation set in, instinctively stoical.

"You didn't do it on purpose," little-Smith told Hanema. Foxy wondered why he, Thorne's friend, had stayed outdoors, with the guilty. The patterns of union were many.

"But I did," Piet said. "I deliberately tripped the poor jerk. The way he bumps with his belly gets me mad."

Gallagher said, "He doesn't understand the game." Gallagher would have been handsome but for something narrowed about the mouth, something predetermined and closed expressed by the bracketlike creases emphasizing the corners: prim tucks. Amid the whiskery Sunday chins his jaws were smooth-shaved; he had been to mass.

She said, "I think you're all awfully rough with each other."

"C'est la guerre," little-Smith told her.

Ken, in the lull, was practicing shots, perfecting himself. Foxy felt herself submerged in shadows and cross-currents while he was on high, willfully ignorant, hollow and afloat. His dribbling and the quivering rattle of the rim irritated her like any monologue.

Hanema was beside her. Surprisingly, he said, "I hate being a shit and that's how it keeps turning out. I beg him to come play and then I cripple him."

It was part confession, part brag. Foxy was troubled that he would bring her this, as if laying his head in her lap. She shied, speechless, angered that, having felt from an unexpected angle his rumored force, his orphan's needful openness, she had proved timid, like Angela.

The gravel driveway splashed again. An old maroon coupe pulled in, its windshield aswarm with reflected branches and patches of cloud. Janet Appleby got out on the driver's side. She carried two sixpacks of beer. Georgene Thorne pushed from the other door holding in her arms a child of a cumbersome age, so wadded with clothes its legs were spread like the stalks of an H. By the scorched redness of its cheeks the child was an Appleby.

Little-Smith and Hanema quickly went to greet them. Gallagher joined Ken at shooting baskets. Not wishing to eavesdrop, yet believing her sex entitled her to join the women, Foxy walked slowly down the drive to them as little-Smith caperingly described Freddy's unfortunate finger—"*le doigt disloqué.*"

Georgene said, "Well, I've told him not to try sports when he's potted." Her upper lids were pink, as if she had been lying in the sun.

Piet Hanema told her, "But I asked him especially to come, so we could have four on a side." Such a sad broad face, growing old without wisdom, alert and strained.

"Oh, he would have come anyway. You don't think he'd sit around all Sunday afternoon with just *me*."

"Why not?" Piet said, and Foxy imagined hostility in his eyes as he gazed at her. "Don't you want to go inside and see how he is?"

"He's all right," she said. "Isn't Angela with him? Let them alone. He's happy."

Janet and Harold were conferring urgently, in whispers. Their conversation seemed logistical, involving schedules and placement of cars and children. When the Appleby infant seized a cat on the lawn and tried to lift it by its hindquarters, as if spilling a bag of candy out, it was little-Smith who went and pried it loose, while

Janet held her face in this idle moment up to the sun. The cat, calico, with a mildewed eye, ran off and hid in the lilac hedge. Foxy asked Hanema, "Is that yours?"

"The cat or the child?" he asked, as if also aware that the child's parentage seemed in flux.

"The calico cat. We have a cat called Cotton."

"*Do* bring Cotton to the next basketball game," Georgene Thorne said. She added, throwing an athletic arm toward the woods, "I can't see the children for the trees," as if this explained the rudeness of her first remark, with its implied indignation at Foxy's being here at all.

Hanema explained, "She belongs to the dairy down the road but the children sometimes feed it. They let the damn thing into the house full of fleas and now I have them."

Freddy Thorne came out of the house. His little finger was bandaged to a green plastic picnic spoon. The pad of his fingertip rested prettily in the bowl and the curve of the handle made a very dainty fit. That Angela had improvised this strengthened Foxy's sense of illicit affection between these two. Freddy was plainly proud.

"Oh Freddy," Janet said, "it's just gorgeous." She was wearing white slacks so snug they had horizontally wrinkled along her pelvis. The nap of her turquoise velour jersey changed tint as it rounded the curve of her breasts; as she moved her front was an electric shimmer of shadow. The neck was cut to reveal a slash of mauve skin. Her lips had been painted to be a valentine but her chalky face needed sleep. Like her son she was thin-skinned and still being formed.

Freddy said, "The kid did it."

Constantine's young neighbor explained, "At camp last summer we had to take First Aid." His voice emerged reedy and shallow from manhood's form: a mouse on a plinth.

Eddie Constantine said, "He comes over to the house and massages Carol's back."

Freddy asked, "Oh. She has a bad back?"

"Only when I've been home too long."

Ken and Gallagher stopped playing and joined the grown-ups.

The sixpacks were broken open and beer cans were passed around. "I *despise* these new tabs," little-Smith said, yanking. "Everybody I know has cut thumbs. It's the new stigmata." Foxy felt him grope for the French for "stigmata."

Janet said, "I can't do it, I'm too weak and hung. Could *you?*" She handed her can to—Ken!

All eyes noticed. Harold little-Smith's nose tipped up and his voice rose nervously. "Freddy Thorne," he taunted. "Spoonfinger. The man with the plastic digit. *Le doigt plastique.*"

"Freddy, honestly, what a nuisance," Georgene said, and Foxy felt hidden in this an attempt to commiserate.

"No kidding," Constantine said, "how will you get in there? Those little crevices between their teeth?" He was frankly curious and his eyes, which Foxy for a moment saw full on, echoed, in the absence of intelligence, aluminum and the gray of wind and the pearly width low in the sky at high altitudes. He had been there, in the metallic vastness above the boiling clouds, and was curious how Freddy would get to where *he* had to go.

"With a laser beam," Thorne said, and the green spoon became a death ray that he pointed, saying *zizz* between his teeth, at Constantine, at Hanema, at herself. "Zizz. Die. Zizz. You're dead."

The people nearest him laughed excessively. They were courtiers, and Freddy was a king, the king of chaos: though struck dead, Foxy refused to laugh. At her back, Georgene and Piet, ignoring Freddy, exchanged words puzzling in their grave simplicity:

"How are you?"

"So-so, dollink."

"You've been on your sunporch."

"Yes."

"How was it? Lovely?"

"Lonely."

Overhearing, Foxy was rapt, as when a child she listened to her parents bumbling and grunting behind a closed door, intimacy giving their common words an exalted magic.

Ben Saltz's voice overenunciated; his moving lips had an air of isolation, as if they were powered by a battery concealed in his beard. He was saying, "All kidding aside, Freddy, they really can do great things now with nontactile dentistry."

"Whoops," Freddy Thorne said, "that lets tactile types like me out," and he slapped the biform seat of Janet's tense white pants. She whirled from cozying with Ken to give Freddy a look less of surprise than of warning, a warning, Foxy felt, that had to do less with the pat than with its being witnessed.

Saltz seized the chance to latch on to Ken. "Tell me, if you can spare a minute, have you felt the effects of laser beams in biochemistry yet? I was reading in the *Globe* the other week where they've had some success with cancer in mice."

"Anybody can do miracles with mice," Ken stated, ruefully staring down at Janet's backside. He was not comfortable, Foxy had noticed years ago, talking to Jews; he had competed unsuccessfully against too many.

"Do me a favor," Saltz went on, "and tell me about DNA. How the blazes, is the way my thinking runs, how the blazes could such a complex structure spontaneously arise out of chaos?"

"Matter isn't chaos," Ken said. "It has laws, legislated by what can't happen."

"I can see," Saltz said, "how out in our western states, say, the Grand Canyon is the best example, how a rock could be carved by erosion into the shape of a cathedral. But if I look inside and see a lot of pews arranged in apple-pie order, in rows, I begin to smell a rat, so to speak."

"Maybe," Ken said, "you put those pews there yourself."

Ben Saltz grinned. "I like that," he said. "I like that answer." His grin was a dazzling throwback, a facial sunburst that turned his eyes into twinkling slits, that seized his whole face like the snarl on the face of a lion in an Assyrian bas-relief. "I like that answer a lot. You mean the Cosmic Unconscious. You know, Yahweh was a volcano god originally. I think it's ridiculous for religious people to be afraid of the majesty and power of the universe."

Angela called from the porch, "Is anybody except me chilly? Please come into the house, anybody."

This signaled some to go and some to stay. Eddie Constantine crushed his beer can double and handed it to Janet Appleby. She placed it above her breast, as if it were a tin corsage. He crossed to his Vespa and, passing close to Foxy, tapped her stomach. "Suck in your gut." Those were his words. The neighbors' boy got on the Vespa behind him, clinging possumlike. Constantine kicked off, and a spray of stones leaped from his rear wheel as he went down the drive and banked into the road beyond the lilac hedge, which was losing transparence to the swelling of buds. The cat raced from the hedge in terror and ran silently across the lawn, elongating. Children were emerging from the darkening woods. Half of them were crying. Really, it was only Frankie Appleby crying. Jonathan Smith and Whitney Thorne had tied him to a tree with his own shoelaces and then couldn't undo the knots so they had to cut them and now he had no shoelaces and it wasn't his *fault*. His feet stumbled and flopped to illustrate and Harold little-Smith ran to him while Janet his mother stood cold, plump and pluming, on the porch gazing to where the sun, a netted orange, hung in the thin woods. Across the lawn came the rosy Hanema girls and a beautiful male child like a Gainsborough in the romantic waning light, curly black hair and a lithe self-solicitous comportment. With a firm dismissing nod Gallagher took this luxurious child by the hand and led him to their car, the gray Mercedes from whose tall clean windows Foxy had first viewed Tarbox. Saltz and the Thornes moved to go in. In the narrow farmhouse doorway the two men, one bearded and one bald, bumped together and Thorne unexpectedly put his arm, the arm with the crippled green-tipped hand, around the Jew and solidly hugged him sideways. Saltz flashed upward his leonine grin and said something to which Thorne replied, "I'm an inde-structible kind of a prick. Let me tell you about dental hypnosis." The pleasant house accepted them. Foxy and Ken moved to go.

"Don't all leave," Angela begged. "Wouldn't you like to have a *real* drink?"

Foxy said, "We must get back," truly sad. She was to experi-ence this sadness many times, this chronic sadness of late Sunday afternoon, when the couples had exhausted their game, basketball or beachgoing or tennis or touch football, and saw an evening weighing upon them, an evening without a game, an evening spent among flickering lamps and cranky children and leftover food and the nagging half-read newspaper with its weary portents and atrocities, an evening when marriages closed in upon themselves like flowers from which the sun is withdrawn, an evening giving like a smeared window on Monday and the long week when they must perform again their impersonations of working men, of stockbrokers and dentists and engineers, of mothers and housekeepers, of adults who are not the world's guests but its hosts.

Janet and Harold were arguing in whispers. Janet whirled and proclaimed, "Sweet, we *can't.* We *must* rescue Marcia and Frank, they're probably *deep* in conversation." She and little-Smith collected their scrambled children and left in her maroon car. As they backed from the driveway, the sinking sun for an instant pierced the windshield and bleached their two faces in sunken detail, like saints under glass.

"Good-bye," Piet Hanema said politely from the porch. Foxy had forgotten him. He seemed so chastened by the finger incident that she called to him, "Cheer up."

Safe in their MG, Ken said, "Zowie, I'm going to be stiff tomorrow."

"But wasn't it fun?"

"It was exercise. Were you terribly bored?"

"No. I *loved* Angela."

"Why?"

"I don't know. She's gracious and careless and above it all at the same time. She doesn't make the *demands* on you the others do."

"She must have been a knockout once."

"But not now? I must say, your painted friend Janet with her hug-my-bottom sailor pants does *not* impress me aesthetically."

"How does she impress you, Fox?"

"She impresses me as less happy than she should be. She was meant to be a jolly fat woman and somehow missed."

"Do you think she's having an affair with Smith?"

Foxy laughed. "Men are so observant. It's so obvious it must be passé. I think she had an affair with Smith some time ago, is having one with Thorne right now, and is sizing you up for the future."

His flattered languid answering laugh annoyed her. "I have a confession," she said.

"You're having an affair with Saltz. God, Jews are ponderous. They *care* so much. The Cosmic Unconscious, Jesus."

"No. But almost as bad. I told Angela we wanted to have her husband look at our house."

His voice withdrew, acquired a judging dispassion. "Did you set a date?"

"No, but I think we should now. You should call. She didn't think he'd be interested anyway."

Ken drove swiftly down the road they already knew by heart, so both leaned a little before the curve was there. "Well," he said after silence, "I hope his basketball isn't a clue as to how he builds houses. He plays a pretty crusty game."

Ruth, standing beside the bed with almost a woman's bulk, was crying and by speaking woke him from a dream in which a tall averted woman in white was waiting for him at the end of a curved corridor. "Daddy, Nancy says the dairy cat got an animal downstairs and the hamster's not in his cage and I'm afraid to look."

Piet remembered the *eek eeik* by which he had learned to lull himself to sleep and slid from the bed with fear lumping in his stomach. Angela sighed moistly but did not stir. The floor and stairs were cold. Nancy, huddled in her pink nightie on the brown living-room sofa in the shadowless early-morning light, removed her thumb from her mouth and told him, "I didn't mean to, I didn't mean to, it was a 'stake!"

His mouth felt crusty. "Mean to what? Where's the animal?"

The child looked at him with eyes so pure and huge a space far bigger than this low-ceilinged room seemed windowed. The furniture itself, surfacing from the unity of darkness, seemed to be sentient, though paralyzed.

He insisted, "Where is the animal you told Ruthie about, Nancy?"

She said, "I didn't mean to," and succumbed to tears; her

smooth face disintegrated like a prodigy of embalming suddenly exposed to air, and Piet was numbed by the force that flowed through the hole her face made in the even gray light.

Ruth said, "Crybaby, crybaby, sit-and-wonder-whybaby," and Nancy plugged her face again with her thumb.

The little animal, sack-shaped, lay belly up in the center of the kitchen linoleum. The dairy cat watched at a distance, both cowardly and righteous, behind the rungs of a kitchen chair. Its quick instinctive work had been nicely done. Though scarcely marked, the hamster was dead. Its body yielded with a sodden resilience to the prodding of Piet's finger; its upper lip was lifted to expose teeth like the teeth of a comb and its eyes, with an incongruous human dignity, were closed. A trace of lashes. The four curled feet. The lumpy bald nose.

Ruth asked, though she was standing in the kitchen doorway and could see for herself, "Is it him?"

"Yes. Sweetie, he's dead."

"I know."

The adventure was easy to imagine. Ruth, feeling that her pet needed more room for running, suspecting cruelty in the endless strenuousness of the wheel, not believing with her growing mind that any creature might have wits too dim to resent such captivity, had improvised around his tiny cage a larger cage of window screens she had found stacked in the attic waiting for summer. She had tied the frames together with string and Piet had never kept his promise to make her a stronger cage. Several times the hamster had nosed his way out and gone exploring in her room. Last night he had made it downstairs, discovering in the moon-soaked darkness undreamed-of continents, forests of furniture legs, vast rugs heaving with oceanic odors; toward morning an innocent giant in a nightgown had admitted a lion with a mildewed eye. The hamster had never been given cause for fear and must have felt none until claws sprang from a sudden heaven fragrant with the just-discovered odors of cat and cow and dew.

Angela came downstairs in her blue bathrobe, and Piet could not convey to her why he found the mishap so desolating, the dim-witted little exploration that had ended with such a thunderclap of death. The kitchen linoleum, the color of grass, felt slick beneath him. The day dawning outside looked stale and fruitless and chill, one more of the many with which New England cheats spring. Angela's concern, after a glance at him and Ruth and the body of the hamster, was for Nancy; she carried her from the living room into the relative brightness of the kitchen. Squeamishly Piet enfolded the russet corpse, disturbingly dense and, the reins of blood slackened, unstable, in a newspaper. Nancy asked to see it.

Piet glanced at Angela for permission and unfolded the newspaper. KENNEDY PRAISES STEEL RESTRAINT. Nancy stared and slowly asked, "Won't he wake up?"

Ruth said, her voice forced through tears, "No stupid he will not wake up because he is dead and dead things do not wake up ever ever ever."

"When will he go to Heaven?"

All three looked to Piet for the answer. He said, "I don't know. Maybe he's up there already, going round and round in a wheel." He imitated the squeaking; Ruth laughed, and it had been her he had meant to amuse. Nancy's anxious curiosity searched out something he had buried in himself and he disliked the child for seeking it. Angela, holding her, seemed part of this same attempt, to uncover and unman him, to expose the shameful secret, the childish belief, from which he drew his manhood.

He asked Nancy roughly, "Did you see it happen?"

Angela said, "Don't, Piet. She doesn't want to think about it."

But she did; Nancy said, staring at the empty floor where it had happened, "Kitty and Hamster played and Hamster wanted to quit and Kitty wouldn't let him."

"Did you know the hamster was downstairs when you let Kitty in?"

Nancy's thumb went back into her mouth.

"I'm sure she didn't," Angela said.

"Let me see him once more," Ruth said, and in disclosing to her the compact body like a stiffening heart Piet saw for himself how the pet had possessed the protruding squarish bottom of the male of its species, a hopeful sexual vanity whose final denial seemed to

Piet a kind of relief. With Ruth he knew now the strange inner drying, a soft scorching, that follows the worst, when it has undeniably come true. She went off to school, walked down the crunching driveway in her yellow Easter coat to await the yellow school bus, with all her tears behind her, under a cloudy sky that promised no rain.

Piet had promised her a new hamster and a better cage. He buried the old hamster in the edge of the woods, near a scattering of scilla, little lillies of a wideawake blue, where the earth was soft and peaty. One shovelful did for the grave; two made it deep. The trees were beginning to leaf and the undergrowth was sketchy, still mixed, its threads of green, with winter-bleached dead stalks delicate as straws, as bird bones. In a motion of the air, the passionless air which passively flows downhill, spring's terror washed over him. He felt the slow thronging of growth as a tangled hurrying toward death. Timid green tips shaped like tiny weaponry thrust against nothing. His father's green fond touch. The ungrateful earth, receptive. The hamster in an hour of cooling had lost weight and shape to the elements. All that had articulated him into a presence worth mourning, the humanoid feet and the groping trembling nose whose curiosity, when Ruth set him out on her blanket, made her whole bed lightly vibrate, had sunk downward toward a vast absence. The body slid nose down into the shoveled hole. Piet covered him with guilty quickness. In the nearly five years they had lived here a small cemetery had accumulated along this edge of woods: injured birds they had vainly nursed, dime-store turtles that had softened and whitened and died, a kitten slammed in a screen door, a chipmunk torn from throat to belly by some inconclusive predator who had left a spark of life to flicker all one long June afternoon. Last autumn, when the robins were migrating, Nancy had found one with a broken back by the barn, groveling on the asphalt basketball court in its desire to fly, to join the others. Lifted sheerly by the beating of its heart, it propelled itself to the middle of the lawn, where the four Hanemas gathered in expectation of seeing it take wing, healed. But the bird was unhinged, as Piet's own father with his shattered chest and spine would have been unhinged had his lungs let him live; and the children, bored by the bird's poor attempt to become a miracle, wandered away. So only Piet, standing helpless as if beside a party guest who refuses to leave, witnessed the final effort, an asymmetric splaying of the dusty wings and a heave that drove the robin's beak straight down into the sweetish weedy shadowy grass. The bird emitted a minute high cry, a point of noise as small as a star, and relaxed. Only Piet had heard this utterance. Only Piet, as now, attended the burial.

Angela came across the lawn to him where he stood with the shovel. She was dressed in an English-appearing suit of salt-and-pepper tweed; today, Tuesday, was her day to be a teaching parent at Nancy's nursery school. "How unfortunate," she said, "that of all of us it had to be Nancy who saw it happen. Now she wants me to take her to Heaven so she can see for herself that there's room for her, and a little wheel. I really do wonder, Piet, if religion doesn't complicate things worse than they'd have to be. She can see that I don't believe it myself."

He stooped beside the shovel and assumed the manner of an old yeoman. "Ah," he said, "thet's all verra well for a fine leddy like yerself, ma'am, but us peasants like need a touch o' holy water to keep off the rheumatism, and th' evil eye."

"I de*test* imitations, whether you do them, or Georgene Thorne. And I detest being put in the position of trying to sell Heaven to my children."

"But Angel, the rest of us think of you as never having left Heaven."

"Stop trying to get at me and sympathize with the child. She thinks of death all the time. She doesn't understand why she has only two grandparents instead of four like the other children."

"You speak as if you had married a man with only one leg."

"I'm just stating, not complaining. Unlike you, I don't blame you for that accident."

"Ah, thank ye kindly, ma'am, and I'll be makin' a better hamster cage today, and get the poor kid a new hamster."

"It's not Ruth," Angela said, "I'm worried about." These were the lines drawn. Angela's heart sought to enshrine the younger child's innocence; Piet loved more the brave corruption of the older, who sang in the choir and who had brusquely pushed across the sill of fear where Nancy stood wide-eyed.

Angela and Nancy went off to nursery school together. Piet drove the pick-up truck into downtown Tarbox and at Spiros Bros. Builders & Lumber Supply bought five yards of galvanized cage mesh, a three-by-four-piece of ¾″ plywood, twenty feet of 2″ pine quality knotless stock, a half pound of 1½″ finishing nails, and the same quantity of the finer gauge of poultry staples. Jerry Spiros, the younger of the two brothers, told Piet about his chest, which since Christmas had harbored a congestion that ten days in Jamaica did not clear up. "Those fucking blacks'd steal," Jerry said, "the watch right off your wrist," and coughed prolongedly.

"Sounds like you've been sniffing glue," Piet told him, and charged the hamster-cage materials to the Gallagher & Hanema account, and threw them into the back of his truck, and slammed shut the tailgate that said WASH ME, and drove to Indian Hill, taking the long way around. He swung by his office to see if Gallagher's gray Mercedes was there. Their office was a shacklike wing, one-story, upon an asphalt-shingled tenement, mostly unoccupied, on Hope Street, a little spur off Charity, a short cut to the railroad depot. Charity, the main business street, met Divinity at right angles, and Divinity carried up the hill, past Cogswell's Drug Store. The church bulked white on the green.

Huge airy thing. Twenty-four panes in each half window, forty-eight in all, often while Pedrick wrestled he counted them, no symbolism since when it was built there weren't that many states in the Union, Arizona, Oklahoma, Indian Territory. The lumber those people had. To burn. Waste? Gives the town a sense of itself. Dismal enough otherwise. On this heavy loveless day everything looked to need a coat of paint. The salt air corrupts. In Michigan barns stayed red for ages.

The green was hourglass-shaped, cut in two by a footpath, the church's section pinched off from the part holding the backstop and basepaths. Swinging left along the green's waist, Piet looked toward the Constantines' side yard hoping to see Carol hanging out wash with upstretched arms and flattened breasts. At Greek dances, leading the line, hair in spit curls, slippered toe pointed out, the neighbors' boy linked to her by a handkerchief, lithe. Lower classes have that litheness. Generations of hunger. Give me your poor. Marcia brittle, Janet fat. Angela drifty and that Whitman gawky, a subtle stiffness, resisting something, air. Eddie's Vespa but no Ford, Carol's car. He home and she shopping. Buying back liniment. *I ache afterwards.* Funeral home driveway held a Cadillac hearse and a preschool child playing with pebbles. Growing up in odor of embalming oil instead of flowers, corpses in the refrigerator, a greenhouse better, learn to love beauty, yet might make some fears seem silly. Death. Hamster. Shattered glass. He eased up on the accelerator.

Forsythia like a dancing yellow fog was out in backyards and along fences and hedges and garages, the same yellow, continuous, dancing yard to yard, trespassing. Forgive us. Piet drove on down Prudence Street past the Guerins'. Nicely restored, six thou, one of their first jobs in Tarbox, Gallagher not so greedy then, Adams and Comeau did all the finish work, nobody under sixty knows how to hang a door. The whole frame had sagged. Dry rot. The uphill house sill buried in damp earth. They had threaded a reinforcing rod eighteen feet long through the summer beam up through a closet to an ironshod A-brace in the attic. Solid but still a touch off true. *Why don't you want to fuck me?* Good question. Loyalty to Georgene, offshoot loyalty, last year's shoot this year's limb, mistress becomes a wife. Sets. Determined set of Georgene's chin. Not always attractive. Coke-bottle eyes, nude like rancid butter, tarpaper grits, Freddy's spies. Piet's thoughts shied from a green plastic spoon.

Downhill a mailman gently sloped away from the pull of his bag. Blue uniform, regular hours, walk miles, muscles firm, live forever. At the corner two dogs were saying hello. Hello. Olleh.

He drove along Musquenomenee Street, along the river, tidal up to the factory waterfall, low at this moment, black salt mud gleaming in wide scummy puddled flats, the origin of life. Across the river were high-crowned streets of elms and homes with oval windows and leaded fanlights built in the tinkling decades of ice wagons. Knickers, mustaches, celluloid collars: nostalgic for when he had never been. Piet saw no one. No one walked now. The silver maples were budding in reddish florets but the elms in tan tassels. Rips in a lilac sky. Nature, this sad grinding fine, seed and weed.

His spirits slightly lifted as he passed the Protestant cemetery, fan-shaped acres expanding from a Puritan wedge of tilted slate stones adorned with winged skulls and circular lichen. Order reigned. Soon cemeteries and golf courses the last greenswards. Thronging hungry hoardes, grain to India. On the golf course he spotted two lonely twosomes. Too early, mud, heavy lies, spikes chew up the green, proprietors greedy for fees, praise restraint, earth itself hungry, he had thrown it a sop. Pet. Pit. He drove through pastel new developments, raw lawns and patchwork façades, and up a muddy set of ruts beside which hydrants and sewer ports were already installed, in obedience to town ordinances, to his site on Indian Hill.

The bulldozer had arrived. This should have pleased him but the machine, a Case Construction King with hydraulic back hoe and front loader, crushed him with its angry weight, its alarming expense. Twenty-five dollars to move it in, twenty-two fifty per hour with the driver, a large coveralled Negro from Mather. Sitting on his jarring throne, he conveyed the impression that the machine's strength was his strength, and that if the gears ceased to mesh he would himself swing down and barehanded tear the stumps from the outraged red earth. By no extension of his imagination could Piet believe that he had helped cause this man and machine to be roaring and churning and chuffing and throttling here, where birds and children used to hide. Yet the Negro hailed him, and his young foreman Leon Jazinski eagerly loped toward him across the gouged mud, and the work was going smoothly. Stumps whose roots were clotted with drying mud and boulders blind for aeons had been heaped into a towering ossuary that must be trucked away. Now the Negro was descending, foot by foot, into the first cellar hole, diagrammed with string and red-tipped stakes. This house would have the best view, overlooking the fan-shaped cemetery toward the town with its pricking steeple and flashing cock. The other two would face more southerly, toward

Lacetown, an indeterminate area of gravel pits and back lots and uneconomic woods strangely intense in color, purple infused with copper; and should bring a thousand or two less. Piet saw the first house, the house where he stood, pine siding stained redwood and floor plan C, seeded terrace lawn linked by five fieldstone steps to the hardtopped driveway of the under-kitchen garage, smart flagstone stoop and three-chime front doorbell, baseboard oil-fired forced-hot-water heating and brick patio in the rear for summer dining and possible sunbathing, aluminum combination all-weather sash and rheostated ceiling fixtures set flush, efficient kitchen in Pearl Mist and Thermopane picture window, as bringing $19,900, or at a knockdown eighteen five if Gallagher panicked, a profit above wages paid even to himself, one-fifty weekly, of three or four, depending on how smoothly he dovetailed the subcontractors, which suddenly didn't seem enough, enough to placate Gallagher, enough to justify this raging and rending close at his back, this rape of a haven precious to ornamental shy creatures who needed no house. Builders burying the world God made. The two-headed tractor, the color of a school bus, trampled, grappled, growled, ramped. Blue belches of smoke flew upward from the hole. The mounted Negro, down to his undershirt, a cannibal king on a dragon dripping oil, grinned and shouted to Piet his pleasure that he had not encountered ledge.

"This is the soft side of the hill," Piet shouted, and was not heard. He felt between himself and the colored man a continental gulf, the chasm between a jungle asking no pity and a pampered rectilinear land coaxed from the sea. The Negro was at home here, in this tumult of hoisted rocks, bucking reversals of direction and shifting gears, clangor and fumes, internal combustion, the land of the free. He was Ham and would inherit. Piet tried to picture the young couple who would live in this visualized home and he did not love them. None of his friends would live in such a home. He stooped and picked a bone from its outline in the earth, where the grid of the dozer's tread had pressed it, and showed it curiously to Jazinski.

"Cow bone," Leon said.

"Doesn't it seem too delicate?"

"Deer?"

"Don't they say there was an Indian burying ground some-where on this south side?"

Jazinski shrugged. "Beats me." Leon was a weedy, hollow-chested young man originally from Nashua, New Hampshire. He was one of the three men that Gallagher & Hanema kept on the payroll all year long. The other two were venerable carpenters, Adams and Comeau, that Piet had inherited from Ed Byrd, an excessively amiable Tarbox contractor who had declared bank-ruptcy in 1957. Piet had himself singled out Jazinski from a doz-en summer laborers two summers ago. Leon had a good eye and a fair head, an eye for the solid angle and the overlooked bind and a sense for the rhythmic mix of bluff and guess whereby a small operator spaces men and equipment and rentals and prom-ises to minimize time, which is money. Gallagher, who discreetly craved the shoddy—vinyl siding versus wood, pressed wallboard panels versus plaster—had intended to lay Jazinski off last winter; Piet had begged him to hold the boy, offering to drop his own salary to one-twenty-five, fearing that something of himself, his younger self, would be lost if they failed to nurture a little longer Leon's uneducated instinct for the solid, the tight, the necessary.

Piet felt that the bone in his hand was human. He asked Leon, "Have you seen any arrowheads turn up? Beads, bits of pot?"

Leon shook his slow slender head. "Just crap," he said. "Mother Earth."

Embarrassed, Piet said, "Well, keep your eyes open. We may be on sacred ground." He let the bone, too small to have been a thigh, perhaps part of an arm, drop. On Leon's face, downcast beneath a blond eave of hair, Piet spied the smudge of a sneer. In his tone that meant business, the warmth withdrawn, Piet asked, "When can we pour? Early next week?"

"Depends." The boy was sulking. "I'm here all by myself, if Adams and Comeau could stop diddling with that garage . . ."

"They're not to be hurried."

"Waterproofing the foundation takes at least a day."

"It has to be done."

"If it wasn't, who'd be the wiser?"

Piet said swiftly, seeing he must pounce now, or the boy would be a cheat forever, "We would. And in a few years when the house settled and the basement leaked everybody would. Let me tell you about houses. Everything outs. Every cheat. Every short cut. I want the foundation damp-proofed, I want polyethylene under the slab, I want lots of gravel under the drain tile as well as over it, I want you to wrap felt around the joints or they'll sure as hell clog. Don't think because you cover something up it isn't there. People have a nose for the rotten and if you're a builder the smell clings. Now let's look at the drawings together."

Leon's avoiding cheek flushed under the discipline. He gazed at the hole growing in the earth and said, "Those old clunkers have been a month on a garage me and two kids could have put up in a week."

Piet's pedagogic spurt was spent. He said wearily, "They're winding up, I'll go over and see if they can't be up here by to-morrow. I'll call for a load of gravel this afternoon and see if we can set up Ready-Mix over in North Mather for next Monday, do the three at once, that'll give you a day each, I'll help myself if we can't squeeze some trade-school kids out of Gallagher." For an hour, using as a table a boulder under the low boughs of a great oak that would overshadow the patio, he and Leon analyzed the blueprints bought by mail from an architectural factory in Chicago. Piet felt the younger mind picking for holes in his, testing, resenting. It grew upon him as they plotted their campaign together that Leon disliked him, had heard enough about his life to consider him a waster, a drinker, an immigrant clown in the town's party crowd, unfaithful to his wife, bored by his business. This appraisal blew coolly on Piet's face as he traced lines and dimensions with his broad thumbnail and penciled in adjustments demanded by this sloping site. Leon nodded, learning, yet did not let up this cool pressure, which seemed part of the truth of these woods, where the young must prey upon the not-so-young, the ambitious upon the preoccupied. Piet was impatient to leave the site.

In parting, he turned for a moment to the Negro, who had retired with a lunch box and thermos bottle to the edge of the

excavation. The sliced sides showed a veined logic of stratifica-
tion. Pages of an unread book. Impacted vegetable lives. Piet asked
him, "Do you ever find Indian graves?"

"You see bones."

"What do you do when you see them?"

"Man, I keep movin'."

Piet laughed, feeling released, forgiven, touched and hugged
by something human arrived from a great distance, imagining behind the casually spoken words a philosophy, a night life.

But the Negro's lips went aloof, as if to say that laughter would
no longer serve as a sop to his race. His shoulder-balls bigger than
soccer balls. His upper lip jeweled with sweat. A faint tarry tigerish smell. Piet, downwind, bowed.

Pardon me, Dr. King.

Piet left the two men in the clearing and drove into town, to
the far end of Temperance Avenue, where Adams and Comeau
were building a garage at the rear of a house lot. Comeau was thin
and Adams was fat, but after years of association they moved as
matched planets, even at opposite corners of the garage revolving,
backs turned, with an unspoken gravitational awareness of the
other. Passing to the toolbox, on a board between sawhorses, they
crossed paths but did not bump. Neither acknowledged Piet. He
stood in the empty rectangle that awaited a track-hung spring-lift
garage door; he inhaled the scent of shaved lumber, the sense of
space secured. Except for the door, the structure seemed complete.
Piet cleared his throat and asked, "When do you gentlemen
think we can call it quits here?"

Adams said, "When it's done."

"And when might that be? I don't see a day's work here, just
the door to come."

"Odds and ends," Comeau told him. He was applying a plane to
the inside of the window sash, though the sash was factory-made.
Adams was screwing in L-shaped shelf brackets between two
studs. Adams smoked a pipe and wore bibbed overalls with as
many pockets as a hardware store has drawers; Comeau's blue
shirts were always freshly laundered and cigarettes had stained his
fingers orange. He added, "Once we finish up, the widow'll have

to manage herself." The property belonged to a young woman whose husband, a soldier, had been killed—knifed—by the German boy friend of his girl friend in Hamburg.

"It ought to be left neat," Adams said.

Piet, inspecting, paused at a detail of the framing. A two-by-four diagonal brace intersected a vertical stud and, though the angle was not an easy one, and this was rough work, the stud had been fitted as precisely as a piece of veneer. Waste. Piet felt as if he had been handed a flower; but had to say, "Leon needs you on the hill to knock together the basement forms."

"Jack be nimble," old Comeau said, shaking out a match. It was their nickname for Jazinski.

"Door isn't come up yet from Mather," Adams said.

Piet said, "I'll call them. If it isn't brought this afternoon, come up to the hill tomorrow morning anyway. This is a beautiful garage for the widow, but at six-fifty an hour enough is enough. She'll have boy friends who can put up shelves for her. I must get back to the hill."

As he walked around the garage to the street, he heard Comeau, who was still planing at the window, say, "Greedy Gally's on his back."

Piet drove home. The square yard and house were welcoming, empty. He carried the wood and wire he had bought into his basement workshop, which he hadn't used all winter. He cut some segments of the 2″ pine but discovered that the warpage of the rolled wire was so strong that a cumbersome system of braces would be needed to hold the sides straight. So he formed in his mind another design, using the warp of the wire as a force, and rooted a parabolic curve of mesh on either side of the plywood with the poultry staples, and then cut an oval of wire to seal the cage shut. But one end had to be a door. He improvised hinges from a coat hanger and fitted sticks for the necessary stiffness. As he worked, his hands shook with excitement, the agitation of creation that since childhood had often spoiled his projects—birdhouses, go-carts, sand castles—in the final trembling touches. The cage, completed, seemed beautiful to him, a transparent hangar shaped by laws discovered within itself, minimal, invented,

Piet's own. He foresaw Ruth's pleased surprise, Angela's grudging admiration, Nancy's delight and her insistence on crawling inside this child-sized shelter. He carried the cage upstairs to the kitchen and, needing to share his joy of accomplishment, dialed the Thornes' number. "Is this the Swedish bakery?" It was their formula, to which she could say No.

Georgene laughed. "Hi, Piet. How *are* you?"

"Miserable."

"Why?"

He told her about the hamster and the dismal work on Indian Hill, but could not specifically locate the cause of his depression, his sense of unconnection among phenomena and of falling. The lack of sun and shadows. Angela's aloofness. The Negro's snub. The slowness of spring to come.

Georgene said, "Poor Piet. My poor little lover."

He said, "Not much of a day for the sunporch, is it?"

"I've been in the house cleaning. I'm having the League Board tonight and Irene frightens me, she's so efficient and worthy."

"How's Freddy's finger?"

"Oh, fine. He took it out of the spoon yesterday."

"I felt crummy about that. I don't see why I should want to hurt him since in a way, without knowing it of course, he lets me have you."

"Is that the way you think of it? I thought *I* let you have me."

"You do, you do. Thank you. But why do I have such a hatred of him?"

"I have no idea." Always, over the telephone, there was the strangeness of their not being able to touch, and the revelation that her firm quick voice could be contentious.

He asked politely, "Could I—would you like me to come visit you for a minute? Just to say hello, we don't have time to make love. I must get back to the hill."

Her pause, in which they could not touch, was most strange. "Piet," she said, "I'd love you to—"

"But?"

"But I wonder if it's wise right this noon. I've had something happen to me."

Pregnant. By whom? There was a mirror above the telephone table and in it he saw himself, a pale taut-faced father, the floor tipped under him.

She went on, hesitating, she who had confided everything to him, her girlish loves, her first sex with Freddy, when they made love now, her periods, her mild momentary yearnings toward other men, everything, "I think I've discovered that Freddy is seeing Janet. I found a letter in the pocket of a suit I was taking to the cleaner's."

"How careless of him. Maybe he wanted you to find it. What did it say?"

"Nothing very much. It said, 'Let's break it off, no more phone calls,' et cetera, which might mean anything. It could mean she's putting on pressure for him to divorce me."

"Why would she want to marry Freddy?" He realized this was tactless and tried to disguise it with another question. "You're sure it's her?"

"Quite. She signed it J and anyway her handwriting is unmistakable, big and fat and spilly. You've seen it on her Christmas cards."

"Well. But sweet, it's been in the air for some time, Freddy and Janet. Does it really shock you?"

"I suppose," Georgene said, "there's something called female pride. But more than that. I'm shocked by the idea of divorce. If it comes to that I don't want him to have anything to throw back at me, for the children to read about in the paper. It wouldn't bother Freddy but it would me."

"So what does this do to us?"

"I suppose nothing, except that we must be very careful."

"How careful is careful?"

"Piet. I'm not going to tell you how much you mean to me. I've said that in ways a woman can't fake. I just don't think I could enjoy you today and I don't want to waste you. Also it's too near noon."

"Have you confronted Freddy with your discovery?" The man in the mirror had begun to squint, as his pang of fear relaxed into cunning.

Georgene, growing franker, said, "I'm too chicken. He'll tell Janet, then she'll know *I* know, and until I have some plan of action I'd rather just *know*."

"I'm touched by how much Freddy means to you."

"Vell, honeybunch, he *is* my husband."

"Sure enough. You picked him, he's all yours. Except I don't see why I must be sacrificed because Freddy is naughty."

"Maybe he is because I am. Because we are. Anyway you sound as though you rather *want* to be sacrificed."

"Tell me when I can see you."

"Oh love, anytime, just not today. I'm not myself."

"Sweet Georgene, forgive me. I'm being very stupid and full of threatened egotism."

"I *love* your egotism. Oh hell. Come on over now if you want, she isn't brought back from nursery school until twelve-thirty."

"No, of course not. I don't want it unless you feel right about it. You feel guilty. You feel you've driven poor old God-fearing monogamous Freddy into the arms of this harlot."

"I *like* Janet. I think she's quite funny and gutsy. I think Frank is impossible and she does quite well considering."

Piet liked Frank; he resisted the urge to quarrel. Every new assertion of Georgene's, as she relaxed into the certainty that he would not come, advanced his anger. "Anyway," he said, "I just heard the noon whistle blow. I don't want Judy coming back from school saying, 'Mommy, what's that lump under the covers? It smells like Nancy's daddy.'" Smells: the woods, the earth, the Negro's skin, the planed pine of the garage, the whiskey on Bea Guerin's breath.

"Piet. Am I putting you off? I do want you."

"I know. Please don't apologize. You've been a lovely mistress."

She ignored his tense. "When I found the note, the first thing I wanted to do was call you and—what? Cry on your shoulder. Crawl into bed beside you. It was Monday night, Freddy was at Lions'. Suddenly I was terrified. I was alone in a big ugly house with a piece of paper in my hand that wouldn't go away."

"Don't be terrified. You're a lovely doubles partner and a fine wife for Freddy. Who else could stand him? If he lost you it would be the worst thing that's happened to him since he flunked medical school." Did she notice his unintended equation of her with dentistry—both practical, clean, simple, both a recourse? By this equation was Angela something difficult that he, Piet, had flunked? "Anyway," he went on, "I don't think either Freddy or Janet have it in them these days to give themselves much to anybody."

She said, "It's so sad. You call to be reassured and end up by reassuring me. Oh my Lord. Bernadette's VW is coming up the drive. Nursery school let out early. Is today a holiday?"

"April twenty-third? The paper said Shakespeare's birthday. He's three hundred and ninety-nine years old."

"Piet. I must run. There's a lot we haven't said. Let's see each other soon."

"Let's," Piet said, and her kiss ticked as he had halfway returned his receiver to the cradle. The man in the mirror was hunched, a shadow ready to spring, sunless daylight filtering into the room behind him. He looked, he thought, young, his crow's feet and the puckering under his eyes smoothed into shadow. A fragment came to him of the first conversation he and Georgene had had as lovers. She had been so gay, so sporting, taking him upstairs to her bed that fresh September day, he could hardly believe he was her first lover. Reflected autumnal brilliance had invaded her house and infused with warmth her exotic furniture of bamboo and straw rosettes and batik and unbleached sailcloth. Gaudy Guatemalan pillows heaped against the kingsized headboard had surprised him. *Here? In Freddy's very bed?*

It's my bed too. Would you rather use the floor?

No, no. It's luxurious. Whose books are all these?

Freddy's pornography, it's disgusting. Please pay attention to me.

I am, Jesus. But . . . shouldn't we do something about not making a little baby?

Sweetie. You're so naieef. You mean Angela doesn't take Enovid yet?

You do? It works?

Of course it works, it's wonderful. Welcome, Georgene said, *to the post-pill paradise.*

Piet remembered, standing alone in his low-ceilinged living

room, where the wallpaper mourned its slanting visitor the sun and the spare neat furniture reflected his and Angela's curiously similar austerity of taste, how Georgene's cheeks, freckled from a summer of sunbathing, had dryly creased as she made this joke. Her manner had been a feathery teasing minimizing his heart's clangor, and always until now she had brought to their affair, like a dowry of virginal lace, this lightness, this guiltlessness. If she was now sullied and spoiled because of Freddy's dabbling, where would he find supplied such absolution? That first time, had she bathed? No, it became her habit when he revealed he liked to kiss between her thighs. And had her easy calm gaiety been a manner she had contrived to suit some other crimp in his manner of bestowing love, perhaps an untoward seriousness that threatened her marriage? His praise had amused her; she had always responded that all women liked to make love, that all women were beautiful, like a toilet bowl, when you needed one. But by daylight he had discovered on her rapt Roman face an expression, of peace deeper than an infant's sleep, that the darkness of night had never disclosed on the face of his wife. Furtive husbandly visitant, he had never known Angela as he had often known his lovely easy matter-of-fact morning lay. The line of her narrow high-bridged nose a double arabesque. Her white hairs belying her body's youth. Her bony bit of a tail.

Her receding hollowed the dull noon. Tipped shoots searched for wider light through sunless gray air. The salami he made lunch from was minced death. He went at last to his office. His telephone voice grew husky, defeated. Garage doors of the type needed were out of stock in Mather and were being ordered from Akron. The price of gravel had gone up two dollars a ton and a truckload could not be delivered before Friday. The urban renewal in Boston had sucked the area dry of carpenters and six phone calls turned up only two apprentices from a trade school twenty miles away. Spring building had begun and he had been slow. Gallagher's silences, though his conversation was commiserating, breathed accusation.

Piet had met Matt in the army, in Okinawa, in 1951. There, then, in that riverless flatland of barracks and sand, of beer in blank cans and listless Luchuan prostitutes, where the danger of death in battle was as unreal as the homeland whose commercial music twanged in the canteens, Piet was attracted by Matt's choir-boy prankishness, his grooming, his black hair and eyes, his freedom from the weary vocabulary of dirt and disdain, his confident ability to sell. He had sold Piet on himself as a short cut to architecture and, both discharged, had brought him to New England, into this life. Piet's loyalty was lately strained. He found Matt grown brittle, prim, quick to judge, Jesuitical in finance. He dreamed of corrupting whole hillsides, yet wished to keep himself immaculate. He secured his wife and only child behind a wall of Catholicism. In the little transparent world of couples whose intrigues had permeated and transformed Piet, Matt stood out as opaquely moral.

When the phone on his desk rang, Piet feared it would be Georgene, seeking a reconciliation. He hated paining Matt with his duplicity; he thought of Matt with the same pain as he thought of his father, that ghost patiently circling in the luminous greenhouse gloom, silently expecting Piet to do right, to carry on.

It was not Georgene but Angela. Nancy at nursery school had burst out crying because of the hamster. The child suddenly saw with visionary certainty that its death had been her fault. *Daddy said*, she said. Her hysterics had been uncontrollable. Angela had carried her from the room and, since she was teaching, the class ended early. They did not go home. There was nothing to eat at home but ham. In hopes of distracting Nancy with syrup and ice cream, Angela had taken her to eat at the Pancake House in North Mather. Now the child, sucking her thumb and running a slight fever, had fallen asleep on the sofa.

Piet said, "The kid sure knows how to get herself sympathy."

"But not from her own father, evidently. I didn't call just to touch you with this, though as a matter of fact I do think you handled it stupidly. Stupidly or cruelly. I called to ask you to meet Ruth after school and drive to the pet shop in Lacetown for a new hamster. I think we should do it *instantly*."

Magic. The new hamster by sleight of hand would become the old one, the one moldering nose-down underneath the scilla. A religion of genteel pretense. The idea of a hamster persists, eternal. Plato. Piet was an Aristotelian. He said he couldn't possibly do it this afternoon, he had a thousand things to do, the first quarter's accounts to check, he was trying to move the houses on the hill, a million details, the construction trade was going to hell. He was heavily conscious of Gallagher listening. Softer-voiced, he added, "I wasted half the morning making a new cage. Did you notice it in the kitchen?"

Angela said, "Oh is that what it is? We didn't know what it was for. Why is it such a funny shape? Nancy thought it was a little prison you were going to put *her* in."

"Tell the kid I love her lots and to shape up. Good-bye."

The books showed less than the twenty per cent Gallagher liked to clear. Spiros Bros. had attached to their monthly statement a printed threat to stop the account; the balance owed was $1189.24. Gallagher liked to let bills run long, on the theory that money constantly diminished in value. The figures made a gray hazy net around Piet and to compound his claustrophobia the Whitman woman, who had come to basketball uninvited, phoned and asked him to come look at her house. He didn't want the job, he didn't like working for social acquaintances. But in his hopeless mood, to escape the phone and the accounts and Gallagher's binding nearness, he got into the truck whose tailgate said WASH ME and drove down.

The marshes opened up on his right, grand in the dying day. A strip of enameled blue along the horizon of the sea. Colored tiles along a bathtub. The first drops of a half-hearted rain, cold and dry, struck the backs of his hands as he climbed from the truck. The lilacs by the door of the Robinson place were further along that those of Piet's own roadside hedge. More sun by the sea. More life. Tiny wine-colored cones that in weeks would be lavender panicles of bloom. Drenched. Dew. Salt. Breeze. Buttery daffodils trembled by his cuffs, by the bare board fence where they enjoyed reflected warmth. Piet lifted the aluminum latch, salt-corroded, and went in. Even under close clouds, the view was prodigal, a heart-hollowing carpeted span limited by the purity of dunes and ocean. He had been wrong, overcautious. It should be Angela's.

· · ·

Ken Whitman's field of special competence, after his early interest in echinoid metabolism, was photosynthesis; his doctoral thesis had concerned the 7-carbon sugar sedoheptulose, which occupies a momentary place within the immense chain of reactions whereby the five-sixths of the triosephosphate pool that does not form starch is returned to ribulose-5-phosphate. The process was elegant, and few men under forty were more at home than Ken upon the gigantic ladder, forged by light, that carbon dioxide descends to become carbohydrate. At present he was supervising two graduate students in research concerning the transport of glucose molecules through cell walls. By this point in his career Ken had grown impatient with the molecular politics of sugar and longed to approach the mysterious heart of CO_2 fixation—chlorophyll's transformation of visible light into chemical energy. But here, at this ultimate chamber, the lone reaction that counterbalances the vast expenditures of respiration, that reverses decomposition and death, Ken felt himself barred. Biophysics and electronics were in charge. The grana of stacked quantasomes were structured like the crystal lattices in transistors. Photons excited an electron flow in the cloud of particles present in chlorophyll. Though he had ideas—why chlorophyll? why not any number of equally complex compounds? was the atom of magnesium the clue?—he would have to put himself to school again and, at thirty-two, felt too old. He was wedded to the unglamorous carbon cycle while younger men were achieving fame and opulent grants in such fair fields as neurobiology, virology, and the wonderful new wilderness of nucleic acids. He had a wife, a coming child, a house in need of extensive repair. He had overreached. Life, whose graceful secrets he would have unlocked, pressed upon him clumsily.

As if underwater he moved through the final hour of this heavy gray day. An irreversible, constricted future was brewing in the apparatus of his lab—the fantastic glass alphabet of flasks and retorts, the clamps and slides and tubes, the electromagnetic scales sensitive to the hundredth of a milligram, the dead experiments probably duplicated at Berkeley or across the river. Ken worked on the fourth floor of a monumental neo-Greek benefaction, sooty without and obsolete within, dated 1911. The hall window, whose sill held a dreggish Lily cup, overlooked Boston. Expressways capillariously fed the humped dense center of brick red where the State House dome presided, a gold nucleolus. Dusty excavations ravaged the nearer ground. In the quad directly below, female students in bright spring dresses—dyed trace elements—slid along the paths between polygons of chlorophyll. Ken looked with a weariness unconscious of weariness. There had been rain earlier. The same rain now was falling on Tarbox. The day was so dull the window was partly a mirror in which his handsomeness, that strange outrigger to his career, glanced back at him with a cocked eyebrow, a blurred mouth, and a glint of eye white. Ken shied from this ghost; for most of his life he had consciously avoided narcissism. As a child he had vowed to become a saint of science and his smooth face had developed as his enemy. He turned and walked to the other end of the hall; here, for lack of space, the liquid-scintillation counter, though it had cost the department fifteen thousand, a Packard Tri-Carb, was situated. At the moment it was working, ticking through a chain of isotopically labeled solutions, probably Neusner's minced mice livers. A thick-necked sandy man over forty, Jewish only in the sleepy lids of his eyes, Neusner comported himself with the confidence of the energetically second-rate. His lectures were full of jokes and his papers were full of wishful reasoning. Yet he was liked, and had established forever the spatial configuration of one enzyme. Ken envied him and was not sorry to see, at four-thirty, his lab empty. Neusner was a concertgoer and winetaster and womanizer and mainstay of the faculty supper club; he traveled with the Cambridge political crowd and yesterday had confided to Ken in his hurried emphatic accents the latest Kennedy joke. *One night about three a.m. Jackie hears Jack coming into the White House and she meets him on the stairs. His collar is all rumpled and there's lipstick on his chin and she asks him, Where the hell have you been? and he tells her, I've been having a conference with Madame Nhu, and she says, Oh, and doesn't think any more about it until the next week the same thing happens and this time he says he was sitting up late arguing ideology with Nina Khrushchev* . . . A sallow graduate student was tidying up the deserted labs. A heap of gutted white mice lay like burst grapes on a tray. Pink-eyed cagefuls alertly awaited annihilation. Neusner loved computers and statistical theory and his papers were famous for the sheets of numbers that masked the fantasy of his conclusions. Next door old Prichard, the department's prestigious ornament, was pottering with his newest plaything, the detection and analysis of a memory-substance secreted by the brain. Ken envied the old man his childlike lightness, his freedom to dart through forests of evidence after such a bluebird. Neusner, Prichard—they were both free in a way Ken wasn't. Why? Everyone sensed it, the something wrong with Ken, so intelligent and handsome and careful and secure—the very series expressed it, an unstable compound, unnatural. Prichard, a saint, tried to correct the condition, to give Ken of himself, sawing the air with his papery mottled hands, nodding his unsteady gaunt head, whose flat cheeks seemed rouged, spilling his delicate stammer: *The thing of it, the thing of it is, Wh-Whitman, it's just t-tinkering, you mustn't s-s-suppose life, ah, owes us anything, we just g-get what we can out of the b-bitch, eh?* Next to his lab, his narrow office was a hodgepodge encrusted with clippings, cartoons, snapshots of other people's children and grandchildren, with honorary degrees, gilded citations, mounted butterflies and framed tombstone tracings and other such detritus of the old man's countless hobbies. Ken halted at the door of this living scrapbook wistfully, wanting a moment of encouragement, wondering why such a sanctified cell would never be his. The old man was unmarried. In his youth there had been a scandal, a wife who had left him; Ken doubted the story, for how could any woman leave so good a man?

Inspiration came to him: Prichard's virtues might be a product of being left, a metabolic reduction necessary to growth, a fruitful fractionation. Inspiration died: he looked within himself and encountered a surface bafflingly smooth. On Prichard's cluttered desk today's newspaper declared, ERHARD CERTAIN TO SUCCEED ADENAUER.

Morris Stein was waiting for him with a problem, an enzyme

that couldn't be crystallized. Then it was after five. He drove home expertly, a shade arrogantly, knifing along the Southeastern Expressway like a man who has solved this formula often, changing lanes as it suited him, Prichard and Neusner and Stein revolving in his head while automobiles of differing makes spun and shuffled, passed and were passed, outside his speeding windows. He wondered about the people in Tarbox, how Hanema could drive that filthy clanking pick-up truck everywhere and the Applebys stick with that old maroon Mercury when they had the money. He wondered why Prichard had never won the Nobel and deduced that his research was like his hobbies, darting this way and that, more enthusiasm than rigor. He thought of photosynthesis and it appeared to him there was a tedious deep flirtatiousness in nature that withheld her secrets while the church burned astronomers and children died of leukemia. That she yielded by whim, wantonly, to those who courted her offhand, with a careless ardor he, Ken, lacked. *The b-b-bitch.*

The smokestacks and gasholders of South Boston yielded to the hickory woods of Nun's Bay Road. He arrived home before dark. Daylight Saving had begun. Alone in the living room Cotton was curved asleep in the sling chair from Design Research. Ken called Foxy's name. She answered faintly from the porch. Someone had torn away the boards that had sealed the French doors. She sat on a wicker chair, a tall gin drink in her hand, looking through rusted porch screens toward the sea. The sky was clearing after the brief rain. Dark-blue clouds thin as playing cards seen edgewise duplicated the line of the horizon. The lighthouse was tipped with an orange drop of final sun. He asked her, "Aren't you cold?"

"No, I'm warm. I'm fat."

He wanted to touch her, for luck, for safety, as when a child in Farmington after a long hide in the weeds shouts *Free!* and touches the home maple. Gazing in the dying light across the greening marsh, she had a tree's packed stillness. Her blond hair and pink skin and brown eyes were all one shade in the darkness of the porch. With a motion almost swift, the light had died. Bending to kiss her, he found her skin strange; she was shivering. Her arms showed goosebumps. He begged her, "Come in the house."

"It's so pretty. Isn't this what we're paying for?"

He thought the expression strange. They had never given much thought to money. Advancement, distinction: these were the real things. As if having overheard his thoughts, she went on, "We all rather live under wraps, don't we? We hardly ever really open ourselves to the loveliness around us. Yet there it is, every day, going on and on, whether we look at it or not. Such a splendid waste, isn't it?"

"I'm going in to make a drink." She followed him in and told him about her day. She had weeded and raked in the side yard. She had decided she wanted roses, white and red mixed, along the blind southern wall of the servants' wing. The Plymouth agency had called and said her car—a secondhand station wagon they had bought for her, since without a vehicle she was virtually a prisoner at this end of the beach road—would be ready Thursday, with license plates and an inspection sticker. Ken had forgotten about this car, though obviously she needed it. In Cambridge they had done so long without any car at all. Just before lunchtime Irene Saltz, with tiny Jeremiah in a papooselike arrangement on her back, had dropped in on her way back from the beach. She was a conservationist and distressed that the winter storms had flattened a number of dunes. Any town but Tarbox would ages ago have put up fences and brush hedges to hold the sand. She asked Foxy to join the League of Women Voters and drank three cups of coffee. With such a monologuist for a husband, you probably have to develop another erotic outlet, but the trouble with people who have poured themselves into good works is they expect you to do the same, pour away, even if they have husbands as handsome, charming, and attentive as, dear, yourself . . . Ken sipped his drink and wondered what she was driving at. In the living-room light she looked pale, her ears and nostrils nipped pink. She was high on something.

What else happened? Oh, yes, in the middle of her nap, and by the way she had gotten to volume two of Painter's life of Proust, which looked to be much the duller, since Proust was no longer having his childhood, Carol Constantine had called, inviting them to a May Day party; it sounded rather orgiastic. And finally she had got up her nerve and called this man Hanema to come look at the house.

"When will he come?"

"Oh, he came."

"And what did he say?"

"Oh he said fifteen thousand, more or less. It depends on how much you want to do. He'd like to see us with a full basement but a crawl space with I think he said plastic film over the earth might do for the kitchen half. He prefers hot-water heat but says hot air would be cheaper since we can put the ducts right in the walls we're going to have to build anyway. You'll have to talk to him yourself. Everything seemed to depend on something else."

"What about the roof and the shingles?"

"New roof. He thinks we can patch the shingles for now."

"Does this fifteen thousand include doing anything to those ugly upstairs dormers and that leaky skylight?"

"We didn't go upstairs. Of course he knows the house already. He thought the big issue was the basement. He was rather quaint and cute. He kept talking about babies crawling around on a nice warm floor and glancing at my tummy."

Ken felt a weight descend but persisted. "And the kitchen?"

"He sees about four thousand there. He wants to knock out the pantry partition and have new everything except the sink. He agreed with me, the slate sink must be kept. But the plumbing should be done over top to bottom. And the wiring. Have some more bourbon, baby."

She took his glass and smoothly, like a sail pushed by wind, moved toward the kitchen. "Very weak," he said, and, when she returned with the drink, said, "Well. But did you like him?"

Foxy stood a moment, her pale mouth shaped as if to hum. "I can manage him. He seemed a little forlorn today. His daughter's pet hamster was eaten by a neighbor's cat." Ken remembered Neusner's tray of gutted mice and wondered how some men still could permit themselves so much sentiment.

"You're the one," Ken said, "who'll have to deal with him."

She again moved with that airy quickness, as if she had considered a possibility and dismissed it. "I don't think he wants the job. He and your friend are building new houses for the population explosion."

"Gallagher's not my friend especially. Did Hanema recommend any other contractor?"

"I asked him to. He said there wasn't anybody he'd trust us with offhand. He was very indecisive. He seemed to feel possessive about this house."

"His wife had wanted it."

"You keep *saying* that." Her reactions had a quickness, her eyes a hard brightness, that was unusual; he felt an unseen factor operating, an unaccounted-for chemical. She had disliked Hanema: this guess, flattering to himself, inevitable in the light of himself, disposed him to the man, and he told her, "I think, why not put him to work? Exert your charm."

She was moving, swiftly, lightly, about the room, taking a kind of inventory perhaps, touching rough surfaces that soon would be smooth, saying goodbye to the ugly mementos, the fan-shaped shell collection, the dried sprigs of beach pea and woolly hudsonia, that had housed her for this while, this pregnant month. She changed the subject. "How was your day?"

He confessed, "I feel bogged down."

She thought, *You need another woman.* She said, "It's too much commuting."

"It's too much mediocre mental grinding. On my part. I should have gone into law. That we can do. The old man has two flat feet for a brain, and everybody in Hartford thinks he's nifty." She laughed, and he looked up startled; his vocabulary became boyish when he thought of Hartford, and he was unconscious of it. He went on sadly, "I was thinking about Prichard today and it made me realize I don't really have it. The flair. It all just looks like a bunch of details to me, which is the way it looks to every boob."

"Prichard's an old man. You're young. Old men have nothing serious to think about." By "serious" she meant the shadow within herself, her child, the dark world of breeding.

"Except death," Ken said, a touching strange thing for him to say. She had pictured him as thinking no more about death than a watch does about running down. She had assumed he from birth had solved it and had worked out her own solution apart from him.

Foxy said eagerly, "Oh no, when you're young you think about that. So when you're old you have nothing to do but be happy for each new day." She drifted to where a scantling shelf horizontal between two studs held a single forgotten amber marble, striped with a swirl of honey-white. She held it in her pink oval palm and tried to see into its center and imagined God as a man so old each day makes Him absolutely happy. She wondered why she could not share God with Ken, it was so innocent, like this marble, meek and small but there. She didn't ask him to believe in more than this. But in his presence she became ashamed, felt guilty of duplicity.

Ken looked up as if awaking. "Who took the boards off the porch doors?"

"He did. Hanema."

"With his bare hands?"

With your bare hands?

Sure. Why not? Why haven't you done this yourselves?

We thought it served some purpose.

It did, but winter's over. Welcome to spring. Now. This should turn, with a little love. Ah, It does. Come on.

Oh. I've hardly ever been on the porch. Are the screens still mendable?

He had taken a loose piece of rusted screening and crumpled it and showed her the orange dust like pollen in his palm. *New screens will be one of the least of your expenses. Alcoa makes nice big panels we can fit into runners along here. And here. Take them down in the fall. In summer this porch is the best room in the house. Grab the breeze.*

But it makes the living room so dark. I was thinking of having it torn away.

Don't tear away free space. You bought the view. Here's where it is.

Do you think we were silly? To buy it.

Not at all. This could be a dandy house. You have the skeleton and the size. All it needs now is money.

It was my husband who fell in love with it. I thought of us living nearer to Boston, in Lexington or Newton.

You know—Instead of finishing, he had jogged up and down on the boards, where the line of the porch sagged, testing.

Yes?

Your porch sill is missing a support. Don't hold any square dances out here.

You started to say something.

Not really.

She had waited.

I was going to say that your view makes me sad, because my wife loved it, and I didn't have the courage to do what your husband has done, take this place on.

Do you think courage is what it took? It may have been more a matter of self-esteem.

Perhaps.

Maybe it's just not your kind of place.

Thank you. I didn't feel it was. I'm not a seaside type. I like to feel lots of land around me, in case of a flood.

I suppose me too. I hate wet feet.

But you're happy here, aren't you? Somebody told me you said you were. It's none of my business, of course.

He had seemed so courtly and embarrassed, so ready to put himself back into the hired-man role, that her tongue hastened to ease his presumption. *Yes, I'm happy enough. I'm a little bored. But I like the town and I like the people I've met.*

You do?

You say that with such surprise.

Don't mean to. I guess I'm past asking myself if I like them or not. They're mine.

And you're theirs?

In a way. Watch out. It can happen to you.

No, Ken and I have always been independent. We've never gotten involved with people. I suppose we're both rather cold.

He had taken out a knife and, having turned his back on her, was prying. *Your window sashes should all be replaced.*

Wouldn't storm windows make that unnecessary?

Some of these frames are too rotten to screw a storm sash into.

I hope—

You hope what?

I was going to say, I hope we can have your wife down, you and your wife, when the house is fixed up. Already I'm frightened she won't approve of what we do to it.

He had laughed—his laugh came from deeper within him than the laugh of most men, was warmer, a bit disconcerting, more invading.

She had tried to defend herself. *I don't know why I should be worried about your wife's approval. She's a lovely person.*

His laugh repeated. *And your husband's a lovely man.*

ii. *Applesmiths and Other Games*

Foxy was both right and wrong about Janet. Janet had never actually slept with Freddy Thorne, though she and Freddy had held earnest discourse about it, and her affair with Harold little-Smith had proved to be unexpectedly difficult to untangle and end.

The Applebys and little-Smiths had moved to Tarbox in the middle Fifties, unknown to each other, though both men worked in securities on State Street, Harold as a broker, Frank as a trust officer in a bank. Frank had gone to Harvard, Harold to Princeton. They belonged to that segment of their generation of the upper middle class which mildly rebelled against the confinement and discipline whereby wealth maintained its manners during the upheavals of depression and world war. Raised secure amid these national trials and introduced as adults into an indulgent economy, into a business atmosphere strangely blended of crisp youthful imagery and underlying depersonalization, of successful small-scale gambles carried out against a background of rampant diversification and the ultimate influence of a government whose taxes and commissions and appetite for armaments set limits everywhere, introduced into a nation whose leadership allowed a toothless moralism to dissemble a certain practiced cunning, into a culture where adolescent passions and homosexual philosophies were not quite yet triumphant, a climate still *furtively* hedonist, of a country still too overtly threatened from without to be ruthlessly self-abusive, a climate of time between, of standoff and day-by-day, wherein all generalizations, even negative ones, seemed unintelligent—to this new world the Applebys and little-Smiths brought a modest determination to be free, to be flexible and decent. Fenced off from their own parents by nursemaids and tutors and "help," they would personally rear large intimate families; they changed diapers with their own hands, did their own housework and home repairs, gardened and shoveled snow with a sense of strengthened health. Chauffered, as children, in black Packards and Chryslers, they drove second-hand cars in an assortment of candy colors. Exiled early to boarding schools, they resolved to use and improve the local public schools. Having suffered under their parents' rigid marriages and formalized eva-sions, they sought to substitute an essential fidelity set in a matrix of easy and open companionship among couples. For the forms of the country club they substituted informal membership in a circle of friends and participation in a cycle of parties and games. They put behind them the stratified summer towns of their upbring-ings, with their restrictive distinctions, their tedious rounds of politeness, and settled the year round in unthought-of places, in pastoral mill towns like Tarbox, and tried to improvise here a fresh way of life. Duty and work yielded as ideals to truth and fun. Virtue was no longer sought in temple or market place but in the home—one's own home, and then the homes of one's friends.

In their first years in Tarbox, the social life of the Smiths and Applebys was passed among older men and women. Neighboring aunts dutifully called and were politely received and, in the end, resolutely snubbed. "How dreary," Marcia would say, "these horsey people are," and as she and Janet became intimate they coined a term, the "big H," to signify all those people, hopefully put behind them and yet so persistently attentive, who did all the right things, a skein of acquaintance and cousinship that extended from Quogue to Bar Harbor. Discovering each other at a horsey party, in Millbrook or Scituate, that each with a great show of wifely resignation had agreed to attend, Janet and Marcia would, by way of greeting, neigh at one another. Janet's delicate nostrilly snort, accompanied by a hoofing motion of one foot, was very piquant; she was slimmer then. In truth, they rarely declined these invitations, though as they failed to return them their number slowly diminished. For among these mocked people, however nasal and wooden-headed, the Applebys and Smiths were given presence on the strength of their names and parents' names; it was years before Tarbox provided them with a society as flattering and nutritious as the scorned "big H."

The Thornes and the Guerins were in Tarbox already, but there was something uncomfortable about both couples, something unexplained and embarrassed about the men—one a dentist, and the other seemingly not employed at all, though frequently in Boston. Both wives were shy; Bea did not drink so much then, and would sit quiet and tensely smiling for an entire evening. When Roger glared, she would freeze like a rabbit. Harold called them *Barbe bleu et Fatime*. They all found Freddy Thorne's smirking pretensions and coziness ridiculous. In those days he still had some hair—wavy fine flax grown long and combed across a bald spot. Georgene was plainly another well-trained, well-groomed filly from the Big H, Philadelphia branch. The couples entertained each other with infrequent stiff dinners, and exchanged maternity clothes—except that Bea was never pregnant.

The people who did throw parties were a decade older and seemed rather coarse and blatant—Dan Mills, the bronzed, limping, and alcoholic owner of the abortive Tarbox boatyard; Eddie Warner, the supervisor of a Mather paint plant, a bullet-headed ex-athlete who could still at beery beach picnics float the ball a mile in the gull-gray dusk; Doc Allen; good old Ed Byrd; a few male teachers in the Tarbox schools, defensive plodders; and their wives, twitchy women full of vicarious sex and rock-and-roll lyrics, their children being adolescent. To Janet they seemed desperate people, ignorant and provincial and loud. Their rumored infidelities struck her as pathetic; their evident heavy drinking disgusted her. She herself had just produced a baby,

Franklin, Jr.—eight pounds, six ounces. The skin of his temples exquisitely pulsed as he sucked her breasts, so that not only the hoarsely joshing voices and unsweet breaths but the imperfect complexions of the "boatyard crowd," as she and Marcia had christened it, offended her; lepers should not insist on dancing. The boatyard crowd, a postwar squirearchy of combat veterans, locally employed and uncollegiate, knew that it was patronized by these younger cooler couples and suffered no regrets when they chose to form a separate set and to leave them alone with their liquor and bridge games and noisy reminiscences of Anzio and Guadalcanal.

Had they been less uncongenial, Janet would hardly have made social overtures to the Saltzes and the Ongs, who moved to opposite ends of the town in 1957 and who at least were college graduates. John Ong, indeed, was supposedly very brilliant. He worked in Cambridge, mathematically deciphering matter, in a program underwritten by the government. He should have been fascinating but his English was impossible to understand. His wife, Bernadette, was a broad-shouldered half-Japanese from Baltimore, her father an immigrant Portugese. She was exotic and boistrous and warm and exhausting, as if she were trying to supply by herself enough gregariousness for two. The Saltzes were killingly earnest but Irene could be fun after the third martini, when she did imitations of all the selectmen and town officials her crusading spirit brought her up against. Ben had only one imitation, which he did unconsciously—a rabbi, with scruffy beard and bent stoop, hands clasped behind him, and an air of sorrowing endurance. But it was not until, in 1958, Hanema and Gallagher set up their office on Hope Street that the final ecology of the couples was established. With these two men, the Irishman and Dutchman, shaped together like Don Quixote and Sancho Panza, began the round of sports—touch football, skiing, basketball, sailing, tennis, touch football again—that gave the couples an inexhaustible excuse for gathering: a calendrical wheel of unions to anticipate and remember, of excuses for unplanned parties. And the two new women, Terry and Angela, brought a style with them, an absent-minded amiability from which the other women were able to imitate the only tone, casual and amused, that could make bearable such a burden of hospitality and intermingling. In 1960 the Constantines moved into their sinister big house on the green; Carol painted, and Eddie flew. As a couple, they had an appealingly dangerous air. And now, in 1963, the Whitmans had moved into the old Robinson place.

These years had seen the boatyard crowd go from decay to disintegration. Two couples had been divorced, the schoolteachers had failed to get tenure and had quit or been dismissed, poor alcoholic Danny Mills had lost his boatyard to the bank and gone to Florida without his wife, whose hard stringy legs had been so quick to master the newest dance step. The only remaining contact with the boatyard crowd was by phone, when one called to ask one of their teen-age daughters to babysit. Their existence, which might have been forgotten entirely, was memorialized by a strange vestige, irksome to Harold and Marcia, within the younger group of couples. There had been, in those first Tarbox years, another couple called Smith, a pair of big-headed, ruddy, humorless social pushers who had since moved to Newton but who were, for a year, present at the same parties the smaller Smiths were invited to. So the modifiers had been coined as a conversational convenience and had outlived the need for any distinction, and become part of Harold and Marcia, though by now few of their friends knew who the big-Smiths had been, or could envision their ponderous, flushed, doll-like faces, always eagerly nodding, like floats in a Shriners parade. It was an annual cause for hilarity when, with that inexorable plodding friendliness that had been their method of attack, the Smiths from faraway Newton Centre favored the Thornes, the Guerins, the Applebys, and their name-twins with a hectographed Christmas letter. In the salutation to Harold and Marcia they unfailingly put "little" in quotes—*to our Tarbox doppelgängers the "little" Smiths.*

The affair among the Applesmiths began—gossip wrongly assumed that Janet initiated things—with Marcia noticing Frank's hands. In turn the beauty of his hands had emerged from their former pudgy look by way of an ulcer diet brought on by the sharp market slump of April and May of 1962. This slump, which more affected Frank's trusts (he had just been promoted from junior officer) than Harold's brokerage business, and which furthermore caught Frank with thousands of his own in electronics and pharmaceuticals, brought the couples closer than usual that spring and summer. It became their custom, Sunday nights, after tennis, to eat together fried clams or lobster fetched in steaming paper bags from a restaurant in North Mather. One night, as they sat on cushions and chairs around the little-Smiths' tesselated coffee table, Marcia became hypnotized by the shapely force with which Frank's fingers, their tips greasily gleaming, manipulated onion rings. His diet had shorn a layer of fat from them, so the length of the fingers, with something especially sculptured about the knuckles and nail sheaths, was revealed as aristocratic; his thumbs were eloquent in every light. Along the fleecy wrists, through the cordlike tributary veins raised on the backs of his hands, down into the tips, a force flowed that could destroy and shape; pruning roses had given Frank's hands little cuts that suggested the nicks a clammer or sculptor bears, and Marcia lifted her eyes to his face and found there, beneath the schoolboy plumpness, the same nicked, used, unconscious look of having done work, of belonging to an onflowing force whose pressure made his cheeks florid and his eyes bloodshot. He was a man. He had a battered look of having been swept forward past obstacles. After this revelation every motion of his altered Marcia's insides with a slight turning, a purling in the flow within her. She was a woman. She sensed now in him a treasurable dreadfulness; and, when they rose to leave and Janet, eight months pregnant, lost her balance and took Frank's quickly offered hand for support, Marcia, witnessing as if never before the swift sympathetic interaction of the couple, felt outraged: a theft had been brazenly executed before her eyes.

Née Burnham, Marcia was the daughter of a doctor and the granddaughter of a bishop. Her detection of a masculine beauty in Frank Appleby at first took the form of an innocent glad lightness in the company of the other couple and a corresponding dreariness on weekends when they were not scheduled to see them—though she usually managed to call Janet and arrange for at least a drink together, or a sail with their boys in the Applebys' catboat. Her possessive and probing fondness was hardly distinguishable from their old friendship, though at dances or at parties where they danced she did feel herself lifted by a willingness to come into Frank's hands. He had never been a dancer, and Marcia, locked into his bumping shuffle, aware of her toes being stubbed and her cool lotioned hand vanishing in the damp adhesion of his grip and his boozy sighs accumulating on her bare neck like the patch of mist a child will breathe onto a windowpane, sometimes watched enviously her husband and Janet or Carol Constantine waltzing from corner to corner around the shadowy rim of the room whose bright dead center she and Frank statically occupied. Harold was an adroit, even flamboyant, dancer, and sometimes after a long set with Frank she would make him take her and whirl her around the floor to relieve the crick in her neck and the ache, from reaching too high, across her shoulder blades. But there was a solidity in Frank that Harold lacked. Harold had never suffered; he merely dodged. Harold read *Barron's* or Ian Fleming on the commuting train; Frank read Shakespeare.

What Marcia didn't know was that she preceded Shakespeare: for Frank the market slump, the sleepless nights of indigestion, the birth of his second child, and his friend's wife's starry glances and strange meltingness were parts of one experience, an overture to middle age, a prelude to mortality, that he answered, in the manner of his father, an ardent amateur Sinologist, by dipping deep into the past, where peace reigned. *When all aloud the wind doth blow/And coughing drowns the parson's saw/And birds sit brooding in the snow* . . . Those vanished coughs, melted snow, dead birds seemed sealed in amber, in something finer than amber, because movement could occur within it. *I'll have a starling shall be taught to speak/Nothing but "Mortimer," and give it him/To keep his anger still in motion:* in Frank's contemplation of such passion, perfectly preserved, forever safe, his stomach forgot itself. He was not a natural reader, couldn't focus on two lines of Dante or Milton, disliked plays on the stage and novels, and found this soothing quality, of flux confined with all its colors, only in Shakespeare.

"Everything is in him," he told Marcia, flirtatiously, for he talked about Shakespeare with no one, especially not Janet, who took his reading as a rebuke of her, for not finishing college, but marrying him instead, "everything we can hope to have, and it all ends badly."

Marcia asked, "Even the comedies?"

"They end in marriage, and Shakespeare's marriage was unhappy."

"I feel," Marcia said, for she was a tight-wound nervous woman who had to have things clear, "you're trying to tell me *we* would end badly."

"Us? You and me?"

So he hadn't meant at all to tell her his own marriage was unhappy. But she went on, "If we . . . started anything."

"Should we start something? I'll buy that idea. Yes." His large red head seemed to settle heavier on his shoulders as the notion sank in. "What about Harold and Janet? Should we consult them first? Let's not and say we did."

He was so clumsy and ironical, she took offense. "Please forget whatever I said. It's a female fault, to try and sexualize friendship. I want you only as a friend."

"Why? You have Janet as a friend. Please sexualize me. It sounds like a good process. With this sloppy marketing running, it's probably the best investment left." They were leaning in the summer heat against the maroon fender of the Applebys' Mercury, after tennis, beside the Gallaghers' rather fortresslike brick house on the back road to North Mather. Matt had got permission to use a neighbor's court. Harold was inside the house, drinking; Janet was home nursing the baby. It had been a girl, whom they had named Catharine, after an aunt Frank remembered as a heap of dusty velvet, knobbed with blood-red garnets.

Marcia said to him, but after laughing enjoyably, "You're shocking, with your doubled responsibilities."

"Double, double, toil and trouble. Janet's been a bitch for nine months plus. Let's at least have lunch together in Boston. I need a vacation. How are your Tuesdays?"

"Car-pool day."

"Oh. Wednesdays I usually have lunch with Harold at the

Harvard Club. All he does is sniff. Shall I cancel him?"

"No, no. Harold hates any change of routine. Let me see if I can get a sitter for Henrietta for Thursday. Please, Frank. Let's understand each other. This is just to talk."

"Of course. I'll tell you of men whose heads do grow beneath their shoulders."

"Othello?"

"Right."

"Frank, listen. I've become fixated on you, I know it's absurd, and I'm asking for your help. As a friend."

"Pre- or post-sexualization?"

"Please be serious. I've never been more serious. I'm fighting for my life. I know you don't love me and I don't think I love you but I *need* to talk. I need it so much"—and here, half artfully, she lowered her face to hide tears that were, after all, real—"I'm frightened."

"Dear Marcia. Don't be."

They had lunch, and lunch often again, meeting at the corners of new glass buildings or in the doorways of flower shops, a toothy ruddy man with a soft air of having done well at school and a small dark efficient woman looking a little breathless, hunting hand in hand through the marine stenches of the waterfront and the jostling glare of Washington Street for the perfect obscure restaurant, with the corner table, and the fatherly bartender, and the absence of business acquaintances and college friends. They talked, touching toes, quickly brushing hands in admonishment or pity, talked about themselves, about their childhoods spent behind trimmed hedges, about Shakespeare and psychiatry, which Marcia's lovely father had practiced, about Harold and Janet, who, as they obligingly continued to be deceived, were ever more tenderly considered, so that they became almost sacred in their ignorance, wonderful in their fallibility, so richly forgiven for their frigidity, demandingness, obtuseness, and vanity that the liaison between their spouses seemed a conspiracy to praise the absent. There was a cottage north of Boston—and thus extra safe and remote from their real lives—belonging to one of Frank's aunts, who hid the key on a little sill behind one of the fieldstone foundation-pillars. To Frank as a child, groping for this key cached here had seemed a piratical adventure, the pillaging of a deep grotto powerfully smelling of earth and creosote and rodent dung. Now the key seemed pathetically accessible, and he wondered how many others, strangers to the family, had used these same bare mattresses, had borrowed these same rough army blankets from the cedar chest, and had afterwards carefully tipped their cigarette ashes into the cellophane sealer slipped from the pack. In the kitchen there had been a dead mouse in a trap. Dying, it had flipped, and lay belly up, dirty white, like a discarded swab in a doctor's office. Frank and Marcia stole some sherry from the cupboard but had not disturbed the mouse. They were not here. The cottage was used only on weekends. From its security amid pines and pin oaks it overlooked the slender peninsula of Nahant. The seaside smell that leaked through the window sashes was more saline and rank that that of Tarbox Beach, where Janet and the children would be sunning. Marcia had felt to Frank strangely small, more athletic and manageable than Janet, without Janet's troubled tolling resonance but with a pleasing pointed firmness that reminded him, in his passage into her body, of the little mistresses of the French court, of Japanese prostitutes that Harold had once drunkenly described, of slim smooth boys who had been Rosalind and Kate and Ophelia. There was in Marcia a nervous corruptibility he had never tasted before. Her thin shoulders sparkled in his red arms. Her face, relaxed, seemed, like an open lens, to be full of his face. "I love your hands," she said.

"You've said that before."

"I loved being in them. They're huge."

"Only relatively," he said, and regretted it, for he had brought Harold into bed with them.

Knowing this, knowing they could never be alone, she asked, "Did I feel different than Janet?"

"Yes."

"My breasts are so small."

"You have lovely breasts. Like a Greek statue. Venus always has little breasts. Janet's—Janet's are full of milk right now. It's kind of a mess."

"What does it taste like?"

"What? Janet's milk?"

"You don't have to tell me."

"No, why not? Sweet. Too sweet, really."

"You're such a gentle man," Marcia said. "I'm not used to being loved so gently." Thus she conveyed, weakening them as lovers but strengthening them as confidants, the suggestion to Frank that he had been too gentle, that Harold was rougher, more strenuous and satisfying with, no doubt, a bigger prick. As if hailing a dim stubby figure on a misted shore, Frank mournfully confronted the endomorph in himself. His demanding deep-socketed mistress, ectomorphic, lay relaxed at his side; their skins touched stickily along her length. The neural glitter of her intelligent face was stilled; a dangling earring rested diagonally forward from her ear lobe, parallel to the line of her cheekbone; the severe central parting of her black hair had been carried off by a kind of wind. Was she asleep? He groped beside the bed, among his under-clothes, for his wristwatch. He would soon learn, in undressing, to leave it lying discreetly visible. Its silent gold-rimmed face, a tiny banker's face, stated that he had already been out to lunch an hour and forty minutes. A sour burning began to revolve in his stomach.

Their affair went two months undetected. It is not difficult to deceive the first time, for the deceived possesses no antibodies; unvaccinated by suspicion, she overlooks latenesses, accepts ab-surd excuses, permits the flimsiest patchings to repair great rents in the quotidian. "*Where* have you been?" Janet asked Frank one Saturday.

"At the dump."

"At the dump for two *hours?*"

"Oh, I stopped at the drug store and talked to Buzz Kappiotis about the tax rate and the firemen's four-per-cent increase."

"I thought Buzz was fishing in Maine." Their cleaning lady was a neighbor.

"I don't mean Buzz, I mean Iggy Galanis, I must be losing my mind."

"I'll say. You're so twitchy in bed you give me insomnia."

"It's my blue-eyed baby ulcers."

"I don't see what you're so nervous about lately. The market's happy again, they've reduced the margin rate. And *how* did your clothes get so rumpled?"

He looked down at himself and saw a long black hair from Marcia's head adhering to the fly of his corduroy pants. Glancing there, he felt the little limb behind the cloth as warm and used, softly stinging. Sun had streamed through the dusty windshield glass onto her skin. He pulled the hair off and said, "From handling the trash cans."

But an affair wants to spill, to share its glory with the world. No act is so private it does not seek applause. In public Frank could scarcely contain his proud and protective feeling toward Marcia; the way at the end of an evening he held her coat for her and slipped it around her was as different from the way he would help Georgene Thorne as receiving the Host is from eating an hors d'oeuvre. All the empty pauses and gropings of this simple social action were luxuriously infused with magic: his fingers in adjusting her collar brushed the nape of her neck; her hands pressed her own lapels secure if they were his hands clasped upon her breasts; her eyes rolled Spanishly; and this innocent pantomime of robing was drenched in reminiscence of their nakedness. Their minds and mouths were committed to stability and deception while their bodies were urging eruption, violence, change. At last the little-Smiths, Harold prattling drunkenly, spilled from the lit porch into the night—a parting glance from Marcia, dark as a winter-killed rose—and the door was finally shut. Janet asked Frank, "Are you having an affair with Marcia?"

"Now there's a strange question."

"Never mind the question. What's the answer?"

"Obviously, no."

"You don't sound convincing. Convince me. Please convince me."

He shrugged. "I don't have the time or the stomach for it. She's not my type. She's tiny and jittery and has no tits. Lastly, you're my wife and you're great. Rare Egyptian! Royal wench! The holy priests bless you when you are riggish. Let's go to bed."

"We have to stack the dishwasher first. Anyway, don't think you've sold me. How does she know so much about Shakespeare all of a sudden?"

"I suppose she's been reading him."

"To please you. To get at me somehow."

"How does that get at you?"

"She knows I never read."

"But you find books in running brooks, sermons in stones, and good in everything."

"Ha ha. That busy little bitch, she keeps telling me she has a secret."

"She says this?"

"Her eyes say it. And her bottom. I used to think of her as so stringy and intellectual, but she's been doing a ton of hip-waggling lately."

"Maybe she's having an affair with Freddy Thorne."

"Take that expression off your face."

"What expression?"

"That amused look. Take it off! Take it off, Frank! I hate it!" And suddenly she was at him, after him with her fists, her struggling weight; he squeezed her against him, regretfully conscious that even now, as her pinned fists flailed his shoulders and her face crumpled into contorted weeping and the sharp smell of perfume was scalded from her, that the expression, of serene superiority, of a beautiful secret continually tasted, was still on his face.

Harold little-Smith could not immediately identify the woman who called him at his office one morning. He and Janet rarely talked on the telephone; it was Marcia and Janet, or Marcia and Frank, who arranged the many things—the tennis and sailing, the Friday-night plays and Saturday-night concerts—that the two couples had done together this summer. The woman's voice said, "I've been in town all morning shopping, the damn stores have *nothing*, and I'm hungry and cross and wondered if you'd like to split a lunch with me. *Not* fried clams, thank you." Just in time, he recognized Janet.

"Janet, really? It's a lovely idea, but this is the day I usually have lunch with Frank. Why don't the three of us have lunch together?"

"That's *not* the idea, Harold. Couldn't you call Frank and cancel it? Think of some good excuse. Tell him you have a girl friend. Don't be afraid of Frank, Harold."

"Who said I was?"

"Well, then. Please. I know it seems funny and pushy, but I must talk to you, and this was the only way I could think of. I knew Wednesday is your day with Frank and that you would be free otherwise."

Still Harold hesitated. He enjoyed a certain freedom of speech and thought because his life, from childhood up, had been outwardly orderly and obedient. Life was a kind of marathon you could run as you please as long as you touched all the checkpoints; his weekly lunch with Frank was one of the checkpoints. They discussed stocks and bonds and hardly ever spoke of their domestic life together in Tarbox.

Janet prompted, "You won't have to *pay* for my lunch, just *have* it with me."

This stung him; he considered himself something of a dandy, an old-fashioned elegant. Last spring, in St. Louis, he had given a girl two hundred dollars to spend the night with him. He told Janet the Ritz, upstairs, at one o'clock, and hung up.

It was strange she should have told him not to be afraid of Frank because it was she Harold had always been afraid of. Any vulgarity that could not be paid off and dismissed intimidated him. Meeting the Applebys the first time, he had wondered why Frank had married such a common girl—fine in bed, no doubt, but why marry her? Though she was from a respectable family (her father owned a pharmaceutical manufacturing firm in Buffalo, and her maiden name was on drugstore shelves across the country) Janet was one of the few women of Harold's social acquaintance who could have been, without any change in physical style, a waitress or a girl in a five and ten (in fact she had worked two summers behind a counter, selling men's jewelry, at Flint & Kent) or a dance-hall hostess. She would some day, some day soon, be fat. Already there was a crease at the front of her ankles, and the flesh of her upper arms was loose, and her hips had a girdled hardness. Not that Harold did not find her attractive. He did, and this went with his fright. Her beauty seemed a gift she would abuse, like a boy with a gun, or squander, like a fool with a fortune. She struck him as a bad investor who would buy high and sell after the drop and take everybody she could down with her. So he walked, up Milk, through the thick of Boston's large codger population, along Tremont, through the Common and the Public Garden, in a pinching mood of caution. The sidewalk was so hot it stung through the soles of his thin black Italianate shoes; yet scraps of velour and highlights of satiny white skin skated through his head, and it was somewhat romantic of him not to have taken a cab. Of the four Applesmiths, Harold was sexually the most experienced. He possessed that trivial air, trivial yet assured and complacent, that women feel free to experiment with, and before his marriage he had slept with enough to lose the exact count. After marriage (he had been old: twenty-six) there had been business trips, and call girls, generally doughy and sullen, with whiskeyish breaths and terrible voices; but he had never betrayed Marcia with a social equal.

After her second martini, Janet said, "Harold, it's about Marcia and Frank."

"They seem very amiable lately."

"I should hope so. I *know* they're seeing each other."

"You know? You have evidence? *Évidence?*"

"I don't need evidence, I *know*. There's a tone about them. He's always bringing her up, casually. 'Did Marcia seem irritable to you tonight?' 'What did you think, dear, of Marcia's dress?' What the fuck do I care about Marcia's dress?"

"But you have no evidence? There's been no confession from Frank? He hasn't asked to leave you?"

"Why should he want to leave me? He's happy. He's milking two cows."

"Janet, you don't put things very gracefully."

"I don't *feel* graceful about it. You evidently do. Evidently you're used to your wife sleeping around."

"I am not. The fact is, I don't believe this. I think there is an attraction between Frank and Marcia, yes. It's natural enough, considering how much we see each other. For that matter, there's an attraction between you and me. *Toi et moi.*"

"This is the first I've heard of it."

"Oh, come on. You know what you are. You know how you look to men. I'd love to go to bed with you."

"You don't put things that gracefully yourself."

"Of course, we won't. We're married now and we've had our flings, our *escapades romantiques*. We have others beside ourselves to think about."

"Well it's the others I'm trying to talk about, Marcia and Frank. You keep talking about you and me going to bed. They *are* going to bed. What are you going to do about it, Harold?"

"Bring me some evidence, and I'll confront her with it."

"What kind of evidence do you expect? Dirty pictures? A notarized diaphragm?"

Ringlets of vibration, fine as watch springs, oscillated on the surface of his Gibson as he laughed; there was an unexpected poetry in the woman, face to face across a table for two, the cloth and the softness of her stirred forward by a passionate worry. Through the windows the trees of the Public Garden were hushed cascades, the great copper beech a glittering fall of lava. Janet said, "All right. How is Marcia in bed for you lately? Less or more?"

How common, really, this was; it smacked of midwifery, of witchery, of womanish cures and auguries, of stolen hairpins and menstrual napkins. The waiter, a gray man polished and bent by service like a spoon, came and Harold ordered without consulting Janet *potage à la reine, quiche Lorraine,* salad, a light dry Chablis. "You're putting me on a diet," she said.

He told her, "In answer to your question. I think more."

"See? She's aroused. She's full of it. Screwing."

He laughed; his Gibson glass was empty and no watchsprings materialized. "Come off it, Janet. You expected me to say less, didn't you?"

"Has it been less?"

"No, I was honest. She's been quite loving lately. Your thesis is that women are polygamous; the more they have the more they want?"

"I don't know, Harold. I've never been unfaithful to Frank, isn't that funny? But I would think, as a woman—"

As a woman: this plump soft phrase out of her mouth gave him the pleasure he felt when, after a party, drunkenly showering, to hear Marcia feign shock he would fasten her bra to his skinny wet chest.

"—that she would feel guilty toward you, and wants to prove to herself that this isn't taking away from her marriage, that she has enough for both; and that furthermore she wants to tell you about it, this wonderful thing about herself, about the whole business. I know that Frank has out of the blue started doing things that *I* never taught him."

The thin wedge of a headache entered Harold's right temple. He reflexively reached for his empty glass, uncertain if Marcia had changed or not, for of those conversations of tranced bodies there is little distinct to recall, only the companionable slow ascent to moon-blanched plateaus where pantomimes of eating and killing and dying are enacted, both sides taking all parts. He found Marcia kittenish, then tigerish, then curiously abstract and cool and mechanical, and finally, afterwards, very grateful and tender and talkative and sticky.

Janet smiled, tipping a little from her glass into his. "Poor Harold," she said. "He hates indiscreet conversations. It's too female, it threatens him. But you know," she went on, having realized he would be good to experiment with, "I can't talk to other women comfortably. I could only have said these things to a man." She stated this with an air of having produced a touching confession for him, but he found it presumptuous and offensive. He thought women should properly talk with women, and men with men, and that communication between the sexes should be a courtly and dangerous game, with understood rules, mostly financial, and strict time limits. Ninety minutes was usually quite enough, and this lunch lasted longer than that.

They agreed to have lunch again, next week, to compare notes. Harold went home to a house more transparent; its privacy had been surrendered. While the Applebys lived in town, on a secluded lane on the far side of the Musquenomenee, in an ample white house of nondescript style whose interior comfort was essentially borrowed or inherited, the little-Smiths had built their own, and designed it in every detail, a flat-roofed redwood modern oriented along a little sheltered ridge overlooking the marsh to the south. The foyer was floored in flagstones; on the right an open stairway went down to a basement level where the three children (Jonathan, Julia, Henrietta) slept and the laundry was done and the cars were parked. Above this, on the main level, were the kitchen, the dining room, the master bedroom, a polished hall where hung reproductions of etchings by Rembrandt, Dürer, Piranesi, and Picasso. To the left of the foyer a dramatically long living room opened up, with a shaggy cerulean rug and two facing white sofas and symmetrical hi-fi speakers and a Baldwin grand and at the far end an elevated fireplace with a great copper hood. The house bespoke money in the service of taste. In the summer evenings he would drive back from the station through the livelong light hovering above the tawny marshes, flooded or dry according to the tides, and find his little wife, her black hair freshly combed and parted, waiting on the longer of the sofas, which was not precisely white but rather a rough Iranian wool bleached to the pallor of sand mixed with ash. A record, Glenn Gould or Dino Lupati playing Bach or Schumann, would be sending forth clear vines of sound from the invisible root within the hi-fi closet. A pitcher of martinis would have been mixed and held chilled within the refrigerator toward this precious moment of his daily homecoming; the tinge of green in the vermouth was intensified by the leafy green, green upon green, ivy and alder and hemlock and holly, crowding through their walls of sliding plate glass. Outdoors on the sparkling lawn, sparkling in the lowering light as the sun slowly approached the distant radar station—exquisite silver disc, always fidgeting— Jonathan, in bathing trunks and a candy-striped shirt, would be playing catch with Julia, or some children of neighboring summer people, tossing a chewed sponge ball, a little pitted moon, back and forth through the revolving liquid branches of the lawn sprinkler. Henrietta, as neat and alert in feature as Marcia herself, in her duckling nightie, bathed, would run toward Harold bare-foot through the cerulean rug to be lifted and hugged and twirled, and Marcia would pour two verdant martinis into glasses that would suddenly sweat, and the ball would fall short and lie crescented by sunlight, soaking, while the children noiselessly argued which would retrieve it and get drenched, and his entire household, even the stray milk butterfly perched on the copper fireplace hood, felt about to spring into bliss, like a tightly wound music box.

He detected small change in Marcia. They had met one sum-mer on Long Island and married the next, and things, more or less, had turned out as charmingly as had been predicted. They had both been in their mid-twenties and were considered by their contemporaries a bit intellectual and cool. They discovered each other to be sensual, but allowed this coolness to characterize their marriage. They never quarreled in public, rarely in private; each expected the other to see clearly into the mechanism of their union and to make without comment the allowances and adjust-ments needed. He excused his occasional call girls as hygienic; he took them as he took, behind the closed bathroom door, without complaint to Marcia, aspirins to relieve his headaches. He could believe that Marcia might be unfaithful to him, but as some kind of service to himself, to save him trouble, to accommodate him with new subtlety. He had married her after most of her friends had married. He had removed her from that crass monied Middle Atlantic society where she had seemed stilted and fragile. He trusted her to be always his. Smiling, she lifted the martini; the gin and her earrings trembled. He sipped; the coolness was delicious.

Without looking it, they were slightly older than most of their friends in Tarbox; Harold was thirty-eight, Marcia was thirty-six.

She did seem, lately, more inventive and solicitous. A ram-shackle boardwalk, in need of repair every spring, had come with their land, with the old summer cottage they had torn down. It led out to a small tidal creek too narrow for most powerboats; here, at high tide, between banks tall with reeds, in water warmer than the sea off the beach, they and their friends and their friends' children could swim. At night, now, this summer, when the tide was right, and the children were asleep, Marcia had taken to inviting him, Harold alone, for a swim before bed, without bathing suits. So they would walk down in moonlight through poison ivy and cut-back sumac, treading warily, and out the often-patched boardwalk, its slats of varied wood like the keys of a gigantic piano, and on the splintery soft dock take off their clothes and stand, husband and wife, naked together, gooseflesh rising, for an instant of nerve-gathering before plunging from the expectant summer air into the flat black water alive with reeds. Beside him her flitting breasts, arching arms, upturned face gashed by black licks of her hair bubbled through the blanched foam and slopping clammy slick. The water's million filaments sucked from his nerve ends the flecks of city filth. Our first love, our love of the elements, restored to him his youngest self. Sometimes, at high tide, like a laboring Cyclopean elephant a powerboat would come crowding up the channel with its searchlight and they would squat like aborigines under the dock in the root-riddled mud until the boat passed. And they would dry each other, Harold and Marcia, she toweling even his fumbly dripping genitals, thinking how innocently part of him they seemed, and not a harsh jutting second life parasitic upon him. As she ran ahead up the boardwalk, clutching her clothes to her breasts, her buttocks would be dancy in the steady moon. If in bed they made love, with salty bodies and damp hair, she praised his ardor—"so fierce"—and expertness—"oh, you know me so well"—as if a standard of comparison, someone gentle and clumsy, had appeared. And she would blurt "I love you" with a new emphasis, as if the "you" were darkened by the shadow of an unspoken "nevertheless."

At their next lunch Janet had nothing to offer but complaints about Marcia's constantly calling up and suggesting they do things together, as couples—sail, swim, play tennis, go to meetings. She was even trying to get her interested in the Tarbox Fair Housing Committee, which Irene Saltz and Bernadette Ong were organizing. "I said to her, 'But there isn't a single Negro in town,' and she said, 'That's the point. We're culturally deprived, our children don't know what a Negro looks like,' and I said, 'Don't they watch television?' and then I said, getting really mad, 'It seems to me awfully hard on the Negro, to bring him out here just so your children can look at him. Why don't they instead look at the Ongs on a dark day?' I shouldn't have said that, I think Bernadette's great; but there's something basically snotty about this committee. It's all because other towns have one. Like a drum-and-bugle corps."

Janet seemed old to Harold, though she was years younger than he, old and double-chinned and querulous, vexing herself with what he knew to be Marcia's simple gregariousness, her innocent need to be doing. He changed the subject. "What were you and Piet talking about so earnestly at the Thornes' party?"

Her valentine mouth, its lipstick flaking, frowned. "He was telling me his wife doesn't give him shit. He tells every woman."

"He's never told Marcia."

"She's never told you. Piet's been aching to break out for a long time and I don't know what's holding him back. Georgene's right there waiting."

It was fascinating, seeing his friends through a whole new set of windows. "And Freddy Thorne?" he asked delicately. He had long wondered if Janet had slept with Freddy.

Janet said, "Freddy's my friend. He understands women."

"And that's all you choose to say."

"That's all I have to say. We've never gone to bed, I'm fond of Freddy, he's harmless. Why are you men so mean to him?"

"Because you women are so nice to him."

Amused to discover himself jealous, Harold studied his fingers, which he set parallel to the table silver, and asked, "Do you think the Hanemas will get a divorce?" He liked Angela, one of the few women in town who could speak his language. He loved her upward-searching diffidence, her motherly presiding above their summer-evening gatherings. Everyone rather loved Angela.

"Never," Janet said flatly. "Piet's too tame. He's too thick in the conscience. He'll stick it out with those three, picking up whatever spare ass he can. The bad thing about a cockteaser like Angela is she turns her man loose on the world and lets a lot of other women in for trouble. Piet can be very winning."

"You speak as one who knows. *Elle qui sait.*"

"There've been overtures, nothing drastic. Among his other problems, he's shy."

"Poor Piet," Harold said, uncertain why, though Janet nodded in agreement.

That weekend, he asked Marcia, after a party, when both were drunk, "Do you love me?"

"I love you, Harold, but please not tonight. We're both too drunk and sleepy. Let's have a nap instead sometime tomorrow." Tomorrow was Sunday.

"I didn't mean to make love, I meant, honestly, *après douze années très heureuses*, aren't you pretty bored with me? Don't you ever think of what it would be like with other men?"

"Oh, maybe a little. Not very consciously." She was wearing a chiffon nightie the color of persimmon, and as she crawled into bed her dark limbs looked monkeyish. Getting into bed demanded nimbleness of her because the bed was high; also it was high and hard, because they found such a mattress best for lovemaking. The little-Smiths' bedroom, as they had designed it, was a shrine, a severe sacred space; its furniture consisted of little more than two teak bureaus, a reading lamp built into the headboard, a mirror on a closet door, a philodendron, and for a rug the hide of a zebra that Harold's grandfather had shot on safari with Teddy Roosevelt. When she was settled in, he turned off the light. The darkness was purple, and high in the window the marsh moon amid moving clouds seemed to swing back and forth like the bob of a pendulum.

"Tell me,' he said. "You won't hurt my feelings."

"OK. Ask me the men."

"Have you ever wanted to go to bed with Piet Hanema?"

"Not really. He reminds me too much of a fatherly elf. He's too paternal and sympathetic. Once at the Guerins we were left alone in the room with the bigger fireplace and he began to stroke my back and it felt as if he wanted to burp me. I think Piet likes bigger women. Georgene and Bea and I are too small for him."

"Freddy Thorne."

"Never, never. He's so slippery and womanish, I think sex is all talk with him anyway. Janet responds to him better than I do; ask her."

"You know I can't talk to Janet. Her vocabulary puts me off."

"It's getting worse lately, isn't it?"

"And Frank?"

Patterns of light—long lozenges of moonlight laid across the zebra rug and a corner of the bed; a rod of electric light coming from the hallway through the crack their door was left ajar, to comfort the children; a dim bluish smear on the ceiling from a carbon streetlight on the beach road, entering by the foyer transom—welled from the purple darkness as Harold held his breath, waiting for Marcia's answer.

It came very casually, in a voice half asleep. "Oh, Frank's been a friend too long to think about that way. Besides, he has whiskey breath and an ulcer. No, thanks." When, still studying their placid guests of light, he made no reply, she stirred and asked, "Why? Do you want Janet?"

He laughed quite loudly and said, "*Mon Dieu,* no! That girl's pure trouble."

"She's very hostile to me lately."

"I think," Harold said, snaking his arm around her and snuggling his genitals into the curved warmth of her backside, "we should make an effort to see less of the Applebys. Let's have the Guerins over sometime. Maybe with some new people like the Constantines. The wife seems pretty hip."

Marcia made no response, and he nudged her, and she said, "The Guerins are so depressing."

Janet was gayer at their next lunch, and looked five years younger. The day was one of those very hot days toward the end of August when to a woman summer seems a lover leaving, to be embraced with full abandon: appearances are past mattering; love disdains nothing. Sweat mars her makeup and mats her hairdo. Her arms swim freely in air. The steaming city streets crammed with secretaries have the voluptuousness of a seraglio. Janet wore an armless cotton dress printed with upside-down herons on a turquoise ground and swung herself along as if nothing in the natural world, no thrust of sun or thunderclap, could do her harm. Her feet, naked in sandals, were dusty, and Harold wondered, walking along Federal Street beside her in the heat, what it would be like to suck each dirty one of her ten toes clean. He took off his coat and swung it over his shoulder like a tough; they ate in a cafeteria whose glass doors were open at either end like sluice gates. Noise poured through him, backfiring trucks and the clatter of cutlery and the shouting of orders and the words of the girl across from him, with her sweating round face and eroded lipstick. She said, "How was *your* weekend?"

"Fine. You should know. We saw you every minute of it, except when somebody had to go to the bathroom."

"I know, isn't it boring? Frank and Marcia mooning at each other and exchanging ever so teeny-tiny little tender glances."

"You *do* exaggerate that."

"Balls, Harold. Frank absolutely gets choleric when he can't have Marcia as his tennis partner. And when they're across the net from each other, all those cute little pat shots, I could puke. He's always 'swinging by.' 'I'll swing by the Smith's to pick up Frankie.' 'I just swung by Smitty's to drop off the variorum Shakespeare, and they had me in for a drink.' It turns out 'they' was Marcia and you were off at a town Republican meeting. Harold, *why* are you a conservative?—it's such a pose."

He endured this tirade pleasurably, as if it were a massage or a shower. "But you still have nothing definite."

"How definite must definite be? Harold, he knows too much. He knew you were going to Symphony with the Gallaghers Saturday night. He knew Julia sprained her shoulder diving off the dock Thursday. When I talk to Marcia and tell him what she said he doesn't bother to listen because he's heard it all already. He knows you and she go skinny-dipping down by your dock and then fuck."

"Doesn't everybody know that? The dock part of it. The other doesn't invariably follow."

"How would everybody know? You think your friends have nothing better to do than splosh around the marshes with binoculars?"

"Marcia might tell Bea, or Georgene, or even Irene, in passing."

"Well she doesn't tell me and I'm her best friend supposedly. Frank tells me. Frank."

"I asked her the other night if she was having an affair with Frank."

Janet bit into her pastrami-on-a-roll and stared above the bun. "And she said?"

"I forget exactly what she said. We were both sleepy. She said he was too old a friend and had an ulcer."

"Two good reasons for it. Every woman has a nurse complex. And why not sleep with a friend? It's better than sleeping with an enemy. I've never understood why people are so shocked when somebody sleeps with his best friend's wife. Obviously, his best friend's wife is the one he sees most *of*."

"Well, she convinced me." He tried to state his heart's case. "We're not that unhappy, for her to do me dirt."

"Very well. She's as pure as Snow White and the stains in Frank's underpants are accidents of nature. Let's forget them. Let's talk about us. Why don't you like me, Harold? I like you. I like the way your nose comes to two points, like a very pale strawberry. Why don't you take the afternoon off and walk me through the Common over to Newbury Street and look at pictures? You understand pictures. What's this new gimmick of making things look like comic strips?"

She put her hand palm up on the tabletop; it was moist, a creased pink saucer of moisture on the silver-flecked formica. When he put his hand in hers, the gesture, amid the clatter and breeze of the cafeteria, felt hugely inflated: two immense white hands, like the mock-up of a beefburger, advertising love. With the other hand she was mopping up bits of pastrami with the final bite of the roll. "That's a delectable idea," he said, "but I can't. We're taking off Friday for Maine over Labor Day, so I have only one day left at the office. I need this afternoon. It's called Pop Art. It's also called hard-edge."

"So you'll be gone all weekend?" She withdrew her hand to wipe her fingertips, one by one, on a paper napkin. Her face seemed forlorn; her eye shadow had run, making her look theatrically tired.

Harold said, "Yes, and we're staying a few days past the holiday, so I'll miss next week's lunch with you. *Je regrette*."

"Do you?" In parting she told him, this blowzy stacked woman in upside-down herons, with a wave of her shapely swimmer's arm, "Have a *good* time with Marcia," the emphasis insolent. Then they went out of opposite ends of the cafeteria, she toward her maroon car in the Underground Garage, he toward his office on Post Office Square, glad to be released.

The family place in Maine overlooked a mottled blue harbor choked with glinting sails, swinging buoys, and surprising rocks that all jutted from the water at the same angle, testifying to a geological upheaval aeons ago. The largest rocks supported grass and shrubs and were therefore islands. The water was icy-cold and the beaches, far from the endless dunes of Tarbox, were niggardly arcs of shingle and brownish grit strewn with rack. Yet Harold, who visited Tarbox Beach only once or twice a summer, here swam before every breakfast. He was always happy in Maine. He ate the lobster and potato salad his mother set before him and read brittle paperback mysteries and old explorer's accounts in splotched bindings and sailed through the slapping spray and needled his sisters and brothers-in-law and slept soundly, having made love to Marcia like a sailor in from months at sea. She seemed his whore. She crouched and whimpered above him, her nipples teasing his lips. She went down on him purring; she was a minx. This was new, this quality of prostitution, of her frankly servicing him, and taking her own pleasure as a subdivision of his. Her slick firm body was shameless yet did not reveal, as her more virginal intercourse once had done, the inner petals drenched in helpless nectar. She remained slightly tight and dry. He did not wonder from whence this change in her chemistry had been derived, since he found it an improvement: less tact was demanded of him, and less self-control. Perhaps he abused her, for in the second half of their vacation, abruptly beginning on Labor Day night, she refused him. Afterwards she told Frank that suddenly she couldn't stand the confident touch of Harold's all-too-knowing hands. "He seemed a lewd little stranger who acted as if he had bought me." To have him inside her was distasteful: "like food in my mouth I couldn't swallow." Perhaps, in Maine, Marcia had experimented with corruption too successfully. Carrying within her like a contraceptive loop her knowledge of her lover, she had inflicted a stark sensuality upon her husband and then been dismayed by his eager submission to it. She realized she could serve several men in one bed, many men in one night—that this possibility was part of her nature; and she fled into an exclusive love for Frank. Making love to Harold suddenly lost seriousness. What they did with each other's bodies became as trivial as defecation, and it was not until months later, when his form was charged with the tense threat of his leaving her, that the curse of squeamishness was removed from their physical relations.

The little-Smiths returned to Tarbox Thursday night. Harold was conscious of having broken the string of appointments with Janet and doubted, without conscious regret, that there would be any more. Her theory had been wrong and may have never been more than a pretext. Growing up with three sisters had left him with little reverence for female minds. He had seen his sisters turn from comfortably shouting slugging animals into deceptive creatures condemned to assure their survival without overt aggression; their sensibilities were necessarily morbid. Janet was at best a poor reasoner and at worst a paranoid. About to go fat and lose her looks, stuck with a bilious and boring husband, she had turned desperately to a man in no way desperate. Brokers reaped in fair and foul weather, and Marcia had demonstrated a new versatility and violence in her love of him.

He did expect Janet to call him at his office Friday and, when no call came, was annoyed at the extent to which he permitted himself to listen for it. All day, as he rooted through the earth-bound stack of waiting mail and obsolete stock fluctuations, a signal from outer space kept tickling his inner ear. He remembered her strange way of wearing cloth, so that it came loose from her body and fluttered in the mind's eye. Perhaps they would see them this weekend. He hoped she wouldn't attempt a scene. Her indignation was so—fluffy. His secretary asked him why he was smiling.

Saturday morning, Marcia drove up to the center of Tarbox to talk to Irene Saltz about the Fair Housing group; Marcia had agreed to be on the education committee, whose chief accomplishment so far had been to give the high-school library a subscription to *Ebony*. "It might take hours, you know how she talks. Can you feed yourself and the children if I don't make it back by noon? There's some pastrami in the freezer you can heat up. The directions are on the package. The important thing is to boil it with the cellophane *on*."

They had been up drinking with the Thornes and the Hanemas the night before, and Harold was content to putter about gingerly, tucking away the props of high summer, folding the collapsed and torn plastic wading pool, coiling hose and detaching the sprinkler. Jonathan rummaged the football from a closet and he and Harold tossed it back and forth until a playmate, pudgy Frankie Appleby, arrived, with his mother. Janet was wearing snug blue denim slacks, an orange-striped boating jersey, and an unbuttoned peach-colored cashmere sweater, hung on her shoulders like a cape. "Where's Marcia?" she asked, when the boys were out of earshot on the lawn.

"In town conferring with Irene. Where's Frank?"

"He told me he was getting a haircut. But he didn't want to take Franklin because he might go to the drugstore and have to talk politics." She snorted, a sardonic equine noise, and stamped her foot. She was caught beneath a bell of radiance; the mistless sharp light of September was spread around them for miles, to the rim of the marshes, to the bungalow-crowded peninsula of East Mather and the ghostly radar dish, cocked toward the north. Janet was hollow-eyed and pale and ripe with nervous agitation, a soft-skinned ripeness careless of itself.

Harold said, "You think he's lying."

"Of course he's lying. Must we stand out here? The sun hurts."

"I thought you were a sun lover. *Une amoureuse du soleil.*"

"Not today. I'm sick at what I have to do."

"To whom?"

"To youm."

Harold opened for her the door that entered from the lawn the lower level of the house, where the children slept and the laundry was done. The laundry room smelled of cement and soap and, this morning, sourly, of unwashed clothes heaped around the dryer.

The gardening and carpentry tools and shelves of paint and grass seed and lime were ranged along the other wall, which reeked of gasoline from the power mower. Amid these fragrances Janet took a stance and said, "While you were away in Maine my car broke down, the transmission, so I had to go shopping in Frank's Corvair. I like the Lacetown IGA and on the way back that officious old Lacetown cop, the one with the gold teeth, stopped me for gliding through the stop sign, you know, just this side of the lace-making museum. What made me so mad, I was almost in Tarbox, where they never arrest you. Anyway, in looking through the glove compartment for the registration, underneath all the maps, I found this." She brought from her purse a piece of smudged white paper folded quarto. Harold recognized the indigo rim of Marcia's stationery. The notepaper had been given her as a wedding present, embossed with a monogram of her new initials, by a Southampton aunt, boxes of it; Marcia had laughed, thinking it hideously pretentious, the essence of everything she had married Harold to escape, and used it so seldom, once the thank-you notes were written, that after twelve years it was not used up. Indeed, he wondered if Janet had not somehow stolen a piece, it was so unlike Marcia to write on it. He reached and Janet held the folded paper back from him. "Are you sure you want to read it?"

"Of course."

"It's awfully conclusive."

"Damn you, give it to me."

She yielded it, saying, "You'll hate it."

The handwriting was Marcia's.

Dear Frank, whom I want to call dearest but can't—

Back from the beach, a quick note, for you to have while I'm in Maine. I drove home from our view of Nahant and took the children to the beach and as I lay there the sun baked a smell of you out of my skin and I thought, That's him. I smelled my palms and there you were again and I closed my eyes and pressed myself up against the sun while Irene and Bernadette chattered on and on and the children called from the ocean—there was ex-

traordinary surf today. I feel today left you sad. I'm sorry the phone rang—like icy water being poured over us—and that I teased you to stay longer. I do tease. Forgive me, and believe that I cherish our times together however unsatisfactorily abbreviated, and that you must take me as you can, without worry or self-blame. Love satisfies not only technically. Think of me in Maine, wishing you beside me and happy even in this wish, my "wanton's bird."

In love and haste,
M.

The signature was hers, the angular "M" of three strokes emphatically overstruck; but the body of the letter was written with a flowing smoothness not quite familiar, as if she had been drunk or tranced—it had been years since he had examined her handwriting. He lifted his eyes from the paper, and Janet's face held all the dismay he was still waiting to feel.

"Well," he said, "I've often wondered what women think about while they're sunbathing."

"Oh Harold," she cried, "if you could see your *face*," and she was upon him, had rushed into his unprepared embrace so swiftly he had to pull Marcia's letter free from being crumpled between them. The blue-bordered note fluttered to the cement floor. His senses were forced open, admitting the scouring odors of cement and *Tide;* along the far wall the sunburned lawn flooded the window with golden stitchwork, like a Wyeth. Janet's chest and hips, pillows sodden with grief, pressed him against the enameled edge of the dryer; he was trapped at the confluence of cold tears and hot breath. He kissed her gaping mouth, the rutted powder of her cheeks, the shying trembling bulges of her shut eyes. Her body his height, they dragged each other down, into a heap of unwashed clothes, fluffy ends of shirtsleeves and pajama pants, the hard floor underneath them like a dank bone. Sobbing, she pulled up her sweater and orange-striped jersey and, in a moment of angry straining, uncoupled her bra, so her blue-white breasts came tumbling of their own loose weight, too big to hold, tumbled like laundry from the uplifted basket of herself, nipples buttons, veins seaweed green. He went under. Her cold nails contemplated the tensed sides of his sucking mouth, and sometimes a finger curiously searched out his tongue. Harold opened his eyes to see that the great window giving on the lawn was solidly golden; no child's watching shadow cleft it; voices glinted from a safe distance, the dock. His face was half-pillowed in dirty clothes smelling mildly of his family, of Jonathan and Julia and Henrietta and Marcia. He was lying on ghosts that had innocently sweated. Janet's touch fumbled at his fly and he found the insect teeth of the zipper snug along her side. *Tszzzc:* he tugged and the small neat startled sound awoke them.

"No," she said. "We can't. Not here."

"One more kiss," he begged.

There was a wetness to her mouth, as her breasts overflowed his hands, whose horizon his tongue wished to swim to. She lifted away. "This is crazy." She kneeled on the cement and harnessed her bosom in cups of black lace that reminded him of the doilies in his grandmother's home in Tarrytown. It had been her side of the family that had known Teddy Roosevelt, who had taken Grandpa hunting. "The kids might barge in any second," Janet said, pulling down her jersey. "Marcia might come back."

"Not if she and Frank are copulating out by the dump."

"You think they'd do it to*day?*"

"Why not?" Harold said. "Big reunion, she's back from Maine with the horned monster. *Avec le coucou.* They've set us up for them to be gone for hours. Haircuts. Fair housing."

She adjusted her peach sweater so it again hung like a cape. Standing, she brushed the smudges on the knees of her slacks, from having kneeled. He remained sprawled on the laundry, and she studied him as if he were an acquisition that looks different in the home from in the store. She asked, "You really never suspected her until just now?"

"No. I didn't think she had the guts. When I married her she was a tight little mouse. My little girl is all growed up."

"You're not shocked?"

"I am desolated. But let's talk about you."

She adjusted her clothes with thoughtful firmness. "That was an instinctive thing. Don't count on me for anything."

"But I *do.* I adore you. *Ta poitrine, elle est magnifique.*"

As if the compliment had adhered, she removed a piece of lint from her jersey. "They're pretty saggy now. You should have known me when I was nineteen."

"They're grand. *Please* come upstairs with me." He felt it was correct, in asking her, to stand; and thus their moment of love was reduced to a flattened heap of laundry. Having surrendered all evidence, he was at her mercy.

Janet said, "It's impossible. The children." Lamely her hands sketched multiple considerations.

"Can't we ever get together?"

"What about Marcia and Frank?"

"What about them? Are they hurting us? Can we give them, honestly, what they give each other?"

"Harold, I'm not that cool. I have a very jealous moralistic nature. I want them to be punished."

"We'll all be punished no matter how it goes. That's a rule of life, people are punished. They're punished for being good, they're punished for being bad. A man in our office, been taking vitamin pills all his life, dropped dead in the elevator two weeks ago. He was surrounded by healthy drunks. People are even punished for doing nothing. Nuns get cancer of the uterus because they don't screw. What are you doing to me? I thought you were offering me something."

"I was, I did, but—"

"I accept."

"I felt sorry for you, I don't know what it was. Harold, it's too corrupt. What do we do? Tell them and make a schedule of swap nights?"

"You *do* de-romanticize. Why tell them anything? Let's get something to tell first. Let's see each other and see how it goes. Aren't you curious? You've *made* me want you, you know; it was you who chased me through all those hot Boston streets in your sexy summer dresses. Janet, don't you want me at all for myself? Am I only a way of getting back at Frank?" He glided the back of his hand down the slope of her left breast, then of the right. From the change in the set of her face he saw that this was the way. Touch her, keep touching her. Her breasts are saggy and want to be touched. Don't give her time to doubt, she hates what she knows and doesn't want the time. Don't pause.

She spoke slowly, testing the roof of her mouth with the tip of her tongue and fingering each button on the way down his shirt. "Frank," she told him, "is going to New York the first part of next week."

"*Quelle coïncidence!* Also next week Marcia was talking about going to Symphony Tuesday night and doing Junior League good deeds Wednesday morning and maybe spending the night in town. I think she should be encouraged to, don't you? Poor saint, that long hour in and out."

Janet gazed over his shoulder; her mouth, whose long out-turned upper lip was such a piquant mismatch with her brief plump lower, tightened sadly. "Has it really come to that? They spend whole nights together?"

"Don't bridle," he said, telling himself, *Don't pause.* "It's a luxury, to fall asleep beside the beloved. *Un luxe.* Don't begrudge them." He continued stroking.

"You know," Janet said, "I *like* Marcia. She's always cheerful, always has something to say; she's often got me out of the dumps. What I think I must mind is not Frank so much—we haven't been that great in bed for years, poor guy, let him run—as that *she* would do this to me."

"Did you hear what I said about Tuesday night?"

"I heard."

"Which of us should get the babysitter?"

So that fall Harold and Janet slept together without Frank and Marcia's knowing. Harold at first found his mistress to be slow; his climax, unmanageably urged by the visual wealth of her, was always premature. Not until their sixth time together, an hour stolen in the Applebys' guest room, beneath a shelf of Chinese-temple paraphernalia and scrolls inherited from Frank's father, did Janet come, pulling in her momentous turning Harold virtually loose from his roots, so that he laughed at the end in relief at having survived, having felt himself to be, for a perilous instant, nothing but a single thunderous heartbeat lost in her. He loved looking at her, her nude unity of so many shades of cream and pink and lilac, the soles of her feet yellow and her veins seaweed-green and her belly alabaster. He found an unexpected modesty and elusiveness in her, which nourished his affection, for he enjoyed the role of teacher, of connoisseur. It pleased him to sit beside her and study her body until, weary of cringing, she accepted his gaze serenely as an artist's model. He was instructing her, he felt, in her beauty, which she had grown to disparage, though her bluntness and forwardness had clearly once assumed it, her beauty of fifteen years ago, when she had been the age of his St. Louis mulatto. Harold believed that beauty was what happened between people, was in a sense the trace of what had happened, so he in truth found her, though minutely creased and puckered and sagging, more beautiful than the unused girl whose ruins she thought of herself as inhabiting. Such generosity of perception returned upon himself; as he lay with Janet, lost in praise, Harold felt as if a glowing tumor of eternal life were consuming the cells of his mortality.

The autumn of 1962, the two couples were ecstatically, scandalously close. Frank and Marcia were delighted to be thrown together so often without seeking it. Janet and Harold in private joked about the now transparent stratagems of the other two lovers. These jokes began to leak out into their four-sided conversations. To the Sunday-night ritual of fetched-in food had been added weekday parties, drinks prolonged into scrambled dinners, arranged on the pretext of driving the children (Frankie Jr. and Jonathan detested each other; Catharine was too much of a baby to respond to Julia's and Henrietta's clumsy mothering) back and forth to each other's houses. While the women cooked and fussed and preened around them, Frank and Harold with bottomless boozy searchingness would discuss Shakespeare, history, music, the bitchy market, monopolies, the tacit merger of business and government, the ubiquity of the federal government, Kennedy's fumblings with Cuba and steel, the similarity of JFK's background to their own, the differences, their pasts, their fathers, their resentment and eventual appreciation and final love of their fathers, their dislike and dread of their mothers, sex, their view of the world as a place where foolish work must be done to support fleeting pleasures. "Ripeness is all," Frank would sometimes say when silence would at last unfold its wings above the four spinning heads intoxicated by an intensity of friendship not known since childhood.

Or Janet would say, knowing they expected something outrageous from her, "I don't see what's so very wrong about incest. Why does everybody have a tabu about it? I often wanted to sleep with my brother and I'm sure he wouldn't have minded with me. We used to take baths together and I'd watch him get a hard on. He did something on my belly I thought was urination. Now he runs my father's antibiotic labs in Buffalo, and we can't."

"Sweetheart," Harold said to her, leaning forward above the round leather coffee table in the Applebys' lantern-hung living room, "that's the reason. That's why it's so tabu. Because everybody wants to do it. Except me. I had three sisters, and two of them would have stood there criticizing. *Trois sœurs est trop beaucoup.*"

Marcia sat up sharply, sensing a cause, and said, "I was just reading that the Ptolemies, you know, those pharaoh types, married brothers and sisters right and left and there were no pinheads produced. So I think all this fear of inbreeding is Puritanism." Her earrings scintillated.

"Cats do it," Frank said. "Sibling cats are always fucking."

"But are fucking cats," Janet asked, "always sibling?"

"I once talked," Harold said, determined to quarrel with Marcia, "to a banker who did a lot of financing for the Amish around Lancaster P-A, and he told me they're tiny. *Trés, trés petits.* They get smaller every generation. There's inbreeding for you, Marcia. They're no bigger than you are."

"She's a nice size," Frank said.

Marcia said to Janet, "I agree with *you.* I have a dreamy younger brother, he played the oboe and was a pacifist, and it would be *so* nice to be married to him and not have to explain all the time why you are the way you are, somebody who knew all the family jokes and would be sensitive to your *phases.* Not like these two clods."

"Vice versa," Harold persisted, "do you know why Americans

are getting bigger at such a phenomenal rate? Nutrition doesn't explain it. Exogamy. People marry outside the village. They fly clear across the continent, to Denver, to St. Louis, to marry."

Marcia asked, "Why on earth St. Louis? Denver I can see."

Harold continued, flushing at his slip (neither of the women knew of the mulatto, but Frank did), "The genes are fresh. It's cross-fertilization. So the advice 'Love thy neighbor' is terrible advice, biologically. Like so much of that Man's advice."

"He said love, He didn't say lay your neighbor," Janet said.

"I want my dreamy brother," Marcia said, pouring herself some more bourbon and twitteringly pretending to cry.

"Ripeness is all," Frank said, after a silence.

Or else they would sit around the rectangular tesselated coffee table in the little-Smiths' living room with its concealed rheostated lighting and watch Harold, bare-handed, gesticulating, conduct sides of Wagner's *Tristan*, or Mozart's *Magic Flute*, or Britten's *War Requiem*. Frank Appleby liked only baroque music and would sit stupefied, his eyeballs reddening and his aching belly protruding, while Harold, whirling like a Japanese traffic cop, plucked the *ting* of a triangle from the rear of the orchestra or with giant motions of embrace signaled in heaving oceans of strings. Janet hypnotically watched Harold do this and Marcia watched Janet curiously. What could she be seeing in this manic performance? How could a woman who nightly shared Frank's bed be even faintly amused by Harold's pathetic wish-fulfillment? One night, when the Applebys had gone, she asked Harold, "Are you sleeping with Janet?"

"Why? Are you sleeping with Frank?"

"Of course not."

"In that case, I'm not sleeping with Janet."

She tried a new tack. "Aren't you awfully tired of the Applebys? What ever happened to our other friends?"

"The big-Smiths moved to Newton."

"They were never our friends. I mean the Thornes and the Guerins and the Saltzes and the Gallaghers and the Hanemas. You know what Georgene told me the other day? She said Matt has had a nibble on the Robinson place, that Angela had wanted. A couple from Cambridge."

"How does Georgene come by all her information? She's become a real expert on the Hanemas. *Un spécialiste vrai.*"

"Don't you think Freddy and Angela are fond of each other?"

"*Tu es comique*," Harold said. "Angela will be the last lady in town to fall. Next to yourself, of course."

"You think Georgene has Piet?"

"Well. She has a very indulgent smile on her face when she looks at him."

"You mean like Janet has when she looks at you?"

"*Tu es trop comique.* She's twice my size."

"Oh, you have big—"

"Parts?"

"Ideas of yourself, I was going to say."

The other couples began to call them the Applesmiths. Angela Hanema, who never dreamed, dreamed she went to the Applebys' house carrying a cake. On the front porch, with its six-sided stained-glass welcoming light, she realized she couldn't get in the front door because the house was full of wedding invitations. Marcia little-Smith came around the side of the house, in shorts and swinging a red croquet mallet, and said, "It's all right, my dear, we're going to be very happy." Then they were all, a crowd of them, walking along a country path, in some ways the path down to the dock, Angela still carrying the cake on upraised palms before her, and she said to Frank Appleby, "But can you get the insurance policies straightened out?" which was strange, because in waking life Angela never gave a thought to insurance. With a gargantuan wink he assured her, "I'm floating a bond issue," and that was all she could remember, except that both sides of the path were heavily banked with violets, hyacinth, and little blue lilies. She had coffee with Georgene the next morning after nursery school, and, feeling uneasy with Georgene lately, in nervousness told her the dream. Georgene told Bea and Irene, while Piet, who had heard the dream at breakfast, was telling Matt Gallagher at the office. So Bernadette Ong heard the dream from two directions, from Irene at a Fair Housing executive meeting and from Terry Gallagher after a rehearsal of the Tarbox–North Mather–Lacetown Choral Society; the thirsty singers commonly went back to the Ongs afterwards for a beer.

But it was Bea, Bea whose malice was inseparable from her flirtatiousness, in turn inseparable from her sterility and her tipsiness, Bea who told Marcia. Marcia was puzzled and not amused. She did not for a moment believe that Janet and Harold were sleeping together. She did not think Harold was up to it; a certain awe of Janet, as of all big women, had been heightened by falling in love with this woman's husband. She had not suspected that from outside the couples might appear equal in complicity. She was shocked, frightened. She told Harold; he laughed. They told the Applebys together, and it was Janet who laughed, Frank who showed annoyance. "Why can't people mind their own dirty business?"

"Instead of our dirty business?" Harold said gaily, the double tip of his nose lifted, Marcia thought, like a bee's behind.

"Our language!" she said, nettled.

"Come on, *mon petit chou*," he said to her, "Angela can't help what she dreams. She's the most sublimated woman we know. Bea can't help it that she had to tease you with it. Her husband beats her, she can't have children, she has to make her mark somehow."

Janet was in a lazy mood. "She must ask to be beaten," she said. "She picked Roger so he must have been what she wanted."

"But that's true of all of us," Harold said. "*Tout le monde*. We get what we unconsciously want."

Marcia protested, "But they must think we do *every*thing, which seems to me so sick of *them*, that they can't imagine simple friendship."

"It *is* hard to imagine," Harold said, wondering if to smile would be too much. They were all on the verge. He looked at Janet, sleepily leaning with a cigarette in the Applebys' yellow wing chair, her silk blouse veined by its shimmer and her skirt negligently exposing her stocking-tops and fasteners and bland known flesh, and thought how easy, how right, it would be to take her upstairs now, while these other two cleared away the glasses and went to their own bed.

Frank said, "They're starved. Their marriages have gone stale and anything that tickles their nose they think is champagne. We enjoy relaxing with each other and musn't let them make us self-conscious about it." He cleared his throat to quote. "The mutable, rank-scented many."

This speech conjured a malicious night all about them. Marcia's eyes, watching Frank, were dark, dark like stars too dense to let light escape, and she felt her being as a pit formed to receive this blood-slow soft-handed man whose own speech, more and more as she was his mistress, was acquiring Shakespearian color and dignity. *Tickles their nose is champagne.* He had called them back from the verge. The little-Smiths left at one-thirty and drove through the town whose burning lights, bared in November, seemed to be gossiping about them. From their bedroom window the marsh, rutted and tufted along the ebbed canals, appeared a surface of the moon and the onlooking moon an earth entire in space. Restless, apologetic, they made love, while miles away across the leafless town the other couple, also naked, mirrored them.

Full confession waited until winter. Snow fell early in New Hampshire, and during Christmas vacation the Hanemas, the Applebys, the Thornes, the Gallaghers, and the little-Smiths went north to ski with their older children. The lodge bulletin board was tacked thick with pictures of itself in summer, of canoes and couples pitching quoits and porch rails draped with wet bathing suits. Now packed snow squeaked on the porch steps, a sign forbade ski boots in the dining hall, the dinner was pea soup and baked ham and deep-dish apple pie, the children afterwards thumped and raced in the long hall upstairs, between the girls' bunk room and the boys', and downstairs their parents basked by the fireplace in the afterglow of exercise. Whiskey hurried to replace the calories fresh air had burned from their bodies. Georgene methodically turned the pages of *Ski*. Freddy murmured on the sofa to Janet, who looked discontented. Frank played Concentration with his son and Jonathan little-Smith, and was losing, because he was concentrating upon a rotating inner discomfort, perhaps the ham, which had had a thick raisin sauce. Gaily rattling ice cubes, Harold was mixing a drink for Angela, whose fine complexion had acquired on the bitter slopes an unearthly glow, had reached an altitude beyond decay; she looked more twenty-two than thirty-four. Marcia was listening to Matt Gallagher explain the Vatican's likely verdict, now that the ecumenical council was adjourned, on artificial birth control: "Nix. They won't give us sex, but they may give us meat on Fridays." Marcia nodded understandingly—having a lover deepened her understanding of everything, even of Matt Gallagher's adherence to the letter of an unloving church—and glanced toward Terry. Terry, sitting cross-legged on the floor in black stretch pants, carefully picked through a chord sequence on her lute; it was a gourd-shaped, sumptuous instrument, whose eight strings produced a threadbare distant tone. Matt had bought it for her for Christmas, in line with the policy of conspicuous consumption that had led to the Mercedes, and perhaps with a more symbolic intent, for its blond lustre and inlaid elegance seemed sacramental, like their marriage. Piet lay beside her on the rug gazing at the taut cloth of her crotch. The seam had lost one stitch. Conscious of Georgene sulking at his back, he rolled over and did a bicycling exercise in air, wondering if with Catholics it was different, remembering his long-ago love for Terry, unconsummated, when he and Matt were newly partners. Whitney and Martha Thorne, Ruth Hanema, Tommy Gallagher with his Gainsborough fragility, and Julia Smith in raven pigtails watched a World War II movie starring Brian Donlevy. The channel, from Manchester, was weakly received. The game of Concentration broke up. Frank needed more bourbon to soothe his stomach. In twos and threes the children were led upstairs or out to the gas-heated cottages beneath the bone-white birches. A bridge game among strangers beside the fireplace broke up. Georgene Thorne, a tidy woman with feather-cut graying hair and a boyish Donatello profile, nodded while leafing through *House & Garden* and followed her children out to their cabin to sleep. Freddy blew her a smirking kiss. Walking down the squeaking path alone, she thought angrily of Piet—his flirting, his acrobatics—yet knew it was in the bargain, she had got what she wanted. Her breath was white in the black air. The unseen lake gave a groan and crack, freezing harder. The black birch twigs rattled. Harold and Marcia tried to organize word games—

Botticelli, Ghosts—but everyone was too suffused with physical sensations to play. The television set, unwatched, excited itself with eleven-o'clock news about UN military action in the Katanga province of the Congo; and was switched off. Piet begged Terry Gallagher to give them a concert, and so she, watching as if from beyond her own will her white bewitched fingers assume each position on the frets, played the one melody she had mastered, "Greensleeves." They tried to sing with her but had forgotten the words. Her head was tilted; her long black hair fell straight from one side. She finished; Matt, with a military swiftness, stood; and the Gallaghers went outdoors to their cabin. In the momentary opening of the door, all heard a snowplow scraping along the upper road. High in a dusty corner a cuckoo clock, late, sounded eleven. Angela, stately, her fair cheeks flaming, now stood, and Piet, muscled like a loose-skinned dog that loves to be scratched, followed her upstairs to their room. This left the Applesmiths and Freddy Thorne.

The elderly young couple that ran the lodge came in from doing a mountain of dinner dishes and thriftily turned off all the lights but one and separated the fireplace logs so that the fire would die. Their smiles of good will as they faced their guests were wretchedly enfeebled by contempt. "Good night now."

"Good night."

"Night."

"*Bon soir.*"

Yet for an hour more, in semidarkness and the growing cold, Freddy held forth, unable to let go of a beauty he had felt, of a goodness the couples created simply by assembling. "You're all such beautiful women. Marcia, why do you laugh? Jesus Christ, every time I try to tell people something nice to their face they laugh. People hate love. It threatens them. It's like tooth decay, it smells and it hurts. I'm the only man alive it doesn't threaten, I wade right in with pick and mirror. I love you, all of you, men, women, neurotic children, crippled dogs, mangy cats, cockroaches. People are the only thing people have left since God packed up. By people I mean sex. Fucking. Hip, hip, hooray. Frank, do you believe in the difference between tragedy and comedy? Tell me, for fuck's sweet sake. This is a serious question."

Frank said carefully, rumbling from the slumped position that seemed to ease his stomach, "I believe in it as a formal distinction Shakespeare believed in. I wouldn't make anything absolute of it."

"Frankfurt, that is beautiful. That's just where any medium intelligent man of the world would come down. That's where you and I differ. Because I do. I believe there are tragic things and comic things. The trouble is, damn near everything, from the yellow stars on in to the yummy little saprophytes subdividing inside your mouth, are tragic. Now look at that fire our penny-pinching hosts broke up to save a nickel. Tragic. Listen to the wind. Very tragic. OK, so what's not tragic? In the western world there are only two comical things: the Christian church and naked women. We don't have Lenin so that's it. Everything else tells us we're dead. Think about it; think about those two boobies bounding up and down. Makes you want to laugh, doesn't it? Smile at least? Think of poor Marilyn Moronrow; her only good pictures were comedies, for Chrissake."

"And the Christian church?" Marcia asked, glancing sideways at Frank as if nervously to gauge his pain.

"Christ, I'd love to believe it," Freddy said. "Any of it. Just the littlest bit of it. Just one lousy barrel of water turned into wine. Just half a barrel. A quart. I'll even settle for a pint."

"Go ahead," Janet told him, lazily. "Believe it."

"I *can't*. Marcia, stop checking on Frank. He's hyperalgesic, he'll live. Come on, this is a real gut talk. This is what people are for. The great game of truth. Take you and that fuzzy big-throated purply sweater; you're terrific. You look like a tinted poodle, all nerves and toenails, a *champeen*, for Chrissake. If your grandfather hadn't been the Bishop of East Egg you'd have made a terrific whore. Janet, you're a funny case. Sometimes you have it, right up the alley, all ten pins, and other times you just miss. Something pruney happens around your mouth. Tonight, you're really on. You're sore as hell about some silly thing, maybe Harold's snubbing you, maybe you have the red flag out, but you're right there. You're not always right there. Where would you rather be? Jesus, you're in every drugstore, and people tell me it's a hell of a good laxative, though I've never needed one myself, frankly."

"We've diversified," Janet told him. "We do a lot with antibiotics now. Anyway it wasn't a laxative, it was mineral oil."

"More power to it. You've lost some weight, that's a shrewd move. For a while there you had something bunchy happening under your chin. You know, honey, you're a fantastic piece—I say this as a disinterested party, girl to girl—and you don't have to wear all those flashy clothes to prove anything. Just you, fat or skinny, Janet Applesauce, that's all we want for dessert; we *love* you, stop worrying. As I say, you're all gorgeous women. It killed me tonight, it really tumified me, seeing old Terry Tightcunt sitting there with her legs spread and her hair down jerking off that poor melon. Have you ever noticed her mouth? It's enormous. Her tongue is as big as a bed. Every time I work on her molars I want to curl up in there and go to sleep."

"Freddy, you're drunk," Marcia said.

"Let him alone, I like it," Harold said. "*Je l'aime.* Freddy's aria."

"Oh God," Frank said, "that men should put an enemy in their mouths to steal away their brains."

Janet said, "Freddy, enough of us. Tell us about Angela and Georgene."

"Beautiful girls. Beautiful. I'm not kidding. You all knock Angela—"

"We *don't*," Marcia protested.

"You all knock that saint, but she has absolutely the most eloquent ass I've ever seen except on an ostrich."

"Giraffes have beautiful behinds," Harold said.

"Out of your class, I would think," Frank told him.

Harold turned, nose upturned, and said, "You hippopotamus. You ox."

Janet said, "Boys."

Freddy went on, "And *didn't* she look lovely tonight? Angela."

Harold, who had a nasal bass voice of which he was proud, imitated the singing of an aria: "And didn't she, di-hi-hidn't she, look lovely, luh-hu-hovilee tonight. A-aaaaangela, lala!"

Freddy appealed to the two women. "Tell me straight. You're

women. You have nice clear Lesbian eyes. Didn't she look about twenty, a virginal twenty, those eyes full of sky, that fantastic skin all rosy, Jesus. I mean, you're both beauties, I'm telling you straight, but she's my ideal. I idolize her. I look at that ass and I think Heaven. Twenty miles of bluebirds and strawberry whip."

The two couples laughed in astonishment. Freddy blinked for orientation; the whiskey in his glass had magically replenished itself. Marcia said, "Freddy, and Georgene? You haven't mentioned your wife."

"A healthy child," Freddy said. "She cooks well, she plays tennis well. In bed"—he squinted estimatingly and wiggle-waggled his hand—"so-so. *Comme ci comme ça*. I like it to be long, to take forever, have a little wine, have some more wine, fool around, try it on backwards, you know, let it be a *human* thing. She comes too quick. She comes so she can get on with the housework. I gave her the *Kama Sutra* for Christmas and she wouldn't even look at the pictures. The bitch won't blow unless she's really looped. What did the Bard say? To fuck is human; to be blown, divine."

Freddy, as usual, had gone beyond all bounds of order; the Smiths and Applebys made restless motions of escape. Janet stood and tossed the contents of her ashtray into the smoldering fireplace. Frank collected the cards scattered by Concentration. Harold rested his ankles on the sofa arm and elaborately feigned sleep. Only Marcia, twiddling one of her earrings, retained an appearance of interest.

Freddy was staring at the far high corner of the lodge, where above the cuckoo clock hung a dusty mass of cobwebs with the spectral air of an inverted reflection in water. He said, "I've seen the light. You know why we're all put here on earth?"

From the depths of his spurious sleep, Harold asked, "Why?"

"It just came to me. A vision. We're all put here to *humanize* each other."

"Freddy, you're so stupid," Marcia said, "but you *do* care, don't you? That *is* your charm. You care."

"We're a subversive cell," Freddy went on. "Like in the catacombs. Only they were trying to break out of hedonism. We're trying to break back into it. It's not easy."

Janet giggled and put her hand across Frank's lips before they could pronounce, as they were going to, "Ripeness is all."

Then fatigue and defeat were among them unannounced. The room was cold. Silence stood sentry. Freddy rose sluggishly, said, "See you on the slopes," and took himself outdoors to his cabin. The black lake beyond the chalky birches seemed an open mouth waiting for attention. The liquorish sweat of his chest froze into a carapace; his bare scalp contracted. He hastened along the squeaking path to Georgene, her forgiveness a dismissal.

Still the two couples were slow to go upstairs. Freddy's sad lewdness had stirred them. Marcia and Janet rotated, picking up glasses and aligning magazines, and sat down again. Frank cleared his throat; his eyes burned red. Harold crossed and recrossed his legs, dartlike in stretch pants, and said, as if on Frank's behalf, "Freddy is very sick. *Très malade*." Behind the fire screen the embers of the parted logs formed a constellation that seemed to be receding. The silence grew adhesive, impossible. Marcia pushed herself up from the sofa, and Janet, moving in her peach sweater and white slacks like a dancer intently gliding out of the wings toward her initial spring and pirouette, followed her to the stairs, and up. Both couples had rooms upstairs in the lodge. Frank and Harold listened below to the gush and shudder of activated plumbing, and switched off the remaining light. Again Frank cleared his throat, but said nothing.

In the upstairs hall, with its row of sleeping doors, Harold felt his arm touched. He had been expecting it. Frank whispered, mortified and hoarse, "Do you think we have the right rooms?"

Harold quickly said, "We're in nine, you're in eleven."

"I mean, do you think you and I should switch?"

From the elevation of his superior knowledge, Harold was tempted to pity this clumsy man groveling in lust. Daintily he considered, and proposed: "Shouldn't the ladies be consulted? I doubt if they'll concur."

A single bulb burned in the hallway and by this all-night light Frank's forward-thrust head looked loaded to bursting as he tried not to blurt. He wetly whispered, "It'll be all right. Janet's often said she's attracted to you. Take her. My blessing. What the hell. Let copulation thrive."

Harold feigned arch bemusement. "And Marcia? Does she want you?"

The other man nodded miserably, hastily. "It'll be all right."

The doors each of Rooms 9 and 11 were open a crack.

Harold remembered Janet's naked arms swinging moist along the gritty mica-starred streets of summer Boston, and could not resist tormenting his rival a moment longer. "Uh—do you and Janet work this"—he rotated his hands so the fingers and thumb reversed positions in air—"often?"

"Never. Never before. Come on, yes or no. Don't make a production of it. I'm sleepy and my stomach hurts."

In Frank's inflection there was a rising note of the bigger man whom Harold feared. There was also this, that from his desk at the bank Frank had thrown Harold, as broker, a wealth of commissions. The deposit of secrets Harold held in his head felt tenuous, no longer negotiable. Frank's big horned head was down. The two doors waited ajar. Behind one lay Marcia, with whom stretched side by side he shared every weary night; behind the other, Janet, whose body was a casket of perfume. He saw that the deceit he had worked with her would now lose all value. But there is always a time to sell; the trick of the market is to know when. Janet waited like a stack of certain profit. He carefully shrugged. "Why not? *Pourquoi non?* I'd love to. But be gentle." This last was strange to add, but here in the fragile wallboard and linoleum hall he had felt, as Frank's lifted head released a blast of muggy breath, the man's rank heaviness. Harold feared that his nervous lithe wife could not support such a burden; then remembered that she had sought it many times. The sight of Frank—his donkeyish outcurved teeth, his eyeballs packed with red fuses— became an affront; Harold turned to the door of Room 9, and touched it, and it swung open as if the darkness were expectant.

The latch clicked. A light from beyond the snow-heaped porch roof broke along the walls confusedly. Janet sat up in bed and her words, monosyllabic, seemed matches struck in a perilous inner space. "You. Why? Why now? Harold, it's wrong!"

He groped to the bed and sat on the edge and discovered she was wearing a sweater over her nightgown. "It was your husband's idea. I merely gave in. They'll think this is our first time."

"But now they'll *know*. They'll watch us. Don't you *see?* You should have acted shocked and said you wouldn't dream of any such thing. Frank knows when he's drunk, he wouldn't have minded. I'm sure it's what he expected. Oh God, Harold." She huddled tight against him sexlessly. His arms encircled her rounded back, sweatered like an invalid's.

"But I wanted you, Janet."

"But you can have me anytime."

"No, not anytime. When else could I be with you all night?"

"But how can you enjoy it, with those two a door away?"

"They're not hurting me. I like them both. Let them have what happiness they can."

"I can't stand it. I'm not as cool as you are, Harold. I'm going right in there and break it up."

"No."

"Don't take that bossy tone. Don't try to be my father. I'm all agitated."

"Just lie in my arms. We don't have to make love. Just lie in my arms and go to sleep."

"Don't you feel it? It's so *wrong*. Now we're really corrupt. All of us."

He lay down beside her, on top of the covers. The snow at the window had brightened. "Do you think it matters," he asked, "on the moon?"

"Somehow," Janet said, "it's *her*. She'll have this on me now."

"Marcia? No more than you have on her."

"But she completed college and I didn't."

He laughed in surprise. "I see. She completed college, therefore she knows more about erotic technique than you, therefore she's getting more out of Frank than you could get out of me. Right now she's doing the Fish Bite, followed by the astraddle position as recommended by the Bryn Mawr hygiene department."

Janet put her arms back beneath the covers and sniffed. "That's not it at all. But it seems to be what *you* think."

He supposed that, in his irritation at her lack of ardor, he had hopelessly offended her. All lost, he sighed through his nose.

After a pause she asked him, in the diffident voice of a salesgirl faced with an indecisive customer, "Why don't you get under the covers?"

So he did then travel through a palace of cloth and sliding stairways toward the casket of perfume that she spilled upon him from a dozen angles, all radiant. The radiator by the washstand purred in its seven parallel throats. She was, Janet, opaque, pale, powdery, heavy, sweet, cuffing, motherly; she roughly bid him rest with his narrow face between her breasts, his tongue out-thrust like a paralyzed lizard's.

While for Frank, a space away, Marcia was transparent, glid-ing, elusive, one with the shadows of the room; he enlarged, enlarged until she vanished quite and the darkness was solid with himself, then receded, admitting her silvery breathless voice say-ing lightly, "How lovely. Oh. Fuck. How lovely. Fuck. Fuck."

Between the couples, in Room 10, Piet and Angela Hanema slept back to back, oblivious, Piet dreaming of mortised tenons unpleasantly confused with the interlocking leap and slide and dipped shoulder of a ski lesson he had had that afternoon, Angela dreaming of nothing, skippingly, of children without names, of snow falling in a mountainous place where she knew she had never been, of a great lion-legged table supporting an empty but perfect blue vase of *mei ping* form—dreams when she awoke she would not remember.

Harold would not forget the cool grandeur of Janet that night, or the crescent of light on her fat shoulders above him, or the graciousness of her submission to the long work of his second climax. Fatigue, and the distracting question posed by their open privacy, made him uncharacteristically slow. She lay beneath him with the passiveness of the slaughtered, her throat elongated, her shoulders in shadow.

"I'm sorry," he said. "I'm taking forever."

"It's all right. I like it."

"Shall I stop?"

"Oh no. No."

The mournful tranquillity of her voice so moved him he at-tained the edge, fell from suspense, and released her from bondage. She turned and slept. As if he and she were on a seesaw, her dead weight lifted him into insomnia. The snow beyond the window was insistently brilliant, a piece of overexposed film. The pillow supporting her tangled hair seemed a second snow. Each time Harold closed his eyes he saw again the mountainside, the stunted ice-burdened pines at the top beside the lift shed, the troughs of ice, the slewing powder, the moguls packed by many turnings; and felt tense effort twitch his legs. His shins ached. Music, translucent sheets of it as in Debussy, was trying to break through to him, in the gaps between her breaths. He turned and fitted his body to hers. With a child's voice she sighed, "Oh no, lover, not again."

Dozing, he woke toward dawn. A footstep snapped in the hall. Marcia. His forsaken wife, abused and near madness, was seeking him. Janet's unfamiliar corpulence curled unconscious beside him, making him sweat. Like a spy unsticking an envelope, he removed himself carefully from her bed. The fabric of the night itself was showing fragility, crumbling into the brown particles of distinct visual detail—dashes of dirt embedded in the floorcracks, his own narrow feet chafed across the instep by his ski boots, Janet's silk glove liners drying on the radiator like tiny octupi, a jar of hand lotion on her bare pine bureau cupping moonglow. Of the clothes he had entered this room in, he took time to put only his pants and sweater back on. The hall creaked again, nearer this door. He lightly pulled it open, his face a mask of tenderness.

There was Frank, coming from the lavatory, bug-eyed and mottled beneath the all-night bulb. At the sight of Harold his eyes underwent a painful metamorphosis, becoming evasive and yet defiant and yet ashamed and defenseless in sickness.

Harold whispered, "What's up?"

"Stomach. Too much booze."

"*Et ma femme? Dorme-elle?*"

"Like a rock. How about Jan-Jan?"

"*La même.*"

Frank pondered, revolving his condition through his mind. "It's like a ball of tar in there I can't break up. I finally threw up. It feels better. Maybe I'm nervous."

"Do you want to go back to your own room?"

"I suppose we should. The kids will soon be up and might come in."

"Good night, sweet prince. May flights of angels, et cetera."

"Thanks. See you on the slopes."

"*Oui*. See you on the slopes." Harold tried to think of the French for "slopes," couldn't, and laughed as if an irony had been belatedly uncloaked.

Janet had been stirred awake by Harold's leaving and the whispering in the hall and knew it was Frank returning to her bed, though she feigned sleep. Perhaps in this moment began her irritated certainty of being wronged. Janet was a woman in whom early beauty had bred high expectations. Their disappointment brought with it a soured idealism, an idealism capable only of finding the world faulty. She decided that with Harold's acquiescence in the end of deception she had been betrayed. Marcia had entered adultery freely whereas Janet had thrown herself upon Harold to assuage their despair. A cynical ménage cheated her of such justification. Each liaison with Harold had been an installment of vengeance; a pattern of justice was being traced in the dark. But her affair had proved to be not a revenge but a convenience, and Janet's idealism asked of life more than a rectangular administration of reassurance and sex. Deeper than her moral reservations lurked the suspicion that Marcia was more sensual than she, better in bed. Janet did not see why she should submit to two inadequate and annoying men so that Marcia could respectably be a nymphomaniac. The woman, whom Janet had always considered dry and dowdy, was really diabolical, and it irked Janet to know that, in the likely event of a scandal, she would get all the sympathy, and Janet all the blame.

The inadequacy and annoyingness of the men emerged as soon as Janet made resistance. They were sitting, the weekend after their swap, in the Applebys' living room, with its round leather coffee table and its shelves of inherited uniform sets: red Balzac, ochre Scott, D'Annunzio in gold-stamped white calfskin, Mann in the black Knopf editions, green Shaw by Dodd, Mead. This wall of books, never touched, absorbed their smoke and conversation. Snow, the first storm to visit Tarbox that winter, was sealing them in. Frank had made a hot rum punch and they were drunk. He said at midnight, "Let's go upstairs."

"No," Janet said.

"I don't mean with *me*," Frank explained. "You can have *him*."

"I find both of you distinctly resistible."

"Janet!" Harold said, not so surprised, since she had slept with him Wednesday and afterwards told him her feelings.

"I think it's too corrupt," she said. "Don't you, Marcia?"

Marcia pinched her left earring, as if it had chimed. "Not if we all respect each other."

"I'm sorry," Janet said. "I can't respect any of you. I especially can't respect a woman who has to have so many men."

"Only two," Frank protested.

"I'm sorry, Marcia. I honestly think you should put yourself in the hands of a doctor."

"That'll make *three* men," Harold said. He was inwardly betting that Janet's resistance was a kind of mist that seemed solid from a distance but proved negotiable as you moved into it: like golf in the fog.

"You're suggesting I should be *fixed?*" Marcia asked.

"I don't mean a physical doctor, I mean a therapist. An analyst. Frank has told me everything about your affair and I think the way you went after him was scarcely normal. I'm not speaking as the injured wife, I'd say the same if it was any man. In fact it probably could have *been* any man."

"Darling Janet," Marcia said, "I love your concern. But I didn't go after Frank. We came together because you were making him miserable. You were giving him an ulcer."

"His stomach has gotten ten times worse in these last months."

"So, I imagine, have you. From Harold's description of your strip-tease in the laundry room I'm amazed to discover you're so fastidious."

Janet turned to Harold. "You told her?"

He shrugged and touched his left earlobe. "She told *me* everything. I didn't want her to feel guilty."

Janet began to cry, stonily, without any concessive motions of her arms or hands.

Marcia lit a cigarette and stared at the other woman dry-eyed.

"Don't you worry," she said. "I wouldn't take Frank if you begged me. Tonight or any night. I want you to have him until you've ground him down to nothing. I've been keeping him afloat for half a year and frankly I'm tired to death of it. The *last* thing I expect is thanks from *you*."

Janet said nothing and both men pleaded for her.

"It was the bear market gave me the ulcer," Frank said, "not anything Jan-Jan did."

"She's *nice* in bed," Harold told his wife. "*Belle en lit*."

Marcia told Frank, "Fuck her, then. Take her upstairs and fuck her and don't come creeping to me with your third-rate Shakespeare bits. I'm sick to tears of these big dumb women that don't do a damn thing except let the world lick their lovely derrières. Divorce me," she said to Harold. "Divorce me and marry her if she has such hot tits. Let me not to the blah blah blah admit impediments, isn't that it, Frank? This is the end. You, me, the whole rotten works." She stood, gauging the dismay in the faces suddenly beneath her.

"Marcia," Harold said. "Stop bullying Janet with your foul language."

"She's not bullying me," Janet said. "I agree with her."

"I'll heat up the punch," Frank said. "Or would anybody like a beer?"

"Frank, you're a prince," Harold said. "But if we're not going to bed I really could use the sleep. We have one of the Mills girls babysitting and she's having midyears at B.U."

Frank said, "That Exeter friend of mine who's buying the Robinson place teaches at B.U."

"I hear he's handsome," Janet said.

Marcia, feeling her scene slide away from her, said, "I can't stand any of you and I hate this dreary house." She went to the front hall for her coat, which was mousy and old. Harold followed, knowing that she had brought a diaphragm in her purse and wondering if now she would use it at home. But the little-Smiths had waited too long to leave and both the Applebys, first Frank and then Janet too, had to wade through the snow and push Harold's Porsche to get it started down the driveway. The taillights slithered back and forth insolently in escaping and Janet said, "I hope that's the last we ever see of them. They're little and, I know they can't help it, they're poisonous. Isn't it a lovely night, Frank? I don't think I've noticed the weather once since we got involved with those people." In the spaces between the trees, dimly lit by their distant porchlight, flakes were hurrying to touch them, lightly, lightly, dying as they did. But in the hot front hall, as she bent over to tug off her galoshes, Frank patted her and she straightened, fierce, and said to him, "Don't you *dare* touch me. It's her you want. You go to her. Just go. *Go.*"

Janet wished powerfully not to be frigid. All her informal education, from Disney's *Snow White* to last week's *Life*, had taught her to place the highest value on love. Nothing but a kiss undid the wicked apple. We move from birth to death amid a crowd of others and the name of the parade is love. However unideal it was, she dreaded being left behind. Hence she could not stop flirting, could not stop reaching out, though something distrustful within her, a bitterness like a residue from her father's medicinal factory, had to be circumvented by each motion of her heart. Liquor aided the maneuver.

For some weeks the Applebys and little-Smiths stayed apart. Marcia and Janet each let it known there had been a fight. The other couples tactfully did not invite them to parties together. When Harold phoned Janet she said, "I'm sorry, Harold, I loved being with you, person to person, man and woman, you really know how to make a woman feel it. But I think doing it with couples is terribly messy, and I'll have to hang up the next time you call. Think of the children if of nobody else." When Frank called Marcia, she said, "I do want to be with you, Frank, just *with* you, anywhere. I want it worse than any man can imagine. But I'm not, simply *not*, going to give Janet any more ammunition. If I felt you loved me that would be one thing; but I realized that night in the lodge when you left my bed how committed you still are to her, and I must think now about protecting myself. She'd destroy me if she could. I don't mean to be melodramatic; that's her style, not mine. I'm not saying good-bye to you. When you and she get yourselves straightened out, I'd *adore*

to see you again. You're the love of my life, unfortunately."
Frank could not escape the impression that she was asking him to
get a divorce. Meanwhile, our advisory capacity in Vietnam was
beginning to stink and the market was frightened, frightened yet
excited by the chance of expanding war. Basically business was
uneasy with Kennedy; there was something unconvincing about
him.

One January Saturday all the Tarbox couples went into Boston
for dinner at the Athens Olympia and to see a hockey game:
Bruins vs. Red Wings. Both the little-Smiths and Applebys declined to go, under the mistaken impression that the other couple
was going. This left them alone in Tarbox together, and it naturally followed that since Jonathan and Frank Jr. had Saturday ski
lessons together at the hill in East Mather, under the radar station,
the fathers arrange for Frank Sr. to bring them both back at
four-thirty; and that, once at the little-Smiths, he accept the offer
of a drink, and then another, and then at six, egged on by the
giggling little-Smiths, he call Janet at home with the suggestion
that she get a sitter and pick up some pizza and come on down.
For much of what they took to be morality proved to be merely
consciousness of the other couples watching them.

Janet called back in ten minutes saying she couldn't find a
sitter; the hockey expedition had taken them all. Harold got on
the phone and told her to bring Catharine with her and they
would put her to sleep on the cot in Henrietta's room.

Holding the bulky baby in one arm and a steaming paper bag in
the other, Janet arrived at seven-thirty. She wore a knee-length
mink coat, a coat she had owned since early marriage but that,
pretentious and even comical in Tarbox, usually hung idle in a
mothproofed bag. Beneath the coat, she was wonderfully dressed:
in a poppy-orange silk blouse and blue jeans shrunk and
splotch-bleached like a teen-ager's and white calf-length boots she
pulled off to reveal bare feet. Seeing her pose thus clothed in his
long living room (on the shaggy cerulean rug her toes were rosy
from the cold, the insteps and sides of her feet lilac white, her
heels and the joints of her toes dusted with pollen), Harold felt
his entire frame relax and sweeten. Even Marcia was moved, to

think her husband had once possessed such a splendid mistress. Frank stepped toward her solicitously, as if toward an invalid, or a genie that might disappear.

From seven to eight they drank. Between eight and nine they put the children to bed. Franklin Jr., secretly afraid he would wet the sheets, refused to sleep in the same bed with scornful Jonathan. They gave him instead the cot in Henrietta's room. This left Catharine Appleby, her cheeks as red as permeated wineskins, to go into the great high square sacred marital bed, on top of a rubber sheet. Janet lay down and crooned to the baby while Marcia put the cooled-off pizzas in the oven. Harold read Frankie Junior a Little Golden Book entitled *Minerals,* while Frank watched Jonathan contemptuously settle himself under the covers with a Junior Detective Novel entitled *The Unwanted Visitor.* From nine to ten the grown-ups ate, from ten to eleven they talked, from eleven to midnight they danced. Harold put an old Ella record on their hi-fi and to the tunes of "These Foolish Things" and "You're the Top" and "I've Been Around the World" the pair of couples rotated, Harold and Janet sliding smoothly around the edges, Frank and Marcia holding to the center of the derugged floor. The sliding glass doors giving on the view of the marsh doubled their images, so that a symmetrical party seemed in progress, the two linked couples approaching and withdrawing from two others like blots on a folded paper, or like visitors to a violet aquarium who, seeing no fish, move closer to the glass and discover the watery shadows of women and men.

Marcia, almost motionless, watched Harold's hand confidently cup Janet's derrière as he waltzed her from corner to corner; Janet, whirling, glimpsed Marcia bending closer into Frank's static embrace as he rumbled at her ear. His face was glossy, suffused with drink. The hand of his not on her back was tucked in between her chin and his chest and Janet knew, while Harold's thighs slithered on her thighs, that a single finger of Frank's was hypnotically stroking the base of Marcia's throat, down to the tops of her breasts. It was a trick he had, one of the few. She whirled, and the hand of Frank's not at her throat was unzipping the back of Marcia's dowdy black dress. Then from another angle

Janet saw held between Marcia's lips like a cigarette the slitted drag of cruelty that came to her face, Janet had noticed, whenever she was very tired or very much at ease. To Marcia, Janet's eyes staring from across the room seemed immense, so dilated they contained the room in their circle of vision as a metal lawn ball contains, distorted and compressed, an entire neighborhood. Frank's delicate hand uncoupled her bra snaps; his single finger slipped further down her breasts. Her body slightly dissolved. She felt herself grow. "I've flown around the world in a plane," Ella, purple spirit, sang, "I've settled rev-o-lutions in Spain." Janet, dizzy from being whirled, felt tipped back by an insistent pressure, knoblike and zippered, amid a lizardly slithering, and thought it sad that Harold should appear a fool before these cruel two other people when she, alone with him, in an ideal seclusion, could have forgiven so well his conceited probing and insinuations of skin. As her image of herself expanded, milk and pollen and poppies, up to the parallel redwood boards of the ceiling inset with small round flush lights rheostated dim, it seemed to Janet that mothering had always been her specialty.

So it was she, when the music stopped, who said, "I'm sleepy and dizzy. Who's going to take me to bed?" Frank in the center of the room made no move, and Harold stayed at her side.

To make space for themselves the two couples had to rearrange the children. Catharine Appleby, her heavy flushed head lolling, was moved into bed with dainty six-year-old Julia Smith; and the door to Jonathan's room (he had fallen asleep with the light on and *The Unwanted Visitor* face down on the blanket) was closed, so no noise from the master bedroom would wake him. The two white sofas were pushed together to make a second bed. It seemed very strange to Janet, as strange as a visit to Sikkim or high Peru, to journey forth, between three and four that morning, toward their own home; to bundle their two oblivious children in borrowed blankets and carry them across the little-Smith's stone-hard lawn to their two dark cars; to hiss farewells and exchange last caresses through clothes that upon resumption felt like fake and stiff and makeshift costumes; to drive behind Frank's steady taillights through a threadbare landscape patched with pieces of dry half-melted snow; to enter a deserted house carrying children like thieves with sacks of booty; to fall asleep beside an unfamiliar gross man who was also her husband; to feel the semen of another man still moist between her thighs; to awaken and find it morning and the strangeness banished with no traces save a congested evasive something in Frank's grateful eyes and a painful jarring, perhaps inaccurate overlay printing, in the colors of the Sunday comics section.

This pattern, of quarrel and reunion, of revulsion and surrender, was repeated three or four times that winter, while airplanes collided in Turkey, and coups transpired in Iraq and Togo, and earthquakes in Libya, and a stampede in the Canary Islands, and in Ecuador a chapel collapsed, killing a hundred twenty girls and nuns. Janet had taken to reading the newspaper, as if this smudgy peek into other lives might show her the way out of her own. Why was she not content? The other three were, and there was little in her religious background—feebly Presbyterian; her father, though a generous pledger, had been rather too rich to go to church, like a man who would have embarrassed his servants by appearing at their party—to account for her inconvenient sense of evil. She suspected that Marcia and Harold and Frank, having completed college, knew secrets, and used her. She felt her flesh prized by them. She was their sullen treasure. Once, serving them scrambled eggs in her home after midnight, wearing a bathrobe over a nightie (she had gone to bed with a headache and a temper and had come back downstairs again after an hour of listening to their three-cornered laughter), Janet had leaned over the kitchen table with the frying pan and Frank had stroked her from one side and Harold from the other and Marcia, watching, had smiled. She had become their pet, their topic. They could not understand her claustrophobia and indignation, and discussed her "problem" with her as if it might lie anywhere but with them, the three of them.

"Did you ever see," Harold asked, as they sat around the round grease-stained leather table, "your parents making love?"

"Never. The nearest thing to it, some Sunday mornings the door to their bedroom would be locked."

"Dear Janet," Marcia said. "Poor dear Janet. Tiptoeing in her Sunday-school dress down that long silent hall and pushing, pushing at that locked door."

"Shit," Janet said. "I never pushed at anything. Speak for yourself."

"Dear me," Marcia said. "I suppose that should hurt."

"Bad girl, Janet," Harold said. "You pushed me into the laundry."

"Because you looked so *mis*erable." Janet tried not to cry, which she knew would encourage them.

"Let Jan-Jan alone," Frank said. "She's a lovely broad and the mother of my heirs."

"There's Frank," Marcia said to her husband, "giving himself heirs again." Their intimacy had forced upon each a rôle, and Marcia had taken it upon herself to be dry and witty, when in fact, Janet knew, she was earnest and conscientious, with humorless keen emotions. Janet looked at her and saw a nervous child innocently malicious.

"You don't have to defend Janet to me," Harold told Frank. "I love her."

"You desire her," Marcia corrected. "You've cathected in her direction."

Harold continued, shinily drunk, his twin-tipped nose glinting, "She is the loveliest goddam p—"

"Piece," Marcia completed, and scrabbled in her bent pack of Newports for a cigarette.

"*Pièce de non-résistance* I've ever had," Harold finished. He added, "Out of wedlock."

"The horn, the horn, the lusty horn," Frank said, "is not a thing to laugh to scorn," and Janet saw that the conversation was depressing him also.

Harold went on with Janet, "Were your first experiences with boys under bushes interesting or disagreeable? *Intéressant ou désagréable?*"

"Buffalo boys didn't take me under bushes," Janet said. "I was too fat and rich."

Marcia said, "*We* were never really *rich*. Just respectable. I thought of my father as a holy man."

"Saint Couch," Harold said, and then repronounced it, *"San' Coosh!"*

"I thought of mine," Janet said, growing interested, beginning to hope they could teach her something, "as a kind of pushover. I thought my mother pushed him around. She had been very beautiful and never bothered to watch her weight and even after she got quite large still thought of herself as beautiful. She called me her ugly duckling. She used to say to me, 'I can't understand you. Your father's such a handsome man.'"

"You should tell it to a psychiatrist," Marcia said, unintended sympathy lighting up her face.

"No need, with us here," Harold said. *"Pas de besoin, avec nous ici.* Clearly she was never allowed to work through homosexual mother-love into normal heterosexuality. Our first love-object is the mother's breast. Our first gifts to the beloved are turds, a baby's turds. Her father manufactures laxatives. Oh Janet, it's so obvious why you won't sleep with us."

"She sleeps with me," Frank said.

"Don't brag," Marcia said, and her plain warm caring, beneath the dryness, improved Frank's value in Janet's eyes. She saw him, across the small round raft crowded with empty glasses and decanters, as a fellow survivor, scorched by the sun and crazed by drinking salt water.

"Why must you ruin everything?" he suddenly called to her. "Can't you understand, we all love you?"

"I don't like messy games," Janet said.

"As a child," Harold asked, "did they let you play in the buffalo mud or did you have an anal nanny?"

"Anal nanny," Marcia said. "It sounds like a musical comedy."

"What's the harm?" Frank asked Janet, and his boozy dishevelment, his blood-red eyes and ponderous head rather frightened her, though she had lulled him to sleep, her Minotaur, for ten years' worth of nights. He shouted to all of them, "Let's do it! Let's do it all in the same room! Tup my white ewe, I want to see her whinny!"

Harold sighed daintily through his nose. "See," he told Janet. "You've driven your husband mad with your frigidity. I'm getting a headache."

"Let's humanize each other," Frank pleaded.

Marcia turned on him, possessive of his mind. "Frank, don't quote Freddy Thorne. I'd think you'd have more intellectual self-respect."

Yet it was Freddy Thorne who sensed the trouble, and who tried to turn it to his own advantage. "I hear there's a snake in Applesmithsville," he said to Janet.

"Where's that?" They were in her house, at the April party given to welcome the Whitmans to town. Janet was distracted by her duties as hostess; she imagined that people and couples needed her everywhere. Piet Hanema was lying all over the stairs and down came Foxy Whitman from the bathroom, with him looking up her skirt. She must take Foxy aside and explain about Piet.

"Oh," Freddy answered, demanding her attention, "here and there, everywhere. All the world is Applesmithsville." In the corner, by the wall of uniform sets, John Ong, his ageless face strained and courteous, was listening to Ben Saltz painstakingly jabber; Janet thought that a woman should go over and interpose herself, but with this alternative she turned herself a little closer into Freddy Thorne's murmur. Why does his mouth, she wondered, if he's himself such a dentist, look so toothlesss? "They're feasting off you, Jan-Jan," he told her. "You're serving two studs and Marcia's in the saddle."

"Spare me your vulgar fantasies, Freddy," Janet said, imitating Marcia. "Contrary to what seems to be the popular impression, Harold and I have never slept together. The possibility has been mentioned; but we decided it would be too messy."

"You're beautiful," Freddy told her. "The way you look me right in the eye handing out this crap is beautiful. Something you don't realize about yourself, you really have it. Not like these other cunts. Marcia doesn't have it, she's trying to jiggle herself into having it. Bea's trying to drink herself into it. Angela's trying to rise above it. You're right there. Do me a favor though and don't fib to jolly old Freddy."

Janet laughed; his words were like the candyish mouthwash by his porcelain dental chair—unswallowable but delicious. She asked, "And Georgene? Does she have it?"

"She's OK in a tennis dress, don't knock the kid. She fucks and she can cook, so what the hell. I'm not proposing marriage."

"Freddy, don't make me hurt your feelings."

"You want out, right?"

"In a way, in a way not. I'm, what's the word, not ambidextrous?"

"Ambivalent. Androgynous. Androdextrorogerogynous."

"We have *fun* with the Smiths, just sitting and talking, neither Frank or I have ever had really close friends before. You can't imagine just friendship, can you?"

He patted his bright bald head and in sudden exultation vigorously rubbed it. "Between you and me, yes. It's what a fish feels for the fish he's eating. You want out, I can get you out. Have a little affair with me and that circus you're supporting will pack up and leave town. You can be your own girl again."

"How little is little?"

"Oh"—his hands did one squeeze of an invisible accordion—"as much as suits. No tickee, no washee. If it doesn't take, it doesn't take. No deposit on the bottle, Myrtle."

"Why do you propose this? You aren't very fond of me. It's Angela you want."

"A, I don't, and B, I am, and C, I like to help people. I think you're about to panic and I hate to see it. You're too *schnapps* for that. You wear clothes too well. Terrific dress you have on, by the way. Are you pregnant?"

"Don't be silly. It's an Empire line."

"Now wouldn't it be awful to get knocked up and not know which was the father? Hey. Are you on the pills?"

"Freddy, I'm beginning to hate this conversation."

"Okey-doke-doke. Let it simmer. As Khrushchev said when he put the missiles on Cuba, nothing ventured, nothing gainski. I'm there if you think you can use me."

"Thank you, Freddy. You're a nice man." Janet's conscience pricked her; she added, "Yes."

"Yes how?"

"Yes, in answer to your question, I am on the pills. Marcia isn't yet. She's afraid of cancer."

Freddy smirked and made a ring with his thumb and forefinger. "You're golden," he told her. "You're the last of the golden girls." He put the ring to his mouth and fluttered his tongue through it.

Janet considered his offer seriously. As she picked her way through the tangle of her party it seemed not so implausible. Freddy would know his way around a woman. Marcia and Frank and Harold would be horrified. Harold's vanity would be unforgivably piqued. Love chases love. These things happen. Piet was making out with poor little Bea Guerin. Frank was grotesquely Twisting (his digestion!) opposite Carol Constantine. Eddie on the sofa was demonstrating with his circling hands to Bernadette Ong the holding pattern of air traffic over LaGuardia and Idlewild, and why the turboprops and private planes were brought down sooner than the pure jets, the beautiful new 707s and DC-8s, and why with every new type of commercial aircraft several hundred passengers will die through pilot error, and why the starlings and gulls at Logan are a special menace; and finally he brought his narrow curly-haired head down safely onto her silk shoulder and appeared to sleep. The guests of honor felt out of it. Foxy queasy, the Whitmans left early. When everyone had left except the little-Smiths, and they were sitting around the table having the dregs of the liqueurs, Janet asked Marcia, "Did Freddy Thorne seem attractive to you tonight?"

Marcia laughed; the glitter of her earrings clashed on the surface of her face. "Heavens, no. He asked me if I was happy in Applesmithsville."

"What did you say?"

"I was very frosty. He went away. Poor Georgene."

"He asked me, too. In fact"—Janet was not sure if this was a tactic, but the Benedictine made it seem one—"he offered to have an affair with me."

"He really is a fantastic oaf," Frank said. Brandy was the worst thing for him, and he was on his third glass.

Harold swirled his Grand Marnier thoughtfully. "Why are you telling us this?"

"I don't know. I was so surprised at myself, that it didn't seem like such a bad idea. Since he's lost all of his hair, he's rather handsome, in a sinister way."

"In a mealy-mouthed way," Marcia said. She sipped anisette.

"Janet, you disgust me," Harold said. "How can you unload this *merde* on three people who adore you?"

"I half-adore her," Marcia said.

"Two point five people who adore you," Harold said. "*Deux point cinq.*"

"I don't know," Janet said. "I guess I want to be talked out of it. I don't see why you men look so offended. It might bring Georgene in and don't we need some new blood? It seems to me we've said everything we have to say about sixty times. We know all about Frank's ulcer and Frank's father who avoided getting an ulcer by learning all about China and how Shakespeare doesn't work as well as China, maybe he's more acid; I *do* advise Maalox. We know all about what saints her father and grandfather the bishop were from Marcia, and how she hated Long Island and loves it up here away from all those dreary clubby types who kept playing badminton with martini olives. We know all about Harold's prostitutes, and the little colored girl in St. Louis, and how neither of us are quite as good . . ."

"Any funny business with Freddy," Frank said, bloating with menace, "and it's get thee to a nunnery. I'll divorce you."

"But then," Janet told him, "I'd have to drag all of us out into the open, and we'd look so funny in the newspapers. Things are so hard to explain that are perfectly obvious to friends."

"It's obvious to me," Freddy Thorne said to her the following weekend, when they were alone in the kitchen late at a dinner party given by the Guerins, "you never were in love with Harold, you went after him to even the score with Marcia." In the intervening week she had had a dental appointment, and in the gaps of prophylaxis he had wheedled from her her version of the full story.

"Freddy, how can you judge?" She helped herself to a piece of cream-cheese-laden celery left over from the hors d'oeuvres. "How can you hope to get inside people's lives this way? Harold when he and I are alone is something you can't imagine. He can be irresistible."

"We all can," was the answer. "Resistibility is a direct function of the female decision to resist or not to." He seemed to be sweating behind the thick eyeglasses that kept misplacing his eyes. Freddy had trouble seeing. He had recently installed a new drill with a water-spray attachment, and during her appointment his glasses had often needed to be wiped.

"Freddy," she told him, "I don't like being pried and poked at. You must make a woman your friend first."

"I've been your friend since you moved to town." He stroked her arm, left bare by the black-lace blouse. Candlelight shuddered in the other room, where the others were chattering. "On second thought," Freddy murmured on, "I think you took Harold on not to hurt the other two but to oblige them, to win their affection. For a magnificent piece who's also rich, you're damn unsure of yourself."

"For a near-sighted boob who's also a dentist, you're damn sure of yourself. Speaking of which, stop trying to make the Whitman girl. She's pregnant."

"Praise be. More men to man America's submarines. She doesn't know it yet, but she's a swinger. Women with that super-heated skin are usually fantastic in the sack. Their hearts beat harder."

"You're such a bastard," said Janet, whose skin, though strikingly pale, was rather grainy and opaque.

Freddy was right, she later reflected, in that obligingness had become a part of it; they had reached, the Applesmiths, the boundary of a condition wherein their needs were merged, and a general courtesy replaced individual desire. The women would sleep with the men out of pity, and each would permit the other her man out of an attenuated and hopeless graciousness. Already a ramifying tact and crossweave of concern were giving their homes an unhealthy hospital air. Frank and Harold had become paralyzed by the habit of lust; she and Marcia, between blow-ups, were as guarded and considerate with one another as two defaced patients in an accident ward.

In the following week she had a porcelain filling replaced, and Freddy called her on the phone every noon, always inviting her to sleep with him. But he never named a place where they could go, never suggested a definite time; and it dawned upon her that he had no serious physical intention: the verbal intimacy of gossip satisfied him. Meanwhile Harold, begging her to resume with him, had gone to the trouble of acquiring the key to a Beacon Street bachelors' apartment that was empty all day. Curious as to how bachelors live, she went there with him the Friday before the Sunday when Piet broke Freddy's little finger. At a glance she gathered that the inhabitants were homosexuals. The furnishings too beautifully harmonized; bent wicker and orange velvet prevailed. One of the men painted, or, rather, did collages juxtaposing magazine advertisements and war headlines, deodorized nudes with nacreous armpits and bombed peasants flecked with blood, green stamps and Robert McNamara and enraptured models in striated girdles, comic-strip cannons pasted at the crotch. It was quite ugly and malicious, yet the room was impossible to shock and the magnolias on the south of Beacon were about to flower. Harold was polite, timid, fatherly, reminiscent, touching. She allowed him to slide her from her clothes and, rising quickly, came with him and then, after a cigarette and wine, let him come again, let him gather himself into his groin and hurl himself painlessly into the dilated middle amplitudes of herself. Trembling as if whipped, he licked her eyelids and sucked her toes, one by one. The sensation felt hysterically funny. The next day, Saturday, she wrote Freddy a letter:

Freddy dear—
I am grateful for your caring. Truly. But my future, I am more than ever convinced, lies with Frank. So your phone calls must stop. After today I will hang up on your voice. May we continue to be pleasant, and friends? Please, I don't want to change dentists, you have all my records.
Fondly,
J.

She mailed it to his cottagelike office on Divinity Street. He received it Monday, read it smiling, was not disappointed, considered burning it on the gas flame in his lab but, the amorous keepsakes of his life having been few, instead crumpled the envelope into the wastebasket and tucked the letter into his coat pocket, where Georgene found it that evening, while he was at Lions. The next day she confessed her terror to Piet, and irrevocably offended him.

So Foxy was both right and wrong about Janet. She overestimated Janet's freedom, and had mistaken the quality of Freddy Thorne's sexuality. Though he seemed aggressive toward women, he really sought to make alliance with them. But then summer overwhelmed Foxy's speculations about the love life of others, and swept her as if out to sea, to a vantage where the couples on the shore of Tarbox looked like a string of colored beads.

Piet Hanema was sent out of the room and they decided he was Ho Chi Minh. Frank Appleby wanted him to be Casanova but Irene said the person couldn't be fictional. Frank told Irene that Casanova had been as real as you and I but everyone agreed they had no feeling for him. Irene suggested Vice-President Johnson. Everyone protested that he was much too dreary. Terry Gallagher came up with Ho Chi Minh and it seemed perfect. Good for Terry: ever since getting her lute, she was much more with it. More human. All spring she had been taking lute lessons from an old woman in Norwell. She had let her long black hair down; her wide lips were tucked up at the corners as if she were holding a coin or candy in her mouth. Looking at Terry, Eddie Constantine suggested that Piet be Joan Baez, but the rest voted to stick with Ho Chi Minh, and Georgene went to the foot of the Saltzes' stairs to call Piet down.

It was the last Sunday night in June. The tight wine-colored cones of the lilacs that Piet had noticed as he hesitated by Foxy Whitman's gate had loosened and expanded with the first hot week of May into papal miters of bloom, first the lavender and then the taller, holier, more ascetic white, ensconced amid heart-shaped leaves whose green was suddenly cheap. The lilacs faded and dried, and bridal wreath drooped, gathering dust, by every garage door and drive. Sagitta, most exquisite of constellations, flew unmoving between the Swan and Eagle, giant jeweled airplanes whose pilots are Deneb and Altair; the Milky Way wandered like a line of wash in the heat-bleached sky. Desultory parties, hardly organized, social weeds, sprang up to fill the pale nights bloated by Daylight Saving, parties mixed of tennis leftovers and sunburned half-couples and cold salami and fetched pizza and Bitter Lemon and sandy stray forgotten children lulled asleep by television's blue flicker. *President Kennedy's triumphal tour of Western Europe today subsided to quiet talks in Sussex, England . . .*

The Saltzes, great birdwatchers and walkers, as if Nature were a course they were cramming, had gone down late to the beach, to see the sandpipers and to swim. Irene suffered from sun poisoning and ventured out at midday protected in floppy hats and long-sleeved jerseys, and went swimming only toward evening. Up by the far rocks she and Ben had found the Hanemas, all four of them, with the Whitmans, the two of them. Ken liked to snorkel, and the Hanema children had been fascinated by his equipment. The beach here by the rocks dropped off steeply enough for diving. Piet was giving Ruth, in face mask and foot fins, a lesson while Nancy, anxious for her sister and envious, cried. Ken and Angela stood together, an almost godlike couple, untroubled, invulnerable, gazing at the horizon, where a sailboat race was suspended, gaudy spinnakers bellied. Foxy, in a skirted lemon-yellow maternity swimsuit, lay supine on a smooth rock, eyes shut, smiling. Irene was envious of everyone's happiness and ease beneath the same sun that gave her a painful rash. They had all been here since noon. Impulsively, yet with some small hope of inducing the Whitman woman, so complacently uncommitted, to work on one of her causes (pre-primary education, fair housing, soil conservation), she invited them back for a drink. The Saltzes lived near the green, in a narrow asbestos-shingled house visible from the Constantines. The Constantines saw the cars and came over. They brought Terry Gallagher with them. Carol, who had taken ballet and who sewed and wove and painted, also played the guitar, and that summer the two women sometimes met for duets. At Eddie's prompting, Ben Saltz phoned the Applebys, who were having the little-Smiths and Thornes over for a pick-up meal, and

half of this party showed up—Frank, Marcia, and Georgene. By
now it was after eight. Before the light died, Eddie took Angela,
of all people, on his Vespa to the Italian place on Route 123 and
they brought back five pizzas. Reëntering the Saltzes' narrow
living room, Angela looked glorious, flushed from the wind and
the fear and the effort of balancing the cardboard boxes. She
wore a damp towel tucked around the waist of a wet black bathing suit, and when she bent forward to bite a point of pizza slice
Piet could see her nipples. His wife. Where he had sucked. Not
thinking it would be so long a party, they had brought their
children along. Ruth, her wide eyes watering, watched streams of
television with the older Saltz boy Bernard, and Nancy fell asleep
in little Jeremiah's room. Irene loved word games. By eleven-
thirty, when Ken Whitman was studying the laces of his sneakers
and Frank Appleby's eyes had rolled inward upon his digestion
and Janet had phoned twice to make sure that he and Marcia had
not gone off alone somewhere and to ask him how ever were they
supposed to get Freddy Thorne out of the house, the crowd at
the Saltzes' had played four games of Ghosts, two of Truth, and
three of Botticelli. This left Impressions. Eddie Constantine had
gone out first and with only one wrong guess, Burl Ives, identified
himself as the late Pope John. It took Georgene somewhat longer
to discover that she was Althea Gibson. Then Piet volunteered
because he wanted to go to the john and to check on Nancy (*I
will never grow up and I will never ever in my whole life die.*
Her hair was tangled and stiff; her aqua bathing suit, riding up in
sleep, had exposed of her bottom half-moons sparkling with sand.
Piet mourned the child's body but the tug of bright life downstairs held him helpless here. *Sleep. Forgive us in your sleep.*) and
they made him Ho Chi Minh.

At the foot of the stairs he tapped Georgene's flank with the
side of his hand for old time's sake while gazing straight ahead.
He came into the living room; he wore a sweater and plaid bathing trunks; his bare feet looked knobbed and splayed on the floor
and in Foxy's eyes his naked legs wore a pale fur halo. "What
kind of landscape am I?" he asked.

"Jungle," Georgene said.

"Rice paddies," said Marcia little-Smith.

Terry Gallagher said, "Torn."

Piet asked, "A torn landscape?"

"Maybe I mean pacified."

Angela closed her eyes. "I see a temple, with reddish pillars, and an idol with its head knocked off, overgrown with vines, and someone has been doing mathematical calculations with chalk on the broad part of one thigh."

"Sexy," Eddie Constantine said.

Georgene said, her chin hardening, "No fair couples using ESP."

Piet asked, "Anybody else? Foxy? Ken?"

Ken said, "I get Indiana, I don't know why."

Everyone laughed, except Foxy, who nodded. "He's right. Something quiet and gray and ordinary," she said. "Oregon? South Dakota?"

Frank Appleby said, "You mean North Dakota."

"No hints," Carol Constantine protested. She was sitting on the floor in the position of one weaving, or praying, or playing Monopoly. Her legs were folded under a green lily pad of a ballerina's skirt from which her torso rose like a stem. Her waist was remarkably thin and pliant and her nostrils, long slits, seemed always to be inhaling.

Piet asked, "What flower?"

"Poppy."

"Poppy."

"Nodding pogonia," Irene Saltz said. "Or maybe a fringed orchis."

"A fringed orchis in the shade of an enormous Chinese tulip tree," Frank Appleby said.

Carol said to Marcia, "I don't think Frank understands the game. He hints."

Foxy Whitman said, "I see something gray. Mistletoe."

"I keep getting gray out of you," Piet said to her, with strange edge, and asked Angela, "Flower? Ken?"

"Daisy fleabane," Ken said, perhaps antagonistically, staring at his feet. Did he mean it?

Angela said, "No flower or any flower. A single lily presented by a child to the major's wife on a fête day."

"A wilted gardenia in a busboy's lapel," Terry Gallagher said, and smiled broadly when they all burst into compliments. They felt her developing, coming to bloom.

Georgene said, "A thistle. From an official point of view."

Piet complained, "I can't even tell if you like this person or not."

"What sex are you getting?" Carol asked him. Her face, though composed and smooth, held contentious points of shadow—at the nostril wings, at the corners of her mouth, beneath her pouting lower lip, where there seemed to be a smudge. Piet saw that she lengthened the line of her lids with eye shadow, and realized that her eyes were small and rather close together, so close together that in certain flitting lights her stilted dignity of stance appeared that of a cross-eyed person. He felt better about her, less fascinated. Her hair was a dull brown nothing color done up in a pony tail she was too old for.

"Male," he answered. "But it doesn't seem to matter. His maleness isn't his claim to fame."

"Unlike who?" Carol coolly asked.

Piet obligingly blushed. "What—what period of painting?"

"Art Nouveau," Angela said promptly.

"Spanish cave," Foxy said, also prompt.

Frank Appleby rolled his eyes inward and groaned. "All I get is what Carol doesn't want me to get."

"What's that?" Carol asked.

"Soviet posters."

"No," Carol said, "I don't mind that. It's not very good, but I don't mind it."

Irene Saltz asked her, "Who appointed you referee?"

"Medical-textbook illustrations," Ken Whitman said firmly, "with a rice-paper overlay leaf."

"Good," someone said politely, after a pause.

"Terry and the Pirates," Eddie Constantine said.

Carol said, "I'm sorry, I think you're all horrible. He's definitely Yves Tanguy. And maybe Arshile Gorky."

"He's a playwright," Frank told her.

"That's Maxim," she told him.

Ken, remembering the success of some of his other puns, asked innocently, "Who was Maxim Ize?"

Foxy winced.

"A Jewish expansionist," Eddie said. "Whoops, no offense intended, Ben."

Patiently Piet asked, "Any other painters or periods of painting?"

"I don't think," Marcia said, "they ever work out very well. They're too literal. Stretch our minds, Piet."

Into this Piet read Frank's becoming bored, and asked him, "Frank, what play by Shakespeare am I?"

Frank revolved the question uncomfortably inside him, and after a swallow of brandy pronounced, "*Anthony and Cleopatra,* from the viewpoint of Octavius."

Marcia in a helpful wifely way prompted, "What about *Titus Andronicus?*"

"Too messy," Frank said. "This man is efficient."

Foxy Whitman—she had stopped off at her house to change from her tentlike maternity bathing suit into a more flattering shift, a canary-yellow muu-muu that tapped and hugged her hidden shape—was fighting for attention. "What about an *Othello* in which Iago is right?"

Frank said, "He's always right," and brayed.

Ben Saltz, looking tired, got to his feet and asked, "Who wants some more beer? Brandy? We have lots of gin but we're out of Bitter Lemon."

Georgene said, "Piet, you're taking much too long. We've given you beautiful answers and you spurn us."

"You've confused me, you're all so beautiful. I keeping thinking about Ken's medical textbook."

"Ignore it," Foxy said.

"All right: what beverage?"

"Tea."

"Tea."

"Souchong more than orange pekoe."

"Tea with nutmeg," Angela said.

"Angela, you really like this person, don't you?" It was Terry asking.

"I have to, he's my husband."

"I hate tea," Piet said. "I hate tea with nutmeg."

"You've never had it," Angela told him.

"Don't be too sure." The others hushed, to give them space to quarrel. Piet hastily moved on: "What kind of food?"

"Rice."

"Rice, but you want more," Ben said, returning with beer in two brown nonreturnable bottles.

Piet asked, "Boiled or fried?"

Angela said, "Boiled. It's purer."

Marcia said, "Delicately fried."

Terry closed her eyes and said, "A BLT on burnt toast."

Frank Appleby said, "To hell with you all. I'll say what comes to me. A monk barbecue."

Carol cried, all her lithe lines electric, her feet thrusting from under her skirt, "Frank, you're a pig! You've given it to him!"

Piet said in great relief, "I'm No-go Diem."

The voices of the others flocked: "Ngo, you're not." "Close, but no sitar." "Close? He couldn't be wronger." "Right church, wrong side of the aisle." This last was Georgene, reaching out to him; her help was accepted while she was spurned.

Piet arrived: "Ho Chi Minh." In a glad clatter the game collapsed. The beer went around. Terry Gallagher and Ken Whitman stood with one motion and looked at each other, surprised by unison.

"It's treasonous," Piet was saying, "how affectionate your impressions were. This enemy of our democracy, all those flowers and delicate grays." His complaint was directed, Georgene felt, toward Angela and Foxy.

"*You* asked flowers."

"You never asked animals. A whiskery weasel."

"A very thin panda."

"Why hate him? He's what they want." This was Irene, who had been uncharacteristically silent.

"*Chacun à son goût*, as Harold would say if he were here," Marcia said with quaint loyalty.

"I thought that was good of me to remember him being a busboy in Paris," Terry said. "Thanks, people, but I must go. We went to early mass this morning and poor Matt's been showing houses all afternoon."

"I second that," Ken said. "Fox, come."

But the momentary impression, of Terry and Ken standing together as a handsome couple, tall and dark-haired and grave, led the others to tease Foxy.

"Oh please," Carol begged. "Stay for one more."

"We'll let Foxy be it."

"Foxy's it. It, Foxy."

"All pregnant women leave the room."

Foxy looked toward Ken; he read on her face a touching indecision. This boozy catty crowd tempted her; their own house was full of mosquitoes and uncompleted carpentry. Yet she was tired, and his wife, and faithful. She said, "No, I'd just be stupid. I don't really understand the game."

"Oh, but you do, you do."

"The game is to be yourself."

"Your impressions are lovely."

"We'll pick somebody simple. Margaret Truman. *Not* Jackie. It'll take ten minutes."

She wavered, and Ken spoke to her across the calling heads with perfect kindness, yet his voice frightened her; his appearance had no roundness. An immaculate cutout seemed wired for sound. "I'm dead, Fox, but you stay and play. Marcia can drop you off."

"Oh," she said, "but that's not right. Marcia has Harold to worry about. I'll go with you."

They all said, "You can't. You're it. Stay."

"Stay," Ken told her, and turned to leave, and she felt herself cut off, her roundness rejected; her shape offended him. She had asked him to rescue her from indecision and he had petulantly set her adrift. Angered, she agreed to stay, and went upstairs, where Piet had been. He had left no clues.

It did not take them long to decide, June having been so fertile of news: Pope John had died, Quang Duc had immolated himself, Valentina Tereshkova had become the first woman in space, John Profumo had resigned, the Lord's Prayer had been banned in the American public schools. Soon Georgene was at the foot of the stairs, calling, "E-liz-a-beth! Elizabeth Fox Whitman, come right down here!" It was the voice of her Wilmington aunt.

Like a rebuked child Foxy entered the living room; its human brightness seemed savage. The darkened rooms upstairs, rooms of pinned-up maps and scattered toy tracks, of silently sleeping children and docile plumbing fixtures, had been a better world. She thought of her bedroom and the moon that shared her insomnia. The blank pillow beside Ken's head was her. Here, Ken and Terry Gallagher were gone. Frank Appleby was asleep, his feet in sandals cocked up on the Saltzes' fake-colonial coffee table, his mouth ajar and raggedly snoring. Foxy also heard whispering in the kitchen and counted Eddie Constantine and Irene missing. The six survivors, four of them women, looked weary and forbearing and she realized she should have gone home with Ken. The game was exhausted, they were merely being polite, to make her feel loved and part of them. She must quickly guess and go.

"What—what kind of ocean am I?" Foxy wasn't sure if the rules forbad using associations others had used, and she wanted to be creative, sensitive, unique. On the nubbly sofa next to his wife, Piet Hanema gazed down into his glass.

"What kind of ocean?" Carol echoed. "How odd. Choppy, I guess."

"Sometimes choppy," Marcia said. "Sometimes very still and tranced. Sometimes even a big wave."

"Untracked," Piet said.

"Untracked?"

"Ships go back and forth across you and leave no trace. You accept them all. They don't impress you."

"A piece of ocean," Ben said, grinning, "with a mermaid in it."

Carol said, "No direct hints."

Suddenly immersed in timidity, Foxy asked, "Angela? Any ocean?"

"Not an ocean," Angela said. "A sad little pond."

"Sad?"

"Kind of scummy," Georgene said: a startling flat insult, but everyone, especially the men, laughed, agreeing.

"Well. What time of day?"

"Two in the morning."

"Eleven a.m., with rumpled sheets."

"Any time. All day."

Again, this unkind laughter. A slow blush caked Foxy's face. She wanted to like this person she was, in spite of them.

Angela tried to rescue her. "I see this person around nine at night, going out, into the city lights, kind of happy and brainless."

"Or maybe even," Marcia added, "at four-thirty in the afternoon, walking in a park, without a hat, smiling at the old men and the squirrels and the babies."

"And the bobbies," Piet said.

Carol sang, "We're getting too spe-ci-fic," and glanced toward the whispering kitchen with that abrupt head turn ballerinas use in pirouettes.

English, Piet's implication was. Queen Elizabeth, scummy? Virginia Woolf? *The Waves*. But those rumpled sheets. Perhaps an effeminate seedy man. Cecil Beaton. Alec Guinness, Piet's saying back and forth across an ocean, an actor's parts. But a scummy pond? How stupid she was being. Afraid to guess wrong, self-conscious, stuck. The furnishings of the Saltzes' living room pressed in upon her emptiness: velvety dark easy chairs wearing doilies on their forearms, maple magazine racks of *Scientific American* and *Newsweek* and *Look*, inquisitive bridge lamps leaning over the chairs' left shoulders, Van Gogh sunning on the walls, wedding pictures frozen on the top of an upright piano with yellow teeth, an evil-footed coat rack and speckled oblong mirror in the dark foyer, narrow stairs plunging upward perilously, children climbing each night in a fight with fear. Her mother's Delaware second cousins had lived in such houses, built narrow to the street and lined with hydrangea bushes where a child could urinate or hide from her third cousins. The Jews have inherited the middle class—nobody else wants it. "What social class?" Foxy asked.

"Too direct," Carol said.

"Lower," Georgene said.

"Middle lower," Piet said. "Some airs and graces."

"Transcending all classes," Angela told her. "Lower than low, higher than high."

"You sound," Ben Saltz said to Angela with a pedantic mannered twinkle, "like a Gnostic devotee."

"What a nosty suggestion," Marcia said.

"Oh, I *don't* understand how we *know* about this person, she seems so *common!*" Foxy cried.

"She has hidden talents," Piet said.

"He or she," Carol corrected.

Foxy asked, "What bird am I?"

"Of paradise," Angela said.

"Sparrow."

"Soiled dove."

"Soiled dove is good."

"I envision," Piet said, "a rather tall bird, with a shimmer on its breast. A cockatoo?"

"You're a cowbird," Georgene told Foxy.

Piet turned on Georgene. "How unfair!"

Georgene shrugged. "Using other people's nests."

It was like, Foxy felt, being naked and not knowing it, like being dead on the autopsy table and yet overhearing the remarks, the cold ribaldry. She wanted to be with Ken, to take the wakening presence within her and flee; she had sinned. "What figure am I in the Bible? I know you're going to say Delilah."

"No," Piet said, "you're too hard on yourself. Maybe you're Hagar."

"No," Ben said, "she's Abishag. Abishag was the girl who they brought in to David, when he was dying, to give him some heat. *Vecham leadoni hamelekh*, in the Hebrew."

"And what happened?" Marcia asked.

"*Vehamelekh loh yada-ah*. The king knew her not."

"Ben," Marcia said, "I think it's marvelous, the way you can rattle it off. Hebrew."

"I studied it for ten years. We were conservative."

"Even those little skullcaps?"

"Yarmulkes." His grin was leonine, thrilling, his teeth brilliant within his beard. "Summers I was sent to Camp Ramah."

Foxy asked, "Georgene?"

"I don't know the Bible. I would have said Delilah. Or Magdalen, except that seems presumptuous."

"I see her as one of those Jerusalemites who never got into the Bible," Angela said. "She just couldn't be bothered. She was flirting with a Roman soldier when the Cross went by."

"What a terrible woman," Foxy said. "A scummy pond, a cowbird."

"You've been listening only to Georgene," Piet said. "Georgene's being moralistic tonight."

"You don't like her either. Angela and Ben are the only ones who like her." Saying this made Foxy jealous, for she did not want Ben and Angela to be linked, she vaguely wanted Ben—not the real Ben, but the echoes he evoked—to be her own Jew.

The whispering from the kitchen had ceased.

"This is going on too long," Carol said, and stood up, stiff from long sitting, her throat and wrists stringy, tense. She did not quite dare go into the kitchen; she took a step toward the open doorway and sharply called, "Come help us, you two. She's stuck."

"I quit," Foxy said. "Who am I? I'm sure I've never heard of myself."

"You have, you have," Piet urged; he wanted her to do well, he was embarrassed for her.

"I'm some dreary little starlet and I never notice their names."

"At the moment," Piet told her, "you're a star."

"At the moment. Julie Andrews. Liz Taylor."

"No. You're on the wrong track."

"Phooey," Foxy said. "I was so proud of those. They're both English. I'm not Dame May Whitty?"

"You're being silly," Carol told her.

"Think big," Piet said. "Think world."

Ben said, "Ask some more questions."

They were all prompting, hissing at the balky child in the Christmas recitation. Georgene's hard eyes were plainly pleased. Marcia said, "Ask Frank what Shakespeare play you are. I'll wake him up." Marcia glided to where Frank lay deflated and sunk in the corner of the fat sofa and, wifely, whispered into his ear until his lids parted and his eyes, open, stared sorely ahead. Foxy felt his eyes, in mid-dream, gaze through her.

"Frank, help," she said. "What Shakespearian play am I?"

"*Troilus*," he said, and his eyes closed.

"I've never read it," Foxy said.

"I think you're the sonnets," Marcia said.

"In Russian and English *en face*," Piet said, and everybody, everybody, laughed.

"Oh, you're all too clever," Foxy told them. "I'm totally lost now. I was working on Princess Margaret." Their laughter renewed itself; she said, "I hate you all. I want to go home. I want to give up."

"Don't give up," Piet said. "I know you know it. You're trying too hard."

Ben asked her, "What's the opposite of a princess?"

"A ragpicker. Oh. A flowergirl. Eliza Doolittle. But I thought you couldn't use fictional people."

"You can't. You're not Eliza," Georgene told her. "What's the opposite of a virgin?"

Angela said, "I think Foxy should give up if she wants to."

"She's too close to give up," Carol said.

Irene Saltz, smoothing back her hair, returned to the living room. Her black eyebrows were shapely as wingbeats. She told Carol, "Eddie said to tell you he's gone home. He has to fly tomorrow and went out through the kitchen door."

"Typical," Carol said, and brightened. Her spine as she sat on the floor became again a flower stem, slender, erect. She begged Foxy, "Try one more impression."

With a surrendering sigh, Foxy asked, "What flower?"

The answers were elaborate, since they wanted her now to guess, to know.

"A tiger lily," Carol said, "transplanted from a village garden to a city street."

"Why would anyone bother to do that?" Georgene asked. "I see something coarse but showy. A poppy."

"But Ho Chi Minh was a poppy," Piet told her.

"Yes. There may be an affinity," Georgene said, and turned on him those slightly bulging indignant eyes which, with her cultivated tan and graying hair, belonged to the caustic middle-aged woman she would become. Foxy remembered Georgene's silence during the candlelit dinner at the Guerins, a secretive and contented silence which had seemed, that uncomfortable night, to share, to be of the same chemical nature as, Foxy's pregnancy. Since then this woman had aged unkindly.

Irene said, "I don't know who it is." When Carol whispered the name into her ear, she snapped: "Eglantine."

"In Japan," Angela said, "after our bombs, wasn't there a flower that came out of nowhere and flourished in the radioactive area? I see this person like that, as turning our modern poison into a kind of sweetness."

Foxy said gratefully, "Angela, that's nice. I don't feel so badly now about being this person."

"Devil's paintbrush," Marcia said. "Or something hothousy."

"You know how sometimes," Ben Saltz said, "in weeding around the house, you come to a plant, such as Queen Anne's lace or those spindly wild asters, that is obviously a weed but you don't have the heart to pull because for the time being it's very ornamental?"

Angela said, "We're all like that."

Georgene said, "Speak for yourself, dollink."

"A geranium that's moved from sill to sill to catch the sun," Piet said. "A hyacinth that's sold in a plastic pot. Sometimes a Lady Palmerston rose. Foxy, have you ever noticed, in a greenhouse, how they put cut carnations in a bucket of ink to dye them? That's how they make those green ones for St. Patrick's Day. I think you're a yellow carnation they made drink purple ink, so you're this incredible black, and people keep touching you, thinking you must be artificial, and are amazed that you're an actual flower. As you die, you'll bleed back to yellow again." His flat taut-featured face became this much-touched flower fading.

Carol said, "There's a carefree toughness we're not suggesting."

"Let's do books," Marcia said, impatient. "*Moll Flanders*, by Ian Fleming."

"*Phineas Finn*," Angela said, "abridged for *Playboy*."

"*Little Red Riding Hood*," Ben said, "by the Marquis de Sade."

"*Stop*," Foxy begged. "I give up. I'm very stupid. Angela. Tell me."

"You're Christine Keeler," Piet told her.

In the silence, Foxy's stomach growled.

"That . . . tart? I am? Oh. I'm so *sorry*." Without willing it, without wanting it, not knowing at what instant she passed, averting her head, into tears, Foxy began in fatigue and confusion to cry; and it was clear to all of them, except Angela and Ben, that as they had suspected she was seeing Piet.

iii. *Thin Ice*

Ａs in sleep we need to dream, so while waking we need to touch and talk, to be touched and talked to. *Foxy?*

Yes, Piet? Their simple names had a magic, the magic of a caress that searches out the something monstrous and tender in the genitals of another.

Do you think we're wrong?

Wrong? The concept seemed to swim toward her out of another cosmos of consideration. *I don't know. I don't think so.*

How good of you!

Not to think so?

Yes, yes, yes. Yes. Don't ever think so. Make it right for me. Hey. I dreamed about you last night. I never have before. It's funny, the people you dream about. It's a club with the stupidest rules. I'm always dreaming about Freddy Thorne and I can't stand him.

What did I do in your dream? Was I erotic?

Very chaste. It was in a department store, with a huge skylight overhead. You were a salesgirl. I stopped in front of your counter, without knowing what I wanted.

A salesgirl, am I? She had this mode, of contentious teasing, to vent a touchy pride. *And what do you suppose I am selling?*

It wasn't that atmosphere at all. You were very prim and distant and noncommittal, the way you can be; even though I couldn't say anything, you bent down behind the counter, out of sight, as if to find something, and I woke up with a killing erection.

Sometimes insomniac that summer, Piet, lying in bed beside sleeping Angela, would lift his hand and study its shape stamped black on the window of light-blue panes framed by cruciform mullions. His hand seemed one lifted out of the water in the instant before the final sinking. Angela's heedless slow breathing seemed a tide on the skin of the depths to which he could sink. He missed the squeaking, like glints of light, of the hamster's wheel. He had been shy and circumspect with Foxy, a hired man in her house, and had not intended to desire her. But she had moved with him through the redesign of this old wreck, outdoors to indoors, detail to detail, with a flirting breezy eagerness that had oddly confounded him with the naked wood, where she touched it.

Here there could be shelves.

Or cabinets.

Don't you like open shelves better? Doors are so self-righteous. Then they stick or stop shutting.

They make magnetic catches now that are pretty foolproof. Open shelves are a temptation. You have a cat, you're going to have children. You need spaces you can close. I have two old finish carpenters whose cabinets can be quite handsome.

Did they come from Finland together?

One "n" finish. Their names are Adams and Comeau.

And you want to make work for them.

Piet was taken aback; this woman seemed, as she moved this way and that in her antique kitchen, in her tapping billowing maternity smock, lighter than other women, quicker in exploring him, as if he appeared before her not as himself but as another, whom she had once known well, and still directed some emotion toward. He told her guardedly, *They care, I like them to do work for people who care.*

She turned and held up her arms to the view as if to an ikon and turned again and said urgently, *I want open shelves, and open doorways, and everything open to the sea and the sea air. I've lived my whole life in clever little rooms that were always saving space,* and swept from her narrow kitchen with her lemon-colored smock swinging coolly about her, the high fair color of her face burning. Piet saw she was going to be trouble.

Georgene asked him, "Why have you taken the job? You told me you had to build ranch houses."

They were beside the Ongs' tennis court on Sunday morning. Piet had given up church so that Angela could accept a challenge teasingly given by Freddy Thorne. Piet missed that hour of seated mulling and standing song. Also his head was pinched in tightened icy bands of last night's gin. The challenge, delivered loudly by Freddy at the Constantines' last night, had been for Angela to play him at singles; but then this morning Bernadette was already returning with her three sons from early mass, so the Ongs had to be invited to play, on their own court. The court had been carved from a sloping field adjoining their newly built house. The exotic and expensive house, all flat eaves and flagstones and suspended stairways, designed by an architect John knew in Cambridge, an associate of I. M. Pei, was a puzzling reminder, for the self-important young couples of Tarbox, of John Ong's incongruous prestige. John himself, a small bony butternut-colored man, in love with everything American from bubble chambers to filtered cigarettes, was a tennis enthusiast without aptitude; he invariably played in freshly pressed whites, complete to the wrist band, and a green eyeshade. His dainty popping strokes, accompanied by himself with a running comment of encouraging cries and disappointed coos, were rudely smashed away by his Occidental friends. Bernadette, however, was a walloper. She and Freddy, who stood comically flatfooted and served patball like a child, opposed John and Angela, whose game was graceful and well schooled and even, except at the net, where she had no sense of kill. Piet and Georgene, watching, talked. They spoke at what seemed normal pitch but took care not to be overheard.

He answered her, "Ranch houses are so boring. They all look alike."

There was in Georgene a store of clubwomanly indignation. "So do teeth," she said. "Teeth all look alike. Stocks and bonds all look alike. Every man works with things that look alike; what's so special about you? What makes you such a playboy? You don't even have any money."

Ever since childhood, being scolded had given Piet cerebral cramps; that the world was capable at any point of its immense surface of not loving him seemed a mathematical paradox it was torture to contemplate. He said, "The rest of you have money for me."

"That *is* your style, isn't it? You take. You take, and bow, and leave." Her face was in profile, one-eyed and prim, like the Jack of Diamonds. Sun-glisten salted her chin.

"It was *you*," he told her, having waited until a flurry of strokes and exclamations from the game concealed his voice, "who said we must be careful. Because of Janet's letter, remember? I needed you that day and you shut me out."

"That was months ago. I said to be careful, not to call it off."

"I don't like being told to be careful."

"No, of course you don't, you don't have to be. Angela knows damn well what you're up to but prefers not to see it."

Angela, hearing her name, turned her head. Piet called to her, "Georgene's admiring your style." To Georgene he said, smiling as if chatting, "And what about you and yours? Did you ever confront him with the letter?"

"Yes. Eventually."

"And what did the dear man say?"

She turned her tennis racket between her knees and studied the strings. Rough and smooth. Rough, smooth. "I forget. He wriggled out of it somehow. He said it was a purely paternal thing, that he had been trying to help Janet get out of the Applesmith mess, and she was too neurotic, she had turned on him. It was pretty plausible, from the way her note was worded."

"And then in relief you went to bed with him."

"Yes, as a matter of fact."

"And it was splendid."

"Not bad."

"You each had seven orgasms and read Henry Miller to each other between times."

"You see it very clearly."

"Working from your many vivid descriptions."

"Piet. Stop being a bastard. I'm tired of being a bitch. Come see me. Just for coffee."

"Just for coffee is as bad as for screwing if we're caught."

"I miss you."

"Here I am."

"You have somebody else, that's it, isn't it?"

"Dollink," he said, "you know me better than that."

"I can't believe it's that Whitman girl. She's just too stiff and pretty-pretty for you. She's not your type."

"You're right. It's not her. It's Julia little-Smith."

"Foxy's too tall for you, Piet. You make yourself ridiculous."

"Not only am I poor, I'm a midget. How did a high-class chick like you ever get mixed up with me?"

Georgene contemplated him coldly. Beyond her green eyes and high-bridged nose, wire mesh of the tennis court; beyond, the slope of summer grass whitening where wind touched it. Waves. Lattices. Combine and recombine. Dissolution. She whispered. "I wonder. It must have been purely chemical." The sadness of lust swept numbly up from below Piet's belt. They had come together. Time and again. Larches, tarpaper. Her purple turban.

A final point, and the game was over. Angela and John Ong, winners, walked to the sidelines shining with sweat. John spoke, and Piet didn't understand what he was saying; the vowels, all flattened toward "a," were strung together with clattering consonants. Piet, squinting upward, felt intelligence wildly straining toward him from behind that smooth golden mask. "He says he has no wind any more," Bernadette said for him. She was broad in the shoulders and pelvis and her face had the breadth of a smile even when she was not smiling. Piet loved the Ongs: they let him use their tennis court, they never patronized him, their presence in Tarbox was as contingent as his own. John lit a cigarette and

suffered a fit of dry coughing, and Piet was surprised that the
coughs were intelligible. An elemental vocabulary among all men.
The cough, the laugh, the sob, the scream, the fart, the sigh.
Amen.

John said, bent double by coughing, "Oo two now," meaning
the other two couples must play. The Ongs walked together
toward their house, amid their trio of petitioning boys.

The Hanemas faced the Thornes. Georgene had put on sunglasses; the rest of her face looked chiseled. The sun was high.
Sheen skated on the green composition court. Angela served; her
serves, though accurate, lacked pace and sat up pleasantly fat to
hit. Georgene's return, one of her determined firm forehands,
streaked toward Piet as he crouched at the net; anger had hurried
her stroke slightly and the ball whacked the net at the height of
his groin and fell dead on her side.

"Fifteen love," Angela called, and prepared, on tiptoe, to serve
again.

Piet changed courts. Opposite him Freddy Thorne wore loud
plaid shorts, a fairyish pink shirt, a duck bill hat for his bald head,
fallen blue socks, and rubbery basketball sneakers that seemed too
large. Freddy pointed his feet outward clownishly and hoisted his
racket to his shoulder like a baseball bat. Angela, having laughed
and lost rhythm, double-faulted.

"Fifteen all," she called, and Piet faced Georgene again. A
fluid treacherous game. Advantages so swiftly shifted. Love became hate. *You give me my shape.* Georgene, eyeless, braced for
the serve, gauged it for her forehand, took back the racket, set
her chin, stepped forward, and Piet, gripping his handle so hard
it sweated, bit down on a shout for mercy.

"Daddy. Am I pretty?"

Piet's jaw ached with a suppressed yawn. He had thought his
job was done. He had watched Nancy brush her teeth and read
with her for the twentieth time *Where the Wild Things Are* and
recited with her, what they did more and more rarely, a good-
night prayer, a little litany of blessings into which Piet never
knew whether or not to insert the names of his parents. He felt

that they too, along with her maternal grandparents, should be remembered by the child; but their unalterable deadness disturbed her. So usually Jacobus and Marte Hanema went unblessed, and their unwatered ghosts in Heaven further withered. "Yes, Nancy, you are very pretty. When you grow up you will be as pretty as Mommy."

"Am I pretty now?"

"Aren't you being a silly? You are very pretty now."

"Are other girls pretty?"

"What other girls?"

"Martha and Julia." Topless little females shrieking in the icy water of Tarbox Bay. Round limbs sugared with sand. Squatting in sunset glaze to dam the tide.

Piet asked her, "What do *you* think?"

"They're ugly."

"They're pretty in their way and you're pretty in your way. Martha is pretty in a Thorne way and Julia is pretty in what way?"

"Smith way."

"Right. And Catharine in what way?"

"In an Applebay."

"In an Appleby way. And when Mrs. Whitman has her baby it will be pretty in a Whitman way." It was wrong to use the innocent ears of a child, but it gave Piet pleasure to say Foxy's name, to hold it in his mouth and feel his body suffused with remembrance of her. Angela, sensitive beyond her conscious understanding, showed irritation with his talk, so carefully casual, of the Whitmans, and the name had become subliminally forbidden in the house.

Nancy understood the game now. Her round face gleeful in the pillow, she said, "And when Jackie Kenneny has her baby it will be pretty in a Kenneny way."

"*Right.* Now go to sleep, pretty Nancy, or you will be grumpy and lumpy in the morning."

But there was in this child, more than in her blunt Dutch-blooded sister Ruth, that thing female which does not let go. "But am I the prettiest?"

"Baby, we just said, everybody is pretty in her own way and

nobody wants them to change because then everybody would be alike. Like turnips." He had left a martini-on-the-rocks beside his chair downstairs and the ice would be melting, spinning water into the jewel-clear gin.

Nancy's face was distorted by the effort not to cry. "But I'll *die*," she explained.

He groped for her thought. "You think if you're the prettiest God won't let you die?"

She wordlessly nodded. Her thumb had found its way to her mouth and her eyes darkened as if she were sucking from it ink.

"But pretty people must die too," Piet told her. "It wouldn't be fair to let only ugly ones die. And nobody looks ugly to people who love them."

"Like mommies and daddies," she said, removing and replacing her thumb in an instant.

"Right."

"And boy friends and girl friends."

"I suppose."

"I know your girl friend, Daddy."

"You do! Who?"

"Mommy."

Piet laughed. "And who's Mommy's boy friend?" Symmetry. The child said, "Martha's daddy."

"That awful man?"

"He's funny," Nancy explained. "He says poo."

"You mean if I said poo I'd be funny too?"

She laughed: the noise was pulled bubbling from deep near the door to the kingdom of sleep. "You said poo," she said. "Shame on Daddy."

A silence fell between them. The lilac leaves, flourishing, flowerless, had reached to the height of Nancy's window and, heart-shaped, brushed her screen. Fear tapped, scraped. Piet did not dare leave. "Are you really worried about dying, baby?"

Solemnly Nancy nodded. "Mommy says I'll get to be an old, old lady, and then die."

"Isn't that nice? When you're a very old lady you can sit in your rocking chair and tell all your great-great-grandchildren how once you had a daddy who said poo."

The desired laugh rose toward the surface of the child's shadowed face, and without a sound submerged. She was gazing into the horror he had conjured up. "I don't want to be an old lady! I don't want to be big!"

"But already you're bigger than you were. Once you were no bigger than my two hands. You don't want to be that small again. You couldn't talk or walk or anything."

"I do too, Daddy. Go away, send Mommy."

"Nancy, listen. You won't die. That little thing inside you that says 'Nancy' won't ever ever die. God never lets anybody die; he lifts them up and takes them into Heaven. That old thing they put in the ground isn't you at all."

"I want Mommy!"

Piet, sickened, saw that Angela, in her simplicity, had made this doctrine of hope, the only hope, strange and frightful to the child. "Mommy's doing the dishes downstairs."

"I want her."

"She'll come and give you a kiss when you're fast asleep."

"I want her now."

"And you don't want Daddy?"

"*No.*"

Sometimes in these warm pale nights, as the air cooled and the cars on the road beyond the lilac hedge swished toward Nun's Bay trailing a phosphorescence of radio music, Angela would turn to Piet while he lay willing to yield himself to fatigue. It seemed crucial that he make no motion of desire toward her; then, speaking no word, as if a visitant from space had usurped his wife's body, Angela would press herself against him and with curved fingers curiously trace his sides and spine. Unspeaking also, lest the spell break, he would dare mirror her caress, discovering her nightgown, usually an opaque and entangling obstacle, transparent, rotten, sliding and falling from her flesh like deteriorated burial cloth from a body resurrected in its strength. She showed behind and between her legs a wealth of listening curves and damps. She tugged her gown to her throat and the bones of her fingers confided a glimmering breast to his mouth, shaped by an *ah* of apprehension; when with insistent symmetry she rolled onto her back to have him use the other, his hand discovered her mons Veneris swollen high, her whole fair floating flesh dilated outward toward a deity, an anyoneness, it was Piet's fortune to have localized, to have seized captive in his own dark form. The woman's beauty caressed the skin of his eyes; his shaggy head sank toward the ancient alleyway where, foul proud queen, she frothed most. His tongue searched her sour labia until it found them sweet. She pulled his hair, *Come up.* "Come inside me?" He realized, amazed, he who had entered Foxy Whitman the afternoon before, that there was no cunt like Angela's, none so liquorish and replete. He lost himself to the hilt unresisted. The keenness of her chemistry made him whimper. Always the problem with their sex had been that he found her too rich to manipulate. She touched his matted chest, *wait,* and touched her own self, and, mixed with her fluttering fingers, coming like a comet's dribble, he waited until her hand flew to his buttocks and, urging him to kill her, she gasped and absolved herself from tension.

He said, "My dear wife. What a nice surprise."

She shrugged, flat on her back on the sweated sheet, her bare shoulders polished by starlight. "I get hot too. Just like your other women."

"I have no other women." He stroked and smoothed the outflowing corona of her hair. "Your cunt is heavenly."

Angela motioned him off and rolled away to sleep; it was their custom since the start of their marriage to sleep nude after making love. "I'm sure," she said, "we're all alike down there."

"That's not true," Piet told her, "not true at all." She ignored his confession.

He had been shy and circumspect with Foxy and had not wanted to desire her. He would spend most of each day on Indian Hill with the three ranch houses, which rose in quick frames from the concrete foundations: an alphabet of two-by-fours, N and T and M and H, interlocked footings and girders and joists and flooring and studs and plates and sills. Piet, hammer in hand, liked to feel the bite taken into gravity. The upright weight-bearing was a thing his eye would see, and a house never looked as pretty again to him as it did in the framing, before bastard materials and bastard crafts eclipsed honest carpentry, and work was replaced by delays and finagling with subcontractors—electricians like weasels, grubby plumbers, obdurate motionless masons.

So, many days, it was not until three or four o'clock that he rattled down the beach road to the Robinson place. The worst problem, the lack of a basement, had been solved first. The servants' wing, four skimpy dormered bedrooms and a defunct kitchenette, had been torn down, enabling a back hoe to dig a hole ten feet deep to the edge of the kitchen, in two days. Four college boys with hand shovels had taken a week to dig under the length of the kitchen and hallway area and break through to the existing furnace hole beneath the living room. For a few days, while concrete was poured and spread (the operation coincided with an early-June heat wave; the scene in the cave beneath the house, boys stripped to the waist and ankle-deep in sludge, was infernal), half of Foxy's home rested on a few cedar posts and Lally columns footed on cinder block. Then, above the basement where the wing had been, Piet built a modified annex of one story, two rooms one of which could be a nursery and one a playroom, with a screened-in sunporch overlooking the marsh, connected to the kitchen by a passageway where gardening tools could be kept. Before June's end Foxy had ordered six rose bushes from Vos & Sons' greenhouses, and had had them set along the butt end of the new wing, and was trying with Bovung and peat moss to nurse them to health in a clayey earth still littered with splinters and scarred by tractor-tire tracks.

In five July days, a roofer's crew stripped the lumpy leaky accumulation of shingles and hammered down a flat snug roof.

The old sagging porch was torn away. Light flooded the living room, whose walls, as the hot-air ducts from the new furnace were installed, were covered with wire lath and plastered by an old Czech from Lacetown, with his crippled nephew: the last plasterers south of Mather. These major renovations, substantially completed by August, cost Ken Whitman eleven thousand dollars, of which only twenty-eight hundred came to Piet's firm, and only a few hundred adhered as profit. The rest went for material, for rough labor, for the skilled labor of Adams and Comeau, to the heating contractor, the concrete supplier, the plumbing subcontractor. Kitchen improvement—new appliances, additional plumbing, cabinets, linoleum—came to another three thousand, and Piet, pitying Whitman (who never asked for pity, who comprehended the necessities and expenses with a series of remote nods, as the house at each transformation became less his and more Foxy's), held his own charges close to cost. As everyone, especially Gallagher, had foreseen, the job was a loser.

But it gave Piet pleasure to see Foxy, pregnant, reading a letter beside a wall of virgin plaster, her shadow subtly golden. And he wanted her to be pleased by his work. Each change he wrought established more firmly an essential propriety. At night, and in the long daytime hours when he was not yet with her, he envisioned her as protected and claimed by sentinels he had posted: steel columns standing slim and strong in the basement, plaster surfaces of a staring blankness, alert doors cleverly planed to hang lightly in old frames slumped from plumb, a resecured skylight, now of double thickness and freshly flashed, above her sleeping head. He saw her as always sleeping when he was not there, her long body latent, ripening in unconsciousness. Sometimes, when he came in midafternoon, she would be having a nap. The sea sparkled dark in the twisting channels. Lacetown lighthouse trembled in the distance and heat. High summer's hay smell lay thick upon the slope, full of goldenrod and field mice, down to the marsh. Beside the doorway there were lilac stumps. No workmen's cars were parked in the driveway, only her secondhand Plymouth station wagon, hymnal blue.

He lifted the aluminum gate latch. He examined the unfinished framing of the annex, noted two misnailed and split pieces of cross-bridging between joists, walked around the front of the house where the porch had been and an unconcluded rubble of mud and hardened concrete splotches and dusty hundredweight paper bags and scraps of polyethylene film and insulation wool now was, and, continuing, tapped on the side door, a door that seemed to press outward with the silence it contained. Within, something made the house slightly tremble. It was Cotton, the

Whitmans' heavy-footed caramel tom. Piet entered, and the cat, bowing and stretching and purring in anticipation of being picked up, greeted him amid the holy odor of shavings.

Foxy was above him. With a stealth meant to wake her slowly, Piet moved through the unfinished rooms, testing joints with his pocket knife, opening and shutting cabinet doors that closed with a delicate magnetic suck. Above him, a footstep heavier than a cat's sounded. Furiously Piet focused on the details of the copper plumbing installed beneath the old slate sink, suspended in mid-connection, where the plumbers had left it, open like a cry. She was beside him, wearing a loosely tied bathrobe over a slip, her face blurred by sleep, her blond hair moist on the pillowed side of her head. *They said they'd be back.*

I was trying to figure out why they had quit.

They explained it to me. Something about a male threader and a coupling.

Plumbers are the banes of this business. Plumbers and masons.

They're a vanishing breed?

Even vanishing they do slowly. You and Ken must be tired to death of living in the middle of a mess.

Oh, Ken's never here in the day and it's fun for me, to have men bringing me presents all day long. Adams and Comeau and I sit around the coffee table talking about the good old days in Tarbox.

What good old days?

Apparently it's always been a salty town. Look, would you like something to drink? I've woken up with a terrible thirst, I could make lemonade. That only needs cold water.

I ought to get back to the office and give the plumbers a blast.

They promised they'd be back so I'd have hot water. Do you mind if it's pink?

Pink lemonade? I prefer it. My mother used to make it. With strawberries.

In the good old days, Adams and Comeau tell me, the trolley car ran along Divinity Street and all the drunks would pile out because this was the only un-dry town between Boston and Plymouth. Even in the middle of a blizzard this would happen.

Funny about the trolley cars. How they came and went.

They used to make me sick. That awful smell, and the motorman's cigars.

Speaking of messes, what about where your porch was? Do you see that as lawn, or a patio, or what?

I'd love a grape arbor. Why is that funny?

You'd lose all the light you've gained. You'd lose your view from those windows.

The view bores me. The view is Ken's thing. He's always looking outward. Let me tell you about grape arbors.

Tell me.

When I was growing up one summer, the summer before Pearl Harbor, my parents wanted to get out of Bethesda and for a month we rented a brick house in Virginia with an enormous grape arbor over bricks where the ants made little hills. I must have been, what? '41, seven. Forgive me, I'm not usually so talkative.

I know.

I remember the little offshoots of the vines had letters in them, formed letters, you know. She made an A with her fingers. *I tried to make a complete collection. From A to Z.*

How far did you get?

I think to D. I never could find a perfect E. You'd think in all those vines there would have been one.

You should have skipped to F.

I was superstitious and I thought I couldn't. I inhibited myself all the time.

Piet grimaced and considered. The lemonade needed sugar. *It seems to be going out. Inhibition. In a way, I miss it.*

What a sad thing to say. Why? I don't miss it at all. Ever since I got pregnant I've become a real slob. Look at me, in a bathrobe. I love it. Her lips, in her clear pink complexion, looked whitish, as if rubbed with a chapstick. *Shall I tell you a secret?*

Better not. Tell me, what shade of white do you want your living-room woodwork? Flat white, glossy, ivory, or eggshell?

My secret is really so innocent. For years I wanted to be pregnant, but also I was afraid of it. Not just losing my figure, which was too skinny to care about anyway, but my body being somehow an embarrassment to other people. For months I didn't tell anybody except Bea Guerin.

Who told everybody else.

Yes, and I'm glad. Because it turns out not to matter. People just don't care. I was so conceited to think that people would care. In fact they like you a little better if you look beat-up. If you look used.

You don't look very used to me.

Or you to me.

Do men get used? They just use.

Oh, you're so wrong. We use you all the time. It's all we know how to do. But your saying that fits with your missing inhibition. You're very Puritan. You're quite hard on yourself. At first I thought you fell down stairs and did acrobatics to show off. But really you do it to hurt yourself. In the hope that you will. Now why are you laughing?

Because you're so clever.

I'm not. Tell me about your childhood. Mine was dreary. My parents finally got a divorce. I was amazed.

We had a greenhouse. My parents had Dutch accents I've worked quite hard not to inherit. They were both killed years ago in an automobile accident.

Yes, of course. Freddy Thorne calls you our orphan.

How much do you see of Freddy Thorne?

No more than I must. He comes up to me at parties.

He comes up to everybody at parties.

I know that. You don't have to tell me.

Sorry. I don't mean to tell you anything. I'm sure you know quite enough. I just want to get this job done for you so you and your baby can be comfortable this winter.

Her lips, stunned a moment, froze, bloodless, measuring a space of air like calipers. She said, *It's not even July.*

Time flies, he said. It was not even July, and he had never touched her, except in the conventions of greeting and while dancing. In dancing, though at least his height, she had proved submissive to his lead, her arm weightless on his back, her hard belly softly bumping. He felt her now expectant, sitting composed in a careless bathrobe on a kitchen chair, aggressive even, unattractive, so full of the gassy waitingness and pallor of pregnancy.

He said casually, *Good lemonade*, in the same moment as she sharply asked, *Why do you go to church?*

Well, why do you?

I asked first.

The usual reasons. I'm a coward. I'm a conservative. Republican, religious. My parents' ghosts are there, and my older girl sings in the choir. She's so brave.

I'm sorry you're a Republican. My parents worshipped Roosevelt.

Mine were offended because he was Dutch, they didn't think the Dutch had any business trying to run the country. I think they thought power was sin. I don't have any serious opinions. No, I do have one. I think America now is like an unloved child smothered in candy. Like a middle-aged wife whose husband brings home a present after every trip because he's been unfaithful to her. When they were newly married he never had to give presents.

Who is this husband?

God. Obviously. God doesn't love us any more. He loves Russia. He loves Uganda. We're fat and full of pimples and always whining for more candy. We've fallen from grace.

You think a lot about love, don't you?

More than other people?

I think so.

Actually, I never think about love. I've left that to your friend Freddy Thorne.

Would you like to kiss me?

Very much, yes.

Why don't you?

It doesn't seem right. I don't have the nerve. You're carrying another man's child.

Foxy impatiently stood, exclaiming, *Ken's frightened of my baby. I frighten him. I frighten you.* Piet had risen from his chair and she stood beside him, asking in a voice as small as the distance between them, *Aren't we in our house? Aren't you building this house for me?*

Before kissing her, yet after all alternatives had been closed to him, Piet saw her face to be perfectly steady and clean of feeling, like a candleflame motionless in a dying of wind, or a road straight without strategies, like the roads of his native state, or the canals of Holland, and his hands on her body beneath the loose robe found this same quality, a texture almost wooden yet alive and already his; so quickly familiar did her body feel that there was no question, no necessity, of his taking her that afternoon— as a husband and wife, embracing in the kitchen, will back off because they will soon have an entire night, when the children are asleep, and no mailman can knock.

Outdoors again, amid the tracked clay, the splinters, the stacked bundles of raw shingles, the lilac stumps, Piet remembered how her hair, made more golden by the Tarbox sun, had been matted, a few damp strands, to her temple. She had averted her blushing face from his kiss as if to breathe, exhaling a sigh and gazing past his shoulder at a far corner of the unfinished room. Her lips, visually thin, had felt wide and warm and slippery; the memory, outdoors, as if chemically transformed by contact with oxygen, drugged Piet with a penetrating dullness.

His life with Angela suffered under a languor, a numbness that Georgene had never imposed. His blood brooded on Foxy; he dwelled endlessly upon the bits of her revealed to him—her delicate pubic fleece, her high-pitched coital cries, the prolonged and tender and unhoped-for meditations of her mouth upon his phallus. He became an obsessed inward housekeeper, a secret gardener.

I didn't know you'd be blond here too.

What would I be? You're red.

But you're so delicate. Transparent. Like the fuzz on a rose.

She laughed. *Well I've learned to live with it, and so must you.*

He lived dimly, groping, between those brilliant glimpses when they quickly slipped each other from their clothes and she lay down beside him, her stretched belly shining, and like a lens he opened, and like a blinded skier lost himself on the slopes of her presence. July was her fifth month; her condition forced upon their intercourse homely accommodations. Since bending was awkward, she would slide down in the bed to kiss him. *Do you really like that?*

Love it.

Is there a taste?

A good taste. Salty and strong. A bit of something bitter, like lemon.

I'm afraid of abusing you.

Don't be. Do.

She never came. However gladly she greeted him, and with however much skill he turned her body on the lathe of the light, shaping her with his hands and tongue, finally they skidded separate ways. *Come in me.*

Are you ready?

I want you in me.

He felt her inner music stall. Her cunt was young, snug. A kind of exasperation swept him forward toward the edge, and as she whimpered he ejaculated, and sighing she receded. But in her forgiving him and his forgiving her, in her blaming herself and his disagreeing, in their accepting the blame together, their love had exercise and grew larger. Her brown eyes, gazing, each held in miniature the square skylight above him. She apologized, *I'm sorry. I can't quite forget that it's you.*

Who should I be?

Nobody. Just a man. I think of your personality and it throws me off the track.

Does this happen with Ken?

No. Sometimes I come first. We've known each other so long we're rather detached, and just use each other. Anyway, as I guess I've told you, we don't make much love since I've gotten big.

That seems strange. You're lovely this way. Your skin is glossy, even your shape seems right. I can't imagine making love to you with a flat tummy. It wouldn't be you. You'd lack grandeur.

Ken is strange. He wants sex to stay in a compartment. He married me, and that solved the problem, as far as he was concerned. He never wanted me to have a baby. We had enough money, it was just his selfishness. I was never his wife, I was his once-a-week whore for all those years.

I'm jealous.

Don't be. Piet, don't feel bad about my not coming. I feel love too much with you, is the problem.

You're kind, but I honestly fear I'm second-rate at this. Like my skiing and my golf. I began too late.

Horrible man. I hate you when you fish for compliments. As all the ladies must tell you, you're incredible. You're incredibly affectionate.

Any man you took to bed with all his clothes off would be affectionate.

No. At least, I've only known three men, and the other two weren't especially.

Not the Jew? She had told him about the Jew.

He laughed at me. Sometimes he hurt me. But then I had been a virgin and probably he couldn't help hurting me. Probably he wouldn't hurt me now.

Do you want him now?

I have him now. Is that awful to say? I have him in you, and you besides. It's better. He was perverse, Piet.

But you're perverse too.

Her brown eyes childishly widened. *How? You mean*—her fingertips touched her lips, then his penis—*that? But why is that perverse? Don't you like it?*

I love it. It binds us so close, though, I'm frightened.

Are you? I'm glad. I was afraid only I was. Piet. What will the world do to us?

Is it God or the world you care about?

You think of them as different? I think of them as the same.

Maybe that's what I mean when I say you're perverse. Her face so close to his seemed a paradigm, a pattern of all the female faces that had ever been close to him. Her blank brow, her breathing might have belonged to Angela; then Foxy turned her head on the pillow so her pink face took the light from above, the cold blue light of the sky, and was clearly not Angela, was the Whitman woman, the young adulteress.

She was frightened, brazen, timid, wanton, appalled by herself, unrepentant. Adultery lit her from within, like the ashen mantle of a lamp, or as if an entire house of gauzy hangings and partitions were ignited but refused to be consumed and, rather, billowed and glowed, its structure incandescent. That she had courted him; that she was simultaneously proud and careless of her pregnancy; that she would sleep with him; that her father had been an inflexible family-proud minor navy deskman; that her mother had married a laundromat entrepreneur; that by both birth and marriage she was above him in the social scale; that she would take his blood-stuffed prick into the floral surfaces of her mouth; that there had been a Jew she had refound in him; that her mind in the midst of love's throes could be as dry and straight-seeking as a man's; that her fabric was delicate and fragile and burned with another life; that she was his slave; that he was her hired man; that she was frightened—compared to these shifting and luminous transparencies, Angela was a lump, a barrier, a boarded door. Her ignorance of the affair, though all the other couples guessed it, was the core of her maddening opacity. She did not share what had become the central issue of their lives. She was maimed, mute; and in the eggshell-painted rooms of their graceful colonial house she blundered and rasped against Piet's taut nerves. He was so full of Foxy, so pregnant with her body and body scents and her cries and remorses and retreats and fragrant returnings, so full of their love, that his mind felt like thin ice. He begged Angela to guess, and her refusal seemed willful, and his gratitude to her for permitting herself to be deceived turned, as his secret churned in sealed darkness, to a rage that would burst forth irrationally.

"Wake up!"

She had been sitting reading a book in lamplight, and blinked. Her eyes, lifted from the bright page, could not see him. "I am awake."

"You're *not*. You're drifting through life in a trance. Don't you feel what's happening to us?"

"I feel you getting meaner every day."

Bruised moths bumped and clung to the lampshade above her shoulder. "I'm upset," he said.

"What about?"

"About everything. About that pinchy-mouthed gouger Gallagher. About the crappy ranch houses on the hill. About Jazinski: he thinks I'm a drunk. About the Whitman job. I'm losing my shirt for the bastard and he isn't even grateful."

"I thought you enjoyed it, tripping down there every day to visit the little princess."

He laughed gratefully. "Is that what you think of her?"

"I think she's young. I also think she's arrogant. I think she'll be mellowed eventually, I think having a baby will do her good. I don't think she needs your paternal attentions especially."

"Why do you think my attentions are paternal?"

"Whatever they are. Can I go back to my book? I don't find Foxy Whitman or this conversation that interesting."

"God, you are smug. You are so fantastically above it all you stink."

"Listen, I promise I'll make love to you tonight, just let me get to the end of this chapter."

"Finish the fucking book for all I care. Stuff it. Give yourself a real literary thrill."

She heard the appeal in his violence and tried to lift her head, but the hooked print held her gaze. Absent-mindedly she asked, "Can't you relax ten minutes? I have five more pages."

He jumped to his feet, strode two steps to the mirror above the telephone, strode back. "I need to go out. I need a party. I wonder what the Applesmiths are doing. Or the Saltines."

"It's eleven o'clock. Please hush."

"I'm dying. I'm a thirty-four-year-old fly-by-night contractor. I have no sons, my wife snubs me, my employees despise me, my friends are all my wife's friends, I'm an orphan, a pariah."

"You're a caged animal."

"Yes." He took an aggressive stance, presenting himself before her with fists on hips, a bouncy close-set red-haired man whose rolled-up shirtsleeves revealed forearms dipped in freckles. "But Angel, who made the cage, huh? Who? *Who?*"

He meant her to fling him open and discover his secret, to be awed and enchanted by it, to decipher and nurture with him its intricate life. But, enclosed in the alternative world—a world exotic yet strict, mixing a lover's shamelessness and a father's compassion—arising from her lap, she did not respond. The book was an old college text, little appreciated at the time, stained by girlish annotations and translucent blots of the oil she and her roommates had used under their sunlamp, the Modern Library edition of *The Interpretation of Dreams*.

Janet Appleby had confessed to Angela on the beach that she was seeing a psychiatrist. Angela explained it to Piet: "It's just twice a week, for therapy, as opposed to real analysis. Frank's all for it, though it was her idea. She described coming home about three a.m. from the little-Smiths after a terrible scene with Marcia and suddenly knowing that she needed help, help from somebody who isn't a friend or a lover or has any reason to care about her at all. She's only been a few times but already she's convinced she doesn't know why she does what she does. She never loved Harold, so why did she go to bed with him? She told herself it was because she felt sorry for him but he didn't feel sorry for himself especially so who was she kidding? And why now, even though they've all stopped sleeping with each other, or at least she and Harold have, can't they stay away from the other couple every weekend? She says now they've somehow acquired the Thornes, too, especially Freddy—"

"That jerk," Piet said.

"—and it's a real mess. Onion rings and gin. The Thornes never go home, apparently. Georgene just sits and drinks, which she never used to do, and Freddy writes an endless pornographic play on his knee."

"So Janet has to go to a psychiatrist because Georgene drinks?"

"Of course not. Because she thinks she, Janet, is neurotic."

"Define neurotic."

Janet had a variety of bikinis and semi-bikinis and Piet pictured her making her confession while lying belly down on the sand, her top untied to give her back an unbroken tan, her cheek pillowed on a folded towel, her breasts showing white when she lifted up on her elbows to explain better or to survey her children.

Angela said, "You know what neurotic is. You do things you know not why. You sleep with women when you're really trying to murder your mother."

"Suppose your mother's already been murdered?"

"Then maybe you're trying to bring her back to life. The ego tries to mediate between external reality and the id, which is our appetites. The ego carries all this bad news back and forth, but the id refuses to listen, and keeps trying to do whatever it wanted to do, even though the ego has turned its back. I don't explain it very well, because I don't understand it, but dreams are a way of letting out these suppressions, which mostly have to do with sex, which mostly has to do with your parents, who have become a superego and keep tormenting the ego from the *other* side. You know all this, everybody does."

"Well, do you see anything unnatural about Janet sleeping with Harold now and then? Frank can be a real boor; would you like to go to bed with him for the rest of your life, night after night?"

"It's not a question of natural or unnatural or right or wrong. It's understanding why you do things so you can stop doing them. Or enjoy doing them. Certainly Janet does not make herself happy. I don't think she enjoys her children very much, or sex, or even her money. She could be great, you know. She has everything."

"But it's just those people who are unhappy. The people with everything are the ones who panic. The rest of us are too busy scrambling."

"Piet, that's a very primitive attitude. You're saying the rich can't get through the needle's eye. The first shall be last."

"Don't poke fun of the Bible. What's your stake in all this hocus-pocus with egos and ids? Why are you so defensive? I suppose you want to go to a psychiatrist too."

"Yes."

"The hell you will. Not as long as you're my wife."

"Oh? You're thinking of getting another wife."

"Of course not. But it's very insulting. It implies I don't give you enough sex."

"There is no such implication."

"I give you more than you want."

"Exactly. Maybe a psychiatrist could tell me why I don't want more. I do and I don't. I hate myself the way I am. It's doing awful things to both of us."

Piet was taken aback; he had inwardly assumed that Angela knew best, that the amount of sex she permitted was the proper amount, and the surplus was his own problem, his own fault. He asked her, "You don't think our sex life is right?"

"It's awful. Dreadful. You know that."

He tried to pin this estimate down. "How would you rate it on a scale of one to ten?"

"Two."

"Oh come *on*, it's not *that* bad. You can be gorgeous."

"But so rarely. And I don't use my hands or mouth or anything. I'm sick. I need help, Piet. I'm turning you into a bully and a cheat and myself into one of those old maids everybody says you wouldn't believe how beautiful she once was." Blue-eyed, she began to cry. When she cried, it made her face look fat, like Nancy's. Piet was touched. They were in the kitchen, she with vermouth and he with gin-and-Bitter-Lemon, after putting the girls to bed. Against the tiny red florets of the kitchen wallpaper Angela's head, nicely oval, with summer braids and bun, did have a noble neatness that was maidenly. He then realized that in a sociable way she was preparing him for another night without lovemaking. Confessing her frigidity sanctioned it.

He protested, "But everybody loves you. Any man in town would love to go to bed with you. Even Eddie Constantine flirts with you. Even John Ong adores you, if you could understand him."

"I know. But I don't en*joy* knowing it. I don't want to go to bed with *any*body. I don't feel I'm a woman really. I'm a kind of cheerful neuter with this sex appeal tacked on as a kind of joke."

"My poor Angel. Like having Kick Me on your back."

"Exactly. I really thought, listening to Janet, how much we're alike. A lot of coziness and being nice to creeps and this disgusted emptiness at heart. We both come from good families and have big bottoms and try to be witty and get pushed around. Do you know she keeps sleeping pills by her bed and some nights doesn't bother to count how many she takes?"

"Well you don't do that."

"But I could. It sounded very familiar, the way she described it. I love sleep, just delicious nothing sleep. I'd love not to wake up."

"Angela! That's sinful."

"The big difference between Janet and me is, I repress and she tries to express. No?"

"Don't ask *me*."

"I'm sure you've had an affair with her and know just what I mean. Tell me about us, Piet."

"You are a scandalous wife. I have never slept with Janet."

"In a way, I want you to. In a Lesbian way. I felt very drawn, lying beside her on the beach. I think I must be Sapphic. I'd love to have a girls' school, where we'd all wear chitons and play field hockey and sit around listening to poetry after warm baths."

"If you have it all analyzed, you don't need an analyst."

"I don't. I'm just guessing. He'd probably say the reverse was true. I can't stand being touched by other women, for instance. Carol Constantine is always patting, and so does Bea. He might say I'm *too* heterosexual, for America the way it is now. Why did nobody marry me, for example, until you came along? I must have frightened them away."

"Or your father frightened them away."

"Do you want to know something else sick? Can you take it?"

"I'll try."

"I masturbate."

"Sweetie. When?"

"More in the summer than in the winter. I wake up some mornings between four and five, when the birds are just begin-ning, or a trailer truck goes by on the road, and the sheets feel terribly sensitive on my skin, and I do it to myself."

"That sounds pretty normal. Do you imagine anybody, any particular man?"

"Not very clearly. It's mostly sensation. You're the only man

I've ever known, so if I picture anyone it's you. Now why don't I wake the real you up?"

"You're too considerate and shy."

"Oh balls, Piet. Just balls."

"You must stop talking to Freddy Thorne at parties. Your language is deteriorating."

"*I'm* deteriorating. I don't know how to act in this sexpot."

"Sexpot?"

"Tarbox."

"A sexpot is a person, not a place."

"This one's a place. Get me out or get me to a doctor."

"Don't be silly. The town is like every other town in the country. What you're saying is you're too good for this world. You're too fucking good for any of us."

"Don't raise your voice. I hate that high voice you put on."

"Of course you hate it, you're supposed to hate it. You hate me, why not hate my voice?"

"I don't hate you."

"You must, because I'm beginning to hate you."

"Ah. Now you're saying it."

"Well, I don't quite mean it. You're gorgeous. But you're *so* self-centered. You have no idea what I'm like inside—"

"You mean you're having an affair and you want me to guess the woman?"

"No I don't mean that."

"Foxy Whitman."

"Don't be grotesque. She's pregnant and adores her icy husband and gives me a professional pain in the neck besides."

"Of course—but why do I imagine it? I know it's neurotic but every time you go down there and come back so affectionate to me and the children I think you've been sleeping with her. I watch her face and feel she has a secret. She's so tender and gay talking to me. She knows me all too well, they've only been in town since March."

"She likes you. Maybe she's a Lesbian too."

"And it's not just Foxy, it can be Janet or Marcia or even Georgene—I'm madly jealous. And the more jealous I get the less

I can bring myself to make love to you. It's sad. It's miserable. Your telephone was busy for half an hour yesterday and I made myself a martini at eleven in the morning, imagining it was some woman."

Her oval face yearned to cry some more but a sophisticated mechanism produced a half-laugh instead. Painfully Piet looked toward the floor, at her bare feet; neither of her little toes touched the linoleum. His dear poor blind betrayed Angel: by what right had he torn her from her omnipotent father? Each afternoon, an hour before quitting, old man Hamilton would walk down his lawn between his tabletop hedges, trailing pipesmoke, bringing a quart bottle of Heineken's and Dixie cups for the workmen. Piet told her, "I don't have Appleby's money. I can't afford it."

She asked, "Isn't there some way I can earn it? I could go into Boston this fall and get enough education credits to teach at least at a private school. Nancy will be away all day in the first grade; I must do *some*thing with my time. I can begin therapy, just twice a week, with the education courses. Oh, Piet, I'll be a wonderful wife; I'll know *every*thing."

It grieved Piet to see her beg, to see her plan ahead. She was considering herself as useful, still useful to him, exploring herself bravely toward a new exploitation when to him she was exhausted, a stale labyrinth whose turnings must be negotiated to reach fresh air and Foxy. Foxy asleep, moonlight lying light along her bones and diagonally stroking the down of her brow: at this vision his stomach slipped, his skin moistened, numbness stung his fingertips and tongue. There was a silver path beneath the stars. Obliviously Angela barred his way. "No," broke from him, panicked as he felt time sliding, houses, trees, lifetimes dumped like rubble, chances lost, nebulae turning, "*no;* sweetie, don't you see what you're doing to me? Let me *go!*"

At his high voice her face paled; its eager flush and the offer of its eyes withdrew. "Very well," she said, "go. What are you going to, may I ask?"

Piet opened his mouth to tell her, but the ice shelling his secret held.

Angela diffidently turned her back. "Your routines," she told him, "are getting less and less funny."

"Daddy, wake up! Jackie Kenneny's baby died because it was born too tiny!"

Nancy's face was a moon risen on the horizon of his sleep. Her eyes were greatly clear, skyey in astonishment. Red tear ducts the tone of a chicken's wattle. Slaughter. The premature Kennedy had been near death for two days. Nancy must have heard the news over television. "I'm sorry," he said. His voice was thick, stuffed and cracked. August was Piet's hay-fever season. Strange, he thought, how pain seeks that couple out. Not wealth nor beauty nor homage shelters them. Suffering tugging at a king's robe. Our fragile gods.

"Daddy?"

"Mm."

"Was the baby scared?" Fear, a scent penetrating as cat musk, radiated through the flannel perfume of her infant skin. He had been dreaming. His brother. His brother frozen under glass, a Pope's remains, Piet apologetic about not having stayed and helped him, been his partner, in the greenhouse. *Is het koud, Joop?* Frozen by overwork, gathering edelweiss. He turned and explained, to the others, *Mijn broeder is dood.* Yet also Foxy was in the dream, though not visibly; her presence, like the onflow of grace, like a buried stream singing from well to well, ran beneath the skin of dreaming as beneath reality, a living fragility continually threatened.

"The baby was too little to be scared. The baby never knew anything, Nancy. It had no mind yet."

"He wants his mommy!" Nancy said, stamping her foot. "He cries and he cries and nobody listens. Everybody is *happy* he hurt hisself."

"Nobody is happy," Piet told her, returning his cheek to the pillow, knowing the child was right, nobody listens. The window against whose panes his upheld hand was silhouetted at night as a monstrous many-horned shape now, at dawn, gave on the plain sweet green of leaves, heart-shaped lilac and feathery, distant elm. Space, it seemed, redeems. Piet reached outwards and pulled Nancy toward him, into the mediating warmth that remained of his sleep. She fought his embrace, feeling its attempt to dissolve and smother the problem. Her wide face studied him angrily, cheated. Freckles small as flyspecks had come to her nose this summer, though they had thought she had inherited her mother's oily brunette skin. Angela's serene form pricked by his own uneasy nature. Flecks of lead in the condensed blue smoke of her irises. Sea creatures. Vague light becomes form becomes thought becomes soul and dies. The retina retains nothing. Piet asked, "Where's Mommy?"

"Up. Get up, Daddy."

"Go talk to Mommy about the Kennedy baby while Daddy gets dressed." Last night he had attempted to make love and though Angela had refused him he had slept nude. He did not wish his body to frighten the child. "Go downstairs," he said. "Daddy feels funny."

"Are you drunk?" She had learned the word and felt threatened by it; once Frank Appleby had crawled into her playpen and shattered a plastic floating duck, and the next day they had explained to her that he had been drunk.

"No. I *was* drunk, and now I wish I hadn't been. My head hurts. I feel sad about the Kennedy baby."

"Mommy said I would never die until I was an old old lady wearing earrings."

"That's absolutely right."

But— It was unspoken. Impatiently needing to urinate, he threw back the covers; his body filled her eyes and they overflowed into tears. He said, "But the little baby was even smaller than you?"

She nodded helplessly.

Piet kneeled and hugged her and recognized in his arms the mute tepid timbre he had often struck from Angela's larger form. He said urgently, "But the baby came out too soon, it was a mistake, God never meant it to live, like a big strong chubby girl like you." His nakedness in air, the stir of her skin in his arms, was gently leading his penis to lift. A cleft or shaft of sun.

Nancy pulled from his arms and shouted from the head of the stairs, "God should have teached the baby not to come out!"

Angela called, "Piet, are you up?"

"Be down in three minutes," he answered. He half dressed and shaved and finished dressing. Today was to be a deskwork day. From the bedroom windows his square lawn looked parched. A droughty summer. Prevailing winds shifting. Icecaps melting. The great forests thinning. On Indian Hill clouds of dust coated the constructions, seeped into the unfinished frames cluttered by leaning plywood and loose electric cable. Here and there in the woods a starved maple turning early. The crickets louder at night. But from Foxy Whitman's windows the marshes, needing no rain, sucking water from the mother sea, spread lush and young, green as spring and carved like plush by the salt creeks' windings. Some afternoons, the tide high, the marshes were all but submerged, and Piet felt the earth reaching for the moon. Atlantis. Ararat.

The narrow farmhouse stairs descended through two landings and stopped a step from the front door, in a hall so cramped the opening door banged the newel post. On Piet's right, in a living room which the crowding lilacs left rather dark and where like sentinels in castellar gloom the empty glasses used last night by the little-Smiths and Saltzes and Guerins were still posted on arms and edges of furniture, Nancy and Ruth were watching television. A British postal official, relayed by satellite, supercilious and blurred, was discussing yesterday's seven-million-dollar robbery of a London mail train, the biggest haul in history—"not counting, of course, raids and confiscations which should properly be termed political acts, if you follow me. As far as we can determine, there was nothing political about these chaps." Television brought them the outer world. The little screen's icy brilliance implied a universe of profound cold beyond the warm encirclement of Tarbox, friends, and family. Mirrors established in New York and Los Angeles observed the uninhabitable surface between them and beamed reports that bathed the children's faces in a poisonous, flickering blue. This poison was their national life. Not since Korea had Piet cared about news. News happened to other people.

On his left, in the already sun-flooded kitchen, Angela laid out breakfast plates on four rectangular mats. Dish, glass, spoon, knife. Her nipples darkly tapped her nightie from within. Her hair was down, swung in sun as she moved, blithe. She seemed to Piet to be growing ever more beautiful, to be receding from him into abstract realms of beauty.

He said to her, "Poor Nancy. She's all shook up."

Angela said, "She asked me if the Kennedy baby was up in Heaven with the hamster going round and round in the wheel. Honestly I wonder, Piet, if religion's worth it, if it wouldn't be healthier to tell them the truth, we go into the ground and don't know anything and come back as grass."

"And are eaten by cows. I don't know why all you stoics think death is so damn healthy. Next thing you'll get into a warm bath with your wrists slit to prove it."

"Oh, you do like that idea."

Nancy came into the kitchen sobbing. "Ruthie says—Ruthie says—"

Ruth followed, flouncing. "I said God is retarded." She sneered at Nancy, "*Baaby*."

"Ruth!" Angela said.

"Retarded?" Piet asked. It was an adjective her generation applied to everything uncooperative. *The retarded teacher kept us all after class. This retarded pen won't write. Frankie is a re-tard.*

"Well He is," Ruth said. "He lets little babies die and He makes cats eat birds and all that stuff. I don't want to sing in the choir next fall."

"I'm sure that'll make God shape up," Piet said.

"I don't see why the child should be forced to sing in the choir every Sunday," Angela told him, standing bent as Nancy cried into her lap. Her hair overhung the child. Mothering. Seeking the smothering she had fled from in Piet. Loves her more than me. Each to each. Symbiosis.

"For the same fucking reason," Piet told Angela, "that I must spend my life surrounded by complaining females." He ate breakfast surrounded by wounded silence. He felt nevertheless he had done a good deed, had rescued Nancy from the grip of death.

Better anger than fear. Better kill than be killed.

He drove to the office, rattling down Charity, parking on Hope. A space today, lately often not. Talk of the need for a stoplight at the corner where Divinity turned. Confusing to out-of-towners. Too many cars. Too many people. Homosexuality the answer? The pill. Gallagher was talking on his phone, Irish accent emergent. "We've got thirty-three rooms, Sister, and removing a lone partition would give us a grand refectory." Piet heated water on their electric coil and made instant coffee. Maxwell. Faraday. He settled at his desk to concentrate on deskwork. Lumber $769.82, total, overdue, if has escaped your previous notice please remit, since a sound credit rating, etc. His nasal passages itched and his eyes watered. Another scratchy August day. Foxy far. Hours away. Her laughter, her fur. *To visit the little princess. Too pretty-pretty for you.* His own phone rang.

"Allo, dollink." It had been a month since they had talked.

"Hello." He used his flat contractor's voice.

"Are you surrounded? Is Matt there?"

"No. Yes." They had recently installed in their crowded space a corrugated-glass divider (ASG mfg., 1″ thickness overall) which set Gallagher apart and made him appear, subtly, the head of the office. But the partition was thin and without a client in his cubbyhole Gallagher kept the door open, to create a breeze. He needed a breeze, or his shirt would wrinkle. He had walled himself in without a window. In there with him were an electric clock, a Ford-agency calendar, a colored zoning map of Tarbox, an aerial photograph of the downtown and beach area, an overall map of Plymouth County, a Mandarin-orange street directory of Tarbox, the pale-blue annual town reports back to 1958, a thin red textbook entitled *Property Valuation*, a thumbed fat squat black missal. While Piet worked, when he did, at a yellow oak desk salvaged from a high school and littered with molding samples and manufacturers' catalogs, Gallagher's desk was military gray steel and clean except for a pen set socketed in polished serpentine, a blotter, framed photographs of Terry and Tommy, and two telephones. Behind his head hung framed his license from the Board of Registration of Real Estate Brokers and Salesmen. He had just purchased for their firm the fifty-odd acres and the thirty-odd rooms of an estate in Lacetown with iron deer on the lawn. He had intended to develop the grounds piecemeal but had since got wind of an order of nuns who were seeking to relocate a novitiate. As he exultantly told Piet, the Church doesn't haggle. In the meantime their tiny office supported among its debts a hundred-thousand-dollar mortgage; it felt precarious. But gambling was Gallagher's meat, and having dared the deal increased the amount of psychic space he occupied. Piet feared Georgene's voice was coming through too strong; he huddled the receiver tight against his ear.

"Don't worry, I'll hang up in a minute," she said. "I just had a crazy impulse to call and find out how you were doing. Is that presumptuous? I still have some rights, don't I? I mean you and me, we *were* something real, weren't we?

"I understand you," Piet said.

"You can't really talk, can you?"

"That sounds correct."

"Well, if you'd call me once in a while this wouldn't happen. We hear you had a little party last night and I felt very hurt we weren't invited. The way Irene let it slip out was positively malicious."

"The orders," Piet said uncertainly, "are slow coming through this time of year. The government's buying up a lot of west-coast fir."

"Piet, I miss you so much, it's killing me. Couldn't you just come for coffee on your way to somewhere else sometime? Like this morning? It's perfectly safe. Whitney's off at camp and Irene took Martha and Judy down to the beach. I told her I had a plumber coming. It's true, our pressure's down to nothing. Don't ever live on a hill. Can't you come, please? Just to talk a *little* bit? I promise I won't be pushy. I was *such* a bitch at the Ongs'."

"The estimate looks discouraging."

"I'm *mis*erable, Piet. I can't stand living with that man much longer. He gets worse and worse. I'm losing all sense of myself as a woman."

"I thought he did good work."

Georgene laughed, a brisk, slightly formal noise. "I'm sure Matt isn't fooled at all. The games you two play down there. No, if you must know, he does lousy work. Freddy's lousy in bed, that's what you want to hear, isn't it? That's what you always wanted to hear. I lied to you. I protected him. He can't manage anything until he's drunk and then he's sloppy and falls asleep. He wilts. Do you understand what I'm saying?"

"We're speaking of upright supports."

"It's *so* sad. It makes me so *ashamed*. I have no self-confidence at anything any more, Terry and I lost six-two, six-three to Bernadette and Angela yesterday, I suppose she told you, crowing about it."

"No."

"*Please* come over. I'm *so* blue, so *blue*. I won't pry, I promise. I know you have somebody else but I don't care any more. Was I ever that demanding? Was I? Didn't I just take you as you came?"

"Yes." Gallagher loudly rustled papers and tapped shut a steel desk drawer.

"God, I hate the sound of my voice. I hate it, Piet. I hate to beg. It's taken me weeks to bring myself to make this call. You don't have to go to bed with me, I promise. I just need to have you to myself for half an hour. For fifteen minutes."

"We're behind schedule now, I'm afraid."

"Come, or I'll tell Freddy about us. I'll tell Freddy and Angela everything. No. Forget Angela. I'll tell Foxy. I'll waltz right down there and plump myself down and tell her the kind of bastard she's mixed herself up with."

"Let me call you back. I'll look at my schedule again."

She began to cry; Georgene's crying, rare, was an unlovely and unintelligent sound, and Piet feared it would fill the little office as it filled his skull. "I didn't know," she sobbed, "I'd miss you this much, I didn't know . . . you were into me . . . so deep. You knew. You knew just what you were doing to me, you bastard, you marvelous poor bastard. You're making me suffer because your parents were killed. Piet, I didn't kill your parents. I was in Philadelphia when it happened, I didn't know them, I didn't *know* you . . . oh, forgive me, I have no idea what I'm saying . . ."

"In the meantime," Piet said, "watch out for seepage," and hung up.

There was an inquisitive silence behind him. He responded, "Bea Guerin. She thinks her house might be settling. She doesn't trust those cedar posts I put in because we used metal in the Whitman renovation. I think she's hysterical. It's too bad, all she needs is a baby. Which reminds me, Matt, something I wanted your opinion on. Angela thinks she needs to go to a psychiatrist."

As Piet had hoped, the second statement caught Matt's attention; the truth is always more interesting than the lie. "Angela's the sanest woman I know," Matt said.

"Ah, Matt," Piet answered, "in this fallen world, being sane and being well aren't the same thing." Gallagher uncomfortably frowned; it was part of his Catholicism to believe that all theological references in private conversation must be facetious. Piet had developed with Gallagher a kidding pose, a blarneyish tone, useful in both acknowledging and somewhat bridging the widening gap between them. Gradually they were finding each other impossible. Without an act, a routine, Piet would hardly have been able to talk to Gallagher at all. "And surely she's no saner than Terry," he said.

"Terry. She's gone gaga over the lute. She's in Norwell twice a week and now she wants to take pottery lessons from the woman's husband."

"Terry is very creative."

"I suppose. She won't play for *me*. I don't know how to treat Terry these days."

Piet abruptly volunteered, "Actually, what Angela needs is a lover, not a psychiatrist."

Matt's brittle face, his jaw so smooth-shaven it seemed burnished, hardened at this; his mouth tightened. He felt in Piet's train of association possible news for himself. Yet he was curious; he was human, Freddy Thorne would have pointed out. He asked, "You'd let her?"

"Well, I'd expect her out of decency to try to conceal it. I'd simply not pry. If it came into the open, I'd of course have to be sore."

They were talking through the doorway; Matt was framed by corrugated glass. The office was so small there was no need to raise their voices. Matt said, "Piet, if I may say so—"

"You may, my good fellow. An honest man's the noblest work of God."

"You seem quite jealous of her. Terry and I have always been struck by you two as a couple, how protective and fond you are of each other, while pretending the opposite."

"Do we pretend the opposite?" Piet was offended, but Matt was too intent to notice.

"Terry and I," he said, "don't have your room for maneuver. Fidelity can't be a question. Do you know that, in the view of the Church, marriage is a sacrament administered by the couple themselves?"

"Maybe some of the sacrament should be giving the other some freedom. Why all this fuss about bodies?" Piet asked. "In fifty years we'll all be grass. You know what would seem like a sacrament to me? Angela and another man screwing and me standing above them sprinkling rose petals on his back." Piet held up his hand and rubbed thumb and forefinger. "Sprinkling blessings on his hairy back."

Gallagher said, "Mother and father."

"Whose?"

"Yours. As you described that I pictured a child beside his parents' bed. He loves his mother but knows he can't handle her so he lets the old man do the banging while he does the blessing."

Again offended, Piet said, "Everybody's so damn psychoanalytical all of a sudden. Let me ask you something. Suppose you discovered Terry wasn't going off for music lessons."

"I'd refuse to discover it," Gallagher answered with catechetical swiftness, and smiled. The smiles of the Irish never fail to strike a spark; they have the bite in their eyes of the long oppressed. The flint of irony. He told Piet, "You have a kind of freedom I don't have. You can be an adventurer where I can't. I have to have my adventures here." He laid his hand flat on the steel desk. His hand was hair-backed. Big pores. Coarse dogma.

Piet said, "And they make me damn nervous. What the hell are we going to do with that rotten old castle in Lacetown? That partition you were telling the sister about can't just be knocked out. It's weight-bearing."

Matt told him, "You shouldn't be in this business, you're too conservative. You don't have the nerves for it. What you got to realize, Piet, is that land can't lose. There's only so much of it, and there are more and more people."

"Thanks to the Pope."

"You have more children than I do."

"I don't know how you do it, it's a miracle."

"Self-control. Try it."

This was Piet's day to fight. That Gallagher, with his wife off with some old potter, felt able to deliver instruction so angered Piet that he rose from his creaky swivel chair and said, "Which reminds me, I better get over to the hill and see if they're using wood on the houses or cardboard like you tell them to."

Matt's face was a crystal widening toward the points of the jaws, his shaved cheeks and flat temples facets. He said, "And check on Mrs. Whitman while you're at it."

"Thanks for reminding me. I will."

Stepping outdoors onto treeless Hope Street, Piet was struck by the summer light so hard that his eyes winced and the world looked liquid. It was all, he saw, television aerials and curbstone grits, abortive—friendships, marriages, conversations, all aborted, all blasted by seeking the light too soon.

On Indian Hill the three ranch houses had reached a dismal state of incompletion. The frames, sheathed in four-by-eight sheets of plywood, were complete but the rooms within were waiting for electricians and plumbers and plasterers. Cedar shingles lay on the damp earth in costly unbroken stacks. Jazinski was watching two trade-school boys nail shingles and Piet was annoyed by his idle supervision. He told him, "Get a hammer," and spent the morning beside him, aligning and nailing cedar shingles over insulating foil. The cedar had an ancient fragrance; the method of aligning the shingles, by snapping a string rubbed with chalk, was agreeably primitive. Sun baked Piet's shoulders and steamed worry from him. It was good to work, to make weatherproof, to fashion overlapping fishscales. He was Noah; the skinny-armed young Polack swinging his hammer in unison beside him perhaps was a son. Piet tried to converse with Leon, but between hammer blows the boy responded with pronouncements that, sullen yet definite, were complete in themselves, and led nowhere.

On the death of the Kennedy baby: "That crowd has everything but luck. Old Joe can't buy them luck." On the Catholic religion: "I believe in some kind of Supreme Being but none of the rest of it. My wife agrees, I was surprised." On the progress of the job: "It's waiting on the plumbers now. I guess two have been already sold. The families want to move in by the start of school. Do you want to give the plumbers a ring, or shall I?" On the colored Construction King operator, whom Piet remembered fondly, for having shown him cheerfulness on a day of death: "I feel this way about it. If they measure up they should be treated like everybody else. That don't mean I want to live next door to them." On the future: "I may not be here next summer. I'm looking around. I have responsibilities to myself."

"Well, Leon, maybe next summer I won't be here, and you can be me."

The boy said nothing, and Piet, glancing over, wondered how his arms could remain so stringy and pale, like those of a deskworker, though he worked all summer in the sun.

In the rhythmic silence Piet began to talk with Foxy in his head. He would take her a flower from the roadside—a stalk of chicory, with flowers as blue as the eyes of a nymphomaniac. *For me?*

Who else?

You're so tender. When you're not with me I remember the passion but I forget the affection.

He would laugh. *How could I not be affectionate?*

Other men could. I guess. I've not had much experience.

You've had enough, I'd say.

What can you see in me? I'm getting huge, and I never come for you, and I'm not good, or witty, like Angela.

I find you quite witty.

Should we go up to bed?

Just for a moment. To rest.

Yes. To rest.

I love your maternity clothes. The way they billow and float. I love the way your belly is so hard and pushes at me. In another month it'll start kicking.

Do you really like me this way? Look, I'm getting veins in my legs.

Beautiful blue. Blue blond furry rosy Foxy.

Oh Piet. Take these awful Paisley things off. I want to kiss you.

As you like.

Leonine he would lie back. Eyelids lowered, her dusty-rose cheek dented by the forcing apart of her jaws, her sleeping face would eclipse that gnarled choked part of him a Calvinist whisper by his cradle had taught him to consider vile. Touch of teeth like glints of light. Her fluttered tongue and lips' encirclement. Her hair spun air between his lifted thighs, nipples and fingernails, muddled echoes of blood. He would seek the light with one thrust and she would gag; penitent he would beg *Come up* and her tranced drained face swim to his and her cold limp lips as he kissed them wear a moony melted stale smell whose vileness she had taken into herself. All innocent they would lock loins, her belly gleaming great upon his, and though short of breath and self-forsaken she would not quite come; this had happened and would happen again that summer of the solar eclipse.

Three weeks ago, it had been ninety per cent at their latitude. An invisible eater moved through the sun's disc amid a struggle of witnessing clouds. The dapples of light beneath the elm became crescent-shaped; the birds sang as in the evening. Seen through smoked glass the sun was a shaving, a sideways eyebrow, a kindergarten boat riding a tumult of contorted cumulus. The false dusk reversed; the horns of the crescents beneath the trees pointed in the opposite direction; the birds sang to greet the day. Not a month before, he had first slept with Foxy.

Only one other time had been so ominous: the Wednesday in

October of 1962 when Kennedy had faced Khrushchev over Cuba. Piet had had a golf date with Roger Guerin. They agreed not to cancel. "As good a way to go as any," Roger had said over the phone. Stern occasions suited him. As Piet drove north to the course, the Bay View, he heard on the radio that the first Russian ship was approaching the blockade. They teed off into an utterly clear afternoon and between shots glanced at the sky for the Russian bombers. Chicago and Detroit would go first and probably there would be shouts from the clubhouse when the bulletins began coming in. There was almost nobody else on the course. It felt like the great rolling green deck of a ship, sunshine glinting on the turning foliage. As Americans they had enjoyed their nation's luxurious ride and now they shared the privilege of going down with her. Roger, with his tight angry swing, concentrating with knit brows on every shot, finished the day under ninety. Piet had played less well. He had been too happy. He played best, swung easiest, with a hangover or a cold. He had been distracted by the heavensent glisten of things—of fairway grass and fallen leaves and leaning flags—seen against the onyx immanence of death, against the vivid transparence of the sky in which planes might materialize. Swinging, he gave thanks that, a month earlier, he had ceased to be faithful to Angela and had slept with Georgene. It had been a going from indoors to outdoors; they met at beaches, on porches, beneath translucent trees. Happy remembering her, picturing her straight limbs, Piet sprayed shots, three-putted, played each hole on the edge of an imaginary cliff. Driving home, he heard on the car radio that the Russians had submitted to inspection and been allowed to pass. He had felt dismay, knowing that they must go on, all of them, Georgene and Angela and Freddy and himself, toward an untangling less involuntary and fateful. He had been fresh in love then.

Leon said: "That sun is brutal. I like winter myself. My wife and I thought we'd try skiing this year."

Noon passed, and one. The connective skin between thumb and palm, where the hammer rubbed, smarted as if to blister. Piet left Leon and drove into town, through town, on down the beach road. Dusty flowers, chicory and goldenrod, a stand of late daisies, flickered at the roadside, but he was in too much of a hurry to stop. *I wanted to bring you a flower but it seemed too urgent so I just brought you myself.*

Of course. What a nice present.

Her house was empty. No Plymouth station wagon, no workman's truck, was in the driveway. The door was unlocked. The hall rug awry. Cotton slept in the blue sling chair. The work was nearly done, the plastering completed even to the sweeping up. A round thermostat and square light switch on the smooth wall side by side. Rough edges. Books of wallpaper samples lay face up on the sanded and sealed floor. A folder of paint shades was propped against a pine baseboard. In the kitchen all that was needed was white paint and for the dishwasher on order to arrive. Sawdust and earth smells still lived in the house. Salt air would wipe them away. She had promised to invite Piet and Angela down when the house was finished. The wallpaper books were open to samples that were not Angela's taste. Big pastel splashes. Vulgar passion.

Where was she? She never shopped at this hour, her nap hour. Had he only dreamed of possessing her? The tide was low and the channels seen from the kitchen windows were ribbons glittering deep between banks of velvet clay. Three red deer were bounding across the dry marsh to the uninhabited shrub island. The days to hunting season were finite. The crystalline sky showed streaks of cirrus wispy at one end, like the marks of skates braking. Miscarriage. Doctors, workmen returning. Without her here he felt the house hostile, the walls of their own will rejecting him. Too soon, too soon. He became anxious to leave and, driving back toward town, turned on an impulse up the Thornes' long driveway.

The Saltzes and the Constantines, maliciously called the Saltines by the other couples, had jointly bought a boat, the Applebys' catboat, with a six-horsepower motor, and after a Saturday or Sunday of sailing would drink beer and California sauterne in their damp bathing suits and have other couples over. The Sunday night before Labor Day a crowd collected in the Constantines' messy Victorian manse. The couples were excited and wearied by tennis; this was the weekend of the North Mather Court Club Open Tournament. Annually the North Mather men, rangy automobile salesmen and insurance claims agents who exerted themselves all winter long on two domed courts grassed with plastic fiber, easily eliminated even the best of the Tarbox men, such as Matt Gallagher; but, contrariwise, the North Mather wives wilted under the assault of their Tarbox counterparts. Invariably Georgene and Angela, Terry and Bernadette dominated the female finals, and for weeks before Labor Day their telephones jangled as the men of North Mather, centaurs in search of Amazons, beseeched the fabulous Tarbox women to be their partners in mixed doubles.

None of the Saltines played. A delicate social line had early hardened and not been crossed. Instead, today they had taken Freddy Thorne, who played terribly, out into the Bay for skin diving. It amused him to keep his wetsuit on. His appearance in the tight shiny skin of black rubber was disturbingly androgynous: he was revealed to have hips soft as a woman's and with the obscene delicacy of a hydra's predatory petals his long hands flitted bare from his sleeves' flexible carapace. This curvaceous rubber man had arisen from another element. Like a giant monocle his Cyclopean snorkeling mask jutted from his naked skull, and his spatulate foot flippers flopped grotesquely on the Constantines' threadbare Oriental rugs. When he sat in a doilied armchair and, twiddling a cigarette, jauntily crossed his legs, the effect was so outrageous and droll, monstrous and regal that even Piet Hanema laughed, feeling in Freddy's act life's bad dreams subdued.

"Read us your play," Carol Constantine begged him. She wore a man's shirt over an orange bikini. Something had nerved her up tonight; a week ago, she had dyed her hair orange. "Let's all take parts."

All summer it had been rumored that Freddy was writing a pornographic play. Now he pretended not to understand. "What play?" he asked. Beneath the misted snorkel mask he missed his customary spectacles. His eyes were blind and furry; his lipless mouth bent in upon itself in a pleased yet baffled way.

"Freddy, I've *seen* it," Janet Appleby said. "I've seen the cast of characters."

With the dignity of a senile monarch Freddy slowly stared toward her. "Who are you? Oh, I know. You're Jan-jan Applesauce. I didn't recognize you out of context. Where are your little friends?"

"They're in Maine, thank God."

"Don't be your usual shitty self, Freddy," Carol said, sitting on the arm of the chair and draping her gaunt arms around his rubber shoulders. The action tugged open her shirt. Piet, sitting cross-legged on the floor, saw her navel: a thick-lidded eye. Carol caressed Freddy's air hose, hung loose around his neck. "We want to do your play," she insisted.

"We can make a movie of it," Eddie Constantine said. He flew in spells; he had been home three days. His growth of beard suggested a commando, cruel and sleepless. He held a beer can in each hand. Seeing his wife draped across Freddy, he had forgotten who he was fetching them for, his vacant eyes the tone of the same aluminum. Abruptly, as if tossing a grenade, he handed a can to Ben Saltz, who sat in the corner.

"I want to be the one who answers the door," Carol said. "Don't all dirty movies begin with a woman answering the door?"

Ben sat staring, his dark eyes moist with disquiet. He had recently shaved, and looked enfeebled, slack-chinned, mockingly costumed in sailing clothes—a boat-neck jersey, a windbreaker, a white officer's cap, and suntans cut down to make shorts, fringed with loose threads. Ben's calves were heavily, mournfully hairy. Piet glimpsed himself in that old-fashioned male shagginess but his own body hair was reddish, lighter, gayer, springy. Ben's lank hairs ran together to make black seams, like sores downrunning into the tops of his comically new topsiders, cup-soled, spandy-bright. Except for his sunburned nose, Ben's skin was pasty and nauseated. He had pockmarks. His wounded love of Carol weighed on the air of the room and gave the couples an agitated importance, like children in safe from a thunderstorm.

"What's a dirty movie?" Freddy asked, blinking, pretending to be confused.

"*Tom Jones,*" Terry Gallagher said.

Angela rose up unexpectedly and said, "Come on Carol, let's undress him. I know he has the play in his pocket."

"You think he takes it underwater with him?" Piet asked mildly, exchanging with Foxy a quizzical look over Angela's uncharacteristic display of flirtatious energy. They had become, these two, the parents of their spouses, whose faults they forgave and whose helplessness they cherished from the omniscient height of their adultery.

Foxy had come to the party without Ken, but with Terry Gallagher. Ken and Matt, having been easily beaten in North Mather, had played consolation singles together all afternoon on the Ongs' court. The two men, uncomfortable among the couples, were comfortable with each other. Foxy and Terry shared tallness and an elusive quality of reluctance, of faintly forbidding enchantment, reflected, perhaps, from their similar husbands. But Foxy was Snow White and Terry Rose Red—something Celtic strummed her full lips, her musical hands, the big muscles knitting her hips to her thighs. She stood tall and joined in the rape, asking Janet, "Where are his pants? You told me he always carries it in his pants."

"Upstairs," Carol said brokenly, wrestling with Freddy's flailing arms, struggling to undo his jacket's rusty snaps. "In Kevin's room. Don't wake him up."

Janet, who had been in therapy two months now, watched the struggle and pronounced, "This is childish."

Angela tried to pin Freddy's ankles as he slid from the chair. One of his flippers kicked over a tabouret holding a crammed ashtray and a small vase of asters. Angela brushed up the ashes and butts with two copies of *Art News*, Eddie carefully poured beer over Freddy's head, and Ben Saltz sat dazed by the sight of Carol, her hair a color no hair in nature ever was, writhing nearly nude in the man's black embrace. The rubber of his suit squeaked as her bare skin slid across his lap. Her shirt had ridden up to her armpits; her orange top twisted, and a slim breast flipped free. Crouching on the carpet, Carol quickly readjusted herself, but kneeled a while panting, daring to look nowhere. All these people had seen her nipple. It had been orangish.

In the front parlor, reached through a doorway hung with a

beaded curtain, Irene Saltz's voice was saying, "I can't believe you know what you're saying. Frank, I *know* you, and I *know* that you're a human being." She was drunk.

His voice responded, heated and pained. "It's *you* who want to keep them down, to give them on a platter everything everybody else in this country has had to work for."

"Work! What honest work have you ever done?"

Janet Appleby shouted toward them, "He's worked himself into an ulcer, Irene. Come on in here and take your husband home, he looks sick."

The Constantines' house was large, but much of its space was consumed by magniloquent oak stairways and wide halls and cavernous closets, so that no single room was big enough to hold a party, which then overflowed into several, creating problems of traffic and acoustics. Janet was not heard, but Frank's voice came to them from the parlor clearly. "The federal government was never meant to be a big mama every crybaby could run to. Minimal government was the founders' ideal. States' rights. Individual rights."

Irene's voice in argument was slurred and even affectionate. "Frank, suppose you were Mrs. Medgar Evers. Would you want to cry or not?"

"Ask any intelligent Negro what the welfare check has done to his race. They hate it. It castrates. I agree with Malcolm X."

"You're not answering me, Frank. What about Medgar Evers? What about the six Birmingham Sunday-school children?"

"They should have the protection of the law like everybody else, like everybody else," Frank said, "no more and no less. I don't approve of discriminatory legislation and that's what the Massachusetts Fair Housing Bill is. It deprives the homeowner of his right to chose. The constitution, my dear Irene, tries to guarantee equality of *opportunity*, not equality of status."

Irene said, "Status and opportunity are inseparable."

"Can't we shut them up?" Eddie Constantine asked.

"It's sex for Irene," Carol told him, standing and buttoning her shirt. "Irene loves arguing with right-wing men. She thinks they have bigger pricks."

Janet's lips opened but, eyes flicking from Carol to Freddy to

Ben, she said nothing. Self-knowledge was turning her into a watcher, a hesitater.

Terry Gallagher came down the Constantines' grand staircase holding a single often-folded sheet of paper. "It's nothing," she said. "It's not even begun. It's a cast of characters. Freddy, you're a fake."

Freddy protested, "But they're beautiful characters."

Amid laughter and beer and white wine, through the odors of brine and tennis sweat, the play was passed around. It bore no title. The writing, beginning at the top as a careful ornamental print, degenerated into Freddy's formless hand, with no decided slant and a tendency for the terminal strokes to swing down depressively.

DRAMATIS PERSONÆ

Eric Shun, *hero*
Ora Fiss, *heroine*

Cunny Lingus, *a tricksome Irish lass*
Testy Cull, *a cranky old discard*

Anna L. Violation ⎫
Ona Nism   ⎬   *nymphs*
Labia Minoris   ⎭

Auntie Climax, *a rich and meaningful relation*

ACT I

Eric *(entering):* !
Ora *(entered):* O!

"That's not fair," Janet said. "Nobody is really called Ora or Ona."

"Maybe the problem," Piet said, "is that Eric enters too soon."

"I was saving Auntie Climax for the third act," Freddy said.

Terry said, "I'm so glad Matt isn't here."

Foxy said, "Ken loves word games."

"Good job, Freddy," Eddie Constantine said. "I'll buy it." He clapped Ben Saltz on the back and held the paper in front of Ben's eyes. Ben's face had become white, whiter than his wife's sun-sensitive skin. Foxy went and, awkwardly pregnant, knelt beside him, tent-shaped, whispering.

Piet was busy improvising. The crude energy the others loved in him had been summoned. "We need more plot," he said. "Maybe Ora Fiss should have a half-brother, P. Niss. Peter Niss. They did filthy things in the cradle together, and now he's returned from overseas."

"From Titty City," Eddie said. He was of all the men the least educated, the least removed in mentality from elementary school. Yet he had lifted and hurled thousands of lives safely across the continent. They accepted him.

Janet said, "You're all fantastically disgusting. What infuriates me, I'm going to have to waste a whole twenty-dollar session on this grotesque evening."

"Leave," Carol told her.

Piet was continuing, gesturing expansively, red hair spinning from his broad arms. "Ora is frightened by his return. Will the old magic still be there? Dear God, pray not! She takes one look. Alas! It is. 'Ora!' he ejaculates. 'Mrs. Nism now,' she responds coldly, yet trembling within."

"You're mixing up my beautiful characters," Freddy complained.

"Let's play some new game," Carol said; she squatted down to gather the residue of the spilled ashes. Her slim breasts swung loose in Piet's eyes. Welcome to Titty, somber city of unmockable suckableness: his heart surged forward and swamped Carol as she squatted. Love for her licked the serial bumps of her diapered crotch. Her bare feet, long-toed, stank like razor clams. Her painted hair downhung sticking drifting to her mouth. She stood, ashes and aster petals in her lily palm, and glared toward the corner where, beneath a Miró print, Foxy was ministering with words to the immobilized Ben Saltz.

"Let's not," Freddy Thorne said to her. "It's good. It's good for people to act out their fantasies."

Angela leaped up, warm with wine, calling Freddy's bluff, and announced, "I want to take off all my clothes!"

"Good, good," Freddy said, nodding calmly. He stubbed out his cigarette on his own forehead, on the Cyclopean glass mask. It sizzled. His wise old woman's face with its inbent lips streamed with sweat.

Piet asked him, "Shouldn't you take that outfit off? Don't you eventually die if the skin can't breathe?"

"It's me. Piet baby, this suit *is* my skin. I'm a monster from the deep."

Angela's hand had halted halfway down the zipper at the back of her pleated white tennis dress. "No one is watching," she said. Piet touched her hand and redid the zipper, which made a quick kissing sound.

"Let her go, it's good," Freddy said. "She wants to share the glory. I've always wanted to see Angela undressed."

"She's beautiful," Piet told him.

"Jesu, I don't doubt it for a sec. Let her strip. She wants to, you don't understand your own wife. She's an exhibitionist. She's not this shy violet you think you're stuck with."

"He's sick," Foxy told Carol, of Ben, in self-defense.

"Maybe," Carol said, "he'd like to be left alone."

"He says you all gave him lobster and rum for supper."

Ben groaned. "Don't mention." Piet recognized a maneuvering for attention, an economical use of misery. But Ben would play the game, Piet saw, too hard in his desire to succeed, and the game would end by playing him. The Jew's fierce face was waxen: dead Esau. Where his beard had been it was doubly pale.

"Shellfish," Eddie explained to all of them. "Not kosher."

Carol said sharply, "Foxy, let him sit it out. He can go upstairs to a bed if he has to."

"Does he know where the beds are?" Freddy asked.

"Freddy, why don't you put that mask over your mouth?" Carol's skin was shivering as if each nerve were irritated. The holiday eve was turning chilly and the furnace had been shut off for the summer. Her lips were forced apart over clenched teeth like a child's after swimming and, touched and needing to touch her, Piet asked, "Why are you being such a bitch tonight?"

"Because Braque just died." Her walls were full of paintings, classic prints and her own humorless mediocre canvases, coarse in their coloring, modishly broad in their brushwork, showing her children on chairs, the Tarbox wharf and boatyard, Eddie in a turtleneck shirt, the graceless back view of the Congregational Church, houses, and trees seen from her studio windows and made garish, unreal, petulant. Cézanne and John Marin, Utrillo and Ben Shahn—her styles muddled theirs, and Piet thought how provincial, how mediocre and lost we all are.

Carol sensed that he thought this and turned on him. "There's something I've been meaning to ask you for a long time, Piet, and now I've had just enough wine to do it. Why do you build such ugly houses? You're clever enough, you wouldn't have to."

His eyes sought Foxy's seeking his. She would know that, hurt, he would seek her eyes. Their glances met, locked, burned, unlocked. He answered Carol, "They're not ugly. They're just ordinary."

"They're hideous. I think what you're doing to Indian Hill is a disgrace."

She had, slim Carol, deliberately formed around her a ring of astonishment. For one of their unspoken rules was that professions were not criticized; one's job was a pact with the meaningless world beyond the ring of couples.

Terry Gallagher said, "He builds what he and Matt think people want to buy."

Freddy said, "I *like* Piet's houses. They have a Dutch something, a fittingness. They remind me of teeth. Don't laugh, everybody, I mean it. Piet and I are spiritual brothers. I put silver in my cavities, he puts people in his. Jesus, you try to be serious in this crowd, everybody laughs."

Angela said, "Carol, you're absurd."

Piet said, "No, she's right. I hate my houses. God, I hate them."

Janet Appleby said, "Somebody else died last month. A poet, Marcia was very upset. She said he was America's greatest, and not that old."

"Frost died last January," Terry said.

"*Not* Frost. A German name. *Oh*. Marcia and Harold would know it. None of us *know* anything."

"I thought you'd start to miss them," Freddy said to her.

Janet, sitting on the floor, sleepily rested her head on a hassock. She had switched from twice-a-week therapy to analysis, and drove into Brookline at seven-thirty every weekday morning. It was rumored that Frank had commenced therapy. "We need a new game," she said.

"Freddy, let's play Impressions," Terry said.

"Let's think up more names for my play," he said. "They don't have to be dirty." He squinted blindly into space, and came up with, "Donovan U. Era."

"You had that prepared," Janet said. "But Harold the other night did think of a good one. What was it, Frank?" With a rattle of wooden beads, the couple had returned from the political parlor. Frank looked sheepish, Irene's eyebrows and lips seemed heavily inked.

"León MacDouffe," Frank pronounced, glancing toward Janet, wanting to go home.

Carol said, in the tone of a greatly removed observer, "Irene, your husband looks less and less well. I think he should go upstairs but nobody else has bothered to agree. It makes no difference to me but we can't afford to have our rug ruined."

Irene's expression as she studied Ben was strange. Maternal concern had become impatient and offended. Delilah gazed upon the Samson she had shorn. In the room's center Eddie Constantine, a small effective man without religion or second thoughts, wiry and tanned and neatly muscled, vied in his health for her attention; a beer can glinted in his hand and his gray eyes could find the path through boiling Himalayas of cloud. As he gazed at her it dawned on the room that she was worth destroying for. Though pale and heavy, she had a dove's breasted grace. Irene asked, "Why can't he go upstairs in his own house a few doors away?"

"I'll take him," Eddie said and, going and thrusting his head under Ben's arm, expertly hoisted him up from the chair.

The sudden motion, like a loud noise to the sleeping, led Ren'u conversational faculty to roll over. "I'm very interested in this," he said distinctly. "What should the aesthetics of modern housing be? Should there be any beyond utility and cost?"

Gleefully Freddy Thorne chimed in, "Did the peasants who put up thatched huts worry about aesthetics? Yet now we all love the Christ out of thatched huts."

"Exactly," Ben said. He sounded like himself, and was reasoning well, but the sounds floated from his ghostly mouth at half-speed. "But perhaps a more oral and sacramental culture has an instinctive sense of beauty that capitalism with its assembly-line method of operation destroys. *Commentary* this month has a fascinating—"

"Greed," Carol said vehemently, "modern houses stink of greed, greed and shame and plumbing. Why should the bathroom be a dirty secret? We all do it. I'd as soon take a crap in front of all of you as not."

"Carol!" Angela said. "That's even more wonderful than my wanting to take off my clothes."

"Let's play Wonderful," Freddy Thorne announced, adding, "I'm dying in this fucking suit. Can't I take it off?"

"Wear it," Piet told him. "It's you."

Foxy asked, "How do you play Wonderful?"

"You," Freddy told her, "you don't even have to try."

Terry asked, "Is it at all like Impressions?"

Ben said, his weight full on Eddie now, his colorless face turned to the floor, "I'd like to discuss this seriously some time. Super-cities, for example, and the desalinization of seawater. I think the construction industry in this country is badly missing the boat."

"Toot, toot," Eddie said, pulling on an imaginary whistle cord and hauling Ben toward the doorway.

Irene asked, "Shall I come along?" Her expression was again indecisive. To be with her husband was to be with her lover. The romantic Semitic shadowiness of her lower lids contended with pragmatic points in her eyes and lips seeking their good opinion, these heirs of the Puritans.

Eddie looked at her acutely, estimated her ripeness, chose his path, and said decisively, "Yes. I'll get him over there and you put him to bed." So all three made exodus from the musty room, through the huge space-wasting hallway smelling in all weathers of old umbrellas, into the leaf-crowded night splashed by blue streetlamps.

Carol swung her arms, relieved and seething. The Applebys exchanged solicitous confidences—Frank's stomach, Janet's head—and also left, reluctantly; their manner of leaving suggested that this was an end, an end to this summer of many games, that they were conscious of entering now an autumn of responsibilities, of sobered mutuality and duty. Only Freddy Thorne begged them not to go. He had peeled himself out of his skin-diving suit and stood revealed in a soaked T-shirt and crumpled bathing trunks. The skin of his legs and arms had been softened and creased by long enclosure like a washerwoman's palms. The Applebys' leaving left Freddy and Piet alone with many women.

Foxy rose, stately in yards of ivory linen, seven months gone, and said, "I should go too."

"Sweetheart, you can't," Freddy told her. "We're going to play Wonderful."

Foxy glanced at Piet's face and he knew that whatever was written there she would read, *Don't go*. He said, "Don't go."

Terry asked Freddy, "How do you play?" Piet pictured Gallagher, grim as a mother, waiting up for her, and wondered how she dare not go, dare sit there serene. Women have no conscience. Never their fault. The serpent beguiled me.

Freddy licked his lips, then answered weakly, "Each of us names the most wonderful thing he or she can think of. Carol, where's the fucking furnace? I'm freezing."

She fetched from another room an Afghan blanket; he wrapped it around himself like a shawl. "Freddy," she said, "you're getting old."

"Thank you. Now please sit down and stop swishing, Carollino. Eddie and Irene are just putting Ben to bed. They'll be back in a minute. And what if they aren't? The world won't stop grinding. Imagine Eddie's off on a flight to Miami. *Che sarà, sarà*, I keep telling everybody."

"Explain," Terry said, "the point of Wonderful."

"The point is, Terrycloth, at the end of the game we'll all know each other better."

Angela said, "I don't *want* to know any of you better."

Foxy said, "I don't want any of you to know *me* better."

Piet asked, "Where's the competitive element? How can you win or lose?"

Freddy answered Piet with oracular care. He still wore the giant monocle and was drunk, drunker than anyone except Angela, white-wine-drunk, a translucent warm drunkenness whose truth lifts the mind. "You can't lose, Piet. I'd think you'd like that for a change. You know, Peterkins—may I speak my heart?—"

"Oh do, brother, do!" Piet holy-rolled on the floor. "Say it, brother, say it!"

Freddy spoke solemnly, trying to be precise. "You are a paradox. You're a funny fellow. A long time ago, when I was a little boy studying my mommy and my daddy, I decided there are two kinds of people in the world: A, those who fuck, and, B, those who get fucked. Now the funny thing about you, Petrov, is you think you're A but you're really B."

"And the funny thing about you," Piet said, "is you're really neither."

Before he began sleeping with Foxy, when Freddy, however unknowingly, held Georgene as hostage, Piet would not have been so quick to answer, so defiant. Freddy blinked, baffled by feeling Piet free, and more openly an enemy.

"If you two prima donnas," Terry said, "would stop being hateful to each other, we could play Wonderful."

"I think more wine would be wonderful," Carol said. "Who else?"

"Me," Angela said, extending a shapely arm and an empty glass. "I must face Georgene in the finals tomorrow."

"Where *is* Georgene?" Piet asked Freddy politely, afraid he had overstepped a moment before, saying "neither."

"Resting up for the big match," Freddy answered, apparently forgiving.

"We really must go soon," Foxy said to Terry.

"Us too," Piet told Angela. In her rare moods of liberation she held for him the danger that she would disclose great riches within herself, showing him the depths of loss frozen over by their marriage.

Carol poured from the Almadén jug, making of it a dancer's routine. Six glasses were refilled. "OK," Freddy said. "Carol has begun by saying that more wine is wonderful."

"I didn't say it was the most wonderful thing I could think of. I still have my turn."

"All reet-o, take it. You're the hostess; begin."

"Must I start?"

All agreed yes, she must, she must. As Carol stood barefoot in silence, Angela asked of the air, "Isn't this exciting?"

Carol decided, "A baby's fingernails."

Gasps, *ah*, awed, then parodies of gasps, *aaah*, greeted this.

Freddy had provided himself with a pencil and wrote on a small piece of paper, the back of his folded play. "A baby's fingernails. Very well. Please explain."

"I must explain?"

"Well. I mean the whole process, all the chemistry. I don't understand it, which may be why it seems wonderful. You know," she went on, speaking to Foxy, who alone of the women did not absolutely know, "the way it produces out of nothing, no matter almost what we do, smoke or drink or fall downstairs, even when we don't want it, this living *baby*, with perfect little fingernails. I mean," she went on, having scanned all their faces and guessed she was not giving enough, "what a lot of *work*, somehow, ingenuity, *love* even, goes into making each one of us, no matter what a lousy job we make of it afterwards."

Piet said, "Carol, how sweet you are. How can anyone so sweet hate me and my nice little houses?" He felt she had taken the opportunity to repair her image; she was aware of having appeared a hennaed bitch and, deserted by the Saltzes and her husband, needed love from those left around her, and perhaps especially from him, who like her had been born lower in the middle class than these others.

She said, "I *don't* hate you. On the contrary, I think you have too much to give people to waste it the way you do."

After a mild silence Angela said, "I can't tell if that's an insult or a come-on."

"We have a baby's fingernails," Freddy Thorne said. "Who's next?"

"Let's have a man," Terry Gallagher said.

Piet felt singled out, touched, by her saying this. Let's. She reposed on the floor, a tall woman, legs bent under her broadened haunches and the knit of her hips. Her lips held a coin. Her dark hair's harp-curve hung down. Once he loved her, too shy then to know they are waiting. Vessels shaped before they are filled. He drank more of the wine of a whiteness like that of the sun seen through fog, a perfect circle smaller than the moon. The eclipse. Love doomed? Foxy was watching him sip, her pink face framed by pale hair fluffed wide by seabathing. Sometimes her belly tasted of salt. Bright drum taut as the curve of the ocean above the massed watchsprings of blond hair. Her navel inverted. Their lovemaking lunar, revolving frictionless around the planet of her womb. The crescent bits of ass his tongue could touch below her cunt's petals. Her far-off cries, eclipsed.

"Piet, you go," Angela said.

His mind skimmed the world, cities and fields and steeples and seas, mud and money, cut timbers, sweet shavings, blue hymnals, and the fuzz on a rose. Ass. His mind plunged unresisted into this truth: nothing matters but ass. Nothing is so good. He said, "A sleeping woman." Why sleeping? "Because when she is sleeping," he added, "she becomes all women."

"Piet, you're drunk," Carol said, and he guessed he had spoken too simply from himself, had offended her. The world hates the light.

Freddy's mouth and eyes slitted. "Maybe sleeping," he said, "because awake she threatens you."

"Speak for yourself," Piet said, abruptly bored with this game and wanting to be with his sleeping children; maybe they, Ruth and Nancy, were the women he meant, drenched and heavy with sleep like lumps of Turkish delight drenched in sugar. "A sleeping woman," he insisted.

"Containing a baby's fingernails," Freddy Thorne added. "My, we're certainly very domestic. Horizonwise, that is. Terry?"

She was ready, had been ever since her smile became complacent. "The works of J. S. Bach."

Piet asked jealously, "Arranged for the lute?"

"Arranged for anything. Played anyhow. That's what's so wonderful about Bach. He didn't know how great he was. He was just trying to support his seventeen children with an honest day's work."

"More domesticity," Angela murmured.

"Don't you believe it," Piet told Terry. "He wanted to be great. He was mad to be immortal." In saying this he was still involved with Carol, arguing about his houses, her paintings, apologizing, confessing to despair.

Terry said serenely, "He feels very unself-conscious and—ordinary to me. Full of plain daylight. It's wonderful to have him in your fingers."

"Keep it clean," Freddy said, writing. "The works of J. S. Bach, not necessarily for stringed instruments. Angela."

"I'm about to cry," Angela said, "you're all so sure of what's good. I can't think of anything wonderful enough to name. The children, I suppose, but do I mean *my* children or the fact of having children, which is what Carol already said? Please come back to me, Freddy. Please. I'm not ready."

Foxy said, "The Eucharist. I can't explain."

"Now it's Freddy's turn," Piet said. It had been a double rescue: Foxy Angela, he Foxy. Exposure was, in the games Freddy invented, the danger. The danger and the fruit.

Freddy rested his pencil and with a groping mouth, as if the words were being read from a magic text materializing in air, said, "The most wonderful thing I know is the human capacity for self-deception. It keeps everything else going."

"Only in the human world," Carol interjected. "Which is just a conceited little crust on the real world. Animals don't deceive themselves. Stones don't."

Angela sat up: "Oh! You mean the world is *everything?* Then I say the stars. Of course. The stars."

Surprised, frightened—he seemed to sink in the spaces of her clear face—Piet asked her, "Why?"

She shrugged: "Oh. They're so fixed. So above it all. As if somebody threw a handful of salt and that's how it stays for billions of years. I know they move but not relative to us, we're too small. We die too soon. Also, they *are* beautiful—Vega on a summer night, Sirius in winter. Am I the only person who ever looks at them any more? One of my uncles was an astronomer, on my mother's side, Lansing Gibbs. I think there's an effect named after him—the Gibbs effect. Maybe it's a galaxy. Imagine a galaxy, all those worlds and suns, named after one man. He was very short, some childhood disease, with pointed teeth and bow legs. He liked me, even when I got taller than him. He taught me the first-magnitude stars—Vega, Deneb, Antares, Arcturus . . . I've forgotten some. As a girl I'd lie on the porch of our summer place in Vermont and imagine myself wandering among them, from life to life, forever. They're wonderful."

"Angela," Foxy said. "You're lovely."

"Angela can be lovely," Piet admitted to them all, and sighed. It was past time to go.

"Freddy, tell us about self-deception," Terry said. Freddy looked elderly and absurd, huddled in his shawl. In the slots of his flippers his toenails were hideous: ingrown, gangrenous, twisted toward each other by the daily constriction of shoes.

Freddy told them, "People come to me all the time with teeth past saving, with abscesses they've been telling themselves are neuralgia. The pain has clearly been terrific. They've been going around with it for months, unable to chew or even close their jaws, because subconsciously they don't want to lose a tooth. Losing a tooth means death to people; it's a classic castration symbol. They'd rather have a prick that hurts than no prick at all. They're scared to death of me because I might tell the truth. When they get their dentures, I tell 'em it looks better than ever, and they fall all over me believing it. It's horseshit. You never get your own smile back when you lose your teeth. Imagine the horseshit a doctor handling cancer has to hand out. Jesus, the year I was in med school, I saw skeletons talking about getting better. I saw women without faces putting their hair up in curlers. The funny fact is, you don't get better, and nobody gives a cruddy crap in hell. You're born to get laid and die, and the sooner the better. Carol, you're right about that nifty machine we begin with; the trouble is, it runs only one way. Downhill."

Foxy asked, "Isn't there something we gain? Compassion? Wisdom?"

"If we didn't rot," Freddy said, "who'd need wisdom? Wisdom is what you use to wave the smell away."

"Freddy," Piet said, tenderly, wanting to save something of himself, for he felt Freddy as a vortex sucking them all down with him, "I think you're professionally obsessed with decay. Things grow as well as rot. Life isn't downhill; it has ups and downs. Maybe the last second is up. Imagine being inside the womb—you couldn't imagine this world. Isn't anything's existing wonderfully strange? What impresses me isn't so much human self-deception as human ingenuity in creating unhappiness. We believe in it. Unhappiness is us. From Eden on, we've voted for it. We manufacture misery, and feed ourselves on poison. That doesn't mean the world isn't wonderful."

Freddy said, "Stop fighting it, Piet baby. We're losers. To live is to lose." He passed the sheet of paper over. "Here it is. Here is your wonderful world." The list read:

> Baby's fingernails
> woman (zzzz)
> Bach
> Euch.
> ☆ ☆ ☆
> capac. for self-decep.

Foxy said sharply, "I won't believe it. Everything people have ever built up, Freddy, you'd let slide and fall apart."

"I do my job," he answered. "It's not the job I would have chosen, but every day I put on that white coat and do it."

White coat. The antiseptic truth. He has learned to live in it. I have not. Better man than I. Piet felt himself falling in a frozen ridged abyss, Freddy's mind. Foxy silently held out her hand toward him; Terry turned to him and recited, "Hope isn't something you reason yourself into. It's a virtue, like obedience. It's given. We're free only to accept or reject."

Angela stood and said, "I think we're all pretty much alike, no matter what we think we believe. Husband, I'm drunk. Take me home."

In the hall, with its elephantine scent of umbrellas, Piet playfully poked Freddy in the stomach and said, "Tell Georgene we missed her."

Freddy's response was not playful; his blurred face menacingly bloated beneath the glare of his subaqueous mask. "She chose not to come. You have any message for her?" The cold fact of his knowing seemed to flow across Piet's face.

"No, just give her all our loves," Piet said nimbly, able to skim and dodge at this level, where actions counted, and no submission to death was asked. He doubted that Freddy knew anything. Georgene had wept after sleeping with him again after her long hiatus of innocence, but Piet had tested her strength before and knew she could withstand all pressure of grief, all temptation to confess. Freddy's tone of menace was a bluff, a typical groping gesture in the murk. His element. Piet jabbed again: "Shouldn't you be going home to her now?" Freddy was making no show of leaving with the four others.

"She's asleep," he said. A woman asleep. As ominous as wonderful. Rather than come to a gathering where her lover might be, she had chosen to sleep. Nursing her misery. Piet felt her captive within the murk of this man, her husband, and regretted having visited her again.

Carol had fallen silent, listening for Eddie's return. Now she roused herself to say good night. She and Freddy, both dressed to swim, waved together from the sallowly lit side porch. Down the side street the Saltzes' narrow house was dark but for a bulb left burning at the rear of the downstairs. Tarbox was settled to sleep. The waterfall by the toy factory faintly roared. A car screeched its tires by the rocks at the base of the green. A jet rattled invisibly among the stars. Its sound was a scratch on glass. A final flurry of good nights. Foxy and Terry, limping shadows on the blue September street, went to the Gallaghers' Mercedes. Without glancing backward she twiddled the fingers of her left hand: farewell until I touch you. Angela said softly, "Poor Foxy, why didn't Terry have the sense to take her home hours ago?"

Insulted, Piet asked, "You thought she wanted to go?"

"Of course, she was exhausted. Isn't she due next month?"

"Don't ask me. How should I know?"

"Once in the middle of that endless game—and by the way you and Freddy should *not* work out your private difficulties in front of us ladies; it's *not* that fascinating or delightful—I happened to glance over at her and she looked completely desolated."

"I didn't notice."

"She was so beautiful when she came to this town and we're turning her into a hag."

The shade of the brick pavement under the streetlamps was the purple of wine dregs. Piet noticed a small round bug scurrying along in a crevice: a citizen out late, seen from a steeple. No voice to call him home. Motherless, fatherless. *Onvoldaan.* Too much wine had unfocused the camera of Piet's head; he lifted his eyes and saw beyond the backstop screen his church bulking great, broad and featureless from the rear, a stately hollow blur.

Piet heard about Ben's losing his job from three directions. Angela was told after nursery school, where she had agreed to teach Tuesdays and Fridays, though Nancy now went to the public first grade. Irene herself told her; it came out flat, handed to Angela in a voice like a printed card. "I suppose you've already heard. Ben's changing jobs."

"No! I hadn't heard at all. How exciting! Where is his new job? I hope it won't mean you're leaving Tarbox."

"Well, that part of it is still a bit up in the air. But he has definitely given them his resignation."

"Good for him," Angela said, having been forced into inanity by the constraint of Irene's manner; the impulse of condolence had to be forcefully suppressed. Angela told Piet, "She looked ghastly. Ravished. All of a sudden, you know how pretty she's been looking this summer, she was a weighed-down Jewish middle-aged woman. Her eyes were absolutely black telling me and, you know, *too* steady. Quite hard. I felt she was *bargaining* with me."

"I never knew," Piet said, unable to feign much surprise, for he had already been told the news, "exactly what Ben did anyway."

"He miniaturized, sweetie. For the space program. It was secret exactly what." She was setting out the places for the girls' supper; she was at her most companionable while making meals. They themselves were to have dinner at the Guerins tonight.

"I meant," Piet said, "how good was he at it? Was he just a technician, or was his work more theoretical?"

"He loves theory in conversation."

"Which makes me wonder. From what Irene used to imply, the whole Mariner Venus probe belonged to Ben. At the least he was in the same league with John Ong. Now it turns out his company can can him virtually the minute the poor bastard wanders from the straight and narrow."

"Oh, you think the Saltine business had something to do with it?"

"Obviously. Everything to do with it. The Constantines ran him ragged. Neither one of them ever sleeps and Eddie only flies forty hours a month, by regulation. Even Irene was letting slip that Ben was missing the early train." Piet was putting forward as conjecture what Georgene had passed on to him as fact, as reported by Freddy.

"I can't believe it was that bad."

"You're so *god*dam innocent, Angel. You can't believe that anybody has more sexual energy than you. These four would stay up all night swapping off. Carol loves having two men at the same time; before Ben she was sleeping with that kid Eddie used to bring to basketball."

"How do you know all this?"

He said quickly, "Everybody knows it."

Angela thought, pausing in ladling chicken soup into two chaste bowls. "But would she *take* both at once?—I mean, is there room? And where would it happen? In her studio, with all those messy tubes of paint? What would Irene do while this acrobatic act was going on?" Her blue eyes flickered with the attempted vision; Piet was pleased to see her interested. But he could not locate, among all the males they knew, the man with whom he would share her. Thorne was too awful, and Whitman too pure.

The next Tuesday, Angela came back from nursery school late, the sky of her eyes scintillating, and said, "You were right. It was the Constantines. Irene took me home for a cup of tea, only it turned out to be bourbon, and told me everything. She's extremely bitter about it. She refuses to see the Constantines at all, though Carol keeps coming over and wants to talk it out. Irene admits it was partly her fault, and Ben should have known enough to control it himself, but she says it was just terribly exciting for them, they had always been so serious about everything, and had never really been close friends with another couple before. She and Ben just thought it was *wonderful*, the way the Constantines lived by a wholly different philosophy, and were always so relaxed and game for everything, and ate whenever it occurred to them, and would stay up all night if they felt like it. She says, to give them credit, that Carol and Eddie can be terribly charming, and in a way they're not to blame, it's how they are, amoral. In a way, she says, she's even grateful for the summer, it was an experience she's glad she's had, even though it nearly wrecked her marriage and they apparently are really strapped for money now. She admitted she lied to me about changing jobs. Ben has no other job."

"Of course not. Did she go into the mechanics of it at all? I mean, what was the effect on Ben so bad they had to fire him?"

"She didn't really, except to admit he wasn't merely late, some days evidently he wouldn't go in at all, especially after they got the boat, when they'd go for these long all-day cruises. Once they actually made it to Provincetown, can you imagine, in this old catboat made for playing around the marshes in. Irene said she was terrified half the time, but Eddie apparently is a very clever sailor. I love the picture—Irene in that huge floppy purple hat and long-sleeved blouse, and Ben fighting seasickness all the way. Like two owls and two pussycats in a beautiful pea-green boat.

To Provincetown! My father and uncle used to take a crew of six, and even then the children weren't allowed along. And of course Ben doesn't really have any stomach for alcohol either, so even when he did go in to work he'd be too sick to work often, and he doesn't have a private office, just a glass cubicle, so there was no hiding it."

"What about the sex? Did she go into that?"

"She got very cagey, and I didn't want to press her; I felt so flattered and bewildered by it all, just sitting there and getting this torrent. I wonder why she decided to tell *me?*"

"You're our town conscience. Everybody must placate you."

"Don't be sarcastic. She did imply it wasn't what I may have heard from other sources. She said that Eddie could be very appealing—as if she had felt this appeal but hadn't of course succumbed. If you've succumbed, it's no longer an appeal, is it?"

"You're the expert," Piet told her. He was offended by how fully vicarious experience seemed to satisfy her.

"The evenings they all spent together she described as being all *talk.* Freddy Thorne and sometimes Terry were there. She went out of her way, I thought, to let me know that the night she and Eddie put Ben to bed and all the lights in their house looked out she and Eddie were really in the kitchen talking about Ben's job; even by then he had gotten a pretty drastic warning."

"But no sex. Booze and boats undid him."

"Irene didn't precisely *say*, but the suggestion was certainly *not*. She even—I was dumbfounded, it coming from Irene—called Carol a cockteaser. As if she *should* have gone to bed with Ben, and didn't, or didn't often enough, I don't know. It's pretty messy and sad. When you think of the children especially. Most of it apparently happened at the Constantines' house because it was easier for the Saltzes to leave Bernard, who stays up forever reading anyway, to sit for his brother, but after midnight Irene would sometimes feel guilty enough to go home, leaving Ben talking with Eddie. They would talk everything—space, computers, public versus private schools, religion. Eddie is so lapsed he begins to scream whenever he thinks at all about the Church."

"And then Carol would lay them both."

"Piet, I don't want to diminish your high estimate of Carol but I really think that's unlikely. Maybe in Okinawa whorehouses, but in somebody's home who we know . . . it's grotesque."

"Love, she's human. She could take one in her mouth."

The sky of Angela's eyes flashed. "That's what you want me to do, isn't it?"

"No, no, no," he said. "Good heavens, no. That's sodomy."

Foxy had a rather different story, Carol's as confided to Terry Gallagher. Terry and Carol shared music; Foxy and Carol once in a while drew together, with one of the exquisite Constantine girls, Laura or Patrice, posing in leotards. "She says," she said, "that the Saltzes just moved in on them. That they were outcasts in the town, and terribly lonely, and when they saw that she and Eddie would accept them, there was just no moderation. That Ben had had a *very* sheltered and old-fashioned upbringing, in a Hebrew ghetto in Brooklyn—"

Piet laughed. "I can just see Carol saying 'Hebrew.' " Foxy was a fair mimic and unconsciously colored her retellings with something of the lilt of the telling. Piet's head lay on her lap, and the heartbeat of her unborn infant was next to his ear.

"—a Hebrew ghetto, and was just *starved* for, well, a little swinging. Carol's point, and she's very convinced about this, is that until the Constantines came to town the Saltzes had been excluded by the 'nice' couples, the Guerins who live just a block away on Prudence Street, and the darling Thornes, and the extremely lovely Applesmiths, and the ever-fashionable Hanemas, not to mention the delightfully up-and-coming Gall—"

"Not true. We always asked Ben to basketball. They don't ski or play tennis, whose fault is that? They were always at large parties. The Dutch are more of a minority in this town than Jews."

"Well, this is what Carol's impression was, presumably from Irene." Absent-mindedly as she talked Foxy was stroking Piet's hair. "Your hair is quite unsmoothable."

"Is it thinning out? Will I get bald like Freddy? Red-haired men do. It's Jehovah's rebuke to our vigor. Don't stop. I am *very* hurt that Irene, whom I've always adored, thought we were all anti-Semitic."

"Well evidently she did. Does. She was furious when the elementary school put Bernard in a Christmas pageant. As Joseph yet. According to Terry, Carol is positive that Irene was the real moving spirit behind the couples' getting together. The Saltzes' marriage has been on the rocks for years. They were staying together because of Bernard, and then Jeremiah was a mistake. Irene had a kind of nervous breakdown over it."

"I remember her as so lovely, pregnant. I do love pregnant women."

"So I see."

"According to Carol according to Terry, what is or was Irene's complaint about Ben?"

"She feels he has no ambition, no drive. Her father came up the hard way in the garment business. Anyway, Piet, who knows why women like some men and don't like others? Chemistry? Carol's story is that Irene took a fancy to Eddie and lit out after him the way she lights into everything—Fair Housing, or the nursery school, or conservation. He became a cause."

"I love the way you say 'cozz.' Honeh chile, ah loves it."

"How do you say it? Cawss. Like the way you say 'haas' for 'house.' "

"OK, I'm an immigrant. Anyway, your description sounds more like Terry than Carol. Carol would say 'She wanted him' or something with the same awesome simplicity and then look daggers. 'She vowed to *have* him.' 'She thenceforth consecrated herself to sharing his pallet.' "

"She wouldn't at all. She'd say, 'The bitch went into heat and got herself screwed.' "

"Oh, my mistress. Your language. Skeerooed."

"Don't jiggle your head like that. You'll induce me."

"It's true, Irene has been promoted by all this to full-fledged bitch status. She used to be somebody you talked to early at cocktail parties to get her out of the way."

"Carol says she and Eddie used to sit after the Saltzes had left and laugh, Irene was being so blatant."

"Then he'd go down the street and laugh out of the other side of his mouth. I love the idea of Eddie Constantine being a worthy project like school integration or the whooping crane. The most worthless man I know. To think we all entrust our lives to him. What did Carol say she and Ben did to combat this assault on the young aviator's virtue?"

"She says she pitied Ben but, frankly, never found him attractive."

"She excluded him. One more Wasp."

"Yes," Foxy said, "she did mention that, that she was the only Wasp in the ménage. Eddie apparently hates Wasps, and is always testing her. Scaring her when he drives the car, and things like that."

"I thought she was a lapsed R.C."

"*He* is. *She* was a Presbyterian." Her fingers had trespassed from his hair to the sensitive terrain of his face, taut planes she explored as if blind. "Furthermore," she said, in a voice whose musical shadows and steeps had become, like the flowing sight of her and her perfumed weight, a body his love inhabited, "furthermore, and stop looking at me like that, she doesn't think what he did with them has anything to do with Ben's losing his job. Carol thinks he was just poor at it, which in a way I can believe, since the times he's talked to Ken—"

"Ken and Ben, they don't know when," Piet said.

"—the times he talked to Ken, after expressing all this interest in biochemistry, and the secret of life and whatnot, Ken says he shows no real comprehension or much interest beyond the superficial sort of thing that appears in *Newsweek*. He's really looking for religious significance, and nothing could bore Ken more. What was his word?—eclectic. Ben has a thoroughly eclectic mind."

"*My* theory is," Piet said, closing his eyes the more keenly to sense Foxy's circumambient presence, her belly beside his ear, her fingers on his brow, her thighs pillowing his skull, "that the Saltzes went into it so Ben could learn about aviation from Eddie and improve his job in the aerospace complex. That once they got into that smelly old house, Carol being a nymphomaniac, she had to get laid, and rather than stand around watching, Eddie gave Irene a bang, and she said to herself, 'What the hell! This is fun!' "

"Well, without everything being spelled out, that's more or less Carol's story too."

"Carol and I, we think alike."

"Oh, don't *say* that!" Foxy urgently begged, touching his lips, recalling them to the incomparable solemnity of their sin.

Angela brought home new refinements of Irene's version. "She took me aside after nursery school almost in tears and said Carol's been spreading around the story that she, Irene, felt ostracized in town because she was Jewish. She wanted me to know this was perfectly untrue, that she and Ben agree they've always been very warmly treated, and they'd be very upset to have their friends think they thought otherwise. She says Carol is *extremely* neurotic, that Kevin is the way he is because of how she's treated him. Whenever she wants to paint she locks him in his room and some mornings he screams so much the neighbors have complained. Irene also said her point about Bernard's being in the Christmas play has been deliberately misunderstood. She never said they shouldn't put on a Christmas pageant; she just thinks to be fair they should have some kind of Hanukkah observance too."

"Yeah," Piet said, "and why not make the kids celebrate Ramadan by not eating their box lunches?"

Angela, who had been considering Irene's cause seriously, from the standpoint of an hereditary liberal, told Piet, "I don't know why you bother to go to church, it seems to do you less and less good."

Georgene threw a lurid borrowed light upon the mystery. Over the phone, she told Piet, "Freddy's been talking to Eddie—"

"Freddy and Eddie, they're always ready," Piet said. Gallagher was off talking to the nuns who were about to buy the mortgaged estate in Lacetown, and Piet was alone in the office.

"Don't interrupt. Eddie told him that Ben late at night used to talk about the work he was doing on these rockets—is there a thing called the Titan?—and the ridiculous waste and backbiting between the different departments and government representatives, and some of the ideas they were working on with solid propellants and self-correcting guidance systems, which I guess Ben helped with, and Eddie was shocked, that Ben would be telling him all this. He thinks if he told *him* he must have told others, and the government got wind of it, and had him released."

"Don't you think Ben would put any spy to sleep that tried to listen to him?"

"Freddy thinks that Eddie might have been the one to turn Ben in. I mean, he *is* in aeronautics, so he would know who to report him to."

"Why would he want to ruin his wife's lover? You think Eddie minds?"

"Of course he minds. That woman has put him through hell. She's insane. She's an utter egotist."

"More hell than vice versa?"

"Oh, much more. Eddie's just a little boy who likes to play with engines."

"Huh. I distrust all little-boy theories of male behavior. They rob us of our sinful dignity."

"Hey. When are you coming to see me again?"

"I just did."

"That was a month ago."

"Time flies."

"God this is humiliating. The hell with you, Piet Hanema."

"What have I done?"

"Nothing. Forget it. Good-bye. I'll see you at parties."

"Wait."

She had hung up.

The next day she called again, imitating a secretary. "I just wanted to report, sir, in regard to our conversation as of yesterday a.m., that two men in suits and hats were seen surveying and then entering the Saltz residence on West Prudence Street, Tarbox."

"Who told you this?"

"A patient of Freddy's told him, very excited. Who would wear hats in Tarbox but FBI agents? Apparently the entire town knows about Ben."

"Do you think he'll be electrocuted like the Greenbergs or traded to Russia for Gary Powers?"

"Ha ha. Ever since you've been sleeping with Foxy you've been high as a kite. You're riding for a fall, Piet. This time I am *not* going to catch you."

"I have not been sleeping with that extremely pregnant and very chaste lady. Hey. I dreamed about you last night."

"Oh. A nice dream?"

"Not bad. It was in a kind of wine cellar. Freddy was running for selectman this fall and you took me down into the cellar to show me the champagne you were going to use if he won. Then down there, surrounded by old wicker furniture, you asked me to smell the new perfume you were wearing behind the ear. You said, very proudly, you had bought it at Cogswell's Drug Store. I put my face deep into your hair and you gently put your arms around me and I realized you wanted to make love and woke up. Somehow you had much longer hair than yours. You had dyed it red."

"It wasn't me at all. You bastard."

"It was, Georgene. You talked just like yourself, in that reedy indifferent voice, about Freddy's chances of winning."

"Come see me, Piet."

"Soon," he promised.

That evening, Angela said, "Irene was almost funny today. She said that Ben with nothing to do keeps entertaining these two young Mormons. They think they're a lost tribe of Israel, so it's really like a family reunion with Ben."

"What Mormons?"

"You must have noticed them walking around town, what do you *do* all day? Two young men with suits and broad-brimmed Western-style hats on. Apparently it's part of every Mormon's life to go out and proselytize some benighted area. That's us. We're Hottentots as far as they're concerned."

"I heard they were FBI men."

"Irene says that's what everybody thinks. She says Carol has been spreading it all around that Ben betrayed government secrets."

"That woman is losing her marbles. Carol."

"I saw her in the A & P today and she couldn't have been sweeter. She said Eddie wants to take me for another ride on his Vespa."

At the center of this storm of gossip, the destroyed man raked leaves, made repairs and painted within his house, took his sons to the beach on clear weekend afternoons. Summer over, the beach was restored to the natives, who ran their dogs along the running surf and tried to raise kites above the sea of dunes. The clouds changed quality, changed from the puffy schooners of hot weather to grayer, longer bodies, with more metal in them. The horse trailers of North Mather stables parked in the Tarbox lot and teen-age girls galloped across the dun-colored flats of low tide. Here one Sunday morning in mid-October, Piet, walking with Ruth—since he had not gone to church today she had not sung in the choir—saw Ben Saltz at a distance, holding little Jeremiah by the hand, stopping with Bernard to examine shells and instructive rubbish in the wrack. Piet wanted to approach Ben, to express fellow-feeling, but he dreaded the man as he dreaded the mortally diseased. His own life felt too precarious to be drawn into proximity with a life that had truly broken through. Angela thought they should have the Saltzes over, just the two couples, for a relaxed dinner. Piet resisted, then consented; but Irene coolly refused. She and Ben had agreed that, since they were not in a financial position to repay hospitality, they would not accept any. By tacit agreement among the other couples the Saltzes were no longer invited to parties, which would have been painful for them and have embarrassed the Constantines. Still Piet yearned to peer into the chasm, to spy out the face of catastrophe. He went out of his way at all hours to drive by their house. The Saltzes' lights went dark early at night; the Constantines' defiantly blazed. They were seeing a lot of the Guerins, the Thornes, and the Gallaghers. In the mornings, the older children—Bernard, Laura—of each household set off to school along parallel paths across the much-traversed green; before evening they returned together, talking more seriously than children should have to.

One windy weekday afternoon Piet, rounding the green in his pick-up truck, saw Ben putting up storm windows. They were stacked, a leaning deck of great glass cards, at the side of the house, and Ben was puzzling over the numbers. Wanting to hail him, yet afraid to slow down and be caught, Piet gave himself only a glimpse; but it was a glimpse, shockingly, of happiness. Ben was letting his beard grow back. His archaic profile as it bent to the Roman numerals chiseled on the upper edges of the storm windows seemed asleep and smiling. His air was of a man who deserved a holiday like any other, who had done something necessary and was now busy surviving, who—Piet's impression was—had touched bottom and found himself at rest, safe.

Piet dreamed, at this same time of his life, that he was in an airplane, a big new jet. The appointments, in beige and aqua, of the immense tubular interior were vivid to his eyes, though he had never ridden in such a plane. Since the army, he had flown rarely; the last time had been two years ago, to visit his brother in Michigan. The plane to Detroit had been a sooty-engined Electra, shivering in flight like an old hound. Now the luxurious plane of his dream was gliding as if motionless through the sky; the backs of heads and hands receded tranquilly down the length of aqua-carpeted aisle. The pilot's voice, too musical and southern to be Eddie Constantine's, jubilantly announced over the loudspeaking system, "I think we've slipped it, folks!" and through his little rubber-sealed porthole Piet saw a wall of gray cloud, tendrilous and writhing, slowly drift backward, revealing blue sky. They had evaded a storm. Then the plane rocked and jerked in the bumpy air currents; it sank flatly through a gap in atmosphere, grabbed for something, missed, slipped, and tilted. The angle of tilt increased; the plane began to plunge. The huge hull rushed toward the earth. The delicately engineered details—the luminous stenciled seat numbers, the chrome rivets holding the tinted head napkins—stayed weirdly static amid the rising scream of the dive. Far down the aisle, a stewardess, her ginger hair in a high stiff coiffure, gripped the seats for support, and the curtains hiding the first-class section billowed. Otherwise there was no acknowledgment of the horror, no outcry. Piet thought, *The waste.* Such ingenious fragility utterly betrayed. The cost. The plane streamed straight down. The liquid in Piet's inner ear surged, froze. He knew there could be no pulling from this dive and awoke in darkness, convinced of his death.

Angela's breathing was moist and regular beside him. Her body tilted the mattress toward the middle. Her honeyish pungent female smell monopolized the warm bed. Vague light limned the ridges of the pleated linen shade of the lamp on the bureau by the window. His house. A trim ship motionless on the swell of the night. He raised his hand from beside his cheek. Its black silhouette showed cornute against the cruciform mullions and blue panes. His hand. He made the fingers twiddle. He was alive. Yet, having faced the full plausibility of his death—the screaming air of the dream had been so willing to swallow him, so voraciously passive—he was unable to reënter the illusion of security that is life's antechamber. Heavy as lead he lay on the thinnest of ice. He began to sweat. A ponderous creeping moisture coated his skin and, like a loose chain dangling from his stomach, nausea, the clumsy adrenal nausea of panic, threatened to wrench him inside out. Nimbly he turned and lay on his back.

He had experienced this panic before. Antidotes existed. Picture snow. Picture a curved tent secure against the rain. Pretend the blankets are shelter. Think of skin. Piet tried to lull himself with bodies of women he knew. Foxy's powdery armpits and petaled cleft simpler than a rose. The freckled boniness below Georgene's throat. Her factual nakedness and feather-cut hair full of gray, dulled his lust to see it, perhaps lovelessness let them come always together. Unlike Angela's ambrosial unsearchable. Carol's lissome waist and nerved-up dancer's legs. Bea Guerin's swarmy drunken breasts, nectar sweat between. The rank elastic crotch of the step-ins of Annabelle Vojt who, though both were virgins, would allow him, in that rain-pattered cavity of a car parked amid nodding weedy hay, to kiss there, and exploringly tongue, applying mind to matter, his face upside-down between her thighs, his broad back aching, crickets trilling, her tranced fingers combing his uncombable hair. Of pious family, in the hamburger heat, the radio down but glowing, she would sometimes wordlessly remove the secret wall of silk, heaving with a motion that disturbed him by being expert her pelvis up free from the car seat and tugging her pants down from behind; to that mute silver flicking and heave, leaping arched from memory like a fish, he held tight a second, then it too, with the other pale bodies, proved too slippery to ride into sleep. He was too agitated to sink. Nerves and atoms whirled and scintillated within him. Hollow-boned like a bird, he would forever hover, retasting the same sourness.

Angela's even breathing broke pace; she turned with a slithering turmoil of sheets, and the stride of her unconscious sighing resumed.

Horribly awake, Piet tried to pray. His up-pouring thoughts touched nothing. An onyx dust of gas above his face. Something once solid had been atomized. *Thou shalt not covet. Whosoever lusteth in his heart.* Pedrick's foolish twisting. A dour desert tribe: Dead Sea. Pots broken by a shepherd boy. Orange dust. One more dismal sect. Mormons. Salt Lake. Hymnals unopened all week stink of moldy paper: unwrapping a fish. Forgive me. Reach down and touch. He had patronized his faith and lost it. God will not be used. Death stretched endless under him. Life a scum, consciousness its scum. Piet lay as a shimmering upon an unfounded mineral imperviousness. His parents were twin flecks of mica squeezed in granite. No light touched them into light. The eternal loss of light: in the plane's plunge, not knowing he was dreaming, honest to his bones, he had phrased it so to himself, like any unchurched commuter whose day takes a bad turn. Why tease God longer? Busy old fellow has widows and orphans to interview, grieving Tehranese, still benighted. Bite down on death. Bite down. No screaming within the plane. All still in falling. Stoic grace learned from movies. Hope of heaven drains the sky. No Hottentot he. Away with the blindfold. Matter mostly nothing, a titter skinning a vacuum. Angela sleeps in the cradle of the stars, her uncle's web. Nothing sacred. Triune like cock and balls: Freddy Thorne. Oh Lord, this steepness of sickness, this sliding. Patient parents thumbing home seeds in peat had planted a tree whose fruit he had fed to women. The voracious despair of women had swallowed God.

From his height of fear Piet saw his life dwindled small, distinct. The three new houses, sold, on Indian Hill as from a helicopter. Now Gallagher wanted acres more, saw himself a developer, a builder of cities. Gallagherville. Terrytown. Hanema Plaza. Angela Place. Maps, prospecti, underground garages, a grateful Commonwealth votes its thanks. Sir Matthew Galleyslave, having given employment to thousands, true prince of the Church, dinner at the White House starring Pablo Casals and Ruby Newman. *And Mr. President, this is my partner.* That flinty Irish smile, stiff-backed, wall-eyed. Jack: *This cunning little fellow? May I pet him?* Another voice, more musical: *Does he bite?*

Feeling his thoughts expand into nonsense, Piet went tense with gratitude, with eager anticipation of sleeping, and snapped wide awake again, his heart churning. He needed to touch something. He could never rise with Gallagher because he needed to touch a tool. Grab the earth. The plane had plunged and he had been without resources, unchurched, unmanned. He needed to touch Foxy, her nipples, her belly, in oblique moonlight. Her head was full of braid and crosses. She believed. She adored his prick. With billowing gauzy width she had flung herself onto him, was his, his woman given to him.

Angela obliviously stirred, faintly moaned. Piet got out of bed and went downstairs for a glass of milk. Whenever he was most lovesick for Foxy, that summer, he would go to the refrigerator, the cool pale box full of illuminated food, and feed something to the void within. He leaned his cheek against the machine's cold cheek and thought of her voice, its southern shadows, its playful dryness, its musical remembrance of his genitals. He spelled her name with the magnetized alphabet the girls played with on the tall blank door. FOXY. PIET L VES FOXY. He scrambled the letters and traveled to bed again through a house whose familiar furniture and wallpaper were runes charged with malevolent magic. Beside Angela, he thought that if he were beside Foxy he could fall asleep on broken glass. Insomnia a failure of alignment. A rumbling truck passed, vanishing.

The weight of this stagnant night. Fear scurried inside him, seeking a place to stop. How Annabelle would spread her legs as if imperiously to seize his entire face in the lips of her young swamp. Foxy's delicately questioning sideways glint: a dry mind that sized him up through veils of rapture. His daughters' anxious great eyes: in a sense what a mercy to die and no longer torment his children with the apparition of their father. The death of another always a secret relief. Tides of life swing up to God for slaughter. Slum clearance. Dearest Lord do shelter Foxy my shyest candleflame from this holocaust Thy breath. Amen. Revolving terror scooped the shell of him thin. A translucent husk emptied of seed, Piet waited to be shattered.

The Chinese knife across the eye. The electric chair dustless in the tiled room. The earthquake that snaps cathedral rafters. The engorged mineral ocean. The knotted silk cord. The commando's piano wire. The crab in the intestine. The chicken bone in the windpipe. The slippery winter road. The misread altimeter. The firing squad crushing out its Spanish cigarettes in the baked clay courtyard, another dull dawn, exhaling philosophically. The boy from Ionia. The limp-limbed infant smothered in his crib. The rotting kidney turning the skin golden. The shotgun blast purging the skull of brains. The massive coronary. The guillotine. The frayed elevator cable. The booming crack and quick collapse of ice: in Michigan on the lakes the fishermen would ride their jalopies to the bottom in the air bubble and with held breaths ascend to the jagged light. The threshing machine. The random shark. Puffy-tongued dehydration. Black-faced asphyxia. Gentle leprosy. Crucifixion. Disembowelment. Fire. Gas in the shower room. The scalper's hurried adze. The torturer's intent watchmaker's face. The pull of the rack. The suck of the sea. The lion's kittenish gnawing. The loose rock, the slipping boot, the dreamlike fall. The anger of kings. The bullet, the bomb, the plague, the wreck, the neglected infection, the mistaken reaction. The splintered windshield. The drunken doctor's blunder shrugged away. The shadow of fragility on the ice, beneath the implacably frozen stars: the muffled collapse, the opaque gasp, the unresisted plunge.

"Angela?" His voice sounded alien, dragged from a distance. "Could you wake up a little and put your arm round me? I've had a nightmare."

She half-woke and half-obeyed, turning toward him but sinking into sleep again on her stomach; her arm tried to reach him but lapsed at her side. He listened for the glinting of the hamster's wheel and instead heard the refrigerator shudder and break into purring.

Dear Piet—

The tide is coming in high and so blue it seems ink. A little boy in a red shirt has been anchored in a rowboat off the island ever since my second cup of coffee. I have been thinking about us and there seems a lot to say until I sit down and try to write it. When we were together yesterday I tried to explain about Ken and me and "coming" but you chose to be haughty and hurt—my lover, don't be. How timid I feel writing that odd word "lover." And ridiculous too. But you must have a name and what else are you of mine?

Ken is my husband. I love him as such. I feel right, is what I tried to say, making love to him. There is no barrier between us except boredom which is not so serious since life is such a daily thing anyway. With you there are many barriers—my guilt of course, a true shyness and fear of seeming inadequate compared with the other women you've had, our fear of being discovered, a sometimes (I suggest) needless impatience and hurry in you, your annoying habit of mocking yourself and waiting to be contradicted, and even your extreme lovingness toward me, which I find sometimes dismaying, let me confess. To all this add the libidinous vagaries of the pregnant state. These barriers are piled high, so my not coming, dear Piet, does not mean I do not go high with you. I go very high. Do not ask me to say more. Do not ask me to deny my pledge to Ken—which I felt at the time and still feel is sacred above and beyond all discomfort and discontent—or try to compete. There is no competition. I do not understand why I have taken you into my life at this time of all times but the place you occupy is one you have created and you must not be insecure in it.

I have brought this letter outside to the sun, me in my underwear, casually enough, since none of my bathing suits fit. I trust the plumbers not to suddenly arrive. The boy in red has gone away. I don't think he caught anything. Rereading this, it seems so poorly expressed, so self-protective and hedgy, I wonder if I will give it to you. Your sleepy but fond

Foxy

Undated and not always signed, Foxy's letters accumulated in the back of a Gallagher & Hanema office filing cabinet, under the carbon paper, where Gallagher would never look. They were of varying shapes and sizes. Some consisted of as many as four sheets smoothly covered on both sides with a swift upright script. Others, holding a few hurried words, were mere scraps passed wadded into Piet's hand at parties. Orderly, superstitious, Piet saved them all, and fitfully read them through in the numb days following his night of dread. He read them as an insignificant person seeks himself in a fable whose hero is a remote ancestor.

My lover!—

My whole house breathes of you—the smell of planed wood is you, and the salt wind is you, and the rumpled sheets whose scent is sweetest and subtlest—of us—is you. I have been all open windows and blowing curtains and blue view these last hours—so much yours I must write and tell you, though Ken is downstairs waiting to go to the little-Smiths. In a few minutes I will see you. But surrounded by others. Accept this kiss.

Other letters were more expansive and discursive, even didactic. Piet felt in them an itch to shape him, to rectify and justify.

Holy Firecracker Day

My dear lover—

I have gone far down the beach, the public end, past the holiday crowds (Italian grandmothers with aluminum chairs sit-

ting right in the surf, skirts up to their knees and knitting in their laps) to where none of our mutual friends might ambush me. It is curiously different down here, cliffy and pebbly, and windier and the water choppier than the sheltered stretch where our lovely Tarbox matrons and their offspring dabble. Lacetown lighthouse seems very close in the haze. Now and then a pair of Boston or Cape fairies go by in their skimpy trunks—Freddy calls them ball-huggers—holding hands. Otherwise I am alone, a pregnant and therefore pass-proof lass with a crinkled New Yorker on her knees for a writing pad, coining funny phrases for her lover, who thinks he is a Jew.

I explained badly about Peter. You are not he, the coincidence of your names notwithstanding. For years he has ceased to be a name for me, just a shadow, a shadow between me and my parents, between me and Ken. He didn't love me—I amused him, awkward and innocent shiksa as I was. I was a toy for him (toy/goy), and the frightening thing I discovered, I liked it. I loved being used/abused. There was nothing he could do that did not intensify my love for him, even his terrible mood of coldness, the scorn that wished me away. He needed to be alone more than I could let him be alone. It was all very young and uncontrolled and must have been influenced for each of us by how our parents had behaved. My father's absences had been cruel for my mother and as long as Peter was not absent from me, even if his language was foul, I was grateful. Or perhaps I was attracted to just that pride, a kind of mechanical selfishness, in which he resembled my father. Do you know, he has become famous? His picture was in Time a year or so ago, with a junk sculpture he had welded. He still lives in Detroit. With his mother, unmarried. So I had years when I could have flown to him, years of being childless with Ken, and I didn't. It would have been like eating chocolate sundaes again.

You and I are different, surely. With you I feel for the first time what it is like _not_ to be young. With you I feel that I at last have exercised my right of _choice_—free of habit or command or compulsion. In a sense you are my first _companion_. Our sweet sin is strangely mixed with the sweetness of pregnancy—perhaps Ken *waited too long to make me pregnant and now that it is here I have turned toward someone else with the gratitude. I trust you and fear you. I feared Peter, and trust Ken. The conjunction is uniquely yours.*

Am I proposing marriage? Scheming woman!! Nothing of the kind—I am so securely tied to Ken I dare open myself to you as I might to a stranger in a dream, knowing I was all the time securely asleep beside my husband. Please do not fear I will try to take you from Angela. I know even better than you how precious she is to you, she and the home you have made together, how well, truly, you are wed. Isn't it our utter captivity that makes us, in our few stolen afternoons together, so free? My hand is tired and shakes. Please don't leave me yet. My flying Dutchman— contradiction in terms?

Later.

I went down to swim—delicious, like being inside a diamond, the water at Woods Hole was much warmer—and examined the pebbles. Did you know, I once took a term of geology? I recognized basalt and quartz, the easy ones, black and white, God and the Devil, and then a lot of speckly candyish stones I mentally lumped as "granite." So much variety! And what a wealth of time we hold in our hands in the smoothness of these stones! I wanted to kiss them. Remembering your smoothness. I do love the beach. I wonder if I was ever myself until Ken moved me into sight of the sea.

Then, to my horror, who should come along but Janet and Harold! Damn!! It was I who was embarrassed, and they who should have been. They were brazen as always—they had left Frank and Marcia back with the children and what was I doing way up here in Fairyland? I told them the walk was necessary exercise and that I wanted to sketch the Lacetown lighthouse. They noticed that I had been writing a letter and were very twinkly and jolly and I think genuinely like me but seemed depressingly corrupt. Who am I to pass judgment? Yet I seem very righteous within myself still and virtually cried, as you saw, when I turned out to be Christine Keeler.

Still later.

I fell asleep. So strange to wake in floods of light, mouth bloated and hair full of sand. I must go home. Ken is tennising with Gallagher and Guerin and I don't know who the fourth is. You? Answer to a riddle: the fourth of July.

Piet, have I explained anything? I think I wanted somehow to untangle us from those others, to spare you that woeful wild look that comes into your eye when it's time to be back on the job or you imagine the phone in your office ringing. In a way, because you suspect a Heaven somewhere else (like Harold's French: a constant appeal to above), you live in Hell, and I have become one of the demons. I don't want this, I want to be healing—to be white and anonymous and wisecracking for you, the nurse I suppose my father said I was too good to be. I worry that you'll do something extravagant and wasteful to please your funny prickly conscience. Don't. Have me without remorse. Remorse is boring to women. Your seducing me is fine. I wouldn't have missed it for the world. Better you than Freddy Thorne.

Which is a way of concealing that falling asleep on the sand has sexed me up. I crave your strength and length, and remain,

Your mistress

Oh blessed, blessed Piet—

How tactless, how worse than tactless <u>wrong</u> I was to use you today as an audience for my feelings about Ken. How comic your anger was—you seemed amazed that I <u>had</u> feelings about him—and how sad, in the end, your effort to turn your anger into a joke. It is one of your charms that you make both too much and too little of yourself, with a swiftness of alternation that is quite hypnotic. But your departure left me depressed and with a need to try again.

When I said that he and I had been married seven years whereas you and I had known each other a few months it was not a criticism—clearly your newness in many ways works to your advantage. But in the mysterious (as much to me as to anyone) matter of my sexual response, it is an advantage in Stage I, a dis- in Stage II. Maybe men like new women while women perform best with men they know. There is something of trust in this—there really is, whenever you spread your legs, the flitting fear you are going to be hurt—and something of the sad (why do I find it sad?) fact that with women personality counts for less in sex than with men. In actual sex as opposed to all the preamble. A dull familiar trustworthy tool is all we ask. Female genitalia are extremely stupid, which gets us into many a fix our heads would get us out of.

Why must I apologize to you for continuing to enjoy my husband? You have woken me from my seven years' sleep and Ken benefits. Isn't it enough for your ego to promise you that you exist in dimensions where Ken is blank? And that his ignorance of our affair, of what consumes my inner life, makes him seem a child, a child behind glass, a child willfully behind glass. He has never been very curious about life, above the molecular level. He is a masked man who climbs a balcony to be with me at night. I discover in myself a deep coldness toward him. In this coldness I manipulate our bodies and release the tension you have built in me.

Yet do let me love him as I can. He is my man, after all. Whereas you are only a man. Maybe the man. But not mine.

I suppose I am confused. Having decided, long before we slept together, to have you, I determined to keep you each in place, in watertight compartments. Instead, the two of you are using my body to hold a conversation in. I want to tell you each about the other. I live in fear of calling out the wrong name. I want to confide you to Ken, and Ken to you—he is unhappy about his career, and apprehensive about our unborn child, and turns to me more often now than since our first year of marriage. Of course, I am so safe. He pierces me saying, You can't impregnate the pregnant. You can't kill the dead. Compared to you it is mechanical but then Ken's career is to demonstrate how mechanical life is.

Yours is to build and blessed lover you have built wonderfully in me. I breathe your name and in writing this I miss your voice, your helpful face. Do you really think we bore God? You once told me God was bored with America. Sometimes I think you underestimate God—which is to say, you despise the faith your fear of death thrusts upon you. You have struck a bad bargain and

keep whittling away at your half. You should be a woman. The
woman in the newspaper holding a dead child in her arms knows
God has struck her. I feel Him as above me and around me and in
you and in spite of you and because of you. Life is a game of lost
and found. I must start Ken's supper. Unapologetic love. Love.

Piet turned with relief from these narcissistic long letters to a
small scrap asking: *Are you still sleeping with Georgene?*

After she had told him about the Jew, he had told her about
Georgene. In September her instinct, or gossip, informed her that
he had resumed. In truth, there had been the unplanned lapse on
the day the Kennedy infant died, and in the month and a half
since, only three visits, and these largely spent in tentative exploration of the new way out. He found Georgene sulky, passive,
flat-stomached, and sexually unadventurous. Whether in Freddy's
bed or outdoors under the sun, Piet was so nervous and watchful
he had difficulty maintaining an erection. Foxy's note seemed a
warning, a loud snap in the dark. He saw Georgene once more,
early in October: the shedding larch needles pattered steadily on
the tarpaper, the sun was wan, her chin trembled, her eyes in tears
refused to confront his. He left her with no doubt that he would
not come soon again, blaming Angela's suspiciously *gemütlich*
intimacy with Freddy, Freddy's threatening manner lately, Piet's
strained relations with Gallagher and increased work load, Georgene's own well-being—surely the essence of an affair was mutual
independence, and Georgene had sinned, endangering herself, by
becoming dependent. Her firm chin nodded but still her green
eyes, though he seized her naked shoulders in his hands, refused to
gaze into his. To Foxy's question he answered No, he had not
slept with Georgene since soon after the Whitmans came to town
and he had first glimpsed Foxy slamming her car door after
church. He retrospectively dated his love from this glimpse. He
admitted that Georgene remained his friend, and—with such a
husband, who could blame her?—now and then called him at his
office; Piet admitted this on the chance that Foxy already knew,
via Matt and Terry. Thus, in being deceived, Foxy closer approached the condition of a wife.

RIDDLES

1. *What is five feet nine, Episcopalian, and about to burst?*
2. *What is smaller than a box car but bigger than mortality?*
3. *What is five feet ?, clever with its hands, has red hair, big feet, and foreign origins?*
4. *What is smaller than a breadbox but gives satisfaction anyway?*

4. Right. Where are you, lover?
3. An auburn kangaroo doing needlepoint, Huh!
2. A bed.
1. Foxy Whitman.

As they aged in their affair her notes became briefer and more playful; as fall progressed he was able to see her less. The renovations within her home were completed, and Gallagher had obtained a lucrative rush contract, the enlargement of a local restaurant in antique style. So Piet was compelled to spend long days rough-hewing factory-planed beams and fabricating seventeenth-century effects in green lumber. The owners of the Tarbox Inne, a pair of pushing Greek brothers, wanted the new wing ready for operation by November. The trips were tedious and frequent to Mather for old bricks, to Brockton for hand-wrought iron, to Plymouth for research into details of colonial carpentry: *the side bearers for the second story being to be loaden with corne, &tc., must not be pinned on, but rather eyther lett in to the studds, or borne up with false studds, & soe tenented in at the ends. In this story over the first, I would have a particion, whether in the middest or over the particion vnder, I leave it to the carpenters. I desire to have the sparrs reach downe pretty deep at the eves to preserve the walls the better from the wether. I would have the howse strong in timber, though plaine & well brased. I would have it covered with very good oake-hart inch board . . .* Trying to turn these ethical old specifications into modern quaintness demoralized Piet. The fraudulent antiquation of the job seemed prophetic of the architectural embalming destined for his beloved unself-conscious town, whose beauty had been a by-product of neglect. Maddeningly, he could not get to Foxy, and absurdly he hoped for her unmistakable silhouette to bloom on the streets of strange towns, in the drab alleyways leading to construction-supply yards. Every blue station wagon stopped his heart; every blond blur in a window became a broken promise. Now and then they did meet in spots away from Tarbox—in a Mather bar where fluorescent beer advertisements described repetitive parabolas, in a forest preserve west of Lacetown where huge mosquitoes clustered thick as hair on her arms whenever they paused in walking to embrace, on a wild beach north of Duxbury where the unsoftened Atlantic surf pounded wrathfully and the high dunes were littered with rusting cans, shards of green glass, and abandoned underpants. The danger of being discovered seemed greater out of town than in it, within the maze of routines and visiting patterns they could predict; and as Foxy's time drew near she became reluctant to drive far. Outside of Tarbox they seemed to themselves merely another furtive illicit couple, compelled toward shabby seclusion, her pregnancy grotesque. Within her breezy home they seemed glorious nudes, symphonic vessels of passion. Their dream was of a night together.

Piet—Ken has to go to a conference—in New York, Columbia—this Tuesday/Thursday. Could you possibly get free to see me, or shall I go to Cambridge and stay with friends— with Ned and Gretchen—for these days? Ken wants the latter— doesn't want me left alone—but I can argue him down if there's a reason—is there? I ache and need to be praised by you. My bigness is either horrible or a new form of beauty—which?

He could not get free. The restaurant wing was in the finish stage and he and Adams and Comeau had to be there ten hours a day. And now that the foliage was down, the beach road seemed transparent. He was timid of driving his truck past the Thornes' watching hill to the Whitmans' house, visible in fall from the little-Smiths'. At night, also, he was barred from seeing her, by a new turn in their social life: Angela in her fascination with psychiatry had taken up with the Applebys and Freddy Thorne, which involved both the Thornes. Georgene's brittle, slightly hyperthyroid eyes, when it emerged in conversation that Ken Whitman was going to be away, flicked toward Piet with the narrowing that appeared on her face when set point was deuced. Piet told Foxy to go to Cambridge, to place herself above gossip and to remove his temptation to do something desperate, revealing, and fatal.

Damn! My mother has decided to come hold my hand through "the adventure" so she will be in the house from Monday on. Could you go to church tomorrow?

After church, on the hill, beneath the penny eye of the weathercock, Piet walked down the gray path past the iron pavilion toward the reddish rocks by which Foxy had parked. Standing waiting with an alert appearance of politeness, she was vast, a full sail in pale wool, one of the high tight turbans fashionable that fall covering her hair and making her face appear stripped and sleek. He felt pulled into her orbit; he yearned to embrace, to possess forever, this luxurious ball, this swollen woman whose apparition here recalled his first impression, of wealth and an arrogant return home.

"Hi."

"Hi. Why the solemn face?"

"You look so good. You look grand."

"So do you, Mr. Hanema. Is that a new suit?"

"New last fall. You didn't know me then. Is that a new hat?"

"It's called 'a hat to meet your mother at the airport in, to show her you're doing all right.' "

"It's very successful."

"Is it too severe? I'd take it off but it's pinned."

"It's great. It brings out the pampered pink of your face."

"God, you're hostile."

"I may be hostile, but I adore you. Let's go to bed."

"Wouldn't that be a relief? Do you know how many days it's been since we made love?"

"Many."

"Nineteen. Two Tuesdays ago."

"Can we elude your mother?" Piet's palms and the area of his lips had gone cold; he felt here at the town's center that he was leaning inwards like a man on the edge of a carrousel.

Foxy said, "I can if you can get away from Angela and Gallagher."

"They're a vigilant pair these days. Jesus, I hate not seeing you. I find myself—"

"Say it." Perhaps she thought he was going to confess another woman.

"Terrified of death lately."

"Oh, Piet. Why? Are you sick?"

"It's not practical death I'm worried about, it's death anytime, at all, ever."

She asked, "Does it have to do with me?"

He had not thought so, but now he said, "Maybe. Maybe I'm frightened of you having your baby and everything changing."

"Why should it?"

He shrugged. "You'll be a mother. It won't be my child. It just won't work, you'll be too torn."

She was blank, still. Sunday was gathered around them, the sky a rung bell, cars in all colors hurrying home. Against her silence he suddenly pleaded, "I need to see you, woman. I need to see your belly."

They were exposed in sunlight and traffic, and she decided to turn to her car. "Call me," she said. "Can you call tomorrow before nine? Mother's plane comes in at ten-thirty." She thought. "No. You can't. Ken is going into Boston with me, so he'll be at the house." She thought again. "I'll try to call your office when I go shopping in the afternoon. But you'll be at the Inne." She paused a third time, having been listening to herself. "Damn, this is shitty," she said. "I *want* you to see me. I want to be with you all the time. I want to own you."

As if this last admission had confirmed and justified him in his sense of certain loss, Piet waved his hand generously, meaning it couldn't be helped. "Your wanting it," he told her, "is what matters to me. We'll keep in touch. Be nice to your Mom."

Her white-gloved hand appeared to flinch on the car-door handle. "I must go," broke from her. In full view of the town, he comically bowed, and saw she was wearing, for the good of her legs, elastic stockings dusty rose in color.

"Charrming," he said, "to be seeing ye sae fair on so fair a morrning, Mrs. Whitman."

"Likewise, I'm sure, Mr. Hanema," she replied, her brown eyes alive in the trap of their plight.

The brilliant October days brimmed for him with her absence. On the evenings when there was no party, no gathering, Piet and Angela sat at home in the stifling atmosphere of his longing. "Stop sighing."

Piet looked up surprised from a page of *Life:* saffron-robed monks protesting. "I'm not, am I?"

"Well, your breathing is unpleasant."

"Sorry. I'll try to stop breathing."

"What's bothering you? The Tarbox Inne?"

"Nothing. I just feel restless. What's in the refrigerator?"

"You've already looked. You'll get fat, the way you nibble. Why don't you go out and look at the stars? I can't stand that sighing."

"Will you come out with me?"

"In a minute." She was absorbed in her book, the new Salinger, with an endless title and a mustard jacket whose front and back were identical. "They're about to have a revelation." At what point in their courtship was it, years ago, on the Nun's Bay cliffs, that she had astonished him by knowing the stars, her uncle having been an astronomer? Her cheek to his so he could follow her pointing hand, she had taught him. Find the bright stars first. Then travel between them. Imagine straight lines. The dew touching them through the blanket. Her father's windowlights marching across the grass but dying among the shrubs trimmed like table tops. Her warm breath telling of legends above them.

He left her beneath the lamp and ventured across the crunching driveway into the yard's darkness, green-veined like black marble. The high-pitched thrum of cicadas encircled him. The clear night threatened frost. The rigid cascade of stars had been dealt a sideways blow: Vega the queen of the summer sky no longer reigned at the zenith, having yielded to paler Deneb and to a faint house-shaped constellation. Cepheus. In Andromeda Piet searched for the very dim stir of light that Angela had once pointed out to him as another galaxy altogether, two million light years distant. Through oceans of onyx its light had traveled to him. Mirrorwise his gaze, followed shortly by his death, would travel outward in an eternal straight line. Vertigo afflicted him. Amid these impervious shining multitudes he felt a gigantic slipping; sinking upwards, he gripped the dim earth with his eyes. The leaves of a broken lilac branch, dead and unable to girdle their stems and fall, hung unstirring in windowlight. He pictured Foxy, a vapor, a fur, a memory of powdery armpits, lips dry then wet, the downy small of her back where his thumbs would massage the ache of carrying a child, her erect coral nipples teased by his fingernails, the guarded blur of her gaze. She became formless and undefended beneath the sorrowful confiding of his seed. *I abuse you.*

No. Don't stop.

I'll come.

Do. I can't this time. Do, Piet.

Truly? You like it? She nodded, silent, her mouth full. Her tongue fluttered him into heat; her hand helped. *Oh. Sweet. Swallow me.* She swallowed him.

The leaves of the broken lilac branch, dead and unable to girdle their stems and fall, hung unstirring in windowlight. Behind glass Angela calmly turned a page. Above his square yard the burning dome seemed splintered by a violent fleeing. Give me now her by whom You have fled.

Piet that night fell asleep promptly, but awoke in the early morning, hours before dawn, feeling cheated, having been unable to dream. Angela lay oblivious beside him. He brought her hand to his penis but it slipped away. With his own skilled hand he lightened himself of desire; yet still he could not relax and sink. He remembered from childhood a curling warm darkness he could snuggle backwards into, at the touch of a soft blanket, of a furry toy, of rain overhead, of voices below. Now, at midpoint of his life's arc, this first darkness had receded beyond recovery and the second, the one awaiting him, was not yet comfortable. Sudden faces, totally unknown, malevolent, flicked through his mind as it sought to erase itself into sleep. Detailed drawings of unbuilt buildings, clear in every pinion and cornice, were momentarily laid flat upon his unsteady inner surface. Again and again his racing heart checked his mind's intended dissolution. He itched to thump Angela awake; the desire to confess, to confess his misery, his fornication with Foxy, rose burning in his throat like the premonition of vomit. After many turnings and futile resettlings he crept downstairs, outdoors.

The stars had wheeled out of all recognition. They were as if seen from another earth, beyond the Milky Way, rich in silence and strangeness. Treading lightly upon the rime-whitened grass, ice to his bare soles, he finally located, southward above the barn ridge with its twin scrolled lightning rods, a constellation gigantic and familiar: Orion. The giant of winter, surprised in his bed. So the future is in the sky after all. Everything already exists. Piet returned to his snug house satisfied that a crisis in his love for Foxy had passed, that henceforth he would love her less.

iv. *Breakthrough*

Foxy felt that her mother's presence in the house formed a dreadful, heavensent opportunity to confess that she had a lover. No practical benefit could follow from such a confession, and her mother, in the blithe, efficient complacence bestowed upon her by remarriage and middle age, exerted no pressure to confess; rather, she assumed that the marriage she had chosen for her daughter was going all the smoother now that its one blemish, childlessness, was about to be removed. This assumption annoyed Foxy; the world's downward skid seemed to her greased by such assumptions. Confession to the contrary ballooned against the roof of her mouth. Foxy had carried her secret alone too long. Her two hidden burdens had grown parallel, and now the guilty one also demanded to emerge, to show itself, to be satisfied by a wider environment, a sunlit hemisphere of consultation and sympathy.

Yet her mother was in the house two weeks, and Foxy proved awkwardly retentive. Her delicate flush masked an inconvenient toughness. The baby was late. There were jokes, too many, about the possibility of quintuplets like those born in South Dakota the previous month. Ken and Foxy's mother—Constance Price Fox

Roth, she begged them to call her Connie—got along all too nicely. They dressed in the same way: in costumes rather than clothes. Ken had outfits for every occasion, for going to work, for being at work, for being at home casually, for being at home less casually, for walking on the beach, for playing tennis, for playing touch football with the other young husbands of Tarbox on fall Sunday afternoons; he owned a closet of suits graded by sobriety, madras and linen and tweedy sports jackets, sweaters of many weights, chinos and jeans in all degrees of wear, several types of sneakers, even a foulard and a smoking jacket for the at-home occasion pitched to just this formality. In the same style, Foxy's mother, now wealthy, changed at every turn of the day. Between five-thirty and six, when the two women could make themselves a drink and settle to waiting for Ken's arrival from Boston, Connie would slip into one of her quieter cocktail dresses and Foxy in her exhausted maternity tent would be obliged to covet her mother's figure; though thickening at the waist and shrinking at the hips, it was still more compact and orthodoxly sexy than Foxy's languorous, flat-footed, overall own. Too keenly Connie would await Ken. He had grown handsomer in the years since Foxy's parents had approved him, the same years in which Foxy had grown numb to his handsomeness. The elegant height held so uprightly, the shapely long skull now becomingly touched at the temples with gray, the gray gaze bold as a child's. Connie was impressed by Ken's professional distinction, which Foxy had come to see as an anticlimax to their long student wait, a cheat. Mrs. Roth was intrigued by what Foxy dismissed as aspects of Ken's essential coldness—the dash and abruptness with which he performed some actions, such as driving his car, ending a conversation, or acquiring this house. "I *love* the house, Liz," she told her daughter. "The view is *so* New England." Her accent sounded exaggeratedly southern to Foxy; her ceaseless emphases suggested a climacteric society where politeness has absorbed the deeper passions and become a charade. Yet beneath this flossy alien creature with teased and skillfully tinted hair, this second wife chosen to reign over mountains of laundromat quarters, there was the prior woman, the war wife and young mother, with her straggling dull bun, her serge dresses and low-heeled shoes, her scorched ironing board and her varnished Philco crackling with news from both oceans, her air of brave fatigue, her way of suddenly dropping her hands and revealing dread. Foxy thought she could find this woman if she needed her.

Mrs. Roth continued with proprietary enthusiasm: "It's a *castle*. How sweet and ambitious of Ken to have wanted it just for the two of you."

"And the baby."

"Oh, of course, for the baby, *how* could I forget the *ba*by? The cherub is why I'm here!"

Foxy said, of the house, "It was a wreck of an old summer place when we moved in. We got a rather cute local contractor to make it livable. The walls, the porch, the kitchen and the little wing beyond are all new. We had to excavate a cellar."

Foxy's mother, squinting through the smoke of the red-filtered cigarette, the aged skin of her throat betrayed by the lifting of her head, surveyed Piet's work. Foxy's heart felt displaced upward by an inward kicking. "I don't know, Liz. It seems a bit fussy. All this old-fashioned blank plaster just *isn't* you and Ken."

"You need something solid on the marshes," Foxy said defensively, "to keep out the wind."

Wishing to be tactful, and sensing a sudden need for tact, Mrs. Roth said, "I'm sure as you live here you'll make it more cozy," and changed the subject. "Speaking of the wind, Libby, do you know—it's fresh on my mind, my book circle has been reading Greek mythology, it seems to be the literary rage this year—the ancient Greeks and all those people apparently thought women were *fertilized by it? The wind!*"

Foxy laughed. "Do you remember, Mother, in Bethesda, old Miss Ravenel always sitting rocking in her breezeway?" Every day, she steered the conversation to reminiscence of Bethesda.

"*Do* I?" Connie cried. "Of course, That's what she was waiting for, to be fertilized!" The laughter in the big bare-walled room sounded thin; each woman had proved fertile but once.

Ken liked his mother-in-law's presence in the house because it kept Foxy entertained at home, away from the gatherings of the couples he had taken to describing to her as "your friends."

When they did go out, it was the three of them together, and Foxy's mother, in crackling purples, with a white silk stole she kept flicking and adjusting, was a social success, half-chaperon, half-fool. Freddy Thorne and she hit it off especially well. After the little-Smiths' Halloween party, held the night after the holiday and without masks, she said to Foxy, "I must say, he seems terribly *up* on things, to be only a *den*tist. He was fascinating on modern psychology and myths. Don't you, among your gay friends, find him one of the most sympatico?"

"Frankly, Mother, no. I find him insidious and odious."

"Truly? Of course, his mouth is unfortunate, but then no man will truly seem handsome set against Ken." She spoke gropingly, for in two weeks she had begun to sense Ken's curious absence, the deadening in Foxy that his presence caused. He was off this morning playing tennis, having served breakfast to himself and set his dishes nicely rinsed, as a kind of rebuke, in the slate sink. "Who *do* you like?" she asked.

"Well," Foxy said, "mostly the women, sad to say. Terry Gallagher, she's the tall one with straight dark hair who couldn't be coaxed into playing her lute even though she brought it, and in a way Janet Appleby. She's the plump one who toward the end got quite drunk and did the impersonation of her psychiatrist."

"I thought she should be happier than she is."

"She thinks that too. And of the couples, I quite like the Hanemas and don't mind the Guerins. I can't communicate with Roger but Bea, even though she's a show-off about it, I think is genuinely affectionate. *Their* tragedy is, they can't have any children."

"The Hanemas. Not that horrid little redheaded man who ran around slapping everyone's behind and doing handstands?"

"That is Piet, yes. His wife is lovely. Very kind and serene and amused."

"I didn't notice her. But I must say, as a group, you all seemed *very* sympatico with each other. You're fortunate to have found friends you can have *fun* with. Your father and I had no such circle. We were alone; alone with you. It's good, to be able to let off steam."

"Ken thinks we *make* steam. Ken thinks we know each other

too well. It's true, one man of a couple we know has lost his job because of their involvement with another couple."

"Which was he?"

"They don't come any more. His name was Ben Saltz. They were Jewish." Helplessly, incriminatingly, Foxy blushed.

Her mother gave no sign of remembering, with her, Peter. Rather, she said, tidily dousing her cigarette in her slopped coffee saucer, "It must have been a combination of circumstances."

"The woman he was in love with was there last night. Carol Constantine. Piled red hair with dark roots and a very thin waist. She paints. I've been thinking of buying a painting from her, after your chilling remarks about our bare walls."

"I noticed her. Stunning now, but she'll soon go brassy. She knows it, too. And she can expect precious little mercy from that dandy little husband of hers."

"Eddie? We don't take him very seriously."

"You should. He is a very vain and ruthless young Italian. I told him to his face, I'd be happy to ride in any airplane he was piloting; he was too conceited to crash."

"Mother! Aren't you wicked, flirting with these men young enough to be your sons?"

"I wasn't flirting, I was alarmed. And so is his poor emaciated wife."

"Speaking of couples," Foxy asked, homesick for Washington, "how are the Kennedys?"

"People say, better than they used to be. He used to be notorious, of course."

"She looks less anxious in the newspapers lately. At her Greek beach."

"A *dreadful* misfortune, their premature child. But I suppose being Catholics they have some way of turning it all to the good. One more angel up there, tra la."

"You don't think we Episcopalians have these ways."

"Dear good Elizabeth." Her mother's hand reached tentatively to touch hers, and their wedding rings lightly clashed, gold to gold. "I must confess I've stopped thinking of myself as anything. Roth scorns it all, of course. It was mostly a navy thing with your father."

"Does he still go to church?"

"I've never thought to ask him, and now it's been years since I've seen him. He's in San Diego, I may never see him again. Think of that."

Foxy refused to think of it. Carefully she asked, "Is it true, what everybody said, they almost got divorced?"

"The Kennedys. We don't see many government people, but yes, you do hear that sort of thing. Not divorced, of course; they'd have to buy an annulment, I suppose from Cardinal Spellman. Of course, with his back, he's *not* as active as apparently he was." Mrs. Roth rested her elbows on the table edge and wearily smoothed the skin beneath her eyes. "Why do you ask?"

Foxy said, "I'm curious about divorce." In turning her head to mute this admission she read the banner headline of the newspaper left neatly folded at Ken's empty place: DIEM OVERTHROWN. Diem. *Dies, diei, diei, diem.* "I wonder sometimes if Ken and I shouldn't get one."

The planet turned while Foxy waited to hear which woman would respond, her mother or Mrs. Roth. "Seriously?" Which was it?

Foxy sought cover. "Not very," she said very lightly. "The thought comes and goes. Since coming out here I have too much time to myself. Once the baby arrives I'll be all right."

"Well I *won*der," her mother said. "But if you're not happy why didn't you end things when there was no one else involved? You lived alone with Ken how many years was it? Seven?"

"I didn't *know* I wasn't happy till I moved here. Oh mother, it's such a mess—so *sad.* He's everything I could want but we don't make *con*tact."

"Oh, child. Cry, yes. I'm so sorry."

"He's so good, Mother, he's so goddam *good.* He doesn't *see* me, he doesn't *know* me."

"Are you sure?"

"Oh, yes, yes. I've been seeing another man and Ken doesn't have a clue. A *clue.*"

"What other man?" Mrs. Roth asked sharply. "Truly seeing?"

"It doesn't *matter* what other man. A man. Oh, God, yes, seeing to sleep with."

"The child is his?"

"No, Mother, the child is *Ken's*."

This admission was the worst; as Foxy sobbed into crumpled whiteness, sobbed toward her own lap beyond the pinkness of her fingers supporting her face, she saw that this was the worst, that had the child been Piet's there would be a rationale, she would not be so purely beyond the pale.

"Well," the other woman at last found tongue to say, "it must stop."

Foxy felt the power of tears; behind the silver shield of them she advanced against her mother, refusing her an easy victory, demanding to be rescued. "But if I could *stop* I wouldn't have started. It was so wrong in the first place. It wasn't his idea it was *mine*. What I'm most afraid of isn't hurting Ken it's hurting *him*, of using his love for me to make him *marry* me."

"The man, I take it, is married also?"

"Of course he is, we're all married out here."

"Has he expressed a wish to marry you?"

"No. Yes. I don't know. It's not possible."

"Well, my advice is certainly to break it off. But I'd be the last person to say that divorce is always catastrophic."

"Oh, but it would be. He loves his wife."

"He says this?"

"He loves us both. He loves us all. I don't want to be the bitch who took advantage of him."

"Such elevated morality. In my day it was the woman who was taken advantage of. If it's the man I think it is, he'll land on his feet."

"Who do you think it is?"

"The contractor. The tall Irishman, I forget his name, who danced with you last night."

"Matt Gallagher?" Foxy laughed. "He's a good dancer but, Mother, he's just like Ken, only not as bright."

Connie blushed, hearing in her daughter's laugh how wrong her guess had been. She said, weakly, "He's the only one tall enough for you," and then, stronger, having found the right line, "Sweetheart, I don't *want* to know who the man is. If I knew the man, I'd be obliged to tell Ken. I'd rather know what dissatisfies you. To me, Ken seems perfect."

"I know he seems that to you. You've made that clear."

"And he a*dores* you. Is it the sex?"

"The sex is all right."

"You have climaxes?"

"Mother. Of course."

"Don't be so short. I didn't begin to enjoy my body until I was past thirty."

"Well I must say I don't much enjoy my body in this condition. I can't bend in the middle and my legs hurt." She abruptly stood and swept back and forth carrying plates and cups, making her mother call to her on the fly.

"How can this other man have continued with you when you are carrying this child?"

Foxy shrugged. "He never knew me when I wasn't carrying this child. It didn't seem to matter that much. He's very tender about it. His wife has stopped having children. She believes in overpopulation."

"Oh, Liz, he sounds *so* unstable to me. You have *such* unfortunate taste."

"You ask me about Ken. I think what's wrong with him is that I didn't choose him. You chose him. Daddy chose him. Radcliffe and Harvard chose him. All the world agreed he was right for me, and that's why he's not. Nobody *knew* me. Nobody *cared*. I was just something to be bundled up and got out of the way so you and Daddy could have your wonderful divorce." The accusation was so grave she sat down at the table again. Beneath her crowded heart there was an unaccustomed burning.

Her mother massaged the moist red spaces below her eyes, and answered huskily, "Is that how it looked to you? It wasn't that way, we didn't think, but I'm so sorry, Liz, so sorry. We both loved you so, you had always been so brave for us, all those dull years your bright voice, your prettiness, we were terrified over what you were doing to yourself with Peter."

"But, Mother"—their hands on the table avoided touching, remembering the grotesque click of wedding rings—"I knew that. I knew Peter. I knew it would end of itself, you shouldn't have stepped in. I lost all dignity. This other man and I. I know it will end. He'll leave me. He'll move on. Don't tell Ken about it. Please."

"I never *thought* to tell Ken. He wouldn't know what to do with it; he might panic. You know, Liz, I'm not totally a garish old fool. I can see Ken's limits. He's like your father, he needs a form for everything. But within the rules, I think he's remarkable. He's worth treasuring."

"He is, I do treasure him. It's just so devastating, to have a husband whose job is to probe the secrets of life, and to feel yourself dying beside him, and he doesn't know it or seem to care."

"He cares, I'm sure."

"He cares about his equipment and I'm part of it."

Mrs. Roth came to attention again. "You honestly believe," she said, "that you and this other man can end it? It hasn't gone too far?"

The breakfast debris on the table, orange rinds and eggshells and newspaper, seemed to Foxy to epitomize the contents of the world. Small wonder the child was reluctant to emerge. Its weight within her—the fetus had dropped over a week ago, and its movements, once a faint fluttering, had grown tumultuous—felt leaden, panicked, betrayed. Foxy answered her mother. "It may be ended already. We've hardly talked since you came. We haven't—been together really, for five weeks."

Mrs. Roth's fingertips crept up her face and now stroked, as if treasuringly, the shape of her eyeballs beneath shut lids. "Dear Libby," she said, not looking. "What I most remember from that terrible Bethesda house was the radio dial glowing, and your lovely flaxen hair, that I combed, and combed."

"Gone, Mother, gone," Foxy airily stated, rising and startling in the small of her back an untypical, musical phrase of pain.

Just ten now, still stocky yet dawningly comely, Ruth was given to placid self-communings in her room, which she kept extremely neat. For her birthday Piet had given her a full-length mirror, a doorway to vanity, a father's doting and perhaps intrusive gift. He had grown shy, wary of intruding on her. When he ventured into Ruth's room, he glanced at the mirror to detect signs of its use and surprised his own sharp reflection, looking pouchy and thievish. Surrounded by her mirror, by the splashy flowers of the wallpaper she had chosen herself, by collections, each to its shelf, of books, seashells, bottlecaps, and the foreign dolls sent to her by Angela's parents from the harbors of their winter cruises, by a turquoise-oceaned map of the world and a green-and-white Tarbox High football banner, by Scotch-taped Brownie snapshots she had taken herself of her parents arm-in-arm, of the hamster who had died, of the lilac hedge in bloom, of her friends at the beach but none of her sister—so surrounded, Ruth would sit at the fold-down desk Piet had built for her and do her homework, or make entries in her laconic diary of weather and excursions, or maintain her scrapbook of figures carefully scissored from *Life* and the *National Geographic*, an assortment including Sophia Loren, Queen Elizabeth II of England, a Russian spacedog, a huge stone Pharaoh threatened with immersion by the Aswan Dam, a naked Nigerian bride, a Pakistani mother bewailing the death of her child by earthquake, Jacqueline Kennedy, a vocal group called the Beatles.

On days like this Monday when Piet returned home before Angela, he felt his daughter busy above him; she was bused back from school by four. The silence behind her closed door, broken when she rearranged objects or crooned to herself hymns learned at choir, intimidated him; he had scrubbed her diapers and warmed her bottles and now his only function was to safeguard her privacy, to make himself unobtrusive. He reread the newspaper and considered replacing the rotten boards of his own barn and instead made himself an early gin-and-Bitter-Lemon. Now that the tavern addition was completed, and christened with a formal banquet attended by all three selectman and fire chief Kappiotis, who fell asleep, there was not enough for Piet to do. Gallagher had sold the estate in Lacetown to the nuns, but a Watertown firm whose director's brother was a priest had been awarded the fat reconstruction contract. They were told the bids had been considered blind; all Gallagher's charm with the sisters had been wasted. They were down to a single job, converting the old Tarbox house on Divinity into offices and apartments suitable for rental. Old Gertrude Tarbox, having constructed for herself a paradise of hoarded paper and tin, was in September carted off to a nursing home, at the command of cousins living in Palo Alto, through the agency of a New Bedford bank. Piet's job—replacing clapboards, removing partitions, sanding floors, dressing up ratty surfaces with decorator panels of vinyl surfaced to counterfeit wood—was scarcely enough to occupy Adams and Comeau and Jazinski, who, being employees paid by the hour, were entitled to work first. So Piet was often idle. He drank deep of the sweetened gin and tried not to think of Foxy; since she had hidden behind her mother she was in his mind like a canker that memory's tongue kept touching. The summer seemed dreamlike and distant. She had vanished—the slam of a car door after church. He missed the thrift of a double life, the defiant conservation. Faithful, he was going to waste. Attenuated hours spread lifeless around him. He drank to kill time.

Angela came home brimful of Irene. "You know what that woman has done? She's gotten a paying job at the Lacetown Academy for Girls, starting next Monday, today a week, which means I have to do the whole kindergarten by myself."

"Tell her you can't do it."

"Who said I can't? If I can't go to a psychiatrist at least I can run a dozen children by myself, without Irene's kibbutzy theories getting in my way."

"You *want* to do it."

"What's so surprising about that? I don't want to very much. I don't think children this small are my meat really, but I do want to see how teaching after all these years strikes me. I mean, wouldn't you like it if I could bring home a little money?"

"You're afraid I can't support you."

Angela bent and rubbed her cheek against his temple softly, yet hastily, the brush of a wing about to fly. "Of course you can. But I'm a person too. My children are growing up." She whispered:

"Nancy goes all morning without sucking her thumb, unless something happens to remind her." She whispered because she had brought the child home, and Nancy was on the stairs, wondering if she dared go bother Ruth.

"What else did Irene say? You've been gone forever. Has Ben found a job yet?"

"No, I'm not even sure he's looking. But she was full of news. She keeps a beady black eye on the Constantines across the way and says they've taken up with the Guerins. Roger and Bea are over there every night, and what Irene thinks, you have to hear it from her to get the humor of it, is that the attraction is between the like halves of the couples." She drew a box in air with her fingers to explain. "Carol and Bea are attracted to each other, and Roger and Eddie."

"Well does she think they're putting this attraction into practice? I'm having another drink. Would you like one?"

"Bourbon, not gin. Piet, summer's over. She doesn't quite dare say so. But she thinks Carol is capable of anything physically and Bea *does* have this very passive streak. She's always been a kind of a woman's woman, in a way; she *flirts* with women, and gives them little pats."

"But it must be a huge step," Piet said, though knowing that heterosexually it was not so, "between that kind of current and taking off your clothes and doing the stuff."

Angela took her musky gold drink from his hand; as she sipped her eyes went bluer, gazing toward scenes she had been told of. "But," she said, "we're none of us getting younger and if it's something you've always wanted aren't the inhibitions less and less? Things keep getting less sacred."

Piet said, pouring lucid gin for himself, "Roger *is* homosexual, sure, but his charm has always been his refusal to admit it. Except in his manner to women, which is either rude or excessively polite."

"I think there's a difference," Angela said, "between being homosexual and being angry at females. Has Roger ever, on the golf course say, made a pass at you?"

"No. But he *is* very comfortable, and can't *stand* being stuck behind a female foursome. But I think Eddie's the mystery. How can Irene accuse her lover of a few months ago of being a working fairy?"

"Well, for one thing, she didn't exactly, and for another she is quite hurt and bitter. When I sort of asked her this, all she'd say was that Eddie could be very per*sua*sive. I don't know what it meant, but she said it three or four times."

Piet asked her, "Where does your friend Freddy Thorne fit in this new arrangement?"

"Oh, well Freddy's the one who brought them together; the Guerins and Constantines had almost nothing to do with each other until Freddy. I guess he's over there pretty much, stirring the brew."

"Poor Georgene."

Angela asked, alert, her upper lip lifted, her wet teeth aglint, "Why poor Georgene?"

"On general principles. Married to that evil jerk."

"You can't really think he's evil. He just loves a mess. Anyway, Georgene's been *very* frosty to me ever since school started. Once Irene goes, it wouldn't surprise me if Georgene stopped doing her day."

"What else did Irene have on her teeming mind?"

"Let me remember. John Ong is apparently sick. Something with his chest; the doctors have told him to quit smoking and he won't. He can't."

"My Lord. Cancer?"

"Nobody knows. Of course, he's older than any of us, it just hasn't showed, because he's Asiatic."

"Is he in the hospital?"

"Not yet. And, oh yes, of course. This will please you. Foxy Whitman has had her baby."

The air compressed; a sense of suffocation was followed by a carefree falling independent of space. Piet asked, "When?"

"Sometime this weekend. I think on Sunday. You saw her Friday night at the little-Smiths'. Maybe dancing with Matt Gallagher brought it on. He's awfully bouncy."

"Why hasn't anybody told us before?"

"Piet, you're taking it so *personally*. You're not exactly the next of kin. I *am* surprised that Matt didn't mention it at work. Terry must have heard, if she's Foxy's best friend."

"Matt and I don't communicate much at work these days. He's sulking because we lost the nunnery. But that's very nice. She had gotten enormous. Boy or girl?"

"Boy. Seven pounds something. Should we send flowers? I like Foxy, but we don't seem quite at the flower-sending stage."

"Oh, send her some. Loosen up. You can't take them with you, Angel. Flowers don't grow in Heaven, they only spring from dung."

Angela grimaced, puzzled by his hostile patter, and left the kitchen, calling, "Ru-uth! Come down and be sociable. Nancy wants to play Fish."

Alone, Piet tried to grasp the happiness distinct yet unsteady within him. She was safe. The child had been a boy. Foxy's luck had held. He wanted to be very close to her, to creep into the antiseptic white room where she lay, deflated and pink, invisibly bleeding, breathing in unconsciousness, her pale mouth askew, her hair adrift. He saw hothouse flowers—lush gladiolas, display dahlias, beribboned hyacinths fragrant of greenhouse earth packed tight by mossy thumbs, red cut roses leaning heavy-headed and coolly rank. He glimpsed the glass of water standing stale-beaded beyond her blurred face, and the cartoon cards of congratulation, and a candy bar concealed half-eaten in an enameled drawer. And in a chamber beyond this possessive daydreaming waited the realization that, in giving birth without notifying him, she had been guilty of an affront and in that guilt promised him freedom. Once, uncoming, she had masturbated against his thigh squeezed between hers. *Is this too awful for you?*

No, of course not, no. Youth must be served.

Don't tease. I'm shy enough with you as is.

With me, your lover? Shy?

Just am.

It's so touching, how hard women must work.

Touch my nipples.

Gladly.

More gently. I'm almost there.
Come. His thigh was beginning to ache and tingle, the circulation hampered. *Oh come. Good. Terrific. Wow.*

On top of the refrigerator was a wooden salad bowl brimming with Halloween candy that Ruth and Nancy had begged. To celebrate, to lend substance to, his happiness Piet took down the bowl and gobbled a handful of imitation corn; he rarely ate candy, out of fear for his teeth.

Though Foxy had made the appointment three weeks ago, while still in the hospital, for this Friday at one, Freddy Thorne seemed startled by her appearance in his office. Until now she had kept her Cambridge dentist, but toward the end of her pregnancy her teeth had begun to twinge, and with the baby nursing her mobility was lessened. No one, not even Piet, denied that Freddy was a competent dentist. Yet she could not escape the feeling, entering his inner office, that by coming to him, in his absurd cottage tucked beside the post office on Divinity Street, when there were other competent dentists in town, she was, emboldened by motherhood, playing the game that Tarbox had taught her, the game of tempting her fate.

He wore a white jacket and, an inch or more in front of his regular glasses, a pair of rectangular magnifying lenses. The sanctum was fanatically clean, from the circular napkin on the swinging tool tray to the scrubbed blush of Freddy's palms, uplifted in surprise or blessing, in front of his backwards white jacket. A square black clock said twelve after one. His first appointment after lunch. She had nibbled around ten; the baby had scattered her habits of sleep and eating. It reassured her that like all normal dentists Freddy ran behind schedule. "Well look who's here!" he said when she entered. "Lovely day," he murmured while he adjusted her into the chair. Now he asked, as her mouth obediently opened, "Which is the area of discomfort?" Three persons had spoken: the first a frivolous prying man she knew, the second a polite bored acquaintance, the third a wholly alien technician.

"Here," she said. She pointed with her finger from outside her cheek and with her tongue from within. Freddy held the pick and mirror crossed at his chest as she explained. "The upper, molar I suppose it is. I get a twinge when I eat candy. And over here, on the other side, I can feel a hole where a filling used to be. Also all the books say, and my mother in*si*sted, my teeth would fall out because the calcium went into the baby."

"Did you take calcium pills?"

"Iron, I know. I took whatever Doc Allen gave me."

Freddy said, "With a modern diet calcium displacement isn't usually a problem. Primitive women *do* tend to lose their smiles. Shall we have us a look?" His touch with the exploratory picks was delicate. A steel point touched a nerve once, and tactfully feathered off. Mint on his breath masked the odor of whatever he had eaten for lunch, perhaps veal. His perfumed fingers were in her mouth, and, like many things she had abstractly dreaded, like childbirth, like adultery, the reality was more mixed than she had imagined, and not so bad.

"You have strong teeth," he said. He made precise pencil marks on one of those dental charts that to Foxy as a child had seemed a wide-open scream. Curious, his choice of "strong" over "nice" or "good."

She counted the marks and said, "*Four* cavities!" Always in dental chairs she wanted to talk too much, to fend the drill away from her mouth.

"You're in respectable shape," he told her. "Let's begin with the upper right, the one you've been feeling."

He removed an injecting needle from a tray of blue sterilizer. She told him, "I don't usually bother with Novocain."

"I want you to today." His manner was mild and irresistible; where was that sloppy troll she knew from parties? With the secondary lenses in place, his eyes were totally elusive. Freddy became a voice and a touch. He said, "This is a new gadget," and his fingers exposed a spot on her upper gum where, with a tiny hiss, something icy was sprayed. Thus numbed, she did not feel the stab of the needle.

They waited for the Novocain to take effect. Freddy busied

himself behind her back. She yawned; Toby had been fed at two and awakened again at five. Her feet on the raised metal tread looked big and flat and pale in ballet slippers. Above her feet a large window curtained in dun sacking framed an abstract view: the slate roof of the Tarbox post office descended in courses of smaller to greater from a ridge of copper flashing set smack, it seemed, against the sky. The day was balmy for this late in November. Small tugging clouds darkened Tarbox with incongruous intensity when they crossed the sun. She wondered why Piet had sent no flowers. Freddy shuffled tinkling metal and his receptionist, a pug-nosed girl with skunk-striped bangs, passed back and forth between the anteroom and a nether room in which Foxy could glimpse a table, a Bunsen burner, a tattered chart dramatizing dental hygiene for children, and the end of a cot. Nearer, on a chest of enameled drawers, a small blond radio played colorless music interrupted now and then by a characterless male voice, a voice without a trace of an accent or an emotion. Foxy wondered where such music originated, whether in men or machines, and who supplied it so inexhaustibly to dentists' offices, hotel lobbies, and landing airplanes. Ken called it toothpaste music.

Freddy cleared his throat and asked, "Is your mother still here? Will she be coming tonight?" The Thornes were giving a black-tie party tonight. To Foxy it meant that after weeks of seclusion she would at last again see Piet.

"No, we put her on a plane Tuesday. At last."

"Did Ken not enjoy having his mother-in-law in the house?"

"He minded it less than I did. I'm used to being a hermit."

"She seemed jolly."

"She is. But I haven't really had much to do with her since college. I'm too old to have a mother."

"She enjoyed the baby." It was not quite a question.

"She made the noises. But people that age, I discover, aren't very flexible, and it took a lot of my energy to keep the baby off of her nerves. She kept changing clothes and trying to reminisce while I wobbled up and down stairs." As the moment for Freddy to use the drill neared, Foxy's mouth watered, fairly bubbled with the wish to tell him everything—the musical first pains, the narrowing intermittences, the dreamlike unconcern of the doctors and nurses, the anesthesia like a rustling roaring wing enfolding her, the newborn infant's astonishingly searching gaze, her wild drugged thought that he more resembled Piet than Ken, and the miraculous present fact that she, slim Foxy, was a good nurser, a tall tree of food.

Freddy said, "She seemed in no hurry to go back to her husband."

"Yes, I wondered about that. She spoke very loyally of 'Roth,' when she thought of him. I think she sees her life as a kind of Cinderella story, rescued at the end, and now that she's living happily ever after, she's bored."

"She found Ken congenial." Again, it was not quite interrogative.

"Very."

Freddy had not expected so curt a response; delicately balked, he licked his lips and volunteered, "She also seemed attracted to me."

"Oh, Freddy, we all are."

The receptionist, who had been tinkling in the corner with the sterilizer, flashed a naughty smile behind Freddy's back. Sensing teasing, he became dryer in manner. "We discussed fertility; did she tell you?" The receptionist left the room.

"Breathlessly. All about myths."

"In part. We concluded, as I remember, that women could as easily be fertilized by the wind as by men, if they believed in it. That all conception is immaculate, on the handiest excuse." That blurred smirk: what was she supposed to imagine it implied?

Foxy said, "How silly. We're obviously helpless."

"Are you?"

"Otherwise why would there be so many only children? I *hated* being an only child. My father just wasn't there. We had plenty of electric fans."

"Did you?" He had lost track of the joke, the wind.

"One in every room. I know I certainly don't intend my child to be only." There it was: just when Foxy had decided for the hundredth time that Freddy was contemptible, she found she had been drawn out.

He asked, "Numb yet?"

She said, "Almost. What's that cot for?" She gestured toward the nether room, to fling the conversation from herself. A small cloud crossed the sun and dipped them into momentary shadow as if into intimacy. The music was mechanically doing "Tea for Two." She was suddenly hungry for English muffins.

"Not what you think," Freddy said.

"I don't think anything. I'm just asking."

"Instead of lunch sometimes I take a nap."

"I've wondered how you keep going with all those parties. But what did you think I thought?" She made silent motions indicating the young receptionist, doing her doll stare and touching her forehead for the skunk bangs, and, folding her hands beside her face, sleep. She formed a kissing mouth to cement her meaning.

"No," Freddy whispered. "That I give abortions."

Shocked, stifled by shock, Foxy wanted to flee the chair. "I *never* thought that."

"Oh, but dentists do. It's a perfect set-up. They have everything, the chair, anesthetic, instruments . . ."

She judged he was saying these things to enlarge himself in her eyes, to inflame with innuendo her idea of him. If he had gone to medical school, he had aspired to power over life and death; having failed, having settled for dentistry, a gingerly meddling at the mouth of life, he still aspired. She put him down: "I don't want to hear about it."

He answered, "You must be numb now," and began to drill. Upside down, his warm cheek close against her head, Freddy resolved into a pair of hairy nostrils, a dance of probing fingers, and glinting crescents of curved glass. His aura was maternal, soapy. Foxy relaxed. Her breasts began to sting and she anticipated release, leaving this office, collecting the baby in his vanilla Carry-Cot at Bea Guerin's, driving down the winding beach road to her empty house, undoing her upper clothes, and giving her accumulated richness over to that tiny blind mouth so avid to suck. He had begun on the right breast this morning, so it would be the left this noon. Twenty minutes, and the Novocain would be wearing off, and she could make a lunch of leftover salad and a tuna sandwich. How innocently life ate the days. How silly she was, how Christianly neurotic, to feel beneath the mild mixed surface of aging and growing, of nursing and eating and sleeping, of love feigned and stolen and actual, a terror, a tipping wrongness, a guilt gathering toward discharge. Poor Freddy, their ringleader, was revealed as a competent dentist. "Lady Be Good" was played. Beneath the red blanket of her closed eyelids Foxy saw that she must soon break with Piet, and felt no pain.

In mid-melody the radio music stopped.

The characterless male voice, winded, hurried, as if called back to the microphone from a distance, pronounced, "A special bulletin. Shots have been heard in Dallas in the vicinity of the Presidential motorcade. We repeat. Gunshots have been reported in Dallas in the vicinity of President Kennedy's motorcade."

There was a second of sharp silence. Then the needle was returned to the groove and the toothpaste music smoothly resumed "Lady Be Good." The black clock said 1:36.

Freddy held the drill away from her mouth. "You hear that?"

She asked him, "What does it mean?"

"Some crazy Texan." He resumed drilling. The pitch of speed lifted impatiently. The star of heat pricked its cloud of spray, and hurt. Freddy sighed mint. "You may spit."

The receptionist, wide-eyed from having overheard the radio, came in from the anteroom to whip the silver and to listen. "Do you think it was Communists?" the girl asked. The music halted again. She signed herself with the cross. On the slates opposite, a small flock of pigeons, having settled near the post office chimney for warmth, clumsily swirled and lifted. The bulletin was repeated, with the additional information that the motorcade had definitely been fired *at*. Three shots had been counted. The pigeons gripped flight in their dirty wings and beat away, out of Foxy's sight. The girl brought a pellet of silver in a chamois pad and set it on the impeccable circular napkin of Freddy's tool tray. Freddy rolled it tighter with his fingertips. The blunder of resuming the music was not repeated. Words spaced by silence filled in the solid truth. The President had been shot at, the President had been hit, he had been hit in the head, his condition was critical, a priest had been summoned, the President was dead. By two o'clock, all of this was known. Amid medicinal whiffs, Freddy had swabbed Foxy's cavity and flanked the tooth with cotton and clamps and pressed the silver filling tight. Foxy had waited in the chair ten additional minutes to hear the worst. Kennedy dead, she left. The nurse was crying, her eyes still held wide, as if like a doll's unable to close unless she lay down. Foxy, grateful to her for showing emotion, patted her hand, a cool tap in passing. Living skin seeks skin. The girl blurted, "We didn't even vote for him, my family, but would have the next time."

Freddy seemed distended and titillated by this confirmation of chaos. Escorting Foxy out through the anteroom, he said in the hall, "This fucks up our party, doesn't it?"

"You must cancel," Foxy told him. She would not see Piet tonight.

"But I've bought all the *booze*," Freddy protested.

Foxy went out into Freddy's tiny front yard, which held a crabapple tree skeletal and spidery without leaves. The post office flag was already at half-mast. Divinity Street was so silent she heard an electric sander working well down the block. Through the plate-glass windows of the pizza shop and the Tarbox *Star* and the shoe-repair haven that was also a bookie joint, she saw shadows huddled around radios. She thought of the little blond radio's embarrassed fall from its empyrean of bland music, of the receptionist's navy-blue eyes lacquered by tears, of Freddy's stupid refusal to mourn, mistaken and contemptible, yet—what was better in herself? She tried to picture the dead man, this young man almost of her generation, with whom she could have slept. A distant husband had died and his death less left an emptiness than revealed one already there. Where grief should have dwelt there was a reflex tenderness, a personal cringing. At Cogswell's corner she glanced up toward the Congregational Church and her heart, blind lamb, beat faster. The Plymouth was parked by the rocks; she must hurry to the baby. Striding uphill through the spotty blowing sunlight, Foxy imagined her son's avid toothless mouth. Her left breast eagerly ached. She tested the right side of her mouth and found it still numb. Would her lopsided smile frighten him? Then it seemed to her that the cocky pouchy-eyed corpse had been Piet and the floor of her stomach fell and the town around her gripped guilt in its dirty white gables and tried to rise, to become a prayer.

The Thornes decided to have their party after all. In the late afternoon, after Oswald had been apprehended and Johnson sworn in, and the engines of national perpetuity had demonstrated their strength, Georgene called all the houses of the invited and explained that the food and liquor had been purchased, that the guests had bought their dresses and had their tuxedos cleaned, that she and Freddy would feel lonely tonight and the children would be *so* disappointed, that on this terrible day she saw nothing wrong in the couples who knew each other feeling terrible together. In a way, Georgene explained to Angela, it would be a wake, an Irish wake, and a formal dinner-dance was very fitting for the dead man, who had had such style. Do come. Please. Freddy will be very hurt, you know how vulnerable he is.

The fashion that fall was for deep décolletage; Piet, arriving at nine, was overwhelmed by bared breasts. He had been reluctant to come. His superstitious nature had groped for some religious observance, some ceremony of acknowledgment to gallant dead Kennedy, though he was a Republican. He knew Freddy would be blasphemous. Further, he felt unwell: his tongue and gums had developed a rash of cankers, and since Foxy had become inaccessible Angela had also ceased to make love to him, and his tuxedo was old, a hand-me-down from his father-in-law, and unfashionably wide-lapelled, and the black shoulders showed his dandruff. Entering the Thornes' living room he saw naked shoulders and flaringly bared bosoms floating through the candlelight, haunting the African masks, the gaudy toss pillows, the wickerwork hassocks and strap-hinged Spanish chests and faded wing chairs. Logs burned in the fieldstone fireplace. The bar table of linen and glasses and bottles formed an undulant field of reflected fire. Janet

Appleby wore an acid-green gown whose shoelace straps seemed unequal to the weight squeezed to a sharp dark cleavage like the vertical crease of a frowning brow. Marcia little-Smith, in a braless orange bodice, displayed, as she reached forward, earrings shuddering, to tap a cigarette into a copper ashtray each dent of which was crescental in the candlelight, conical tits hanging in shadow like tubular roots loose in water. Georgene wore white, two filmy breadths of cloth crossed to form an athletic and Attic binder, her breasts flattened boyishly, as if she were on her back. Carol Constantine had stitched herself a blue silk sheath severely narrow at the ankles and chastely high in front but scooped in the back down to her sacral vertebrae. Irene Saltz—for the Saltzes had come, partly renewed confidence brought on by Irene's job, partly impish insistence on Freddy's part—had put on a simple cocktail dress of black velvet; its oval neckline inverted the two startled arcs of her eyebrows as she jealously, anxiously surveyed the room for the whereabouts of Ben and Carol and Eddie. Piet was touched by her. Like him, she felt it was wrong to have come. She had lost weight. Humiliation flattered her.

Bea Guerin drifted toward him with uplifted face; her bosom, sprinkled with sweat, was held forward in a stiff scarlet carapace like two soft sugared buns being offered warm in the metal vessel of their baking. "Oh Piet," she said, "isn't it awful, that we're all here, that we couldn't stay away, couldn't stay home and mourn decently?" With lowered lids he fumbled out a concurrence, hungering for the breasts that had risen to such a roundness their upper rims made a dimpled angle with Bea's chest-wall. *Why don't you want to fuck me?* Her lifted upper lip revealed the little gap between her front teeth; she laid a trembling hand on his arm, for balance, or as a warning. *You're surrounded by unkind people.* Embarrassed, he sipped his martini, and the cankers lining his mouth burned.

He said, "I hear you're seeing a lot of the Constantines."

"They're bores, Piet. Roger enjoys them, but they're self-centered bores. After a while one minds their not having gone to college."

"Who does Roger enjoy most, Eddie or Carol?"

"Don't be wicked, Piet. I don't mind it from these others, but I hate it from you. You're not wicked, why pretend?"

"Answer my question."

"Carol can be fun," Bea said, "but she's *so* cold. Cold and crude. I think—this is terribly sad—I think she was honestly in love with Ben, terribly in love, and never let herself know it, and now she can't admit it, it's too un*dig*nified, and does the *cruelest* imitations of him."

"But Ben is so boring."

"Piet, I don't think they noticed, they're such bores themselves. Oh, it's awful, everybody is so boring. Roger is so ex*treme*ly boring."

"You think I wouldn't be?"

"Not for a while, sweet Piet. Not for a long while. But you don't like short women, it's *so* Napoleonic of you."

Piet laughed and gazed over Bea's head. Where was Foxy? He searched the flickering room in vain. He felt that in her staying away she had achieved over him a moral ascendancy that completed the triumph, the royal disregard, of her giving birth to a son. Pity sucked at him; he felt abandoned, small. He asked Bea, "Where are the Gallaghers?"

"Matt told Georgene they were going with their children to a special mass. She said he was polite over the phone but just barely."

"Matt is getting very independent. And the Ongs?"

"John was too sick."

"How sick is he?"

"Freddy says he's dying," Bea said, the curve of her cheek a Diana's bow in candlelight. Dying. Before coming to the party Piet and his daughters had watched, on television, the casket being hauled from the plane amid the spotlights of the air field: a long gleam on the polished wood as sudden as a bullet, the imagined airless privacy within, the flooding lights without, the widow blanched amid rapid shadows, the eclipsing shoulders of military attachés. The casket had tipped, bumped. Bea said to Piet, "You haven't asked where are the Whitmans."

"Oh, aren't they here?"

"Piet, you're *so* obvious. I have *no* idea where they are, but you've been looking over my head *all* this time. It's not very flattering."

"I was thinking I should get another drink." To quench panic. The refrigerator. The stars.

"Piet," Bea said swiftly, softly, seeing he was pulling away. "I could love you, if you'd let me."

At the drinks table Carol was flirting simultaneously with Harold and Frank. "Frank," she said loudly in a voice that did not quite dare call the party to attention, to make an occasion, "give us a Shakespeare quote. Nobody knows quite what to say."

"Good night, sweet prince?" Angela offered. It startled Piet to see her there, her fine oval skull and throat suspended in the hovering light, shadows fluctuating on her white shoulders, the scalloped neckline, the discreet parabola of pearls.

Frank Appleby, red-eyed, considered and said, "Ambition's debt is paid."

Carol asked, "Is that a quote?"

"From *Julius Caesar*. What a dumb floozy." He gave Carol a crunching shoulder hug that Piet feared would shatter her brittle blue sheath.

"What about"—Harold little-Smith interrupted himself with a giggle—"For Oswald is an honorable man?" Enjoying the laughter of the others, he went on, "I *really* had to laugh, the news came in just as I was having dessert, *gâteau avec des fraises*, with three of my most Republican associates, including, Frank—this will amuse you—young Ed Foster, who as Frank knows thinks Bob Taft was turning pink at the end. *Un peu de rose au fin.* Naturally everybody's first assumption, including the broadcasters, who are all liberals of course—"

Carol interrupted, "Harold, are you *really* a conservative?"

Janet spoke up. "Harold and Frank are different. Frank's a Federalist; he honestly *loves* the Founding Fathers. Harold's an ultramontane; with him it's just a form of swank."

"*Merci pour votre mots très incisifs.* May I please continue? Well, naturally everybody assumed that a *right*-wing crackpot had done it. You remember at first there was a lot of melancholy fill-in about Dallas the Birchers' paradise, et cetera; we were all very pious and tut-tutty."

"Is that French?" Carol asked.

"But then, around two-thirty, when I'd got back to the office and the stuff on Oswald had begun to filter through, young Ed called up absolutely ec*static* and said, 'Did you hear? It wasn't one of ours, it was one of *theirs!*'" Perhaps because all those listening had experienced the same reversal of prejudice, there was less laughter than Harold had expected.

Frank offered, "Ever since McCarthy cracked up, all the real wolves have been on the left."

Freddy said, "One thing I'm absolutely certain of, he wasn't in it alone. There were too many shots. The whole fucking thing was too successful."

He was unanimously pooh-poohed. Janet said, "Freddy, you see conspiracies in everything."

"He thinks," Angela stated, "we're all a conspiracy to protect each other from death."

"To shut out the night, I think I said."

Piet was impressed that Freddy remembered anything of what he said. Shapelessness was growing bones. Feeding on calcium stolen from Piet's own slack and aimless life. Lately Freddy had taken to staring at Piet too hard, meaningfully.

"One conspiracy I'll let you all in on is," Harold little-Smith said, "when the market opens again, buy. Business was *not* happy with Kennedy, and it's going to *love* Johnson. He's just the kind of old bastard business is happy under."

Carol with her long bare back shivered. "That gross sad man. It was like the high-school shot putter accepting the class presidency, all humility and rotten grammar. Freddy, are you going to let us dance?"

"Whatever my guests think is proper. I don't know how to act, frankly. I've never had my President assassinated before. I was a baby when they did Lincoln in. Honest Abyface."

Ben Saltz overheard and came up to them. His face above his beard appeared to Piet shell-white, a grinning fragment from an exploded past. "And yet," he informed Freddy, "this country since 1865 has an unenviable record for political violence. *Four* presidents, plus the attempts on Truman and both Roosevelts— as you know, Teddy was actually wounded, in his unsuccessful campaign in 1912—not to mention Huey Long. There isn't a country west of the Balkans with any kind of the same record. The Prime Ministers of England go everywhere with a single body-guard."

"We fought for the right to bear arms," Frank said.

Carol was saying, "Ben will dance with me, won't you, Ben? Wouldn't you like to dance with me?"

His carved lion's smile appeared, but his eyes remained dubious, frightened, human. Carol twitchily seized Harold's arm and said, "If Ben's scared to, Harold will, won't you, Harold? Dance with me. After Janet's been so mean about your elegant politics. Freddy, put on music." She turned the chill pallor of her back on Piet.

Ben too, in a trim tuxedo that looked rented, turned his back, and spoke to Angela. Piet heard his wife ask, ". . . like her teaching by now?"

Ben's voice, doleful and clear, responded, ". . . gratifying to me to see her using her mind after all these years, being at least to some extent intellectually challenged."

Georgene was standing in the middle of the room with the air of a hostess undecided between duties. Piet approached her and let her sip his drink. "Carol is terribly high," he said.

"Well, take her to bed. You know where it is."

"I wouldn't dream of it. She'd scratch. But I wonder whose inspiration it was to have the Saltzes and Constantines together."

"Freddy's, of course."

"But you made it stick. Freddy has a lot of ideas that you let wither."

Georgene's righteous clubwoman's temper flared. "Well really Piet, it's too tedious, if people aren't going to have their affairs in private." We were different, she was saying, we were secret, and brave, and better than these corrupt couples. She went on aloud, roughly pushing her fingers through her graying hair, as if combing out larch needles, "I seem to be the only person I know left who has any sense of privacy."

"Oh. That's an interesting remark."

"It's not meant to be."

"Sweet Georgene, what *are* you doing with all this privacy, now that I'm not around?"

"Oh," she said, "men come and go. I can't keep track of them all. They've worn a path through the woods." She asked, "Do you care?"

"Of course. You were wonderful for me."

"What happened then?"

"It began to frighten me. I felt Freddy knew."

"What if he did? I was handling Freddy."

"Maybe I'm not being entirely honest."

"I know you're not," Georgene said, "you never are," and, like a playing card being snapped, showed him her edge and dealt herself away. Let women in, Piet thought, and they never stop lecturing. Pedagogy since the apple. Be as gods.

Roger Guerin came up to him. His brows were knit tight and he was wearing a frilled and pleated dress shirt, with ruby studs and a floppy bow tie in the newest fey fashion. He asked, "Put your golf clubs away yet?"

Piet said, "There may be one more warm weekend."

Eddie Constantine came up to them crouching. "Hey Jesus," he said, "have either of you looked down Marcia's dress yet? She's nose cones down to her navel."

"You've always known they were there," Piet told him.

"Believing isn't seeing. God, we were in the kitchen talking about some cruddy thing, air pollution, and I kept looking down and they kept bobbling around, I got such a hard-on I had to dive in here to level off."

Roger laughed, too loudly out of his tiny mouth, like one who has learned about laughing late in life, and Piet realized he was standing here as an excuse, that the point of Eddie's anecdote had been to amuse and excite Roger. My cock, he had been secretly saying, is big as a fuselage. Women, he had been saying, are dirt.

"How about Janet?" Roger asked him. "Held by those two little shoestrings."

Eddie drew closer, still in his scuttling position, to the other man, stiff-standing. "It looks to me the way they're squeezed she's carrying a second backside, in case the first wears out." The beauty of duality. A universe of twos. "Hey Roger, do you want to know what crazy Carol did the other night? We were . . . you know . . . in my lap . . . up . . . and what does the bitch do but swing her leg way the hell back and stick her foot in my mouth! It was great, I damn near puked. Get Bea to try it."

Piet moved off and gently, by standing expectant, detached Janet from the little-Smiths and Freddy Thorne. The glass in her hand held a few melted ice cubes; he touched it to take it from her. She did not resist, her head was bowed. In the hushed space walled by their bodies Piet asked, "How goes it, Jan-Jan? How's your beautiful shrink?"

"That bastard," she said, without looking up, "that son of a bitch. He won't tell me to stop seeing Harold."

"We all thought you'd stopped seeing Harold ages ago. Ever since your goodness and health regime."

Now she did look up. "You're nice, Piet. Naïve but nice."

He asked her, "Why is it your psychiatrist's job to tell you to stop seeing Harold?"

"That's what *he* says," she said. "Because I love him, that's why. He's a fat old Kraut with a brace on one leg and I love him, he's a total fink but I adore him, and if he gave even the simplest kind of a fart about me he'd tell me to stop sleeping with Harold. But he won't. He doesn't. The old re-tard."

"What *does* the man tell you?"

"I've been going now five months and the only hint he's ever dropped is that because of the pharmaceutical business every time I take a pill I'm having intercourse with my father, it's his seed. I said to him, What am I supposed to do when I get a headache and need two aspirin, dial a prayer?"

"Dear lovely Janet, don't cry. Tell me instead, should Angela go? Ever since you started, she's wanted to go. What's my duty as a husband?"

"Don't let her. Get her a lover, send her to Yugoslavia, anything but this. God, it's degrading. It'll get her all mixed up and she's so serene. She doesn't know how neurotic she is."

"She's beginning to. She tells me she feels too detached, as if she's already dead."

"Mm, I know that feeling. Angela and I are somewhat alike."

"Yes, that's what she says too. She says you both have big bosoms and it makes you both melancholy."

"Let Angela speak for herself. I'm not sure I like being somebody's twin. Are you going to get me another bourbon or not?"

While Piet was at the drink table, Freddy Thorne sidled up to him and said, "Could we talk a moment? Alone."

"Freddy, how exciting! Just little old me and big old you?"

"Notice I'm not smiling."

"But I can see your skull smiling through, behind those poodgy lips."

"How much have you had to drink?"

"Never ask an Irishman that question at a wake. Eh cup quaffed fer sorree's sake isn't nae cup at all. Stop standing there looking portentous. I have to take Janet her drink. I think I'm falling in love with Janet."

But by his return with the drink, Janet was deep in conversation with Harold, and Piet let himself be led to a corner by Freddy, the corner behind the unstrung harpframe.

"Piet," Freddy said, biting the word short. "I'll give you this cold turkey. I know about you and Georgene."

"Cold turkey? I thought that was how dope addicts broke the habit. Or am I thinking of the day after Thanksgiving?"

"I told you that night at the Constantines to lay off. Remember?"

"Was that the night you were Chiang Kai-shek?"

"And just now I see you and she having a cozy-type talk in the middle of the room. Righty-right?"

"I don't care what they say at the State Department, I think we should let you invade. Unleash Freddy Thorne, I'm always saying, as our many mutual friends will testify."

Freddy said nothing. Piet found the lack of any answer a frightening void. He asked, "How do you think you know this?" When again no answer came, he asked, "What do you think you know?"

"She told me herself. You and she were lovers."

"Georgene?"

"Well, did she lie?"

"She might have, to get back at you for something else. Or you might be lying to me. When is this supposed to have happened?"

"Don't play games. You know when."

"All right. I confess. It happened last summer. We were tennis partners. I lost my head, her pretty white dress and freckles and all, I flung her right down on the service line and we conceded the set six-love. I'm sorry. I'm sorry, I'm sorry, I'm sorry." His mouth felt very dry, though his third martini was light in his hand: empty, flown, the olive a tame green egg.

Freddy tried, with some success, to gather himself into a menacing mass, a squinting cloud, his narrow hairless skull majestic. When he frowned, forked wrinkles spread back on his pate. "I'm going to hurt you," he told Piet, and stalked toward the kitchen, for more ice.

Angela, seeing Piet shaken, left Ben lecturing to air and came to her husband and asked, "What were you and Freddy saying? You're pale as a ghost."

"He was telling me I must have my teeth straightened. Ow. My mouth hurts."

"You won't tell me. Was it about me?"

"Angel, you've got it. He asked me for the honor of your hand. He said he's been in love with you for years."

"Oh, he always says that."

"He does?"

"It's his way of bugging me."

"But you like it. I can tell by your face that you like hearing crap like that."

"Why not? Why are you so mean about Freddy? What has he ever done to you?"

"He threatens my primitive faith," Piet told his wife.

Foxy came into the room with Ken. She wore a strapless silver gown. Her breasts were milk-proud. There was a slow luminous preening of her upper body as she turned, searching for Piet in the mad shadows. The Whitmans' entrance at the front door had disturbed the air of the house, for the candleflames now underwent a struggle and the furniture and walls seemed to stagger and billow. She had come for him. She had abandoned her house and warm baby on this tragic night solely to seek him out, to save him from harm amid this foul crowd. He heard her explain to Georgene, "We had the sitter all lined up and thought we'd come for a little while just to make it worthwhile for her—she's Doc Allen's daughter and we don't want to discourage her when we're just beginning, we've never *needed* sitters before. Then after she came we sat around for the longest while unable to tear ourselves away from the television."

"What's happening now?" Roger's deep voice inquired.

"Oh," Foxy said, "mostly old film clips. What are really heartbreaking are the press conferences. He was so quick and sassy and, I don't know, attentive. He somehow brought back the *fun* in being an American." Piet saw that as she spoke she held close to her husband's arm, sheltering. Ken stood erect and pale in impeccable black. His studs were onyx.

"I loved him," Bea Guerin cried, in a flung voice whose woe seemed distant within it, a woe calling from an underworld, "I could never have voted for him, I really don't believe in all those wishy-washy socialist things he wanted, I think people must be themselves even if it's only to suffer, but I *loved* the way he held himself, and dressed, never wearing a hat or an overcoat, I mean."

"The terrible sadness," Frank Appleby said, "of those strange wall eyes."

Marcia asked, "Were they really wall? I thought it was just he was always reading a Teleprompter."

Music translucently flooded the room. Doris Day, "Stars Fell on Alabama." Freddy loved Doris Day. Freddy was all heart and as American as apple pie and Swapsies.

"Freddy!" Carol cried. "You angel! Where's Roger?" The Thornes' rug of interwoven rush rosettes was rolled to the legs of the satin chaise longue, and Carol and Roger, she lithely, he stiffly, danced. "Oh," she cried, "your hand is icy!"

"From holding a drink," he muttered, scowling, embarrassed, and on the bony stem of her naked back set his hand edgewise, curled in a limp half-fist like a sleeping child's.

The others watched uneasily. In moving to get his wife and himself a drink, Ken Whitman fastidiously skirted the bare floor and, waiting for Freddy to bring ice from the kitchen, talked softly with Janet. Ben Saltz moved to be beside Foxy. Her gestures expressed pleasure at seeing him again, after his long absence from parties; then, in response to words of his, she looked down at her flat soft stomach and obligingly, not displeased, enjoying in his Jewishness the ghost of Peter, blushed. Angela touched Piet's arm and asked, "Shall we dance?"

"Do you want to? It seems blasphemous, waltzing on the poor guy's grave."

"It does, it is, but we must. It's terrible taste, but we can't let Roger and Carol do it alone. They're getting too embarrassed."

She was familiar and thick and pliant in his arms; he had never learned proper steps and in the course of their marriage she had learned to follow his vague stridings lightly, as if they made a pattern, her thighs and pelvis gently cushioned against his. Their heights were equal. She rarely wore perfume, so her hair and skin released a scent unspecific but absolutely good, like water, or life, or existence itself, considered in contrast to the predominant vacuum between the stars.

"Where," he asked her, "are Irene and Eddie?"

"In the kitchen talking about air pollution."

"They are the *smuggest* couple," Piet said. "After all that fuss. I hope you take Irene's injured confidences henceforth with a lick of salt." He meant a saltlick, a large cake such as were mounted in the barnyards of Michigan dairy farms, but it came out sounding like a tiny amount, less than a grain.

"Well Ben," Angela said, "is talking to your ex-pregnant girl friend, so Irene *had* to go back to Eddie."

"That's too complicated," Piet said, trying to match his feet to the change of tempo as "Stars Fell on Alabama" became "Soft as the Starlight." "And the other lady is surely ex-pregnant but she was never my girl friend."

"I was kidding. Don't resist me like that. Relax. Glide."

"I hate this party, frankly. When can we go home?"

"Piet, it's the sort of party you love."

"I feel we're insulting Kennedy."

"Not at all. Yesterday, he was just our President way down in Washington, and now he belongs to all of us. He's right here. Don't you feel him?"

He looked into her blue eyes amazed. There was an enduring strangeness to Angela that continued through all disillusions to enchant him. Perceiving this, he resented his subtle bondage, and burned to tear Foxy from Ben, to trample on his bushy face with boots. Ineptly he stepped on Angela's toe.

Now Ken and Janet joined them on the dance floor, and Freddy and Irene. Above his black shoulder the twin circumflex of her perfect eyebrows seemed a lifted wingbeat. Her hair was parted precisely in the middle. Eddie Constantine came as if to capture her but at the last moment veered off and cut in to dance with Angela. Piet went and asked Georgene, standing gazing by the table of lightened bottles and dirtied glasses.

In his arms she asked him, "Do you think it's too early for the ham? We bought some salmon but no Catholics have come."

He accused her: "You and your noble privacy. Your husband just lowered the boom on me."

"Freddy? What on earth for?"

"For having an affair with you."

"Don't tease. Our times together were very precious, at least to me."

"Tease! He said you yourself told him everything. Postures, dates, phases of the moon."

"That's such a lie. I've *never* admitted anything about us, though he's tried to get me to often enough. It's the way he works. I hope *you* didn't admit anything."

"I didn't, but it was sheer perversity. I assumed he had me cold."

"He talks to Carol and Janet all the time; maybe one of them has made him think he knows something."

"Are you sure he doesn't? Are you sure you didn't tell him some night before dropping off to sleep, figuring I was a lost cause anyway, and needing something to even some score with, like an affair he'd had with Carol."

"Carol? Do you know this?" He loved feeling her experience fear in his arms; there was a dissolution of the bodily knit indistinguishable from sexual willingness.

"No. But he's over there all the time, and Carol's not too fussy.

Not," he added hastily, "that Freddy isn't a gorgeous hunk of man."

She ignored his unkind parody of tact, asking instead, "And you? *Are* you a lost cause?"

"Soft as the Starlight" became "It Must Have Been Moonglow."

"Well," Piet said carefully, "more and more, as Freddy acts as if he knows."

"Oh, Freddy. He doesn't want to know *any*thing, he just wants people to *think* he knows *every*thing. But if I'm not worth the trouble to you, there's no use talking, is there, Piet?" With her quick athletic firmness she put her hands on his arms and pushed herself out of his embrace. "Only don't come running to *me* the next time you need a little change of ass." Watching her retreat, he realized that all these months, all through Foxy, he had been considering Georgene still his mistress.

Foxy was across the room dancing with Frank Appleby. They moved together placidly, without reference to the beat, silver locked in lead's grip. "Wrap Your Troubles in Dreams" became the song. Marcia was at hand and, slithery quick, she nestled against his damp shirtfront, asking, "Piet, what's happened to you? You're not funny like you used to be."

"I never was trying to be funny."

"You were too. You were so delighted to be with us, at the beach, skiing, anywhere. Now you've stopped caring. You think we're ugly, silly people."

"Marcia, I love you. I bet you were class secretary in school."

"Is it your work? What are you doing now that it's too cold to put up any more cozy little horrors on Indian Hill?"

"We've been saved by the bell. Just the other week we got a big inside job on Divinity. They hauled off Gertrude Tarbox to a nursing home and the bank in New Bedford that held the mortgage is turning the house into offices. We've taken out three truckloads of *National Geographics*." Telling Marcia this troubled him, for he had been working in this house all day, alone, operating a big sander on the floors of what had once been a chandeliered dining room. Lost in the hypnotic whine and snarl of the machine, fascinated by the disappearance of decades of dirt and paint, by this reversal into clean wood, he had been ignorant of the President's assassination until Jazinski returned at three from a mysteriously long lunch hour. Deafened by the sander, Piet had let the bullet pass painlessly through him.

Marcia asked irritably, "Why does anyone need office space in Tarbox?"

"Oh, you'd be surprised. There's a crying shortage downtown. Insurance companies, chiropractors. AA wants to set up a branch here. This isn't the idyllic retreat you moved to, Marcia. We're sadly suburban. There's going to be a big shopping center between here and Lacetown. Isn't Frank on the committee to squeeze more train service out of the poor old New Haven, or the MBTA, or the Lionel Company, or somebody?"

"Piet, when are you going to get away from Gallagher? Frank and Harold were talking at lunch in Boston to a man who knows the South Shore and he expects Gallagher to go bankrupt. The banks own him twice over and he keeps gambling. If the nuns hadn't bailed him out last summer he couldn't have met another payment."

"No, sweetie, you don't understand. Matt can't lose. We live in an expanding universe." To quiet her, to quell her critical spirit, he dipped his hand to her buttocks; they were narrow and nipped-in like the responsive little wheels at the front of a tractor. At a guiding touch from him she brought her body closer, so close his lips shrank from the cold aura of her dangling earring. He murmured, "How *is* Frank, speaking of the MBTA?"

"The same. Maybe worse. Simply going to bed doesn't soothe him any more. He needs to get out from under that heavy neurotic bitch."

"Oh hell, we all need to get out from under."

"Not me. I need Harold. To hurt me. He's beautifully cruel, don't you think?"

"Beautifully?"

"And yet gallant, in an old-fashioned way. I'm his, but he respects my independence. I think we're a very nice old-fashioned couple, don't you?"

"Antique. Victoria and Prince Albert. But let's talk about me.

Don't I need to get out from under Angela?"

"Oh Piet," Marcia said impatiently, "without Angela, you'd die."

Struck empty by this, unable to answer, he sang with the gauze-voiced record into the curled cool shell of her ear, "*Castles may tum*ble, that's *fate* after *all*, life's really *fun*ny that *way*."

She mistook his mood and flattened her body more sinuously against his. Her fingertips found the small hairs at the back of his neck, her pelvis lifted an inch. This a woman twice spoken for: he glanced around the room for rescue. Ken was still dancing with Janet. His temples looked gray as they circled near a candle. Freddy had replaced Eddie with Angela. Eddie and Irene had gone to stand against the wall, talking. Frank Appleby was making himself another drink. Foxy had fled. Doris Day's song became "Moonglow." Harold, catching Piet's eyes, came over, dug his fingers into Marcia's sleeping arm so cruelly her olive skin leaped white between his nails, and said, "Now on the idiot box they're talking about giving him an eternal flame. *Une flamme éternelle.* For Christ's sake, he wasn't the Unknown Soldier, he was a cleverly manufactured politician who happened to catch a nobody's bullet. *Chérie, es-tu ivre?*"

Marcia said huskily, having slept against Piet's body, now awoken, "Yes."

"Then come with me. *Pardonnez-nous*, Piet."

"Gladly. I'll go catch a bullet." Piet made his fourth martini, silvery. Foxy. Was she in the woods? Where was Ben? Not among the men dancing. Like a moth to flame was she to Jews. Abram over Lot. Ben's fingers, deft from miniaturizing, gliding down the tawny long insides of her stocking-topped thighs to fumble in the nigger-lipped pale fur there. Her clitoris welling through a milky film slowly, ruby rosy, watchsprings in a pansy shape. All shadowy smiling distances, Foxy would stretch and guide. Ben leonine, in the concealing shade of a Thorne-owned bush. Beyond these black windows she had opened to another lover.

Piet turned in pain from the window and it seemed that the couples were gliding on the polished top of Kennedy's casket. An island of light in a mourning nation. "Close Your Eyes." "Cuh-

lozzz yur eyeszz": the velvet voice from Hollywood whispered
an inch inside Piet's ear. The olive egg in his martini had been
abandoned by its mother high and dry. His cankers hurt, especially the one his tongue had to stretch to reach, low and left on
the front gum, at the root of his lip. A maze of membranes, never
could have evolved from algae unassisted. God gave us a boost.
He felt he shouldn't have another drink. No supper, empty stomach. Marcia's slithering had stirred him. Half-mast, subsided,
lumpy. His kidneys signaled: the sweetness pealing of a silent
bell: relieve me. The Thornes' bathroom. There Georgene would
wash herself before and after. Said his jizz ran down her leg, too
much of it, should screw Angela more. Hexagonal little floor
tiles, robin's-egg toilet paper, posh purple towels. *Welcome to
the post-pill* . . . Sashaying from the shower nude, her pussy of
a ferny freshness. The grateful lumpiness following love. Well
done, thou good and faithful. Turning up the familiar stairs, his
black foot firm on the swaying treads, he glanced into the dark
side room, where a few obscure heads were watching a weary
flickering rerun of the casket's removal from the belly of the
airplane. Ben was there, bent forward, his profile silvered as in
Sunday-school oleographs, facing Sinai. Roger and Carol, sharing a hassock. Frank sucked a cigar whose smoke was charged
with the dartings of light as casket became widow, widow became Johnson, Johnson became commentator. Ghouls. Foxy
must be in the kitchen. The paneled bathroom door was closed.
Tactfully he tapped. Her musical voice called, "Just a min-ute."
Piet said, "It's me," and pushed. The door gave. She was sitting
on the toilet in her uplifted silver gown, startled, a patch of blue
paper like a wisp of sky in her hand. The pressure of the oval seat
widened her garter-rigged and pallid thighs; she was perched
forward; her toes but not her heels touched the hexagonal tiles of
the floor. "I love you" was pulled from him like a tooth. The
mirror above the basin threw him back at himself. His flat taut
face looked flushed and astonished, his mouth agape, his black tie
askew.
Foxy said in a whisper reverberant in the bright tiled space,
"You're mad to be in here." Then with incongruous deliberation
she patted herself, let the paper drop into the oval of water below,

and, half-turning on the seat, depressed the silver handle. Sluggishly the toilet flushed: Georgene used to complain about the low water pressure on the hill. Foxy rose from the vortex and smoothed her gown downward. Facing him, she seemed tall, faintly challenging and hostile, her closed lips strangely bleached by pale pink lipstick, newly chic. He made sure the door behind them was shut, and moved past her to urinate standing. With a pang, initially reluctant, his golden arc occurred. "God," he said, "it's a relief to see you alone. When the hell can we meet?"

She spoke hurriedly, above his splashing. "I wasn't sure you wanted to. You've been very distant."

"Ever since you've had the baby I've been frightened to death of you. I assumed it was the end of us."

"That's not true. Unless you want it to be true."

"The fact is, all fall I've been frightened of everything. Death, my work, Gallagher, my children, the stars. It's been hideous." A concluding spurt, somewhat rhetorical, and a dismissive drying shake. He tucked himself in. "My whole life seems just a long falling."

"But it's *not*. You have a good life. Your lovely family, your nice square house, me if you want me. We can't talk here. Call me Monday. I'm alone again."

He flushed, but the water closet had not filled. "Wait. Please. Let me see your breasts."

"They're all milky."

"I know. Just for a moment. Please. I do need it."

They listened for steps on the stairs; there were none. Music below, and the television monologue. Her mouth opened and her tongue, red as sturgeon, touched her upper lip as she reached behind her to undo snaps. Her gown and bra peeled down in a piece. Fruit.

"Oh. God."

She blushed in answer. "I feel so gross."

"So veiny and full. So hard at the tops, here."

"Don't get them started. I must go home in an hour."

"And nurse."

"Yes. What funny sad lines you're getting here, and here. Don't frown, Piet. And gray hairs. They're new."

"Nurse me."

"Oh darling. No."

"Nurse me."

She covered one breast, alarmed, but he had knelt, and his broad mouth fastened on the other. The thick slow flow was at first suck sickeningly sweet. The bright bathroom light burned on his eyelids and seemed to dye his insides a deep flowing rose, down to the pained points of his knees on the icy tile. Foxy's hand lightly cupped the curve of the back of his skull and now guided him closer into the flood of her, now warned by touching his ear that he was giving her pain. He opened his eyes; the nipple of her other breast jutted cherry-red between ivory fingers curled in protection; he closed his eyes. Pulses of stolen food scoured his tongue, his gums; she toyed with his hair, he caressed her clothed buttocks. She was near drowning him in rose.

Knocks struck rocklike at the unlocked door inches behind them. Harsh light flooded him. He saw Foxy's free hand, ringed, grope and cup the sympathetic lactation of the breast jutting unmouthed. She called out, as musically as before, "One moment, please."

Angela's lucid polite voice answered, "Oops, sorry, Foxy. Take your time."

"All ri-ight," Foxy sang back, giving Piet a frantic look of interrogation. Her bare breasts giant circles. A Christian slave stripped to be tortured.

His body thundered with fear. His hands were jerking like puppets on strings but his brain took perspective from the well-lit room in which he was trapped. There was no other door. The shower curtain was translucent glass, two sliding panels; his shape would show. There was a little window. Its sill came up to his chest. Realizing the raising of the sash would make noise, he motioned Foxy to flush the toilet. As she bent to touch the silver handle the shape of her breasts changed, hanging forward, long-tipped udders dripping cloudy drops. He undid the brash catch and shoved up the sash as the water closet again, feebly, drained. Setting one black dancing slipper on the lip of the tub, he hoisted himself into the black square of air headfirst. Trees on this side of the house, elms, but none near enough to grasp. His hands could touch only vertical wood and freezing air pricked by stars. Too late he knew he should have gone feet first; he must drop. This the shady rural side of the house. Soft grass. The toilet had quieted and left no noise to cover the sounds of his scrambling as he changed position. Foxy thought to turn both faucets on full. By logic she must next open the door to Angela. Piet backed out of the window. Foxy was standing by the roaring faucets staring at him and mopping herself with a purple washcloth and resecuring the bodice of her silver gown. He imagined she smiled. No time to think about it. He stood on the slick tub lip and got a leg through the little window and doing a kind of handstand on the radiator cover maneuvered the other leg through also. Button. Caught. Ah. There. He slid out on his chest and dangled his weight by his hands along Thorne's undulate shingles. Loose nails, might catch on a nostril, tear his face like a fish being reamed. Air dangled under his shoes. Ten feet. Eleven, twelve. Old houses, high ceilings. Something feathery brushed his fingers gripping the sill inside the bathroom. Foxy begging him not to dare it? Angela saying it was all right, she knew? Too late. Fall. No apologies. Pushing off lightly from the wall with his slippers and trying to coil himself loosely against the shock, he let go. Falling was first a hum, then concussion: a harpstring in reverse. His heels hit the frost-baked turf; he took a somersault backwards and worried about grass stains on his tuxedo before he thought to praise God for breaking no bones. Above him, a pink face vanished and a golden window whispered shut. They were safe. He was sitting on the brittle grass, his feet in their papery slippers stinging.

The silhouette of the trunk of the elm nearest him wavered; a female voice giggled. "Piet, you're such a show-off," Bea Guerin said.

Ben Saltz's orotund voice pronounced, "That was quite a tumble. I'm impressed."

Piet stood and brushed dirt from his clothes. "What are you two doing out here?"

"Oh," Bea said, and her offhand accents seemed, out of doors, disembodied, "Ben brought me out here to watch a satellite he miniaturized something in go by overhead."

"A tiny component," Ben said. "My old outfit developed it, with maybe one or two of my bright ideas. I thought it might be passing right about now, but all we've seen is a shooting star."

"So lovely," Bea said, and to Piet, still dizzy, the tree was talking, though the scarlet of her dress was growing distinct, "the way it fell, flaring all greeny-blue, like a match being struck, then nothing. I hadn't seen a comet since a child."

"That wasn't a comet," Ben said. "That was a meteor, an inert chunk of matter, of space dust you might say, burning up with friction upon contact with our atmosphere. Comets are incandescent and have elliptical orbits."

"Oh Ben, you're wonderful, you know everything, doesn't he, Piet? But now tell us, whatever were you and Foxy *doing?*"

"Why do you say Foxy?"

"We saw her close the window. Didn't you?"

"Are you sure it was Foxy? I thought it was Angela."

"Angela, poo. Of course it was Foxy, that lovely honey hair. Were you making love? In the bathroom?"

"Boy, that takes nerves of iron," Ben said. "Not to mention pretty well-padded bodies. I've tried it in a boat and it just wasn't my style, very frankly."

"Don't be silly," Piet said. "Of course we weren't. You two are grotesque." Perhaps anger could dissolve this unexpected couple.

"Why is that *silly?*" Bea cried in a soft raising wail, as when she had mourned Kennedy. "Everyone knows about you and Foxy. Your truck is parked down there all the time. We think it's *nice.*"

"My truck hasn't been there for months."

"Well my dear, she's hardly been in a condition to."

"You know," Ben said, "I wonder about that. Forbidding intercourse during pregnancy. I suspect it will turn out to be one more pseudo-medical superstition, like not breast-feeding because it wasn't sanitary, which they sincerely believed in the Thirties. I *made* Irene breast-feed, and she's grateful."

"You're a wonderful husband, Ben," Piet said. "Now you're making her work and she's grateful again."

Bea put her hand, trembling, on his forearm. "Now don't be

sarcastic to Ben, just because you yourself are embarrassed. We won't tell anybody we saw you jump. Except Roger and Irene."

"Well, who shall I tell about you and Ben necking out here?"

"You may tell one person," Bea said, "those are the rules, but you mayn't tell Angela, because she'll tell Freddy Thorne, and then everybody will know. I'm freezing."

All three, they went back into the house together. Doris Day was singing "Stardust." Angela was coming downstairs from the bathroom. She asked, "Where have *you* all been?"

Piet told her, "Ben says he made one of the stars out there, but we couldn't find it."

"Why were you looking under the trees? I *won*dered who was mumbling outside; I could hear you from the bathroom." Suspended halfway up the stairs, she shimmered like a chandelier. Now that he had safely rejoined the party, Piet was piqued by Bea's assumption that Angela told Freddy Thorne everything. Wanting to ask his wife if this were true, he asked her instead, "How much have you drunk?"

"Just enough," she answered, descending. Parting an invisible curtain with her hands, she floated past him.

Piet hurried on; he had questions to ask of every woman. He kept tasting cloying milk. Foxy was in the kitchen, talking to Janet, who turned her back, so the lovers could talk. He asked Foxy hoarsely, "Make it OK?"

"Of course," she whispered.

He went on, "Did I imagine it, or were you standing there smiling at me?"

She glanced about to see they were not being overheard. "You were so manic, it was like a silent comedy. I wanted to tell you not to be silly and kill yourself, but we couldn't make any talking noises, and anyway you were clearly in love with the idea of jumping."

"In love! I was terrified, and now my right knee is beginning to hurt."

"You were terrified of Angela. Why? After all, so your husband is in the bathroom with another woman. It's not the end of the world. Maybe you were helping me get something out of my eye."

Piet drew on his impoverished reserves of moral indignation. "I'm shocked," he said, "that you would laugh. With all our love in the balance."

"I tried to catch your hand at the last minute; but you let go." Her smile became artificial, feral. "We better stop talking. Freddy Thorne has a fishy eye on us and here comes Harold Little."

Harold, petitely storming, his slicked-down hair mussed in pinfeathers in back, said, continuing a conversation begun elsewhere, "If I believed in the omnipotent Lord Jesus, I'd say this was punishment for his letting our one staunch ally in Southeast Asia get nailed to please the pansy left in this country. *La gauche efféminée.*"

"Oh Harold," Foxy said, mothering, "in," "don't talk like that, you're imitating somebody else. Cardinal Richelieu. You think we'll think you're cute if you go right-wing. We think you're cute now. Don't we, Piet?"

"Harold," Piet asked, "have you thought of asking the young widow for her hand? You and Madame Nhu would make a lovely couple. You both have a fiery way of expressing yourselves."

"You both speak French," Foxy added.

"The trouble with this *merde*-heap of a country," Harold said, sullenly flattered by their teasing, "there's no respectable way to not be a liberal."

Piet said, "Why, look at me. I'm not a liberal. Look at all your fellow brokers. They swindle the poor and pimp for the rich. Nothing liberal about that."

"They're idiots." In French: "*Idiots.*" Harold told Piet, "You never venture outside of this bucolic paradise, so you don't know what imbeciles there are. They really *care*," he said, "about the difference between driving a Buick and a Cadillac."

"That's too hideous to believe," Piet said and, seeing Carol alone by the harpframe, went over to her. "What have you been telling that jerk Freddy Thorne?"

"I don't know," she said, "but I'll tell you this, Piet Hanema. He was about the only person who kept coming around when the rest of you were ostracizing Eddie and me because of poor old Irene. Poor old Irene my ass. Did you see her take Eddie into the kitchen as soon as they got here?"

"You beauty. Let's dance." Doris Day was now singing "Under a Blanket of Blue." Carol's back beneath his hand was extensively naked, bony and supple and expressive of the immense ease with which in bed his hairy long arms could encircle and sooth her slender nerved-up dancer's nakedness. His thumb grazed the edge of one shoulder blade; his palm lay moist across her spine's raised ridge; his fingertips knew the fatty beginnings of her sides. Pliant sides that would downslip, gain muscle, and become the world's wide pivot and counterthrusting throne, which in even a brittle woman is ample and strong. With a clothy liquidity Carol was yielding herself up, grazing easily the length of him. The bodies of women are puzzle pieces that can fit or not, as they decide. Imperceptibly Carol shaded the tilt of her pelvis so his penis felt caressed. She rubbed herself lightly from side to side, bent her neck so he could see her breasts, blew into his ear. The music stopped. She backed off, her face frowningly dilated, and sighed. She told him, "You're such a bastard," and walked away, naked from nape to waist. Mermaid. Slip from his hands like a piece of squeezed soap.

Such a bastard. When he had been told, at college, coming in late from a date that had left his mouth dry and his fly wet and his fingertips alive with the low-tide smell of cunt, about his parents' accident, his thought had been that had he been there, been there in Grand Rapids in any capacity, his presence would have altered the combination of events, deflected their confluence, enough to leave his mother and father alive. In the same way, he felt guilty about Kennedy's death, when Jazinski told him of it, in the silence of the sander.

Irene Saltz floated toward him, her eyebrows arched above bright tears, scintillant in candlelight. "Are you happy, Irene?" he asked her.

"I still love him, if that's what you're asking," she said.

"You want to be laughed at," Piet told her, "like me. We're scapegoat-types."

Triumphantly upheld by Freddy flanked by Georgene and Angela, the ham, the warm and fat and glistening ham, scotched and festooned with cloves, was fetched in from the kitchen. Bea Guerin, her washed-out hair, paler than wind, done up loosely in a psyche knot, followed holding a salad bowl heaped full of oily lettuce, cucumber slices, avocados, tomatoes, parsley, chives, chicory, escarole. Their blessings were beyond counting. With a cruciform clashing of silver Freddy began to sharpen the carving knife. Out of the gathering audience Frank Appleby boomed, "Upon what meat does this our Caesar feed, that he is grown so great?"

Georgene explained, "I had salmon for the Catholics but since none of them came I'll give it to the children for lunch."

Freddy's eyeglasses flickered blindly as he carved; he was expert. Nobody but Freddy could cut slices so thin. "Take, eat," he intoned, laying each slice on a fresh plate a woman held out to him. "This is his body, given for thee."

"Freddy!" Marcia little-Smith cried. "That's disgusting."

"Don't you think," Bea Guerin asked, her voice pure and plaintive and proud of sounding lost, "we should be fasting or something?"

"Fasting or fucking," Freddy Thorne said, with surgical delicacy laying on another slice.

Ken Whitman watched silent from near the wall, beneath an African mask. Ben Saltz, eagerly hunchbacked, fetched radishes and bread to the buffet table. Carol carried two bottles of burgundy black as tar in the candlelight. Piet, being passed a plate, chewed but without saliva; his mouth felt full of ashes that still burned. Suddenly old, he sought a chair. His knee did hurt.

Still limping, he visited Foxy the following Tuesday, when the nation resumed normal life. The three days of omnipresent mourning had passed for these couples of Tarbox as three tranced holidays each alike in pattern. The men each afternoon had played touch football on the field behind the Applebys, by Joy Creek, while the women and children stayed indoors watching television in the library. During dull stretches of the Washington ceremonies or the Dallas postmortems (Piet and his children, just back from church, were watching when Oswald was shot; Ruth calmly turned and asked him, "Was that real?" while Nancy silently stuck her thumb in her mouth) some of the women would come outdoors and arrange themselves in Frank's hay and watch their men race red-faced up and down the hummocky field, shouting for the ball. These days on the verge of winter were autumnally fair, struck through with warmth until the swift lengthening of the shadows. At game's end, that long weekend, the men and children would drink from paper cups the cider someone (the Whitmans, the little-Smiths) had brought from the orchard along the beach road, and then there would be a general drift indoors, to cocktails and a long sitting around the television set while the children grew cranky and raided Janet's supply of crackers, peanut butter, raisins, and apples. Run and rerun as if on the revolving drum of insomnia, Haile Selassie and General De Gaulle bobbed together down Pennsylvania Avenue, Jack Ruby's stripper drawlingly allowed that his temper could be mean, Lee Oswald, smirking, was led down a crowded corridor toward a lurching hat and wildly tipping cameras. The widow and one of the brothers, passing so near the camera they blurred, bent obliquely over an indeterminate tilted area of earth and flowers. The dome was distant in the southern sunshine. Amid drumrolls, the casket gleamed and was gone. The children came crying, bullied by others. Another drink? It was time to go home, but not yet, not quite yet. It was evening before they packed the children into the cars. The space in the cars as they drove home was stuffy with unasked questions, with the unsayable trouble of a king's murder, a queasy earthquake for little children, a funny stomach-gnawing only sleep eased. School and Tuesday came as a relief.

Piet parked his truck in plain sight in the driveway. The Whitmans' surviving lilacs were leafless and his eyes winced in the unqualified light. Every season has a tone of light we forget each year: a kitchen with frosted windows, a leaf-crowded side porch, the chalky noons of spring, the chill increase, as leaves fall, of neutral clarity. October's orange had ebbed in the marshes; they stretched dun gray to the far rim of sand. The tide was low; the sea lay sunken in the wider channels like iron being cast. Foxy answered his second ring.

Opening the door, she looked delicate, as if recovered from an illness, or as if she had just chastised herself with a severely hot bath. "Oh. You. Wonderful."

"Is it? Are you alone? I've come to see the baby."

"But not me?"

Yet, once inside, on the loop rug, he embraced and held her as if there were no baby, as if there were no one alive in this sunken barren world but themselves. Beneath her coarse house smock, between her lifted breasts and bony pelvis, a defenseless hollow felt placed against his memory of her swollen belly. A snuffling aggrieved sound, less crying than a scratching at some portal of need, arose in the living room. Foxy clung to him in a pose of weeping, and reflexively he bent his head into her hair to kiss the side of her neck, and now her tongue and fingers, as if released from the timidity of long absence, tremblingly attempted to seize him, but blind as bees in a room of smoke they darted to absurd places—his unshaven chin, his jingling pockets, an eye that barely closed in time, a ticklish armpit her ardor could not unlock. He told her, "The baby's crying."

Together they went to where in the living room the baby lay breathing in a bassinet. A pearly quiet blessed its vicinity and the windows giving on the frost-charred marsh seemed to frame images thrown from within, by a magic lantern centered on the infant's untinted soul. Foxy asked, "Do you want to hold him?" and pulled the infant gently up and unceremoniously passed him to Piet's hands. Piet, cupping his broad palms under their sudden unsteady burden, let himself be astounded by, what he had forgotten, the narrowness of the buttocks, the feverish mauve skull. For a second the child appraised him with stern large eyes the color of basalt; then the irises crossed and the muscles in his forehead bulged like elastic levers to squeeze the eyebrows down. The baby began to cry. Fearing his noise would betray their secrecy, Piet returned him to Foxy. Brusquely, she jiggled the bundle against her bosom.

Piet asked, "What is his name?"

"You must know it."

"Angela told me but I've forgotten. An old-fashioned name, I thought. For such a modern couple."

"Tobias."

"That's not the cat?"

"Cotton is the cat. Tobias was Ken's grandfather."

"Why didn't you name him after Ken's father?"

"Ken apparently doesn't like his father."

"I thought his father was perfect, the perfect Hartford lawyer."

"He is. But Ken was very definite, I was surprised."

"Ken is full of surprises, now and then, isn't he? A fascinating fellow."

"Are you trying to sell him to me?"

Piet asked her, "Why are we fencing?"

Foxy said, "I don't know. The baby upsets you."

"I love the baby. I love you as a mother."

"But not as a mistress any more?"

"Well"—embarrassment gnawed his stomach—"you're not ready yet, are you?"

"I shouldn't make love for two more weeks but I think I could stand a little show of affection. Why are you so remote?"

"Am I?" How could he tell her, of the quietness he had found here, the sere marsh filling the windows, the serene room he had carved, its plaster walls spread wide like a wimple, of the pearly aura near the baby, of Foxy's own subdued dry grace, dry as if drained of sleep and self-concern—of this chaste charmed air and his superstitious reluctance to contaminate it? He confessed, "I just wonder if I have any business being here now."

"Why not now? What business did you ever have? I was never your wife. You came here for an extramarital screw, that was fine, I gave it to you, I loved it. Now what? I've made myself dirty by having a baby." Piet felt she too much enjoyed such tough talk, that it was something revived, on the excuse of him, from deeper in her experience. She stood with legs apart, bent forward a bit from the waist, Tobias held tight but unacknowledged in her arms. Her raised voice had lulled him to sleep. Piet loved her maternal clumsiness, her already careless confidence that the child was hers to handle.

He asked her, "How can you want me? You have this marvelous little package. You have Ken who gave it to you."

"He doesn't like it. He doesn't like the baby."

"Impossible."

Foxy began to cry. Her hair, lusterless in the dull late light, hung forward over the child. "It frightens him," she said. "I frighten him. I've always frightened him. I don't blame him, I'm a mess, Piet."

"Nonsense." His inner gnawing was transmuted into a drastic sunk feeling; he had no choice but to go to her, put his arms around her and the child, and say, "You're lovely."

Her sobbing would not stop. Her situation, including his concession and his sheltering arms, seemed to anger her increasingly. "Don't you like talking to me?"

"Of course I do."

"Don't you like talking to me at all? Don't you ever want to do anything with me except go to bed? Can't you wait a few more weeks to have me?"

"Please. Fox. Don't be so silly."

"I was afraid to take ether for fear I'd cry out your name. I go around the house saying 'Piet, Piet' to this innocent baby. I dragged poor Ken to that hideous party just to see you and you risked killing yourself rather than be found with me."

"You exaggerate. There was very little risk. I did it as much to protect you as myself."

"You're still limping from it."

"It was all that football."

"Oh, Piet. I'm beginning to nag. Don't leave me absolutely yet. You're the only thing real I have. Ken is unreal. This marsh is unreal. I'm unreal to myself, I just exist to keep this baby alive, that's all I was put here for, and it makes me *mad*."

"Don't be mad," he begged; but he himself felt anger, to be so pressed and sunk he could not spare breath to explain that for them to keep seeing each other now would be evil, all the more in that it had been good. They had been let into God's playroom, and been happy together on the floor all afternoon, but the time had come to return the toys to their boxes, and put the chairs back against the wall.

   · · ·

Ken came home from work looking more tired than she had seen him since graduate-student days. He carried a sheaf of mimeographed pre-prints and flopped them down on the hall table. "There's been a breakthrough in photosynthesis," he told her. "They've figured out something involving ferredoxin—it seems to be the point of transition between the light and dark reactions."

"What's ferredoxin?"

"A protein. An electron carrier with a very low redox potential."

"Who's figured it out?" He almost never talked to her about his work, so she was anxious to respond fruitfully. For his return she had put on a lemony cocktail dress, celebrative. Their child was six weeks old today.

"Oh," he sighed, "a couple of Japs. Actually, they're good men. Better than me. I've had it." He dropped himself into the armchair, the leather armchair they had steered up and down apartment-house stairs all over Cambridge. Feeling their life slip backwards, she panicked.

"Let *me* see," Foxy said, and went, all wifely bustle and peremptoriness, to the hall table to prove him wrong. The pamphlet on top was titled *Neurophysiological Mechanisms Underlying Behavior: Emotions and the Amygdala.* The one underneath was *Experimental Phenylketonuria: Pharmacogenetics of Seizures in Mice.* She looked no further.

To our Tarbox doppelgängers the "little" Smiths—

Another Yuletide finds us personally well and prosperous yet naturally saddened by the tragic and shocking events of this November. Man is truly "but as grass." A different sort of sadness entered our household when this September we saw young Tim, our precocious and precious baby of a few short years ago, off for his freshman year at St. Mark's. He has been home for weekends, very much the "young man," but it will be joyous to have him under the manse roof these holidays—even if he has, to our decibel's dismay, taken up the electric guitar. Meanwhile Pat, Audrey, and Gracelyn continue happily in the excellent Newton

public schools. Pat, indeed, has been honored with (and that
sound you hear is our buttons "popping" with pride)

"God," Marcia said, "the way she crawls right over poor Kennedy to tell us they can afford St. Mark's."

"To our decibel's dismay," Janet said, and both went helpless
with laughter.

The evenings before Christmas are gloomy and exciting in
downtown Tarbox: the tinfoil stars and wreaths hung from slack
wires shivering audibly in the wind, the silent crêche figures
kneeling in the iron pavilion, the schoolchildren shrieking home
from school in darkness, the after-supper shoppers hurrying
head-down as if out on illicit errands and fearful of being seen,
the Woolworth's and Western Auto and hardware stores wideawake with strained hopeful windows and doors that can't help
yawning. This year the civic flags were at half-mast and some
stores—the old jeweler's, the Swedish bakery—had forsaken the
usual displays. In the brilliantly lit and remorselessly caroling five
and ten, Piet, shopping with his daughters for their present to
Angela, met Bea Guerin at the candle counter. At the sight of
her small tipped head, considering, her hair stretched to shining,
his heart quickened and his hands, heavily hanging, tingled. She
turned and noticed him; her instinctive smile tightened as she
gauged his disproportionate gladness at seeing her.

Ruth and Nancy wandered on uncertainly down an aisle of
kitchen gadgets. Their faces looked dirty in the crass light; his
daughters seemed waifs lost and sickened in this wilderness of
trash. Their puzzled greed exasperated Piet. He let them go down
the aisle and knew that they would settle on a package of cute
Pop-pattern dish towels and a red-handled sharpener that would
be lost by New Year's.

Innocent of children, Bea seemed strangely young, unsullied.
She wore a green wool cape and elfish suède shoes. She held a box
of long chartreuse tapers. More than young, she seemed unattached, a puckish interloper meditating theft. Piet approached her
warily, accusing, "Candles?"

"Roger likes them," she said. "I find them eerie, really. I'm afraid of fire."

"Because you live in a wooden house? We all do."

"He even likes real candles on the tree, because his family had them. He's such an old fogey." Her face, upturned toward him in the claustrophobic brightness, was grave, tense, homely, frightened. Her hairdo pulled her forehead glossily tight. His parents' house had held prints of Dutch paintings of girls with such high shining brows.

"Speaking of your house—"

Nancy had returned to him and pulled at his thumb with an irritating hand tacky from candy. "Daddy, come look with us."

"In a second, sweet."

"Come look with us *now*. Ruthie's teasing me, she won't let me *say* anything." Her face, round as a cookie, was flyspecked with freckles.

"I'll be right there," he told her. "You go back and tell Ruthie I said not to act like a big shot. You each are supposed to find your own present for Mommy. Maybe you can find some pretty dish towels."

Against her better judgment Nancy obeyed and wandered back to her sister. Piet said to Bea, "Poor child, she should be in bed. Christmas is cruel."

Having no children, she was blind to their domination, and her eyes expressed admiration of his patience, when in truth he had slighted an exhausted child. Bea prompted him, "Speaking of my house—"

"Yes," Piet said, and felt himself begin to blush, to become enormously red in this bath of plastic glare, "I've been wondering, would you mind, some morning or afternoon, if I came around and inspected the restoring job I did for you four years ago? I experimented, hanging the summer beam from an A-brace in the attic, and I'd like to see if it settled. Has your plaster cracked anywhere?"

Something by the side of his nose, some cruelly illuminated imperfection, held her gaze; she said slowly, "I haven't noticed any cracking, but you're welcome to come and look."

"But would you *like* me to?"

Bea's face, its almost lashless lids puffily framing her eyes at a slight slant, became even more of a child's, a child's piqued by Christmas greed yet hesitant, distrustful of gifts.

"Once," he prompted, "you would have liked me to."

"No, I would like you to; it's just"—she groped, and her eyes, a paler blue than Angela's, lifted to his—"a house, you know."

"I know it's a house. A lovely house. Tell me what would be a good morning?"

"Today's Thursday. Let's do it after the weekend. Monday?"

"Tuesday would be better for me. Monday's my catch-up day. Around ten?"

"Not before. I don't know what's the matter with me, I can't seem to get dressed in the mornings any more."

"Daddy. She is *being* a *pesty* crybaby and I am *not* being a *big shot.*" Ruth had stormed up to them, trailing tearful Nancy, and Piet was shocked to see that his elder daughter was, though not yet as tall as Bea, of a size that was comparable. While her father had been looking elsewhere she had abandoned the realm of the miniature. In this too strong light he also saw that her heated face, though still a child's, contained the smoky something, the guarded inwardness, of womanhood.

Bea beside him, as if licensed now to know his thoughts, said proprietarily, "She'll be large, like Angela."

At the New Year's Eve party the Hanemas gave, Foxy asked Piet, "Who is she?"

"Who is who?" They were dancing in the trim colonial living room, which was too small for the purpose. In pushing back the chairs and tables Frank Appleby and Eddie Constantine had scarred the eggshell-white wainscoting. The old pine floorboards creaked under the unaccustomed weight of the swaying couples, and Piet feared they would all be plunged into his cellar. Giving the party had been more Angela's idea than his; lately she, who used to be more aloof from their friends than he, seemed to enjoy them more. She had even persuaded poor Bernadette Ong to come, alone. John was still in the hospital.

"The woman who's taken my place," Foxy said. "Your present mistress."

"Sweet Fox, there isn't any."

"Come off it. I know you. Or has Angela turned into a hot ticket?"

"She *is* more amiable lately. Do you think she has a lover?"

"It's possible, but I'm not interested. The only person in Tarbox who interests me is you. Why don't you call me any more?"

"It's been Christmas. The children have all been home from school."

"Phooey to the children. They didn't bother you all summer."

"There's one more now." He feared he had hurt her, hit out roughly. He petted her wooden back and said teasingly, "Don't you really like any of our friends? You used to love Angela."

"That was on the way to loving you. Now I can't stand her. Why should she own you? She doesn't make you happy."

"You're a hard woman."

"Yes."

Demurely she lowered her lids and danced. Her body, its placid flats and awkward stiffness, was obscurely his, a possession difficult to value now that the bulge, the big jewel, of her belly was gone.

He said at last, "I think we *should* talk. It would be nice to see you." Betrayal upon betrayal. Dovetailing, rising like staging.

"I'm home all the time."

"Is Ken going back to work Monday?"

"He never stops working. He went to Boston every day of his vacation except Christmas."

"Maybe he's seeing a woman."

"I wish he would. I deserve it. But I'm afraid he's seeing a cell. He's beginning modestly."

He laughed and without bringing her visibly closer to him tightened the muscles of his arms for her to feel as an embrace. If Piet had a weakness, it was for feminine irony. "I'm dying to see you," he said, "but I'm afraid of being disappointing. Don't expect too much. We'll just talk."

"Of course, what else? You can't fuck a young mother."

"I think you enjoy misunderstanding me about that. I love your baby."

"I don't doubt it. It's me you don't love."

"But I do, I do, too much I do. I was in you so deep, loved you so terribly, I'm scared of getting back in. I think we were given it once and to do it all over again would be tempting fate. I think we've used up our luck. It's be*cause* I love you, be*cause* I don't want you to be hurt."

"All right, shut up for now. Freddy and Georgene are both looking."

The music, Della Reese, stopped. Piet pushed away from Foxy, relieved to be off, though she did look, standing deserted in a bouffant knee-length dress the milky green of cut flower stems, like the awkward proper girl from Maryland, leggy and young, she had often described to him, and he had never quite believed in.

He heard from the kitchen Bea's clear plaintive voice rising and falling within some anecdote, calling him. But in the narrow front hallway Bernadette Ong's broad shoulders blocked him. "Piet," she said plangently. "When do I get my duty dance?"

He took a grave tone. "Bernadette. How is John doing? When is he coming home?"

She was tipsy, for she took a step and her pelvis bumped him. Her breath smelled bronze. "Who knows? The doctors can't agree. One says soon, the other says maybe. With the government insurance covering, they may keep him there forever."

"How does he feel?"

"He doesn't care. He has his books. He talks to Cambridge on the phone now."

"That's good news, isn't it?" Piet edged toward the stairs.

She stepped again and barred him from touching the newel. "Maybe yes, maybe no. I don't want him back in the house the way he was, up all night fighting for breath and scaring the boys half to death."

"Jesus. Is that how it was?"

Bernadette, her body wrapped in silk, a toy gold cross pasted between her breasts, heard a frug record put on the phonograph and held wide her arms; Piet saw her dying husband in her like a larva in a cocoon. Nervously acrobatic, he slid past her and up a step of the stairs. "I'll be down in two seconds," he said, and needlessly lied, since she would assume he must go to the toilet, "I thought I heard a child cry."

Upstairs, captive to his lie, he turned away from the lit bathroom into the breathing darkness where his daughters lay asleep. Downstairs the voices of Angela and Bea alternated and chimed together. His wife and his mistress. In bed Bea had enraptured him, her skin sugary, granular, the soles of her feet cold, the grip of her vagina liquid and slim, a sly narrowness giving on a vastness where his drumming seed quite sank from sight. Her puffy eyelids shut, she sucked his fingers blindly, and was thus entered twice. She seemed to float on her bed at a level of bliss little altered by his coming and going and thus worked upon him a challenge; at last she confessed he was hurting her and curled one finger around the back of his ear to thank him. She was his smallest woman, his most passive, and his most remote, in these mournful throes, from speech or any question. He had felt himself as all answer. When the time for him to leave at last was acknowledged she wrapped herself quickly in a bathrobe showing, in the split second of standing, that her breasts and buttocks hung like liquid caught in too thin a skin. Ectoplasm.

He crouched where his two daughters' breathing intersected. Nancy's was moist and scarcely audible. Might fall through into silence. The frail web of atoms spinning. The hamster in his heavenly wheel. There. It. Is. Ruth's deeper, renewed itself with assurance, approached the powerful onward drag of an adult. The hauling of a boat upriver. Full steam. Boys soon. Bathroom jokes, Nancy Drew, drawings attempting bosoms: teen-age. The time she was Helen Keller for a school project, bumping through the bright house blindfold, couldn't get her to take it off. Frightening herself. Must do. So brave in choir, bored. Her breathing stuttered, doubled tempo. A dream. His leaving. He crouched deeper between their beds and held her damp square hand. Her breathing eased. Her head changed position. Sleeping beauty. Poison apple. **I am your only lover. All who follow echo me. Shadows. Sleep.**

The music downstairs stopped. Frug, nobody could do it yet, too old to learn. Nancy's breathing eluded his listening. Instead a most gentle of presences tapped at the window whose mullions were crosses. Snow. A few dry flakes, a flurry. This winter's shy first. The greenhouse at home banked deep in snow. A rusty warmth of happiness suffused him, joy in being rectangularly enclosed, alive with flowers growing, captive together, his mother at the far end tying ribbons tight with needling fingers, school vacation on, all need to adventure suspended.

Distantly, a gun was fired. Downstairs, his friends, voice by voice, launched "Auld Lang Syne." Though his place as host was with them, Piet remained where he was, crouching above the ascending din until it subsided, and he could again pick up the fragile thread of Nancy's breathing, and the witnessing whisper of the snow.

The visit to Foxy proved disappointing. It was a blowy earachy winter Monday; the truck rattled bitterly as he drove down the beach road and the radio through its static told of Pope Paul being nearly trampled in Jerusalem. The house was cold; Foxy was wearing a heavy sweater and a flannel nightie and furry slippers. She moved and spoke briskly, angrily, as if to keep warm. The offending marshes, which permitted the wind to sweep through the walls he had woven for her, were scarred by lines of salty gray ice rubble rimming the tidal channels. Gusts visibly walked on the water. She asked, "Would you like some hot coffee?"

"Yes, please."

"I'm freezing, aren't you?"

"Is the thermostat up?"

"The furnace is on all the time. Can't you hear it roaring? I'm scared it's going to explode."

"It won't."

"A friend of Ken's who's built his own house on the Cape thinks we were crazy not to excavate a full cellar under the living room."

"It would have meant at least another two thousand."

"It would have been worth it. Look at all the gas I burn buzzing around Tarbox visiting people to keep warm. Janet one day, Carol the next. I know all the dirt."

"What is the dirt?"

"There isn't much. I think we're all tired. Janet was very curious about Ken's boyhood and Carol thinks you're seeing Bea Guerin."

"How sweet of Carol."

"Come into the kitchen for the coffee. It's not so bad there."

"I wonder if wooden-framed storm windows on the marsh side wouldn't help. They have more substance than the aluminum combinations. Or what about shuttering them straight across with the boards that were there?"

"What would happen to Angela's view?"

This humorousness remembered the times she had lain in his arms remarking on her double theft, of Angela's man and Angela's house. In the less chilly kitchen, where the Whitmans had reinstated the electric heater, she said, "You'd laugh to see me at night, Ken on one side and Toby on the other. It's the only way I can keep warm."

Though he knew that her description was intended to pique his jealousy, he did feel jealous, picturing her asleep between her husband and son, her fanning spread of moonlit hair tangent to them both. Knowing that his interest in her child irked her, he asked, "How *is* the young master?"

"Strapping. He's two months old now and looks like Ken's father. That same judicial grimace."

"Two months," Piet said. He was wearing workboots and a lumberjack shirt underneath his apricot windbreaker. She gave him coffee in a mug, without a saucer, as if to a handyman. He felt tongue-tied and coarse, and found her large brown eyes uncomfortably alert. Listening for the phone, another lover? Of course not, she had a child. The mother in her den.

She looked at him intently. The unbiased winter light showed a small sty distorting the shape of her left eyelid. She said, "Two months is more than six weeks."

He groped for the significance of six weeks. "Oh. Terrific. But—do you want to? With me, I mean."

"Do you want to with me, is more the question."

"Of course. Of course I do, I love you. Obviously. But should we? Start everything up again. It frightens me, frankly. Haven't we paid our debt to society? Getting over you once was hard enough."

He feared she might mock him, but she nodded solemnly instead. Foxy's hair was not blond clear through like Bea's but blond in part, of many shades—oak, honey, ash, even amber—and darker with beach weather by. She lifted her head. There was a pink cold sore beneath one nostril. "I frighten you?"

"Not you. It. It would be *wrong* now."

"All right, then go. Go, Piet. Thanks for everything. It's been swell."

"Don't. Don't be hard." In waiting for her to begin to cry, he felt his own eyes warm. The scene must be played.

She seized the high, the haughty, rôle. "I don't know how a dismissed mistress should act. They didn't teach us at Radcliffe. Maybe I took the wrong courses. I'm sure I'll be better at it next time."

"Don't," he begged. Rays were being hurled from her dry eyes, and he hunched to dodge these spears.

"Don't what?" she asked. "Don't make a scene? Don't be a bitch? When all the poor little workingman has done is come into your house and charmed the pants off of you and let you fall in love with him, don't embarrass the poor baby, don't make yourself a nuisance. I won't, Piet love, I won't. Just go. Git. Go to Bea. Go back to Georgene. Go way back to Angela. I couldn't care less."

Her eyes, they wouldn't cry, and he must do something, anything, to smother their icy dry rays, that were annihilating him. He asked, "Can't we lie down together?"

"Oh," she said, and flounced herself, but her sweater and heavy nightie refused, amid the ghosts of summer's billowing, to fling, and the kitchen presences, stove, oven, sink, and windows, retained their precise shape, like unimpressed judges. "You'll make one more stab at it, as a favor. Forget it, I'm not that hard up."

But the integrity of her eyes had cracked, she had been brought to tears. He heard his voice grow wise and warm, reaching into the reserves of darkness he and Foxy had shared. "I want to rub your back, and hear about your baby."

She smoothed the skin beneath her eyes. "I think you're right about us," she confessed. "I just don't want to know exactly when it's happening."

This was, his release, of her many gifts to him the most gracious. In an hour, he knew, in good conscience he would be free. He asked, "Shall we go upstairs? We'll need covers over us."

She said, "We must leave the door open, to hear the baby. He's asleep in the nursery." Piet rejoiced that concern for her child was dovetailing with relinquishment of him.

The upstairs was even colder. In bed she kept her wool nightie on and he his underclothes; he rubbed the smooth planes of her back and backside until she seemed asleep. But when he stopped she rolled to face him, reached down to touch him, in Paisley underpants, and asked as if she could be refused, "Would you like to come inside me?"

"Terribly, actually."

"Gently."

Yes, she had been stretched by the child; the precious virginal tightness had fled. He offered to kiss her breasts, though a stale milky smell disturbed him; her fingers pushed his face away. She must save herself for the baby. Her long body beneath his felt companionable, unsupple, male. His mind moved through images of wood, patient pale widths waiting for the sander, intricate joints finished with steel wool and oil, rounded pieces fitted with dowels, solid yet soft with that placid suspended semblance of life wood retains.

A weight fell on the bed; Piet's heart leaped. Foxy's cheek against his stretched in a smile. It was the cat, Cotton. Purring, the animal nestled complacently into the hollow on top of the blankets between the lovers' spread legs. "I have two lovers," Foxy said softly, but fear had been touched off in Piet, and its flare illuminated the world—the Gallagher & Hanema office on Hope

Street, the colonial farmhouse on Nun's Bay Road, the unmistakable pick-up truck blatantly parked in the Whitmans' drive. He must hurry. He asked her, "Can you make it?"

"I don't think so. I've too many emotions."

"Then let me?"

She nodded stiffly and with a few unheeding, gay and forceful strokes he finished it off, holding her pinned through the distracting trembling with which she greeted his coming and which at first he had mistaken for her own climax. He left his lust as if on a chopping block miles within her soft machine. She looked at him with eyes each holding the rectangle of the skylight. "So quick?"

"I know. I'm lousy at love. I must go."

He dressed rapidly, to avoid the discussion and recapitulation he knew she desired. It was good, he thought, that the last time was bad for her. Her slowness to come, he saw now, had always been a kind of greed. As he carefully opened the door behind the lilacs, the baby began to cry in the nursery wing.

Outdoors was as still as a house in that interval after the last subcontractors have left and before the occupants have moved in and the heat is turned on. The woods toward the little-Smiths' house, purple diluted with rime, moved no more under the wind than frost-ferns on glass. No cars passed on the beach road. A single gull knifed across his vision, and he heard behind him Foxy begin to cry. His palms tingling against the wheel, he backed the truck around and headed toward the center of Tarbox. Through the leafless trees peeked a gold weathercock. As the cab warmed, he whistled along with the radio music, exhilarated once again at having not been caught.

Perhaps that day he discovered a treasure of cruelty in himself, for alone with Bea later that week, late in the afternoon, he struck her. She had been above him on all fours, a nursing mammal, her breasts pendulous, with a tulip sheen, and as if to mark an exclamatory limit to happiness he had cuffed her buttocks, her flaccid sides, and, rolling her beneath him, had slapped her face hard enough to leave a blotch. Seeing her eyes incredulous, he had slapped her again, to banish all doubt and establish them firmly on this new frontier. Already he had exploited her passivity in all positions; the slap distracted his penis and he felt he had found a method to prolong the length of time, never long enough, that he could inhabit a woman.

Bea's left eye slitted against a third blow and when it didn't come widened with the surprise of recognition. "That's what Roger does."

"So people say."

"I thought it was because he couldn't make love normally, because I didn't excite him otherwise. But that's not so of you."

"No, it's in you. You invite it. You're a lovely white hole to pour everything into. Jizz, fists, spit." He spat between her breasts and lifted his arm as if to club her.

Her eyes, so washed-out they were scarcely blue, widened in alarm and she turned her head sideways on the shadowy pillow. "It makes me wonder if I'm insane," she said. "That I do this to people. Eddie twists my wrist all the time. Please, Piet, I'd really rather you wouldn't. Use me but don't hurt me if you don't absolutely have to. I don't really like it. Maybe I should."

"Oh I know, I know, you must hate it, forgive me," Piet said, hiding his face in Bea's throat and hair. "Do forgive me." Yet he was pleased, for in abusing her he had strengthened the basis of his love, given his heart leverage to leap. He loved any woman he lay with, that was his strength, his appeal; but with each woman his heart was more intimidated by the counterthrust of time. Now, with Bea, he had made a ledge of guilt and hurled himself secure into the tranquil pool of her body and bed. High above the sound of children throwing snowballs as they returned from school in the dusk, Bea sucked his fingers, and her nether mouth widened until he was quite lost, and he experienced orgasm strangely, as a crisisless osmosis, an ebbing of light above the snow-shrouded roofs. Death no longer seemed dreadful.

The phone rang and surprised him by being Foxy. In the month since their unsatisfactory coitus in the cold house, she had not called, and had hardly spoken at parties. She had faded into the tapestry of friends. She asked, "Piet, is Gallagher there?"

"Yes he is," he cheerfully sang.

"Could you go out to a pay phone and call me?"

"Now?"

"Piet. Please. We must talk." Her voice had a distant chafed quality, and he pictured a handkerchief balled in her fingers.

"As you wish." He added a firm, man-to-man "Right." He felt Gallagher listening behind the corrugated glass partition, though his door was closed. Increasingly Gallagher's door was closed. Each morning, coming to his office, Piet found that the walls had been slightly narrowed in the night. Beside his desk hung a calendar, from Spiros Bros. Builders & Lumber Supply, showing a dripping golden retriever mouthing a green-headed mallard; as Piet worked at his desk he could feel the dog's breath pushing on his ear.

He went out into the valentine brightness of plow-heaped snow and entered an aluminum phone booth smelling of galoshes. A single dried-up child's mitten lay on the change shelf, unclaimed. The Whitmans' number rang three, four, five times unanswered. He pictured Foxy lying dead, a suicide, having called him in the clouded last moment of waking and then sinking in coma onto her bed, her long hair spilling, the child crying unheard. The phone was picked up; as if a window had been opened Piet saw, across the street, through the besmirched phone-booth glass, four men rocking a car, trying to push it free.

"Hello." Foxy's voice was cool, impersonal, unfocused.

"It's me. What took you so long to answer the phone?"

Her voice, relieved, collapsed—but not, he felt, all the way. "Oh. Piet. You're so quick to call back."

"You told me to be."

"I was with Toby."

"What's up?"

She hesitated. "I just wondered how you were. I had a spell of missing you, and realized that I'd been resisting calling you just to punish you and you weren't being punished, so what the hell."

He laughed, reassured yet suspicious, for he did not remember her as a waverer. "Well, I *was* being punished, but I figured unless we had something to tell each other it was right we didn't talk. I admired your tact." In her silence he hurried on. "I get your letters out and read them now and then." This was a lie; he had not done this for months; they seemed, all those blue barbs and squiggles, dead thorns the sharper for being dead.

As if sensing this, she laughed. "But I *do* have something to tell you. Good news, you'll be pleased. The house is warm now, and it wasn't your fault. When they installed the furnace the man had put the thermostat too near some hot-water pipes in the wall, so the thermostat thought the house was warm when only *it* was, and kept shutting off. Ken and Frank Appleby figured it out one drunken night. The Applesmiths have been coming over lately."

"Oh, sweet, but it *is* my fault. I was the general contractor, I should have noticed. But I was distracted by making love to you."

"Did you like making love to me? I was never sure, I'm awfully virginal somehow."

"Virginal and whorish together. I adored making love to you. It was somehow it. But don't you feel better now in a way? You can look Angela in the face, and me Ken."

"I never minded Angela. I had a mysterious feeling she approved."

The subject displeased him; he did not like Angela to be dismissed. He felt his mistresses owed it to him to venerate her, since he had taken it upon himself to mock her through their bodies. "And how is Toby? Are you enjoying him?"

"Pretty much. He lifts up his head and seems to listen to what I say. Unlike his father."

"Aren't you enjoying Ken?"

"Not much."

"And this is all you called me for? Got me out here in the snow for?"

"No." The syllable seemed a metallic sound the receiver had made purely by itself. When Foxy's voice resumed, it had collapsed all the way; he felt, listening, that he was skating on a crystal surface, the pure essence of her that God's hands had held before thrusting it into a body, her soul. "Piet. My period is two weeks late. And it would have to be you."

"Me what?" But of course he instantly knew. That cold house, that scared last piece. The chopping block. The hostage.

As she spoke, her voice made soft tearing noises, caused by the skating action of his listening. "It's not just the lateness, it's a whole chemical something, a burny feeling down low that I remember from carrying Toby."

"Would you feel it so soon?"

"It's been a month."

"So soon after giving birth, aren't your insides naturally mixed up?"

"But I had two periods."

"And it can't be Ken?"

"Not really, no." He thought her phrasing strange. She added, "He uses those things."

"Sometimes they break."

"Not Ken's. Anyway, it's not been that often. I depress him since the baby. And he's worried about his work. Not only Jews but now the Japanese are getting ahead of him."

"But *how* often?"

"Twice when it could have been, except for the thing, and once just recently, when I hoped it would bring my period on."

"And you *do* have the burny feeling?"

"Yes. And agitation. Insomnia. Piet, Piet, I'm so sorry, it's so stupid."

"Why did you let me that day, if—"

"I don't know, you didn't act like you were going to do it, and my old diaphragm doesn't fit, and—"

"I assumed you used pills. Everybody else does."

"Oh, *does* everybody else? You've taken a poll."

"Don't be petulant."

"Don't you be. About the pills, not that it matters, Ken doesn't trust them. He thinks it's all too intricate, they may trigger off something."

"Bang," Piet said. "Bang, bang."

Foxy was going on, "And if you must know, if you must know how naïve I am, I thought that I was nursing made me safe." Her tears crackled and rasped in the receiver cold against his ear.

He laughed. "That old wives' tale? I keep forgetting about you,

you're a Southern woman, raised on recipes learned at Aunt Jemimah's knee."

"Oh," her wet pale voice gasped, "it's good to hear you laugh at me. I've been in hell. I called you this morning to keep from going crazy and then when you called back I was too frightened to answer, and then I lied. I just lie and lie, Piet."

"It's something we all get good at," he said. The receiver was such a little weight in his hand, chill and stiff and hollow, he wondered why he could not hang it up and walk away free, why it was clamped to him as the body is clamped to the soul.

Foxy was asking, "What shall we do?"

In the illusion of giving advice he found some shelter, right angles and stress-beams of sense they could inhabit. "Wait a few more days," he told her. "Take hot baths, as hot as you can stand them. If it still doesn't come on, go to a doctor and take the rabbit test. Then at least we'll know."

"But I *can't* go to Doc Allen. For one thing he'd be shocked that I was pregnant again so soon. He might tell some of his boatyard friends."

"Doctors never tell anything. But didn't you and Ken have a doctor in Cambridge? Go to him if you'd rather. But not quite yet. It might come on still. Angela is sometimes three weeks, sometimes five; she's terribly casual. It's a miracle I haven't knocked her up."

Though he had been serious, Foxy laughed. "Poor Piet and his women," she teased, "picking his way through the phases of the moon. I guess I turned out to be the dud."

"The opposite of dud, I'd say," and he glimpsed in himself amid the terror pleasure that she had proved doubly fertile, that she had shown him capable of bringing more life to bud upon the earth.

She asked, "Will you call me? Please. You won't have to *do* anything, I'll take care of it myself somehow—absolutely; no, don't say anything. But it *is* lonely. Lonely, Piet."

He promised her, "I'll call you tomorrow." A last word felt needed, a blessing to unclamp the receiver from his hand and ear. He stammered in fear of sounding pompous as he unlocked to her all the wisdom he possessed. "Foxy. After years of thought, I have come to this conclusion: there are two kinds of situation in the world, those we can do something about and those we can't, like the stars and death. And I decided it's a great waste, a sin in fact, to worry about what we can't help. So take a hot bath and relax. We're in the hands of Allah."

His not daring saying "God" disgusted him. But Foxy, lulled as if she had not listened, said singsong, "Call me tomorrow, Piet, and I bet it will have gone away like a silly dream, and we can go back to our nice comfortable estrangement."

So "estrangement" was the last word. He hung up and saw that the men had extricated the car from the white gutter, and all of Charity Street, alive with the rasping of shovels, seemed a sacred space, where one could build and run and choose, from which he was estranged.

Now began a nightmare of daily phoning, of small false hopes (the burning sensation seemed less distinct today, she had felt a uterine strangeness after this morning's scalding bath, a medical reference book at the Tarbox Library admitted of many post-partum menstrual irregularities) and of cumbersomely advancing certainty. The first rabbit test came back from the lab negative; but the Cambridge doctor explained that this early in the game there was only a ninety per cent accuracy, and implied disapproval of her haste. A curt, hawk-faced man with golfing trophies in his consulting room, he may have diagnosed at a glance her symptoms and recognized the plague, this not uncommon infection of decent society's computations with blind life's long odds, that to Foxy and Piet seemed so isolating. For a whole night of sleeplessness she lay trembling with the good news that she could not deliver to Piet until morning. But the one-in-ten chance dilated fascinatingly as Foxy refused to let go of her microscopic captive and surrender and bleed. Piet battered her over the phone, begged at her with his patience, his refusal to blame her: he had resigned from being her lover, he had lain with her to say good-bye, he was happy with his rare and re-

mote wife, he had been gulled by Foxy's naïveté, she had no
claim upon him—none of this he needed to say, it was assumed.
She apologized, she ridiculed herself, she offered to take her
child, her existing child, and vanish from the town; but for the
time being he and he only knew her secret, only he could share
with her the ordeal of these days. The sound of his voice was the
one thing on earth not alien to her. They agreed to meet, out of
pity for each other and a desire, like that of boxers clinching, to
draw near to the presence, each to the other, that was giving
them pain. In Lacetown there was an IGA whose large parking
lot the plows would have cleared; behind the building, where
the trucks unloaded, few cars parked. Of their friends only
Janet sometimes shopped here. They would be safe.

Friday. A heavy mauve sky. A few dry flakes. His heart leaped
at the sight, alone on the asphalt, beneath the close clouds, of the
Whitmans' black MG. He parked his truck near the store inciner-
ator barrel and walked across empty parking spaces. Foxy rolled
down her window. A flake caught in her left eyebrow. He said,
"I thought Ken took this car to Boston."

"He took the train today, because they forecast a storm. Get
in."

Inside, having slammed the door, he said, "He's always thinking, Ken."

"Why do you dislike him? This isn't his fault."

"I don't dislike him. I admire him. I envy him. He has a college
degree."

"I thought you were going to say he has *me*." They laughed, at
her, at themselves, at them all. In leaving the limits of Tarbox
they had acquired a perspective; their friends and their houses
seemed small behind them. Only they, Foxy and Piet, were life-
size. Only they had ceased flirting with life and had permitted
themselves to be brought, through biology, to this intensity of
definition. Their crisis flattered them like velvet backdrop. She sat
awkwardly sideways in the bucket seat behind the wheel, her
knees touching the gearshift, her legs long in yellow wool slacks,
her hair loose over the shoulders of her Russian general's coat.

He said, "You look pretty good," and patted her thigh. "After our frantic phone conversations I thought you'd look more of a wreck."

She grinned; her nose and chin seemed whittled by the pressure of the coming storm. Snowflakes were making a thin white line along the rubber window sealer. On the loading platform of the IGA a solitary boy in a clerk's apron was stacking cardboard boxes, his breath a commotion of vapor. "Oh," she said, feinting. "We women can keep up appearances."

"I take it there's not much doubt left."

She nodded, as delicately as if a corsage were fastened near her chin. Dances. Girls in cars after dances. It had been a generation since he had sat like this. Foxy said, "Not in my mind. I'm driving in this afternoon to have another rabbit test. I was supposed to. The storm may cancel it."

"Not with you at the wheel." As if rationalizing his laugh, he added, "Funny how that one-in-ten chance didn't go away."

"You always said we'd press our luck too far."

"I'm sorry that the time that did it wasn't better for you."

"I remember it very clearly. How we moved from room to room, the cat jumping on the bed. It's all so silly, isn't it? Adultery. It's so much *trouble*."

He shrugged, reluctant to agree. "It's a way of giving yourself adventures. Of getting out in the world and seeking knowledge."

She asked, "What do we know now, Piet?"

He felt her, in the use of his name, drawing near, making of this desperate meeting an occasion of their being together, a date. He hardened his voice: "We know God is not mocked."

"I was never mocking God."

"No. Your God is right there, between your legs, all shapeless and shy and waiting to be touched. It's all right, Fox. I don't mean to complain. It's partly I suppose that I find you so attractive; I didn't expect to, it makes me crabby. It seems so much beside the point for me to still want you."

She adjusted her legs more comfortably; a knee touched his, and quickly pulled away. "You expected to hate me?"

"A bit. This has been hell, these ten days. Compared to your voice on the phone, you seem happy."

"That's the worst of it. I am happy. I'm happy to be carrying your child. My whole system wants to go ahead and have it."

"You may not have it. May not, may *not*."

"Oh of course. Absolutely. I agree."

But her face had withdrawn into sharpness. A moan caught in his throat; he lurched at her, fumbling, afraid of her face. Her breath was hot, her cheek cold with tears; her body within her massive coat sought to conform to his, but the bucket seats and floor shift prevented them. He backed off and read hastily in her distorted face absolution, permission to scour from her insides all traces of their love. "But how?" he asked. "Sweden? Japan? How do people *do* these things?" Beyond her mussed hair a lane of leafless maples made an embroidered edge upon the snowing sky.

"It's sad, isn't it?" she asked. "We don't seem to know the right people. I know there are abortionists *every*where, waiting for customers, and here am I, and there's no way to get us in touch."

"What about Ken? He knows doctors."

"I can't tell Ken."

"Are you sure? It would make things possible. You could fly to Japan even. He could give a guest lecture."

"He's not that good."

"I was joking."

"I know. Piet, I'll do anything to get rid of this except tell my husband about us. He couldn't handle it. He's too—complacent. And in a way I'm too complacent too. I knuckled under once and I won't again. I won't beg, or apologize for us when we were so *right*. I'd rather risk death. That sounds more arrogant than it is. You could tell Angela you slept with me and the two of you would absorb it, be better for it after a while, but our marriage just isn't built that way. We're not that close. We made a very distinct bargain, one that doesn't allow for either of us making mistakes this big. It would shatter Ken. Am I making any sense?"

He saw that she would not tell her husband, just as months ago she would not install closed cabinets. She was the customer; he must work with her whims. "Well, what about telling him it's his and going ahead and having another little Whitman? It might have red hair but there must be a red-haired gene in one of you."

She spoke with care, after biting the tip of her tongue. Women whose tongues won't stay in their mouths are the sexiest. "It's possible. But it seems to me, if you picture the little child, getting bigger day by day, me watching him as he looks less and less like Ken and more and more like Piet Hanema, as he starts swinging from banisters and nailing pieces of wood together, we'd be giving ourselves a lifetime of hell. I'd rather take the hell in a stronger dose and get it over with."

"My poor Fox." He leaned and kissed her nose. Her red hands lay inert in the lap of her greatcoat; possibly she shrugged.

A maroon Mercury coupe like Janet Appleby's slowly wheeled through the lot. But the driver was unknown, an elderly Lacetown citizen with grizzled jaws and a checked hunter's cap. He stared at them—white-ringed raccoon eyes—and continued his circling arc through the lot and out the other side. The apparition had given them both heartstop, and contaminated their hiding place. The boy stacking boxes was gone from the platform. "We better go," Piet said, "or they'll find us frozen in each other's arms."

At home, sheltered from the blizzard amid the sounds of Angela's cooking and his daughters' quarrelsome play, Piet struggled to see his predicament as relative, in any light but the absolute one that showed it to be a disaster identical with death. Pregnancy was life. Nature dangles sex to keep us walking toward the cliff. Slip-ups are genially regarded. Great men have bastards: Grover Cleveland, Charlemagne. Nobody cares, a merry joke, brown beer, the Lord of Norfolk salutes his natural son. One more soul: three billion plus one. Anyway she would probably move to Berkeley or Los Alamos and he'd never see it. Down the drain. Piet Hanema, father of a new nation. To your health. He sipped the double martini and a boiling soughing dread like pigswill welled up to meet the gin. Ken. His dread had to do with Ken's face, the strange trust its faintly rude blankness imposed, the righteousness of the vengeance it would seek. Sickened, slipping, Piet saw that he lived in a moral world of only men, that only men demanded justice, that like a baby held in a nest of pillows from falling he had fallen asleep amid women. He had been dumbstruck to hear Foxy speak slightingly of Ken. In Piet's mind there was no end of Ken, no limit to the ramifying offense of inflicting a child upon Ken's paternity. Paternity a man's cunt. Vulnerable. Gently. His father potting geraniums with stained thumbs, the perspective of the greenhouse implying an infinity of straight lines. He had preferred as a child the dead-ended warm room at the end where his mother sat broad-lapped among looping ribbons. There was a mandate in his father's silences he had shied from. Straight man, his mouth strange from dentures. Ah God, how glad he was that they were gone, all things considered.

All things are relative. As a boy in trouble he would think of something worse. It would be worse than not making the football squad to get polio. It would be worse than not getting invited to Annabelle Vojt's party to accidentally shoot Joop in the eye and have him blind forever. It would be worse to be dead than to be in this box. Would it? In a manner analogous to dying he had trespassed into a large darkness. In Foxy's silken salty loins he had planted seed that bore his face and now he wished to be small and crawl through her slippery corridors and, a murderer, strike. God forgive. No: God do. God who kills so often, with so lordly a lightness, from diatoms to whales, kill once more, obliterate from above, a whip's flick, a finger down her throat, erase this monstrous growth. For Thine is the kingdom.

Ken's face, barely polite. Pale from ambition and study. Piet's guts groveled again; he sipped silver to kill them. The bullet. The sleepy firing squad. The terrible realm where life leaps up from impeccable darkness. God's premeditated deed. Clay mixed with spit. Foxy's sly cunt, coral the petals, more purple within, her eyes like twin bells hung on a tree, tinkled by every wind. Yet she suffered, beneath the woman there was an animal, a man like him, an aged child rather, judging, guessing, hoping, itching. How monstrous to have a thing attach and fester upon you like a fungus. His balls sympathetically crawled. Poor soft Foxy. Erase. Pluck, Lord. Pluck me free.

He drank. The final sweetness of truly falling. Bea. Scared to call, she might guess. She knew some things. Had seen him leap from the window, Foxy's head golden in the bathroom light. In her bed he had left unconfessed only that last drab Monday visit when, trespassing unwittingly upon Ken's paternity, conjuring into the world another responsible soul, he had made himself legally liable. Disgrace, jail, death, incineration, extinction, eternal namelessness. The laughter of their friends. The maledictions of newspapers. He saw Bea smiling, her breasts melted, her body a still pool, his prick suspended in her like a sleeping eel, and knew why he loved her: she was sterile. His semen could dive forever in that white chasm and never snag.

His solitude became desolate. The blizzard crooned mournfully, a thing without existence, a stirring. He emptied his glass and went into the kitchen. His daughters and wife were arranging valentines. He had failed to get Angela one. Ruth and Nancy at school had received fuzzy hearts, mooning cows, giraffes with intertwined necks. Ruth was arranging the best on top of the refrigerator. Reaching up, her figure was strikingly lithe. His coming into the kitchen for more gin intruded upon a triangular female rapport especially precious to little Nancy. She turned her face, shaped like a rounded cartoon heart, upwards toward him, giggled at the approach of her own impudence, and said, "Daddy's ugly."

"No, Daddy not ugly," Ruth said, putting her arm about his waist. "Daddy pwetty."

"He has awful nostrils," Nancy said, moving closer and looking up.

Ruth continued the baby talk in which her impulse of love sought disguise. "Daddy has the beeyeutifullest nostwils," she said, "because he came from Howwand long ago."

Piet had to laugh. "What about my feet?" he asked Nancy.

"Acky feet," she said.

Ruth hugged him tighter and stroked his furry arm. "Loberly feet," she said. "Mommy has silly feet, her little toes don't touch the ground."

"That's considered," Angela said, "a sign of great beauty."

"You know something, Mommy?" Ruth said, abandoning Piet's

side and the baby voice. "Mrs. Whitman has *flat* feet, because at the beach this summer Frankie Appleby and Jonathan Smith were being detectives and following people and her footprints had no dent on the inside, you know, where the curvy place, whatever it's called—"

"Arch," Angela said.

"—where the arch is. It was like she was wearing sneakers only with toes." The child glanced over at her father. True, even so unkind an evocation of Foxy gave him pleasure. Slouching flat-footed broad, big with his baby. His tall cockpit.

"How fascinating," Angela said. Her hands busily sparkled amid the leaves of their supper salad. "What else have you noticed about feet?"

"Mr. Thorne has a green toenail," Ruth said.

"Daddy's toes," Nancy said, gazing up impudently from beneath Angela's protection, "are like Halloween teeth," and Piet saw that he represented death to this child: that what menaced and assaulted the fragility of life was being concentrated for her in his towering rank maleness; that this process would bring her in time to Ruth's stage, of daring to admire and tame this strangeness; and at last to Angela's, of seeking to salvage something of herself, her pure self, from the encounter with it. He loved them, his women, spaced around him like the stakes of a trap.

Ruth said, "Mommy, make Nancy stop insulting Daddy. Daddy's handsome, isn't he?"

Piet stooped and picked Nancy up; she shrieked and kicked in mixed pleasure and fear. A peppery whiff of red candy hearts was on her breath. Rotting her fine teeth. Angry, he squeezed her harder; she squealed and tried to fight down, all fear now.

"I don't know if Daddy's exactly *handsome*," Angela was saying. "He's what people call attractive." She added, "And nice, and good." He set Nancy down, pinching her unseen. She stared upward at him, now knowing something she would never forget, and could never express.

Perhaps as a sequitur of the tenderness of their being together with their children and their valentines, perhaps simply excited by their snugness within the blizzard, Angela led him to bed early and, like a warm cloud descending, made love to him sitting astride, in the classic position of Andromache consoling Hector.

Saturday morning their phone rang; Foxy spoke breathily, with her lips against the mouthpiece. "Is Angela right there?"

"No," Piet said, "she's out shoveling with the kids. What would you have said if she had answered?"

"I would have asked her if she was wearing a short or a long dress to the Heart Fund dance."

"It's really risky, you know. She's just beginning to be less suspicious of you."

"I had to talk to you, I'm sorry. I thought you'd be at the Gallaghers last night. Why didn't you come?"

"We weren't invited. Who was there?"

"Everybody. Except you and the Saltzes and the Ongs. There was a new couple who seemed stuffy and young."

"Matt didn't say anything to me. Anyway. What's up with you?"

"The test. It was positive. There's no doubt, Piet."

"Oof." He was fascinated, as he sank into this fact, by the delicacy of his furniture, the maple telephone table with tapering legs, the mirror in its acanthus frame of chipped gilt. These things had been fashioned by men without care, with no weight on their hands. He marveled at himself, that he had ever found the energy, the space, to set two sticks together.

Into his leaden silence she cried, "Oh Piet, I've become such a burden."

"No," he lied. "I still think of you as very light and kind."

"At any rate—hang up if Angela comes in—I think I've hit on something."

"What?"

"Freddy Thorne."

Piet laughed. "Freddy can bore it out of you. That's called an abortion."

"All right. I'll hang up. I won't bother you again. Thanks for everything."

"No. Wait," he shouted, fearing the receiver would already be away from her ear. "Tell me. Don't be so touchy."

"I'm in hell, darling, and I don't like being laughed at."

"That's what hell is like."

"Wait until you know."

He prompted her, "Freddy Thorne."

"Freddy Thorne once told me that dentists commit abortions. They have all the tools, the chair, anesthetic—"

"A likely story. And?"

"And last night at the Gallaghers, you know how he gets you into a corner to be cozy, I brought the subject around, and asked him if he knew any who did it."

"You told him you were pregnant."

"No. Heaven forbid. I told him I knew somebody who was, a perfectly nice girl from Cambridge who was desperate."

"True enough."

"And—are you sure Angela isn't listening?—"

"I'll go to the window and see where she is." He returned and reported, "She's down the driveway shoveling like a woman inspired. She's been in a very up mood lately. She was excited by the storm."

"*I* wasn't. I was driving in and out of Cambridge to donate my urine. Then we had to struggle over to the Gallaghers."

"And Freddy Thorne looked at you with that fuzzy squint and knew fucking damn well it was *you* who were pregnant."

"Yes. He did. But he didn't say so."

"What did he say? He consulted his abortion schedule and gave you an appointment."

"Not exactly. He said a very spooky thing. All this by the way was in the kitchen; the others were in the living room playing a new word game, with a dictionary. He said he'd have to meet the girl and the man."

"That *is* spooky. The girl *and* the man."

"Yes, and since if I'm the girl, he must guess you're the man, I could only conclude he wants to see *you*."

"You're concluding too much. Freddy just isn't that organized. He's playing games. Blind man's bluff."

"I didn't feel that. He seemed quite serious and definite. More his dentist self than his party self."

"You bring out the dentist in Freddy, don't you? I don't want to see him. I don't like him, I don't trust him. I have no intention of putting us at his mercy."

"Whose mercy do you suggest instead?"

The front door was pushed open. Deftly Piet replaced the receiver and faced the hall as if he had been just looking in the mirror. Nancy stood there, swaddled with snowy clothes. Her cheeks were aflame. Wide-eyed she held out to him on one wet leather mitten what he took to be a snowball; but it was half-gray. It was a frozen bird, with a gingery red head and a black spot on its chest, a tree sparrow caught by the blizzard. Crystals adhered to its open eye, round as the head of a hatpin. In a businesslike manner that anticipated his protests, the child explained, "Mommy found it in the snow all stiff and I'm going to put it on the radiator to get warm and come alive again even though I know it won't."

The Heart Fund dance was held annually at the Tarbox Amvets' Club, a gaunt cement-block building off Musquenomenee Street. The club contained a bar and two bowling alleys downstairs and a ballroom and subsidiary bar upstairs. A faceted rotating globe hurled colored dabs of light around and around the walls, speeding at the corners, slowing above the windows, crisscrossing in crazy traffic among the feet of those dancing. No matter how cold the weather, it was always hot in the Amvets'. Whenever the doors opened, steam, tinted pink and blue by neon light, rolled out to mix with the exhaust smoke pluming from parking cars.

This year the dance was indifferently attended by the couples Piet knew. Carol Constantine was a graceful Greek dancer, and while the patriarchs and wives benignly watched from card tables laden with *keftedes* and *dolmathes* and black olives and *baklava*, she would lead lines hand in hand with their sons—grocers, electronic technicians, stockbrokers. Carol had the taut style, the archaic hauteur, to carry it off. But Irene Saltz was on the board of this year's Heart Fund, and the Constantines had gone into Boston with the Thornes and Gallaghers to see the Celtics play. The Hanemas had come mostly out of loyalty to Irene, who had confided to them (don't tell *any*one, es*pe*cially not Terry Gallagher) that these might be their last months in Tarbox, that Ben had been offered a job in Cleveland. The Whitmans were at a table with the Applesmiths, and the Guerins had brought the new couple. Their name was Reinhardt. They looked smooth-faced and socially anxious and Piet barely glanced at them. He only wanted, as the colored dots swirled and the third-generation Greek girls formed their profiled friezes to the Oriental keening of the bouzouki, for the American dancing to begin, so he could dance with Bea. Angela was sluggish from all her shoveling, and Foxy looked rigid with the effort of ignoring him. Only Bea's presence, a circle like the mouth of a white bell of which her overheard voice was the chiming clapper, promised repose. He remembered her as a calm pool in which he could kneel to the depth of his navel. When the teen-aged musicians changed modes, and his arms offered to enclose her, and they had glided beyond earshot of their friends, she said, gazing away, "Piet, you're in some kind of trouble. I can feel it in your body."

"Maybe it's in your body." But she was not drunk, and held a little off from him, whereas he had had three martinis with dinner at the Tarbox Inne, and was sweating. He wanted to smear her breasts against his chest and salve his heart.

"No," she said, singsong, refusing to yield to the questioning pressure of his arms, "it's in you, you've lost your usual bounce. You don't even stand the same. Didn't I once tell you the unkind people would do you in?"

"Nobody's been unkind. You're all too kind. In that same conversation, which I'm surprised you remember, you asked me if I didn't want to—"

"I do remember. Then you did, and didn't come back. Didn't you like it?"

"God, I loved it. I love you. The last time was so lovely. There was no longer any other place to go."

"Is that why you haven't called?"

"I couldn't. You're right, there *is* something in my life right now, a knot, an awful knot. If it ever untangles, will you have me back?"

"Of course. Always." Yet she spoke from a distance; in sorrow he squeezed her against him, pressed her like a poultice against that crusty knot in his chest where betrayal had compounded betrayal. Frank Appleby, dancing with the Reinhardt girl, accidentally caught Piet's eye, and biliously smiled. Lost souls. Hello in hell. Frank, having no mistress pregnant, seemed infinitely fortunate: advantages of an Exeter education. Whitewash.

Bea backed off, broke their embrace, gazing at something over his shoulder. Piet turned, frightened. Foxy had come up behind them. "Bea, it isn't *fair* for you to mono*p*olize this ado*r*able man." She spoke past Piet's face and her touch felt dry and rigid on his arm. Maneuvering him to dance, she said, her voice sharp, her pale mouth bitter, "I've been commissioned by your wife to tell you she's sleepy and wants to go home. But hold me a minute." Yet her body felt angular and uneasy, and they danced as if linked by obligation. She was wearing, uncharacteristically, a cloying perfume, overripe, reminiscent of rotting iris; by the contrast Piet realized Bea's scent had been lemony. She had floated, a ghost, in his arms.

Freddy Thorne's office smelled of eugenol and carpet cleaner and lollypops; holding Nancy by her plump tugging hand, Piet remembered his own childhood dread of that dental odor—the clenched stomach, the awareness of sunlight and freedom outside, the prayer to sleep through the coming half-hour. In Freddy's walnut magazine rack old *Time* and *Newsweek* covers showed Charles De Gaulle and Marina Oswald. Both looked haggard. Freddy's pug-nosed receptionist smiled reassuringly at the nervous child, and Piet's heart, though tracked to run head-on into Freddy, was shunted by a flick of gratitude into love of this girl. A crisp piece, young. Like eating celery, salting each stalk as it parted. Had Freddy ever? He doubted it. He was full of doubt of Freddy; just to picture the man filled him with a hopeless wet heaviness, like wash in a short-circuited machine.

Piet's left palm tingled with shame. He envied little Nancy her fear of merely pain. As he tried to read a much-creased *Look*, his daughter rubbed against him. The wrong way. Two cats. Electricity is fear. Pedrick had once said you could picture God as electromagnetic waves. He missed the poor devil's struggling, ought to go again. Nancy whispered, and he could not hear. Exasperated by her numb bumping, he said "What?" loudly.

The child cried "Shh!" and her hand darted to his lips. He embarrassed her. She had come to trust only her mother. Angela would normally have taken her to this appointment but today there was a meeting after nursery school and Piet, faced with fate's challenge, reluctantly accepted. *Whose mercy do you suggest instead?* Now indecision and repugnance fluttered in him and only fatigue scaled his dilemma down to something that could be borne. Like waiting outside the principal's office. Old Orff, a fierce Lutheran. Despised the Dutch. Servile Calvinism. Sir, I'm sorry, just awfully sorry, I didn't know—*You didn't know anypody wutt be vatching?* Caught swinging on the banisters in the brick-and-steel stairwell. Nancy whispered more distinctly, "Will he use the busy thing?"

"It's called the drill. Only if you have any cavities."

"Can you see some?" She opened her mouth wide—a huge mouth, his mouth.

"Sweetie, I can't see any, but I'm not a dentist. If you do have any cavities, they will be little ones, because you have such little teeth, because you're such a little girl."

He tickled her, but her body was overheated and preoccupied and did not respond. "Tell him not to do it," she said.

"But he *must*, that's Dr. Thorne's job. If we don't let him fix things now, they will be much worse later." He put his face close to hers. Like a round white blotter she absorbed his refusal to rescue him; and, refusing in turn to cry, she imprinted him with courage. They went together into Freddy's inner office.

Once there, in the robin's-egg-blue reclining chair, with the water chuckling in the bowl beside her ear and Dr. Thorne joking overhead with her father, Nancy somewhat relaxed, and let the dentist pick his way along the reverberating paths of her teeth. "Two," he pronounced at last, and made the marks on his chart, and judged, "Not so bad."

"Two cavavies?" Nancy asked. "Will they hurt?"

"I don't think so," Freddy answered unctuously. "Let us see how quiet you can be. The quieter you are outside, the quieter you are inside, and the quieter you are inside, the less you'll notice the drill."

Piet remembered the dove-gray handbook on hypnotism by Freddy's bed, and would have made a jabbing joke about amateur psychology, but his need for mercy restrained him, and he instead asked humbly, "Should she have Novocain?"

Freddy looked down at him. "They're very little," he said.

Nancy withstood the first drilling in silence; but when Freddy began the second cavity without a pause a guttural protest arose in her throat. Piet moved to the other side of the chair and took her agitated hand in his. He saw into the child's mouth, where between two ridged molars the drill, motionless in its speed, stood upright like a potted flower. Her tongue arched against the point of intrusion and Piet had to restrain her hand from lifting to her mouth. Her guttural complaint struggled into a scream. Her eyes, squared in shape by agony, opened and confronted her father's. Piet burst into sweating; perspiration raced across his chest, armpit to armpit. The coral space of gum between Nancy's lower lip and lower incisors was a gorge of saliva and drill spray. Her back arched. Her free hand groped upwards; Piet caught it and held it, pleading with Freddy, "Let's stop."

Freddy leaned down upon the now convulsive child. His lips thinned, then opened fishily. He said "Ah," and let the drill lift itself away, done with. "There now," he told Nancy, "that wasn't worth all that fuss, was it?"

Her cheeks soaked, she spat into the chuckling bowl and complained, "I wanted only *one*."

"But now," her father told her, "they're both done with and now comes the fun part, when Dr. Thorne puts in the silver!"

"Not fun," Nancy said.

Freddy said, "She's not easily got around, is she? Her mother's daughter." His smirk appeared pleased.

"You shouldn't have plunged in so ruthlessly."

"They were *tiny*. Scratches on the enamel. She frightened herself. Is she apprehensive at home?"

"She has my distrustful nature. The older girl is more stoical, like Angela."

"Angela's not stoical, that's *your* theory. My theory is, she suffers." Freddy's smile implied he enjoyed access to mines of wisdom, to the secret stream running beneath reality. What a sad jerk, really. His skunk-striped assistant came in to spin the silver.

Nancy's ordeal was over. As Freddy inserted and smoothed her fillings, Piet brought himself to ask, "Could we talk afterwards for a moment, in private?"

Freddy looked up. His eyes were monstrously enlarged by the magnifying lenses that supplemented his ordinary glasses. "I'm running behind on my appointments today."

"OK, forget it." Piet was relieved. "It didn't matter. Maybe some other time."

"Now, Handyman. Don't be persnickety. I can fit a minute in."

"It might take two," Piet said, his escape denied.

Freddy said, "Allee allee done free, Nancy. You go with Jeannette and maybe she can find you a lollypop." He ushered Piet into the small side room where his old yellow porcelain chair and equipment were kept for emergency use and cleanings. The window here looked upward over back yards toward the tip of the Congregational Church, a dab of sunstruck gold. Freddy in his sacerdotal white seemed much taller than Piet. Piet blushed. Freddy wiped his glasses and waited; years of malice had enriched that sly congested expression.

"We both know a lady—" Piet began.

"We both know several ladies."

"A tall lady, with long blondish hair and a maiden name that's an animal."

"A lovely lady," Freddy said. "I hear she's wonderful in bed."

"I haven't heard that," Piet said. "However, she and I were talking—"

"Not in bed?"

"I think not. Over the phone, perhaps."

"I find phones, myself, so unsatisfying."

"Have you tried masturbation?"

"Piet my pet, I don't have much time. Spill it. I know what it is, but I want to hear you spill it."

"This lady has told me, or maybe she told somebody else who told me, that you know gentlemen who can perform operations of a nondental nature."

"I might. Or I might not."

"My guess is you might not." Piet made to shoulder past him to the closed door.

Freddy stayed him with a quiet touch, a calibrated technician's touch. "But if I might?"

"But do you? I must trust you. Answer yes or no."

"Try yes."

"Then, sweet Freddy, this lady needs your friendship."

"But old Piet, pious Piet, *friend* Piet, you speak of *her*. What about you and me? Don't *you* need my friendship too?"

"It's possible."

"Probable."

"OK. Probable."

Freddy grinned; one seldom saw Freddy's teeth. They were small and spaced and tartarish.

Piet said, "I hate this game, I'm going. You're bluffing, you bluffed her into getting me to betray us. You stink."

The bigger man stayed him again, holding his arm with injured warmth, as if their years of sarcasm and contempt had given him the rights affection claims. "I'm not bluffing. I can deliver. It's not easy, there's some risk to me, but it would be clean. The man's an idealist, a crackpot. He believes in it. In Boston. I know people who have used him. What month is she in?"

"Second. Just."

"Good."

"It really is possible?" The good news was narcotically spreading through Piet's veins; he felt womanish, submissive, grateful as a dog.

"I said *I* can deliver. Can *you* deliver?"

"You mean money? How much does he ask?"

"Three hundred. Four hundred. Depends."

"No problem."

"For the man, no. What about me?"

"You want money too?" Piet was happy to be again confirmed in his contempt for Freddy. "Help yourself. We'll raise it."

There was a fumbling at the door; Freddy called out, "*Uno momento*, Jeanette."

But it was Nancy's scared voice that answered: "When do we go, Daddy?"

Piet said, "One more minute, sweetie-pie. Go into the waiting room and look at a magazine. Dr. Thorne is giving me an X-ray."

Freddy smiled at this. "You've become a very inventive liar."

"It goes with the construction business. We were discussing money."

"No we weren't. Money isn't discussed between old friends like you and me. Surely, old friend, we've gone beyond money as a means of exchange."

"What else can I give you? Love? Tears? Eternal gratitude? How about a new skin-diving suit?"

"Boy, you do make jokes. You play with life and death, and keep making jokes. It must be why women love you. Piet, I'll give it to you cold turkey. There's an unbalanced matter between us: you've had Georgene—right?"

"If she says so. I forget how it was."

"And I, on the other hand, though I've always sincerely admired your bride, have never—"

"Never. She'd never consent. She hates you."

"She doesn't hate me. She's rather attracted to me."

"She thinks you're a jerk."

"Watch it, Handlebar. This is my show and I've had enough of your lip. I want one night. That's very modest. One night with Angela. Work it out, fella. Tell her what you have to. Tell her everything. Confession is good for the soul."

Piet said, "You're asking the impossible. And I'll tell you why you are: you have nothing to deliver. You are a slimy worthless creep."

With crooked forefingers Freddy made gay quick horns at his scalp. "You put 'em there, buddy. You're the expert. I'm just a gullible middle-class grubber who as far as we know hasn't made a career of screwing other men's wives." Freddy's hairless face became very ugly, the underside of some soft eyeless sea creature whose mouth doubles as an anus. "You dug this grave by yourself, Dutch boy."

Again Piet moved toward the door, and this time he was not prevented. He hauled it open, and hopped back, startled; Nancy, having disobeyed, was standing there listening. Her lips were pursed around the stem of a lollypop and her eyes, though she had no words, knew everything.

When over the phone Piet told Foxy of Freddy's proposition, she said, "How funny. I had assumed he and Angela did sleep together, or at least *had*."

"On what basis had you assumed this?"

"Oh, how they act together at parties. Very relaxed. Chummy."

"As far as I know, she's never been unfaithful."

"Are you bragging or complaining?"

"You're in a jolly mood. What do you suggest our next step should be?"

"Me. I don't have a next step. It's up to Angela, isn't it?"

"You're kidding. I can't put this to her."

"Why not?" Impatience surmounted fatigue in her voice. "It's not such an enormous deal. Who knows, she might enjoy getting away from you for a night."

He'll hurt her, Piet wanted to explain. Freddy Thorne will hurt Angela. He said, "But it means telling her all about us."

"I don't see why. If she loves you, she'll do it simply because you ask. If you do it right. She's your wife, let her earn it. The rest of us have been keeping you entertained, let her do something for the cause."

"You're tough, aren't you?"

"I'm getting there."

"Please, Fox. Don't make me ask her."

"I'm not *making* you do anything. How can I? It's between

you and her. If you're too chicken, or she's too holy, we'll have to work at Freddy some other way, or do without him. I could try throwing myself on the mercy of my Cambridge doctor. He's not a Catholic. I could say I was going to have a nervous breakdown. It might not be a lie."

"You honestly think it's possible for me to ask her? Would you do it, to save Ken?"

"I'd do it to save *me*. In fact, I already offered."

"You offered what? To sleep with Freddy?"

"Don't let your voice get shrill like that. It's unbecoming. Of course I did, more or less. I didn't pull up my skirt; but what else do I have for him? What else do men and women ever talk about? He turned me down. Rather sweetly, I thought. He said I reminded him too much of his mother, and he was afraid of her. But it may have given him the idea of having Angela. I think what he really wants is to get at *you*."

"Because of Georgene?"

"Because you've always scorned him."

"You don't think he just honestly wants *her?*"

"Please don't try to squeeze compliments for your wife out of me. We all know she's magnificent. I have no idea what Freddy honestly wants. All I know is what *I* honestly want. I want this damn thing to stop growing inside of me."

"Don't cry."

"Nature is *so* stupid. It has all my maternal glands working, do you know what that means, Piet? You know what the great thing about being pregnant I found out was? It's something I just couldn't have imagined. You're never alone. When you have a baby inside you you are not *alone*. It's a *person*."

He had already told her not to cry. "You really think . . . she might?"

"Oh for God's sake, she's human like everybody else, I don't know what the hell she'll do or won't do. You still seem to think there's a fate worse than death. She's your divine wife, settle it between yourselves. Just let me know how it comes out, so I can work on something else. I thought I'd done pretty well to get Freddy Thorne for us."

"You did. You're being very brave and resourceful."

"Thank you for the compliment."

Piet told her, "I'll try. You're right. I don't expect it to go. She may ask for a divorce instead, but if it does, Foxy, love—"

"Yes, love."

"If we do get out of this, it has to be the end of our—of us."

"Obviously," Foxy said, and hung up.

A morning later, Nancy described her first dream, the first remembered dream of her life. She and Judy Thorne were on a screened porch, catching ladybugs. Judy caught one with one spot on its back and showed it to Nancy. Nancy caught one with two spots and showed it to Judy. Then Judy caught one with three spots, and Nancy one with four. Because (the child explained) the dots showed how old the ladybugs were!

She had told this dream to her mother, who had her repeat it to her father at breakfast. Piet was moved, beholding his daughter launched into another dimension of life, like school. He was touched by her tiny stock of imagery—the screened porch (neither they nor the Thornes had one; who?), the ladybugs (with turtles the most toylike of creatures), the mysterious power of numbers, that generates space and time. Piet saw down a long amplifying corridor of her dreams, and wanted to hear her tell them, to grow older with her, to shelter her forever. For her sake he must sell Angela.

"Angel?"

"Mm?" They were in the dark, in bed, nearly asleep. They had not made love; Piet had no intention of making love to anyone ever again.

"Would you believe it," he asked, "if I told you I was in deep trouble?"

"Yes," she answered.

Surprised, he asked, "What sort of trouble?"

"You and Gallagher aren't getting along any more."

"True. But that's the least of it. I can work things out with Matt once I get myself straightened out."

"Do you want to talk about it? I'm sleepy but can wake myself up."

"I can't talk about it. Can you accept that?"

"Yes."

"Could you believe it if I told you you could help me greatly by doing a specific thing?"

"Like getting a divorce?"

"No, not that at all. Have you been thinking about that?"

"Off and on. Does that alarm you?"

"Quite. I love my house."

"But that's not the same as loving me."

"I love you too. Obviously." The word echoed dryly and he felt them drifting farther from the point, the question. Perhaps there was a way of making it also seem a drifting, a detail of fate. "No," he said, "the thing you could do for me would only take one night."

"Sleep with Freddy Thorne," she said.

"Why do you say that?"

"Isn't that right?"

In the softness of the dark Piet could find no breath to make an answer; he lay on the bed like a man lying on water, only his eyes and nostrils not immersed. Finally he repeated, "Why do you say that?"

"Because he's always told me he would get into bed with me some day. For years he's been wanting to get a hold over you. Now does he have it?"

Piet answered, "Yes."

"And is that what he wants?"

His silent nodding made the bed slightly shudder.

"Don't be shocked," Angela went on, in a voice soft as the dark, "he's been working on it for years, and would tell me, and I imagined I should laugh. What I always thought strange, was that he never just *asked* me, on his own merits, but assumed it had to be worked by bullying you. I don't love him, of course, but he can be appealing sometimes, and I've been unhappy enough with you so that it might have happened by itself, if he'd just been direct. Do you want to know something sad?"

He nodded again, but this time the trembling of the bed was a theatrical effect, deliberately managed.

She told him, "He's the only man in town who's ever been attracted to me. Eddie Constantine took me for that ride on his Vespa and never followed it up. I'm just not attractive to men. What's wrong with me?"

"Nothing."

"Well something must be. I'm not on anybody's wavelength. Not even the children's, now that Nancy's no longer a baby. I'm very alone, Piet. No. Don't touch me. It sometimes helps but it wouldn't now. I really don't seem to be quite *here;* that's why I meant it about psychiatry. I think I need a rather formal kind of help. I need to go to a school where the subject is myself."

He sensed a bargain forming in the shadows. The far lamps along Nun's Bay Road, the wavy-branched lilacs and vase-shaped elms, leafless, and the reflecting snow made patterns of light along the walls that would never occur in summer. He said, "Why not? If things straighten out."

Angela repeated, "If. One question. I'm incredibly curious, but I'll ask just one. Do you trust Freddy? To keep his end of this bargain."

"I don't know why, I do. He needs to impress me as a man of honor, maybe."

"He wants me only once?"

"That's what he said."

She laughed a syllable and turned her back on him. "I don't seem to arouse very strong passions in men." Her words were muffled but her accent sounded ironical.

He lifted himself on an elbow to hear her better. Was she crying? Would she die?

She answered his lurch, "I'd rather not do it here in town. There are too many cars and children to keep track of. Aren't the Thornes coming on the Washington's Birthday ski weekend?"

"Sure. They never miss anything."

"Well, the children will all be in the bunk rooms and we'll

probably be along the same hall. You've slept with Georgene?"

He hesitated, then saw that they had passed into another room of their life altogether, and admitted, "In the past."

"Well then. It's all very neat. No, Piet, don't touch me. I really must go to sleep."

The ski lodge still displayed on its bulletin board photographs of itself in summer, as if to say, *This is me, this soft brown lake, these leafy birches, not the deathlike mask of ice and snow in which you find me.* The defunct cuckoo clock still haunted the high corner misted with cobwebs, the television set crackled with ignored news, the elderly young proprietors came and went with ashtrays and ice trays, trailing an air of disapproval. The rates had been raised. The raisin sauce on the ham was less generous. A quartet of strangers played bridge, and the Tarbox couples played word games on the floor. Whiskey warmed their bodies with a triumphant languor—they were survivors, the fortunate, the employed, the healthy, the free. The slopes today had been brilliant, under the holiday sun that daily looped higher. The conditions had been icy at the top, powdery in the middle of the mountain and along the shaded trails, corny on the broad lower slopes, and slushy by the base lodge, where mud was beginning to wear through. The potent sun, the prickling scintillating showers of dry snow abruptly loosened from the pine branches overhanging the trails, the heavyish conditions, the massive moguls carved by two months of turning and edging all freighted the skiers' bodies with a luxurious lassitude. They began to retire earlier than they had last year, when Freddy Thorne regaled the Applesmiths with his fantasies. Now Jonathan little-Smith, nearly thirteen, was livelier than his parents, and made Frankie Appleby, two years younger and cranky from drowsiness, play one losing game of chess after another. The only way to get him to bed was for Harold and Marcia to go themselves, out to the gas-heated cottage where Julia and Henrietta already were sleeping. The Applebys promptly followed. This year both couples were in cottages—at opposite ends, Janet had insisted, of the row. Then the Guerins, though Freddy huggingly begged Roger to stay for another drink, and Bea cast wise swarming glances of farewell to Piet, went out into the night, barren of a moon, to their hissing cottage. This left the Gallaghers, Hanemas, and Thornes. The Whitmans did not ski. Eddie Constantine, promoted to ever greater responsibilities, was piloting a wonderful new jet, three-engined and hot, the Boeing 727, to San Juan. The Saltzes, who had announced this as the winter when they would take up skiing, were now authoritatively rumored to have accepted the Cleveland offer, to be leaving Tarbox; and instantly they had become pariahs. After some constrained banter Matt Gallagher primly coughed and announced that *he* was going to bed. The emphasis of "he" implied that Terry had been formally given freedom. She, who under circumstances confided only to Carol Constantine had stopped taking pottery lessons, promptly stood and said that so was *she*. When the Hanemas and Thornes were alone, disposed as couples face to face on the two sofas opposed across a maple coffee table stacked with back copies of *Ski* and *Vogue*, Freddy said to Piet, "You and Matt don't seem to have much to say to each other these days."

Piet told him, "He does his end, and I do mine."

Freddy smiled fishily. "Not much doing at your end these days, is there, Handball?"

"There will be soon. As soon as the frost breaks we'll be going back to Indian Hill. Six houses this summer is the plan." A year ago he would not have given Freddy the satisfaction of so full a response, almost an apology.

Angela sat up and parted an invisible drape with her hands. "Well. Is this the night?" Her face looked fevered from sun and windburn, and her eyes had been so steeped in unaccustomed exercise and the beauty of the day that the irises and pupils were indistinguishable. She had changed her ski costume for a looseknit mauve sweater and white pants flared at the ankles; she was barefoot. She had become Janet Appleby.

Georgene stood and said, "I'm not going to listen to this. I'm going to go to bed and lock the door and take a sleeping pill. You three do whatever you want. Don't involve *me*." She stood as if waiting to be argued with.

Freddy said, "But Georgie-pie, you started everything. This is just my tit for your tat. What's sauce for the goose, et cetera."

"You're contemptible. All of you." Her long chin flinty, she crossed through the light of several lamps to the stairs. The day's sun had already become on her face the start of a tan.

While she was still within earshot, Freddy said, "Oh hell. Let's call it off. I was just curious to see your reactions."

Angela said, "No, sir. There's some kind of a bargain and we're going to keep our side. We better go up now because all that fresh air is getting to me and I'll soon fall asleep."

Piet found he could not look at either of them: he felt their faces, blurs in his upper vision, as deformed, so deformed that if he dared to lift his eyes to them he might involuntarily whimper or laugh. He told his stockinged feet, "Let's give Georgene a minute to get into her room. Freddy, should you get your toothbrush or anything?"

Freddy asked, "She's on the pill, isn't she?"

"Of course. Welcome to paradise." Piet stayed sitting on the sofa as they went up. Angela kissed him good night on his cheek; his head refused to move. Her lips had felt weirdly distinct, the parted carved lips of a statue, but a statue warmed by fire. He dared look at her only as she disappeared up the stairs, gazing straight ahead, her gentle hair unbound from the scarlet ear-warmer she wore skiing. Freddy followed, his white hands held lamely at his chest, his mouth open as if to form a bubble.

The upstairs hall was hushed. A single light bulb burned. Georgene's door looked tight shut. The Gallaghers in the room adjacent could be heard murmuring. On silent bare feet Angela led Freddy into her room, and then without their touching excused herself to go back into the hall, to the lavatory. When Freddy in turn returned from the lavatory, she was in her nightie, simple cotton such as a child might wear, a green flower stitched at the neckline. The room's single window overlooked a shallow deck that in summer would be a sunporch; the banister supported baroque shapes of snow sculpted by the melting of the day and the night's refreezing. Within the room there was a double bed with a brass-pipe headboard, a porcelain washstand stained by the hot-water faucet's tears, a five-and-dime mirror, an old rocking chair painted Chinese red, a pine bureau painted bile green, a black bedside table nicked by alarm-clock legs and holding a paperbound copy of *Beyond the Pleasure Principle* and a gay small lamp whose shade was orange. When Angela, who had been brushing down her hair amid serene explosions of static, bent to turn out this lamp, the light pierced the simple cloth and displayed her silhouetted bulk, the pucker of her belly; her big breasts swayed in the poppy glow like sluggish fish in an aquarium of rosewater. The light snapped off and a ghost replaced her. Her voice from a frame of fluffed black hair asked Freddy, "Don't you want to take off your clothes?"

Snowlight from the window picked out along the rim of her hair those tendrils looped outwards by the vigor of the brushing. She had expanded expectantly. Freddy felt the near presence of her blood-filled body as an animal feels the nearness of water, of prey, or of a predator. He said, "Love to, but how would you feel about a drink first? You haven't anything in the suitcase, a little Jack Daniels, say?"

"We brought some bourbon but it's downstairs. Shall I go down and take it from Piet?"

"Jesus, no. Don't go near him."

"Do you really need a drink? I think you've had plenty."

The lining of his mouth felt scratchy, as if he had chewed and swallowed a number of square blocks. This ungainly squareness had descended, still abrasive, to his stomach. Her long-awaited nearness had crystallized his poisons. He said, "I see you're still reading Freud."

"I love this one. It's very severe and elegant. He says we, all animals, carry our deaths in us—that the organic wants to be returned to the inorganic state. It wants to rest."

"It's been years since I read it. I think I doubted it at the time." Paralyzed, he felt her unbuttoning his shirt. He was immobilized by the vision of a drink—amber, clouded with ice—and the belief that its smoky golden distillation would banish his inner kinks. He let her part the halves of his shirt and fumble at his fly until, irritated at her own inexpertness, she turned away. She went to the window, glanced out quickly, peeled off her nightgown, and jackknifed herself, breasts bobbling, into the tightly made bed. "Oh, it's icy," she cried, and pulled the covers over her face. "Hurry, Freddy": the call came muffled.

He imagined Piet downstairs with the whiskey bottle, in the long room golden from the fire, and undressed down to his underwear, and got into the bed.

"Hey," Angela said. "You're cheating."

"You scared me by saying the bed was so cold."

"Well. Let's warm it up." She touched him in front. "Oh. You're not excited."

"I'm in shock," Freddy told her, stalling, adjusting the covers. The tightly made sheets had virginally resisted his entry, and then tangled, exposing him behind.

"Piet never—" Angela stopped. Had she been going to say, "—is not excited"? She instead said, "I don't move you."

"You stun me. I've always loved you."

"You don't have to say that. I'm nothing special. Sometimes I look at myself in the mirror Piet gave Ruth and I see this knotty veiny fat peasant woman's body with tiny red feet and a dear little oval head that doesn't go with the rest. Piet calls me a dolphin." She remembered that he called her this in bed, when she turned her rump upon her husband and, holding him in herself, exposed her curved back to his smoothing rough hands.

"How are you and Piet getting along?"

She realized Freddy wanted to talk, and foresaw that talk would make her sleepy. She tickled the gap between his undershirt and pants elastic while answering, "Better, really. He's been bothered about something lately, but I think basically we're more *fun* for each other than we've been for years. I think it's taken me a year to forgive him for not letting me have the Robinson place. The Whitman place, I should say. Those people haven't made much of an impression on me." She lifted his shirt and snuggled against his bare chest.

"But—how do you reconcile this?" Freddy asked.

"With what?" His dumbstruck silence led her to laugh; fatty warm points, her breasts, shimmered against him, and the jiggled bed complained. "You and me in bed? He told me I should do it. The Hamiltons are always obedient wives. Anyway, I was curious what it would be like. And I must say, Freddy, you're being passive. Take off these insulting clothes."

She managed to lower his elastic waistband—unlike Piet's Paisley, he wore little-boy Jockey briefs. When he was naked, she explored with pinches his sides and the tops of his arms. "Freddy Thorne," she said, "you are pudgy." Her fingers went lower. "And still little," she accused. Delicate and tepid, his genitals lay in her hand like three eggs, boiled and peeled and cooled, she was carrying to the table. The sensation made Angela languorous. She hadn't dreamed men could be this calm with women. She could never have held Piet so long. Even asleep. Their sweetest phase. Not tucked safe inside like women. Committed to venture. More injurable.

Testingly Freddy placed his hand on her back, as if they were dancing. Her skin felt dark to him, oily and Negroid: flat wide muscles glidingly wedged into one another, massive buttocks like moons heaved from an ancient earth. Her body's bland power dismayed him. That Angela, the most aloof of women, whose shy sensitive listening had aroused in his talking tongue the eager art of a drill probing near pulp, should harbor in her clothes the same voracious spread of flesh as other women afflicted Freddy, touching his way across the smooth skin black as lava, with the nausea of disillusion. Her hand under his balls seemed about to claw. He begged, "Let's talk." He longed for her voice to descend from silence, to forgive him.

She asked, "Is there anything you'd like me to do? Anything special?"

"Just talk. Aren't you curious about what the bargain is?"

"No. It feels too scary to me, I don't want to hear it. I feel we've all gone too far to know everything. It's awful of me, but I've never wanted to know about Piet and his women. For me it's no more part of him than his going to the bathroom. You can't realize this, but he's terribly pleasant around the house."

"Tell me about it. I never can picture you and Piet fucking."

"How funny of you, Freddy. You've idealized me or mixed me up with somebody else. Piet and I don't"—she couldn't manage the word, out of consideration, it seemed, for *him*—"as often as he'd like, but of course we do. More and more, in fact."

"Have you ever slept with anyone except Piet?"

"Never. I thought maybe I should."

"Why?"

"So I'd be better at it."

"For *him*. Shit. Let's face it, Angela. You married a bastard. A bully boy. He's pimping for you. He's got you so intimidated you'll shack up with anybody he tells you to."

"You're not anybody, Freddy. I more or less trust you. You're like me. You want to teach."

"I used to. Then I learned the final thing to teach and I didn't want to learn any more."

"What final thing?"

"We die. We don't die for one second out there in the future, we die all the time, in every direction. Every meal we eat breaks down the enamel."

"Hey. You've gotten bigger."

"Death excites me. Death is being screwed by God. It'll be delicious."

"You don't believe in God."

"I believe in that one, Big Man Death. I smell Him between people's teeth every day."

He was hoping to keep her at a distance with such violence of vision but she nudged closer again, crowding him with formless warmth. Her toes engaged his toes; her chin dug into his chest, the hard bone to the right of the heart. "Piet's terrified of death," she said, snuggling.

Freddy told her, "It's become his style. He uses it now as self-justification. He's mad at the world for killing his parents."

"Men are so romantic," Angela said, after waiting for him to tell her more. "Piet spends all his energy defying death, and you spend all yours accepting it."

"That's the difference between us. Male versus female."

"You think of yourself as female?"

"Of course. Clearly I'm homosexual. But then, of the men in town, who isn't, except poor old Piet?"

"Freddy. You're just leading me on, to see what I'll say. Be sincere."

"I am sincere. Anybody with a little psychology can see I'm right. Think. Frank and Harold. They screw each other's wives because they're too snobbish to screw each other. Janet senses it; she's just their excuse. Take Guerin and Constantine. They're made for each other."

"Of course, Roger—"

"Eddie's worse. He's a suc*cess*ful sadist. Or Gallagher and Whitman. Spoiled priests. Saltz and Ong, maybe not, but one's moving and the other's dying. Anyway, they don't count, they're not Christian. Me, I'm worst of all, I want to be everybody's mother. I want to have breasts so everybody can have a suck. Why do you think I drink so much? To make milk."

Angela said, "You've really thought about this, haven't you?"

"No, I'm making it all up, to distract your attention from my limp prick; but it works, doesn't it? Piet stands alone. No wonder the women in town are tearing him to pieces."

"Is that why you've always hated him?"

"Hated him, hell. I love him. We both love him."

"Freddy, you are not a homosexual and I'm going to prove it." She pushed herself higher in bed, so her breasts swam into starlight and her pelvis was above his. She lifted a thigh so it rested on his hipbone. "Come on. Put it in me."

He had kept a half-measure of firmness, but the slick warmth of her vagina singed him like a finger too slowly passed through a candleflame.

Feeling him grow little again, she asked again, "What can I do?"

He suggested, "Blow me?"

"Do what? I don't know how."

Pitying her, seeing through this confession into a mansion of innocence that the Hanemas, twin closed portals, had concealed, Freddy said, "Skip it. Let's gossip. Tell me if you think Janet still goes to bed with Harold."

'She made a big deal of getting cottages at opposite ends of the row."

"Merely thirty or so yards, not very far even in bare feet, if your heart's in it. My thought about Janet is, being her father's daughter, she really believes in cures. She had the baby, then she took a lover, then she went into analysis; and still she wears that headachy expression."

"I want to go into analysis," Angela told him. Her voice was slow and her weight now rested all on the bed, depressing it in the middle so that Freddy had to resist rolling closer toward her. His voice stroking, his hand on her halo of hair, he talked to her about analysis, about himself, about Marcia and Frank, Irene and Eddie, about John Ong's cancer, about the fate of them all, suspended in this one of those dark ages that visits mankind between millennia, between the death and rebirth of gods, when there is nothing to steer by but sex and stoicism and the stars. Angela, reminded by his tone and rhythm of her parents and uncle talking, of the tireless Gibbs pedantry, the sterile mild preachiness descended from the pilgrims, in which she had been enwombed, and from which Piet had seemed to rescue her, dozed, reawoke, heard Freddy still discoursing, and fell irrevocably asleep. He, having held her at bay and deepened his shame and completed his vengeance, felt himself grow strong and adamant and masturbated toward her belly, taking care not to defile her. Then both, parallel, floated toward dawn, their faces slacker than children's.

Downstairs, Piet, having poured himself one more bourbon, had grown cold beside the dying fire, and bored, and outraged. He tried to use his parka as a blanket but it was too small. He tiptoed up the stairs, listened at his own door, and tapped at Georgene's. He tested the lock. It gave. Georgene, though at first overwhelmingly indignant about being discarded by her lover, betrayed by her husband, and treated like an insignificant counter in this game, accepted Piet into her bed, because there was really nowhere to sit, and it was cold. She vowed to him she would not make love. Piet agreed. But, as he lay meekly beside her, his proximity and the danger of insomnia conspired to render her resolve unreal. He offered to rub her back. She invited him into her body. As always, though many distorting months had intervened, they came together; her face snapped sideways as if slapped, a welling softness merged with his clangor, her thighs flared to take him more fully, and he knew that he had exaggerated his trouble, that fate could be appeased.

v. *It's Spring Again*

Iɴ Bᴏsᴛᴏɴ Cᴏᴍᴍᴏɴ there is a somber little pavilion surrounded by uneven brick paving and cement-and-slat benches for band concerts. Here Piet waited for Foxy to come down from a dentist's office in a mustard-colored six-story office building on Tremont Street. By this the middle of March few other idlers were present in the park. Some children in snowsuits were snuffing caps on the lip of the dry wading pool; a gray squirrel raced staccato across the dead grass, at intervals pausing as if to be photographed or to gauge the danger expressed by the muted gunshot sound of the caps. Piet's own scuffing footsteps sounded loud. There was a mist in which the neon signs along Tremont and Boylston distinctly burned. Sooty wet pigeons veered arrogantly close to the heads of hurrying passersthrough. Trees overhead, serene fountains of life labeled *Ulmis hollandicis,* dangled into the vaporous air drooping branchlets dotted with unbroken buds, having survived the blight to greet another year. The wheel turned. Time seemed to Piet as he waited a magnificent silence: the second hand of his watch circling the dial daintily, the minute hand advancing with imperceptible precision. He almost adored the heartlessness that stretched him here for hours, untouched by any news. RUBY GUILTY, TO DIE, said a discarded tabloid being mulched by footsteps into the mud and ice bordering the path. The palm of Piet's left hand tingled thunderously whenever he read the headline, or heard a child shout.

Freddy and Foxy had arranged the matter between them so efficiently Piet felt excluded. Neither wished to explain the arrangements to him. Foxy, pale on Charity Street, her nostrils pinched by wind, a tearing bag of groceries bulky in her arms, told him, "You don't have to do a thing. I'd rather you didn't even know when it happens. Just tell me one thing now. Is it what you want? You want this child destroyed?"

"Yes." His simplicity shocked her; she turned paler still. He asked, "What are the alternatives?"

"You're right," she said coldly, "there are none," and turned away, the bag tearing a bit more in her arms.

She explained the plan to him later, reluctantly, over the phone. Ken had to go to Chicago three days for a biochemical symposium, in the middle of March, beginning on a Wednesday, the eighteenth. Wednesday was also Freddy's day off, so he could take her up to Boston to the idealist who for three hundred fifty dollars would perform the abortion. Freddy would stay with her and drive her back home to Tarbox. Alone in her home at the far end of the beach road, she would need only to feed herself and Tobias, who slept twelve hours a day. Georgene would come by in the mornings and evenings, and Foxy would be free to call her any time. If complications ensued, she could be admitted to the Tarbox hospital as a natural abortion, and Ken would be told the child had been his.

Piet objected to Georgene's knowing.

Foxy said, "She already knows there was some kind of hideous bargain. It's Freddy's decision, and he's entitled to it. If anything were to happen to me, you must realize, he'd be an accessory to murder."

"Nothing will happen to you."

"Let's assume not. Georgene can drop around in a way neither you or Freddy can. Marcia goes up and down that road all day. It is especially important that *you* stay away. Forget I exist." She would not tell him the address of the abortionist until she had talked to Freddy again. "Freddy's afraid you'll do something dramatic and crazy."

"And are you?"

"No." Her tone was not kind.

Freddy called him that afternoon, gave him the address on Tremont, absolutely forbade his coming in with them, and tried to discourage his keeping watch from the Common. "What can you do?" Freddy asked. He answered himself scornfully: "Pray. If she's had it, son, she's had it." The ambiguity of "had it," the suggestion of a finite treasurable "it" that Foxy could enclose and possess, as one says "had him" of sleeping with a man, the faint impression that Foxy was competing for a valuable prize, sent ghosts tumbling and swirling through Piet, the ghosts of all those creatures and celebrities who had already attained the prize. He longed to call it off, to release Freddy from his bargain and let Foxy swell, but that wouldn't do; he told himself it had gone beyond him, that Freddy and Foxy would push it through regardless: they had become gods moving in the supernature where life is created and destroyed. He replaced the receiver physically sick, his hand swollen like a drowned man's, the brittle Bakelite more alive than he.

Yet last night, playing Concentration with his two daughters, knowing he had set a death in motion, he cared enough to concentrate and win. Piling up cards under Nancy's eyes filling with tears. She had thought the game hers. A little beginner's luck had told her she owned a magic power of selecting pairs. Piet had disillusioned her. A father's duty. But so jubilantly. Ruth had watched his vigorous victory wonderingly.

A snuffly bum approached him, hand out, whiskers like quills. Piet shied from being knifed. The other man confusedly flinched, palm empty. Piet settled to listening; he was being asked for something. Dime. Derelict wanted a dime. His voice retreated behind the whiskers toward the mumbled roots of language. Piet gave him a quarter. "Gahblessyafella." Angel in disguise. Never turn away. Men coming to the door during the Depression. His mother's pies. Bread upon the waters. Takes your coat, give him your cloak. Asks a mile, go twain. Nobody believes. Philanthropy a hoax to avoid Communism. As a child he wondered who would eat wet bread. Tired old tales. Loaves and fishes, litter. Keep your Boston clean. He found himself hungry. A lightness in his limbs, strange sensation, how does it know food? Strange angels, desires. Come from beyond us, inhabit our machines. Piet refused his hunger. If he ran to the cafeteria burning at the corner, Foxy would die. He did without. His mother's beautiful phrase. *Well sen, do wissout.* Her floury arms upreaching to the pantry shelf. Glory. An engine of love ran through him, flattened his gut. Never again. *Moeder is dood.*

Cruel hours passed. The pavilion, the frost-buckled bricks, the squirrels posing for snapshots, the hurtling gangs of hoodlum pigeons, the downhanging twigs glazed with mist to the point of dripping became the one world Piet knew: all the others—the greenhouse, the army, the houses and parties of his friends in Tarbox—seemed phantom precedents, roads skimmed to get here. Hunger questioned his vaporous head, but he went without. Might miss Foxy's moment. The knife. Ask for a dime, give a quarter. Fifteen-cent profit. He was protecting his investment. His being expanded upward in the shape of a cone tapering toward prayer. Undo it. Rid me of her and her of it and us of Freddy. Give me back my quiet place. At an oblique angle she had intersected the plane of his life where daily routines accumulated like dust. Lamplight, breakfast. She had intruded a drastic dimension. He had been innocent amid trees. She had demanded that he know. Straight string of his life, knotted. The knot surely was sin. Piet prayed for it to be undone.

Overhead the elm branches were embedded in a sky of dirty wool: erosion deltas photographed high above the drained land: stained glass. Footsteps returning from lunch scuffed everywhere in the Common distinctly, as if under an enclosing dome. A small reddish bug crawled along an edge of brick. Happened before. When? His head tilted just so. Exactly. His mind sank scrabbling through the abyss of his past searching for when this noticing of an insect had happened before. He lifted his eyes and saw the Park Street church, stately. He looked around him at the grayly streaming passersthrough and all people seemed miraculous, that they could hold behind their glowing faces the knowledge that soon, under the whitewash-spattered sky, they would wither or be cut.

Church. Tolled. Three. He weakened, broke faith with himself, ran for coffee and one, no two, cinnamon doughnuts. When he emerged from the cafeteria the yellow sky between the buildings was full of Foxy. Coffee slopping through the paper cup and burning his fingers, he ran up Tremont, convinced of hopeless guilt. But Freddy's car, his yellow Mercury convertible, the canvas top mildewed from being buttoned up all winter, was still parked, half on the sidewalk, down a narrow alley off the street, near a metal door painted one with the mustard wall yet whose hinges, rubbed down to the bare steel, betrayed that it could be opened. So she was not gone. He went back across Tremont to the pavilion's vicinity and ate.

His feet grew numb. Boston danker than Tarbox: oily harbor lets in the cold sea kiss. More northern. To his dread for Foxy attached a worry that he would be missed at home. Gallagher, Angela, each would think the other had him. The sun slipped lower behind the dome of sky, to where the walls were thinner. Sunshine luminous as tallow tried to set up shadows, touched the tree plaques and dry fountains. In this light Piet saw the far door down the alley open and a dab that must be bald Freddy emerge. Dodging through thickening traffic, Piet's body seemed to float, footless, toward the relief of knowing, as when he would enter the Whitmans' house by the doorway crowded with lilacs and move through the hallway fragrant of freshly planed wood toward the immense sight of the marshes and Foxy's billowing embrace. Freddy Thorne looked up from unlocking his car door, squinting, displeased to see him. Neither man could think to speak. In the gaping steel doorway a Negress in a green nurse's uniform and silver-rim spectacles was standing supporting Foxy.

She was conscious but drugged; her pointed face, half-asleep, was blotched pink and white as if her cheeks had been struck, and struck again. Her eyes paused on Piet, then passed over him. Her hair flowed all on one side, like wheat being winnowed, and the collar of her Russian-general greatcoat, a coat he loved, was up, and buttoned tight beneath her chin like a brace.

Freddy moved rapidly to her side, said "Six steps," and, his mouth grimly lipless, one arm around her waist, the other beneath her elbow, eased her toward the open car door as if at any jarring she might break. The Negress in silence closed the metal door upon herself. She had not stepped into the alley. Piet's running had attracted the curiosity of some pedestrians, who watched from the sidewalk at the alley mouth yet did not step toward them. Freddy lowered Foxy into the passenger's seat, whispering, "Good girl." With the usual punky noise of car doors hers swung shut. She was behind glass. The set of her mouth, the tension above the near corner predicting laughter, appeared imperfectly transported from the past, a shade spoiled, giving her face the mysterious but final deadness of minutely imitated wax effigies. Then two fingertips came up from her lap and smoothed the spaces of skin below her eyes.

Piet vaulted around the front of the car. Freddy was already in the driver's seat; grunting, he rolled his window some inches down. "Well, if it isn't Piet Enema, the well-known purge."

Piet asked, "Is she—?"

"Okey-doak," Freddy said. "Smooth as silk. You're safe again, lover."

"What took so long?"

"She's been lying down, out, what did you think, she'd get up and dance? Get your fucking hand off the door handle."

Perhaps roused by Freddy's fury of tone, Foxy looked over. Her hand touched her lips. "Hi," she said. The voice was warmer, drowsier, than hers. "I know you," she added, attempting, Piet felt, irony and confession at once, the irony acknowledging that she knew very well this intruder whom she could not quite name. Freddy rolled up the window, punched down both door locks, started the motor, gave Piet a blind stare of triumph. Delicately, taking care not to shake his passenger, he eased the car down off the curb into the alley and into the trashy stream of homeward traffic. A condom and candy wrapper lay paired in the exposed gutter.

Not until days later, after Foxy had survived the forty-eight hours alone in the house with Toby and the test of Ken's return from Chicago, did Piet learn, not from Freddy but from her as told to her by Freddy, that at the moment of anesthesia she had panicked; she had tried to strike the Negress pressing the sweet, sweet mask to her face and through the first waves of ether had continued to cry that she should go home, that she was supposed to have this baby, that the child's father was coming to smash the door down with a hammer and would stop them.

After she confessed this to him over the phone on Monday, his silence stretched so long she laughed to break it. "Don't take it upon yourself that you didn't come break down the door. I didn't want you to. It was my subconscious speaking, and only after I had consciously got myself to the point of no return, and I could relax. What we did was right. We couldn't do anything else, could we?"

"I couldn't think of anything else."

"We were very lucky to have brought it off. We ought to thank our, what?—our lucky stars." She laughed again, a perfunctory rustle in the apparatus.

Piet asked her, "Are you depressed?"

"Yes. Of course. Not because I've committed any sin so much, since it was what you asked me to do, what had to be done for everybody's sake, really. But because now I'm faced with it again, *really* faced with it now."

"With what?"

"My life, Ken, this cold house. The loss of your love. Oh, and my milk's dried up, so I have that to feel sorry for myself about. Toby keeps throwing up his formula. And Cotton's gone."

"Cotton."

"My cat. Don't you remember him?"

"Of course. He always greeted me."

"He was here Wednesday morning catching field mice on the edge of the marsh and when I came back that night he was gone. I didn't even notice. Thursday I began to call, but I was too weak to go outdoors much."

Piet said, "He's out courting."

"*No*," Foxy said, "he was fixed," and the receiver was rhythmically scraped by her sobs.

He asked her, "Why didn't you talk to me more, before we did it?"

"I was angry, which I suppose is the same as being frightened. And what did we have to say? We'd said it. You were too chicken to let me have it as if it were Ken's, and I've always known I could never get you away from Angela. No, don't argue."

He was obediently silent.

She said, "But what now, Piet? What shall we expect of each other?"

He answered, after thought, "Not much."

"It's easier for you," she said. "You'll always have somebody else to move on to. Don't deny it. Me, I seem stuck. You want to know something horrible?"

"If you'd like to tell it."

"I can't stand Ken now. I can hardly bear to look at his face, or answer when he talks. I think of it as *him* who made me kill my baby. It's *just* the kind of thing he'd do."

"Sweet, it wasn't him, it was *me*."

Foxy explained to him, what he had heard often before, how Ken, in denying her a child for seven years, had killed in her something only another man could revive. She ended by asking, "Piet, will you ever come talk to me? Just talk?"

"Do you think we should?"

"Should, shouldn't. Of course we shouldn't. But I'm down, lover, I'm just terribly, terribly down." She pronounced these words with a stagy lassitude learned from the movies. The script called for her to hang up, and she did. Losing another dime, he dialed her number from the booth, the booth in front of Poirier's Liquor Mart, where one of their friends might all too likely spot him, a droll corpse upright in a bright aluminum coffin. At Foxy's house, no one answered. Of course he must go to her. Death, once invited in, leaves his muddy bootprints everywhere.

Georgene, faithful to Freddy's orders, came calling on Foxy that Monday, around noon, and was shocked to see Piet's pick-up truck parked in the driveway. She felt a bargain had not been kept. Her understanding had been that the abortion would end Foxy's hold over Piet; she believed that once Foxy was eliminated her own usefulness to Piet would reassert itself. She prided herself, Georgene, on being useful, on keeping her bargains and carrying out the assignments given her, whether it was obtaining a guest speaker for the League of Women Voters, or holding her service in a tennis match, or staying married to Freddy Thorne. She had visited Foxy late Wednesday night, twice on Thursday, and once on Friday. She had carried tea and toast up to the convalescent, changed Toby's spicy orange diapers, and seen two baskets of clothes and sheets through the washer and dryer. On Friday she had spent over an hour vacuuming the downstairs and tidying toward Ken's return. Her feelings toward Foxy altered in these days of domestic conspiracy. Georgene, from her first glimpse, a year ago at the Applebys' party, of this prissy queenly newcomer, had disliked her; when Foxy stole Piet from her this dislike became hatred, with its implication of respect. But with the younger woman at her mercy Georgene allowed herself tenderness. She saw in Foxy a woman destined to dare and to suffer, a younger sister spared any compulsion to settle cheap, whose very mistakes were obscurely enviable. She was impressed with Foxy's dignity. Foxy did not deny that in this painful interregnum she needed help and company, nor did she attempt to twist Georgene's providing it into an occasion for protestation, or scorn, or confession, or self-contempt. Georgene knew from living with Freddy how surely self-contempt becomes contempt for others and was pleased to have her presence in Foxy's house accepted for what it was, an accident. Wednesday night, Foxy dismissed her with the grave tact of a child assuring a parent she is not afraid of the dark. She was weepy and half-drugged and clutched her living baby to her like a doll, yet from a deep reserve of manners thanked Georgene for coming, permitted her bloody bedsheets to be changed, accepted the injunction not to go up and down stairs, nodded gravely when told to call the Thornes' number at any hour, for any reason, even senseless fright. Thursday morning, Georgene found her downstairs, pale from lack of sleep; she had been unable to breast-feed the baby and had had to come downstairs to heat up a bottle. Obedient, she had not attempted the return trip upstairs, and with one blanket had made a bed for them both on the sofa. Imagining those long moon-flooded hours, the telephone offering a tempting release from solitude, Georgene secretly admired the other's courage and pride. She helped her upstairs and felt leaning upon her, naked under its robe and slip, the taller, less supple, rather cool and dry and ungainly body her lover had loved. Imagined love flowed from her. The current was timidly returned. They were silent in unison. They moved together, in these few days, whose weather outside was a humid raw foretaste of spring less comfortable than outright winter, through room upon room of tactful silence. They did not speak of Piet or of Freddy or of the circumstances that had brought them together except as they were implied by Georgene's inquiries into Foxy's physical condition. They discussed health and housework and the weather outside and the needs of the infant. Friday afternoon, the last day Georgene was needed, she brought along little Judy, and in the festive atmosphere of recovery Foxy, now fully clothed, served cookies and vermouth and persuaded Georgene, after her exertions of cleaning, to smoke an unaccustomed cigarette. Awkwardly they lifted their glasses as if to toast one another: two women who had tidied up after a mess.

Georgene had not been asked to return on Monday. But she was curious to know how Foxy had weathered the weekend, had put off Ken. She would ask if Foxy needed any shopping done. Seeing Piet's truck in the driveway, she experienced a compounded jealousy, a multiple destruction within her: the first loss was her tender comradeship with the other woman. Of Piet she expected nothing except that he continue to exist and unwittingly illumine her life. She had willed herself open to him and knew that the chemistry of love was all within her, her doing. Even his power to wound her with neglect was a power she had created and granted; whatever he did he could not escape the province of her freedom, her free decision to love. Whereas between her and Foxy a polity existed: rules, a complex set of assumed concessions, a generous bargain posited upon the presumption of defeat.

Georgene seldom visited the middle ground between female submission and sexless mastery, so her negotiated fondness for Foxy was rarer for her, more precious perhaps, than her love for Piet, which was predetermined and unchanging and somewhat stolid. Foxy's betrayal found her vulnerable. She was revealed to herself as not merely helpless but foolish. Helplessness has its sensual consolations; foolishness has none. She pushed through the door without knocking.

Piet and Foxy were sitting well apart, on opposite sides of the coffee table. Piet had not removed the zippered apricot suède windbreaker he wore to jobs, and the stub of a yellow pencil was tucked behind his ear. The morning marsh light struck white fire from the hem of Foxy's frilled nightie and froze into ice her pale hand holding a cigarette from which spiraled smoke sculptural as blue stone. Coffee equipment mixed arcs of china and metal and sun on the low teak table between them. Georgene felt she had entered upon a silence. Her indignation was balked by her failure to surprise them embracing. Nevertheless, Piet was embarrassed, and half rose.

"Don't get up," Georgene told him. "I don't mean to interrupt your cozy tryst."

"It wasn't," he told her.

"Just a meeting of souls. How beautiful." She turned to Foxy. "I came to offer to do your shopping and to see how you were doing. I see you're back to normal and won't be needing me any more. Good."

"Don't take that tone, Georgene. I was just telling Piet, how wonderful you were."

"*He* wasn't telling *you?* I'm hurt."

"Why are you angry? Don't you think Piet and I have a right to talk?"

Piet moved forward on his chair, grunting, "I'll go."

Foxy said, "You certainly will not. You just got here. Georgene, have some coffee. Let's stop playing charades."

Georgene refused to sit. "Please don't imagine," she said, "that I have personal feelings about this. It's none of my business what you two do, or rather it wouldn't be if my husband hadn't saved your necks at the risk of his own. But I *will* say, for your own good, unless you're planning to elope, it is very sloppy to have Piet's pick-up truck out where Marcia could drive by any minute."

"Marcia's at her psychiatrist in Brookline," Foxy said. "She's gone every day from ten to two, or longer, if she has lunch with Frank in town."

Piet said, wanting to have a conversation, a party, "Is Marcia going too? Angela's just started."

Georgene asked him, "How on earth can *you* afford it?"

"I can't," he said. "But Daddy Hamilton can. It's something the two of them cooked up."

"And what were you two cooking up, when I barged in?"

"Nothing," Piet told her. "In fact we were having some trouble finding things to say."

Foxy asked, "Why shouldn't I talk to the father of my child?"

Piet said, "It wasn't a child, it was a little fish, less than a fish. It was nothing, Fox."

"It was *something,* damn you. You weren't carrying it."

Georgene was jealous of their quarrel, their display of proud hearts. She and Freddy rarely quarreled. They went to sleep on one another, and kept going to parties together, and felt dreary all next day, like veteran invalids. Only Piet had brought her word of a world where vegetation was heraldic and every woman was some man's queen. That world was like, she thought, the marsh seen through the windows, where grasses prospered in salty mud that would kill her kind of useful plant. "I honestly think," she heard herself saying, "that one of you ought to move out of Tarbox."

They were amazed, amused. Foxy asked, "Whatever for?"

"For your own good. For everybody's good. You're poisoning the air."

"If any air's been poisoned," Piet told her, "it's your husband that's done it. He's the local gamesmaster."

"Freddy just wants to be human. He knows you all think he's ridiculous so he's adopted that as his act. Anyway, I didn't mean poison. Maybe the rest of us are poisoned and you two upset us with your innocence. Think of just yourselves. Piet, look at her.

Why do you want to keep tormenting her with your presence? Make her take her husband back to Cambridge. Quit Gallagher and go somewhere else, go back to Michigan. You'll destroy each other. I was with her at the end of last week. It's not a little thing you put her through."

Foxy cut in drily. "It was my decision. I'm grateful for your help, Georgene, but I would have gotten through alone. And we would have found a way without Freddy, though that *did* work out. As to Piet and me, we have no intention of sleeping together again. I think you're saying you still want him. Take him."

"That's *not* what I'm saying! Not at all!" There had been some selfless point, some public-spirited truth she had been trying to frame for these two, and they were too corrupt to listen.

Piet said, joking, "I feel I'm being auctioned off. Should we let Angela bid too?"

He was amused. They were both amused. Georgene had entertained them, made them vivid to themselves. Watching her tremblingly try to manage her coffee cup, a clumsy intruder, they were lordly, in perfect control. Having coaxed the abortion from their inferiors, they were quite safe, and would always exist for each other. Their faces were pleasant in sunlight, complacent in the same way, like animals that have eaten.

Georgene took a scalding sip of coffee and replaced the cup in its socket on the saucer and sat primly upright. "I don't know what I'm trying to say," she apologized. "I'm delighted, Foxy, to see you so happy. Frankly, I think you're a very gutsy girl."

"I'm *not* happy," Foxy said, protesting, sensing danger.

"Well, happier. I am too. I'm *so* glad spring is here, it's been a long winter up on my hill. The crocuses, Piet, are up beside the garage. When can we all start playing tennis?" She stood; there was no coat to slow her departure. On all but the coldest days of winter, Georgene wore no more than a skirt and sweater and a collegiate knit scarf. It was warming, on a January afternoon when the sun had slipped through a crack in the sky, to see her downtown dressed as if for a dazzling fall afternoon, leading snowsuited Judy over hummocks of ice, hurrying along full of resolution and inner fire.

. . .

Town meeting that spring smelled of whiskey. Piet noticed the odor as soon as he entered the new high-school auditorium, where orange plastic chairs designed to interlock covered the basketball floor solidly between the bleachers and the stage, beneath the high fluorescent emptiness hung with cables and gymnastic riggings. A few feet above the swamp of faces hovered a glimmering miasma of alcohol, of amber whiskey, of martinis hurriedly swallowed between train and dinner, with the babysitter imminent. Piet had never noticed the scent before and wondered if it were the warm night—a thawing fog had rolled in from the sea and suddenly dandelions dotted the football field—or if the town had changed. Each year there were more commuters, more young families with VW buses and Cézanne prints moving into developments miles distant from the heart of historical Tarbox. Each year, in town meeting, more self-assured young men rose to speak, and silent were the voices dominant when Piet and Angela moved to town—droning Yankee druggists, paranoid clammers, potbellied selectmen ponderously fending off antagonisms their fathers had incurred, a nearsighted hound-faced moderator who recognized only his friends and ruled all but deafening dissents into unanimity. At the first meeting Piet had attended, the town employees, a shirtsleeved bloc of ex-athletes who perched in the bleachers apart from their wives, had hooted down the elderly town attorney, Gertrude Tarbox's brother-in-law, until the old man's threadbare voice had torn and the microphone had amplified the whisper of a sob. Now the employees, jacketed, scattered, sat mute and sullen with their wives as year after year another raise was unprotestingly voted them. Now the town attorney was an urbane junior partner in a State Street firm who had taken the job as a hobby, and the moderator a rabbit-eared associate professor of sociology, a maestro of parliamentary procedure. Only an occasional issue evocative of the town's rural past—the purchase of an old barn abutting the public parking lot, or the plea of a farmer, a fabulous creature with frost-burned face and slow tumbling voice, that he be allowed to reap his winter rye before an S-curve in the Mather road was straightened—provoked debate. New schools and new highways, sewer bonds and zoning by-laws

all smoothly slid by, greased by federal grants. Each modernization and restriction presented itself as part of the national necessity, the overarching honor of an imperial nation. The last opponents, the phlegmatic pennypinchers and choleric naysayers who
had absurdly blocked the building of this new school for a
decade, had died or ceased to attend, leaving the business of the
town to be carried forward in an edifice whose glass roof leaked
and whose adjustable partitions had ceased to adjust. There was
annual talk now of representative town meeting, and the quorum
had been halved. Among Piet's friends, Harold little-Smith was
on the Finance Committee, Frank Appleby was chairman of the
committee to negotiate with the Commonwealth for taxpayer-
subsidized commuter service, Irene Saltz was chairlady of the
Conservation Commission (and charmingly coupled her report
with her resignation, since she and her husband were with sincere
regret moving to Cleveland), and Matt Gallagher sat on the
Board of Zoning Appeals. Indeed, there was no reason why Matt,
if he believed the hint of the Polish priest, could not be elected
selectman; and Georgene Thorne had narrowly missed—by the
margin of a whiff of scandal—election to the school board.

Politics bored Piet. The Dutch in his home region had been
excluded from, and had disdained, local power. His family had
been Republican under the impression that it was the party of
anarchy, they had felt government to be an illusion the governed
should not encourage. The world of politics had no more substance for Piet than the film world, and the meeting of which he
was a member made him as uncomfortable as the talent auditions
at a country fair, where faces strained by stolen mannerisms lift in
hope toward wholly imagined stars. Piet went to town meetings
to see his friends, but tonight, though the Hanemas had arrived
early, it happened that no one sat with them. The Applesmiths
and Saltzes sat up front with the politically active. On the stage,
as observers, not yet citizens, sat the young Reinhardts, whom
Piet detested. The Guerins and Thornes had entered and found
seats by the far doors and Piet never managed to catch either
woman's eye. Bernadette Ong and Carol Constantine came late,
together, without husbands. Most strangely, the Whitmans did

not attend at all, though they had now lived in Tarbox long enough to be voting citizens. At Piet's side Angela, who had to rush into Cambridge after nursery school every day and then fight the commuter traffic home, was exhausted, and kept nodding and twitching, yet as a loyal liberal insisted on staying to add her drowsy "Ayes" to the others. The train service proposal, at the annual estimated budget cost of twelve thousand dollars, on the argument that the type of people attracted to Tarbox by creditable commuter service would enrich the community inestimably, unanimously passed. The self-righteous efficiency of the meeting, hazed by booze, so irritated Piet, so threatened his instinct for freedom, that he several times left the unanimous crowd to get a drink of water at the bubbler in the hall, where he imagined that the town building inspector evaded his gaze and refused to return his hello. When the meeting, after eleven, was adjourned, he saw the other couples huddling by an exit, planning a drink at one of their homes. Harold's eager profile jabbered; Bea slowly, dreamily nodded. Angela mocked Piet's premonition of exclusion and said she wanted to go home and sleep. Before psychiatry, she would have equivocated. Piet could only yield. In the car he asked her, "Are you dead?"

"A little. All those right-of-ways and one-foot strips of land gave me a headache. Why can't they just do it in Town Hall and not torment us?"

"How did psychiatry go?"

"Not very excitingly. I felt tired and stupid and didn't know why I was there."

"Don't ask *me* why you're there."

"I wasn't."

"What do the two of you talk about?"

"Just *I'm* supposed to talk. He listens."

"And never says anything?"

"Ideally."

"Do you talk about me? How I made you sleep with Freddy Thorne?"

"We did at first. But now we're on my parents. Daddy mostly. Last Thursday it came out, just popped out of my mouth, that he always undressed in the closet. I hadn't thought about it for years. If I was in their bedroom about something, he'd come out of the closet with his pajamas on. The only way I could see him *really* was by spying on him in the bathroom."

"You spied. Angel."

"I know, it made me blush to remember it. But it made me *mad*, too. Whenever he'd be in there he'd turn on both faucets so we couldn't hear him do anything."

We: Louise, her seldom-seen sister, a smudged carbon copy, two years younger, lived in Vermont, husband teaching at a prep school. Louise married early, not the rare beauty Angela was, smudged mouth and unclear skin, probably better in bed, dirtier. He thought of Joop. His pale blond brother, flaxen hair, watery eyes, younger, purer, had carried on the greenhouse, should have married Angela, the two of them living together in receding light. Leaving him dirty Louise. Piet asked, "Did Louise ever see his penis? Did you and she ever talk about it?"

"Not really. We were terribly inhibited, I suppose, though Mother was always talking about how glorious Nature was, with that funny emphasis, and the house was full of art books. Michelangelo's, the ones on Adam, are terribly darling and limp, with long foreskins, so when I saw you, I thought—"

"What did you think?"

"I'll try to work it out with *him* what I thought."

The Nun's Bay Road was, since it had been widened, unlike the beach road, straight and rather bare, more like a Midwestern road, sparsely populated by a shuttered-up vegetable stand and, high on a knoll, a peeling gingerbread mansion with a single upstairs light burning, where a widower lived. Joop had had more Mama's eyes and mouth. Washed-out, unquestioning, shattered. He felt Angela beginning to doze and said, "I wonder if I ever saw my mother naked. Neither of them ever seemed to take a bath, at least while I was awake. I didn't think they knew a thing about sex and was shocked once when my mother in passing complained about the spots on my sheets. She wasn't really scolding, it was almost kidding. That must have been what shocked me."

"The one good thing Daddy did," Angela answered, "was to tell us to stand up straight when we began to get breasts. It made him furious to see us hunch over."

"You were ashamed of them?"

"Not ashamed so much, it just feels at first as if you can't *manage* them. They stick out and wobble."

Piet pictured Angela's breasts and told her, "I'm very hurt, that you talk about your father when I thought *I* was your problem. To be sure, he *is* the one paying for it."

"Why does that make you so angry? He has money and we don't."

The wheels of their car, her cream-colored Peugeot, crunched on gravel. They were home. Squares of windowlight transfixed shrubbery in misted crosshatch. The lawn felt muddy underfoot, a loose skin of thaw on winter's body. A maple sapling that had taken root near the porch, in the bulb bed, extended last summer's growth in glistening straight shoots red as thermometer mercury. Beside the black chimney the blurred moon looked warm. Gratefully Piet inhaled the moist night. His year of trouble felt vaporized, dismissed.

Their babysitter was Merissa Mills, the teen-age daughter of the ringleader of the old boatyard crowd, who years ago had divorced his wife and moved to Florida, where he managed a marina and had remarried. Merissa, as often with children of broken homes, was determinedly tranquil and polite and conventional. She said, "There was one call, from a Mr. Whitman. I wrote down the number." On a yellow pad of Gallagher & Hanema receipt forms her round bland hand had penciled Foxy's number.

Piet asked, "*Mr.* Whitman?"

Merissa, gathering her books, gazed at him without curiosity. Her life had witnessed a turmoil of guilt she was determined not to relive. "He said you should call him no matter how late you got back."

"He can't have meant *this* late," Angela told Piet. "You take Merissa home and I'll call Foxy in the morning."

"No!" In sudden focus Piet saw the two women before him as identical—both schooled prematurely in virtue, both secluded behind a willed composure. He knew they were screening him from something out there in the dark that was his, his fate, the fruit of his deeds. His tongue streaked tranced down the narrow path still open. "We may still need Merissa. Let me call Ken before we let her go."

Angela protested, "Merissa has school tomorrow and I'm exhausted." But her voice lacked fiber; he walked through it to the phone, his palms tingling. His movements, as he picked up the receiver and dialed, were as careful as those of a leper whose flesh falls off in silver shards.

Ken answered on the second ring. "Piet," he said. It was not said as a greeting; Ken was giving something a name.

"Ken."

"Foxy and I have had a long talk."

"What about?"

"The two of you."

"Oh?"

"Yes. Do you deny that you and she have been lovers since last summer?"

Ken's silence lengthened. An impatient doctor faced with a procrastinating hope. Piet saw that there was no glimmer, that the truth had escaped and was all about them, like oxygen, like darkness. As a dying man after months of ingenious forestallment turns with relief to the hope of an afterlife, Piet sighed, "No, I don't deny it."

"Good. That's a step forward."

Angela's face, forsaken, pressed wordless against the side of Piet's vision as he listened.

"She also told me that she became pregnant by you this winter and you arranged to have the pregnancy aborted while I was in Chicago."

"Did she though? While you were in the Windy City?" Piet felt before him an adamant flatness upon which his urge was to dance.

"Is that true or false?" Ken persisted.

Piet said, "Tell me the rules of this quiz. Can I win, or only lose?"

Ken paused. Angela's face, as something of what was happening

dawned on it, grew pale, and anxiously mouthed the silent syllable, *Who?*

Less disciplinary, a shade concessive, Ken said, "Piet, I think the
best thing would be for you and Angela to come over here
tonight."

"She's awfully tired."

"Could you put her on the phone, please?"

"No. We'll come over." Hanging up, he faced the rectangle
of slightly darker wallpaper where until recently a mirror had
hung. Angela had transferred it to Nancy's room because the
child expressed jealousy of her father's birthday gift of a mirror
to Ruth. He told Angela, "We must go," and asked Merissa, "Can
you stay?" Both acquiesced; he had gained, in those few seconds
over the phone, the forbidding dignity of those who have no
lower to go. His face was a mask while his blood underwent an
airy tumult, a boiling alternation of shame and fear momentarily
condensing into those small actions—a sticky latch lifted, a
pocket-slapping search for car keys, a smile of farewell at Merissa
and a promise not to be long—needed to get them out of the
house, into the mist, on their way.

By way of Blackberry Lane, a winding link road tenderly
corrupted from Nigger Lane, where a solitary escaped slave had
lived in the days of Daniel Webster, dying at last of loneliness and
pneumonia, the distance from the Hanema's house to the Whitmans was not great. Often in summer Piet after his afternoon's
work would drive his daughters to the beach for a swim and be
back by supper. So Piet and Angela had little time to talk; Angela
spoke quickly, lightly, skimming the spaces between what she had
overheard or guessed. "How long has it been going on?"

"Oh, since the summer. I think her hiring me for the job was a
way of seeing if it would happen."

"It occurred to me, but I thought you wouldn't use your work
like that, I thought it was beneath your ethics to. Deceive me, yes,
but your men, and Gallagher . . ."

"I did a respectable job for her. We didn't sleep together until toward the end. It was after the job was done, when I had no reason to have my truck parked there, that it began to seem not right."

"Oh, it did seem not right?"

"Sure. It became very heavy. Religious, somehow, and sad. She was so pregnant." It pleased Piet to be able to talk about it, as if under this other form he had been secretly loving Angela, and now could reveal to her the height and depth of his love.

She said, "Yes, that is the surprise. Her being pregnant. It must be very hard for Ken to accept."

Piet shrugged. "It was part of her. I didn't mind it if she didn't. Actually, it made it seem more innocent, as if that much of her was being faithful to Ken no matter what we did with the rest."

"How many times did you sleep with her in all?"

"Oh. Thirty. Forty."

"Forty!"

"You asked." She was crying. He told her, "Don't cry."

"I'm crying because you seemed happier lately and I thought it was *me* and it's been *her*."

"No, it hasn't been her." He felt under him a soft place, a hidden pit, the fact of Bea.

"No? When was the last time?"

The abortion. She mustn't know. But it was too big to hide, like a tree. In its shade the ground was suspiciously bare. He said, "Months ago. We agreed it would be the last time."

"But after the baby had been born?"

"Yes. Six or so weeks after. I was surprised she still wanted me."

"You're so modest." Her tone was empty of irony, dead. A mailbox knocked cockeyed, toppling backwards forever, wheeled through their headlights. Ghosts of mist thronged from the marshes where the road dipped. Angela asked, "Why did you stop?"

Having withheld truth elsewhere, Piet lavished frankness here. "It began to hurt more than it helped. I was becoming cruel to you, and I couldn't *see* the girls; they seemed to be growing up without me. Then, with her baby, it's being a boy, it seemed somehow clear that our time was past." He further explained: "A time to love, and a time to die."

Her crying had dried up but showed in her voice as a worn place, eroded. "You did love her?"

He tried to tread precisely here; their talk had moved from a thick deceptive forest to a desert where every step left a print. He told her, "I'm not sure I understand the term. I enjoyed being with her, yes."

"And you also enjoyed Georgene?"

"Yes. Less complexly. She was less demanding. Foxy was always trying to educate me."

"And any others?"

"No." The lie lasted as they dipped into the last hollow before the Whitman's little rise.

"And me? Have you ever enjoyed being with me?" The desert had changed; the even sand of her voice had become seared rock, once molten, sharp to the touch.

"Oh," Piet said, "Jesus, yes. Being with you is Heaven." He hurried on, having decided. "One thing you should know, since Ken knows it. At the end, after I figured our affair was over, Foxy got pregnant by me, don't ask me how, it was ridiculous, and we got Freddy Thorne to arrange our abortion for us. His price was that night with you. It sounds awful, but it was the only thing, it was great of you, and it absolutely ended Foxy and me. It's done. It's over. We're just here tonight so I can get reprimanded."

They were at the Whitmans'. With the motor extinguished, Angela's not answering alarmed him. Her voice when it came sounded miniature, dwindled, terminal. "You better take me home."

"Don't be silly," he said. "You *must* come in." He justified his imperious tone: "I don't have the guts to go in without you."

Ken answered their ring. He wore a foulard and smoking jacket: the host. He shook Piet's hand gravely, glancing at him from those shallow gray eyes as if taking a snapshot. He welcomed Angela with a solicitude bordering on flirtation. His man's voice and shoulders filled comfortably spaces where Foxy alone had seemed adrift and forlorn. He took their coats, Angela's blue second-best and Piet's little apricot jacket, and ushered the couple down the rag-rugged hall; Angela stared all about her, fascinated by how the house that should have been hers had been renovated. She murmured to Piet, "Did *you* choose the wallpaper?" Foxy was in the living room, feeding the baby in her lap. Unable to rise or speak in greeting, she grinned. Lit up by her smile, her teary face seemed to Piet a net full of gems; lamplight flowed down her loose hair to the faceless bundle in her lap. The array of bottles on the coffee table glittered. They had been drinking. In the society of Tarbox there was no invitation more flattering than to share, like this, another couple's intimacy, to partake in their humorous déshabille, their open quarrels and implicit griefs. It was hard for these couples this night to break from that informal spell and to confront each other as enemies. Angela took the old leather armchair, and Piet a rush-seat ladderback that Foxy's mother, appalled by how bleak their house seemed, had sent from Maryland. Ken remained standing and tried to run the meeting in an academic manner. Piet's itch was to clown, to seek the clown's traditional invisibility. Angela and Foxy, their crossed legs glossy, fed into the room that nurturing graciousness of female witnessing without which no act since Adam's naming of the beasts has been complete. Women are gentle fruitful presences whose interpolation among us diffuses guilt.

Ken asked them what they would like to drink. The smoking jacket a prop he must live up to. Outrage has no costume. Angela said, "Nothing."

Piet asked for something with gin in it. Since tonic season hadn't begun, perhaps some dry vermouth, about half and half, a European martini. Anything, just so it wasn't whiskey. He described the smell of whiskey at the town meeting, and was disappointed when no one laughed. Irked, he asked, "Ken, what's the first item on your agenda?"

Ken ignored him, asking Angela, "How much did you know of all this?"

"Ah," Piet said. "An oral exam."

Angela said, "I knew as much as you did. Nothing."

"You must have guessed something."

"I make a lot of guesses about Piet, but he's very slippery."

Piet said, "Agile, I would have said."

Ken did not take his eyes from Angela. "But you're in Tarbox all day; I'm away from seven to seven."

Angela shifted her weight forward, so the leather cushion sighed. "What are you suggesting, Ken? That I'm deficient as a wife?"

Foxy said, "One of the things that makes Angela a good wife to Piet, better than I could ever be, is that she lets herself be blind."

"Oh, I don't know about that," Angela said, preoccupied with, what her shifting in the chair had purposed, pouring herself some brandy. It was five-star Cognac but the only glass was a Flintstone jelly tumbler. Foxy's housekeeping had these lapses and loopholes. Admitted to her house late in the afternoon, Piet would see, through the blond rainbow of her embrace, breakfast dishes on the coffee table unwashed, and a book she had marked her place in with a dry bit of bacon. She claimed, when he pointed it out, that she had done it to amuse him; but he had also observed that her underwear was not always clean.

Unable to let Angela's mild demur pass unchallenged, she sat upright, jarring the sleeping bundle in her lap, and argued, "I mean it as a compliment. I think it's a beautiful trait. I could never be that way, the wise overlooking wife. I'm jealous by nature. It used to kill me, at parties, to see you come up with that possessive sweet smile and take Piet home to bed."

Piet winced. The trick was not to make it too real for Ken. Change the subject. A mild man innocently seeking information, he asked the other man, "How did you find out?"

"Somebody told him," Foxy interposed. "A woman. A jealous woman."

"Georgene," Piet said.

"Right," Foxy said.

Ken said, "No, it was Marcia little-Smith. She happened to ask me the other day downtown what work was still being done on the house, that Piet's truck was parked out front so often."

"Don't be ridiculous, that's what the two of them cooked up to say," Foxy told Piet, "Of course it was Georgene. I knew when she found us together last week she was going to do something vicious. She has no love in her life so she can't stand other people having any."

Piet disliked her slashing manner; he felt they owed the couple they had wronged a more chastened bearing. He accused her: "And then you told him everything."

The gems in her face burst their net. "Yes. Yes. Once I got started I couldn't stop. I'm sorry, for you, and then not. You've put me through hell, man."

Angela smiled toward Ken, over brandy. "They're fighting."

He answered, "That's their problem," and Piet, hearing the unyielding tone, realized that Ken did not view the problem, as he did, as one equally shared, a four-sided encroachment and withdrawal. Ken's effort, he saw, would be to absolve, to precipitate, himself.

Angela, frightened, with Piet, of the other couple's rising hardness, inquired softly, her oval head tilted not quite toward Foxy, "Georgene found you together a week ago? Piet told me it was all over."

Foxy said, "He lied to you, sweet."

"I did *not*." Piet's face baked. "I came down here because you were miserable. We didn't make love, we hardly made conversation. We agreed that the abortion ended what should have been ended long ago. Clearly."

"Was it so clear?" Eyes downcast. Velvety mouth prim. He remembered that certain subtle slidiness of her lips. Her demeanor mixed surrender and defiance. Piet felt her fair body, seized by his eyes, as a plea not to be made to relive the humiliation of Peter.

Ken turned again on Angela. "How much *do* you know? Do you know the night of the Kennedy party they were necking in the upstairs bathroom? Do you know he was having both Georgene and Foxy for a while and that he has another woman now?"

"Who?"

Angela's quick question took both Whitmans aback; they looked at each other for a signal. Piet saw no sign from Foxy. Ken pronounced to Angela's face, "Bea."

"Dear Bea," Angela said, two fingertips circularly lingering on the brass stud second from the top along the outer edge of the left leather arm. Pain so aloofly suffered. The treachery of Lesbians. Dress in chitons and listen to poetry. Touch my arm. Hockey.

Piet interposed, "This is gossip. What evidence do you two have?"

"Never mind, Piet," Angela said aside.

Ken resumed the instructor's role; lamplight showed temples of professorial gray as he leaned over Angela. "You know about the abortion?" His face held a congestion his neat mouth wanted to vent. A pudgy studious boy who had been mocked at recess. *Never tease, Piet, never tease.*

Piet asked Foxy, "Why doesn't he lay off my wife?"

Angela nodded yes and with a graceful wave added, to Ken, "It seems to me they did that as much for you as for themselves. A cynical woman would have had the child and raised it as yours."

"Only if I were totally blind. I know what a Whitman looks like."

"You can tell just by listening," Piet said. "They begin to lecture at birth."

Ken turned to him. "Among the actions I'm considering is bringing criminal charges against Thorne. You'd be an accessory."

"For God's sake, why?" Piet asked. "That was probably the most Christian thing Freddy Thorne ever did. He didn't have to do it, he did it out of pity. Out of love, even."

"Love of who?"

"His *friends*." And Piet pronouncing this felt his heart vibrate with the nervousness of love, as if he and Freddy, the partition between them destroyed, at last comprehended each other with the fullness long desired, as almost had happened one night in the Constantines' dank foyer. Hate and love both seek to know.

Ken said, and something strange, a nasty puffing, an adolescent sneer, was afflicting his upper lip, "He did it because he likes to meddle. But that's neither here nor there. It's been done, and I see no way back through it."

Angela understood him first. She asked, "No way?"

Ken consented to her implication. "I've had it. To be technical: there are reactions that are reversible and those that aren't. This feels irreversible to me. Simple infidelity could be gotten around, even a prolonged affair, but with my *child* in her belly—"

"Oh, don't be so superstitious," Foxy interrupted.

"—and then this monstrous performance with Thorne . . ."

Angela asked him, "How can you judge? As Piet says, in context, it was the most merciful thing."

Piet told him, "She wrote me long letters, all summer, saying how much she loved you." But even as he pleaded he knew it was no use, and took satisfaction in this knowledge, for he was loyal to the God Who mercifully excuses us from pleading, Who nails His joists of judgment down firm, and roofs the universe with order.

As Ken spoke, still standing above them like a tutor, his voice took on an adolescent hesitancy. "Let me try again. It's clear I don't count for much with any of you. But this has been quite a night for me, and I want to have my say."

"Hear, hear," Piet said. He waited happily to be crushed, and dismissed.

"In a sense," Ken went on, "I feel quite grateful and benevolent, because as a scientist I supposedly seek the truth, and tonight I've gotten it, and I want to be worthy of it. I don't want to shy from it."

Piet poured more gin for himself. Foxy blinked and jostled the baby; Angela sipped brandy and remained on the edge of the huge leather chair.

"In chemistry," Ken told them, "molecules have *bonds;* some compounds have strong bonds, and some have weaker ones, and though now with atomic valences we can explain why, originally it was all pragmatic. Now listening to my wife tonight, not only what she said, the astonishingly cold-blooded deceptions, but the joyful fullness with which she spilled it all out, I had to conclude we don't have much of a bond. We should, I think. We come from the same kind of people, we're both intelligent, we can stick to a plan, she stuck with me through a lot of what she tells me now were pretty dreary years. She told me, Piet, she had forgotten what love was until you came along. Don't say anything. Maybe I'm incapable of love. I've always assumed I loved her, felt what you're supposed to feel. I wanted her to have my child, when we had room for it, I gave her this house—"

Foxy interrupted, "You gave yourself this house."

Piet said, "Foxy."

Ken's hands, long-fingered and younger than his body, had been groping into diagrams on a plane in front of him; now they dropped rebuked to his sides. He turned to Piet and said, "See. No bond. Apparently you and she have it. More power to you."

"*Less* power to them, I would think," Angela interposed.

Ken looked at her surprised. He had thought he had been clear. "I'm divorcing her."

"You're not."

"Is he?"

Angela had spoken to Ken, then Piet to Foxy. She nodded, gems returning to her pink face, burning, eclipsing the attempted gaze of recognition, the confession of hopelessness, toward Piet. He was reminded of Nancy in the instant of equilibrium as she coped with the certain knowledge that she was going to cry, before her face toppled, broke like a vase, exposing the ululant tongue arched in agony on the floor of her mouth.

"If you divorce her, I'll have to marry her." Piet felt the sentence had escaped from him rather than been uttered. Was it a threat, a complaint, a promise?

Drily Foxy said, "That's the most gracious proposal I've ever heard." But she had named it: a proposal.

"Oh, my God, my God," Angela cried. "I feel sick, sick."

"Stop saying things twice," Piet told her.

"He doesn't love her, he doesn't," Angela told Ken. "He's been trying to ditch her ever since summer."

Ken told Piet, "I don't know what you should do. I just know what *I* should do."

Piet pleaded, "You can't divorce her for something that's over.

Look at her. She's repentant. She's confessed. That's your child she's holding. Take her away, beat her, leave Tarbox, go back to Cambridge with her, anything. But no reasonable man—"

Ken said, "I am nothing if not reasonable. I have legal grounds six times over."

"Stop being a lawyer's son for a second. Try to be human. The law is dead."

"The point of it is," Ken said, sitting down at last, "she's not repentant."

"Of *course* she is," Piet said. "*Look* at her. Ask her."

Ken asked gently, as if waking her from sleep, "Fox, are you? Repentant?"

She studied him with bold brown eyes and said, "I'll wash your feet and drink the water every night."

Ken turned to Piet, his experiment successful. "See? She mocks me."

Foxy stood tall, placed the infant on her shoulder, and rapidly drummed its back. "I can't stand this," she announced, "being treated as a *thing*. Excuse me, Angela. I'm truly sorry for your grief, but these *men*. All this competitive self-pity." She paused by the doorway to retrieve a blanket from a chair, and in the motion of her stooping, in the silence of her leaving, Tobias burped.

At the little salutary hiccup, so portentously audible, Angela's shoulders jerked with laughter. She had hidden her face in her hands. Now she revealed it, as if, her own acolyte, she were reverently unfolding the side wings of a triptych. It was a face, Piet saw, lost to self-consciousness, an arrangement of apertures willing, like a sea anemone, to be fed by whatever washed over it. "I want to go home," she told Ken. "I'm tired, I want a bath. Is everything settled? You're going to divorce Foxy, and Piet's going to divorce me. Do you want to marry me, Ken?"

He responded with a gallantry that confirmed Piet in his suspicion, from infancy on, that the world was populated by people bigger and wiser, more graceful and less greedy, than he. Ken said, "You tempt me. I wish we had met years ago."

"Years ago," Angela said, "we would have been too busy being good children." She asked Piet, "How shall we do? Do you want to move out tonight?"

Piet told her, "Don't dramatize. Nothing is settled. I think we all need to get some daylight on this."

Ken asked, "Then you're already backing out on your offer?"

"What offer?"

Ken said, "Piet, there is something you should know about us, you and me, that for some reason, modern manners I suppose, I don't seem able to express, and that I don't think this discussion has made clear to you, from the way you're sitting there smiling. I hate your guts." It sounded false; he amended it, "I hate what you've done to me, what you've done to Foxy."

Piet thought Angela would defend him, at least vaguely protest; but her silence glided by.

Ken went on, "In less than a year you, you and this sick town, have torn apart everything my wife and I had put together in seven years. Behind all this playfulness you *like* to destroy. You love it. The Red-haired Avenger. You're enjoying this; you've *enjoyed* that girl's pain."

Bored with being chastised, Piet rebelled. He stood to tell Ken, "She's your wife, keep her in your bed. You had lost her before you began. A man with any self-respect wouldn't have married her on the rebound like you did. Don't blame me if flowers didn't grow in this" —at the mouth of the hall, following Angela out, he turned and with whirling arms indicated to Ken his house, the Cambridge furniture, the empty bassinet, mirroring windows, the sum of married years—"test tube." Pleased with his rebuttal, he waited to hear Angela agree but she had already slammed the screen door. Outside, in sudden moist air, he stepped sideways into the pruned lilacs and was stabbed beneath an eye, and wondered if he were drunk, and thus so elated.

The car hurtled through mist. Angela asked, "Was she that much better in bed than me?"

Piet answered, "She was different. She did some things you don't do, I think she values men higher than you do. She's more insecure, I'd say, than you, and probably somewhat masculine.

Physically, there's more of *you* everywhere; she's tight and her responsiveness isn't as fully developed. She's young, as you once said."

The completeness of his answer, as if nothing else had convinced her that he had truly known the other woman, outraged Angela; she shrieked, and kneeled on the rubber car floor, and flailed her arms and head in the knobbed and metal-edged space, and tried to smother her own cries in the dusty car upholstery. He braked the Peugeot to a stop and walked around its ticking hood to her side and opened her door. As he pulled her out she felt disjointed, floppy as a drunk or a puppet. "Inhale," he said. The beach road dipped here, low to the marsh, and the mist was thick, suffused with a salinity that smelled eternal. Angela recovered her composure, apologized, tore up some wands of spring grass and pressed them against her eyelids. A pair of headlights slowly trundled toward them in the fog and halted.

A car door opened. Harold little-Smith's penetratingly tipped voice called, "All right there?"

"We're fine, thanks. Just enjoying the sea breeze."

"Oh, Piet. It's you. Who's that with you?"

"Angela.'

"Hi," Angela called, to prove it.

Piet called to the others over the glistening car roof, "How was the party?"

Harold guiltily answered, "It wasn't a party, just a beer. *Un peu de bière.* Carol looked for you but you'd gone out the other exit."

"We couldn't have come, thanks anyway," Piet said, and asked, "Who's that with *you?*"

"Marcia. Of course."

"Why of course?"

Marcia's voice piped through the fog. "Cut it out, Piet. You're a dirty old man."

"You're a doll. Good night, all."

"Good night, Hanemas." The pair of red tail lights dwindled, dissolved. In the silence then was the sighing of the sea rising in the marsh channels, causing the salt grass to unbend and rustle and suck. Her shrieks had been animal, less than animal, the noise of

a deranged mechanism. Piet could hardly believe that the world
—the one-o'clock mist, the familiar geography of Tarbox—
could reconstitute itself after such a shattering. But Merissa, as
Angela thanked her and told a lie about their going out again
("Their baby was having colic and they panicked; it's their first,
you know."), noncommitally gathered together her books, having been reading in the light of television. As Piet drove her home
she exuded a perfume of tangerines and talked about the dreadful
earthquake in Anchorage. Returning, he found his downstairs
lights off and Angela upstairs in the bathtub. The veins in her
breasts turquoise, the ghost of a tan distinct on her shoulders and
thighs, she was lying all but immersed, idly soaping her pudenda.
She scrubbed circularly and then stroked the oozy hair into
random peaks and then shifted her body so that the water washed
over her and erased the soap. Her breasts slopped and slid with
the pearly-dirty water; her hair was pinned up in a psyche knot,
exposing tenderly the nape of her neck.

Piet said, "Pardon me, but I must sit down. My stomach is a ball
of acid."

"Help yourself. Don't mind me."

He opened himself to the toilet and a burning gush of relief
mixed with the fascinating sight of her toes—scalded, rosy, kittenish nubs. Foxy had long prehensile toes; he had seen her one
night at the Constantines' hold a pencil in her foot and write
Elizabeth on the wall. He asked Angela, "How do you feel?"

"Desperate. If you'll pass me the razor, I'll slash my wrists."

"Don't say things like that." A second diarrheic rush, making
him gasp, had postponed his answer an instant. Where could so
much poison have come from? Did gin kill enzymes?

"Why not?" Angela rolled a quarter-turn. The water sloshed
tidally. "That would save you all the nuisance of a divorce. I
don't think my father's going to let me be very generous."

"Do you think"—a third, reduced rush—"there's going to be
such a thing? I'm scared to death of that woman."

"I heard you propose to her."

"She made it seem that way. Frankly, I'd rather stay married to
you."

"Maybe I'd rather not stay married to you."

"But who do you have to go to?"

"Nobody. Myself. Somehow you haven't let me be myself. All these parties you've made me go to and give so you could seduce the wives of all those dreary men."

He loved hearing her talk with such casual even truth; he loved agreeing with her, being her student. "They *are* dreary. I've figured out there are two kinds of jerks in this town, upper-middle-class jerks and lower-middle-class jerks. The upper went to college. My problem is, I'm sort of in the middle."

She asked, "What did you think of Ken?"

"I hated him. A real computer. Put in some data and out comes the verdict."

"I don't know," Angela said, moving her legs gently apart and together and apart in the water. "I think he showed more courage than any of us have."

"Talking about divorce? But he has no intention of divorcing her. All he cares about is frightening her and me and you and protecting his schoolboy honor."

"She didn't seem frightened to me. It's just what she wants. Why else would she tell him so much, all night?"

Now a coldness cut into his voided bowels. He wiped himself and flushed; the odor in the little room, of rotten cinnamon, embarrassed him before his wife. She held a washcloth to her face and moaned through it, "Oh God, oh my God."

He asked her, "Sweet, why?"

"I'll be so alone," she said. "You were the only person who ever tried to batter their way in to me."

"Roll over and I'll scrub your back." Her buttocks were red islands goose-bumped from heat. A slim bit of water between. Her back an animal brown horizontally nicked by the bra strap and starred by three dim scars where moles had been removed. "It won't happen," he told her, smoothly soaping, "it won't happen."

"I shouldn't even let you stay the night."

"Nothing will happen," he told her, making circles around and around her constellation of scars.

"But maybe something should happen," she told him, her voice small in submission to his lulling laving. But when he quit, and she stood in the tub, Angela was colossal: buckets of water fell from the troughs among her breasts and limbs and collapsed back into the tub. Her blue eyes seemed wild, her bare arms flailed with an odd uncoördination. Tears glazed her cheeks while steam fled her skin in the coolness of their eggshell bedroom. "Something *should* happen, Piet. You've abused me horribly. I've asked for it, sure, but that's my weakness and I've been indulging it."

"You're beginning to talk like your own psychiatrist."

"He says I have no self-respect and it's true. And neither do you. We were with two people tonight who have some and they rolled right through us."

"It was his inning. I've had mine."

"Oh, I can't *stand* you when your face gets that stretched look. That's the thing you don't know. How your face looked tonight. When you said you'd have to marry her, there was this incredible, I was stunned, happiness, as if every question ever had been answered for you."

"That can't be true. I don't want to marry her. I'd rather marry Bea Guerin. I'd rather marry Bernadette Ong."

"You've slept with Bernadette."

"Never. But she's bumped me and her husband's dying." He laughed. "Stop it, angel. This is grotesque. I have no desire to marry Foxy, I love you. Compared to you, she's such a bitch."

Her neck had elongated; though exactly her height, he felt he was looking up at her—her thoughtful pout so tense her nostrils were flared, the breasts over which she had defensively flung an arm. "You like bitches," she said. Another thought struck her: "Everybody we know must think I'm an absolute fool."

He calculated he must do something acrobatic. Having removed all his clothes but his Paisley shorts, Piet threw himself on his knees and wrapped his arms around her thighs. The hearthbricks were cold, her body still steamy; she protestingly pushed down on his head, blocking an amorous rise. Her vulva a roseate brown. Parchment. Egypt. Lotus. "Don't make me leave you," he begged. "You're what guards my soul. I'll be damned eternally."

"It'll do you good," she said, still pushing down on his head.

"It'll do Foxy good too. You're right, Ken is not sexually appealing. I tried to get the hots for him tonight and there was nothing, not a spark."

"God, don't joke," he said. "Think of the girls."

"They'll be fine with me."

"They'll suffer."

"You used to say they should suffer. How else can they learn to be good? Stop nibbling me."

Embarrassed, he got to his feet. Standing two feet from her, he removed his undershorts. He was tumescent. "God," he said, "I'd love to clobber you."

She dropped her arm; her breasts swung free, livid and delicate as wounds. "Of course you would," she said, confirmed.

His fist jerked; she flinched and aloofly waited.

Through the April that followed this night, Piet had many conversations, as if the town, sensing he was doomed, were hurrying to have its last say in his ear. Freddy Thorne stopped him one rainy day on Divinity Street, as Piet with hammer and level was leaving the Tarbox Professional Apartments, once Gertrude Tarbox's shuttered hermitage. "Hey," Freddy said, "what have you done to me? I just got a paranoid letter from Ken Whitman about the, you know, the little pelvic orthodonture we performed. He said he had decided not to take legal action at the present time, but, cough, cough, reserved the intention to do so. The whole thing was psychopathically formal. He cited four laws I had broken chapter and verse, with the maximum penalties all neatly typed out. He's anal as hell. Wha' hoppen, Handlebar?"

Piet, who lived now day and night behind glassy walls of fear, clinging each evening to the silence of the telephone and to Angela's stony sufferance, while his children watched wide-eyed and whimpered in their sleep, was pleased to feel that at least he had been redeemed from Freddy Thorne's spell; the old loathing and fascination were gone. Freddy's atheism, his evangelical humanism, no longer threatened Piet; the dentist materialized in the drizzle as a plump fuzzy-minded man with a squint and an old woman's sly mouth. A backwards jacket peeked white under his raincoat. If any emotion, Piet felt fondness, the fondness a woman might feel toward her priest or gynecologist or lover—someone who has accepted her worst. Piet decided not to tell him that Georgene had betrayed them to Ken; he owed the Thornes that much. He said instead, "Foxy broke under the tension and blurted it all out to him the night of town meeting."

And he described briefly the subsequent confrontation of the two couples.

"The old mousetrap play," Freddy said. "She wants you bad, boy."

"Come on, she was hysterical. She couldn't stop crying."

Freddy's lips bit inward wisely. "When that golden-haired swinger has hysterics," he said, "it's because she's punched the release button herself. You've been had, friend. Good luck."

"How worried about Whitman are you?"

"Semi-semi. He's not going to press anything, with Little Miss Vulpes pulling the strings."

"Freddy," Piet said, "you live in a fantasy world of powerful women. I haven't heard from her since. In fact, I'm worried. Could you possibly send Georgene down to see how things are?"

"I think Georgene's errand days are over," Freddy said. "She really blew up after finding you and Foxtrot together; I had a vicious creature on my hands for a few days. The less you and she see each other, the better we'll all be. Keerect?"

"Is that why we're not being invited to parties any more?"

"What parties?"

Georgene phoned him Friday afternoon, while he was leafing through Sweet's Light Construction Catalogue File, looking for flanged sheathing. Two of the houses on Indian Hill had complained about leaks last winter, and Piet wanted to improve the new houses, whose foundations were already being bulldozed. Gallagher sat listening in his cubbyhole, but Piet let Georgene talk. Her clubwoman's quick enunciation, and the weather outside hinting of tennis and sunporches again, made him sentimental and regretful. He could see larches leaning, remembered the way the inside tendons of her thighs cupped and her pupils contracted as her eyelids widened and how afterwards she would tell him he gave her her shape. "Piet," she said, in syllables from which all roughnesses of love and innuendo had been burred, leaving a smooth brisk sister, "I drove down to the Whitmans today, Freddy mentioned you were worried, and there's nobody there. It doesn't look as if anybody has been there for a while. Four newspapers are bunched up inside the storm door."

"Does Marcia know anything?"

"She says there hasn't been a car in the drive since Tuesday."

"Did you look inside a window?" The open oven. The gobbled sleeping pills. The hallway where a lightbulb has died above a pair of ankles.

"Everything looked neat, as if they had tidied up before going away. I didn't see the bassinet."

"Have you talked to Carol or Terry? Somebody must have the answer. People just don't vanish."

"Easy, dollink, don't panic, you're not God. You can't protect the Whitmans from what they want to do to each other."

"Thanks. Thanks for the pep talk. And thanks a bushel for telling Whitman in the first place."

"I told him almost nothing. I admit I did, more or less maliciously, ask him why your truck was parked down there, but then he jumped all over me with questions, he was really hungry for it. Clearly he had half guessed. I *am* sorry, though. But, Piet—are you listening?—it made me mad the way I came in there that Monday all anxious to be Sue Barton and somehow I was turned into the cleaning lady who invites herself to tea."

He sighed. "OK, forget it. Truth will out, it may be best. You're a good woman. A loyal wife and dutiful mother."

"Piet—I wasn't right for you, was I? I thought we were so good, but we weren't?"

"You were a gorgeous piece of ass," he told her patiently. "You were too good. You made it seem too easy and right for my warped nature. Please forgive me," he added, "if I ever hurt you. I never meant to."

It was Gallagher, of all people, who had the answer. Having overheard this conversation, he called Piet into his inner office, and there, as the late light died in measured segments, without turning on a lamp, so his broad-jawed pentagonal face became a murmuring blur, told Piet of a strange scene. Early Tuesday morning, earlier than the milk, Ken Whitman had appeared at their house. He was soaked and rumpled and sandy; he had spent the night walking the beach in the mist and had taken a cramped nap in his MG. Silent, Piet guiltily remembered how Monday night he had slept warm beside Angela, as soundly as the just, amid irrelevant dreams about flying. Ken explained himself. He had come to the Gallaghers because Matt was the one man in Tarbox he could respect, the only one "uninvolved." Also Terry, he tried to say, could understand Foxy, perhaps. What did he mean? Were they alike? They were both "proud." Here Matt hesitated, caught in private considerations, or debating with himself how much Piet should be told. But having commenced, his Irish blood demanded the tale should continue fully. Piet pictured that early-morning kitchen, the postcard print of Dürer's praying hands framed above the stainless-steel sink, Terry's rough bright tablecloth and the bowls she had clumsily turned, three drowsy mouths sipping coffee, and heard himself being discussed, deplored, blamed. Ken asked them what he should do. Both of course told him to go back to Foxy; he loved her, they had a son now to think of, they were a handsome couple. Everybody, Terry said, lapses—or is tempted to. Piet suspected Matt had added the qualification in his own mind. But they found Ken adamant. Not vindictive. He spoke of the people concerned as of chemical elements, without passion. He had thought it through by the side of the ocean and could make no deduction but divorce. Terry began to cry. Ken ignored her. What he was curious to know from *them* was whether or not they thought Piet would divorce Angela to marry Foxy. If they thought yes, then the sooner the better. If they thought Piet would be "bastard enough"—Matt tactfully paused before releasing the expressions —to "let her stew," then maybe they at least should wait, merely separate. He was going to go back to Cambridge, she should stay in the house. Would they keep an eye on her? Of course they would. Terry then gave him a long lecture. She said that he and Foxy had been different from the rest of them because they had no children, and that because of this they were freer. That, despite what the Church said, she did not think a marriage sacred and irrevocable until the couple produced a third soul, a child. That until then marriage was of no different order than kissing your first boy; it was an experiment. But when a child was created, it ceased to be an experiment, it became a fact; like papal infallibility or the chromatic scale. You must have such facts to build a world on, even if they appeared arbitrary. Now Ken might still feel free, he seemed very slow to realize that he had a son—

Piet asked, "She told him that?"

"Yes. She's never liked Whitman much."

"How nice of Terry."

Terry had gone on, Ken might imagine he was free to make decisions, but Piet certainly wasn't. He loved his children, he needed Angela, and it would be very wrong of Ken to try to force him, out of some absurd sense of honor that hasn't applied to anybody for centuries, to give up everything and marry Foxy. Piet just wasn't free.

"And how did Ken take all this?"

"Not badly. He nodded and thanked us and left. Later in the morning Terry went over to see Foxy, since Ken has somehow chosen us, and she was packing. She was perfectly calm, not a hair out of place. She was going to take the baby and go to her mother in Washington, and I assume that's where she is."

"Thank God. I mean, what a relief she's all right. And that she's out of town."

"You honestly haven't heard from her?"

"Not a whisper."

"And you haven't tried to reach her?"

"Should I have? No matter what I said, that would only have meant to her that I was still in the game and confused things. What's your advice?"

Matt spoke carefully, picking his words in such a way that Piet saw he was no friend; one did not have to speak so carefully to friends. Matt had grown to dislike him, and why not?—he had grown to dislike Matt, since he had first seen him, in a pressed private's uniform, his black button eyes as shiny as his shoes: an eager beaver. "Terry and I of course have discussed this since, and there is one thing, Piet, we agree you should do. Call his bluff. Let them know, the Whitmans, either by phone to Ken or by letter to Foxy, you surely can find her mother's address, that you will *not* marry her in any case. I think if they know that, they'll get back together."

"But is that necessarily good? Them coming back together to make you and Terry and the Pope comfortable? Georgene just told me I shouldn't try to play God with the Whitmans."

The other man's skull, half-lit, lifted in the gloom, one tightly folded ear and the knot of muscle at the point of the jaw and the concavity of his temple all bluish-white, for beyond the office window the carbon-arc streetlight on Hope Street had come on. Piet knew what had happened and what would: Matt had misjudged the coercive power of his moral superiority and would retreat, threatened by Piet's imperfect docility, into his own impregnable rightness. Matt slammed shut a steel desk drawer. "I don't like involving myself with your affairs. I've given my advice. Take it if you want this mess to have a decent outcome. I don't pretend to know what you're really after."

Piet tried to make peace; the man was his partner and had transmitted precious information. "Matt, frankly, I don't think I'm calling any of the shots any more. All I can do is let things happen, and pray."

"That's all you ever do." Matt spoke without hesitation, as a reflex; it was one of those glimpses, as bizarre as the sight in a three-way clothing-store mirror of your own profile, into how you appear to other people. *The Red-haired Avenger.*

At home Angela had received a phone call. She told him about it during their after-supper coffee while the girls were watching *Gunsmoke.* "I got a long-distance call today, from Washington," she said, beginning.

"Foxy?"

"Yes, how did you know?" She answered herself, "She's been calling you, though she told me she hadn't."

"She hasn't. Gallagher told me today where they both were. Ken apparently went over there Tuesday and told his sad story."

"I thought you knew that. Terry told me days ago."

"Why didn't you say so? I've been worried sick."

"We haven't been speaking." This was true.

"What did the lovely Elizabeth have to say for herself?"

Angela's cool face, slightly thinner these days, tensed, and he knew he had taken the wrong tone. She was becoming a disciplinarian. She said, "She was very self-possessed. She said that she was with her mother and had been thinking, and the more she thought"—Angela crossed her hands on the tabletop to control their trembling—"the more she felt that she and Ken should get a divorce now, while the child was still an infant. That she did not want to bring Toby up in the kind of suppressed unhappiness she had known as a child."

"Heaven help us," Piet said. Softly, amid motionless artifacts, he was sinking.

Angela lifted a finger from the oiled surface of the cherrywood dining table. "No. Wait. She said she called not to tell me that, but to tell me, and for *me* to tell *you*, that she absolutely didn't expect you to leave me. That she"—the finger returned, weakening the next word—"loves you, but the divorce is all between her and Ken and isn't because of you really and puts you under no obligation. She said that at least twice."

"And what did you say?"

"What could I? 'Yes, yes, no, thank you,' and hung up. I asked her if there was anything we could do about the house, lock it or check it now and then, and she said no need, Ken would be coming out weekends."

Piet put his palms on the tabletop to push himself up, sighing. "What a mercy," he said. "This has been a nightmare."

"Don't you feel guilty about their divorce?"

"A little. Not much. They were dead on each other and didn't know it. In a way I was a blessing for bringing it to a head."

"Don't wander off, Piet. I didn't have anything to say to Foxy but I do have something to say to you. Could we have some brandy?"

"Aren't you full? That was a lovely dinner, by the way. I don't know why I adore lima beans so. I love bland food."

"Let's have some brandy. Please, quick. *Gunsmoke* is nearly over. I wanted to wait until the children were in bed but I'm all keyed up and I can't. I must have brandy."

He brought it and even as he was pouring her glass she had begun. "I think Foxy's faced her situation and we should face ours. I think you should get out, Piet. Tonight. I don't want to live with you any more."

"Truly?"

"Truly."

"This does need brandy, then. Now tell me why. You know it's all over with Foxy."

"I'm not so sure, but that doesn't matter. I think you still love her, but even if you don't, they mentioned Bea, and if it's not Bea it's going to be somebody else; and I just don't think it's worth it."

"And the girls? It's not worth it for them either?"

"Stop hiding behind the girls. No, actually, I *don't* think it's worth it for them. They're sensitive, they know when we fight, or, even worse I suppose, don't fight. Poor Nancy is plainly disturbed, and I'm not so sure that Ruth, even though she inherited my placid face, is any better."

"I hear your psychiatrist talking."

"Not really. He doesn't approve or disapprove. I try to say what I think, which isn't easy for me, since my father always knew what I should think, and if it bounces back off this other man's silence—I hardly know what he looks like, I'm so scared to look at him—and if it still sounds true, I try to live with it."

"Goddammit, this is all because of that jackass Freddy Thorne."

"Let me finish. And what I think is true is, you do not love me, Piet Hanema. You do not. You do *not*."

"But I do. Obviously I do."

"Stop it, you *don't*. You didn't even get me the house I wanted. You fixed it up for her instead."

"I was paid to. I adore you."

"Yes, that says it. You adore me as a way of getting out of loving me. Oh, you like my bosom and bottom well enough, and you think it's neat the way I'm a professor's niece, and taught you which fork to use, and take you back after every little slumming expedition, and you enjoy making me feel frigid so you'll be free—"

"I adore you. I need you."

"Well then you need the wrong thing. I want out. I'm tired of being bullied."

The brandy hurt, as if his insides were tenderly budding. He asked, "Have I bullied you? I suppose in a way. But only lately. I wanted *in* to you, sweet, and you didn't give it to me."

"You didn't know how to ask."

"Maybe I know now."

"Too late. You know what I think? I think she's just your cup of tea."

"That's meaningless. That's superstition." But saying this was to ask himself what he contrariwise believed, and he believed that there was, behind the screen of couples and houses and days, a Calvinist God Who lifts us up and casts us down in utter freedom, without recourse to our prayers or consultation with our wills. Angela had become the messenger of this God. He fought against her as a raped woman might struggle, to intensify the deed. He said to her, "I'm your husband and always will be. I promise, my philandering is done, not that there was awfully much of it. You imagine there's been gossip, and you're acting out of wounded pride; pride, and the selfishness these fucking psychiatrists give everybody they handle. What does he care about the children, or about your loneliness once I'm gone? The more miserable you are, the deeper he'll get his clutches in. It's a racket, Angel, it's witchcraft, and a hundred years from now people will be amazed that we took it seriously. It'll be like leeches and bleeding."

She said, "Don't expose your ignorance to me any more. I'd like to remember you with some respect."

"I'm not leaving."

"Then I am. Tomorrow morning, Ruthie has dancing class and she was going to have lunch with Betsy Saltz. Nancy's blue dress should be washed and ironed for Martha Thorne's birthday party. Maybe you can get Georgene to come over and do it for you."

"Where could you go?"

"Oh, many places. I could go home and play chess with Daddy. I could go to New York and see the Matisse exhibit. I could fly to Aspen and ski and sleep with an instructor. There's a lot I can do,

Piet, once I get away from you." In her excitement she stood, her
ripe body swinging.

The upsurge of music in the dark living room indicated the end
of the program. Cactuses. Sunset. Right triumphant. He said, "If
you're serious, of course, I'm the one to go. But on an experimental basis. And if I'm asked politely."

Politeness was the final atmosphere. Together they settled the
girls in bed, and packed a suitcase for Piet, and shared a final
brandy in the kitchen. As he very slowly, so as not to wake the
sleeping girls, backed the pick-up truck down the crunching
driveway, Angela made a noise from the porch that he thought
was to call him back. He braked and she rushed to the side of his
cab with a little silver sloshing bottle, a pint of gin. "In case you
get insomnia," she explained, and put the bottle dewy in his palm,
and put a cool kiss on his cheek, with a faint silver edge that must
be her tears. He offered to open the door, but she held the handle
from the other side. "Darling Piet, be brave," she said, and raced,
with one step loud on the gravel, back into the house, and doused
the golden hallway light.

He spent the first weekend in the Gallagher & Hanema office,
sleeping under an old army blanket on the imitation-leather sofa,
lulling his terror with gin-and-water, the water drawn from the
dripping tap in their booth-sized lavatory. The drip, the tick of
his wristwatch left lying on the resounding wood desk, the sullen
plodding of his heart, the sash-rattling vibration of trucks changing gears as they passed at all hours through downtown Tarbox,
and a relentless immanence within the telephone all kept him
awake. Sunday he huddled in his underwear as the footsteps of
churchgoers shuffled on the sidewalk beside his ear. His skull
lined like a thermos bottle with the fragile glass of a hangover, he
felt himself sardonically eavesdropping from within his tomb.
The commonplace greetings he overheard boomed with a sinister
magnificence, intimate and proud as naked bodies. On Monday
morning, though Piet had tidied up, Gallagher was shocked to
find his office smelling of habitation. That week, as it became
clear that Angela was not going to call him back, he moved to the
third floor of the professional apartment building he himself had

refashioned from the mansion of the last Tarbox. The third floor
had been left much as it was, part attic, part servants' quarters.
The floorboards of his room, unsanded, bore leak stains shaped
like wet leaves and patches of old linoleum and pale squares where
linoleum had been; the oatmeal-colored walls, deformed by the
slant of the mansard roof outside, were still hung with careful
pastels of wildflowers Gertrude Tarbox had done, as a young
single lady of "accomplishments," before the First World War.
When it rained, one wall, where the paper had long since curled
away, became wet, and in the mornings the heat was slow to
come on, via a single radiator ornate as lace and thick as armor.
To reach his room Piet had to pass through the plum-carpeted
foyer, between the frosted-glass doors of the insurance agency
and the chiropractor, up the wide stairs with an aluminum strip
edging each tread, around past the doors of an oculist and a
lawyer new in town, and then up the secret stair, entered by an
unmarked door a slide bolt could lock, to his cave. A man who
worked nights, with a stutter so terrible he could hardly manage
"Good morning" when he and Piet met on the stairs, lived across
the stair landing from Piet; besides these two rooms there was a
large empty attic Gallagher still hoped to transform and rent as a
ballroom to the dancing school that now rented the Episcopal
parish hall, where Ruth took her Saturday morning lessons.

Though work on Indian Hill had begun again, with hopes for
six twenty-thousand-dollar houses by Labor Day, Jazinski could
manage most problems by himself now. "Everything's under
control," Piet was repeatedly told, and more than once he called
the lumberyard or the foundation contractors to find that Gallagher or Leon had already spoken with them. So Piet was often
downtown with not much to do. On Good Friday, with the stock
market closed, Harold little-Smith stopped him on Charity Street,
in front of the barber shop.

"Piet, this is a terrible. *C'est terrible.* What did the Whitmans
pull on you?"

"The Whitmans? Nothing much. It was Angela's idea I move
out."

"*La belle ange?* I can't buy that. You've always been the

perfect couple. The Whitmans now, the first time I met them I could see they were in trouble. Stiff as boards, both of them. But it makes me and Marcia damn mad they've screwed you up too. Why can't *tout le monde* mind their own business?"

"Well, it's not as if I had been totally—"

"Oh, I know, I know, but that's never really the issue, is it? People use it when they need to, because of our moronic Puritan laws."

"Who used who, do you think, in my case?"

"Why, *clairement*, Foxy used you. How else could she get rid of that zombie? Don't be used, Piet. Go back to your kids and forget that bitch."

"Don't call her a bitch. You don't know the story at all."

"Listen, Piet, I wouldn't be telling you this just on my own account, out of my own reliably untrustworthy neo-fascist opinion. But Marcia and I stayed up till past three last night with the Applebys talking this over and we all agreed: we don't like seeing a couple we love hurt. If I weren't so hung, I'd probably put it more tactfully. *Pas d'offense*, of course."

"Janet agreed too, that Foxy was a bitch and I'd been had?"

"She was the devil's advocate for a while, but we wore her out. Anyway, it doesn't mean a fart in Paradise what we think. The thing is, what are you going to do? Come on, I'm your friend. *Ton frère.* What are you going to do?"

"I'm not doing anything. Angela hasn't called and doesn't seem to need me back."

"You're waiting for her to call? Don't wait, go to her. Women have to be taken, you know that. I thought you were a great lover."

"Who told you? Marcia?" Harold's twin-tipped nose lifted as he scented a remote possibility. Piet laughed, and went on, "Or maybe Janet? A splendid woman. Why I remember when she was a prostitute in St. Louis, the line went clear down the hall into the billiard room. Have you ever noticed, at the moment of truth, how her whole insides kind of *pull?* One time I remember—"

Harold cut in. "Well I'm glad to see your spirits haven't been crushed. Nothing sacred, eh Piet?"

"Nothing sacred. *Pas d'offense.*"

"Marcia and I wanted to have you over for a drink sometime, and be serious for a change. She's all in a flap about it. She went over to your house, and Angela was perfectly polite, not a hair out of place, but she wouldn't unbend."

"Is that what Marcia likes, to bend people?"

"Listen, I feel I've expressed myself badly. We care, is the point. Piet, we *care*."

"*Je comprends. Merci. Bonjour.*"

"OK, let's leave it at that," Harold said, miffed, sniffing. "I have to get a haircut." His hair looked perfectly well-trimmed to Piet.

The invitation to a drink at the little-Smith's never came. Few of the friends he and Angela had shared sought him out. The Saltzes, probably at Angela's urging, had him to dinner by himself, but their furniture was being readied for moving, and the evening depressed Piet. Now that they were leaving, the Saltzes could not stop talking about themselves as Jews, as if during their years in Tarbox they had suppressed their race, and now it could out. Irene's battle with the school authorities over Christmas pageantry was lengthily recounted, her eyebrows palpitating. The fact of local anti-Semitism, even in their tiny enlightened circle of couples, was urgently confided to Piet. The worst offenders were the Constantines. Carol had been raised, you know, in a *very* Presbyterian small-town atmosphere, and Eddie was, of course, an ignorant man. Night after night they had sat over there arguing the most absurd things, like the preponderance of Jewish Communists, and psychoanalysts, and violinists, as if it all were part of a single conspiracy. Terrible to admit, after a couple of drinks they would sit around trading Jewish jokes; and of course the Saltzes knew many more than Eddie and Carol, which was interpreted as their being ashamed of their race, which she, Irene, certainly, certainly was *not*. Piet tried to tell them how he felt, especially in the society of Tarbox, as a sort of Jew at heart; but Irene, as if he had furtively petitioned for membership in the chosen race, shushed him with a torrent of analysis as to why Frank Appleby, that arch-Wasp, always argued with her, yet couldn't resist arguing with her, and sought her out at parties. In fairness, there were two people among their "friends" with whom she had never felt a trace of condescension or fear; and one was

Angela. The other was Freddy Thorne. "That miserable bastard," Piet groaned, out of habit, to please; people expected him to hate Freddy. The Saltzes understood his exclamation as a sign that, as all the couples suspected, Freddy and Angela had for ages been lovers.

Piet left early; he missed the silence of his shabby room, the undemandingness of the four walls. Ben put his hand on his shoulder and smiled his slow archaic smile. "You're down now," he told Piet, "and it's a pity you're not a Jew, because the fact is, every Jew expects to be down sometime in his life, and he has a philosophy for it. God is testing him. *Nisayon Elohim.*"

"But I clearly brought this on myself," Piet said.

"Who's to say? If you believe in omnipotence, it doesn't matter. What does matter is to taste your own ashes. Chew 'em. Up or down doesn't matter; *ain ben David ba elle bador shekulo zakkai oh kulo chayyav.* The son of David will not come except to a generation that's wholly good or all bad."

Piet tried to tell them how much he had liked them, how Angela had once said, and he had agreed, that the Saltzes of all the couples they knew were the most free from, well, crap.

Ben kept grinning and persisted with his advice. "Let go, Piet. You'll be OK. It was a helluva lot of fun knowing you."

Irene darted forward and kissed him good-bye, a quick singeing kiss from lips dark red in her pale face, rekindling his desire for women.

Later in the week, after cruising past her house several times a day, he called Bea. He had seen her once downtown, and she had waved from across the street, and disappeared into the jeweler's shop, still decorated with a nodding rabbit, though Easter was over. Her voice on the phone sounded startled, guilty.

"Oh, Piet, how are you? When are you going back to Angela?"

"Am I going back? She seems more herself without me."

"Oh, but at night it must be terrible for her."

"And how is it for you at night?"

"Oh, the same. Nobody goes out to parties any more. All people talk about is their children."

"Would you—would you like to see me? Just for tea, some afternoon?"

"Oh, sweet, I think not. Honestly. I think you have enough women to worry about."

"I don't have any women."

"It's good for you, isn't it?"

"It's not as bad as I would have thought. But what about us? I was in love with you, you know, before the roof fell in."

"You were lovely, so alive. But I think you idealized me. I'm much too lazy in bed for you. Anyway, sweet, all of a sudden, its rather touching, Roger needs me."

"How do you mean?"

"You won't tell anybody? Everybody's sure you're keeping a nest of girls down there."

"Everybody's wrong. I only liked married women. They reminded me of my mother."

"Don't be uppity. I'm trying to tell you about Roger. He lost a lot of money, one of his awful fairy investment friends in Boston, and he really came crying to me, I loved it."

"So because he's bankrupt I can't go to bed with you."

"Not bankrupt, you *do* idealize everything. But scared, so scared—oh, I must tell somebody, I'm bursting with it!—he's agreed to adopt a child. We've already been to the agency once, and answered a lot of insulting questions about our private life. The odd thing is, white babies are scarce, they have so many more Negroes."

"This is what you've wanted? To adopt a child?"

"Oh, for years. Ever since I knew I couldn't. It wasn't Roger, you know, it was me that couldn't. People poked fun of Roger but it was *me*. Oh, Piet, forgive me, I'm burdening you with this."

"No, it's no burden." Floating, he remembered how she floated, above the sound of children snowballing, as evening fell early, through levels of lavender.

She was sobbing, barely audibly, her voice limp and moist, as her body had been. "It's so rotten, though, that you need me and I must say no when before it was I who needed you, and you came finally."

"Finally. Bea, it's great about the adoption, and Roger's going to the poorhouse."

A laugh skidded through her tears. "I just can't," she said, "when I've been given what I've prayed for. The funny thing is, you helped. Roger was very frightened by you and Angela breaking up. He's become very serious."

"He was always serious."

"Sweet Piet, tell me, I was never very real to you, was I? Isn't it all right, not to? I've been dreading your call so, I thought it would come sooner."

"It should have come sooner," he said, then hastened to add to reassure her with, "No, you were never very real," and added finally, "Kiss."

"Kiss," Bea faintly said. "Kiss kiss kiss kiss kiss."

Sunday, bringing his daughters back from a trip to the Science Museum in Boston, Piet was saddened by the empty basketball court. This was the time of year when the young married men of Tarbox used to scrimmage. Whitman was gone, Saltz had moved, Constantine was flying jets to Lima and Rio, Thorne and little-Smith had always considered the game plebeian. Weeds were threading through a crack in the asphalt and the hoop, netless and aslant, needed to be secured with longer screws. Angela greeted them outdoors; she had been picking up winter-fallen twigs from the lawn, and sprinkling grass seed in the bare spots. Seeing the direction of his eyes, she said, "You should take that hoop down. Or would you like to invite your gentlemen friends to come play? I could tolerate it."

"I have no gentlemen friends, it turns out. They were all your friends. Anyway, it would be artificial and not comfortable, don't you think?"

"I suppose."

"Mightn't Ruth ever want to use the hoop?"

"She's interested right now in being feminine. Maybe later, when they have teams at school; but in the meantime it looks hideous."

"You're too exquisite," he said.

"How was your expedition? Artificial and not comfortable?"

"No, it was fun. Nancy cried in the planetarium, when the machine made the stars whirl around, but for some reason she loved the Transparent Woman."

"It reminded her of me." Angela said.

Piet wondered if this bit of self-disclaiming wit was the prelude to readmitting him into their home. Sneakingly he hoped not. He felt the worst nights of solitude were behind him. In loneliness he was regaining something, an elemental sense of surprise at everything, that he had lost with childhood. Even his visits to Angela in their awkwardness had a freshness that was pleasant. She seemed, with her soft fumbling gestures and unaccountable intervals of distant repose, a timid solid creature formed from his loins and now learning to thrive alone. He asked her, "How have you been?"

"Busy enough. I've had to reacquaint myself with my parents. My mother says that for ten years I snubbed them. I hadn't thought so, but maybe she's right."

"And the girls? They miss me less?"

"A little less. It's worst when something breaks and I can't fix it. Ruth was very cross with me the other day and told me I was stupid to lose their Daddy for them by being so pushy in bed. I guess Jonathan or Frankie at school had told her I was bad in bed, and she thought it must mean I didn't give you enough room. Oh, we had a jolly discussion after that. Woman to woman."

"The poor saint. Two poor saints."

"You look better."

"I'm adjusting. Everybody lets me alone, which in a way is a mercy, since I don't have to play politics. The only people I talk to all day some days are Adams and Comeau; we're doing some cabinets for a new couple toward Lacetown."

"I thought you were on Indian Hill."

"Jazinski and Gallagher seem to be managing that. They're working straight from canned plans that don't fit the slope at all."

"Oh. They had me over, with some North Mather people I hated. Money sort of people. Horsey."

"Matt's on the move."

"Terry seemed very bored."

"She'll be bored from here on in. And you? Bored? Happy? Fighting off propositions from our gentlemen friends?"

"A few feelers." Angela admitted. "But nothing serious. It's a different kettle of fish, a separated woman. It's scarier for them."

"You do think of us as separated?"

Rather than answer him, she looked over his shoulder, toward the corner of woods where scilla was blooming and where he had buried Ruth's hamster and where the girls, in a burst of relief at being released from the confinement of their father's embarrassingly rattly and unwashed pick-up truck, had, still in their Sunday expedition clothes, sought their climbing tree, a low-branching apple stunted among maples. Angela's face was recalled to animation by remembered good news. "Oh Piet, I must tell you. The strangest nicest thing. I've begun to have dreams. Dreams I can remember. It hasn't happened to me for years."

"What kind of dreams?"

"Oh, nothing very exciting yet. I'm in an elevator, and press the button, and nothing happens. So I think, not at all worried, 'I must be on the right floor already.' Or, maybe it's part of the same dream, I'm in a department store, trying to buy Nancy a fur hood, so she can go skiing in it. I know exactly the size, and the kind of lining, and go from counter to counter, and they offer me mittens, earmuffs, galoshes, everything I don't want, but I remain very serene and polite, because I know they have them somewhere, because I bought one for Ruth there."

"What sweet dreams."

"Yes, they're very shy and ordinary. *He* doesn't agree, or disagree, but my idea is my subconscious tried to die, and now it's daring to come back and express things I want. Not for myself yet, but for others."

"He. You're having dreams for *him*. Like a child going wee-wee for her daddy."

She retreated, as he desired, into the enchanted stillness that, in this square yard, this tidy manless house, he liked to visit. "You're such a bully," she told him. "Such a jealous bully. You always dreamed so easily, lying beside you inhibited me, I'm sure."

"Couldn't we have shared them?"

"No, you do it alone. I'm discovering you do everything alone. You know when I used to feel most alone? When we were making love." The quality of the silence that followed demanded she soften this. She asked, "Have you heard from Foxy?"

"Nothing. Not even a postcard of the Washington Monument." His lawn, he saw, beside the well and barn, had been killed in patches where the ice had lingered. Hard winter. The polar cap growing again. The hairy mammoths will be back. "It's kind of a relief," he told Angela.

The girls returned from the woods, their spring coats smirched with bark. "Go now," Nancy said to Piet.

Ruth slapped at her sister. "Nancy! That is *not* very nice."

"I think she's trying to help," Angela explained. "She's telling Daddy it's all right to go now."

"Mommy," Nancy told her, her plump hand whirling with her dizzy upgazing, "the stars went round and round and round."

"And the *baby cried*," Ruth said.

Nancy studied, as if seeking her coördinates, and then sprang at her sister, pummeling Ruth's chest. "Liar! Liar!"

Ruth bit her lower lip and expertly knocked Nancy loose with a sideways swerve of her fist. "*Baby cried*," she repeated, "*Hurting Dad*dy's *fee*lings, making him *take* us out *ear*ly."

Nancy sobbed against her mother's legs. Her face where Piet would never be again. Convolute cranny, hair and air, ambrosial chalice where seed can cling. "I'm sure it was very exciting," Angela said. "And that's why everybody is tired and cranky. Let's go in and have supper." She looked up, her eyes strained by the effort of refusing to do what was easy and instinctive and ask Piet in too.

Bernadette Ong bumped into Piet on the street, by the door of the book store, which sold mostly magazines. He was entering to buy *Life* and she was leaving with a copy of *Scientific American*. Her body brushing his felt flat, hard, yet deprived of its force; she was sallow, and the Oriental fold of upper-lid skin had sagged so that no lashes showed. She and Piet stood beneath the book-store awning; the April day around them was a refraction of apical summer, the first hot day, beach weather at last, when the high-school students shove down the crusty stiff tops of their convertibles and roar to the dunes in caravans. Above downtown Tarbox the Greek temple on its hill of red rocks was limestone white and the gold rooster blazed in an oven of blueness. Bernadette had thrown off her coat. The fine chain of a crucifix glinted in the neck of a dirty silk blouse. Descending into death, she had grown dingy, like a miner.

He asked her, immediately, guiltily, how John was, and she said, "About as well as we can expect, I guess." From her tone, her expectations had sunk low. "They keep him under drugs and he doesn't talk much English. He used to ask me why nobody visited him but that's stopped now."

"I'm so sorry, I thought of visiting him, but I've had my own troubles. I suppose you've heard Angela and I are separated."

"No, I hadn't heard. That's *terrible*." She pronounced it "tarrible"; all vowels tended in her flat wide mouth toward "a." *Whan do I gat my duty dance?* "You're the last couple I would have thought. John, as you've probably guessed, was always half in love with Angela."

Piet had never guessed any such thing. Impulsively he offered, "Why don't I visit him now? I have the time, and aren't you on your way back to the hospital?"

The Tarbox Veterans' Memorial hospital was two miles from the center of town, on the inland side. Built of swarthy clinker bricks, with a rosy new maternity wing that did not quite harmonize, it sat on a knoll between disused railroad tracks and an outlay of greenhouses (Hendrick Vos & Sons—Flowers, Bulbs, and Shrubs). Behind the hospital was a fine formal garden where no one, neither patients nor nurses, ever walked. The French windows of John Ong's room opened to a view of trimmed privet and a pink crabapple and a green-rusted copper birdbath shaped like a scallop shell, empty of water. Wind loosened petals from the crabapple, and billowed the white drapes at the window, and made the coarse transparent sides of the oxygen tent beside the bed abruptly buckle and snap. John was emaciated and, but for the hectic flushed spots, no larger than half dollars, on each cheekbone, colorless. So thin, he looked taller than Piet had remembered him. He spoke with difficulty, as if from a diminished pocket of air high in his chest, near the base of his throat. Only unaltered was the quick smile with which he masked imperfect comprehension. "Harya Pee? Wam weller mame waller pray terrace, heh?" Bernadette plangently translated: "He says how are you Piet? He says warm weather makes him want to play tennis."

"Soon you'll be out there," Piet said, and tossed up and served an imaginary ball.

"Is emerybonny?"

"He asks how is everybody?"

"Fine. Not bad. It's been a long winter."

"Hanjerer? Kiddies? Feddy's powwow?"

"Angela wants to come see you," Piet said, too loud, calling as if to a receding car. "Freddy Thorne's powwow has been pretty quiet lately. No big parties. Our children are getting too big."

It was the wrong thing to say; there was nothing to say. As the visit grew stilted, John Ong's eyes dulled. His hands, insectlike, their bones on the outside, fiddled on the magazine Bernadette had brought him. Once, he coughed, on and on, an interminable uprooting of a growth with roots too deep. Piet turned his head away, and a robin had come to the lip of the dry birdbath. It became clear that John was drugged; his welcome had been a strenuous leap out of hazed tranquillity. For a moment intelligence would be present in his wasted face like an eager carnivorous power; then he would subside into an inner murmuring, and twice spoke in Korean. He looked toward Bernadette for translation but she shrugged and winked toward Piet. "I only know a few phrases. Sometimes he thinks I'm his sister." Piet rose to leave, but she sharply begged, "Don't go." So he sat fifteen more minutes while Bernadette kept clicking something in her lap and John, forgetting his guest, leafed backwards through *Scientific American*, impatiently skimming, seeking something not there. Rubber-heeled nurses paced the hall. Doctors could be heard loudly flirting. Portentous baskets and pots of flowers crowded the floor by the radiator, and Piet wondered from whom. McNamara. Rusk. The afternoon's first cloud darkened the crabapple, and as if held pinned by the touch of light a scatter of petals exploded toward the ground. The room began to lose warmth. When Piet stood the second time to break away, and took the other man's strengthless fingers into his, and said too loudly, too jokingly, "See you on the tennis court," the drug-dilated eyes,

eyes that had verified the chaos of particles on the floor of matter, lifted, and dragged Piet down into omniscience; he saw, plunging, how plausible it was to die, how death, far from invading earth like a meteor, occurs on the same plane as birth and marriage and the arrival of the daily mail.

Bernadette walked him down the waxed hall to the hospital entrance. Outdoors, a breeze dragged a piece of her hair across her eye and a sun-shaped spot on the greenhouses below them glared. Her cross glinted. He felt a sexual stir emanate from her flat-breasted body, her wide shoulders and hips; she had been too long torn from support. She moved inches closer, as if to ask a question, and the nail-bitten fingers rising to tuck back the iridescent black strand whose windblown touch had made her blink seemed to gesture in weak apology for her willingness to live. Her smile was a grimace. Piet told her, "There *are* miracles."

"He rejects them," she said, as simply as if his assertion, so surprising to himself, had merely confirmed for her the existence of the pills she administered daily. A rosary had been clicking.

The adventure of visiting the dying man served to show Piet how much time he had, how free he was to use it. He took long walks on the beach. In this prismatic April the great Bay was never twice the same. Some days, at high tide, under a white sun, muscular waves bluer than tungsten steel pounded the sand into spongy cliffs and hauled driftwood and wrack deep into the dunes where tide-change left skyey isolated pools. Low tide exposed smooth acres that mirrored the mauves and salmons and the momentary green of sunset. At times the sea was steeply purple, stained; at others, under a close warm rain sky, the no-color of dirty wash; choppy rows hurried in from the horizon to be delivered and disposed of in the lick and slide at the shore. Piet stooped to pick up angel wings, razor-clam shells, sand dollars with their infallibly etched star and the considerate airhole for an inhabiting creature Piet could not picture. Wood flecks smoothed like creek pebbles, iron spikes mummified in the orange froth of oxidation, powerfully sunk horsehoe prints, the four-tined traces of racing dog paws, the shallow impress of human couples that had vanished (the female foot bare, with toes and a tender isthmus linking heel and forepad; the male mechanically shod in the waffle intaglio of sneaker soles and apparently dragging a stick), the wandering mollusk trails dim as the contours of a photograph overdeveloped in the pan of the tide, the perfect circle a blade of beach grass complacently draws around itself—nothing was too ordinary for Piet to notice. The beach felt dreamlike, always renewed in its strangeness. One day, late in an overcast afternoon, with lateral flecks of silver high in the west above the nimbus scud, he emerged from his truck in the empty parking lot and heard a steady musical roaring. Yet approaching the sea he saw it calm as a lake, a sullen muddy green. The tide was very low, and walking on the unscarred ribs of its recent retreat Piet percieved—diagnosed, as if the sustained roaring were a symptom within him—that violent waves were breaking on the sand bar a half mile away and, though little of their motion survived, their blended sound traveled to him upon the tranced water as if upon the taut skin of a drum. This effect, contrived with energies that could power cities, was his alone to witness; the great syllable around him seemed his own note, sustained since his birth, elicited from him now, and given to the air. The air that day was warm, and smelled of ashes.

In his loneliness he detected companionship in the motion of waves, especially those distant waves lifting arms of spray along the bar, hailing him. The world was more Platonic than he had suspected. He found he missed friends less than friendship; what he felt, remembering Foxy, was a nostalgia for adultery itself—its adventure, the acrobatics its deceptions demand, the tension of its hidden strings, the new landscapes it makes us master.

Sometimes, returning to the parking lot by way of the dunes, he saw the Whitmans' house above its grassy slope, with its clay scars of excavation and its pale patches of reshingling. The house did not see him. Windows he had often gazed from, euphoric and apprehensive, glinted blank. Once, driving past it, the old Robinson house, he thought that it was fortunate he and Angela had not bought it, for it had proved to be an unlucky house; then realized that they had shared in its bad luck anyway. In his solitude he was growing absent-minded. He noticed a new woman downtown— that elastic proud gait announcing education, a spirit freed from the peasant shuffle, arms swinging, a sassy ass, trim ankles. Piet hurried along the other side of Charity Street to get a glimpse of her front and found, just before she turned into the savings bank, that the woman was Angela. She was wearing her hair down and a new blue cape that her parents had given her, as consolation.

How strange she had been to be jealous of his dreams, to accuse him of dreaming too easily! Perhaps because each night he dosed himself with much gin, his dreams now were rarely memorable —clouded repetitive images of confusion and ill-fittingness, of building something that would not stay joined or erect. He was a little boy, in fact his own father, walking beside his father, in fact his own gandfather, a faceless man he had never met, one of hundreds of joiners who had migrated from Holland to work in the Grand Rapids furniture factories. His thumbs were hugely callused; the boy felt frightened, holding on. Or he was attending John Ong's funeral, and suddenly the casket opened and John scuttled off, behind the altar, dusty as an insect, and cringing in shame. Such dreams Piet washed away along with the sour-hay taste in his mouth when, before dawn, he would awake, urinate, drink a glass of water, and vow to drink less gin tomorrow. Two dreams were more vivid. In one, he and a son, a child who was both Nancy and Ruth yet male, were walking in a snowstorm up from the baseball diamond near his first home. There was between the playground and his father's lower greenhouses a thin grove of trees, horsechestnut and cherry, where the children would gather and climb in the late afternoon and from which, one Halloween, a stoning raid was launched upon the greenhouses that ended with an accounting in police court and fistfights for Piet all November. In the dream it was winter. A bitter wind blew through the spaced trunks and the path beneath the snow was ice, so that Piet had to take the arm of his child and hold him from slipping. Piet himself walked in the deeper snow beside the tightrope of ice; for if both fell at once it would be death. They reached the alley, crossed it, and there, at the foot of their yard beside the dark greenhouses, Piet's grandmother was waiting for them, standing stooped and apprehensive in a cube of snowless-ness. Invisible walls enclosed her. She wore only a cotton dress and her threadbare black sweater, unbuttoned. In the dream Piet wondered how long she had been waiting, and gave thanks to the

Lord that they were safe, and anticipated joining her in that strange transparent arbor where he clearly saw green grass, blade by blade. Awake, he wondered that he had dreamed of his grandmother at all, for she had died when he was nine, of pneumonia, and he had felt no sorrow. She had known little English and, a compulsive housecleaner, had sought to bar Piet and Joop not only from the front parlor but from all the downstairs rooms save the kitchen.

The second dream was static. He was standing beneath the stars trying to change their pattern by an effort of his will. Piet pressed himself upward as a clenched plea for the mingled constellations, the metallic mask of night, to alter position; they remained blazing and inflexible. He thought, *I might strain my heart*, and was awakened by a sharp pain in his chest.

Foxy was back in town. The rumor flew from Marcia little-Smith, who had seen her driving Ken's MG on the Nun's Bay Road, to Harold to Frank to Janet to Bea and Terry in the A & P and from there to Carol and the Thornes, to join with the tributary glimpse Freddy had had of her from his office window as she emerged that afternoon from Cogswell's Drug Store. The rumor branched out and began to meet itself in the phrase, "I know"; Terry, acting within, as she guessed at her duties, the office of confidante that Ken had thrust on the Gallaghers that dawn a month ago, phoned and gingerly told Angela, who took the news politely, as if it could hardly concern her. Perhaps it didn't. The Hanemas had become opaque to the other couples, had betrayed the conspiracy of mutual comprehension. Only Piet, as the delta of gossip interlaced, remained dry; no one told him. But there was no need. He already knew. On Tuesday, in care of Gallagher & Hanema, he had received this letter from Washington:

Dear Piet—

I must come back to New England for a few days and will be in Tarbox April 24th, appropriating furniture. Would you like to meet and talk? Don't be nervous—I have no claims to press.

Love,

F.

After "press" the word "but" had been scratched out. They met first by accident, in the town parking lot, an irregular asphalt wilderness of pebbles and parked metal ringed by back entrances to the stores on Charity Street—the A & P, Poirier's Liquor Mart, Beth's Books and Cards, the Methodist Thrift Shop, even, via an alleyway sparkling with broken glass, the Tarbox Professional Apartments. He discovered himself unprepared for the sight of her—from a distance, the candence of her, the dip of her tall body bending to put a shopping bag into her lowslung black car, the blond dab of her hair bundled, the sense of the tone of muscle across her abdomen, the vertiginous certainty that it was indeed among the world's billions none other than she. His side hurt; his left palm tingled. He called; she held still in answer, and appeared, closer approached, younger than he had remembered, smoother, more finely made—the silken skin translucent to her blood, the straight-boned nose faintly paler at the bridge, the brown irises warmed by gold and set tilted in the dainty shelving of her lids, quick lenses subtler than clouds, minutely shuttling as she spoke. Her voice dimensional with familiar shadows, the unnumbered curves of her parted, breathing, talking, thinking lips: she was alive. Having lived with frozen fading bits of her, he was not prepared for her to be so alive, so continuous and witty.

"Piet, you look touchingly awful."

"Unlike you."

"Why don't you comb your hair any more?"

"You even have a little tan."

"My stepfather has a swimming pool. It's summer there."

"It's been off and on here. The same old tease. I've been walking on the beach a lot."

"Why aren't you living with Angela?"

"Who says I'm not?"

"She says. She told me over the phone. Before I wrote you I called your house; I was going to say my farewells to you both."

"She never told me you called."

"She probably didn't think it was very important."

"A mysterious woman, my wife."

"She said I was to come and get you."

He laughed. "If she said that, why did you ask why wasn't I living with her?"

"Why aren't you?"

"She doesn't want me to."

"That's only," Foxy said, "half a reason."

With this observation their talk changed key; they became easier, more trivial, as if a decision had been put behind them. Piet asked her, "Where are you taking the groceries?"

"They're for me. I'm living in the house this weekend. Ken's promised to stay in Cambridge."

"You and Ken aren't going to be reconciled?"

"He's happy. He says he works evenings now and thinks he's on to something significant. He's back on starfish."

"And you?"

She shrugged, a pale-haired schoolgirl looking for the answer broad enough to cover her ignorance. "I'm managing."

"Won't it depress you living there alone? Or do you have the kid?"

"I left Toby with Mother. They get along beautifully, they both think I'm untrustworthy, and adore cottage cheese."

He asked her simply, "What shall we do?" adding in explanation, "A pair of orphans."

He carried her bag of groceries up to his room, and they lived the weekend there. Saturday he helped her go through the empty house by the marsh, tagging the tables and chairs she wanted for herself. No one prevented them. The old town catered to their innocence. Foxy confessed to Piet that, foreseeing sleeping with him, she had brought her diaphragm and gone to Cogswell's Drug Store for a new tube of vaginal jelly. As he felt himself under the balm of love grow boyish and wanton, she aged; his first impression of her smoothness and translucence was replaced by the goosebumped roughness of her buttocks, the gray unpleasantness of her shaved armpits, the backs of her knees, the thickness of her waist since she had had the baby. Her flat feet gave her walking movements, on the bare floor of Piet's dirty oatmeal-walled room, a slouched awkwardness quite unlike the casually springy step with which Angela, her little toes not touching the floor, moved through the rectangular farmhouse with eggshell trim. Asleep, she snuffled, and restlessly crowded him toward the edge of the bed, and sometimes struggled against nightmares. The first morning she woke him with her hands on his penis, delicately tugging the foreskin, her face pinched and blanched by desire. She cried out that her being here with him was wrong, wrong, and fought his entrance of her; and then afterwards slyly asked if it had made it more exciting for him, her pretending to resist. She asked him abrupt questions, such as, Did he still consider himself a Christian? He said he didn't know, he doubted it. Foxy said of herself that she did, though a Christian living in a state of sin; and defiantly, rather arrogantly and—his impression was—prissily, tossed and stroked back her hair, tangled damp from the pillow. She complained that she was hungry. Did he intend just to keep her here screwing until she starved? Her stomach growled.

They ate in the Musquenomenee Luncheonette, sitting in a booth away from the window, through which they spied on Frank Appleby and little Frankie lugging bags of lime and peat moss from the hardware store into the Applebys' old maroon Mercury coupe. They saw but were not seen, as if safe behind a one-way mirror. They discussed Angela and Ken and the abortion, never pausing on one topic long enough to exhaust it, even to explore it; the state of their being together precluded discussion, as if, in the end, everything was either too momentous or too trivial. Piet felt, even when they lay motionless together, that they were skimming, hastening through space, lightly interlocked, yet not essentially mingled. He slept badly beside her. She had difficulty coming with him. Despairing of her own climax, she would give herself to him in slavish postures, as if witnessing in her mouth or between her breasts the tripped unclotting thump of his ejaculation made it her own. She still wore the rings of her marriage and engagement, and, gazing down to where her hand was guiding him into her silken face, her cheek concave as her jaws were forced apart, he noticed the icy octagon of her diamond and suffered the realization that if they married he would not be able to buy her a diamond so big.

She did not seem to be selling herself; rather, she was an easy and frank companion. After the uncomfortable episode of tagging the furniture (he was not tempted to touch her in this house they had often violated; her presence as she breezed from room to room felt ghostly, impervious; and already they had lost that prerogative of lovers which claims all places as theirs) she walked with him Saturday along the beach, along the public end, where they would not be likely to meet friends. She pointed to a spot where once she had written him a long letter that he had doubtless forgotten. He said he had not forgotten it, though in part he had. She suddenly told him that his callousness, his promiscuity, had this advantage for her; with him she could be as whorish as she wanted, that unlike most men he really didn't judge. Piet answered that it was his Calvinism. Only God judged. Anyway he found her totally beautiful. Totally: bumps, pimples, flat feet, snuffles, and all. She laughed to hear herself so described, and the quality of her laugh told him she was vain, that underneath all fending disclaimers she thought of herself as flawless. Piet believed her, believed the claim of her barking laugh, a shout snatched away by the salt wind beside the spring sea, her claim that she was in truth perfect, and he hungered to be again alone with her long body in the stealthy shabby shelter of his room.

Lazily she fellated him while he combed her lovely hair. Oh and lovely also her coral cunt, coral into burgundy, with its pansy-shaped M, or W, of fur: kissing her here, as she unfolded fom gateway into chamber, from chamber into universe, was a blind pleasure tasting of infinity until, he biting her, she clawed his back and came. Could break his neck. Forgotten him entirely. All raw self. Machine that makes salt at the bottom of the sea.

Mouths, it came to Piet, are noble. They move in the brain's court. We set our genitals mating down below like peasants, but when the mouth condescends, mind and body marry. To eat another is sacred. *I love thee, Elizabeth, thy petaled rankness, thy priceless casket of nothing lined with slippery buds.* Thus on the Sunday morning, beneath the hanging clangor of bells.

"Oh Piet," Foxy sighed to him, "I've never felt so taken. No one has ever known me like this."

Short of sleep, haggard from a month of fighting panic, he smiled and tried to rise to her praise with praise of her, and fell asleep instead, his broad face feverish, as if still clamped between her thighs.

Sunday afternoon was his time with the children; at Foxy's suggestion the four of them went bowling at the candlepin alleys in North Mather. Ruth and Nancy were wide-eyed at the intrusion of Mrs. Whitman, but Foxy was innocently intent on bowling a good score for herself, and in showing the girls how to grasp the unwieldy ball and keep it out of the gutters. When it went in, Ruth said, "*Merde.*"

Piet asked her, "Where did you learn that word?"

"Jonathan little-Smith says it, to keep from swearing."

"Do you like Jonathan?"

"He's a fink," Ruth said, as Angela had once said of Freddy Thorne, *He's a jerk.*

On the second string Piet bowled only 81 to Foxy's 93. She was competition. The outing ended in ice-cream sodas at a newly reopened roadside ice-cream stand whose proprietor had returned, with a fisherman's squint and a peeling forehead, from his annual five months in Florida. To Piet he said, putting his hand on Ruth's head, "This one is like you, but this little number"—his brown hand splayed on Nancy's blond head—"is your missus here all the way."

Foxy had planned to fly back to Washington late Sunday, but she stayed through the night. "Won't Ken guess where you've been sleeping?"

"Oh, let him. He doesn't give a damn. He has grounds enough already, and anyway the settlement's pretty much ironed out. Ken's not stingy with money, thank God. I've got to admit, he's the least neurotic man I ever met. He's decided this, and he's going to make it stick."

"You sound admiring."

"I always admired him. I just never wanted him."

"And me?"

"Obviously. I want you. Why do you think I came all this way?"

"To divide the furniture."

"Oh who cares about furniture? I don't even know where I'm going to be living."

"Well, I suppose I *am* up for grabs."

"I'm not so sure. Angela may just be giving you a holiday."

"I—"

"Don't try to say anything. If you're there, you're there; if not, not. I must make myself free first. I'll be away for a long time now, Piet. Six weeks, two months. Shall I never come back?"

"Where are you going?"

"I don't know yet. Ken's father thinks it should be a western state, but a friend of ours in Cambridge went to the Virgin Islands and that sounds like more fun than some desert ranch full of Connecticut menopause patients whose husband shacked up with the secretary."

"You're really going to go through with it?"

"Oh," she said, touching his cheek in the dark curiously, as if testing the contour of a child's face, or the glaze on a vase she had bought, "absolutely. I'm a ruined woman."

Later, in that timeless night distended by fatigue, demarcated only by a periodic rising of something within him yet not his, a surge from behind him that in blackness broke beneath him upon her strange forked whiteness, Foxy sighed, "It's good to have enough, isn't it? Really enough."

He said, "Sex is like money; only too much is enough."

"That sounds like Freddy Thorne."

"My mentor and savior."

She hushed his lips with fingers fragrant of low tide. "Oh don't. I can't stand other people, even their names. Let's pretend there's only us. Don't we make a world?"

"Sure. I'm a ticklish question, and you're the tickled answer."

"Oh sweet, I do ache."

"You think I don't? Oooaaoh."

"Piet."

"Oooaauhooaa."

"Stop it. That's a horrible noise."

"I can't help it, love. I'm in the pit. One more fuck, and I'm ready to die. Suck me up. Ououiiiyaa. Ayaa."

Each groan felt to be emptying his chest, creating an inner hollowness answering the hollowness beneath the stars.

She threatened him: "I'll leave you."

"You can't. Try it yourself. Groan. It feels great."

"No. You're disciplining me. You're under no obligation to marry me, I'm not so sure even I want to marry you."

"Oh, do. Do. Uuoooiiaaaugh. Oh, mercy. You are tops, Fox."

"Mmmmooh. You're right. It does relax."

He repeated, "Oh, mercy," and, as the wearying wonder of her naked sweated-up fucked-out body being beside his sank in, said with boneless conviction, "Ah, you're mine." She put her blurred cheek against his. The tip of her nose was cold. A sign of health. We are all exiles who need to bathe in the irrational.

Monday morning, sneaking downstairs, they met the other tenant of the third floor returning, a small bespectacled man in factory grays. Freezing on the narrow stair to let them pass, he said, "G-g-g-gu-ood mur-mur—"

Outdoors, in the parking lot, beside the glittering MG, Foxy giggled and said, "Your having a woman scared the poor man half to death." Piet told her No, the man always talked like that. The world, he went on, doesn't really care as much about lovers as we imagine. He saw her, said his farewell to her, through a headachy haze of ubiquitous, bounding sun; her pale brave face was lost, lightstruck. He saw dimly that her eyes above their blue hollows had been left soft by their nights, flowers bloomed from mud. Called upon by their circumstances to laugh joyfully, or to weep plainly, or to thank her regally for these three slavish days, or even to be amusingly stoical, he was nothing, not even polite. She gave him her hand to shake and he lifted it to his mouth and pressed his tongue into her palm, and wished her away. He leaned into the car window and blew on her ear and told her to sleep on the plane. Nothing had been concluded; nothing wanted to be said. When, after a puzzled flick of her hand and the sad word "Ciaou," learned from movies, her MG swerved out past the automatic car-wash and was gone, he felt no pang, and this gravel arena of rear entrances looked papery, like a stage set in daylight.

Loss became real and leaden only later, in the afternoon. Walking along Divinity Street with an empty skull and aching loin muscles, he met Eddie Constantine, back from the ends of the world. Eddie was rarely in town any more, and perhaps Carol had just filled him in on a month's worth of gossip, for he gleefully cried in greeting, "Hey, Piet! I hear you got caught with your hand in the honeypot!"

One Sunday in mid-May Piet took his daughters to the beach; the crowd there, tender speckled bodies not yet tan, had herdlike trapped itself between the hot dunes and the cold water, and formed, with its sunglasses and aluminum chairs, a living ribbon parallel to the surf's unsteady edge. Nancy splashed and crowed in the waves with the three Ong boys, who had come with a grim babysitter; Bernadette's final vigil had begun. Ruth lay beside Piet unhappily, not quite ready to bask and beautify herself like a teen-ager, yet too old for sandcastles. Her face had thinned; the smoky suggestion across her eyes was intensifying; she would be, unlike her mother, a clouded beauty, with something dark and regretted filtering her true goodness. Piet, abashed, in love with her, could think of no comfort to offer her but time, and closed his eyes upon the corona of curving hairs his lashes could draw from the sun. Distant music enlarged and loomed over him; he saw sandy ankles, a turquoise transistor, young thighs, a bikini bottom allowing a sense of globes. *How many miles must a man . . .* Folk. Rock is out. . . . *the answer, my friends . . .* Love and peace are in. As the music receded he closed his eyes and on the crimson inside of his lids pictured globes parting to admit him. He was thirsty. The wind was from the west, off the land, and tasted of the parched dunes.

Then the supernatural proclaimed itself. A sullen purpling had developed unnoticed in the north. A wall of cold air swept south across the beach; the wind change was so distinct and sudden a unanimous grunt, *Ooh*, rose from the crowd. Single raindrops heavy as hail began to fall, still in sunshine, spears of fire. Then the sun was swallowed. The herd gathered its bright colors and hedonistic machinery and sluggishly funneled toward the boardwalk. Brutal thunderclaps, sequences culminating with a splintering as of cosmic crates, spurred the retreat. The livid sky had already surrounded them; the green horizon of low hills behind which lay downtown Tarbox appeared paler than the dense atmosphere pressing upon it. A luminous crack leaped, many-pronged, into being in the north, over East Mather; calamitous crashing followed. There was a push on the boardwalk; a woman screamed, a child laughed. Towels were tugged tight across huddling shoulders. The temperature had dropped twenty degrees in five minutes. The beach behind Piet and his children was clean except for a few scoffers still lolling on their blankets. The plane of the sea ignited like the filament of a flash bulb.

A moment before Piet and his daughters reached the truck cab, the downpour struck, soaking them; rain slashed at the cab's windows and deafeningly drummed on the metal sides. WASH ME. The windshield had become a waterfall the wipers could not clear. Bits of color scurried through the glass, and shouts punctured the storm's exultant monotone. In their space of shelter his daughters' wet hair gave off an excited doggy smell. Nancy was delighted and terrified, Ruth stoical and amused. At the first slight relenting of the weather's fury, Piet put the truck in gear and made his way from the puddled parking lot, on roads hazardous with fallen boughs, via Blackberry Lane, flooded at one conduit, toward the crunching driveway of Angela's house. In the peril his dominating wish had been to deliver his daughters to their mother before he was overtaken: he must remove his body from proximity with theirs. He refused Angela's offer of tea and headed into the heart of Tarbox, unaware that the year's great event had begun to smolder.

The cloudburst settled to a steady rain. Houses, garages, elms and asphalt submitted to the same gray whispering. Thunder, repulsed, grumbled in retreat. Piet parked behind his building and there was a sudden hooting. The Tarbox fire alarm launched its laborious flatulent bellow. The coded signal was in low numbers; the fire was in the town center. Piet imagined he scented ginger. Quickly he ran upstairs, changed out of his bathing suit, and came down to the front entrance. On Divinity Street people were running. The ladder truck roared by with spinning scarlet light and firemen struggling into slickers, clinging as the truck rounded Cogswell's corner. The fire horn, apocalyptically close, repeated its call. The section of the town leeward from the hill was fogged with yellow smoke. Piet began running with the rest.

Up the hill the crowds and the smoke thickened. Already fire hoses, some slack and tangled, others plump and leaking in graceful upward jets, filled the streets around the green. The Congregational Church was burning. God's own lightning had struck it. The icy rain intensified, and the crowds of people, both old and young, from every quarter, watched in chilled silence.

Smoke, an acrid yellow, was pouring neatly, sheets of rapidly crimping wool, from under the cornice of the left pediment and from the lower edge of the cupola that lifted the gilded weathercock one hundred twenty-five feet into the air. Down among the Doric columns firemen were chasing away the men of the church who had rushed in and already rescued the communion service, the heavy walnut altar and pulpit, the brass cross, the portraits of old divines, stacks of old sermons that were blowing away, and, sodden and blackening in the unrelenting rain, a few pew cushions, new from the last renovation. As a onetime member of the church Piet would have gone forward to help them but the firemen and police had formed a barricade through which only the town dogs, yapping and socializing, could pass. His builder's eye calculated that the bolt had struck the pinnacle, been deflected from the slender lighting-rod cable into the steel rods reinforcing the cupola, and ignited the dry wood where the roofline joined the straight base of the tower. Here, in the hollownesses old builders created for insulation, between the walls, between the roof and the hung plaster ceiling of the sanctuary, in the unventilated spaces behind the dummy tympanum and frieze and architrave of the classic façade, amid the hodgepodge of dusty storage reachable by only a slat ladder behind the disused choir loft, the fire would thrive. Hoses turned upon the steaming exterior surfaces solved nothing. The only answer was immediate axwork, opening up the roof, chopping without pity through the old hand-carved triglyphs and metopes. But the columns themselves were forty feet from porch to capital, and no truck could be worked close enough over the rocks to touch its ladder to the roof, and the wind was blowing the poisonously thickening smoke straight out from the burning side into the throats of the rescuers.

A somewhat ironical cheer arose from the theater of townspeople. Buzz Kappiotis, his swollen silhouette unmistakable, had put on a smoke mask and, ax in hand, was climbing a ladder extended to its fullest to touch the great church's pluming rain gutter. Climbing slower and slower, his crouch manifesting his fear, he froze in a mass of smoke, disappeared, and reappeared inching down. A few teen-agers behind Piet booed, but the crowd, out of noncomprehension or shame, was silent. Another fireman, shiny as a coal in his slicker, climbed to the ladder's tip, swung his ax, produced a violet spurt of trapped gas, so his masked profile gleamed peacock blue, and was forced by the heat to descend.

Now flames, shy flickers of orange, materialized, licking their way up the cupola's base, along the inside edges of the louvered openings constructed to release the sound of the bell. The bell itself, ponderous sorrowing shape, a caped widow, was illumined by a glow from beneath. Jets of water arched high and fell short, crisscrossing. Spirals of whiter smoke curled up the painted cerulean dome of the cupola but did not obscure the weathercock turning in the touches of wind.

The fire signal sounded a third time, and engines from neighboring communities, from Lacetown and Mather, from as far away as Quincy and Plymouth, began to arrive, and the pressure generated by their pumps lifted water to the flickering pinnacle; but by now the tall clear windows along the sides had begun to glow, and the tar shingles of the roof gave off greasy whiffs. The fire had spread under the roof and through the double walls and, even as the alien firemen smashed a hundred diamond panes of glass, ballooned golden in the sanctuary itself. For an instant the Gothic-tipped hymnboards could be seen, still bearing this morning's numerals; the Doric fluting on the balcony rail was raked with amber light; the plush curtain that hid the choir's knees caught and exploded upwards in the empty presbytery like a phoenix. Gone was the pulpit wherein Pedrick had been bent double by his struggle with the Word. The booing teen-agers behind Piet had been replaced by a weeping woman. The crowd,

which had initially rushed defenseless and naked to the catastrophe, had sprouted umbrellas and armored itself in raincoats and
tarpaulins. There was a smell of circus. Children, outfitted in
yellow slickers and visored rainhats, clustered by their parents'
legs. Teen-age couples watched from cars cozy with radio music.
People crammed the memorial pavilion, clung to the baseball
screen. The gathered crowd now stretched far down each street
radiating from the green, Divinity and Prudence and Temperance, ashen faces filling even the neon-scrawled shopping section.
Rain made dusk premature. The spotlights of the fire trucks
searched out a crowd whose extent seemed limitless and whose
silence, as the conflagration possessed every section of the church,
deepened. Flames, doused in the charred belfry, had climbed
higher and now fluttered like pennants from the slim pinnacle
supporting the rooster. With yearning parabolas the hoses arched
higher. A section of roof collapsed in a whirlwind of sparks. The
extreme left column began to smoulder like a snuffed birthday
candle. Through the great crowd breathed disbelief that the rain
and the fire could persist together, that nature could so war with
herself: as if a conflict in God's heart had been bared for them to
witness. Piet wondered at the lightness in his own heart, gratitude
for having been shown something beyond him, beyond all blaming.

He picked up a soaked pamphlet, a sermon dated 1795. *It is the*
indispensable duty of all the nations of the earth, to know that the
LORD he is God, and to offer unto him sincere and devout
thanksgiving and praise. But if there is any nation under heaven,
which hath more peculiar and forcible reasons than others, for
joining with one heart and voice in offering up to him these
grateful sacrifices, the United States of America are that nation.

Familiar faces began to protrude from the citizenry. Piet spotted the Applebys and little-Smiths and Thornes standing in the
broad-leafed shelter of a catalpa tree near the library. The men
were laughing; Freddy had brought a beer. Angela was also in the
crowd. She had brought the girls, and when they spoke to him it
was Ruth, not Nancy, who was weepy, distressed that the man
Jesus would destroy His church, where she had always wiped her

feet, timid of the holy, and had dutifully, among children who were not her friends, sung His praise, to please her father. Piet pressed her wide face against his chest in apology; but his wind-breaker was soaked and cold and Ruth flinched from the unpleasant contact. "This is too damn depressing for them," Angela said, "we're going back." When Nancy begged to stay, she said, "The fire's nearly out, the best part is over," and it was true; visible flames had been chased into the corners of the charred shell.

Nancy pointed upward and said, "The chicken!" The rooster, bright as if above not only the smoke but the rain, was poised motionless atop a narrow pyre. Flames in little gassy points had licked up the pinnacle to the ball of ironwork that supported the vane's pivot; it seemed it all must topple; then a single jet, luminous in the spotlights, hurled itself higher and the flames abruptly vanished. Though the impact made the spindly pinnacle waver, it held. The flashbulbs of accumulating cameras went off like secondary lightning. By their fitful illumination and the hysterical whirling of spotlights, Piet watched his wife walk away, turn once, white, to look back, and walk on, leading their virgin girls.

Pedrick, his wiry old hair disarrayed into a translucent crest, recognized Piet in the crowd, though it had been months since he had been in the congregation. His voice clawed. "You're a man of the world. How much in dollars and cents do you estimate it will take to replace this tragic structure?"

Piet said, "Oh, if the exterior shell can be salvaged, between two and three hundred thousand. From the ground up, maybe half a million. At least. Construction costs increase about eight per cent a year." These figures bent the gaunt clergyman like a weight on his back; Piet added in sympathy, "It *is* tragic. The carpentry in there can never be duplicated."

Pedrick straightened; his eye flashed. He reprimanded Piet: "Christianity isn't dollars and cents. This church isn't that old stump of a building. The church is people, my friend, people. *Hu*man *be*ings." And he waggled a horny finger, and Piet saw that Pedrick too knew of his ouster from his home, his need to be brought into line.

Piet told him in return, "But even if they do save the shell, the walls are going to be so weakened you'll have to tear it down anyway." And as if to bear him out, fresh flames erupted along the wall on the other side and leaped so high, as the hoses were shifted, that a maple sapling, having ventured too close to the church, itself caught fire, and dropping burning twigs on the shoulders of spectators.

The crowd churned to watch this final resurgence of the powers of destruction, and Piet was fetched up against Carol Constantine. She carried an umbrella and invited him under it with her, and two of her children, Laura and Patrice. Her show of sorrow touched him. "Oh Piet," she said, "it's too terrible, isn't it? I loved that church."

"I never saw you in it."

"Of course not, I'm a Presbyterian. But I'd look at it twenty times a day, whenever I was in our yard. I'd really be very religious, if Eddie weren't so anti-everything."

"Where is Eddie? On the road?"

"In the sky. He comes back and tells me how beautifully these Puerto Rican girls lay. It's a joy to see him leave. Why am I telling you all this?"

"Because you're sad to see the church burn."

The gutted walls stood saved. The pillars supported the pediment, and the roof beam held the cupola, but the place of worship was a rubble of timbers and collapsed plaster and charred pews, and the out-of-town firemen were coiling their hose, and Buzz Kappiotis was mentally framing his report, and the crowd gradually dispersing. Carol invited Piet in for a cup of tea. Tea became supper, spaghetti shared with her children. He changed from his wet clothes to a sweater and pants, too tight, of Eddie's. When the children were in bed it developed he would spend the night. He had never before slept with a woman so bony and supple. It was good, after his strenuous experience of Foxy, to have a woman who came quickly, with grateful cries and nimble accommodations, who put a pillow beneath her hips, who let her head hang over the side of the bed, hair trailing, throat arched, and who wrapped her legs around him as if his trunk were a stout trapeze by which she was swinging far out over the abyss of the world. The bedroom, like many rooms in Tarbox that night, smelled of wet char and acidulous smoke. Between swings she talked, told him of her life with Eddie, his perversity and her misery, of her hopes for God and immortality, of the good times she and Eddie had had long ago, before they moved to Tarbox. Piet asked her about their affair with the Saltzes and whether she missed them. Carol seemed to need reminding and finally said, "That was mostly talk by other people. Frankly, she was kind of fun, but he was a bore."

Larry & Linda's Guest House
Charlotte Amalie, St. Thomas, V.I.
May 15

Dearest Piet—

Just to write your name makes me feel soft and collapsing inside. What am I doing here, so far from my husband, or my lover, or my father? I have only Toby, and he, poor small soul, has been sunburned by his idiot mother who, accustomed to the day-by-day onset of the Tarbox summer, has baked both him and herself in the tropical sun, a little white spot directly overhead no bigger than a pea. He cried all night, whenever he tried to roll over. Also, this place, advertised as "an inn in the sleepy tradition of the islands of rum and sun" (I have their leaflet on the desk, the very same one given to me by a Washington travel agent), is in fact two doors up from a steel band nightclub and the slanty little street where blue sewer water runs is alive most of the night with the roar of mufflerless VW's and the catcalls of black adolescents. So I have fits all night and droop all day.

Just then a maid with slithery paper sandals and a downcast lilt I can hardly decipher as English came in. From the way she stared at Toby it might have been a full-grown naked man lying there. I don't suppose too many tourist types bring babies. Maybe they think babies come to us in laundry baskets, all powdered and blue-eyed and ready to give orders.

Peace again. The girl cuddled him at my urging and made the beds and pushed some dust here and there and left and he went back to sleep. Trouble is, his mother is sleepy too. Outside the street is incandescent but in here sun lies slatted like yellow crayon sticks on the gritty green floor—Piet, I think I'm going to love it here, once I stop hurting. On the ride from the airport in I wanted to share it with you—just the way they build their houses, corrugated iron and flattened olive oil cans and driftwood all held together by flowering bougainvillaea, and the softness of the air, stepping from the plane in San Juan, like a kiss after fucking—oh lover, forgive me, I am sleepy.

After her restorative nap, the fair-haired young soon-to-be divorcee swiftly arose, and dressed, taking care not to abrade her sunburned forearms and thighs and (especially touchy) abdomen, and changed her youngling's soiled unmentionables, and hurled herself into the blinding clatter of the tropical ville in a heroic (heroinic?) effort to find food. No counterpart of the Tarbox A & P or Lacetown IGA seems to exist—though I could buy bushels of duty-free Swiss watches and cameras. The restaurants not up on the hills attached to the forbidding swish hotels are either native hamburgeries with chili spilled all over the stools or else "gay" nightclubs that don't open until six. At this time of year most of the non-Negroes seem to be fairies. Their voices are unmistakable and everywhere. I finally found a Hayes-Bickford type of cafeteria, with outrageous island prices, up the street near the open market, which meets my apparently demanding (sweet, I'm such an old maid!) sanitary standards, and gives me milk for Toby's bottle in a reassuring waxpaper carton. Larry and Linda aren't much help. They are refugees from New York, would-be actors, and I have the suspicion she rescued him from being gay. He keeps giving me his profile while she must think her front view is the best, because she keeps coming at me head on, her big brown bubs as scary as approaching headlights on a slick night. I was shocked to learn she's five years younger than me and I could see her tongue make a little determined leap to put me on a first-name basis. They seem waifs, rather. They talk about New

York all the time, how horrible it was etc., love-hate as Freddy Thorne would say, and are in a constant flap about their sleepy elusive unintelligible help. Though the evening meals Linda puts on are quite nice and light and French. American plan—they give you breakfast and supper, forage as best you can in between. $18 per diem.

But it's you, you I think about, and worry about, and wonder about. How grand we were, me as a call girl and you as a gangster in hiding. Did I depress you? You seemed so dazed the last morning, and pleased I was going, I cried all the way into B.U., and let Ken take me to lunch at the faculty club and cried some more, so the tables around us became quite solemn. I think he thought I was crying for him, which in a way I was, and I could see him fighting down a gentlemanly impulse to offer to call it all off and take me back. He has become so distinguished and courtly without me—his female students must adore him. He had bought a new spring suit, sharkskin, and seemed alarmed that I noticed, as if I were wooing him again or had caught him wooing someone else, when all the time you were flowery between my legs and I was neurotically anxious because we had left Toby in Ken's lab with his technicians and I would go back up the elevator and find him dissected. Horrible! Untrue!! Ken was very cute with the baby, and weighed him in milligrams.

Days have passed. My letter to you seemed to be going all wrong, chattery and too "fun" and breezy. Rereading I had to laugh at what I did to poor Linda's lovely bosom—she and Larry are really a perfectly sweet phony fragile couple, trying to be parental and sisterly and brotherly all at once to me, rather careful and anxious with each other, almost studiously sensual, and so lazy basically. I wonder if ours was the last generation that will ever have "ambition." These two seem so sure the world will never let them starve, and that life exists to be "enjoyed"—barbarous idea. But it is refreshing, after our awful Tarbox friends who talk only about themselves, to talk to people who care about art and the theater (they invariably call it, with innocent pomp, "the stage") and international affairs, if that's what they are. I've forgotten what else "affair" means. They think LBJ a boor but feel better under him than Kennedy because K. was too much like the rest of us semi-educated lovables of the post-Cold War and might have blown the whole game through some mistaken sense of flair. Like Lincoln, he lived to become a martyr, a memory. A martyr to what? To Marina Oswald's sexual rejection of her husband. Forgive me, I am using my letter to you to argue with Larry in. But it made me sad, that he thought that somebody like us (if K. was) wasn't fit to rule us, which is to say, we aren't fit to rule ourselves, so bring on emperors, demigods, giant robots, what have you. Larry, incidentally, has let me know, during a merengo at the Plangent Cat, which is the place down the street, that his sexual ambivalence (AC or DC, he calls it) is definitely on the mend, but I declined, though he does dance wonderfully, to participate in the cure. He took the refusal as if his heart hadn't been in it.

Which brings us to you. Who are you? Are you weak? This theme, of your "weakness," cropped up often in the mouths of our mutual friends, when we all lived together in a magic circle. But I think they meant to say rather that your strengths weren't sufficiently <u>used</u>. *Your virtues are obsolete. I can imagine you as somebody's squire, maybe poor prim fanatic Matt's, a splendid redheaded squire, resourceful, loyal, living off the land, repairing armor with old hairpins, kidding your way into castles and inns, making impossible ideals work but needing their impossibility to attach yourself to. Before I knew you long ago Bea Guerin described you to me as an old-fashioned man. In a sense if I were to go from Ken to you it would be a backwards step. Compared to Ken you are primitive. The future belongs to him or to chaos. But my life belongs to me now, and I must take a short view. I am not, for all my vague intellectual poking (about as vague as Freddy's, and he knew it), good for much—but I know I could be your woman. As an ambition it is humble but explicit. Even if we never meet again I am glad to have felt useful, and used. Thank you.*

The question is, should I (or the next woman, or the next) subdue you to marriage? How much more generous it would be to let you wander, and suffer—there are so few wanderers left. We are almost all women now, homebodies and hoarders. You married Angela because your instinct told you she would not possess you. I would. To be mastered by your body I would tame you with my mind. Yet the subconscious spark in me that loves the race wants instead to give you freedom, freedom to rape and flee and to waste yourself, now that the art of building belongs entirely to accountants. Ever since you began to bounce up to my empty house in your dusty pick-up truck and after an hour rattle hastily away, I have felt in you, have loved in you, a genius for loneliness, for seeing yourself as something apart from the world. When you desire to be the world's husband, what right do I have to make you my own?

Toby is crying, and Linda is here. We are taking a picnic to Magen's Bay.

Night. The steel band down the street makes me want to go outdoors. What I wrote this afternoon please read understanding that its confusions are gropings toward truth. I am unafraid to seek the truth about us. With Ken I was always afraid. Of coming to the final coldness we shared.

You would have loved it where we went. Coral sand is not like silica sand; it is white and porous and <u>breathes</u>, and takes deep sharp footprints. My feet look huge and sadly flat. The shells are tiny and various, baby's fingernails for Carol. Remember that night? I was so jealous of Angela. Magen's Bay has sea-grape bushes for shade. I am getting a tan. Linda has talked me into a bikini. We roof Toby's basket with mosquito netting and he is turning caramel through it. I have learned to drive on the left-hand side of the road and am mastering my routines. The lawyers are dreadful. You would hate the process. Marriage is something done in the light, at noon, the champagne going flat in the sun, but divorce is done in the dark, where insects scuttle, in faraway places, by lugubrious lawyers. But at the end of the main street where it stops selling watches there is an old square Lutheran church smelling of cedar, with plaques in Danish, where I went Sunday. The congregation was plump colored ladies who sang *even the hymns of rejoicing wailingly. The sermon, by a taut young white man, was very intellectual—over my head. I liked it. The Negroes are lovely, softer than the Washington ones I rather dreaded as a child, without that American hardness and shame. I even like the fairies—at least they have made a kind of settlement and aren't tormenting some captive woman. The boats in the harbor are fascinating. Linda has rummaged up a baby carriage and I push Toby a half-mile each way along the quay. My father would tell me about boats and I find I still know a ketch from a yawl. I marvel at the hand-carved tackle on the old fishing boats from the more primitive islands. Not a bit of metal, and they hold together. The clouds are quick, translucent, as if Nature hardly intends them. When it rains in sunlight, they say, the Devil is beating his wife.*

Are you well? Are you there? If you have gone back to Angela, you may show this to her. Think of me fondly, without fear. Your fate need not be mine. I will write again, but not often. There are things to do even here. Linda has put me in charge of the morning help, for a reduction in fee, and has begun to confess to me her love life. *I am your*

Foxy

P.S.: Larry says that man is the sexiest of the animals and the only one that foresees death. I should make a riddle of this.
P.P.S.: At the Plangent Cat down the street I have danced now with Negroes, greatly daring for a Southern girl—the last one who touched me was the nurse in the dentist's office. They are a very silky people, and very innocently assume I want to sleep with them. How sad to instinctively believe your body is worth something. After weeks of chastity I remember lovemaking as an exploration of a sadness so deep people must go in pairs, one cannot go alone.
P.P.P.S.: I seem unable to let this letter go. A bad sign?

John Ong died the same day that France proposed another conference to restore peace to Laos, and Communist China agreed

to loan fifteen million dollars to Kenya. Piet was surprised by the
length of the obituary in the Globe: born in P'yongyang, political
refugee, asylum in 1951, co-discoverer in 1957, with a Finn, of
an elementary particle whose life is measured in millionths of a
second, list of faculty positions, scientific societies, survived by
wife and three sons, Tarbox, Mass. Private services. No flowers.
Their friend. Piet walked through the day lightened, excited by
this erasure, by John's hidden greatness, imagining the humming
of telephone wires among the couples he and John had once
known. The same covey of long-haired boys gathered on Cogswell's corner after three, the same blue sky showed through the
charred skeleton of the burnt church, topped by an untouched
gold rooster.

That same week, on an errand of business, trying to locate
Jazinski, who seemed now to hold all of Gallagher's plans and
intentions in his head, Piet went to the boy's house, an expanded
ranch on Elmcrest Drive, and saw Leon's new golf bag in the
garage. Not only were the clubs gleaming new Hogans but the
handle of each was socketed in one of those white plastic tubes
that were the latest refinement in fussy equipment: pale cannons
squarely aimed upward. The bag, black and many-pocketed, was
tagged with the ticket of a new thirty-six-hole club, in South
Mather, that Piet had never played on. Piet, who played with an
originally odd-numbered set filled in with randomly purchased
irons whose disparate weights and grips he had come to know like
friends, recognized that he must yield to the force expressed by
this aspiring bag, mounted on a cart the wheels of which were
spoked like the wheels of a sports car. When Leon's pretty wife,
her black hair bobbed and sprayed, answered the side door, he
read his doom again in her snug cherry slacks, her free-hanging
Op-pattern blouse, the bold and equalizing smile that greeted her
husband's employer, qualified by something too steady in the
eyes, by a curious repressing thoughtful gesture with the tip of
her tongue, as if she had often heard Piet unfavorably discussed.
Behind her (she did not invite him in; his reputation?) her
kitchen, paneled with imitation walnut and hung with copper
pâté molds, seemed the snug galley of a ship on its way to
warmer waters.

And before May was out Gallagher called Piet in for a serious talk. Matt asked if Piet thought Leon was ready to supervise construction, and Piet answered that he was. Matt asked if Piet didn't feel that over the last year their ends—sales and building—had begun to pull in opposite directions, and Piet responded that he was proud of how promptly the first three houses on Indian Hill had sold. Matt admitted this, but confessed that instead of these half-ass semi-custom-type houses he wanted to go into larger tracts—there was one beyond Lacetown he was bidding for, low clear land swampy only in the spring—and try prefab units, which would be, frankly, a waste of Piet's talents. Personally, he thought Piet's real forte was restoration, and with Tarbox full of old wrecks he would like to see Piet go into business for himself, buying cheap, fixing up, and selling high. Piet thanked him for the idea but said he saw himself more as a squire than a knight. Matt laughed uneasily, hearing another voice or mind emerge from Piet's disturbingly vacant presence. By the time a partnership dissolves, it has dissolved. In consideration for his half of their tangible assets—including a few sticks of office furniture, an inventory of light equipment and carpentry tools and the pick-up truck, a sheaf of mortgages held on faith, and a firm name that sounded like a vaudeville team (here Matt laughed scornfully, as if they had always been a joke)—he offered Piet five thousand, which to be honest was goddam generous. Piet, rebellious as always when confronted with pat solutions, suggested twenty, and settled for seven. He had not imagined himself getting anything, having forfeited, he felt, by his weekend with Foxy, all his rights. To placate his guilt he satisfied himself that Gallagher, who knew the value of their parcels better than he, would have gone higher than seven. They shook on it. The points of Gallagher's jaw flinched. He said earnestly, sellingly, that he wanted Piet to understand that this had nothing to do with Piet's personal difficulties, that he and Terry still believed that he and Angela would be reconciled. Piet was touched by this deceitful assurance for, though Matt had come to relish hard dealing, his conception of himself did not permit him, usually, to lie.

Meanwhile, across the town, Bea Guerin delighted in her

adopted baby, its violet toenails, its fearless froggy stare. It was a colored child. "Roger and I have integrated Tarbox!" Bea exclaimed breathlessly over the phone to Carol. "You know we're the last crusaders in the world, it's just that we couldn't bear to wait!" Bernadette Ong awoke to widowhood as if the entire side on which she had been sleeping were torn open, a mouth the length of her, where her church's balm burned like salt; she had respected John's desire to be buried without religion, and was bathed in a recurrent guilt whose scalding was confused with the plucking questioning hands of her children. "Daddy's gone away. To a place we can't imagine. Yes, they'll speak his language there. Yes, the Pope knows where it is. You'll see him at the end of your lives. Yes, he'll know you, no matter how old you've grown." She had been beside the bed when he died. One moment, there was faint breathing; his mouth was human in shape. The next, it was a black hole—black and deep. The vast difference haunted her, gave the glitter of the mass a holocaustal brilliance. Marcia little-Smith received a shock; having twice invited the Reinhardts to dinner parties and been twice declined, she went to visit Deb Reinhardt, a thin-lipped Vassar graduate with ironed hair, who told her that she and Al, though they quite liked Harold and Marcia in themselves, did not wish to get involved with their friends, with that whole—and here her language slipped unforgivably—"crummy crowd." So the Reinhardts, and the young sociologist who had been elected town moderator, and a charmingly yet unaffectedly bohemian children's book illustrator who had moved from Bleecker Street, and the new Unitarian minister in Tarbox, and their uniformly tranquil wives, formed a distinct social set, that made its own clothes, and held play readings, and kept sex in its place, and experimented with LSD, and espoused liberal causes more militantly than even Irene Saltz. Indignantly the Applesmiths christened them "the Shakers."

Georgene Thorne suffered a brief vision. Heartsick over Piet's collapse, and her final loss of him, and her own rôle in bringing it about, she had turned to her children, and as the weekend weather softened took Whitney and Martha and Judy on long undesired expeditions to museums in the city and wildlife sanctuaries well inland and unfamiliar beaches far down the coast. At one beach she was walking in from the parking area with her children when the laughter of a couple knee-deep in the icy ocean struck her as half familiar. The man was old and bearded and goatish, with knotted yellow legs, skimpy European-style bathing trunks, and a barrel chest coated in gray fur; coarsely hooting, rapacious, he was splashing seawater at a shrieking tall slender woman with tossing dark hair, girlish in a black bikini, Terry Gallagher. The man must be her lute teacher's husband, the potter. Georgene steered her children down the beach past some eclipsing rocks and never breathed a word of this glimpse to anyone, not even to Freddy, not even to Janet Appleby, who, in the course of their confidential outpourings following the discovery of Janet's note to Freddy, had become her closest friend.

Janet too had her secrets. One Saturday afternoon late in May, driving home from the little-Smiths', she noticed Ken's MG parked in the Whitmans' driveway, and impulsively stopped. She walked around the nursery wing, where Foxy's roses were budding, and found Ken at the front of the house, burning brush. In the light off the flooding marsh his hair was white. At first she talked in pleasantries, but he sensed in her, because he had always liked her, a nervous stalled fullness unbalanced by the beauty of the day. She moved the conversation toward his state of mind, to the loneliness she presumed was his and, unstated beyond that, the shame; and then she offered, not in so many words but with sufficient clarity, to sleep with him, now, in the empty house. After consideration, and with equal tact and clarity, he declined. It was the best possible outcome, "I've been burned, you see; I can't be hurt," had been the basis of her offer; and his refusal was phrased to enhance rather than diminish her notion of her worth: "I think we both need time to generate more self-respect." There was an island of brambles, hawthorn and alder, in the marsh too small to support even a shack, and as they watched, a cloud of starlings migrating north passingly settled here; even before the last birds of the flock alighted, the leaders lifted and fled. So their encounter, amid the quickening and the grass-smoke and the insect-hum and the tidewater overflowing its rectilinear channels, was sufficient consummation, an exercise for each of freedom. The first breath of adultery is the freest; after it, constraints aping marriage develop. Janet and Ken were improved for having stood, above the glorious greening marsh, in this scale, fit to live in such an expanding light. Their faces seemed each to each great planetary surfaces of skin and tension, overflowing dazzlingly at the eyes and mouths. She lowered her gaze; wind unsmoothed his hair. Her offer had been instructive for him; his refusal for her. For years they treasured these minutes out of all proportion to their circumspection.

The couples, though they had quickly sealed themselves off from Piet's company, from contamination by his failure, were yet haunted and chastened, as if his fall had been sacrificial. Angela, unattached now, was a threat to each marriage, and, though the various wives continued for a time to call on her politely, to be rebuffed by her coolness and distance, and to return home justified in their antipathy, she was seldom invited to parties. Indeed, parties all but ceased. The children as they grew made increasingly complex and preoccupying demands. The Guerins and Thornes and Applebys and little-Smiths still assembled, but rather sedately; one night, when once Freddy would have organized a deliciously cutting psychological word game, to "humanize" them, they drew up two tables and began to play bridge; and this became their habit. The Gallaghers, without the link of the Hanemas, drifted off to consort with the realtors and money-men of the neighboring towns, and took up horse riding. The Saltzes sent cards to everyone at Christmas. The Jazinskis have moved to an old house near the green and become Unitarians. Doc Allen has learned, the newest thing, how to insert intrauterine loops. Reverend Pedrick, ecstatic, has been overwhelmed by contributions of money, from Catholics as well as Congregationalists, from Lacetown and Mather as well as Tarbox, toward the rebuilding of his church. The fire was well publicized. One national foundation, whose director happened to be reading the *Herald* over breakfast at the Ritz that Monday, has offered to match private contributions dollar for dollar, and reportedly federal funds are available for the restoration of landmarks if certain historical and aesthetic criteria can be met. But the rumor in town is that the new building will be not a restoration but a modern edifice, a parabolic poured-concrete tent-shape peaked like a breaking wave.

The old church proved not only badly gutted but structurally unsound: a miracle it had not collapsed of itself a decade ago. Before the bulldozers and backhoes could munch through the building, the rooster was rescued by a young man riding a steel ball hoisted to the tip of an enormous crane. The elementary-school children were dismissed early to see the sight. Up, up, the young rider went, until he glimmered in the sun like the golden bird, and Piet Hanema, who in his unemployment was watching, and who knew what mistakes crane operators could make, held his breath, afraid. Gently the ball was hoisted and nudged into place; with surprising ease the young man lifted the gilded silhouette from its pivoted socket and, holding it in his lap, was swiftly lowered to the earth, as cheers from the schoolchildren rose. The weathercock measured five feet from beak to tailfeathers; the copper penny of his eye was tiny. As the workman walked across the green to present it to Pedrick and the two deacons waiting with him, the clustering children made a parade, a dancing flickering field of color as they jostled and leaped to see better the eye their parents had told them existed. From Piet's distance their mingled cry seemed a jubilant jeering. The grass of the domed green was vernally lush. The three stiff delegates of the church accepted the old emblem and posed for photographs absurdly, cradling the piece of tin between them; the man on Pedrick's right had hairy ears, the one on his left was a jeweler. The swarming children encircled them and touched the dull metal. The sky above was empty but for two parallel jet trails.

Affected by this scene of joy, seeing that his life in a sense had ended, Piet turned and realized he was standing where he had first glimpsed Foxy getting into her car after church, the spot where later they had met in the shadow of her mother's arrival, her tall body full, she in her pale turban; and he was glad that he would marry her, and frightened that he would not.

Is it too severe? I'd take it off but it's pinned.

It's great. It brings out the pampered pink of your face.

God, you're hostile.

I may be hostile, but I adore you. Let's go to bed.

Wouldn't that be a relief? Do you know how many days it's been since we made love?

Many.

Now, though it has not been many years, the town scarcely remembers Piet, with his rattly pick-up truck full of odd lumber, with his red hair and corduroy hat and eye-catching apricot windbreaker, he who sat so often and contentedly in Cogswell's Drug Store nursing a cup of coffee, the stub of a pencil sticking down from under the sweatband of his hat, his windbreaker unzipped to reveal an expensive cashmere sweater ruined by wood dust and shavings, his quick eyes looking as if they had been rubbed too hard the night before, the skin beneath them pouched in a little tucked fold, as if his maker in the last instant had pinched the clay. Angela, who teaches at a girls' school in Braintree, is still seen around, talking with Freddy Thorne on the street corner, or walking on the beach with a well-tailored wise-smiling small man, her father. She flew to Juárez in July and was divorced in a day. Piet and Foxy were married in September. Her father, pulling strings all the way from San Diego, found a government job for his new son-in-law, as a construction inspector for federal jobs, mostly military barracks, in the Boston-Worcester area. Piet likes the official order and the regular hours. The Hanemas live in Lexington, where, gradually, among people like themselves, they have been accepted, as another couple.

A Note about the Author

*JOHN UPDIKE was born in 1932, in Shilling-
ton, Pennsylvania; he attended Harvard College and
the Ruskin School of Drawing and Fine Art, in Oxford, England. From 1955 to 1957 he was a staff
member of* The New Yorker, *to which he has contributed stories, essays, and poems. His previous
novels are* The Poorhouse Fair (*1959*), Rabbit, Run
(*1960*), The Centaur (*1963*), *and* Of the Farm
(*1965*). *He lives with his wife and four children in
Massachusetts.*

A Note on the Type

The text of this book was set on the Linotype in Janson, a recutting made direct from type cast from matrices long thought to have been made by the Dutchman Anton Janson, who was a practicing type founder in Leipzig during the years 1668–87. However, it has been conclusively demonstrated that these types are actually the work of Nicholas Kis (1650–1702), a Hungarian, who most probably learned his trade from the master Dutch type founder Kirk Voskens. The type is an excellent example of the influential and sturdy Dutch types that prevailed in England up to the time William Caslon developed his own incomparable designs from these Dutch faces.

The book was composed, printed, and bound by Kingsport Press, Inc., Kingsport, Tennessee.